The Nature of Cognition

The Nature of Cognition

edited by Robert J. Sternberg

A Bradford Book
The MIT Press
Cambridge, Massachusetts
London, England

This book was set in Sabon by Achorn Graphic Services, Inc. and was printed and bound in the United States of America.

Library of Congress Cataloging-in-Publication Data

The nature of cognition / edited by Robert J. Sternberg.
   p.   cm.
"A Bradford book."
Includes bibliographical references and indexes.
ISBN 0-262-19405-8 (hardcover : alk. paper).—ISBN 0-262-69212-0 (pbk. : alk. paper)
  1. Cognition.   2. Mental representation.   I. Sternberg, Robert J.
BF311.N37   1998   97-47622
                                                                          CIP

Contents

Preface

The study of cognition has become essential not only for those interested in cognitive science, in general, and cognitive psychology, in particular, but for almost all those with an interest in the mind. In psychology, cognition is now recognized to play a central role in social psychology (the study of social cognition), developmental psychology (the study of cognitive development), clinical psychology (the study and implementation of cognitive therapy), educational psychology (the study of cognition in the classroom), cognitive neuroscience (the study of the cognitive processes related to brain functioning), and practically every other area of psychology as well. In philosophy, cognition is realized to be the most central topic that philosophers of mind from Plato to Saul Kripke and Hilary Putnam have pondered. Even many economists are now recognizing that they will never really understand consumer behavior until they let go of models of the completely rational "economic man and woman" and take into account how people really think. In anthropology, cognitive anthropology has become a major subfield, and in linguistics, more and more linguists are recognizing the close interrelation between thought and language.

How does a psychologist, a philosopher, an economist, an anthropologist, a linguist, or anyone else learn about the nature of cognition? If one is a college sophomore, one may take an introductory cognition course and use a textbook organized around the standard *substantive topics* that cognitive scientists or cognitive psychologists study (see, e.g., Sternberg, 1996), topics that include areas such as perception, memory, knowledge, representation, problem solving, and the like. The presentation is usually in terms of major empirical findings and, sometimes, major theories. If one is past the sophomore level, however, this form of presentation can at times be unsatisfying, geared as it is to a college student who is just starting to think about the mind as an object of study.

For those past the sophomore year, another approach is perhaps more fruitful—a presentation in terms of *conceptual themes*. This book takes that approach. *The Nature of Cognition* is the first book, to my knowledge, to introduce cognition at a higher level for those beyond the sophomore year—in terms of the major conceptual themes that underlie any serious study of cognition.

Because the focus of the book is on enduring conceptual themes rather than particular hot theories and findings that come and go, the book may have a more lasting quality than the typical college textbook.

Many different approaches could be taken to the use of themes as the basis for a book on cognition. The approach I have taken emphasizes Georg Hegel's (1931) concept of the *dialectic*. This idea—that knowledge proceeds from a thesis to an antithesis to a synthesis—is presented in more detail in chapter 1. But the basic idea throughout this text is to present the main themes of the study of cognition in terms of the dialectic, presenting opposing viewpoints—theses and antitheses such as heredity versus environment—that are then recognized to require a synthetic integration. In this way, readers learn to think about issues in the way scholars of cognition have thought about them, rather than in a way that sophomores in college typically think about them.

The book is divided into six parts, each dealing with different aspects of the nature of cognition.

Part I, General Issues in Cognition, contains three chapters dealing with the philosophical and psychological foundations of the study of cognition. In particular, chapter 1, by Earl Hunt, considers what constitutes a theory of thought. Chapter 2, by Robert J. Sternberg, deals with a dialectical basis for understanding the study of cognition and problems in the study of cognition such as the mind-body problem. Chapter 3, by Daniel N. Robinson, deals with rationalism versus empiricism in cognition.

Part II, Representation and Process in Cognition, contains four chapters. Chapter 4, by Timothy P. McNamara, addresses single-code versus multiple-code theories in cognition. Chapter 5, by Peter A. Frensch and

Axel Buchner, addresses domain-generality versus domain-specificity in cognition. Chapter 6, by John F. Kihlstrom, explores conscious versus unconscious cognition. And chapter 7, by Brian H. Ross and Valerie S. Makin, deals with the issue of prototype versus exemplar models in cognition.

Part III, Methodology in Cognition, contains five chapters that deal with alternative ways of studying cognition. Chapter 8, by Patricia A. Carpenter and Marcel Adam Just, addresses computational modeling of high-level cognition versus hypothesis testing. Chapter 9, by Elizabeth A. Phelps, addresses the issue of brain versus behavioral studies of cognition. Chapter 10, by Michael Kahana and Geoffrey Loftus, discusses two alternative dependent variables, response time and accuracy, in human memory. Chapter 11, by Stephen J. Ceci, Tina B. Rosenblum, and Eduardus DeBruyn, compares laboratory and field approaches to cognition. And chapter 12, by Raymond S. Nickerson, deals with basic versus applied research.

Part IV explicitly addresses various kinds of cognition. It contains six chapters. Chapter 13, by Dennis R. Proffitt, addresses inferential versus ecological approaches to perception. Chapter 14, by Arthur S. Reber, Rhianon Allen, and Paul J. Reber, deals with implicit versus explicit learning. Chapter 15, by Randall W. Engle and Natalie Oransky, compares multi-store and dynamic models of temporary storage in memory. Chapter 16, by Steven Sloman, addresses the question of rational versus arational models of thought.

Chapter 17, by P. N. Johnson-Laird, discusses formal rules versus mental models in reasoning. Chapter 18, by Thomas O. Nelson, compares cognition with metacognition.

Part V deals with group and individual differences in cognition. Chapter 19, by Michael Cole, deals with culture-free versus culture-based measures of cognition. Finally, chapter 20, by Elena L. Grigorenko, discusses issues underlying the dialectic of heredity versus environment as bases of cognitive abilities, in general, and intellectual abilities, in particular.

I am grateful to Amy Brand at The MIT Press for contracting and helping me develop the book, to all the authors for agreeing to write, and to the U.S. Office of Educational Research and Improvement (grant #206R50001) for supporting my own research in cognition.

This book is dedicated to the memory of Amos Tversky, who represents consummately that ideal scholar of cognition whose deep understanding of the issues that underlie the field so greatly enriched the field, and all of us in it.

References

Hegel, G. W. F. (1931). *The phenomenology of mind* (2nd ed., J. B. Baillie, Trans.). London: Allen & Unwin. (Original work published in 1807.)

Sternberg, R. J. (1996). *Cognitive psychology.* Ft. Worth, TX: Harcourt Brace College Publishers.

I

General Issues in Cognition

1

What Is a Theory of Thought?

Earl Hunt

Revolutions Old and New

The study of human thought is one of the most active areas of scientific psychology today. Offhand, I know of seven journals with *cognition* in their titles, and I am sure there are more. Most of the articles in these journals are elaborations on ideas introduced in the 1950s, ideas that have been collectively described as the "cognitive revolution" in psychology (Baars, 1986). As the twenty-first century is about to begin, many people think we are on the brink of a second cognitive revolution, which may be as profound as the first. Why?

There are two types of scientific revolution. New ideas can be developed that cause scientists to reexamine old data in new ways and to do new experiments they would not have thought of using older ways of thinking. Alternatively, new technologies may open up new sources of data, making it physically possible for scientists to test old theories in new ways. Such developments often lead to a shift in the original theories. New ideas provide incentives for the development of techniques, which, when used to uncover new data, lead to new theories. Let us call these types of revolutions *idea* or *data driven*. The cognitive revolution that took place in the 1950s was clearly idea driven; the new experiments were done because the new ideas suggested them. The revolution that is being talked about today is data driven, based on the development of new techniques for the *in vivo* measurement of brain processes in both humans and other animals. Probably the most dramatic of these techniques are the methods of brain-imaging techniques that allow us to take pictures of both structures and metabolic processes in the brain without opening the skull (Posner & Raichle, 1994). Other biotechnologies, such as molecular genetic analyses, are also important. The dramatic development in biotechnology has opened up a world of data that psychologists simply could not view before.

As we enter this revolution, two questions lie before us. Will the new sources of data require new ideas about cognition, or even psychology in general, or will the new data lead to evolutionary rather than revolutionary changes in our present theories? Will the new data sources and techniques sweep away the old, as chemistry swept away alchemy, or will two parallel but related fields of scientific inquiry exist, one based on the cognitive neurosciences and one based on the procedures that scientific psychology has used since the 1950s? In order to answer these questions we have to get a grasp on what psychological theories can and should be. That is the issue addressed in the current chapter.

The Philosophy behind Psychology: Are There Separate Laws for Mind and Body?

Two Theories of Dualism
The philosophical puzzle that has dominated virtually all studies of thought is, What is the relationship between the brain and the mind? The great French philosopher, Descartes (1637/1970) believed that brain and mental activity had to be considered separately because although they must interact, he was unable to see how (Bechtel, 1988; Dennett, 1992). To see how complex the issues are, let us look at an empirical question in social cognition: the influence of alcohol upon interpersonal perception.

In our society alcohol is widely used as a facilitator for social activities connected to sexual behavior. The drug is served at functions ranging from singles bars to marriage celebrations. Why? Is heightened sexual awareness an automatic reaction to the drug itself or are there more indirect mechanisms at work? Are we dealing with the brain or the mind?

Some of alcohol's effects are indirect. Men who believe that they have drunk alcohol, even though they have not, show increased sexual responsiveness in their social behavior and attitudes.[1] This behavior cannot be due to the physiological effects of the drug, because the men did not receive it. Furthermore, this could not be a conditioned response, based on previous associations of the smell of alcohol with an unconditioned physiological response to the drug, because at the physiological level alcohol consumption decreases both penile and vaginal arousal. It seems that arousal can be dissociated from actual consumption but not from the belief in having consumed (George & Norris, 1991). Shakespeare correctly said that alcohol "provokes the desire, but it takes away the performance" (*MacBeth*, act 2, scene 1).

George and Norris's (and Shakespeare's) observation about alcohol's lowering the performance is an assertion about how a pharmacologically defined agent influences a physiologically defined state of behavior. The effect of the drug on sensory receptors involved in sex can also be studied by the neurosciences. The remark about beliefs is a bit harder to understand. Consider a somewhat more subtle finding: when men see a woman drinking they perceive her as being more sexually available than she would be otherwise (George, Gournic, & McAfee, 1988). In order for a man to think this way, a man has to have a concept of a woman's mind. In physical terms the man's brain must contain an internal representation of the information in the woman's brain. Whether the man's representation is accurate or not is not the issue.[2] The point is that the representation exists. Why does it exist, and what variables cause it to take the particular structure it has?

The example illustrates the mind-body problem, which is probably the most important single issue facing the philosophy of the mind. The example also touches on two other major issues. Alcohol produces a certain subjective feeling, a *qualia* in the philosopher's terms, that may enter into future actions. The nature of a *qualia* cannot be tied directly to a physical state. Why will alcohol cause one man to initiate a tender, romantic interlude whereas another attempts aggressive and even brutal sex? How the arousal is translated into behavior depends upon the man's subjective experience of his physical state, strained through a complex of beliefs about the world.

The men's beliefs about women's desires illustrate the next problem in the philosophy of the mind. Our brain, a physical organ, somehow represents things outside of itself. In philosophical terms, the brain state has an intention. To what extent should a theory of cognition be concerned with intentions? To what extent can a theory of thought be divorced from what we are thinking about?

Opinions differ dramatically on this issue. Simon says, in a discussion arguing for the use of computer programs to construct models of human mental activity, "I have discussed the organization of the mind without saying anything about the structure of the brain" (Simon, 1981, p. 97). The argument that Simon gave for doing so was that several quite different physical devices might give rise to the same sorts of intellectual accomplishments. Computers have been programmed to do many tasks that when performed by humans are considered intellectual accomplishments. Playing chess and solving algebraic problems are good examples. Other intellectual tasks are quite complex, language being perhaps the most extreme example. Simon argues that such complex actions can only be accomplished in a few ways and perhaps in only one way. Therefore, if we manage to program a computer to play chess (which has been done) or comprehend free-form text (which has yet to be done), we may well have discovered how human thought proceeds. Simon argues for a sharp distinction between the brain as a physical system and the programs the brain executes, and he urges us to concentrate our attention on the programs.

In opposition, Francis Crick states: "The brain does not make a distinction between hardware and software, as a computer does. Theories [of thought] that have made this distinction are unfortunate" (Crick, 1994, p. 179). Crick goes to great length to argue for theories of cognition that are strictly tied to biology, which implicitly forces him to argue for the study of simple cognitive acts, such as visual word detection, rather than complex acts, such as paragraph comprehension.

Can these views be reconciled? Descartes's concept of dualism was based on the idea that the mind and body have separate existences and follow different laws. Modern philosophers call this attitude *substance dualism*. Simon specifically disavows substance dualism. He does advocate what I will call *pragmatic dualism*: the belief that although the mind does depend on brain processes, the connections are so convoluted, and we know so little about them, that it makes sense to try to develop laws of mental action that are defined independently of the brain.

Pragmatic dualists argue that scientific psychology can go about its business without having to wait for advances in the neurosciences. Looked at this way, pragmatic dualism seems to be a sort of holding strategy, in which we develop a temporary set of laws of mental action in anticipation of later developments that will supersede purely psychological theories with theories based on the neurosciences. This state of affairs could arise at different times in different areas of cognition. For instance, although Crick's general discussion is of the concept of conscious thought, virtually all the specific studies he cites deal with visual cognition. It might be most profitable to deal with vision entirely from the field of neurosciences, while dealing with language comprehension in terms of psychological mechanisms that have no known neural basis. More generally, we can approach topics in cognition from the perspective of reduction to the neurosciences, total pragmatic dualism, or some mix of the two approaches. What is required is a set of rules to decide when a particular approach is useful and when it is not.

Science Studies Systems

Plato is usually credited with the observation that scientific studies should "carve nature at its joints." More precisely (but less picturesquely), Sperber and Wilson (1986) say: "In science a definition is motivated when it groups together propositions which are systematically linked in nature" (p. 173). The word *systematically* is key. In mathematics, and in the sciences, a system is a set of mutually dependent variables that take on different values over time. The state of the system is defined by the values of the variables. A closed system is a system in which the state at time t can be predicted perfectly from knowledge of the state at any previous time, t'. A scientific law can be thought of as a statement of the rules of transition from one state to another within a closed system. For instance, Newtonian mechanics define a system in which the location of objects at the next instant in time is determined by their current location and motion and the forces acting upon them.

A system is open if its next state cannot be predicted perfectly, given knowledge of its current state. The usual interpretation of an open system is that the variables being observed are a subset of the variables in some larger, closed system. Because the observer does not know all the variables in the larger system, the variables that actually are being recorded may sometimes change in unpredictable ways.[3]

In practice, the only completely closed system is the universe itself, which we believe maintains a set relationship between its geometry and the distribution of matter and energy in it (Krause, 1995). This system is hardly manageable. However, different bits of the universe are sufficiently separate from each other so that they can be regarded as disconnected. Scientists try to study systems that are sufficiently closed to be predictable and sufficiently small to be understandable. To continue the physical example, Newton is (mythically?) supposed to have conceived of the law of gravity when he saw an apple fall. An apple is a relatively massive object, with respect to normal wind and air pressure, so when it falls it usually falls directly toward earth. Thus the apple-earth system is a reasonably close approximation of abstract Newtonian mechanics. If Newton had drawn his inspiration from watching a leaf fall, his theories might never have been developed. The leaf-earth system is much more open than the apple-earth system because air resistance does have a major effect on the leaf's fall. The law of gravity could be uncovered using the leaf-earth system, but to do so one would have to resort to statistical studies to show how leaves fall on the average, ignoring the effects of unmeasured variables in the open system.

Newton's apple may well be mythical, but there are ample, well-documented historical examples of the importance of defining manageable, closed systems. The study of astronomy was not possible until the Babylonians realized that the heavens and the clouds should be thought of as separate systems (Boorstin, 1983). What are the analogous distinctions that should be made in the study of thinking? This question is central to the pragmatic dualist approach.

Cognitive Psychology as the Study of Information-Processing Systems

An Example

In order to define the systems that influence thought, we need to undertake a closer analysis of what thought is. One model is that thinking is the manipulation of an *internal representation* of real or imagined events that are external to the thinker. Physically, internal representations are brain states. Logically, they are symbolic representations of the external world, in the same sense that a map is a symbolic representation of geographic objects and relationships. If an internal representation is to be of any use it must be changeable so a thinker can manipulate it to determine "what if." These internal manipulations save us from actually poking around in a possibly dangerous world. Finally, there must be a link between thought and action, for if there were no action what would be the use of thinking? Suppose a tree could divine the intentions of a lumberjack. What could the tree do about them?

Another model for a theory of thinking comes from the study of brain activity. We can learn a good deal about the elementary processes of perception, memory, and imagination that underlie thought by looking at how different brain structures and processes are involved in different types of cognitive acts. For instance, psychologists today make a strong distinction between working memory for events that occurred in the past few seconds or minutes and long-term memory for events that occurred hours, days, or even years ago. This distinction is based in part on the observation that certain types of brain injuries can affect one of these functions but not the other. These two approaches to thought are complementary, but not identical. The nature of the complement is illustrated in the following anecdote.

At the outset of a sabbatical of mine some years ago, a realtor was showing me an apartment for rent. When we entered it, I smelled gas and cautioned the realtor, a smoker, not to light a cigarette. In any reasonable sense of the word, I thought. What was the formal relationship between my thinking and the physical actions that occurred?

Figure 1.1 depicts what happened. My brain contained an internal representation of the physical state of the room and the habits of my companion. Processes internal to the brain constructed a second brain state that depicted a potential explosion. For each brain state there was an interpretation in terms of correspondence between properties of the brain state and a property of the external world. Further brain processes operated on the first and second states to produce a third state that initiated the external warning to my companion.

In principle, it would also be possible to explain my actions by specifying the physical changes that occurred in my nasal passages, brain, and

Figure 1.1
Depiction of the mental events and communicative acts that occurred when I smelled gas in an apartment.

eventually my vocal apparatus. The idea of explaining mental actions by cataloging the accompanying physical events is appealing because it would be a major step toward unifying the mental and biological sciences. Nevertheless, relying exclusively on a physical theory of thought has definite drawbacks. The obvious one is impracticality. Although there have been major advances in the brain sciences in the last 50 years, we are not even close to being able to explain all the physiological events involved in even the slight amount of thinking that I did when I smelled the gas. For example, advances in brain imaging in the early 1990s have been used to locate the brain areas that are active when we look at and comprehend a single written word (Posner & Raichle, 1994). Based on this work, it seems reasonable to expect that within a few years we will locate those areas of the brain that are involved in normal reading. However, there is little chance that this research will let us discriminate between brain activities involved in reading Shakespeare and those involved in reading the sports pages.

Suppose we could get a description of the sequence of neural activities involved in a single thought? The brain has approximately 10^{11} neurons (Thompson, 1995). Even if we could track the state of every neuron in the brain we could not understand the resulting record. When we talk about brain activity, we will always have to resort to a higher-order language. A good analogy is the way in which computer systems designers understand very large programs, such as operating systems, the programs used to supervise air traffic, or those used to monitor money flow between banks. These programs can contain millions of lines of code, executed simultaneously on thousands of machines. It would be physically possible to print out and examine the individual instructions, but no human being could comprehend so much detail.

In order to avoid being overwhelmed with details, system designers break the programs down into functional modules—subprograms that pass well-defined messages back and forth between themselves. Different languages are required to talk about actions within and across modules, because talking about everything in terms of elementary machine operations would overwhelm the system engineers. Because a million-line (10^6) program is orders of magnitude simpler than the brain, it seems likely that the same principle will be required in thinking about thought.[4] "What are the systems appropriate for studying cognition?" can be reframed as "What different levels of models do we need to formulate a theory of thought?"

An anthropologist interested in human cognition (or perhaps a novelist) might object to my approach thus far. From the viewpoint of understanding how my realtor and I functioned as social beings, the talk about brain states is close to irrelevant. To the anthropologist and novelist, the important things to understand are our beliefs and knowledge systems: what we know and what we think we know about the way our world works. Therefore, I warned the realtor because I, like most human beings, wanted to avoid disasters and because I believed that the joint presence of natural gas and a flame would lead to an explosion. (Note that the example does not require that I understood the nature of combustion. All that is asserted is that I believed that the combination of gas and match is bad news.) To give a grander-scale example, historians say that in 1938 Neville Chamberlain *believed* that Hitler would cease his aggressive policies if Germany were allowed to occupy Czechoslovakia and that in 1990 Saddam Hussein *believed* that George Bush was bluffing when Bush demanded that Iraqi forces retreat from Kuwait. To understand what happened next, historians, and most of us, appeal to causal laws stated in terms of what the objects of thought are about, not how neurons become active.

A theory of thought based on content would be stated as rules, describing the sequences by which thoughts trigger each other, without any commitment to how the sequencing occurs. For instance, my actions in the apartment could be explained by the rule

R1 If the state of the gas indicator is "on" and the description of a companion includes the term *smoker,* then issue a warning.

Rule R1 is not a useful theory of behavior, because it simply restates what happened. A better set of rules, still tied to the content of thought, would be

R2 If the gas indicator is "on," mark that an explosive potential is present.
R3 If an explosive potential is present, set a marker to eliminate fire hazards.
R4 If a smoker is present and fire hazards are to be eliminated, issue a no-smoking warning.

We now have the rudiments of a theory, in the sense that some general principles have been established that can account for behavior in a variety of situations. Variants of R2 could be developed that would apply R3 and R4, which actually do the work, to situations involving gunpowder, spilled gasoline, and anything else I believed might explode.

This approach to content-based theories can be extended to cover virtually all human behaviors. The key idea, which goes back to Aristotle and Plato, is that humans respond to specific situations either by executing a memorized rule for that situation or by classifying the current situation as a member of a class of situations and then responding in a way that is appropriate for the class. Therefore, a theory of a person's thought should state what general classes of things that person knows about, what rules are used to associate instances with classes, and what responses are seen as appropriate when a class member is encountered. In the language of philosophy, theories of thought that are thus stated deal directly with the intention of thought, and that is what thinking is about.

Such an approach is pragmatic dualism in its most extreme form. Unfortunately, because scientists are materialists, they place considerable value on the goal of reducing psychological theories to biological terms. However, there is no point in trying to connect events in my brain to my knowledge that flames can ignite natural gas; one may as well attempt to explain the flight of a baseball in terms of quantum mechanics. Physicists are confident that there is a direct link between quantum mechanics and the flight of a baseball, but the link is so long and tortuous that we simply cannot think about it. Newtonian physics provides us with an intermediate language that is highly useful in dealing with the movement of physical bodies above the atomic level. Specific motions, like that of the baseball, can be described by appeal to general concepts in the Newtonian language. The Newtonian concepts themselves can then be explained in terms of theories of subatomic physics. Consider the concept of a solid body. At the subatomic level, there is no such thing because subatomic particles can be located only up to a probability distribution. At the Newtonian level, the bat hits the ball or it doesn't, and a theory that says that yes, you can locate an object in space and time, can be used to explain what happens next. Cognitive psychologists need the same sort of language to explain specific thoughts in terms of general concepts that, themselves, may be linked to brain processes.

A Computational View of Cognition

Following the lead of numerous authors, Pylyshyn (1984, 1989) has referred to content-based and biologically based explanations of human thought as *knowledge* and *physical* levels of thought. Because *knowledge* has some additional connotations, I will use the more neutral term *representational-level theory*. So long as we believe in materialism we must assume that an omnipotent, omniscient theorist could derive representational-level theories from physical levels of information. However, given our limited ability to observe and comprehend, it appears that the worlds of thoughts and neural events behave as separate systems, with at best poorly understood links between them. A great deal of the modern study of cognition depends on the insight that representational-level and neural-level events can be linked through the development of intermediate, *computational* theories of thought. This insight is based upon a rather sophisticated notion both of thinking and computation as activities that are carried out by physical symbol systems (Newell, 1980).

To understand Newell's "physical symbol system" it helps to look at a thinking device whose inner workings can be observed directly, rather than one, like humans, whose inner workings are a bit mysterious. Computers are used to calculate the trajectories of objects in flight, varying from space shuttles to artillery rounds. Consider an object that has been in free fall toward Earth for t seconds. What is its current height above the Earth? Applying Newton's laws of motion, the appropriate equation is

(1) $h(t) = h(0) - 1/2gt^2$,

where $h(0)$ is the starting height, $h(t)$ is the height at time t, and g is the gravitational constant. Height, time, gravity, and motion are properties of the world; whereas h, t, g, multiplication, and subtraction are terms in the symbolic system that represent properties of the physical system.

Suppose that a computer is used to calculate $h(t)$. A computer is a physical device that manipulates electrical signals standing for the symbols in the equation. A *machine* consisting of an engineer, a pencil, and paper is also a device for manipulating physical objects (marks on paper) that stand for the abstractions in the symbolic system. Both are physical symbol systems. The computer and the engineer-paper-pencil devices are general purpose computing systems in the sense that they can, in principle, compute any computable function that is defined by a symbol system. (Ignore for the moment the practicality of making some computations.) In order to actually compute something, the physical device must be given a set of instructions, stated in terms of actions it can take for manipulating its physical manifestation of the symbols in the symbol system. For instance, a possible set of instructions for computing the position of a body in free fall is

1. Write down the value of $h(0)$.
2. Write down the value of t.

3. Multiply the number found in step 2 by itself.
4. Write down the value of the gravitational constant.
5. Multiply the number found in step 3 by the number found in step 4.
6. Divide the number found in step 5 by 2.
7. Subtract the number found in step 6 from the number found in step 1.
8. Mark the number found in step 7 as the answer.

Steps 1 through 8 define a *program* or *algorithm* for computing position after free fall. Note that the algorithm is not stated in terms of the physical machine, because the physical operations that achieve the primitive functions *writing down, multiplying,* and *subtracting* have not been specified. Either a computer or an engineer with a pencil and paper could execute steps 1 through 8 because they can do physical operations that correspond to the primitive functions of the algorithm. Therefore, there is a correspondence between the two machines at the algorithmic level. Because the algorithm is an accurate representation of the physical events during free fall, both machines are models of the physical world and of each other at the representational level. On the other hand, the physical operations of writing down something on paper and changing the numbers stored in a computer are quite different, so there is no correspondence between the two machines at the physical level.

Correspondence can exist at the representational level without existing at the algorithmic level. For example, consider an alternative algorithm for free fall

$1'$ Compute $x = \ln(t) + \ln(t) + \ln(g) - \ln(2)$.
$2'$ Compute $h(t) = h(0) + e^x$, where e is the Naperian constant.
$3'$ The number computed in step 2 is the answer.

Rules 1 through 8 and rules $1'$ through $3'$ will compute exactly the same mathematical function. Suppose that we programmed two physically identical computers, one using rules 1 through 8, the other using rules $1'$ through $3'$. By definition these computers could be thought of as models of each other at the physical level. They would not be models of each other at the computational level, but they would be identical at the representational level. Neither computer would be a model of the engineer and pencil at the physical level. However, the first computer but not the second would be a model of the engineer at the programming level, and both computers, with their programs, would be models of the engineer at the representational level.

The cognitive revolution of the 1950s was based on the insight that cognition can be modeled at the computational level without any commitment to modeling at the physical level. Returning to my anecdote about the gas leak in the apartment, suppose that someone produced a robot fire marshal, suitably equipped with gas detectors and computing circuits. Could this machine be offered as a psychological explanation of my behavior? It depends upon what you mean by an explanation.

A superficial examination of the robot's computing circuit would quickly rule out the robot as an explanation at the physical level. My brain operates on neural circuitry; the robot's would operate using electronic technology. The two are vastly different. Determining whether or not we were representational level models of each other would be similarly straightforward. Do we issue the same set of warnings over a wide range of situations? The qualifier *wide range* is important. Recall that I argued that I probably operate as a general classifier, telling people not to smoke when "combustibles" are present. Therefore, showing that the robot and I behaved the same way in the presence of gas leaks would be necessary but not sufficient evidence of modeling. The robot might be a specialized gas detector. The argument for the robot as a model of the mind gets stronger as we investigate more situations; gunpowder storage rooms, gasoline dumps, and hydrogen leaks (where we should both fail to issue a warning because humans cannot sense the presence of hydrogen).[5]

The crux of the argument is that there are three qualitatively different classes of systems of thought: systems at the physical, computational, and representational level. (The reason for saying "classes of system" is that there may be separate systems within a level. For instance, the physical systems for auditory and olfactory perception are distinct.) The physical and representational levels can be directly tied to observation; we can see, photograph, feel, or touch their elements. The elements of computational level systems cannot be so observed. Computational-level models of thought are inherently functional models, dealing with generalized functions, such as short- and long-term memory, that can only be observed through their manifestations in specific instances. In some sense, computational models are models of systems that cognitive psychologists made up. Nevertheless, computational models are quite important.

Sublevels within the Computational System: The Black Box Problem in Engineering Terms

Before arguing for the importance of a computational-level theory, a closer look at computational systems is in order. This examination requires an aside to present some results from computer science and the mathematics of computation. I ask the reader to bear with me. The connection to psychology will be made in the following section.

Computation depends upon three linked but separate ideas: *mathematical function, algorithm*, and *system architecture*. A *mathematical function* maps from a set of input objects, called the *domain,* to a set of output objects, called the *range.* For example, the function *square root of* maps the positive real numbers into the positive reals; the function *largest integer contained in* maps the real numbers into the integers. The idea of a function is applicable outside of conventional mathematics. Consider the infinite set S of all strings of English words. Let E be the (infinite) subset of S whose elements are those strings of words that are also sentences in English. For example, "Mary likes the salad" and "salad the Mary likes" are both in S, but only the first string is in E. A parser for English f_E is a function that maps from S into the set $\{1, 0\}$. Let s be some string in S. The value of $f_E(s)$ is 1 if s is a member of E, and 0 otherwise.

An *algorithm* for the function f is a computing procedure that calculates f. In general, there will be several algorithms for computing any one function. The earlier examples of two ways of calculating free fall illustrate this point.

Because an algorithm is a procedure, the existence of an algorithm implies the existence of a machine that can execute the algorithm. We may think of an algorithm as a series of primitive operations that are within the capability of the computing machine. In the trajectory example, the first algorithm (rules 1–8) can only be executed by a machine that contains, as primitive operations, the operations of adding, subtracting, multiplying, and dividing, plus the operations of storing a number in a temporary memory area. The second algorithm also requires a machine that has addition, subtraction, and temporary storage as primitive operations, but multiplication and division have been replaced by the use of logarithms. Therefore the second algorithm requires a machine that either contains a logarithm calculator as a primitive device or contains a table of logarithms in a permanent memory, distinct from whatever resources are required to hold temporary information relevant to the problem at hand.

The design of the computing machine that executes an algorithm is called its *system architecture*. This term includes the primitive operations used by the algorithm and any necessary communications between them that are dictated by the nature of the machine itself. The system architecture of the machine provides its "programmer," which could be a person or evolution (if the machine is the human mind), with tools used to define algorithms. These tools are computational modules to be used by the algorithm, but are not part of the algorithm. The designer of an algorithm regards the modules provided by the system architecture as sealed units (conventionally, a black box). The designer knows what functions a module computes and the resources required, including time, to do the computations, but does not know what the internal operations of the module are. There is an analogy between the system architecture and algorithmic levels of description of a computation and the description of a carpenter's workroom and the procedures that the carpenter follows to build a particular piece of furniture.

One of the fundamental results connecting logic to mathematics is the finding that any computable function[6] can be computed by a device containing just two computing modules, one of which computes the logical function NOT and the other either the logical function AND or OR. This means that you cannot in general discriminate between two system architectures on the basis of the functions that they can compute, providing that both architectures contain these modules and that they have some way of storing intermediate results. This problem, called the *black box problem*, is an important one for psychology. Here is an expanded version.

Suppose that you are presented with two black boxes, one containing a computer with system architecture *A* and the other a computer with system architecture *B*. You are assured that system architectures *A* and *B* are at least complicated enough to meet the minimum conditions for modularity just described. How can you devise a test to see which box contains which architecture?

A method that will *not* work is to present the computers' programmers with a list of functions and see which computer could execute which function, because programmers for both systems *A* and *B* would be able to write algorithms to compute any computable function. It might be the case that for a particular function the programmer for system *A* would write a simple algorithm, whereas the programmer for system *B* would write a complicated one. However, you cannot tell the difference from outside the box, because all you can see is what goes into the box (the element from the domain of the function) and what comes out (the element from the range). What you see is the result of the combination of system architecture and algorithm, so you cannot evaluate either in isolation. For those familiar with computers, this statement is an abstract version of the observation that any computer can compute any computable function.

The difference between system architectures is in the efficiency with which the computation can be executed. When a designer (or evolution) sets out to design algorithms that are efficient for the particular machine at hand, the algorithm designer needs to know what sort of resources are required by each module. Two are of particular importance: time and interference patterns.

Because the elementary computing modules of every machine are physical devices, they will take time to complete whatever function they compute. Two differently defined modules may compute exactly the same function, but vary in the time that they take to compute different instances of the required mapping. Take an adding module, such as is found in every modern computer. It may be somewhat surprising to those who have not thought about it, but there are several ways to add! In the standard "right-to-left" algorithm taught in U.S. schools, addition proceeds from right to left (least to most significant digits) and terminates when there are no carries and all nonzero digits have been processed. Thus it takes longer to add 7456 and 9843 than to add 3 and 6. This is called *serial addition*. In *parallel addition*, addition is carried out in a two-step operation that assumes that all digits are potentially nonzero. First, each pair of digits is added together, and then the carries are shifted and added in. Thus, 3 + 6 would be added as 0003 + 0006, and it would take exactly as long to add 3 and 6 as it would take to add 7456 and 9843. An outsider performing the black box experiment could not distinguish between system architectures using serial and parallel addition modules by determining what numbers the two boxes could add, but could distinguish between the architectures by determining whether or not the time taken to do addition varied with the number of digits in the addends.

Using interference patterns to identify system architectures is a bit trickier. The underlying idea is that any computing module will require resources to be effective and that its effectiveness will decrease if its resources are reduced. Actual computers again provide an example. The earliest commercial computers had a single arithmetic-processing unit that did everything, including controlling the printer. Suppose that such a computer was used to balance a company's books and to print a report on the status of various branches of the company. Two different algorithms might be used.

Algorithm A
A1 Compute the report for one branch: store the results. Compute the report for the next branch: store the results. Continue until the books have been balanced for each branch.
A2 Compute the summary report for the entire company.
A3 Print the report for each branch, and then the summary report.

Algorithm B
B1 Compute the report for each branch. As soon as a branch report has been computed, store the results and print the part of the final report associated with that branch.
B2 After calculating all branch reports calculate the summary report.
B3 Print the summary report.

Algorithm A does calculation and printing in series; algorithm B interleaves calculating and printing. An old-fashioned computer, circa 1958, would have taken exactly the same amount of time to execute each of the two algorithms because early computers could not compute and print at the same time. Note that this is not because of the modules the machines had but because of the way that they were hooked together. In modern computing systems separate computing modules control printing and program computations. A computing system with this architecture can benefit from algorithms that interleave computing and printing. Returning to the black box experiment, you could discriminate between the old and the new architectures by seeing which black box computers benefited from interleaving.[7]

The example just given is of competition for a common process. Interference between operations can also occur because of competition for some sort of power resource. Resource competition is difficult to illustrate in modern computers because the modules of these machines generally either operate with sufficient power or they do not operate at all. However, resource competition occurs all the time with other machines. For example, why do you get poorer gasoline mileage from your automobile if you drive with the air conditioner on? The answer is that the air conditioner draws power from the engine, so the engine must generate more energy to go a fixed distance, at a fixed speed, with the air conditioner on than with it off. It would be possible to design an automobile in which the air conditioner had its own source of power. The clever driver could discriminate between these two system architectures by experimentation, without ever looking under the hood.

Our main interest here is psychology, so why is this excursion worthwhile? We try to infer both the algorithms and system architecture of the mind by seeing what functions people can compute and how efficiently they compute them. This insight was a major part of the cognitive revolution of the 1950s. The next section illustrates the point, by using the concepts developed here to isolate and study manageable systems in the brain and mind.

Psycholinguistics as an Illustration of the Need for Different Levels of Psychological Theories

I have argued that cognition has to be studied simultaneously at the neuroscientific, computational, and representational levels. Language has been chosen to illustrate the argument because it is a uniquely human bit of cognition and because, by definition, all readers of this article read and so will be familiar with the phenomena to be discussed. However, the reader should keep in mind the purpose of the section. I have chosen examples to illustrate the importance of different types of theories in psychology. The discussion is certainly not intended to be a comprehensive coverage of psycholinguistics.

Neuropsychological Studies of Language

A great deal of what we know about the brain processes that support language comes from neuropsychology, the study of brain-injured individuals. During the nineteenth century, case studies reported by the physicians Paul Broca, Carl Wernicke, and others showed a clear association between loss of speech function and injuries in the left temporal region of the brain. These observations have been confirmed many times over the years. During the mid twentieth century, Roger Sperry and his collaborators carried out a series of studies on *split brain* patients, persons whose hemispheres have been disconnected during necessary medical procedures.[8] This work has since been carried on by numerous other investigators. Because the left visual field projects to the right hemisphere, and vice versa, problems can be presented to such a patient in just one visual hemifield and thus are processed by one side of the brain or the other. The split brain studies generally confirmed what the earlier clinical studies had suggested: language functioning is largely, although not exclusively, located in the left hemisphere (Gazzaniga, 1985).

This is an interesting but fairly gross observation. Even the nineteenth-century physicians drew finer conclusions. They noticed that patients with lesions in the anterior part of the left temporal lobe showed severe problems in the production of speech (Broca's aphasia), whereas patients with lesions in the posterior left temporal lobe exhibited problems in comprehension but were able to produce fluent, although not always sensible, speech (Wernicke's aphasia). Because the anterior lesions were located close to areas known to control motor movements and the posterior lesions were located near areas associated with auditory perception, Wernicke interpreted the two types of aphasia as evidence for separate brain systems associated with the production and comprehension of language.

Modern analyses (e.g., Zurif, 1990) come to quite a different conclusion. The modern view is that Broca's aphasia is characterized by loss of grammatical function, which then disrupts speech production because the appropriate words are not available for insertion into the output string at the right time. (Wernicke's aphasia is less studied, and less well understood, but it is clear that patients with posterior lesions show more sensitivity to grammar than patients with anterior lesions.) The modern conclusion is based on two additional sources of evidence. The first is that Broca's aphasics, who are diagnosed by their production difficulties, have difficulty comprehending sentences when the interpretation depends upon syntactic analysis. For instance, Broca's aphasics, but not Wernicke's aphasics, are unable to determine who did what to whom upon hearing a sentence such as "The girl whom the boy is pushing is tall." On the other hand, Broca's aphasics can comprehend "The apple that the boy is eating is red," where semantic analysis permits only one possible interpretation.

The recent experiments on sentence comprehension would certainly be understood by the nineteenth-century physicians, who might have had a fleeting moment of regret that they did not think of doing these studies themselves! A second source of evidence for grammatical difficulties that Zurif cites would be more foreign to their way of thinking, because it is based on performance on a nonlinguistic task whose interpretation depends upon a theoretical analysis of language itself. To explain it, a brief excursion into linguistics is needed.

Modern linguists distinguish between open and closed classes of words. An open class is one that can be added to as the need arises, without making any fundamental change in the language itself. For instance, nouns are an open class that we can add to as the need arises. Nineteenth-century English had no word for television. Closed class words serve grammatical functions. Examples are the articles and prepositions. Closed class words appear to function as units that are more difficult to analyze into components than open class words are. If people without brain injury are asked to cross out target letters in a printed text they are more likely to miss letters in closed than in open class words. To illustrate, if *t* is the target letter you would expect an intact person to be more likely to miss the *t* in *the* than the *t* in *toe*. Wernicke's aphasia patients make similar errors, but Broca's aphasics do not. Zurif (1990, pp. 188–190) argues that this discrepancy demonstrates that damage to the anterior left temporal lobe damages a process that involves rapid, automated access to key grammatical terms and that this process is part of normal language processing.

Note what has happened here. The early observations and their interpretation depend only upon a sort of folk psychology view of language that distinguishes between reception and production. The distinction between understanding based on syntactical and semantic processing, and even more the notion of closed class words as being psychologically different from nouns, is based upon a sophisticated view of how language works as a communication system quite apart from the brain processes that make it work. In fact, the motivation for doing both the sentence comprehension and the closed class perception studies depended upon the development of a computational-level view of what a language is and how one can be analyzed.

Computational Models of Language

Most of today's research on the psychology of language, including but not limited to psycholinguistics, is either directly based on or has been tremendously influenced by the ideas of Noam Chomsky, a professor at the Massachusetts Institute of Technology. These ideas, introduced in the late 1950s and early 1960s (Chomsky, 1957, 1963), constituted one of the cornerstones of the cognitive revolution in the behavioral sciences.

Prior to Chomsky's work most studies of psycholinguistics were based on a more or less intuitive view of language, as the set of utterances spoken by people in a particular linguistic community; e.g., the set of all sentences that speakers of modern English (or Spanish or Urdu) speak. Chomsky proposed a new definition that shifted emphasis from a naturalistic study of the words and sentences that do appear in a language to the rules that define what words and sentences might appear. He defined a language as a set of surface terms, called the lexicon, that might appear in a sentence, and a set of rules, that define how words must be arranged to form a proper sentence.

Consider the trivial "language" L1, consisting of the following sentences:

(2) L1 = {"Lions attack elephants," "Elephants attack lions", "Lions scare elephants," "Elephants scare lions"}.

The sentences in this language can be generated by the following set of *rewriting rules*. First, define the set of *nonterminal symbols,*

(3) V = {S, N, V, NP, VP}

and the set *T* of terminal symbols,

(4) T = {elephants, lions, attack, scare}.

The terminal symbols, loosely the words in the lexicon, are the terms that appear in utterances. These are the hooks that tie the language to external, nonlinguistic reality. A lion, as a concept, is not a linguistic term. The nonterminal symbols are grammatical categories, here a sentence, noun phrase, verb phrase, noun, and verb. The special term, *S* ("sentence"), called the *head symbol,* refers to the set of all possible utterances in the language. Jointly, the symbols are called the *lexicon* of a language.

The lexicon is augmented by a finite set of rules, called the *grammar* of a language. A grammar for L1 is

(5) S → NP VP

NP → N

VP → V NP

N → {elephants, lions}

V → {attack, scare},

where the arrow means, "May be rewritten as," and the notation $x →$ {$a, b, \ldots$} indicates that the symbol on the left hand side of the arrow may be rewritten as any member of the set of symbols on the right. A string of terminal symbols is said to be a well-formed expression in L1 if the string can be generated by successively applying the rewriting rules of R1, starting at *S* and continuing until the target string is generated. The sentences in (2) can be generated using the categories of (3) and rules of (5). So can sentences of the form "Elephants attack elephants," where the first and second occurrences of an *N* term are identical.

To generalize the example, according to Chomsky's definition a language is defined by lexicon consisting of a finite set of terminal and nonterminal symbols, one of which must be the head symbol, *S*, and a finite set of rewriting rules. On the surface, a language may appear to be the set of sentences it contains, but the real definition is in the grammar and the lexicon, i.e., in the syntactic part of the language.

One of the reasons that Chomsky argued for the primacy of syntax is that the grammar of a language is finite, and hence knowable, whereas the set of sentences in a language is infinite, and hence not knowable. For instance, English (and all other natural languages) permit embedded sentences, as in "The rat the cat scared ate the cheese." This lets us say, "The rat the cat the dog chased scared ate the cheese" and ad infinitum. Whether or not we would actually say or comprehend such a sentence is not a linguistic issue, although it is an interesting psychological one. The linguistic point is that native speakers regularly and easily distinguish grammatical and ungrammatical sentences, even though they have never heard them.

To back up a little, the example illustrates an algorithm for generating and analyzing sentences. The argument is that native speakers of a natural language incorporate in their minds rules analogous to, but much more complicated than, the rules in the example. The basic point, though, is simple. There is a strong distinction between syntactic rules, which determine the structure of an utterance, and semantic rules, which connect the terms in the utterances to the world outside the language. Given this analysis, the distinction between open and closed word classes begins to make more sense. Open word classes contain semantic references to the external world. A functional language has to allow for open references in order to deal with new things. On the other hand, the set of words used solely to mark linguistic structures must be closed because adding a new function word would require a change in the grammatical rules of the language. Such changes do occur, and languages do change their function words, but this is a much slower process than the change in topics indicated by changes in nonfunction words. Natural language can be modified to talk about new things, without having to modify the structure of the language itself.

In the computational terms we used earlier, Chomsky and most modern linguists argue that the human mind, as a computing device, contains separate modules for carrying out syntactic and semantic analyses. This computational assumption makes the agrammatical speech of Broca's aphasia more sensible. Evidently, injury to the posterior temporal lobe can damage the syntactical analysis module. The same distinction has also motivated a much more recent, but clearly related finding. Electroencephalography (EEG) is a technique for recording the electrical activity in the brain using electrodes placed on the scalp. EEG analyses have shown that the brain produces one type of electrical pattern (Event-Related Potential, ERP) when a person hears a semantically anomalous sentence, such as "The senator lectured the pudding" and another type of ERP signal when the listener hears a syntactically anomalous sentence, such as "The senator lectured the boringly" (Osterhout & Holcomb, 1992). A computational-level theory of language was required in order to make sense of known neuroscience data (the pattern of deficit in Broca's aphasia) and to motivate further neuroscientific studies of language, such as the EEG research.

Language users do not just judge whether a string of words is well formed; they actually (although usually not consciously) determine interword relations. How else would we be able to distinguish between "John loves Mary" and "Mary loves John"? At least at present, there is little chance that we could study how this is done at the level of brain processes. However, these sorts of questions can be examined at the computational level. An example is uncovering the strategies that are used to parse and comprehend sentences.

Consider a person reading the sentence

(6) Sally found out the answer to the difficult physics problem was in the book.

The initial part of this sentence, "Sally found out the answer to the difficult physics problem," is itself a well-formed sentence with *Sally* as the subject, *found out* as the verb, and *answer* as the object. In the full sentence the embedded sentence, the "answer to the difficult physics problem was in the book," replaces "answer to the difficult physics problem" in the object position. How do readers or listeners distinguish between these options?

Garrett (1990) describes three possibilities. One is that the comprehender waits until the sentence is completed and then conducts a full analysis of his or her memory of what was said. This method is economical in information-processing terms but has the disadvantage of imposing a burden on short-term memory. A second possibility is that the most likely syntactical structure is constructed, on a word-by-word basis. In this case recomputation is required if and only if unanticipated disambiguating information is developed. In example 6 the initial analysis would identify *answer* as the object of the verb, and recomputation would be required upon reading the second verb (*was*), which indicates a more complex structure. This method would be an economical strategy because sentences such as (6) are somewhat unusual. Most of the time a noun phrase immediately following a verb is the object of the verb. Finally, it is possible that when readers encounter the noun phrase *the answer* they initially begin constructing both syntactical analyses, in parallel. Erroneous or unlikely constructions are dropped when disambiguating information is encountered (the *was* in example 6) or when short-term memory is overloaded.

McDonald, Just, and Carpenter (1992) report a psychological study intended to discriminate among these alternatives. First, they classified participants as having low, medium, or high memory spans for reading, on the basis of a previously developed test of a person's ability to hold words in short-term memory while continuing to read or hear a sentence. The participants then read sentences in which the first section was ambiguous and the ambiguity was resolved in a later section. An example is

(7)   The experienced soldiers warned about the dangers conducted the midnight raid.

In this sentence "The experienced soldiers warned" could mean either that the experienced soldiers warned someone or that the experienced soldiers were themselves warned, by some unspecified person. The phrase cannot be disambiguated until the second verb, *conducted*, is encountered. McDonald et al. found that people with high memory spans read the disambiguating part (*conducted the midnight raid*) relatively slowly and were likely to comprehend the sentence correctly. People with low memory span did not slow down while reading the disambiguating information and showed poor sentence comprehension. The authors concluded that readers with high memory span considered both interpretations of *soldiers warned* and then selected the correct one after reading the rest of the sentence, whereas the low memory-span readers, who did not have sufficient memory capacity to carry forward two interpretations, considered only one, usually assuming that *soldiers warned* meant that the soldiers did the warning. Upon encountering the disambiguating information, the low memory-span readers did not realize that it could be used to disambiguate the earlier phrase, because at that point they were unaware that an ambiguity had occurred. Therefore they seem to have ignored the information in the final phrase and, as a result, to have made quite a few errors in comprehension.

I do not want to put the McDonald, Just, and Carpenter study forward as the final word on this topic. As Garrett (1990) points out, there are many models of sentence processing. Deciding between the evidence for them would take us too far afield. What we are more concerned with is the logic of the study. McDonald et al.'s work was defined purely at the computational level. Furthermore, the laboratory procedures they used did not mirror the normal way in which discourse occurs. They used the rapid single visual presentation (RSVP) procedure for presenting text, in which the words in a sentence are presented one at a time, on a computer screen. Disconnected sentences were presented, rather than coherent text. The dependent variables that were recorded, the time to read a word and the percentage of sentences correctly interpreted, are computational rather than biological variables. Finally, the concept of memory span is clearly a system architecture concept. McDonald et al. made no attempt to tie memory span while reading to any particular brain region or process. Instead they treated memory span as a functional capacity of the mind.

The vast majority of studies in psycholinguistics, and for that matter in cognitive psychology in general, are defined at the computational level. A computational model of the mind is defined, and an experimental paradigm is developed to evaluate that model. If the model accurately describes a system that exists in the human mind, orderly relationships will be found, as occurred for McDonald et al. Cognitive psychologists, including myself, believe that studies of this sort make a valuable contribution to our understanding of human cognition, even if the studies do depend upon observations of how people behave in an unnatural laboratory setting, and even if no attempt is made to tie the observations to brain processes.

Language Use at the Representational Level

Representational models deal with "the real world," the content of what people are thinking about rather than the brain processes or computational procedures they use to do the thinking. To illustrate, I will examine a bit of recent history.

In 1989 the Indian author Salman Rushdie published a novel called *The Satanic Verses,* an allegorical study of Islamic traditions. One passage in the novel infuriated Islamic clerics, to the point that the Ayatollah Ruholla Khomeini, then probably the most prominent Islamic theologian in the world,[9] urged Muslims to kill Rushdie. The Ayatollah meant his threat to be taken literally, and it was. Rushdie went into hiding and as of this writing (March, 1998) he remains there, making only a very few public appearances. His books are banned in many Islamic countries, and some distributors of *The Satanic Verses* have been killed.

What did Rushdie say that raised such an uproar? The offending passage is an interchange between one of the novelist's protagonists, who represents the prophet Mohammed, and the angel Gabriel. In the novel Gabriel asserts that the entire Koran was dictated by God (Allah), including a section that is known as the Satanic verses. According to Islamic tradition, these verses, which are not part of the Koran, were actually dictated by Satan, who fooled Mohammed. Subsequently, Gabriel upbraided Mohammed and gave him the true word of Allah, which is now in the Koran. The Ayatollah and other fundamentalists concluded that Rushdie had questioned the authenticity of the Koran, which is an act of blasphemy (Pipes, 1990). To a non-Islamic, however, the book is merely an allegory and the offending passages well within the bounds of normal literary license.

Similar differences in reactions to the written word can occur in the West. When commenting on the Rushdie incident, former U.S. president Jimmy Carter observed that *The Life of Brian,* a 1970s movie, was deeply offensive to sincere Christians (including President Carter) because it was a crude and unsympathetic spoof of the life of Jesus. The same movie had something of a cult following among some intellectuals, who decried attempts to drive it out of theaters in the United States.

The different reactions people have to *The Satanic Verses* and *The Life of Brian* cannot be understood on linguistic grounds alone. A person's reaction to these accounts depends on the ideas represented in the text, not their linguistic form, and the way in which these ideas fit into a person's belief system. The psychological action, if you will, is neither at the brain process or computational level of thought. The interesting relationships are at the representational level.

No one would argue this point. Clearly, what a person makes of a text depends on what that person believes. But can we say anything more general? It turns out that we can but that to do so we must turn from a purely representational discussion to a discussion at the computational level. To illustrate, it will be a good idea to move away from such highly charged situations as the Salman Rushdie case and to concentrate on some more prosaic examples of language comprehension.

Spillich, Vesonder, Chiesi, and Voss (1979) had people listen to a "radio broadcast" of a fictitious baseball game. The listeners then answered questions about the broadcast. Spillich et al. found that people who were familiar with baseball (fans) remembered game-relevant events, such as the number of men on base when a particular play was made. People who were not baseball fans remembered as much information as the fans did, but they did not remember as much game-relevant information and they remembered more game-irrelevant statements, such as a comment about the weather. The fans focused their attention on what they thought was important, whereas the nonfans did not have any way to focus attention.

Lawrence (1986) looked at comprehension in a different setting. She studied the decisions made by sentencing magistrates in Australian courts. (These magistrates hear minor criminal cases, roughly equivalent to the American concept of a misdemeanor.) Williams found that the magistrates would first make a determination of the type of case in front of them in somewhat nonlegal terms. For instance, in shoplifting cases they would focus on whether the perpetrator was best described as simply greedy; acting in order to fulfill a real need, such as obtaining food for children; or behaving compulsively, without any need for the goods taken. This determination was made from a number of cues, such as the type of goods taken and the person's apparent need for these goods. Stealing jewelry would be seen as an indication of greediness, food as an indication of need, and items of little value as an indication of confusion. Once magistrates had determined the type of cases they (thought they) were dealing with they proceeded to develop appropriate sentences, which could vary from fines to references to social welfare agencies.

This type of behavior exhibited by the fans and the magistrates, which has been observed in many situations, is usually explained by recourse to the concept of a schema. A schema is seen as a sort of "fill-in-the-blanks" form that is maintained in the mind and that is called up to handle particular situations. A baseball schema, for instance, directs one's attention to events that are appropriate for a baseball game. A greedy shoplifter schema directs a magistrate's attention to some facts of a shoplifting case and not others. According to schema theory, most understanding of text involves recognizing what schema is appropriate and then fitting the text to the schema. In order to understand how a person is going to react to a text, you have to know what schema they have and the situations in which they believe each schema is appropriate.

Although not all people who study comprehension utilize the concept of a schema, all agree that texts are interpreted in the light of prior knowledge. Walter Kintsch's (1988, 1994; van Dijk & Kintsch, 1983) work on text comprehension provides a good example of this sort of reasoning. Kintsch argues for two separate stages in text understanding. In the first stage, the sentences in a text are translated into logical propositions and the logical propositions are knit together to form a model of the text. The text model is then formed into a situation model, which represents the comprehender's understanding of what is going on. The idea can be grasped by the following example, which is mine rather than Kintsch's but has been chosen to illustrate his ideas.

The text is an adaptation of an "Uncle Remus" children's story. The bear and the fox have just caught Brer Rabbit, who says,

(8)   Please, please, don't throw me in the briar patch.

Kintsch assumes that an unspecified sentence processor can translate this sentence into a mental representation consisting of logical propositions. If the propositions are written in the form "Verb (Subject, Object, Indirect Object)," sentence 8 becomes

(9)   Request (Rabbit, Not (throw (Bear, Rabbit, in briar patch)), Bear).

Previous sentence analyses will have produced a text representation that might look like this:

(10)   Cause (Catch (Bear, Rabbit), Frighten (Rabbit))

The rabbit is frightened because the bear caught him. The new sentence augments this by saying that because the rabbit is frightened, he asks not to be thrown into the briar patch,

(11)   Cause (Frighten (Rabbit), Request (Rabbit, Not (throw (Bear, Rabbit, in briar patch)) Bear)).

This interpretation is consistent with what has been said in the text. In fact, though, a person experienced at listening to Uncle Remus stories will know that the rabbit lives in the briar patch and that the bear is not exactly a rocket scientist. Combining the expert knowledge with the knowledge presented in the text produces a situational model that is quite different from (11). It is

(12)   Cause ((Desire (Rabbit, escape)) AND (Believe (Rabbit, stupid (Bear))) AND (Wish (Bear, harm (Rabbit))), Request (Rabbit, Not (throw (Bear, Rabbit, in briar patch)), Bear)).

The rabbit requests not to be thrown into the briar patch because he believes that the bear wishes him harm and that the bear is stupid enough to think that he (the rabbit) will be harmed by being thrown into the briar patch.

Kintsch has developed these ideas into an elaborate description of how situational models can be built up from texts. Once again, it would not be appropriate to go into the details here. What is important is the relation between Kintsch's work and representational-level models. Kintsch's theory of comprehension is a computational-level explanation that is intended to apply to a number of different situations at the representational level. For instance, in various applications he has considered how people understand fables, such as the preceding one, newspapers and elementary science texts. His model provides a common psychological analysis, at the computational level, for situations that from the viewpoint of an anthropologist are quite different from each other at the representational level.

Kintsch's work also illustrates the point made earlier about studying manageable systems. Kintsch was interested in how the information presented in individual sentences is incorporated into a person's understanding of a text. He acknowledges that at a lower (but still computational) level, text understanding must depend on lexical and sentence comprehension processes, but he does not depend upon their details for his analyses. Instead, he simply assumes that people somehow make the transition from the surface form of sentences to logical propositions. He then goes on to explain how we fit together separate logical propositions in order to develop a coherent representation of what a text really means.

A Summary of the Three Levels of Cognitive Theories

Social and behavioral scientists are often accused of simply proving the obvious. At other times they are accused of obscuring the obvious. Suppose that some cognitive psychologists were attending a cocktail party, and were asked to explain what they do. What would be the reaction to cognitive psychologists who worked at the neuroscience, computational, or representational levels of explanation?

The cognitive neuroscientist would have little trouble commanding respect. When a cognitive neuroscientist says that he or she is trying to find out where in the brain we analyze sentences, most people at a cocktail party will accept this as a reasonable goal. Studies that relate behavior to biological processes are "normal science" in the layperson's eyes. Although the lay public may not follow the technical details, the worthiness of the pursuit will not be challenged. Representational-level studies seem to smack more of social science or education. If a social scientist at a cocktail party says that he or she is studying the relation between, say, religious beliefs and attitudes toward social welfare programs, the other people at the cocktail party will understand what has been said, although they may question whether or not the answer isn't obvious. People think that their personal knowledge gives them some expertise at the representational level, which it may, but they acknowledge that they have very little idea of the internal processes of their brains.

Investigators whose work depends solely on computational-level concepts are more likely to be seen as arcane. It seems that theory is being piled on theory, without any tie to either biological concepts or to the realities of thinking in the world. Instead, the professors seem to be making up a world of laboratory-bound thought and then showing that they can find regularities of thinking within this world. This may be so, but who cares?

My own answer should be clear by now. Making a direct link between the neurosciences and representational-level thought would require linking brain processes to the content of thought, rather than to computationally defined acts of thinking. There is no prospect of doing this at the present moment, simply because we do not have the technology. I am not sure that even if we did have the technology, we could ever understand the results. The explanation that links the events in a lawyer's brain to the convolutions of a lawyer's argument might be so complex that scientists, who are human beings, could not understand it. Therefore we need computational theories, simply so that we can manage the data.

Arguments against the Three-Level Approach to Cognition

The argument for a three-level approach to cognition is not universally accepted. Not surprisingly, the strongest objections are directed at the computational level. Biological structures and thoughts about concrete objects are real; they make contact with the external world. The computational level of mental action is something that cognitive psychologists have made up. Is it really needed? Although I think it is, the arguments that it is not are worth considering.

Replacing Computational Concepts with Neuroscience Concepts
Probably the most publicized argument against the use of computational-level models comes from those interested in cognitive neurosciences. Once again we may quote Crick. According to him, the "astonishing

hypothesis" is that consciousness and all the thinking that goes with it are the product of neurons, and therefore the primary business of the scientific study of thought has to be the reduction of cognitive behavior to neurology. He says, "One may conclude, then, that to understand the various forms of consciousness we first need to know their neural correlates" (Crick, 1994, p. 10).

Crick is not opposed to studies of computational-level concepts of cognition when they are linked to physiological investigations. Indeed, he quotes with approval several such studies. It does seem reasonable to conclude that Crick would assign very low priority to studies of higher-order thinking, such as problem solving in chess and algebra, that are undoubtedly produced by brain action, but by such a complicated path that we cannot hope to trace it out at any time in the near future. Consistent with this view, Crick spends most of the rest of his book "explaining consciousness" by concentrating on studies of the neurological processes and anatomical structures involved in visual perception, on the grounds that this is one of the few situations where we have enough knowledge of the underlying biology to have a chance of understanding how we become aware of something. The message that cognitive psychology should stand on the neurosciences is clear, indeed.

The problem with this approach is that studies at the biological level cannot be interpreted without some sort of theory of cognition at the information-processing level. I do not think Crick would object to this statement, as long as the tie to the neurosciences is clear. What is further from his thinking is the argument that we need purely computational-level concepts because we simply could not make the leap from neurosciences to representational-level thinking. There is a counterargument to to this idea.

Advocates of computational-level models are careful to dissociate themselves from the idea that the computer, as a physical device, is being used as a model for the brain. Nevertheless, there is no doubt that the design of computers has provided a metaphor for many of the cognitive models studied since the 1950s. From time to time there have been suggestions that rather than use a computing metaphor psychologists should try to develop computational models using primitive elements that have some biological justification. This idea was actually put forward before the cognitive revolution began, when McCulloch and Pitts (1943) showed that the logic circuits required in computing machines could be constructed from elements that behaved like idealized neurons. The idea of using a network of neuronlike elements to mimic human perceptions and cognition was elaborated upon by a number of authors during the 1950s and 1960s, but they were clearly not in the mainstream of the 1950 to 1960 cognitive revolution. In the 1980s and 1990s the idea resurfaced, under the rubric *connectionism*. Some people (e.g., Rumelhart, 1989) argue that connectionism will provide the language that can tie molecular neuroscience findings about brain mechanisms to molar computational models of high-level thinking.

The basic idea of connectionism is that thinking is to be mimicked by computations in a network of neuronlike elements. Figure 1.2 shows one such element: a threshold detector. The threshold detector receives multiple inputs from other elements, weights them, and transmits a signal to other threshold detector units if the weighted sum of the inputs exceeds the unit's threshold level. Figure 1.3 shows a network of such elements that can compute the function Exclusive Or (XOR). This example is important because it can be shown that any logical function can be computed by combining the logical function NOT and XOR. Since networks can compute NOT and XOR, there must exist neural-like networks for all the computable functions.

What a network computes will be a function of the number of nodes and the weights that establish the strength of connections between each pair of nodes. One of the more interesting ideas of connectionism is the

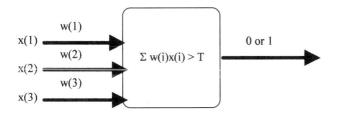

Figure 1.2
A threshold detection unit. The unit receives input [$x(i) = 1$ or 0] from the elements on the left and computes a weighted sum. The unit outputs a 1 if the weighted sum exceeds a threshold, f. The output is 0 otherwise.

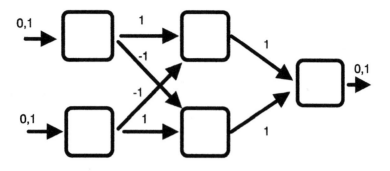

All units are linear units with a threshold of zero

Figure 1.3
A network of threshold detection elements (with threshold 0) that can compute
the logical function Exclusive Or. The network consists of two input units, two
interior (hidden) units, and an output unit. The output unit will register a 1 if
and only if one, but not both, of the input units are set to 1. All units are linear
units with a threshold of zero.

notion of a trainable network. A trainable network is constructed by assigning the initial weights arbitrarily. An example stimulus is then shown
to the network, and its response recorded. If the desired response is obtained, nothing is done. If the desired response is not obtained, a learning
algorithm is applied to adjust the weights in a manner that makes it
more likely that the desired response will be obtained if the stimulus is
re-presented. This procedure can be repeated over and over again until
the desired level of performance is obtained. When networks are used
to simulate human performance, the "desired level" is determined by a
comparison to human performance. For instance, in principle it would
be possible to train a network to agree with a person's classification of
photographs of scenes as being "attractive" or "unattractive." Once this
was done, you could argue that the resulting network was a theory of
the person's aesthetic judgments. Furthermore, if you were willing to argue that the individual nodes in the network were really analogous to
neurons, and that the learning mechanism was biologically justifiable,
you could claim that higher-order perception had been derived from principles of neuroscience.

Proponents of connectionist approaches believe that some form of connectionism will provide the biologically justifiable language we need to link the neurosciences to models of higher-order cognition. Their enthusiasm cannot be gainsaid, for connectionist models have been developed to mimic very high levels of cognition indeed. For instance, Thagard (1990) has reported a connectionist model that mimicked the tactical decision making of a naval commander during a battle, and Holyoak and Thagard (1989) have reported connectionist simulations of analogical reasoning. At a lower level, connectionist models have been used to model the computations performed by specific neural systems or that are required for very simple learning situations (Hawkins & Bower, 1989). A certain amount of enthusiasm for the approach is clearly in order. On the optimistic side, connectionism might provide the language needed to connect low-order and high-order cognition.

Nevertheless, caution is also in order. Connectionist modeling has, at present, three drawbacks. In order to develop and understand these models, a good deal of mathematical sophistication is required. One observer (himself a well-known mathematical psychologist) has remarked that if connectionism becomes the dominant mode of theorizing, cognitive psychologists will have to take tensor calculus or early retirement (Hintzman, 1990). This is not an idle threat. Since the 1970s, mathematical training has dropped out of many graduate psychology programs, and if connectionism becomes the dominant mode for thinking about thinking, it is entirely possible that conventional psychologists will have to yield the field to cognitive neuroscientists. Although this change might create an employment problem for psychologists, it would not necessarily impede our development of better theories of thought.

Two related problems are more serious. When connectionist models are used to simulate "lower-order" thinking, such as classical conditioning in animals, the connection between the models and realistic neuroscience is fairly direct. The connection becomes more tenuous when the models are applied to higher-order thought, such as analogical reasoning or human memory. For instance, a class of connectionist models known as Hopfield networks can simulate some interesting phenomenon associated with the formation of abstractions, such as the development of a general concept of *dog* given experience with specific examples of dogs.

Hopfield networks require symmetric connections between elements, so if element *A* feeds into element *B*, element *B* feeds back into element *A* (Hertz, Krogh, & Palmer, 1991). Crick (1994) points out that the nervous system simply is not built that way. This contradiction is not necessarily damning. To return to a point made earlier, all science involves the construction and study of ideal systems that do not exactly mirror the part of the world we are trying to understand. We have to remember that connectionist networks bear a loose resemblance to a biological network and that we are not sure how tight the resemblance must be to produce a realistic model of thought.

Finally, connectionist networks do provide one truly unique puzzle for those interested in the logic of scientific explanations. Suppose that a learning procedure is used to construct a connectionist network that mimics some interesting human behavior, such as scene classification. If the network contains more than about twenty elements, the connections may be so convoluted that a human, looking at the network, cannot tell how it computes whatever function it is computing. The theorist then faces a dilemma. Because the network mimics human behavior, the theorist can be sure that the right function is being computed. Because the theorist understands the learning algorithm used to construct the network, the theorist understands how the network came to be. However, the theorist does not know how the network computes whatever it is computing. Has this exercise in modeling increased our understanding of the original human behavior?

The Situated Cognition Objection to the Three-Level View

Having stated the case for making psychology derivative of the neurosciences, let us turn the argument around. Is it possible to study cognition solely by studying thought at the representational level? A more extensive quote from Simon sets the stage:

I have discussed the organization of the mind without saying anything about the structure of the brain. . . .

The main reason for this disembodiment of mind is of course the thesis that I have just been discussing. The difference between the hardware of a computer and the "hardware" of the brain has not prevented computers from simulating a wide spectrum of kinds of human thinking . . . just because both computer and brain, when engaged in thought, are adaptive systems that seek to mold themselves to the shape of the task environment. (Simon, 1981, p. 97)

This passage contains three important ideas. The first is that the mind can be studied without studying the brain, which is precisely the opposite conclusion that Crick reached. The second is that computer simulation has produced adequate models of the mind. This claim is empirical and has to be examined on a case-by-case basis. The third, which is our immediate concern, is that the reason different physical devices can be cognitive models of each other is that they must adapt to similar environments.

As has been noted earlier, Simon has argued that the human mind is, at the information-processing level, a rather simple device and that its apparent complexity is produced by the complexity of its environment. It follows from this argument that in order to reveal the general computational processes the mind uses, you ought to study relatively simple cognitive situations that will reveal those processes. In general, that is what cognitive psychologists have done. They have developed a large number of paradigms that are supposed to isolate pure cases of cognitive actions, and then they have performed laboratory studies to develop laws of behavior in those paradigms. The hope is that the results will generalize to situations outside the laboratory. This tradition dates back to Hermann Ebbinghaus's development of nonsense syllable learning in the nineteenth century and has since led to literally thousands of studies of cognition in controlled environments.

Some people think this emphasis on pure principles of thought throws the baby out with the bathwater. In the mid-1980s a number of scholars developed a different approach, called the study of *situated action*. There seem to have been multiple sources for the development of the situated action approach to cognition. Frequent citations are made to earlier work by J. J. Gibson (1950, 1979), who argued that perception was guided by direct responses to complex properties in the visual world, rather than being constructed from the sensation of elementary physical properties of the light falling on the retina. To me, though, the analogies seem strained, and I must admit that I find some of Gibson's own comments opaque. One thing is clear, though. In their everyday lives people display reasoning abilities that go well beyond what one would expect of them, based upon formal examinations of these same abilities. Greeno (1989) offers an elegant example. He described a situation in which a member of a weight watchers' group was told that the normal recipe for a dessert calls for 3/4 pound of cottage cheese but that the weight watcher recipe calls for 2/3 of the normal recipe's amount. How much cheese is required? It is somewhat discouraging, but most adults with high school educations have considerable difficulty with this sort of problem, when it is posed as one in fractional arithmetic. The weight watcher simply avoided arithmetic. She put a pound of cottage cheese on the table, formed it into a disk, cut the disk into quarters, separated one-quarter out so that three-quarters remained, and then took two of the remaining quarters. This is only one of many examples that can be offered to show that people who "can't do math" formally are quite capable of developing localized computing methods that work in the store and on the job (Lave, 1988; Scribner, 1984).

The advocates of situated cognition argue that these examples show that most thinking depends on specialized responses to environmental demands. The situationist claims that people make opportunistic use of any locally available computing aids, such as the way the weight watcher used a disk of cheese to avoid applying abstract arithmetical procedures. What does this mean for a theory of cognition?

Advocates of situated cognition display little concern for biological issues because they regard the (normal) human brain as being sufficiently malleable to deal with any cultural situation that exists. Here they have a point: if humans cannot do a task then human cultures do not evolve to require it. However, they go further by arguing that cognition is based on a collection of special problem-solving methods that are defined at the representational level, rather than on the translation of particular situations into instantiations of general classes of problems and then applying problem-solving rules associated with the general class. Of course, as Greeno clearly points out, it is still true that the brain represents every situation and that thinking is a manipulation of the symbolic representation inside the head. Such manipulations are limited by the information-processing characteristics of the brain, but, as an (often unstated) assumption, advocates of situated cognition believe that this is not a tight limitation. In the situated cognition view the brain provides tools for the mind, such as pattern recognition and short-term memory capacities, but it does not provide instructions for using them. Instead people, through experience, develop instructions for using their mental tools to solve specific problems.

It follows that if you want to study thinking at the representational level you must embark on an anthropological-educational program, developing microtheories of cognition in a particular situation. The idea that chess playing can play a role in cognitive psychology analogous to the role of fruit flies in genetics is rejected; if you study chess, you learn how people play chess. Going further, advocates of situated cognition believe that it is futile to search for any experimental paradigm that could play the role of *Drosophila*. Cognition is not like genetics, so cognitive psychologists cannot have fruit flies.

This argument has an important practical consequence. If advocates of situated cognition are correct, general thinking skills do not exist. Pushing this position to its extreme would have profound consequences for the educational establishment. Society's commitment to school-based education assumes the closely related premises that general-thinking skills can be taught out of the context in which they are to be used and that information acquired in school contexts will be translated to applications outside the schools. To the extent that cognition must be situated, learning to think cannot be so dissociated from practice.

What Might Future Theories Look Like?

Cognitive psychologists seem to be torn between the views of people such as Crick, who would replace them with neuroscientists, and those such as Greeno, who would replace them with cognitive anthropologists. I would like to argue for an intermediate position.

In discussing the role of information-processing theories of thought it is necessary to distinguish between architectural-level theories and computational-level theories. Architectural-level theories deal with static processes of the mind, such as the functional capacities of immediate and long-term memory. I have argued earlier that this sort of theory is required in order to guide neuroscientific investigations. Therefore, this work has to be continued, but it is only sensible to link it closely to the neurosciences.

The issues posed by studies intended to reveal the algorithms of thought are more difficult to resolve. Newell (1980) is undoubtedly correct in saying that the mind is a physical symbol system, and it is appropriate to ask what programs this physical symbol system uses. How general these programs are is an empirical question. Early in the cognitive revolution, Newell and Simon (1972) proposed a "general problem-solving" program as a model of human thought in many different areas. This approach may have been overly optimistic. On the other hand, I do not think that we have unique problem-solving procedures for every problem we encounter.

What are the implications for a research agenda? Perhaps, most important, I suggest a certain amount of healthy skepticism about the generality of findings based on studies of paradigms that have been designed to reveal the key operations of an entirely algorithmic theory. Board games such as chess and checkers, for instance, do represent pure cases of zero-sum games,[10] in which the consequence of any course of action could, in principle, be determined in advance if one had sufficient computing power. Therefore chess, checkers, and similar games provide interesting forums for investigating certain types of computational algorithms for decision making. The claim that such situations are representative of normal human decision making is, to put it mildly, questionable. Findings about how people play chess (or solve the "missionaries and cannibal" problem, or any of a number of other popular paradigms in cognitive psychology) cannot automatically be generalized to other situations.

On the other hand, when a connection can be made between a laboratory paradigm and ecologically valid applications of thought, then the laboratory paradigm is something to be treasured and studied. The connection must be made by verifiable, empirically supported theories of why the laboratory task mimics the extralaboratory situation. I am not inveighing against laboratory studies of thought. I am inveighing against the study of paradigms that are used solely because traditions (and powerful advocates) have encouraged their use in the past.

Theories of thought at different levels have to be connected to each other. The brain provides the biological capacities that determine the mind's cognitive architecture. The architecture, in turn, provides the functional tools that experience (and occasionally biology) organize into symbolic problem-solving programs, and these programs operate upon our representations of external problems. Each level of thought constrains the other; mental architecture has to have a biological basis, our problem-solving procedures cannot demand functional capacities that people do not have, and, somehow, our problem-solving procedures must be sufficient to solve the problems that people demonstrably do solve. So long as we keep these connections in mind, we can study human thought at any one of the three levels. When cognitive psychologists begin to develop theories and procedures for testing theories that operate at one level of thought while ignoring the level next door, the psychologists are on the road, not to disaster, but to trivialization.

Notes

This chapter is an abridgement of the introductory chapter in my forthcoming book, *Thoughts on Thought*.

1. In the experiment, people drank tonic water with a very small amount of gin floating on top of it. Thus they smelled the alcohol, although they ingested a tiny amount.

2. George et al. conclude that it is not.

3. Following mathematical developments in the 1980s, some mathematicians and philosophers have argued that certain systems are chaotic and that prediction of such systems is inherently impossible (Gleick, 1988). An extended discussion of this concept is far beyond the scope of this book, but I will state the idea and its problems briefly. The classic notion of a closed system is that the location of a system (defined by the simultaneous values of all of its variables) is a point on a fixed time line. Thus if we knew the location $X(t)$ at some time t we should be able to predict the location $X(t') = f(X, d)$ at some time $t' = t + d$ in the future. The problem is that in any actual situation the determination of $X(t)$ will contain some error, e, so if we record $X(t)$ when the system is actually in state $X(t) + d(t)$, $d(t)$ takes on value x with probability $p(x|e)$, where p is a probability function with dispersion parameter e. (For instance, if p were the normal function, e would be the standard deviation.) Virtually all measurement procedures in the sciences assume that the system's equation, $f(X, d)$, is such that the smaller the error in location is at time t the smaller the error of prediction is at time $t + d$. That is, the difference between $f(X, d)$ and $f(X + e, d)$ should be a monotonically increasing function of e. In the 1980s mathematicians discovered that there are some functions where this is not true. These are called chaotic functions. It is impossible to predict the future location of a chaotic system (one for which f is a chaotic function) if there is any error of measurement. Furthermore, we know, from Heisenberg's principle of uncertainty, that at the subatomic level it

is fundamentally impossible to measure location and velocity without error. Combining these facts, some observers have argued that a materialistic approach to the study of the mind is fundamentally impossible (Penrose, 1991). Echoing a comment by Churchill & Sejnowski (1992, p. 2), I know of no even moderately convincing evidence that this is a serious concern.

4. This estimate is based on the facts that there are 10^6 lines of code in the program and 10^{11} neurons in the brain. However, it is not clear how to compare individual neurons to individual lines of code in computer programs. In mathematical terms, neurons map vectors representing their input into a single binary digit, representing the state of electrical transmission along the axon. A line of computer code can represent a more complicated mathematical function. On the other hand, neurons also have a storage function, in the structure of the membrane, and the communication paths between neurons are much more complicated than data transmission channels in a computer.

5. The last example, incidentally, illustrates the difference between artificial intelligence and simulation of cognitive processes. An artificial intelligence robot should detect all potentially explosive situations; a psychological simulation robot should succeed or fail in those situations where humans succeed or fail.

6. There are noncomputable functions, but it is not clear that their existence has any relevance at all for psychology. A classic one is the so-called Cretan paradox. A Cretan approaches a Greek and says, "I am lying." Should the Greek believe the Cretan? An omniscient statement evaluator would map from the set C of all statements that the Cretan is capable of making into the set {1, 0}, where 1 means "the statement is true" and 0 means "the statement is false." Therefore the function is definable. It is not computable, because if the statement is false it is true, and if it is true it is false, so an algorithm would flip back and forth between evaluations of true and false. Occasionally it is claimed that because there are functions that humans can define but computers cannot solve, the attempt to model human thinking by machines is inherently faulted because the machines are limited to the computable functions. But aren't humans similarly limited?

7. Users of desktop computers may claim that my description cannot be right, because if you try to print while doing word processing or spreadsheet computing the machine appears to hang up during printing. "Hanging up" means that the computer is unresponsive to input from the keyboard. There is a resource conflict, but not between the central processor of the computer and the printer controller. In many of the systems marketed in the mid-1990s some of the same circuits were used by the printer controller, the module that read input from the keyboard, and the module that controlled the display unit.

How much a computing system can benefit from interleaving depends upon the nature of the computations and printing to be done. If the time required to compute a section report is exactly the same as the time required to print it, the interleaved algorithm will take a little more than half the time the serial algorithm does. Savings are reduced if there is an imbalance, with the effect that the computing unit is sometimes idle while printing is being conducted or vice versa.

8. The operation is performed in order to limit the spread of epileptic seizures from one side of the brain to the other.

9. The Ayatollah's writings had sparked the Iranian revolution. At the time the Ayatollah, though not part of the government, was the de facto ruler of Iran.

10. These are games in which wins for one player exactly mirror losses for the other.

References

Baars, B. J. (1986). *The cognitive revolution in psychology*. New York: Guilford.

Bechtel, W. (1988). *Philosophy of mind: An overview for cognitive science*. Hillsdale, NJ: Erlbaum.

Boorstin, D. J. (1983). *The discoverers*. New York: Random House.

Chomsky, N. (1957). *Syntactic structures*. The Hague, Netherlands: Mouton.

Chomsky, N. (1963). Formal properties of grammars. In R. D. Luce, R. R. Bush, & E. Galanter (Eds.), *Handbook of mathematical psychology* (Vol. 3, pp. 323–418). New York: Wiley. Churchland, P. S., & Sejnowski, T. J. (1992). The computational brain. Cambridge, MA. MIT Press.

Crick, F. (1994). *The astonishing hypothesis*. New York: Scribner.

Dennett, D. C. (1992). *Consciousness explained*. Boston: Little, Brown.

Descartes. R. (1970) Discourse on Method. In E. S. Haldane & G. R. T. Brown (Eds.), *The philosophical works of Descartes* (Vol. 1, pp. 178–291). Cambridge, England: Cambridge University Press. (Original work published 1637.)

Garrett, M. F. (1990). Sentence processing. In D. N. Osherson & H. Lasnik (Eds.), *Language: An invitation to cognitive science* (Vol. 1, pp. 135–175). Cambridge, MA: MIT Press.

Gazzaniga, M. (1985). *The social brain*. New York: Basic Books.

George, W. H., Gournic, S. J. & McAfee, M. P. (1988). Perceptions of postdrinking female sexuality: Effects of gender, beverage choice, and drink payment. *Journal of Applied Social Psychology, 15*, 1295–1317.

George, W. H., & Norris, J. (1991). Alcohol, Disinhibition, Sexual Arousal, and Deviant Sexual Behavior. *Alcohol Health & Research World, 15*, 133–138.

Gibson, J. J. (1950). *The perception of the visual world*. Boston: Houghton Mifflin.

Gibson, J. J. (1979). *The ecological approach to visual perception*. Boston: Houghton Mifflin.

Gleick, J. (1988). *Chaos: Making a new science*. New York: Penguin.

Greeno, J. G. (1989). Situations, models, and generative knowledge. In D. Klahr & K. Kotovsky (Eds.), *Complex information processing: The impact of Herbert A. Simon* (pp. 285–318). Hillsdale, NJ: Erlbaum.

Hawkins, R. D., & Bower, G. H. (1989). *Computational models of learning in simple neural systems.* San Diego, CA: Academic Press.

Hertz, J., Krogh, A. & Palmer, R. G. (1991). *Introduction to the theory of neural computation.* Redwood City, CA: Addison-Wesley.

Hintzman, D. L. (1990). Human learning and memory: Connections and dissociations. *Annual Review of Psychology, 41,* 109–139.

Holyoak, K. J., & Thagard, P. (1989). Analogical mapping by constraint satisfaction. *Cognitive Science, 13,* 295–355.

Hunt, E. *Thoughts on Thought.* Forthcoming.

Kintsch, W. (1988). The role of knowledge in discourse comprehension: A Constructionist-integration model. *Psychological Review, 95,* 163–182.

Kintsch, W. (1994). Text comprehension, memory, and learning. *American Psychologist, 49,* 294–303.

Krause, L. M. (1995). *The physics of Star Trek.* New York: Basic Books.

Lave, J. (1988). *Cognition in practice.* Cambridge, England: Cambridge University Press.

Lawrence, J. A. (1986). Expertise on the bench: Modeling magistrates' judicial decision making. In M. T. H. Chi, R. Glaser, & M. J. Farr (Eds.), *The nature of expertise* (pp. 229–259) Hillsdale, N.J.: L. Erlbaum Associates.

McCulloch, W. S., & Pitts, W. (1943). A logical calculus of ideas immanent in nervous action. *Bulletin of Mathematical Biophysics, 5,* 115–133.

McDonald, M. C., Just, M. A., & Carpenter, P. A. (1992). Working memory constraints on the processing of syntactic ambiguity. *Cognitive Psychology, 24,* 56–98.

Newell, A. (1980). Physical symbol systems. *Cognitive Science, 4,* 135–183.

Newell, A., & Simon, H. A. (1972). *Human Problem Solving.* Englewood Cliffs, NJ: Prentice-Hall.

Osterhout, L., & Holcomb P. J. (1992). Event-related brain potentials elicited by syntactic anomaly. *Journal of Memory and Language, 31,* 785–806.

Penrose, R. (1991). *The emperor's new mind: Concerning computers, minds, and the laws of physics.* Oxford, England: Oxford University Press.

Pipes, D. (1990). *The Rushdie affair: The novel, the Ayatollah, and the West.* New York: Carol.

Posner, M. I., & Raichle, M. E. (1994). *Images of mind.* San Francisco: Freeman.

Pylyshyn, Z. W. (1984). *Computation and cognition: Toward a foundation for cognitive science.* Cambridge, MA: MIT Press.

Pylyshyn, Z. W. (1989). Computing in Cognitive Science. In M. I. Posner (Ed.), *Foundations of cognitive science* (pp. 51–91). Cambridge, MA: MIT Press.

Rumelhart, D. E. (1989). The architecture of the mind: A connectionist approach. In M. I. Posner (Ed.), *Foundations of cognitive science* (pp. 133–160). Cambridge, MA: MIT Press.

Scribner, S. (1984). Studying working intelligence. In B. Rogoff & J. Lave (Eds.), *Everyday cognition: Its development in social context* (pp. 9–40). Cambridge, MA: Harvard University Press.

Simon, H. A. (1981). *The sciences of the artificial* (2nd ed.). Cambridge, MA: MIT Press.

Sperber, D., & Wilson, D. (1986). *Relevance: Communication and cognition.* London: Basil Blackwell.

Spillich, G. J., Vesonder, G. T., Chiesi, H. L., & Voss, J. L. (1979). Text processing of domain related information for individuals with high and low domain knowledge. *Journal of Verbal Learning and Verbal Behavior, 18,* 275–290.

Thagard, P. (1990). Explanatory coherence and naturalistic decision making. *Proceedings of the Twelfth Annual Conference of the Cognitive Science Society* (p. 1064). Hillsdale, NJ: Erlbaum.

Thompson, R. F. (1995). *The brain: A neuroscience primer.* New York: Freeman.

van Dijk, T. A., & Kintsch, W. (1983). *Strategies of discourse comprehension.* New York: Academic Press.

Zurif, E. B. (1990). Language and the brain. In D. N. Osherson & H. Lasnik (Eds.), *Language: An invitation to cognitive science.* Cambridge, MA: MIT Press.

2

A Dialectical Basis for Understanding the Study of Cognition

Robert J. Sternberg

How does a student of Spanish learn that *te amo* means "I love you" in Spanish? It depends, of course, on whom you ask. At one time, many psychologists might have said that it was by being rewarded, or reinforced, for making the right connection (and it is easy enough to think of a variety of ways in which such rewards might be forthcoming). Some psychologists would still take this point of view. Today, more psychologists might say that it is by having a propositional network that has in the past represented the idea of "I love you" in terms of those English words at a node within the propositional network and that now incorporates *te amo* into this node. Other contemporary psychologists might view the information as being encoded into a connection between two nodes, rather than at a node. And still other psychologists might reject all these explanations, arguing that we learn what the phrase means when we engage in the activity represented by the phrase.

The way we attempt to understand concepts (such as *te amo*), interpret contemporary ideas, and determine what seems reasonable (or unreasonable) about these concepts is shaped by our contemporary context of ideas (our Zeitgeist) and by the past ideas that have led up to the present ones. Today, we might consider many psychological ideas that were proposed recently to be outrageous, many other ideas proposed millennia ago to be reasonable, and still other intervening ideas to be surprising but appealing in some ways. This introductory chapter attempts to provide both the historical and the more contemporary context for many of the current perspectives in the study of the nature of cognition and to discuss how these perspectives have come and gone through a process of dialectical evolution (Kalmar & Sternberg, 1988; Sternberg, 1995, 1996).

First, I will discuss some of the ideas that were historical precursors to the study of cognition as a discipline. After discussing these early roots, I turn to some major schools of thought in the history of modern cognitive theory and research.

The Dialectical Progression of Ideas

Much of psychological thinking about cognition or anything proceeds in cycles, spiraling through the centuries of human thought. Philosophers, psychologists, and other people may propose and believe strongly in one view for a while (a thesis); then a contrasting view comes to light (an antithesis); and after a while, the most attractive or reasonable elements in each are melded into a new view (a synthesis), which then gains acceptance. This new integrated view then serves as the springboard (thesis) for a new contrasting view (antithesis) and eventually yet another melding (synthesis) of views. This process of evolving ideas through theses, antitheses, and syntheses was first termed a *dialectic* by Georg Hegel (1807/ 1931).

Dialectical progression depends on having a critical tradition that allows current beliefs (theses) to be challenged by alternative, contrasting, and sometimes even radically divergent views (antitheses), which may then lead to the origination of new ideas based on the old (syntheses). Western critical tradition is often traced back to the Greek philosopher Thales (624–545 B.C.), who invited his students to improve on his thinking, a stance not easy for any teacher to take. In addition, Thales did not hesitate to profit from knowledge accumulated in other parts of the world, far removed from Greece. Today, when we critique the ideas of our predecessors—proposing antitheses to their theses—we accept Thales' invitation to make progress by building upon or springing away from old ideas. Of course, even when we reject outdated ideas, those ideas still move us forward, serving as the valuable springboards for new ideas—the theses to our innovative antitheses.

A Brief Intellectual History: Western Antecedents of Psychology

Where and when did the study of cognition begin? Arguably, however far back our historical records may go, these documented accounts do not trace the earliest human efforts to understand the ways in which we humans think. In a sense, the mythical origins of psychology are in the ancient Greek myth of Psyche, whose name was synonymous with the vital "breath of life," the soul, believed to leave the body at death. The Greek term *thymos* was a motivational force generating feelings and actions, and to this day, the Greek root *thym-* is used as a combinative form to mean feelings and motivations. The Greek word *nous* (an organ responsible for the clear perception of truth) is an uncommon English word for the mind, particularly for highly reasoned or divinely reasoned mentation. Thus, according to the archaic Greeks, the body and the mind are somewhat distinct, although the mind, perhaps influenced by external causes, does cause activity of the body. The dialectic of mind versus body has its roots, at the very latest, in ancient Greece.

Ancient Classical Greece and Rome (600–300 B.C.)

The study of cognition traces its roots to two different approaches to human behavior: philosophy and physiology. In the contemporary world, these two fields seem dialectically opposed—philosophy using more armchair speculation and physiology using more systematic empirical investigation, often via laboratory science. In ancient Greece, however, the approaches of these two fields did not differ much. Both fields used the more philosophical approach of introspective contemplation and speculation as a means of seeking to understand the nature of the body and the mind—how each works and how they interact. In ancient Greece, many philosophers and physiologists believed that understanding could be reached without having or even pursuing supporting observations.

As the fields of philosophy and physiology diverged, they continued to influence the way in which psychology was to develop. Several strands intertwine as important philosophical precursors to the dialectics of modern psychological thought about cognition: whether the mind and body are separate entities; whether knowledge is innate or is acquired through experience; what contributes to learning and the acquisition of knowledge; and how speculation and theory development, on the one hand, and observation and data gathering, on the other, are used in seeking an understanding of the truth.

The ancient Greek physician (and philosopher) Hippocrates (ca. 460–377 B.C.), commonly known as the father of medicine, left his mark on the then overlapping fields of physiology and philosophy. What sharply distinguished him from archaic Greek philosophers and physicians was his unorthodox idea that disease was not a punishment sent by the gods. Hippocrates also used unorthodox methods—empirical observations—to study medicine. Contrary to the mode of the day, he studied animal anatomy and physiology directly, using both dissection and vivisection as means of study. Thus, he moved the study of living organisms toward the empirical. He was not entirely empirical in his methods, however, for he often assumed that what he had observed in animals could be generalized to apply to humans. He did not, however, confirm that the animal and human structures and functions were indeed parallel (Trager, 1992).

Hippocrates was particularly interested in discovering the source of the cognizing mind. He saw the mind as a separate, distinct entity that controls the body. This belief that the body and the mind (or "spirit," or "soul") are qualitatively different, *mind-body dualism,* is the view that the body is composed of physical substance but that the mind is not. Unlike his archaic Greek ancestors, Hippocrates proposed that the mind resides in the brain. Hippocrates induced this conclusion by observing that when either side of the head was injured, spasms were observed in the opposite side of the body (Robinson, 1995). Thus, with regard to the dialectic of the causes of thought and behavior, Hippocrates held that the agent of control is within the body, not in external forces, whether gods or demons. He also presaged modern psychology by speculating that physiological malfunctions rather than demons cause mental illness—again turning away from divine intervention as a cause of human behavior.

Two younger contemporaries of Hippocrates also considered the location of the mind to be within the body: Plato (ca. 428–348 B.C.) agreed that the mind resides within the brain; his student Aristotle (384–322 B.C.) located the mind within the heart. These two philosophers profoundly affected modern thinking about cognition. Of the many, far-reaching aspects of Platonic and Aristotelian philosophies, there are three key areas in which the dialectics between these two philosophers are particularly relevant to modern psychology: the relationship between the mind and the body, the use of observation versus introspection as a means for discovering truth, and the original source for our ideas.

Plato and Aristotle differed in their views of the mind and body because of their differing views regarding the nature of reality. According to Plato, reality resides not in the concrete objects of which we are aware through our body's senses, but in the abstract forms these objects represent. These abstract forms exist in a timeless dimension of pure abstract thought. Thus, reality is not inherent in any particular chair we see or touch, but in the eternal abstract idea of a chair that exists in our minds.

The objects our bodies perceive are only transient and imperfect copies of these true, pure, abstract forms. In fact, Plato's reason for locating the mind in the head was based on his introspective reflections on these abstract forms, rather than on any observations of physiology or behavior: the head must contain the seat of the mind because the head resembles a sphere—a perfect abstract form. Thus, to Plato, the body and mind are interactive and interdependent but are essentially different, with the mind superior to the body. We reach truth not via our senses but via our thoughts.

Aristotle, in contrast, believed that reality lies only in the concrete world of objects that our bodies sense. To Aristotle, Plato's abstract forms—such as the idea of a chair—are only derivations of concrete objects.

Aristotle's concrete orientation set the stage for *monism,* a philosophy regarding the nature of the body and mind, based on the belief that reality is a unified whole, existing in a single plane, rather than the two planes specified by dualism. According to monism, the mind (or soul) does not exist in its own right but merely as an illusory by-product of anatomical and physiological activity. Thus, the study of the mind and the study of the body are one and the same. We can understand the mind only by understanding the body.

Their differing views regarding the nature of reality led Plato and Aristotle also to disagree about how to investigate their ideas. Aristotle's view that reality is based on concrete objects led him to research methods based on the observation of concrete objects—and of actions on those objects. Thus, Aristotle (a naturalist and biologist, as well as a philosopher) was an *empiricist*, believing that we acquire knowledge via empirical evidence, obtained through experience and observation. The Aristotelian view is associated with empirical methods, by which we conduct research—in laboratories or in the field—on how people think and behave. Aristotelians tend to induce general principles or tendencies, based on observations of many specific instances of a phenomenon.

Plato's views lie at the opposite end of the dialectical continuum. For Plato, empirical methods have little merit because true reality lies in the abstract forms, not in the imperfect copies of reality observable in the world outside our minds. Observations of these imperfect, nonreal objects and actions would be irrelevant to the pursuit of truth. Instead, Plato suggested a *rationalist* approach, using philosophical analysis in order to understand the world and people's relations to it. For Plato, rationalism is consistent with his dualistic view of the nature of the body and mind: we find knowledge only through using the mind, through reason and speculation about the ideal world, not about the corporeal world of the body. Rationalists, therefore, tend to be much less drawn to inductive methods. Rather, they usually tend to deduce specific instances of a phenomenon, based on general principles.

Aristotle's view, then, leads directly to empirical psychological research, whereas Plato's view foreshadows theorizing that might not be grounded in extensive empirical observation. Each approach has merit, of course, and thus a synthesis of the two views is necessary in scientific and other forms of thought. Rationalist theories without any connection to observations have little validity, but mountains of observational data without an organizing theoretical framework have little meaning and therefore little use.

In addition to differing both in their views of the relationship between the mind and body and in their methods for finding truth, Plato and Aristotle differed in their views regarding the dialectic of the origin of ideas. Where do ideas come from? Aristotle believed that ideas are acquired from experience. Plato, on the other hand, believed that ideas are innate and need only to be dug out from the sometimes hidden nooks and crannies of the mind.

In the dialogue the *Meno*, Plato claims to show that the rules of geometry already resided within the mind of a slave boy, who needed only to be made aware of these innate ideas, not to be taught these ideas from the world outside of the boy's mind. That is, through dialogue, Socrates (the protagonist in this and other Platonic dialogues) helps the boy bring into awareness his innate mental concepts of these pure forms. Today, many people still debate whether abilities and dispositions such as language or intelligence are innate (a thesis) or are acquired through interactions with the environment (an antithesis). The most plausible solution is that a synthesis of both experience and innate ability contribute to many aspects of cognition and other psychological constructs.

The Early Christian Era (A.D. 200–450) and the Middle Ages (A.D. 400–1300)

The dialectics of monism versus dualism, empiricism versus rationalism, and innate versus acquired abilities continued in Europe, even throughout the early Christian Era and the Middle Ages. These epochs were not, however, a golden age for empirical science. Even some rationalists did not thrive during this time. The basis of philosophical discourse was faith in a Christian God and in scriptural accounts of phenomena. Neither empirical demonstrations nor rationalist arguments were considered valid or even permissible unless they illustrated what was already dictated to be true on the basis of religious faith and official doctrine. Whatever contradicted these beliefs was heretical and unacceptable—to the point where the freedom and even the life of the doubter were at risk.

Great Christian philosophers of this era, such as Saint Augustine of Hippo (354–430 A.D.), a bishop in Roman Africa, were much more interested in the afterlife than in life itself. They urged people to seek a desirable afterlife, rather than a desirable life. Unlike Plato, they were relatively doctrinaire and not fully open to the critical tradition. However, they agreed with Plato that the main basis for thought was introspection, not observation. Like Plato, they considered the concrete, material objects and phenomena of the world to be of interest primarily for what they symbolically represented, not for any empirical value that might lead to knowledge.

The critical tradition is widely accepted in most societies today, but dogmatists of all kinds—political extremists, jingoists, chauvinists, and other ideologues—continue to accept as true only those ideas and observations that conform to their prior and often rigid beliefs, and people continue to die for opposing such rigid beliefs. Such attitudes diverge from contemporary notions of science, in which it is believed that, ultimately, the truth will come out, whether or not it conforms to our present convictions and beliefs.

It is easy to believe that only extremists fall prey to the neglect or rejection of the critical tradition. Unfortunately, we are all susceptible to such tendencies. For example, everyone is susceptible to the phenomenon of confirmation bias, whereby we sometimes cling to ideas in the face of contradictory evidence. In fact, although most of us, including scientists, cherish our belief that we are open to new ideas and that we are willing to change our minds when faced with contradictory evidence, most of us hesitate to embrace ideas that challenge some of our core beliefs. We see confirmation bias in dictators and their mindless subjects, but often not in ourselves.

After centuries of medieval dogmatism, some thinkers tried to provide a synthesis that integrated empiricism and faith. Saint Thomas Aquinas (1225–1274), the theologian and philosopher, was an avid student of and commentator on Aristotle and his works. He attempted to synthesize a sort of "Christian science," wherein empiricist philosophy was bounded by the dictates of Christian theology. According to Aquinas, reasoning also is important and acceptable because, in his view, such reason will lead to God. Aquinas's acceptance of reason as a route to truth opened the way for those who followed him yet did not share his religious dogma.

According to Aquinas's precariously perched empirical-rational-religious approach, humans are at the juncture of two universes, the corporeal and the spiritual (similar to Plato's mind-body dualism). The goal for humans is to understand the life of the body through the life of the spirit. Science must therefore take a backseat to religion. As the Middle Ages drew to a close, particularly in the eleventh and twelfth centuries, many changes heralded the arrival of the Renaissance: the first modern universities were founded, ancient Greek medical and natural-science texts were translated, and some experimental techniques were advanced.

The Renaissance (Rebirth) of Criticism (A.D. 1300s–1600s) and the Nascence (Birth) of Science

As critical thought was reborn throughout Europe, modern views of science were born. During the Renaissance, the focus of philosophical thinking shifted from God to humankind, and from the afterlife to the present life. The established Roman Catholic Church remained a strong force both philosophically and politically, but the focus of philosophical thinking veered away from Christian doctrine's emphasis on God and the afterlife back to a renewed interest in humankind and the here and now. Science as we know it was born, and direct observation was established as the basis of knowledge.

Another name for the Renaissance (rebirth) is the Awakening, and during this period, the intellectual movement known as humanism awoke after centuries of slumber. Renaissance humanism investigated the role of humans in the world, centering on humans "as the measure of all things." Humanists exalted the role of humans in nature, which contrasted with the previous exaltation of God. Humanism grew out of the rediscovery and revival of ancient classics of Greek and Roman philosophy, literature, mathematics, medicine, and the natural sciences, which had been ignored, submerged, or even destroyed during the Middle Ages.

Revolutionary thinkers in mathematics and physics led the way toward empirical science as we know it today. Modern astronomy was heralded when Polish astronomer Nicolaus Copernicus (1473–1543) proposed his heliocentric theory, which argued that the sun and not the earth is at the center of our solar system. This theory contradicted the traditional Ptolemaic geocentric theory and the then official church doctrine. Later in this era, Italian astronomer, mathematician, and physicist Galileo Galilei (1564–1642) was branded a heretic and placed under lifelong house arrest by the Roman Catholic Church. His unorthodox use of scientific observation rather than religious faith as the basis for his conclusions earned him suspicion and contributed to his arrest.

During the Middle Ages, theory—Christian religious theory—was the engine that drove all attempts to understand human nature. The guidance by theory that sometimes occurs in science today differs from the extreme guidance by theory as it occurred during the Middle Ages: With moderate guidance by theory, the theory forms a path that is harder to swerve from than to stay on. However, with some effort, we can leave what has become a blind alley. In the Middle Ages, the role of theory was more like that of a train track, and any departure from the track meant sheer disaster and sometimes death for those who veered.

During the Renaissance, strict guidance by religious theory came under attack. Francis Bacon (1561–1626) proposed an antithesis to the medieval point of view: scientific thinking must be purely empirical—not guided by theory at all. Bacon believed that theories color our vision and thereby get in the way of our perceiving the truth. He therefore asserted that studies of nature and of humankind must be wholly unbiased and atheoretical.

Many contemporary scientists studying cognition and other phenomena seek to synthesize the two extreme views on the role of theory. Theory should guide and give meaning to our observations; yet our theories should be formed, modified, and perhaps even discarded as a result of our observations. The progress of the study of cognition or of any other science depends on a continual interaction between theory and data.

Beginnings of the Modern Period (1600s–1800s)

Descartes and Locke (1600s–1750)   The dialectic of theory versus data continued in the seventeenth century, when René Descartes (1596–1650) sharply disagreed with the glorification of the empirical methods espoused by Bacon and his intellectual predecessor Aristotle. Descartes agreed with Plato's rationalist belief that the introspective, reflective method is superior to empirical methods for finding truth. Cartesian rationalist philosophy contributed much to the modern philosophy of mind (a grandparent of psychology), and Descartes's views had numerous other implications for psychology.

Like Plato, Descartes believed in both mind-body dualism (that the mind and the body are qualitatively different and separate) and innate (versus acquired) knowledge. According to Descartes, the dualistic nature of the mind (nonmaterial, incorporeal, spiritual) and the body (material) separates humans from animals. For humans, the mind and its powers are supreme: *cogito, ergo sum* (Latin for "I think, therefore I am"). According to Descartes, the mind has great influence over the body, but the body still has some effect on the mind. Thus, Descartes is considered both mentalistic (viewing the body as subordinate to the mind) and interactionistic, in that he held that there was two-way interaction between the mind and body.

On the other side of the dialectic, the British empiricist philosopher John Locke (1632–1704) believed that the interaction between the mind and body is a symmetrical relationship between two aspects of the same unified phenomenon. The mind depends on sense experience processed by the body for its information, whereas the body depends on the mind for the storage and later usage of processed sense experience. Locke and other British empiricists also shared Aristotle's and Bacon's reverence for empirical observation. Locke's Aristotelian (and perhaps anti-Cartesian) valuing of empirical observation naturally accompanied his view that humans are born without knowledge—and must therefore seek knowledge through empirical observation. Locke's term for this view is *tabula rasa,* meaning "blank slate" in Latin: life and experience "write" knowledge upon us.

Mill and Kant (1750–1800)   Locke's philosophical successor was James Mill (1733–1836), who took British empiricism to its philosophical extreme. As a radical associationist, Mill believed that events occurring close to one another in time become associated in our minds, so that they can later be recalled in tandem by memory. Mill suggested that the mind can be viewed in entirely mechanistic terms. According to Mill, the laws of the physical universe can explain everything, including the activity of the mind. The idea of a separate mind or soul that exists independent of the body therefore is both unnecessary and wrong. This extreme version of monism is sometimes referred to as *reductionism,* in that it reduces the role of the mind to the status of a mere cog in a larger physiological machine. The important thing is therefore the environment and how the sense organs of the body—eyes, ears, and so on—perceive it. In one form of reductionism, the individual responds mechanistically, with all knowledge starting at the level of sensations and working up to the mind, which is merely the next step in the "intellectual assembly line" (Schultz, 1981).

In the eighteenth century, the debates about dualism versus monism and about empiricism versus rationalism had peaked. German philosopher Immanuel Kant (1724–1804) began the process of dialectical synthesis for these questions. He redefined the mind-body question by asking how the mind and body are related, rather than whether the mind is in control.

Instead of phrasing the problem in terms of duality or unity, Kant proposed a set of faculties, or mental powers: the senses, understanding, and reason. He believed that the faculties, working in concert, control and provide a link between the mind and body, integrating the two. Loosely speaking, Kant's faculty of the senses is closest to the idea of the body, his faculty of reason parallels the concept of the mind, and his faculty of understanding bridges the two. Faculties of the mind also figured prominently in psychology later on, when early twentieth-century psychologists tried to define and understand more clearly what the faculties of the mind might be. The debate still lives on today.

In terms of rationalism versus empiricism and whether knowledge is innate or is passively acquired through experience, Kant firmly declared that a synthesis of both rationalism and empiricism is needed whereby the two ways of thinking work together in the quest for truth. Kant called the empirically acquired experiential knowledge *a posteriori knowledge* (from the Latin meaning "from afterward"); we gain this knowledge after we have experience.

On the other hand, Kant recognized that some knowledge ("general truth") exists regardless of individual experience. Kant referred to this general truth as *a priori knowledge;* such knowledge exists whether or not we become aware of it through our own experiences. A key example of a priori knowledge is our knowledge of time. We know a priori to link together our fleeting sensations over time into a seemingly continuous stream of experience. However, for us to observe any cause-effect relationship over time, we must have a posteriori knowledge of the related preceding and consequent events. According to Kant's synthesis, understanding requires both a posteriori, experience-based knowledge (thesis) and a priori, innate concepts (antithesis), such as knowledge of the concept of time and causality, which permit us to profit from our experiences. In this way, understanding evolves both through nature (innate) and through nurture (experience).

Of course, Kant did not settle these debates once and for all. Questions probing the nature of cognition and reality have not been and probably never will be settled for good. In fact, two influential books have appeared within the past decade that continue the dialectic about the mind-body issue. D. Dennett (1991) takes a reductionist view, saying that there is no mind without the physical body. R. Penrose (1989), on the other hand, allows for a consciousness not linked to the physical realm.

Scholars will probably always wrestle with aspects of these problems. Kant did, however, effectively redefine many of the issues with which philosophers before him had grappled. Kant's enormous impact on philosophy interacted with nineteenth-century scientific exploration of the body and how such exploration worked to produce profound influences on the eventual establishment of psychology as a discipline in the 1800s.

Merging of Philosophy and Physiology into Modern Psychology (1800s–1900s)

Clearly, the study of cognition has much in common with other disciplines. The issues that have faced and continue to face philosophers, physicians, and other scholars also confront all those studying cognition. We have seen this confrontation in dialectics described earlier regarding the nature of the mind and body and regarding the sources of knowledge. So intertwined are the issues confronted by philosophers, physicians, and psychologists that in the 1800s (about the same time that Hegel proposed his idea of the dialectic), when psychology was starting out as a field, it was viewed by some as a branch of philosophy and by others as a branch of medicine. As psychology increasingly became a scientific discipline focused on the study of the mind and behavior, nineteenth-century philosophy merged increasingly with the study of physiological issues pertaining to sensory perception.

Gradually, the psychological branches of philosophy and of medicine diverged from the two parent disciplines and then merged to form the distinct unified discipline of psychology. Today, although psychology, philosophy, and medicine are essentially discrete, they are not completely so, for many psychological questions remain rooted in both philosophy (such as the nature of the mind and its relation to the body) and medicine (such as the biological causes of behavior).

The Diverging Perspectives of Modern Psychology

Building on dialectics of the past, the study of cognition has hosted a wide variety of intellectual perspectives on the human mind and how it should be studied. In order to understand cognition as a whole, one needs to be familiar with the schools of thought that are precursors to and that have evolved as bases in psychology for the field of cognition. The main early psychological perspectives build on and react to those perspectives that came before; the dialectical process that appeared throughout the history of thought about cognition also threads through modern psychology, starting with approaches that focus on mental structures and continuing with approaches that focus on mental functions, or on mental associations.

Structuralism, Functionalism, Pragmatism, and Associationism: Early Dialectics in Psychology

Structuralism   The goal of structuralism, generally considered to be the first major school of thought in psychology, was to understand the structure (configuration of elements) of the mind by analyzing the mind into its constituent components or contents. When structuralism was a dominant school of psychological thought, scientists in other fields were similarly analyzing materials into basic elements and then studying combinations of these basic elements—chemists were analyzing substances into their constituent chemical elements, biologists were analyzing the biochemical constituents of cells, physiologists were analyzing physiological structures, and so on. Although structuralism is no longer a dynamic force in psychology, it is important for having taken the first steps toward making psychology a systematic, empirical science and for establishing some of the dialectics of contemporary psychology—for example, the dialectic between molecular analysis of behavior, on the one hand (the position of structuralism), and global analysis, on the other.

An important proponent of structuralism was German psychologist Wilhelm Wundt (1832–1920). Wundt believed that psychology and the study of cognition should focus on immediate and direct, as opposed to mediated (interpreted), conscious experience. For example, suppose that one looks at a green, grassy lawn. To Wundt, the concepts of *lawn* or even of *grass* would be irrelevant. Even one's awareness of looking at a grassy lawn would not have particularly interested Wundt. These conceptually mediated experiences are too far removed from the mental elements of one's experience, which one infers from the more important (to Wundt) immediate experience of seeing narrow, vertical, spiky, green protrusions of varying lengths and widths, amassed closely together on a two-dimensional surface. It was to these elementary sensations that Wundt gave his attention.

For Wundt, the optimal method by which a person can be trained to analyze these sensory experiences is introspection, looking inward at pieces of information passing through consciousness—a form of self-observation. Today, we would call introspection subjective, but it did not seem so to the structuralists of the time.

Wundt's student, Edward Titchener (1867–1927), held views that we would consider generally similar to Wundt's. Titchener believed that all consciousness can be reduced to three elementary states: sensations—the basic elements of perception; images—the pictures we form in our minds to characterize what we perceive; and affections—the constituents of emotions such as love and hate.

During most of his life, Titchener was a strict structuralist; he used structuralist principles in his teaching, research, and writings at Cornell University. Toward the end of his life, however, Titchener began to diverge from Wundt. He open-mindedly listened to alternative views (particularly the criticisms by functionalists, described in the following section), which suggested that structuralists had proposed too many sensations. Titchener eventually came to argue that psychology should study not merely the basic elements of sensation, but also the categories into which these sensations can be grouped (Hilgard, 1987).

Titchener's change of mind illustrates an important point about psychologists in particular and about scientists in general. Outstanding scientists do not necessarily adopt a particular viewpoint in the dialectical cycle and then stick with it for the rest of their lives. The thinking of most scientists and other good thinkers (see, e.g., Basseches, 1984; Labouvie-Vief, 1980, 1990; Pascual-Leone, 1987; Riegel, 1979) evolves dialectically; they reject or build on their earlier work (and the work of others), in the creation of what they hope will be their lasting contributions to scientific or other kinds of thinking. Truly outstanding scientists or other thinkers are not immune to criticism and change; instead, they consider antitheses to their own theses, and they formulate their own syntheses, incorporating the alternative views into their own thinking. Early in his career, Titchener had been considered dogmatic, but he had the intellectual strength and fortitude to allow his thinking to evolve and change.

Functionalism: An Alternative to Structuralism   The roots of structuralism were in Germany, but its countermovement, functionalism, was rooted in America—the first U.S.-born movement in psychology. It could be said that the key difference between structuralists and functionalists lay not in the answers they found, but in the fundamentally different questions they asked. Whereas structuralists asked, "What are the elementary contents [structures] of the human mind?" functionalists asked, "What do people *do,* and *why* do they do it?" Structure versus function thus constituted the basis of the dialectic that distinguished the two schools of thought.

Another way of viewing the difference between structuralism and functionalism is to say that structuralists viewed the human or other organism as an object that passively receives sensations to analyze. Functionalists, in contrast, viewed humans and others as more actively engaged in their sensations and actions. The functionalist addresses the broad question of how and why the mind works as it does, by seeking functional relationships between specific earlier stimulus events and specific subsequent response behaviors. Psychologist and educator James Rowland Angell (1869–1949), whose criticism of structuralism was instrumental in swaying Titchener to change his views, suggested three fundamental precepts of functionalism (Angell, 1907): (1) the study of mental processes, (2) the study of the uses of consciousness, and (3) the study of the total relationship of the organism to its environment.

Even given these precepts, the functionalist school of thought never had the unity that structuralism had. Functionalists were unified by the kinds of questions they asked, but not necessarily by the answers they found or by the methods they used for finding those answers. We might even suggest that they were unified in believing that a diversity of methods could be used, as long as each method helped to answer the particular question being probed.

Functionalists' openness to diverse methodologies broadened the scope of psychological methods. Among the various approaches used by functionalists was animal experimentation, perhaps prompted by Charles Darwin's revolutionary ideas on evolution.

Pragmatism: An Outgrowth of Functionalism   Because functionalists believed in using whichever methods best answered the researcher's questions, it seems natural for functionalism to have led to pragmatism. Pragmatists believe that knowledge is validated by its usefulness: what can you *do* with it? Pragmatists are concerned not only with knowing what people do, but also with what we can do with our knowledge of what people do.

A leader in guiding functionalism toward pragmatism was William James (1842–1910)—physician, philosopher, psychologist, and brother of author Henry James. The chief functional contribution of William James to the field of psychology is a single book: his landmark *Principles of Psychology* (James, 1890/1983). Today, many regard James as among the greatest psychologists ever, although James himself seems to have rejected psychology later in his life.

James minced no words in his criticism of structuralism's detail-oriented approach, snidely commenting that structuralism's nit-picking approach "taxes patience to the utmost, and could hardly have arisen in a country whose natives could be *bored*" (p. 192). James is particularly well known for his pragmatic theorizing about consciousness, emphasizing that the function of consciousness is to enable people to adapt to the environment and to give them choices for operating within that environment.

Another of the early pragmatists has profoundly influenced my own evolution of thinking about psychology, as well as the thinking of many others. John Dewey (1859–1952), along with Angell, mentioned earlier, is credited with laying out the formal defining principles for the philosophical school of functionalism. Dewey was important to psychology for his contribution to functionalism, as well as for his stimulation of new ideas in others. Dewey is remembered primarily, however, as a philosopher of education; his pragmatic functionalist approach to thinking and schooling heralded many of the current notions in cognitive and educational psychology. Much of what cognitive and educational psychologists say today reiterates what Dewey said early in the twentieth century.

Dewey (1910, 1913, 1922), ever the pragmatist, emphasized motivation in education. If no one inspires you to learn, the chances are that you will not learn very well. To learn effectively, you need to see the point of your education—the practical use of it. One way to interest you in education is to give you more opportunity to select your own problems rather than always to tell you what problems to solve. Perhaps most important, you should learn by experimentation and by doing, rather than merely by being told facts, so that you can learn to think for yourself and to use information intelligently. Dewey also practiced what he preached: he opened an elementary school at Columbia University, which taught according to his precepts (Hilgard, 1987).

Dewey's practical applications of psychological principles were not universally well received, due to one of the many dialectics underlying the study of cognition and other aspects of the mind. Many psychologists felt that true scientists should avoid diverting their attention from the study of underlying principles merely to address some immediate applications of those principles. Other scientists believed, and still do, that basic research ultimately leads to many of the most practical applications. To this day, scientists disagree regarding how much of scientific research should be basic research and how much should be applied research. Ideally, we would have a synthetic balance between research that is basic and research that is applied.

In addition to the question of applied versus basic research, many of the dialectics that first emerged via functionalism and structuralism were fundamental to the development of the psychology of cognition. In particular, functionalism expanded the scope of the fledgling academic discipline to comprise a range of methodological techniques far wider than the structuralists ever would have permitted. Although functionalism, like structuralism, did not survive as an organized school of thought, its influence remains widespread in psychological specializations that stress both flexibility of research methods and practicality.

Associationism: An Integrative Synthesis Associationism, like function-alism, was less a rigid school of psychology than an influential way of thinking. In general, the main interests of associationism are the middle-level to higher-level mental processes, such as those of learning. Associationism examines how events or ideas can become associated with one another in the mind, to result in a form of learning. This focus on rather high-level mental processes runs exactly counter to Wundt's insistence on studying elementary sensations.

For example, with repetition, concepts such as *thesis, antithesis,* and *synthesis* will become linked in one's mind so often that they will become inextricably associated with one another. To put it another way, one will have learned that the dialectical process involves a thesis, an antithesis, and a synthesis. Learning and remembering thus depend on mental association.

Associationism itself has been associated with many other theoretical viewpoints. Traveling backward in time, its principles can be traced directly to James Mill; even further back, we find Locke's view that the mind and the body are two aspects of the same unified phenomenon, a view rooted in Aristotle's ideas. Subsequent contemporary views were also founded on associationism. Consequently, it is difficult to categorize associationism as belonging strictly to one era.

An influential associationist was the German experimenter Hermann Ebbinghaus (1850–1909), the first experimenter to apply associationist principles systematically. Ebbinghaus prided himself on using much more rigorous experimental techniques (counting his errors, recording his response times, etc.) than Wundt used during introspection. On the other hand, Ebbinghaus used himself as his only experimental subject, just as Wundt had done. In particular, Ebbinghaus used his self-observations to study and quantify the relationship between rehearsal and recollection of material.

Psychologists' views about introspection have evolved since the days of Ebbinghaus and Wundt, but many dialectical controversies remain regarding its use. Some psychologists discount most self-observations as being fruitless for gathering empirical data because many of our thought processes are unconscious or at least not available to our conscious minds (Nisbett & Wilson, 1977). Others consider self-observations valuable for generating hypotheses but useless in evaluating hypotheses. Still others view subjects' introspective self-analyses while they perform a task to be an invaluable source of confirmatory data (Ericsson & Simon, 1980). Even those who value self-observations as a tool for empirical study disagree regarding when to obtain the observational data. Some contend that if observations are obtained during the performance of a task, the very act of observing the task performance changes it. Others argue that inaccurate (or at least imperfect) recall interferes with self-observations obtained after the task performance has ended.

Ebbinghaus's ideas were elaborated by Edwin Guthrie (1886–1959), who observed animals instead of himself. Guthrie proposed that two observed events (a stimulus and a response) become associated through their close temporal contiguity. That is, the stimulus and the response behaviors/events become associated because they continually occur at about the same time. In contrast, Edward Lee Thorndike (1874–1949) held that the role of "satisfaction," rather than of Guthrie's temporal contiguity, is the key to forming associations. Thorndike (1905) termed this principle the *law of effect:* A stimulus will tend to produce a certain response (the *effect*) over time if an organism is rewarded (the *satisfaction*) for that response.

In considering the methods of Ebbinghaus, Guthrie, and Thorndike, we see that the associationists followed the functionalist-pragmatic tradition of using various methods in their research. In fact, Thorndike can be tied directly back to his functionalist mentor, William James. James even encouraged Thorndike to conduct his experiments on animals, offering his own house as the locale for some of Thorndike's earliest studies of animals' learning to run through mazes.

Twentieth-Century Perspectives on Psychology

Origins of Behaviorism

Other researchers, who were contemporaries of Thorndike, used animal experiments to probe stimulus-response relationships in ways that differed from those of Thorndike and his fellow associationists. These researchers straddled the line between associationism and the emerging field of behaviorism. Some of these researchers, like Thorndike and other associationists, studied responses that were voluntary (though perhaps lacking any conscious thought, as in Thorndike's work), but others studied responses that were involuntarily triggered, in response to what appear to be unrelated external stimuli.

In Russia, Nobel Prize–winning physiologist Ivan Pavlov (1849–1936) studied involuntary learning behavior of this sort, beginning with his observation that dogs salivated in response to the sight of the lab technician who fed them before the dogs even saw whether the technician had food. To Pavlov, this response indicated a form of learning, termed *classically conditioned learning*, over which the dogs had no conscious control. In the dogs' minds, some type of involuntary learning was linking the technician with the food (Pavlov, 1955).

Behaviorism

Behaviorism, an American school of psychology, may be considered an extreme version of associationism, which focuses entirely on the association between environmental contingencies and emitted behavior. Behaviorism was born as a dialectical reaction against the focus on personally subjective mental states found in both structuralism and functionalism. Instead, behaviorism asserts that the science of psychology should deal only with observable behavior. According to strict, extreme ("radical") behaviorists, any conjectures about internal thoughts and ways of thinking are nothing more than speculation, and although they might belong within the domain of philosophy, they certainly have no place in psychology. This behaviorist view originates in the philosophical tradition of logical positivism, which asserts that the only basis for knowledge is sensory perceptions; all else is idle conjecture.

Watson's Groundwork

The man usually acknowledged as the father of radical behaviorism is American psychologist John Watson (1878–1958). Watson, like British empiricist James Mill, had no use for internal mental contents or mechanisms. Still, although Watson disdained key aspects of functionalism, he was clearly influenced by the functionalists in his emphasis on what people do and what causes their actions. In fact, arguably, behaviorism depends more on the study of functions in behavior than functionalism ever did!

Behaviorism also differed from previous movements in psychology by shifting the emphasis of experimental research from human to animal subjects (although animal studies have been used since the days of Hippocrates). Historically, much behavioristic work has been conducted (and still is) with laboratory animals such as rats. Watson himself preferred animal subjects. He believed that with animal subjects, it is easier to ensure behavioral control and to establish stimulus-response relationships while minimizing external interference. Indeed, the simpler the organism's emotional and physiological makeup, the less the researcher needs to worry about any of the interference that can plague psychological research with humans as subjects. Many nonbehavioral psychologists wonder whether animal research can be generalized to humans (i.e., applied more generally to humans instead of just specifically to the animals that were studied). In response, some behaviorists would argue that the study of animal behavior is a legitimate pursuit in its own right, and all behaviorists would assert that we can learn useful principles that generalize to other species, including humans.

Hull's Synthesis with Pavlovian Conditioning

An American behavioral psychologist who tried to connect the involuntary learning studied by Pavlov with the voluntary learning studied by Watson and Thorndike was Clark Hull (1884–1952). Hull had always shown a predilection for synthesis; even his dissertation synthesized strict experimental psychology with theoretical analyses of thought processes, particularly in regard to the learning of concepts. Although Hull's work was virtually ignored for nearly a decade, during which he became quite discouraged (see Hilgard, 1987), his work on learning eventually became among the most widely cited work of his time. Hull's ideas also enriched the field of psychology with ideas from such diverse fields as physiology and evolutionary biology (see Robinson, 1995).

Above all, Hull was particularly influential for his belief that the laws of behavior can be quantified, as are laws in other scientific disciplines such as physics. Hull's (1952) final presentation of his theory of behavior contains numerous mathematical postulates and corollaries. Hull's interest in mathematical precision also led to his development of an early computational device, which he used in his psychological research and which used punch cards for statistical calculations.

Skinner's Radicalism

In modern times, radical behaviorism has seemed almost synonymous with one of its most radical proponents, B. F. Skinner (1904–1990). For Skinner, virtually all of human behavior, and not just learning, can be explained by behavior emitted in response to environmental contingencies, which can be studied effectively by observing animal behaviors. Skinner applied the behaviorist model to almost everything, from learning to language acquisition to problem solving, and even to the control of behavior in society. As a consequence, he was criticized for overgeneralizing the applicability of his data by making pronouncements about what would be good for society as a whole, based largely on data from learning in animals.

Skinner also entered domains typically reserved nowadays for philosophers. For example, in his novel *Walden Two* (Skinner, 1948), Skinner depicts a utopian society run entirely on behaviorist principles. He also argues that *ought* and *should* are meaningless concepts outside of a specific environment. The environment controls behavior, and thus the setting in which a person is raised determines what he or she should do.

The following passage illustrates how behaviorists view social interactions in terms of the specific observable rewards that might be derived from a conversational interchange; they avoid references to the elusive, unobservable aspects of social relationships.

The [Walden] Code [by which the utopia's members agree to abide] even descends to the level of the social graces. . . . We've tried a number of experiments to expedite and improve personal relations. For example, introductions in Walden Two are solely for the purpose of communicating information; we don't wait to be introduced before speaking to a stranger, nor do we bother to make introductions if no relevant information is to be communicated. (B. F. Skinner, 1948, p. 163)

This deterministic view calls to mind the original radical conception of behaviorism, as proposed by Watson, which states that any behavior can be shaped and controlled:

Give me a dozen healthy infants, well-formed, and my own specified world to bring them up in, and I'll guarantee to take any one at random and train him to become any type of specialist I might select—doctor, lawyer, artist, merchant—chief and yes, even beggarman and thief, regardless of his talents, penchants, tendencies, abilities, vocations, and race of his ancestors. (Watson, 1930, p. 104)

Many psychologists disagree with the behaviorist view. For example, in a debate between Watson and psychologist William McDougall, McDougall says,

I come into this hall and see a man on this platform scraping the guts of a cat with hairs from the tail of a horse; and, sitting silently in attitudes of rapt attention, are a thousand persons who presently break out into wild applause. How will the Behaviorist explain these strange incidents: How explain the fact that the vibrations emitted by the cat-gut stimulate all the thousand into absolute silence and quiescence; and the further fact that the cessation of the stimulus seems to be a stimulus to the most frantic activity? (Watson & McDougall, 1929, p. 63)

Gestalt Psychology

Of the many dialectical critics of behaviorism, Gestalt psychologists may be among the most avid. According to Gestalt psychology, we best understand psychological phenomena when we view them as organized, structured wholes, not when we break them down into pieces. Actually, this movement was not only an antithetical reaction against the behaviorist tendency to break down behaviors into stimulus-response units, but also against the structuralist tendency to analyze mental processes into elementary sensations. The maxim "the whole is different from the sum of its parts" aptly sums up the Gestalt perspective. The name of the approach comes from the German word *Gestalt* (now an English word). The German word does not have an exact synonym in English, although it is something close to "whole unitary form," "integral shape," or "fully integrated configuration" (Schultz, 1981). The movement originated in Germany, the fount of structuralism, and later spread to the United States, the fount of behaviorism, and to other countries.

Gestalt psychology is usually traced to the work of German psychologist Max Wertheimer (1880–1943), who collaborated with compatriots Kurt Koffka and Wolfgang Köhler to form a new school of psychology, with an emphasis on understanding wholes in their own right. The Gestaltists applied this framework to many areas in psychology. For example, they proposed that problem solving cannot be explained simply in terms of automatic responses to stimuli or to elementary sensations. Instead, new insights emerge in problem solving; people simply form entirely new ways to see problems.

Given some of the criticisms of the vagueness of the Gestalt perspective, many psychologists now believe that the most fruitful approach to understanding psychological phenomena is to synthesize analytic and holistic strategies. Cognitivists are among the many who use both analytic and holistic strategies.

Cognitivism

Finally, we reach cognitivism, the conceptual basis of this book. Cognitivism is the belief that much of human behavior can be understood if we understand first how people think. The contemporary cognitivist examines the elementary structuralist contents of thought, the functionalist processes of thought, and the Gestaltist holistic results of thinking. The cognitivist, like the Gestaltist, may well conclude that indeed the whole is different from the sum of its parts. At the same time, however, cognitive psychologists attempt to determine precisely which mental mechanisms and which elementary elements of thought make that conclusion true. Cognitivists would study the way in which we perceive the gestalt of the chapter or of the Seurat painting, but they also would want to determine precisely how we perceive it as such.

Early cognitivists, for example, Miller, Galanter, and Pribram (1960) argued that traditional behavioristic accounts of behavior were inadequate precisely because they said nothing about—indeed, they ignored—how people think. Subsequent cognitivists Allen Newell and Herbert Simon (1972) proposed detailed models of human thinking and problem solving from the most basic levels to the most complex (such as playing chess). Ulric Neisser (1967) was especially critical in bringing cognitivism to prominence. Neisser defined cognitive psychology as the study of how people learn, structure, store, and use knowledge. The cognitive approach has been applied in a variety of areas of psychology—including everything from thinking to emotion to the treatment of various psychological syndromes, including depression. Cognitive psychologists use a variety of methods to pursue their goal of understanding human thought, such as the study of reaction times, the study of people's subjective reports as they solve problems, and computer simulations.

Today, cognitivism incorporates many aspects of the biological approach to cognition. A direct descendant of evolutionary theory, for example, is behavioral genetics, which attempts to account for behavior by attributing it to the synthetic influence of particular combinations of genetic and environmental influences. A behavioral geneticist might attempt to explain, for example, the genetic and environmental elements contributing to general or specific cognitive abilities.

Another psychobiological approach is to determine which specific regions of the brain are responsible for the origination, learning, or expression of particular behaviors, feelings, or kinds of thoughts. For example, Roger Sperry (1920–1994) tried to determine what kinds of thinking occur in each of the two halves of the brain. These and other insights into our minds and bodies—and the interactions between the two—have synthesized the methods and the data from cognitive psychology and biological psychology.

In the 1960s cognitivism was just coming of age, and behaviorism seemed to be on its way out. Today, cognitivism is popular, and many fields within psychology have adopted a cognitive perspective. This perspective, too, may someday fade in importance and yield to other perspectives. The dominant perspective of the future may be unimaginable today. Psychology is a dynamic science, precisely because it is ever evolving in its dialectical perspectives on the puzzles of human behavior.

Acknowledgments

Preparation of this chapter was supported under the Javits Act Program (Grant #R206R50001) as administered by the Office of Educational Research and Improvement of the U.S. Department of Education. Grantees undertaking such projects are encouraged to express their professional judgments freely. This chapter, therefore, does not necessarily represent positions or policies of the government, and no official endorsement should be inferred. This chapter draws in part on Sternberg (1995, 1996).

References

Angell, J. R. (1907). The province of functional psychology. *Psychological Review, 14,* 61–91.

Basseches, M. A. (1984). Dialectical thinking as an organized whole. In M. L. Commons, J. D. Sinnott, F. A. Richards, & C. Armon (Eds.), *Beyond formal operations* (pp. 216–238). New York: Praeger.

Dennett, D. (1991). *Consciousness explained.* Boston: Little, Brown.

Dewey, J. (1910). *How we think.* Boston: Heath.

Dewey, J. (1913). *Interest and effort in education.* New York: Houghton Mifflin.

Dewey, J. (1922). *Human nature and conduct: An introduction to social psychology.* New York: Holt.

Ericsson, K. A., & Simon, H. A. (1980). Verbal reports as data. *Psychological Review, 87,* 215–251.

Hegel, G. W. F. (1931). *The phenomenology of mind* (2nd ed., J. B. Baillie, Trans.). London: Allen & Unwin. (Original work published 1807.)

Hilgard, E. R. (1987). *Psychology in America.* Orlando, FL: Harcourt, Brace, Jovanovich.

Hull, C. L. (1952). *A behavior system: An introduction to behavior theory concerning the individual organism.* New Haven, CT: Yale University Press.

James, W. (1983). *Principles of psychology.* Cambridge: Harvard University Press. (Original work published New York: Holt, 1890.)

Kalmar, D. A., & Sternberg, R. J. (1988). Theory knitting: An integrative approach to theory development. *Philosophical Psychology, 1,* 153–170.

Labouvie-Vief, G. (1980). Beyond formal operations: Uses and limits of pure logic in life span development. *Human Development, 23,* 141–161.

Labouvie-Vief, G. (1989). Modes of knowledge and the organization of development. In M. L. Commons, J. D. Sinnott, F. A. Richards, & C. Armon (Eds.), *Beyond formal operations: Vol. 2. Comparisons and applications of adolescent and adult development models* (pp. 158–179). New York: Praeger.

Miller, G. A., Galanter, E. H., & Pribram, K. H. (1960). *Plans and the structure of behavior.* New York: Holt, Rinehart, & Winston.

Neisser, U. (1967). *Cognitive psychology.* New York: Appleton-Century-Crofts.

Newell, A., & Simon, H. A. (1972). *Human problem solving.* Englewood Cliffs, NJ: Prentice-Hall.

Nisbett, R. E., & Wilson, T. D. (1977). Telling more than we can know: Verbal reports on mental processes. *Psychological Review, 84,* 231–259.

Pascual-Leone, J. (1987). Organismic processes for neo-Piagetian theories: A dialectical causal account of cognitive development. *International Journal of Psychology, 22,* 531–570.

Pavlov, I. P. (1955). *Selected works*. Moscow: Foreign Languages Publishing House.

Penrose, R. (1989). *The emperor's new mind: Concerning computers, minds, and the laws of physics*. New York: Oxford University Press.

Riegel, K. F. (1979). *Foundations of dialectical psychology*. New York: Academic Press.

Robinson, D. N. (1995). *An intellectual history of psychology* (3rd ed.). Madison, WI: University of Wisconsin Press.

Schultz, D. (1981). *A history of modern psychology* (3rd ed.). New York: Academic Press.

Skinner, B. F. (1948). *Walden II*. New York: Macmillan.

Sternberg, R. J. (1995). *In search of the human mind*. Orlando, FL: Harcourt Brace College Publishers.

Sternberg, R. J. (1996). *Cognitive psychology*. Orlando, FL: Harcourt Brace College Publishers.

Thorndike, E. L. (1905). *The elements of psychology*. New York: Seiler.

Trager, J. (1992). *The people's chronology*. New York: Holt.

Watson, J. B. (1930). *Behaviorism* (rev. ed.). New York: Norton.

Watson, J. B., & McDougall, W. (1929). *The battle of behaviorism*. New York: Norton.

3

Rationalism versus Empiricism in Cognition

Daniel N. Robinson

We must not corrupt our hope, To prostitute our past-cure malladie To empiricks.
—Shakespeare, *All's Well That Ends Well*

A mere rationalist (that it to say, in plain English, an Atheist of the late Edition).
—Robert Sanderson, *Preface to Ussher's Power Princes* (1670)

A Word about Words

That most enduring of metaphysical problems—the problem of knowledge—expresses itself in any number of subsidiary problems at once ontological, methodological, lexical, logical, psychological. Barring total and unbridled skepticism, the claims of philosophy, of science, and of ordinary common sense are regarded as true or false, valid or infirm statements about what there is. But to take a position (an *ontological* position) on what there is presupposes a well-tested method by which to make such discoveries. It is also to locate the findings or facts within some larger or more general context and in a manner that satisfies ordinary or disciplinary standards of intelligibility and criteria of meaning. The complementary and competing tenets of empiricism and rationalism at once arise from and give bulk to the problem of knowledge. And, as *knowledge* (itself a term of art) is presumably what the cognitive "sciences" are about, the historical evolution and philosophical dimensions of these two *isms* cannot be safely ignored by students of these subjects.

That a seventeenth-century commentator thought of rationalism as but atheism "of the late Edition," as Shakespeare's character would spare hope itself from the machinations of the "Empirick," illustrates the historical instability of terms when used for purposes of learned name-calling. Accordingly, a word or two might profitably be devoted to the words themselves.

Empiricism was generally a pejorative term until well into the nineteenth century. In his *History of India* James Mill himself would write of "Mere observation and empiricism," declaring such to be "not even the commencement of science" (1818, vol. I, chap. II, sec. ix, p. 399). The English *empirick* and French *empirique* were formed from the Latin *empirici,* itself derived from the Greek *empeirikoi,* who were ancient doctors committed to observation and more or less hostile to or bereft of theory. The Greek *empeiria* translates more or less indifferently as "knowledge," "skill," or "experience," but typically connotes an ability or competence that is *acquired* in an essentially trial-and-error fashion or through persistent practice. Thus was the *Empeirikos* distinguished from the *Dogmatikos,* the latter's therapeutic practice being based on a rational system of health and disease. Ancient sources established the now traditional contrast between the followers of Pythagoras and those of Hippocrates as being theory bound and observation bound respectively. In time, philosophical partisans would conspire with comic playwrights and the skeptical intelligentsia to dub every species of dullard as a mere or brute empiric; as one who, in the felicitous prose of Sir Thomas Browne, "stares about with a gross rusticity."

By the middle of the nineteenth century, however, and chiefly as a result of the "textbook" empiricistic philosophers (John Locke, George Berkeley, David Hume, John Stuart Mill) empiricism would be widely understood as a metaphysical position on the ultimate source of all knowledge, namely, *experience.* This *epistemological empiricism,* as it might be called, was deployed in defense of a *methodological empiricism* advocated by Francis Bacon early in the seventeenth century and rendered canonical in Newton's *Regulae philosophandi.*

Rationalism has had a more winding lexical history and resists clear definition even at this date. If in the salient innings of the "long debate" the empiricist is understood as conferring epistemological authority on experience, then the rationalist might be most readily recognized as one who resists this, but on several different grounds. The rationalist, for example, might agree (as did Immanuel Kant) that all knowledge *arises* from experience but that it must itself take place within a (logically) p rational or intuitive framework. On this account, rationalism is to ve understood as a metaphysical theory about the necessary preconditions for experience and therefore for all that experience might yield. Accordingly, for the claims of the empiricist to be valid, a form of rationalism must be presupposed. With hesitation this form of rationalism will be referred to here as *analytical rationalism*.

Related to but distinct from analytical rationalism is what might be called *teleological rationalism*. A congeries of experiences can rise no higher than a mere buzz unless it is possible to locate these experiences within an intelligible context, unless one can come to grasp the very point of the sensed happenings. Aristotle famously included "final" causes in his theory of explanation, insisting that a complete understanding of any observed event must include a comprehension of the goals or purposes proximately and ultimately served by the events. The distinction between experience and understanding, then, is the distinction between isolated and incoherent perceptions and those experiences that have been integrated into a rational *schema* that discloses the that-for-the-sake-of-which the events took place in the first instance.

Finally, rationalism has been defended as a counter to skepticism, and particularly forms of skepticism deriving their force from the (allegedly) deceptive and untrustworthy operations of the senses. Satisfied that the merely factual *ephemera* of daily experience have nothing in common with truth itself, Plato (ca. 428–348 B.C.) produced philosophical masterpieces in defense of the rational, theoretical, contemplative life. The world of the senses supports only the life of the cave dweller whose firmest epistemic convictions have no more substance than the projected shadows on which they are based. Once liberated, the truth seeker moves toward the light of reason and discovers that all prior understandings were illusory. Ultimate truths are unchanging, relational, abstract. They are inaccessible to the senses, the latter having commerce only with what is transitory and thus without essential being. The Platonic defense of rationalism is thus based on a prior theory regarding essential being or real existence. Rationalism in this sense might be best classified as *ontological rationalism*.[1]

In the balance of this essay different versions of empiricism and rationalism are considered and are given qualifying labels where clarity demands.

Framing the Issues

The answer to the question, Was Aristotle an empiricist or a rationalist? is, yes. A student in Plato's Academy for twenty years, Aristotle (384–322 B.C.) was thoroughly acquainted with the philosophically rich and deep challenges to the claims of experience. The very inconstancy of the perceptible world was indelibly recorded by Heracleitus's famous maxim, "No one can enter twice into the same stream." Not only is the flux of matter incessant, but the senses too, as material organs and processes, suffer similar vicissitudes. If the aim of a genuinely philosophical or scientific understanding is the discovery of what truly is and the underlying lawful principles, the senses can only be a distraction and a path to self-deception. It is something of a declaration of independence, then, when Aristotle begins his monumental *Metaphysics* with the well-known passage "All men by nature desire to know. An example of this is the delight we take in our senses" (*Metaph.*, 980a22).[2] The juxtaposition here between wanting to be knowing or knowledgeable *(eidenai)* and a love of the senses *(tOn aisthEseOn agapEsis)*[3] calls into question traditional skepticism about empirical sources of knowledge.

It is in his *Metaphysics,* chiefly book 4, that Aristotle pauses to consider the reach and limits of various epistemological resources. He reviews several of the commoner charges against the senses: something may taste sweet to one person and bitter to another; a strong man finds light the same weight that a weak man finds heavy; the very same person experiences the same object differently at different times; different animals (ourselves included) experience the same physical stimulus differently; alterations in conditions of the body—as in instances of disease—radically alter certain perceptions. To proclaim the authority of experience is finally to submit truth to some sort of vote or plebescite, for must not the experiences of the many count more than those of the few? Would not the insane many judge the sane few to be diseased (1009b5–10)? Innumerable kindred examples tell against any general theory offering experience or perception as the ultimate arbiter of truth. Thus, where experience is the official guide, philosophy's vaunted goal becomes no more than "chasing birds on the wing" *(ta petomena diOkein;* 1009b40).

Aristotle's counters to these claims are measured and sometimes not entirely transparent. He agrees that it is an error to equate truth *(alEtheia)* with appearances *(phainomena),* but it is also a mistake to equate the latter with perception itself *(aisthEsis).* When the proper object of sense (sound for hearing ear, light for vision, contact for touch) is delivered to a healthy sensory organ, the resulting sensation faithfully records the stimulus. However, the mental impression derived from such a sensation may under various circumstances be a false representation of the stimulus and the sensory response to it (1010b1–5).

Aristotle distinguishes between the physical response of a sense organ to its adequate stimulus, and the phenomenal impression that arises. After all, one can dream of events that are making no contact whatever with the senses. In such instances, it would be foolish to charge the senses with inventing or distorting reality, for the senses are not involved at all. The first step, then, in answering skeptical charges against empirical knowledge is to distinguish between *aisthEsis* and *phainomena.* Moreover, although it is true that things undergo changes of a quantitative sort, reflecting more or less of an attribute under conditions of growth and decay, this does not invariably alter their qualitative or essential nature. The sense in which Coriscus is a man is essential; the sense in which he is musical is not. Thus, in one sense the musical Coriscus is different from the Coriscus who has yet to master the lyre, but in the essential respects he is not. Though it be granted that quantitative changes are ever present, "it is by the *form* that we recognize everything" (1010a25–27) and the form *(eidos)* does not invariably change. Indeed, even in the matter of quantitative alterations, these are common only among the earthly flotsam confronted in daily life that are, after all, "a practically negligible part of the whole (cosmos)" (1010a35–40). Aristotle was a confident empiricist!

This much said, it is necessary to acknowledge that statements about reality or statements *regarding what is (peri tOn ontOn)* are not to be confined to sensible things, for the senses are indeed limited and, in any case, cannot comprehend either the essence of things or their causes. In

Aristotle's theory of knowledge, an object or event is not fully known or understood until all of the causal modalities on which its being depends have been unearthed; the "textbook" material, formal, efficient, and final causes. To know is to comprehend both the whatness and the whyness of a thing: its matter, its form, and its purpose. Thus, for example, the soul is the form of the (material) body. Only a certain (essential kind of) material entity can be ensouled or animated. To be thus animated is to be able to achieve those ends that identify a form of life as a given form of life. Coriscus is not essentially musical, but, if he is an instance of *anthropos,* he is essentially rational.

Aristotle's theory of what might be called a scientific understanding or knowledge of things is developed in his *Posterior Analytics.* The main point of this theory for present purposes is that scientific knowledge is *demonstrative:* to understand anything scientifically is to recognize it as an instance of a universal class or the effect of a universal law and therefore to understand that the "because of which the object is" just *is* its explanation. Where this is so, "it is not possible for it to be otherwise" (*Post. Anal.,* 70b10–15). Of course none of this comprehension falls within the ambit of mere observation, and this establishes the limit of empirical modes of knowing. Direct observation provides extensive and generally quite accurate knowledge of the attributes of events and things in the world. Through associative principles, recurring observations build up a store of memories and nurture useful habits of both body and mind, for, as he says, "frequency creates nature" (*On Memory,* 452b5–6).

However, it is reserved for a rational being to comprehend the principles underlying the order of things and to discover the general laws by which events invariably occur or do so for the most part. Smith and Jones both know that the angles of a square add up to 360°. Thus, they both "know" that square X contains 360°. Smith knows it as a result of (empirical) measurement. Jones knows it as the necessary conclusion of a deductive argument whose major premises are the axioms of geometry. Clearly, Smith and Jones know the same fact but know it in quite different senses (*Post. Anal.,* 71a25–30). Ultimate knowledge includes not only an accurate account of what a thing is but also and more significantly the very *reason* behind it. "If the art of ship-building were in the wood, there would be ships by nature" (*Physics,* 984a17–25). One knows fully what a ship is not through an empirical inquiry into its material composition or the shape of it but through a rational awareness of its intended function and the anticipation of this that guided the designers and builders. If the orderly and functional adequacy of triremes discloses a purpose, it is clear that the order of nature is not purposeless. Rationality is the means by which one might locate, as it were, the reason behind the cause. Understood in this light, rationality is not some add-on or ex post facto supplement to what is fundamentally an empirical enterprise. Rather, it is the overarching framework within which observations become integrated, meaningful, and systematic. Aristotle was a committed rationalist!

Nominalism, Realism, and the Problem of Universals

Plato's debts to Pythagoras are now incalculable, but it is fair to say that a Pythagorean subtext fortifies if it does not actually generate the Platonic ontology of *true forms*. Moreover, though Plato's less than distinct philosophical "stages" reveal shifting loyalties to this ontology, there is no significant departure from the principle that truth, if there is such, is universal.[4] Accordingly, the essence of a thing—that which makes it what it is and not something else—is its sharing in the universal thing*ness*. Aristotle rejects the theory of forms and claims further that Socrates himself never affirmed it: "Socrates did not make the universals or the definitions exist apart; his successors, however, gave them separate existence and this [these separately existing universals] was the kind of thing they called Ideas" (*Metaph.*, 1078b29–32).

Nonetheless, medieval commentators, both Eastern and Western, focused on the so-called problem of universals and in the process put empiricism and rationalism on something of a collision course. This is a long and complex chapter in intellectual history and one that can be compressed only with caveats and reservations. It is enough for present purposes to note that the central epistemological issue of medieval philosophy turned on the question of whether sensible particulars exhausted the domain of the knowable, or whether such particulars triggered an a priori set of universal cognitions. Philosophical arguments were much in the service of what were taken to be theological matters of far greater consequence. If one is to know God, then the question naturally arises as to whether such knowledge is limited to the mere empirical facts of the Creation.

Except for the daring few—notably William of Ockham (ca. 1300–1349)—the most influential religious philosophers of the period took the Creation itself to be the product of a rational plan and to be emblematic of abstract and universal truths accessible to reason. The senses respond to the particulars, but the rational mind is able to move from the contents of perception to those universal truths immanent in these. What reason thus unearths is not a fabrication, for the rational abstraction is no lie ("Abstrahentium non est mendacium"). Defenders of the thesis that such rational abstractions discovered ontologically real universals—quasi-Platonic "forms," as it were, from which particulars derived their utterly dependent ontological standing—would come to bear the misleading label *realists*.

Those, such as Ockham,[5] who argued that there is only knowledge of particulars and that all general or universal categories are but class names within which particulars are included, came to be called *nominalists*. On the nominalist account, universals do not exist outside the mind *(extra animam)* of the cognizer but are constructed within the mind by frequent association and a mental disposition to generalize across similar experiences. Ockham was especially aware of the part played by language in creating mental constructs then taken to have some real rather than lexical existence. In this respect his analytical philosophy prefigured much found later in Locke and in Hume. Indeed, the more familiar disputes between eighteenth- and nineteenth-century empiricists and rationalists continued, if in a somewhat different key, the scholastic debates that had raged between realists and nominalists a half-millennium earlier.

Empiricism, Materialism, and Skepticism

The modern defense of empiricism, in the form of a developed theory of knowledge, began with *An Essay Concerning Human Understanding* (1690/1956) by John Locke (1632–1704). There were earlier works of course, including works of philosophical rigor and influence. One need only consider Francis Bacon's *Novum organum* among the seventeenth-century rallying cries in defense of observational and experimental modes of inquiry. But Locke's *Essay* would come to be the locus classicus of those issues and arguments on which successive generations of empiricistic philosophers refined their thinking and rested their claims. It was written by the same author whose political treatises had given the rhetoric of rights a sound philosophical foundation, the same author who would extend triumphant Newtonianism into the realms of psychological and social phenomena. Locke's *Essay* would come to have a nearly scriptural authority among the *philosophes* of the French Enlightenment and the leading thinkers of colonial and revolutionary America. Its relentless defense of experience as the source of all epistemic authority served purposes beyond those of philosophy itself. "Nothing is more indisputable," Jean Le Rond D'Alembert would write in his introduction to Denis Diderot's *Encyclopedia,* "than the existence of our sensations. Thus, in order to prove that they are the principles of all our knowledge, it suffices to show that they can be [exist]" (1751/1963, p. 7).

It is worth noting that the *Essay* does not advance a radical empiricism. Locke acknowledges that the understanding possesses different degrees of confidence, marking out different modes of knowing. He dubs these *intuitive, demonstrative,* and *sensitive.* That a circle is not a triangle is something known immediately and with certainty. It is known intuitively in that neither learning nor practice nor calculation nor argument is necessary to establish the truth of it. One who would discredit such intuitive knowledge, says Locke, "has a mind to be a skeptic" (1690/1956, bk. 4, chap. 2, sec. 1, italics in original). It is also certain that two triangles, with equal bases and constructed between parallel lines, are equal. Although this knowledge is certain, however, it is not immediate. Rather, it calls for a demonstrative argument, specifically the one developed by Euclid. What intuitive and demonstrative knowledge have in common is their certainty, though only the former is immediately apprehended. Framing such knowledge—all knowledge—is the awareness that a thing *necessarily* cannot be and at the same time not be. There is this "first act of the mind" (bk. 4, chap. 1, sec. 2), as Locke calls it. It is the "Law of Contradiction" itself and does not (because it could not) arise from experience. In all, then, Locke grants innate powers, intuitions, and original acts to the mind, finding these in the very nature of mind itself rather than in sources external to it. Sensitive knowledge, however, is a different matter. What is thus known is never certain, never necessary. The contingent facts of the world are known by way of sensation, for, absent sensory experience, the mind with respect to these facts is a tabula rasa. It is with respect to knowledge of this kind that Locke answered the question, How comes the mind to be furnished? with a one-word reply: *experience.*

It was Locke's aim in the *Essay* to begin to develop a science of the mind patterned on Newtonian science and theory. The Lockean *elementary sensations,* which combine to form simple ideas, themselves the combinatory elements of more complex ideas, are held together by associative mechanisms. The match between this sort of mental mechanics and the corpuscular world of Newton, with its gravitational binding forces, is both obvious and suggestive. But with the usual persistence the problem of knowledge arose for Locke as he considered the faithfulness with which experience recorded the actual facts of the physical world. Locke's solution was his famous division of the known into primary and secondary qualities, a distinction anticipated by both Galileo Galilei and Robert Boyle. Where the elementary components of a thing are densely packed, the object is hard and is experienced as being hard. Similarly, the shape and extent of palpable and visible objects are as they are perceived to be. The "primary qualities" are those properties perceptually attributed to things that are in fact possessed of the things themselves. Here there is no qualitative transformation imposed by the mediating steps between objects and the percipient's experience of them.

What of colors or odors or tastes? Whatever it is that gives rise to the experience of "blue" is not something that is blue at the ultimate corpuscular level of physical being. Rather, there is something in the physics of the matter that, when acting upon the sensory organs with their own special material composition, gives rise to perceived qualities reflecting this interaction. The secondary qualities of bodies are those contingent on being perceived by a given sort of percipient. When an object is seen as blue or is tasted as sweet, therefore, the sensory report is not a faithful recording of properties of the object, but the result of an interaction leading to the experiential representation of a physical property that is not directly perceived. In Locke, then, one finds the seeds of *phenomenalism* planted, and an unintended revival of the ancient skepticisms that are based on the premise that unmediated knowledge of the external world is impossible.

It is not coincidental (though it is also not logically mandated) that empiricistic philosophies support or are fortified by a materialistic psychology. To take experience as the ultimate arbiter on matters of fact is to install the organs of perception as the sole avenues along which facts gain entry into the mind. It was a veritable maxim among Scholastics of the Ockhamistic stripe that "Nothing is in the mind which was not first in the senses" ("Nihil in intellectu quod erat non prius in sensu"). And, by a kind of ontological reciprocity, the same line of thinking tends to conclude in a more radical materialism according to which the contents of the cosmos are solely material. Knowledge claims not grounded in sensory commerce with the material world thereby become, quite literally, nonsense. The ethereal realms of the religious imagination are and must be among the first casualties of the war on abstractions.

The materialistic features of Locke's psychology are present throughout the *Essay* but are not advanced stridently. Locke was a physician, a fellow of the Royal Society, and a committed Newtonian. Like the cleric Pierre Gassendi, Descartes's contemporary critic and enthusiastic defender of Epicurean materialism, Locke saw no incompatibility between the tenets of Christian faith and an ontology based on the assumption that God constituted the physical universe *physically*. Others, needless to say, found in the very coherence of such teaching good reason to reject all theories that went beyond the material facts. It was in opposition to these skeptical tendencies that George Berkeley (1685–1753) offered as a remedy *A Treatise concerning the Principles of Human Knowledge* (1710/1963). The position ably defended by Berkeley is that all the Lockean qualities are "secondary" in that the concept of a property or quality of a thing presupposes its being experienced. And, as any and every material object is but a congeries of such properties, there can be no independently subsisting material world at all. "To be is to be perceived" ("Esse est percipi"), declares Berkeley, as a last word on the pretensions of materialism (1710/1963, part I, sec. 3; p. 31).

Berkeley's achievement was but the stretching of empiricism to the end of its conceptual tether. If all that is knowable is reached solely by way of experience, then what is finally known are the experiences themselves or, as Berkeley put it, ideas in the mind. It is nothing less than a contradiction, argued Berkeley, to claim to know that of which one has no idea. Claims of knowledge, then, refer not to objects in some external and independent duchy of material things, but to objects of thought, to *ideas*. Nor are these replicas of material things, for an idea can only be like another idea and certainly not like something physical. The idea of a square is not a square idea, nor is the idea (experience) of a heavy object a heavy idea. Ontologically, there are in the end only ideas and spirits as independently existing, and the material world of objects owes its utterly dependent subsistence to these. In the process of developing this surprising thesis, however, Berkeley provided additional support for mediational theories of knowledge; theories that yield yet another species of skepticism, for what they deny is any possibility of direct, nonrepresentational knowledge of the external world.

The philosophical culmination of these tendencies was reached in David Hume's (1711–1776) *A Treatise of Human Nature* (1739/1973), his *An Enquiry concerning Human Understanding* (1758/1965), and his *Essays Moral, Political and Literary*.[6] Perhaps the most influential philosopher in the English-speaking world, Hume mounted precise and formidable defenses of an empirical epistemology, an associationistic theory of cognitive psychology, a utilitarian theory of ethics, and a sentimentalist theory of aesthetics and morality. Because all epistemic, moral, political, and aesthetic conjectures and debates proceed on the basis of human understanding, it becomes necessary to examine the detailed nature and structure of that understanding. For this one must have a method of inquiry sufficiently independent of the forms and habits of thought that are the subject of the inquiry itself. Thus the subtitle of the *Treatise* is "An ATTEMPT to introduce the experimental Method of Reasoning INTO MORAL SUBJECTS." This "experimental" method calls for repeated observations and the recognition that the most reasonable explanation of any phenomenon is the one compatible with the most frequently associated conditions. When *A* and *B* are constantly conjoined in experience, with *B* reliably following *A* in time, it is a fixed tendency of the mind to regard *A* as the cause of *B*. There are no certainties in the domain of contingent fact, so the most reasonable conjectures (here following Locke) are those grounded in probabilities based on a history of relevant experiences.[7]

The universal causal laws of the universe, long regarded as rationalism's chief line of defense, are conceived, according to Hume, as a result of associational principles and related mental dispositions. Hume is not skeptical about causation itself, but he is at pains to develop an adequate psychological theory to account for our *conception* of causation. To speak of causes is not to identify something obtaining between perceived antecedents and perceived consequences. Rather, it is for the mind itself to comprehend such conjunctions as causally related. The more reliable the conjunction, the firmer the belief, for the belief accumulates with rising probabilities. Just as in the following century J. S. Mill (fully in the patrimony of Hume) concluded that a universal truth can refer only to that which is exceptionless in experience, Hume systematically reduced the claims of rationalism either to veiled tautologies or to experience and the complex ideas formed out of it.

If all knowledge is dependent upon experience, this must include as well moral and aesthetic knowledge or what is more aptly called moral and aesthetic judgment. The reference of such judgments is not to be found in the external actions or objects but in the mind of the percipient. To *believe* something to be good or bad, beautiful or ugly, is not to have a given order of ideas or impressions but "their feeling to the mind . . . [B]elief is something felt by the mind" (Hume, 1758/1965, sec. 5, part 2). The man in love declares the object of his affection to be nothing less than a "divine creature," though she is nonetheless found to be utterly mortal by a different man. Parents confer virtues on their own children not always obvious to others. "Nature," after all, "has given all animals a like prejudice in favour of their offspring" (Hume, 1777/1988, p. 162). In all, moral and aesthetic qualities are not properties of things but are imputed to things by a mind that is either habitually or instinctually so inclined, though this correct but controversial thesis will not easily be made palpable "to negligent thinkers" (p. 163).

"Essentialism" and Personal Identity

Heaven waxeth old, and all the spheres above
Shall one day faint, and their swift motion stay:
And Time itself in time shall cease to move:
Only the Soul survives, and lives for aye.
—John Davies, *Nosce teipsum* (1599)

[W]hat we call a *mind* is nothing but a heap or collection of different perceptions, united together by certain relations, and suppos'd, tho' falsely, to be endow'd with a perfect simplicity and identity.
—David Hume, *Treatise*

The venerable ontology of *substances* is invoked to account for the continuity of identity amidst change.[8] The position of the so-called essentialist is that attributes inhere in *something* and that the essential something survives even as its surface (accidental) attributes undergo generation or corruption. Essentialism poses a challenge to the empiricist to the extent that the abiding essence of a thing is (rationally or intuitively) knowable despite its variability at the empirical level. The most vivid form of the challenge comes about as a result of personal identity: the continuity of one's own identity in the face of daily and even momentary changes in all of the material components of one's physical being. Beneath the skin all is a shifting storm of processes leading to the birth and death of myriad cells, the onset and termination of myriad physiological and chemical processes. Through it all, however, Smith remains the same *person;* hence the theory according to which Smith's *self* is a *substantial* entity in which various properties inhere.

Locke was to focus on the issue of personal identity and attempt to deal with it in a manner consistent with his empiricistic psychology. The Lockean "self" and the continuity of consciousness are featured in the second edition of the *Essay* in the chapter "Identity and Diversity," written in response to Molyneux's suggestion that a new edition address the matter of the *principium Individuationis*. For the (Newtonian) Locke, the ultimate constituents of the physical world are corpuscles; those of the mental world, sensations. Neither ensemble is a *substance*. Thus,

personal identity—that is, the sameness of a rational being—consists in consciousness alone, and, as far as this consciousness can be extended backwards to any past action or thought, so far reaches the identity of that person. So that whatever hath the consciousness of present and past actions, is the same person to whom they belong . . . *self* is not determined by Identity . . . of Substance, which it cannot be sure of . . . but only by Identity of consciousness. (1690/1956, bk. 2, chap. 27, secs. 16–23)

Locke is prepared to grant that consciousness may be said to inhere in some sort of substance, but we can know nothing of it, for such cannot be the subject of experience. Nor is he convinced at all that said "substance" is not a *material* substance, for surely, "GOD can, if he pleases, superadd to Matter a Faculty of Thinking . . . since we know not wherein Thinking consists" (1690/1956, bk. 4, chap. 3, sec. 6). It is in virtue of a particular physical organization that certain powers and properties come into being and qualify a given entity as the sort of thing it is. It is not enough that there be such powers and properties; they must be integrated within a given identifiable system. Neither speech nor rationality is sufficient to establish a human being. Thus, Prince Maurice's Brazilian parrot fails to be a *man* on Locke's account, even if the bird does qualify as a rational animal. The failure is a failure of the *body*. What we have is a rational *bird*, whatever its discursive powers.[9] Nor would speech and rationality establish (or individuate) a given *person*, for the person one is finally is no more than the contents of a given consciousness: a constellation of memories over a span of time within the ambit of consciousness. What makes Smith the person he is, therefore, is not something "essential" grounded in substance but something psychological grounded in experience.[10]

The radical implications of Locke's theory include that there is no continuing personal identity and therefore no (substantial) self to be held morally responsible. Alas, one may at the same time be and not be the same person. It is even imaginable that indefinitely many men might be the same person, something Locke illustrates by way of the "prince and the cobbler" example. After the mind of the elegant, affluent, and refined prince enters the cobbler's body there is no other conclusion possible but that the same princely *person* is now within a different *man*. The person is a shifting and unstable item, forged out of experiences, something of a cultural artifact, a product of memory and those processes that connect experiences over a span of time. What was long taken to be one's abiding character is replaced by the protean personality.

It did not take long for criticisms and alarms to be sounded. John Sergeant in his *Solid Philosophy Asserted* (1697/1984, p. 47) notes that Locke's theory leads to the inevitable conclusion that "the Individuality of Man [must] alter every moment." Henry Lee observes (1702/1978, p. 88) that on Locke's account we can "as wisely bury our Friends when fast *asleep*, as when they are *dead*. For when . . . *asleep* . . . they are not *conscious*" and are thus not persons. Lee goes on to note that persons cannot even be tried for crimes on this theory.

For how can any judge or jury be certain, that a man (during the Commission of any Fact, or entering into any Covenants) was sleepy or broad awake, sober or mad, sedate or passionate. . . . For any of these . . . circumstances may so alter the State of the Case, as to denominate him a *different* person.

Undaunted, Hume both develops and criticizes the Lockean theory, concluding that the "heap . . . of perceptions" constitutive of mind was all he could find when he undertook a search for his *self*. Rejecting Locke's "memory" theory of identity on the grounds that one's personal identity can be extended beyond what memory provides, Hume applies his "relation of cause and effect" as a corrective. Impressions give rise to ideas, these then producing other impressions: "One thought chases another, and draws after it a third, by which it is expell'd in its turn." The analogy of a parade formation is illustrative. Each of the marchers can be replaced by another marcher, but with the overall formation preserved. The relation of *cause and effect* is what preserves the "identity": as each perception within the bundle enters into associative bonds with others, the functional consequence is that ideas hold together in unique ways, not unlike the functional organization of the march. Thus, it is the *same march* even as the individual participants are replaced, as long as the replacements enter into the drill in proper fashion. Hume offers another analogy: the soul is like a republic or commonwealth whose citizens come into being and pass away, but with each generation retaining the same republic even as the laws and constitutions change. It is "in like manner that the same person may vary his character and disposition, as well as his impressions and ideas, without losing his identity" (1739/1973, bk. 1, pt. 4, sec. 6, p. 281). The causal connections within the pool of impressions and ideas constitute the basis of the continuity of the person, for all identity depends finally and solely on the relations among ideas.

By the middle of the nineteenth century the essential terms of the long debate were articulated well enough for the increasingly independent discipline of psychology to be developed along more or less distinct lines. The claims of empiricism were given their most authoritative post-Humean expression in the writings of John Stuart Mill (1806–1873), who provided both a rationale and a methodology for what would become an independent and "scientific" (experimental) psychology.[11]

Intuitionism and Rationalism: The Measured Reply

The target of Locke's *Essay* was not simply Descartes's (alleged) theory of *innate ideas* but an entire pattern of thought indebted to both Scholasticism and Neoplatonism. Locke's contemporaries included the influential group of Cambridge Platonists, who argued in behalf of a priori and rational principles of knowledge and for essentially deductive systems of morality. As for Cartesian innate ideas, perhaps the less said the better, for Descartes explicitly denied ever having advanced such a theory in the form that invited (and has since invited) criticism.[12] Actually, it was the empiricistic side of Descartes's philosophy of mind (or psychology) that led him to dub certain ideas as innate rather than derived from experience. One example of this is the idea of *matter* itself. Supposing all knowledge of externals to be mediated by the senses, Descartes reached the (phenomenalist) conclusion that what is *directly* known must be the sensation or perception itself. Assuming further that the facts of the world have no access to consciousness except by way of the senses, it follows that all of the contents of consciousness must be sensations, perceptions, ideas—anything *but* material objects. Nonetheless, everyone regards the objects of the external world as material entities causally related to our perceptions of them. The idea of matter, however, cannot be derived from anything mental (i.e., sensations, perceptions, ideas), so it must arise from a native power or disposition of the mind triggered by experiences of a certain kind. This disposition allows us to form ideas that link our perceptions to the external world. Understood this way, then at least with respect to knowledge of the external world, "there is nothing in our ideas which is not innate to the mind" (Descartes, 1648/1987, p. 304). Had Descartes the prescience to describe such knowledge in terms of "primary and secondary qualities," Locke might have been spared a hundred pages of text.

For all of the squalls of controversy there are few empiricists or rationalists in the periods under consideration who have not subscribed to one or another form of "intuitionism." Behind the notion is the recognition that something about mind (body, brain, consciousness, perception) is constituted in such a way as to receive or convert or translate the bare physical events of the external world in such a way to render them meaningful, intelligible, and useful. The debate, then, tends to center on just what it is that performs such functions, whether the performance is at the expense of truth, and whether the right way to address such questions is by way of further observation or through systematic and rational analysis.

Hume's most acute and influential contemporary critic was Thomas Reid (1710–1796), whose *An Inquiry into the Human Mind* (1764/ 1863b) remains a compelling defense of one species of intuitionism and a trenchant analysis of the assets and liabilities of empiricistic theories of mind. This father of Scottish "commonsense" philosophy would be the principal target of John Stuart Mill's critique of "intuitionism" and a central figure in that part of Scottish thought that influenced Kant and other German Enlightenment writers.[13] A brief sketch of several of Reid's major criticisms and principles is useful as an introduction to rationalistic psychology in the modern era.

Against what he took to be the very basis of skepticism, namely, that all knowledge of the external world is representational, Reid affirms the theory of *direct realism.* He rejects the view (dubbed by Reid the *ideal* theory) that percipients never know things themselves but only the "idea" of things that the mind represents in the form of "images" of things. Reid insists that there is actually no evidence of this and that such a theory could only apply to visual perception; there can be no image of an odor! Moreover, a close analysis of the theory of visual images finds it hopelessly defective.

In chapter 6 ("Of Seeing") of his *Inquiry* Reid develops this theory in the section he titles "The Geometry of Visibles," where he anticipates Riemannian geometry by decades. The main line of argument here may be summarized as follows: Objects in the external world are projected on the spherical surface of the cornea and then to the bottom of the eye, which is also spherical. If, in fact, "ideas" of external objects are, to use Hume's term, *copies* of these sensory impressions, the perceived object (e.g., a rectilinear triangle) should appear spherical, which it does not. Were it the case that what is visually perceived are copies made of objects projected onto the surface of a sphere, the *visual* perceptual outcomes would differ radically from what is reported by touch. Tangibly straight lines would be seen as curved, tangible straight triangles would be spherical, and so on. Such projected forms within Reid's geometric system are nonetheless based on a deductive geometric system as coherent and defined as Euclid's. However, within this system the angles of triangles sum to more than 180°; parallel lines intersect at two loci; the only visibly straight lines are circumferential lines spanning the sphere. Were all these features common to ordinary visual perception, it is this geometry and not Euclid's that would have been developed first. True, perceived objects in this system are projected onto a very small area of the retina where differences between Euclidean and non-Euclidean forms are negligible, but this perceptual ability further supports the general *realist* thesis according to which animals are constituted in such a way as to give them valid information of the facts of the external world. The caterpillar, observes Reid, will climb over a thousand leaves until it finds one that is right for its needs, the results here pragmatically defeating the skeptic's challenge.

Reid observes that apart from the idle speculations of philosophers, no one has ever doubted the difference between objects perceived in the external world and our ideas about them. The concept of *illusion* presupposes nonillusory knowledge of the external world and the fact of daily success in dealing with the external world indicates that organisms are designed in such a way as to have realistic contact with the world about them. Surely the difference between the lion now making an impression on the visual organ, and one's idea of a lion, is rather more substantial than the Humean account, according to which the former is just more lively or vivid. On the question of just how it is that percipients, whose knowledge of objects in the external world is in fact the result of complex sensory processes, do perceive the objects themselves and not the intervening processes, Reid does not pretend to have an answer. There is no logical reason why food is digested in the stomach rather than in the foot. The order of nature predates logic. All knowledge has a starting point: the "common notions" of the ancient mathematicians in the matter of formal systems, the principles of "common sense" in the matter of objective knowledge of the world. Knowledge itself presupposes any number of truths that cannot be derived from more basic precepts. Reid notes that external objects stimulate sensory structures whose responses are the natural signs of these objects. What is perceived, however, are not these, but the objects themselves. By its very constitution and in a way that is not and perhaps cannot be known, the mind is able to go from the physiological signs of such things to the things thus signified. Governing all such transactions are what Reid with reluctance calls the "principles of common sense," taking these to be what we (and in some cases the animal kingdom in general) are under an obligation to take for granted. Hume doubts much, but not his own sensations, and this because he *can't*.

In "Essay-Three" (chapters 4–7) of his *Essays on the Intellectual Powers of Man* (1785/1863a), Reid examines personal identity and the Lockean and Humean reduction of *self* to experience and mental associations. He makes short work of Locke's memory theory. Needless to say, all but the insane have the strongest conviction that their personal identities stretch back as far as their memories reach, but it is not memory that achieves the identity. Recalling oneself to have been defeated at the Battle of Waterloo is not what makes one Napoleon. Then taking a page from Berkeley's *Alciphron,* Reid illustrates the formal defects of the Lockean account. Imagine a young officer (dubbed *B*) decorated for valor in battle and recalling when years earlier he had been a boy (dubbed *A*) punished for taking fruit from the orchard. Consider now an aged general (dubbed *C*) remembering his decoration for valor but having no recollection whatever of punishment in childhood. Assuming the self to be nothing more than whatever is present in consciousness, including all that memory can reach, $A = B$, $B = C$, but $A \neq C$. Thus does the identity collapse.

It is worth noting, especially in light of efforts to salvage the Lockean theory of self, that Reid had a deeper understanding of Locke's reasoning on this subject than later commentators were and current commentators are, wont to recognize or, alas, share. Recall Locke's three modes of knowing (intuitive, demonstrative, and sensitive), now in relation to personal identity: Personal identity cannot be known by demonstration, for in that case knowledge of the self would be logical and derived from principles and would be available only to those skilled in demonstrative sciences. It also cannot arise as a result of sensory experience, for there is nothing in experience per se that identifies its subject; rather, the subject identifies the experience. Moreover, as the stream of consciousness is ever changing, consciousness cannot provide the grounds of a continuing personal identity. Nor (as Hume had shown) can one's personal identity be projected into the future and, in that imagined place, be distinguished from one's personal identity in the past. Accordingly, on Locke's own epistemology, this leaves only an *intuitive* knowledge of one's personal identity, which is Reid's position.

Reid's critique of Hume is different, for Hume's theory of personal identity is different from Locke's (Robinson & Beauchamp, 1978). The "bundle of perceptions" that turn up when Hume undertakes a search for his *self* are held together by causal relations in the mind, and it is the uniqueness of these relations that generate a unique self. Reid devotes less space to this proposition, largely because he has already satisfied himself that the Humean account of causality is itself defective. Reid judges the regularity ("constant conjunction") theory of causation to be discredited in common experience; no one thinks that day is the cause of night or vice versa merely because the two are "constantly conjoin'd" in experience. Further, the concept of causality cannot be got from the perception of external events (as Hume himself has argued). What, then, is its source? On Reid's account, the notion of a cause is probably an inference developed very early in life and drawn from the immediate recognition of ourselves as having active powers. That is, someone's (infant's) recognition of his or her having the ability to bring certain events about (bringing a thumb to the mouth) conduces to the notion of a power. Absent this notion, there would be no basis upon which to rest the assumption that events external to oneself are similarly (i.e., causally) brought about. But the possession of active power presupposes the intuitive awareness of oneself as the source of one's actions. Thus, for there to be causal relations in experience there must be a prior conception of causality; for there to be a conception of causality there must be an awareness of active power; for there to be active powers there must be an intuitive awareness of oneself as the source of one's actions. Conclusion: a (substantial) *self* is presupposed in both the Lockean and Humean theories of personal identity. This species of intuitionism has been something of a fixture in rationalistic philosophies, and it becomes a central feature of them through the influence of Kant.

If Locke may be said (but only with needed reservation) to have endorsed the ageless maxim "Nihil in intellectu quod non fuerit prius in sensu," then the shortest path to the intuitionist's or rationalist's critique is by way of Gottfried Wilhelm Leibniz's, "Nisi intellectus ipse": nothing is in the intellect except the intellect itself.[14] In his *New Essays on the Understanding* (1765/1982), Leibniz (1646–1716) closely examines the controversies arising from the works of Descartes and his continental critics (notably Pierre Gassendi) and from Locke's *Essay*. His defense of innate ideas is grounded in the claim that certain established principles of thought itself cannot be gleaned from experience and must be granted if the mind is to be receptive to experience itself. There is, then, that same intuitionism in Leibniz that is found in Reid and that comes to be fully developed in Kant's *Critique of Pure Reason*.

The Kantian "a priori"

Immanuel Kant (1724–1804), along with Descartes and Leibniz, was one of the "textbook" rationalists. He claimed that he had been shaken out of his philosophical complacency—that he had been awakened from his "dogmatic slumber"—by David Hume. The question that remains unanswered is whether thus awakened Kant thereupon defeated or completed what might be called Hume's project. It is in the *Critique of Pure Reason* (1781/1965) that Kant tests the claims of empiricism and the limits of reason in the matter of what is knowable.[15] A review of his position begins with a clarification of terms.

As Kant would use the word, *transcendental* refers to that which transcends the level of (empirical) observation. *Pure,* too, is contrasted with that which is given in experience and thus refers to what is nonempirical. *Analytic* and *synthetic* refer to the truth conditions of propositions. A proposition is synthetic when what it affirms is subject to empirical modes of verification. A proposition is analytic when the meaning of the subject term is included in the meaning of the predicate; for example, unmarried men are bachelors. The truth of analytic propositions is established independently of experience and is in this logical sense prior to any and all empirical modes of confirmation or test. Thus, what is analytically true is true a priori. Understood in these terms, Hume's central thesis, consistent with the tenets of empiricism, is that the truth of a synthetic proposition can never be established a priori. Kant's criticism then succeeds just in case there is at least one synthetic proposition the truth of which is known a priori.[16]

Granting Hume's claim that all knowledge arises from experience, Kant notes nonetheless that all knowledge is not *grounded* in experience, for experience itself needs a grounding. Under the heading of the "Analytic of Concepts," Kant develops his "transcendental deduction" and lays the foundation for what is finally a theory of knowledge: "We are already in possession of concepts which are of two quite different kinds, and which yet agree in that they relate to objects in a completely *a priori* manner, namely, the concepts of space and time as forms of sensibility, and the categories as concepts of the understanding" (1787/1965, B118).[17]

In referring to the concepts of space and time as forms of sensibility Kant registers the logically necessary conditions for there to be experience of any sort at all. Neither time nor space is given in experience, so both concepts are *pure* (i.e., nonempirical). Yet, both are necessarily related to "objects" and are so related to each other "in a completely *a priori* manner." They are, then, *pure intuitions (Anschauungen)*, not derivable from experience but necessarily grounding experience. The famous Kantian *categories* are the pure concepts of the understanding that exhaust the forms of knowing, as time and space exhaust the forms of sensibility. They are reduced to tabular form (table 3.1) at B106 and analyzed in detail under the heading "Transcendental Doctrine of Judgment," in chapter 1, "The Schematism of the Pure Concepts of Understanding."

Within this fourfold table Kant includes the *schemata*, or frameworks, within which all knowledge can be had. The categories are not supplied by experience—nothing in experience qualifies as "necessary," for example—and therefore are pure. They are also logically prior to

Table 3.1
Kant's Table of Categories

I. Quantity	II. Quality	III. Relation	IV. Modality
Unity	Reality	Inherence and subsistence	Possibility-impossibility
Plurality	Negation	Causality and dependence	Existence-nonexistence
Totality	Limitation	Community	Necessity-contingency

Sources: From Kant (1785/1965, chap. 1, A137–150, B176–189).

cognitive encounters of any kind, whether with the world of fact or the formal world of abstractions. No number of discrete events can be added to yield "all." Rather, numerosity itself presupposes a framework, or schema, for categorical distinctions between and among unity, plurality, and totality. Similarly, absent the (pure) concept of causality, there could be no basis upon which temporally coincidental events could be thus classified.

The points of compatibility between Kant and Hume are numerous and suggestive. Kant grants, for example, that all empirical knowledge is mediated by sensory processes and is thus representational and not direct. What is known empirically are *phenomena*, but the things they really are in themselves are the *noumena*. The understanding is able to conclude from the existence of phenomena *that* something must stand behind them, but cannot know *what* it is. Kantian epistemology, therefore, breeds its own and even more daunting variety of skepticism. On the Kantian account empirical knowledge bears the stamp of merely contingent mechanisms of perception, the fidelity of whose representations can never be known; and the necessary *forms* of knowledge—the categories—are logically unassailable but at the same time entirely empty of content. None of this supports the more radical "sociologies of knowledge" now so influential. Kant's categories are not established by anything about us that is *human* as such; they are rather the formal framework within which there *can* be concepts of the understanding for anything that has understanding. Note, then, that Kant is not defending a version of epistemological relativism; quite the contrary. Rather, he is establishing the boundary conditions beyond which neither perception nor reason can reach.

Rationalism and Empiricism—Are There Implications for Cognitive Psychology?

Considering only the half-century of Piagetian research on children's concepts ("schemata") of necessity and of universals ("totality") the influence of Kantian epistemology on cognitive psychology becomes quite apparent. But there are far more foundational aspects of the historic dialogue between the major representatives of these two schools. Indeed, radically different implications can be and have been drawn from the same treatises. It is sufficient within the aims of this essay merely to illustrate the point.

Consider first the issues raised by language. A radically empiricistic account of language is advanced by behavioristic psychologists, notably B. F. Skinner in his *Verbal Behavior* (Skinner, 1957). On this account, language is an acquired behavior that, though complex, is subject to the same "operant" analysis as bar pressing or bicycle riding. Critics of this thesis, notably the linguist Noam Chomsky, have countered with nativistic theories according to which the structural or grammatical features of language express "prewired" features of the brain. Despite widely varying practices of child rearing, children begin to frame statements grammatically at about the same age the world over; and this occurs notwithstanding the strong tendency of parents to "reinforce" not the structure of such utterances but their content (Chomsky, 1959).

The tendency within contemporary cognitive psychology is to understand an issue of this sort as, to use the overworked and misleading term, *empirical*. The strategy then is to study little linguists in early stages of development and record their linguistic achievements, carefully assessing the environmental influences. But it is clear that the existence of language must depend on powers and capacities present before any relevant experience, powers whose absence would make it impossible for language to be learned at all. Perhaps the shortest proof of this was supplied by Reid in the eighteenth century:

I think it is demonstrable that, if mankind had not a natural language, they could never have invented an artificial one by their reason and ingenuity. For all artificial language supposes some compact or agreement to affix a certain meaning to certain signs; therefore there must be compacts or agreements before the use of artificial signs; but there can be no compact or agreement without signs, nor without language; and therefore there must be a natural language before any artificial language can be invented: Which was to be demonstrated. (Reid, 1764/1863b, p. 93)

At the foundation of Reid's argument is the recognition that language is the means by which human communities enter into shared practices and cooperative ventures. His account is ethological, social, and realistic. Contrast this with the popular program within contemporary cognitive science, the program that strives to explain such achievements by proposing "processes" and models that allegedly mimic human cognition. If human language is inextricably bound up with social plans and purposes, and is thus grounded in uniquely human cultures of thought and value, what explanatory power is likely to reside in noncultural, noncontextual devices?

Such so-called functionalist accounts would advance cognitive science by establishing systems whose hardware and software configurations—*modularity,* as Minsky calls it (Minsky, 1981)—generate just those "functions" identified as sufficient for one or another cognitive achievement. The modularity theory of mind would explain complex achievements by recourse to some number of subsidiary functions performed by identifiable modules, presumably without any need for mentalistic or folk-psychology terms. But the functions themselves are so laced with these very folk understandings that, stripped of them, the ensemble of modules might just as well be found in a hardware store. In this connection arguments of the sort advanced by, for example, S. Stich (1983) to the effect that such folk concepts as belief and desire are reducible to the operations of identifiable modules, take on the character of Molière's *vis dormativa.* It is entirely unclear in such accounts just what would be achieved if, in fact, the operation of some modular mechanism generated states recognizable *by believers* as "belief" states.

In the matter of beliefs, orthodoxy and heterodoxy presuppose a cultural ethos and are unintelligible in any other terms. The exception to this is the (Reidian) belief each actor has in the potential efficacy of his own actions, Reid insisting that no one undertakes what he truly believes to be beyond his powers (save for some symbolic purpose, as in futile gestures). But belief thus understood now requires the very agency and *self* at once central to folk-psychology explanations of significant actions and anathema to the reductionist.

In like fashion, for it is a fashion, there are "neurocognitive" projects of one sort or another, fortified by the thick book of fact compiled by neurology and the neural sciences over the past century and especially in the most recent decades. It is with restrained irony that one reads criticisms of the rationalist tradition by those whose own neurophilosophy more or less follows, even if blindly, in the Kantian tracks.[18] It may well be that nervous systems are structured in such a way as to permit the elaboration of ever more complex states. The standard functionalist argument, however, accepts that what makes a system worthy of cognitive ascriptions is nothing necessarily material or physical about it. Rather, it is its ability to realize some program that serves as the formal basis for its functioning. On this account, a system is a cognitive system when its functions, for all philosophically or conceptually valid purposes, are taken to be grounded in a priori principles indistinguishable from *pure intuitions and concepts of the understanding*. In the absence of such (prewired? hardwired?) formal and a priori organization, the events in the external world could never be relevantly connected; they could not even be *events*. Presumably there is or will be sufficient technology to produce programs and machines able to realize them in such a manner as to recover the Kantian categories, one and all. What conclusions would follow from this, other than that all problems become problems in virtue of certain "pure concepts" that provide the necessary context for cognition itself? That is, what would be yielded other than a needlessly clumsy rediscovery of the main themes of Kant's first *Critique*?

Suppose, further, that it can be shown that highly evolved nervous systems, by way of the richness of the connections within them, have sufficient resources to generate "Kantian" forms of cognition; that they can, as it were, compute modal categories, causal relationships, and so forth. Again, it is not clear what of consequence would follow. Surely Kant at least suspected that his own philosophical undertakings required a functioning brain. But a functioning brain is not what determines the categories, nor is it the necessary precondition for their elucidation.

The question must remain open as to the extent to which scientific inquiry and experimental findings can vindicate or defeat a developed philosophical theory, a systematic philosophy. To some extent the task of philosophy is the clarification of concepts and testing the implications derived from them when they are deployed in one or another set of propositions. It is not philosophy that legislates what will or will not qualify as fact, and it is not experimental science that legislates how a body of fact is most coherently and defensibly interpreted. Accordingly, nothing in the most recent century of experimental psychology bears directly (or could bear directly) on the larger philosophical claims of empiricist and rationalist philosophers. To think that the laboratory is the court of last recourse in such matters is to beg, not settle the matter. The scientific undertaking itself is a vindication of rationalism's most consistent claim, namely, that there are answers to all meaningful questions and that the rational and judicious mind stands as the final arbiter when conflicting answers arise.

The general point was offered with clarity and economy by Werner Heisenberg:

If we go beyond biology and include psychology in the discussion, then there can scarcely be any doubt but that the concepts of physics, chemistry, and evolution together will not be sufficient to describe the facts. . . . [W]e . . . start from the fact that the human mind enters as object and subject into the scientific process of psychology." (Heisenberg, 1959)

As for the implications of empiricism, it is worth recalling the *radical empiricism* of William James, radical because it rules out nothing that has been featured in the human experience.[19] James's version of empiricism takes the shifting, cluttered, and chaotic world of human experience as the undoing of each and every "block universe" minted by the confident theorist.

Notes

1. Needless to say, Plato's own position on this matter was not constant. The supremacy of the rational in such dialogues as the *Meno*, the *Republic*, and the *Laws* is cogently challenged by the ontological powers of *eros* in the *Symposium* and the *Phaedrus*.

2. Passages in Aristotle are located by the traditional Bekker numbers given in most editions of the works of Aristotle so that readers can find passages in whatever edition they are using. In most instances citations in the present chapter are

taken from *The Complete Works of Aristotle,* edited by Jonathan Barnes (1984). Greek terms are taken from the Greek text provided by the Loeb Classics editions.

3. In transliterating the Greek capital letters are used for long vowels and lowercase letters for short vowels; e.g., eta *(E)* and epsilon *(e);* omega *(O)* and omicron *(o).*

4. Plato's early period covers the years when Socrates was still alive and when Plato may have been composing such early dialogues as the *Protagoras, Meno,* and *Gorgias.* That he later completely abandoned the theory of the "forms" is arguable, for it is featured in the late dialogue the *Theaetetus.*

5. Germane to the issues under consideration here is Ockham's "Seven Quodlibeta" *(Quadlibeta septem).* Question 13 of *Quadlibet I* is "Whether that which is known by the understanding first according to a primacy of generation is the individual." A redaction of the seven is given in MkKeon's *Selections from Medieval Philosophers.*

6. The *Enquiry* appeared with this title in the 1758 edition of Hume's *Essays and Treatises on Several Subjects.* It had been earlier published (1748) as *Philosophical Essays concerning Human Understanding.* The main purpose of the *Enquiry* was to compensate for the relative indifference shown his *Treatise* of 1739 by putting that work's central arguments in a more accessible form. For a quarter of a century Hume wrote, revised, and added to a collection of *Essays Moral, Political and Literary* (1740–1776), the final and fully edited version appearing posthumously in 1777.

7. Hume's consideration of probabilities is most keen in book 1, part 3, sections 2 and 12, and part 4, section 1 of the *Treatise.* In Locke's *Essay* (bk. 4, chaps. 15–16) "degrees of probability" are discussed within the context of juridical reasoning. Juries run the gamut from total assenting belief to total doubt. The basis for this must be ideas about the relevance and reliability of certain combinations of facts. Belief, then, varies in strength with degrees of probability, and these degrees are established empirically. For a thorough analysis of the history of probabilistic thinking and the place of Locke's and Hume's writings therein, consult Lorraine Daston, *Classical Probability in the Enlightenment* (1988).

8. The concept of *substance* has been variously understood and expressed. For Aristotle the essence *(ousia)* of a thing is that of which attributes are predicated but is not itself a predicate of anything else. For Descartes man is essentially a "thinking thing" *(res cogitans),* this essence being irreducible to the material composition of the body. Thomas Reid (1710–1796) expresses the more general sense of *substance* as "an unchanging subject of thought."

9. See Yolton's *Thinking Matter* (1983) for the sources and inferences of this eighteenth-century predilection regarding language.

10. The Lockean and Humean positions are different and call for different critical appraisals. In corrections to the first edition of his *Treatise,* where Hume seeks to qualify certain arguments developed in the body of the text, he is especially vexed by the question of personal identity. He says, "I find myself involv'd in

such a labyrinth, that, I must confess, I neither know how to correct my former opinions, nor how to render them consistent" (p. 633). On the general issue, see also D. N. Robinson and T. L. Beauchamp (1978).

11. For a discussion of Mill's psychology and its place within the modern history of the discipline, see D. N. Robinson (1982, chap. 2; 1995, pp. 263–270). Wundt, of course, is the widely acknowledged father of experimental psychology, but within the empiricistic tradition Mill's works—chiefly his *A System of Logic* (1843) and *An Examination of Sir William Hamilton's Philosophy* (1865)—supplied the most detailed and developed philosophical context within which a scientific psychology might evolve.

12. Replying to a broadsheet posted by Regius in 1647, Descartes defends himself against the criticism thus: "I have never written or taken the view that the mind requires innate ideas which are something distinct from its own faculty of thinking. I did, however, observe that there were certain thoughts within me which neither came to me from external objects nor were determined by my will, but which came solely from the power of thinking. . . . So I applied the term 'innate' to the ideas . . . in order to distinguish them from others, which I called 'adventitious' or 'made up'" (Descartes, 1648/1987, p. 303).

13. On Mill's focus on Reid's *Inquiry,* see Robinson (1982, chap. 2). Scottish and specifically Reid's influence on Kant is closely examined by Manfred Keuhn (1987).

14. Leibniz undertakes a detailed criticism of Lockean empiricism in his *New Essays on the Understanding.* Though completed in 1704, the work was not published until 1765. Leibniz withheld it owing to the recency of Locke's death (1704) and at a time when the Newton-Leibniz controversy needed no further fuel. The form of the treatise is a dialogue between Philalethes and Theophilus. It is in book 2, chapter 1 (p. 110) that the "nisi intellectus ipse" passage is offered as a counter to the maxim, though the maxim itself is not found as such in Locke's *Essay.* Indeed, after declaring that "an exception [to the maxim] must be made of the soul itself and its states" (p. 110), Theophilus notes that his position "agrees pretty well" with Locke, "for he looks for a good proportion of ideas in the mind's reflection on its own nature."

15. The first edition of the *Critique of Pure Reason* appeared in 1781. It is the second edition (1787) that was authoritatively translated by Norman Kemp Smith and first published in 1929 and reprinted thereafter. All references here are to the 1929 translation.

16. Still illuminating on this point is L. W. Beck's 1967 essay, which reaches the conclusion that Hume's empiricistic argument succeeds only if Kant's rationalistic argument is assumed to be true.

17. By convention the letters *A* and *B* refer to the first and second editions, and the numbers to the pagination in these respective editions.

18. For instructive examples of this, see P. S. Churchland and T. J. Sejnowski (1989) and D. M. Armstrong (1981).

19. See his *Essays in Radical Empiricism* (1912).

References

Aristotle (1984). *The complete works of Aristotle* (2 vols., Jonathan Barnes, Ed.). Princeton, NJ: Princeton University Press.

Aristotle (1933). *Metaphysics* (Hugh Tredennick, Trans.). Cambridge, MA: Harvard University Press.

Armstrong, D. M. (1981). *The nature of mind and other essays.* Ithaca, NY: Cornell University Press.

Beck, L. W. (1967). Once more unto the breach: Kant's answer to Hume again. *Ratio, 9,* 33–37.

Berkeley, G. (1963). *A treatise concerning the principles of human knowledge.* La Salle, IL: Open Court. (Original work published 1710.)

Chomsky, N. (1959). [Review of Skinner's *Verbal behavior.*] *Language, 35,* 26–58.

Churchland, P. S., & Sejnowski, T. (1989). Neural representation and neural computation. In *Neural connections, mental computations* (L. Nadel et al., Eds.). Cambridge, MA: MIT Press.

D'Alembert, Jean Le Rond (1963). *Preliminary discourse to the encyclopedia of Diderot* (Richard Schwab, Trans.). Indianapolis: Bobbs-Merrill. (Original work published 1751.)

Daston, L. (1988). *Classical probability in the Enlightenment.* Princeton, NJ: Princeton University Press.

Descartes, R. (1987). *Comments on a certain broadsheet* (Dugald Murdoch, Trans.; original work published 1648). In vol. 1, J. Cottingham, R. Stoothoff, & D. Murdoch (Trans.), *The philosophical writings of Descartes* (pp. 293–311). Cambridge, England: Cambridge University Press.

Heisenberg, W. (1959). *Physics and philosophy.* London: George Allen & Unwin.

Hume, D. (1965). *An enquiry concerning human understanding.* In Ralph Cohen (Ed.), *The essential works of David Hume.* New York: Bantam. (Original work published 1758.)

Hume, D. (1973). *A treatise of human nature* (L. A. Selby-Bigge, Ed.). Oxford, England: Oxford University Press. (Original work published 1739.)

Hume, D. (1988). *Essays moral, political and literary* (Eugene Miller, Ed.). Indianapolis: Liberty Fund Press. (Original work published 1777.)

James, W. (1912). *Essays in radical empiricism.* New York: Longmans Green.

Kant, I. (1965). *Critique of pure reason* (Norman Kemp Smith, Trans.). New York: St. Martin's Press. (Original work published 1787.)

Kuehn, M. (1987). *Scottish common sense in Germany.* Montreal: McGill-Queen's University Press.

Lee, H. (1978). *Anti-scepticism.* London: Clavil & Harper. New York: Garland. (Original work published 1702.)

Leibniz, G. W. (1982). *New essays on the human understanding* (Abridged ed., P. Remnant & J. Bennett, Trans. & Eds.). Cambridge, England: Cambridge University Press. (Original work published 1765.)

Locke, J. (1956). *An essay concerning human understanding.* Chicago: Henry Regnery. (Original work published 1690.)

Mill, J. *History of India* (1818). London: Longmans Green.

Mill, J. S. (1843). *A System of Logic.* London: Longmans Green.

Mill, J. S. (1979). *An examination of Sir William Hamilton's philosophy.* (Original work published 1865.). In J. M. Robinson (Ed.), *Collected works* (Vol. 9). Toronto: University of Toronto Press.

Minsky, M. (1981). K-lines. In D. Norman (Ed.), *Perspectives on cognitive science* (pp. 87–103). A theory of memory. NJ: Ablex.

MkKeon, R. (1930). *Selections from the medieval philosophers* (Vol. 2, pp. 351–421). New York: Scribner's.

Reid, T. (1863a). *Essays on the intellectual powers of man* (Original work published 1785). In Sir William Hamilton (Ed.), *The works of Thomas Reid* (6th ed.) Edinburgh, Scotland: Maclachlan & Stewart.

Reid, T. (1863b). *An inquiry into the human mind.* (Original work published 1764.) In Sir William Norton (Ed.), *The works of Thomas Reid* (6th ed., pp. 87–103). Edinburgh, Scotland: Maclachlan & Stewart.

Robinson, D. N. (1982). *Toward a science of human nature: Essays on the psychologies of Mill, Hegel, Wundt and James.* New York: Columbia University Press.

Robinson, D. N. (1995). *An intellectual history of psychology* (3rd ed.). Madison: University of Wisconsin Press.

Robinson, D. N., & Beauchamp, T. (1978). *Personal identity: Reid's answer to Hume. Monist, 61,* 326–339.

Sergeant, J. (1984). *Solid philosophy asserted.* New York: Garland. (Original work published London: R. Clavil, 1697.)

Skinner, B. F. (1957). *Verbal behavior.* New York: Appleton-Century, Crofts.

Stich, S. (1983). *From folk psychology to cognitive science: The case against belief.* Cambridge, MA: MIT Press.

Yolton, J. (1983). *Thinking matter.* Minneapolis: University of Minnesota Press.

II

Representation and Process in Cognition

4

Single-Code versus Multiple-Code Theories in Cognition

Timothy P. McNamara

I begin this chapter by having the reader answer two simple questions:

1. How many windows does your home have?
2. In two or three sentences, explain the causes of the U.S. Civil War.

The experiences I have while answering these questions differ dramatically. To answer the first question, I visualize my house, one side at a time, and count the windows. The knowledge I use to answer the question seems to represent the properties of my house in a direct, perceptual manner. In contrast, I am able to answer the second question by retrieving, in a pretty much unconscious manner, the relevant information from memory. Certainly, I do not need to visualize scenes from the Civil War to answer the question. Complexities aside, the major question that I examine in this chapter is this: Is the knowledge that I use to answer the first question the same kind of knowledge as the knowledge that allows me to answer the second? If so, why are my experiences so different; and if not, what is the nature of each kind of knowledge?

The goal of this chapter is to explore a fundamental problem in cognitive psychology, namely, how our knowledge of the world is represented in the mind. Specifically, I hope to provide a tutorial review of two major classes of theories of knowledge representation. According to one class of theories, human knowledge is represented in an abstract format, called *propositions*. The other major class of theories accepts that much of human knowledge can be represented propositionally but rejects the claim that all knowledge is so represented. According to these theories, a significant portion of knowledge is represented in a perceptual format, often referred to as *images* or more generally as *analogical representations*. In this chapter, I will refer to the first class of theories as *single-code theories* and to the second class of theories as *multiple-code theories.*

The plan of this chapter is as follows. I begin by discussing the nature of mental representation. In that section, I explore what mental representations are and why cognitive scientists believe that they exist. In the second section, I examine single-code and multiple-code theories of knowledge representation. The third section of the paper reviews the so-called imagery debate of the 1970s and the early 1980s. Although this debate focused on issues more narrow than those examined in this chapter, it produced several general lessons for researchers interested in knowledge representation. The fourth and final section summarizes the discussion.

The Nature of Knowledge Representations

What Are Mental Representations?

A *representation* is something that stands for something else. The words of any human language are examples of a form of representation because they stand for objects, events, and ideas. Words are an abstract representation because the relation between a word and the object or the idea it represents is arbitrary; words in other languages can refer to the same objects and ideas, and with few exceptions the referent of a word cannot be predicted from its auditory or visual form. I will refer to representations of this kind as *symbolic.* A representation can also be concrete. For example, the silhouette in figure 4.1 is a representation of a falcon taken from an encyclopedia of birds (Terres, 1980). This silhouette could be used by a beginning bird watcher to identify a falcon in flight. An important characteristic of this representation is that it represents a falcon in a direct, perceptual way: falcons often display long, thin tails in flight, and so does the silhouette. I will refer to these representations as *analogical.*

A *mental representation* is a structure in the mind that preserves information about objects or events in the world. For example, you have a mental representation of the spatial layout of your bedroom, and this representation preserves relative locations of objects in the space. This mental representation supports a number of abilities, including imagining the room from different viewpoints, estimating distances from memory,

Figure 4.1
A depiction of a bird. (Reprinted from Terres, J. K. [1980]. *The Audubon Society Encyclopedia of North American Birds.*

navigating in the dark, and so on, all of which depend on mental processes that operate on the spatial representation. As we shall see later, the fact that you can imagine what your room looks like does not imply that the mental representation is analogical. The mental representation may be very abstract.

Are Mental Representations Necessary?

There are many reasons to posit the existence of mental representations. One of the more important reasons is that human behavior cannot be explained without specifying how individuals represent the world to themselves. The contemporary history of this idea can be traced to Chomsky's (1959) critique of behaviorist accounts of language acquisition (e.g., Skinner, 1957). As an example, consider the following anecdote. Recently, I was driving around Nashville trying to find a plumbing store, and I ended up driving several miles out of my way because I thought I could exit from the interstate highway onto a cross street, Fessler's Lane, when in fact there was no exit. To explain my behavior, one must appeal to ideas of the following kind: "McNamara was looking for a plumbing store because he wanted to fix his sink," "McNamara thought that he could exit the highway onto Fessler's Lane," and so forth. One must know how I interpreted the world and represented it mentally to understand why I did what I did. My belief that I could get to Fessler's Lane from the interstate highway is especially enlightening because it makes no sense at all given the physical arrangement of the highways and cross streets. This belief is sensible only if one knows that I *mis*represented crucial information about the roads of Nashville.

In summary, the concept of mental representation is fundamental to the cognitive sciences. The controversial questions have to do with how information is represented, whether different types of information (e.g., visual vs. verbal) are represented in different ways, and whether theories of mental representation can be tested experimentally. These are the questions we shall examine in this chapter.

Single-Code versus Multiple-Code Theories of Knowledge Representation

When we say that a person "knows" something, there are at least two senses in which we use the term (e.g., Ryle, 1949). One kind of knowledge can be verbalized, visualized, or declared in some manner, and for these reasons has been called *declarative knowledge.* A second type of knowledge consists of skills, cognitive operations, knowledge of how to do things, and has been called *procedural knowledge.* If I ask when you were born, what you had for breakfast this morning, or what the Eiffel tower looks like, you will be able to respond in a way that allows you to communicate an answer, even though the response may require drawing a picture. In contrast, if I ask how you are able to ride a bicycle or how you are able to understand what I write in this passage, you will not be able to give a satisfactory answer, and, certainly, another person could not learn from the answer how to perform the activity.

There is a growing consensus in cognitive psychology that a complete theory of knowledge representation must explain both declarative knowledge and procedural knowledge (e.g., Anderson, 1993, and Squire, 1992; but see Ratcliff & McKoon, 1996, for an alternative point of view). This incipient consensus did not exist, however, when many influential theories of knowledge representation were originally proposed. Consistent with the scope of these theories, the scope of this chapter will be limited to declarative knowledge. Hence, the term *single-code theories* will be used to refer to single-code theories of declarative knowledge. This usage is consistent with usage in the field, even though it misrepresents a few theories of knowledge representation (e.g., Anderson's, 1976, original ACT theory, which used propositions to represent declarative knowledge and productions [condition-action rules] to represent procedural knowledge).

Single-Code Theories

Single-code theories might just as well be called propositional theories because all of the major single-code theories of knowledge representation are propositional theories (e.g., Anderson, 1976; Collins & Loftus, 1975; Fodor, 1975; Kintsch, 1974; Norman, Rumelhart, & LNR Research Group, 1975; Quillian, 1967). According to these theories, human knowledge is represented in terms of a single code: propositions.

A proposition is the smallest unit of knowledge that can stand as an assertion, the smallest unit that can be true or false. For example, consider the sentence "Bush declared war against the oil-rich country of Iraq, which was led by Saddam Hussein." This sentence contains three propositions:

1. Bush declared war against Iraq.
2. Iraq has an abundance of oil.
3. Saddam Hussein was the leader of Iraq.

Propositions are not the same as words; they are best thought of as ideas that can be expressed in words. The same three propositions could be expressed in another language, such as Spanish, using different words and somewhat different grammar: "Bush declaró la guerra contra el rico país petrolero de Iraq, el cual era liderado por Saddam Hussein." In fact, a proposition has been characterized as the meaning that is preserved under paraphrase or translation. To divorce propositions from the words used to express them, it is customary to use special notation to designate propositions. For example, using a variant of Kintsch's (1974) notation, the three propositions in the Bush sentence can be written as follows:

1′. (DECLARE-WAR, Bush, Iraq)
2′. (OIL-RICH, Iraq)
3′. (LEADER-OF, Saddam Hussein, Iraq)

The first word in each proposition expresses the *relation*, and the next one or two words are called *arguments* of the proposition.

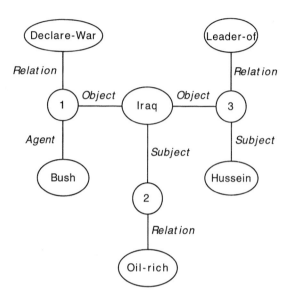

Figure 4.2
A propositional network representation of the sentence "Bush declared war against the oil-rich country of Iraq, which was led by Saddam Hussein."

Propositional representations are often depicted in networks, and there are many schemes for doing so (e.g., Anderson, 1976; Norman et al., 1975). The example in figure 4.2 represents a combination of several of these methods. In this network, the circles represent the propositions, the ellipses represent relations and arguments, and the lines represent the associations between them. The circles and ellipses are commonly called *nodes,* and the lines are called *links.* The only spatial relation of importance in the network is whether or not things are connected to each other.

There are many retrieval schemes associated with propositional networks, but most are based on a concept of spreading activation (e.g., Anderson, 1976, 1983; Collins & Loftus, 1975; Quillian, 1967). Specific properties of this process vary from theory to theory, but the general features are that the retrieval of an item from memory consists of activating its internal representation, the activation of a node spreads through the links to other nodes in the network, and the time required to retrieve an item from memory is inversely related to its activation level; that is, more active items in memory are retrieved faster than less active ones.

Single-code—in particular, propositional—theories have been proposed for several reasons. First, there is general agreement that propositions can represent any well-specified set of information, which implies that propositional representation is a general formalism for representing human knowledge. The power of propositional representations is a major reason that single-code theories have been proposed: why use two (or more) codes if one will do the job? A second attraction of propositional theories, especially in the domain of meaning representation, is that propositions preserve the meaning but not the surface form of a sentence or utterance. For example, there is no way to recover from a propositional representation whether an idea was expressed in an active or a passive sentence. This feature is attractive because research on memory for language has shown again and again that people remember the gist of a passage much better than properties of the language used to express it (e.g., Bransford, Barclay, & Franks, 1972; Sachs, 1967). A third attractive feature of propositional theories is that propositions support in a natural way the making of inferences. Propositional representations are powerful, and when they are combined with appropriate inferential machinery, they almost certainly have sufficient computational power to explain human cognition (Anderson, 1976). Importantly, the inferential rules are simplified because propositions only represent what is essential to judge the validity or the plausibility of an inference; irrelevant details are omitted from a propositional representation. For example, in a propositional representation the active sentence "The President kissed the woman" and the passive sentence "The woman was kissed by the President" would be represented in the same way. Hence, the same inferential rules could be used for both; there is no need to have separate rules for active and passive sentences.

The empirical evidence in support of propositional theories is strong (e.g., Anderson, 1976; Kintsch, 1974; Ratcliff & McKoon, 1978). For instance, in one of Ratcliff and McKoon's (1978) experiments, subjects studied a series of sentences, such as these:

4. The host mixed a cocktail but the guest wanted coffee.
5. The driver bruised a hip and the passenger strained a knee.
6. A gust crushed the umbrella and rain soaked the man.

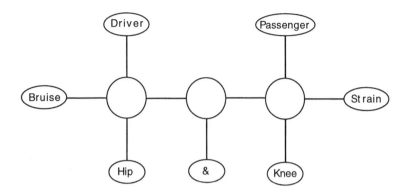

Figure 4.3
A simplified propositional network representation of the sentence "The driver bruised a hip and the passenger strained a knee."

After reading a set of sentences, subjects received a recognition test in which they saw a series of words on a computer display and had to decide whether each had been in the set of sentences. Ratcliff and McKoon were interested in the speed of responding on a particular item (e.g., *passenger*), depending on what item had appeared on the previous trial (e.g., *hip* vs. *knee*).

Figure 4.3 contains a network representation of the propositional structure of sentence 5. This network represents the major conceptual relations in the sentence but omits details to keep the diagram simple. The proposition attached to & corresponds to the proposition defined by the conjunction of the simple propositions in the sentence. Notice that distances between concepts in the same proposition are less than distances between concepts in different propositions; compare, for example, *knee-passenger* to *hip-passenger*. According to the retrieval assumptions outlined earlier, more activation will accumulate at *passenger* when it is preceded, or *primed*, by *knee* than when it is primed by *hip*. Thus, if sentences are mentally represented in terms of propositions, then responses to a target word should be faster when it is primed by a word from the same proposition than when it is primed by a word from a different proposition. This facilitation is called *associative priming*.

The experiments showed clearly that priming was determined by propositional relations. Mean response times were 550 ms when a word was primed by a word from the same proposition, but 595 ms when it was primed by a word from a different proposition. Crucially, same and different proposition pairs were separated in the sentences by the same number of words. Another important finding in these experiments was that distance in the surface form of the sentence had no effect on priming. For example, no more priming occurred between *hip* and *passenger* than between *hip* and *knee*. These results argue strongly that mental representations of even simple sentences preserve propositional relations but not perceptual properties of the stimulus. Similar results have been obtained in tests of generic (i.e., "semantic") memory (e.g., McNamara, 1992; McNamara & Altarriba, 1988).

Multiple-Code Theories

The fundamental tenet of multiple-code theories is that one code is not enough: the properties of human behavior are too rich to be explained in a single form of representation (e.g., Anderson, 1983; Kosslyn, 1980; Paivio, 1971, 1983). Although these theories differ in many important ways, the common thread that ties them together is that they include, in one form or another, analogical representations.

Analogical representations preserve properties of objects and events in an intrinsic manner. Intrinsic representations are those in which the representational system has the same inherent constraints as the system being represented (McNamara, 1994; Palmer, 1978). Figure 4.1 is a representation of a falcon in flight, and it preserves visually salient and distinctive properties of the birds in a concrete way. In fact, spatial properties of the birds are preserved in the same spatial properties of the representation. Analogical representations need not be so concrete, however. There is evidence that neurons in the motor cortex of primates represent the direction of movement of an arm by firing rate: the firing rate of a neuron gradually increases as the direction of movement approaches the neuron's preferred direction, and then falls off as the direction of movement goes past the preferred direction (Georgopoulos, Schwartz, & Kettner, 1986). This direct, nonarbitrary relation between the thing being represented—direction of movement—and the thing doing the representing—neuronal firing rate—is a signature of analogical representation.

Why have multiple-code theorists argued for analogical representation? A significant (if not scientific) argument is that many conscious experiences beg for an explanation in terms of analogical representations and processes. Bugelski (1970) and Paivio (1969), among others, were struck by how visual imagery improved paired-associate learning. These researchers would not accept that the experience of imagery and the effects it had on learning and memory could be explained in terms of propositional, verbal, or associative codes.

The evidence consistent with analogical representations and processes, and, hence, multiple-code theories, is too extensive to be reviewed here (see Finke, 1986; Kosslyn, 1980; Shepard & Cooper, 1982). General interest in analogical representations and processes was probably stimulated more by Shepard and Metzler's (1971) experiments on mental rotation than by any other single source. Shepard and Metzler found that the time to judge whether or not two line drawings depicted the same three-dimensional object was a linear function of the difference in angular rotation between the two figures. Shepard and Metzler concluded that mental rotation was analogical: the mental events occurring during imagined rotation were very similar to the mental events occurring during the perception of actual rotation. Subsequent experiments by Cooper and Shepard strongly supported this conjecture because they showed that the process of imagined mental rotation actually passed through intermediate states that corresponded to the intermediate states of actual rotation (see Shepard & Cooper, 1982).

Another influential (but controversial—see Pylyshyn, 1981) line of research examined mental scanning of images. In an experiment reported by Kosslyn, Ball, and Reiser (1978), subjects studied a map of a fictitious island (figure 4.4). After subjects had memorized the island and were able to visualize it with their eyes closed, they took part in a task in which they had to scan from one location to another. The experimenter named a starting location (e.g., the grass hut) and then named a destination (e.g., the tree). The subjects' task was to imagine a black dot moving from the starting location to the destination and to press a response button as soon as the dot arrived at the destination. The map was not visible during this test phase; subjects imagined the dot moving on a mental image of the map. The major finding was that scan time increased as a linear function

Figure 4.4
A replica of the map used by Kosslyn, Ball, & Reiser (1978) in the experiment on image scanning. (Reprinted from Kosslyn, S. M., Ball, T. M., & Reiser, B. J. [1978]. Visual images preserve metric spatial information: Evidence from studies of image scanning. *Journal of Experimental Psychology: Human Perception and Performance, 4,* 47–60.)

of distance on the map (figure 4.5). This result points to another correspondence between the representations and the processes used in imagery and those used in perception. Scanning a mental image seems to require the same or similar mental processes as those required in scanning an actual object, map, or scene.

These and other findings indicate that one important function of mental imagery may be to preserve information that is not recognized as important at the time of an experience and to provide means by which this implicit knowledge can be made explicit. Apparently, for example, I never recognized the potential importance of the number of windows in my house and, consequently, did not encode that information in an explicit manner (e.g., "my house has 22 windows"). However, my experiences in and around my house produced a sufficiently rich spatial representation that I was able to infer the number of windows by applying a

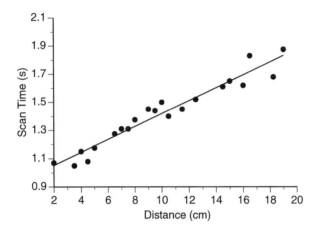

Figure 4.5
Image-scanning time plotted as a function of Euclidean distance on the map.

counting process to the spatial representation. Put another way, mental imagery may comprise the mind's attempt to re-create the world as it was previously experienced.

The Imagery Debate

Mental imagery was a mainstay of psychology in the early development of the field (e.g., James, 1890). However, research on and even discussions of mental imagery were effectively killed by the rise of behaviorism in the early twentieth century (e.g., Watson, 1913). As Brown (1958, p. 93) colorfully put it: Watson "mercifully closed the bloodshot inner eye of American psychology."

It was not until the late 1960s and early 1970s that imagery began to be investigated scientifically. The revival of interest in mental imagery was stimulated by research on the role of imagery in human learning and memory (e.g., Bower, 1972; Bugelski, 1970; Paivio, 1969). This research demonstrated that mental imagery typically facilitated learning and memory: for example, words that readily evoked mental images (e.g., *alligator*) were usually remembered better than words that did not (e.g., *force*). This research was sound, but the concept of the mental image was not well defined. According to Bugelski (1970), an image was an indirect reactivation of former sensory or perceptual information. Paivio (1969, p. 243) defined an image as a symbolic process linked to associative experiences involving concrete objects and events. Visual images were, according to Paivio, functionally related to visual perception and were specialized for representing spatial information.

Sixty years following the publication of Watson's (1913) paper on behaviorism, and on the heels of Bower's (1972), Bugelski's (1970), and Paivio's (1969) articles, Pylyshyn (1973) published a stinging critique of then current conceptualizations of imagery. Pylyshyn asked whether the mental image could be a primitive explanatory construct in cognitive psychology. His answer was that it could not. Pylyshyn did not doubt that people experienced mental imagery; nor did he claim that studying mental imagery was a waste of time. Rather, Pylyshyn doubted whether mental images were a different kind of mental representation from propositions. He argued that mental images were generated from a more fundamental representation (propositions, or something similar) and were not themselves functional in human cognition.

Pylyshyn's (1973) article ignited a raging debate in cognitive psychology on the nature of mental representation. Initially, the debate centered on whether mental images were functional in cognition or were generated from something more primitive (e.g., Kosslyn & Pomerantz, 1977; Pylyshyn, 1973); the debate then turned to the question of whether theories of knowledge representation could be tested in behavioral experiments (e.g., Anderson, 1978; Pylyshyn, 1979); finally, the debate centered on whether mental imagery was affected by tacit knowledge (e.g., Kosslyn, Pinker, Smith, & Shwartz, 1979; Pylyshyn, 1981). Although many cognitive psychologists may think that this debate generated more heat than light, I believe that it produced several essential lessons for future generations of scientists. In the next few paragraphs, I will summarize a few of the more important ones.

One of Pylyshyn's (1973) arguments was that the representations and processes that are functional in cognition may not be consciously accessible and that just because something is consciously accessible does not guarantee that it is functional. So, for example, the mental images of my house that I experience while trying to count the windows may not be primitive mental representations that are analyzed by some counting process but, rather, products of those mental representations and processes used to count the windows in my house. Put another way, mental imagery may be the very thing in need of explanation, not the thing providing the explanation. A corollary of this principle is that researchers must distinguish between what people normally do and what they must do to solve a problem. People may report the use of imagery because that is the way they normally go about solving a problem, not because the information is inaccessible in other ways.

A second lesson that emerged from the imagery debate is that theories of mental representation cannot be tested without specifying the mental processes that operate on the representation (e.g., Anderson, 1978; Pylyshyn, 1979). Mental representations exist in a representational system that includes mental processes. Experiments test the entire system, not just the representations or the processes. The concept of a representational system can be illustrated with a concrete example. Consider judgments of the spatial relations between geographical landmarks: many people believe that San Diego, California, is west of Reno, Nevada, when in fact the opposite is true (Stevens & Coupe, 1978). An analogical model might specify that spatial relations are represented in mental images and that these images may, on occasion, be incorrect (e.g., San Diego may be represented in the image as west of Reno). According to a propositional model, the error may be caused by inferential processes that operate on incomplete but accurate propositional representations (e.g., San Diego is in California, Reno is in Nevada, and California is west of Nevada; therefore, San Diego must be west of Reno).

This principle *does not* imply that a theory of representation can be perfectly mimicked by another theory of representation as long as the mental processes are chosen judiciously (cf. Anderson, 1978). Perfect behavioral mimicry is possible only if the two forms of representation are isomorphic (i.e., preserve the same distinctions and differ only in notation). This constraint will be violated, however, by any reasonable pair of alternative theories because theories of representation are proposed to distinguish events that are not distinguished by other theories or to blur events that are distinguished by other theories; in other words, alternative theories are designed to be nonisomorphic. Another problem with mimicry is that representational systems are not usually equivalent and cannot be made to be equivalent in general, at the level of complexity (Pylyshyn, 1979). Complexity will reveal itself in certain behavioral measures, such as processing time. Finally, alternative representational systems will differ, in the long haul, in explanatory adequacy. Data alone will not be able to adjudicate between theories of cognition; no finite amount of data can uniquely determine a theory of any natural phenomenon. The evaluation of a theory also depends on how well the theory explains the relevant phenomena (e.g., Pylyshyn, 1981). The explanatory adequacy of a theory is evaluated by looking at how general the theory is, how well the theory captures important generalizations in other areas, how constrained the theory is in terms of the number of free parameters, and so on. Scientists must distinguish curve fitting, which may be empirically perfect but is conceptually vacuous, from true scientific explanation.

The third and final principle is that progress will be made in understanding cognitive phenomena only if converging operations are applied diligently (e.g., Garner, Hake, & Eriksen, 1956). Converging operations can be used within a level of analysis, as when two or more tasks (e.g., recognition and recall) are used to test theoretical predictions, or between levels of analysis, as when behavioral measures are combined with neurophysiological measures. The goal of converging operations is to force theoretical commitments in one domain of investigation that must be honored in other domains. A successful theory is one that successfully explains human behavior in the multitude of ways it is manifested and does so with a minimum number of unprincipled modifications.

It is natural to ask, however, whether Pylyshyn's (1973) original challenge was answered: Is the mental image a primitive explanatory construct in cognitive psychology? On this issue, there is probably still disagreement in the field, although the consensus seems to be closer in spirit to the claims made by proponents of imagery than to the claims made by its opponents.

One of Pylyshyn's (1973) most important arguments was that images were not "pictures in the head." His analysis is intact: there is uniform agreement now that images are conceptually interpreted, not raw sensory information that must be reperceived by the "mind's eye" (cf. Bugelski, 1970). Experimental investigations of imagery have documented that images have internal structure and are constructed in working memory.

Reed (1974), for example, showed that some parts of an imagined figure could be recognized more quickly than other parts, indicating that the internal representation of the figure had hierarchical structure. Studies by Kosslyn, Cave, Provost, and von Gierke (1988) indicate that mental images of letters and letterlike patterns are generated part by part in sequences that correspond to how the patterns are drawn.

It is also widely recognized that we may never know whether images as they are experienced are generated from another form of representation, such as propositions, or are constructed from primitive analogical components. However, it is also recognized that this issue may not be important (Kosslyn & Pomerantz, 1977). The crucial issue is whether mental imagery is produced by mental representations and processes that must produce and use analogical representations to solve the problems that they have been marshaled to solve. To illustrate what is at stake here, consider one of Pylyshyn's (1981) criticisms of Kosslyn, Ball, and Reiser's (1978) image-scanning experiment: Pylyshyn argued that subjects might have been trying to re-create what it would be like to scan from location to location on the map, rather than actually using the analogical process of scanning on an analogical representation of the map. This distinction is vital: according to Pylyshyn's analysis, subjects were using their tacit knowledge about space to do what they were told to do by the experimenter; according to Kosslyn et al., subjects were actually processing an analogical representation in an analogical manner.

Finke and Pinker (1983) responded to this criticism by designing an experiment in which there were no explicit demands to use mental images but in which scanning was an effective way to perform the task. In their experiment, subjects first saw a display of dots, like the one in figure 4.6A. The dots were then removed, and in their place appeared an arrow, like the one in figure 4.6B. The subjects' task was to decide whether the arrow pointed at any of the dots in the original display (the correct answer was yes in 4.6B and no in 4.6C). The independent variable was the distance between the tip of the arrow and the dot at which it pointed. This task is quite different from the one used by Kosslyn et al. (1978). Subjects were not instructed to scan from one place to another; their task was to decide whether or not the arrow pointed at any of the dots. Cru-

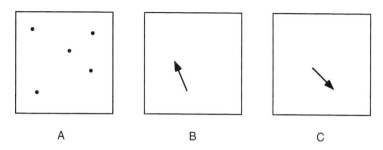

Figure 4.6
Examples of stimuli used by Finke & Pinker (1983).

cially, Finke and Pinker found the same linear relation between distance and decision time as had Kosslyn, Ball, and Reiser (figure 4.7).

In recent years, several investigators have picked up Pylyshyn's gauntlet and turned to neurophysiological studies to resolve the imagery debate. For example, Kosslyn, Thompson, Kim, and Alpert (1995) measured cerebral blood flow with positron-emission tomography (PET) while subjects were engaged in imagery tasks. The results showed that the primary visual cortex was activated when subjects closed their eyes and visualized objects and that the location of maximal activation in the brain was di-

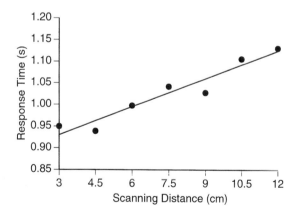

Figure 4.7
Response time as a function of the distance between the tip of the arrow and the dot in Finke and Pinker's (1983) experiment. (Adapted from Finke & Pinker, 1983, figure 1.)

rectly related to the size of the image generated. These and related findings (e.g., Farah, 1985; Farah, Péronnet, Gonon, & Giard, 1988; Kosslyn et al., 1993, Parsons et al., 1995) indicate that the representational system activated by visual imagery is used in visual perception, and at very early stages, when vision almost certainly relies on analogical representations (e.g., Tootell, Silverman, Switkes, & De Valois, 1982).

The analogical nature of imagination has also been revealed in investigations of the primate motor system. Georgopoulos and his colleagues (e.g., Georgopoulos et al., 1986) showed that the angular direction of a monkey's arm movements could be predicted by the activity of neurons in the motor cortex. In effect, the pattern of activity over a collection of neurons points (in an abstract frame of reference) in the direction of the arm movement. This discovery was exploited by Georgopoulos, Lurito, Petrides, Schwartz, and Massey (1989), who trained monkeys to move a handle in the direction 90° to the left of a stimulus. The crucial finding was that the collection of neurons encoding the direction of movement initially pointed at the stimulus and then "rotated" continuously until it pointed in the direction 90° to the left of the stimulus. All of this happened before the monkey actually moved his arm. Georgopoulos and his coworkers seem to have found a neural implementation of mental rotation (figure 4.8).

Stimulus

Time

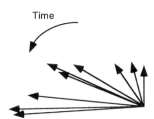

Direction
of Arm Movement

Figure 4.8
Neuronal population vector plotted as a function of time. The vector summarizes the directional tendency of a population of neurons in the motor cortex. Initially, the vector points in the direction of the stimulus; it then rotates continuously and points in the direction of the arm movement. All of this neural activity occurred before the arm was actually moved. (Adapted from Pellizzer & Georgopoulos, 1993, figure 4.)

In summary, the results of brain-imaging studies of humans and of single-unit recording studies of monkeys provide compelling evidence of the existence of analogical representations and processes in the primate brain (also see Kosslyn, 1994). It is difficult to countenance a single-code theory of knowledge representation in the presence of these findings.

Summary and Conclusions

To understand why people act in the ways that they do, one must know how people mentally represent their physical, social, and emotional worlds. Hence, the topic of mental representation has always been and will always be a central one in cognitive science.

Theories of the mental representation of knowledge have appeared in many forms and differ in many important ways. Nevertheless, these theories can be divided into two categories. According to single-code theories, human knowledge is represented in a single format, usually identified as propositions. Propositions are abstract representations of ideas and are not tied to any particular sensory modality. Propositional systems are computationally powerful, and for this reason, some cognitive scientists doubted whether any other form of internal representation was necessary. The other category of theories is multiple-code theories. According to these theories, human knowledge is represented in several types of codes, the most common of which are propositional and analogical codes. Analogical representations preserve information in a direct perceptual way, are linked to particular sensory modalities, and play a crucial role in many tasks, but especially those whose solution requires the reenactment of previous experiences.

Although these theories seem dramatically different, they were difficult to distinguish empirically. The problem was that single-code theories could explain findings that were attributed to analogical representations and processes. This conundrum, as well as conceptual problems in distinguishing images from propositions, led to a major debate on knowledge representation in cognitive psychology.

Several important lessons were learned from the imagery debate. Two of the more important ones were these: First, because mental representations exist in a representational system that includes mental processes, experiments test representation process pairs, not just representations. Second, progress in cognitive psychology will depend on the sedulous application of converging operations, at the behavioral and neurophysiological levels.

The imagery debate also led to new theoretical and empirical inquiries into the nature of mental imagery. Recent findings have documented functional relations between imagination, perception, and action, and they suggest that analogical representations and processes comprise a representational system separate from the propositional system. This conclusion finds form in the most recent version of Anderson's ACT theory (1993), which explicitly endorses multiple types of knowledge representation. Squire's (1992) views on memory are also of this ilk, in that he posits multiple memory systems with separate functions and anatomical organizations.

The imagery debate is just one of many debates on knowledge representation that have, and will, split the discipline of cognitive psychology. Indeed, the field is in the midst of yet another debate on the nature of human knowledge representation, a connectionist versus information processing debate (e.g., Fodor & Pylyshyn, 1988; McClelland & Rumelhart, 1986; Rumelhart & McClelland, 1986). The issues at stake in this debate, however, are more fundamental than those at stake in the imagery debate. Single-code and multiple-code theorists at least agreed that human cognition consisted of the interpretation, manipulation, and transformation of mental representations. Proponents of connectionism, however, reject most, if not all, of these assumptions. The concept of a mental representation may be so different in future theories that the distinction between single-code and multiple-code theories may be meaningless. Although many students may be frustrated by this kind of instability, for many of us it is what makes cognitive science so exciting.

References

Anderson, J. R. (1976). *Language, memory, and thought.* Hillsdale, NJ: Erlbaum.

Anderson, J. R. (1978). Arguments concerning representations for mental imagery. *Psychological Review, 85,* 249–277.

Anderson, J. R. (1983). *The architecture of cognition.* Cambridge, MA: Harvard University Press.

Anderson, J. R. (1993). *Rules of the mind.* Hillsdale, NJ: Erlbaum.

Anderson, J. R., & Bower, G. H. (1973). *Human associative memory.* Washington, DC: Winston.

Bower, G. H. (1972). Mental imagery and associative learning. In L. Gregg (Ed.), *Cognition in learning and memory.* New York: Wiley.

Bransford, J. D., Barclay, J. R., & Franks, J. J. (1972). Sentence memory: A constructive versus interpretive approach. *Cognitive Psychology, 3,* 193–209.

Brown, R. (1958). *Words and things.* Glencoe, IL: Free Press.

Bugelski, B. R. (1970). Words and things and images. *American Psychologist, 25,* 1002–1012.

Chomsky, N. (1959). [Review of Skinner's *Verbal behavior.*] *Language, 35,* 26–58.

Collins, A. M., & Loftus, E. F. (1975). A spreading-activation theory of semantic processing. *Psychological Review, 82,* 407–428.

Farah, M. J. (1985). Psychophysical evidence for a shared representational medium for mental images and percepts. *Journal of Experimental Psychology: General, 114,* 91–103.

Farah, M. J., Péronnet, F., Gonon, M. A., & Giard, M. H. (1988). Electrophysiological evidence for a shared representational medium for visual images and visual percepts. *Journal of Experimental Psychology: General, 117,* 248–257.

Finke, R. A. (1986). Mental imagery and the visual system. *Scientific American, 254,* 88–95.

Finke, R. A., & Pinker, S. (1983). Directional scanning of remembered visual patterns. *Journal of Experimental Psychology: Learning, Memory, and Cognition, 9,* 398–410.

Fodor, J. A. (1975). *The language of thought.* New York: Thomas Y. Crowell.

Fodor, J. A., & Pylyshyn, Z. W. (1988). Connectionism and cognitive architecture: A critical analysis. In S. Pinker & J. Mehler (Eds.), *Connections and symbols* (pp. 3–71). Cambridge, MA: MIT Press.

Garner, W. R., Hake, H. W., & Eriksen, C. W. (1956). Operationism and the concept of perception. *Psychological Review, 63,* 149–159.

Georgopoulos, A. P., Lurito, J. T., Petrides, M., Schwartz, A. B., & Massey, J. T. (1989). Mental rotation of the neuronal population vector. *Science, 243,* 234–236.

Georgopoulos, A. P., Schwartz, A. B., & Kettner, R. E. (1986). Neuronal population coding of movement direction. *Science, 233,* 1416–1419.

James, W. (1890). *Principles of psychology.* New York: Henry Holt.

Kintsch, W. (1974). *The representation of meaning in memory.* Hillsdale, NJ: Erlbaum.

Kosslyn, S. M. (1980). *Image and mind.* Cambridge, MA: Harvard University Press.

Kosslyn, S. M. (1994). *Image and brain: The resolution of the imagery debate.* Cambridge, MA: MIT Press.

Kosslyn, S. M., Alper, N. M., Thompson, W. L., Maljkovic, V., Weise, S. B., Chabris, C. F., Hamilton, S. E., Rauch, S. L., & Buonanno, F. S. (1993). Visual mental imagery activates topographically organized visual cortex: PET investigations. *Journal of Cognitive Neuroscience, 5,* 263–287.

Kosslyn, S. M., Ball, T. M., & Reiser, B. J. (1978). Visual images preserve metric spatial information: Evidence from studies of image scanning. *Journal of Experimental Psychology: Human Perception and Performance, 4,* 47–60.

Kosslyn, S. M., Cave, C. B., Provost, D. A., & von Gierke, S. M. (1988). Sequential processes in image generation. *Cognitive Psychology, 20,* 319–343.

Kosslyn, S. M., Pinker, S., Smith, G., & Shwartz, S. P. (1979). On the demystification of mental imagery. *Behavioral and Brain Sciences, 2,* 535–581.

Kosslyn, S. M., & Pomerantz, J. R. (1977). Imagery, propositions, and the form of internal representations. *Cognitive Psychology, 9,* 52–76.

Kosslyn, S. M., Thompson, W. L., Kim, I. J., & Alpert, N. M. (1995). Topographical representations of mental images in primary visual cortex. *Nature, 378,* 496–498.

McClelland, J. L., & Rumelhart, D. E. (1986). *Parallel distributed processing* (Vol. 2). Cambridge, MA: MIT Press.

McNamara, T. P. (1992). Theories of priming: I. Associative distance and lag. *Journal of Experimental Psychology: Learning, Memory, and Cognition, 18,* 1173–1190.

McNamara, T. P. (1994). Knowledge representation. In E. C. Carterette & M. P. Friedman (Series Eds.) & R. J. Sternberg (Vol. Ed.), *Handbook of perception and cognition: Vol. 12. Thinking* (pp. 81–117). Orlando FL: Academic Press.

McNamara, T. P., & Altarriba, J. (1988). Depth of spreading activation revisited: Semantic mediated priming occurs in lexical decisions. *Journal of Memory and Language, 27,* 545–559.

Norman, D. A., Rumelhart, D. E., & LNR Research Group (1975). *Explorations in cognition.* San Francisco: Freeman.

Paivio, A. (1969). Mental imagery in associative learning and memory. *Psychological Review, 76,* 241–263.

Paivio, A. (1971). *Imagery and verbal processes.* New York: Holt, Rinehart, & Winston.

Paivio, A. (1983). *Mental representations.* New York: Oxford University Press.

Palmer, S. E. (1978). Fundamental aspects of cognitive representation. In E. Rosch & B. Lloyd (Eds.), *Cognition and categorization.* Hillsdale, NJ: Erlbaum.

Parsons, L. M., Fox, P. T., Downs, J. H., Glass, T., Hirsch, T. B., Martin, C. C., Jerabek, P. A., & Lancaster, J. L. (1995). Use of implicit motor imagery for visual shape discrimination as revealed by PET. *Nature, 375,* 54–58.

Pellizzer, G., & Georgopoulos, A. P. (1993). Mental rotation of the intended direction of movement. *Current Directions in Psychological Science, 2,* 12–17.

Pylyshyn, Z. W. (1973). What the mind's eye tells the mind's brain: A critique of mental imagery. *Psychological Bulletin, 80,* 1–24.

Pylyshyn, Z. W. (1979). Validating computational models: A critique of Anderson's indeterminacy of representation claim. *Psychological Review, 86,* 383–394.

Pylyshyn, Z. W. (1981). The imagery debate: Analogue media versus tacit knowledge. *Psychological Review, 88,* 16–44.

Quillian, M. R. (1967). Word concepts: A theory and simulation of some basic semantic capabilities. *Behavioral Science, 12,* 410–430.

Ratcliff, R., & McKoon, G. (1978). Priming in item recognition: Evidence for the propositional structure of sentences. *Journal of Verbal Learning and Verbal Behavior, 17,* 403–417.

Ratcliff, R., & McKoon, G. (1996). Bias effects in implicit memory tasks. *Journal of Experimental Psychology: General, 125,* 403–421.

Reed, S. K. (1974). Structural descriptions and the limitations of visual images. *Memory & Cognition, 2,* 329–336.

Rumelhart, D. E., & McClelland, J. L. (1986). *Parallel distributed processing* (Vol. 1). Cambridge, MA: MIT Press.

Ryle, G. (1949). *The concept of mind.* London: Hutchinson.

Sachs, J. (1967). Recognition memory for syntactic and semantic aspects of connected discourse. *Perception & Psychophysics, 2,* 437–442.

Shepard, R. N., & Cooper, L. A. (1982). *Mental images and their transformations.* Cambridge, MA: MIT Press.

Shepard, R. N., & Metzler, J. (1971). Mental rotation of three-dimensional objects. *Science, 171,* 701–703.

Skinner, B. F. (1957). *Verbal behavior.* New York: Appleton.

Stevens, A., & Coupe, P. (1978). Distortions in judged spatial relations. *Cognitive Psychology, 10,* 422–437.

Squire, L. R. (1992). Memory and the hippocampus: A synthesis from findings with rats, monkeys, and humans. *Psychological Review, 99,* 195–231.

Terres, J. K. (1980). *The Audubon Society encyclopedia of North American birds.* New York: Knopf.

Tootell, R. B. H., Silverman, M. S., Switkes, E., & De Valois, R. L. (1982). Deoxyglucose analysis of retinotopic organization in primate striate cortex. *Science, 218,* 902–904.

Watson, J. B. (1913). Psychology as the behaviorist views it. *Psychological Review, 20,* 158–177.

5

Domain-Generality versus Domain-Specificity in Cognition

Peter A. Frensch and Axel Buchner

Can you "learn to think" and become a creative problem solver for all sorts of problems? For a creativity-training program (e.g., Crawford, 1966) to make sense, the answer should be yes. Proponents of such a training would need to assume that creative thinking is a teachable skill that generalizes across different domains such as mechanical problems, logistic problems, graphic design problems, political problems, and social problems. However, many people might disagree with the idea that the skill of creative problem solving can be so domain-general. For instance, solving problems in the domain of mechanics and solving problems in the domain of graphic design appear to have little, if anything, in common.

The preceding example captures the essence of the binary concept that we are concerned with in this chapter: domain-generality versus domain-specificity. At a general and abstract level, domain-generality stands for the uniting of a wide range of diverse phenomena by the positing of a relatively small set of general underlying principles. This idea can be found in the thinking of Aristotle, and it is one of the main premises of British empiricism (e.g., George Berkeley, David Hartley, David Hume) and behaviorism (e.g., B. F. Skinner, C. L. Hull, John Watson). More recently, Piaget's (1970) theory in developmental psychology provides a general model of this kind, as does Anderson's (1983) attempt at formulating explanatory principles that apply equally well to all domains of thought, including language, problem solving, and arithmetic.

Domain-specificity, by comparison, stands for the view that the mind consists of different entities whose functioning obeys different rules. Domain-specific ideas can be found, for example, in the epistemologies of Plato, René Descartes, and Immanuel Kant, in the various versions of faculty psychology, and in the psychologies of Edward L. Thorndike, A. D. de Groot, and L. S. Vygotsky. Vygotsky (1978), for instance, argued that

the mind is not a complex network of general capabilities such as observation, attention, memory, judgment, and so forth, but a set of specific capabilities, each of which is, to some extent, independent of others and is developed independently. Learning is more than the acquisition of the ability to think; it is the acquisition of many specialized abilities for thinking about a variety of things. (p. 83)

The binary contrast between domain-generality and domain-specificity has been a predominant force in shaping concepts of the mind for a long time and has been at the center of a wide variety of scientific debates. Table 5.1 illustrates the diversity of the psychological phenomena to which the domain-generality versus domain-specificity issue has been applied. The table displays a collection of selected book chapter and journal titles containing the terms *domain generality* or *domain specificity* that resulted from a PsycLIT search covering publications between 1990 and 1995.

Our primary goal in this chapter is to convey an understanding of what domain-generality versus domain-specificity (henceforth DG-DS) debates are all about. The remainder of the chapter is divided into two main sections. The first section is devoted to a theoretical clarification of the issue of domain-generality versus domain-specificity. In the second section, we summarize and discuss two well-known DG-DS debates, debates centering on the nature of expertise and the nature of human development. We conclude the chapter with a few comments on the usefulness of the binary concept of domain-generality versus domain-specificity for psychological theorizing in general.

Domain-Generality versus Domain-Specificity: Navigating through the Theoretical Morass

Debates on domain-generality versus domain-specificity can be found in many different areas of psychology (see table 5.1) and differ in many aspects, most obviously perhaps in the conceptual questions to which they are applied and in the methods that are deemed acceptable to solve

Table 5.1
Selected recent book chapter and journal titles on domain-generality versus domain-specificity

---

Discovering linguistic differences: Domain specificity and the young child's awareness of multiple languages

Of beasties and butterflies: Evidence for the stability and domain-specificity of individual differences in categorization

The interaction of domain-specific and strategic knowledge in academic performance

An investigation of life satisfaction following a vacation: A domain-specific approach

Anxiety sensitivity: Unitary personality trait or domain-specific appraisals?

How domain-general and domain-specific knowledge interact to produce strategy choices

Domain-specific social judgments and domain ambiguities

Acquisition of domain-specific knowledge in organic amnesia: Training for computer-related work

Theoretical and methodological issues in domain-specific problem-solving research

Acquisition of domain-specific knowledge in patients with organic memory disorders

Investigation of children's three dimensional and domain-specific scale of perceived control

Metacognitive versus traditional reading instructions: The mediating role of domain-specific knowledge on children's text processing

School and peer competence in early adolescence: A test of domain-specific self-perceived competence

---

Source: PsychLIT search covering publications between 1990 and 1995.

the debates. Our first goal in this section is to provide a theoretical framework for understanding DG-DS debates in general, that is, a framework that applies to all debates. Providing such a framework implies, at minimum, answering three interrelated questions: (1) what are the *goals* of DG-DS debates? (2) what is *meant* by domain-generality and -specificity? and (3) what is a *domain?*

Our second goal in this section is to gain an understanding of the wide range of DG-DS debates that is found in the psychological literature. We will suggest that the diversity of DG-DS debates is due to systematic variations in the conceptual questions for which DG-DS debates arise, and we will describe a number of dimensions that capture these variations.

What Are DG-DS Debates All About?

Central to any DG-DS debate is the question of how widely applicable a particular theoretical statement or empirical finding is. Thus, for instance, the empirical phenomenon of negative priming with pictorial material (Tipper, 1985)[1] triggers the question of whether the same results can be obtained with letters (Tipper & Cranston, 1985). The empirical phenomenon that women demonstrate a preference for a certain life goal at age 20 raises the question of whether males show a similar preference (Heckhausen, in press). The fact that providing a verbal summary of the principle underlying a certain problem solution is not helpful for finding the solution to a similar new problem might stimulate asking whether a graphical illustration of the principle would be more useful than the verbal summary (Gick & Holyoak, 1983). Finally, the theory that expert human chess players create elaborated memory retrieval representations (Chase & Ericsson, 1981) might lead to the question of whether the same might be true for expert physicists and psychologists.

DG-DS debates are, thus, concerned with the question of how widely a statement can be applied. As the examples just given demonstrate, asking the width-of-applicability question often defines the empirical approach to be taken as well and thus serves to guide research. Put differently, adopting a DG-DS perspective has theoretical and methodological implications for the way the human mind is studied, defining and generating research problems, and suggesting specific research strategies and methodologies. In some sense, DG-DS debates function as a scientific paradigm in the Kuhnian (1962) sense (Garfield, 1987).

For the DG-DS question to be meaningful, of course, it needs to be tied to a meaningful statement about the functioning of the human mind. Determining the domain-generality or domain-specificity of the statement "the head is round" is not meaningful because the statement "the head is round" does not describe how the mind works. Applying the DG-DS question to the statement "humans can remember only seven phonological sounds in their short-term memory" (Miller, 1956) is meaningful because the latter statement describes the functioning of mind. Technically, we therefore define the goal of DG-DS debates as determining *the width of applicability of a psychological constraint.*

By *psychological constraint* we mean any theoretical statement that is (a) tied to an empirical phenomenon[2] and (b) narrows the number of possibilities of how the human mind (in its broadest sense) may function. Put differently, constraint is any statement that allows one to predict the outcome of mental activity.[3] For example, stating that "expertise correlates with test intelligence" places restrictions on the way the mind functions, and it allows us to predict a person's level of expertise if we know his or her level of test intelligence. On the other hand, stating that "the human mind is complex" does not aid in predicting humans' mental performance.

Building on the definition given earlier, we are now ready to tackle the question of what we mean by domain-generality and domain-specificity. Both of these terms need to be tied to the notion of a psychological constraint. Stating that a particular psychological constraint is *domain-general,* consequently, is stating that the constraint is invariant; that is, it applies to all actions and properties of the human mind. Stating that a constraint is *domain-specific* is stating that it applies to some but not all actions and properties of the mind.

The psychologically interesting question linked to the DG-DS issue is, however, not whether a constraint is domain-general or domain-specific in some absolute sense. Rather, it is *how* specific or *how* general a constraint is. The width of applicability of a constraint should be viewed as a continuum with domain-specific on one end and domain-general on the other. To illustrate, the driving force behind the question of whether the limit of human short-term memory is domain-specific or domain-general, whether it applies to verbal information only or to nonverbal information as well, is to find out how far the constraint can be applied, that is, how invariant the constraint is. Domain-specificity and domain-generality are thus no more than the two endpoints on the applicability continuum.

Defining the DG-DS issue in terms of the width of applicability of psychological constraints, of course, also raises the question of what the *units* of the applicability continuum are. Stated differently, it raises the question of what a *domain* is. If the notion of a domain may refer to phonological and nonphonological information, on the one hand, and to expert knowledge of physics, on the other hand, then any attempt at defining the notion of domain in some absolute objective sense can never hope to succeed. Any specification of what is meant by domain must be tied to the specific psychological constraint under consideration.

For example, the constraint that an expert's knowledge in physics is arranged hierarchically implies physics as a domain. The constraint that belief systems for school success are structured in a certain way implies school as a domain. The constraint that repetition priming can be observed with letters implies letters as a domain. Of course, constraints may imply more than one domain. The constraint that negative priming for visual objects seems to persist unchanged for stimulus-response intervals of up to 6.6 seconds (Tipper, Weaver, Cameron, Berhaut, & Bastedo, 1991) implies both visual objects and the 6.6 seconds as domains. In principle, a domain is anything that a given constraint can potentially be generalized to and from.

It would be wrong to conclude, however, that what is considered a domain depends *only* on the constraint involved. What is considered a domain is affected by many additional factors, most importantly the general paradigm encompassing current psychological explanations (e.g., the information-processing paradigm, behaviorism, action theory), the researcher's individual belief about which goals should guide the psychological enterprise, and the researcher's knowledge of psychology. For example, exploring the nature of human learning from a behaviorist or from an information-processing perspective leads to different notions of what is called a domain. Furthermore, believing that the ultimate goal of psychology is to explain behavior at the neuronal level will lead to very different ideas about what is accepted as a domain than believing that behavior should be explained at a psychological level (see Frensch & Funke, 1995b, for a similar argument). In general, what is considered a domain is a function of various variables, one of which is the nature of a constraint; because it is never possible to know all of these variables, what constitutes a domain is not objectively definable.

In summary and in answer to the three questions raised at the beginning of this section, the goal of any DG-DS debate is to determine the width of applicability of a psychological constraint. Constraints thus form the basis around which DG-DS debates evolve, and they codetermine the meaning of domain. Constraints are also the main source of variability among DG-DS debates. That is, many of the DG-DS debates found in the literature differ in the type of constraint they are applied to. Stated differently, differences in the type of constraint are responsible for the wide range of DG-DS debates encountered in psychology (see table 5.1). Because of the central importance of constraints for the issue of domain-generality versus domain-specificity, we will next consider the nature of constraints in more detail.

Classifying Constraints

Low-Level versus High-Level Constraints   Constraints can be formulated at many different levels of abstraction, ranging from behavioristic couplings of stimuli and responses near one end of the continuum (low-level constraints) to general evolutionary considerations near the other end (high-level constraints). Furthermore, constraints can be formulated at the level of task analysis, the level of implementation, or the metalevel (Marr, 1982; Rosenthal, 1988). Constraints can thus refer to the cognitive processing of the mind, to the neuronal implementation of cognitive processing, and to the general conditions that underlie different learning objectives.

For example, repeated exposure to aversive stimuli that cannot be avoided reduces the probability that a person (or an animal) will learn to avoid the aversive stimulus once avoiding it is possible (Hiroto, 1974). This phenomenon has been termed *learned helplessness*. It constrains the possibilities of how the human mind may function, as does the much more general and abstract idea that the mind is composed of a large number of psychological mechanisms each dedicated to a specific problem, the solution of which was of benefit in the evolutionary development of humans (e.g., Cosmides & Tooby, 1987, 1989).

Internal versus External Constraints   Constraints can be formulated with regard to either the functioning of the human mind itself (internal constraints) or the relation between environment and mind (external constraints). Simon (1995), for instance, argues that internal constraints are "the natural laws that determine the structure and behavior of any artificial or living object" (p. 99), whereas external constraints are "the initial and boundary conditions under which the object exists" (p. 100). Similarly, Chomsky (1975) envisions external constraints as partially specifying a function that maps sets of environments onto sets of mental representations. External constraints are thus regularities in the mind-environment mapping that are, according to Simon (1995), partly responsible for the evolution of the mind and are necessary to guarantee the mind's existence. Internal constraints, by comparison, are architectural reasons for the nonrandom functioning of the mind, reasons that lie in the organism itself.

External constraints are, for example, the oxygen in the air or the range of the color spectrum available in the environment; these facts shape the way mind works. In a different environment, present human minds might not work at all. By comparison, priming (e.g., Neely, 1991) and negative priming (e.g., Tipper, 1985) phenomena reflect internal constraints that have to do with the inability of the mind's architecture to terminate its processing abruptly.

Process versus Structure Constraints   Many theorists have made the distinction between process and structure constraints (e.g., Keil, 1990a; Maratsos, 1992). Structure constraints concern knowledge structures and can hold that a particular structural relation is favored over others, that some structural relations cannot occur, and so on. The idea of experts' hierarchical knowledge representations (e.g., Chi, 1989) falls under the rubric of structure constraint. By contrast, the notion of process constraints applies to the processing that occurs within an organism.[4] For instance, Treisman's feature integration theory of attention (Treisman & Gelade, 1980) holds that simple features in the visual field such as color or line orientation are registered early, automatically, and in parallel, whereas visual objects, that is, combinations of features "glued" together by focal attention (such as a red vertical line), have to be scanned serially, one after another.

Structure and process constraints may coexist in a field and even complement each other. For instance, according to the so-called multiple memory systems view, the general faculty of memory must be divided into a number of substructures, such as declarative and procedural memory (e.g., Cohen & Squire, 1980). The fact that amnesiacs can learn certain motor skills but cannot recall having acquired them may then be accounted for by assuming that procedural, but not declarative, memory is spared in amnesia. The transfer-appropriate processing approach as developed by Roediger and his coworkers (e.g., Roediger, 1990) ignores memory structures and specifies that performance on memory tests benefits to the extent that the cognitive operations involved in the test recapitulate those engaged during initial learning. For instance, simply reading a word improves its later identification under difficult viewing conditions relative to generating the word from its antonym (e.g., "hot-?; answer: cold"). However, generating the word from its antonym (i.e., processing its semantic content) improves later recognition of a read word (Jacoby, 1983).

Static versus Dynamic Constraints   Many empirical and theoretical statements in psychology make conditional assertions such as "Given x, then y will result," correlational statements such as "If the independent variable, x, increases, then the dependent variable, y, will increase," or quantitative statements such as "$y = a \times x^{-b}$." The latter, for instance, is known as the power law of practice, which specifies that the time to solve a task, y, is a power function of the amount of practice on the task, x, and some constants a and b. These three statements describe structural static constraints of the mind, although the third statement goes further in specifying the system than the former, especially when the parameters a and b are known or estimated quantities.

Static constraints, thus, are statements that relate two aspects of the mind or behavior to each other without reference to time. The human mind is an adaptive system, however; it can learn. As a consequence, static constraints can capture only part of the functioning of the mind. Dynamic constraints, by comparison, are statements that characterize the transition between different mind states. The need for dynamic constraints is nowhere more obvious than in human development. For instance, Piaget's conception of developmental stages is a dynamic constraint because it limits the possible developmental patterns that can occur. Indeed, the constructing of theories of human development can be viewed as an attempt to understand the dynamic constraints that govern change in the operation of the human mind (see next section).

Innate versus Acquired Constraints   Distinguishing innate from acquired constraints is problematic, as Keil (1990a) observes, given the many arguments about the intrinsically interactional nature of development (e.g., Johnston, 1988; Lehrman, 1953; Lerner, 1983). Nothing is strictly innate or learned, the argument goes, because there must always be an organism in which learning takes place and an environment to be learned. Use of the term *innate* remains controversial, but somewhat less so with respect to constraints because constraints are partly based on the notion of interaction itself. For instance, following Chomsky (1975), one can envision innate constraints as partially specifying the function that maps sets of environments onto sets of mental representations. In this view, the mapping function and the constraints that it embodies may be innate. Innate constraints, thus, tie certain events in the environment to specific states of the human mind. Any spoken word, for instance, can only be "interpreted" by the mind as an utterance, nothing else.

Innate constraints can also be inherent in the functional "hardware" of the human mind, determining the architecture of the mind. Thus, as stated earlier, empirical demonstrations of repetition priming (e.g., Neely, 1991) and negative priming (e.g., Tipper, 1985) reflect internal properties of the cognitive system that may be present from birth or that may mature at a later date.

Acquired constraints, by contrast, can neither be present at birth nor maturationally predetermined. They emerge out of acquired knowledge and capture the notion that what one has learned in turn constrains how easily what kinds of things can be learned next. Proactive inhibition (Underwood, 1957) is an almost paradigmatic example of a set of empirical phenomena demonstrating the existence of acquired constraints.

The Consequences of Contrasting Constraint Dimensions
The discussion of the various types of constraints has important consequences for the domain-generality versus domain-specificity issue. First, constraint distinctions may have important bearings on how one conducts research and formulates theoretical ideas on the DG-DS issue. De-

pending on the sorts of constraints one thinks are at work, one may adopt very different research styles. Thus, internal and change constraints may push one to examine empirically a set of completely artificial stimuli and to search for process models of learning. A famous example is Ebbinghaus, who took the pains to memorize thousands of nonsense syllables in order to investigate the processes of learning, retention, and forgetting (Ebbinghaus, 1885/1966). Structural and change constraints may force one to focus on structural descriptions of natural knowledge at different points in development, and so on.

Second, and perhaps more important, the discussion of various types of constraints makes it obvious that any general attempt to characterize the working of the human mind in its entirety as domain-general or domain-specific is doomed to fail. Some constraints may be conceived of as domain-general and others may be conceived of as domain-specific. Given that many different constraints together—some domain-specific, some domain-general—shape the mind's processing of even the most minor event or task, the perhaps most interesting question is how the various constraints interact to produce the appearance of a uniform, meaningful human mind (e.g., Sternberg, 1989).

Summary

We began this section by asking what the general goal of any DG-DS debate is and what is meant by domain-generality, domain-specificity, and domain. The goal of any DG-DS debate is to determine how widely any psychological constraint can be applied. Domain-generality is an absolute concept and implies that the constraint is invariant; that is, it applies to all actions and properties of the human mind. Domain-specificity, by comparison, is a relative, rather than absolute, concept, implying that the constraint applies to some, but not all actions and properties of the mind. Finally, domain is viewed as a relative and subjectively defined concept that partly depends on the constraint under consideration.

Because DG-DS debates evolve around constraints, constraints are at the center of DG-DS debates. We broadly defined constraint as any theoretical statement tied to an empirical phenomenon that narrows the number of possibilities of how the human mind may operate. Constraints come in many different forms but can be reasonably well described in terms of the five partially overlapping dimensions discussed. The type of constraint determines whether asking the DG-DS question is meaningful to begin with, and it strongly influences both the theoretical goal of research and the research strategy. In the next section, we exemplify the diversity of DG-DS debates in psychological theory and research by summarizing two important and well-known debates.

Domain-Generality versus Domain-Specificity: Two Debates

In this section, we briefly describe and discuss two of the best-known DG-DS debates in psychology, debates focusing on the characteristics of human expertise and the nature of human development. Our discussion of the debates is guided, albeit rather informally, by four main questions: First, what are the constraints that each of the debates centers on? Second, which views on the domain-generality and domain-specificity of these constraints have been formulated? Third, what are the empirical phenomena that most directly speak to the DG-DS issue? And fourth, what were the reasons for preferring domain-specific or domain-general views? We begin with what is arguably the most famous of the recent DG-DS controversies.

The Nature of Expertise
At the most general level, the study of expertise seeks to understand what distinguishes outstanding individuals in any area from less outstanding individuals. As Ericsson and Smith (1991) argue, theoretical conceptions of expertise favor one of four possible explanations: innate/domain-general, innate/domain-specific, acquired/domain-general, and acquired/domain-specific. The four different explanations reflect the basic belief that expertise is either predominantly influenced by inherited qualities or is a function of learning and that it can either be attributed to general characteristics of the individual or to specific aspects. In research on the nature of expertise, the DG-DS issue has thus played a major role.

The theoretical discussion in the first section of this chapter has taught us that any general statement of the form "Expertise is domain-general" or "Expertise is domain-specific" is neither meaningful nor helpful. The question of domain-generality versus domain-specificity is meaningful only in the context of particular psychological constraints. Accordingly, a variety of constraints on the nature of expertise have been formulated in the past, most of them implicitly, rather than explicitly. Perhaps two of the best-researched constraints can be informally formulated as follows: (1) "Experts perform better than novices" and (2) "The organization of an expert's knowledge base is hierarchical."

Asking the DG-DS question for the two constraints means determining how far (i.e., across how many domains) they can be applied. Empirical research focusing on the first constraint has typically been searching for performance correlations across different knowledge domains (e.g., chess playing, physics), whereas research focusing on the second constraint has usually been trying to establish functional equivalence of experts' knowledge bases in different knowledge domains. Consequently, much of the former research has been correlational in character (e.g., Ceci & Liker, 1986), whereas much of the latter research has been experimental (e.g., Chi, Feltovich, & Glaser, 1981). In the following, we limit ourselves primarily to a discussion of research on the first constraint.

Early research on the domain-general versus domain-specific nature of the first constraint tended to lean toward the domain-general view. The general assumption was that stable characteristics of the individual determined whether the individual demonstrated outstanding performance in any domain or not. Innate general characteristics are, for example, intelligence and personality; acquired general characteristics are, for instance, general problem-solving strategies. Because expertise was due to stable individual characteristics, the argument went, people who performed outstandingly in one domain would do so in a different domain as well.

This domain-general view of expertise seemed appropriate because it corresponded to early informal and formal observations of experts.[5] Galton (1869), for instance, identified eminent individuals in a wide range of fields and then studied their familial and genetic origins. He reported strong evidence for eminence's being limited to a relatively small number of families stemming from common ancestors, and inferred that expertise was domain-general and genetically determined.

Similarly, summaries of biographical data obtained by de Groot (1965) and Elo (1978) also indicated that experts in the area of chess did not represent a random sample from the general population. Elo's (1978) comprehensive sample of 180 highly skilled players showed that 63% of the players had obtained at least some education at the university level, as had 38% of their parents. Also, 40% of the players reported as their profession chess journalism, a profession that seemed to require at least some verbal ability, which, in turn, has been shown to be one of the better indicators of general intelligence (Sternberg, 1985). In addition, 96% of the players reported proficiency in at least two different languages, with 25% reporting proficiency in five or more languages, again indicating that the sample was unlikely to be randomly derived from the general population.

In contrast to these formal and informal observations, however, methodologically sound empirical studies have had a difficult time demonstrating the domain-generality of expertise. First, the relations between expertise and intelligence and between expertise and basic cognitive abilities have not been demonstrated consistently. Second, expertise has not been found to correlate with stable personality characteristics. Third, expertise can apparently not be explained by the positing of general problem-solving strategies.

For example, tests measuring general intelligence have been remarkably unsuccessful in accounting for individual differences in levels of performance in the arts and sciences and advanced professions, as measured by social indicators (e.g., money earned, status) and judgments (e.g., prizes, awards) (Tyler, 1965). Ceci and Liker (1986), for instance, reported correlations in the range of $r = .04$ to $r = .07$ between a measure of general intelligence and several measure of expertise in the area of horse race handicapping.

Other research motivated by the belief that expertise reflects some basic cognitive ability involving attention, memory, general speed of reaction, or command of logic has been similarly unsuccessful. For example, Guilford (1967) reported disappointingly low correlations between expertise and basic cognitive individual characteristics, such as speed of mental processing. More recent attempts (Baron, 1978; Carroll, 1978; Cooper & Regan, 1982; Hunt, 1980) have also yielded inconclusive results. For instance, research on individual differences in general memory performances has found low correlations of memory performance across different types of material and methods of testing (Kelley, 1964). Doll and Mayr (1987), comparing some of the best chess players in West Germany with normal subjects of similar age, found no evidence that expertise in chess was related to performance on spatial tasks.

Of the research that has focused not on intelligence or general cognitive abilities, but on other stable, or innate, characteristics of the individual, that by Cattell (1963; Cattell & Drevdahl, 1955) is perhaps the best example. Cattell tried to determine whether the personality profiles of eminent researchers in physics, biology, and psychology could be distinguished from those of teachers and administrators in the same fields and from those of the general population. Compared with all other groups, top researchers were found to exhibit a consistent profile, being more self-sufficient, dominant, emotionally unstable, introverted, and reflective. Despite these hints at possible personality patterns, the idea to account for expertise in terms of general personality characteristics has been largely unsuccessful (Ericsson & Smith, 1991). Indeed it becomes difficult to rule out the possibility that certain personality characteristics have not been acquired as a result of many years of extensive practice.

Expertise does not seem to be based on the availability of general problem-solving strategies either. This particular conclusion has been supported by recent work in artificial intelligence, where researchers are trying to develop nonhuman systems that can mimic intelligent human task performance in a variety of domains (e.g., Feigenbaum, 1989). Most of the early work in artificial intelligence in the late 1950s and early 1960s was based on the assumption that domain-general problem-solving heuristics and domain-general rules of learning were the most important ingredients of an expert system (for a review see Sternberg & Frensch, 1989). Perhaps the most prominent enterprise conducted in this spirit was the General Problem Solver (Ernst & Newell, 1969). This computer program was designed to translate and then represent internally the components of a certain problem and then to solve it by applying certain problem-solving heuristics based on the idea of means-ends analysis.

Early failures to write programs that could compete with human experts (particularly in the area of chess; Berliner, 1978) have led researchers to acknowledge that domain-independent expert systems do not exist. Rather, different expert systems have to be created for different domains, at least partly because the nature and structure of knowledge differs from one domain to another (Duda & Shortliffe, 1983; Hayes-Roth, Waterman, & Lenat, 1983).

As a result of the difficulties linking empirically any stable domain-general individual characteristics to measures of expertise, recent research on the nature of expertise has turned to domain-specific explanations. The turn toward domain-specific explanations has been brought about as much by the failure to establish empirical links between individual characteristics and expertise as by empirical findings that directly demonstrate domain-specificity in expertise. As a result, most modern researchers have come to accept, more or less, a domain-specific view of expertise, and they have concentrated their efforts on finding skill-related differences within, rather than outside, expertise domains, such as chess playing, physics, electronics, and so on.

Modern experimental efforts in the knowledge-based domain-specific tradition date back at least to de Groot. In one of his studies, de Groot (1965) showed two groups of chess players (five grandmasters and five experts) a set of unfamiliar positions and asked them to think out loud while choosing a move. The verbal statements were recorded by hand. De Groot's subjects ranged from grandmasters, some of the best players in the world, to club players. The results were rather surprising: although the grandmasters chose better moves than the less skilled players and did so in less time, the two groups did not differ on any of the quantitative indices of their move selection processes. That is, both groups considered roughly the same number of potential moves and initial base moves. Also, they did not differ in how far they were looking ahead to find the best move. Still, four of the five grandmasters ended up choosing the objectively best move whereas none of the experts did so.

It appeared that the major difference between the two groups of players was simply that the grandmasters did not waste any time exploring moves and move constellations that did not lead anywhere, instead concentrating their time and efforts on the exploration of promising moves, whereas the less skilled players wasted much time exploring moves that were not even candidates for the grandmasters' search processes. De Groot (1965) hypothesized that the experts' larger knowledge base guided their better selection of moves.

More recently, the ideas formulated by de Groot were extended by Chase and Simon (1973a, 1973b), who proposed a somewhat more sophisticated theory of chess playing. Chase and Simon studied three chess players (a master, a class-A player, and a beginner) in a variety of experimental situations. They found that the master's ability to recall briefly presented meaningful chess positions was better than the class-A player's and the novice's. Furthermore, the master reproduced the board perfectly in three of four trials, whereas the class-A player typically required one or two more trials than the master. The beginner needed up to 14 trials to reproduce the entire board configuration.

When random configurations were recalled, however, the results changed dramatically. Now, there were no differences in the number of pieces correctly recalled among the three players. Furthermore, the first-trial performance of all three subjects was even poorer than the first-trial performance of the beginner on meaningful chess configurations.

Chase and Simon (1973b) interpreted these results in the following way, roughly following the conclusions arrived at earlier by de Groot (1965) and Jongman (1968): the superior ability of experienced over less experienced chess players to recall briefly presented meaningful chess patterns cannot be explained by superior storage capacity. That is, masters cannot keep more chess pieces in their short-term memory than can less experienced players. Rather, their superiority is based upon a knowledge of a vast number of basic, meaningful chess patterns, called chunks, that are stored in long-term memory. Each of these patterns can be quickly identified and can be accessed in long-term memory through a label. When faced with the memory task, expert players match the chess configuration they perceive on the board with their long-term memory chunks. When they find a match, they retrieve the label for the pattern and store this label in short-term memory. At recall time, they can then use the label to access and retrieve the pattern from long-term memory.

This line of reasoning also explains why experience does not aid recall performance for randomly generated chess patterns. In this case, matching long-term memory chunks simply do not exist. Therefore, the individual chess pieces, rather than labels of chunks, have to be memorized.

Consequently, because their short-term memory capacity is not different from that of less experienced chess players, masters do not perform any better than beginners on random chess patterns.

De Groot's (1965) and Chase and Simon's (1973a, 1973b) subsequent findings were largely responsible for steering the interest of expertise researchers away from domain-general search-related issues and toward domain-specific perceptual- and knowledge-based issues. The exploration of domain-specific explanations of expertise has come to heavily dominate research, not only in the area of chess playing, but in many other areas as well (e.g., electronics, physics, managerial problem solving, and problem solving in international relations; see contributions in Frensch & Funke, 1995a, and Sternberg & Frensch, 1991).

Summary   The theoretical treatment of the nature of expertise has been guided rather directly by the domain-generality versus domain-specificity distinction. Two of the best-researched constraints are (1) "Experts perform better than novices" and (2) "The organization of an expert's knowledge base is hierarchical." Early views on the former constraint reflected the belief that stable domain-general individual characteristics were responsible for outstanding performance. Lately, these views have been replaced by the opposite assumption, namely, that expert performance is determined by domain-specific factors. Theoretical accounts of this aspect of the nature of expertise have thus drifted from one extreme view to the other and have left little ground for intermediate positions.

Interestingly, research on the second constraint has come to exactly the opposite conclusion, namely that the hierarchical nature of an expert's knowledge base organization can be found across many different expertise domains (e.g., Chi et al., 1981). The fact that applying the DG-DS question to different constraints within the same general research area can lead to completely different conclusions, of course, strengthens our earlier argument that any DG-DS debate can only be understood in the context of a particular constraint. By the same token, it demonstrates nicely Sternberg's (1989) general claim that researchers need to address the interaction of domain-specific and domain-general aspects of cognitive functioning.

Human Development

The study of human development is the study of change. One would like to know, for example, why the vocabulary explosion of children consistently occurs at around 18 months (Smith, 1926), why 30-month-olds so rarely and 36-month-olds so consistently succeed in using scale maps to locate hidden objects (DeLoache, 1987), and why 5-year-olds almost never and 10-year-olds almost always understand conservation of liquid quantity (Piaget, 1952).

Virtually all theoretical accounts of human development center, explicitly or implicity, on the notion of constraints. The general argument is that the uniformity of development cannot be understood without reference to some underlying constraints that govern the changes that take place in the human mind. As Peirce (1931–1935, vol. 1, p. 121) so succinctly put it,

suppose a being from some remote part of the universe, where the conditions of existence are inconceivably different from ours, to be presented with a United States Census Report which is for us a mine of valuable inductions, so vast as almost to give that epithet a new signification. He begins, perhaps, by comparing the ratio of indebtedness to deaths by consumption in counties whose names begin with different letters of the alphabet. It is safe to say that he would find the ratio everywhere the same, and thus his inquiry would lead to nothing. The stranger to this planet might go on for some time asking inductive questions that the Census would faithfully answer without learning anything except that certain conditions were independent of others. . . . Nature is a far vaster and less clearly arranged repertoire of facts than a census report; and if men had not come to it with special aptitudes for guessing right, it may well be doubted whether in the ten or twenty thousand years that they may have existed their greatest mind would have attained the amount of knowledge which is actually possessed by the lowest idiot. But, in point of fact, not man merely, but all animals derive by inheritance (presumably by natural selection) . . . classes of ideas which adapt them to their environment.

Theories of human development can thus be viewed—in our terminology—as descriptions of the dynamic constraints that govern change in the operation of the human mind. Much of the theoretical debate on the nature of human development has centered on three questions: First, what are the exact constraints governing development? Second, are these constraints innate or acquired? Third, how domain-specific are the constraints? The issue of domain-generality versus domain-specificity, thus, has been a major issue in the study of human development.

Despite their general acceptance of constraints governing development, theories of human development differ markedly in which sorts of constraints they posit and in the scope they ascribe to constraints. In principle, the DG-DS issue could be, and indeed has been applied to, dynamic constraints ranging from the very specific to the very abstract. For example, one might ask whether particular lexical acquisition constraints, such as the whole object constraint, the taxonomic constraint, or the mutual exclusivity constraint (Markman, 1990) apply to nonlanguage domains as well. Alternatively, one might ask whether all developmental constraints that exist apply in general or apply only to one or several domains. The most important debates have centered on the latter; we therefore concentrate in the following on DG-DS debates at a relatively abstract level.

Historically, most of the prominent older and more recent theoretical views on development fall into one of the four different categories that are created by crossing the binary concepts of the innate versus acquired constraint with the domain-general versus domain-specific. Theories of human development, thus, emphasize the role either of domain-specific innate constraints, domain-general innate constraints, domain-specific acquired constraints, or domain-general acquired constraints.[6]

Emphasis on Domain-Specific Innate Constraints   The most extreme proponents of a domain-specific/innate constraints view see human development as driven by innate constraints, where the details of the constraints differ qualitatively across domains. Fodor might be attributed with such a view when he argues that "all concepts are innate" (Fodor, 1981) or when he claims that cognitive development consists of increasing access to preexisting structures rather than the differentiation and elaboration of knowledge structures (Fodor, 1972, 1975). Fodor (1972, p. 93) writes,

Classical developmental psychology invites us to think of the child as a realization of an algebra which can be applied, relatively indifferently, to a wide variety of types of cognitive integrations, but which differs in essential respects from the mathematics underlying adult mentation. The alternative picture is that the child is a bundle of relatively special purpose computational systems which are formally analogous to those involved in adult cognition but which are quite restricted in their range of application, each being more or less tightly tied to the computation of a specific sort of data, more or less rigidly endogenously paced, and relatively inaccessible to purposes and influences other than those which conditioned its evolution. Cognitive development, on this view, is the maturation of the processes such systems subserve, and the gradual broadening of the kinds of computations to which they can apply.

In support of this view, one can find many cases in perception where domain-specific constraints dominate development, such as the development of binocular vision (Aslin & Smith, 1988) or of speech perception (Eimas, Miller, & Jusczyk, 1987). However, these cases are rarely disagreed upon any longer. Even empiricists who seek to explain development in terms of domain-general constraints usually acknowledge domain-specificity at the sensory level. Thus, of much more interest and more hotly debated are claims that locate domain-specific innate constraints at the more central, knowledge- and belief-laden aspects of cognition, such as intuitive physics and intuitive folk psychology (Keil, 1990a). Here, the current wisdom appears to be that young children's expectations concerning the behavior of objects and people may be guided by domain-specific innate constraints.

However, there are still many controversies among even those favoring a domain-specific innate-constraints view of intuitive physics and folk psychology. For example, Carey (1985) suggests that intuitive physics and folk psychology may be the only domains guided by domain-specific innate constraints and that all other theoretical beliefs emerge out of these two domains. Keil (1989), in contrast, argues for domain-specific constraints in a much larger number of theoretical domains.

Emphasis on Domain-General Innate Constraints   Perhaps the most prototypical proponent of a domain-general/innate constraints view on understanding change, be it in development or learning, was Hull (1943), who argued for a small set of axioms governing all of human learning. In this view, human development is guided by a few general principles that apply across domains. Although Hull's influence has waned, the same principled argument for domain-generality can be observed in more recent information-processing theorists, such as Anderson (1983), or in even more recent connectionist theorists, such as McClelland and Rumelhart (1986). Anderson (1983), for example, acknowledges the necessity of domain-specific sensory systems, but argues,

The most deeply rooted preconception guiding my theorizing is a belief in the unity of human cognition, that is that all higher cognitive processes, such as memory, language, problem solving, imagery, deduction, and induction, are different manifestations of the same underlying system. This is not to deny that there are many powerful special-purpose 'peripheral' systems for processing perceptual information and coordinating motor performance. However, behind these lies a common cognitive system for higher level processing. Moreover, the essence of what it is to be human lies in the principles of this core, higher level system. . . . The unitary position should not be confused with the belief that the human mind is simple and can be explained by just one or two principles. However, it is general-purpose, that is one can use the same data structures and processes in programs for language and for problem solving. (pp. 1–5)

Anderson's theoretical view on the domain-generality of change constraints is mirrored by his construction of production systems to model many facets of human functioning and learning. Production systems consist of a large number of if-then rules whose application is governed by a small set of laws of operation. Developmental psychologists that share Anderson's use of production systems as models of human performance and learning, and his theoretical views, include, for instance, Klahr (1984), Salthouse (1991), and Siegler (1986). Siegler (1986), for example, states,

Are the mechanisms specifically designed for language learning (e.g. a specific language acquisition device) or are they the same mechanisms that lead to other types of learning (e.g. a general ability to induce rules)? My personal suspicion is that widely applicable learning mechanisms produce most forms of language learning. . . . Thus, children's acquisition of language rules can be viewed as simply one manifestation of a basic human rule-learning ability, no different from any of the others except for the massive amount of opportunities the world affords for practice and learning through observation. (pp. 179–180)

A conceptually similar argument, albeit for a different developmental age trend and at a different constraint level, is made by Salthouse (1991). Salthouse argues that much, if not all, of the developmental declines that occur from middle to older age on many measures of cognitive performance are due to a general slowing of people's information processing. The slowing is expression of a domain-general innate constraint that is most likely located at the neurological level.

Newport (1989) gives a very striking example of how a critical period in development—typically viewed as evidence for the maturation of domain-specific systems—can be explained on the basis of domain-general innate constraints and thereby greatly enhances the attractivity of this particular theoretical position. Newport argues that the critical period in the acquisition of (the syntax of the native language) is tied to the development of domain-general constraints in the amount of information that can be stored. According to this explanation, young children are able to store only component parts of syntactical information whereas older children can store the entire linguistic stimulus. However, by storing only part of the syntactic stimulus, so the argument goes, younger children are better able to locate the relevant syntax information than are older children. Consequently, learning of natural language is easier for younger than for older children.

Emphasis on Domain-Specific Acquired Constraints   Whereas the two preceding views are logically sufficient to explain human development, this view, as the following view, is not. Domain-specific acquired constraints cannot explain all of development because they cannot explain how initial learning gets off the ground. Thus, the domain-specific solidus/acquired constraints assumption always needs to be accompanied by one or both of the two innate views discussed.

In general, accounts of human development that fall into this category typically rely on structure constraints, rather than process constraints, assuming that the child's initial acquisition of knowledge occurs in the same manner across domains. With additional experience, however, the knowledge already acquired exerts an influence on the knowledge to be acquired. The exact effect the old knowledge exerts on the new can either be the same across domains, as in the domain-general/acquired constraints view, to be presented in the next section, or it can differ for different domains, as for the present account.

Perhaps one of the best examples of the domain-specific/acquired constraints view can be seen in Quine's discussion of concept development (Quine, 1977). Quine views the child as developing different *similarity spaces* in different domains, due to different theories about the domains that, in turn, lead to different knowledge representations. Although Quine is not explicit about whether the constraints underlying knowledge representation in different domains are qualitatively different, such a view is at least consistent with his general argument.

Similarly, Chi's (1989) work comparing experts and novices in different knowledge domains also suggests that the constraints governing change can be different in different domains. For example, Chi (1989) reports that knowledge about dinosaurs contains many heavily connected sets of causal beliefs, whereas knowledge of chess might involve spatial, rather than causal, relations. Again, the exact details of the constraints governing knowledge acquisition in the two domains are not specified in detail, however, and it is therefore not entirely clear whether they are really domain-specific or domain-general.

Keil (1986) offers yet another example of an empirical finding that appears to at least be consistent with a domain-specific/acquired constraints view on development. Keil can show that for some well-defined concepts and word meanings, children shift from representations based on domain-general tabulations of all typically co-occurring characteristic features to representations based on only a few critical features. This characteristic-to-defining shift, as Keil terms it, seems to occur in relatively the same manner within domains but appears to be very different between domains.

From the examples discussed thus far, it should be clear that accounts of human development based on domain-specific acquired constraints can be rather different from accounts based on domain-specific innate constraints. First, innate constraints typically cover a wider range than acquired constraints that might apply only to very specific knowledge areas. Second, innate constraints apply in the same manner to all people; they tend to be universal, whereas acquired constraints can differ for different people and for people living in different cultures. Cross-cultural research on expertise (e.g., Scribner, 1983) is consistent with the acquired constraints view.

Emphasis on Domain-General Acquired Constraints   In the early 1970s, the prevailing view on human development appeared to be that it could be largely understood in terms of domain-general acquired constraints. Many theorists viewed the growth of knowledge as enabling the emergence of new structures that could in turn exert influences on the acquisition of new knowledge. The manner in which old knowledge affected the acquisition of new knowledge was thereby viewed as identical across all developmental domains. Piaget (1929, 1970), for example, viewed the domain-general constraints as emerging out of existing knowledge when it reached a critical mass.

Despite the general theoretical agreements, there was much controversy about the details of the constraints. For example, Bruner's enactive-iconic-symbolic sequence of development (Bruner, Olver, & Greenfield, 1965) was seen as sharply contrasting with Piaget's sensorimotor-preoperational-concrete operational stages. Vygotsky's (1965) and Werner's (1948) views were even more different.

Piaget's views, as one example of a primarily domain-general acquired constraints view of development, have not fared well. According to Case (1992), some of the reasons for the dismantling of Piagetian theory have been empirical and some theoretical. For example, the formulation and presentation of Piagetian theory made it difficult to test it empirically. Furthermore, when tested empirically it could not always be supported. For instance, many short-term training studies on Piagetian tasks exerted an impact on one class of task without exerting an influence on a structurally related class of tasks (Gelman, 1969). Also, children's intellectual development, when measured across many tasks, contexts, and domains, was much more uneven than the theory would permit (Beilin, 1971; Gelman & Baillargeon, 1983).

A further reason for the dismantling of Piagetian theory was the rise of domain-specific innate constraints views on development that allowed for qualitative changes occurring differently for different domains and not in an across-the-board fashion. Even highly similar developmental patterns, such as seen in stage changes according to Piagetians, could be explained in terms of these views. Stage changes could, for example, be viewed as caused by the maturation of new structures that were either dependent or independent of prior knowledge.

Criticisms of Piagetian views, however, have not necessarily led to abandoning the domain-general/acquired constraints view altogether. Case (1992), for example, has argued rather persuasively in favor of a new neo-Piagetian view of development that combines classic Piagetian as well as cognitive information-processing views. Case argues that with increasing age, automatization and chunking processes (e.g., Anderson, 1983; Frensch, 1991, 1994) increase overall processing efficiency and thereby free working memory capacity, which in turn allows new modes of thinking to emerge. Similar views based on the domain-general/ acquired constraints assumption have been formulated by Halford (1980; for a summary see Levin, 1986).

Summary   The binary concept of domain-generality versus domain-specificity has driven much of past and present theorizing about the nature of human development. Views of development have ranged from an emphasis on domain-specific innate constraints to an emphasis on domain-general acquired constraints. However, except perhaps for some proponents of domain-general acquired constraints (e.g., Piaget), theories have typically acknowledged that the four different views on human development are not mutually exclusive. That is, most theorists have assumed that development is driven by an interaction of different types of constraints, even though the emphasis on what was considered the most important type of constraints has differed among theories.

At present, one cannot detect a widely held consensus on the issue of domain-generality and domain-specificity in the field of human development; too different are the various theoretical views. Nevertheless, a few commonalities seem to emerge. First, it is generally acknowledged that there exists a certain number of highly domain-specific innate constraints (e.g., for the visual and auditory systems and for language) that guide the development of primarily sensory and perceptual systems. Second, views emphasizing primarily domain-general acquired constraints have run out of steam; the consensus, if there is one, appears to be that domain-generality is more likely to be the result of innate rather than acquired constraints. Third, and perhaps most important, it is now generally acknowledged that human development is the result of an interaction of constraints, some of which are very specific and some of which are very general. This particular conclusion, of course, is one we have encountered in our discussion of the previous debate as well.

General Comments on the Debates

The two debates discussed differ in many respects. They differ in terms of the psychological constraints they consider, in research strategies, in what is considered support for particular domain-specific or domain-general views, in how broad or narrow domain-specific mechanisms can be, and so on. Nevertheless, our discussion of the debates highlights some important aspects common to most DG-DS debates. First, it nicely demonstrates that applying the DG-DS question has both theoretical and empirical implications, reflecting a search for the width of applicability of psychological constraints and also guiding the corresponding empirical research. These two aspects are clearly visible in both debates.

Second, both debates are primarily oriented toward domain-generality or domain-specificity of relatively high-level, abstract constraints. For example, the DG-DS debate on the nature of human development has been primarily concerned with the question of whether *all* of the dynamic constraints that govern development are domain-specific or domain-general. More recently, however, a shift in orientation has occurred—visible, for instance, in the debate on human development—toward acknowledging that any interesting psychological phenomenon involves the interaction of many different constraints, that is, constraints differing on the five dimensions outlined earlier. This shift has led to a wealth of new DG-DS debates, debates that are sometimes concerned with very specific, and sometimes rather obscure, constraints (for examples see table 5.1).

Third, the acknowledgment that every psychological phenomenon is the result of an interaction among many different constraints has not (yet) led to the general insight that it is the interaction of constraints that needs to be addressed empirically. Despite the plea of some theorists (e.g., Sternberg, 1989), debates continue, as the two debates discussed do, to center on individual constraints with little attention to the way in which different constraints interact.

Fourth, both debates focus on the endpoints of the width-of-applicability dimension of a constraint. DG-DS debates generally continue to be couched in terms of the domain-generality versus domain-specificity opposition, without paying much attention to the more important question of where exactly on the width-of-applicability dimension a particular constraint might be located. Theorizing has been, and is still, characterized by an either-or mentality; constraints are viewed as either domain-specific or domain-general, without much thought of what exactly domain-general or domain-specific means.

Conclusions

Our primary goal in this chapter has been to convey an understanding of what the domain-generality versus domain-specificity issue is all about. We have defined the goal of DG-DS debates as determining how widely any psychological constraint can be applied. We broadly defined constraint as any theoretical statement tied to an empirical phenomenon that narrows the number of possibilities of how the human mind may operate. Domain-generality is an absolute concept and implies that the constraint is invariant, that is, that it applies to all actions and properties of the human mind. Domain-specificity, by comparison, is a relative, rather than absolute, concept, implying that the constraint applies to some but not all actions and properties of the mind. Domain we viewed as a relative and subjectively defined concept that partly depends on the constraint under consideration.

We discussed two DG-DS debates that have figured prominently in psychology, debates centering on the nature of human expertise and human development. Common to both debates is an emphasis on relatively high-level constraints, a focus on the two endpoints of the width-of-applicability dimension, and a general failure to acknowledge that domain-general and domain-specific constraints may coexist in descriptions and explanations of empirical phenomena (or else these debates would not have started in the first place).

Why is it, then, that despite the shortcomings of DG-DS debates in the past and present, the issue continues to influence much of our thinking about how the human mind works? One possible reason is the unwavering hope that we will be able (one day!) to describe mind in a parsimonious manner, with a few general principles. This hope is misguided, we argue, for at least two reasons. First, our chances of capturing the functioning of the mind by positing a few underlying principles is, as history tells us, equal to nil.

Second, parsimony is usually achieved at the expense of precision. Thus, even if one were able to find truly domain-general principles that characterize the functioning of mind, these principles would probably be of little use to predicting individual behavior in a particular situation, or even the "modal" behavior of a person given a sample of situations. In all likelihood, they would be of little use for certain practical purposes as well, such as the construction of programs of intervention in certain behaviors.

Does this mean then that DG-DS debates are obsolete, serving no purpose? To the contrary, these debates are meaningful and helpful *if* they focus on determining the width of applicability of thoroughly defined psychological constraints. They are not meaningful if they concentrate on contrasting only the two endpoints of the width-of-applicability dimension.

Determining the exact location on the width-of-applicability dimension is important for at least two reasons. First, it helps researchers to find the proper level of psychological explanation. For instance, if we discover that negative priming can be observed with letters, words, line drawings, complex drawings, and photographs, then we may consider the constraint to be domain-general in the sense that it applies to all these types of visual materials. We may then propose a mechanism that explains negative priming for "visual materials" and not just one for letters, one for words, and so on.

Second, determining the width of applicability may have important practical consequences, addressing, for instance, the feasibility of intervention programs. Knowing that the ability to find creative solutions to problems in the domain of mechanics has nothing in common with the ability to be creative in the domain of graphic design, to return to the example we gave at the beginning of this chapter, has obvious consequences for the way creativity-training programs need to be constructed.

Thus, DG-DS debates are meaningful to the extent that they focus on the width-of-applicability question. This insight needs to be supplemented by the further insight, however, that most, if not all interesting psychological phenomena are affected by the interactions of many constraints varying in width of applicability and that explanation of behavior can only be achieved if these interactions are understood. Sternberg (1989) writes that "researchers should be asking in what ways representation and processing are domain-general and in what ways they are domain-specific, and why. Researchers need to explore the interactions between general and specific aspects of functioning" (p. 115). We could not have said it any better!

Notes

1. Negative priming refers to the phenomenon that responses to recently ignored stimuli may be slower and less accurate than responses to new stimuli.

2. By empirical phenomenon we mean an empirical effect that has been observed repeatedly and not just once. A singular empirical finding may be due to chance. It need not reflect an empirical effect that can be measured reliably, and thus, asking the DG-DS question may be a waste of time and resources. In other words, the establishing of reliable effects should preceed the asking of the DG-DS question.

3. This definition is reminiscent of several other definitions that can be found in the literature. For example, Keil (1990b) conceives of constraint as "any factors ... that result in nonrandom selection of the logically possible characterizations of an informational pattern" (p. 136). Maratsos (1992) argues that "in its widest sense, constraint would apply very broadly to what organisms do, and how they think" (p. 4). Simon (1995), referring to internal constraints, argues that "The natural laws that determine the structure and behavior of an object, natural or artificial, are its internal constraints" (p. 99).

4. The relation between process and structure is complicated by the problematic distinction between the two. Newell (1972), for example, pointed out that computer programs are completely ambiguous as to whether they should be considered a process or structure.

5. When we refer to the domain-generality or domain-specificity of expertise or simply to expertise in the following text, we are referring to domain-generality or -specificity of the first constraint, as stated earlier in the text. Any use of the shorter expression is strictly for simplicity's sake.

6. The following discussion summarizes many arguments that can be found in Keil (1990a, 1990b).

References

Anderson, J. R. (1983). *The architecture of cognition.* Cambridge, MA: Harvard University Press.

Aslin, R. N., & Smith, L. B. (1988). Perceptual development. *Annual Review of Psychology, 39,* 435–473.

Baron, J. (1978). Intelligence and general strategies. In G. Underwood (Ed.), *Strategies in information processing* (pp. 403–450). London: Academic Press.

Beilin, H. (1971). Developmental stages and developmental processes. In D. R. Green, M. P. Ford, & G. B. Flamer (Eds.), *Measurement and Piaget.* New York: McGraw-Hill.

Berliner, H. (1978). A chronology of computer chess and its literature. *Artificial Intelligence, 10,* 201–214.

Bruner, J. S., Olver, R. R., & Greenfield, P. M. (1965). *Studies in cognitive growth*. New York: Wiley.

Carey, S. (1985). *Conceptual change in childhood*. Cambridge, MA: MIT Press.

Carroll, J. B. (1978). How shall we study individual differences in cognitive abilities? Methodological and theoretical perspectives. *Intelligence, 2*, 87–115.

Case, R. (1992). Neo-Piagetian theories of child development. In R. J. Sternberg & C. A. Berg (Eds.), *Intellectual development* (pp. 161–196). Cambridge, MA: Cambridge University Press.

Cattell, R. B. (1963). The personality and motivation of the researcher from measurements of contemporaries and from bibliography. In C. W. Taylor & F. Barron (Eds.), *Scientific creativity: Its recognition and development* (pp. 119–131). New York: Wiley.

Cattell, R. B., & Drevdahl, J. E. (1955). A comparison of the personality profile (16 PF) of eminent researchers with that of eminent teachers and administrators, and of the general population. *British Journal of Psychology, 46*, 248–261.

Ceci, S. J., & Liker, J. K. (1986). A day at the races: A study of IQ, expertise, and cognitive complexity. *Journal of Experimental Psychology: General, 115*, 255–266.

Chase, W. G., & Ericsson, K. A. (1981). Skilled memory. In J. R. Anderson (Ed.), *Cognitive skills and their acquisition* (pp. 141–189). Hillsdale, NJ: Erlbaum.

Chase, W. G., & Simon, H. A. (1973a). The mind's eye in chess. In W. G. Chase (Ed.), *Visual information processing* (pp. 215–281). New York: Academic Press.

Chase, W. G., & Simon, H. A. (1973b). Perception in chess. *Cognitive Psychology, 4*, 55–81.

Chi, M. T. H. (1989). How inferences about novel domain-related concepts can be constrained by structural knowledge. *Merrill-Palmer Quarterly, 36*, 27–62.

Chi, M. T. H., Feltovich, P. J., & Glaser, R. (1981). Categorization and representation of physics problems by experts and novices. *Cognitive Science, 5*, 121–152.

Chomsky, N. (1975). *Reflections on language*. New York: Pantheon.

Cohen, N. J., & Squire, L. R. (1980). Preserved learning and retention of pattern-analyzing skill in amnesia: Dissociation of knowing how and knowing that. *Science, 210*, 207–210.

Cooper, L. A., & Regan, D. T. (1982). Attention, perception and intelligence. In R. J. Sternberg (Ed.), *Handbook of human intelligence* (pp. 123–169). Cambridge, MA: Cambridge University Press.

Cosmides, L., & Tooby, J. (1987). From evolution to behaviour: evolutionary psychology as the missing link. In J. Dupre (Ed.), *The latest on the best: Essays on evolution and optimality* (pp. 277–306). Cambridge, MA: MIT Press.

Cosmides, L., & Tooby, J. (1989). Evolutionary psychology and the generation of culture, part I. *Ethology and Sociobiology, 10*, 19–29.

Crawford, R. P. (1966). *The techniques of creative thinking; How to use your ideas to achieve success.* New York: Hawthorn Books.

de Groot, A. D. (1965). *Thought and choice in chess.* The Hague, Netherlands: Mouton.

DeLoache, J. S. (1987). Rapid change in the symbolic functioning of young children. *Science, 238,* 1556–1557.

Doll, J., & Mayr, U. (1987). Intelligenz und Schachleistung—eine Untersuchung an Schachexperten. [Intelligence and achievement in chess—A study of chess masters.] *Psychologische Beiträge, 29,* 270–289.

Duda, R. O., & Shortliffe, E. H. (1983). Expert systems research. *Science, 220,* 261–268.

Ebbinghaus, H. (1966). *Über das Gedächtnis.* Amsterdam: E. J. Bonset. (Original work published 1885.)

Eimas, P. D., Miller, J. L., & Jusczyk, P. (1987). On infant speech perception and the acquisition of language. In S. Harnad (Ed.), *Categorical perception* (pp. 161–195). New York: Cambridge University Press.

Elo, A. (1978). *The rating of chessplayers, past and present.* New York: Arco.

Ericsson, K. A., & Smith, J. (1991). Prospects and limits of the empirical study of expertise: An introduction. In K. A. Ericsson & J. Smith (Eds.), *Toward a general theory of expertise: Prospects and limits* (pp. 1–38). Cambridge, MA: Cambridge University Press.

Ernst, G. W., & Newell, A. (1969). *GPS: A case study in generality and problem solving.* New York: Academic Press.

Feigenbaum, E. A. (1989). What hath Simon wrought? In D. Klahr & K. Kotovsky (Eds.), *Complex information processing: The impact of Herbert A. Simon* (pp. 165–182). Hillsdale, NJ: Erlbaum.

Fodor, J. A. (1972). Some reflections on L. S. Vygotsky's Thought and Language. *Cognition, 1,* 83–95.

Fodor, J. A. (1975). *The language of thought.* New York: Thomas Y. Crowell.

Fodor, J. A. (1981). The current status of the innateness controversy. In J. A. Fodor (Ed.), *Representations: Philosophical essays on the foundations of cognitive science.* Cambridge, MA: MIT Press.

Frensch, P. A. (1991). Transfer of composed knowledge in a multi-step serial task. *Journal of Experimental Psychology: Learning, Memory, and Cognition, 17,* 997–1016.

Frensch, P. A. (1994). Composition during serial learning: A serial position effect. *Journal of Experimental Psychology: Learning, Memory, and Cognition, 20,* 423–442.

Frensch, P. A., & Funke, J. (Eds.) (1995a). *Complex problem solving: The European perspective.* Hillsdale, NJ: Erlbaum.

Frensch, P. A., & Funke, J. (1995b). Definitions, traditions, and a framework for understanding complex problem solving. In P. A. Frensch & J. Funke, (Eds.),

Complex problem solving: The European perspective (pp. 3–26). Hillsdale, NJ: Erlbaum.

Galton, F. (1869). *Hereditary genius.* New York: Macmillan.

Garfield, J. L. (1987). Introduction. In J. L. Garfield (Ed.), *Modularity in knowledge representation and natural-language understanding* (pp. 17–23). Cambridge, MA: MIT Press.

Gelman, R. (1969). Conservation acquisition: A problem of learning to attend to relevant attributes. *Journal of Experimental Child Psychology, 7,* 167–187.

Gelman, R., & Baillargeon, R. (1983). A review of some Piagetian concepts. In J. H. Flavell & E. M. Markman (Eds.), *Handbook of child psychology. Vol. 3. Cognitive development.* New York: Wiley.

Gick, M. L., & Holyoak, K. J. (1983). Schema induction and analogical transfer. *Cognitive Psychology, 15,* 1–38.

Guilford, J. P. (1967). *The nature of human intelligence.* New York: McGraw-Hill.

Halford, G. (1980). Toward a redefinition of cognitive developmental stages. In J. Kirby & J. B. Biggs (Eds.), *Cognition, development and instruction* (pp. 39–64). New York: Academic Press.

Hayes-Roth, F., Waterman, D. A., & Lenat, D. B. (1983). An overview of expert systems. In F. Hayes-Roth, D. A. Waterman, & D. B. Lenat (Eds.), *Building expert systems* (pp. 3–29). Reading, MA: Addison-Wesley.

Heckhausen, J. (in press). *Developmental regulation in adulthood: Age-normative and sociostructural constraints as adaptive challenges.* Cambridge, MA: Cambridge University Press.

Hiroto, D. S. (1974). Locus of control and learned helplessness. *Journal of Experimental Psychology, 102,* 187–193.

Hull, C. L. (1943). *Principles of behavior.* New York: Appleton-Century-Crofts.

Hunt, E. (1980). Intelligence as an information processing concept. *Journal of British Psychology, 71,* 449–474.

Jacoby, L. L. (1983). Remembering the data: Analyzing interactive processes in reading. *Journal of Verbal Learning and Verbal Behavior, 22,* 485–508.

Johnston, T. D. (1988). Developmental explanation and the ontogeny of birdsong: Nature/nurture redux. *Behavioral and Brain Sciences, 11,* 617–773.

Jongman, R. W. (1968). *Het oog van de meester.* Amsterdam: Van Gorcum.

Keil, F. C. (1986). On the structure-dependent nature of stages of cognitive development. In I. Levin (Ed.), *Stage and structure: Reopening the debate* (pp. 144–163). Norwood, NJ: Ablex.

Keil, F. C. (1989). *Concepts, kinds, and cognitive development.* Cambridge, MA: Bradford Books.

Keil, F. C. (1990a). Constraints on the acquisition and representation of knowledge. In M. W. Eysenck (Ed.), *Cognitive psychology: An international review* (pp. 197–219). Chicester, England: Wiley.

Keil, F. C. (1990b). Constraints on constraints: Surveying the epigenetic landscape. *Cognitive Science, 14,* 135–168.

Kelley, H. P. (1964). Memory abilities: A factor analysis. *Psychometric Society Monographs, 11,* 1–53.

Klahr, D. (1984). Transition mechanisms in quantitative development. In R. J. Sternberg (Ed.), *Mechanisms of cognitive development.* San Francisco: Freeman.

Kuhn, T. S. (1962). *The structure of scientific revolutions.* Chicago: University of Chicago Press.

Lehrman, D. (1953). A critique of Konrad Lorenz's theory of instinctive behavior. *Quarterly Review of Biology, 28,* 337–363.

Lerner, R. (1983). *Development and plasticity.* New York: Academic Press.

Levin, I. (Ed.) (1986). *Stage and structure: Reopening the debate.* Norwood, NJ: Ablex.

Maratsos, M. (1992). Constraints, modules, and domain specificity: An introduction. In M. R. Gunnar & M. Maratsos (Eds.), *Modularity and constraints in language and cognition: The Minnesota Symposia on child psychology* (Vol. 25, pp. 1–23). Hillsdale, NJ: Erlbaum.

Markman, E. M. (1990). Constraints children place on word meanings. *Cognitive Science, 14,* 57–77.

Marr, D. (1982). *Vision.* New York: Freeman.

McClelland, J. L., & Rumelhart, D. E. (Eds.) (1986). *Parallel distributed processing: Explorations in the microstructure of cognition.* Cambridge, MA: MIT Press.

Miller, G. (1956). The magical number seven, plus or minus two: Some limits on our capacity for processing information. *Psychological Review, 63,* 81–97.

Neely, J. H. (1991). Semantic priming effects on visual word recognition: A selective review of current findings and theories. In D. Besner and G. Humphreys (Eds.), *Basic processes in reading: Visual word recognition* (pp. 264–336). Hillsdale, NJ: Erlbaum.

Newell, A. (1972). A note on process/structure distinctions in developmental psychology. In S. Farnham-Diggory (Ed.), *Information processing in children.* New York: Academic Press.

Newport, E. (1989). Maturational constraints on language learning. *Cognitive Science, 14,* 11–28.

Peirce, C. S. (1931–1935). *Collected papers of Charles Sanders Pierce* (6 vols.). (C. Hartshorne & P. Weiss, Eds.) Cambridge, MA: Harvard University Press.

Piaget, J. (1929). *The child's conception of the world.* New York: Harcourt Brace.

Piaget, J. (1952). *The child's concept of number.* New York: Norton.

Piaget, J. (1970). Piaget's theory. In P. H. Mussen (Ed.), *Carmichael's manual of child psychology* (3rd ed., Vol. 1). New York: Wiley.

Posner, M. I. (1988). Introduction: What is it to be an expert? In M. T. H. Chi, R. Glaser, & M. J. Farr (Eds.), *The nature of expertise* (pp. xxix–xxxvi). Hillsdale, NJ: Erlbaum.

Quine, W. V. O. (1977). Natural kinds. In S. P. Schwartz (Ed.), *Naming, necessity and natural kinds*. Ithaca, NY: Cornell University Press.

Roediger, H. L. (1990). Implicit memory. Retention without awareness. *American Psychologist, 45,* 1043–1056.

Rosenthal, V. (1988). Does it rattle when you shake it? Modularity of mind and the epistemology of cognitive research. In G. Denes, C. Semenza, & P. Bissiacchi (Eds.), *Perspectives on cognitive neuropsychology* (pp. 31–58). Hove, England: Erlbaum.

Salthouse, T. A. (1991). Mediation of adult age differences in cognition by reductions in working memory and speed of processing. *Psychological Science, 2,* 179–183.

Scribner, S. (1983). Studying working intelligence. In B. Rogoff and J. Lave (Eds.), *Everydays cognition: Its development in social context* (pp. 9–40). Cambridge, MA: Harvard University Press.

Siegler, R. S. (1986). *Children's thinking.* Englewood Cliffs, NJ: Prentice Hall.

Simon, H. A. (1995). Artificial intelligence: An empirical science. *Artificial Intelligence, 77,* 95–127.

Smith, M. E. (1926). *An investigation of the development of the sentence and the extent of vocabulary in young children. University of Iowa Studies in Child Welfare, 3* (5).

Sternberg, R. J. (1985). *Beyond IQ: A triarchic theory of human intelligence.* Cambridge, MA: Cambridge University Press.

Sternberg, R. J. (1989). Domain-generality versus domain-specificity: The life and impending death of a false dichotomy. *Merrill-Palmer Quarterly, 35,* 115–130.

Sternberg, R. J., & Frensch, P. A. (1989). Intelligence and cognition. In M. Eysenck (Ed.), *International Review of Cognitive Psychology* (Vol. 1, pp. 57–103). Chichester, England: Wiley.

Sternberg, R. J., & Frensch, P. A. (Eds.) (1991). *Complex problem solving: Principles and mechanisms.* Hillsdale, NJ: Erlbaum.

Tipper, S. P. (1985). The negative priming effect: Inhibitory priming by ignored objects. *The Quarterly Journal of Experimental Psychology, 37A,* 571–590.

Tipper, S. P., & Cranston, M. (1985). Selective attention and priming: Inhibitory and facilitatory effects of ignored primes. *The Quarterly Journal of Experimental Psychology, 37A,* 591–611.

Tipper, S. P., Weaver, B., Cameron, S., Berhaut, J. C., & Bastedo, J. (1991). Inhibitory mechanisms of attention in identification and localization tasks: Time course and disruption. *Journal of Experimental Psychology: Learning, Memory, and Cognition, 17,* 681–692.

Treisman, A., & Gelade, G. (1980). A feature integration theory of attention. *Cognitive Psychology, 12,* 97–136.

Tyler, L. E. (1965). *The psychology of human differences.* New York: Appleton-Century-Crofts.

Underwood, B. J. (1957). Interference and forgetting. *Psychological Review, 64,* 49–60.

Vygotsky, L. S. (1965). *Thought and language.* Cambridge, MA: MIT Press.

Vygotsky, L. S. (1978). *Mind in society.* Cambridge, MA: Harvard University Press.

Werner, H. (1948). *Comparative psychology of mental development* (2nd ed.). New York: International Universities Press.

6

Conscious versus Unconscious Cognition

John F. Kihlstrom

Conscious and Unconscious Cognition

The cognitive revolution made the study of consciousness respectable again, if only in the form of studies of attention, primary memory, and imagery. The legitimation of consciousness was not inevitable, however: one of the dirty secrets of cognitive psychology is that many of those who practice it can get along perfectly well without displaying any interest in consciousness at all. Flanagan (1991) has pointed out four reasons for this state of affairs:

Positivistic Reserve: Cognitive psychology inherited some of the methodological assumptions of the behaviorism it replaced, in particular an emphasis on publicly observable behavior as the window into the mind. Because consciousness is inherently private, as well as somewhat metaphysical, it still seems somehow beyond the pale of a science of the mind.

Piecemeal Approach: Furthermore, even among those cognitive psychologists who affirm an interest in consciousness, there is a tacit assumption that an understanding of consciousness will emerge, in a bottom-up fashion, from studies of individual phenomena. Many cognitive psychologists have made their careers by studying the phenomena of consciousness, such as attention, episodic memory, and imagery, without ever referring to consciousness itself. The effect has been to marginalize consciousness, as a topic that, perhaps like pornography, is too embarrassing to discuss in polite company even if we might admit privately that it's something we're really interested in.

Conscious Inessentialism: To make things even worse, the doctrine of computational functionalism, which underlies so much contemporary modeling of cognitive processes and systems, assumes that we can produce a perfectly adequate description of human information processing solely in terms of the functional relations between stimulus inputs and response outputs, with perhaps a hidden layer or two in between. After all the effort to get past behaviorism, this apparent throwback to the connectionism of Edward L. Thorndike and the radical formulations of B. F. Skinner renders consciousness, once again, inessential to the study of the mind.

Epiphenomalist Suspicion: Finally, many of those computational functionalists who, however grudgingly, admit that consciousness is part of the human experience, nonetheless argue that consciousness is the end product of cognitive functioning, and plays no causal role in human experience, thought, and action—thus rendering us merely conscious automata. For example, connectionist analyses of cognition state or imply that conscious awareness is the last thing that happens, after the network has settled into a steady state—that is, after all of the interesting and important work is done. The thrust of this argument is that while we humans may happen to be conscious, nothing much hangs on this fact, and things wouldn't be any different if we weren't conscious at all.

All this sounds pretty bad if one is interested in consciousness, but the upside is that conscious inessentialism and the epiphenomenalist suspicion, taken together, provide cognitive psychologists with ample motivation for exploring the psychological unconscious—that is, the idea that conscious experience, thought, and action are influenced by percepts, memories, and other mental states inaccessible to phenomenal awareness and independent of voluntary control. So it is one of the ironies of contemporary cognitive psychology that many of those who might have made a science of consciousness have instead gravitated, knowingly or not, toward a science of the mind that gives precedence to unconscious processes.

Automatic versus Controlled Processing

So far as modern psychology is concerned, the psychological unconscious began life as a kind of mental wastebasket: it was the repository for unattended inputs, memories rendered unavailable by decay or displacement, and latent knowledge not currently being utilized by the cognitive system. Consider the multistore *modal models* of memory of the sort proposed by Waugh and Norman (1965) and Atkinson and Shiffrin (1968), depicted schematically in figure 6.1 (for a review, see Healy & McNamara, 1996).

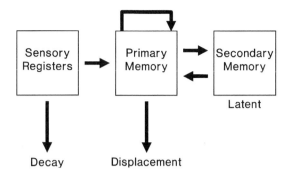

Figure 6.1
Schematic description of the three-store modal model of memory, with the psychological unconscious reserved for items lost from the sensory registers by decay or from primary (short-term) memory by displacement, or residing in a latent state in secondary (long-term) memory.

Although its advocates rarely discussed the topic as such (a reflection of the piecemeal approach described by Flanagan), the modal model essentially identifies consciousness with attention and short-term memory. Thus, mental representations enter short-term memory when attention is paid to them; only at this point are they accessible to phenomenal awareness (Posner, 1980, 1982)—a condition they retain only so long as they are rehearsed. From this perspective, debates about unconscious processing generally take the form of questions about how much information can be processed preattentively (Neisser, 1967).

The earliest *filter* theories (e.g., Broadbent, 1958) proposed that attentional selection occurred early in cognitive processing and was based on perceptual features. According to these models, preattentive semantic analysis was not possible, and so there could be no preconscious processing of meaning. Consider, for example, the dichotic listening paradigm, in which the subject is presented with a different auditory message in each ear, but told to attend to only one of them. Treisman's (1960) discovery of semantic intrusions from the unattended channel in dichotic listening led to the replacement of the filter with an *attenuator,* so unattended information is not completely filtered out. Still, the implication was that semantic processing occurred only after information had passed through an attentional bottleneck—hence, no preattentive semantic processing. Finally, there emerged a number of *late selection* theories of attention (Deutsch & Deutsch, 1963; Norman, 1968), which allowed for full semantic processing of the unattended channel, permitting attentional selection to be based on the pertinence of information to ongoing tasks. The question of preattentive semantic processing came to a head with Marcel's (1983) demonstration of masked semantic priming and with the subsequent debate (e.g., Holender, 1986) over whether semantic processing could occur in the absence of attention and conscious identification.

At about the same time, however, theories of attention underwent a shift from filter to capacity theories (Kahneman, 1973; Posner, 1980; for an account of this shift, see Kahneman & Treisman, 1984). According to this view, attention is equated with mental effort, cognitive resources are held to be limited, and the perceiver's ability to process information depends on the resources required by the task(s) at hand. If these tasks are undemanding, several can be carried out simultaneously, so long as there is no structural interference between them. The success of the capacity view quickly led to a distinction between *automatic* and *controlled* cognitive processes (LaBerge & Samuels, 1974; Posner & Snyder, 1975; Schneider & Shiffrin, 1977; Shiffrin & Schneider, 1977).

As defined by Posner and Snyder (1975), automatic processes are— in a word—*automatic:* they are initiated independently of the person's conscious intentions, and they cannot be terminated until their execution has been completed. Controlled processes, by contrast, are initiated and terminated voluntarily. Moreover, whereas we are phenomenally aware of our controlled processes, automatic processes are executed outside of awareness. Automatic processes might be innate, or they may have become automatized by virtue of extensive practice (Anderson, 1982; LaBerge & Samuels, 1974; Logan, 1988); but the models for automatic processes seem to be the innate, incorrigible stimulus-response connections familiar to psychobiologists: spinal reflexes, which can occur without the involvement of "higher" cortical centers; taxes, the gross orientation responses observed in many invertebrates; instincts, species-specific responses to specific patterns of stimulation; and the habits acquired through classical and instrumental conditioning. In principle, at least, automatic processes are *unconscious* in the strict sense of the term because they are executed outside phenomenal awareness and are independent of voluntary control.

Intentionality and Cognitive Resources

Of course, the positivistic reserve carried over from functional behaviorism still makes many cognitive psychologists nervous about defining their concepts in terms of such private, mentalistic constructs as *awareness* and *intention*. Perhaps for that reason, certain other attributes were quickly added onto the concept of automaticity. So, for example, Posner and Snyder (1975) asserted that automatic processes consumed no attentional resources, while Schneider and Shiffrin (1977) argued that they were carried out in parallel rather than in series. Hasher and Zacks (1979, 1984) elaborated the concept of automaticity still further. According to their definition, a process was automatic if performance was (1) insensitive to intentions; (2) equivalent under intentional and incidental conditions; (3) not modified by training and feedback; (4) invariant with respect to individual differences (e.g., in intelligence); (5) invariant with respect to age; and (6) unaffected by arousal, stress, or the requirements of simultaneous tasks.

Some of these additional properties, especially the idea that automatic processes consume no attentional resources, have become part and parcel of the very notion of automaticity. However, they are better construed as empirical questions than as definitional criteria. There is no a priori reason, for example, why an automatic process should consume no attentional resources; it is easy to imagine a process whose execution, though independent of conscious intention, necessarily requires cognitive resources. Even thermostats draw electricity, as do the furnaces and air conditioners they automatically regulate.

An attempt to break out of the positivistic reserve, and define automatic processes solely in terms of intentionality, has been proposed by Jacoby (1991), in terms of his *process dissociation framework*. According to Jacoby, an automatic process is one that occurs despite the person's intention that it should not do so. For example, if prior study of a word list automatically primes performance on a word stem completion task, this influence would persist even if subjects were specifically instructed to complete word stems with items that were not on the studied list. Thus, intention, not the consumption of resources, is the defining feature of automaticity. Jacoby's process dissociation framework has become enormously influential, at the same time that it has also come under severe criticism. For example, it rests on the assumption that the exclusion task is a pure measure of automatic influence, which may not be true (for other criticisms, see Curran & Hintzman, 1995). However, in the present context what is appealing about the framework is Jacoby's attempt to develop an operational definition of automaticity strictly in terms of subjects' conscious intentions, while relegating such matters as the consumption of cognitive resources to the status of empirical questions.

Toward a Psychology of Zombies?

The distinction between automatic and controlled processes is somewhat muddied by the fact that in principle, even deliberate, conscious actions are mediated by unconscious, automatic processes. Thus, driving a car over a familiar route may be automatic, in the sense that one can carry on a complex conversation while driving and arrive at one's destination without any awareness of various turns, gearshifts, and speed changes made along the way. But the decision to get in the car and drive it from point *A* to point *B* is surely a conscious one. Still, the attractions of conscious inessentialism are so strong that some psychologists and other cognitive scientists have argued that automatic processing dominates mental life and interpersonal behavior. For example, Dennett's (1991) Multiple-Drafts Model, based on a strong version of computational functionalism, explains consciousness as merely a snapshot of one of the many discriminative states that continuously arise between stimulus input and behavioral response. Computers have consciousness in this sense, according to Dennett's theory, and so do zombies. Consciousness is a momentary by-product of a cognitive machinery that is grinding away automatically; it plays no special role in mental life; we might as well be zombies ourselves (and we probably are!).

The embrace of automaticity is particularly visible within social psychology, where some theorists have argued that certain critical interpersonal processes are automatic and thus both unconscious and uncontrollable. Thus, Nisbett and Wilson (1977) have argued that our conscious beliefs are simply after-the-fact explanations that have nothing to do with why we do what we do because our behavior is mediated by processes that are themselves unconscious. Similarly, Berkowitz (1993) has argued that aggressive responses to frustration are automatically triggered by particular cues in the environment; and many theorists concerned with stereotyping and prejudice have concluded that the negative views that men hold of women, whites of blacks, Anglos of Hispanics, and so on, reflect an automatic evocation of negative stereotypes leading to prejudicial behavior (e.g., Devine, 1989; Fazio, Sanbonmatsu, Powell, & Kardes, 1986; Greenwald & Banaji, 1995).

Berkowitz and Devine (1995) have been especially astute in seeing the close relationship between a modern social psychology whose cognitive components are largely automatic and an earlier one based on S-R associationism. Bargh (1997) has brought cognitive social psychology full circle by explicitly embracing Skinner's (1953) rejection of free will and conscious choice as determinants of behavior. At the beginning of his essay he writes that "Much of everyday life—thinking, feeling, and doing—is automatic in that it is driven by current features of the environment . . . as mediated by automatic cognitive processing of those features, and not mediated by conscious choice or reflection" (pp. 2).

And toward the end, he concludes:

Automaticity pervades everyday life, playing an important role in creating the psychological situation from which subjective experience and subsequent conscious and intentional processes originate. Our perceptions, evaluations, and the goals we pursue can and do come under environmental control. Because these perceptual interpretations, likes and dislikes, and reasons for our behavior are not consciously experienced, we make sense of them in terms of those aspects of which we are consciously aware, and our theories as to what would have caused us to feel or act that way. (pp. 50)

Bargh especially seems to be leading us toward a psychology of a special class of zombies, creatures who are not quite unconscious, but for whom consciousness has no function other than to erect personal theories—quite literally afterthoughts—concerning our own experience, thought, and action that are wholly irrelevant to what actually goes on in our minds and our lives. One can only wonder whether, when the reduction of mental life to automatic mental processes (e.g., Dennett, 1991), and then to brain processes (e.g., Churchland, 1995) is complete, there will be any place left for conscious awareness and control in James's (1890/1981, p. 1) science of mental life.

Implicit versus Explicit Memory

No such concerns attach to the concept of *implicit memory* (Graf & Schacter, 1985; Schacter, 1987), which along with automaticity has been largely responsible for the revival of interest in the cognitive unconscious. This is because implicit memory has a specific contrast in *explicit memory*. Explicit memory refers to the conscious recollection of some past event (as revealed, for example, in recall and recognition), whereas implicit memory refers simply to any effect on a person's experience, thought, or action that is attributable to a past event (as revealed, for example, in priming effects), independent of conscious recollection of that event. By acknowledging that there are two expressions of memory, one with and the other without conscious awareness of the past, theories of implicit memory do not seek, even by implication, to banish consciousness to the realm of folk psychology. Moreover, Jacoby's (1991) process dissociation procedure, which evolved in the context of research on implicit memory, asserts a specific role for consciousness in behavior. That is, conscious awareness of the past allows us to exercise conscious control over the automatic influence of the past on our current experience, thought, and action.

Although the explicit-implicit distinction drawn in memory had many precursors in both philosophy and psychology (reviewed by Schacter, 1987), its more immediate sources were experimental studies that revealed evidence of learning and transfer even though subjects had no recollection of what they had learned. For example, Warrington and Weiskrantz (1968) found that while amnesic patients were unable to recall recently presented words, they produced these items at higher than baseline rates when asked to complete stems and fragments with words. Even earlier, Evans and Thorn (1966; see also Evans, 1979) found that subjects displaying posthypnotic amnesia could answer trivia questions based on information acquired while they were hypnotized—a phenomenon they termed *source amnesia* and which has since been explored in amnesic patients as well. Later, Nelson (1978) found that normal subjects

showed savings in relearning paired-associate items that they could neither recall nor recognize from a prior study trial. Finally, Jacoby and
Dallas (1981) found repetition priming effects on the perceptual identification of words that were independent of subjects' conscious recollection
of their prior presentation. In these and other ways, research showed that
implicit memory could be spared even though explicit memory was
grossly impaired; or, alternatively, that implicit memory was in some
sense independent of explicit memory, so the two expressions of memory
could be functionally dissociated in terms of the experimental manipulations that affected them.

Taxonomy of Memory Tasks

Research on implicit memory has suffered from a considerable degree of
terminological confusion (Roediger, 1990a). At roughly the same time
that Graf and Schacter (1985) announced the distinction between explicit
and implicit memory, Johnson and Hasher (1987) and Richardson-
Klavehn and Bjork (1988) articulated a distinction between *direct* and
indirect tests of memory. And even earlier, Cohen and Squire (1980) had
already adopted the distinction, originally drawn by Bergson (1911) and
Ryle (1949), between *knowing that* and *knowing how*—which later became a distinction between *declarative* and *procedural* memory (Squire &
Cohen, 1984) and then evolved into a distinction between *declarative*
and *nondeclarative* memory (Squire & Knowlton, 1995).

It should be noted, however, that the declarative-procedural distinction
refers to two different types of knowledge, rather than two different expressions of memory. As formulated by Winograd (1972, 1975) and Anderson (1976, 1983), declarative knowledge is factual in nature and can
be represented in terms of sentencelike propositions; by contrast, procedural knowledge concerns mental and behavioral operations and can be
represented in a production system of condition-action rules. There is an
assumption that declarative knowledge is available to conscious introspection whereas procedural knowledge is unconscious, but this does not
mean that unconscious influences should be identified with procedural
knowledge. After all, declarative knowledge—in the form of propositional networks and the like—is just as unconscious as procedural knowledge is. We have no direct introspective access to the perception-based

and meaning-based structures that comprise our fund of declarative knowledge—they, too, are known only by inference. What is conscious are the percepts, memories, images, and thoughts that come to mind when unconscious procedural knowledge operates on unconscious declarative knowledge. By identifying declarative knowledge with conscious recollection, and relegating all unconscious influences to the realm of the procedural (or merely nondeclarative), Squire and his colleagues seem to have conflated the technical meaning of declarative, which refers to the format in which knowledge is represented, with the ordinary-language definition, in terms of what knowledge can be reported.

Although the direct-indirect contrast is generally considered to be tantamount to the explicit-implicit one (e.g., Roediger & McDermott, 1993), an interesting classification of memory tasks emerges when the two distinctions are treated as independent (table 6.1; see also Barnhardt, 1993). Thus, explicit and implicit tasks differ from each other in terms of whether they require conscious recollection of some event, whereas direct and indirect tasks differ in terms of whether studied items are presented at the time of the memory test. Recall and recognition tests are both explicit and direct because they require the subject to consciously recollect previously studied items. In stem completion, subjects are presented with the initial letters of a word, while in fragment completion, they are presented with some letters of a word, interspersed with blanks. In either case, when asked to complete the stem or fragment with the first word that comes to mind, they will often do so with an appropriate word from a previously studied list—an effect known as priming. Stem-completion

Table 6.1
Fourfold classification of memory tasks

Memory Task	Explicit	Implicit
Direct	Free recall, cued recall Recognition Savings in relearning (?)	Stem completion Fragment completion Savings in relearning (?)
Indirect	Proactive inhibition Retroactive inhibition	Free association Category generation

Source: After Barnhardt (1993).

and fragment-completion tests are both direct, because they present at the test the same items that were studied; but implicit, because they do not require conscious recollection of the study episode. Proactive inhibition (PI) and retroactive inhibition (RI) tests are explicit because they require conscious recollection (of the interpolated or the original list, respectively), but indirect because these effects reveal memory for items (on the original or the interpolated list, respectively) that are not themselves presented at the test. Semantic priming is both implicit and indirect because the items presented at test are not those presented at study and because subjects are not required to recollect study items at all. The classification of savings in relearning is variable, depending on how the test is presented. If on the relearning trials the subject is told of the relation between the first and second lists, and instructed to use his or her memory of the first list in order to learn the second, the test is both direct and explicit (this is also true for PI and RI). If this information is withheld from the subject, and the second list is presented as if it were new, the test is direct but implicit.

In fact, there is some evidence for dissociations between implicit and indirect memory tasks. For example, Barnhardt (1993) conducted a directed forgetting experiment in which subjects studied two lists, *A* and *B*; between these phases one group of subjects was directed to forget list *A*, while the other was instructed to remember it. Testing list *B* by stem-cued recall showed that administration of the forget cue reduced the PI of list *A* on list *B*; but testing list *A* by stem completion showed no effects of the forget cue on priming. Thus, even though PI is commonly considered to be an implicit memory test, assessment of PI indicated that list-*A* items had been forgotten, while assessment of priming indicated that these same items had been remembered.

This classification of memory tasks, viewed in the context of Barnhardt's (1993) results, reminds us that we know little about the relations among various implicit and indirect tests of memory. In particular, we know little about the relations between priming effects, on the one hand, and procedural knowledge on the other—for the simple reason that the vast bulk of literature on implicit memory focuses on priming. The reason for this is that priming procedures allow investigators to devise explicit and implicit memory tests that are equivalent in terms of the cues presented to the subject at the time of retrieval and differ only in terms of the task to be performed. Thus, in both stem-cued recall and stem completion, subjects are presented with three-letter stems; in the former case, they are asked to use the stems as cues for recall of previously studied list items; in the latter, to complete the stems with the first word that comes to mind. This procedural elegance is missing in tests of procedural knowledge, where—for example—subjects must recall a learning experience for the explicit memory test, but demonstrate what they have learned for the implicit memory test.

Furthermore, it turns out that we know little about priming effects themselves, for the simple reason that the recent literature on priming has been almost completely dominated by studies of repetition effects of the sort observed on lexical decision, perceptual identification, and stem and fragment completion tasks. As will become clear, this strategic choice may have severely distorted our theoretical understanding of the nature of implicit memory.

Theories of Implicit Memory

The currently prominent theories of implicit memory may be arranged in the two-way classification depicted in figure 6.2, depending on whether they postulate single versus multiple memory systems, or whether they emphasize the activation and integration of preexisting knowledge or the acquisition of new knowledge.

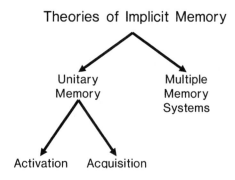

Figure 6.2
Taxonomy of current theories of implicit memory.

The most popular theories among cognitive neuroscientists are those that argue that explicit and implicit memory reflect the operation of separate memory systems, mental modules that have their biological substrates in separate brain systems. For example, Tulving and Schacter (1990) argue that implicit memory is based on several *perceptual representation systems* (PRSs) that store modality-specific representations of the perceptual structure, but not the meaning, of a stimulus. Explicit memory is based on other systems serving semantic and episodic memory. The best evidence favoring the PRS view is provided by the repeated failure to find evidence of priming of impossible figures—two-dimensional projections that cannot be constructed in three-dimensional space. Tulving and Schacter (1990; Schacter, 1995) have so far presented evidence for three different PRSs: a *visual word form system,* which represents the orthographic features of printed words, associated with the extrastriate cortex; a *structural description system,* representing the relations among the parts of objects, associated with the inferior temporal cortex; and an *auditory word form system,* representing acoustic and phonological properties of spoken words, and associated with the perisylvian cortex.

On the other hand, Squire (Squire & Cohen, 1984; Squire & Knowlton, 1995) has argued that explicit memory is based on a *medial-temporal lobe memory system* consisting of the hippocampus and other nearby structures. The two theories are not, of course, incompatible: it may be that the role of medial-temporal structures is to link discrete perceptual representations into an integrated memory of an event.

In contrast to the multiple-system theories of Tulving, Schacter, and Squire, other theories assume (sometimes tacitly) that explicit and implicit memory reflect the operation of a single memory system, the difference between the two expressions of memory being that they make different requirements on that single system. Single-memory-system views of implicit memory come in two forms, depending on whether they emphasize *activation* or *acquisition.* The activation view, exemplified by the work of Mandler (1980; see also Morton, 1969), holds that encoding a memory entails the activation and integration of preexisting knowledge and then the elaboration of this activated material into a representation of the event itself. In this view, implicit memory is the product of activation and integration, whereas explicit memory is the product of elaboration.

The acquisition view essentially holds that encoding entails the formation of a new representation of each experience, and this view comes in two principal forms. According to Roediger's (1990b; Roediger & McDermott, 1993) *transfer-appropriate processing* view, most explicit memory tasks are conceptually driven, whereas most implicit memory tasks are perceptually driven. According to Jacoby's (1991) *process dissociation* view, described earlier, most implicit memory tasks require only automatic processing, whereas most explicit memory tasks require conscious processing as well.

The distinctions among these theories should not be drawn too sharply. For example, the perceptual representations view appears to agree with the transfer-appropriate processing view that implicit memory is mediated by representations of a perceptual, structural, and presemantic nature. And both types of view have difficulty accounting for evidence that implicit memory extends to semantic and conceptual priming of a sort that cannot be mediated by perceptual representations and data-driven processing—for example, semantic priming, observed in both subjects during posthypnotic amnesia (Kihlstrom, 1980) and amnesic patients (Gardner, Boller, Moreines, & Butters, 1973; Graf, Shimamura, & Squire, 1985; Shimamura & Squire, 1984) on tests of free association and category generation. Although Tulving and Schacter (1990) acknowledge that semantic priming cannot be accomplished within a perceptual representation system, such empirical difficulties have gone largely unrecognized by the field as a whole, probably because of its infatuation with repetition priming effects.[1]

Furthermore, the perceptual representations view agrees with the transfer-appropriate processing view that implicit memory reflects the formation of new representations during encoding. Thus, the fate of unfamiliar events in implicit memory becomes critical to distinguishing between both these theories and the activation view proposed by Mandler and others: novel events cannot activate preexisting memory structures and so would seem to require the encoding of entirely new memory traces. An experiment by Diamond and Rozin (1984; but reported informally by Rozin, 1976) was perhaps the earliest attempt to perform this critical test. Amnesic patients and normal controls studied paired associates consisting of disyllabic words, such as *candy* and *number,* and disyllabic pseudowords, such as *canber* and *numdy,* formed by repairing the sylla-bles of the real words. Amnesics were severely impaired on tests of stem-cued recall for both types of items. On a stem completion test, however, the patients showed levels of priming comparable to the controls only on the real words and not the pseudowords.

Diamond and Rozin (1984; Rozin, 1976) interpreted their findings as consistent with the activation view: priming was preserved only when there were preexisting lexical representations of list items to be activated during the study phase. Subsequent studies, however, did demonstrate priming for novel materials—a fact consistent with the acquisition and perceptual representations views and apparently inconsistent with the ac-tivation view (for reviews, see Bowers, 1994; Dorfman, 1994a).

However, as Dorfman (1994a) has noted, these studies did not care-fully analyze the relations between ostensibly novel events and preexisting knowledge. Because perceivers necessarily make sense out of new events in terms of what has been perceived before, percepts of new objects must be constructed based on representations acquired in the past and retained in memory until the present. According to Mandler's (1980) dual-process model of memory, for example, presentation of a word automatically activates sublexical components that make up the word and integrates them into a unified representation; this representation is then effortfully elaborated with respect to other activated structures (e.g., markers repre-senting time, place, and the role of the self; see Kihlstrom, 1995a) to form a representation of the entire episode. Thus, from the activation point of view, the priming of novel materials such as nonwords depends intimately on how these materials are constructed. If they are constructed from com-ponents that have preexisting representations in memory, then priming is possible; if not, then priming should not occur.

To test the activation view, Dorfman (1994a) constructed novel words according to three rules: *morphemic* pseudowords (e.g., *genvive*) were constructed of actual English morphemes (*gen* as in *genius, general,* and *gender; vive* as in *survive, revive,* and *vivify*); *syllabic* pseudowords (e.g., *fasney*) were composed of nonmorphemic syllables (*fas* as in *fasten, fascinate,* and *fascist; ney* as in *chimney, journey,* and *kidney*); and *pseu-dosyllabic* pseudowords (e.g., *erktofe*) were constructed of letter strings that were neither morphemes nor syllables (e.g., *erk* and *tofe*). After a single study trial, the subjects were presented with explicit and implicit memory tests. The explicit test was two-alternative forced choice recognition (2AFC); for the implicit test, the subjects were presented with items from the study list (targets) and control items (lures) and asked which item seemed to be the "better" English word. Across five experiments, Dorfman observed priming consistently for morphemic pseudowords, less consistently for syllabic items, and rarely for pseudosyllabic ones. Similar trends also were obtained with a standard perceptual identification task (Dorfman, 1994b). These findings are consistent with at least a weak version of the activation view: priming occurs more reliably when presentation of an item can activate preexisting knowledge structures.

In the final analysis, it may not be necessary, or even desirable, to choose among the competing theories of implicit memory. It may well be that the nature of implicit memory depends on the resources available to the subject at the time of encoding and retrieval. For example, the use of encoding conditions that do not favor semantic processing at the time of encoding make it unlikely that strong associative or conceptual priming effects will be observed on an implicit memory test. If novel stimuli are formed from sublexical components or their nonverbal analogs, such as the geons postulated by Biederman (1987) as the elementary components of pictorial representations, priming will be based on the activation and integration of preexisting knowledge; but when the construction process avoids such building blocks, priming necessarily will be based on whatever jury-rigged perceptual representation the cognitive system can form. Such a proposal may seem to lack parsimony, but it should be noted that current theories of implicit memory are based almost entirely on studies of repetition priming following impoverished encoding. It is not clear that theoretical parsimony achieved under such restricted research conditions is in fact a virtue.

Extensions of the Explicit-Implicit Distinction to Other Cognitive Domains

Theories aside, it should be understood that the explicit-implicit distinction in memory is primarily phenomenological. That is, explicit and implicit memory are, first and foremost, different expressions of memory for some past event—different in terms of the role played by conscious awareness. Explicit memory involves conscious recollection of a past event, whether deliberate or involuntary; implicit memory entails the influence of such an event on subsequent experience, thought, and action in the absence (or, at least, independent) of conscious recollection. From this point of view, it would seem that the explicit-implicit distinction could be extended to other cognitive domains where the issue of consciousness arises.

Explicit versus Implicit Perception

Many effects often ascribed to implicit memory do not really count as expressions of memory per se—at least, not as expressions of secondary memory, defined as whatever trace remains of an event after the person has stopped attending to it (James, 1890/1991). Thus, in experiments by Marcel (1983) on masked semantic priming, and by Forster (1987) on masked lexical priming, the prime and target are separated by a period of seconds (or less); moreover, the masking conditions prevent the subject from consciously attending to the items in the first place. Under these conditions it seems inappropriate to think of implicit memory, but more natural to think of implicit *perception.* Kihlstrom, Barnhardt, and Tataryn (1992; see also Kihlstrom, 1996) offer a contrast between explicit perception, which entails the subject's conscious perception of the presence, location, form, identity, and activity of some object present in the current environment (or the very recent past), and implicit perception, which (by direct analogy to implicit memory) they define as any effect on experience, thought, and action attributable to a *current* event, in the absence of conscious perception of that event.

Implicit perception, so defined, includes the traditional category of *subliminal* perception, in which stimuli are too weak or too brief to be consciously perceived. It also includes cases where conscious perception is prevented by forward and/or backward masking of a stimulus, as in the classic experiments by Marcel (1983), and where a supraliminal stimulus is unattended, as in cases of dichotic listening or parafoveal viewing (in which a stimulus is presented in the periphery of the visual field). However, implicit perception also subsumes other cases where the stimulus is in no sense subliminal. In blindsight (Weiskrantz, 1986), for example, some patients with damage to the striate cortex no longer have the conscious experience of seeing; nevertheless, they are able to respond at above-chance levels to visual stimuli presented in their scotoma. Similarly, in hypnotic analgesia, subjects do not feel the pain of an aversive stimulus; even so, they show by physiological and other responses that the stimulus has registered outside of conscious awareness (Hilgard, 1977). Finally, "hysterical" patients with functional blindness or deafness complain that they cannot hear or see, but they still respond appropriately to visual or auditory stimuli (e.g., Brady & Lind, 1961; Barraclough, 1966).

Memory for the events of anesthesia provides an opportunity to define the boundary between implicit memory and implicit perception (for reviews, see Cork, Couture, & Kihlstrom, 1997; Kihlstrom, 1993; Merikle & Daneman, 1996). By definition, adequately anesthetized surgical patients have no memory of events that transpired during their surgery; they are, to all intents and purposes, unconscious. Nevertheless, it has been demonstrated that such patients may show priming effects attributable to stimuli presented during surgery. In one experiment, for example, patients were played a tape recording consisting of paired associates of the form *ocean-water* (Kihlstrom, Schacter, Cork, Hurt, & Behr, 1990). On an explicit memory test, they were presented with the cue term and asked to produce the associated response; on an implicit memory test, they were asked to produce the first word that came to mind. The patients showed no cued recall, but they did show priming on the test of free association. Because memory in the present implies perception in the past, in this case preserved implicit memory also provides evidence for implicit perception: some degree of perceptual processing was performed by these unconscious patients (for reviews, see Cork, Couture, & Kihlstrom, 1997; Merikle & Daneman, 1996). The distinction between implicit memory and implicit perception is not simply a matter of the retention interval involved (e.g., seconds versus minutes, hours, or days). Perhaps implicit memory should be confined to those cases where the person was consciously aware of the event at the time of encoding; where such awareness is lacking, the effects—regardless of the retention interval—may be classified as evidence of implicit perception.

Implicit perception, especially in "subliminal" cases, is a continuing hotbed of controversy. Thus, Eriksen (1960) criticized claims of subliminal perception by the New Look theorists and others on the grounds that their procedures for establishing threshold for detection or discrimination were inadequate. In the post-Marcel (1983) era, similar criticisms have been offered by Holender (1986) and by Shanks and St. John (1994). Such criticisms have elicited two different types of response. On the one hand, investigators such as Greenwald (e.g., Greenwald, Klinger, & Liu, 1989; Greenwald, Klinger, & Schuh, 1995) have gone to extreme lengths to establish that their stimuli are incontrovertibly subliminal. Another response has been simply to reject Eriksen's critique, on the ground that it defines implicit perception out of existence (Bowers, 1984). For example, Cheesman and Merikle (1985) argue that subliminal perception occurs in the space between the *subjective threshold* (the point at which the subject's *confidence* in his or her discriminative responses falls to zero) and the *objective threshold* (the point at which the *accuracy* of those choices falls to chance levels). In order to escape the criticism that the subjective threshold is just an underestimate of the true, objective threshold, Merikle and his colleagues further require that there be a qualitative difference between performance above and below the subjective threshold.

The most contentious issue concerning implicit perception is whether it can include semantic analyses of the stimulus (Holender, 1986). Most likely, the answer depends on the means by which conscious perception is denied to the subject. Only in the case of hypnotic blindness is there any evidence for long-lasting semantic priming effects (Bryant & McConkey, 1989). With truly subliminal stimulus presentations, the answer seems to be that the semantic-priming effects of masked stimuli are extremely weak and short lived (Greenwald et al., 1989, 1995). Moreover, they are analytically limited (Greenwald, 1992), in that priming can be produced by single words but not two-word phrases. However, it should be noted that Greenwald's experiments involve presentations that are as close to Merikle's objective threshold as it is possible to get; more substantial semantic priming may be possible with presentations that are closer to the subjective threshold. Semantic priming has not been obtained in the case of general anesthesia, where the stimuli are supraliminal but the subject is unconscious: rather, the best evidence is for repetition priming, which reflects structural processing of a sort that could be mediated by a perceptual representation system. Although such results may disappoint those who advocate subliminal stimulation as a major vehicle for social influence, it should surprise nobody to learn that semantic-priming effects are weak under conditions that afford little opportunity for complex semantic analyses.

Explicit versus Implicit Thought

If there is evidence for implicit perception and memory, why not seek evidence for implicit *thought* as well? Put another way, is it possible to use paradigms initially employed in the study of implicit memory and perception to study the implicit effects of mental representations that are neither percepts nor memories, but rather something more akin to ideas and images? Anecdotal accounts of thinking (e.g., Wallas, 1926) offer such a possibility in their accounts of intuition, a form of metacognition (Nelson, 1996) in which problem solvers feel that a solution to a problem is forthcoming, even though they do not know what that solution is. Formal accounts of problem solving often refer to these intuitions as *feelings of warmth* (e.g., Newell, Simon, & Shaw, 1962/1979); something similar occurs in the *feelings of knowing* observed on semantic memory tasks (Hart, 1965).

Some evidence of implicit thought is provided by a series of experiments by Bowers and his colleagues (Bowers, Regehr, Balthazard, & Parker, 1995; Bowers, Farvolden, & Mermigis, 1990) with a variant of Mednick's (1962) Remote Associate Test (RAT). On the RAT, subjects view a set of three words, such as *goat, pass,* and *green,* and then must generate an associate that all three items have in common (*mountain*). In their experiments, Bowers et al. (1990, 1995) presented subjects with two RAT-like items, one soluble and the other insoluble. If the subject could not produce the answer to the soluble triad, he or she was asked to guess which triad was in fact soluble. Bowers et al. (1990) found that subjects were able to do this at better than chance levels, even though they were not aware of the solution to the triad they selected. Bowers et al. (1990) suggested that this ability was due to a priming effect of the sort observed in implicit memory. That is, processing of the cues activated their corresponding representations in semantic memory, from which activation spread to other, associated representations; some of this activation converged on the representation of the associate common to the three cues. The level of activation attained by this common associate did not cross a threshold required for conscious awareness, but it was sufficient to influence subjects' choice behavior.

Some evidence favoring this spreading-activation account was provided by Bowers et al. (1990) themselves, who observed that their subjects' intuitions were correct above chance levels when the solution preserved its meaning across the three cues, but not when its meaning changed. In the former case, activation accrued at a node representing a single word; in the latter, activation spread to two or more different nodes representing different words with the same spelling. Further evidence for spreading activation was obtained by Shames, Forster, & Kihlstrom (1994), who adapted a paradigm initially developed by Yaniv and Meyer (1987) to study spreading activation in the feeling of knowing. Shames et al. (1994) presented RAT problems, followed by a lexical decision task in which subjects had to decide whether each of a series of letter strings was an English word. When the answers to unsolved RAT items appeared as targets for lexical decisions, response latency was speeded—a priming effect. Interestingly, this priming effect was not observed for RAT items which were solved. Shames et al. (1994) interpreted this difference as a sort of Zeigarnik (1927) effect, reflecting the persistence in memory of uncompleted tasks.

In the experiments of Bowers et al. (1990) and Shames et al. (1994), the subject's task performance (e.g., choosing the soluble triad) is affected by the correct solution to the problem, even though the subject is not consciously aware of what that solution is. This summary fits the generic form of the explicit-implicit distinction as applied to perception and memory. It should be understood, however, that whatever is affecting the subject's behavior is neither an implicit perception nor an implicit memory—for the simple reason that the solution itself is never presented to the subject, but is internally generated. If it is not a percept or a memory, it must be a thought—an *implicit* thought. Application of the explicit-implicit distinction to thinking and problem solving may afford a new perspective on a number of thorny issues (Dorfman, Shames, &

Kihlstrom, 1996; Kihlstrom, Shames, & Dorfman, 1996). For example, whereas intuition may reflect the influence of implicit thought, incubation may reflect the process by which an implicit thought gains strength outside of awareness, and insight the point at which an implicit thought becomes explicit and accessible to conscious awareness.

Unconscious Processes versus Nonconscious Contents

The cognitive study of mind and behavior is concerned with both content and the process—with declarative and procedural knowledge, in the terms of Winograd (1972, 1975) and Anderson (1976, 1983). Within this framework, it is common to argue that although cognitive contents— what we perceive, remember, think, and imagine—are conscious, the processes by which these cognitions arise are not. Thus, the content-process distinction contains within it a distinction between those aspects of cognition that are conscious and those that are unconscious. And, indeed, it seems that there is a class of *automatic* cognitive processes that appear to be unavailable to either the monitoring or controlling functions of consciousness. That is, they operate independent of conscious intention and can be known only through inference. These automatic processes are unconscious in the strict sense of the word.

If procedural knowledge is unconscious, then the contrast between declarative and procedural knowledge would seem to imply that declarative knowledge must be conscious or at least available to conscious introspection. But, as indicated earlier, this is not really the case. Declarative and procedural knowledge, as elements of cognitive architecture, are both unconscious in the strict sense of the term, in that they are unavailable to conscious introspection and can be known only by inference. What are ordinarily conscious are the percepts, memories, thoughts, and other mental states constructed by the operation of procedural knowledge on declarative knowledge structures. The burden of this chapter has been to argue that the psychological unconscious includes, in addition to strictly unconscious knowledge structures that compose the architecture of cognition, mental states corresponding to percepts, memories, and thoughts that influence experience, thought, and action outside of phenomenal awareness and voluntary control.

In contrast to unconscious procedural knowledge, which is unavailable to conscious awareness and control in principle, the declarative knowledge involved in these cognitive states of perception, memory, and thought is available to consciousness in principle, but inaccessible to consciousness under certain circumstances (Tulving & Pearlstone, 1966). Some of these inaccessible mental states may be described as *preconscious*—a term borrowed from Freud (1900/1953) to denote percepts, memories, and thoughts that have been degraded by circumstances affecting either the environment in which cognition takes place (e.g., subliminal presentation, divided attention, or other suboptimal encoding conditions; long retention intervals; or impoverished retrieval cues) or the person him or herself (e.g., brain damage or general anesthesia). Processing of preconscious percepts and memories appears to be analytically limited— in fact, this processing may be restricted to those operations that are performed automatically by the perceptual-cognitive system.

Preconscious percepts, memories, and thoughts reside on the fringes of consciousness. But other percepts, memories, and thoughts are inaccessible to phenomenal awareness even though environmental and personal circumstances would seem to favor awareness of them. The functional deafness and blindness observed in clinical cases of conversion disorder, for example, involve auditory and visual stimuli which are by any standard above the threshold required for conscious perception; the dissociative disorders of memory observed in psychogenic amnesia, fugue, and multiple-personality disorder involve experiences that normally would be memorable. These events are not consciously perceived and remembered, yet they influence the patients' experience, thought, and action outside of phenomenal awareness. In the hypnosis laboratory, otherwise normal subjects experience suggested amnesias, negative hallucinations, and amnesias that bear a phenotypic similarity to those observed in clinical syndromes of conversion and dissociation. These percepts, memories, and thoughts, cannot be classified as either unconscious (because they are available in principle to conscious awareness) or as preconscious (because their underlying representations have not been degraded by impoverished encoding conditions, brain damage, and the like). Following James (1890/1991) and Janet (1907), these mental states may be classified as *subconscious* or *coconscious*.

The phenomena of implicit memory, perception, and thought make it clear that the cognitive unconscious extends beyond the strictly unconscious procedural and declarative knowledge structures that provide the foundations of conscious perception, memory, and thought. Percepts, memories, and thoughts themselves may be inaccessible to consciousness. In the preconscious case, it appears that percepts, memories, and thoughts have not achieved a level of activation necessary for introspective phenomenal awareness. But studies of hypnotic phenomena indicate that consciousness is not a matter of activation levels any more than it is a matter of automaticity. Apparently, consciousness can be divided (Hilgard, 1977), so a stream of thought involving fully activated percepts, memories, and thoughts, as well as controlled, effortful processes, can proceed outside of phenomenal awareness.

The expansive description of the cognitive unconscious offered here should not be misunderstood as an argument for either the epiphenomenalist suspicion or conscious inessentialism. The distinction between conscious and unconscious mental life is fundamental to human cognitive architecture, and it has adaptive significance as well. Because conscious awareness is the prerequisite for conscious control, our ability to reflect on the past, present, and future liberates us from control by both the immediate stimulus and our histories of stimulus contingencies. At the same time, empirical evidence of preconscious and subconscious percepts, memories, and thoughts reminds us that we are not always aware of why we do what we do and that the difference that makes for consciousness is not merely a matter of activation or attentional effort.

Acknowledgments

The point of view represented herein is based on research supported by Grant #MH 35856 from the National Institute of Mental Health. I thank Terrence Barnhardt, Talia Ben-Zeev, Marilyn Dabady, Jennifer Dorfman, and Katharine Shobe for their helpful comments.

Note

1. Another conspicuous omission in the literature on implicit memory is any attempt to connect dissociations between explicit and implicit memory to computa-

tional models of memory such as ACT (Anderson, 1976, 1983) or search of associative memory (SAM; Shiffrin & Raaijmakers, 1992). Such an exercise would be interesting, if only because such models assume a single memory system and operate according to principles of activation. Evidence that ACT or SAM can produce explicit-implicit dissociations of the sort observed in the laboratory would provide additional evidence for the viability of the activation view of implicit memory.

References

Anderson, J. R. (1976). *Language, memory, and thought.* Hillsdale, NJ: Erlbaum.

Anderson, J. R. (1982). Acquisition of cognitive skill. *Psychological Review, 89,* 369–406.

Anderson, J. R. (1983). *The architecture of cognition.* Cambridge, MA: Harvard University Press.

Atkinson, R. C., & Shiffrin, R. M. (1968). Human memory: A proposed system and its control processes. In K. W. Spence & J. T. Spence (Eds.), *The psychology of learning and motivation: Advances in research and theory* (Vol. 2, pp. 89–195). New York: Academic Press.

Bargh, J. A. (1997). The automaticity of everyday life. In R. S. Wyer (Ed.), *Advances in social cognition* (Vol. 10, pp. 1–61). Mahwah, NJ: Erlbaum.

Barnhardt, T. M. (1993). *Directed forgetting in explicit and implicit memory.* Unpublished doctoral dissertation, University of Arizona.

Barraclough, M. (1966). A method of testing hearing based on operant conditioning. *Behavior Research & Therapy, 4,* 237–238.

Biederman, I. (1987). Recognition-by-components: A theory of human image understanding. *Psychological Review, 94,* 115–147.

Bergson, H. (1911). *Matter and memory.* New York: Macmillan.

Berkowitz, L. (1993). Towards a general theory of anger and emotional aggression: Implications of the cognitive-neoassociationistic perspective for the analysis of anger and other emotions. In R. S. Wyer & T. K. Srull (Eds.), *Advances in social cognition* (Vol. 6, pp. 1–46). Hillsdale, NJ: Erlbaum.

Berkowitz, L., & Devine, P. G. (1995). Has social psychology always been cognitive? What is "cognitive" anyhow? *Personality & Social Psychology Bulletin, 21,* 696–703.

Bowers, J. S. (1994). Does implicit memory extend to legal and illegal nonwords? *Journal of Experimental Psychology: Learning, Memory, & Cognition, 20,* 534–549.

Bowers, K. S. (1984). On being unconsciously influenced and informed. In K. S. Bowers & D. Meichenbaum (Eds.), *The unconscious reconsidered* (pp. 227–272). New York: Wiley-Interscience.

Bowers, K. S., Farvolden, P., & Mermigis, L. (1995). Intuitive antecedents of insight. In S. M. Smith, T. M. Ward, & R. A. Finke (Eds.), *The creative cognition approach* (pp. 27–52). Cambridge, MA: MIT Press.

Bowers, K. S., Regehr, G., Balthazard, C. G., & Parker, K. (1990). Intuition in the context of discovery. *Cognitive Psychology, 22,* 72–110.

Brady, J. P., & Lind, D. L. (1961). Experimental analysis of hysterical blindness. *Archives of General Psychiatry, 4,* 331–339.

Broadbent, D. (1958). *Perception and communication.* Oxford, England: Pergamon Press.

Bryant, R. A., & McConkey, K. M. (1989). Hypnotic blindness: A behavioral and experiential analysis. *Journal of Abnormal Psychology, 98,* 71–77.

Cheesman, J., & Merikle, P. M. (1985). Word recognition and consciousness. In D. Besner, T. G. Waller, & G. E. Mackinnon (Eds.), *Reading research: Advances in theory and practice* (Vol. 5, pp. 311–352). New York: Academic Press.

Churchland, P. M. (1995). *The engine of reason, the seat of the soul: A philosophical journey into the brain.* Cambridge, MA: MIT Press.

Cohen, N. J., & Squire, L. R. (1980). Preserved learning and retention of pattern-analyzing skill in amnesia: Dissociation of "knowing how" and "knowing that." *Science, 210,* 207–209.

Cork, R. C., Couture, L. J., & Kihlstrom, J. F. (1997). Memory and recall. In J. F. Biebuyck, C. Lynch, M. Maze, L. J. Saidman, T. L. Yaksh, & Zapol, W. M. (Eds.), *Anesthesia: Biologic foundations* (pp. 451–469). New York: Raven Press.

Curran, T., & Hintzman, D. L. (1995). Violations of the independence assumption in process dissociation. *Journal of Experimental Psychology: Learning, Memory, & Cognition, 21,* 531–547.

Dennett, D. (1991). *Consciousness explained.* Boston: Little, Brown.

Deutsch, J. A., & Deutsch, D. (1963). Attention: Some theoretical considerations. *Psychological Review, 70,* 80–90.

Devine, P. G. (1989). Stereotypes and prejudice: Their automatic and controlled components. *Journal of Personality & Social Psychology, 56,* 680–690.

Diamond, R., & Rozin, P. (1984). Activation of existing memories in the amnesic syndromes. *Journal of Abnormal Psychology, 93,* 98–105.

Dorfman, J. (1994a). Sublexical components in implicit memory for novel words. *Journal of Experimental Psychology: Learning, Memory, & Cognition, 20,* 1108–1125.

Dorfman, J. (1994b, November). Further evidence for sublexical components in implicit memory for novel words. Paper presented at the annual meeting of the Psychonomic Society, St. Louis.

Dorfman, J., Shames, V. A., & Kihlstrom, J. F. (1996). Intuition, incubation, and insight: Implicit cognition in problem-solving. In G. Underwood (Ed.), *Implicit cognition* (pp. 257–296). Oxford, England: Oxford University Press.

Eriksen, C. W. (1960). Discrimination and learning without awareness: A methodological survey and evaluation. *Psychological Review, 67,* 279–300.

Evans, F. J. (1979). Contextual forgetting: Posthypnotic source amnesia. *Journal of Abnormal Psychology, 88,* 556–563.

Evans, F. J., & Thorn, W. A. F. (1966). Two types of posthypnotic amnesia: Recall amnesia and source amnesia. *International Journal of Clinical & Experimental Hypnosis, 14,* 162–179.

Fazio, R. H., Sanbonmatsu, D. M., Powell, M. C., & Kardes, F. R. (1986). On the automatic activation of attitudes. *Journal of Personality & Social Psychology, 50,* 229–238.

Flanagan, O. (1991). *The science of mind* (2nd ed.). Cambridge, MA: MIT Press.

Forster, K. I. (1987). Form-priming with masked primes: The best-match hypothesis. In M. Coltheart (Ed.), *Attention and performance* (Vol. 12, pp. 127–146). Hillsdale, NJ: Erlbaum.

Freud, S. (1953). *The interpretation of dreams.* In J. Strachey (Ed.), *The standard edition of the complete psychological works of Sigmund Freud* (Vols. 4 and 5). London: Hogarth Press. (Original work published 1900.)

Gardner, H., Boller, F., Moreines, J., & Butters, N. (1973). Retrieving information from Korsakoff patients: Effects of categorical cues and reference to the task. *Cortex, 9,* 165–175.

Graf, P., & Schacter, D. L. (1985). Implicit and explicit memory for new associations in normal and amnesic subjects. *Journal of Experimental Psychology: Learning, Memory, & Cognition, 11,* 501–518.

Graf, P., Shimamura, A. P., & Squire, L. R. (1985). Priming across modalities and priming across category levels: Extending the domain of preserved function in amnesia. *Journal of Experimental Psychology: Learning, Memory, & Cognition, 11,* 385–395.

Greenwald, A. G. (1992). New Look 3: Unconscious cognition reclaimed. *American Psychologist, 47,* 766–779.

Greenwald, A. G., & Banaji, M. R. (1995). Implicit social cognition: Attitudes, self-esteem, and stereotypes. *Psychological Review, 102,* 4–27.

Greenwald, A. G., Klinger, M. R., & Liu, T. J. (1989). Unconscious processing of dichoptically masked words. *Memory & Cognition, 17,* 35–47.

Greenwald, A. G., Klinger, M. R., & Schuh, E. S. (1995). Activation by marginally perceptible ("subliminal") stimuli: Dissociation of unconscious from conscious cognition. *Journal of Experimental Psychology: General, 124,* 22–42.

Hart, J. T. (1965). Memory and the feeling-of-knowing experience. *Journal of Educational Psychology, 56,* 208–216.

Hasher, L., & Zacks, R. T. (1979). Automatic and effortful processes in memory. *Journal of Experimental Psychology: General, 108,* 356–388.

Hasher, L., & Zacks, R. T. (1984). Automatic processing of fundamental information: The case of frequency of occurrence. *American Psychologist, 39,* 1372–1388.

Healy, A. F., & McNamara, D. S. (1996). Verbal learning and memory: Does the modal model still work? *Annual Review of Psychology, 47,* 143–172.

Hilgard, E. R. (1977). *Divided consciousness: Multiple controls in human thought and action.* New York: Wiley-Interscience.

Holender, D. (1986). Semantic activation without conscious identification in dichotic listening, parafoveal vision, and visual masking: A survey and appraisal. *Behavioral & Brain Sciences, 9,* 1–23.

Jacoby, L. L. (1991). A process dissociation framework: Separating automatic from intentional uses of memory. *Journal of Memory & Language, 30,* 513–541.

Jacoby, L. L., & Dallas, M. (1981). On the relationship between autobiographical memory and perceptual learning. *Journal of Experimental Psychology: General, 110,* 306–340.

James, W. (1991). *Principles of Psychology* (2 vols). Cambridge, MA: Harvard University Press. (Original work published 1890.)

Janet, P. (1907). *The major symptoms of hysteria.* New York: Macmillan.

Johnson, M. K., & Hasher, L. (1987). Human learning and memory. *Annual Review of Psychology, 38,* 631–668.

Kahneman, D. (1973). *Attention and effort.* Englewood Cliffs, NJ: Prentice-Hall.

Kahneman, D., & Treisman, A. (1984). Changing views of attention and automaticity. In R. Parasuraman & D. R. Davies (Eds.), *Varieties of attention* (pp. 29–61). New York: Academic Press.

Kihlstrom, J. F. (1980). Posthypnotic amnesia for recently learned material: Interactions with "episodic" and "semantic" memory. *Cognitive Psychology, 12,* 227–251.

Kihlstrom, J. F. (1993). Implicit memory function during anesthesia. In P. S. Sebel, B. Bonke, & E. Winograd (Eds.), *Memory and Awareness in Anesthesia* (pp. 10–30). New York: Prentice-Hall.

Kihlstrom, J. F. (1996). Perception without awareness of what is perceived, learning without awareness of what is learned. In M. Velmans (Ed.), *The science of consciousness: Psychological, neuropsychological, and clinical reviews* (pp. 23–46). London: Routledge.

Kihlstrom, J. F. (1997). Consciousness and me-ness. In J. Cohen & J. Schooler (Eds.), *Scientific approaches to the question of consciousness* (pp. 451–468). Hillsdale, NJ: Erlbaum.

Kihlstrom, J. F., Barnhardt, T. M., & Tataryn, D. J. (1992). Implicit perception. In R. F. Bornstein & T. S. Pittman (Eds.), *Perception without awareness* (pp. 17–54). New York: Guilford.

Kihlstrom, J. F., Schacter, D. L., Cork, R. C., Hurt, C. A., & Behr, S. E. (1990). Implicit and explicit memory following surgical anesthesia. *Psychological Science, 1,* 303–306.

Kihlstrom, J. F., Shames, V. A., & Dorfman, J. (1996). Intimations of memory and thought. In L. Reder (Ed.), *Implicit Memory and Metacognition* (pp. 1–23). Hillsdale, NJ: Erlbaum.

LaBerge, D., & Samuels, S. J. (1974). Toward a theory of automatic information processing in reading. *Cognitive Psychology, 6,* 293–323.

Logan, G. (1988). Toward an instance theory of automatization. *Psychological Review, 95,* 492–527.

Mandler, G. (1980). Recognizing: The judgment of prior occurrence. *Psychological Review, 87,* 252–271.

Marcel, A. (1983). Conscious and unconscious perception: Experiments on visual masking and word recognition. *Cognitive Psychology, 15,* 197–237.

Mednick, S. (1962). The associative basis of the creative process. *Psychological Review, 69,* 220–232.

Merikle, P. M., & Daneman, M. (1996). Memory for unconsciously perceived events: Evidence from anesthetized patients. *Consciousness & Cognition, 5,* 525–541.

Morton, J. (1969). Interaction of information in word recognition. *Psychological Review, 76,* 165–178.

Neisser, U. (1967). *Cognitive psychology.* New York: Appleton-Century-Crofts.

Nelson, T. O. (1978). Detecting small amounts of information in memory: Savings for nonrecognized items. *Journal of Experimental Psychology: Human Learning & Memory, 4,* 453–468.

Nelson, T. O. (1996). Consciousness and metacognition. *American Psychologist, 51,* 102–116.

Newell, A., Simon, H. A., & Shaw, J. (1979). The process of creative thinking. In H. A. Simon, *Models of thought* (pp. 144–174). New Haven, CT: Yale University Press. (Original work published 1962.)

Nisbett, R. E., & Wilson, T. D. (1977). Telling more than we can know: Verbal reports on mental processes. *Psychological Review, 84,* 231–259.

Posner, M. (1980). Orienting of attention. *Quarterly Journal of Experimental Psychology, 32,* 3–25.

Posner, M. (1982). Cumulative development of attentional theory. *American Psychologist, 37,* 168–179.

Posner, M. I., & Snyder, C. R. R. (1975). Attention and cognitive control. In R. So-so (Ed.), *Information processing and cognition: The Loyola Symposium* (pp. 55–85). Hillsdale, NJ: Erlbaum.

Richardson-Klavehn, A., & Bjork, R. A. (1988). Measures of memory. *Annual Review of Psychology, 39,* 475–543.

Roediger, H. L. (1990a). Implicit memory: A commentary. *Bulletin of the Psychonomic Society, 28,* 373–380.

Roediger, H. L. (1990b). Implicit memory: Retention without remembering. *American Psychologist, 45,* 1043–1056.

Roediger, H. L., & McDermott, D. B. (1993). Implicit memory in normal human subjects. In F. Boller & J. Grafman (Eds.), *Handbook of neuropsychology* (Vol. 8, pp. 63–131). Amsterdam: Elsevier Science.

Rozin, P. (1976). A psychobiological approach to human memory. In M. R. Rosenzweig & E. L. Bennett (Eds.), *Neural mechanisms of memory and learning* (pp. 3–48). Cambridge, MA.: MIT Press.

Ryle, G. (1949). *The concept of mind.* London: Routledge & Kegan Paul.

Schacter, D. L. (1987). Implicit memory: History and current status. *Journal of Experimental Psychology Learning, Memory, & Cognition, 13,* 501–518.

Schacter, D. L. (1995). Implicit memory: A new frontier for cognitive neuroscience. In M. S. Gazzaniga (Ed.), *The cognitive neurosciences* (pp. 815–824). Cambridge, MA: MIT Press.

Schneider, W., & Shiffrin, R. M. (1977). Controlled and automatic human information processing. *Psychological Review, 84,* 1–66.

Shames, V. A., Forster, K. I., & Kihlstrom, J. F. (1994). *Implicit problem-solving.* Unpublished manuscript, University of Arizona.

Shanks, D. R., & St. John, M. F. (1994). Characteristics of dissociable learning systems. *Behavioral & Brain Sciences, 17,* 367–447.

Shiffrin, R. M., & Raaijmakers, J. (1992). The SAA retrieval model: A retrospective and prospective. In A. F. Healy, S. M. Kosslyn, & R. M. Shiffrin (Eds.), *Essays in honor of William K. Estes.* Vol. 1: *From Learning theory to connectionist theory* (pp. 69–86). Hillsdale, NJ: Erlbaum.

Shiffrin, R. M., & Schneider, W. (1977). Controlled and automatic human information processing: Pt. 2. Perceptual learning, automatic attending, and a general theory. *Psychological Review, 84,* 127–190.

Shimamura, A. P., & Squire, L. R. (1984). Paired-associate learning and priming effects in amnesia: A neuropsychological study. *Journal of Experimental Psychology: General, 113,* 556–570.

Skinner, B. F. (1953). *Science and human behavior.* New York: Free Press.

Squire, L. R., & Cohen, N. J. (1984). Human memory and amnesia. In J. McGaugh & N. Weinberger (Eds.), *The neurobiology of learning and memory* (pp. 3–64). New York: Guilford.

Squire, L. R., & Knowlton, B. J. (1995). Memory, hippocampus, and brain systems. In M. Gazzaniga (Ed.), *The cognitive neurosciences* (pp. 825–837). Cambridge, MA: MIT Press.

Treisman, A. M. (1960). Contextual cues in selective listening. *Quarterly Journal of Experimental Psychology, 12,* 242–248.

Tulving, E., & Pearlstone, Z. (1966). Availability versus accessibility of information in memory for words. *Journal of Verbal Learning & Verbal Behavior, 5,* 381–391.

Tulving, E., & Schacter, D. L. (1990). Priming and human memory systems. *Science, 247,* 301–306.

Wallas, G. (1926). *The art of thought.* New York: Franklin, Watts.

Warrington, E. K., & Weiskrantz, L. (1968). New method for testing long-term retention with special reference to amnesic patients. *Nature, 228,* 628–630.

Waugh, N. C., & Norman, D. A. (1965). Primary memory. *Psychological Review, 72,* 89–104.

Weiskrantz, L. (1986). *Blindsight.* Oxford, England: Oxford University Press.

Winograd, T. (1975). Frame representations and the procedural-declarative controversy. In D. Bobrow & A. Collins (Eds.), *Representation and understanding: Studies in cognitive science* (pp. 185–210). New York: Academic Press.

Winograd, T. (1972). *Understanding natural language.* New York: Academic Press.

Yaniv, I., & Meyer, D. E. (1987). Activation and metacognition of inaccessible stored information: Potential bases for incubation effects in problem solving. *Journal of Experimental Psychology: Learning, Memory, & Cognition, 13,* 187–205.

Zeigarnik, B. (1927). Das Behalten von erledigten und unerledigten Handlungen [Memory for completed and uncompleted tasks). *Psychologie Forschung, 9,* 1–85.

7

Prototype versus Exemplar Models in Cognition

Brian H. Ross and Valerie S. Makin

Introduction

Categories are essential for intelligent thought and action. When faced with a new object, situation, or problem, people often access knowledge to *classify* it as being of a certain type and then use their knowledge of this type to determine how to deal with it. An unfamiliar object is classified as a pen, and our knowledge of the category of pens is used to help us know how to write with it. Thus, categories allow us to access and use relevant knowledge, even for items we have never encountered before.

Given the importance of categories, a critical research question is to understand how category knowledge is represented. A particular focus of research in this area has been on the representation of knowledge used for classification. A number of possibilities exist, but the two that have been most prominent, and which form the basis for this chapter, are the *prototype view* and the *exemplar view*. A brief example may help to clarify these two views. Suppose you saw an unfamiliar animal and classified it as a dog. The prototype view would claim that you used knowledge about dogs *in general* to classify this new animal—in particular, your knowledge consists of a kind of average of dog features, built up from having seen many dogs in the past. The exemplar view would claim that this dog evoked memories of one or more specific earlier dogs and that you used the similarity of the new animal to your memory of dog exemplars to decide that this new animal was a dog.

This distinction of prototypes versus exemplars has been a central one within research on classification, leading to a variety of research findings, as will be discussed in this chapter. In addition, similar contrasts have been made in many other research areas. The general issue is whether the knowledge underlying cognitive performance is a general abstraction built up from earlier experiences or is a function of more specific instances.

Preliminary Remarks

The goal of this chapter is to contrast two very different views of categories, partly to see the advantages of each, but mainly to better understand how categories might be represented and used. We will begin by explaining what categories are, the domains to be considered, and how the models will be used.

Concepts and Categories   A *concept* is a mental representation of a class (e.g., dogs, professors), which includes our knowledge about such things. A *category* is the set of examples picked out by a concept. However, these two terms are often used synonymously to refer to both the mental representation and the set of examples it picks out.

Domains   Many ideas about categorization have come from considering biological categories, such as birds. However, these categories are not designed to allow a clear discrimination of hypotheses, so much of the experimental work to distinguish theories has used artificial categories that are learned in the laboratory. The prototype-exemplar controversy has often relied on such artificial categories for deriving distinctive predictions, and much of the work we review will be with artificial categories. However, we will try to stress the connection to more natural categories as well.

Models and Model Classes   A specification of a model requires presenting its representation and its processes. In this chapter, the representations will usually consist of a set of features, such as color or shape, with a particular value for each feature, such as red or square. This general representational scheme allows an easier comparison between the prototype and exemplar models, though much work has also been done with dimensional representations, in which the feature values are ordered, such as for height or darkness (e.g., Nosofsky, 1986). In addition, some recent work examines more complex representations than sets of features, such as structured representations in which the features are organized by representing particular relations among them, such as *next-to, supports,* or *causes* (e.g., Goldstone, 1994).

The prototype and exemplar views are really classes of models, rather than two specific models. That is, people can believe that there is abstracted knowledge about each category that is gained from experience and yet propose very different prototype models. For example, the models might differ on how the abstraction occurs, what information is retained, or how the information from different features of the items is combined (e.g., Barsalou, 1990; Reed, 1972). All of these could reasonably be called prototype models, yet they might make substantially different predictions. Similarly, exemplar models may make different predictions, with some exemplar models being more similar to certain prototype models than to some models in their own class (Medin, 1986). Barsalou (1990) even argued that the models are not distinguishable, especially if one focuses on representation alone: for any prototype model, one could construct an exemplar model that mimics it, and vice versa.

Although it may be impossible to compare the entire class of prototype models to the entire class of exemplar models, it is useful to discuss the general properties of each class and to compare particular models in each class. In this chapter, we will first compare the most prominent views of prototype and exemplar models, both to give a better understanding of the research area and to illustrate the strengths and weaknesses of many members in each class of models. Following this discussion, we will consider more complex mixed views. We will now elaborate on the two prominent prototype and exemplar models.

The Prototype versus Exemplar Distinction

History

Many early ideas of categories assumed that each category could be defined by a set of necessary and sufficient features (this idea was termed the *classical view* by Smith & Medin, 1981). By this account, one determines classification by checking whether the new instance has all of the necessary properties to be in the category. If it does, it is classified as a member of the category; otherwise, it is not. The classical view does seem to be a reasonable account for a small number of well-defined categories, such as square. Any closed figure with four equal sides and four equal angles is a square, and all squares have these properties. However, this classical view fails to explain many of the research findings that categories are often "fuzzy" or ill defined. For example, some members of a category are rated as being more typical exemplars than other members, and the typical members are classified more quickly than are atypical members (e.g., Smith, Shoben, & Rips, 1974). A robin is a more typical bird than is a penguin. An accurate representation of people's categories has to allow for differences in the typicality of exemplars. However, if the category representation has only necessary and sufficient features, then an instance either has these features and is a category number, or it does not have these features and is not a category member. Thus, typicality differences cannot be explained by the classical view.

Prototype Model

The prototype view (see Rosch, 1973, 1975; also Hampton, 1993, 1995) assumes that there is a summary representation of the category, called a *prototype*, which consists of some central tendency of the features of the category members. Classification is determined by similarity to the prototype. When a new instance is encountered, its similarity to the prototype is computed (in terms of feature matches), and if the similarity is greater than some threshold criterion, it is considered a category member. If the instance is to be classified into one of several possible categories, it is assigned to the category whose prototype it most closely matches. This idea of representing a concept as its central tendency has a long tradition in psychology (e.g., Galton, 1883).

Details of the prototype representation and the similarity computation are often vague, but Hampton (1993) presented a recent explicit version of the prototype theory that captures the main ideas. In this view, the similarity to the prototype is computed as a weighted sum of the features, with the weights determined by the importance of the feature for that concept. More formally (adapting Hampton's, 1995, eq. 1), let item t be the test item. Let $S(A, t)$ be the similarity of t to category A, which for a prototype view means the similarity of t to the prototype of A:

$$S(A, t) = \sum_{i=1}^{n} (w_i \times v_{it}) \tag{7.1}$$

where w_i is the weight of the ith feature in the prototype, and v_{it} is the extent to which item t possesses the feature i ($0 \leq w_i, v_{it} \leq 1$). The prototype is assumed to consist of the central tendency of the features of the category instances, so this formula computes similarity to the center of the category, weighted by the importance of the features. For determining classification among contrasting categories, item t would be assigned to the category whose prototype it most closely matched, perhaps using Luce's Choice Rule, with the probability of assigning item t to category A:

$$p \text{ (item } t \text{ in category } A) = \frac{S(A, t)}{S(A, t) + \sum_{j \neq A} S(j, t)} \tag{7.2}$$

Table 7.1 uses a simple numerical example (in which the weights are all equal) to show how this computation is done.

For the purposes of this chapter, there are two important points about prototype models. First, the similarity computation is an *additive* function across the features. Thus, low similarity on some features can be compensated for by high similarity on other features. Second, the same summary representation, the prototype, is used to classify each instance of a category.

Evidence for the Prototype View   The prototype view predicts a large number of robust effects in category research, just a few of which will be discussed here (see Smith & Medin, 1981; Medin & Smith, 1984). First, as mentioned with regard to problems of the classical view, there are differences in typicality of the category members. Some category members are rated as better, or more typical (such as robin for the category *birds*) than are other category members (e.g., penguin). The prototype view would predict that those members with more characteristic features (or more of the heavily weighted features) would be viewed as

Table 7.1
Numerical example of classification under prototype and exemplar theories

Study exemplar	Category	Features* 1	2	3	4
1	*A*	1	1	1	1
2	*A*	1	1	0	0
	Prototype A	1	1	.5	.5
3	*B*	1	0	0	0
4	*B*	0	0	0	1
	Prototype B	.5	0	0	.5
Test item *t*		0	1	1	1

Classification under Prototype Theory

Using equation 7.1 (with $w_i = 1$, and v_{it} is the extent to which the test exemplar and prototype feature values match),

$$S(A, t) = 0 + 1 + .5 + .5 = 2; \quad S(B, t) = .5 + 0 + 0 + .5 = 1.$$

Therefore, the test instance has greater similarity to category *A*.
Using Luce's Choice Rule (equation 7.2),

$$p(\text{item } t \text{ in category } A) = \frac{2}{2 + 1} = .67.$$

So test item *t* would be classified in category *A* under the prototype theory, with .67 probability.

Classification under Exemplar Theory

Using equation 7.4, and letting all $m_i = m$ for simplicity, we calculate the similarity of each exemplar in category *A* to test item *t*, $S(a_i, t)$,

$$S(a_1, t) = m \times 1 \times 1 \times 1 = m; \quad S(a_2, t) = m \times 1 \times m \times m = m^3.$$

The similarities for category *B* are

$$S(b_3, t) = m \times m \times m \times m = m^4; \quad S(b_4, t) = 1 \times m \times m \times 1 = m^2.$$

Using equation 7.3,

$$S(A, t) = m + m^3; \quad S(B, t) = m^4 + m^2.$$

So here, too, the test item *t* is more similar to category *A*.
Using Luce's choice rule (equation 7.2),

$$p(\text{item } t \text{ in category } A) = \frac{m + m^3}{m + m^3 + m^4 + m^2} = \frac{1 + m^2}{1 + m^2 + m^3 + m}.$$

Table 7.1 (continued)

As m varies from 0 to 1, this quotient varies from 1.0 to .5. As an example, if $m = .2$, indicating much attention was being paid to each feature, then

$$p(\text{item } t \text{ in category } A) = \frac{1 + .2^2}{1 + .2^2 + .2^3 + .2} = .83.$$

So test item t would be classified in category A under the exemplar theory, with .83 probability (assuming $m_i = m = .2$).

*Features in this example are binary values, with an intermediate value of .5 assumed for simplicity; the prototype is assumed to be the arithmetic mean of the exemplar features.

better category members. Second, these differences in typicality lead to large differences in classification performance. For example, typical category members (whether they are presented as names or as pictures) are classified faster than less typical members (e.g., Murphy & Brownell, 1985; Rips, Shoben, & Smith, 1973). Even in artificial categories, more typical members are learned earlier and classified faster (Rosch & Mervis, 1975). Third, people often have trouble deciding whether an item is a member of a particular category (McCloskey & Glucksberg, 1978). For example, is a television in the furniture category? If items were classified by well-defined rules, such unclear cases would not occur. However, if classification depends upon similarity to a prototype, it is likely that the low similarity of some items will make it hard to decide about their classification. Fourth, in some experiments, a prototype that had not been presented at study can be classified as well or even better than the category members pertaining to that prototype, which were seen often during study (Posner & Keele, 1968, 1970). All of these results suggest that there is a summary representation that captures the structure of the category as a whole.

Problems with the Prototype View   Although the prototype view does predict an impressive array of results, it has two major difficulties in accounting for a variety of additional findings (see Medin & Ross, 1989; Nosofsky, 1992; Ross & Spalding, 1994, for fuller presentations). First, people appear to use more information than just similarity to prototypes for classifying new instances. For example, if two instances are equally similar to a prototype, the one that is more similar to studied instances will be classified more accurately (e.g., Whittlesea, 1987). In other cases, test instances that are less similar to a prototype may be more accurately classified if they are very similar to a studied instance (e.g., Brooks, 1978; Medin & Schaffer, 1978). Second, people not only know the central tendency of features within a category, but discern and use other statistical properties of the features, such as the range of values of each feature (e.g., Rips, 1989) or the correlations of features with each other (e.g., Malt & Smith, 1984). The standard prototype view has no way to account for such effects because the prototype consists of the central tendency of each feature (calculated independently of the other features). In addition to problems accounting for data, the prototype view has never presented a clear learning theory—how is information about instances combined to form a prototype? There appears to be an assumption of a type of associationist learning view, but the learning of prototypes has not been detailed. (See Galton, 1883, for an interesting example of this, in which pictures of faces are overlapped to get a prototypical face.)

The problems that the prototype view encounters are due to its two important characteristics mentioned earlier: a single summary representation is used to classify all instances, and similarity is computed as an additive function over features. The single summary representation makes it difficult to be sensitive to both the typicality of the test instance and its similarity to studied instances. The use of an additive function makes it impossible to take into account information about relations among features, such as correlations. The exemplar view, which we examine next, has neither of these characteristics.

Exemplar Model

Exemplar models assume that categories consist of a set of exemplars and that the classification of new instances is by their similarity to these stored exemplars. We focus here on the most prominent exemplar model, the *context model* of Medin and Schaffer (1978). This model has been extended in a series of well-known papers by Nosofsky (e.g., 1986). Other prominent exemplar views include those of Brooks (1978, 1987) and Hintzman (1986).

Under the exemplar view, the representation of the category is not a single summary representation, but rather a collection of instance representations. For now, we consider the representations to be particular instances, though we discuss other possibilities later. Each instance consists of a set of feature values with the same features for all instances, but with the values varying. The context model makes two important process assumptions. First, the similarity of the new instance to previously learned instances is a *multiplicative* function of the similarity of their features. Thus, instances that match well on all features have much higher similarity than do instances that match well on only some features. One very dissimilar feature may lead to a low similarity, even if the other features match well. Second, the classification is determined by comparing the similarity of the new instance to all previously learned instances in each category and then classifying it to the category that has the greatest overall similarity, using the same decision rule as in equation 7.2.

The context model of Medin and Schaffer (1978) is a simple exemplar model for binary-valued features, in which the similarity of the test item t to the category A, $S(A, t)$, is not its similarity to the prototype, but the sum of its similarity to each exemplar of the category:

$$S(A, t) = \sum_{a \in A} S(a, t) \tag{7.3}$$

This computation of similarity does not appear to be very different from that of the prototype view, because the prototype is the central tendency of the exemplars. What makes it different is that the computation of similarity to each exemplar uses a multiplicative rule, rather than the additive rule of equation 7.1:

$$S(a, t) = \prod_{i=1}^{n} s_i \tag{7.4}$$

where $s_i = 1$ if the ith features of items a and t match, and $s_i = m_i$ if they mismatch. The last section of table 7.1 applies this exemplar model to a simple classification example, as was done for the prototype model.

The exemplar and multiplicative similarity assumptions mean that the previously stored exemplars that are highly similar to a new instance will largely determine its classification. Thus, rather than a single summary representation, as in the prototype view, the exemplar view can be thought of as weighting those instances most similar to the current instance being classified (the exemplar model of Hintzman, 1986, does this explicitly). Note that the exemplar view makes claims about the types of information used for classification and how the decision is made; however, there is no claim that the instances themselves are consciously available for this classification.

Evidence for the Exemplar View   Although it may seem counterintuitive, the exemplar model can account for all of the results presented as evidence for the prototype view. First, according to the exemplar view, some instances are more typical than other instances, both because typical instances usually occur more frequently (so there are more exemplars of typical instances) and because typical instances tend to be highly similar to other instances (Rosch & Mervis, 1975). For example, robins are similar to many other songbirds (sparrows, thrushes, etc.), whereas atypical birds like penguins and ostriches have few similar instances. Second, the differences in classification performance that result from typicality occur for related reasons. For example, if classification time is a function of how quickly one finds a highly similar instance in the category, then typical instances will be classified faster, both because of their greater frequency and their high similarity to more category members. Third, exemplar models can even predict that prototypes that are not seen during learning may be classified more accurately at test than previously studied instances under some circumstances (see Hintzman & Ludlam, 1980, for one derivation). The reason is that the prototype test item may be highly similar to a number of instances, so its classification, according to the exemplar model, will be getting high weight from multiple instances, whereas, the classification of studied items will usually be getting weight from just one instance.

The exemplar view also deals well with the two problems mentioned for the prototype view. First, the effect of instance similarity on classification is obviously not a problem for the exemplar view, because that is the primary assumption of the view. Second, the exemplar view provides a simple way for implicitly keeping track of much additional information about the features of the category members (e.g., range, correlation). If the individual instances are stored, then various statistics can be computed as they are needed. For example, in the category of birds, singing is negatively correlated with beak size (larger beaks generally go with larger birds, which are less likely to sing). Even if one had never thought about this correlation, it is implicitly encoded in the set of exemplars that one has experienced, so it could influence the classification (especially because of the multiplicative similarity function).

Problems for the Exemplar View   The main problems for the exemplar view are not problems in fitting data, but conceptual problems. First, by claiming that categories are collections of instances, the exemplar view seems to take away the "categoriness" of categories. That is, why are these instances members of the same category? Although the prototype view does not address this issue directly, it does so implicitly by using central tendencies of the feature values; the category members are assumed to be related to the prototype through similarity, although their degree of similarity may vary. The flexibility of the exemplar view, which is important in helping to account for the data, has the disadvantage of making it difficult to understand why these items cohere as a category (Murphy & Medin, 1985). Second, many people question the claim that abstractions are *never* used to help classify an unfamiliar instance. Even proponents of exemplar views agree that people do know abstractions about categories (e.g., birds have wings), but they argue that this knowledge is not used for classification. However, if people do have such knowledge about category members, might there not be times when it is used to aid classification? Third, it is not clear how to apply the exemplar view to some of the issues in category research, such as hierarchical effects or basic levels, to be discussed later.

Final Comments on the Exemplar View   In most experimental contrasts, the exemplar view provides a better fit for the data than does the prototype view (Medin & Smith, 1984; Nosofsky, 1992). The main advantages of the exemplar view, we believe, are the two characteristics that we contrasted with the prototype view. First, the use of multiple representations for a category allows for *selective* use of knowledge. That is, the most relevant information is accessed and used because the most similar exemplars greatly determine the classification. Second, rather than an additive function to combine feature information, the exemplar view uses a multiplicative function. Although the exact mathematical form is not crucial, it is important that the model does not *independently* combine information but takes into account *relational* information. The use of multiplicative similarity, combined with multiple representations, provides much greater sensitivity to relational information for classification. A prototype model has great difficulty in keeping track of all the possible statistics that might influence classification (feature correlations, variances, forms of distributions, frequencies), and updating such summary statistics with each new exemplar would be very difficult. The exemplar model overcomes these problems by keeping this information distributed across the exemplars and only making use of it when necessary.

Combining Exemplar and Prototype Models

Some readers may wonder whether the exemplar and prototype models are really competitors—perhaps they are both true. For example, one common idea is that an exemplar representation characterizes categories with very few instances, but as more instances are experienced, an abstraction is formed to represent the category. If both specific and abstract representations are used, then one needs to address such issues as how the abstractions are formed and what determines when each representation is used. In this section, we discuss some possible combined views and also consider an alternative parallel distributed processing (PDP), or connectionist, view. First, we mention some empirical evidence that favors a combined model.

Empirical Evidence for a Combined View
The empirical evidence is of two general types. First, several studies have shown that even when people use an exemplar strategy to classify new exemplars, they may end up learning something more general about the category (Medin & Edelson, 1988; Medin & Florian, 1992; Ross, Perkins, & Tenpenny, 1990; Spalding & Ross, 1994). For example, Ross et al. (1990) examined exemplar-based abstractions in a series of experiments involving classification of fictitious people into groups. A sample

Table 7.2

Sample stimuli from one category of Ross et al.'s exemplar-based abstraction experiments (Phases of Experiments)

---

1. Study (Each subject would learn both of these study exemplars for this category)

Study Exemplar *A* likes ice cream   Study Exemplar *B* likes to read Westerns
                   buys nails   buys a swimsuit

2. First test: Classification (Each subject would see one of these test exemplars)

Test Exemplar *A*   likes sherbet   *or* Test Exemplar *B*   likes to read Cowboy
                    buys wood   and Indian stories
                    buys a towel   buys wood
                                                                buys a towel

3. Final test: Feature ranking

                                       buys a chisel
                                       buys sunglasses
                                       2 filler features

Source: Adapted from Ross, Perkins, & Tenpenny (1990).

of their materials is presented in table 7.2. Each exemplar shown during the study phase consisted of two features, and there were two exemplars per category. Subjects were obliged to use an exemplar-based strategy to learn the categories because each instance had different features. At test, subjects were given one new instance from each category to classify. A test exemplar consisted of three features from within the same category—one reminding feature and two related features. The reminding feature was highly similar to a feature that had appeared in one of the study exemplars (e.g., the reminding feature *likes sherbet* of test exemplar *A* was highly similar to the feature *likes ice cream* in study exemplar *A*). Each related feature was associated with a feature that had appeared in one of the two study exemplars. By associated, we mean that the features often occur together as part of a more general theme. To illustrate, the related feature *buys wood* is associated with the feature *buys nails* from study exemplar *A* as part of a carpentrylike theme. The other related feature, *buys a towel,* is associated with the feature *buys a swimsuit* in study exemplar B as part of a beach or swimming theme. The same related features occurred with both possible test exemplars of a category (i.e., test exemplar *A* and *B* both had these same two related features). However, it was hypothesized that the reminding feature would prompt subjects to think back to a specific study exemplar, causing them to make an explicit comparison between the test exemplar and the previously studied exemplar as part of their classification process. Generalized knowledge about the commonalities between the two exemplars would then be stored as part of the category knowledge. For example, the test exemplar A (consisting of features *likes sherbet, buys wood, buys a towel*) would remind subjects of study exemplar A (with features *likes ice cream, buys nails*), leading subjects to encode the similarities of the features *likes ice cream* and *likes sherbet,* along with *buys nails* and *buys wood,* as generalizations about this category. In this case, the exemplar abstractions would be a fondness for frozen desserts and the purchase of carpentry materials. Subjects receiving test exemplar B would instead encode the similarities of the features *likes to read Westerns* and *likes to read Cowboy and Indian stories,* along with *buys a swimsuit* and *buys a towel,* leading to very different generalizations about the category (concerning reading preference and the beach-swimming theme). The important point about this design was that all subjects studied the same study exemplars and saw the same related features in the test exemplar (*buys wood* and *buys a towel*). The hypothesis was that the reminding feature would make subjects think back to different study exemplars, and that the related features would lead to different generalizations about the category (either carpentry or beach).

This link between novel test exemplars and prior study exemplars was confirmed in a feature-ranking test. Subjects were presented with a listing of four features for each category and were asked to rank the features according to the likelihood of their occurrence within that category. Two of the features (*buys a chisel, buys sunglasses*) were from the same generalization or theme (carpentry and beach, respectively) as the related features that had appeared in the study and test exemplars, while the other two features were filler features. Subjects ranked the related feature that had been common to both the test instance that they had seen and an earlier study instance as being more central to that particular category, despite the equal frequency of the two related features (*buys wood, buys a towel*) within the category. Specifically, subjects who had been presented with test exemplar A ranked the feature *buys a chisel* as being more likely to occur, while those who had classified test exemplar *B* gave a higher ranking to the feature *buys sunglasses*. This finding indicated that subjects were using generalized knowledge about feature commonalities among exemplars in their category judgments. This knowledge was learned from the use of specific studied exemplars for classifying new instances, thereby blending the exemplar and prototype views of categorization (Ross & Kennedy, 1990, showed similar results in problem solving).

The second type of evidence for a combined view is that a number of studies have found circumstances under which each view may predict the data better. As one example, Malt (1989) directly contrasted the two views with a new reaction time procedure and found evidence for both prototype and exemplar classifications. In particular, she asked whether categorization reaction time to a test instance was facilitated by its similarity to the preceding test instance. If the current test instance had been activated in the immediately preceding trial to help classify the previous test instance, then one might expect a faster classification response to the current test instance (because it would still be somewhat activated from the previous trial). On the other hand, if exemplar representations were not used in classification, then one would not expect a faster response to the current test instance. Malt showed that the faster classification response occurred under some conditions but not others. Her findings support the idea that classification may consist of a mixture of exemplar and prototype strategies. As another example, in Medin, Dewey, and Murphy (1983), subjects studied yearbook photographs under instructions intended to focus them on exemplar-level information (such as different first names) or on category-level information (such as last names for two different families). For our purposes, the important result was that whether the exemplar or prototype model provided a better fit depended upon the instructions: generalization did not occur automatically but depended on how people learned the information.

The empirical results from these studies suggest that people may encode and use both specific and generalized representations. Some theorists also argue that exemplars and abstractions may represent points along a continuum and that the same set of processes could use either type (or both types) of representation in classifying new instances (e.g., Elio & Anderson, 1981; Estes, 1986; Homa, 1984). We now turn to some models that combine exemplars and abstractions.

Combined Models

In this section, we consider three types of models that include a combination of exemplar and more prototypelike information but do so in very different ways: a selective attention exemplar model, an exemplar-based abstraction view, and Anderson's (1991) rational model.

Selective Attention in Exemplar Models   Before examining explicit combined models, we first point out that exemplar models are not as "exemplarlike" as the name would suggest. In particular, under some circumstances, they can end up with abstractions. The exemplar models all have a selective attention parameter, such as m_i (see equation 7.4 and table 7.1). The reason is simple—some features or dimensions are attended to more than others, so the encoding of each exemplar cannot be considered to be a simple copy of the instance, but rather one in which some aspects may have been attended to more than others. If a particular feature is not encoded, then it does not matter if a new instance matches or mismatches on this feature. More specifically, if a feature is not attended to, then its mismatch value, m_i, is near 1 (showing that the mismatching value is about the same as a matching value). If a feature is not attended to, then one can think of the exemplar representation as an abstraction over this feature, because the value for that feature does not influence the similarity.

Selective attention is crucial in exemplar models—it allows a represented exemplar to be a partial abstraction rather than a complete representation of an exemplar. Extensions to the context model have emphasized the role of attention weights in classification. Nosofsky (1986), in addition to extending the context model to include dimensional representations, showed that people often weight the dimensions to optimize classification performance. Kruschke (1992) added a connectionist learning of attention weights to Nosofsky's model to show how such attention weights might be learned. (Another interesting adaptation is presented in Lamberts, 1994.)

Exemplar-Based Abstractions   Not only might selective attention weights lead people to learn an abstract "exemplar"; the use of exemplars may lead to abstractions. The *exemplar-based abstraction* view (Brooks, 1987; Jacoby & Brooks, 1984; Medin & Edelson, 1988; Medin & Florian, 1992; Ross et al., 1990; Spalding & Ross, 1994) assumes that many categorizations are made using exemplars but that the effect of using exemplars leads to an abstraction that may also be stored and used for categorizing later instances. Thus, if a current situation reminds you of an earlier one, using the previous experience to determine your current action may cause you to learn something about dealing with situations of this type, in addition to what you learn about the two particular incidents. The results of Ross et al. (1990) that were discussed earlier (and presented in table 7.2) are one illustration of exemplar-based abstraction.

When a current instance reminds one of a previous instance, the two representations may be compared and the similarities and differences noted. The idea is that the similarities provide an abstraction over these two instances—the similar features are the commonalities between the two instances and include features that are likely to be important for the category. These similar features represent a type of "local" abstraction that can be stored and used later for classifying instances. By local abstraction, we mean that the abstraction is made over a small (in this case, two) number of instances, not over the entire set of category members, as in prototype models. These abstractions will often be far more specific than the prototype would be, because they include information that applies to these two instances but that may not be true of the category in general. However, if these abstractions are used later in classifying another instance, a still more general abstraction may be made, consisting of the commonalities between the first local abstraction and the new instance.

It is worth noting three points about these exemplar-based abstractions. First, the exemplar used for classifying the new instance is not simply any category instance, but one of which the person was reminded. Remindings are usually greatly influenced by all types of similarities, including superficial ones (e.g., Ross, 1984), so the two instances compared are likely to be similar in some ways that are not crucial for the category.

This fact means that the abstractions will often include many features that are not category relevant but that have consistently co-occurred with particular category-relevant features. Second, this scheme will result in the category representation consisting of both exemplars and abstractions (at varying levels of generality). Thus, there will not be a single summary representation. Third, even once abstractions have been learned, the classification of new instances will use a variety of category knowledge— sometimes earlier instances (leading to exemplar-based abstractions), sometimes exemplar-based abstractions (leading to more general abstractions), and sometimes both. Which knowledge is used depends upon the similarity of the knowledge to the test instance.

This exemplar-based abstraction view is one way in which both prototypes and exemplars may coexist and provide input to classification. Under this approach, abstractions are formed from comparisons made during classification, but no information is discarded, because exemplars are also stored and used.

Rational Model   Anderson (1991) has proposed a very different category learning model which arises from his rational analysis of cognition view (Anderson, 1990). Limited space prohibits a full exposition of this *rational model,* but the main point is that category structure evolves to allow the best performance possible for predicting features. (This assumption also includes classification because the category label is considered one of the features.) During learning, exemplars get grouped together into clusters. Each cluster of exemplars has a central tendency that represents that particular cluster, like a miniprototype. For each new exemplar, the model determines whether to add it to an existing cluster or start a new cluster. This determination is made by calculating the similarity of the new item to each of the various clusters, using a multiplicative similarity rule, much like the context model. The item is then assigned to that cluster to which it is most similar. The assignment is also affected by the size of the clusters and the likelihood that instances group together. When predicting a feature for a new instance, such as the category label, the model does not simply find the most similar cluster and use that to make the prediction. Rather, it uses *all* the clusters, weighting the prediction of each cluster by the probability that the instance would be assigned to that cluster. In addition, this same scheme can be used not only for classifying new instances, but for predicting any unknown feature of a new instance.

How does this model relate to exemplar and prototype models? Nosofsky (1991) presented a number of interesting findings. Of most interest here, the model has a parameter, called the coupling parameter, that influences how much grouping of items occurs. If this coupling parameter is set to 0, then no grouping occurs, and each item is a separate cluster. Nosofsky showed that under these circumstances, the rational model becomes isomorphic to the context model of the exemplar view. When the coupling parameter is set to 1 and the category label similarity is high (so that exemplars with the same category label are likely to be grouped together), then the model leads to a clustering of all exemplars with the same label (i.e., the experimenter-defined category members are grouped together), and this cluster is represented by a summary representation. (The rational model is not a prototype model as defined here, because a multiplicative similarity calculation is used.)

For intermediate values of the coupling parameter, the rational model can be viewed as a combination of exemplar and prototype models. If members of a category occur in multiple clusters, then the central tendencies of these clusters can be viewed as multiple prototypes of the category. (We are simplifying here by assuming that the cluster items are all from one category and by ignoring the multiplicative similarity.) Although the idea of having multiple prototypes is not new, the rational model provides a principled way of determining which prototypes would be formed (Nosofsky, 1991).

The rational model provides an interesting combination of exemplar and prototype approaches, but it has been criticized on a number of fronts. Murphy and Ross (1994; Ross & Murphy, 1996) found little evidence for its core assumption that all categories are used in making predictions for a new feature. In addition, Murphy (1993) raised a number of conceptual problems that remain unresolved. However, see Anderson and Fincham (1996) for a recent version of the rational model that addressed some of these issues.

Other Ways of Combining Prototype and Exemplar Information

In addition to models that explicitly include both prototypes and exemplars, there are alternative ways in which people's classification might be influenced by both specific and general properties of the category instances. Three possibilities are mentioned here: PDP views, different structures for distinct levels of categories, and different types of categories.

PDP Models of Categorization   Until now, we have focused on models in which the knowledge being stored can be thought of as abstractions or exemplars, with each representation stored separately from the other representations. The *connectionist*, or *PDP*, approach argues instead that the representation of knowledge is distributed across many connection weights in a network and that there is no representation of the category (neither abstractions nor exemplars), except as embedded in the many connection weights between units. We do not have space to provide the details of such models, but they are explained in a variety of papers (e.g., Gluck & Bower, 1988; Knapp & Anderson, 1984; McClelland & Rumelhart, 1986).

The PDP model does technically have a single summary representation—namely, the whole network—that is used for classifying new instances, so it may seem to be prototypelike, but it also has many exemplarlike properties. Although the entire network is used to classify, the particular input determines which connection weights have the most influence, a characteristic more like the selective use of knowledge found in exemplar models. The response to any item relies extensively on the correlations among features in the instances that have been experienced, not the additive combination of features proposed by the prototype view. These properties allow it to overcome both of the major difficulties with the prototype view. First, although the PDP model does show sensitivity to typicality, it also is sensitive to exemplar similarity, especially if the test instance is atypical or the studied instances are very dissimilar from one another (Knapp & Anderson, 1984). Second, the reliance on correlations of features occurs because of the connectionist learning mechanism, and this allows the model to be sensitive to the within-category correlations that pose difficulties for the prototype model. In addition, these models provide an explicit learning mechanism in which each new instance leads to specifiable changes in the connection weights.

Despite these advantageous properties, no current connectionist model has been able to account for as wide a variety of categorization data as the exemplar models do. Nosofsky, Kruschke, and McKinley (1992) argued that the failure to represent the category in terms of exemplars is a major problem for connectionist models. More generally, we believe that many of the categorization results suggest the importance of having multiple representations for a category. This problem does not mean that connectionist ideas are not useful in modeling classification. Kruschke (1992) has produced impressive fits of data by combining an error-driven connectionist learning process for learning the selective attention weights with a model that has exemplar representations (see also Nosofsky et al., 1992).

Different Category Levels A different way to think about the combination of prototype and exemplar views is that they may each apply in different circumstances. We illustrate this possibility by using a robust and important idea in the category literature: basic levels. Objects can be classified at various levels of specificity. For example, a particular piece of fruit might be classified as a fruit, as an apple, or as a McIntosh apple. Similarly, a particular item of furniture might be considered a piece of furniture, a chair, or a desk chair. Rosch and her colleagues (Rosch, Mervis, Gray, Johnson, & Boyes-Braem, 1976) demonstrated that one level, the *basic level,* is psychologically privileged. This corresponds to the apple and chair levels in the examples given, with the next highest level (fruit, furniture) being called the *superordinate* level and the next lowest level (McIntosh apple, desk chair) being called the *subordinate* level. The basic level is "privileged" in that people are most likely to use this level in naming; people are faster to verify objects at this level; people learn basic level concepts earlier; and so forth. (See Lassaline, Wisniewski, & Medin, 1992, for an extended review of the many findings supporting the basic level, as well as some criticisms.)

We do not wish to delve into the many details of the basic-level debate, except to point out a speculative possibility, raised in Ross and Spalding (1994), that different levels may have different types of category structures (i.e., prototype or exemplar). Consider the categories of fruit, apple, and McIntosh apple. The subordinate level of McIntosh apples seems well suited to be represented by a prototype. Although people might remember a particular McIntosh apple, it seems unlikely that such exemplars are used for classifying new McIntosh apples. Instead, perhaps the many highly similar McIntosh apples we have seen are all mushed together in some summary representation that is used for classifying new instances. However, the superordinate level of fruit does not seem so amenable to a prototype representation. One could have a fruit prototype consisting of some typical fruit, such as apple, or of the central tendency of fruits, but is that really going to be helpful in classifying pineapples, bananas, and kiwis? Apples may be usual fruits, but using them as the summary representations of all fruits is going to make classification difficult. Instead, perhaps we have a set of disjunctive concepts, such as apple, plum, nectarine, and so on and something is classified as a fruit if it is any one of these (e.g., Murphy & Smith, 1982). Such a representation would be disjunctive, as exemplar models are, but the exemplars here would be categories, not instances. Interestingly, American Sign Language explicitly includes such types of categories—for example, *fruit* may be expressed by signing "apples and oranges and bananas and etc." (Newport & Bellugi, 1978).

If the subordinate level uses prototypes and the superordinate level consists of exemplars, what about the basic level, with items such as apple or chair? One possibility is that it consists of prototypes of the categories that are used by the superordinate level. Thus, there may be prototypes of apple, banana, and so forth. These prototypes might be formed from combining the instances that went into the subordinate level prototypes (McIntosh apples, Delicious apples, etc.). This idea seems fine for some categories, such as apples, but perhaps less useful for categories in which the subordinates vary greatly, such as chair. Another possibility for such categories is that they consist of multiple prototypes derived from the subordinate level (e.g., desk chairs, easy chairs, recliners, lawn chairs, etc.), which would be more exemplarlike. It may be that both of these possibilities for representing categories at the basic level are true, with some basic-level categories represented as prototypes and others as disjunctions of subordinate prototypes.

Although this account of varying representation by category level is clearly speculative, it suggests another way in which prototype and exemplar representation may be combined. As a further conjecture, these representations could result from exemplar-based abstractions; that is, similar instances lead to prototypes derived from that cluster of instances.

Different Types of Categories   As we have seen, there may be no general answer to whether categories are represented as prototypes or exemplars—it may be a combination of these, with either both kinds of representations used, or at least each type of representation used in different cases. In addition to the combined models and the speculation about different representations at different levels, other research suggests that the representations may even depend upon the content of the category (e.g., Homa, 1984). For example, Medin, Wattenmaker, and Hampson (1987) showed that the summing of independent features (as in the additive combination rule) applies for some categories, such as whether a particular person is honest (where the features would be observed behaviors of the person), but the multiplicative rule applies to other categories, such as whether the features allow an object to be used as a hammer. Also, Wattenmaker (1995) argued that there may be fundamental differences in the structure of representations used for social categories (e.g., traits, such as honesty) and for objects.

A very different example of how category representations may vary according to category content would be *ad hoc*, or *goal-derived*, categories (Barsalou, 1983, 1991). Unlike common taxonomic categories, ad hoc categories, such as *things to eat on a diet* or *things to take out of your house in case of a fire* are constructed in the course of meeting some goal. In a variety of interesting experiments, Barsalou showed that ad hoc categories often do have a summary representation, but rather than a central tendency or average, the representation is an ideal. For example, among diet foods, the ideal would be a food with zero calories.

Before ending this discussion of combined models, it is worth noting that in addition to prototypes and exemplars, another common representation for categories, as mentioned earlier, is rules or definitions (the classical view of concepts). Rules are a more specific type of summary representation in which category membership is assigned only if all the features are true. The early work in hypothesis testing (e.g., Bruner, Goodnow, & Austin, 1956) focused largely on how such rules are acquired. Although a simple rule model will not account for many findings, a number of suggestions have been made for augmenting this idea with additional knowledge or conditions (e.g., Medin & Smith, 1984; Nosofsky, Palmeri, & McKinley, 1994).

Conclusions

This section on combined models of prototype and exemplar information suggests that there may be ways to combine the advantages of summary representations with the advantages of more specific representations. Summary representations make use of more of the data, whereas exemplar representations are more sensitive to correlations and the particulars of the instance to be classified. The exemplar-based abstraction view and the rational model provide specific ways in which more general representations may be formed from exemplars. The PDP model includes a means by which both types of information may be represented together. Finally, the discussions of levels of categories and different types of categories are speculations about how representations may vary between categories.

Use of Categories

Classification is rarely your ultimate goal when you are faced with an unfamiliar object or new situation. If an approaching animal is classified as a dog, the classification is not sufficient to allow you to know what to do. Rather, you need to access your knowledge about dogs to make a prediction about whether it would be best to flee or not. Classifying a situation, a math problem, or a person, for example, is a first step in allowing you to know how to deal with the entity. In addition to classification, category knowledge plays a critical role in a variety of other cognitive activities, such as explanation, conceptual combination, communication, and inference. The use of categories for inference is particularly important and has been the subject of an increasing amount of research (e.g., Anderson, 1991; Gelman & Markman, 1986; Heit, 1992; Murphy & Ross, 1994; Osherson, Smith, Wilkie, Lopez, & Shafir, 1990;

Ross & Murphy, 1996). Given the importance of inference in category research, it is useful to consider what the prototype, exemplar, and combined views might claim about how inferences are made following classifications. The exact way in which inferences would be made under each view has not yet been detailed by researchers, but we can sketch out enough of the process to examine the differences between the views. We consider the particular case in which some features are presented and an unobserved feature has to be predicted. (In this case, we view prediction as a simple but common type of inference.) For example, one sees an animal and has to predict its ferocity or one sees the silhouette of a bird and has to predict what food it might eat. Although any differences in predictions for this simple type of category use may not definitively discriminate among the views of category representation that we have discussed, we do think it important that the use of categories be considered in the debate on category representations.

Prototype View   The prototype view assumes that the summary representation of the category would be used to make inferences about unobserved features. So, if the presented features on an item caused it to be classified as a member of category X (i.e., it was similar enough to the prototype of category X), then the prototype of category X would be used to predict the unobserved feature. Assuming that the features are considered independently (as they are in classification because of the additive combination), then the prediction would be the central tendency of that feature for category members. That is, if the average dog ferocity were "friendly" and a new animal were classified as a dog, then the predicted ferocity would be "friendly."

The advantage of this prototype prediction process is that the prediction uses a central tendency derived from all of the category instances. If one has no additional information on which to base a prediction, the best guess one can make is the central tendency. Thus, if all you know is that a particular animal is a dog, then the average dog ferocity is the best prediction to make.

The disadvantage of relying on the prototype is that predictions may sometimes depend on more specific clusterings of information. For example, the predicted ferocity of a new dog might be very different if it were a spaniel than if it were a pit bull. On could argue that the new dog would be classified more specifically than dog, such as a spaniel, but that poses three problems. First, as discussed in the previous section, the data suggest that *dog* is the basic level, so dogs are usually classified first as dogs, not as a particular kind of dog (Rosch et al., 1976; Tanaka & Taylor, 1991). Second, using subordinate-level information would necessitate the representation of additional prototypes at this lower level. This arrangement would then require a means of knowing when to use each type of representation for prediction. Such a proposal may be a correct one for prediction, but it has not yet been worked out in any detail for a prototype view. Third, if more specific subcategories are used, then those prototypes are constructed from fewer data. That may be necessary, but one also needs to realize that many predictions about dogs do seem to be true of many dogs, such as tail wagging or coldness of noses. Subcategory prototypes could also lead to correct predictions, but they would be more influenced by unusual observations because the prototypes would be based on fewer data. Thus, although it seems that predictions might sometimes be made on the basis of subordinate-level information, the prototype view does not yet include a means of deciding what level of knowledge is used for making different predictions.

Exemplar View   The exemplar view uses the same processes to predict features as it uses to classify instances. However, one compares the presented features of the new instance to previously learned instances, causing similar instances within each category to be more influential in the prediction. This means that the predicted feature would not be a simple central tendency of all category members, but a weighted central tendency, with the weight of each instance a function of its similarity to the new instance. Thus, in a similarity comparison to the features of a new dog, dog exemplars that were very similar would be most weighted. The resulting predicted feature would then be a weighted central tendency of those similar instances. For example, the predicted ferocity of a new dog would depend on its similarity to other dog instances. If the similarity comparison led to high weights on various spaniels, then the predicted ferocity would be low, whereas if it led to high weights on various pit bulls, then the predicted ferocity would be high.

The advantage of this exemplar prediction process is that the most similar instances are used to make the feature prediction. Thus, any within-category correlations can be captured at this more specific level. Even though most birds do not eat rodents, if a new bird were much like hawks and falcons that one had seen, then one might predict it would eat rodents. Brooks (1987) pointed out how the distribution of knowledge across instances allows learning correlations of features, which may be especially useful for prediction.

The main disadvantage of using exemplars in this way is that a prediction based principally on a small number of exemplars has the danger of being affected by unusual observations. To the extent that a small number of exemplars are highly weighted for the prediction, then one or two unusual observations may lead to a very inaccurate prediction. However, there is some evidence from categorization studies that people do highly weight a few very similar exemplars when making a prediction (Brooks, Norman, & Allen, 1991).

Combined Views   The prototype view of inference has the advantage of using data from all exemplars but the disadvantage of being insensitive to within-category correlations. The exemplar view has the opposite problem—it is sensitive to these correlations, but the inference may be based on few data. A final possibility to be considered is how a combined view, in which both exemplars and summary representations are stored, may be utilized to make such inferences. For illustration, consider the exemplar-based abstraction view, which has both exemplars and any abstractions built up from comparisons that have occurred during classification and use of new instances. Such a combined view may make use of both types of representations for inferences. For instance, suppose a prediction of a feature value for a new instance makes use of both exemplars and abstractions (i.e., both are weighted enough to influence the judgment). Then if there were agreement about the predicted feature value, the inference could be made with confidence. Without agreement, some further process might be required, such as a more detailed consideration of the source of conflict or the use of further representations. The multiple representations and the selective access of knowledge in this combined view could lead to very different knowledge being used as a function of the new instance. For example, if the novel instance were typical, then it would be likely to activate both abstractions and exemplars. In contrast, if the instance were atypical, then there would be a greater likelihood that the exemplar representations would dominate. Clearly, much needs to be detailed about such a combined view for inference, but it does allow the use of many data (both specific and abstracted) for typical instances, while relying on fewer but more specific data for atypical instances.

The goal of this section on the use of categories has been to point out that we need to consider more than just classification performance when discussing how categories are represented. Research on categories has focused mainly on classification, but the use of categories for prediction appears to be a fruitful area, both for expanding our understanding of categorical knowledge and for examining the implications of classification theories.

Specificity and Generality in Cognition

We have been focusing on prototypes versus exemplars in categorization, but the general issue is a broader one that touches upon many areas of cognition: what knowledge do people access and use to accomplish particular cognitive tasks? In many situations, as in categorization, it seems likely that people have knowledge about both specific occurrences and more general regularities. Examining this issue in other areas of cognition may extend our understanding of the work in categorization and provide us with a clearer perspective of how specific and general representations play a role in other cognitive tasks.

In other research areas, a wide variety of results can be interpreted as aids to understanding the relation between specific instances and more general or abstract representations. As one illustration of this idea, many research projects examine basic perceptual and attentional processes, such as word recognition and automaticity. Many researchers assume that people use abstract representations to accomplish such tasks. For example, identifying a briefly presented word would appear to rely on a general representation of that word, abstracted from many experiences with that word. However, such identification is also affected by the specifics of earlier episodes (e.g., Jacoby & Brooks, 1984). Even the automaticity built up from much practice in a domain may not necessarily result from the refining and tuning of a general procedure, but rather from accessing more and more exemplars (Logan, 1988). In Logan's theory, the response to each item is determined by a race among the independent exemplars that closely match it. He showed that many aspects of the data that have been taken as evidence for general procedures can also be accounted for by his exemplar model. In addition, this exemplar model makes unique predictions that have since been confirmed (e.g., Logan, 1992). These projects indicate that even when it seems "obvious" that some abstract representation underlies performance, exemplar-based knowledge may be used.

This influence of specific experiences extends to many complex behaviors as well. Much research has examined how schemas such as event scripts might underlie comprehension and memory (e.g., Bower, Black, & Turner, 1979; Schank & Abelson, 1977). However, these large abstract representations are often not flexible enough to easily address the wide range of situations people experience. A different possibility is that our understanding of even routine events might be tied to more specific experiences (Schank, 1982). Case-based reasoning, a large area of research in artificial intelligence, is based upon this idea of using specific earlier experiences to help perform cognitive tasks. Such research has produced a number of different computer programs that can give advice, solve problems, or help in design tasks (see Kolodner, 1993). Even psychological studies of expertise sometimes reveal that performance that appears to be based on a deep general understanding of the domain is sometimes based on a deep *specific* understanding. For example, chess masters have much general knowledge about the game, but they may also rely on their memories of moves in specific games when deciding what move to make.

An additional illustration of the investigation of specific and general knowledge can be seen in research examining the learning of simple rules. Sometimes when people are given generalizations or rules to help them accomplish some task, specific instances still affect their performance. For example, Allen and Brooks (1991) provided people with rules for making a simple categorization and then had them practice with particular instances. Although the rule was simple, and learners were able to use it, test items that were similar to the practice items were often classified using the practice instances, not the rule. Rothkopf and Dashen (1995) found a related effect in which extended practice using particular instances led to the rules being "specialized" in terms of the exemplars. In more complex domains, such specialization of abstract principles is common. As one example that we have all had experience with, algebraic principles taught using word problems become specialized by the content of the word problems. If people hear just the first few words of a word problem, such as "The riverboat . . . " they often can quickly tell what type of problem it is and begin to access the schemas for solving these problems (e.g., Blessing & Ross, 1996; Hinsley, Hayes, & Simon, 1977). Although the principles may have been taught more abstractly, extended practice with riverboat word problems can lead to specialization of the abstract principles.

In all of these cases, there is a general tension between two forces. On the one hand, it is important to take advantage of the regularities within a domain in order to perform both efficiently and effectively. To the extent that there are rules or generalizations that apply to most instances, using an abstract representation allows one to function in a way that is usually appropriate, even when new instances are dissimilar to previously learned instances. On the other hand, using specific instances has a number of advantages as well (see Medin & Ross, 1989, for a thorough discussion). Exemplar representations can encode complex interactions within categories, such as feature correlations, as discussed earlier. Even if a generalization is sufficient for classifying and responding to a specific instance, an exemplar representation might facilitate the process if the instance has a set of features that has often co-occurred in previously learned exemplars. Abstract representations provide wide coverage, whereas specific representations allow faster and more varied responses.

Summary and Conclusions

In this chapter, we have presented a brief overview of the controversy about prototype and exemplar views in categorization. We began by considering two specific models to illustrate the advantages and disadvantages of each view. The next section considered the evidence that both types of representations might be used, and presented several models and ways of combining the representations. We then moved away from classification to consider how categories might be used to make inferences. Finally, we discussed research that contrasts the use of general and specific representations in other cognitive tasks. So, what does it all mean for the distinction between prototype and exemplar theories?

Overall, we believe that the evidence favors a view in which both exemplars and more abstract representations are used in categorization. The exemplar view includes two properties important in many category-related tasks: multiplicative similarity and multiple representations. Multiplicative similarity, which could also be used with prototype views, leads to a much greater weighting of similar representations. The availability of multiple representations, when combined with multiplicative similarity, means that the access and use of knowledge will tend to be selective. This selectivity allows the exemplar view to make use of complex co-occurring patterns of features in the instances. In contrast, the prototype view does not have this selectivity, but it does respond on the basis of all the category exemplars and thus is not influenced by particular idiosyncratic patterns that may have no category relevance. If there are regularities in a category that occur across many instances, it seems useful to encode these regularities for aiding the classification and use of new instances. Which view does a better job classifying and predicting may depend upon the category structure and the task, but each provides important category knowledge.

Although our understanding of categorization is far from complete, there does seem to be some consensus for having both specific and more general representations. As we encounter and encode new instances, their representations may sometimes influence later classification and category use. At the same time, our use of earlier instances allows us to recognize and abstract more general information, which may also be used in subsequent category judgments. Category representations are then built up from this interaction between the selective use of the most similar representations and the codification of regularities among the representations. This continual interplay between specific and general representations, as characterized by exemplar and prototype theories, may prove to be an integral part of category knowledge, performing a critical role in both categorization and other cognitive processes.

Acknowledgments

We thank Gordon Logan and Gregory Murphy for comments on an earlier version of this chapter. Preparation of this chapter was partially supported by NSF Grant SBR 97-20304.

References

Allen, S. W., & Brooks, L. R. (1991). Specializing the operation of an explicit rule. *Journal of Experimental Psychology: General, 120,* 3–19.

Anderson, J. R. (1990). *The adaptive character of thought.* Hillsdale, NJ: Erlbaum.

Anderson, J. R. (1991). The adaptive nature of human categorization. *Psychological Review, 98,* 409–429.

Anderson, J. R., & Fincham, J. M. (1996). Categorization and sensitivity to correlation. *Journal of Experimental Psychology: Learning, Memory, and Cognition, 22,* 259–277.

Barsalou, L. W. (1983). Ad hoc categories. *Memory & Cognition, 11,* 211–227.

Barsalou, L. W. (1990). On the indistinguishability of exemplar memory and abstraction in category representation. In T. K. Srull & R. S. Wyer Jr. (Eds.), *Advances in social cognition: Vol. 3. Content and process specificity in the effects of prior experiences* (pp. 61–88). Hillsdale, NJ: Erlbaum.

Barsalou, L. W. (1991). Deriving categories to achieve goals. In G. H. Bower (Ed.), *The psychology of learning and motivation* (Vol. 27, pp. 1–64). San Diego, CA: Academic Press.

Blessing, S. B., & Ross, B. H. (1996). Content effects in problem categorization and problem solving. *Journal of Experimental Psychology: Learning, Memory, and Cognition, 22,* 792–810.

Bower, G. H., Black, J. B., & Turner, T. J. (1979). Scripts in memory for text. *Cognitive Psychology, 11,* 177–220.

Brooks, L. (1978). Nonanalytic concept formation and memory for instances. In E. Rosch & B. B. Lloyd (Eds.), *Cognition and categorization* (pp. 169–211). Hillsdale, NJ: Erlbaum.

Brooks, L. (1987). Decentralized control of categorization: The role of prior processing episodes. In U. Neisser (Ed.), *Concepts and conceptual development: Ecological and intellectual factors in categorization* (pp. 141–174). Cambridge, England: Cambridge University Press.

Brooks, L. R., Norman, G. R., & Allen, S. W. (1991). Role of specific similarity in a medical diagnostic task. *Journal of Experimental Psychology: General, 120,* 278–287.

Bruner, J. S., Goodnow, J. J., & Austin, G. A. (1956). *A study of thinking.* New York: John Wiley & Sons.

Elio, R., & Anderson, J. R. (1981). The effects of category generalizations and instance similarity on schema abstraction. *Journal of Experimental Psychology: Human Learning and Memory, 7,* 397–417.

Estes, W. K. (1986). Array models for category learning. *Cognitive Psychology, 18,* 500–549.

Galton, F. (1883). *Inquiries into human faculty and its development.* London: Macmillan.

Gelman, S. A., & Markman, E. M. (1986). Categories and induction in children. *Cognition, 23,* 183–209.

Gluck, M. A., & Bower, G. H. (1988). From conditioning to category learning: An adaptive network model. *Journal of Experimental Psychology: General, 117,* 227–247.

Goldstone, R. L. (1994). The role of similarity in categorization: Providing a groundwork. *Cognition, 52,* 125–157.

Hampton, J. A. (1993). Prototype models of concept representation. In I. Van Mechelen, J. A. Hampton, R. S. Michalski, & P. Theuns (Eds.), *Categories and concepts: Theoretical views and inductive data analysis* (pp. 67–95). London: Academic Press.

Hampton, J. A. (1995). Testing the prototype theory of concepts. *Journal of Memory and Language, 34,* 686–708.

Heit, E. (1992). Categorization using chains of examples. *Cognitive Psychology, 24,* 341–380.

Hinsley, D. A., Hayes, J. R., & Simon, H. A. (1977). From words to equations: Meaning and representation in word problems. In M. A. Just & P. A. Carpenter (Eds.), *Cognitive processes in comprehension* (pp. 89–106). Hillsdale, NJ: Erlbaum.

Hintzman, D. L. (1986). "Schema abstraction" in a multiple-trace model. *Psychological Review, 93,* 411–428.

Hintzman, D. L., & Ludlam, G. (1980). Differential forgetting of prototypes and old instances: Simulation by an exemplar-based classification model. *Memory & Cognition, 8,* 378–382.

Homa, D. (1984). On the nature of categories. In G. H. Bower (Ed.), *The psychology of learning and motivation* (Vol. 18, pp. 49–94). Orlando, FL: Academic Press.

Jacoby, L. L., & Brooks, L. R. (1984). Nonanalytic cognition: Memory, perception, and concept learning. In G. H. Bower (Ed.), *The psychology of learning and motivation* (Vol. 18, pp. 1–47). Orlando, FL: Academic Press.

Knapp, A. G., & Anderson, J. A. (1984). Theory of categorization based on distributed memory storage. *Journal of Experimental Psychology: Learning, Memory, and Cognition, 10*, 616–637.

Kolodner, J. L. (1993). *Case-based reasoning.* San Mateo, CA: Morgan Kaufmann.

Kruschke, J. K. (1992). ALCOVE: An exemplar-based connectionist model of category learning. *Psychological Review, 99*, 22–44.

Lamberts, K. (1994). Flexible tuning of similarity in exemplar-based categorization. *Journal of Experimental Psychology: Learning, Memory, and Cognition, 20*, 1003–1021.

Lassaline, M. E., Wisniewski, E. J., & Medin, D. L. (1992). Basic levels in artificial and natural categories: Are all basic levels created equal? In B. Burns (Ed.), *Percepts, concepts, and categories: The representation and processing of information* (pp. 327–378). Amsterdam: North-Holland.

Logan, G. D. (1988). Toward an instance theory of automatization. *Psychological Review, 95*, 492–527.

Logan, G. D. (1992). Shapes of reaction time distributions and shapes of learning curves: A test of the instance theory of automaticity. *Journal of Experimental Psychology: Learning, Memory, and Cognition, 18*, 883–914.

Malt, B. C. (1989). An on-line investigation of prototype and exemplar strategies in classification. *Journal of Experimental Psychology: Learning, Memory, and Cognition, 15*, 539–555.

Malt, B. C., & Smith, E. E. (1984). Correlated properties in natural categories. *Journal of Verbal Learning and Verbal Behavior, 23*, 250–269.

McClelland, J. L., & Rumelhart, D. E. (1986). A distributed model of human learning and memory. In J. L. McClelland & D. E. Rumelhart (Eds.), *Parallel distributed processing: Explorations in the microstructures of cognition: Vol 2. Psychological and biological models* (pp. 170–215). Cambridge, MA: MIT Press.

McCloskey, M. E., & Glucksberg, S. (1978). Natural categories: Well-defined or fuzzy sets? *Memory & Cognition, 6*, 462–472.

Medin, D. L. (1986). Comment on "Memory storage and retrieval processes in category learning." *Journal of Experimental Psychology: General, 115*, 373–381.

Medin, D. L., Dewey, G. I., & Murphy, T. D. (1983). Relationships between items and category learning: Evidence that abstraction is not automatic. *Journal of Experimental Psychology: Learning, Memory, and Cognition, 9*, 607–625.

Medin, D. L., & Edelson, S. M. (1988). Problem structure and the use of base-rate information from experience. *Journal of Experimental Psychology: General, 117*, 68–85.

Medin, D. L., & Florian, J. E. (1992). Abstraction and selective coding in exemplar-based models of categorization. In A. F. Healy, S. M. Kosslyn, & R. M. Shiffrin (Eds.), *From learning processes to cognitive processes: Essays in honor of William K. Estes* (Vol. 2, pp. 207–234). Hillsdale, NJ: Erlbaum.

Medin, D. L., & Ross, B. H. (1989). The specific character of abstract thought: Categorization, problem-solving, and induction. In R. J. Sternberg (Ed.), *Advances in the psychology of human intelligence* (Vol. 5, pp. 189–223). Hillsdale, NJ: Erlbaum.

Medin, D. L., & Schaffer, M. M. (1978). Context theory of classification learning. *Psychological Review, 85*, 207–238.

Medin, D. L., & Smith, E. E. (1984). Concepts and concept formation. *Annual Review of Psychology, 35*, 113–138.

Medin, D. L., Wattenmaker, W. D., & Hampson, S. E. (1987). Family resemblance, conceptual cohesiveness, and category construction. *Cognitive Psychology, 19*, 242–279.

Murphy, G. L. (1993). Theories and concept formation. In I. Van Mechelen, J. A. Hampton, R. S. Michalski, & P. Theuns (Eds.), *Categories and concepts: Theoretical views and inductive data analysis* (pp. 173–200). London: Academic Press.

Murphy, G. L., & Brownell, H. H. (1985). Category differentiation in object recognition: Typicality constraints on the basic category advantage. *Journal of Experimental Psychology: Learning, Memory, and Cognition, 11*, 70–84.

Murphy, G. L., & Medin, D. L. (1985). The role of theories in conceptual coherence. *Psychological Review, 92*, 289–316.

Murphy, G. L., & Ross, B. H. (1994). Predictions from uncertain categorizations. *Cognitive Psychology, 27*, 148–193.

Murphy, G. L., & Smith, E. E. (1982). Basic-level superiority in picture categorization. *Journal of Verbal Learning and Verbal Behavior, 21*, 1–20.

Newport, E. L., & Bellugi, U. (1978). Linguistic expression of category levels in a visual-gestural language: A flower is a flower is a flower. In E. Rosch & B. Lloyd (Eds.), *Cognition and categorization* (pp. 49–71). Hillsdale, NJ: Erlbaum.

Nosofsky, R. M. (1986). Attention, similarity, and the identification-categorization relationship. *Journal of Experimental Psychology: General, 115*, 39–57.

Nosofsky, R. M. (1991). Relation between the rational model and the context model of categorization. *Psychological Science, 2*, 416–421.

Nosofsky, R. M. (1992). Exemplars, prototypes, and similarity rules. In A. F. Healy, S. M. Kosslyn, & R. M. Shiffrin (Eds.), *From learning theory to connectionist theory: Essays in honor of William K. Estes* (Vol. 1, pp. 149–167). Hillsdale, NJ: Erlbaum.

Nosofsky, R. M., Kruschke, J. K., & McKinley, S. C. (1992). Combining exemplar-based category representations and connectionist learning rules. *Journal of Experimental Psychology: Learning, Memory, and Cognition, 18*, 211–233.

Nosofsky, R. M., Palmeri, T. J., & McKinley, S. C. (1994). Rule-plus-exception model of classification learning. *Psychological Review, 101*, 53–79.

Osherson, D. N., Smith, E. E., Wilkie, O., Lopez, A., & Shafir, E. (1990). Category-based induction. *Psychological Review, 97,* 185–200.

Posner, M. I., & Keele, S. W. (1968). On the genesis of abstract ideas. *Journal of Experimental Psychology, 77,* 353–363.

Posner, M. I., & Keele, S. W. (1970). Retention of abstract ideas. *Journal of Experimental Psychology, 83,* 304–308.

Reed, S. K. (1972). Pattern recognition and categorization. *Cognitive Psychology, 3,* 382–407.

Rips, L. J. (1989). Similarity, typicality, and categorization. In S. Vosniadou & A. Ortony (Eds.), *Similarity and analogical reasoning* (pp. 21–59). Cambridge, England: Cambridge University Press.

Rips, L. J., Shoben, E. J., & Smith, E. E. (1973). Semantic distance and the verification of semantic relations. *Journal of Verbal Learning and Verbal Behavior, 12,* 1–20.

Rosch, E. (1973). On the internal structure of perceptual and semantic categories. In T. E. Moore (Ed.), *Cognitive development and the acquisition of language* (pp. 111–144). New York: Academic Press.

Rosch, E. (1975). Cognitive representations of semantic categories. *Journal of Experimental Psychology: General, 104,* 192–233.

Rosch, E., & Mervis, C. B. (1975). Family resemblances: Studies in the internal structure of categories. *Cognitive Psychology, 7,* 573–605.

Rosch, E., Mervis, C. B., Gray, W., Johnson, D., & Boyes-Braem, P. (1976). Basic objects in natural categories. *Cognitive Psychology, 8,* 382–439.

Ross, B. H. (1984). Remindings and their effects in learning a cognitive skill. *Cognitive Psychology, 16,* 371–416.

Ross, B. H., & Kennedy, P. T. (1990). Generalizing from the use of earlier examples in problem solving. *Journal of Experimental Psychology: Learning, Memory, and Cognition, 16,* 42–55.

Ross, B. H., & Murphy, G. L. (1996). Category-based predictions: Influence of uncertainty and feature associations. *Journal of Experimental Psychology: Learning, Memory, and Cognition, 22,* 736–753.

Ross, B. H., Perkins, S. J., & Tenpenny, P. L. (1990). Reminding-based category learning. *Cognitive Psychology, 22,* 460–492.

Ross, B. H., & Spalding, T. L. (1994). Concepts and categories. In R. J. Sternberg (Ed.), *Handbook of perception and cognition: Vol. 12. Thinking and problem solving* (pp. 119–148). San Diego, CA: Academic Press.

Rothkopf, E. Z., & Dashen, M. L. (1995). Particularization: Inductive speeding of rule-governed decisions by narrow application experience. *Journal of Experimental Psychology: Learning, Memory, and Cognition, 21,* 469–482.

Schank, R. C. (1982). *Dynamic memory: A theory of reminding and learning in computers and people.* Cambridge, England: Cambridge University Press.

Schank, R. C., & Abelson, R. P. (1977). *Scripts, plans, goals, and understanding: An inquiry into human knowledge structures.* Hillsdale, NJ: Erlbaum.

Smith, E. E., & Medin, D. L. (1981). *Categories and concepts.* Cambridge, MA: Harvard University Press.

Smith, E. E., Shoben, E. J., & Rips, L. J. (1974). Structure and process in semantic memory: A featural model for semantic decisions. *Psychological Review, 81,* 214–241.

Spalding, T. L., & Ross, B. H. (1994). Comparison-based learning: Effects of comparing instances during category learning. *Journal of Experimental Psychology: Learning, Memory, and Cognition, 20,* 1251–1263.

Tanaka, J. W., & Taylor, M. E. (1991). Object categories and expertise: Is the basic level in the eye of the beholder? *Cognitive Psychology, 23,* 457–482.

Wattenmaker, W. D. (1995). Knowledge structures and linear separability: Integrating information in object and social categorization. *Cognitive Psychology, 28,* 274–328.

Whittlesea, B. W. A. (1987). Preservation of specific experiences in the representation of general knowledge. *Journal of Experimental Psychology: Learning, Memory, and Cognition, 13,* 3–17.

III

Methodology in Cognition

8

Computational Modeling of High-Level Cognition versus Hypothesis Testing

Patricia A. Carpenter and Marcel Adam Just

Computational modeling in cognitive science and artificial intelligence has profoundly affected how the human mind is viewed and how it is studied. This chapter examines some recent contributions of computational modeling to the analysis of high-level human cognition, particularly language, problem solving, reasoning, and learning. We will situate computational modeling within the broader framework of cognitive science by discussing four topics:

1. *AI's approach.* This section describes how computational approaches contribute to the understanding of theoretical issues in cognitive science. We will illustrate the point by describing how the computer chess programs, including Deep Blue, compare and contrast with human chess expertise.

2. *Cognitive architectures.* We will argue that computational modeling has shaped the concept of cognitive architecture. We will briefly describe three types of architectures: symbolic, connectionist, and hybrid, and we will consider how the concept of cognitive architecture frames the issue of modularity.

3. *Computational models.* We will describe some computational models and architectures that address high-level cognition, including sentence and text comprehension and intelligent tutoring in mathematics, and the use of modeling in the analysis of neuropsychological impairments and individual variation.

4. *Evaluating models and modeling.* We will describe some of the issues that arise in evaluating the adequacy of computational models in comparison to evaluating verbal models. We will also discuss some of the strengths and weaknesses of the modeling approach to understanding human cognition.

Before we describe specific models, it is useful to consider modeling as a scientific approach and how it relates to other approaches. We will argue that computational modeling as an approach reflects a shared assumption about scientific goals and methods. *The assumption is that it is useful to specify cognitive mechanisms in detail by using computational systems and to test the sufficiency of those mechanisms for performing some task in ways that are analogous (at some level) to human performance.* The goal of providing a detailed mechanistic account (using computational formalisms) distinguishes modeling from some other approaches, such as verbal models, mathematical formalisms, or flowchart models, that may indicate the general sequence and type of processes without specifying their representation or processing characteristics. Specifically, the modeling approach contrasts with the hypothesis-testing approach to scientific inquiry. The hypothesis-testing approach poses either-or questions, such as Does some factor have a significant effect or not? or Is some characteristic present or not? Such questions and the associated approach are ultimately compatible with modeling because modeling builds on such empirical findings. But the modeling doesn't start with the yes-no question or stop with the single piece of information. Rather, a model begins by focusing on the mechanisms that might underlie a particular process. Also, the computational format enables more precision and more complexity in specifying such mechanisms than does a verbal description. Perhaps more subtly, the computational approach promotes a different view of the theoretical issues and goals of cognitive science than those views promoted by the hypothesis-testing approach.

AI's Approach: An Example from Chess

The primary focus of the chapter is on computational models that have taken account of human cognitive constraints, rather than the broader domain of artificial intelligence (AI), the study of the principles by which computers achieve complex goals. Nevertheless, it is useful to consider AI's approach more abstractly. Our argument is that such models can provide insights into human cognition that are analogous to the insights that come from the comparative study of different species in perception.

Different computational models may be contrasted with each other and with what is known about the human system to provide a more abstract view of what mechanisms are sufficient for complex problem solving, their strengths and weaknesses, and their relations to the overall constellation of computer and human abilities.

Human Chess Experts

A timely illustration of this point comes from the research on chess. Human chess experts use relatively shallow searches, averaging only three or four moves deep, and even that search is highly guided by their recognition of the larger patterns associated with good moves (Charness, 1991; Chase & Simon, 1973). This characterization of chess expertise arose from research showing that experts (but not novices) could rapidly encode and reproduce chess board configurations, as long as the configurations were legal and meaningful; their advantage over the novice evaporated if the configurations were not legal (Chase & Simon, 1973; de Groot, 1965). The interpretation of such data was that experts acquire tens of thousands of patterns through their experience in playing chess, much as a reader learns to rapidly recognize words. The board's configurations evoke a small set of appropriate possible moves that are then evaluated. By contrast, searching through all of the possible outcomes of a variety of legal moves would run into the cognitive bottleneck of working memory limitations, as well as whatever time limitations were imposed by the playing conditions. Although recognition, search, and evaluation are all components of chess expertise (and of problem solving more generally), this research indicates that recognition has a much larger role than search in the human expert's performance.

How Chess Programs Work

In contrast to the human expert, some of the most successful chess-playing programs rely on extensive searches of possible moves and possible countermoves; move time can be minimized by optimizing search speed and organization. Beginning with the earliest chess-playing programs in the 1950s, brute force methods have been relatively successful in chess, although they do not work as well for games such as Go or Backgammon, which involve higher branching factors (more choices at each decision point). Most successful chess programs rely on both deep searches (following the consequences of a particular path) and wide searches (considering many different possible paths), searching all alternatives at a node except those that can be mathematically eliminated as having nothing to do with the solution. Such searches require keeping track of several pieces of information, including what has been tried, the best move in each position, and the depth to which a subtree of possible moves is searched (Berliner & Eberling, 1989). Then these alternatives must be compared and evaluated to select the best move. So, chess programs exploit search and evaluation more than recognition. Obviously, the storage and computation demands of this type of exhaustive search would be mentally too costly for the human. For the machine, search speed is highly dependent on the hardware.

These contrasting architectural features contributed to the fascination of the 1996 and 1997 chess tournaments between IBM's Deep Blue program and the world chess champion, Gary Kasparov. Deep Blue's 32 parallel processors evaluated millions of positions a second, allowing it in 1996 to win the first of the six matches and draw game three. Kasparov's victories in the last three games emerged from his metaskill, his ability to analyze Deep Blue's type of understanding, and adapt his own playing to his conception of Deep Blue's approach (Byrne, 1996). Kasparov and his advisor claimed that Deep Blue evidenced an understanding of the game, a nascent form of intelligence, although of a different character than that of the human's, concluding "Somewhere out there, mere tactics are translating into strategy. This is the closest thing I've seen to computer intelligence. It's a weird form of intelligence, the beginning of intelligence" (Weber, 1996). Although for Deep Blue, search and evaluation processes played a much bigger role than recognition, it was able to challenge the skills arising from a different architecture, the human's. In the 1997 rematch, Deep Blue's search power was increased by a factor of two, so that it evaluated 200 million moves per second. Kasparov's first win was equalled by Deep Blue's win in game two. This was followed by three draws. Then Deep Blue won the sixth game after only 19 moves, and Kasparov was forced to concede to the machine.

The chess matches also highlight the issue of the nature of intelligence and how we will know it when we see it in computational devices. Playing expert-level chess was accepted as a benchmark of artificial intelligence at an earlier time, and the media attention paid to the Kasparov–Deep Blue matches suggests that chess is still a benchmark for journalists and perhaps for the general public. However, 40 years have intervened since computers first started performing complex problem solving, and chess' as a benchmark usefulness has been questioned by some. One reason is that chess is a computational task, albeit an incredibly complex one for humans. But whether Deep Blue (or its successors) shows evidence of intelligence is not the main reason for discussing the match. Rather, the point is to illustrate how the comparison and contrast of different computational architectures (in this case, Deep Blue's and Kasparov's) can stimulate a more abstract view of what mechanisms may enable complex behavior. The argument is that computational models, even pure artificial intelligence models, help crystallize the dimensions that underlie intelligence, including human intelligence. In this chapter, we will focus on computational models that, more directly than Deep Blue, simulate the mechanisms in human cognition.

Cognitive Architectures

One of the impacts of computational modeling is its influence on the broader view that is taken toward defining the goals of cognitive science. In particular, modeling has made the cognitive architecture of the mind a central concern (Pylyshyn, 1991). *Computer architecture* is an earlier metaphor that referred to the design of a computer system in architectural terms, by specifying the system's basic components or resources (memories, processing units, instruction sets, communication channels) and their organization. *Cognitive architecture* refers to the design of the mind in analogous terms. Like a computer architecture, a cognitive architecture permits many different procedures and data structures to be constructed and used within it, but the nature of the procedures and data structures is constrained by (and cannot be defined independently of) the architecture. In this section, we will describe three architectures—symbolic, connectionist, and hybrid—that combine features of both symbolic and connectionist architectures.

Symbolic architectures

Modern computational modeling of cognition was initially grounded in the symbolic architectures, which trace their ancestry to digital computers in the post–World War II era and the 1950s research on complex problem solving, such as proving logic theorems, recognizing patterns, and game playing. It was with symbolic models that researchers first saw the ability of a computer model to demonstrate complex, high-level processing beyond numerical calculation, and hence, to be capable of revealing aspects of human thought. An abstract characterization of a computational system is the notion of a symbol system. A symbol system has patterns that provide access to distal symbol structures, has a memory, and has operations that transform input symbols into output symbols (Newell, Rosenbloom, & Laird, 1989).

Perhaps the most fundamental contribution of symbolic computational modeling has been the *physical symbol system hypothesis,* explicitly stated by Newell and Simon (1976, p. 118), that "a physical symbol system has the necessary and sufficient means for general intelligent action." Problem solving, deductive reasoning, and language processing are examples *par excellence* of symbolic domains, and the ability of computer simulations to model such processes was interpreted as an existence proof of the broader claim that a symbol system is at the center of human intelligence. Many of the concepts at the heart of symbolic computational modeling are the same ones that enabled the construal of the human mind as a complex information-processing system, such as the concepts of hierarchies, variables, heuristic strategies, and the fundamental concept of a symbol and the associated idea of combinatorial expressive power that comes from organizing symbols, as in natural language (Lindsay, 1991).

Production Systems   One of the key types of symbolic architecture is the *production system* (Hunt, 1989; Newell & Simon, 1972). A production system has several components, but at the heart of it are the productions, which are *if-then* rules. The *if* part states a condition and the *then* part gives an action that should be taken if the condition is satisfied. For example, a production might be "If there is the problem 2 + 2 = ?, then say 4." The productions encode the knowledge of the domain, in this case, a math fact. A production system also has a database that represents the state of the external world or what is in the individual's immediate memory. The productions are described as "firing" when the condition side elements (the *if* side) match the elements in the database. So if the model encodes the problem "2 + 2 = ?" the *if* side of a production will be matched, and the production will fire and retrieve the action, namely, the sum of 4. According to this construal, if certain conditions arise in working memory, then the associated cognitive actions are performed.

One of the useful properties of production systems is that the productions are modular forms of knowledge, more modular than the way comparable knowledge would be coded in a conventional program. Consequently, new knowledge can be added without drastically changing the system's performance. For example, in the case of math knowledge, each new math fact (2 + 2 = 4, 2 + 3 = 5, 2 + 4 = 6, etc.) could be coded by a separate production without altering the productions that represent other math facts. (This is just an illustration of its potential modularity.)

In a production system, the flow of control emerges from the content of the productions interacting with the environment. The elements that are already present in working memory or newly created will determine which production fires next. If only one production is assumed to fire at a time (which is not true in all production system architectures), then there must be some conflict resolution process that selects which production will fire from among those that are potentially enabled.

A production system architecture can be viewed as a general set of principles, a theoretical and methodological toolkit, that can be used to construct models of various specific tasks. The development of individual models depends not only on the constraints imposed by the architecture, but also on an analysis of the task that specifies what processes occur and what representation would be plausible. It is the performance and characteristics of the individual models that are then related to the analogous human performance.

An Example   Production system architectures have been used to model many types of processes, such as language understanding, problem solving, complex spatial reasoning, and so on. To provide a concrete example of one, consider a "toy" model that constructs a syntactic representation of a sentence. This toy model would actually be one part of a larger system that processed language. Its goal is to take the successive words of a sentence and develop a phrase-structure representation that specifies which constituents represent noun phrases, which represent the verb phrases, and so on. For example, one production recognizes the syntactic category of words such as *the* and *a* (articles) that are followed by nouns; its action is to represent that such combinations are noun phrases. The production could be expressed as "Article + Noun → Noun Phrase." The noun phrase, in turn, could be part of the action side for another production, such as "Noun Phrase + Verb Phrase (intransitive) → Clause." (For those readers who have studied linguistics, note that each production corresponds to a context-independent rewrite rule: Allen, 1995.)

Table 8.1 gives a sample set of productions that has been simplified by eliminating some of the implementational details. These productions would do a syntactic-based parse of some simple sentences, such as "The dog bit one cat," if implemented with a lexicon that coded the syntactic

Table 8.1
Sample parsing productions

P1	((Article) + (Noun))	→	(Noun Phrase)
P2	((Number) + (Noun))	→	(Noun Phrase)
P3	(Noun)	→	(Noun Phrase)
P4	(Verb(intransitive))	→	(Verb Phrase)
P5	((Verb(transitive)) + (Noun Phrase))	→	(Verb Phrase)
P6	((Noun Phrase) + (Verb Phrase))	→	(Clause)

A Trace of the Sequence of Productions in Parsing the Sample Sentence
"The dog bit one cat."

P1	((Article) + (Noun))	→	(Noun Phrase)
P1	((The) + (dog))	→	(The dog)
P2	((Number) + (Noun))	→	(Noun Phrase)
P2	((one) + (cat))	→	(one cat)
P5	((Verb(transitive)) + (Noun Phrase))	→	(Verb Phrase)
P5	((bit) + (one cat))	→	(bit (one cat))
P6	((Noun Phrase) + (Verb Phrase))	→	(Clause)
P6	((The dog) + (bit (one cat)))	→	((The dog) (bit(one cat)))

and semantic properties of individual words (such as *the, one, dog, bit, wild, cat,* etc.). This system is still incomplete in that there is no representation of the feedforward expectations; for example, when a reader encounters a transitive verb, an expectation is set up for a noun-phrase object. Nevertheless, the sample model conveys how a production system works.

One interesting aspect of such a model is that it makes salient the step-by-step processing from the beginning state of the problem to the goal state, in this case, from the first word to the representation of the entire sentence. The latter part of table 8.1 shows the successive productions that would be evoked by the successive words in the sample sentence in the sample parsing model.

All of the possible ways to get from a starting point to a goal constitute a theoretical construct called a *problem space* (Newell & Simon, 1972). In the sample parsing model, a noun phrase can begin either with an article or a quantifier or with neither; so there are at least three possible paths to this node in the problem space. (The problem space is equivalent to a transition network grammar.) The sequence of operations can be thought of as a path through the problem space. The productions evoke the successive operations, going from one state to the next in the problem space. The trace of the successive processes of the model can sometimes be compared to traces of the human's successive processes (as inferred from data such as the participant's eye fixations or think-aloud comments). In fact, we will show that the temporal characteristics of readers' eye fixations as they go through a sentence are well captured by a model that has a production system architecture.

The productions' actions involve operations that can be interpreted symbolically, such as creating representations, modifying them, and associating one element with another. There are several aspects of the example production system that are not invariant characteristics of this architecture. First, the representations used in the example are composed of unitary symbols, but it is possible to use representations that consist of features. Second, in the example, the production only fired if the condition side perfectly matched the elements in working memory. However, the system might allow productions to fire if there are "partial matches" between the condition in the production and the elements in the database.

Third, the action was described as occurring in a single cycle of processing, when the production fired. However, actions can occur gradually over successive cycles rather than in a single cycle, as in connectionist models. Fourth, the production system can be a serial one, as illustrated here, in which only one production fires at a time. Alternatively, some production system architectures allow multiple productions to perform at least some actions in parallel (Holland, Holyoak, Nisbett, & Thagard, 1986; Thibadeau, Just, & Carpenter, 1982).

The rule-based formalism of production systems has been extraordinarily useful in artificial intelligence, not only in theoretical models but also in AI applications, including expert systems. *Expert systems* are programs for performing practical tasks, such as prescribing antibiotics or configuring computers, that require expertise but not necessarily subtle insights (Charniak & McDermott, 1985). The production rules encode the various contingencies that represent the relevant features of the problems and actions associated with certain configurations of conditions. However, neither the representation nor the processing is necessarily intended to be analogous to those of a human expert. In fact, some expert systems are intended as aids to the human decision maker. We will revisit the contrast between expert systems and psychological models in a later section on intelligent tutoring. Here, the point is simply that this approach has had a major role in both cognitive science and AI applications.

Connectionist Architectures

Another type of architecture encompasses connectionist models, which are networks of parallel-computing elements in which each element (or node) has an associated activation value that is computed from the values of its input. These elements are often conceptualized as being subsymbolic—either features, microfeatures, or uninterpretable primitives. The elements are interconnected through connections that have numerical weights to indicate the strength and polarity (positive or negative) of the relation between the connected elements. An important property of connectionist models is that the operations are numerical ones, representing only increments or decrements in activation or connection weights, rather than operations that can be interpreted symbolically.

A familiar example of a connectionist model is the *interactive activation model* (IAM) of word recognition (McClelland & Rumelhart, 1988), which was developed to explain why people are more accurate at detecting a letter (such as "A") in a word (e.g., "WART") than in a comparable nonword (e.g., "RAWT"). The model has representations of individual letters and words. The connection weights between the letter representations and the word representation are higher than the weights between letters and a representation of an arbitrary nonword. A graphic depiction of this type of model is shown in figure 8.1. The nodes represent networks that process information at successively more abstract levels, with feed-forward and feedback links. If a word is presented, the activation of its letters feeds forward to increase the activation of the word representations, which immediately feeds back activation to the letter

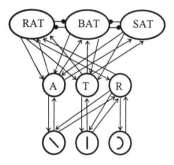

Figure 8.1
A schematic depiction of the various levels in a typical connectionist model, patterned after the interactive activation model (IAM) of word perception that proposes a mechanism that accounts for why the letters of a word are perceived faster and more accurately than the letters of a nonword (McClelland & Rumelhart, 1988). The nodes, representing features, letters, and words, are linked by feedforward and feedback connections. There are also interword inhibitory connections because the encoding of the word *rat* is incompatible with encoding *bat* or *sat* in the same location. When a word is presented, the activation from letter features and letters feeds forward to the activation of the word representation, which in turn feeds back activation to the letter and letter feature levels. By contrast, for nonwords there is no higher-order unit to activate, and so the letters constituting a nonword cannot receive activation from the word level. Thus, words and their constituent letters are perceived faster and more accurately than nonwords and their constituent letters.

level, improving their discriminability from other letters. For example, activation from the letters "R," "A," "T" begin to activate the word "RAT" and almost instantaneously, activation from "RAT" feeds back to increase the activation of the individual letters, as shown in figure 8.1. In the nonword condition there is no higher-level word representation to feed back activation to the letter-level representation. Indeed, the feedback from the word representations to the letter level is crucial to the empirical effect called "the word superiority" effect (Richman & Simon, 1989). This model has the nodes, feedforward and feedback links, and numerical operations that characterize this connectionist architecture.

Connectionist models trace back at least to the 1950s and Rosenblatt's research on *perceptrons,* which were parallel visual-recognition devices. As Minsky and Papert (1969) noted about the initial explorations of the approach, "The popularity of the perceptron as a model for an intelligent, general-purpose learning machine has roots, we think, in an image of the brain itself as a rather loosely organized, randomly interconnected network of relatively simple devices" (p. 18). In the meantime, researchers have found that the brain is not loosely organized in the sense that the networks are not randomly interconnected. Nevertheless, the link between connectionist models and this view of the brain's organization persists. Indeed, it is the emergent structure of the connectionist networks and the highly structured organization of the brain that now appears to provide a rationale for thinking that this type of model may help mediate between cognitive science and neural science.

Since the initial exploration of connectionist models, the incorporation of several powerful mechanisms has greatly extended the scope and usefulness of this architecture. One set of such mechanisms includes various learning algorithms that are not themselves intended to be models of human learning, but that, nevertheless, allow a model's links to acquire weights that reflect the contingencies among the stimuli that the model processes. For example, with one such learning algorithm, called *backpropagation,* the weights between elements that result in some "correct" output are gradually increased, and the weights between elements that are incorrect are decreased. Over successive cycles, the model's weights are tuned to reflect the contingencies in the stimulus set. This acquisition phase may be prior to the main simulation and not constitute part of what is being modeled, except indirectly. Another powerful mechanism is the inclusion of multiple levels of *hidden units,* levels of representations between the input level and the output level. The pattern of weights, the number of units, and the connectivity of the hidden units can strongly influence a model's properties and, in fact, can be crucial to a model's success. The so-called hidden units can be ultimately the source of the model's ability to reflect very complex contingencies in the environment, and they are often the source of some of the more interesting emergent properties.

There has been a tendency for some cognitive scientists to align themselves with the symbolic or connectionist approach and, in some cases, to devalue the other approach. Although connectionist models have already proven themselves to be useful formalisms for modeling perceptual processes, their ultimate role or sufficiency for modeling high-level cognitive processes, such as language and problem solving, is not clear (e.g., Smolensky, 1988; Touretzky, 1988). One major issue has been whether connectionist models are sufficiently powerful to capture the expressiveness and recursion inherent in language (see Bever, 1992; Fodor & Plyshyn, 1988; Kim, Marcus, Pinker, Hollander, et al. 1994; Pinker & Prince, 1988; and others in *Cognition,* 1988, and *Brain and Behavioral Science,* 1988). However, because the development of new computational formalisms is an active research area, the assessment of the ultimate contribution of the approach is a matter of conjecture. Moreover, there is an increasing number of hybrid models that incorporate significant features from both approaches.

Hybrid Models

An increasing number of computational models combine features of connectionist and symbolic architectures. Hybrid models may achieve the power of symbolic models with some of the attractive features of the connectionist systems (Bechtel & Abrahamsen, 1991). For example, in some connectionist models, featural elements (or subsymbolic units) are functionally bound together so that they act as a symbol, which is the equivalent of a symbolic representation. In one type of linguistic inference model, the units that correspond to a single referent are bound together through synchronous firing (Shastri & Ajjanagadde, 1993). Also, some symbolic architectures incorporate some of the attractive properties of the connectionist approach. In a hybrid architecture that we will discuss in more detail, the symbolic elements have activation levels associated with them, and productions take actions by manipulating activation levels (Thibadeau et al., 1982). Hence, there is not an absolute dichotomy between the two approaches. As we will show in the "Computational Models of Higher-Level Processing" section, the two architectures are completely compatible abstractions, which suggests that a wise scientific strategy is to figure out their interrelation, rather than to choose between them.

The concept of a cognitive architecture has made it possible to reconsider a variety of other specific issues in light of each other and in light of the larger system that encompasses them all. Some of these issues are new, but some have roots that long predate computational modeling (such as whether representations are discrete or analog and whether short-term memory is structurally separate from long-term memory). One such issue we will consider next is what constitutes a basic module in the architecture.

Sharpening Conceptual Issues: Cognitive Modules
The concept of cognitive architecture has sharpened the debate relevant to several issues, and one example is the issue of cognitive modularity. It has sometimes been proposed that the mind might consist of a set of cognitive modules, each of which is an autonomous subsystem. The processing of each module is hypothesized to be uninfluenced by certain classes of information that may be present elsewhere in the system (Fodor, 1983; Garfield, 1987). This lack of influence, called *informational encapsulation,* is the single most distinguishing operating characteristic of a cognitive module. One of Fodor's examples is the encapsulation of visual motion perception from certain types of kinesthetic information. When a person nudges her own eye with her finger, she sees the world moving. The information about the finger movement is apparently not available to or not used by the processes that interpret input from the retina, even though some part of the cognitive system "knows" the motion is not real. The rationale Fodor offers for encapsulation is that modular systems have to operate rapidly (without allocating time to consider all possible rele-

vant information), somewhat like a reflex. Fodor considers the syntactic processing of language to constitute a module that is encapsulated from nonsyntactic information, such as the pragmatic context or background world knowledge. These other information sources are ultimately brought to bear on the interpretation of a sentence—not on the syntactic processing itself (according to modularity theory)—but at some later stage. Of course, an important consideration is that modularity can only be defined with respect to a time period (Carpenter, Miyake, & Just, 1995). A process that is encapsulated for 10 to 20 ms may be interactive when viewed from the vantage of a 50 to 100 ms unit. More generally, if the analysis has a 50-ms resolution, then a finer interval of encapsulation (say 10 ms) is not detectable and perhaps not meaningful. One of the contributions of empirical research on eye fixations during reading has been to demonstrate that readers spend more time on certain types of anomalous words and phrases before going on to the successive words and phrases (Carpenter & Daneman, 1981; Carpenter & Just, 1983; Just & Carpenter, 1980). Consequently, any encapsulation must be brief relative to the time to comprehend a whole sentence. In addition, this issue has been addressed by various computational models.

Fodor's encapsulation hypothesis is an example of how the perspective of cognitive architecture has influenced the framing of some important concepts. The issue of what constitutes a module and its relation to behavior has been illuminated by computational models in the context of cognitive neuropsychology where the problem of identifying cognitive modules has relied on the interpretation of behavioral dissociations. The logic of interpreting behavioral dissociations is as follows: if after a particular lesion, patient X shows a behavioral deficit (an inability to perform the task) whenever process x is required and no other deficits, and following some different lesion, patient Y shows a deficit whenever process y is required and no other deficits, then the processes of x and y can be dissociated from each other. In addition, x and y are typically at the "same" level of analysis and represent relatively fine descriptions (how "fine" is an issue). For example, two such candidate "modules" are the processes for representing the pictorial features of a visual image versus the processes for mentally rotating and manipulating an image.

Although the logic sounds compelling, there are both practical and theoretical difficulties in linking behavioral deficits to cognitive modules (see Kosslyn & Van Kleeck, 1990; Miyake, Carpenter, & Just, 1995; Shallice, 1988). Computational modeling has contributed to understanding those difficulties by demonstrating that the mapping between the behavioral impairment and the module need not be straightforward. Indeed, communication between two "modules" in connectionist architectures with feedforward and feedback mechanisms *should not* result in completely dissociable behavioral impairments (Farah & McClelland, 1991). The explorations of the model's behavior demonstrated that the mapping between behavior and the interpretation vis-à-vis potential modules requires much more specification than what a verbal description provides. Later, we will consider another computational perspective on the issue of cognitive modules.

Computational Models of Higher-Level Processes

In this section, we will briefly describe several architectures and models of higher-level cognition, focusing on two key characteristics: the mechanisms they propose and the way in which the model is mapped onto human performance. A second goal of this section is to illustrate some of the domains in which modeling has been pursued, from language comprehension, to intelligent tutoring, to the analysis of neuropsychological deficits and individual differences.

The Capacity-Constrained Activation Theory

One of the more interesting and important issues for psychology is to determine what internal limits account for the obvious and pervasive constraints on thinking. Even as simple a task as mental multiplication of multidigit numbers is effortful and errorful, because it requires that symbolic operations be executed at the same time as partial products are being retained in working memory. Such limits, which can be construed as capacity constraints on working memory, are the bottleneck in the operational throughput of thought. Part of what must emerge in cognitive research is a theory of the architectural constraints on various resources.

Working memory plays a central role in all forms of complex thinking, such as reasoning, problem solving, and language comprehension. However, its function in language comprehension is especially evident because comprehension entails integrating the meanings of a sequence of words and phrases whose processing is distributed over time. Our own recent research (Just & Carpenter, 1992) examines the implications of an architecture that limits the amount of total resources available for processing the successive words of a sentence and maintaining the partial products as needed.

The theory of the capacity-constrained architecture is that of an activation-based production system, 3CAPS; the acronym stands for capacity-constrained concurrent activation-based production system. As is the case with conventional production systems, the procedural knowledge in 3CAPS consists of a set of modules called productions, each of which is a condition-action contingency that specifies what symbolic manipulation should be made when a given pattern of information arises in working memory. However, 3CAPS deviates in at least three ways from conventional production systems in that it uses mechanisms common to activation-based parallel models. First, each representation has an activation level that reflects the accessibility of the representation in working memory. An activation level changes when a production either causes it to increase or decrease in increments or when there is a global deallocation of activation, as will be described. Only if the activation level of an element is above some threshold is it effectively "in" working memory and, consequently, available to enable a production to fire. Second, the processing is graded, in that the productions do their work gradually, over several cycles of the production system's operation, each time incrementally changing the activation level of an element, by repeatedly propagating activation from a source element to an output element. This propagation occurs reiteratively over successive processing cycles, until the activation of the output element reaches some threshold or some other event stops the production from firing. Third, 3CAPS allows multiple productions to fire in parallel in a given cycle, as long as their conditions are met.

The 3CAPS architecture provides one tantalizing solution to the question of how symbolic and connectionist models relate to each other. At

Table 8.2

Gaze durations of a typical reader (in ms)

```
384    267              884      300      333     333              517
```
Another answer to the ever-intriguing question of pyramid construction has been suggested.
```
      267     283        200  350 283 283 733     333 266    183     467  200
```
The Egyptian Engineer of 5,000 years ago may have used a simple wooden device called a
```
 1201          333        367  1151    583      568          417  267 183   217
```
weightarm for handling the 2½ to 7 ton pyramid blocks. The weightarm is like a lever or beam
```
 600 167 200 617        383             300        550 234 217  200      650    117
```
pivoting on a fulcrum. Hundreds of weightarms may have been needed for each pyramid.
```
      267     367      250 283       234 384     216    350      267     250  433
```
Weightarms may have been used to lift the blocks off the barges which came from the upriver
```
 899      300        400        217 217 633  83  383          634        350    333
```
quarries. Also, they would be needed to transfer the blocks to skid roads leading to the base and for
```
 333      267 267  550        317        350 100 350    317         367  333
```
lifting the blocks onto sledges. The sledges were hauled up greased tracks to the working levels.
```
 267      766        350      350 217    333  300      333        333      350   400
```
Again, weightarms were used to pick up the blocks from the sledges and put them on skidways
```
             316            437    2150
```
where workers pulled them to their placements.

Source: From Carpenter and Just (1983, p. 278).

the highest levels, 3CAPS looks like a production system, with symbolic conditions and actions; for example, one such production might relate an earlier noun phrase to a verb. However, successively nested within a condition are other conditions and actions. At the lowest levels, these nested condition-action relations are connectionist networks, such as a network for word encoding and lexical access.

This architecture can be further illustrated by considering how the model accounts for the time a reader spends on successive words of a text, as shown in table 8.2. Above each word is the gaze duration (the total time of successive fixations on a word) for a typical college student reading a technical article on pyramids from a news magazine (Carpenter & Just, 1983; Just & Carpenter, 1980). This reader (who was asked not to reread) spent 384 ms on the opening word; he then spent 1201 ms on the initial mention of the topic word, *weightarm*, at the beginning of line 3, 899 ms on *quarries* (end of sentence 5), and 2150 ms at the end of the paragraph. We can analyze the word-level, phrase-level, clause-level, and sentence- and text-level factors that influence the duration of such gazes, averaged over a large number of texts and readers (Carpenter & Just, 1983). This analysis shows that the time readers spend on a

word strongly reflects the properties of the word (its length and frequency). These measures reflect the operation of the lower levels of the
hierarchy (word encoding and lexical access), processes initiated and
largely terminated before the next word is encoded. Other processes (such
as the syntactic-binding processes that identifies the words *The dog* as a
noun phrase) may be initiated when the first word is encoded, but only
completed when both words have been represented. Finally, at the highest
levels, processes such as relating the whole sentence to the representation
of the whole situation, may be initiated when the important thematic
words are encoded, but may only be completed after the entire sentence
is read. The principle stating that processes at multiple levels are initiated
and completed as soon as possible is the principle of *immediacy* (Just &
Carpenter, 1980), and it characterizes much of cognitive thought. Thus,
to account for the processing at these many levels, one needs an architecture in which the various levels of productions (from word encoding to
text-level representation) are cascaded and nested.

Figure 8.2 shows a schematic depiction of the kinds of processes generated during the left-to-right processing by a typical reader (such as the
one whose fixations are shown in table 8.2). On line 1, the reader fixates
the word *Another,* encodes it, and retrieves its meaning; these low-level
processes are represented by short feedforward and feedback arrows. At
the same time, some weak expectations are generated about the possible
upcoming syntactic category because *Another* must modify a noun. These
expectations are represented by arrows pointing to the next word or
words. On line 2, the next three words are encoded and syntactically
and semantically related to each other. The word *answer* is a noun and
compatible with the syntactic expectations and makes sense with the semantics, so activation is fed back to the representation of the initial
phrase, represented by a feedback arc. In addition, the words *to the* begin
a prepositional phrase, setting up an expectation that at some point there
will be a head noun. The expectation is represented by a large feedforward arc pointing to some future positions. In step 3, the reader encodes
the phrase *ever intriguing,* represents it as a modifier in the prepositional
phrase being constructed, and feeds back activation to the developing
representation. In line 4, the reader encodes *question,* which is a possible
head for the prepositional phrase, and so feeds back activation to that

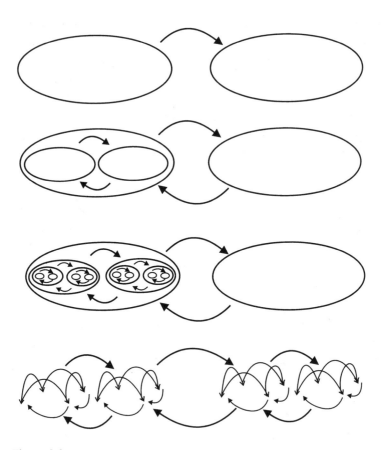

Figure 8.2

A schematic depiction of the patterns of feedforward and feedback activation that occurs as a reader goes from left to right in reading a text, such as the passage in table 8.2 about pyramid construction. As an example, consider the processes underlying the first four gazes shown in table 8.2. Each line shows the word or words that are being encoded, whereas the surrounding words are represented by blanks. The short arcs that feedforward and back to that lexical concept represent visual encoding and lexical access of the word being fixated. Weaker and more distant relations are represented by arcs that point farther ahead or farther back. Each line represents a successive gaze on the sentence. The point is that as the sentence is read, there is a cascaded series of processes that cuts across multiple levels, from encoding, to lexical access, to constructing a representation of a phrase or a clause, and even to forming causal models or scientific explanations. Thus, at the lowest levels, the 3CAPS reading model resembles a connectionist model of word recognition; however, this level is embedded within increasingly higher levels that represent syntactic, semantic, text-level, and schematic processes.

part of the representation and may set up the weak expectation that the entire subject phrase has been encoded. The point of illustrating these successive steps is to show that multiple and overlapping cascaded processes are initiated at each word and phrase.

This example also allows us to explain one way of viewing the relation between the two major proposed architectures, the connectionist and symbolic, as represented by a production system. As figure 8.2 shows, one might view each sequential operation as initiating a cascaded set of processes that, at the lower levels, looks remarkably like the word perception model described earlier. However, this word encoding only addresses one, low-level set of processes, whereas cognition cascades these processes, building up to larger and slower processes, such as those concerned with syntactic, semantic, and text-level processes and on up to referential and schematic processes. At the highest levels, reading a whole introductory sentence might set up certain expectations about how the explanation will proceed, and it might cause the reader to retrieve some relevant facts. Naturally, the higher levels will tend to take longer, their processes will appear to be serial, and their activation basis may be less apparent, though no less real. Thus, at each level, the presence of certain types of elements will initiate certain types of expectations (or actions), which sounds much like the mechanisms underlying symbolic production systems.

This architecture suggests that it is, in part, the abstractness, or grain size, of the analysis that appears to differentiate symbolic and connectionist formalisms. Figure 8.3 gives a schematic depiction of how 3CAPS mediates the transition from symbolic architectures (at the top) to neural nets (at the bottom), with the cascaded hybrid model depicted in the middle. At the highest level, the 3CAPS architecture closely resembles the classic symbolic architecture of production systems that consist of condition-action rules and which Newell and Simon (1972) and others have found so useful in accounting for complex problem solving. At this level, the productions are condition-action rules. In complex problem-solving domains, the total time for the actions of such productions to reach threshold is relatively long, and such cognitive actions are very resource demanding. By contrast, at the more embedded levels of 3CAPS, the productions begin to resemble the structures in the connectionist

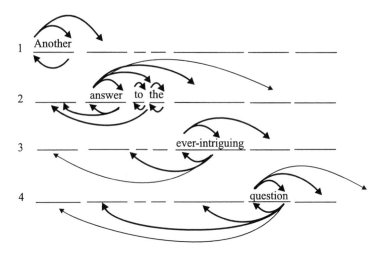

Figure 8.3
A schematic depiction of the various levels in 3CAPS, showing how its connectionist architecture spans between the symbolic production-system architecture and low-level neural networks. 3CAPS itself is a nested, activation-based formalism (which is well represented at the second level). One of the embedded levels can be seen to resemble the interactive activation model, described earlier. At the lowest level, we have represented the parallel, embedded neural circuits that are represented by symbols in 3CAPS. At higher levels, the architecture reveals its relation to that of production systems. The difference is that production systems typically are not activation based and do not operate in parallel; nor do they have resource constraints. The graphic depiction suggests that 3CAPS spans the levels of these formalisms, which may represent different levels of abstraction.

interactive-activation model of word recognition. The intermediate models contain productions expressing processes at many grains, for example, from letter and word encoding to sentence processing. The low-level productions, represented here as embedded loops, are rapid and require few resources. At the bottom of figure 8.3 we have depicted something like the neural nets. The point of including the neural net is to indicate that the nodes and links in the higher levels are isomorphic to neural circuits. The spatial and temporal pattern of relations at this finer level gives rise to what is represented by the nodes and links at the higher level. Thus, 3CAPS claims that the cognitive architecture is a nested and cascaded unified system and that the distinctions between symbolic and connectionist architectures partly represents a difference in the grain size of the theoretical analysis.

Capacity Constraint   A central feature of 3CAPS is its capacity constraint, the claim that all of thinking from the lowest to highest levels is limited by resource consumption. Specifically, 3CAPS proposes that a limited pool of activation mediates both processing and storage. In language, there are resources for language processing and storage; in spatial reasoning, there are separable resources for spatial reasoning and storage. If on some cycle of processing, the total demand for activation for both storage and processing exceeds the allowable maximum, then either processing or storage can be scaled back. The scaling back on processing means that less activation is available during a particular cycle of processing, so processing slows down. The scaling back on storage means that less activation is available to maintain activated elements, allowing them to fall below threshold and effectively be forgotten. Storage in working memory is fueled by activation because the strength of each representational element is determined by its associated activation level. An element can represent a word, a phrase, a proposition, a grammatical structure, a thematic structure, an object in the external world, and so on. The use of the activation level construct here is similar to its widespread use in connectionist models in that it is used as a way to gradually operate on information. The activation is used for information maintenance, and it is also the commodity that underlies computation. The computations are performed within a production system architecture, in which productions manipulate symbols by modifying their activation levels or by constructing new elements. That is, the computations occur over time (cycles of computational operation) in which some action element's activation level is increased or decreased in increments. Thus, one measure of the model's performance is the number of cycles it takes to complete some computation. Processes that take more cycles to be completed can be considered more difficult, and the cycle count can be related to the processing time of the human.

A Model of Sentence Processing   An example of the application of this approach has been in accounting for the profile of processing times when people are reading sentences that vary in linguistic complexity (Just & Carpenter, 1992). College students take longer to read sentences that are linguistically more complex, such as "The senator that the reporter attacked defended the expenditures in the hotel." Much of the additional time occurs at the verbs because the comprehender must figure out who is doing what to whom. Moreover, in this linguistic construction, the process is complicated by the fact that the nouns play different semantic roles in the two clauses. By contrast, a superficially similar sentence in which the nouns have the same roles is understood more quickly, such as "The senator that attacked the reporter defended the expenditures in the hotel." Like the human reader, the computational model processes the successive words of a sentence, developing a representation of the syntactic and semantic relations that can later be interrogated to answer questions, such as "Who did the attacking?" The mapping process for this model is between the cycle count of its computations on words and phrases and the processing time profile of human readers on successive words and phrases of a sentence. The model accounts for the differences between the processing times for different types of sentences, as shown in figure 8.4.

The model also provides an account of one of the dimensions of differ- ence among individuals, proposing that it be conceptualized as different amounts of activation available for processing and storage. Less skilled readers can be modeled as having less activation available for computing and storing the results of those computations than do more skilled read- ers. The lower amount of activation can result in less maintenance if the shortage is borne by the storage function; this results in a functional loss of information during processing. Alternatively, the shortfall can be borne by the computational function, resulting in a slowdown in pro- cessing, or it can be borne by both functions. Although the current imple- mentation of the capacity-constrained model uses an intermediate point in this trading relation, it is possible that different tasks or individuals may occupy different locations on this function. Thus, this computational approach provides an account of certain types of processes that take more time, whether due to the task or to the individual's skill.

Modules Revisited   This model also provides some insight into the issue we raised earlier concerning cognitive modularity. Before explaining the model's point, we will describe one issue that has been proposed to reflect on modularity. The issue concerns the ability to use semantic information

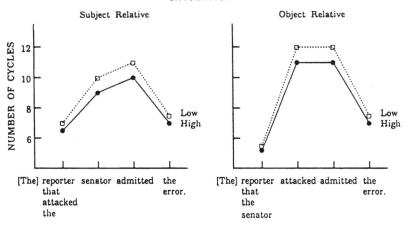

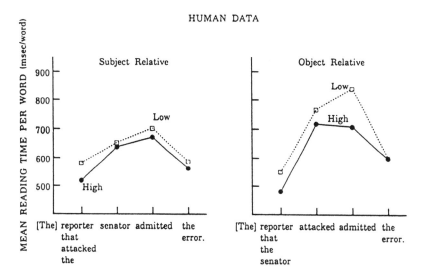

Figure 8.4
The number of cycles expended on various parts of two kinds of sentences (called subject relative and object relative) when the model, CC READER, is operating with more or less working memory capacity. The bottom graph presents the human data for comparison with the simulation. The data is word-by-word reading time. Notice how both the model and humans tend to spend more cycles/time on the harder parts of the sentences, namely around the verbs of the main clause and the relative clause. Comparing the cycle count to the distribution of human processing times is one way to assess whether the model has captured the significant aspects of the processing. (From *A capacity theory of comprehension: Individual differences in working memory,* by Just & Carpenter. Copyright 1992 by the American Psychological Association. Figure 9, p. 140, reprinted with permission.)

to immediately resolve a temporary syntactic ambiguity. For example, consider the ambiguity that is encountered on the third word of the sentence fragment "The defendant examined . . . " This fragment is ambiguous between the past tense interpretation and the less frequent reduced relative clause interpretation, as in "The defendant [who was] examined . . . " However, in a fragment such as "The evidence examined . . . " the inanimacy of *evidence* can, in principle, rule out the active past-tense interpretation, because *evidence* can't do any examining. We say "in principle" because if syntactic processing were truly modular and informationally encapsulated, as Fodor's proposed architecture would have it, then the inanimacy information about *evidence* would in fact not penetrate into the syntactic processing.

An ingenious experiment supported Fodor's proposal by analyzing the time readers spent on fixating successive words of these different types of sentences (Ferreira & Clifton, 1986). The reasoning behind the study was that if readers did take the inanimacy of *evidence* into account during their initial syntactic analysis, then they should not be surprised (surprise indexed by taking additional time) if the initial sentence fragment were followed by something consistent only with the less-frequent reduced relative-clause interpretation (e.g., "The evidence examined by the lawyer . . . "). The results showed that there was just as much "surprise" when the noun was a word such as *evidence* as when it was a word such as *defendant,* suggesting that readers ignore the semantic cue provided by *evidence* during their initial syntactic processing. The initial study favored a modular architecture, at least for syntactic analysis. However, an alternative architectural framework provides a different account of the result. The failure of the inanimacy cue to influence the syntactic processing could just as well be the result of a capacity constraint, rather than being caused by a structural encapsulation. It could be that the semantic cue is not taken into consideration during the first-pass syntactic analysis because there is a lack of resources to do so.

In a subsequent study we found that the initial "syntactic impenetrability" result holds only for subjects who are not the most skilled readers (Just & Carpenter, 1992). Those who have more language skills and resources treated the inanimacy information as a cue, just as they treated a syntactic marker as a cue. Each cue alone and the two cues together

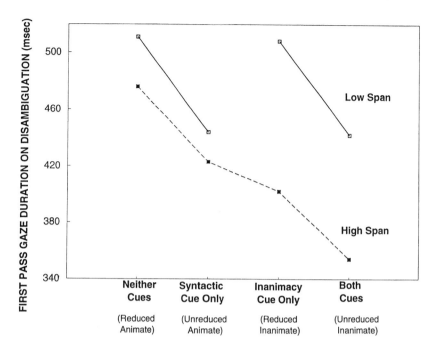

Figure 8.5

A graph of the first-pass reading time on the disambiguating phrase (e.g., *by the lawyer*) for both more skilled (high-span) and less skilled (low-span) college readers. For the low-span readers, only the explicit syntactic cue (i.e., *who was*) facilitates reading time on the disambiguation. By contrast, for the high-span readers, the explicit syntactic cue and the inanimacy cue (i.e., *evidence* vs. *defendant*) both facilitate first-pass gaze duration, and the effect of the two cues together is additive. The difference between the two groups suggests that syntactic information is not necessarily isolated from semantic influences. (Data are adapted from Just & Carpenter, 1992.)

reduced the processing time. Figure 8.5 shows the difference in the initial gaze on the disambiguation for the two groups. For the more skilled readers (the high span), each cue (the syntactic cue and the inanimate noun) reduces processing time and both cues together result in the shortest processing time. By contrast, for the less skilled readers (the low span) only the syntactic cue facilitates the processing of the disambiguation initially. The difference between the groups on this very specific part of the sentence suggests that syntactic processing isn't modular by virtue of some "hardwired" property of the system; otherwise there would be no individual differences in the cue use. The capacity constraint of 3CAPS provides an account for why a semantic cue enters into the first-pass analysis of some readers but not of others, whereas a completely modular architecture cannot accommodate the individual differences.

Although we have described the comprehension models in some detail, the 3CAPS architecture is not limited to language comprehension. In fact, the general approach applies as well to spatial problem solving (Just & Carpenter, 1985). Spatial problem solving draws on processes that show some similarities to those involved in language comprehension, but, at least among college students, spatial skill is fairly independent of language skill (Shah & Miyake, 1996). That is, one can be skilled at language and unskilled at spatial problem solving or vice versa. Moreover, this general architecture has been used to model working memory processes in human-machine interaction (Byrne, 1994), text memory (Goldman & Varma, 1995), and mechanical reasoning (Fallside & Just, 1994). The models differ depending on the domain represented, but they share the structural and processing assumptions that constitute the core of the 3CAPS architecture.

Intelligent-Tutoring Systems

Intelligent-tutoring systems illustrate how computational modeling has been integrated into large-scale domains, and consequently, how modeling has expanded the scope of theoretically driven research (Sleeman & Brown, 1982). The characteristics of the more successful intelligent-tutoring systems reveal cognitive science's concern with the human learning system, as well as computer science's concern with the representation and access of information. In this case, the information is the domain to be learned. The tutoring systems developed since the 1980s respond adaptively to the student's queries and mistakes by incorporating an explicit model of the student, and in that way, intelligent-tutoring systems differ from the educational software known as computer-assisted instruction (CAI), which typically do not explicitly model the student.

Intelligent Tutoring versus Expert Systems   Another way to see the psychological content in a tutoring system is to contrast a successful tutor with the structure of an expert system. An expert system might contain all of the information needed for problem solving, but not necessarily in a form that lends itself to understanding how a student might approach the problem, and so it cannot be the basis of a tutor. The contrast between the expert system and the tutor is highlighted in the case history of the development of a medical diagnosis tutor that was initially based on an expert system, MYCIN (Clancey, 1984). MYCIN, a successful expert system that aided in medical diagnosis, consisted of a set of rules that probabilistically related a list of medical symptoms with their potential diagnoses. Although it had knowledge that was useful for medical diagnosis, the knowledge wasn't usefully represented to serve as the basis of a medical tutor. Medical students found the rules difficult to understand and integrate. In order to move from being an expert system to being a tutor, the system had to be radically revised to reflect the learner's previous knowledge of the relations among diseases, symptoms, and tests. The new tutoring system included a plausible representation of the learner's knowledge as well as the abstract hypothesis-generation and management strategies to guide the learning (Clancey, 1986). This case history clarifies the distinction between an arbitrarily organized knowledge base, which may be at the heart of an expert system, and a psychological model. The psychologically based tutoring model must be more than a representation of the knowledge to be acquired. Although the tutor must have a characterization of the problem domain, it must also characterize the learner's knowledge and thought processes, and it must incorporate some model of the tutoring process itself, such as how to sequence the information, monitor the student's responses, and intervene with certain feedback.

ACT-R and Intelligent Tutoring One of the more theoretically grounded tutoring systems has been developed by Anderson and his colleagues, using Anderson's ACT-R theory, which is a production system architecture (Anderson, Corbett, Fincham, Hoffman, & Pelletier, 1992; Anderson, Corbett, Koedinger, & Pelletier, 1995). The symbolic nature of ACT-R has been used in tutoring systems that span from beginning programming (LISP and Pascal) to high school math (algebra and geometry). The tutors are based on a thorough analysis of the domain that underlies the model, which consists of a set of productions that express the individual steps to be taken to solve particular types of problems. The tutor then works by trying to match its representation of a problem to the student's actions. At each point in the solution, the tutor is capable of generating a set of productions that constitute a correct solution path. If the student takes an action that is off this path, then the computer can provide feedback and instruction. The tutor is also available as a help facility if the student requests an explanation. Some of the tutoring research has focused on how soon feedback should be presented about an error (the consensus has been soon) and what type of information should be given to improve learning rates.

After over a decade of research with various types of tutors, Anderson et al. (1995) described several of the cognitive principles of the tutoring design that characterize their approach. One principle relevant to a cognitive theory expresses the commitment to a production system architecture. This is both a commitment to the idea that cognitive skills can be decomposed and that individual productions provide the appropriate grain size for a theoretical analysis in the tutoring domain. In this theory, the ability to learn, remember, and appropriately apply these productions constitutes the procedures of the cognitive skill, whether it is geometry or the LISP programming language. The theory claims that the learner starts with declarative instructions in a domain (such as geometry); through guided practice, this declarative knowledge is converted into procedural knowledge (the representations evoked in skilled problem solving). The productions that link conditions and actions are then strengthened, making problem solving less error prone and more rapid. The claim of Anderson and his group is that the complexity of learning results from the complexity of the domain but that the learning of each individual production is quite simple.

The research is interesting not only for its theoretical insights into the nature of teaching and learning, but also because of the practical issues that arise in interfacing a theoretical model with the realities of high school classrooms. For example, one assessment suggested that computer tutors are sometimes highly successful with high school students who don't typically enjoy classroom math, but for sociological reasons as much as cognitive ones. Part of the appeal of the intelligent tutor arises from the fact that such tutors are perceived as being high tech, and therefore, desirable. Another important point is that tutors do not replace high school teachers, and the tutor's effectiveness depends on the teacher in the high school classroom. Also, the role of the tutor varies with the students' level and the domain. With the more motivated and mature college students, the programming tutors have operated more as self-paced, stand-alone systems.

At first glance, it might seem that a practical measure of a tutoring system's success is how well people learn with it. However, the interpretation of such a measure is not simple, in part because the baseline isn't obvious. Should the tutor's performance be compared to the learner's achievements with a human teacher, and if so, what about the fact that the two teaching methods may take different amounts of time? Should a tutor be compared to a self-paced course? Any such comparisons in real life may involve additional complicating factors, such as who takes the courses. Nevertheless, in one evaluation of the LISP-programming language-tutoring system, college students acquired it in 30% less time and scored 43% better on a final exam than students who were learning on their own (Anderson, Boyle, & Reiser, 1985). The success of these computer tutors represents an interrelated set of claims concerning how a domain is mentally represented, how it should be physically conveyed, how learning is best accomplished in terms of the feedback and contingencies, and appropriate ways to facilitate and guide that learning. We have described the tutoring project in some detail because it illustrates how a family of computational models can constitute not only a theoretical contribution to cognitive science, but also have a large impact in a complex, practical domain.

Cognitive Lesioning

Just as certain types of animal models have permitted physiological studies that cannot be performed with humans, so computational models have permitted analogous *cognitive-lesioning* experiments. Animal-lesioning experiments involve temporary or permanent disabling of that portion of an animal's brain tissue believed to underlie a given mental function and then examination of the effect on the animal's performance. Computational modeling permits a theoretical counterpart, in which a particular resource is withdrawn to various degrees, and the ensuing performance of the model is observed. This method can be used to associate a given clinical syndrome (say, a particular language dysfunction such as an aphasia) with the disabling of a particular resource in a computational model. A disabling that selectively affects performance in the appropriate way (producing only those performance dysfunctions associated with the syndrome) provides a theoretical account of the disorder.

Agrammatic Aphasia   One example of the lesioning approach in the domain of sentence comprehension arises in accounting for the errors of aphasic patients. Haarmann and Kolk (1991) developed and then lesioned a computational model of language processing in order to simulate the performance of agrammatic aphasics. Patients with this syndrome are so named because their speech is typically dysfluent, even telegraphic and lacking in morphological markers. Their language difficulty also extends to comprehension; such patients have difficulty interpreting sentences purely on the basis of syntactic information, without lexical cues as to who is the actor of the sentence, as in, "The man who greeted the woman smiled," compared to sentences in which the lexical content cues the actor, as in, "The man who petted the dog smiled." Haarmann and Kolk made cognitive lesions that affected the time course of the entry and residence of various representational elements (generated by a sentence parsing mechanism) in working memory. The model assumed that the representations of the constituents of the phrase all had to be in an activated state in working memory at the same time in order for the phrasal unit to be processed as such. On the basis of the differential performance of four different computational models that varied in whether lesion affected the timing of either individual words or of entire phrases, they proposed that agrammatic aphasia arises from an inability to simultaneously retain the components of a phrasal unit (noun phrase or verb phrase) in working memory long enough to construct the representation of the phrase. Thus, the computational model suggested that a timing disorder in processing could be the cause of agrammatic aphasia, an attribution that was seldom previously made in the literature. Furthermore, by varying the severity of the temporal dysfunction in the model (which introduced an asynchrony in the parsing of the phrase units), the models provided an account of the differential severities of agrammatic aphasia.

A related account of the comprehension errors associated with aphasia has been instantiated in the capacity-constrained architecture system described earlier. The model claims that there is a pathological reduction in the activation resources needed to support comprehension that underlies aphasics' impairments. This results in the inability to process complex information and at the same time retain the intermediate products of those computations that are activated (Haarmann, Just, & Carpenter, 1997). In the model, various sentence constituents, such as the noun phrase and the verb phrase of a clause, must be simultaneously active in working memory in order to be linked in the internal representation. If they are not active, the comprehender might have only some fragmentary representation of the sentence, which could allow him or her to answer some types of questions but not all. However, a drastic reduction in processing resources means that often constituents that should be related are not simultaneously activated. Differing amounts of activation loss can be used to model differential degrees of severity (with fewer resources available for more severely impaired individuals). Thus, the frequency and type of errors can be mapped between the versions of the model and various neuropsychological patient groups.

Individual Differences   The cognitive-lesioning approach is a more general tool that is not limited to modeling neuropsychological data. This approach can be construed as the systematic manipulation of some computational parameters that can be used to study proposed population differences (of which clinical vs. unimpaired populations is one example), as well as individual differences on task performance. Consequently, the logic of the technique is applicable to the study of normal individual differences or to the analysis of other population effects, such as age-related changes in cognitive function in the elderly (Salthouse, 1988). It is also applicable to the analysis of development. For example, one computational model has used this approach to study of the acquisition of simple math computation facts, such as 7 + 4 = 11 (Siegler & Shipley, 1995). These facts can either be retrieved or calculated. A simulation based on changes in the distribution of the speed, accuracy, and novelty of each strategy, as well as their changes with experience, provided an excellent account of how children's strategies for retrieving or calculating such numerical facts vary and develop.

This approach can also be used to study normal individual differences among adults, as illustrated by a computational model of a widely used reasoning task called the Raven Progressive Matrices Test (Carpenter et al., 1990). The Raven test consists of a series of 3 × 3 visual analogies. In each analogy, one cell is missing, and the participant's task is to choose one of eight alternatives that would complete the analogy. The 36 problems vary enormously in error rates, from negligible errors for earlier problems in the test to almost negligible correct solutions for later problems. A task analysis of the problems indicated that a small number of relatively familiar relations govern the construction of most of the analogies. For example, three common relations were series progression (e.g., 1 dot, 2 dots, 3 dots), figure addition or subtraction (e.g., triangle + star = triangle with superimposed star), and a constant relation (e.g., the same figure occurs in all three cells of a row or column). Figure 8.6 presents

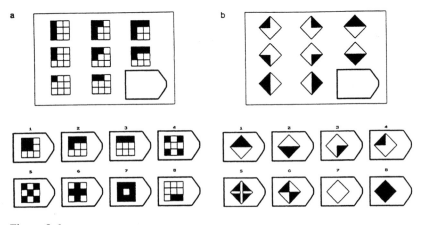

Figure 8.6
Two figural analogy problems illustrating the types of relations found in the Raven Advanced Matrices Test (not actual test items). 8.6A shows a progression in number of darkened elements in each row and column. 8.6B shows figural addition (row 1 + row 2 = row 3). (From *What one intelligence test measures: A theoretical account of the processing in the Raven Progressive Matrices Test*, by Carpenter, Just, & Shell. Copyright 1990 by the American Psychological Association. Figure 4, p. 409, reprinted with permission.)

examples typical of the visual analogy problems that instantiate these rules. The most "complex" rule was one in which an element occurred in two of the three cells of a row or column; this rule was necessary to solve many of the problems associated with the highest error rates.

The sources of difficulty were computationally examined by constructing a set of computational models, using the CAPS architecture, that consisted of a few modules, as shown in figure 8.7. The perceptual encoding productions made pairwise comparisons between figures in a row in order to detect similar and different basic features. The rule induction productions used these features to trigger various rules relating the figures in a row, such as the ones just described. Another set of productions generated a desired target for the missing figure and then checked the alternatives to determine their match to it. Manipulating the parameters of the model indicated that its ability to solve harder problems was influenced by two main features. One was the ability to keep track of multiple relations (rules) within a row or column. By systematically varying the number of rules that could be maintained in working memory, the model was able to solve only the simpler problems or almost all of the problems. A second feature that contributed to the performance was the presence of a control structure that allowed the model to backtrack and try different comparisons to induce relations. The need to backtrack and keep track of one's position in a hypothesis space is a type of executive function that seemed to be required to solve the more difficult problems, but not the easier ones. Thus, the differences between these models provided one possible account of what was needed to solve most of the problems compared to what was needed to solve only the simpler problems. These examples illustrate how simulation modeling can be used to investigate the effects of process variation among individuals, among tasks, and between populations.

A Unified Theory of Cognition

One of the dimensions that differentiates various modeling efforts is the scope of the family of models developed within the architecture. Some models account for a relatively circumscribed domain, perhaps a single task. Other models (such as 3CAPS and the ACT-R math tutors) are part of a family that together account for a broad and complex domain. At

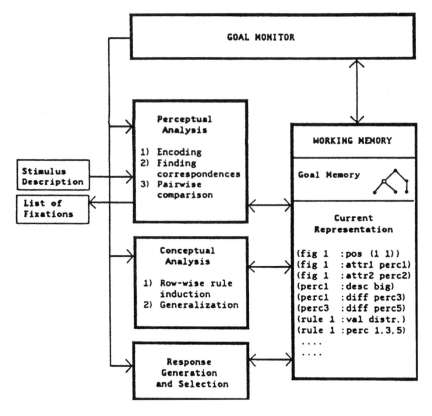

Figure 8.7
A block diagram of the modules in the computational model that solved the difficult problems in the Raven Advanced Matrices Test. One module encodes the perceptual features of the figures (from a symbolic description list). Another module matches the attribute values among the figures in a row to induce relations and rules, such as progression, constant value, or figure addition. A third module induces the characteristics of the missing item and identifies the best match from among the foils associated with the problem. What distinguishes this model from the one that can solve the easier problems is the existence of a goal memory, a module that keeps track of what features have already been matched and can try different attributes as the basis for inducing regularities. (From *What one intelligence test measures: A theoretical account of the processing in the Raven Progressive Matrices Test* by Carpenter, Just, & Shell. Copyright 1990 by the American Psychological Association. Figure 10, p. 420, reprinted with permission).

the far end of this spectrum would be a single architecture that could accommodate all cognitive domains. This ambitious goal was espoused by Allen Newell (1990), who also developed a candidate architecture.

Twenty Questions   To understand one of Newell's reasons for proposing this scientific goal, it is useful to consider a paper that he wrote in the early 1970s called "You Can't Play 20 Questions with Nature and Win" (Newell, 1973). The paper's thesis was that experimental psychologists were treating the research enterprise as a version of the children's "20-questions game." The 20 questions were the implicit questions that generate the dichotomies that permeate cognitive science. For example, is an internal representation propositional or imaginal? Is the retrieval from long-term or short-term memory? Is attention spatially based or object based? and so on. Newell argued that such dichotomies yield only one bit of information and, moreover, that the resulting bits of information do not cumulate to yield a unified theory of cognition. In that way, psychology would not "win" the 20-questions game with nature. Newell proposed the alternative strategy of beginning with a theory of the cognitive architecture, using what we already know about the overall characteristics of the human cognitive system, and then using this theory to guide and integrate the empirical research. Newell suggested making the computational architecture an integral component of the research enterprise. In his own career, Newell developed several candidate architectures, and his most ambitious was SOAR.

SOAR   SOAR is a production system architecture developed by Newell, Laird, and Rosenbloom, within which symbolic processing of many types can be modeled, such that the models exhibit performance characteristics similar to those of human beings (Newell, 1990; Waldrop, 1988a, 1988b). From the vantage of artificial intelligence, SOAR integrates two main thrusts of AI that received much attention in the past several decades and that we mentioned in conjunction with the chess research. One is the heuristic search techniques used in novel problem-solving domains, including means-ends analysis, that is, searching how to reduce the difference between some current state and some desired goal. The second thrust is the use of more specific but more powerful heuristics that can be evoked through recognition. The knowledge is something like what an expert might possess about a very specialized situation, knowledge that is useful but applies to a narrow range of circumstances. Similarly, SOAR can perform like a general problem solver, and it can function as a knowledge-laden expert system. From the psychological vantage point, the SOAR project uses the same set of mechanisms to account for many disparate types of cognitive performance, such as immediate, speeded responses to displays (comparable to deciding whether to go or stop when a stop-light changes color), solving elementary algebra equations, and learning a cognitively based skill, such as learning to read inverted text. A large community of researchers have adopted this architecture in which to develop their computational models, and so the cumulative range of the models is large and growing.

The evaluations of SOAR's performance depends upon the particular model and domain; several focus on the time course of processing, attempting to relate the system's temporal characteristics to human performance characteristics. One review (Lindsay, 1991) described SOAR's successes as well as such incompletenesses as its lack of integration with sensory or motor systems. Moreover, some of its claims have been criticized (Cooper & Shallice, 1995). One of Cooper and Shallice's objections is that SOAR's complexity makes it difficult to know which features are central and which are implementational details. This issue has been raised frequently with respect to computational models and is not itself unique to SOAR or intrinsically a problem. But Cooper and Shallice also argue that some of SOAR's successes are due to noncentral properties. They conclude that the architecture fits better in the problem-solving domain to which it traces its intellectual roots, rather than as a general architecture for all of cognition. However, the scope of a theory and its empirical support are often negatively correlated. Exactly what point in the trading relation is optimal for scientific progress is an interesting issue. Perhaps because of its ambition and scope, SOAR has been difficult for the field to digest. But it captures a number of key insights and its scope is one of the features that makes it merit more attention.

In summary, in this section we have described several architectures, some of the ways in which they have been compared to human performance, and the domains in which they have been developed. The domains were chosen, in part, to illustrate the scope of the computational modeling approach, which goes beyond the claims and contributions of individual computational models to include a more general claim about how cognitive theories can and should be expressed. In the next section, we will examine how such computational models are evaluated.

Evaluating Models and Modeling

Computational modeling has not only changed how theoretical models are constructed in psychology, but also, as a second-order impact, it has changed how models are evaluated. Before considering the changes in evaluation, it is useful to have some benchmark, and as our benchmark we will consider verbal models.

Models: Computational versus Verbal

Two of the major reasons that researchers use computational models are to push the predictive aspects of a theory and to determine whether the model provides a sufficient account of some aspect of human cognition. A computational model is most useful when the proposed mechanisms and their interaction with the environment are too complex to make predictions without actually testing some operational version. In other words, the computational model is most useful if the verbal description is insufficient to generate predictions. This claim understates a computational model's usefulness because verbal models and computational models typically yield different types of predictions. A verbal model often only enables predictions about the direction of the main effects or interactions. By contrast, a computational model may enable quantitative predictions. Thus, the evaluation of a model is hard to compare to that of its verbal counterpart because verbal models typically don't result in comparable predictions.

A verbal model typically yields some hypothesis that is evaluated, in part, using hypothesis-testing statistics, such as the ubiquitous ANOVA, and so forth. The stated goal of conventional statistical evaluation is the rejection of the null hypothesis. However, even in the context of standard

verbal models, hypothesis rejection is an incomplete evaluation procedure. On one hand, if the hypothesis is not rejected, it can be due to an
insensitive experiment, and on the other hand, if the null hypothesis is
rejected, there is no intrinsic information about the directions for improving the theory.

Another issue that arises in evaluating verbal (and computational)
models is the issue of scalableness: would the model scale up from a circumscribed task to a larger domain? Often researchers give at least an
informal assessment of a verbal model's current and potential scope.
Thus, the evaluation of even verbal models of any complexity is not entirely standardized or circumscribed, and the hypothesis-testing approach
treats only the tip of the iceberg in model evaluation and construction.
That approach may only seem satisfactory because there is an implicit
but presumably richer theoretical framework, as well as additional information in the data, that can guide the ultimate interpretation.

Evaluating Computational Models

The picture is not simpler when evaluating computational models. The
model's ability to perform a task is evidence that its mechanisms are sufficient, and sufficiency is a useful criterion, particularly if one considers
the vagueness or absence of specification that may mask the limitations
of a verbal model. Nevertheless, cognitive scientists are typically interested in more evidence than sheer sufficiency before accepting a claim
that the model's processes resemble those of the human. Such supporting
evidence requires mapping between some aspect of the model's performance and the human performance. In some cases, the mapping is fairly
direct. For example, the aphasia models described earlier provide error
measures that can be related to human error rates for particular sentence
types. If a computational model takes a certain number of steps or some
processing time (such as number of cycles) to perform a task, the measures can be related to the corresponding profile of human times (with
some assumptions about scaling). Some models (and behavioral studies)
provide traces of the intermediate stages of processing that can be compared. For example, in the analogical reasoning model of the Raven test,
the computational model's simulated eye fixations were compared to the
successive gazes of the human problem solvers. In some cases, however,

the mapping between a model's performance and human behavior is considerably less direct.

There is often a trade-off between the scope of the model and its fidelity to known (or hypothesized) human mechanisms. Models of a complex domain, such as reading a newspaper or solving a whole array of different types of problems, employ at least some mechanisms that are not in close correspondence to those of humans. The lack of close correspondence may not obviate the model's usefulness at a more molar level. One advantage of modeling is that these issues are easier to make explicit in evaluating computational models; analogous issues may be left implicit for the verbal model counterparts.

Computational modeling, like other forms of scientific modeling, is fundamentally analogical in character, involving a comparison between some features of the natural phenomenon (the "scope" of the model) and some features of the model. The features of the model that are ignored at evaluation are those that are somehow deemed to be less central. An example of such a mapping in a noncomputational domain is a mechanical model of the way the human heart pumps blood. The evaluation of the model should focus on its central functional characteristics, such as the hydrodynamics of the fluid flow, and not on properties less central to the pumping function, such as its composition. In addition, the mapping must be explained. The theorist using the mechanical heart would explain which of its features are important, how the mechanical model works, and the ways in which its operation corresponds to those of the heart. Some of the difficulty in evaluating computational modeling occurs at this juncture, namely, figuring out how the computational model operates, what the mapping is to the human mechanism, and whether the match is compelling. Ideally, the computational model is supported by data that show that the model operates in important ways that resemble the target and that the claimed features are indeed the ones responsible for its correspondence. Thus, the evaluation has both qualitative and quantitative aspects. If the comparison is illuminating and the model is successful, then the evaluation moves on to other complex criteria, such as the model's completeness across the levels of explanation of a phenomenon, its generality across phenomena, and its generativity to as-yet-undiscovered phenomena.

Sensitivity Analysis

An important step in the evaluation of a computational model is a *sensitivity analysis,* which identifies which aspects of the model are necessary, sufficient, or irrelevant for the qualitative aspects of the performance. One way to do the sensitivity analysis is to compare alternative versions of the same model (VanLehn, Brown, & Greeno, 1984), somewhat like the logic of the cognitive-lesioning studies we described earlier. In fact, such analyses are seldom included with the initial, journal presentation of a model because a sensitivity analysis is not as straightforward. There is no algorithmic prescription for doing a sensitivity analysis. For a model of any complexity, the sensitivity analysis requires understanding not only the initial model in great depth, but also performing informative studies. In several recent examples in the literature the computational model is so complex that the model itself becomes a topic of study. For example, the importance of sensitivity analysis has been emphasized by McCloskey (1991) with respect to the connectionist models that have both hidden layers and that use back propagation in order to learn. He suggests that in the absence of a sufficiently detailed explanation of how effects arise, a computational model might be likened to animal models used in physiological research. Researchers may find that the animal's system responds like a human's without really knowing why. The animal model is useful, but it isn't a theory. McCloskey suggests that the model itself must become an object of study that leads to some type of explication of its important properties. Its status as an explanation becomes dependent on a type of examination accessible to only certain subgroups of researchers. On the other hand, this objection to such theories may be a matter of degree, and the analogy to some unknown animal model is not an inevitable consequence of its complexity. A theory that accounts for a wide range of behaviors, but is inscrutable to all but a few, is still a potentially useful scientific contribution. One might legitimately decide that its status is not yet convincingly demonstrated, without rejecting it as necessarily invalid.

It is interesting to note that the complexity and understandability of computational models complicate the evaluation of models in other domains besides cognitive science and that analogous debates to those in cognitive science have arisen in mathematics concerning the proofs generated through AI techniques. Wagman (1991) describes the theorem-proving work on the four-color conjecture, which had previously eluded the best mathematical minds of this century. Its solution was dependent on the work of Appel and Haken, in conjunction with AI work. A difficulty in accepting this proof arose for some mathematicians because the AI component was essentially too complex and long to be adequately checked by mathematicians. At least one philosopher of science objected that such an AI proof inherently lacks the properties of a rigorous proof. But Wagman points out that the objection might be also seen as a resistance to change in the customary ways of thinking. Similarly, a complex computational model is not intrinsically unacceptable as a psychological theory, although it may be difficult to accept its account without an adequate understanding of the nature of its claims.

Evaluating Modeling as an Approach

In preceding sections, we have described some of the features and contributions of computational modeling to cognitive science. We argued that computational approaches have sharpened the theoretical issues and have helped to shape the agenda of cognitive science. In addition, computational models have served as specific proposals in a variety of cognitive domains, from tasks such as reading texts, through the performance of neuropsychological patients, high school math-tutoring systems, and human-computer interaction. In this section, we briefly propose some of the dimensions along which to evaluate the contributions and limitations of the modeling approach.

One obvious advantage of modeling is that it is useful to specify the mechanisms of cognition, as opposed to remaining with a less precise description of its properties. There are other advantages that reflect something of the computational approach. The computational model makes the task requirements clear and allows at least a sufficiency statement of one way in which the task can be accomplished. The requirement to specify such details can also be a rich source of ideas about many aspects of the system being modeled. The need to specify processes can stimulate the researcher to think about processes that hadn't been considered before the model was made to work through a set of problems, so modeling itself is a generative exercise, an ongoing cycle of theory development, enrichment, modification, and evaluation. Computational models invite cognitive-lesioning types of studies, in order to explore spaces represented by various parameters and models. In this way, they discourage thinking in terms of simple binary contrasts.

Computational models make good experimental participants, albeit in some inhuman ways. They are patient with the experimenter and don't fatigue. Considering the model as an experimental participant also provides some insight into some of its limitations. Computational models require specification in ways that can be overlooked with human participants. A computational model won't read instructions in order to understand what will be expected. This information must somehow be explicitly represented, even if the understanding processes aren't of major interest. Also, a computational model will never have been subjected to the same types of social interactions as have humans; it will never experience its physical environment through the same sensory apparatus or act on its environment through the same types of effector organs. Research on perceptual and effector systems in robotics indicates that such differences do not preclude the usefulness of computational approaches. Nevertheless, these differences do shape the applicability and the usefulness of the approach. Like most other scientific theoretical and methodological enterprises, computational modeling has limitations.

Although we have focused on the influence that the modeling approach has exerted on theory, it has also had some influence on empirical research methods. The modeling approach is particularly compatible with behavioral methods that trace a sequence of processes. Such process-tracing methods include the verbal reports of a participant during problem solving (see Carpenter et al., 1990; Ericsson & Simon, 1980) and the locations and durations of the sequence of eye fixations during problem solving and reading (Carpenter & Just, 1983; Just & Carpenter, 1985), or successive steps in problem solving, as in the tutoring system. A simulation model provides a way to describe the successive steps in the solution of a problem and, consequently, a way to map the model's predictions onto dynamic measures of performance.

What may be the ultimate impact of computational models on cognitive science? Based on case studies of competing theories throughout science's history, Thagard (1978) argued that the assessment of the worth of competing scientific theories has been determined by three main criteria. One is the ability to unify many different classes of fact. Depending on the scope of the cognitive domain and how we view the scope of the modeling enterprise, computational modeling has had anywhere from some to a lot of success. Although no one theory has yet been accepted as a unified theory of the mind, as a group, models have articulated mechanisms sufficient to account for a wide range of complex cognitive abilities. So, one might conclude that by the first criterion, computational modeling is a strong contender as a successful set of theories.

Mitigating against extreme comprehensiveness is Thagard's second criterion—the simplicity of the theory. According to this criterion, theories with fewer special assumptions should be preferred over those with more. Unfortunately, most computational models of any scope are very complex, and as we argued earlier, this characteristic complicates their communication to the broader community as well as the evaluation of their contribution. On the other hand, it is even difficult to apply the same yardstick to other types of models because typically they do not have comparable scope or detail.

The third criterion that Thagard argued influenced the success of a scientific theory is the presence of an analogy, such as the analogy between atomic structure and the solar system. Such analogies may impact on the theory's ease of application and communicability. This property may also contribute to the impact computational models have had in cognitive science. Computational theories build on the inherent analogy to the computational systems that initially inspired them.

Acknowledgments

The writing of this chapter was supported by contract N00014-96-1-0322 from the Office of Naval Research, NIMH Research Scientist Awards MH-00661 and MH-00662, and the A. W. Mellon Foundation. We thank Henk Haarmann, Paula Koseff, and Sashank Varma for their comments on the chapter.

References

Allen, J. (1995). *Natural language understanding.* Menlo Park, CA: Benjamin/ Cummings.

Anderson, J. R., Boyle, C. R., & Reiser, B. J. (1985). Intelligent tutoring systems. *Science, 228,* 456–462.

Anderson, J. R., Corbett, A. T., Fincham, J., Hoffman, D., & Pelletier, R. (1992). General principles for an intelligent tutoring architecture. In V. Shute, & W. Regian (Eds.), *Cognitive approaches to automated instruction* (pp. 81–106). Hillsdale, NJ: Erlbaum.

Anderson, J. R., Corbett, A. T., Koedinger, K., & Pelletier, R. (1995). Cognitive tutors: Lessions learned. *The Journal of Learning Sciences, 4,* 167–207.

Bechtel, W., & Abrahamsen, A. (1991). *Connectionism and the mind: An introduction to parallel processing in networks.* Cambridge, MA: Basil Blackwell.

Berliner, H., & Ebeling, C. (1989). Pattern knowledge and search: The SUPREM architecture. *Artificial Intelligence, 38,* 161–198.

Bever, T. G. (1992). The demons and the beast: Modular and nodular kinds of knowledge. In R. G. Reilly, & N. E. Sharkey (Eds.), *Connectionist approaches to language processing* (pp. 213–252). Hove, England: Erlbaum.

Byrne, M. (1994, August). Integrating, not debating, situated action and computational models: Taking the environment seriously. Paper presented at *Sixteenth Annual Meeting of the Cognitive Science Society,* Atlanta, GA.

Byrne, R. (1996, February 19). A collision of brains and brawn. *New York Times,* p. C8.

Carpenter, P. A., & Daneman, M. (1981). Lexical retrieval and error recovery in reading: A model based on eye fixations. *Journal of Verbal Learning and Verbal Behavior, 20,* 137–160.

Carpenter, P. A., & Just, M. A. (1983). What your eyes are doing while your mind is reading. In K. Rayner (Ed.), *Eye movements in reading: Perceptual and language processes* (pp. 275–307). New York: Academic Press.

Carpenter, P. A., Just, M. A., & Shell, P. (1990). What one intelligence test measures: A theoretical account of the processing in the Raven Progressive Matrices Test. *Psychological Review, 97,* 404–431.

Carpenter, P. A., Miyake, A., & Just, M. A. (1995). Language comprehension: Sentence and discourse processing. *Annual Review of Psychology, 46,* 91–120.

Charness, N. (1991). Expertise in chess: The balance between knowledge and search. In K. A. Ericsson & J. Smith (Eds.), *Toward a general theory of expertise.* Cambridge: Cambridge University Press.

Charniak, E., & McDermott, D. (1985). *Introduction to artificial intelligence.* Reading, MA: Addison-Wesley.

Chase, W. G., & Simon, H. A. (1973). The mind's eye in chess. In W. G. Chase (Ed.), *Visual information processing*. New York: Academic Press.

Clancey, W. J. (1984). Methodology for building an intelligent tutoring system. In W. Kintsch, J. R. Miller, & P. G. Polson (Eds.), *Method and tactics in cognitive science* (pp. 51–83). Hillsdale, NJ: Erlbaum.

Clancey, W. J. (1986). Qualitative student models. In J. F. Traub, B. J. Grosz, B. W. Lampson, & N. J. Nilsson (Eds.), *Annual Reviews of Computer Science* (Vol. 1, pp. 381–450). Palo Alto, CA: Annual Reviews.

Cooper, R., & Shallice, T. (1995). SOAR and the case for unified theories of cognition. *Cognition, 55,* 115–149.

de Groot, A. D. (1965). *Thought and choice in chess*. The Hague, Netherlands: Mouton.

Ericsson, K. A., & Simon, H. A. (1980). Verbal Reports as data. *Psychological Review, 87,* 215–251.

Fallside, D. C., & Just, M. A. (1994). Understanding the kinematics of a simple machine. *Visual Cognition, 1,* 401–432.

Farah, M. J., & McClelland, J. L. (1991). A computational model of semantic memory impairment: Modality specificity and emergent category specificity. *Journal of Experimental Psychology: General, 120,* 339–357.

Ferreira, F., & Clifton, C. (1986). The independence of syntactic processing. *Journal of Memory and Language, 25,* 348–368.

Fodor, J. A. (1983). *The modularity of mind*. Cambridge, MA: MIT Press.

Fodor, J., & Pylyshyn, Z. (1988). Connectionism and cognitive architecture: A critical analysis. *Cognition, 28,* 3–71.

Garfield, J. (Ed.). (1987). *Modularity in knowledge representation and natural-language understanding*. Cambridge: MIT Press.

Goldman, S. R., & Varma, S. (1995). CAPing the construction-integration model of discourse comprehension. In C. A. Weaver, S. Mannes, & C. R. Fletcher (Eds.), *Discourse comprehension: Essays in Honor of Walter Kintsch* (pp. 337–358). Hillsdale, NJ: Erlbaum.

Haarmann, H. J., Just, M. A., & Carpenter, P. A. (1997). Aphasic sentence comprehension as a resource deficit: A computational approach. *Brain and Language, 59,* 76–120.

Haarmann, H. J., & Kolk, H. H. J. (1991). A computer model of the temporal course of agrammatic sentence understanding: The effects of variation in severity and sentence complexity. *Cognitive Science, 15,* 49–87.

Holland, J. H., Holyoak, K. J., Nisbett, R. E., & Thagard, P. R. (1986). *Induction: Processes of inference, learning, and discovery*. Cambridge, MA: MIT Press.

Hunt, E. (1989). Cognitive science: Definition, status, and questions. *Annual Review of Psychology, 40,* 603–629.

Just, M. A., & Carpenter, P. A. (1980). A theory of reading: From eye fixations to comprehension. *Psychological Review, 87,* 329–354.

Just, M. A., & Carpenter, P. A. (1985). Cognitive coordinate systems: Accounts of mental rotation and individual differences in spatial ability. *Psychological Review, 92,* 137–172.

Just, M. A., & Carpenter, P. A. (1992). A capacity theory of comprehension: Individual differences in working memory. *Psychological Review, 99,* 122–149.

Kim, J. J., Marcus, G. F., Pinker, S., Hollander, M., et al. (1994). Sensitivity of children's inflection to grammatical structure. *Journal of Child Language, 21,* 173–209.

Kintsch, W. (1988). The role of knowledge in discourse comprehension: A construction-integration model. *Psychological Review, 95,* 163–182.

Kosslyn, S. M., & Van Kleeck, M. (1990). Broken brains and normal minds: Why Humpty-Dumpty needs a skeleton. In E. L. Schwartz (Ed.), *Computational neuroscience* (pp. 390–402). Cambridge, MA: MIT Press.

Lindsay, R. K. (1991). Symbolic-processing theories and the SOAR architecture. *Psychological Science, 2,* 294–302.

McClelland, J. L., & Rumelhart, D. E. (1988). *Explorations in parallel distributed processing: A handbook of models, programs, and exercises.* Cambridge, MA: MIT Press.

McCloskey, M. (1991). Networks and theories: The place of connectionism in cognitive science. *Psychological Science, 2,* 387–395.

Minsky, M., & Papert, S. (1969). *Perceptrons: An introduction to computational geometry.* Cambridge, MA: MIT Press.

Miyake, A., Carpenter, P. A., & Just, M. A. (1995). Reduced resources and specific impairments in normal and aphasic sentence comprehension. *Cognitive Neuropsychology, 12,* 651–679.

Newell, A. (1973). Production system: Models of control structures. In W. G. Chase (Ed.), *Visual information processing* (pp. 463–526). New York: Academic Press.

Newell, A. (1990). *Unified theories of cognition.* Cambridge, MA: Harvard University Press.

Newell, A., Rosenbloom, P. S., & Laird, J. E. (1989). Symbolic architectures for cognition. In M. Posner (Ed.), *Foundations of cognitive science.* Cambridge, MA: MIT Press.

Newell, A., & Simon, H. A. (1972). *Human problem solving.* Englewood Cliffs, NJ: Prentice-Hall.

Newell, A., & Simon, H. A. (1976). Computer Science as empirical inquiry: Symbols and search. *Communications of the Associations for Computer Machinery, 19,* 113–126.

Pinker, S., & Prince, A. (1988). On language and connectionism: Analysis of a parallel distributed processing model of language acquisition. *Cognition, 28,* 73–193.

Pylyshyn, Z. W. (1991). *Architectures for Intelligence* (K. VanLehn, Ed., pp. 189–223). Hillsdale, NJ: Erlbaum.

Richman, H. B., & Simon, H. A. (1989). Context effects in letter perception: Comparison of two theories. *Psychological Review, 96,* 417–432.

Salthouse, T. A. (1988). Initiating the formalization of theories of cognitive aging. *Psychology and Aging, 3,* 3–16.

Shah, P., & Miyake, A. (1996). The separability of working memory resources for spatial thinking and language processing: An individual differences approach. *Journal of Experimental Psychology: General, 125,* 4–27.

Shallice, T. (1988). *From neuropsychology to mental structure.* New York: Cambridge University Press.

Shastri, L., & Ajjanagadde, V. (1993). From simple associations to systematic reasoning: A connectionist representation of rules, variables, and dynamic bindings using temporal synchrony. *Behavioral and Brain Sciences, 16,* 417–494.

Siegler, R. S., & Shipley, C. (1995). Variation, selection, and cognitive change. In T. Simon & G. Halford (Eds.), *Developing cognitive competence: New approaches to process modeling* (pp. 31–76). Hillsdale, NJ: Erlbaum.

Sleeman, D. H., & Brown, J. S. (Eds). (1982). *Intelligent tutoring systems.* London: Academic Press.

Smolensky, P. (1988). On the proper treatment of connectionism. *Behavioral and Brain Sciences, 11,* 1–74.

Thagard, P. (1978). The best explanation: Criteria for theory choice. *Journal of Philosophy, 75,* 76–92.

Thibadeau, R., Just, M. A., & Carpenter, P. A. (1982). A model of the time course and content of reading. *Cognitive Science, 6,* 157–203.

Touretzky, D. S. (1988). On the proper treatment of thermostats. *Behavioral and Brain Sciences, 11,* 55–56.

VanLehn, K., Brown, J. S., & Greeno, J. (1984). *Method and tactics in cognitive science* (W. Kintsch, J. R. Miller, & P. G. Polson, Eds., pp. 235–262). Hillsdale, NJ: Erlbaum.

Wagman, M. (1991). *Artificial intelligence and human cognition: A theoretical intercomparison of two realms of intellect.* New York: Praeger.

Waldrop, M. M. (1988a). Toward a unified theory of cognition. *Science, 241,* 27–29.

Waldrop, M. M. (1988b). SOAR: A unified theory of cognition. *Science, 241,* 296–298.

Weber, B. (1996, February 19). A mean chess-playing computer tears at the meaning of thought. *New York Times,* p. A1.

9

Brain versus Behavioral Studies of Cognition

Elizabeth A. Phelps

Few psychologists today would disagree with the statement that cognitive processes are related to brain function. However, if you asked psychologists whether studying the brain will help us understand cognition, you might get a range of opinions (e.g., Johnson-Laird, 1980; LeDoux & Hirst, 1986). In this chapter, I will attempt to address two related questions. First, can we learn about cognition from studying the brain? Second, is it necessary to study the brain to explain cognitive behavior? In order to address the first question, I will provide examples of research examining cognitive behaviors using three commonly used techniques for studying brain function in humans. For each technique, I will review the background and methodology and discuss some of its advantages and disadvantages. I hope to demonstrate that our understanding of cognition can be informed by the study of the brain.

The second question is a little more difficult. Although one can argue that a type of research is informative, to say it is necessary implies that achieving our goals as cognitive psychologists is intertwined with the study of the brain. At the end of the chapter, I will discuss the role of brain research in our understanding of cognition. I hope to convince you that brain research is a useful and necessary step in our study of cognition, but that success in understanding the brain-behavior relationship is dependent on the quality of the behavioral research and our ability to describe cognition on a behavioral level.

Discovering the Organization of Cognition: The Search for Dissociations

The subject matter of cognitive psychology has been the structure and organization of knowledge (Anderson, 1985). Over the years, psychologists studying cognition have proposed models of how mental functions, such as language, attention, perception, memory, and intelligence, are organized. The primary tool available to psychology for discovering the structure of cognition has been to observe behavior in controlled environments. Through observing the cause-and-effect relationship between stimuli and behavior (or the correlation between behaviors) cognitive psychologists are able to identify some of the components of mental functions, thus providing insight into their structure.

For example, several early studies demonstrated that when subjects are briefly presented a set of stimuli and are asked to report them back, they can usually recall 7 ± 2 items, or "chunks," of information indicating a limited capacity short-term memory (Miller, 1956). The duration of this short-term memory was shown to be less than 18 seconds without rehearsal (Brown, 1958; Peterson & Peterson, 1959). In a classic study, Sperling (1960) was able to show that in addition to this limited capacity short-term memory we also have an even shorter sensory memory whose capacity is not so limited. Sperling briefly presented subjects with an array of 12 letters (three rows of 4 letters) and asked them to report the letters back when the display was removed. When subjects were asked to report all of the letters (the *whole-report* procedure), they could usually report about 5 or 6 items, consistent with a limited capacity short-term memory. However, when the subjects were asked to report only a portion of the items, such as a single row of letters (the *partial-report* procedure), they were very accurate even though they were not told which row to report until *after* the array was removed from the screen. Subjects could accurately report any portion of the array if cued immediately at stimulus offset, indicating that for a brief period of time subjects had all of the information available to them. Although Sperling could show that subjects had access to the entire array for a period of time, this time interval was clearly shorter than the amount of time it took to report the whole array, because subjects began to fail after about 6 items. In fact, if subjects were asked to report a single row of letters as little as 1/2 second following the offset of the array, they often could not accurately report the entire row, suggesting that the duration of this sensory memory was less than a second. Given his results with the *partial report* procedure, Sperling proposed that in addition to a limited capacity short-term memory, there is also a very brief sensory store (called iconic memory) whose capacity may be unlimited.

In this example, Sperling used two different procedures, the *whole-report* and *partial-report* procedures (the independent variable), and looked for differences in the accuracy of the subjects' reports (the dependent variable). He also examined the time from array offset to cue (a second independent variable). By manipulating these factors and looking for differences (or dissociations) in accuracy performance, he was able to hypothesize the structure of iconic memory. This type of study is typical in cognitive psychology. The goal of most studies is to manipulate an independent variable and look for a dissociation in the dependent variable. By examining the relation between the levels of independent variables and dissociations on dependent measures, cognitive psychologists are able to break cognition into its component parts, providing clues to its structure. Typical independent variable manipulations in cognition include stimulus characteristics, stimulus presentation, and instructions. Typical dependent variables include speed (reaction time) and accuracy. Although there are certainly exceptions, most cognitive research has relied on dissociations in performance on dependent measures to discover the organization of cognitive functions.

The strategy behind brain studies examining cognition is not that different. The primary difference between brain and behavioral studies is that a different type of independent or dependent variable is used, depending on the technique. For example, in a drug study, a researcher might use the same dependent measure as a typical cognitive study (e.g., reaction time), but the independent variable would differ (e.g., the presence or absence of the drug). With other techniques, such as neuroimaging, the independent variables are the same as those used in typical cognitive studies (e.g., stimulus type), but the researcher is looking for dissociations on a different type of dependent measure (i.e., brain activation). In all studies examining brain-behavior correlates of cognitive functions, either the dependent or the independent variable is one that would also be used in traditional behavioral studies. Just like more typical cognitive studies, the dissociations we see in these brain studies can help as break cognition into its component parts and provide insight into its organization.

Techniques in Human Brain Research: Three Examples of Brain Research Informing Cognitive Psychology

Lesion Studies

Background and Technique   The oldest and most widely used technique to study brain function in humans is the lesion (brain injury) study. Lesion studies have been of interest to psychologists almost since the beginning of cognitive psychology. In the late 1800s, at about the same time Wilhelm Wundt was setting up his psychology laboratory in Germany, Paul Broca of France and Carl Wernicke of Germany were describing components of language processing based on language dysfunctions suffered by individuals with brain injuries to the left frontal and temporal lobes (see Benson, 1993, for a review). Specifically, Broca described impaired speech production with normal comprehension following damage to the left posterior frontal lobe in an area now called *Broca's area,* and Wernicke described a separate deficit in language comprehension with normal production following damage to the left anterior temporal lobe. In the United States around the mid-1800s, Harlow described the famous patient Phineas Gage, who showed a marked change in personality and reasoning ability following an accident with a railroad spike in which he suffered frontal lobe damage (see Damasio & Anderson, 1993, for a review). Based on the study of Gage, Harlow suggested that personality and reasoning may be independent of traditional measures of intelligence, because Gage performed normally on tasks considered to be related to intelligence. Although Broca, Wernicke, and Harlow are not usually thought of as early researchers in the field of cognitive psychology, they were studying cognitive behaviors (language, intelligence, and reasoning) and providing insight into their organization.

One reason Broca, Wernicke, and Harlow may not have received credit as early cognitive psychologists is the technique they employed. Lesion studies in humans do not use the experimental method in the strict sense, in that the researcher cannot manipulate the independent variable. The independent variable used in these studies is the naturally occurring lesion to an individual's brain. The dependent variables are the same type of behaviors assessed in more traditional cognitive studies. After an individual is identified as having a lesion, the researcher can compare his or her behavior to that of normal control subjects, but the assignment of subjects to conditions is not random. For this reason, the lesion method in humans is sometimes called "quasi-experimental," in that the researcher can relate behaviors to lesions, but cannot manipulate the lesions themselves (Snodgrass, Levy-Berger, & Haydon, M. 1985). In a typical study, a researcher identifies a group of patients with similar lesions and a control group, who are usually normal subjects matched with the patients on some relevant characteristics such as age and level of education. The two subject groups are the levels of the independent variable. The researcher then presents both groups of subjects with the same stimuli and instructions and looks for differences between patients and controls on behavioral measures, such as accuracy or reaction time (the dependent variable). Like the more traditional behavioral studies, the dissociations in performance between patients and controls can give clues to the organization of cognitive function.

Example: Identifying Memory Systems   One area of cognitive research where lesion studies have had an impact in recent years is memory. When the layperson thinks about memory, what comes to mind is the ability to recollect events from the past at will. Most early memory research studied this ability to consciously recollect events (usually words), and it described phenomena such as forgetting curves, memory capacity, and the effect of stimulus type on performance. Although these topics are still studied today, memory research has expanded considerably and some of the new research topics in memory were inspired by the study of a patient referred to as H.M.

   H.M. was a young man with severe epilepsy who underwent surgical removal of his medial-temporal lobe (including the hippocampus) in an effort to control his epilepsy (Scoville, 1954). The surgery was successful in curbing the epilepsy but unfortunately left H.M. with a more serious problem: an apparent inability to acquire new long-term memories (he was able to remember events prior to his surgery and had normal short-term memory). At first it was thought that the part of the brain removed from H.M. must have contained the neuronal seat of all memory acquisition. However, two psychologists, Milner and Corkin, started to study H.M. and discovered that although he couldn't tell you he remembered anything, there were things he did seem to remember (Milner, Corkin, & Teuber, 1968). He could learn to do simple tasks, such as rotary pursuit (tracking a moving object) and mirror drawing (tracing the mirror image of an object). H.M. could learn these simple skills in spite of fact that he could not recollect ever having practiced them. This dissociation in H.M.'s performance between memory for events and retention of skills led researchers to begin breaking down memory into types, such as *declarative* (for events) and *procedural* (for skills). Like behavioral studies of memory, the research with H.M. helped dissociate components of a cognitive function. These studies with H.M. encouraged memory researchers to study other memory-impaired patients with naturally occurring lesions (due to a number of etiologies, including encephalitis, anoxia, and Korsakoff's syndrome) in an effort to further break down the components of memory.

Additional dissociations in memory performance between amnesics and controls were discovered in the 1970s, when Warrington and Weiskrantz (1970, 1974) demonstrated that amnesics have other intact memory abilities. They showed amnesic and normal control subjects lists of words. As expected, amnesics were impaired in recognizing the previously presented words. However, if the subjects were not asked to recognize the words, but were simply asked to generate the first words that come to mind when given the first three letters, the amnesic subjects showed the same advantage for previously presented words as did normal controls. In other words, amnesics performed normally when memory for the words was assessed without conscious effort, or implicitly, but were impaired when asked explicitly to recognize the previously presented words. This research suggested yet another type of memory, called *implicit memory,* that could be separated from our ability to recollect events at will, which is now called *explicit memory*. This dissociation of *implicit* and *explicit memory* led researchers to study the different characteristics of these memory types. It was discovered that manipulations that benefit one type of memory did not necessarily affect performance based on another memory type (Graf, Mandler, & Haden, 1982).

The studies with amnesic patients have led to a large body of research on implicit memory in both amnesics and normal subjects, which has changed the direction of memory research in general. Although the distinctions among skill memory, explicit memory, and implicit memory found in amnesics were not completely new to psychologists—William James had discussed all of these components a century ago (see Burkhardt & Bowers, 1981)—the compelling evidence for dissociations seen in H.M. and other amnesic patients propelled memory researchers once again to examine different types of memory. This has led researchers to propose that there are several interacting memory systems that are part of normal memory (e.g., Schacter & Tulving, 1994). The goal of memory research in recent years has been to understand the characteristics of these different systems. This is an example where the interaction between brain and behavioral studies has significantly influenced our approach in the study of a cognitive behavior.

Advantages and Disadvantages of Lesion Studies in Humans   The primary advantage of lesion studies in humans is that the evidence for dissociations is compelling. If one of the goals of cognitive psychology is to discover the components and organization of cognitive abilities, then showing that certain individuals can lack some cognitive abilities, but not others, is very strong evidence that these must be dissociable processes. In other words, observing how the system breaks down can provide clues as to how it must be put together. Another advantage of lesion studies in humans is that the dependent variables in these studies are the same as those used in traditional cognitive studies, that is, behavioral data. For this reason, it is relatively easy for psychologists to evaluate the results.

However, there are many disadvantages to lesion studies in humans, which should be taken into consideration when interpreting results with brain-damaged patients. First, the assignment of subjects to conditions is not random. Lesion studies are dependent on accidents of nature to occur. There is no control over who will be in your brain-damaged group. It may be the case that individuals who suffer brain damage may not be normal in other ways, aside from the primary behavioral deficit. This is true for H.M., who in addition to his surgery, had a lifetime of epilepsy, which may have affected his cognition in other ways. It is not appropriate to assume that brain-damaged individuals are similar to unimpaired controls except that they lack a single cognitive ability, because there are many other uncontrolled variables.

A second disadvantage is sample size. Often lesion studies rely on a single patient, or a case study, as evidence for a dissociation. Although case studies can be useful, it is hard to know how to generalize from an N of 1. It is especially hard to generalize from an N of 1 when the behavior in question varies a lot between individuals. Even when a group of subjects with similar lesions and behavioral deficits can be identified, the sample size tends to be smaller than normal behavioral studies.

A third disadvantage is the difficulty in identifying groups of patients with similar lesions and behavioral symptoms. Because the experimenter has no control over the lesion, the brain injuries, even for individuals with the same etiology and symptoms, may vary extensively. For this reason, it is difficult to know if variability in the patient group is due to variability in the behavior or the variability in the location or extent of injury.

Finally, a whole set of additional problems is encountered if a researcher tries to make behavioral links with specific brain areas. When a brain lesion leads to a behavioral deficit, it is difficult to know the precise role of the brain area. Imagine if you knew radios played music, but did not know anything about how radios worked. If you one day removed the battery and discovered that music was no longer played, would you assume the battery makes music? Just because a lesion in a brain area leads to a behavioral deficit, this does not mean the brain area "does" that behavior. When trying to discover brain-behavior relations, you must use caution and converging evidence from other techniques when describing the precise function of specific brain regions.

In spite of all the disadvantages of lesion studies, it is clear from their history that they provide a useful tool in the study of cognition. Discovering dissociations in behaviors is the primary tool in discovering the organization of cognition, and lesion studies show us behavioral dissociations. Although the interpretation of lesion studies can be problematic at times, at the very least they provide hints for cognitive components that can be explored further with behavioral studies in normal subjects.

Event-Related Potentials

Background and Technique   Event-related potentials (ERP) provide noninvasive measurements of electrical activity on the scalp that are linked to the presentation of stimuli (or events) (see Allison et al., 1986, for a detailed description). Although it may seem curious to study the outside of the head to learn about what goes on inside, the notion that studying the scalp can inform us about brain-behavior correlates is actually a very old one. In the late 1800s, Franz Joseph Gall, a skilled neuroanatomist, proposed that the mind consists of an interacting set of distinct mental functions (or *faculties*) and that each faculty is mediated by a specific, localized region of the brain. The idea that localized brain regions underlie different behaviors may seem intuitive at the present time, but in Gall's day this was actually a somewhat radical proposal. Unfortunately, Gall's theorizing went further when he proposed that the shape of the skull is related to the shape of the underlying brain and that by studying the shape of the skull (through feeling the scalp) one can learn about an individual's mental faculties (this study was later called phrenology). Although Gall's early idea that the localized regions of the brain may be related to different behaviors has been borne out by extensive research, there does not appear to be a close link between brain morphology and skull shape. Studying the shape of the skull has taught us little about the brain-behavior relationship.

ERP researchers study another aspect of the scalp, its electrical activity, which has been shown to be related to underlying brain function. Although the topic of this chapter is not brain physiology, a few basics are necessary to understand ERPs. The brain consists of a large number of nerve cells or neurons (approximately 10^{12}). There are several different types of neurons, the types differentiated from each other by a precise organization that varies among different structures and layers. When active, these neurons communicate by changes in electrical potentials across the cell membrane (postsynaptic potentials), which are generated by ionic current flow (see Carlson, 1986, for a review). These electrical potentials can be recorded by electrodes located in extracellular space or by electrodes located in electrically conductive material that is in contact with that space. Because the brain and its coverings (the skull, muscle, and scalp) are electrically conductive materials, electrical potentials measured on the scalp can reflect the electrical activity of the underlying neurons.

ERPs measure the changes in electrical potentials that occur in conjunction with an event, for example, seeing a word. In an ERP study, a number of electrodes are placed on the subject's head in a variety of locations. These electrodes measure electrical potentials. The potentials measured from the scalp are generated by the aggregate activity of the underlying brain tissue. The electrodes on the scalp measure potentials by comparing the difference in electrical activity between two electrodes. In most ERP studies, the electrical potentials are measured in relation to a single reference electrode, often placed on the subject's earlobe or chin. This allows the researcher to see a relative change in electrical activity and compare electrical activity across different regions of the scalp. In a typical study, a number of electrodes are placed on the subject's scalp in a variety of predetermined locations (usually between 8 and 32). The subject is then given a task, for example, seeing faces or objects and responding whenever a particular object is presented. For each stimulus presented, a wave form is generated for each electrode, which shows the change in electrical potential (in relation to the reference electrode), starting with stimulus onset. The measurement is the summation of electrical activity at that point on the scalp. In order to get a consistent signal for each stimulus type, the wave forms are averaged over several trials (usually more than 20). Most of the measurements of interest in ERP research occur within 500 ms of stimulus onset. The ERP signals generated are usually described by the peaks and troughs in the wave forms and are labeled according to their latency after stimulus onset. For example, a P300 is a positive change in potential (a peak) that occurs 300 ms after stimulus onset, and an N400 is a negative change in potential (a trough) that occurs 400 ms after stimulus onset. After a number of trials, the researcher can compare the averaged wave forms for the different stimulus types (e.g., faces vs. objects) and can look for relative differences in wave forms or potentials across the different locations on the scalp. This dissociation in wave forms or potentials between stimulus types can provide clues to the neural processing underlying the cognitive function. In ERP studies, the independent variables are the same as those in behavioral studies (e.g., stimulus characteristics), but the dependent measure is the change in electrical potentials on the scalp evoked by the stimuli.

Example: Selective Attention   One area of a cognitive psychology where ERP research has had an influence is attention. Research on attention in the modern era began with the information-processing approach to cognition. Early attention research by Broadbent (1954) proposed that attention is like a limited capacity communication channel, much like an electromechanical device. Broadbent suggested that during the allocation of attention a small portion of the information is made available to the senses for conscious evaluation. Although it was clear that attended stimuli are evaluated perceptually and semantically, the fate of unattended stimuli became a topic of debate. Treisman (1969) and Broadbent (1971) hypothesized that although unattended stimuli may be partially processed, the extent of this processing was attenuated (relative to attended stimuli) and limited to gross physical characteristics and highly meaningful semantic information (such as your own name). An opposing view was expressed by Deutsch and Deutsch (1963) and Norman (1968). They proposed that all stimuli that fall on the senses are fully processed for perceptual qualities and meaning and that the role of attention is to select the stimuli relevant to the appropriate response for the task at hand. In contrast to the Treisman-Broadbent approach, the Deutsch-Norman model suggested that processing of unattended stimuli is not attenuated on the sensory or semantic level but that all stimuli are processed equally until the subject must choose a response.

Although the two opposing views both had behavioral data to support the respective models, it was still difficult to resolve this debate because the behavioral data could often be explained by both models (see Lachman, Lachman, & Butterfield, 1979, for a review).

Using ERPs to examine the processing of unattended stimuli was a novel way to address this debate. In an early study, Hillyard, Hink, Schwert, & Picton (1973) looked at the ERP responses to tones presented to both ears. Previous research had shown that abrupt auditory information (such as a tone) will elicit a negative potential at about 100 ms (an N100). In the Hillyard et al. study, subjects were told to attend to the tones in one ear and count the number of tones at a particular pitch.

They were told to ignore the tones in the unattended ear. Hillyard et al. compared the N100 responses to tones presented in the attended and unattended ears and found that the N100 response was 20% to 70% smaller for the unattended tones. Later research demonstrated that the scalp location that showed the maximal N100 response, as well as the maximal change in this response with attention, was near the auditory cortex, suggesting that the attenuation is occurring at the early stages of auditory processing (Woldoroff & Hillyard, 1991). These results provided support for the idea that there is attenuated perceptual processing for unattended stimuli.

In a later study, McCarthy and Nobre (1993) examined the extent of semantic processing for unattended stimuli using ERPs. It had been documented that the ERP response to a word includes an N400 response occurring at frontal or central electrode sites. It is thought that the N400 response has something to do with semantic processing of the word, because it becomes significantly smaller when a word is preceded by a prime that is identical or related in meaning (i.e., either the same word or a highly related word, such as *doctor preceding nurse*). McCarthy and Nobre (1993) used a visual divided attention task where subjects were presented words in the right and left visual fields and were instructed to attend to one of the fields (while focusing on a central fixation point). The task was to respond whenever a member of a target category appeared in the attended visual field. Unbeknownst to the subjects, some of the nontarget words presented to both visual fields (attended and unattended) were words that were preceded by a prime. McCarthy & Nobre found an N400 response for words in the attended field that is smaller for those words that were preceded by a prime, consistent with previous research. However, they did not show any N400 response for words in the unattended field or differences in ERPs between those words in the unattended field that were preceded by and not preceded by a prime, suggesting limited semantic processing for words in the unattended field.

The results of the Hillyard et al., (1973) and McCarthy and Nobre (1993) studies, as well as the results of several other studies (see Hillyard, Mangun, Wolderoff, & Luck, 1995, for a review), suggest that unattended stimuli are not processed to the same extent as attended stimuli, perceptually or semantically. These neuronal responses to attended and unattended stimuli, as measured by ERPs, support the Treisman-Broadbent model, which proposes that the allocation of attention attenuates the processing of information, with the result that attended stimuli are processed more extensively than are unattended stimuli. This is an example in which studies examining brain function helped resolve a theoretical debate in cognitive psychology.

Advantages and Disadvantages of ERP Studies   ERP studies allow a relatively simple, noninvasive peek into the neural mechanisms underlying normal cognition. By studying the scalp, one can learn something about the function of the underlying brain tissue. The biggest advantage to ERPs is that they provide a glimpse into the brain during normal cognitive processing. As the preceding example illustrates, there are times when different models of a cognitive function may be consistent with the behavioral data. In these cases, different neuronal responses, as measured by ERPs, can provide additional data to help choose between the models.

A second advantage to ERPs is that they are informative about very short latency responses. In traditional cognitive studies, reaction time is examined to learn about a behavior, but it is clear that there are several stages of processing that must occur prior to the reaction time response. With ERPs, one can examine the characteristics of different stages of neuronal responses to stimuli, all of which occur prior to the reaction time response. This mental "reaction time" yields several measurements at all stages of processing.

A final advantage of ERPs is that they allow the experimenter to collect both behavioral data and neurophysiological data at the same time. Given this combination, it is possible to correlate behavioral performance to changes in ERP wave forms, providing additional insight into the mechanisms underlying the behavior.

Although ERPs can be informative for some problems, there are several disadvantages that limit their applicability when studying cognition. First, as was mentioned, ERPs measure short latency responses timed to stimulus onset. The potentials measured on the scalp are the summation of responses from a population of neurons to a discrete stimulus. Although the responses of this neuronal population may be uniform at first, over time the responses generally become more diverse. The summation of these later, diverse responses is less likely to yield consistent patterns. For this reason, ERPs can only measure immediate responses to discrete stimuli. This is an advantage when studying a behavior such as attention, but this technique would not be as useful when studying higher cognitive functions, such as reasoning, which take more time and may not be tied to a discrete stimulus.

A second disadvantage is that a large number of trials is needed for each stimulus type in order to get a consistent averaged wave form. Any time a large number of trials is used, there are problems with practice effects, fatigue, and motivation. Once again, for some types of behavioral studies, these factors may be more important than for others, but any study where previous exposure to a stimulus (or stimulus type) could bias future processing would not be appropriate for ERP research.

A third disadvantage of ERPs is that only gross localization of the source of the neuronal signal is possible. It is often assumed that the neural generator of the scalp recording is the neural tissue closest to the electrode, but this is not necessarily the case (see Allison, Wood, & McCarthy, 1986). The potential measured on the scalp is the summation of all electrical activity at the electrode site. Several factors can influence the electrical signal that summates on a given electrode, including the orientation of the nerve cells, the shape of the tissue, the shape of the tissue between the source of the electrical activity and the electrode, and other neuronal activity occurring prior to or simultaneously with stimulus onset. It is possible, depending on the orientation of neurons, that a large neuronal response may occur that does not yield *any* change in scalp potentials. For these reasons, it is best to think of wave forms as clues to changes in neuronal processing, but to avoid trying to draw conclusions about the precise functioning and location of the underlying neural tissue.

Finally, a big disadvantage to ERP studies, for researchers interested in cognition, is that the type of data (wave forms or maps of differences in potentials across the scalp) is unfamiliar to most cognitive psychologists. Most cognitive researchers are not used to looking at wave forms, and it takes some education and practice to know what to look for when evaluating ERP studies. For this reason, it has been difficult for ERP studies to integrate with traditional cognitive psychology to the same extent as have lesion studies.

There are several limitations in studying cognitive processing with ERPs, but these are similar to limitations that occur when reaction time is used as a dependent measure. In both cases, multiple trials are needed for a reliable response, the response must be tied to the onset of a discrete stimulus, and the pattern of responses doesn't necessarily say anything in particular about the cognitive process but must be interpreted in light of the stimulus manipulations and previous research. Nevertheless, there are times when reaction times are uniquely informative about cognitive processes, and this is also true for ERPs.

Functional Neuroimaging

Background and Technique One of the most exciting advances in brain research in recent history is *functional neuroimaging*. Functional neuro-imaging refers to a recently developed set of techniques for studying the brain-behavior correlates of cognition. There are two main techniques used in functional neuroimaging: *positron-emission tomography* (PET) and *functional magnetic resonance imaging* (fMRI). Both of these techniques have been around for only a short time (in fact the first fMRI study, Belliveau et al., was not published until 1991), but they have had rapid growth and acceptance in cognitive psychology. Before explaining the methodology used in these techniques, I will very briefly review the physiology behind the measurements for these two techniques.

Both PET and fMRI measure indices of blood flow in the human brain. The idea that blood flow in the brain is related to neuronal activity has been around since the 1890s, but no one is certain as to the nature of this response. Nevertheless, there is considerable evidence that blood flow to an area of the brain is an indication of neuronal activity (see Raichle, 1994, for more details). The method used to measure blood flow differs between the two techniques. In PET, blood flow is measured by injecting the subject with a radioactive isotope, oxygen 15 (^{15}O), immediately prior to the behavioral task. In the minute following the injection, the radioactive agent accumulates in the brain in direct proportion to local blood flow. The PET camera (a doughnut-shaped set of radiation detectors that circle the subject's head) can image the blood flow by counting the radiation, providing a map of blood flow during the behavioral task. The half-life for ^{15}O is very short (2 minutes) and the entire sample is decayed within 10 minutes, at which point another image can be acquired (see Posner & Raichle, 1994, and Raichle, 1994, for more details).

FMRI uses a less direct measure of blood flow, but it is naturally occurring so there are no injections or radiation. In MRI studies, the subject's head is placed in a large, doughnut-shaped magnet, which assures that a large number of protons in the brain are in a similar resting state (e.g., upright). The subject is then given a brief energy pulse, which temporally perturbs these protons. A scanning device outside the head records the energy that is released as these protons return to their resting state. Protons belonging to different types of molecules emit different patterns of energy as they return to their resting state. FMRI takes advantage of the natural magnetic properties of oxygenated and deoxygenated hemoglobin. The oxygenation of hemoglobin varies with local blood flow. FMRI produces a map of local blood flow in the brain by measuring the differences in magnetic susceptibility of protons in oxygenated and deoxygenated hemoglobin. Because the measure of blood flow is less direct in fMRI, the signal is often referred to as *activation,* instead of blood flow (see Cohen, Noll, & Schneider, 1993, for more details). Although the differences between PET and fMRI imaging techniques are significant and can influence experimental design and interpretation of results, there are similarities in the logic behind the techniques and there is evidence that they lead to similar patterns of brain activation in behavioral studies (McCarthy, Blamire, Rothman, Grnetter, & Shulman, 1993). For this reason, I will refer to them as a single technique, functional neuroimaging, for the remainder of the chapter.

The logic behind functional neuroimaging studies of cognition relies on the subtraction method initially introduced by Donders in the mid-1800s and reintroduced and extended by Sternberg (1969; see Posner & Raichle, 1994, for more details). Using this technique, Donders tried to learn about the timing of mental processes by measuring the reaction time of components of a task and subtracting this from the overall reaction time for the task. For example, Donders was interested in the amount of time it takes to discriminate between two lights. He first asked subjects to press a key whenever they saw a light. The time required to perform this task was used as a baseline simple reaction time without discrimination. He then asked subjects to respond whenever they saw one of two lights. Donders hypothesized that the time required to perform this second task would include the time required to make a simple response to a light, as well as the time required to discriminate between the two lights. By subtracting the time required for the simple reaction time task, from the time required for the discrimination task, Donders found that the additional time required for the discrimination was 50 ms. Using an extension of this logic, called the additive factors method, Sternberg (1969) was able to hypothesize about the nature of mental searches of active (short-term) memory. Although the subtraction method is not without its critics, it has been used extensively in cognitive psychology.

Functional neuroimaging borrows the idea that one can isolate mental functions by subtracting out component processes. However, in functional neuroimaging the goal is not to isolate the time required for mental processes, but rather the neuronal tissue active during these processes. An example of a typical neuroimaging study is an early PET study by Petersen, Fox, Posner, Mintun, & Raichle, (1988). In this study, subjects were given two tasks. In the *repeat* condition, the subjects were presented a word and were asked to repeat it (e.g., *chair-chair*). In the *generate* condition, the subjects were presented a word and were asked to generate another word that represented a use for the presented word (e.g., *cake-eat*). Repeating a word requires the subjects to see a word, read a word, and speak a word. Generating a use for a word requires all of these components, as well as forming semantic associations and selecting an action. In the Petersen et al. study, functional images were acquired while subjects performed both tasks. In order to acquire reliable measurements, each task needed to be performed several times during image acquisition. The average signal acquired during repeating words was then subtracted from the average signal acquired during generating words. The remaining significant differences in signal (i.e., areas of activation) were plotted on a mean image of the subjects' brains. These areas of activation were displayed as colored regions on brain images and were localized in specific brain regions. The activated regions are the areas that were relatively more active during the *generate* condition than the *repeat* condition. These brain regions are thought to be involved in the additional cognitive processing required when generating a use for a word.

Although the subtraction method has some difficulties, it is the primary method used to assess activation in the brain in functional neuroimaging studies. In these studies, the independent variables manipulated are similar to those used in traditional cognitive studies, but the dependent variable is the activation observed in different areas of the brain. By examining the relative differences in activation between tasks, it is possible to gain insight into the neural basis of cognitive processes.

Example: Mental Imagery   Functional neuroimaging is a relatively new tool for studying brain-behavior correlates in cognition, but it has already had an influence in the debate about the nature of mental imagery. It is well known that subjects can easily form an image of an object, such as a chair or the letter *f*, when instructed to do so. Researchers can then ask questions about this imagined object, and the subject can give specific answers based on the image. But what is the nature of the information the subject is using to perform these tasks? Is it similar to an actual visual image that the subject can scan in order to make the appropriate response? Or is it a set of principles or rules about the imagined object that the subject must search in order to make the appropriate response? These two opposing views have been debated by psychologists Pylyshyn and Kosslyn for a number of years. Pylyshyn (1981) argues that people have tacit knowledge (i.e., learned without effort and unavailable to conscious evaluation) of the structure of objects that can be used when performing mental imagery tasks. This has been called the *propositional* view of mental imagery because it assumes this knowledge is in the form of a list of properties about objects, as opposed to an internal visual image. The opposing view, called the *analogue* approach, was proposed by Shepard (1978) and Kosslyn (1981), who argue that when performing imagery tasks the mind constructs an internal analogue of the actual object that is visual in nature. In support of his view, Kosslyn cites data showing that reaction time on mental imagery tasks, such as scanning and rotation, corresponds to the actual spatial characteristics of the object, suggesting the subjects are mentally manipulating images with spatial qualities. Pylyshyn argues that although there are situations where reaction time on imagery tasks seems to correspond to spatial variables of the actual objects, this correspondence does not hold up in all circumstances. He suggests that when the time required for imagery tasks does correspond to the spatial characteristics of the objects, it is likely the result of the subjects' tacit or propositional knowledge of the objects that allows them to simulate the use of visual-spatial representations. Like the example with selective attention presented earlier, this is a situation in which both views can explain the behavioral data and additional evidence is needed to help resolve the debate.

In an effort to find evidence of visual processing during an imagery task, Kosslyn et al. (1993) conducted a PET study. It is well known, through lesion studies with humans and animal models, that certain areas of the brain are specialized for the processing of visual information, particularly the visual cortex. In this study, Kosslyn attempted to demonstrate that some areas of the visual cortex that are active in perception are also active during imagery (Kosslyn et al., 1993, experiment 2). Subjects were shown letters constructed in a grid. After subjects became familiar with these letters, they were asked to perform three different tasks. In the *imagery* condition, subjects were shown a grid and were asked to image a specific letter (e.g., *F*). An *X* was then flashed in the grid, and subjects were asked to indicate if the *X* fell within the image of the letter. In the *perception* condition, subjects were shown a degraded version of the letter on the grid. An *X* was flashed on the grid, and subjects were asked to indicate if the *X* fell within the letter. In the *baseline* condition, subjects saw a grid. An *X* was flashed on the grid, and subjects were asked to indicate when the *X* appeared. PET images were acquired during all three tasks, and three subtractions were conducted: *imagery-perception, imagery-baseline,* and *perception-baseline*. Although there were activations in all of these subtractions that are meaningful to the interpretation of the results, the finding of primary interest is that there were common areas of activation observed in the visual cortex in both the imagery-baseline and the perception-baseline subtractions. The imagery-perception subtraction did not show this activation because presumably this area was active in both tasks.

The activation of the visual cortex during visual imagery is a strong indication that subjects are constructing internal visual images during imagery tasks. These data support the analogue approach to visual imagery. Although there are also lesion data to support the analogue view of imagery (see Farah, 1995), this is an example in which functional neuroimaging has informed cognitive theory.

Advantages and Disadvantages of Functional Neuroimaging   The primary advantage of functional neuroimaging studies, and the reason for its rapid growth into a significant tool in the field, is the type of data collected. Although ERPs provide a glimpse into brain processing through wave forms, functional neuroimaging provides colored maps of precisely where in the brain the processing occurs. These colored maps have been popular with the media and are appealing in an intuitive sense. One can imagine that parts of the brain "light up" during cognitive processing, and the data from functional neuroimaging studies provide a picture of this occurring. Functional neuroimaging is a safe, noninvasive technique to measure localized brain functioning in normal subjects.

A second advantage of functional neuroimaging studies is that they provide a great deal of data about the cognitive processes being measured. Usually when conducting a functional neuroimaging study, the researcher has a hypothesis, based on previous research with this or other techniques, about a specific area of the brain that might be activated. Although the researcher may or may not see the hypothesized area of activation in the subtraction, there are almost always several additional areas of activation that appear. The additional areas may be due to uncontrolled variables in the two subtracted tasks or may reflect unanticipated aspects of the cognitive function being examined. In some cases, these additional areas of activation can provide new insight into the cognitive behavior.

A third advantage of functional neuroimaging studies is that behavioral data can also be collected along with activation data (although speaking during imaging studies is often difficult due to movement of the head). These behavioral data can be compared to changes in activation to provide additional evidence for brain-behavior correlates of cognition.

There are several disadvantages of functional neuroimaging studies that need to be considered when drawing conclusions from this type of data. First, these techniques are very new and there are still several unresolved issues. For instance, the precise relation between activation and brain function is unclear. There are situations where, based on studies with other techniques, one might expect to see activation in a particular brain region, but activation does not appear. On the other hand, it is often the case that activation does appear in unexpected brain regions. These results may be informing us about fallacies in our previous theories of brain function or may be due to artifacts of activation studies. In addition, there are still significant debates about the proper method for analyzing data (see McCarthy, Puce, Luby, Belgar, & Allison, 1996). Although the resulting pictures of activation are very clean and appealing, there are several stages of data analysis that go into generating these pictures. There is still no general agreement on which techniques for analyzing data are the best and most reliable.

A second disadvantage to functional neuroimaging studies is the reliance on the subtraction methodology. Blood flow in the brain varies considerably across regions. Without a baseline condition to subtract from cognitive tasks, the images generated may not reflect task-specific activation. However, choosing the right baseline subtraction task requires knowledge about the mental operations involved in different tasks. This is a situation where a good understanding of the task and the cognitive behavior is necessary. If an inappropriate baseline task is chosen, then the activation data may reflect something other than the cognitive operations of interest. Some researchers are beginning to have more than one baseline condition in order to control for different, unintended variables. Such concern is essential because the quality of activation data, and the conclusions that can be drawn from them, are completely dependent on choosing the appropriate baseline task.

A final disadvantage of functional neuroimaging studies is also listed earlier as an advantage: the amount of data that is generated. Cognitive psychologists are used to seeing discrete differences in behavioral-dependent measures. With activation data, a large number of colored areas are plotted on the brain, and the researcher is supposed to conclude something about the neural basis of cognition from these data. Not only is the type of data unfamiliar, but there are usually several areas of activation, even though only a few proposed cognitive operations are being measured. It is sometimes difficult for cognitive psychologists to know what to make of these data. Even if the activation observed is expected and consistent with previous results, it is not always clear how showing that a particular area of the brain is active informs us about cognitive processing. In order to make sense of these data, a good understanding of the cognitive behavior is necessary.

Functional neuroimaging is a technique that actually allows the researcher to look inside the brain of individuals during cognitive behaviors. Given its short history, it is clear that functional neuroimaging is in its infancy as a technique for assessing brain function. It is likely that within the next few years, some of the difficulties mentioned here may be resolved. Still, functional neuroimaging, more than any technique discussed thus far, requires a good understanding of cognition in order to be informative. At its current rate of progression it is likely that we will have more activation data than cognitive explanations for these data. If this is the case, we may end up listing activations with no real understanding of their significance or end up choosing inappropriate baseline tasks. Hopefully, the growth of functional neuroimaging will be intertwined with the study of cognition so that this powerful technique can be used to enhance our understanding of brain function, as well as the structure of cognition.

Conclusions about Brain and Behavioral Studies of Cognition

In the beginning of this chapter, I set out to address two questions. The first was whether we can learn about cognition from studying the brain. I hope the examples I provided of the different techniques convinced you that studying the brain can inform our understanding of cognition. Although it is impossible to know if the issues presented in the examples would have eventually been resolved with behavioral studies, brain studies were able to address these questions first. The goal cognitive psychologists are attempting to achieve—an understanding of the mind—is extremely difficult to reach. There is no reason not to use every available technique to help achieve this goal.

I also hope that the review of the techniques gave you a better understanding of how brain research in cognition is conducted. Although I could not cover all the relevant techniques (e.g., drug studies, magnetoencephalography, and models derived from nonhuman animals), I tried to cover the three most commonly used to study cognitive behaviors. With the background information presented in the review of the techniques, you should at least have the necessary tools to be an "educated consumer" when evaluating studies you may encounter.

The second question I set out to address was whether it is necessary to study the brain to explain cognitive behavior. In my opinion the answer is yes, but let me present some of the history of this debate before trying to persuade you that my opinion is correct.

The relationship between the mind and the body (or the brain) has been debated since the days of the early philosophers (see Churchland, 1986, for a review). Although in earlier times, the debate concerned the question of whether the body has anything to do with the mind, in more recent times it has been generally accepted that the mind is somehow related to the brain. However, even with the acceptance of the relationship between the two entities, it is still a matter of debate whether or not studying the brain can tell us anything about the mind. The primary argument against studying the brain to learn about the mind relies heavily on the computer analogy for cognitive processing, which became popular about the same time computers were first starting to be widely used (see Miller, Galante, & Pribram, 1960). This analogy suggests that the brain can be thought of as the hardware of a powerful computer (such as the hypothesized Turing machine; Miller et al., 1960). Presumably this hardware, if given the correct instructions, or software, could perform any task. In this analogy, the performance of the task, or the behavior, is thought to result solely from the instructions in the software, independent of the architecture of the hardware (which, presumably, with the right software, could perform other tasks). The software in this case outlines the structure and organization of cognition, and, it is argued, the hardware is irrelevant when trying to understand the organization of the software. This argument is expressed succinctly by Johnson-Laird in his 1980 book *Mental Models,* where he states that

Psychology (the study of programs) can be pursued independently from neurophysiology (the study of the machine and machine code). The neurophysiological substrate must provide a physical basis for the processes of the mind, but granted that the substrate offers the computational power of recursive functions, its physical nature places no constraints on the patterns of thought. (p. 9)

This argument suggests that studying the brain to help understand cognition is misguided.

In my opinion, there is one major flaw with the computer analogy. It assumes that the brain is a computational machine with the power of recursive functions, or in other words, a relatively simple machine with the theoretical ability to perform any task. If this is the case, why has the brain never performed certain tasks, despite good efforts by several people to reprogram it? For instance, no matter how hard I try, I will never be able to have perfect memory or read this entire book in less than a minute, and neither will anybody else. The software presumably should be malleable, but the brain will not allow it. The brain is an extremely complex structure that shows a remarkable degree of similarity across individuals and, in some respects, across species. Furthermore, the organization of the brain is orders of magnitude more complex than that of the hypothesized computers described by Miller et al. (1960) and Johnson-Laird (1980). Although in theory, computers, with the right software, should be able perform operations thought of as cognitive, this does not mean that the brain works in a similar manner. Rather, humans have evolved with a detailed brain structure and a pattern of processing information that is consistent across individuals. To suggest that this regularity in brain structure is irrelevant to the characteristics of behavior not only goes against evolutionary theory, but is also inconsistent with data we all are familiar with showing that there are predictable changes in information processing when the brain state is altered through drugs or damage. If the brain were a simple computational machine, one would not expect behavior to break down in such predictable and precise ways when the brain is altered.

It is my opinion that a true understanding of cognition requires at least some explanation of the origin of cognitive behaviors, which lies in brain function. Understanding the brain-behavior correlates of cognition not only will inform our efforts to understand cognition at a behavioral level, but will also allow us to have a more complete description of cognitive processing. The structure and organization of knowledge are intimately tied to the structure and organization of the brain, and it would be extremely difficult to have a good understanding of cognition on one level of analysis (i.e., behavior) without some insight into other levels of analysis (i.e., brain function).

However, I believe success in understanding brain correlates of cognition is dependent on the quality of behavioral research. Without at least a rudimentary understanding of cognitive behaviors, it is difficult to know what questions to ask with even the most sophisticated techniques for studying brain function. Although our understanding of cognition on the behavioral level may be altered by data from brain studies, without some understanding of the behavioral components of cognition, it is impossible to ask meaningful questions in brain studies or to make sense of the results. Studies of brain function rely on cognitive theory to help guide the research. For this reason, I think it is a mistake to study the brain without close attention to the behavioral data. With the growing interest in the field of cognitive neuroscience (the study of brain-behavior correlates of cognition), I believe an increased emphasis needs to be placed on the growth and quality of behavioral research. Without a good understanding of cognitive behaviors, the study of brain function underlying the behaviors would be extremely difficult. It is my hope that progress in the behavioral study of cognition will proceed as rapidly as our ability to study the cognitive correlates of brain function.

References

Allison, T., Wood, C. C., & McCarthy, G. (1986). The central nervous system. In M. G. H. Coles, E. Donchin, & S. W. Porges (Eds.), *Handbook of physiology* (pp. 5–25). New York: Guilford Press.

Anderson, J. R. (1985). *Cognitive psychology and its implications* (2nd ed.). New York: W. H. Freeman.

Belliveau, J. W., Kennedy, D. N., McKinstry, R. C., Buchbinder, B. R., Weisskoff, R. M., Cohen, M. S., Vevea, J. M., Brady, T. J., & Rosen, B. R. (1991). Functional mapping of the human visual striate cortex by magnetic resonance imaging. *Science, 254,* 716–719.

Benson, D. F. (1993). Aphasia. In K. M. Heilman & E. Valenstein (Eds.), *Clinical neuropsychology* (3rd ed., pp. 17–36). New York: Oxford University Press.

Broadbent, D. E. (1954). The role of auditory localization in attention and memory span. *Journal of Experimental Psychology, 47,* 191–196.

Broadbent, D. E. (1971). *Decision and stress.* New York: Academic Press.

Brown, J. (1958). Some tests of decay theory of immediate memory. *Quarterly Journal of Experimental Psychology, 10,* 12–21.

Burkhardt, F., & Bowers, F. (Eds.). (1981). *The works of William James* (Vols. 1–3). Cambridge, MA: Harvard University Press.

Carlson, N. R. (1986). *Physiology of behavior* (3rd ed.). Boston: Allyn & Bacon.

Churchland, P. S. (1986). *Neurophilosophy: Towards a unified science of the mind/brain.* Cambridge, MA: MIT Press.

Cohen, J. D., Noll, D. C., & Schneider, W. (1993). Functional magnetic resonance imaging: Overview and methods for psychological research. *Behavior Research Methods, Instruments and Computers, 25,* 101–113.

Damasio, A. R., & Anderson, S. W. (1993). The Frontal Lobes. In K. M. Heilman & E. Valenstein (Eds.), *Clinical Neuropsychology* (3rd ed., pp. 409–460). New York: Oxford University Press.

Deutsch, J. A., & Deutsch, D. (1963). Attention: Some theoretical considerations. *Psychological Review, 70,* 80–90.

Farah, M. J. (1995). The neural bases of mental imagery. In M. S. Gazzaniga (Ed.), *The cognitive neurosciences* (pp. 963–975). Cambridge, MA: MIT Press.

Graf, P., Mandler, G., & Haden, P. E. (1982). Simulating amnesic symptoms in normal subjects. *Science, 218,* 1243–1244.

Hillyard, S. A., Hink, R. F., Schwent, V. L., & Picton, T. W. (1973). Electrical signs of selective attention in the human brain. *Science, 182,* 177–180.

Hillyard, S. A., Mangun, G. R., Woldoroff, M. G., & Luck, S. J. (1995). Neural systems mediating selective attention. In M. S. Gazzaniga (Ed.), *The cognitive neurosciences* (pp. 665–681). Cambridge, MA: MIT Press.

Kosslyn, S. M. (1981). The medium and the message in mental imagery: A theory. *Psychological Review, 88,* 46–66.

Kosslyn, S. M., Albert, N. M., Thompson, W. L., Malkovic, V., Weise, S., Chabris, C. F., Hamilton, S. E., Rauch, S. L., & Buananno, F. S. (1993). Visual mental imagery activates topographically organized visual cortex: PET investigations. *Journal of Cognitive Neuroscience, 5,* 263–287.

Johnson-Laird, P. N. (1980). *Mental models.* Cambridge, MA: Harvard University Press.

Lachman, R., Lachman, J. L., & Butterfield, E. C. (1979). *Cognitive psychology and information processing: An introduction.* Hillsdale, NJ: Earlbaum.

LeDoux, J. E., & Hirst W. (Eds.). (1986). *Mind and brain: Dialogues in cognitive neuroscience.* New York: Cambridge University Press.

McCarthy, G., Blamire, A. M., Rothman, D. L., Gruetter, R., & Shulman, R. G. (1993). Echo-planar MRI studies of frontal cortex activation during word generation in humans. *Proceedings of the National Academy of Sciences, 90,* 4952–4956.

McCarthy G., & Nobre A. C. (1993). Modulation of semantic processing by spatial selective attention. *Electroencephalograhy and Clinical Neurophysiology, 88*, 210–219.

McCarthy, G., Puce, A., Luby, M, Belgar, A., & Allison, T. (1996). Magnetic resonance imaging studies of functional brain activation: Analysis and interpretation. In I. Hashimoto, Y. C. Okada, & S. Ogawa (Eds.), *Visualization of information processing in the human brain: Recent advances in MEG and functional MRI* (pp. 15–31). New York: Elsevier.

Miller, G. A. (1956). The magical number seven plus or minus two: Some limits on our capacity for processing information. *Psychological Review, 63*, 81–97.

Miller, G. A., Galanter, E., & Pribram, K. H. (1960). *Plans and the structure of behavior.* New York: Adams, Bannister, & Cox.

Milner, B., Corkin, S., Teuber, H.-L. (1968). Further analysis of the hipocampal amnesic syndrome: 14 year follow-up of study H. M. *Neuropsychologia, 6*, 215–234.

Norman, D. A. (1968). Toward a theory of memory and attention. *Psychological Review, 75*, 522–536.

Peterson L. R., & Peterson, M. (1959). Short term retention of individual items. *Journal of Experimental Psychology, 58*, 193–198.

Petersen, S. E., Fox, P. T., Posner, M. I., Mintun, M., & Raichle, M. E. (1988). Positron emission tomographic studies of cortical anatomy of single-word processing. *Nature, 331*, 585–589.

Posner, M. I., & Raichle, M. E. (1994). *Images of mind.* New York: Scientific American Library.

Pylyshyn, Z. W. (1981). The imagery debate: Analogue media vs. tacit knowledge. *Psychological Review, 88*, 16–45.

Raichle, M. E. (1994). Visualizing the mind. *Scientific American, 270*, 58–64.

Schacter, D. L., & Tulving, E. (Eds.). (1994). *Memory systems 1994.* Cambridge, MA: MIT Press.

Scoville, W. B. (1954). The limbic lobe in man. *Journal of Neurosurgery, 11*, 64–66.

Shepard, R. N. (1978). The mental image. *American Psychologist, 33*, 125–137.

Sperling, G. A. (1960). The information available in brief visual presentation. *Psychological Monographs, 74* (Whole No. 498).

Snodgrass, J. G., Levy-Berger, G., & Haydon, M. (1985). *Human experimental psychology.* New York: Oxford University Press.

Sternberg, S. (1969). The discovery of processing stages. *Acta Psychologia, 30*, 276–315.

Treisman, A. M. (1969). Strategies and models of selective attention. *Psychological Review, 76*, 282–292.

Warrington, E. K., & Weiskrantz, L. (1970). Amnesia: Consolidation or retrieval? *Nature, 228,* 972–974.

Warrington, E. K., & Weiskrantz, L. (1974). The effect of prior learning on subsequent retention in amnesic patients. *Neuropsychologia, 12,* 419–428.

Woldoroff, M., & Hillyard, S. A. (1991). Modulation of early auditory processing during selective listening to rapidly presented tones. *Electroencephalograhy and Clinical Neurophysiology, 79,* 170–191.

10

Response Time versus Accuracy in Human Memory

Michael Kahana and Geoffrey Loftus

One of the first decisions confronting a behavioral scientist is the choice of a measurement instrument that appropriately captures some relevant aspect of human behavior. Consider a typical memory experiment. A subject is presented with a list of words to remember. Immediately after studying the list, a word is presented, and the subject's task is to judge, as quickly and accurately as possible, whether the word was shown in the studied list. Data in this experiment consist of both the subject's response ("yes" or "no") and the time it took the subject to make the given response (called *response latency, response time,* or *reaction time;* hereafter, RT). Many scientists seem to religiously adhere to the study of either response accuracy or response time; rarely are both investigated simultaneously in a given experimental design. Is this a mistake, or are accuracy and response time perhaps just two sides of the same coin—two measures that can be used interchangeably, depending on which is more convenient in a given experimental design? The goal of this chapter is to attempt to answer this question through a selected review and analysis of some of the basic experimental results and theoretical issues in the area of human memory.

Although interest in RTs has been around for a long time (e.g., Donders, 1868/1969; Helmholtz, 1850), until recently research in human memory has been almost exclusively concerned with measures of response accuracy. In a survey of memory texts published during the 1970s (Baddeley, 1976; Crowder, 1976; Hall, 1971; Kausler, 1974; Murdock, 1974), fewer than 4% of the experiments cited reported data on RTs. Beginning in the late 1960s, however, a whole host of new problems emerged that required the use of RT as the measure of interest: semantic-priming effects (e.g., Meyer & Schvaneveldt, 1971); perceptual priming (Neely, 1981); implicit serial, or sequence, learning (Jiménez, Méndez, & Cleeremans, 1996; Reber, 1967); and short-term memory (Sternberg, 1966)—each of which will be addressed in this chapter. However, it was not until the mid-1970s, when real-time personal computers became standard tools in the psychological laboratory, that the study of RTs became standard in the field. A recent text on human memory (Anderson, 1995) contains a healthy mix of accuracy and RT data.

Not only is there now a heightened interest in RT within cognitive research, but new experimental techniques that combine measurement of processing time and response accuracy have emerged.[1] Later in this chapter, we examine some of these techniques in detail. In discussing the relation between RT and accuracy in human cognition, we will focus primarily on data and theory within the domain of human memory.

Accuracy and Interresponse Times in Free Recall

A first analysis of memory tasks reveals that making a task harder increases error rates and RTs. As a case study, consider the correlation between measures of accuracy and measures of RT in one of the classic verbal memory tasks—*free recall*. In free recall, subjects are presented, one by one, with a set of to-be-remembered items and are then asked to recall as many items as they can remember in any order. The task is "free" because unlike most other memory tasks, the experimenter exerts minimal control over the retrieval process; all cues other than the general cue to recall the list items are internally generated by the subject.

The free recall task is deceptively simple. The experimenter asks the subject a very simple question, but the subject is free to do a great many things. Consider first the nature of the responses. How many list items did the subject recall? In what order were the items recalled? Were any nonlist items recalled? What was the relation between these items and the items in the studied list? How much time elapsed between successive responses? Do these interresponse times vary as a function of the number of items recalled or the length of the list? These questions just begin to point out the wealth of data obtained using this task.

An initial examination of recall accuracy reveals several regularities. Early and late list items are remembered better than items from the middle of the list. The advantage for the first and last few items are referred to as a *primacy* effect and a *recency* effect, respectively. The curve that describes the relation between the position of the items in the list and the probability of recall is termed a *serial position curve*. These results are remarkably stable across subjects, stimulus materials, and many incidental characteristics of the experimental design (Greene, 1992; Murdock, 1962).[2]

It is not sufficient to merely describe these data; the goal of cognitive science is to characterize the memory processes that produce the observed results. Much research has been devoted to understanding the process of free recall, and one successful model of this task is the *Search of Associative Memory* (SAM) model (Raaijmakers & Shiffrin, 1980, 1981; Shiffrin & Raaijmakers, 1992). A central notion in memory research, which is captured in SAM, is that items, processed sequentially or in a common temporal context, become *associated* or linked with one another. In terms of the data, an association between two items, *A* and *B,* simply means that the likelihood of recalling *B* is increased in the presence of *A* (either as an externally or internally provided cue). Is this true in our free recall task? Kahana (1996) reanalyzed data from a number of free recall studies and found that after recall of a given list item, the probability of recalling one of its neighbors (in terms of its position in the studied list) is greatly enhanced. A *conditional response probability* (CRP) function relates the probability of recalling a given item to its distance (in the study list) from the last item recalled. Figure 10.1 (left panel) shows the CRP function for data obtained by Murdock and Okada (1970).

Two aspects of the CRP functions are consistently obtained in studies of free recall: contiguity and asymmetry. Contiguity refers to the finding that items tend to be recalled after other items that were studied in adjacent list positions. For example, item 6 is more likely to be recalled immediately after item 5 than immediately after item 3. Asymmetry refers to the finding that among successively recalled items that were adjacent in the study list, forward transitions (item 5 then item 6) are about twice as likely as backward transitions (item 6 then item 5).

So far, we have just considered accuracy. What can be said of the *interresponse times* (IRTs) between successively recalled items? Like CRP

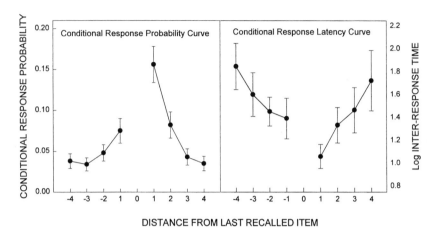

Figure 10.1
Conditional response probability curve (left panel) and conditional response latency curve (right panel) for Murdock & Okada's (1970) study of free recall. Log interresponse time (IRT) is computed as ln (1 + *IRT*). Error bars reflect 95% confidence intervals around each mean. Confidence intervals were calculated using the Loftus & Masson (1994, appendix B) procedure for within-subject designs.

curves, *conditional response latency* (CRL) functions relate IRTs between successively recalled items to their proximity in the original study list. CRL data from Murdock and Okada (1970) are shown in figure 10.1 (right panel). IRTs are short when neighboring list items are recalled successively. IRTs increase as the separation between the items' positions in the study list increases.

The IRT functions mimic the basic result portrayed in the CRP functions—namely, the more likely the transition, the faster the transition. It is tempting to say that both CRP and CRL functions reflect the operation of a single latent construct—associative strength.[3] Nearby items are more strongly associated with each other than are distant items. The stronger the association, the higher the probability and the shorter the IRT between successively recalled items. This is one version of a strength theory of memory—accuracy and IRTs are just two measures of the strength of information stored in memory.

When average accuracy and RT data show similar patterns, we are tempted to hypothesize that these commonalities are indicative of a single underlying process. However, this is not necessarily the case. To take a common example, height and weight show highly similar patterns and yet it is unlikely that they reflect a single underlying variable. Different eating behaviors can affect weight without having any effect on height.

Semantic Clustering

Preexperimental semantic relations among list items also exert a powerful influence on recall order and on recall accuracy.[4] This is often investigated using a *categorized free-recall* task. Subjects study a list of words drawn from a number of different categories (e.g., *airplane, ruby, dog, celery, diamond, car, truck, elephant, tomato, mule, cabbage, boat*). These words are presented in a random order, and subjects are asked to recall the items in any order they like (standard free-recall instructions). The relevant data are the order of recall and the IRTs between successively recalled items. When subjects recall a categorized word list, items belonging to the same category are usually recalled successively and in rapid succession (short within-category IRTs). These categorically related word clusters are separated by long between-category IRTs (Patterson, Meltzer, & Mandler, 1970; Pollio, Kasschau, & DeNise, 1968; Pollio, Richards & Lucas, 1969; Wingfield, Lindfield, & Kahana, 1998).

Although there is substantial data on free recall of categorized lists, there is a paucity of data on the effects of interitem similarity on free recall of random word lists. Unfortunately, studies that have carefully measured interitem similarity and output order in free recall (e.g., Cooke, Durso, & Schvaneveldt, 1986; Romney, Brewer, & Batchelder, 1993) have not simultaneously collected data on IRTs.

Like the data on conditional response probability and latency, semantic cluster effects can be interpreted as reflecting differences in associative strength. Items that are similar in meaning, or members of a common category, are more strongly associated. These items will tend to be recalled together, and the IRTs will be very short. To get from recalling items within a given category to recalling the items in the next category requires subjects to rely on the weaker associations that link all of the experimental items together—associations that stem from the common experimental context in which the items were studied.

Exponential Increase in IRTs

Another feature of the categorized recall is that within-category and be-tween-category IRTs start out fast and slow down with each transition. This finding mirrors a basic result observed in free recall of random word lists: IRTs increase *exponentially* with output position. Figure 10.2 shows the increase in IRTs with output position reported by Murdock and Okada (1970). Rohrer and Wixted (1994) have shown that this finding holds up under variations in list length, presentation rate (of the list items), and a number of other variables.

What causes this increase in IRTs? According to strength theory, items with the strongest representations are recalled first and fastest. The re-maining items, being necessarily weaker, take longer to recall, thus pro-ducing the accelerating interresponse times with output position. Note

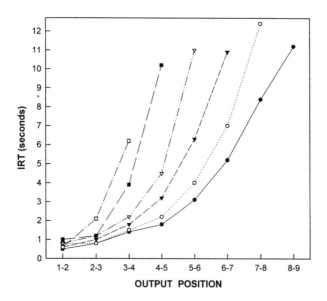

Figure 10.2

This figure shows data from Murdock & Okada (1970) illustrating the exponen-tial increase in IRTs with output position. Subjects in this experiment studied lists of 20 common words presented visually. Vocal responses were tape recorded and IRTs were measured. Each of the six curves in this graph represents a different total number of words recalled (4–9).

that this view does not assume that recalling some items has an effect on recall of subsequent items.

A more cognitively oriented model might propose that another process causes the IRTs to increase. One such model, the *random search-with-replacement* model, has been advocated by Rohrer and Wixted (1994; see also Wixted & Rohrer, 1994). In its simplest form, this is a pure retrieval model. According to this account, recall involves two stages. First, subjects search through recently activated items in memory (termed the *search set*) and sample an item for possible recall. If the item has already been recalled, it is rejected. If it has not already been recalled, the item is recalled. Assuming that it takes time to sample each item, as the ratio of recalled to non-recalled items increases in the search set, the time to recall the remaining items will increase as a consequence of the resampling and rejection of items already recalled. The process of random search with replacement mathematically predicts exponential growth of IRTs (McGill, 1963).

Wixted and Rohrer's (1996) random search with replacement account of IRTs in free recall can be seen as a specific instantiation of the general notion of output interference: that the act of recalling list items impairs access to other list items (cf. Tulving & Arbuckle, 1963). Such interference could be due to the resampling of the recalled items, or to a direct effect of the recalled list items on the accessibility of the not-yet-recalled memories.

Rohrer and Wixted take the generality of the exponential growth of IRTs in free recall as support for the notion of random search with replacement. Although they acknowledge that retrieval in free recall is influenced by many factors not captured in the oversimplistic random search model, they believe that a process akin to resampling is the likely cause of the rapid growth in IRTs with output position. This view is very different from strength theory in that random search with replacement argues that changes in accuracy and RT may be caused by primarily different, though interdependent, memory processes. Nevertheless, without independent evidence for the role of resampling in free recall, it is hard to reject the position that accuracy and RT in free recall are simply two sides of the same memory-strength coin.

Analysis of Memory under Conditions of High Accuracy

We began this chapter by raising the question of whether RT and accuracy are two sides of the same coin. If they are, why not let those who study accuracy live on in blissful ignorance of those who study RT, and vice versa? One reason not to do this revolves around the investigation of well-learned tasks such as reading, speech, naming objects, or performing a practiced motor sequence. In these tasks, people rarely make errors, yet speed may be of the essence. Therefore, to study tasks that are performed essentially without errors, we must consider RTs.

It is probably fair to say that almost all RT research is concerned with tasks where error rates are negligible. Entire areas of cognitive science rely on RTs as their exclusive source of data. For example, one major area of memory research is concerned with the structure of preexperimental semantic representations. These researchers use a variety of techniques including *lexical decision tasks* (LDT; i.e., deciding whether a letter string, such as VOLVAP, is a word) and *sentence verification tasks* (answering yes or no to questions such as "Is a canary a bird?"). RT data from these tasks provide insights into mental processes without making reference to response accuracy.

Even in the case of memory for newly acquired information, there are situations in which performance is relatively error free. Consider the learning of words in a foreign language. Initially subjects will make many errors, but after sufficient repetition, errors will be negligible. Considerable research has shown that RTs speed up dramatically even after accuracy reaches 100%. The reduction in RT with practice is characterized by what is called a *power law* (Newell & Rosenbloom, 1981). In almost any cognitive task, RT varies with practice according to an equation of the form

$$RT = aP^{-b} \tag{10.1}$$

where P is the number of practice trials, and a and b are positive constants that depend on the details of the material, the kind of practice, and the type of learning task. Such regularity summarizes a great deal of data across a variety of domains of cognition and serves as a benchmark that theories must meet.

A nice illustration of the power law can be found in a study by Woltz, Bell, Kyllonen, and Gardner (1996, experiment 3). Woltz et al. examined the contributions of *instance memory* and *rule memory* to the acquisition of a cognitive task. Subjects were given four-digit strings that could be transformed into a single digit by the sequential application of some combination of different rules. Each rule transforms two adjacent digits to a single digit (for example, if two adjacent digits are successive they are transformed into the next item in the sequence: 56 becomes 7; 65 becomes 4). Figure 10.3 shows RT and accuracy as a function of training. Over the two training blocks, RT decreased dramatically and in accord with the power law. Accuracy, on the other hand, remained essentially constant.

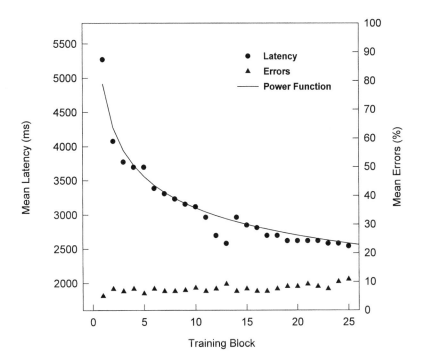

Figure 10.3
Accuracy and latency data in a digit-recoding task (Woltz, Bell, Kyllonen, & Gardner, 1996, experiment 3). The smooth line through the latency data represents the best-fitting power function. These data illustrate what is often called the *power law of learning*.

With practice, subjects got faster at transforming the four-digit strings into single digits. Is this because they were better at using the rules or because they had memory for instances of digit pairs, triples, or quads that they could simply recall? In a final phase of the experiment, subjects were given three types of multidigit strings to recode: strings that were identical with those recoded (i.e., transformed into a single digit) in the earlier training phases (old strings/old rules), new strings based on previously practiced recoding steps (new strings/old rules), and new strings that required new sequences of recoding operations (new strings/new rules). Woltz et al. (1996) found the most improvement for old strings/old rules, an intermediate amount for new strings/old rules, and the least transfer to new strings/new rules. These results were interpreted as evidence for both *instance-based learning* (i.e., learning of particular examples) and *rule-based learning.*

RT and Accuracy in Implicit Sequence Learning and Explicit Sequence Prediction

Sometimes RT (or accuracy) can reveal memory in the absence of intention to retrieve information from a learned episode. This type of memory is referred to as *implicit memory* and distinguished from intentional retrieval, which is termed *explicit memory* (Tulving & Schacter, 1991). Implicit memory has been examined for single items (Jacoby & Dallas, 1981; Tulving, Schacter & Stark, 1982), associations between items (Goshen-Gottstein & Moscovitch, 1995a, 1995b; Graf & Schacter, 1995), and sequences (Reber, 1967).

In studying implicit sequence learning, strings of letters or digits are generated through the use of a finite state grammar (Cleeremans & McClelland, 1991; Reber, 1967). To create the sequence of stimuli, one starts at a given node (figure 10.4) and probabilistically chooses a path to another node. Note that the first node is identical to the last node, so this generative process may be repeated indefinitely. The label of the chosen path is the current stimulus. To introduce some additional noise into the task, on some proportion of trials the stimuli are chosen randomly (i.e., without using the finite state grammar).

In one version of this approach (Jiménez et al., 1996), a simple RT task was employed; letters were shown one by one on the screen, and

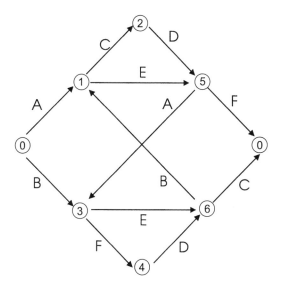

Figure 10.4
Depiction of the artificial grammar used by Jiménez, Méndez, & Cleeremans (1996). An artificial grammar is used to create a sequence of stimuli based on probabilistic rules. To create a sequence, begin with node zero and choose a random path. For simplicity, let us suppose that each path is chosen with an equal probability. If the path from 0 to 1 is chosen, the sequence begins with A. From node 1 there are two possible transitions. If node 5 is chosen, the second element in the sequence is E. This process may repeat indefinitely. Note that the sequence AEFBFDBC is generated by traversing the nodes 015034612. Not all sequences are valid. For example, there is no way to generate the sequence ABCD from this artificial grammar.

subjects pressed the key corresponding to the displayed letter. Unbeknownst to the subjects, there was a probabilistic pattern to the sequence of stimuli (letters). The basic result was that RTs consistently improved over trials. If a new grammar was switched to, RTs slowed down—this shows that the facilitation in performance was not simply due to a learning-to-learn effect. As is generally the case, the facilitation in RTs followed a power law. This improvement has typically been taken as evidence for implicit sequence learning.

Jiménez et al. (1996) introduced a second task in which subjects were instructed to press the key of the letter they thought would follow the probe letter. In this task, accuracy was the primary variable of interest and retrieval was explicit. Interestingly, subjects were able to predict the next letter at a rate substantially better than chance.

Because of the introduction of random letters every so often in the sequence, Jiménez et al. (1996) were able to assess the degree to which prior items in the sequence facilitated subsequent performance. They found that in both the explicit prediction task and the implicit reaction time task, two prior items added significantly to a single prior item, but a third prior item did not significantly improve performance. Contrary to expectations, implicit memory showed the same general pattern as explicit memory. Also, accuracy measures exhibited the same basic pattern of results as RT measures.

Accuracy and RT analysis of the Ranschburg Effect
Sequences of items that contain a repeated element are harder to reproduce than sequences consisting of all unique elements. For example, the sequence of digits 723856391 is harder to recall in order than the sequence 723856491. This finding is known as the *Ranschburg effect*.[5] At first glance, one would expect repetition of a list item to improve rather than worsen memory for ordered lists. A list with a repeated element has fewer different elements to be learned. This is especially evident in the case of words where the pool of possible elements is very large. In addition, we might expect processing the first of the repeated elements to facilitate, or prime, the processing of its repetition.

Rather than just considering subjects' overall ability to reproduce the list, Crowder (1968) and Jahnke (1969, 1970, 1972) examined error rates for individual list elements. They found that repeating elements at separated list positions resulted in impaired memory *only* for the second instance of the repeated element. In a sequence such as 723856391, subjects made more errors on the second of the repeated 3s than on an item from the same position in a control list (containing all unique elements). If, however, an element was repeated successively, subjects were *better* at recalling both repeated elements, but showed no facilitation or impairment in recalling the rest of the list. In a sequence such as 723385691, subjects performed better on the repeated 3s than on items from the same positions in a control list.

Greene (1991) suggested that a guessing strategy might account for the Ranschburg effect. Most studies of the Ranschburg effect employ lists of between 8 and 10 digits with only a single repeated element. When the set of elements is determined (i.e., the digits 0–9), the task only requires that subjects remember which elements belong in which positions. Even with lists of 8 or 9 digits, subjects have most of the information about the list elements, and the task depends primarily on remembering the order. At the end of the list, where performance is generally poor,[6] subjects are most likely to guess. Because only a single element is repeated, it makes sense to guess from among the elements (digits) that they have not already recalled. This will boost performance for all but the repeated items. Because the second repeated item is usually near the end of the list, where poor memory encourages guessing, recall of that element will show greatest impairment relative to the control list. Greene (1991) tested this guessing hypothesis by either encouraging subjects to guess liberally or telling subjects not to guess at all. When encouraged to guess liberally, the Ranschburg effect was enhanced. When guessing was strongly discouraged, the Ranschburg effect was eliminated.

Kahana and Jacobs (1998) wondered if a Ranschburg effect would be obtained using latency (IRTs) rather than accuracy as the variable of interest. Subjects studied lists of nine consonants with or without a single repeated element. The process of studying and recalling elements was repeated until each sequence was reproduced perfectly on three successive trials. On these final three perfect trials, the computer recorded the subjects' IRTs between successive recalls. Relative to a control list with no repeated elements, subjects had longer IRTs to the second repeated element if the repeated elements were spaced apart in the list. In contrast, subjects had shorter IRTs to the second repeated element if the repetitions were in nearby list positions. IRTs to the first of the repeated elements were unaffected by the repetition (as compared with control lists of nonrepeated elements). These results are shown in figure 10.5.

This study demonstrates that the Ranschburg effect, previously only known from accuracy data, can also be revealed using latency data (IRTs). But the latency data make Greene's (1991) guessing account far less appealing. Because the latency data are examined only after accuracy

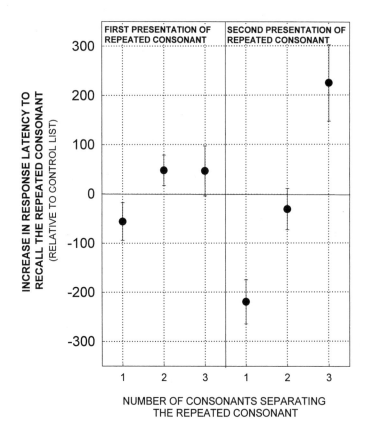

Figure 10.5
Data illustrating the effects of within-list item repetition on reaction times in a sequence recall task (Kahana & Jacobs, 1998). Error bars denote 95% confidence intervals. See text for details.

has reached 100%, it is unlikely that these data are contaminated by guesses. In addition, using lists of nine *consonants* as stimuli makes guessing relatively ineffective. As subjects pass the halfway point in the list, there are 16 possible items for only four remaining positions—guessing is not very helpful under these circumstances. Based on the Kahana & Jacobs study, it seems that the Ranschburg effect is a reliable memory phenomenon that can be revealed using both accuracy and latency measures. Although the parallel finding of Ranschburg interference in both accuracy and RT data may suggest that accuracy and RT are "two sides of the same coin," these two measures provide crucially different kinds of information with respect to the theories of the task.

The Subspan Item-Recognition Task

For a sufficiently easy task, one needn't engage in extensive practice to achieve near perfect accuracy. For example, if you ask someone to remember a five-digit number over a period of time during which there is no distracting information presented, error rates will be negligible. *Memory span* is a term used to denote the number of items that a person can reproduce in the correct order without errors. Lists of items that are shorter than an average person's memory span (about seven digits, six letters, or five words; Crannell & Parish, 1957) are called *subspan* lists, and lists that exceed memory span are termed *supraspan* lists.

Sternberg (1966) examined recognition memory for subspan lists. In the subspan item-recognition task (also called the Sternberg task or the memory-scanning task), subjects are presented with a short list of items (digits, words, letters, etc.). Following a brief delay (typically 1–2 seconds), a probe item is shown, and subjects indicate whether the item was one of the elements of the original list. In Sternberg's original experiments, subjects were well practiced at this task.

Because the list is subspan, there are few errors (less than 5%) and consequently the dependent variable of interest is RT. The effects of numerous experimental manipulations on RT have been investigated. These include variations in list length, probe type (list items versus nonlist items), serial position of the probe item (if it is in the list), or recency of the probe item (if it is not in the list), and the kind of materials used (e.g., letters, digits, words, random polygons, etc.). When a probe item is one of the list items, it is called a *positive* probe (because it warrants a positive, yes response). Similarly, nonlist items are called *negative* probes.[7]

In Sternberg's 1966 paper, two procedures were introduced. In the *varied list* procedure, lists are randomly chosen for each trial and list length varies from trial to trial. In the *fixed list* procedure, a given list of items is prememorized and then repeatedly tested. This process is repeated for prememorized lists of various lengths. Sternberg's results are shown in figure 10.6. Panel A presents data obtained using the varied list procedure, and panel B presents data obtained using the fixed list procedure.

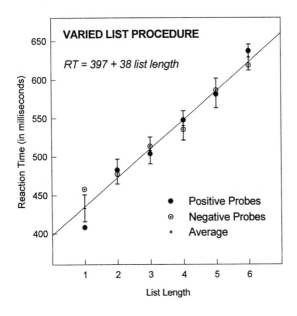

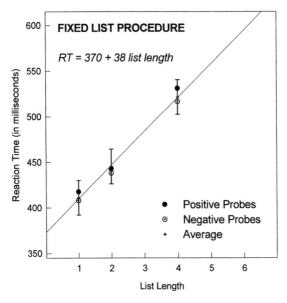

Figure 10.6
Reaction time as a function of list length for Sternberg's (1966) subspan item-recognition experiments. Panel A shows data obtained using a varied list procedure; panel B shows data obtained with a fixed list procedure. In the varied list procedure, items (typically digit, letters, or words) change from trial to trial. In the fixed list procedure, the items are the same for each trial; only the test cue changes. The equations given in each figure characterize the best-fitting line through the average data for positive and negative probes.

In both cases, Sternberg found that mean RT increases linearly with list length. Two features of these data are particularly striking. First, the slopes of positive and negative probes are indistinguishable. Second, the slopes of the linear list-length functions are equivalent for both the fixed list and the varied list procedures.

Sternberg (1966) proposed a simple model to account for these data. He assumed that the probe item is serially compared with each member of the set of items that are activated in memory (the search set). In a *serial* comparison process, a new comparison does not begin until the previous comparison has been completed. This explains why RTs increase linearly with list length (each additional item requires one additional comparison), but why are the slopes identical for positive and negative probes?

Consider what happens if the memory comparison process is *self-termi-nating*. The probe item is compared with each list item until a match is detected or the list is exhausted. This is called a self-terminating search because the comparison process terminates as soon as a match is detected. Consider a list of three items. If given a positive probe (randomly chosen from among the three list items), there is an equal probability of finding a match after one, two, or three comparisons. On average, two comparisons are required. If a negative probe is given, three comparisons are always required (all three list items must be rejected). What happens if the list length is increased from three to four? A positive probe now requires either one, two, three, or four comparisons, resulting in an average of 2.5 comparisons. A negative probe requires all four comparisons to be made. Consequently, increasing the list length by one item results in an increase of 1 comparison for negative items, but only 0.5 comparisons (on average) for positive items. Thus, the slope for negative probes should be twice as great as the slope for positive probes. This is clearly not the case (see figure 10.6).

To explain the equivalence of slopes for positive and negative probes, Sternberg suggested that the serial comparison process is *exhaustive*. Exhaustive search means that the probe item is compared with every item in the search set, and a decision is not made until all comparisons have been made. This idea may seem unrealistic, but if the comparison process is extremely fast and the decision process is noisy and slow, it makes sense to do all of the comparisons prior to making a decision rather than making a separate decision after each comparison (Sternberg, 1969b).

Sternberg (1969a) presented a more complete description of the basic scanning model. The model has four stages: *stimulus encoding, memory comparison, decision,* and *response.* The following claim is critical to the analysis of this model: a given process or stage is not initiated until the previous stage is completed. This claim is reasonable if a stage acts on information produced by a preceding stage that must be available in a fairly complete form (Sternberg, 1998a). Much debate has centered on the validity of this claim (e.g., Hockley & Murdock, 1987; McClelland, 1979). We will return to this issue later in this chapter. A final important detail of the model is that scanning times needn't be fixed. It is often assumed that the time to scan a given item comes from a distribution of possible values. The shape of the distribution (e.g., normal vs. exponential) and its mean and variance are important in generating model predictions (e.g., Luce, 1986, chapter 11).

As discussed previously, recall performance depends crucially on the recency of the items being tested (see "Accuracy and Interresponse Times in Free Recall," p. 324). One may ask how the RT to recognize an item depends on the item's position in the study list. In particular, are subjects faster at recognizing recently presented items? In Sternberg's short-term item-recognition task significant recency effects are often, but not always, obtained (see McElree & Dosher, 1989, and Sternberg, 1975, for reviews). In the clearest case, Monsell (1978) found dramatic recency (i.e., facilitation of positive responses to recent list items) using either letters (experiment 1) or words (experiment 2) as stimuli (figure 10.7). In Monsell's study, the test probe followed the last list item either immediately (right panel) or after a brief delay (left panel). The delay condition required subjects to name a vowel presented immediately after the last list item (this took an average of 500 ms). This step was performed to prevent subjects from rehearsing the list items during the delay period. In an earlier study, Forrin & Cunningham (1973) showed that increasing the length of an unfilled delay between study and test eliminates the recency effect in short-term item recognition. In general, experimental conditions that reduce or eliminate rehearsal tend to produce large recency effects, and those that allow for rehearsal (e.g., Sternberg, 1966) typically have flat serial-position curves.

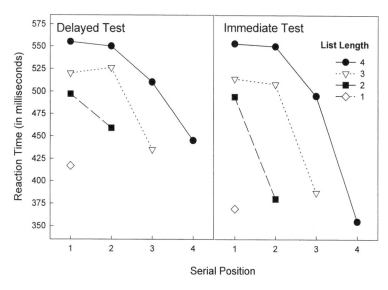

Figure 10.7
Serial position data from Monsell (1978, experiment 1). A fast presentation rate (500 ms/item) was designed to minimize rehearsal. In the immediate test, the probe item immediately followed the presentation of the last list item; in the delayed test a vowel had to be named after the offset of the last list item. As soon as a response was detected, the probe item was presented.

According to Sternberg's serial exhaustive-scanning (SES) model, a response cannot be made until every comparison has been performed. Consequently, the time required to perform the memory scan should be independent of serial position. In light of this, the marked serial position effects obtained by Monsell (1978) and others present a challenge to the Sternberg model. In fact, some authors have rejected the Sternberg model because of this evidence alone. In response, two points need to be made. First, the Sternberg model was designed to explain data obtained under conditions where subjects could freely rehearse highly familiar items (e.g., Sternberg, 1966). Under these conditions, significant serial position effects are consistently absent (Ferrin & Cunningham, 1973). Second, facilitation in performance may be occurring in other stages of the model (Sternberg, 1975). For example, recent items may speed, the encoding of the probe item or the execution of the response—thereby resulting in faster RTs (for a similar argument in the literature on same-different comparisons, see Proctor, 1981). This priming account of the recency effect is difficult to reconcile with the problem of recent negatives. If a probe that was not on the current list was presented as a target on a recent prior list, RTs to respond "no" to the negative probe are significantly increased (e.g., McElree & Dosher, 1989, experiment 2) this finding has proven difficult to reconcile with Sternberg's SES model.

Another challenge to Sternberg's SES model comes from studies that examine list length effects beyond the span of immediate memory. As mentioned earlier, near perfect accuracy is attained either when lists are short (subspan) or through practice (for longer, supraspan, lists). Burrows and Okada (1975) used a prememorized list technique to study RTs in an item recognition task with list lengths far beyond the limits of immediate memory. Their results are shown in figure 10.8. For subspan list lengths (two–six), the slope of the best-fitting line is 37 ms—replicating the classic Sternberg effect. However, a separate line fit to the supraspan lists (lengths greater than eight) yielded a much shallower slope of 13 ms/item. Burrows and Okada also fit a single logarithmic function to their subspan and supraspan data. They found that this function fit all of the data points as well as both the bilinear subspan and supraspan functions, but with fewer parameters. According to the serial exhaustive scanning model, each additional item in the memory set should result in a constant increase in mean RT for both positive and negative probes. These data indicate that the increase in mean RT is not a constant, but varies with list length. This finding is not easily reconciled with the SES model.

So far we have discussed serial position effects (e.g., Monsell, 1978) and list length effects (e.g., Burrows & Okada, 1975) in the context of RT studies of short-term memory. Another major variable that is studied in human memory is repetition. Baddeley and Ecob (1973) wondered what would happen if a single list element in a Sternberg task were repeated. Under these conditions, mean RT is significantly faster for responding to the repeated element than to nonrepeated elements. Like the serial position effects reported by Monsell (1978), these data seem inconsistent with the SES model. If each element must be scanned before a response can be made, it should not matter how many times an element is presented. This critique of the Sternberg SES model assumes that other

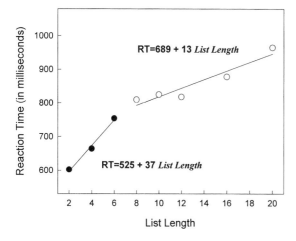

Figure 10.8
Data illustrating the effect of a large range of list lengths on mean reaction time in a probe recognition task (Burrows & Okada, 1975, experiment 2). To achieve nearly errorless performance, lists were "prememorized"; that is, before testing a given list length, the list was already well learned. In the figure, a bilinear function is fit to the data. For short list lengths, the slope of the RT-list length function is similar to results obtained by Sternberg (1966). For longer list lengths, mean RT rises slowly as list length increases (the slope of the best-fitting line is only about 13 ms). As noted by Burrows and Okada (1975), a simple log function fits the data as well as the two linear functions shown here. This raises questions about the linearity of the list length–RT functions reported for short lists.

stages are not influenced by repetition. It is not unreasonable to suppose that the decision stage is executed more quickly when two matches have been registered than when only a single match has been registered.

In the years since the publication of Sternberg's original paper, Sternberg's basic experimental findings have been replicated and extended hundreds of times in studies that manipulated dozens of different experimental variables (see Sternberg, 1975, for a review). Although the data are solid, there has been a long debate about the meaning and interpretation of these findings. Many models have been proposed to account for the basic data, yet none of these models has succeeded in capturing most of the benchmark effects (Sternberg, 1975). Although the simplest version of any model can easily be rejected, the model's creators can often patch things up to correct for the most serious problems. By the 1970s it was already becoming clear that many different types of models can produce identical predictions for data on mean RTs (e.g., Anderson, 1973, Townsend, 1976, 1984).

More recently, attention has shifted from looking at mean RTs to examining the actual shape of the RT distribution. It turns out that although very different types of models can explain the same pattern in the mean RTs, explaining the exact shape of the distribution and how it changes with manipulation of experimental variables is more difficult. Memory theorists have begun to tackle this issue with promising results (Ashby, Tein, & Balakrishnan, 1993; Hockley & Murdock, 1987; Ratcliff, 1978).

The three findings just reviewed, list length, serial position, and repetition effects, all show parallel effects on accuracy and latency. Longer lists are harder to remember than shorter lists. Recently presented items are easier to remember than items presented earlier in the list. Repeated items are easier to remember than nonrepeated items. It may be argued that both the time it takes to recognize an item and the likelihood of successful recognition are reflections of a single construct—the strength of the memory trace.[8] Appealing as this idea may seem, we will later see that the precise nature of the relationship between accuracy and latency may provide important information for testing models of memory.

Task Analysis Using Accuracy and RT Data

If the goal of information-processing research is to break down a complex task into logically distinguishable mental operations and then characterize and model those operations, how do we go about breaking down the complexity of real-world tasks? Among researchers who are concerned with accuracy, the standard method of task analysis is to look for experimental factors (e.g., word frequency or the spacing of repeated elements) that have different effects on different memory tasks or on different aspects of subjects' performance in a given task. Consider the serial position curve in free recall. Presenting the list auditorally results in a larger recency effect (better memory for the last few list items) than does presenting the list visually (this phenomenon is referred to as a *modality effect*). However, the mode of presentation (auditory vs. visual) has no effect on the rest of the serial position curve.[9] This finding is called a *functional dissociation* between the recency and the prerecency part of the serial position curve. Another experimental variable, list length, has no effect on the recency part of the serial position curve but has a substantial effect on the prerecency items. With this second, complementary dissociation, the tasks are said to be *doubly dissociated*. Such double-dissociations are sometimes taken to support the view that recency and prerecency items represent the operation of distinct *short-term* and *long-term memory systems*.[10]

If we are willing to make the assumption that some sets of mental operations are arranged (at least approximately) in nonoverlapping stages (i.e., one stage begins only after the prior stage is done with its processing), we can perform a more sophisticated task analysis using mean RT data. This approach is called the *additive factors* method (Sternberg, 1969a; Sternberg, 1998a). The key to this approach is the factorial experimental design. Two or more factors that are known to affect overall RT are manipulated factorially. If each of the factors selectively affects a different processing stage, then total RT should be given by the sum of the separate effects of each factor on RT. If however, the two factors influence a common stage, total RT will deviate from the sum of the separate effects, and the factors can be said to interact, in a statistical sense.

As an example of the additive factors approach, consider an experiment in which the RT-list length relationship is examined as a function of some other variable: in this case the variable of whether or not the test probe is degraded (made to look blurry) via reduction of contrast or randomizing pixels. Sternberg (1967b) conducted this experiment and his results are shown in figure 10.9. The nearly identical slopes of the two functions indicate a lack of interaction between list length and whether the probe item is degraded: that is, the RT difference between the clean and degraded conditions is approximately the same for each value of list length. In this experiment two factors are varied: list length and probe degradation. Probe degradation simply lowers the RT-list length function by a fixed amount. Statistically, it is said that these factors do not interact (see figure 10.9). Such additivity is predicted by a discrete stage model in which stimulus degradation affects one stage (perhaps encoding) and set size affects another stage (perhaps comparison). If two factors affected the same stage, one would expect to find a statistical interaction (i.e., the

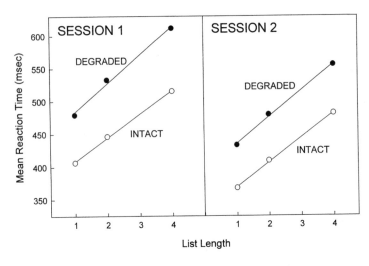

Figure 10.9
Data from Sternberg (1967), illustrating the effect of visually degrading the probe on the RT–list length relation. For both degraded and clean probes, RT is linearly related to list length. There is no interaction, as indicated by the nearly parallel lines for the two conditions. The left panel shows data for the first session of doing the task, and the right panel shows data for the second session. Degree of practice (session 2 versus session 1) does not seem to affect either the slopes of the function or the difference between degraded and intact performance. Rather, practice just speeds everything up (as indicated by the lower intercepts for session 2).

slope of the list length-RT function would be different for degraded and nondegraded stimuli). Sanders (1980) and Sternberg (1998a) reviewed a great deal of evidence from a broad range of factorial RT studies. They found that many variables that would logically be expected to influence different processing stages do have additive effects on RT.

The additive factors method is not without its detractors. An early criticism of the method is that it relies entirely on RT measurements. These measurements may not be comparable across experimental conditions that differ even slightly in accuracy. Pachella (1974) presented a cogent review and critique of the research on RTs during the prior 10 years. As will be described in detail, Pachella pointed out that when you correct for the differences in error rates across conditions, some of the additive effects observed in RT data disappear. This type of error rate correction assumes something called a speed-accuracy trade-off, which will be discussed in the next section.

A subsequent challenge to the additive factors approach came from demonstrations that models that assume continuous transmission of information (i.e., the products of a given stage are constantly available to the next processing stage) can often produce additive effects on mean RT (Ashby, 1982; McClelland, 1979). Roberts and Sternberg (1993) performed a detailed analysis of the McClelland-Ashby model. They found that although the model could predict additive effects on mean RT for some parameter values, the model did not provide a reasonable fit to additivity at the level of the entire RT distribution. Roberts and Sternberg's work exemplifies the recent trend toward fitting RT distributions rather than simply mean RT. Distributional tests provide investigators with significantly greater resolution in distinguishing theories.

In an interesting development in this area, Schweikert (1985) and Roberts (1987) have each expanded the additive factors approach to deal with accuracy and response rate data respectively. Consider a model in which a correct response relies on the completion of two independent processes, A and B. Further, assume that process B must act on the completed output of process A. If processes A and B provide adequate information for a correct response with probabilities $p(A)$ and $p(B)$ respectively, then the probability of a correct response is given by $p(A) \times p(B)$. Converting to logarithms, we can write

$$\log p(A \text{ and } B) = \log p(A) + \log p(B). \tag{10.2}$$

If each of two factors selectively influence each of the two hypothetical processes, one would expect additive effects of the factors on the logarithm of recall probability. This finding has been observed by a number of investigators in a number of different experimental paradigms (see Schweikert, 1985, for a review).

Complications Introduced by the Possibility of Speed-Accuracy Trade-offs

As we have noted, several individuals, most notably Wickelgren and Pachella, wrote of serious difficulties that are entailed when RT studies do not consider variation in error rates across experimental conditions (e.g., Corbett & Wickelgren, 1978; Pachella, 1974; Wickelgren, 1977).

Consider the curves shown in figure 10.10A. This figure introduces the concept of a speed-accuracy trade-off. The general idea is simple: the more time you allot to some task, the better you will do at that task. For instance, if you are typing, you could type slowly and make relatively few errors or, alternatively, you could type more quickly and make more errors. In this example, you, the typist, decide what you will do in terms of trading off additional speed for less accuracy.

In figure 10.10A, *condition 1* and *condition 2* refer to two conditions in some RT experiment. Condition 2 is assumed to be more difficult than condition 1; thus conditions 1 and 2 could, for example, be three- and five-item lists in our familiar item-recognition task. For each condition, probability correct is plotted as a function of what is termed *processing time.* For the moment, processing time, which is measured from the beginning of stimulus onset, is an unobservable construct. The idea here is that the onset of the to-be-processed stimulus (e.g., the probe word in the recognition test) triggers appropriate perceptual and cognitive processing. The more such processing occurs, the more information about the stimulus is obtained. At any given processing time, some specific amount of information has been obtained. Probability correct corresponding to that particular processing time is the probability that with *only the information obtained thus far,* a correct response would be made.

The curves that relate probability correct to processing time are called *speed-accuracy trade-off* (SAT) curves. The greater difficulty of condition 2 compared to condition 1 is embodied in the observation that in order to obtain some fixed level of response probability, more processing time is required for condition 2 than for condition 1. Notice that SAT curves are like typical RT curves (e.g., as in a Sternberg paradigm) rotated by 90°. Whereas in a typical RT function, processing time is plotted as a function of amount of required processing (e.g., of memory list length), in an SAT curve amount of processing (measured in terms of probability correct) is plotted as a function of allotted processing time.

Implications of Only Observing RTs

In a typical RT task, SAT curves are not directly measured. Rather, in a given experimental condition, subjects adopt (implicitly or explicitly) some *criterion* point on the SAT curve (just as when you are typing you

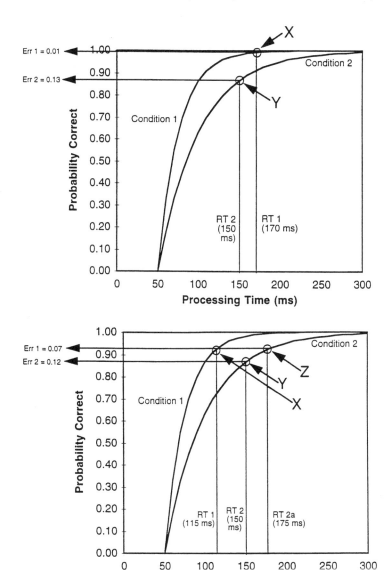

Figure 10.10
Hypothetical speed-accuracy tradeoff (SAT) curves for two conditions. In (A), *X* and *Y* indicate where the speed-accuracy criteria are placed. In (B), *X*, *Y*, and *Z* indicate where the speed-accuracy criteria are placed. In both panels, *RT1* and *RT2* are the RTs for conditions 1 and 2; *Err 1* and *Err 2* are error rates for conditions 1 and 2. In panel B, *RT 2a* shows the RT for condition 2, assuming an error rate equal to the error rate of condition 1.

must decide how fast you are going to type, which, in turn, will produce some corresponding degree of accuracy). The processing time corresponding to this criterion is the observed RT in the experiment, and the probability correct corresponding to this criterion is 1.00 minus the observed error probability in the experiment.[11]

To illustrate the complexities of doing standard RT experiments, consider the curves in figure 10.10A. In condition 1, the criterion point is labeled X. This corresponds to an observed RT of 170 ms, and an observed error rate of .01 (1.00 − .99 probability correct value). In condition 2, the observed RT is 150 ms, and the observed error rate is .13. Clearly, something is amiss. The presumably more difficult condition 2 has a shorter observed RT (150 ms) than does the presumably less difficult condition 1 (170 ms). Thus with RT information only, the experimenter would, incorrectly, conclude that condition 2 is *less* difficult than condition 1.

Fortunately, experimenters would not be quite so naive. Rather, the experimenter would quickly note that the observed error rate in condition 2 (.13) is greater than the observed error rate in condition 1 (.01) and would become suspicious that the shorter observed RT in condition 2 may be due to a speed-accuracy trade-off—that is, in condition 2, observers are (for whatever reason) sacrificing accuracy for increased speed— and it is for this reason that RT is shorter in condition 2 than in condition 1. This would lead the experimenter to suspend judgment about the relative difficulty of the two conditions and rerun the experiment, changing the subjects instructions so as to eliminate this speed-accuracy confounding.

Necessary Conditions for Safe Ordinal Conclusions

Let us imagine that this rerunning produces the data of figure 10.10B. Again, the two speed-accuracy criterion points are labeled X and Y for condition 1 and 2 (ignore point Z for the moment). Now the observed RTs are 115 ms and 150 ms for condition 1 and 2 respectively. Thus, these observed RTs now correctly reflect the greater difficulty of condition 2 compared to condition 1. In addition, the observed error rates are .07 and .12 for conditions 1 and 2, respectively. In short, condition 2 now has both a longer observed RT and a higher observed error rate than does condition 1. Thus, the experimenter could correctly conclude that condition 2 is more difficult than condition 1. In addition, because of the higher observed error rate in condition 2 compared to condition 1, the experimenter would be confident that the longer RT of condition 1 could not have come about because of a speed-accuracy trade-off. To summarize: when one condition (condition 2) produces *both* longer RTs and higher errors than another condition (condition 1), the experimenter can safely conclude that condition 2 is intrinsically harder than condition 1.

Quantitative Interpretational Difficulties
However, the speed-accuracy trade-off problem has not been completely solved even when the data emerge as in figure 10.10B. Suppose the experimenter were interested in the *magnitude by which* the condition-2 processing time exceeded the condition-1 processing time. The best estimate from the figure 10.10B data would be that this value is the difference of the observed RTs, that is, 150 ms − 115 ms = 35 ms. But would this be accurate? No, it wouldn't, because the two conditions differ in terms of error rate as well as in terms of RT.

Suppose the experimenter had been lucky enough that the error rates were identical—say, .07—in both conditions. Now the two speed-accuracy criterion points would be X and Z on figure 10.10B. Note that the RTs corresponding to condition 1 and 2 would be 115 and 175 ms (the latter is labeled as *RT 2a* in the figure). Therefore, the *real* difference between the two conditions—that is, the RT difference with error rates held constant at .07—would be 175 ms − 115 ms = 60 ms. Quantitatively, this is quite a different conclusion from the 35-ms figure that we would have arrived at from the actual data that entailed the different error rates. This means that many patterns of RT data are difficult to interpret when error rates differ among the conditions.

Consider Sternberg's (1966) finding that RT increases linearly with list length in a subspan item recognition paradigm (see figure 10.6). It was this result that led Sternberg to postulate a serial comparison process (i.e., when the probe item is compared with each element of the memory set, one comparison does not begin until the prior comparison has been completed). But, if error rates vary systematically as a function of list length, it is unlikely that the observed linear RT functions would be obtained under conditions in which error rates did not vary with list length (see Pachella, 1974).

Equalizing Error Rates Is Still Not Enough

Suppose one could carefully control error rates so that they were identical in the various conditions. Going back to figure 10.10B, suppose that the speed-accuracy criteria for conditions 1 and 2 were at points X and Z. Note there that the associated RTs of 115 and 175 ms are those associated with a particular error rate—specifically, .07. However, this error rate is *arbitrary;* that is, there is no reason why we should be interested in the RTs associated with this error rate as opposed to any other error rate. It is easy to see that if we observed RTs associated with some other error rate—say .50—then both the RTs associated with the individual conditions and the difference between the two RTs would be different. It is for this reason that more and more investigators have adopted the somewhat time-consuming but more informative strategy of mapping out entire SAT curves for various conditions. The means by which this mapping is done are described in the next section.

An Important Caveat

The foregoing analysis indicates *potential* problems with the RT approach. Suppose, however, that every mental process is characterized by two independent variables: the time it takes (resulting in measured RT) and the information it provides (resulting in measured accuracy). Forcing subjects to respond quickly may still increase errors because a response may be required before the process completes. Yet, left to their own devices, subjects may respond as soon as the necessary processing is complete, and the measured RT may then be directly interpreted as reflecting the time required to perform a given task. There is still considerable debate as to how serious the problems are with the RT approach (see Sternberg, 1998b, appendix A, for a detailed discussion of this point).

SAT Curves in the Study of Human Memory

Schouten and Bekker (1967) introduced an experimental technique to study the SAT function. In this technique, called the *response signal pro-*

cedure, (RSP) subjects are trained to make their response as soon as a signal is given. An SAT curve is constructed by varying the onset time of the response signal. At the very shortest delays, the subjects response is essentially a "guess"; the information processing needed to make a correct response has not begun to become available. As the signal delay increases, the subject has more time, and presumably more information becomes available. Performance increases with the time of the response signal until it reaches some asymptotic value.

As you might imagine, subjects find this task to be quite difficult. To ensure that subjects respond almost immediately after the onset of the response signal requires considerable practice. One of the hardest aspects of this task is withholding a correct response until the signal appears. Some subjects simply cannot do this, and consequently they are excluded from participating.

Before describing the mathematical form of the SAT curve, it is necessary to introduce a special index of performance that is often used in studying detection, discrimination, and recognition. Consider our familiar recognition memory task. This task can be seen as a discrimination task between two sets of items—studied items and nonstudied items. Performance is then characterized in terms of subjects' ability to discriminate studied from nonstudied items. One way of measuring discriminability is by taking the probability of a correct yes response (called a hit) and correcting for the probability of an incorrect yes response (called a false alarm). The way this is done is by first transforming hit rate and false alarm rate to *z scores* (i.e., convert the raw scores into standard scores). The difference between the *z*-transformed hit rate and the *z*-transformed false alarm rate is termed *d prime* (written as *d'*).

Using *d* prime as our measure of performance, it has been shown that SAT curves for individual subjects are well fit by an exponential growth to a limit, given by the equation

$$d' = \lambda(1 - e^{-\beta(t-\delta)}), \ t > \delta. \tag{10.3}$$

The three parameters in equation 10.3, λ (lambda), β (beta), and δ (delta), characterize three phases of information processing. In phase one, $t < \delta$, no information is available. After $t = \delta$, the information rises with rate β (phase 2) until it reaches an asymptotic level of performance (phase 3).

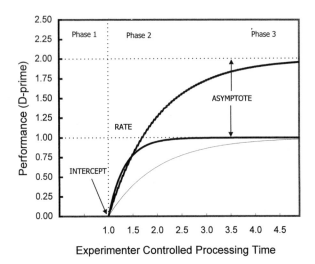

Figure 10.11
Hypothetical speed-accuracy tradeoff (SAT) curve generated by an exponential rise to an asymptote (see equation 9.3). In this figure, all of the curves assume an intercept, δ, set to 1. For the lowest curve (long dash), the rate parameter, β, and the asymptote, λ, are also set to 1. Above this curve, the dark solid curve has a rate parameter of 2. The uppermost curve is defined by a rate parameter of 1 and an asymptote of 2.

Note that we must choose a certain point on the SAT curve to characterize the asymptotic phase. The form of equation 10.3 for different parameter values is shown in figure 10.11.

Reed (1973, 1976) applied this response signal procedure to studying short-term item recognition. McElree and Dosher (1989), following up on Reed's (1976) work, examined SAT curves in the Sternberg task. They conducted two experiments that replicated the standard effects in the literature: asymptotic accuracy varied linearly with list length, and pronounced serial position effects were observed. SAT curves for lists of four and six items are shown in figure 10.12. Analyzing these curves separately for different serial positions and list lengths revealed a surprising result: neither the rate nor the intercept of the SAT curves varied with list length.

According to the classic Sternberg (serial exhaustive-scanning) model, what predictions can one make about the shape of the SAT curves? If each comparison has an equal duration, increasing list length should require more comparisons. Consequently, each added item should cause

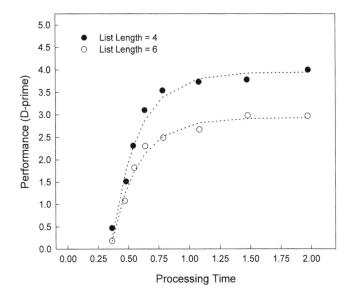

Figure 10.12
Observed average performance (as measured by d-prime) as a function of total processing time for list lengths of four and six. Smooth functions are based on the fits of an exponential rise to an asymptotic function (equation 9.3).

the minimum processing time to increase by the comparison time. This would produce a difference only in the intercept of the SAT curve. Reed's (1976) data ruled out this hypothesis.

Consider a more sophisticated version of the Sternberg model in which the comparison durations vary from trial to trial and from item to item. Because a response cannot be made until all comparisons are complete, longer list lengths will still require more processing time. For the case of a single list, the comparison will be completed very fast for some items and very slowly for other items (with a range of comparison times in between); this variability will result in a gradually increasing SAT curve (assume that subjects guess if they haven't completed all memory comparisons). If there are more items in the list, the likelihood of all of the items having fast comparison rates is quite low, so the SAT curve should rise more gradually as list length increases. As illustrated in McElree and Dosher's (1989) study (see figure 10.12), the rate of increase in the SAT curve does not vary with list length. This finding cannot be reconciled with any known variant of the serial exhaustive-scanning model. However, Ratcliff's (1978) diffusion model, a *parallel* model of RTs, does provide a reasonable account for the basic SAT data (McElree & Dosher, 1989; Ratcliff, 1978). The diffusion model will be discussed in more detail later in this chapter.

Criticisms of the SAT Approach and the Response Signal Procedure

In our earlier discussion, we pointed out some of the potential dangers involved in comparing RTs for conditions in which accuracy varies. It was assumed that variation in accuracy could result from a speed-accuracy trade-off that would disguise true RT differences. As Pachella (1974) pointed out, conditions that yield short RTs often result in lower error rates than conditions that yield long RTs. But the correlation is not 100%. In some cases, error rates vary independently of RT even when subjects are under considerable time pressure to respond (e.g., Sternberg, 1969b).

Given the availability of the response signal procedure as a means of mapping out the effect of experimental variables on the complete SAT curve, it may seem surprising that the field has not completely adopted this approach. Aside from the added complexity of this experimental technique, there have been several potentially serious problems with the RSP that should be pointed out.

The first and most serious problem is that the response signal may alter the way in which information is processed in a given task. Essentially the response signal procedure turns a single task into a dual task. While subjects are busy trying to derive the information needed to make a response, they must be constantly attentive to the response signal. Then, even if they are ready to respond, they must wait until the response signal arrives. This turns a fairly simple task into a relatively complex one, making the task of interest much more difficult to model.

Another important criticism of the response signal procedure is that it cannot distinguish all-or-none processing from continuous accrual of information. If all of the relevant information for a cognitive judgment becomes available at some variable instant in time, SAT curves will still appear to increase smoothly. How, then, can one distinguish between these fundamentally different views of cognition—all-or-none versus continuous processing? Meyer, Irwin, Osman, & Kounios (1988) proposed a variant of the response signal technique, called speed-accuracy decomposition (SAD), as a means of resolving this ambiguity. In the SAD technique, subjects are given regular (no signal) trials randomly interspersed with signal trials. Because subjects don't know if a trial is going to have a signal until the signal arrives, subjects are free to respond as soon as they are ready. On response signal trials, subjects may be responding on the basis of complete information (prior to the onset of the signal) or on the basis of partial information (after the signal is given). By obtaining RT distributions for both response signal trials and regular (no signal) trials, it is possible to determine the separate contributions of complete and partial information to the RTs obtained on the response signal trials. To do this, one must be willing to make certain assumptions about the relationship between responses based on complete and partial information (see Meyer et al., 1988, for details). Although there has been some debate as to the validity of these underlying assumptions (De Jong, 1991, but see Smith, Kounios, & Osterhout, 1997), in the worst case these assumptions leave the investigator with no less information than would be available using the more traditional SAT technique. Evidence obtained using the SAD procedure has shown that under many conditions information is accumulated continuously (e.g., Kounios, 1993; Kounios, Montgomery, & Smith, 1994; Meyer et. al., 1988). However, a recent study of problem solving revealed evidence for all-or-none processing using a SAD procedure (Smith & Kounios, 1996).

Performance Curves to Investigate Visual Information Acquisition

Speed-accuracy trade-off curves, of the sort described in the previous section, can also be used to study relatively low-level processes such as attention and visual information acquisition. When low-level processes are under investigation a simple paradigm can be used in which, on each of a series of trials, the following sequence of events occurs:

1. Usually a trial begins with a warning tone and a fixation point.
2. A stimulus (e.g., a picture) is presented for a variable but short duration (e.g., a duration ranging from 20 to 250 ms).

3. The stimulus is followed by a visual mask that prevents information acquisition from the iconic image that typically follows the visual stimulus. Thus, the time the observer has available to process the stimulus is carefully controlled.

4. Eventually, memory for the presented stimulus is tested. For instance, if pictures were shown as stimuli, memory for the pictures might be tested in a later recognition test.

In this paradigm, memory performance can be plotted as a function of stimulus duration. This form of a speed-accuracy curve is known as a *performance curve*. Performance curves have been generated by numerous researchers to investigate a variety of issues.[12]

An Example: Using Performance Curves to Investigate Effects of Priming

To illustrate how generation of such curves can be instrumental in formulating precise conclusions about the mechanisms by which some variable exerts its effect, consider the phenomenon of *priming*. In general, priming refers to the effect of some *priming stimulus* on the perceptual and cognitive processing of some related *target stimulus* that occurs near in time to the priming stimulus. A classic example is that of a lexical decision task (e.g., Meyer & Schvaneveldt, 1971). In an LDT, an observer is presented with a target letter string that is either a word or a nonword (e.g., NURSE or NIRSE) and must decide, as quickly as possible, whether the letter string is a word or a nonword.

To see the effect of priming in this paradigm, consider the letter string NURSE, to which, of course, the response "word" should be given. A universally reported result is that the RT for correctly responding "word" to the target NURSE is faster when NURSE is preceded by a related word (such as DOCTOR) than by an unrelated word (such as LION). Thus the word DOCTOR is said to *prime* the related word, NURSE. One way or another it shortens the time to correctly respond.

How does priming work? Consider two possibilities:

Possibility 1. The prime acts as if the observer has been given a brief "advance peek" (e.g., a 50-ms advance peek) at the target word. In this case, of course, RT should be 50 ms faster in the primed than in the unprimed condition.

Possibility 2. The prime acts to speed up processing of the target word. In this case, RT should still be faster in the primed compared to the unprimed condition, but by how much is not clear.

In a typical RT experiment, these two possibilities cannot be distinguished, because simply observing a shorter RT to the primed compared to the unprimed condition is consistent with either one. However, Reinitz et al. (1989) investigated priming by observing performance curves. Briefly, their experiment was as follows. On each of a series of trials, a target picture of an object was presented for varying durations and was followed by a visual mask. For instance, the target on one trial might be a guitar. In a *primed condition* the target was preceded by a related word (the word *guitar* in this example), whereas in an *unprimed condition* the target was preceded by an unrelated stimulus (which was either an unrelated word, such as *lamp,* or just a row of Xs; these two unprimed conditions produced identical performances, so we will lump them together and just call them both the *unprimed condition.* Later, memory for the target stimuli was tested in a recognition test.

The results of this experiment took the form of two performance curves: performance as a function of original target stimulus duration for both the primed and the unprimed conditions. Now the two possibilities just sketched make different predictions, which are shown in figures 10.13 A, B.

Possibility-1 Prediction: Horizontally Parallel Curves   Figure 10.13A shows the quite straightforward prediction corresponding to possibility 1: If having a prime is like having an "advanced peek" of, say, X ms at the target stimulus, then the two performance curves corresponding to primed and unprimed conditions should be *horizontally parallel;* that is, the horizontal difference between them should be some constant. The magnitude of the horizontal difference corresponds to the duration that the "advanced peek" is worth. If the data in figure 10.13A were obtained, the experimenter would conclude that possibility 1 is correct and that having a prime is like having an advance peek at the target picture of duration 50 ms (the magnitude of the horizontal difference between the curves). For any performance level achieved in the unprimed condition,

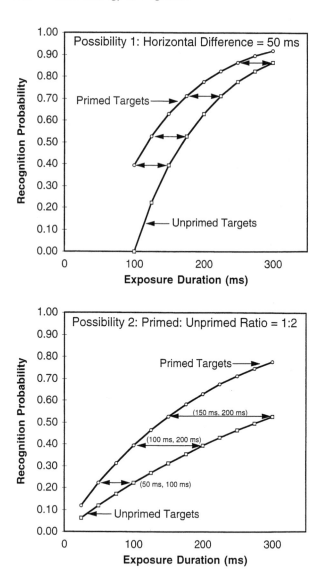

Figure 10.13
Panel (A) illustrates the predictions for possibility 1 (the "advanced peek" possibility). Note that the curves are horizontally parallel, separated by 50 ms. Panel (B) illustrates the predictions for possibility 2 (the "speedup" possibility). Note that the curves are horizontally diverging at a ratio of 1:2. Panel (C) illustrates possibility 2, with duration plotted on a log axis. In this case, the curves are once again horizontally parallel.

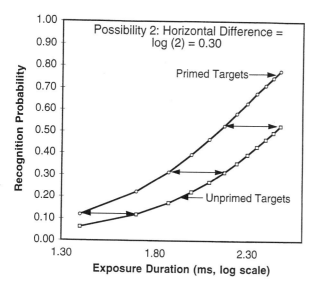

Figure 10.13
continued

the subject needs 50 ms less in the primed condition because of the 50-ms advanced peek provided by the prime.

Possibility-2 Prediction: Constant-Ratio Diverging Curves   The prediction for possibility 2 is a bit more complicated, and it is illustrated in figure 10.13B. The idea here is that if the prime speeds up processing of the target, by some ratio, r, then it should take r times as long to achieve any given performance level for unprimed compared to primed targets. In the illustration of figure 10.13B, $r = 2$; that is, the prime speeds up target processing by a factor of 2. Thus, for instance, to achieve a performance of about .23 requires 50 ms for the primed targets but 100 ms for the unprimed targets. To achieve a performance level of about .40 requires 100 ms for the primed targets, but 200 ms for the unprimed targets, and so on.

One methodological note is of some interest here. Suppose you have a data set corresponding to the primed and unprimed performance curves, and you wish to see whether the data correspond to the prediction of possibility 1 (figure 10.13A) or to the prediction of possibility 2 (figure

10.13B). Testing the possibility-1 prediction is relatively straightforward: you just "slide" the two curves horizontally relative to one another (either physically, using transparencies, or electronically) and see if you can get them to exactly overlap.

Testing the possibility-2 prediction shown in figure 10.13B is not so straightforward. However, there is a trick that allows one to test the possibility-2 prediction in a similarly simple way. This is to plot the curves on a *log duration* axis rather than on a linear duration axis (a linear duration axis, as in figure 10.13B, is the normal way of plotting). Because equal linear *ratios* correspond to equal log *distances,* the possibility-2 prediction is that when plotted on a log duration axis, the performance curves should again be horizontally parallel. This possibility is illustrated in figure 10.13C. How did the data actually come out? The answer to this question is a bit complicated, and we will not describe it in detail here. Suffice it to say that initially possibility 2 was confirmed: that is, at least during the very early stages of perception, priming has the effect of speeding up the rate at which processing takes place.

Models of RT Data in Human Memory

Earlier we asked the following question; Are accuracy and RT two sides of the same coin? We then went on to show that under some circumstances, error rates are negligible and an analysis of RT reveals many interesting features of human behavior. As an example of one particularly well-explored domain, we considered RT data in the Sternberg subspan item-recognition task. Three basic empirical findings emerged from these studies. First, longer lists are associated with longer RTs—we called this a list length effect. Second, in conditions designed to eliminate rehearsal, recent items are recognized more quickly than earlier list items—we called this a recency effect. Finally, repeated items are remembered better than once presented items. Not surprisingly, all of these effects have perfect analogues in the literature on accuracy in recognition memory tasks involving longer lists. The list length effect (in recognition memory) has been known since Strong's 1912 study. Although there is still much debate as to the cause of this effect (See Murdock & Kahana, 1993a, 1993b; Shiffrin et al. 1993), it is found in every type of memory test regardless of whether accuracy or RT is the dependent variable. The beneficial effects of recency are equally ubiquitous in the memory literature. Rubin and Wenzel (1996) and Wixted and Ebbesen (1991) have shown that across a wide range of tasks and materials response accuracy declines as a power function of time, or the number of items intervening between study and test (termed *study-test lag*). In short-term item recognition, Monsell (1978) found a similar type of recency effect in RT data (see figure 10.7). In a continuous recognition task, Hockley (1982) also found dramatic recency effects in RT data.[13] Clearly, recency, repetition, and list length effects are fundamental properties of human memory. It is with this in mind, that we can entertain the possibility that memories vary in the strength of the cue-target match. The amount of information is then a single dimension that has a single SAT function. More information results in faster and more accurate responses.

Unidimensional Strength Theory of Recognition (or Signal Detection Theory)

Consider the familiar item-recognition task (e.g., Sternberg, 1966) as a discrimination between two categories: items that were shown in the list and those that were not. According to *strength theory* (Norman & Wickelgren, 1969) items vary along the dimension of information that distinguishes these two categories (this dimension is sometimes called memory strength). A crucial assumption of the theory is the idea of a noisy system: items within each category may vary greatly in their values along the "strength" dimension. This results in two strength distributions: a distribution for list items and a distribution for nonlist items. Responses are made based on the value of an item along this informational dimension. If an item's strength exceeds some *criterion* value, a positive response is made; otherwise a negative response is made. This theory is considered because it can provide a simple, unified account for both RT and accuracy data in a broad range of recognition memory tasks (Murdock, 1985). Although the model is overly simplistic, the basic ideas it encompasses have become part of almost every current model of human memory (e.g., Hintzman, 1986; Metcalfe, 1982; Murdock, 1982). *Strength theory* is the term used for the application of *signal detection theory* (SDT) to recognition memory tasks (Egan, 1958). In order to see how this theoretical framework can provide an account for both accuracy and RT data, the basic elements of signal detection theory will be briefly introduced (for a more thorough treatment, the reader is encouraged to consult Murdock, 1985).

In a categorization or recognition task, there may be different payoffs associated with incorrectly classifying a nonlist item as a list item (a false alarm) and for correctly classifying a list item as such (a hit). Such differential payoffs are easily modeled by assuming that the criterion can be adjusted to meet the task demands. In a case where we want to avoid false alarms at all costs, we set a high criterion. In a case where we want to maximize hits, but where false alarms aren't too bad, we set a low criterion. Moving the criterion should not affect the discriminability of the two distributions; only the relative numbers of hits and false alarms will change.

A graph that plots hit rate against false alarm rate for different criteria is called a receiver operating characteristic (ROC) curve. According to strength theory, plotting the z-transformed hit rate versus the z-transformed false alarm rate should result in a linear function. If the two distributions have equal variance, the slope of the z-ROC curve should be 1. In the recognition memory task we can vary the criterion by collecting data on *judgements of confidence*. In this technique subjects are asked, "how confident are you that X was on the list?" A typical scale used for confidence judgements is as follows:

−3	−2	−1		1	2	3
High		Low		Low		High
	"No"				"Yes"	

We can now mimic a subject with high criterion by grouping confidence judgments that are less than 3 into the "no" category, leaving only confidence judgements of 3 in the "yes" category. Based on this grouping, our imaginary conservative subject only responds "yes" when our real subject responds "yes" with high confidence. Similarly, we can mimic a subject who is slightly less conservative by grouping confidence judgments that are less than 2 into the "no" category, leaving confidence judgments of 2 and 3 in the "yes" category. Moving the criterion further down, we reach the criterion of our real subject, with positive confidence judgments reflecting "yes" responses and negative confidence judgments reflecting "no" responses. Finally, we can move our criterion yet further down, all the way to the point were only a confidence judgement of -3 is in the "no" category, and all other confidence judgments are grouped in the "yes" category. This hypothetical liberal subject will only withhold a "yes" response when he/she is certain the item was not on the list. If we plot hits against false alarms for each of these hypothetical subjects, we can construct an ROC curve. At the most conservative end of the spectrum, both the hit rate and the false alarm rate will be low because the subject rarely makes "yes" responses. At the most liberal end of the spectrum, both the hit and false alarm rates will be high because the subject almost always makes "yes" responses. The points representing hit rate and false alarm rate for each criteria level (liberal to conservative) traces out the bow-shaped ROC curve (See Swets, 1998 for background information on ROC curves and their applications to some real world problems). Studies of recognition memory (Koppell, 1977; Ratcliff, McKoon, & Tindall, 1994; Yonelinas, 1997) have found that the z-ROC curves are nearly linear but have slopes that are consistently less than 1 (around 0.8 in most studies). The linearity of the z-ROC functions is consistent with the view that strengths of list and nonlist items are distributed normally. The finding that the slope of the z-ROC curve is less than 1 indicates that the variability in the strength of items' representations in memory is greater for list items than for non nonlist items (see Ratcliff, McKoon, & Tindall, 1994)

Strength theory may be extended to deal with RT data in a fairly straightforward manner. If we plot RT as a function of confidence judgment values (which maps directly onto the distance from our yes-no criterion), we find that as we approach the criterion from either direction, RTs increase quite dramatically. According to the *RT-distance* hypothesis, RT increases monotonically as the criterion is approached from either direction (Koppell, 1977; Murdock & Anderson, 1975). Murdock (1985) proposed an extension of strength theory to handle RT data. This model has been shown to fit data on list length effects and recency effects, as well as RT distributions, in both the Sternberg (1966) subspan item-recognition task and in the supraspan study-test recognition paradigm. The power of the RT-distance hypothesis is that it can be applied to any domain of signal detection theory. Maddox and Ashby (1996) incorporated the RT-distance hypothesis into the *generalized recognition theory* of multidimensional categorization tasks (Ashby & Perrin, 1988). In this manner they were able to simultaneously fit both accuracy and RT data in a variety of categorization tasks.

The Diffusion Model

The diffusion model (Ratcliff, 1978; Ratcliff & Van-Zandt, submitted) is an abstract mathematical model of any cognitive task that involves choosing from among a number of sources of information. These tasks include recognition memory as well as multidimensional perceptual discrimination tasks. Consider an application of this model to the basic Sternberg item recognition paradigm. A probe is compared in parallel with a defined (but potentially large) set of items in memory (see figure 10.14). Each memory trace begins with a base level of activation. As time progresses, the activation drifts, or diffuses, with a variable rate toward either a lower or upper boundary. The model is self-terminating on a match (i.e., if an item reaches its upper bound, the model produces a positive response) and exhaustive on nonmatches (i.e., all items must reach the lower bound before a negative response can be made). For appropriately chosen parameter values, this model can produce many of the major findings in the Sternberg paradigm—including both asymptotic accuracy and RT distributions. In addition, it provides a reasonable account of SAT functions (McElree & Dosher, 1991). The diffusion model has also been successfully applied to data on multielement comparisons (Ratcliff, 1981) and choice reaction time[14] (Ratcliff & Van-Zandt, submitted). One criticism of the diffusion model is that it does not explain the basis of the processes it postulates. The model does not explain how items are represented, how they are compared, what causes the variability in drift rates, or even how the upper and lower boundaries are instantiated.

Nonetheless, a diffusion-type mechanism may be incorporated into models that *do* make explicit assumptions about item comparison and representation. Nosofsky and Palmeri (1997) extended Nosofsky's (1986) exemplar-based model of categorization to account for RTs in speeded categorization tasks. In their model, exemplars of items and their associated categories are stored as separate memory traces. A to-be-

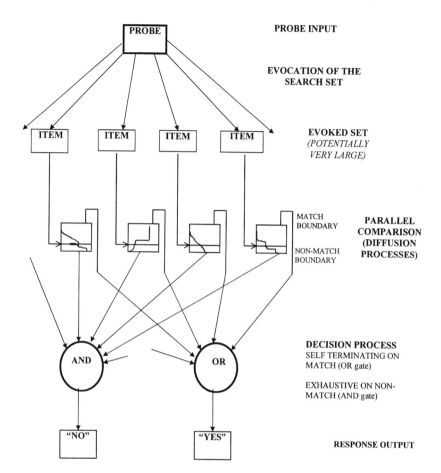

Figure 10.14
An illustration of the diffusion model applied to an item recognition task. The process begins at the top of this figure with the encoding of the probe item. The probe item is then compared, in parallel (i.e., all comparisons begin at the same time), with each of the items in the memory set. Each comparison results in a matching strength value that begins at a *baseline level* and then continuously increases or decreases at a *variable rate*. A positive yes, response is made if any of the comparisons reaches a *match boundary;* a negative, no, response is made if all of the comparisons reach a *nonmatch boundary*. Model parameters include the values of the match and nonmatch boundaries and the mean and variance of the matching strength for each item in the memory set. (Adapted from figure 3, Ratcliff, 1978.)

classified probe item is simultaneously compared with each stored exemplar. The likelihood of successful retrieval is determined jointly by the strength of the exemplar in memory and its similarity to the probe item. Each retrieved exemplar adds evidence in favor of the category with which it has been associated. When a criterion of evidence is reached in favor of a particular category, a response is made. Nosofsky and Palmeri (1997) obtained good fits to both mean RT and to RT distributions.

Connectionist Models

During the last 15 years there has been a surge of interest in connectionist models of memory. These models typically assume that a unit of memory is represented by a pattern of activation across a large number of processing units. The set of activation values across these units defines a vector in a multidimensional space. Given a sufficiently large number of units, the same population of units can be used to store a multitude of items. Interactions among processing units determine the storage of new memories and the dynamics by which the model can reconstruct an entire pattern given a partial input.

Connectionist models of memory and cognition can be subdivided into three major classes: multiple-layer, feedforward models of recognition and categorization (e.g., McClelland, 1979; Usher & McClelland, 1996); autoassociative models of recognition and pattern completion (e.g., Chappell & Humphreys, 1994; Masson, 1995; Metcalfe, 1990); and recurrent, heteroassociative models of sequence memory (e.g., Cleeremans & McClelland, 1991). (See also chapter 8, this volume.)

These models provide mechanisms that give rise to the constructs that are characterized abstractly within models such as the diffusion model or strength theory. In one of the earliest applications of a connectionist model to accuracy and RT data in human memory, Anderson (1973) showed how a simple distributed memory model could account for the basic linear RT functions obtained by Sternberg (1966). Further efforts to model the Sternberg task employed nonlinear models with multiple layers (e.g., McClelland, 1979).

Usher and McClelland (1996) propose a two-layer network model for choice reaction time tasks. The first layer represents the stimulus as a pattern of activation across a set of units. These units send their activation through weighted paths to a second, decision, layer with N units (one for each possible choice). The Usher and McClelland model proposes both recurrent excitatory connections and mutual inhibitory connections between the units in the decision layer. The interplay between the excitatory and inhibitory mechanisms results in a generalized diffusion toward one of two decision bounds. This model encompasses the diffusion model as a special case while providing an even better account of SAT data.

Although the Usher and McClelland model is appropriate for choice reaction time tasks, it cannot do pattern reconstruction or serial recall tasks. To do these tasks, a class of connectionist models known as recurrent, or autoassociative, neural networks have been developed. These models allow for associations between an item and itself (autoassociation) as well as associations among different items (heteroassociations). They follow a simple learning principle called the Hebb rule (after Hebb's, 1949, hypothesis about synaptic plasticity). When two units are coactive the connection between them is strengthened, and when two units have uncorrelated activities the connection between them is weakened. These principles are related to the biological mechanisms of long-term potentiation and long-term depression (Brown & Chattarji, 1995; McNaughton & Morris, 1987; Treves & Rolls, 1994). The network evolves dynamically according to a simple model of neural function (usually a derivative of the classic McCulloch & Pitts, 1943, model). Typically, the activity of a unit is a monotonic function of the weighted sum of the input to that unit.

The Hopfield (1982) model is an example of a simple attractor neural network capable of mimicking human RT and accuracy data in priming experiments (Masson, 1995). Chappell and Humphreys (1994) expanded this approach to explain a number of phenomena in recognition and recall memory tasks. Although there has been some criticism of neural network models of RTs (Ratcliff & Van-Zandt, 1996), these models provide a natural account of both accuracy and RT data across a broad range of cognitive tasks.

Models of accuracy and RT data often assume that a common dimension of information underlies both accuracy and RT judgments. Few models have tackled the difficult problem of fitting SAT functions in a wide range of tasks. The two models that have been largely successful in accounting for SAT data assume variability in the rate with which information continuously accrues (e.g., Ratcliff, 1978; Usher & McClelland, 1996).[15]

Conclusions: Are Accuracy and RT Data Two Sides of the Same Coin?

Superficially, it appears that our review of theory and data concerning accuracy and RT in human memory supports the view that these two measures may reflect a single underlying dimension of information. However, this conclusion leaves us somewhat uneasy. To further examine this question, we have set out to find a few examples of cases in the literature where accuracy and RT have not provided comparable answers.

Sometimes variables that have significant effects on accuracy do not affect RTs (MacLeod & Nelson, 1984). Sternberg (1969b) reported an experiment in which subjects studied a list of items presented either once, twice, or three times. After the list presentation, a single item was presented as a cue to recall the next item in the list. As with the standard item-recognition task, RTs in this task increased linearly with list length, but interestingly, RT was not affected by the number of times the list was presented. In contrast, error rates for the longest list (six items) were quite high (23%) when the list was only presented once, but less than 5% when the list was presented three times. In this study, accuracy differences were not reflected in RT data.

There are fewer cases in the literature where a variable has a significant effect on RT data but no discernible effect on response accuracy (when accuracy is far from ceiling). Sanders, Whitaker, & Cofer (1974) found that in a recognition task, subjects did not suffer from associative interference when measured using accuracy but showed substantial interference when RT was examined. Subjects took as many trials to learn C-D word pairs after learning A-B pairs as they did after learning A-D pairs. In contrast, RTs were significantly slower when tested on the A-D list, presumably because of interference from the A-B pairs learned in the first list.

Santee & Egeth (1982; see also Mordkoff & Egeth, 1993) found that accuracy and latency were affected quite differently from each other in a letter recognition task. Perceptual interference caused by displaying targets very briefly affected accuracy at detection but not latency. In contrast, response competition caused by having to respond to a given target in the face of competing information from another target affected latency of responses but not accuracy.

In a recent study examining accuracy and RT in various types of associative recall tasks, Kahana (1998) found that the order in which a pair of items was studied has no significant effect on accuracy, yet forward recall was significantly faster than backward recall (ART > 400 ms). Accuracy for forward recall was 87.7%, and for backward recall it was 85.1% ($p > .10$). This result makes sense if one assumes that an association is a single integrated unit of information that is unpacked in the order in which it was encoded.

Perhaps the most striking example comes from a *judgment of recency* (JOR) task. In this task, subjects are presented with a short list of items (usually words or letters). Immediately after list presentation, two items are presented and the subject must select the more recent list item. For example, suppose the list consists of items XTLVDGBNW and the probe items are *V* and *N*. In this case, the subject might correctly select *N* as the more recent list item. Muter (1979) and Hacker (1980) independently discovered that RTs in this task are dependent only on the position of the more recent item and not on the relative recency of the two items. From a strength-type theory, we would expect that the difference in the recency of the two items would affect both accuracy and RT data. Data from Hacker's study are shown in figure 10.15. The peculiar finding that the position of the less recent item does not affect RT led Hacker (1980) to propose a self-terminating, backward serial-scanning model of this task. If we scan backward from the end of the list, it will take the same time to find the more recent item regardless of the position of the less recent item (cf. Murdock's, 1974, conveyer belt model of recognition memory).

McElree and Dosher (1993) performed a SAT analysis of the Muter-Hacker JOR task. They succeeded in replicating the Muter-Hacker finding that mean RTs are only affected by the recency of the more recent probe (and not the distance between the two items). The SAT study of the same task showed that there *is* an effect of the relative recency of the two probe items. Specifically, the rate of approach to asymptote was more rapid as the less recent probe was more distant. In contrast, the more recent probe had the expected effects on both the intercept and the

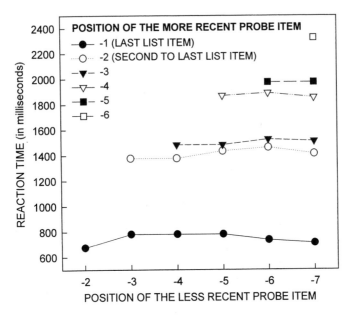

Figure 10.15
Response accuracy and latency in a *judgment of recency* task (Hacker, 1980). Mean correct RT is strongly influenced by the recency of the more recent probe item, but is unaffected by the recency of the less recent probe item. These data conflict with the reasonable prediction that the *relative* recency of the two items influences mean RT. The same basic pattern of data has also been obtained by Muter (1979), Hockley (1984), and McElree & Dosher (1993).

asymptote of the SAT functions. This SAT approach clearly demonstrated that the relative lag of the first list item, which did not affect mean RTs, did have a significant effect on processing rate.

Additional studies using SAT techniques have begun to provide convergent evidence against the idea that memories vary along a single dimension. Rather, SAT studies of human memory have lent support to the view that different types of information are represented in memory (e.g., Murdock, 1974; Underwood, 1983). Gronlund and Ratcliff (1989) compared single-item recognition with associative recognition (recognition that two items were paired together in a list). They found that item information became available before associative information. Ratcliff and McKoon (1989) and Dosher (1984) found that preexperimental relations among items influenced recognition of word pairs or sentences early in processing and that the necessary contextual information did not become available until later stages of processing. Hintzman and Curran (1994) found evidence that item recognition judgments are influenced by a fast-acting familiarity mechanism followed by a slower recall-like retrieval process (c.f., Atkinson & Juola, 1973).

All of these results support the cognitive idea that multiple kinds of information provide us with our "memory strength." In particular, the range of studies reported converge on the need to distinguish between information on item familiarity (the closest idea to the traditional notion of strength), experimentally formed associations between items, and contextual information that binds items and associations to a particular time and place. These different kinds of information are often characterized by different SAT functions. If several different types of information, or memory processes, mediate performance in a task, the accuracy-RT relation would have to be identical for each process in order for accuracy and RT to be measuring the same thing. If each process has a different accuracy-RT relation, it is good cause for studying the effects of experimental variables on both accuracy and RT data.

In recent years the evidence for the involvement multiple processes and types of information in memory tasks has been accumulating. More information implies better accuracy and shorter RT, making accuracy and RT measures highly correlated. But the results of SAT studies have shown that the precise pattern of accuracy-RT effects may teach us a great deal about memory processes. In addressing the question posed in the beginning of this chapter, accuracy and RT cannot be two sides of the same coin unless the cognitive process of interest is a single operation acting on a single type of information. Consequently, consideration of both accuracy and RT data is often critical in distinguishing theories of cognition, and the use of only one of these measures may provide a skewed interpretation of the phenomena of interest.

Notes

1. See, for example, Gronlund & Ratcliff (1989); Hintzman & Curran (1994); Kounios, Osman, & Meyer (1987); McElree (1996); McElree & Dosher (1989, 1993); Meyer, Irwin, Osman & Kounios (1988); Ratcliff & McKoon (1989); Ratcliff & Van Zandt (1996); and Rohrer & Wixted (1994).

2. In these experiments lists are usually made up of between 15 and 40 randomly chosen words. The advantage in recall is for the first 3 to 4 words and the last 6 to 8 words. The size of the recency effect does not depend on the length of the list, the presentation rate, or other variables that generally effect overall memory (Murdock, 1962).

3. Latent constructs are variables (often representing mental processes) that are not directly observed but whose existence is inferred from the data. The idea of association is a latent construct, as is intelligence or morale.

4. See, for example, Brown, Conover, Flores, & Goodman (1991); Cooke, Durso, & Shvaneveldt (1986); and Romney, Brewer, & Batchelder (1993). See Shuell (1969) for a review of the earlier literature.

5. In rapid serial visual presentation (RSVP) of sentences, subjects are impaired at recalling the second presentation of a repeated element. This is known as *repetition blindness* (Kanwisher, 1987). There is some debate as to how repetition blindness is related to the Ranschburg effect: Kanwisher (1987) maintains that the two are distinct phenomena; however, Fagot and Pashler (1995) suggest that the two phenomena may be closely related (see also Whittlesea, et al., 1996).

6. The reader may note that in free recall, performance is *best* at the end of the list. However, in serial or ordered recall, performance is best at the beginning of the list. This makes sense because subjects must start recalling at the beginning in serial recall but are free to recall from the end in free recall.

7. In the recognition memory literature, investigators often call positive probes *old items* and negative probes *new items*.

8. see Murdock (1985) for an attempt to fit such a model to data from the Sternberg task.

9. See Murdock & Walker (1969).

10. For opposing views see Baddeley & Hitch (1974, 1977); Crowder (1982) and Greene (1986, 1992).

11. For an interesting alternative view see Sternberg (1998b).

12. See, for example, Loftus (1985); Loftus & Bell (1975); Loftus, Busey, & Senders (1993); Loftus, Duncan, & Gehrig (1992); Loftus, Johnson, & Shimamura (1985); Reinitz (1990); Reinitz, Wright, & Loftus (1989); Rumelhart (1970); Shibuya & Bundeson (1988); and Townsend (1981).

13. In a continuous recognition task, there is no differentiation between the study and test phases. Stimuli are presented one by one, and as each stimulus appears, subjects respond yes if they think they have seen it before and no if they think it is a new word.

14. In a choice reaction time task a stimulus is presented (e.g., a row of asterisks on a computer screen) and subjects are supposed to make one of several discrete responses according to the qualities of the stimulus (e.g., many or few asterisks). Although a recognition memory task is a kind of two-choice RT task (was the presented word on the list, yes or no?), the term *choice reaction time* is used to

refer to judgments concerning a stimulus that is present rather than judgments concerning one's memory for a stimulus.

15. Hanes and Schall (1996) have found an interesting parallel to the variable rate assumption in single-cell studies of the rhesus monkey.

References

Anderson, J. A. (1973). A theory for the recognition of items from short memorized lists. *Psychological Review, 80,* 417–438.

Anderson, J. R. (1995). *Learning and memory: An integrated approach.* New York: Wiley.

Ashby, F. G. (1982). Deriving exact predictions from the cascade model. *Psychological Review, 89,* 599–607.

Ashby, F. G., & Perrin, N. A. (1988). Toward a unified theory of similarity and recognition. *Psychological Review, 95,* 124–150.

Ashby, F. G., Tein, J. Y., & Balakrishan, J. D. (1993). Response time distributions in memory scanning. *Journal of Mathematical Psychology, 37,* 526–555.

Atkinson, R. C., & Juola, J. F. (1974). Search and decision processes in recognition memory. In D. H. Krantz, R. C. Atkinson, R. D. Luce, & P. Suppes (Eds.), *Contemporary developments in mathematical psychology* (Vol. 1, pp. 242–293) San Francisco: Freeman.

Baddeley, A. D. (1976). The psychology of memory. New York: Basic Books.

Baddeley, A. D., & Ecob, J. R. (1973). Reaction time and short-term memory: Implications of repetition effects for the high-speed exhaustive scan hypothesis. *Quarterly Journal of Experimental Psychology, 25,* 229–240.

Baddeley, A. D., & Hitch, G. (1974). Working Memory. In G. H. Bower (Ed.), *The psychology of learning and motivation: Advances in research and theory* (Vol. 8, pp. 47–90). New York: Academic Press.

Baddeley, A. D., & Hitch, G. (1977). Recency Re-examined. In S. Dornic (Ed.), *Attention and Performance* (Vol. 6, pp. 647–667). Hillsdale, NJ: Erlbaum.

Brown, S. C., Conover, J. N., Flores, L. M., & Goodman, K. M. (1991). Clustering and recall: Do high clusterers recall more than low clusterers because of clustering? *Journal of Experimental Psychology: Learning, Memory, and Cognition, 17,* 710–721.

Brown, T. H., & Chattarji, S. (1995). Hebbian synaptic plasticity. In M. A. Arbib (Ed.), *The handbook of brain theory and neural networks* (pp. 454–459). Cambridge, MA: MIT Press.

Burrows, D., & Okada, R. (1975). Memory retrieval from long and short lists. *Science, 188,* 1031–1033.

Chappell M., & Humphreys, M. S. (1994). An autoassociative neural network for sparse representations: Analysis and application to models of recognition and cued recall. *Psychological Review, 101,* 103–128.

Cleeremans, A., & McClelland, J. L. (1991). Learning the structure of event sequences. *Journal of Experimental Psychology: General, 120,* 235–253.

Cooke, N. M., Durso, F. T., & Schvaneveldt, R. W. (1986). Recall and measures of memory organization. *Journal of Experimental Psychology: Learning, Memory, and Cognition, 12,* 538–549.

Corbett, A., & Wickelgren, W. (1978). Semantic memory retrieval: Analysis by speed-accuracy tradeoff functions. *Quarterly Journal of Experimental Psychology, 30,* 1–15.

Crannell, C. W., & Parish, J. M. (1957). A comparison of immediate memory span for digits, letters and words. *Journal of Psychology, 44,* 319–327.

Crowder, R. G. (1968). Intraserial repetition effects in immediate memory. *Journal of Verbal Learning and Verbal Behavior, 7,* 446–451, 1968.

Crowder, R. G. (1976). *Principles of learning and memory.* Hillsdale, NJ: Erlbaum.

Crowder, R. G. (1982). The demise of short-term memory. *Acta Psychologica, 50,* 291–323.

De Jong, R. (1991). Partial information or facilitation? Different interpretations of results from speed-accuracy decomposition. *Perception & Psychophysics, 50,* 333–350.

Donders, F. C. (1969). On the speed of mental processes. In W. G. Koster (Ed. & Trans.), *Attention and performance* (Vol. 2, pp. 412–431). Amsterdam: North Holland. (Original work published 1868.)

Dosher, B. A. (1984). Discriminating preexperimental (semantic) from learned (episodic) associations: A speed-accuracy study. *Cognitive Psychology, 16,* 519–555.

Egan, J. P. (1958). Recognition memory and the operating characteristic. Technical Note AFCRC-TN-58-51. Indiana University, Hearing and communication laboratory. See Green, D. M., and Swets, J. A. *Signal detection theory and psychophysics.* New York: Wiley.

Fagot, C. & Pashler, H. (1995), Repetition blindness: perception or memory failure? *Journal of Experimental Psychology: Human Perception & Performance, 21,* 275–92.

Forrin, B., & Cunningham, K. (1973). Recognition time and serial position of probed item in short-term memory. *Journal of Experimental Psychology, 99,* 272–279.

Goshen-Gottstein, Y., & Moscovitch, M. (1995a). Repetition priming for newly formed and preexisting associations: Perceptual and conceptual influences. *Journal of Experimental Psychology: Learning, Memory, and Cognition, 21,* 1229–1248.

Goshen-Gottstein, Y., & Moscovitch, M. (1995b). Repetition priming effects for newly formed associations are perceptually based: Evidence from shallow encoding and format specificity. *Journal of Experimental Psychology: Learning, Memory, and Cognition, 21,* 1249–1262.

Graf, P., & Schacter, D. L. (1985). Implicit and explicit memory for new associations in normal and amnesic subjects. *Journal of Experimental Psychology: Learning, Memory, and Cognition, 11,* 501–518.

Greene, R. L. (1986). Sources of recency effects in free recall. *Psychological Bulletin, 99,* 221–228.

Greene, R. L. (1991). The Ranschburg effect: The role of guessing strategies. *Memory and Cognition, 19,* 313–317.

Greene, R. L. (1992). *Human memory: Paradigms and paradoxes,* Hillsdale, NJ: Erlbaum.

Gronlund, S. D., & Ratcliff, R. (1989). Time course of item and associative information: Implications for global memory models. *Journal of Experimental Psychology: Learning, Memory, and Cognition, 15,* 846–858.

Hacker, M. J. (1980). Speed and accuracy of recency judgments for events in short-term memory. *Journal of Experimental Psychology: Human Learning and Memory, 6,* 651–675.

Hall, J. F. (1971). Verbal learning and retention. Philadelphia: Lippincott.

Hanes, D. P., & Schall, J. D. (1996). Neural control of voluntary movement initiation. *Science, 274,* 427–430.

Hebb, D. O. (1949). *Organization of behavior.* New York: Wiley.

Helmholtz, H. von (1853). *Philosophical Magazine, 4,* 313–325. (Original work published 1850.)

Hintzman, D. L. (1986). "Schema abstraction" in a multiple-trace memory model. *Psychological Review, 93,* 411–428.

Hintzman, D. L., & Curran, T. (1994). Retrieval dynamics of recognition and frequency judgments: Evidence for separate processes of familiarity and recall. *Journal of Memory and Language, 33,* 1–18.

Hockley, W. E. (1982). Retrieval processes in continuous recognition. *Journal of Experimental Psychology:Learning, Memory, and Cognition, 8,* 497–512.

Hockley, W. E. (1984). The analysis of reaction time distributions in the study of cognitive processes. *Journal of Experimental Psychology: Learning, Memory, & Cognition, 10,* 598–615.

Hockley, W. E., & Murdock, B. B. (1987). A decision model for accuracy and response latency in recognition memory. *Psychological Review, 94,* 341–358.

Hopfield, J. J. (1982). Neural networks and physical systems with emergent collective computational abilities. *Proceedings of the National Academy of Sciences, U.S.A., 84,* 8429–8433.

Jacoby, L. L., & Dallas, M. (1981). On the relationship between autobiographical memory and perceptual learning. *Journal of Experimental Psychology: General, 110,* 306–340.

Jahnke, J. C. (1969). The Ranschburg effect. *Psychological Review, 76,* 592–605.

Jahnke, J. C. (1970). Probed recall of strings that contain repeated elements. *Journal of Verbal Learning and Verbal Behavior, 9,* 450–455.

Jahnke, J. C. (1972). The effects of intraserial and interserial repetition on recall. *Journal of Verbal Learning and Verbal Behavior, 11,* 706–716.

Jahnke, J. C. (1974). Restrictions on the Ranschburg effect. *Journal of Experimental Psychology, 103,* 183–185.

Jiménez, L., Méndez, C., & Cleeremans, A. (1996). Comparing direct and indirect measures of sequence learning. *Journal of Experimental Psychology: Learning, Memory, and Cognition, 22,* 948–969.

Kahana, M. J. (1996). Associative retrieval processes in free recall. *Memory & Cognition, 24,* 103–109.

Kahana, M. J. (1998). *An analysis of distributed memory models of ordered recall: Effects of compound cueing, target ambiguity, and recall direction.* Manuscript submitted for publication.

Kahana, M. J., & Jacobs, J. (1998). *A response time analysis of the Ranschburg effect: Implications for distributed memory models of serial recall.* Manuscript in preparation.

Kanwisher, N. G. (1987). Repetition blindness: type recognition without token individuation. *Cognition, 27,* 117–43.

Kausler, D. H. (1974). Psychology of verbal learning and memory. New York: Academic Press.

Koppell, S. (1977). Decision latencies in recognition memory: A signal detection theory analysis. *Journal of Experimental Psychology, 3,* 445–457.

Kounios, J. (1993). Process complexity in semantic memory. *Journal of Experimental Psychology: Learning, Memory, and Cognition, 19,* 338–351.

Kounios, J. (1996). On the continuity of thought and the representation of knowledge: Electrophysiological and behavioral time-course measures reveal levels of structure in human memory. *Psychonomic Bulletin & Review, 3,* 265–286.

Kounios, J., Montgomery, E. C., & Smith R. W. (1994). Semantic memory and the granularity of semantic relations: Evidence from speed-accuracy decomposition. *Memory & Cognition, 22,* 729–741.

Kounios, J., Osman, A. M., & Meyer, D. E. (1987). Structure and process in semantic memory: New evidence based on speed-accuracy decomposition. *Journal of Experimental Psychology: General, 116,* 3–25.

Loftus, G. R. (1985). Picture perception: Effects of luminance level on available information and information-extraction rate. *Journal of Experimental Psychology: General, 114,* 342–356.

Loftus, G. R., & Bell, S. M. (1975). Two types of information in picture memory. *Journal of Experimental Psychology: Human Learning and Memory, 104,* 103–113.

Loftus, G. R., Busey, T. A., & Senders, J. W. (1993). Providing a sensory basis for models of visual information acquisition. *Perception & Psychophysics, 54,* 535–554.

Loftus, G. R., Duncan, J., & Gehrig, P. (1992). On the time course of perceptual information that results from a brief visual presentation. *Journal of Experimental Psychology: Human Perception and Performance, 18,* 530–549.

Loftus, G. R., Johnson, C. A., & Shimamura, A. P. (1985). How much is an icon worth? *Journal of Experimental Psychology: Human Perception and Performance, 11,* 1–13.

Luce, R. D. (1986). *Response times.* New York: Oxford University Press.

MacLeod, C. M., & Nelson, T. O. (1984). Response latency and response accuracy as measures of memory. *Acta Psychologica, 57,* 215–235.

Maddox, W. T., & Ashby, F. G. (1996). Perceptual separability, decisional separability, and the identification-speeded classification relationship. *Journal of Experimental Psychology: Human Perception & Performance, 22,* 795–817.

Masson, M. E. J. (1995). A distributed memory model of semantic priming. *Journal of Experimental Psychology: Learning, Memory, and Cognition, 21,* 3–23.

McClelland, J. L. (1979). On the time relations of mental processes: An examination of systems of processes in cascade. *Psychological Review, 86,* 287–330.

McCulloch, W. S., & Pitts, W. H. (1943). A logical calculus of the ideas immanent in nervous activity. *Bulletin of Mathematical Biophysics, 5,* 115–133.

McElree, B. (1996). Accessing short-term memory with semantic and phonological information: A time-course analysis. *Memory & Cognition, 24,* 173–187.

McElree, B., & Dosher, B. A. (1989). Serial position and set size in short-term memory: The time course of recognition. *Journal of Experimental Psychology: General, 118,* 346–373.

McElree, B., & Dosher, B. A. (1993). Serial retrieval processes in the recovery of order information. *Journal of Experimental Psychology: General, 122,* 291–315.

McNaughton, B. L., & Morris, R. G. M. (1987). Hippocampal synaptic enhancement and information storage within a distributed memory system. *Trends in Neuroscience, 10,* 408–415.

Metcalfe, J. (1990). Composite holographic associative recall model (CHARM) and blended memories in eyewitness testimony. *Journal of Experimental Psychology: General, 119,* 145–160.

Metcalfe-Eich, J. (1982). A composite holographic associative recall model. *Psychological Review, 89,* 627–661.

Meyer, D. E., Irwin, D. E., Osman, A. M., & Kounios, J. (1988). The dynamics of cognition and action: Mental processes inferred from speed-accuracy decomposition. *Psychological Review, 95,* 183–237.

Meyer, D. E., & Schvaneveldt, R. W. (1971). Facilitation in recognizing pairs of words: Evidence of a dependence between retrieval operations. *Journal of Experimental Psychology, 90*, 227–234.

Miller, J. (1993). A queue-series model for reaction time, with discrete-stage and continuous-flow models as special cases. *Psychological Review, 100*, 702–715.

Monsell, S. (1978). Recency, immediate recognition memory, and reaction time. *Cognitive Psychology, 10*, 465–501.

Mordkoff, J. T., & Egeth, H. E. (1993). Response time and accuracy revisited: Converging support for the interactive race model. *Journal of Experimental Psychology: Human Perception & Performance, 19*, 981–991.

Murdock, B. B. (1962). The serial position effect of free recall. *Journal of Experimental Psychology, 64*, 482–488.

Murdock, B. B. (1974). *Human memory: Theory and data*. Potomac, MD: Erlbaum.

Murdock, B. B. (1982). A theory for the storage and retrieval of item and associative information. *Psychological Review, 89*, 609–626.

Murdock, B. B. (1985). An analysis of the strength-latency relationship. *Memory and Cognition, 13*, 511–521.

Murdock, B. B., & Anderson, R. E. (1975). In R. L. Solso (Ed.), *Information processing and cognition: The Loyola symposium*. (pp. 145–194) Hillsdale, NJ: Erlbaum.

Murdock, B. B., & Kahana, M. J. (1993a). Analysis of the list-strength effect. *Journal of Experimental Psychology: Learning, Memory, and Cognition, 19*, 689–697.

Murdock, B. B. & Kahana, M. J. (1993b). List-strength and list-length effects: Reply to Shiffrin, Ratcliff, Murnane, and Nobel (1993). *Journal of Experimental Psychology: Learning, Memory, and Cognition, 19*, 1450–1453.

Murdock, B. B., & Okada, R. (1970). Interresponse times in single-trial free recall. *Journal of Verbal Learning and Verbal Behavior, 86*, 263–267.

Murdock, B. B., & Walker, K. D. (1969). Modality effects in free recall. *Journal of Verbal Learning and Verbal Behavior, 8*, 665–676.

Muter, P. (1979). Response latencies in discriminations of recency. *Journal of Experimental Psychology: Human Learning and Memory, 5*, 160–169.

Newell, A., & Rosenbloom, P. S. (1981). Mechanisms of skill acquisition and the law of practice. In J. R. Anderson (Ed.), *Cognitive skills and their acquisition*. Hillsdale, NJ: Erlbaum.

Norman, D. A., & Wickelgren, W. A. (1969). Strength theory of decision rules and latency in short-term memory. *Journal of Mathematical Psychology, 6*, 192–208.

Nosofsky, R. M. (1986). Attention, similarity, and the identification-categorization relationship. *Journal of Experimental psychology: General, 115*, 39–57.

Nosofsky, R. M., & Palmeri, T. J. (in 1997). An exemplar-based random walk model of speeded classification. *Psychological Review, 104,* 266–300.

Pachella, R. G. (1974). The interpretation of reaction time in information processing research. In B. Kantowitz (Ed.) *Human information processing: Tutorials in performance and cognition.* New York: Halstead Press.

Pachella, R. G., & Fisher, D. F. (1969). Effect of stimulus degradation and similarity on the trade-off between speed and accuracy in absolute judgments. *Journal of Experimental Psychology, 81,* 7–9.

Patterson, K. E., Meltzer, R. H., & Mandler, G. (1971). Inter-response times in categorized free recall. *Journal of Verbal Learning and Verbal Behavior, 10,* 417–426.

Pollio, H. R., Kasschau, R. A., & DeNise, H. E. (1968). Associative structure and the temporal characteristics of free recall. *Journal of Experimental Psychology, 76,* 190–197.

Pollio, H. R., Richards, S., & Lucas, R. (1969). Temporal properties of category recall. *Journal of Verbal Learning and Verbal Behavior, 8,* 529–536.

Proctor, R. W. (1981). A unified theory for matching-task phenomena. *Psychological Review, 88,* 291–326.

Raaijmakers, J. G. W., & Shiffrin, R. M. (1980). SAM: A theory of probabilistic search of associative memory. In G. H. Bower (Ed.), *The psychology of learning and motivation: Advances in research and theory,* (Vol. 14, pp. 207–262). New York: Academic Press.

Raaijmakers, J. G. W., & Shiffrin, R. M. (1981). Search of associative memory. *Psychological Review, 88,* 93–134.

Ratcliff, R. (1978). A theory of memory retrieval. *Psychological Review, 85,* 59–108.

Ratcliff, R. (1981). A theory of order relations in perceptual matching. *Psychological Review, 88,* 552–572.

Ratcliff, R., & McKoon, G. (1989). Similarity information versus relational information: Differences in the time course of retrieval. *Cognitive Psychology, 21,* 139–155.

Ratcliff, R., McKoon, G., & Tindall, M. H. (1994). Empirical generality of data from recognition memory receiver-operating characteristic functions and implications for the global memory models. *Journal of Experimental Psychology: Learning, Memory, and Cognition, 20,* 763–785.

Ratcliff, R., & Van-Zandt, T. (1996). *Connectionist and diffusion models of reaction time.* Manuscript submitted for publication.

Reber, A. S. (1967). Implicit learning of artificial grammars. *Journal of Verbal Learning and Verbal Behavior, 6,* 855–863.

Reed, A. V. (1973). Speed-accuracy trade-off in recognition memory. *Science, 181,* 574–576.

Reed, A. V. (1976). List length and the time-course of recognition in immediate memory. *Memory & Cognition, 4,* 16–30.

Reinitz, M. T. (1990). Effects of spatially directed attention on visual encoding. *Perception and Psychophysics, 47,* 497–505.

Reinitz, M. T., Wright, E., & Loftus, G. R. (1989). The effects of semantic priming on visual encoding of pictures. *Journal of Experimental Psychology: General, 118,* 280–297.

Roberts, S. (1987). Evidence for distinct serial processes in animals: The multiplicative-factors method. *Animal learning & Behavior, 15,* 135–173.

Roberts, S., & Sternberg, S. (1993). The meaning of additive reaction-time effects: Tests of three alternatives. In D. E. Meyer & S. Kornblum (Eds.) *Attention and performance XIV: Synergies in experimental psychology, artificial intelligence, and cognitive neuroscience,* pp. 611–653. Cambridge, MA: MIT Press.

Rohrer, D., & Wixted, J. T. (1994). An analysis of latency and interresponse time in free recall. *Memory and Cognition, 22,* 511–524.

Romney, A. K., Brewer, D. D., & Batchelder, W. H. (1993). Predicting clustering from semantic structure. *Psychological Science, 4,* 28–34.

Rubin, D., & Wenzel, A. E. (1996). One hundred years of forgetting: A quantitative description of retention. *Psychological Review, 4,* 734–760.

Rumelhart, D. E. (1970). A multicomponent theory of the perception of briefly exposed visual displays. *Journal of Mathematical Psychology, 7,* 191–218.

Sanders, A. F. (1980). Stage analysis of reaction processes. In G. E. Stelmach & J. Requin (Eds.), *Tutorials in motor behavior* (pp. 331–354). Amsterdam: North-Holland.

Sanders, A. F., Whitaker, L., & Cofer, C. N. (1974). Evidence for retroactive interference in recognition from reaction time. *Journal of Experimental Psychology, 102,* 1126–1129.

Santee, J. L., & Egeth, H. E. (1982). Do reaction time and accuracy measure the same aspects of letter recognition? *Journal of Experimental Psychology: Human Perception & Performance, 8,* 489–501.

Schouten, J. F. & Bekker, J. A. M. (1967) Reaction time and accuracy. *Acta Psychologica, 27,* 143–153.

Schweickert, R. (1985). Separable effects of factors on speed and accuracy: Memory scanning, lexical decision, and choice tasks. *Psychological Bulletin, 97,* 530–546.

Shibuya, H., & Bundsen, C. (1988). Visual selection from multielement displays: Measuring and modeling effects of exposure duration. *Journal of Experimental Psychology: Human Perception and Performance, 14,* 591–600.

Shiffrin, R. M., & Raaijmakers, J. (1992). The SAM retrieval model: A retrospective and prospective. In A. F. Healy, S. M. Kosslyn, and R. M. Shiffrin (Eds.). *From learning processes to cognitive processes: Essays in honor of William K. Estes* (Vol. 1), Potomac, MD: Erlbaum.

Shiffrin, R. M., Ratcliff, R., Murnane, K., & Nobel, P. (1993). TODAM and the list-strength and list-length effects: A reply to Murdock and Kahana. *Journal of Experimental Psychology: Learning, Memory, and Cognition, 19*, 1445–1449.

Shuell, T. J. (1969). Clustering and organization in free recall. *Psychological Bulletin, 72*, 353–374.

Smith, R. W., & Kounios, J. (1996). Sudden insight: All-or-none processing revealed by speed-accuracy decomposition. *Journal of Experimental Psychology: Learning, Memory, and Cognition, 22*, 1443–1462.

Smith, R. W., Kounious, J., & Osterhout, L. (1997). The robustness and applicability of speed and accuracy decomposition: A technique for measuring partial information. *Psychological Methods, 2*, 95–120.

Sternberg, S. (1966). High-speed scanning in human memory. *Science, 153*, 652–654.

Sternberg, S. (1967a). Retrieval of contextual information from memory. *Psychonomic Science, 8*, 55–56.

Sternberg, S. (1967b). Two operations in character-recognition: Some evidence from reaction-time measurements. *Perception & Psychophysics, 2*, 45–53.

Sternberg, S. (1969a). The discovery of processing stages: Extensions of Donders' method. *Acta Psychologica, 30*, 276–315.

Sternberg, S. (1969b). Memory-scanning: Mental processes revealed by reaction-time experiments. *American Scientist, 57*, 421–457.

Sternberg, S. (1975). Memory Scanning: New findings and current controversies. *Quarterly Journal of Experimental Psychology, 27*, 1–32.

Sternberg, S. (1998a). Discovering mental processing stages: The method of additive factors. In D. Osherson (Series Ed.), D. Scarborough & S. Sternberg (Vol. Eds.), *An invitation to cognitive science. Vol. 4: Methods, models, and conceptual issues* (2nd ed., pp. 703–861). Cambridge, MA: MIT Press.

Sternberg, S. (1998b). Inferring mental operations from reaction-time data: How we compare objects. In D. Osherson (Series Ed.), D. Scarborough, & S. Sternberg, (Vol. Eds.), *An invitation to cognitive science. Vol. 4: Methods, models, and conceptual issues* (2nd ed., pp. 365–454). Cambridge, MA: MIT Press.

Strong, E. K., Jr. (1912). The effect of length of series upon recognition memory. *Psychological Review, 19*, 447–462.

Swets, J. A. (1998). Separating discrimination and decision in detection, recognition, and matters of life and death. In D. Osherson (Series Ed.), D. Scarborough, & S. Sternberg, (Vol. Eds.), *An invitation to cognitive science. Vol. 4: Methods, models, and conceptual issues* (2nd ed., pp. 635–702). Cambridge, MA: MIT Press.

Townsend, J. T. (1976). Serial and within-stage independent parallel model equivalence on the minimum completion time. *Journal of Mathematical Psychology, 14*, 219–238

Townsend, J. T. (1981). Some characteristics of visual-whole report behavior. *Acta Psychologica, 47,* 149–173.

Townsend, J. T. (1984). Uncovering mental processes with factorial experiments. *Journal of Mathematical Psychology, 28,* 363–400.

Treves, A., & Rolls, E. T. (1994). Computational analysis of the role of the hippocampus in memory. *Hippocampus, 4,* 374–391.

Tulving, E., & Schacter, D. L. (1991). Priming and human memory systems. *Science, 247,* 301–305.

Tulving, E., Schacter, D. L., & Stark, H. A. (1982). Priming effects in word-fragment completion are independent of recognition memory. *Journal of Experimental Psychology: Learning, Memory, and Cognition, 8,* 336–342.

Underwood, B. J. (1983). *Attributes of memory.* Glenview, IL: Scott, Foresman.

Usher, M. & McClelland, J. L. (1996). *On the time course of perceptual choice: A model based on principles of neural computation.* Manuscript submitted for publication.

Whittlesea, B. W. A., & Podrouzek, K. W. (1995). Repeated events in rapid lists: part 2. Remembering repetitions. *Journal of Experimental Psychology: Learning, Memory, and Cognition, 21,* 1689–1697.

Whittlesea, B. W. A., Dorken, M. D., & Podrouzek, K. W. (1995). Repeated events in rapid lists: part 1. Encoding and representation. *Journal of Experimental Psychology: Learning, Memory, and Cognition, 21,* 1670–1688.

Wickelgren, W. (1977). Speed-accuracy tradeoff and information-processing dynamics. *Acta Psychologica, 41,* 67–85.

Wingfield, A., Lindfield, K., & Kahana, M. J. (1998). Adult age differences in temporal characteristics of category free recall. *Psychology & Aging, 13,* 256–266.

Wixted, J. T. & Ebbesen (1991). On the form of forgetting. *Psychological Science, 2,* 409–415.

Wixted, J. T., & Rohrer, D. (1994). Analyzing the dynamics of free recall: An integrative review of the empirical literature. *Psychonomic Bulletin & Review, 1,* 89–106.

Woltz, D. J., Bell, B. G., Kyllonen, P. C., & Gardner, M. K. (1996). Memory for order of operations in the acquisition and transfer of sequential cognitive skills. *Journal of Experimental Psychology: Learning, Memory, and Cognition, 22,* 438–457.

Yonelinas, A. P. (1997). Recognition memory ROCs for item and associative information: the contribution of recollection and familiarity. *Memory & Cognition, 25,* 747–63.

11

Laboratory versus Field Approaches to Cognition

Stephen J. Ceci, Tina B. Rosenblum, and Eduardus DeBruyn

Imagine the following variation on the well-known game three-card monte. You are presented with three boxes and told that one of them has a $100 bill hidden inside and if you guess which one it is, you get to keep the money. So, you make your selection but are told not to open the box you selected. Then one of the two nonselected boxes is opened, but it is always one that does not contain the $100. Thus, you are left with two unopened boxes, the one you selected and the other one. Now if you are asked whether you want to stick with your original selection before these last two boxes are opened, or whether you want to switch to the remaining unopened box, what should you do? It turns out that the decision is more complex than even some scientists appreciate. (We will return to this problem later.)

Now let's imagine a more dire scenario. Suppose that you are told that you have tested positive for some very rare virus, one that infects only 1% of the population. And further suppose that the test that diagnosed you with this virus is 90% accurate. Therefore, if 100 individuals are tested, half of whom actually do have the virus, the test will correctly detect 45 of the 50 who are infected but it will falsely claim to have detected the virus in 10%, or 5 persons, who are not actually infected. Armed with this knowledge, what are the odds that you actually have this virus considering that you have tested positive (Ceci, Baker-Sennett, & Bronfenbrenner, 1994)?

The statistical solutions to these problems are not exceptionally difficult. The three-box problem requires only a basic knowledge of algebra, and the virus scenario can be solved with knowledge of elementary Bayesian statistics. Yet, these problems often baffle some of the world's best thinkers. According to Piatteli-Palmarini (1991), even Nobel prize physicists do not recognize that with the three-box problem it is always better to switch boxes after being shown the empty box.[1] In fact, when this is explained, some scholars are reportedly enraged, protesting that it should not matter whether or not one switches boxes—the odds associated with any box will always remain 1:3. (If you need to be convinced that by switching boxes you increase the odds from 1:3 to 2:3, do 100 test trials of each strategy and you will discover that switching does indeed double the odds over sticking to your original choice.)

As for the virus problem, graduate students who have studied Bayes's theorem often fail to recognize that this problem requires a consideration of *base rate* (i.e., the virus only affects 1% of the population). In essence, they focus on the sensitivity of the test (90%), neglecting to appreciate that if a virus were totally nonexistent in a given population (i.e., 0% base rate), a test would always yield a false positive result when it indicated the presence of the virus, even if the test's sensitivity were 99.9%. If the virus doesn't exist, then the test must always be wrong when it indicates that an individual has it.[2]

Despite the fact that world-renowned physicists have trouble solving the three-box problem, research with adult gamblers in the United States and Brazil reveals that many of them—most of whom received little formal schooling beyond the fourth grade—accurately perceive the solution to the three-box problem as a variant of a form of gambling they engage in. Does this suggest that these gamblers are smarter than Nobel laureates? Of course not. People are often better at solving problems that reflect important and familiar ecological challenges than they are at solving identical problems that are disconnected from their everyday experiences. It is in the former contexts that they may have acquired the problem-solving skill in question, and often it cannot be spontaneously deployed outside these contexts (Ceci, Baker-Sennett, et al., 1994). The livelihood of a gambler depends upon being able to calculate the option that offers the best odds. Such calculations are not only common in their daily life but essential to it.

Similarly, university students and professionals fail to accurately calculate the odds of being infected with the rare virus, as presented in the second problem-solving scenario. Again, these students and professionals both possess the necessary knowledge of statistics to calculate the odds accurately, yet they fail to do so. Why? As with the Nobel physicists, the students and professionals are not sufficiently familiar with the context in which the problem is presented, and as a result they do not notice important aspects or transfer relevant skills. However, if the same problem is given to engineers who deal with quality control issues, but stated in quality control terms (e.g., "Certain equipment can detect a flaw in a product coming off the production line with an accuracy of 90%; but only 1% of items are actually flawed. So, how often will the equipment be correct when it claims to have detected a flaw?"), most of them quickly produce an approximation to the correct answer (Ceci, Baker-Sennett, et at., 1994). The context in which a problem is presented can be the determining factor in predicting who will generate a correct response.

A corollary of this assertion is that an individual's cognitive potential cannot be accurately assessed without consideration of the context in which the problems have been posed; for example, does the problem's context match the problem solver's representation of knowledge? Perhaps some of what are called learning disabilities are in actuality not neurologically based constraints on cognition but constrained contextual knowledge that inhibits the learner from applying skills already grasped in one context to a different context. And even when neurology is involved in the disability, the route through which it exacts its price on learning may be through constraints on applying what is known in one context to a similar problem in a different context, that is, the inability to transfer. We will have more to say about this topic later. But first we will ask what is meant by context.

Context

The history of twentieth-century cognitive psychology is, in many respects, the history of two paradigms: "pure" cognition, in the absence of context, versus cognition that occurs within some defined context. Representatives of the former paradigm can trace the origin of their work to the earliest psychological research on memory and perception, originating with the first psychological laboratories in Germany run by Wilhelm

Wundt (1866), Gustav Fechner (1878), and Hermann Ebbinghaus (1885). These early explorers, with only a few exceptions, viewed the study of human cognition as a form of pure science, rooted in the same kind of universal principles as classical physics. Their pursuit of universal laws of learning resulted in research on thinking and reasoning that was disembedded from the everyday contexts in which people lived. Such an approach proved valuable in two ways. First, it generated information applicable to and valued in the Zeitgeist in which the research was conducted, namely, theory development and testing. Second, it provided the foundation for the development of a contrasting theoretical approach that examined the contextual differentiation of what many assumed were universal or general laws of learning.

The adherents of the second paradigm studied cognition embedded in the context of prior knowledge and experience. This tradition, originating around the turn of this century (see Ceci, Baker-Sennett, et al., 1994), did not come to wide attention until the early 1930s in the person of Bartlett (1932). Bartlett emphasized the importance of studying cognition in its substantive and social context. For almost two decades Bartlett's theoretical contribution remained unrecognized by his own students, and its scientific power was largely overlooked. It was not until the late 1960s that it experienced a rebirth in the work of Neisser (1976). Since that time, the key role of context in cognitive development has received increasing attention in both theory and empirical work.

Investigators have used the term *context* in two different senses. It was first applied to the mental framework persons bring to a task. Each individual, it is argued, perceives and understands phenomena by means of structured representations of their relevant knowledge. That is, a phenomenon is assimilated into a preexisting knowledge framework (sometimes referred to as *schema* or *representations*), or else a framework must be created or altered to accommodate what is being experienced. The more one knows about a specific domain and the more integrated one's knowledge in this domain is, then the more elaborate one's mental representation will be. For example, knowledge of chess is a type of mental context. As will be seen, the manner in which individuals represent knowledge in a domain such as chess exerts a powerful influence on their problem-solving ability in that domain.

Context has also been used to refer to an aspect of the physical or social environment that is external to the organism (Bronfenbrenner, 1979). Just like the mental context example, aspects of the physical or social context can influence cognition. Later, examples will be described. At this point, however, we call attention to what the two senses of context have in common; namely, both involve, and take into account, the framework, mental and environmental, in which cognition takes place. It is through interaction with persons and objects that individuals develop representations of mental and environmental contexts that either invite or dissuade interaction (i.e., a motivational dynamic). Moreover, through experience mental representations become increasingly elaborated and integrated so that the individual makes more distinctions and classifications that aid cognition. Later, we shall give some concrete examples of the process through which this occurs.

Cognition in and out of Context

As an example of the approach taken by researchers who studied cognition out of context, we can draw on Ebbinghaus's seminal work (1885/ 1913). He created 2300 meaningless syllables that possessed no semantic relationship with the adjacent syllables in the list (e.g., *nin. dalt*). These became known as *nonsense syllables*. Ebbinghaus served as his own subject, as he attempted to memorize these syllables repeatedly. He then plotted his personal retention and forgetting curves. In so doing, he was able to provide general laws regarding how quickly learning occurred, how slowly it was lost, and how well it could be relearned at a later time. Thus began what was to become a systematic study of human memory out of context.

Ebbinghaus argued that if one were to study everyday memory tasks, such as recalling shopping lists or addresses, there might be some individuals who have greater familiarity with such materials than have others, and this would obscure the assessment of their "true" memory ability. He rightly appreciated that the mental context one brings to a task could influence memory and that individuals' varying in their mental contexts introduces "noise" in the search for universal laws. Instead of using materials that may have been represented differently by individuals whose knowledge or mental context differed, Ebbinghaus opted to purge the study of memory of all contextual variation in the hope that doing so would permit him to discover basic or universal laws that governed the underlying memory system. In the preface to his classic volume, Ebbinghaus wrote that the study of memory would eventually need to move outside of the laboratory, and to use meaningful contexts, but his words seem not to have been heard by those who succeeded him, at least not until much later.

Around the turn of this century, a group of investigators began to challenge the view that cognition could be adequately studied out of context (e.g. Henderson, 1903; Whipple, 1915). As already mentioned, this view was most fully and systematically set forth by Bartlett (1932). Today, a large number of researchers are following the Bartlettian tradition of studying memory in various mental and physical contexts (e.g. see edited volumes by Doris 1991; Fivush & Hudson, 1990; Gruneberg Morris, & Sykes, 1989; Light & Butterworth, 1994; Rogoff & Lave, 1984; Winograd & Neisser, 1992). A typical example of this genre is Baddeley's (1988) demonstration that skin divers' recall of words they learned underwater is superior when they are tested in that same context (underwater) than when they are tested on dry land. Apparently, aspects of the physical context that were present at the time of encoding can be replicated at the time of retrieval to serve as implicit cues.

What are the hallmarks of Bartlett's approach? First, he departed from the mechanical view of human memory. In its place, he proposed that memory was a dynamic process in which one's prior beliefs, values, experience, and knowledge were used to make sense of incoming stimuli. He referred to this process as "effort after meaning," by which he meant that human beings attempt to make sense of what they confront in a memory task, deploying their beliefs and knowledge (i.e., mental context) of the world in the process. Bartlett showed that even when verbatim recall is poor, the gist of what was studied may be easily retained, particularly if the subjects tried to "make sense" of it by drawing on their mental context.

For example, Bartlett's subjects were given stories about anomalous events and later asked to recall them. The most famous of them, "The War of the Ghosts," describes two young Indians who, while canoeing, encounter a war party of other Indians, who invite them to join in a raid. One of the young Indians in the canoe declines, but his companion joins and is injured in an ensuing battle. He is taken back to his home, where, after surviving the night, he dies at sunrise. In the course of the story a number of unusual things occur that had little meaning for Bartlett's British subjects. Indeed, these events were completely incomprehensible to Western minds because they hinted at ghosts and unfamiliar symbolism.

Bartlett discovered that when his subjects attempted to recall "The War of the Ghosts," they reconstructed the plot to make it fit with their own beliefs. Through such findings, Bartlett challenged the entire tradition of Ebbinghaus by asserting that memory is not a mechanical input-output (encoding-retrieval) system but a highly dynamic process that often distorts what is presented to make it fit with one's preexisting beliefs and representation of knowledge. Thus, memory cannot be separated from the rest of cognitive and social experience that influence the relevant contexts.

As already mentioned, Bartlett's call to insert context into cognition was not very influential in his time, even among his own students. The reason for traditionally giving context short shrift is not difficult to find. Taking physics as their theoretical model, early psychologists generally preferred universal explanations of cognition, as opposed to those that were situationally bound (Weisz, 1978). They hoped to show that a process operated unchanged across the idiosyncrasies and vicissitudes of context. Consistent with this long-held view, Weisz (1978) asserted that the ultimate goal of science is to find universal principles that "can be shown to hold across physical and cultural setting, time, or cohort" (p. 2). Many others have similarly argued that scientific methods can only succeed if the "operations of invariant mechanisms can be shown" (Banaji & Crowder, 1989, p. 1188).

But in their search for universal cognitive mechanisms, laboratory researchers have misconstrued an important function of all developmental sciences. A distinctive property of the species *Homo sapiens* is its ability to adapt to its environment, to respond differentially to different contexts. This insight led Bronfenbrenner to decry the search for context-invariant mechanisms as illusory:

One can question whether establishing transcontextual validity is . . . the ultimate goal of science. . . . Given the ecologically interactive character of behavior and development in humans, processes that are invariant across contexts are likely to be few in number and fairly close to the physiological level. What behavioral scientists should be seeking, therefore, are not primarily these universals but rather the laws of invariance at the next higher level—principles that describe how processes are mediated by the general properties of settings and of more remote aspects of the ecological environment. (Bronfenbrenner; 1979, p. 128)

Cognitive anthropologists have extended Bronfenbrenner's view by arguing that assessment of cognition in ecologically artificial environments, such as in so-called noise-free psychological laboratories, often obfuscates human intellectual potentials (Lave, Murtaugh, & de la Rocha, 1984; Rogoff, 1984). Indeed, laboratories are not regarded as noise free but are viewed as a different type of context in which cognitive activities take place. For instance, Rogoff (1984) stated that "thinking is intricately interwoven with the context of the problem to be solved. The context includes the problem's physical and the social milieu in which it is embedded . . . including the laboratory context, which is not context-free as researchers frequently assume" (pp. 2–3).

One team of cognitive anthropologists (Lave et al., 1984) examined people's problem-solving capabilities in a meaningful context, that is, grocery shopping. Shopping for groceries is characterized by fairly complex decision processes governed by taste, nutritional value, dietary implications, and aesthetics of particular groceries. In addition, size, brand, price, and quantity are also taken into account when buying comestibles. Lave et al. examined the arithmetic of 25 shoppers with their performance on an extensive paper-and-pencil arithmetic test based on the Torque Project at MIT. Whereas the average score on paper-and-pencil tests reached a modest 59%, shoppers' average arithmetic proficiency in the supermarket reached ceiling level (98%)! The number of years of schooling correlated highly with the paper-and-pencil arithmetic test ($r = .47$), but not with frequency of calculation in the supermarket. Similarly, years since completion of schooling correlated significantly and negatively with test performance but not with frequency of accurate grocery-shopping arithmetic.

To these highly interesting demonstrations by anthropologists we can add a systematic body of psychological research that has examined the influences of various types of physical, mental, social, and emotional contexts. We turn to this literature next.

Physical Context

Ceci and Bronfenbrenner (1985) conducted a study designed to exhibit the effects of environment on cognitive complexity. They asked 10- and 14-year-old children to either charge a motorcycle battery or bake a cupcake for exactly 30 minutes. While the children were waiting to remove the battery cables from the battery or the cupcakes from the oven, they were allowed to play a video game. The video game was located such that whenever the children checked a clock to see if 30 minutes had passed, the experimenter could record this. About half of the children were allowed to charge batteries or bake cupcakes at home; the other half performed their tasks in a laboratory. The children who performed the tasks at home exhibited a U-shaped pattern of clock checking during the 30-minute period. This pattern reflected a high incidence of clock checking for the first 10 minutes, then their hardly looking at all until the last few minutes, when they looked at the clock ceaselessly.

In contrast, children who performed the tasks in the laboratory exhibited a completely different pattern of clock checking, one that was linearly ascending over the 30-minute period. It appeared as if the children who performed in the home setting calibrated their internal clocks. They checked the clock repeatedly the first few minutes to confirm their subjective assessment of time passage, after which they immersed themselves in the video game, free from worrying about the clock. Support for the "setting" of the internal clock enabling the children to run on "autopilot" was obtained in a follow-up study in which clocks were programmed to run faster or slower than real time, and children were still able to recover their U-shaped patterns (Ceci, Baker, Sennett, & Bronfenbrenner, 1994).

Adopting a U-shaped strategy gave the home-tested children two advantages. First, it resulted in the same punctuality as the laboratory-tested children but with 30% less clock checking, a more economical strategy in terms of energy expenditure. Second, once the clocks were calibrated, the home-tested children were able to immerse themselves more deeply in the video game than were the laboratory-tested children. Indeed, a coefficient representing the U-shaped quadratic was associated with superior video game performance.

Familiarity of Task

Ceci et al. (1987) conducted a study highlighting the importance of context on children's cognitive performance, as well as showing the difficulty (and often lack thereof) of transfer from one cognitively isomorphic task (an isomorph is an analogue of the same problem but couched in different terminology or a different context) to another. They instructed children to predict where, on a computer screen, a moving geometrical object would terminate by placing a cross on the screen at that location (by means of a joystick). The object was one of three shapes (square, triangle, or circle), two sizes, and two colors, yielding twelve combinations of features. An additive algorithm (i.e., no interactions) was devised to "drive" the movement of these geometrical figures, such that shape determined vertical movement (squares would go up, circles would go down, and triangles stay horizontal). Dark-colored objects would move right, and light-colored objects would move left. Large objects would move on a lower-left to upper-right diagonal, while small objects would move along the opposite diagonal. Children were given 15 sessions of 50 random trials each to provide probability feedback. Even after 750 feedback trials, however, their prediction accuracy was only 22%.

Next, the same algorithm was used to drive a video game. The geometrical shapes were replaced by butterflies, bumblebees, and birds (same colors and sizes were used). Instead of placing a cross on the screen to predict toward where the shape would migrate, children were asked to place a butterfly net to "capture the prey" by moving a joystick. Children were given points for each capture, and sound effects were added to increase the "reality" of the video game. Children reached ceiling-level performance after 750 trials. In addition, replacing the simple additive algorithm to drive certain figures with a complex curvilinear algorithm did not deter children in a game context from reaching ceiling performance. Children in a disembedded condition (i.e., the geometric shape activity), as predicted, performed extremely poorly. The children were then given the video game context, and after successfully solving it, they were transferred back to the more abstract geometric shape context. An increase in problem-solving efficiency was seen only if the laboratory context was presented within a few hours after the video game context, and if the physical context remained unchanged (i.e., same room, computer, and mouse). This lack of transfer between cognitive isomorphs has also been found among college-aged students (Klayman, 1984), and boundaries of transfer have been demonstrated by, for instance, Nisbett, Fong, Lehman, & Cheng (1988; see also, Detterman, 1992).

In summary, the familiar contexts in these two studies allowed children to exhibit a specific cognitive energy-saving pattern and multicausal reasoning pattern, which would not have been discovered had children been tested exclusively in a different physical context, such as in a laboratory environment.

The context-specific reasoning examples that we have been describing are special instances of what are called *problem isomorphs*. For example, the famous problem about missionaries and cannibals, wherein a single missionary cannot be left alone with more than one cannibal, can be converted into an analogous problem about wives and jealous husbands, in which a wife cannot be left alone with more than one man unless her own husband is present (Gholson et al., 1988). The general finding in the cognitive literature is that cross-task generalization between a problem and its isomorph is usually low: knowing how well individuals can solve one problem is of little help in predicting how well they will solve the same problem in another context even when the two problems are isomorphic.

Perhaps the best-known case of a failure to transfer in isomorphic reasoning is that of Johnson-Laird and Wason's card task that we mentioned earlier (Johnson-Laird, 1983). In this task subjects are asked to decide whether a rule is true. For example, the proposed rule might be "If a card has a vowel on one side, it will have an even number on its other side." The subjects, who are university students, are shown the following four cards—

A, B, 2, 5

—and are asked to turn over only those cards that are critical to verifying the rule. In this example, the best decision is to turn over the 5 and A, as these allow one to disconfirm the rule with the minimum number of card turns. Although university students have great difficulty with this problem, they do much better when the isomorph is framed in the context of a travel game in which one must decide whether to turn over cards that have a picture of a type of transportation or the name of a town on them or whether a traveler can disembark from a plane that lands in a country that has cholera or diphtheria (Kunda & Nisbett, 1986). From a cognitive perspective, there is nothing in these latter two travel iso-morphs to make them easier than the number-letter task. Their underly-ing structure is identical to the one involving the numbers and letters. And yet performance on them is vastly different from performance on the task in its more abstract and less familiar form (Johnson-Laird, 1983; Nisbett et al., 1988).

Knowledge as a Context

In addition to the influence that the physical context exerts on cognition, the amount and type of knowledge people possess about a particular do-main (e.g., sports, cooking, chess, and science) also influences how well they solve problems in a given domain. For example, it has been shown that if a house tour is presented in a house-buying context ("note the large entry-level bathroom off the garage"), it will activate different knowledge structures among professional burglars than it will among prospective home buyers, and significantly different memory performance in these two groups will result (Logie & Wright, 1988). Similarly, depending on whether the identical material is presented in the context of a baseball game, a bird-watching exercise, or a Star Wars game, it can have dramati-cally different consequences because it will activate different bodies of knowledge that can be used to draw different inferences and create differ-ent expectations (Walker, 1987; Coltheart & Walsh, 1988; Means & Voss, 1985).

These kinds of *knowledge effects* (mental contexts) have been the grist for a decade of research on adult expertise. The bottom line of this re-search is that if a problem-solving task requires the use of a well-struc-tured domain of knowledge, then performance is enhanced. Thus, 10-year-old chess experts can recall chess board positions of chess games better than can graduate students who are not chess experts (Chi, 1978), even though their memory for nonchess material is inferior to that of the graduate students. Ten-year-old experts have far greater knowledge of chess strategies than graduate students, and they employ this to code arrays ("I remember the board looked like there had been a Knight's Tour move with a twist"). Interestingly, if the 10-year-old chess experts are shown chess boards that have been randomly formed as opposed to actual games, they do very poorly. The reason is that the random board positions do not allow them to draw on their great knowledge of chess, because the chess pieces in this condition are arranged in such a way that they can not be coded as reflecting some strategy used by chess players.

When considering the role of context in cognition, one must address not only the mental context (i.e., knowledge representation), and the physical context, but also the social and emotional contexts, such as the presence of others with whom one may be working and our implicit theories of self-competence. Is the individual learning or performing the task individually or in the presence of other people? Is the person working competitively against other people in performing a task, or is he or she working collaboratively to perform the task? Is the task one for which an individual's group membership is stereotypically good or poor at solving? Next, we describe research on the effect of social and emotional contexts.

Social Context

The social context in which a problem is tackled relates directly to the question of whether transfer will be easy, difficult, or nonexistent: "Probably the most critical issue in any type of learning is how well the learning transfers from one situation to another" (Reder & Klatzky, 1994, p. 25). It is not known exactly what aspects of context critically affect transfer, but there is some suggestion that working in a social context may foster transfer. One of the few studies to even address this issue was conducted by Gabbert, Johnson, & Johnson (1986). Their study evaluated the differential performance of first graders randomly assigned to a cooperative or individual group. The tasks completed during the training sessions were performed either in cooperative groups or individually. During the two testing days, following the training sessions, all tasks were completed as individuals. The results indicated that for all six of the tasks that were evaluated, the cooperative groups outperformed the individuals. In addition, during the two days of individual testing, the subjects that trained in cooperative groups demonstrated significantly superior transfer on three of the six tasks (Gabbert, et al., 1986).

A more recent study also evaluated how an individual's collaborative work environment can influence the individual's subsequent ability to transfer (Rosenblum, 1995). The subjects in this study were students in two third-grade classes with comparable educational aptitude. Students completed four tasks designed to measure creativity, memory, problem solving, and moral reasoning; these tasks were completed working alone or collaboratively. The results indicated that the students working collaboratively performed as well as or better than the children working individually. The most interesting finding was that performing tasks collaboratively during the first week increased the likelihood that the children would be able to transfer what was learned on the first week's tasks to the second week's isomorphic tasks, which were completed as individuals. Specifically, the students who worked collaboratively demonstrated a significantly better ability to transfer what they learned from the collaborative tasks to the tasks completed alone in the moral-reasoning and problem-solving domains but not in the tasks completed alone in the other two domains.

Socioemotional Context

Claude Steele recently has demonstrated that context can also include the instantiation of stereotypes that a learner harbors during testing. Steele's basic assertion is that when an individual perceives a stereotype threat, i.e., the sense that one is being judged based on stereotype, cognitions and behaviors will be directly affected: "the existence of a [negative] stereotype means that anything one does or any of one's features that conform to it make the stereotype more plausible as a self-characterization in the eyes of others, and perhaps even in one's own eyes" (Steele & Aronson, 1995, p. 797). Steele uses this concept as a foundation for the argument that the performance of African American students on intellectual or academic tasks is highly context dependent; i.e., performance on such tasks may suffer under conditions that elicit stereotype threat.

In order to test this hypothesis, Steele & Aronson (1995) conducted a series of experiments with Stanford University students. All students were instructed to complete very challenging and possibly frustrating items from the verbal Graduate Record Examination. It was deemed necessary that the task be sufficiently challenging in order to elicit the stereotype threat as a possible explanation for an impending failure on the task. The researchers systematically varied whether they led the subjects to believe that the tests were diagnostic of their intellectual ability or not, but in reality the tasks in both conditions were identical. The hypothesis was that black students who believed they were taking a diagnostic test would perform less well on the task than the white students completing the diagnostic test and less well than the black students who completed a test that was not believed to be diagnostic. In other words, the belief that the test was diagnostic of intellectual ability was hypothesized to be sufficient to induce stereotype threat in the black students, which in turn depressed their performance.

The results supported this hypothesis. Black and white students performed equally well on the nondiagnostic test, as did the white students on the diagnostic test. But, as predicted, the black students did demonstrate markedly lower scores on the diagnostic test than the other three groups. It is important to note that all of the results held even after scores on the SATs were controlled for statistically. Therefore, the significant difference in scores that was observed on the experimental task was considered to be a direct result of the testing context, namely, the belief that one's intellectual abilities would be judged based on one's performance on a particular task. "Clearly the diagnostic instructions caused these participants to experience a strong apprehension, a distinct sense of stereotype threat" (Steele & Aronson, 1995, p. 805).

Considerations Regarding IQ and Transfer

The majority of studies that have examined the correlation between IQ and the ability to transfer indicates that the higher the IQ, the more likely the individual is to transfer (Day & Hall, 1988; Ferrara, Brown, & Campione, 1986; Ferretti & Butterfield 1992; Klaczynski & Laipple, 1993). But, when the subjects are experts in the training domain, there appear to be no sizable correlations between IQ and the ability to transfer

(Ceci & Liker, 1986; Ceci & Ruiz, 1992). Below we briefly present several representative studies in this genre.

Klaczynski and Laipple (1993) investigated the relationship in college students between IQ and the ability to transfer. The tasks consisted of causal (i.e. logically required) problems or permission (i.e., allowed but not required) problems (based on the Johnson-Laird [1983] card sort tasks we described earlier). Therefore, there were four possible combinations of source and target problems: causal-causal, causal-permission, permission-permission, and permission-causal. The subjects were told to solve the problems by deciding which cards would help them to prove whether the rule was presented was true or false. After each of the four source problems, all of the subjects were read descriptions for which answers were correct or for which answers were incorrect, and they were given explanations. This activity provided the training for the subjects. After the subject completed each of the four source problems, with training occurring after each problem, they attempted to solve three target problems. During the second session, the subjects completed a short form of the Wechsler Adult Intelligence Scale–Revised (WAIS-R).

The findings indicate that the correlations between problem solving and IQ were highly significant. In general, higher IQ subjects were better able to solve the problems than were lower IQ subjects. But, it was also noted that the domain or context of the source and target problem was significantly related to the subjects' transfer (i.e., to their ability to transfer what was learned from the source problem to the target problem). Correlations between permission source problems and permission transfer problems were highly correlated with IQ, but this did not hold for causal source problems or causal transfer problems. Therefore, as in the Ferrara et al. (1986) study, it appears that the ability to transfer is largely context or domain specific.

Ceci and Liker (1986) have also pursued the connection between IQ, cognitive complexity, and transfer in adults by researching racetrack handicappers. Expert and nonexpert racetrack handicappers were evaluated for their performance in handicapping and predicting probable odds for 10 actual races as well as 50 hypothetical two-horse comparisons (their expertise was determined after they performed the predictions).

Predicting odds and winners was discovered to be a complex cognitive task requiring the use of a nonlinear, multiple-interactions model—essentially the men were calculating regression equations in their heads. It was found that IQ did not correlate with one's ability to predict winners and odds; i.e., expertise was independent of IQ.

The researchers selected 30 men to participate in the study. Each demonstrated a long-term involvement in racing: a minimum of two times/week for at least 8 years. All 30 men were very similar on "background" variables: years of experience at the track, level of education, professional prestige, etc. Each subject was administered a short version of the WAIS to measure their IQ. Both groups, experts and nonexperts had a range of IQ scores representative of the general public: 14 experts (81–128) and 16 nonexperts (80–130). The mean of all IQ scores was 100.0, with a standard deviation of 15.3, which is almost identical to the general population.

The 30 handicappers were to predict which horse would be the "top horse" (i.e., according to odds) at race time and the order of the top three horses' odds at race time for 10 actual races listed in the early form. Two groups emerged, one with 14 experts who correctly picked the top horse for at least nine of ten races and the top three horses at least five out of ten races (i.e., on average were equivalent to paid track experts). The best non expert, on the other hand, picked the top horse only five out of ten races and the top three horses for two out of ten races (Ceci & Liker, 1986, p. 257). The 30 handicappers were then asked to handicap 50 hypothetical races that matched two horses against one another.

The results demonstrated that there was no significant correlation between IQ score and the ability to predict the top horse or the top three horses. Similarly, there was no correlation between IQ and cognitive complexity. In fact, low-IQ experts used more cognitively complex models, including the interactive model variable (IMV), than did the high-IQ experts. The IMV was a variable that consisted of a complex interaction of up to seven factors—this variable was a better predictor of odds for the experts than the nonexperts, when it was placed in a regression equation. The experts were more proficient at using this cognitively complex variable (IMV) than the nonexperts, yet within the expert group there was no difference between high-and low-IQ experts in their frequency of use of the IMV (Ceci & Liker, 1986). Surprisingly, there was also no correlation between performance on any of the WAIS subtest measures and use of cognitive complexity; not even the arithmetic portion, despite the fact that their algorithms required extensive mental arithmetic. Finally, there was also no correlation between IQ and expertise. Therefore, among adult racetrack handicappers, IQ is an insignificant factor in predicting who will be an expert or nonexpert handicapper, who will reason most complexly, and who will be successful at picking the winners.

These findings are highly suggestive of the argument that IQ does not predict or measure cognitive complexity or the ability to solve problems. If it did, one would expect that IQ would then correlate with the ability to use complex cognitive models. This was not the case. More important, this study offers further support for the hypothesis that intelligences can be highly context specific and therefore not demonstrated under certain conditions, whereas the same kind of intelligence is at its peak in other contextual domains: i.e., individuals that scored high on an IQ test were not necessarily any better at predicting odds based on complex cognitive models.

Ceci and Ruiz (1992) further investigated the role of IQ in problem-solving ability by selecting two men, both experts at racetrack handicapping, and asking them to solve a stock market prediction problem based on the computer simulation "Millionaire." One man had a high IQ (WAIS = 121) and was a businessman with an M.A. in mathematics education; the other man had a low IQ (WAIS = 81) and was a retired dockworker with a fifth-grade education. Neither man had previous experience or knowledge about the stock market. This was confirmed with a multiple-choice test designed to test understanding of stock market mechanisms. Both men scored below chance on this test. This was essential, for if one man possessed greater knowledge about the stock market than the other, the results would be confounded by this different level of background experience at the outset of the experiment.

The experimental task was isomorphic to the racetrack handicapping, for which the men had already displayed remarkable expertise. The stock market task employed the same seven-variable interaction term (or "seven-factor equation, with multiple interaction effects [p. 180]") as the racetrack handicapping (IMV). The men were told to predict the probability that one stock would have a higher earning-to-price ratio (P/E ratio) than the other stock. Essentially, this is the same as determining the odds of one horse beating another, as they did in the 50 paired comparisons in the racetrack task. The men were given over 600 trials and only began to perform better than chance after 200 trials. They still had not reached ceiling performance by trial 600. There was also no difference in the ability to transfer from the racetrack to the stock market task based on IQ. Both the high-and low-IQ men displayed virtually identical performance—relatively poor performance. The experimenters then pointed out the similarity between the two tasks, and the men almost immediately attained ceiling performance on the task. In order to test that the men were in fact using the same algorithm as in the racetrack handicapping, the experimenters changed the algorithm in the stock market task without informing the subjects. The men's predictions immediately plummeted to well below chance, indicating that they were in fact using the racetrack algorithm, which was now incorrect.

Transfer did not occur as fully in the stock market simulation as one might have expected, especially if one believes that IQ drives cognitive ability. The men did perform better than chance, but never fully grasped the isomorphism between the two tasks until the experimenters clued them in. Most interestingly, though, there was no difference in performance based on IQ, which indicated that in this context and for these subjects intelligence did not influence their ability to transfer. The men had clearly demonstrated a remarkable ability to handicap horse races, yet they were unable to transfer this cognitive ability to a new domain or context. The specific contextual demands of the stock market task precluded the men from demonstrating their cognitive abilities to design a successful algorithm.

Thus far we have presented evidence for individuals' apparent inability to transfer information to novel domains or contexts. These results could leave one feeling very discouraged about the cognitive capacity of children, college students, and Nobel laureates alike. Is there any evidence to suggest that people *are* capable of applying knowledge to novel contexts? The answer is unequivocally yes, but only if the context is appropriate in the sense of recruiting relevant training skills.

We can find evidence for transfer across contexts in several of the afore-mentioned studies, but the victories are small ones. In general, the transfer of skills or knowledge is minimal, but nevertheless present. Individuals can transfer what is learned in a collaborative setting to a task performed individually; children can generalize from a video game with birds, bum-blebees, and butterflies to a prediction task with only geometric shapes; and when clued in, racetrack handicappers can apply their multiple-inter-actions model, used to predict horse-racing results, to an isomorphic stock market task. This research is not demonstrating an inability to rea-son successfully; rather, it is capturing a "short" in the circuitry for rea-soning across domains.

Perhaps our goal as researchers should be to begin to identify the mech-anisms responsible for allowing successful across-task transfer. What components contribute to an individual's successful transfer? Are people failing to encode knowledge fully or failing to recognize the similarity between isomorphic tasks? The system is breaking down at some point in the chain, and identifying where that occurs would be the first step toward shoring up the strength of our cognitive links.

Conclusion

To conclude, increasingly researchers agree that conceptualizing intelli-gence and cognition as context-free resources is too narrow a view (but for a recent defense of the immutability and domain-generality of intelli-gence argument, see Herrnstein and Murray, 1994). For instance, Shantz (1983) argued for the investigation of a competency-by-task interaction, instead of focusing singularly on either competency or task. She stated that "without any indication as to the relative importance [of task proper-ties] as determiners or their meaning in relation to social-adaptation problems . . . we have little theory of the task (situation) or theory of the task × competency" (p. 525).

Notes

1. The solution to the three-box problem is as follows. The box you chose ini-tially will always have a 1/3 probability of containing the $100 bill. The other two boxes, considered together, have a 2/3 probability of containing the bill. If

the researcher removes an empty box, the remaining box now has a 2/3 probability of containing the bill. Therefore, you should always switch, as you will be switching from your initial choice (1/3 probability) to the new box (2/3 probability). Retaining the initial box will only reveal the $100 one out of every three times you play the game, whereas switching boxes will prove successful two out of every three times (Piatelli-Palmarini, 1991).

2. By the way, the odds that one who has tested positive actually is infected with the virus in our hypothetical example in which the test is 90% accurate and the base rate of the virus in the sample tested is only 1% is not 90% but 8.3%: (.90 × .01)/(.90 × .01 + .10 × .99) = .083. This is an extension of Bayes's theorem:

$$p(A \mid +) = \frac{p(A \text{ and } +)}{p(+)} \; \Box \text{ or } \Box \; p(A \text{ and } +) = p(A \mid +) \times p(+).$$

Similarly,

$$p(+ \mid A) = \frac{p(A \text{ and } +)}{p(A)} \; \Box \text{ or } \Box \; p(A \text{ and } +) = p(+ \mid A) \times p(A).$$

Equating the right sides of the two above equations results in

$$p(A \mid +) = \frac{p(+ \mid A) \times p(A)}{p(+)}.$$

References

Baddeley, A. (1988). *Working Memory*. Oxford Psychology Series, No. 11. Clarendon Press. Oxford, U.K.

Banaji, M., & Crowder, R. (1989). The bankruptcy of everyday memory. *American Psychologist, 44,* 1185–1193.

Bartlett, F. C. (1932) *Remembering*. Cambridge, England: Cambridge University Press.

Binet, A., & Simon, T. (1916). *The development of intelligence in children* (E. S. Kite, Trans.). Baltimore: Williams & Wilkins.

Bronfenbrenner, U. (1979). *The ecology of human development*. Cambridge; MA: Harvard University Press.

Ceci, S. J., Baker-Sennett, G., & Bronfenbrenner, U. (1994). Psychometric and everyday intelligence: Synonyms, antonyms and anonyms. In M. Rutter & D. Hay (Eds.), *Development through life: A handbook for clinicians* (pp. 260–283). Oxford, England: Blackwell Scientific Publications.

Ceci, S. J., Bronfenbrenner, U. (1985). "Don't forget to take the cupcakes out of the oven:" Strategic time-monitoring, prospective memory, and context. *Child Development, 56,* 175–190.

Ceci, S. J., Bronfenbrenner, U., & Baker-Sennett, G. (1994). A tale of two paradigms. In M. Rutter & D. Hay (Eds.), *Development through life: A handbook for clinicians* (pp. 260–283). Oxford; England: Blackwell Scientific Publications.

Ceci, S. J., & Liker, J. K. (1986). A day at the races: A study of IQ, expertise and cognitive complexity. *Journal of Experimental Psychology: General, 115,* 255–266.

Ceci, S. J., & Ruiz, A. (1992). Transfer, abstractness, and intelligence. In D. K. Detterman & R. J. Sternberg (Eds.), *Transfer on trial: Intelligence, cognition, and instruction.* (pp. 168–191). Norwood, NJ: Ablex.

Chi, M. T. H. (1978). Knowledge structures and memory development. In R. Siegler (Ed.), *Children's thinking: What develops?* Hillsdale, NJ: Erlbaum.

Coltheart, V., & Walsh, P. (1988). Expert knowledge and semantic memory. In M. Gruneberg, P. Morris, & P. Sykes (Eds.), *Practical aspects of memory* (pp. 241–277). London: Wiley.

Day, J. D., & Hall, L. K. (1988). Intelligence-related differences in learning and transfer and enhancement of transfer among mentally retarded persons. *American Journal on Mental Retardation, 93,* 125–137.

Detterman, D. (1992). The case for the prosecution: Transfer as an epiphenomenon. In D. Detterman & R. Sternberg (Eds.), *Transfer on trial: Intelligence, cognition, and instruction* (pp. 3–36). Ablex: NJ: Norwood.

Doris, J. L. (Ed.). (1991). *The suggestibility of children's recollections: Implications for their testimony.* Washington, DC: American Psychological Association.

Dorner, D., Kreuzig, H., Reither, F., & Staudel, T. (1983). *Lohhausen: Vom Umgang mit unbestimmtheit und Komplexitat.* Bern: Huber.

Ebbinghaus, H. (1913). Memory H. A. Ruger & C. E. Bussenius, Trans. New York: Teacher's College Press. (Original work published in German as *Uber das Gedachtnis* [on thinking] 1885.).

Eysenck, H. J. (1988). The biological basis of intelligence. In S. H. Irvine & J. W. Berry (Eds.), *Human abilities in cultural context* (pp. 87–104). New York: Cambridge University Press.

Ferrara, R. A., Brown, A. L., & Campione, J. C. (1986). Children's learning and transfer of inductive reasoning rules: Studies of proximal development. *Child Development, 57,* 1087–1099.

Ferretti, Ralph P., & Butterfield, Earl C. (1992). Intelligence-related differences in the learning, maintenance, and transfer of problem-solving strategies. *Intelligence, 16,* 207–223.

Fivush, R., & Hudson, J. (Eds.). (1990). *Knowing and remembering in young children.* New York: Cambridge University Press.

Gabbert, B., Johnson, D. W., & Johnson, R. T. (1986). Cooperative learning, group-to-individual transfer, process gain, and the acquisition of cognitive reasoning strategies. *The Journal of Psychology, 120,* 265–278.

Gholson, B., Eymard, L., Long, D., Morgan, D., Leeming. F. (1988). Problem solving, recall, and transfer. *Cognitive Development, 3,* 37–53.

Gruneberg, M. M., Morris, P., & Sykes, P. (Eds.). (1989). *Practical aspects of memory*. London: Academic Press.

Henderson, C. R., & Ceci, S. J. (1992). Is it better to be born rich or smart? A bioecological analysis. In K. R. Billingsley, H. U. Brown, & E. Derohanes, (Eds.), *Scientific excellence in supercomputing: The 1990 IBM Supercomputing Competition winners* (pp. 705–751). Athens, GA: University of Georgia Press.

Henderson, E. N. (1903). *Psychological monographs, 5*, (23).

Herrnstein, R. & Murray, C. (1994). *The Bell Curve*. NY: Free Press.

Johnson-Laird, P. N. (1983). *Mental Models*. Cambridge, MA: Harvard University Press.

Klayman, J. (1984). *Learning from feedback in probabilistic environments*. Unpublished manuscript, University of Chicago Graduate School of Management.

Kunda, Z., Nisbett, R. (1986). The psychometrics of everyday life. *Cognitive Psychology, 18*, 195–224.

Lave, J., Murtaugh, M., & de la Roche, D. (1984). The dialectic of arithmetic in grocery shopping. I, B. Rogoff and J. Lave (Eds.), *Everyday Cognition*. Cambridge, MA: Harvard University Press. pp. 227–242.

Light, P., & Butterworth, G. (Eds.). (1994). *Context and cognition: Ways of learning and knowing*. Hemel Hempstead: Harvester-Wheatsheaf. U.K.

Logie, R., & Wright, R. (1988). Specialized knowledge and recognition memory performance in residential burglars. In M. M. Gruneberg, P. Morris, & P. Sykes (Eds.), *Practical aspects of memory* (Vol. 2). London: Wiley.

Means, M., & Voss, J. (1985). Star Wars: A developmental study of expert novice knowledge structures. *Memory and Language, 24*, 746–757.

Neisser, U. (1976). *Cognition and reality*. San Francisco: Freeman.

Nisbett, R. E., Fong, G., Lehman, D., & Cheng, P. (1988) *Teaching reasoning*. Unpublished manuscript, University of Michigan, Ann Arbor.

Piatelli-Palmarini, M. (1991, March/April) Probability: Neither rational nor capricious. *Bostonia*, pp. 28–35.

Raven, J. C., J. Court, & J. Raven (1975). *Manual for Raven's Progressive Matrices and Vocabulary Scales*. London: Lewis.

Reder, L., & Klatzky, R. (1994). Transfer: Training for performance. In D. Druckman & R. A. Bjork (Eds.), *Learning, remembering, believing:Enhancing human performance* (pp. 25–56). Washington, DC: National Academy Press.

Rogoff, B. & Lave, J. (Eds.). (1984). *Cognition in a social context*. Cambridge, MA: Harvard University Press.

Rosenblum, T. B. (1995). Collaborative learning: Myth or miracle? Unpublished master's thesis, Cornell University, Ithaca, NY.

Shantz, C. (1983). Social cognition. In J. H. Flavell & E. M. Markman (Eds.), *Handbook of Child Psychology*, Vol. 3. Cognitive Development, pp. 501–566, NY: Wiley.

Walker, C. H. (1987). Relative importance of domain knowledge and overall aptitude or acquisition of domain related information. *Cognition and Instruction* 4, 25–42.

Weisz, J. (1978). Transcontextual validity in developmental research. *Child Development, 49,* 1–12.

Whipple, G. M. (1915). *Manual of mental and physical tests* (Vol. 2). Baltimore: Warwick & York.

Winograd, E., & Neisser, U. (1992). *Affect and accuracy in recall: The problems of flashbulb memories.* New York: Cambridge University Press.

12

Basic versus Applied Research

Raymond S. Nickerson

I do not know the origin of the distinction between basic and applied research; my guess is that it is a relatively recent invention and would not have been recognized by, say, Johanes Kepler, Galileo, or Sir Isaac Newton, or by the founders of experimental psychology. Whatever its origin, the distinction is now a well-known one and not unique to psychology; it is made in all fields in which research is done. It has been the subject of endless debate and not a little contention.

Much of what has been said on the topic can be characterized as a running dispute about the relative merits of each type of research. In many ways the dispute is a tiresome one, with more than a little self-serving rhetoric and intellectual pretentiousness. And like most disputes, this one is won or lost only in the eyes of the disputants, each of whom appreciates the weight of his or her own position and the folly of that of his or her opponents. I do not want to contribute to the dispute here; I want, rather, to make a number of comments that relate to the distinction and some observations that I believe pertain to all research, however one categorizes it in this regard.

That some people work on problems because of what they see as the practical implications of solving them, whereas others do so for other reasons—aesthetics, intellectual challenge—is taken as a given. Moreover, this seems to have been true for a very long time, as a brief detour into the history of mathematics will remind us.

Intellectual versus Practical Motivation in Mathematics

No one knows the extent to which the earliest attempts to count, measure, and compute were motivated by practical as opposed to intellectual or aesthetic interests. It appears to be the case that both types of interest have energized mathematical thinking for a long time, just as they do today; but one can find different opinions among experts regarding the importance of the one type relative to that of the other. The belief that much of the most creative thinking in mathematics has been motivated by an interest in mathematics per se and not by any relationship it may bear to the physical world is held by many mathematicians (Davis & Hersh, 1981; King, 1992). Ulam (1976) expresses the idea this way: "The aesthetic side of mathematics has been of overwhelming importance throughout its growth. It is not so much whether a theorem is useful that matters, but how elegant it is" (p. 274). There is also the view, however, that many areas of mathematics have been developed primarily by people keenly interested in questions about physical reality and that even subjects usually considered pure mathematics often were created in the study of real physical problems (Bell, 1946/1991; Kline, 1980).

It seems that cultures have differed somewhat with respect to how mathematics has been viewed within them. Aesthetics, mysticism, and a general interest in philosophical questions appear to have motivated much of the mathematical thinking of the ancient Greeks. Pythagoras and Euclid treated mathematics as an abstract discipline that existed independently of the material world. The Pythagoreans considered mathematics to be more real, and more nearly perfect, than the world of the senses. Euclid's contempt for the idea that the reason for pursuing mathematics is its practical value is seen in the often-told story of his response to a question from a student regarding what advantage he would gain by learning geometry: Euclid is said to have instructed his slave to give the student three pence, since he must make profit out of what he learns. Boyer and Merzbach (1991) have argued that the Greeks put so much emphasis on deduction and abstraction, and had so little interest in practical applications of mathematics, that they tended to be rather poor observers of the physical world.

A noteworthy exception to this rule was the great mathematician Archimedes, who applied his mathematics to the physical world and especially to practical problems of engineering. His solution of the problem of determining whether a crown recently received from the goldsmith by his king was made of pure gold or a mixture of gold and silver is too well known to warrant retelling. He is reputed to have stalled the Romans' siege of Syracuse for 2 or 3 years by his inventions of various devices and instruments by means of which their efforts to take the city were thwarted. It has been argued that Archimedes' work in physics was unrivaled until the time of Galileo.

Egyptian mathematicians were motivated primarily by the practical demands of land measurement and pyramid building. Trigonometry was created by the Alexandrians, notably Hipparchus and Ptolemy, as a tool for enabling more precise predictions of the movements of the planets and other heavenly bodies. The study of algebra in Arabia may have been stimulated to some degree by the complicated nature of Arabian laws governing inheritance (Boyer & Merzbach, 1991). At least a thousand years before Pythagoras, the Babylonians were considering questions involving the time required for money to double if invested at a specified annual rate of interest (Eves, 1964/1983).

In more recent times, the view that mathematics should be pursued for its own sake is epitomized in a comment made by Hardy (1940/1989) in his *Apology,* which is often quoted as representative of the disdain that (some) pure mathematicians show for the idea that practical utility is an appropriate measure of the merit of their work.

I have never done anything "useful." No discovery of mine has made, or is likely to make, directly or indirectly, for good or ill, the least difference to the amenity of the world. I have helped to train other mathematicians, but mathematicians of the same kind as myself, and their work has been, so far at any rate as I have helped them to do it, as useless as my own. Judged by all practical standards, the value of my mathematical life is nil. (p. 150)

In an even more sweeping statement, Hardy gave essentially the same verdict with respect to higher mathematics generally: "If useful knowledge is, as we agreed provisionally to say, knowledge which is likely, now or in the comparatively near future, to contribute to the material comfort of mankind, so that mere intellectual satisfaction is irrelevant, then the great bulk of higher mathematics is useless" (p. 135).

Others have emphasized the importance of observation of real-world phenomena as a source of mathematical ideas. Sylvester (1869/1956), for example, believed that "[m]ost, if not all, of the great ideas of modern mathematics have had their origin in observation" (p. 1761). Ekeland

(1993), who sees the development of mathematics as part of the general development of science and technology, attributes the growth of analysis to the interest of its developers in celestial mechanics and notes that the book in which Gauss established the foundations of geometry was also a treatise on geodesy.

> Had historical circumstances been different, had there been different needs to satisfy, wouldn't mathematics have been different? If the Earth were the only planet around the Sun and if it had no satellite, we wouldn't have spent so many centuries accumulating observations and building systems to explain the strange movements of the planets among the stars, celestial mechanics wouldn't exist, and mathematics would be unrecognizable. (p. 55)

For present purposes, the most important thing to note relative to the distinction between pure and applied mathematics is the synergistic relationship that has existed between theoretical and practical interests over the history of the discipline. One finds numerous examples of mathematical developments that have come out of work that appears to have been motivated totally by intellectual—what some might call "idle"—curiosity and that has then, surprisingly, turned out to be usefully applied to practical problems. Among the more striking illustrations of this fact are the centuries of work on conic sections that eventually found applications in mechanics, astronomy, and numerous other areas of science.

One also finds many examples of the development of theoretical mathematics getting a push from the desire of people to work on real-world problems for which the then current mathematics did not provide adequate tools. The desire to work on problems of instantaneous change and continuity, which led to the development of the infinitesimal calculus is one well-known case in point; an interest in solving wagering problems that began the development of probability theory is another. Because science has become so dependent on mathematics, the recognition of a need for mathematical tools that do not exist can serve as a powerful motivation for the development of those tools. And the mathematical research done to fill the identified need can lead to developments that not only meet the need but have other unanticipated consequences as well. Even some of the most esoteric developments in mathematics are traceable to practical interests. Bell (1946/1991) puts it this way: "even a rudimentary knowledge of the history of mathematics suffices to teach anyone capable of learning anything that much of the most beautiful and least useful pure mathematics has developed directly from problems in applied mathematics" (p. 130).

In short, theoretical and applied interests appear to have coexisted throughout the history of mathematics. Work that has led to new developments has been motivated sometimes by the one and sometimes by the other. Applied interests have often led to theoretical developments, just as theoretical interests have led to new applications. It has been very much a two-way street. Whether either type of interest has been more important—more productive of new knowledge—than the other, is probably not possible, perhaps not even desirable to try, to say.

The Interdependence of Science and Engineering

Science, like mathematics, has been driven by both theoretical and practical concerns. Moreover, the relationship between science and engineering, or science and technology, has also been a mutually beneficial one. The fact that technology benefits from and builds upon scientific advances—that the knowledge that science produces enables technological developments of many types—is widely recognized. That science benefits greatly from technological advances is perhaps less widely acknowledged but no less true; often technology has led the way.

There are many examples from the past of technology developing relatively independently of science and also many instances of technology motivating scientific investigations and discoveries. Countless instruments and mechanisms of considerable complexity have been built over the centuries in the absence of any deep understanding of the scientific principles involved; often it has been the contemplation of operating devices that has led to scientific inquiry (Chevedden, Eigenbrod, Foley, & Soedel, 1995; McKelvey, 1985). Especially important to science have been advances in the technology of measurement (of both space and time) that have been motivated by such practical concerns as land measurement, the production of calendars, and navigation of the seas.

If we consider such activities as the making of tools, the smelting of metals, and the design of devices to utilize wind and water power as technological activities, then we must see technology as predating science by many millennia. Moreover, we find examples of technological developments that have occurred relatively independently of science even in quite recent times. The steam engine, for example, was built and used-before the theory of its operation got much attention from scientists. This development was in sharp contrast to that of the electrical industry; electricity and magnetism were investigated scientifically for 30 years before they were used much for practical purposes (Schroeer, 1972).

As scientific inquiry has become increasingly sophisticated in many fields, it has also become increasingly dependent on intricate instrumentation. Some types of experimentation in high-energy physics could not occur apart from use of its technologically sophisticated supercolliders. Astronomy has its optical and radio telescopes and space-probing satellites and vehicles. Biology has an array of microscopes capable of providing images of structures too small to be resolved by visible light. All the sciences, even the softest of them, make extensive use of computer technology. The building of such instrumentation requires the kind of understanding of the material world and the principles that govern it that science itself has produced. In short, today the relationship between science and technology is one of dependence that works in both directions. At least since Galileo began looking at the heavens through his first hand-made telescopes, science has both helped technology advance and has waited on technological advances that were essential to its own progress.

The Fuzzy Line between Basic and Applied Research

Like many, perhaps most, dichotomous distinctions, the distinction between basic and applied research lends itself to an oversimplified view of reality. Research projects differ with respect to many attributes or dimensions, and they are not all readily sorted into two mutually exclusive bins, one marked *basic* and the other *applied*. Was the effort to determine the structure of the DNA molecule basic research or applied? What about the current attempt to map the human genome? Or the search for a theory to explain superconductivity and predict what compounds will produce it?

The distinction between basic and applied research often appears to be based on the question of why the research is done—what motivates it. Basic research is said to need no motivation but intellectual curiosity. What one hopes to gain by it is a better understanding of some aspect of the universe. In contrast, applied research typically connotes research undertaken for the express purpose of solving, or helping to solve, some specific practical problem. A well-known example of a research effort that is usually considered applied was the Manhattan Project, which eventuated in the development of the atomic bomb. Another example is the work of Salk and his colleagues that resulted in the development of an effective vaccine for poliomyelitis.

But the motivational basis for the distinction between basic and applied research is problematic. It is not the case that scientists who do basic research have no interest in applications. Perhaps some lack this interest, but many who conduct research classified as basic do so with the firm conviction that the knowledge they are developing will be applied eventually to practical problems even if they are unable to say exactly how. And this conviction may be as important a motivation as intellectual curiosity or any of the other reasons why people do research. Some will argue that conducting basic research aimed at developing a more extensive and precise theoretical understanding of the world and how it works is the most effective way of ensuring a practical impact in the long run. Most of us are probably willing to make the assumption that knowledge is power and that the more we know about the world in general, the greater becomes our ability to influence events in a variety of (desirable and undesirable) ways.

Neither is it the case that scientists who do applied research have no interest in advancing scientific theory or contributing to our knowledge of the world in a fundamental way. Again, perhaps some who do applied work have no interest in making a contribution beyond solving the immediate practical problem on which they are focused, but many see applied research as a way to address specific practical problems *and* to contribute to theory development in the process of doing so. As a matter of historical fact, much of our "basic" knowledge about the universe has been obtained as a result of the work of scientists who were attempting to solve specific practical problems.

In view of all this, one might question whether the distinction between basic and applied research is a legitimate, or useful, one. Perhaps, as Press

(1995) has suggested, the complex relationship that has evolved between basic and applied science and technology is such that they are more appropriately treated as one enterprise. But even if one believed this to be so, the distinction between basic and applied research is not likely to be discarded anytime soon. I believe the distinction is a legitimate and useful one but that it should be thought of as a matter of emphasis rather than as a true dichotomy. I believe, too, that a case could be made for considering basic and applied as orthogonal dimensions, thus recognizing the possibility that research can be more or less basic (in the sense of addressing fundamental questions) and, independently, more or less applied (in the sense of having identifiable practical implications). As the terms are typically used, however, basic and applied mark opposite ends of a single continuum—the more basic, the less applied, and conversely—and, for the sake of discussion, that is, more or less, the connotation used in this essay.

With respect to the relative importance of basic and applied research, one can find a range of perspectives among researchers. One is that theory-motivated research that is not also problem motivated is a luxury that, as a society, we cannot afford, because of the pressing nature of the practical problems we face. Another is that theory-motivated research is the most likely to add to the cumulative knowledge base and therefore prove to be the most useful in the long term. Still another is that intellectual curiosity is the only legitimate reason for doing research and that the question of "importance," at least in the practical sense, should not enter the picture; but I think this is probably not a widely held view.

There can be no doubt that many of the most important applications of scientific discoveries have been unanticipated; they have been serendipitous consequences of research that was addressed to questions far removed from those applications. This fact has sometimes been used as an argument in support of a preference for basic over applied research. But the argument fails on two counts. First, serendipity can occur when one is working on applied problems as well as when one is doing research on questions that have no obvious practical import; it is surely true that research motivated purely by curiosity can lead to surprising consequences, but it is just as surely not true that *only* research motivated purely by curiosity can lead to such consequences. Second, although some basic research yields important unanticipated practical applications, much of it does not, and whether basic research has been more productive than applied research in this regard is not clear. Indeed, it is not entirely clear that research motivated solely by theoretical interests has contributed more to the development of *theory* than has research driven by practical interests as well.

My own view is that to the extent that the distinction between basic and applied research is a meaningful one, the two types must be considered mutually interdependent. Typically, applied research projects draw heavily on the results of earlier basic research; without the knowledge that basic research has produced, neither the harnessing of atomic energy nor the development of the Salk vaccine would have been possible. On the other hand, without applied research many of the results of basic research would have no greater impact than that of satisfying our curiosity somewhat about how the world works in certain respects, if that.

Practical and Theoretical Roots of Experimental Psychology

Unhappily, there are within psychology today attitudes not unlike those that represent the chasm between some pure and some applied mathematicians. On the one hand are those who consider basic research to be more respectable, of higher quality, more noble, and "purer" than applied research and who balk at the notion that they should be expected to justify what they do in practical terms. On the other are those who consider research aimed purely at theoretical questions that do not connect in any apparent way with real-world problems to be useless—the modern-day analogue to the medieval pastime of debating how many angels can dance on the head of a pin.

Fortunately, there are also many psychologists whose attitudes are not represented by these extremes. The work of many of the founders and early molders of psychology as a science was motivated by both theoretical and practical concerns. Alfred Binet, Francis Galton, Edward Thorndike, Raymond Catell, William James, and John Dewey come readily to mind in this regard. I note, too, that many of the leading experimental psychologists during the middle of the current century made both theoretical and practical contributions, the latter, in many cases, in support of the World War II effort. One thinks of Frederic Bartlett, Kenneth Craik, Arthur Melton, Ross McFarland, Leonard Carmichael, and S. S. Stevens, among others, in this context.

Work on effects of stress (e.g., oxygen deprivation, fatigue, and danger) on performance produced both practical knowledge and theoretical advances, as did studies of depth perception, dark adaptation, color coding, camouflage, instrument panel design, map reading, manual tracking, vigilance, and a host of other topics. The tradition of research that addressed both theoretical and practical concerns was continued after the war by numerous outstanding contributors; Donald Broadbent and Paul Fitts were representative of this strong dual interest on either side of the Atlantic.

The question of whether either theoretical or practical interests have been more important than the other in establishing psychology as a science is not answerable, in my view, and debates on the issue are likely to end in standoffs with the strengthening of self-serving opinions on both sides. Each type of interest has motivated psychological research from the beginning, still does, and presumably will continue to do so. It seems to me that research motivated by both types of concern has been, and is likely to continue to be, the most exciting and useful work in the field.

How Research Is Supported

It was once the case that in order to be a full-time scientist, one had either to be independently wealthy or to have a patron; otherwise one had to fit one's science in the cracks, as it were, while devoting most of one's time to earning a living. Recognition of scientific research as something worthy of support by society at large is a relatively recent development.

Most research funding today comes from one of three sources: the federal government (tax dollars), foundations, or private industry. Some government agencies support only research deemed likely to further specific practical objectives for which those agencies have mandates. In the United States, the various military and Department of Defense agencies support research that has implications for military systems. The several institutes within the National Institutes of Health fund research that relates to health issues within their specific areas of responsibility. The National Highway Traffic Safety Agency is especially interested in research that can be expected to help decrease the frequency and severity of motor vehicle accidents. NASA supports research relating to space exploration. And so on.

Some agencies have a mandate to support research not directed at immediate practical applications but at the development of theoretical knowledge in specific areas. The National Science Foundation is perhaps the most notable case in point in the United States. Some agencies support a broad spectrum of activities, ranging from theoretically oriented research on one end to the development and deployment of specific systems on the other. The Department of Defense represents this diversity and has a system of research classification that distinguishes several levels of immediacy or specificity of applicability.

A practical difference between basic and applied research that relates to funding policies and mechanisms is that basic research typically is funded by research grants whereas applied research is more likely to be funded by contracts. Generally speaking, a grant is a vehicle for supporting theoretically oriented field-initiated research. Grants are awarded by the National Science Foundation and the National Institutes of Health, among other federal institutions, and sometimes by private foundations; they typically are awarded to researchers in the academic world who compete for them by writing unsolicited proposals in accordance with general guidelines provided by the granting agencies. The selection process usually involves proposal evaluations by panels of other researchers in the field.

Contracts are the more common vehicle for mission-oriented government organizations—the military services, NASA, the Environmental Protection Agency, for example—and for private industry. In this case, interested prospective researchers, or research organizations, usually submit a proposal in response to a *request for proposal*, the issuance of which is announced in a widely disseminated publication, such as the *Commerce Business Daily*. The request for proposal typically lays out in some detail what the "purchaser" of the research wishes to get from the research project; it may also specify conditions prospective bidders must meet in order to be considered eligible to bid. Proposals are evaluated, and winners selected, by the purchaser; typically the selection is made on the basis of several factors, including the approach that is proposed, the estimated duration and cost of the project, and the ability of the bidder to carry out the research plan on time and within budget (as evidenced by the bidder's qualifications and perhaps past performance).

Grants typically provide the researcher with considerably more latitude than do contracts. The awarding of a grant is, in a sense, a vote of confidence in the researcher's ability to do high-quality research on the problem addressed by the proposal. Once the grant has been awarded, the researcher is given relatively free rein to carry on the research in the way he or she deems best, modifying the plan to take advantage of what is learned as the research proceeds. Technical reports of the research activities and results are expected, usually of the type that can be published in the archival literature of the discipline; progress reports may have to be submitted to the funding agency at specified intervals over the life of the project, but they often are quite informal and need be no more detailed than necessary to keep the funding agency informed of how the project is going.

Contracts tend to be more explicit than grants regarding what the researcher is expected to do. They are likely to contain a *statement of work,* which includes milestones expected to be met on a specified schedule. A contract will probably also specify a list of scheduled *deliverables,* which may include reports, computer programs, and other products. Progress usually is monitored closely—detailed formal progress reports may be required at scheduled intervals, and failures to meet deadlines for milestones or deliverables must be explained; in some cases monetary incentives are provided for performing ahead of schedule or under cost, and penalties are imposed for exceeding time or cost estimates.

This is an oversimplification, but generally speaking there are two types of research organizations in private industry: those that do research on behalf of the corporations themselves (perhaps aimed at product development) and those that do research for hire. The former type is represented by the laboratories within major corporations in automotive, oil, aerospace, chemical, pharmaceutical, computer, and communications industries, among others. The latter type includes research and development organizations—think tanks—that do research under contract for government agencies, foundations, and other industries. Generally, research and development companies specialize by maintaining a staff of professionals in certain areas and taking contracts to do work only in those areas. Not surprisingly, most of the research done in private industry—in either type of industry research organization—is applied work in the sense that it is intended to yield knowledge that will be useful immediately or in the near future in some practical setting.

Applied psychological research is done in both types of industry settings. Many large corporations maintain research groups that work on problems of applied psychology under a variety of rubrics, including human factors, ergonomics, biomechanics, and design. And among research and development companies are many that contain applied psychology groups as well as a few that work exclusively in that area.

Personal Motivations for and Assessments of Research

Why do people choose a career in research? How do those who make this choice decide what field to enter? Having entered a field, how do researchers select specific problems on which to work? All of these questions are themselves legitimate topics for research. Perhaps research has been done on all of them, but I am not familiar with it so will limit my comments here to personal opinion.

Why Do People Do Research?
One thing psychologists know about human motivation is that it usually is complex; seldom can behavior be explained adequately in terms of a single motive. One must assume that this is as true of research as of other forms of behavior. People do research for many reasons; even the individual researcher may be motivated by a number of factors. I believe that at least the following factors are operative, not, of course, all to the same degree in every case.

• Curiosity. Researchers, especially the more effective ones, are curious in the extreme. They have a strong desire to know the answers to questions they believe are answerable by research methods at their disposal.
• The joy of discovery. The joy of discovery is more than the satisfaction of curiosity. Obtaining an answer to a question by consulting a book, or by asking another person, is not satisfying in the same sense as

discovering a fact for oneself; this can be true even, I believe, if what one discovers for oneself turns out to have been discovered already by someone else.

• The aesthetic appeal of science. Many of the most influential scientists have been motivated by a commitment to the idea that the laws by which nature functions are simple and elegant in a deep sense, and they find the attempt to understand this simplicity and elegance gratifying at a very fundamental level. Sullivan (1933/1957) put the matter this way: "science is valued for its practical advantages, it is valued because it gratifies disinterested curiousity, and it is valued because it provides the contemplative imagination with objects of great aesthetic charm. This last consideration is of the least importance, so far as the layman is concerned, although it is probably the most important consideration of all to scientific men [and women]." (p. 7)

• The thrill of the chase. The process of doing research—generating hypotheses, designing experiments, teasing information from data, and interpreting results—is enjoyable to many people because of the intellectual challenge it represents, independently of any consequences the activity produces.

• The possibility of recognition. Researchers are exhibitionists of a sort; which makes us no different, I suspect, from people in other walks of life in this regard. Recognition, especially by peers, for accomplishments has been a major motivation for scientists in all fields over the history of science.

• The possibility of accomplishing something useful or good. The prospect of making a positive contribution to society, of accomplishing something that will improve the quality of life of some people (and not at the expense of others) is, I believe, a powerful motivational factor for many people engaged in research.

• Professional advancement. It must be acknowledged that research can be motivated too by no more lofty motive than that of beefing up one's resume in the interest of improving one's job situation (by means of a raise, promotion, tenure, etc.). I do not mean to disparage this factor—researchers have to make a living like everyone else—but I do believe that, especially in view of the emphasis on publications as the main indicator of accomplishment in the academic world, it can, when it is the predominant motivation, sometimes lead to poorly conceived and executed research.

I suspect that most researchers are driven by some mix of these, and perhaps other, considerations. How well any of us understands why we do research is a question, because another thing that psychologists know about motivation is that we are quite good at deceiving ourselves about our own.

How Do Researchers Decide What Research to Do?

How much time and effort do scientists devote to considering their options for research and deciding what specific problems to tackle? What criteria do they apply to decide that some questions are worth asking and others are not, or in deciding that some are more important than others?

Problem finding—as distinct from problem solving—has been promoted as an important aspect of creativity (Mackworth, 1965; Runco, 1994). As it applies to research, this is sometimes translated as the ability to identify the right *kind* of problem on which to work. The right kind of problem is one that is tractable but not too easy; working on problems that are likely to prove to be unsolvable is risky, and solving easy problems is not considered an accomplishment.

The ideal problem is at the leading edge of some area but not too far ahead of the field. If it is not at the leading edge, it is not likely to be of interest to other scientists; if it is too far ahead of the edge, it will be ignored because no one will understand it. As Cromer (1993) puts it, "A revolutionary insight disconnected from the current consensus is unlikely to be published" (p. 148). If one is to have an impact on a field, one's work must be close enough to current thinking to be of interest to and understandable by other researchers in the area. Apparently, successful scientists have typically sought out, or at least gravitated toward, what are generally seen by their peers as the problems that constitute major challenges to the field at the time (Mansfield & Busse, 1981; Roe, 1952).

Certain specific questions provide a focus for many investigators in a given field. Examples include the search by biologists for the structure of specific (e.g., the DNA) molecules, the search by particle physicists for specific particles (e.g., the Higgs boson) that theory says should exist, and the search by astronomers for the dark matter that is hypothesized to pervade the universe. Sometimes this focus is provided by very practical objectives, such as that of finding an efficient way to use electricity to provide lighting (Conot, 1979) or that of finding materials that will superconduct at relatively high temperatures (Cava, 1990). Sometimes it is provided by strictly theoretical interests.

How Should Researchers Decide What Research To Do?

Nature divulges her secrets grudgingly and generally only if one has asked a precise and well-formed question. In psychology, we do not usually formulate questions very well the first time we try; indeed, we sometimes seem to spend much time fussing about the edges of a problem, convinced there is a problem there but never quite finding our way to the heart of it. We ask questions and proceed to collect data as though we really believed the questions made sense. I suspect we realize, though, that many of the questions we ask are in fact unanswerable—at least until they are formulated with considerably more precision than we have been able to manage heretofore. One could make a case that the real challenge is not to discover the answers, but to find out what the questions should be.

This is not a criticism of psychology as a science. It is rather a reflection of the fact that as a science, psychology is relatively young and its subject matter is complex. One of the indications of the maturity of a science is the precision of the questions it evokes. Of course, all sciences deal with complex subjects in one sense, but there is often a simplicity in the sense that when the question to a complex question is found, everyone in the field will recognize it as *the* correct answer. Discovering the structure of the DNA molecule was a remarkable feat, the culmination of years of work of great complexity; but once it was found, everyone in the field recognized the correctness of the answer. The finding of a new subatomic particle, of a compound that will superconduct at a higher temperature than any other known compound, or of a gene implicated in a specific disease—these are noteworthy accomplishments, not easily achieved, but when done clearly recognizable by everyone in the associated field as answers to the specific questions asked.

Seldom in psychology is there an event comparable to the determination of the structure of a molecule or the discovery of a new particle. What one attempts to do in psychology is to discover relationships between or among variables and to express these relationships as principles or laws of thought and behavior. The variables involved are referred to as variables for good reason and the principles or laws are, at best, approximations, reflecting what can be expected "on average," when all the other factors that can affect thought or behavior are adequately controlled or discounted.

Most answers to questions in psychology are recognized to be *the correct* answers only by some fraction of the researchers working in the field; or to make the point in other words, most questions of theoretical interest have more answers than one at any given time, each supported by some subset of the people working on the question—and usually only tentatively by them. Again, I want to claim that the situation is not an indication that the research being done is of poorer quality than that done in some more mature fields, but rather that it is a reflection of the elusiveness of the subject matter and of the fact that psychology is still young, as sciences go.

How *should* a research psychologist—say one who wishes to do research on cognition—decide what is worth doing? Clearly, all questions are not equally worth asking. But how should the importance of possible research be judged? On what basis should choices among the possibilities be made? What should the criteria be? Should the social significance of the problem to which research might be addressed be a consideration? And, if so, should this concern apply to basic as well as to explicitly applied research? The last question, we can be quite sure, is one that will evoke answers based on strongly held opinions.

Some will argue that potential applications should be considered in any case. This argument may be motivated by the assumption that when the survival of a society is threatened by identifiable problems that research might help solve, it does well to spend most of its limited resources on these problems (Cellarius & Platt, 1972; Platt, 1969; Sperry, 1995). It may be motivated too by the conviction that research that could lead to certain types of undesirable applications should *not* be done, or at least should not be done without the establishment of safeguards against the feared applications.

Others will say that consideration of probable or possible applications should play no role in decisions about the funding of basic research. Basic research, they will argue, should be judged solely on the basis of its prospects for leading to new knowledge regarding questions deemed, by experts in the discipline, to be important to the advancement of the field. Moreover, they will claim—and with good justification, I believe—that it can be difficult to identify the practical effects of specific results of basic research, even after the fact, because the route from the research to the effects can be a long and convoluted one. Effective basic research contributes to the knowledge base in some area. In time, the knowledge base, which is the aggregate result of countless individual research efforts, becomes taken for granted and the critical role that research played in producing it may be forgotten—or the contributions of the many specific research projects may be impossible to trace. There can be little question of the fact that much of the engineering and technological development that goes on today would be impossible apart from the knowledge that past research—basic and applied—has produced. This is true even though it is not always possible to say exactly how important specific research efforts have been in the building of that knowledge base.

I confess to being impressed with the seriousness of some of the problems that contemporary society faces—overpopulation, environmental degradation, resource depletion, violence and crime, massively destructive weaponry, international terrorism, the enormous disparity between living conditions in different parts of the world. . . . And I believe that unless these problems are addressed more effectively in the future than they are being addressed at the present time, research that does not connect in any obvious way to practical matters could become perceived as a luxury that a threatened society can ill afford.

I confess too, though, to deriving considerable personal satisfaction from working on problems for the pure intellectual challenge they represent. I enjoy crossword puzzles, brain teasers, riddles, and conundrums, as well as more substantive intellectual problems for no better reason, that I can discern, than the fact that they are great fun to work on and—occasionally—to solve. And I find many research questions intrinsically interesting even though I would be hard pressed to say how answers to them would find practical applications. Given these predilections, I am more than a little reluctant to support the idea that *only* research with obvious practical implications is worth doing. The satisfaction of our curiosity about how the world works is not, in my view, an unworthy goal.

Nevertheless, if the ultimate goal of research—or at least that of most research—is not to better the human condition in one or another way, I think people who are asked to pay for it have a strong case for being reluctant to do so. I suspect that many researchers who profess no interest in applied problems believe that basic research is justifiable in practical terms on the assumption that research that contributes to the advancement of theory will prove to be useful, in some way, sooner or later. But this is an assumption and should be recognized as such; it does not, I want to argue, absolve the individual scientist from the responsibility of giving some thought to what practical use could conceivably be made of the results of the research he or she is doing, even when that research is explicitly classified as basic. Inasmuch as I believe that research addressed to practical problems can advance theory and contribute to the knowledge base of a discipline, and that theoretically motivated research can yield results useful in applied contexts, I find it easy especially to like research that is explicitly aimed at producing results with both theoretical and practical implications.

In any case, I want to argue that whether the research one proposes to do is basic or applied, one should be able to give compelling reasons for wanting to do it. I do not know how common it is for psychology departments to make the question of how to decide what research to do a priority focus of graduate training. If I were the czar of curriculum, I would make it a requirement that every school that offers a Ph.D. in psychology give a course, mandatory for all Ph.D. candidates, on deciding what research is worth doing or something to that effect. The objective would be to decrease the chances of producing researchers who spend years working on problems for other than critically considered reasons, only to wonder, at some point, why they have devoted their lives to researching *that*.

Such a course would include the study of research that has made a difference, theoretically or practically. It would explore the reasons people do research, the criteria by which research is judged from different perspectives, the various types of rewards and satisfaction researchers can derive from their work, and the importance of being able to explain—to oneself and to others—why the research one is doing is worth the time and effort of doing it, assuming it is. It would cover what various researchers have said about their motivations, about how they have decided what research to do, and about how they have judged their work in retrospect. It would include a fair amount of discussion and debate regarding the pros and cons of proposed research projects.

I would expect that having finished such a course, a student would be able to say what factors he or she would want to consider and weigh in choosing a research direction and specific research projects— to be able to articulate what he or she sees as the defining characteristics of worthwhile research. I would not expect that all students would derive exactly the same set of criteria for deciding what they want to do as researchers; the goal would be that each would have thought deeply about the issue, arrived at least at some tentative conclusions about what makes a research question worth asking that are consistent with their own sets of values, and been convinced that the matter deserves continuing thought.

Societal Motivations for and Assessments of Research

Just as individuals have reasons for doing research, society, presumably, has reasons for supporting it. But why does society—why should society—support research? How does it determine—how should it determine—what research to support? And how does it tell, if it does, whether the research it has supported has been worth the cost?

I do not propose to try to answer these questions here, but I want to call attention to them because I think the individual researcher does well to reflect on them even if the answers to them are not clear. Today research is a highly organized enterprise and it is supported, to a large degree, by public funds. Why the public should be expected to underwrite research and why it should be expected to pay for specific research projects are questions researchers can ill afford to ignore.

Justifying Research

Inasmuch as most researchers are dependent for financial support on a government agency, foundation, or corporation that is in the business of buying or sponsoring research, they must, as a practical matter, convince someone that the research they wish to do is worth doing from the point of view of the sponsoring entity. Moreover, one generally has to convince someone not just that the proposed research is worth doing but that it is more worthy of support than other possible projects competing for the same limited funds.

Sometimes the justification may be in terms of expected return on investment, as when a corporation is asked to commit limited research dollars to an effort intended to lead to a marketable product. When the potential sponsor is a government agency or a foundation, the justification must be consistent with the entity's purposes or mandate. What constitutes a persuasive argument is likely to differ for basic and applied research, but in either case because there is not enough funding to support all the projects researchers would like to undertake, arguments must be put forth so that the decision makers will have some basis on which to allocate available funds.

Should researchers be expected also to justify their research to anyone else, say to the general public, at least when they are asked to do so? I believe they should, for several reasons. First, the general public is the underwriter of research that is supported by tax dollars and has a right to know what its money is buying. Second, whether or not one's research is paid for with public funds, it is being conducted within a cultural context and could have implications for the future of that culture. Third, many writers, beginning perhaps with C. P. Snow, have warned of the risks of an increasing rift between scientifically literate and scientifically illiterate subcultures.

As Hunt (1995) has pointed out, funding decisions are made at more than one level. Although basic research proposals are likely to be evaluated strictly in terms of their scientific merit at the level of a proposal review panel or granting agency, decisions at higher levels regarding the allocation of funds among agencies are likely to favor those perceived to be most responsive to societal needs. "[T]his means that, given equal intellectual preparation, those branches of a science that are seen as responding to a societal need are more likely to be developed than branches that are seen as an intellectual ornament" (p. 266). And how sciences are viewed by high-level policymakers, most of whom are not trained as scientists themselves, must depend, to no small degree, on how effective scientists have been at explaining the societal importance of their work.

It can be argued that the need for explanations of research objectives and rationales becomes more and more acute as the pressures on researchers to specialize narrowly become increasingly strong. Holton (1973) has expressed concern about the divisive and factious effect that increasing specialization can have on society generally. It can lead, as he puts it, to

increasing atomization of loyalties within the intelligentsia. The writer, the scholar, the scientist, the engineer, the teacher, the lawyer, the politician, the physician—each now regards himself first of all as a member of a separate, special group of fellow professionals to which he gives almost all of his allegiance and energy; only very rarely does the professional feel a sense of responsibility toward, or of belonging to, a larger intellectual community. This loss of cohesion is perhaps the most relevant symptom of the disease of our culture, for it points directly to one of its specific causes. (p. 448)

Similarly, Kline (1980) has decried what he sees as a widening schism between mathematics and science, and even within mathematics, that has resulted from the increasing need for specialization that appears to be a natural consequence of advances in the field.

In Bacon's time the concern of mathematicians with physical studies needed no prompting. But today the break from science is factual. In the last one hundred years, a schism has developed between those who would cleave to the ancient and honorable motivations for mathematical activity, the motivations which have thus far supplied the substance and fruitful themes, and those who sailing with the wind investigate what strikes their fancy. Today mathematicians and physical scientists go their separate ways. The newer mathematical creations have little application. Moreover, mathematicians and scientists no longer understand each other, and it is little comfort that, because of the intense specialization, mathematicians do not even understand other mathematicians. (p. 286)

It does not require extraordinary perceptiveness to see a similar increasing specialization within psychology, even within cognitive psychology. And in psychology, as in other fields, specialization has its advantages, but it also has its risks. Among the latter is that of losing the ability to see one's speciality within a broader frame of reference and to communicate the value of one's work to people who do not have the same narrow focus.

If the divide between the scientific community and the general public is allowed to continue to increase, the consequences could be unpleasant for all, but the blame for it would rest with the former group—only the scientifically literate have the capability to close this gap. For these reasons, whether one does basic research or applied, one should, I think, be able to say why his or her research is worth doing and in such a way that the reasons will be understood both by colleagues and by an intelligent layperson. This is not necessarily an easy task. Especially it is not likely to be easy to explain the importance of one's research to others, if one does not have a clear idea of it oneself. At the very least, we should ask *ourselves* why we are doing the research we are doing. If the answer is satisfactory, we should keep doing it; if not, perhaps we should do something else.

Much can be said for the apprenticeship type of training that graduate students typically get by working with an advisor or other senior investigators, but a risk associated with this system is that students may select research problems for no better reason than the fact that someone else has been working on them and consequently fail to learn to think critically about what makes a question worth asking. Mentors should challenge students, I believe, to think hard about what they should do for research and to be able to say clearly why a question they wish to ask by way of research is worth the time and effort that is expected to be required to answer it. (The fact that no one has yet done an experiment that one is considering is a singularly uncompelling reason for doing it oneself.) This is not the same as convincing a student of the importance of a question the professor wants to ask. I am not suggesting that working toward answering the professor's research question is an unworthy goal, but only arguing the importance of encouraging students to think for themselves and helping them develop the ability to do so.

But even if one has a clear and well-conceived opinion regarding why a research problem is important, it may not be easy to convince others, especially those who do not have a lot of relevant background knowledge, of its merits. And one does well to bear in mind that we seem to have a natural tendency to overestimate how intrinsically interesting or important other people will find our own work to be.

Some scientists apparently believe that attempting to communicate effectively about science with people who are not trained in their disciplines is unimportant—perhaps even a waste of their time. This strikes me as an indefensibly elitist attitude and not very wise. Scientists and the general public alike owe an enormous debt to those individuals who understand science, or some aspect of it, at a nonsuperficial level and who have been willing to attempt to communicate what they know to people not trained in their disciplines. This involves not only explaining what science has done and discovered but why research that is currently going on or is planned should be done.

A noteworthy effort to explain the goals and findings of psychological research, basic and applied, to policymakers has been organized by the Federation of Behavioral, Psychological and Cognitive Sciences, a consortium of professional organizations to which many research psychologists belong. The federation sponsors a series of science and public policy seminars presented in Washington, D.C. and attended primarily by congressional staffers and federal government employees. Since 1982, leading researchers have given talks on specific topics, explaining the relevance of psychological research in specific areas to problems of national interest.

About 85 such talks had been given by the end of 1995. Many of the talks are published and distributed by the federation. The following topics are a sample of those addressed in these seminars: psychology and law (Loftus, 1984), television and human behavior (Huston, 1985), cognitive psychology and education (McKeachie, 1986), what we know about teaching reasoning (Glaser, 1989), family violence (Emery, 1989), human factors in flight crew performance (Chidester, 1990), high-stakes decision making in an uncertain world (Swets, 1991), behavioral science and public policy (Horowitz, 1992), and emotion and social judgments (Bower, 1995).

Judging the Value of Research Results

The main way in which we differ cognitively from our prehistoric forebears is probably not with respect to our ability to observe, to reason, to wonder, and to experiment, but with respect to the treasure trove of knowledge and theory that many generations of observing, reasoning, wondering, experimenting individuals have produced. The difference lies in the accumulated knowledge of the species. I know of no convincing evidence that we differ from our ancient forebears in any other significant way.

Some of this accumulated knowledge has resulted from informal observation and reflection. Much of it also has been gained as the result of carefully controlled experimentation. The revolution in approach to the acquisition of knowledge usually associated with Galileo led to the accumulation of more knowledge in the few hundred years between his time and ours than had been gained in all preceding human history. But if the development and continuing use of what we generally refer to as the scientific method has been responsible for this explosion of knowledge, it does not follow that all scientific activity has contributed to this result.

Is there such a thing as dead-end science? Is a certain amount of it unavoidable? If there is such a thing, can the amount of it be decreased without also impeding the progress of useful, productive science? I believe that there is such a thing as dead-end research, some of which is probably avoidable and some probably not. Many problems in psychology are never resolved, and many hypotheses are neither confirmed nor falsified; in time the research community simply loses interest in them and moves on to other questions.

Murdock (1995) suggests that the life span of most topics in the psychology of memory is on the order of ten years. He notes too that many of the results of memory research do not contribute to the cumulative knowledge of the field. "If a study is not a classic, or if it does not get integrated into the current Zeitgeist, then in about ten years it will vanish from the scene only to be rediscovered in some young investigator's doctoral thesis" (p. 117).

What can be said of research on memory may be claimed with equal plausibility of other areas of psychological research. Nor does psychology stand alone in this regard. I have already mentioned Hardy's negative assessment of the practicality of higher mathematics, as a whole. Davis and Hersh (1981) speculate that most of the millions of theorems contained in the mathematical literature are useless dead ends. And King (1992) makes the startling claim that "an ordinary mathematics research paper is read by almost no one except the author and the journal 'referee' who reviewed it prior to publication" (p. 38). (On the other hand, to demonstrate that we are in the realm of opinion here, I note that, in his classic *History of Mathematics*, Cajori [1893/1985] says that the mathematician "takes pride in the fact that his science, more than any other, is an *exact* science, and that hardly anything ever done in mathematics has proved to be useless" [p. 1].)

Supposing, for the sake of discussion, that there is such a thing as dead-end research. Is such research a waste of time and other resources? Does it contribute to the advancement of the science, even if in unintended and unexpected ways? Does it do so invariably? Usually? Only occasionally? I think one would be hard pressed to find incontrovertible answers to these questions. One can find opinions, often strongly expressed, and one can probably build a case for whatever conclusion one wants to draw, but I doubt that one can present evidence that is compelling one way or the other.

Should this be a matter of concern? For scientists? For society? From a societal point of view, how should the value of research results be measured? By the degree to which they contribute to the accumulated knowledge base and thus to our understanding of the world? By the practical utility of the new knowledge that is obtained? By the degree to which research results lead to new questions and thus to further research?

One can make a case for each of these answers, and one can note too that each has its limitations. Knowledge is generally seen as a desirable goal, but there are differences of opinion as to whether we are better off, as a species, with the knowledge of how to build weapons of unimaginably destructive power than we would be without it; not everyone is convinced that the ability to do the kind of genetic engineering that appears to be on the horizon will be an unmitigated blessing. It would be easy to identify other directions that some thoughtful people would question whether research should be allowed to take.

Scientists are given various sorts of recognition. The Nobel prize is undoubtedly the most prestigious recognition to which scientists in many disciplines can aspire, but there are numerous other awards given in recognition of outstanding achievements of researchers in specific fields. One could argue that inasmuch as the criteria for these awards are usually established by scientists and the recipients are typically chosen by them as well, this type of recognition should be considered more reflective of what the scientific community values by way of research results than of the values of society more generally. And one need not be a complete cynic to see that the opportunity periodically to laud individuals for their scientific achievements serves the interests of the scientific community well. Of course, science is not unique in this respect: journalism has its Pulitzer, mathematics its Fields medal, the motion picture industry its Oscar, and so on.

All of these awards are evidence of outstanding achievement, but each represents recognition by a highly specialized subset of society and it serves the purposes, first and foremost, of the subset. This is not to suggest that such recognition is necessarily inconsistent with general societal values but only that it is not constrained to reflect them. It can play a role in shaping them, and it may be that the publicity and ceremonial proceedings that go with the awarding of prizes like the Nobel have done as much as anything else to influence the attitudes of the general public regarding the nature and worth of scientific research. Are there some more objective indicators that could be used to assess the value of research?

One possibility is the effect on other researchers, as indicated, say, by citations of research reports in the scientific literature. (We should note in passing that if citation counts are used, most published reports of psychological research would have to be considered essentially worthless, because the vast majority—like the majority of mathematics papers, if King is right—are cited very few times if at all.) But should large citation numbers be considered evidence of especially worthwhile research? Clearly they are evidence that the cited research has had an influence on other researchers. But what, if any, further conclusions do they permit one to draw regarding the value of the research? Might it not be that, at least in some cases, dead-end research is simply leading to more dead-end research?

The history of science provides numerous examples of poor research that has been widely cited (approvingly) for a time. The "discoveries" of N rays by Blondlot in 1903, of mitogenetic radiation—supposedly given off by growing plants—in the Soviet Union in the 1920s, and of polywater by a Russian chemist in 1961 are well-known cases in point (Cohen, 1985; Franks, 1981; Nye, 1980; Rostand, 1960). Such discoveries have sometimes been hailed by eminent scientists as major scientific advances before being discredited by the weight of accumulating counterindicative evidence. According to Price (1961), the excitement caused among scientists by Blondlot's N rays was quite remarkable:

Nearly one hundred papers on N rays were published in the official French journal *Comptes Rendues* during 1904, representing not only the product of Blondlot and his pupils and assistants but also of other teams of workers growing up in Paris and elsewhere in France. Something like 15 percent of all physical papers in the journal in this period were on this subject. (p. 86)

The French Academy awarded Blondlot the Leconte Prize of 20,000 francs and a gold medal for his N-ray work.

The moral of this story is that the fact that a particular bit of research is widely cited in the literature of a field is no guarantee that it is high-quality research or that it is contributing positively either to the knowledge base of that field or to the solutions of any practical problems. Poor research can be influential in a negative way by leading other researchers down a blind alley. It should be borne in mind too that if a nontrivial number of researchers become focused on a particular theoretical question, their citations of each other can sustain a relatively high citation count for a time, even if they are the only people in the world who find the question of interest. I believe that citation statistics do constitute useful clues to the quality and importance of research, generally speaking, but that they should be interpreted cautiously and in the light of other evidence that the research involved is addressing reasonable questions.

Judging the value of specific research efforts is difficult, especially so when the research we are attempting to judge is our own. There is much evidence from psychological experimentation on egocentric biases that we tend to misjudge our selves in relation to others in ways that show us to advantage. There is little basis for assuming that our assessments of the importance of our own research are immune to such biases. And any tendency to overrate the importance that society in general may attach to a particular research problem can be compounded by the mutual reinforcement that the members of a group of people who are working on it can provide each other

But we must make such judgments as objectively as we can, doing so with criteria that seem reasonable to us. This is another argument for putting a great deal of emphasis, during training, on the question of how to decide what research is worth doing. The individual who has selected a research project because it satisfies criteria that are the result of a critical thought process has a firmer basis for believing in the value of the results it yields than one who has selected the problem for less carefully considered reasons.

One thing about which we can be fairly certain is that categorizing research as basic or applied does not tell us anything about either the quality or the long-term impact of the research so categorized. To the extent that the distinction between basic and applied research is valid, we can safely say that there are many examples of good and poor research, and of consequential and inconsequential research, of both types. To make the point slightly differently, acceptance of the distinction between basic and applied research as a meaningful one does not require that one consider either type to be better or more effective than the other.

Applied Experimental Psychology

It has been my privilege to edit the *Journal of Experimental Psychology: Applied* during its fledgling years. One of the things that makes this task interesting is the broad range of subjects with which incoming manuscripts deal. To be eligible for consideration for publication in *JEP: Applied,* a manuscript must report a study that was based on experimentation and that produced results with clear practical implications. Of special interest are manuscripts reporting experimental work that contributes both to the furtherance of psychological theory and to the solution of a practical problem. There are no limitations with respect to subject matter; no topic that is within the purview of experimental psychology is excluded, so the mailbag is always an adventure.

The following are a few of the subjects addressed by manuscripts received during the first year of the journal's existence: earwitness identification, brainstorming effectiveness, vibrotactile encoding of speech, acquisition of mnemonic skill, negotiation, effectiveness of instructions, ethnicity effects in personnel decisions, conflict management, writer's block, forensic interviewing of children, reading braille, effects of stress on performance, math anxiety, noise and health, aeronautical decision making, AIDS education, memory for advertisements, aircraft navigation displays, and the effects of sleep deprivation on suggestibility. These and countless other topics represent opportunities for psychological experimentation that has both theoretical and practical implications. The tables of contents of other journals that publish primarily applied research, such as the *Journal of Applied Psychology* and *Human Factors and Ergonomics,* also bear witness to the great range of applied problems addressed by research psychologists with an interest in applications.

One of the things that has struck me in the processing of manuscripts for *JEP: Applied* is the fact that many researchers find it difficult to make clear the practical implications of their findings. *JEP: Applied* accepts *only* manuscripts that report experimental studies that have such implications, and the burden is on the author(s) to be explicit regarding what those implications are. The name of the journal is intended to convey this idea, and the editorial in the inaugural issue stresses this requirement. Still, one of the most common criticisms that submitted manuscripts evoke from reviewers is that the reader is not told what practical significance, if any, the findings have. Many investigators among those who consider their research to be applied do not find it easy to say explicitly who, apart from other researchers, should find their findings useful and how they should be able to apply them.

Usually it is not the case that the results have no practical implications, but just that the researcher either considers it unnecessary to articulate them or finds it difficult to do so. I have to wonder to what extent this difficulty reflects a weakness of graduate-training programs. As should be evident by this point, I believe strongly that graduate training should place a great deal of emphasis on the importance of being able to explain why any research, basic or applied, is important enough to justify the time, effort, and other costs of doing it. It is especially important, I want to argue, that investigators motivated to conduct research that is addressed to real-world problems be able to say what (at least some of) the practical implications of their findings are—in terms that can be understood by potential users of those findings. But people who do basic research need to know, too, how to explain why the research they wish to do is worthy of the support the general public, or someone, is expected to provide for it.

Opportunities for Cognitive Research with Both Theoretical and Practical Implications

Several efforts have been made in recent years to identify major research challenges to psychology. Some of the resulting discussions have related primarily to the resolution of theoretical questions; others have focused more on the solution of practical problems. I have been impressed, however, with how much attention has been given in each of the resulting documents to practical problems of the day and to the question of the relevance of psychological research to those problems. I will mention three such efforts.

On the basis of a poll of some 2000 behavioral and social scientists, the Committee on Behavioral and Social Sciences of the National Research Council "delineated 30 topical areas that appear to occupy the leading edges of behavioral and social science research in the United States" (Luce, Smelser, & Gerstein, 1989, p. vii). In the present context, a particularly interesting aspect of the areas identified is the fact that many of them have a practical ring to them: health and behavior, crime and violence, jobs and inequality, macroeconomic policy, international security, and crisis management, to name a few.

Even the chapters with titles that would probably be considered clearly in the basic research camp contain many references to opportunities for applications. The chapter on sensory and perceptual processes, for example, deals with such subtopics as evaluation of design (of visual displays), hearing aids, and tactile aids for people who are deaf. The chapter on the psychobiology of learning and memory mentions education, normal aging, and memory disorders as areas of application. The introduction to the chapter on information and cognitive sciences begins with the identification of several practical reasons for doing research in this area: the problem of adult illiteracy; the challenge posed by the new possibilities for information representation provided by the rapidly moving information technology; and the difficulties experienced by individuals, organizations, and nations that stem from ineffective reasoning. And so on.

A second major effort to identify future research challenges for psychology—to develop a "national research agenda"—was initiated by the convening by the American Psychological Society of a Behavioral Science Summit in 1990 that was attended by representatives from about 70 psychological organizations. As a consequence of this summit and ensuing activities, six major areas were identified as priority areas for research: productivity in the workplace, schooling and literacy, the aging society, drug and alcohol abuse, health, and violence in America (APS Observer, 1992). The effort became known as the Human Capital Initiative, reflecting its focus on people as the country's greatest resource. In addition to the initial research agenda, three reports have resulted from the initiative to date: "The Changing Nature of Work," "Vitality for Life" (Aging), and "Reducing Mental Disorders"; each was produced by a committee composed of participants in the initiative with special interest or expertise in the subject area (APS Observer, 1993a, 1993b, 1996).

A third effort was undertaken by the Committee on Human Factors of the National Research Council (NRC) and resulted in a 1995 report titled "Emerging Needs and Opportunities for Human Factors Research" (Nickerson, 1995). This effort differed from the other NRC effort already mentioned in being much smaller and focused on needs and opportunities for human factors research, human factors being interpreted broadly, but not so broadly as to include all of psychology, or, in particular, research not motivated by practical concerns. This effort emphasized areas of need and opportunity that the committee felt are increasing in practical import because of recent and anticipated changes in technology. The areas identified were productivity in organizations, training and education, employment and disabilities, health care, environmental change, communication technology and telenetworking, information access and usability, emerging technologies in work design, transportation, cognitive performance under stress, and aiding intellectual work.

The work that eventuated in the Human Capital Initiative and the work of the National Research Council's Committee on Human Factors were parallel efforts with little coupling between them; moreover, the two groups involved differed in composition and purpose. Nevertheless there is considerable similarity in the areas of research opportunities they identified. Other attempts to identify major challenges and opportunities for psychological research, basic and applied, in the near-term future include Moray (1995), Nickerson (1992), Smith & Torrey (1996), and Solso & Massaro (1995).

The main point I want to make in calling attention to these efforts is that many (perhaps most) of the problems identified represent opportunities to do research with both theoretical and practical import. In psychology we are a long way from a "theory of everything," there is no dearth of pressing practical problems on which to work, and the overlap between problems that offer a theoretical challenge and those that represent practical needs is great.

Recap

The debate regarding the relative merits of basic and applied research has gone on for a long time and is not likely to end soon. The issue is the kind that sustains debate, I suspect, precisely because it has no resolution. The foregoing comments, which relate to the debate, may be summarized by the following observations.

• People have been motivated to do research for both intellectual and practical reasons for a very long time.

• In both mathematics and science, basic and applied work have been interdependent and mutually reinforcing.

• The line between basic and applied research is a fuzzy one; the same research project can be both basic (in the sense that it addresses fundamental questions) and applied (in the sense that it has identifiable practical implications).

• Psychological research has been motivated by both theoretical and practical concerns from the earliest days of psychology as a science.

• Individuals do research for many reasons, intellectual curiosity and the desire to do some good being only two of them.

• The distinction between basic and applied research is not synonymous with the distinction between good and poor research. it is possible to have good and poor research of both types.

• The distinction between basic and applied research is not synonymous with the distinction between important and unimportant research. It is possible to have important and trivial research of both types.

• The fact that a particular research effort is aimed at advancing theory does not mean that it cannot contribute to the solution of practical problems.

• The fact that a particular research effort is aimed at solving a specific practical problem does not mean that it cannot contribute to our general understanding of the world.

• There are many opportunities for research in psychology, and in cognition in particular, that can contribute to psychological theory while addressing important practical problems.

• Researchers have an obligation to think about their research and to be able to give reasons for why they have chosen to do the research they are doing.

References

APS Observer. (1992, February). Human capital initiative: Report of the National Behavioral Science Research Agenda Committee. [Special issue] *APS Observer.*

APS Observer. (1993a, October). Human capital initiative: The changing nature of work. [Special issue] *APS Observer.*

APS Observer. (1993b, December). Human capital initiative: Vitality for life. [Special issue] *APS Observer.*

APS Observer. (1996, February). Human capital initiative: Reducing mental disorders. [Special issue] *APS Observer.*

Bell, E. T. (1991). *The magic of numbers.* New York: Dover. (Original work published 1946.).

Bower, G. (1995). *Emotion and social judgment.* Washington, DC: Federation of Behavioral, Psychological and Cognitive Sciences.

Boyer, C. B., & Merzbach, U. C. (1991). *A history of mathematics* (2nd Ed.). New York: Wiley.

Cajori, F. (1985). *The history of mathematics* (4th Ed.). New York: Chelsea. (Original work published in 1893.)

Cava, R. J. (1990). Superconductors beyond 1-2-3. *Scientific American, 263*(2), 42–49.

Cellarius, R. A., & Platt, J. (1972). Councils of urgent studies. *Science, 177,* 670–676.

Chevedden, P. E., Eigenbrod, L., Foley, V., & Soedel, W. (1995). The trebuchet. *Scientific American, 273*(1), 66–71.

Chidester, T. R. (1990). *Human factors research: Narrowing the extremes of flight crew performance.* Washington, DC: Federation of Behavioral, Psychological and Cognitive Sciences.

Cohen, I. B. (1985). *Revolution in science.* Cambridge, MA: Harvard University Press.

Conot, R. (1979). *A streak of luck.* New York: Seaview.

Cromer, A. (1993). *Uncommon sense: The heretical nature of science.* New York: Oxford University Press.

Davis, P. J., & Hersh, R. (1981). *The mathematical experience.* Boston, MA: Houghton Mifflin.

Ekeland, I. (1993). *The broken dice.* Chicago: University of Chicago Press. (Original work published in French in 1991.).

Emery, R. E. (1989). *Family violence: Has science met its match?* Washington, DC: Federation of Behavioral, Psychological and Cognitive Sciences.

Eves, H. (1983). *An introduction to the history of mathematics.* Philadelphia: Saunders College Publishing. (Original work published 1964.).

Franks, F. (1981). *Polywater.* Cambridge, MA: MIT Press.

Glaser, R. (1989). *The fourth R: The ability to reason.* Washington, DC: Federation of Behavioral, Psychological and Cognitive Sciences.

Hardy, G. H. (1989). A mathematicians apology. Cambridge, England: Cambridge University Press. (Original work published 1940.)

Holton, G. (1973). *Thematic origins of scientific thought.* Cambridge, MA: Harvard University Press.

Horowitz, F. D. (1992). *From Pandora to panacea with stops between: Travels with behavioral science in the land of public policy.* Washington, DC: Federation of Behavioral, Psychological and Cognitive Sciences.

Hunt, E. (1995). Pulls and pushes on cognitive psychology: The view toward 2001. In R. L. Solso & D. W. Massaro (Eds.), *The science of the mind: 2001 and beyond* (pp. 258–273). New York: Oxford University Press.

Huston, A. C. (1985). *Television and human behavior.* Washington, DC: Federation of Behavioral, Psychological and Cognitive Sciences.

King, J. P. (1992). *The art of mathematics.* New York: Fawcett Columbine.

Kline, M. (1980). *Mathematics: The loss of certainty.* New York: Oxford University University Press.

Loftus, E. (1984). *Psychology and law.* Washington, DC: Federation of Behavioral, Psychological and Cognitive Sciences.

Luce, R. D., Smelser, N. J., & Gerstein, D. R. (1989). *Leading edges in social and behavioral science.* New York: Sage.

Mackworth, N. H. (1965). Originality. *American Psychologist. 20,* 51–66.

Mansfield, R. S., & Busse, T. V. (1981). *The psychology of creativity and discovery.* Chicago: Nelson-Hall.

McKeachie, W. (1986). *Cognitive psychology and education.* Washington, DC: Federation of Behavioral, Psychological and Cognitive Sciences.

McKelvey, J. P. (1985). Science and technology: The driven and the driver. *Technology Review, 88*(1), 38–47.

Moray, N. (1995). Ergonomics and the global problems of the twenty-first century. *Ergonomics, 38,* 1691–1707.

Murdock, B. B. (1995). Human memory in the twenty-first century. In R. L. Solso & D. W. Massaro (Eds.), *The science of the mind: 2001 and beyond* (pp. 109–122). New York: Oxford University Press.

Nickerson, R. S. (1992). *Looking ahead: Human factors challenging in a changing world.* Hillsdale, NJ: Erlbaum.

Nickerson, R. S. (Ed.). (1995). *Emerging needs and opportunities for human factors research*. Washington, DC: National Academy Press.

Nye, M. J. (1980). N-rays: An episode in the history and psychology of science. *Historical studies in the physical sciences, 11,* 125–156.

Platt, J. (1969). What we must do. *Science, 166,* 1115–1121.

Press, F. (1995). Needed: Coherent budgeting for science and technology. *Science, 270,* 1448–1449.

Price, D. J. de S. (1961). *Science since Babylon.* New Haven: Yale University Press.

Roe, A. (1952). A psychologist examines 64 eminent scientists. *Scientific American, 187*(5), 21–25.

Rostand, J. (1960). *Error and deception in science.* New York: Basic Books.

Runco, M. A. (Ed.). (1994). *Problem finding, problem solving, and creativity.* Norwood, NJ: Ablex.

Schroeer, D. (1972). *Physics and its fifth dimension: Society.* Reading, MA: Addison-Wesley.

Smith, P. M., & Torrey, B. B. (1996). The future of the behavioral and social sciences. *Science 271,* 611–612.

Solso, R. L., & Massaro, D. W. (1995). *The science of the mind: 2001 and beyond.* New York: Oxford University Press.

Sperry, R. W. (1995). The impact and promise of the cognitive revolution. In R. L. Solso & D. W. Massaro (Eds.), *The science of the mind: 2001 and beyond* (pp. 35–49). New York: Oxford University Press.

Sullivan, J. W. N. (1957). The limitations of science. New York: Viking Press. Mentor Books. (Originally published 1933.)

Swets, J. A. (1991). *The science of high stakes decision making in an uncertain world.* Washington, DC: Federation of Behavioral, Psychological and Cognitive Sciences.

Sylvester, J. J. (1956). The study that knows nothing of observation. In J. R. Newman (Ed.) *The world of mathematics* (Vol. 3, pp. 1758–1766). New York: Simon and Schuster. (Excerpt of address to British Association, 1869.)

Ulam, S. M. (1976). *Adventures of a mathematician.* New York: Charles Scribner Sons.

IV
Kinds of Cognition

13

Inferential versus Ecological Approaches to Perception

Dennis R. Proffitt

Perception is the most transparent of all human faculties. Perception is effortless. It just happens. Unlike perception, acts of thinking, remembering, speaking, and reasoning often require some effort and planning. Large individual differences in abilities are found for the other faculties, but not for perception. People become famous for being great thinkers, but there are no great perceivers in history. Because of the ease and automaticity of perception, its dazzling complexity is often overlooked. It is only when attempting to explain how perception happens that the incredible difficulty of the feat becomes apparent.

What is the problem? What is perception, and why is it difficult? These questions have typically been answered by representing the problem of perception as is depicted in figure 13.1. Here and throughout this chapter, only visual perception will be discussed; however, this problem representation generalizes to the other sense modalities as well.

In the world there is some object that is perceived. This physical object is called the *distal stimulus,* and to be seen it must be illuminated. Some of the light that strikes it is absorbed and some is reflected, and of the light that is reflected some gets into the observer's eyes. The projected image formed on the back of the eye consists of an array of light having at each point some intensity value and wavelength. This projected image is called the *proximal stimulus*. The proximal stimulus causes receptor cells in the eye to change their activity, and this, in turn, causes a change in the activity of the neurons to which they synapse. This activity flows back through visual tracks to various regions within the brain. As a consequence of all of this—somehow—perception occurs. The percept consists

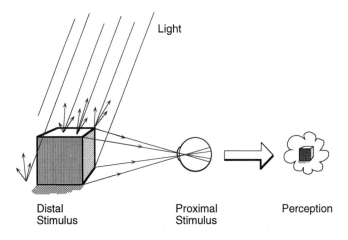

Distal
Stimulus

Proximal
Stimulus

Perception

Figure 13.1
The traditional representation of the problem of perception. A physical object
(distal stimulus) is illuminated, and some of this light is reflected into the eye
causing an image of the object (proximal stimulus) to be formed on the retina.
Photoreceptors respond to this proximal stimulus, thereby evoking perceptual
processes that culminate in an awareness of the object (perception).

of an awareness of the object. Following Restle (1979), in figure 13.1 a
cloud is drawn around the percept to indicate its mental status.

The conundrum inherent within this representation is that perceptions
seem to bear a far closer resemblance to distal stimuli than to the proximal stimuli upon which they are based. For instance, three-dimensional
objects project two-dimensional retinal images, and yet perceptions of
objects are three-dimensional. Physical objects have constant properties,
such as size, shape, and color (spectral reflectance), whereas proximal
images have varying properties. The size of the image on the retina varies
with distance, shape varies with object orientation, and color (reflected
intensity and wavelength) varies with the intensity and spectral distribution of illumination. Proximal stimulation cannot be the sole informational basis for perception. Something must be added to sensory
information to achieve the perceptions we form.

Any information that goes beyond that given in proximal stimulation
must be brought to the occasion of perception by the perceiver. Most
accounts of perception assert that the visual system *infers* the perceptual

world on the basis of both sensory information and assumptions, biases, and knowledge inherent to the perceiver. The reason for postulating inferential processes is the insufficiency of proximal stimulation. There is more to perception than meets the eye.

There is, however, another point of view on the nature of perception that takes exception to everything just stated. Called the *ecological approach* by its creator, Gibson (1979), this theory claims that no inferences are required to account for perception because the effective information for perception is fully sufficient to specify what is perceived. To see how this can be, we need to return to the representation of the problem of perception.

What is the problem? For Gibson, figure 13.1 completely misrepresents the problem of perception. For him, the purpose of perception is not to achieve a mental representation of distal objects. The purpose of perception is to control purposive actions. The information for perception is not the retinal image; rather, it is to be found in the flow of optical information that occurs at a moving point of observation. Gibson argued that perceptions can be based entirely on optical information if, and only if, the observer is allowed to move and explore the environment.

The purpose of this chapter is to describe the main characteristics of both traditional inferential theories of perception and Gibson's ecological approach. Following this discussion an attempt will be made to clarify why it is that both approaches continue to have their influence today, even though they seem quite incompatible. It will be argued that their incompatibility stems, in part, from the fact that proponents of each approach are asking quite different questions. The manner in which a problem is represented determines the form of its solution. It will also be argued that the differences between these positions are, at a metaphysical level, deep and irreconcilable.

Inferential Approaches to Perception

The development of the inferential approach to perception can be traced to Hermann von Helmholtz. Although many early proposals can be found in philosophy, Helmholtz's influence on contemporary theorizing is clear and direct. Helmholtz (1867/1925) coined the term *unconscious inference* to describe the processes by which the perceptual system uses inductive inference to derive perceptual interpretations from incomplete sensory information.

As one of the greatest and most versatile scientists to have ever lived, Helmholtz made important and lasting contributions to such diverse fields as medicine, anatomy, and physiology on the one hand, and physics and mathematics on the other. He also wrote prolifically on the philosophy of science, and in this domain he argued strongly for empiricism, believing that the source of all knowledge—both for the individual and for science—is rooted in empirical experimentation. Science and perception are both deemed to entail inferential processes but of quite different sorts. Science, he noted, is guided by deductive inferences, executed consciously and derived from carefully designed and controlled experiments. Perceptual inferences are unconscious inductions based upon incomplete and inexact experience. They are acquired through happenstance. Helmholtz (1894/1971, p. 505) wrote:

> How young children first acquire an acquaintance with or knowledge of the meaning of their visual images is easily understood if we observe them while they busy themselves with playthings. Notice how they handle them, consider them by the hour from all sides, turn them down or try to break them. This is repeated every day. There can be no doubt that this is the school in which the natural relations among the objects around us are learned, along with the understanding of perspective images and the use of the hands.

Helmholtz proposed that through experiences such as these, the child comes to internalize two things: (1) a knowledge of geometrical optics and (2) implicit assumptions about the nature of the world.

As an example of this sort of approach, consider how one perceives the shape of a book. As represented in figure 13.2, the projected image of a book is ambiguous. The laws of geometrical optics place constraints on what the distal object could be, but still perception is underspecified. An indefinite number of differently shaped objects could project the identical image. However, in experience, the most frequently encountered objects consistent with this projected image have been rectangular solids. Rectangularity is a pervasive constraint in the artifacts that people create, and thus it would be reasonable for the perceptual system to acquire a bias to construe visual images as being rectangular objects whenever such

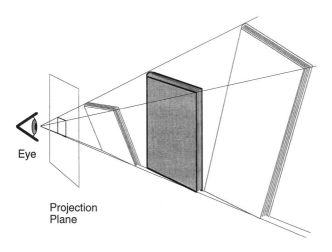

Figure 13.2
An illuminated book projects an image into the eye, and for expository purposes, onto a projection plane in front of the eye. In addition to the book, there are an indefinite number of objects of different shapes and sizes that could project an identical image. Two of these are depicted.

perceptions are possible. This bias would reflect an implicit assumption that rectangular objects were the likely cause of visual images consistent with rectangularity.

Helmholtz's position has become the mainstream in perceptual theorizing (Proffitt & Kaiser, 1998). Within this approach, the problem of perception is grounded in the inherent ambiguity of optical information. Using the optical information available, an internalized geometry, and an appreciation for regularities that have been encountered in experience, the perceptual system is said to make unconscious inferences about the external world. Perceptions are the conclusions of these inferences. In the words of Gregory (1978), a contemporary proponent of this position, "The senses do not give us a picture of the world directly; rather they provide evidence for the checking of hypotheses about what lies before us. Indeed, we may say that the perception of an object *is* an hypothesis, suggested and tested by the sensory data" (p. 13). The work of Adelbert Ames, Jr. (Ittelson, 1968) stands as one of the best examples of perception viewed in this manner.

Ames had a magician's appreciation for the ambiguity of optical information. He knew that through careful contrivance he could evoke illusions of the most elaborate sort. Of these, the most famous is the distorted
room demonstration. As depicted in figure 13.3, a full-size room was
constructed such that with the exception of the front wall, all of the other
walls, the ceiling, and the floor were nonrectangular shapes. In addition,
the walls had windows that were similarly nonrectangular. The dimensions of the room and its windows were determined so that when viewed
from the outside through a viewing hole in the room's front door, the
optical information was consistent with a rectangular room. And, indeed,
a rectangular room is what people saw. Ames's purpose in constructing
his demonstrations was to convince people that what they perceived was
due not only to reality, but also to what they brought to the act of perception. In the case of the distorted room demonstration, he argued that
people bring assumptions about how rooms ought to appear given their
past experience. These assumptions include a strong proclivity to suppose
that rooms and windows are rectangular.

Kubovy (1986) provided a somewhat different twist to the rectangularity bias as it is applied to the Ames distorted room demonstration. He
noted that all of the surfaces in an Ames distorted room meet at edges
that project fork or arrow junctions such as those depicted in figure 13.4.
These junctions are consistent with Perkins's laws. Discovered independently by Perkins (1972, 1973) and by Shepard (1981), these laws state
the conditions under which people will perceive rectangularity when confronted with fork and arrow junctions. The first of Perkins's two laws
states that a fork junction will be perceived to be the projection of the
vertex of a rectangular solid if and only if each of the three angles forming
the Y configuration is greater than 90°. The second law states that an
arrow junction will be perceived to be the vertex of a rectangular solid
if and only if each of the small interior angles is less than 90° and together
they sum to more than 90°. These laws will correctly detect rectangularity
if the object is, in fact, rectangular and is not viewed too peripherally
(Kubovy, 1986). These laws do not, however, assure physical rectangularity as is evidenced by the distorted room demonstration. Kubovy proposed that the reason an Ames distorted room is perceived to be
rectangular is because the presented fork and arrow junctions are consis-

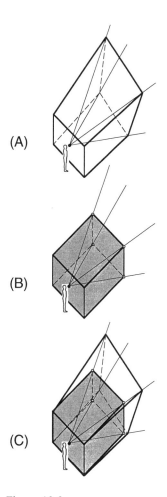

(A)

(B)

(C)

Figure 13.3
An Ames distorted room. Panel A shows a person viewing an Ames room through its viewing hole. Lines of sight are drawn to the room's vertices. Panel B depicts the rectangular room that is perceived. Panel C superimposes the perceived room onto the actual distorted room. Notice that the lines of sight for the perceived and actual room correspond.

tent with Perkins's laws. Kubovy also provided a drawing of an unfamiliar object like that in figure 13.5. Because the junctions in this depiction conform to Perkins's laws, it is perceived to be rectangular. Perkins's laws are a specific instance of how a strong rectangularity bias is operative in perception. It is generally assumed that this bias is based upon the prevalence of rectangularity in the artificial world, and thus, that it has been internalized through experience.

That Perkins's laws are deeply internalized is further supported by a remarkable set of studies by Enns and Rensink (1991). In a visual search

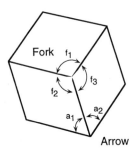

Figure 13.4
Fork and arrow junctions as described by Perkins's laws. For the Y-shaped fork junction, all three angles are greater than 90°. For the arrow junction, the two interior angles are each less than 90°, and together these two angles sum to greater than 90°.

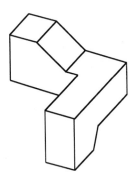

Figure 13.5
An unfamiliar object that appears rectangular in those regions that conform to Perkins's laws.

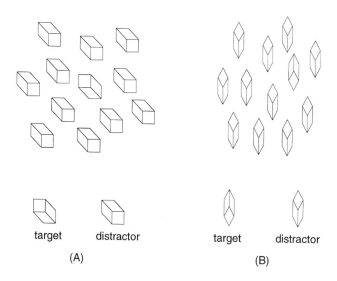

Figure 13.6
A and B presenting arrays of elements in which there is one target that differs from all of the other elements in the array. In (A), the target and distractors conform to Perkins's laws, and the target can be found preattentively. In (B), the target and distractors do not conform to Perkins's laws, and the target is much more difficult to find.

task, they presented figures containing either fork or arrow junctions. As depicted in figure 13.6, target and distractors were identical except that the target was oriented at a 180° angle relative to the array of distractors. When the junctions obeyed Perkins's laws (figure 13.6A), search occurred preattentively, meaning that the time to find the target was unaffected by the number of distractors present, whereas configurations that violated Perkins's laws (figure 13.6B) required slower, more effortful search.

The most comprehensive account of perception viewed as an inferential process is found in Rock's (1983) book, *The Logic of Perception*. In this book, Rock surveyed much of the literature on perception, and everywhere he looked he found evidence for reasoning, problem solving, inference, and knowledge-based assumptions in perception. Consider, for example, lightness perception.

A surface's reflectance value is perceived as its lightness. Dark surfaces absorb more light than do light ones. Given this fact, it might seem that the perceptual system would need only to register the amount of light coming from a surface to determine its lightness. Ignoring such additional complications as surface orientation, the problem is that the luminance emanating from a surface depends upon two things: the amount of light illuminating it and the reflectance value of the surface. If, however, one is presented with two equally illuminated surfaces, then relative lightness could be perceived on the basis of the invariant ratio of luminance emanating from the two surfaces (Wallach, 1948). For instance, if one surface reflects 80% of the light striking it and another surface reflects 40%, then the ratio of their reflected luminance will be 2:1 regardless of how much they are illuminated.

The complication that arises with this ratio account is that surfaces are not always illuminated equally. For example, part of a surface may have a shadow cast upon it. Gilchrist, Delman, and Jacobsen (1983) showed that in perceiving lightness, the visual system must first categorize the edges in the scene. Edges fall into two classes: those due to differences in illumination such as shadows and those due to differences in reflectance values. Rock argued that in perceiving lightness, the perceptual system must go through a multiple-stage process in which inferences are first made in edge classifications, followed by inferences that make use of these edge classifications in determining perceived lightness. When looking at a shadow, for example, the edges of the shadow are detected and an inference is made that it is, in fact, a shadow. Given this inference, the differences in luminance emanating from either side of the edge are attributed to differences in illumination rather than reflectance. As exemplified in this example, an important aspect of Rock's account is that perceptions play a causal role in subsequent perceptions. Perceiving the nature of edges is a necessary precondition for perceiving lightness.

Another example of such perceptual interdependencies is found in traditional accounts of size perception. Rock, like most other theorists, assumed that in order to perceive size, perceived distance must be taken into account. A well-known example of this notion is a demonstration first reported by Emmert (1881). He had observers form an afterimage by looking at a bright light, and then he instructed them to look at near and far surfaces. The afterimage appeared to be localized on whatever surface was being inspected, and thus it was perceived to be located at different observer-relative distances. The visual angle of the afterimage remained constant, whereas its apparent distance varied as the observer looked about. Emmert observed that the apparent size of the afterimage was larger when looking at far surfaces as opposed to nearer ones. From this observation he formulated what has become know as *Emmert's Law,* which states that the perceived size of an afterimage is proportional to its apparent distance. In general, many theorists, as did Rock, assumed that perceived size depends upon perceived distance (c.f. Gogel, 1990, 1993). Notice that the perceptual rules that relate perceived size and distance apply to psychological variables, not to physical ones.

Rather than appealing to perceived variables, there is a greater tendency today to analyze a scene into optical variables that can be geometrically related to distal properties of the scene. This is especially true within the growing field of computational vision, where there is an effort to extract properties of physical objects from their projected images. Computational accounts also differ from Rock's in another way. Instead of postulating that the perceptual system follows rules of inference, computational models instantiate inferential rules without necessarily following them (Epstein, 1995). That is, these models perform as if they were making inferences, even though their algorithms do not embody the inferences themselves. Consider an example. Ullman (1979, 1983) showed how the three-dimensional structure of a rotating object could be derived from its transforming two-dimensional projection so long as the object was assumed to be rigid. The algorithm that he developed does not have within it any reference to the rigidity assumption; rather, the algorithm produces correct interpretations of three-dimensional structure if and only if the images that are presented to it are projections of rigid rotations.

Poggio, Torre, and Koch (1985) looked at a number of problems in vision from a computational point of view and concluded that they were all *ill-posed problems.* They defined this distinction as follows: "A problem is well-posed when its solution exists, is unique and depends continuously on the initial data. Ill-posed problems fail to satisfy one or more of these criteria" (p. 315). Viewing perception as an ill-posed problem motivates a search for intelligent resources capable of making educated guesses in interpreting inputs. Poggio, et al. wrote, "The main idea for 'solving' ill-posed problems, that is for restoring 'well-posedness,' is to restrict the class of admissible solutions by introducing suitable *a priori* knowledge" (p 315). Ullman's (1979) use of a rigidity assumption in his account of extracting three-dimensional structure from motion is a good case in point. If objects can deform as they rotate, then extracting structure from motion is an ill-posed problem. Ullman's rigidity assumption restores well-posedness to the problem. In so doing, his algorithm will yield accurate descriptions of an object's configuration so long as the object is not deforming as it rotates. If the object is deforming, then the algorithm will provide an inaccurate description of its form. This is the hallmark of educated guesses: they are correct with a statistical probability no greater than the likelihood that their assumptions are correct.

Another example of an a priori constraint is Nakayama and Shimojo's (1992) principle of generic sampling. This principle states that the perceptual system assumes that a given object is not being viewed from an accidental vantage point. For example, when looking at a drawing of a square, one perceives it to be a two-dimensional configuration and not one end of a three-dimensional box viewed from a unique vantage point normal to its surface. Almost all perspectives on a box will show more than one of its sides. Only when viewed from a small number of accidental points of view would a box project as a square. The principle of generic views states that the perceptual system assumes that its current vantage point is not an accidental one. Rock (1983) proposed a coincidence explanation principle that attributed to the perceptual system the same sort of assumption.

All of these a priori constraints are consistent with the notion that the perceptual system possesses internalized knowledge about environmental regularities that are usually true. Marr (1982) called such internalized regularities *natural constraints,* meaning that they derive from a knowledge about what sorts of conditions are most likely to occur in the world. This is precisely what Helmholtz had in mind. Through experience— either of the individual or the species—the perceptual system comes to be imbued with knowledge about what is most likely to be present in the world given the evidence extracted from optical information. Perception is an educated guess. It is usually correct, but it is fallible. Illusions such as those seen in the Ames demonstrations are a symptom of its fallibility.

The Ecological Approach to Perception

For Gibson, the positions described in the foregoing discussion are simply muddled, their problem being that they began with a flawed representation of the problem of perception. If perception is represented in the manner depicted in figure 13.1, then it is, indeed, an ill-posed problem. Indeed, the problem is so ill-posed, Gibson argued, that no amount of inference and a priori knowledge will allow a successful restoration of well-posedness. The perceptual system cannot acquire an appreciation for the regularities that uphold in the world without the ability to have perceptions that seemingly require an internalization of these regularities to begin with. Gibson (1979. p. 253) wrote:

Knowledge of the world must come from somewhere; the debate is over whether it comes from stored knowledge, from innate knowledge, or from reason. But all three doctrines beg the question. Knowledge of the world cannot be explained by supposing that knowledge of the world already exists. All forms of cognitive processing imply cognition so as to account for cognition.

Gibson's solution to this paradox was to propose that the information available in optical information is fully sufficient to support perception. There is no need for inference and a priori knowledge because nothing needs to be added to what is given in visual information. Some background into the position is required in order to see how this argument can be made.

Gibson saw his position as having developed from two antecedents. The first was Gestalt psychology, from which he acquired an appreciation for the systems approach to perception and the role of relational variables in specifying perceptual constancies. In regard to the systems approach, the Gestalt psychologists believed that perceptions were irreducible wholes. From a systems perspective, the laws that govern a system cannot be determined from an analysis of its constituent parts. In Gibson's ecological approach, the organism and environment comprise an irreducible system. Relational variables are mathematical relationships that can be extracted from visual information and that specify some persistent property in the environment. Wallach's (1948) aforementioned luminance ratio for specifying surface lightness over changes in illumination is such a relational variable. In Gibson's use, these variables came to be called *higher-order units* of perception.

The second influence was American functionalism as it developed from William James. Like Gestalt psychology, James's functionalism took a systems approach. Perception depended not only upon immediately given information, but also on the context of space and time in which it occurs. Time is clearly of importance for James, with experience being described as a stream of consciousness. Both persistence and change over time are essential properties of experience. Of particular relevance to Gibson's approach is the functionalist's program of understanding biological processes in terms of utility. From this perspective, the purpose of perception is to control actions. The veracity of perceptions is to be evaluated on the basis of whether they lead to appropriate actions, not on whether they correspond to reality objectively defined. The pragmatic definition of truth—truth is what works—makes sense only when embedded within a systems analysis that includes both the organism and the environment.

A clear statement of the functional theory of truth is found in Will's (1978, p. C7) commentary on baseball's Hall of Fame. The hall contains, "a plaque honoring the one American whose achievements of mind rank with those of Aristotle, Newton, Hegel and Einstein." This individual is Alexander Cartwright, and he is credited with setting the distances between bases at 90 feet. Will quoted the sports journalist, Red Smith:

Ninety feet between bases represents man's closest approach to absolute truth. The world's fastest man cannot run to first base ahead of a sharply hit ball that is cleanly handled by an infielder; he will get there only half a step too late. Let the fielder juggle the ball for one moment or delay his throw an instant and the runner will be safe. Ninety feet demands perfection. It accurately measures the cunning, speed, and finesse of the base stealer against the velocity of a thrown ball. It dictates the placement of infielders. That single dimension makes baseball a fine art—and nobody knows for sure how it came to be. (p. C7)

Setting the bases at 90 feet defines a relationship between the relevant surface layout of the baseball field and the behavioral potential and purposes of the ballplayers.

Applying functionalist notions to the content and meaning of perception, Gibson coined the term *affordance* to refer to the functional utility perceived in the visual world. More will be said about affordances, but first his account will be described, beginning with the environment to be perceived.

The environment can be described at many levels depending upon size scale (atomic to light years), time scale (instants to millennia), and purpose. It is the latter constraint that is easy to forget. All descriptions take their form relative to some purpose. For example, a description of a baseball field will take quite different forms depending upon whether the intent is to convey information of geological or baseball-playing relevance. Gibson argued that traditional theories of perception describe the environment in physical or geometrical terms as opposed to ecologically relevant ones.

The environment, as perceived by an organism, is a habitat. A habitat cannot be described without accounting for its relationship to the organism for which it is home. A given environment can be a habitat for a host of different species, and what makes it a habitat differs somewhat for each. An ecological description of the environment implies the mutuality between the organism's way of life and those aspects of the environment that afford these behaviors.

From this perspective, the perceptual environment consists of three things: a medium, substances, and surfaces. The medium of earth is air. Light passes through air, and locomotion is possible through it. Substances are substantial matter through which locomotion is not possible. Media and substances interface at surfaces, and for perception this is where all the action is. Perception informs the organism about surface layout. It is surface layout, not abstract space or geometry, that is perceived. In perceiving the layout of surfaces, the organism perceives the medium and substances that define them.

In order to perceive surface layout, two things must occur. First, the environment must be illuminated, and second, the organism must be allowed to move and explore it. Illumination begins with essentially unstructured parallel rays of light emanating from the sun. This light is scattered somewhat by the earth's atmosphere, but until it strikes surfaces, it contains no structure or information. Upon contact with surfaces, some of the light is absorbed and some is reflected. Reflected light is structured by surfaces, and thus it contains information about them. The problem for the perceptual system is to pick up this information.

In order to perceive the information that is in light, the organism must move and explore the environment. Gibson was in complete agreement with those who argued that the information available in a retinal image is insufficient to support perception. Gibson's response to this insufficiency was not, however, to postulate inferential processes inherent in the perceiver, but rather to argue that the retinal image is not the informational basis for perception. He proposed that optical flow—the change in optical structure that occurs at a moving point of observation—is the effective informational basis for perception.

Consider again the situation of viewing a book as depicted in figure 13.2. The optical information that is present at a single vantage point is ambiguous, as the figure shows; however, if the observer moves his or her head so as to obtain multiple perspectives on the book, then this ambiguity is eliminated. Figure 13.7 shows three images of a book. Each of these images is, by itself, ambiguous. Taken together, however, the three rotated perspectives of the book are sufficient to define the unique three-dimensional structure of its visible surfaces (Ullman, 1979, 1983). The information specifying the book's form consists of invariants extracted from its transforming image. Invariants are mathematical relationships that remain constant as other aspects of optical structure change. Returning to figure 13.7, notice that one of the book's corners has been colored in. In the leftmost image of the book, this corner projects an angle of over 90°; in the middle panel, this angle projects an angle of

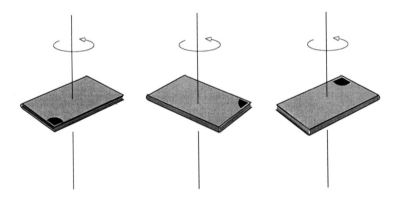

Figure 13.7
Three rotated images of a book. Notice how rotation causes a change in the projected angle for the highlighted vertex of the book.

less than 90°; and in the rightmost panel the angle is again larger than 90°. As the book is observed from different vantage points, this and all other angles change in their projected extent. It can be shown mathematically, however, that these changes in projected structure could be caused by only one rigid three-dimensional structure: a rectangular solid. The mathematics needed to prove this assertion are too complicated to explain here. See Todd (1995) for a review of the literature on perceiving structure from motion.

Consider a second example, of the Ames distorted room depicted in figure 13.3. Ames was able to construct illusory demonstrations such as this because he was able to restrict the viewers' vantage point to a single perspective. Observers looked at the distorted room through a peephole. If the door to the room were opened and observers were permitted to walk about and observe the changing optical structure the room provided, then they would see it accurately as a distorted room. The distorted room projects an image consistent with rectangularity only when viewed from a unique point of observation at the peephole. From every other vantage point, the room projects an optical structure that is totally inconsistent with rectangularity. Figure 13.8 shows this inconsistency from a second vantage point. As is the case generally, three different perspective images of a scene are sufficient to extract the unique three-dimensional structure of its visible surfaces.

Whenever an observer moves, every aspect of a projected scene changes. The changing optical structure that is projected to a moving point of observation is optical flow. Gibson suggested that optical flow contains within it two sorts of information. *Perspective structure* specifies what is changing, whereas *invariant structure* specifies the properties of the scene that remain constant over the change. Perspective structure informs the perceiver about his or her locomotion and changing position relative to the scene. Invariant structure specifies surface layout, including the size, shape, and slant of the surfaces that compose it. Because invariant structure specifies what is constant over change, the extraction of invariant structure requires change. Change is brought about through locomotion or the motions of objects themselves. The optical flow that results is informative about both the invariants of surface layout and the

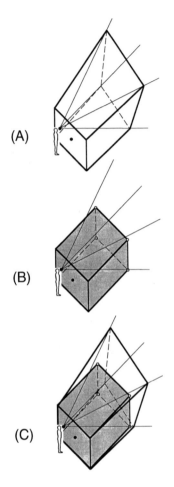

(A)

(B)

(C)

Figure 13.8
An Ames room viewed from a second vantage point. Unlike Figure 3, the lines of sight to the vertices of the perceived and actual room no longer correspond. The second vantage point does not support the perception of a rectangular room.

observer's changing position relative to it. *The perception of the environment and of the self come together.* One is impossible without the other.

Appreciating this mutuality between the perceiver and the environment is essential to understanding Gibson's position. The perception of the world cannot be separated from a perception of self. Consider the perception of size.

As was discussed in the previous section, traditional accounts of perception maintain that distance must be taken into account when perceiving size. Because visual angle varies inversely with distance, it is often supposed that size perception depends upon a prior perception of distance. Gibson stated that this was not so. Size, he argued, could be perceived directly without taking into account distance.

Figure 13.9 depicts an observer looking at an object that has a height, *h,* and that is some distance away, *d.* The altitude of the observer's eye is *i.* If the perceptual system can determine the position of the horizon, then the object's height can be determined as a fraction of the observer's eye height (Sedgwick, 1986). The horizon corresponds to the straight-ahead position in the visual field and is represented in the figure as a line parallel to the horizontal ground at an altitude equal to the observer's eye height. The visual angle from the bottom of the object to the horizon is α, and that from the top of the object to the horizon is β. The distance from the top of the object to the horizon is *j.* Referring to the figure, notice that

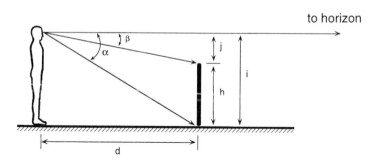

Figure 13.9
An observer looking at an object. The labeled dimensions of this situation are defined in the text.

$i/d = \tan \alpha,$

and thus,

$d = i/\tan \alpha.$

Similarly,

$j/d = \tan \beta,$

and thus,

$j = d \tan \beta.$

Since

$h = i - j,$

then substituting for j,

$h = i - d \tan \beta,$

and substituting for d,

$h = i - i (\tan \beta/\tan \alpha).$

If the object is taller than eye height, then j is added to i, rather than being subtracted.

Critical to this formulation is determining the location of the horizon, but fortunately, its position is given quite robustly in optical information. All projected horizontal lines converge in depth to the horizon. Moreover, whenever the observer moves forward, there is a discontinuity in optical flow such that texture elements above and below the horizon move up or down, respectively. That is, as one moves forward, everything above eye height flows overhead and everything below travels beneath.

The important thing to notice about the final equation is that size can be determined entirely on the basis of optically given visual angles, α and β. Distance need not be taken into account. Again, perception of the environment implies a perception of self. Size is perceived relative to the size of one's body (i).

Another source of information about size is found in texture gradients, as depicted in figure 13.10. For a surface consisting of a relatively uniform texture, there is a compression of projected texture with distance. Even though the projected density of texture increases with distance, the amount of texture occluded at the base of an object is invariant over

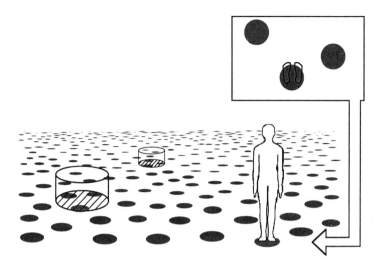

Figure 13.10
A texture gradient. Two cylinders of equal size occlude an equal amount of texture at their bases. The observer can scale the size of these objects to the size of his or her feet by looking down and noticing how much texture they occlude.

displacements on the surface. That is, objects of equal size occlude an equal amount of texture at their base. Texture gradients provide information about relative size but not absolute size unless there is an object of known size on the ground surface. Fortunately, all one needs to do is look down at one's feet in order to scale the texture to this familiar standard.

These are but a few examples of how Gibson's approach can be applied to the perception of environmental properties. In redefining the effective information for perception—from the retinal image to optical flow—Gibson found it to be not nearly so deficient as had been previously thought.

However, the informational basis for perception is not equivalent to the content of perception. We do not perceive information. Instead, we perceive the world and our relationship to it. The content of perception is the functional utility of the surfaces and objects that are encountered. These functional utilities relate the dimensions of objects and surfaces to the behavioral potential of the organism. Gibson coined the term *affordances* to describe these functional utilities.

An affordance specifies what an organism can do with the objects and surfaces that are encountered in the environment. Any given object possesses an indefinite number of affordances; those that are perceived at any moment depend upon the intent of the perceiver. Consider the book you are reading. Its surface layout affords being held. This affordance relates the size and shape of the book to that of your hands. Moreover, the book could also be thrown like a frisbee, used as a club with which to squash a fearsome bug, or placed under the front of a slide projector to raise its projection. The number of possible uses for a book is indefinite, and they do not depend upon its objective conceptual meaning. Gibson (1979, p. 129) wrote: "An affordance cuts across the dichotomy of subjective-objective and helps us to understand its inadequacy. It is equally a fact of the environment and a fact of behavior. It is both physical and psychical, yet neither. An affordance points both ways, to the environment and to the observer." Consider one final example, that being the perception of geographical slant.

The earth's surface is rarely flat, and departures from horizontal are perceived as geographical slant. The magnitude of a hill's slant can be determined from such optical information as texture gradients, motion parallax, and binocular disparity. Even though there is sufficient information to objectively derive slant, people grossly overestimate the inclination of hills in the world (Proffitt, Bhalla, Gossweiler, & Midgett, 1995). When, for example, people stand in front of a 5° hill, they will estimate its inclination to be about 20°, and a 30° hill will be judged to be over 50°. Be that as it may, such overestimations do not cause people to stumble as they commence to walk up or down a hill. Proffitt et al. found that overestimations are only evidenced in explicit judgments of hill slant and that a motoric index of perceived slant is far more accurate. The visual guidance of actions requires accuracy, whereas the conscious awareness of slant is modulated by a person's behavioral potential.

Perceived steepness provides information about the affordances of hills, about whether they can be ascended or descended and with what degree of difficulty. Summarizing the Proffitt et al. findings, a 10° hill is very difficult to ascend for a long distance, and consistent with this it looks very steep. People judge 10° hills to be about 30°. A grassy 30° hill is near the limit of what can be ascended and is too steep to descend due to biomechanical asymmetries in our ascending/descending walking potential. Consistent with this asymmetry, hills steeper than about 25° are judged to be steeper when viewed from the top than from the bottom. Finally, hills appear steeper when we are tired than when we are not. Perceived steepness is not invariant with respect to distal slant alone, but rather it preserves the relationship between locomotor effort and distal slant. Thus, this basic dimension of surface layout—the earth's topography—is perceived as a relationship between the distal inclination of the ground and our behavioral potential.

Concluding Remarks

The differences between the inferential and ecological approaches to perception are profound. By one account, perception is an educated guess; by the other it is a direct pickup of information. In philosophical parlance, the inferential approach is a form of *idealism,* meaning that perceptions are ideas formed by the perceiving mind about the physical world. The ecological approach, on the other hand, is a variant of *realism,* in which perceptions are viewed as corresponding directly to what is in the world. At this level of evaluation, the differences between these two views are irreconcilable.

At another level, however, these approaches can be seen to complement one another. Gibson's approach asks the question, *What* is perception? This question is answered by asserting that perception is an ecological description of the environment based upon the information in optical flow. The inferential approach asks a different question: *How* is perception achieved? Clearly, the answer to these two questions must begin with an analysis of the available information and a search for algorithms that can constrain this information to allow for unique perceptual interpretations.

Answers to what-versus-how questions correspond to what Marr (1982) called computational as opposed to algorithmic theories. A computational theory addresses the question of what the goal of the computation is, that is, what the system is attempting to do and why. Gibson's answer seems the appropriate one: the goal of perception is to discover the affordances of the environment. The algorithmic theory attempts to provide a representation of the system's inputs and outputs and of the algorithms that map one into the other. Of Gibson's approach, Marr (1982, p. 29) wrote:

In perception, perhaps the nearest anyone came to the level of computational theory was Gibson (1966). However, although some aspects of his thinking were on the right lines, he did not understand properly what information processing was, which led him to seriously underestimate the complexity of the information-processing problems involved in vision and the consequent subtlety that is necessary in approaching them.

At least to me, Marr's criticism does not seem fair. Given that Gibson's goal was to provide a theory about what is perceived, problems of information processing were not his concern. Information processing is the province of those seeking to understand how perception is achieved at the level of algorithmic theory.

Marr introduced his distinction between the computational and algorithmic level of analysis with an example of how one might understand a cash register. The computational theory of the cash register would entail a description of what the device does. For example, it needs to accumulate prices in a manner unaffected by the order in which items are presented to it. Moreover, sorting items into groups and paying for each group separately should not affect the total. Enumerating such constraints on the price-totaling process results in a definition of the group-theoretic constraints on addition. Note, however, that nothing has been asserted about how these constraints are actually operationalized in the interior workings of the cash register. The actual device might be a computer or an abacus, because either is capable of performing addition. Neither device possesses internalized knowledge about the group-theoretic constraints on addition, even though both have been constructed in such a way that they cannot violate these constraints.

Gibson's approach does not instruct one on how to build a perceiving machine. Attempts to simulate perception require the evocation of a priori constraints such as those discussed earlier. Recall Ullman's rigidity constraint as applied to an algorithm designed to recover three-dimensional structure from motion information: given that the distal object is assumed to be rigid, then three rotated views of the object are sufficient to derive the three-dimensional form of its visible surfaces. However, the rigidity assumption is no more internalized by Ullman's algorithm than is the group theory of addition internalized by the cash register. In both cases, information processing takes a form that yields veridical outcomes if and only if the assumptions apply. Present a multiplication problem to a cash register, and it will compute a wrong answer. Similarly, present a deforming object to Ullman's algorithm and it will fail.

Whether perception is viewed as entailing inferential processes or not depends upon what sort of problem one is inclined to study. If one is interested in specifying the logic by which optical information is transformed into representations of the world, then indeed, logic will be required. If one wishes to understand what is perceived, then logic becomes unnecessary since we do not perceive logic; we perceive the world. At this level of analysis, the approaches seem compatible; they simply address different questions.

At a metaphysical level, however, the approaches make profoundly different assertions about the nature of mind and of being. By the inferential approach, the perceptual system must guess about the nature of the external world. For Gibson, the nature of the world reveals itself directly in experience. In both cases, what is known reflects upon the knower. In the first case, the knower augments optical information with inferences, assumptions, and a priori knowledge. Within the ecological approach, the knower and the known form an irreducible whole. Knowledge of self and of the world must necessarily come together.

References

Emmert, E. (1881). Grossenverhaltnisse der Nachbilder. *Klinische Monatsblaetter fuer Augenheilkunde, 19*, 443–450. (Translation: Size proportions of after images. *Clinical Monthly Newsletter for Opthalmology.*).

Enns, J. T., & Rensink, R. A. (1991). Preattentive recovery of three-dimensional orientation from line drawings. *Psychological Review, 98*, 335–351.

Epstein, W. (1995). The metatheoretical context. In W. Epstein & S. Rogers (Eds.), *Perception of space and motion: Handbook of perception and cognition* (2nd ed., pp. 1–22). San Diego, CA: Academic Press.

Gibson, J. J. (1966). *The senses considered as perceptual systems.* Boston: Houghton Mifflin.

Gibson, J. J. (1979). *The ecological approach to visual perception.* Boston: Houghton Mifflin.

Gilchrist, A., Delman, S., & Jacobsen, A. (1983). The classification and integration of edges as critical to the perception of reflectance and illumination. *Perception & Psychophysics, 33,* 425–436.

Gogel, W. C. (1990). A theory of phenomenal geometry and its applications. *Perception & Psychophysics, 49,* 105–123.

Gogel, W. C. (1993). The analysis of perceived space. In S. C. Masin (Ed.), *Foundations of perceptual theory* (pp. 113–182). Amsterdam: Elsevier.

Gregory, R. L. (1978). *Eye and brain: The psychology of seeing* (3rd ed.). New York: McGraw-Hill.

Helmholtz, H. von (1925). *Handbook of physiological optics* (Vol. 3, J. P. C. Southall, Trans.). New York: Dover. (Original work published 1867.)

Helmholtz, H. von (1971). The origin and correct interpretation of our sense impressions. In R. Kahl (Ed.), *Selected writings of Hermann von Helmholtz* (pp. 501–512). Middletown, CT: Wesleyan University Press. (Original work published 1894.).

Ittelson, W. H. (1968), *The Ames demonstrations in perception.* New York: Hafner.

Kubovy, M. (1986). *The psychology of perspective and renaissance art.* Cambridge, England: Cambridge University Press.

Marr, D. (1982). *Vision: A computational investigation into the human representation and processing of visual information.* San Francisco: Freeman.

Nakayama, K., & Shimojo, S. (1992). Experiencing and perceiving visual surfaces. *Science, 257,* 1357–1363.

Perkins, D. N. (1972). Visual discrimination between rectangular and nonrectangular parallelepipeds. *Perception & Psychophysics, 12,* 396–400.

Perkins, D. N. (1973). Compensating for distortion in viewing pictures obliquely. *Perception & Psychophysics, 14,* 13–18.

Poggio, T., Torre, V., & Koch, C. (1985). Computational vision and regularization theory. *Nature, 317,* 314–319.

Proffitt, D. R., Bhalla, M., Grossweiler, R., & Midgett, J. (1995). Perceiving geographical slant. *Psychonomic Bulletin & Review, 2,* 409–428.

Proffitt, D. R., & Kaiser, M. K. (1998). The internalization of perceptual processing constraints. In J. Hochberg (Ed.) *Perception and cognition at century's end: Handbook of perception and cognition, 2nd edition.* San Diego: Academic Press. (Will be published this year. Do not yet have page numbers.)

Restle, F. (1979). Coding theory of the perception of motion configurations. *Psychological Review, 86,* 1–24.

Rock, I. (1983). *The logic of perception.* Cambridge, MA: MIT Press.

Sedgwick, H. A. (1986). Space perception. In K. R. Boff, L. Kaufman, & J. P. Thomas (Eds.), *Handbook of perception and human performance: Vol. 1, Sensory processes and perception* (pp. 21.1–21.57). New York: Wiley.

Shepard, R. N. (1981). Psychophysical complementarity. In M. Kubovy and J. R. Pomerantz (Eds.), *Perceptual organization* (pp. 279–341). Hillsdale, NJ: Erlbaum.

Todd, J. T. (1995). The visual perception of three-dimensional structure from motion. In W. Epstein & Rogers (Eds.), *Perception of space and motion: Handbook of perception and cognition* (2nd ed. pp. 201–226). San Diego, CA: Academic Press.

Ullman, S. (1970). *The interpretation of visual motion.* Cambridge, MA: MIT Press.

Ullman, S. (1979). *The interpretation of visual motion.* Cambridge, MA: MIT Press.

Ullman, S. (1983). Recent computational studies in the interpretation of structure from motion. In J. Beck & A. Rosenfeld (Eds.), *Human and machine vision* (pp. 459–480). New York: Academic Press.

Wallach, H. (1948). Brightness constancy and the nature of achromatic colors. *Journal of Experimental Psychology, 38,* 6–13.

Will, G. F. (1978, April 2). The joy of baseball. *Washington Post,* p. C7.

14

Implicit versus Explicit Learning

Arthur S. Reber, Rhianon Allen, and Paul J. Reber

It takes but a moment's reflection to realize that a good bit of our perceptual and cognitive machinery is chugging away without our awareness. Two of our most important accomplishments, natural language acquisition and socialization, take place during early childhood without awareness. It was on this simple premise that the study of implicit learning began back in the 1960s.

Of course, there is not, and never was, any dispute over the existence of unconscious functions and processes. Our digestive systems are all carrying out their roles quite nicely without top-down intervention or awareness. Where the arguments get interesting is in our consideration of processes such as perception, learning, and memory. Here, there is still a lingering sense among many cognitive scientists that consciousness is the presumptive domain, that complex cognitive processes take place within the spotlight of a top-down, modulating awareness. As we develop the material in this chapter, it will become clear that such a position is untenable. Sophisticated perceptual, acquisitional, and memorial processes operate effectively and largely independently of consciousness—although the primary focus of this chapter will be on the acquisitional, or what is known as *implicit learning*.[1] (See Kihlstrom, this volume, where a broader net is cast.)

Implicit learning is the process whereby knowledge is acquired largely independently of awareness of both the process and the products of acquisition. A variety of experimental procedures are in wide use, although all share particular characteristics. In the standard designs, participants are exposed to stimuli that are structured in some fashion and their knowledge of that structure is then assessed. These stimuli may be strings of symbols whose order is determined by a complex set of rules such as the traditional *artificial grammar* (AG) learning tasks (Mathews et al., 1989; A. Reber, 1967, 1993b); sequences of events whose location and order are dictated by repeating patterns (Nissen & Bullemer, 1987; P. Reber & Squire, 1994; Reed & Johnson, 1994), transitional rules (Cleeremans & McClelland, 1991; Jiménez, Méndez, & Cleeremans, 1995), or stochastic principles (A. Reber & Millward, 1968); control systems whose underlying principles are rule governed (Berry & Broadbent, 1984, 1995; Stanley, Mathews, Buss, & Kotler-Cope, 1989); or complex event dependencies based on procedural rules (Lewicki, Czyzewska, & Hoffman, 1987).

Participants in these studies acquire sufficient information about the underlying nature of the displays to be able to (a) judge whether new items follow the rules (A. Reber, 1967, 1993b), (b) solve anagram problems within the stimulus set (A. Reber & Lewis, 1977), (c) respond faster to sequences that follow rules than those that do not (Nissen & Bullemer, 1987; P. Reber & Squire, 1994; Reed & Johnson, 1994), (d) control complex systems, such as a simulated industrial scenario, by anticipating rule-governed reactions (Berry & Broadbent, 1984, 1995), (e) anticipate the location of structured future events (Lewicki et al., 1987), and (f) predict the position of upcoming events (Kushner, Cleeremans, & A. Reber, 1991; Millward & A. Reber, 1972; A. Reber & Millward, 1968). Yet, in all cases, the participants in these studies, who perform so effectively with these complexly structured displays, are largely unaware of what they have learned and find it extremely difficult if not impossible to communicate to others what they so clearly know.

In recent years, the topics of the cognitive unconscious in general and implicit learning in particular have become the focus of intense research. Not surprisingly, a number of issues of interest and importance have emerged, including the following: How cognitively sophisticated is this implicit system? Is implicit knowledge abstract or concrete in nature? What is the representational form of implicit knowledge and associated memories? Does such knowledge tend to be flexible or relatively fixed in form? Are implicit and explicit systems mediated by entirely distinct processing systems, or is there some kind of interaction between them? Are there distinct neuroanatomical systems mediating the implicit and the explicit? How robust is implicitly acquired knowledge? How are implicit and explicit functions differentially affected by particular kinds of neurological or psychiatric disorders? What is the developmental course of implicit learning? In the course of this chapter we will touch upon these issues and survey the evidentiary base for the various claims made.

However, in addition to these "friendly" questions, a number of intriguing challenges to the very existence of a smart cognitive unconscious have been put forward (Dulany, 1991, 1997; Perruchet, 1994; Perruchet, Gallego, & Savy, 1990; Perruchet & Pacteau, 1990; Shanks & St. John, 1994). Although we will try to be fair to the arguments raised by these critics, some of which are quite sophisticated, we are struck by the tenacity with which they maintain that complex cognitive processes do not (cannot?) take place outside of consciousness. So, before we get into the material proper, we would like to take a short historical and philosophical aside and look at the foundations of this perspective.

Some Philosophical Meanderings

If, as we are clearly claiming, the existence of implicit learning is so obvious and the dissociation between the implicit and explicit so compelling, why are there still many thinkers who question the existence of a sophisticated, cognitively rich implicit domain? One possible answer, we would like to suggest, derives from our intellectual history. Western scientific thought is grounded in two classical philosophical traditions, the Cartesian and the Lockean. As noted elsewhere (A. Reber, 1997), John Locke and René Descartes didn't agree on much, but there was one proposition on which they were of one mind: cognition and consciousness are coextensive. That which is cognitive is conscious and vice versa. We are either immediately aware or can be made aware of all of the activities of our cognitive systems. Speaking specifically of Locke, Dennett (1987) put it rather succinctly, "unconscious thinking or perceiving was . . . dismissed as incoherent, self-contradictory nonsense."

By the way, recognizing the importance of this point of view helps us to understand how and why structuralism was such a powerful force in psychology around the turn of the century. Edward Titchener was a devoted Lockean, and so the obvious vehicle for understanding the mind was introspection. If everything mental is, in principle, available to consciousness, then it makes perfect sense to build your empirical edifice around methods rooted in probing awareness. Titchener would not like this chapter.

Although there are no Titchenerian introspectionists about these days, what has struck us in recent years is the likelihood that many contemporary thinkers appear to be operating (perhaps unconsciously) within the Lockean foundations of this tradition. Perruchet and Pacteau (1991, p. 113), in a recent critique of the representation issue in implicit learning, put the matter starkly: "We do not question human abstraction ability, no more than we question the existence of unconscious processes. What we do question is the joint possibility of unconscious abstraction." As noted earlier, there is no dispute over lower-level implicit systems; Perruchet and Pacteau are comfortable with a mechanical, inflexible unconscious. It is when the discussions turn to a sophisticated implicit system, particularly one that capable of abstract representations, that the issue becomes heated. It is worth noting that Perruchet and Pacteau make no in-principle arguments against a smart unconscious. They merely deny it and attempt to challenge the interpretation of the existing database.

In the final analysis, of course, it matters little whether one believes in a sophisticated unconscious. Theory and data will be the adjudicators.

On the Necessity of Both Implicit and Explicit Systems

Three lines of argument point convincingly to the necessity of having implicit learning and memory processes that operate partly or wholly independently of explicit processes. One deals with basic evolutionary considerations, a second with developmental issues, and the third with fundamental aspects of neuroanatomy.

Evolutionary Biology

The argument here is simple, although it has fairly far-reaching entailments (see A. Reber, 1992, 1993b). Consciousness—at least the phenomenologically poignant, self-reflective, top-down, modulatory consciousness that forms the core of our sense of self—is, in an evolutionary sense, something of a Johnny-come-lately, probably only emerging full-blown with the advent of *Homo sapiens.* Hence, there must be functions and processes that operate to acquire information about the world, register and represent such information memorially, and activate the stored knowledge for use in appropriate circumstances without awareness of either the processes or products of these operations. Because evolution is hierarchical and conservative, these systems must continue to exist and function effectively (and more or less insulated from top-down systems) in our species. Nature does not jettison forms and functions that work. Put simply, implicit or nondeclarative functions of learning and memory are a biological necessity.

Further, it is easy to show that by virtue of their evolutionary histories, implicit and explicit learning and memory systems ought to display particular properties that further emphasize the dissociations between them. Specifically, implicit and explicit systems should show differential degrees of robustness in the face of neurological insult, different neuroanatomical characteristics, different distributions of performance in the population, and different life-span progressions. Later, we will discuss each of these properties in more detail.

Developmental Considerations

Just as explicit modes of learning are likely to have emerged slowly over evolutionary history, it is likely that explicit forms of learning also emerge slowly over the course of individual human development. No one would deny that an infant is aware. It is likely to be aware of both internal and external stimulation, such as pain, hunger, and loud noises. In fact, such awareness must be common throughout the animal kingdom, at the very least in all species that possess a central nervous system (Griffin, 1981). However, few would argue that the infant is capable of explicit, consciously goal-directed learning of the same variety displayed by older children and adults. Indeed, the same point might hold for microgenetic development within a number of domains of adult learning (Karmiloff-Smith, 1992).

With the human infant, it is clear that its cognitive armamentarium is quite different from that of the older child and that the young infant's ability to execute top-down explicit processing is but nascent (Piaget, 1936/1977). Thus, early development and learning take place without true explicit guidance and control, although explicit learning and memory do begin to emerge by 11 months (Bauer, 1996). Although earlier learning can be considered limited in that it is confined to direct adaptations to and anticipations of environmental input, the infant in fact accumulates a great deal of knowledge about the world (e.g., Johnson, 1996; Johnson & Nañez, 1995) and about the effects of its own actions on both the physical and social world (e.g., DeCasper & Fifer, 1980; Moon & Fifer, 1990; Rovee-Collier, 1990).

Further, the attainment of explicit-learning mechanisms is unlikely to be a sudden, unheralded shift in development. Instead, there might well be a series of qualitative changes on the road to full development of explicit systems (Karmiloff-Smith, 1992; Piaget, 1974/1976). Therefore, it is necessary to conceive of varieties and levels of awareness in learning, rather than assume a simple explicit-implicit dichotomy. In order for explicit cognitive and executive systems to develop, there must exist implicit information-processing systems that can provide knowledge from which explicit cognitive systems can be constructed and refined over an extended period of time.

Neuroanatomical Considerations

What we currently know about the structure and functioning of the adult mammalian brain suggests that there is neuroanatomical support for different kinds of mnemonic processing. Conscious, explicit learning and memory seem to depend on specific brain structures, whereas implicit learning is likely subserved by different and rather diffuse brain structures. In a normal adult, both types of structures and pathways would generally be activated simultaneously. Hence, what we know about the neuroanatomical necessity of implicit learning comes primarily from studies of persons who have sustained damage to areas subserving explicit processing.

The first critical insight into the neural basis of consciousness in learning and memory came from the assessment of the famous patient H.M. This patient became profoundly amnesic following surgery to control otherwise intractable epilepsy that removed, bilaterally, most of the *medial-temporal lobe* (MTL) including the hippocampus, amygdala, and surrounding cortical regions (Scoville, & Milner, 1957). The striking result of this surgery was a profound anterograde amnesia, which essentially eliminated H.M.'s ability to acquire new explicit knowledge of everyday facts and events while leaving his general cognitive functions largely intact. For example, his memory impairment was such that one half-hour after eating lunch, he could not remember a single item he had eaten or, in fact, that he had eaten at all. This memory impairment was selective for encoding new explicit, long-term memories. His immediate memory (e.g., digit span) was normal, he was able to retrieve explicit memories for childhood, and his postsurgery IQ was above normal.

A number of tasks have now been identified that show specific areas of preserved learning ability in H.M. and other patients with similar neurological damage. In fact, Seger (1994) recently suggested that preserved learning by amnesics on a particular task could be a defining feature of whether that task taps implicit processes. Studies using these tasks will be reviewed later. First, it will be useful to provide some background on the neural structures known to selectively support explicit learning and memory independently of implicit learning and memory.

Patients who have anterograde amnesia, an inability to acquire new explicit, declarative facts, have damage to one or more areas of the media-temporal lobe. Broadly speaking, the overall structure of the MTL system (shown in figure 14.1) is linked to the rest of the brain via two circuits: a cortical circuit and a diencaphalic (subcortical) circuit. The cortical circuit provides the flow of information into and out of the declarative memory system. Projections from throughout the cortical mantle converge on the perirhinal, parahippocampal, and entorhinal cortical areas, and these in turn funnel information into the hippocampal formation. Information about an event or episode that is coded by other parts of the brain (e.g., cortical sensory association areas) is thus introduced into the MTL memory system. These same three cortical areas also project widely back to other processing areas throughout the brain to facilitate the storage and retrieval of long-term memories. The diencephalic circuit of the MTL memory system (comprised of the hippocampal formation, thalamic nuclei, and mamillary bodies) has not been implicated as much in the flow of information between the hippocampus and widespread brain regions,

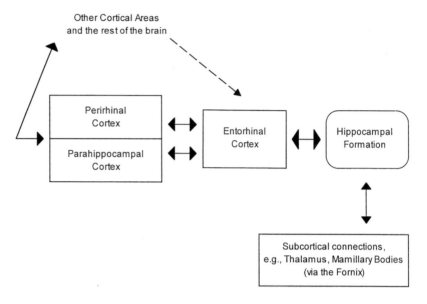

Figure 14.1
Schematic of the medial-temporal lobe memory stytem.

but damage to this circuit (e.g., from a thalamic stroke, tumor, or Korsa-koff's syndrome, an alcoholism-related disorder that results in damage to the mamillary bodies) disrupts the function of declarative memory in the same manner as damage to the cortical circuit so that new, explicit long-term memories are not stored.

This neurological description is only a summary; more detailed discussions of the cytoarchetechtonic structure and connection patterns between these areas are available elsewhere (e.g., Amaral, 1987). Detailed descriptions of the lesion-based studies that have led to the enumeration of the cortical and subcortical elements of the MTL system are also available elsewhere (e.g., Squire, 1992).

Unlike explicit learning and memory, implicit learning and memory do not appear to be supported by a single brain system. Different implicit-learning and memory tasks have been shown to depend on disparate brain areas. Neuroimaging studies implicate the operation of cortical areas in the right occipital lobes in priming (Squire et al., 1992) and the basal ganglia in sequence learning (Grafton, Hazeltine, & Ivry, 1995;

Rauch et al., 1995). Studies using experimental animals have indicated that some habitlike implicit-learning tasks depend on an intact caudate nucleus (Packard, Hirsch, & White, 1989), and classical conditioning of a skeletal-muscular reflex (which can be thought of as a primitive implicit-learning task, at least in nonhumans) appears to depend on the cerebellum (Thompson, 1990). There has also been research on patients with Huntington's and Parkinson's diseases, both of which involve progressive damage to the basal ganglia, demonstrating impairment on some implicit-learning tasks but not on others (Jackson, Jackson, Harrison, Henderson, & Kennard, 1995: Knopman & Nissen, 1987; Knowlton et al., 1996; Pascual-Leone et al., 1993; Willingham & Koroshetz, 1993).

One hypothesis is that implicit learning and memory occur within the cortical areas involved in processing the stimuli for which the learning is occurring, and hence will be found virtually throughout the brain (Ungerleider, 1995). If this proves correct, only with diffuse lesions would one expect global impairments in implicit learning. Focal lesions would result in impairment only on those implicit-learning tasks supported by the affected area, with other implicit-learning functions still being operative. As already suggested, one of the hallmarks of implicit learning is that it is less vulnerable than is explicit learning to neurological damage. If implicit processing is supported by widely divergent and diffuse neural structures, then this robustness is to be expected.

How Implicit Learning Is Studied

Thus, it seems that there is sound evolutionary, developmental, and neurological support for the existence of learning mechanisms that can acquire knowledge without full awareness. What, then, does the experimental literature say about the existence and operation of these mechanisms? As noted above, some half-dozen procedures have been developed for examining implicit learning. All have in common the fact that participants are presented with complex structured stimulus displays but without being told of this fact. Because many of the following theoretical points depend on empirical findings, it will be useful to provide a quick overview of the two studies most frequently used: *artificial grammar* (AG) learning and the *serial reaction time* (SRT) task.

Artificial Grammar Learning

In the standard AG study, participants are presented with strings of letters such as those marked as *learning stimuli* in figure 14.2. These strings are all "grammatical" or "well-formed" in the sense that they can be generated by the finite state device presented in the figure. To appreciate how this AG works, enter at state 1 on the left and follow the arrows, which

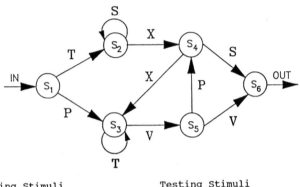

Learning Stimuli		Testing Stimuli			
1.	PVPXVPS	*1.	PTTTVPVS	*26.	SVPXTVV
2.	TSSXXVPS	*2.	PVTVV	27.	PVPXTTVV
3.	TSXS	*3.	TSSXXVSS	28.	PTTVPXVV
4.	PVV	*4.	TTVV	29.	TSXXTVPS
5.	TSSSXXVV	5.	PTTTTVPS	30.	TXXTVV
6.	PTVPXVV	6.	PVV	31.	TSSSSXS
7.	TXXVPXVV	*7.	PTTPS	*32.	TSXXPV
8.	PTTVV	8.	TXXTTVPS	33.	TPVV
9.	TSXXTVPS	9.	TSXXTTVV	*34.	TXPV
10.	TXXTVPS	*10.	PVXPVXPX	*35.	TPTXS
11.	PTVPS	*11.	XXSVT	36.	PVPXTVPS
12.	TXS	12.	TSSXXTVV	*37.	PTVPXVSP
13.	TSXXTVV	13.	TXS	38.	PVPXVV
14.	PVPXTVPS	*14.	TXXVX	39.	PTVPXVPS
15.	TXXTTTVV	*15.	PTTTVT	*40.	SXXVPS
16.	PTTTVPS	16.	TSXXVPS	41.	TXXVV
17.	TSSSXS	17.	PTTTVV	*42.	PVTTTVV
18.	TSSXXVV	*18.	TXV	43.	TSSXXVPS
19.	PVPXVV	19.	PTTVPS	*44.	PTVVVV
20.	TXTVPS	20.	TXXTTVV	*45.	VSTXVVS
		*21.	PSXS	46.	TSXXVV
		*22.	PTVPPPS	*47.	TXXTVPT
		23.	PTTTTTVV	48.	PVPS
		*24.	TXVPS	*49.	PXPVXVTT
		25.	TSSXS	*50.	VPXTVV

Figure 14.2
Examples of learning stimuli and testing stmuli presented to subjects in artificial grammar study. Asterisk indicates a nongrammatical string.

denote permissible transitions from state to state, until state 6 is reached. Because each transition generates a letter, each discrete path through the grammar corresponds to a grammatical string. In some experiments participants memorize these strings, in others they reproduce them, and in others they simply observe them. After the learning phase, participants are informed about the existence but not the nature of the rules and are asked to distinguish novel well-formed or "grammatical" strings from those that violate the constraints of the system. Examples of these testing stimuli are given in figure 14.2. The ability to perform such discriminations in the relative absence of explicit knowledge of the rules is taken as evidence for implicit learning.

Serial Reaction Time

In the classic SRT study, participants sit in front of a computer screen on which a set of four or, in some cases six, locations are marked. Each location is associated with a specific key on the keyboard. On each trial, one location is denoted in some manner usually by having some arbitrary mark such as an "*" occur there. The participants' task is to press the corresponding key as rapidly and accurately as possible. Sequences tend to be of two types. In most studies a relatively simple sequence from 6 to 12 items long is used and is repeated over and over (e.g., 13423124). In other studies a nonrepeating sequence that has a particular rule-governed structure, such as that generated by an AG, is used. In either case, the data consist of participants' reaction times (RTs). Evidence of learning comes from the observation that RTs become shorter as the sequence is practiced but increase dramatically when the structure is changed by introducing a new sequence or shifting to one that is random or follows a new set of rules. As with the AG studies, the implicit element derives from the observation that participants are typically unaware of the nature (and often even the existence) of the structure.

The Core Issues

In the years since the first evidence for implicit learning was presented, a variety of specific issues have emerged as important in understanding the process. In this section, we will review the core issues—ones whose clarification is critical for an understanding of implicit learning and related phenomena.

On Awareness

At first blush, the distinction between implicit and explicit learning would seem to rest on the role of awareness or consciousness. At its simplest, explicit learning is learning with awareness, and implicit learning is its converse. But, alas, this just won't do. What exactly do we mean by awareness? Are there levels of awareness? Is the faint glimmer that something is known different from a fully explicable conscious experience—at least in a way that is phenomenologically interesting? If someone is aware *that* something was learned, is this sufficient for us to conclude that the learning was explicit? Or do we want to insist on their being aware of *what* was learned? Do participants need to be aware of knowledge *when* it is acquired, or can we accept as implicit knowledge that was only brought into consciousness slowly over time or with effort? Do we want to follow the guidance of Berry and Dienes (1993; Dienes & Berry, 1997) that we need to distinguish between subjective and objective thresholds of awareness? Questions like these hint at problems awaiting any attempt to hang implicit learning on the criterion of consciousness, and they have tantalized psychologists and philosophers alike.

At its most primitive, awareness can be defined as a subjective sense that something exists or something is happening—a simple apprehension intimately tied to basic attentional processes. However, from this perspective one could argue that almost all learning is explicit because it takes place when the organism is awake and that human neonates and virtually all animal species are capable of explicit learning. In fact, a few researchers do study learning under conditions of sleep, hypnosis, and anesthesia in order to improve their chances of studying learning that is not explicit (see Kihlstrom, 1990). However, most researchers believe there are important variations in the explicitness of learning.

The question becomes, How can we determine whether we are dealing, in a given experimental setting, with a process that is explicit or one that is implicit? One answer is to impose a rather stark criterion for implicit knowledge: do not conclude that implicit learning has taken place unless you can demonstrate that there is *no* evidence of awareness of what has been learned. Variations on this perspective have been put forward by Brody (1989); Dulany, Carlson, and Dewey (1984); and Shanks and St. John (1994). The basic argument is that conscious processing is the default mode and that only when we can be assured that no such processes are manifest can we conclude in favor of an unconscious process. Taking this hard line has led Dulany (1991) to conclude that there is no evidence for implicit learning at all. Indeed, he suspects that future psychologists will look back on "the metatheory of a cognitive unconscious as a kind of shared madness, a folie à deux milles or so" (p. 116).

There are a lot of reasons for suspecting that this perspective is, if not flat out wrong, certainly unproductive, for it depends on arguments that are suspect. First, it assumes there are clear-cut ways to measure implicit and explicit processes and to know, with certainty, which is which. Second, it is predicated on showing a total absence of explicit functioning before deciding in favor of implicit.

It is easy to show the weakness in this line of reasoning. Let's take a classic case, Kunst-Wilson and Zajonc's (1980) demonstration that the mere exposure effect can operate outside of awareness. In this now classic study, geometric shapes were briefly exposed and participants were then tested for awareness of those shapes using the generally accepted method for assessing awareness, the two-alternative forced choice (2AFC) procedure. Participants were shown pairs of one novel and one old geometric shape and asked to select the one that was presented earlier. Participants responded at chance, levels suggesting no conscious awareness of the original stimuli. They were then shown the pairs again, but this time were asked which of the two they *preferred*. Now participants reliably selected the ones that had been shown earlier, suggesting that we come to prefer the familiar, even while we are unaware of what the familiar is. However, it is not absolutely clear that this process occurs completely unconsciously; the two tasks may have different demand characteristics. The request for a preference may have been seen by the participants as an opportunity to relax their criterion for responding on the basis of a hazy but explicit knowledge base.

Hence, even the most compelling of implicit measures are possibly contaminated by explicit factors. It will do no good to try to hold implicit cognitive functions to the kind of criterion suggested by Brody and others.

This is just as well, for we are better off treating implicit and explicit, not as wholly separable, but rather as aspects of cognitive functioning that are present to some extent in virtually everything interesting that human beings do. Some learning seems to have elements that are compellingly explicit, such as simple problem solving in which individuals generate and test hypotheses about possible solutions. Other learning reflects features that are just as clearly implicit, such as natural language acquisition during early childhood. But it would surely be a mistake to try to argue that even obvious examples such as these are pristine domains of acquisition and representation.

We would rather think of the problem this way. Assume that there is some quantity q that represents total knowledge held and some other quantity x that represents the proportion of knowledge that an individual is aware of. Any time that $q > x$, we can conclude that implicit learning has occurred. There is no need to show that $x = 0$. That is, implicit and explicit knowledge can (and almost certainly do) co-occur in most situations. This functionalist approach to the issue seems sensible. And, as we shall see when we explore specific issues more closely, it is not difficult to set up appropriate laboratory conditions under which the emergence of dissociable implicit and explicit functions can be observed.

To take just one example, Mathews et al. (1989) used a "teach-aloud" technique in an AG-learning experiment. Participants were stopped periodically during the well-formedness task and asked to provide as complete information as possible for a group of yoked participants who would use their instructions to carry out the task but without going through the learning phase. Over the four days of the experiment the separate groups of yoked participants shadowed that of the experimental participants, although never achieving equal levels of performance. However, the most interesting finding was the change that occurred over days. While the experimental participants reached asymptotic levels of performance on day 2, their ability to communicate what they knew increased, and by day 4 the yoked participants were making decisions at approximately their level.

From a folk-psychology point of view, this feels right. Implicit knowledge is acquired naturally and fairly quickly, but bringing it to consciousness and putting it into a form that can be communicated to others takes time and effort. Any quick and dirty attempt to determine thresholds for consciousness, either subjective or objective, in such a situation would misrepresent matters. Intriguingly, this perspective also lies behind arguments put forward about how science itself operates (Polanyi, 1966; A. Reber, 1993a).

Representational Form, or What Is Being Learned in an Implicit-Learning Experiment

The type of consciousness involved in explicit learning entails mental representation of external objects and events. One cannot learn explicitly without the ability to form images or propositional representations of real-world stimuli, which can be executed, recalled, and examined in their absence. So, for example, one cannot explicitly learn that dogs bite without being able to form a dog image or propositional dog representation that is stable and accessible enough to be actively recalled in the absence of a real dog.

However, this is not true of implicit representations, as Claparède (1911/1951) noted in the first clinical report of learning without awareness in an amnesic patient. When first being introduced to the patient, he stuck her hand with a concealed pin. When they later met again, the patient, despite denying she had ever seen Claparède before, refused to shake his hand. Here the mental representation was unavailable, at least in an explicit sense, even in the presence of the individual who was an integral element in the initial episode.

The question of interest here concerns the representational form of implicitly acquired material. There are two broadly competing theories. One, first put forward by A. Reber (1969), maintains that the memorial form of implicit knowledge is abstract, that tacit knowledge is encoded in a manner that it relatively independent of the physical form of the input stimuli. The other, first articulated by Brooks (1978), argues that implicit knowledge is characterized by fairly rigid instantiations based on the physical form of the input stimulus.

The easiest way to appreciate the difference between these two perspectives is to imagine that you had to identify a novel, hairy, four-legged creature that just walked in the room. From the abstractionist's point of view you would call it a dog because its overall configuration corresponded with your deep, abstract representation of a category of critters known as *dogs*. From an instantiationist's perspective, you would call the beast a dog because it reminded you of some specific, memorially encoded instance, say one in which a similar animal was called a dog by your Uncle Harry. Notice that Brooks's version of instantiationism is holistic in nature. The memorial representation is assumed to be encoded as a entire episode and stored as such. There is a third candidate theory as well, one that can properly be classified as a variation on the instantiated model. This approach, championed by Perruchet (1994; Perruchet & Pacteau, 1990), is based on the assumption that the instantiated memories are set up, not as wholes, but as fragments or smaller component parts of the input stimuli. The difference between the two forms of instantiationism is to be found, essentially, in the amount and type of information encoded, not in its form.

It's worth noting that the fragmentary model is, in some sense, predicated on an abstract representation in that encoding the chunks requires that information be integrated across the items used during training. However, it is important to distinguish between abstraction as a process based on scanning multiple inputs and logging information about frequency of occurrence of chunks and abstraction as a process that induces a representation of the rules underlying the stimulus inputs. The former is not a particularly interesting form of abstraction in that the resultant representation is still wedded to the physical form of the stimulus inputs. The latter form is more interesting psychologically, and it is important to determine whether implicit-learning processes are, in fact, capable of inducing such representations.

Most of the experiments designed to examine this issue have used a variation on the AG-learning experiment in which a transfer phase is introduced. In the first of these experiments, A. Reber (1969) had participants memorize letter strings generated by a grammar much like the one in figure 14.2. Participants showed a highly reliable finding: the ability to encode and recall material improved as they learned to exploit the structure in the strings. After a break, experimental participants returned to a task that was changed in one of several ways. In one group, the letters used to present the strings were changed; in a second, the underlying grammar itself was changed; and in a third, both were changed. Participants in each of these groups were compared with a control group that continued to work with strings from the original grammar and letter set. The results were quite clear. Changing the grammar produced a drop in performance. However, changing the letter set had little or no impact, suggesting that participants were setting up abstract mental representations that could be used independently of the surface form of the stimuli.

In recent years, several studies have examined this claim for abstract implicit representations. Most of these have used the procedure of having participants learn using strings instantiated with one letter set and then running the well-formedness phase using a different letter set. In all cases, clear evidence of transfer has been obtained. Mathews et al. (1989) ran participants over four separate sessions; on each session a different letter set was used. They found positive transfer in that these participants continued to perform as well as control participants who worked with the same letter set throughout. Similar results have been reported by Brooks and Vokey (1991); Gomez and Schvaneveldt (1994); Manza and A. Reber (1997); and Shanks, Johnstone, and Staggs (1997). Moreover, Knowlton and Squire (1996) have shown that such transfer also takes place in amnesics who have virtually no recognition memory for the original stimuli. An intriguing variety of transfer has also been shown by Altmann, Dienes, and Goode (1995); J. Howard and Ballas (1980); and Manza and A. Reber (1997), all of whom report cross-modality transfer where stimuli instantiated auditorially can be processed effectively when presented visually and vice versa.

Although these studies certainly suggest that implicit learning yields an abstract representation, this is clearly not the whole story. First, in virtually all the transfer studies, control participants who continue to work with strings made up using the original letters perform somewhat better than participants given novel instantiations. This suggests that there is more to the story than pure abstract representations, for, as Brooks and Vokey (1991) pointed out, in these studies grammaticality and physical similarity are confounded. That is, during testing, the well-formed strings are more physically similar to those used during learning than are those that contain violations. In a series of studies using stimuli that controlled for the physical similarity between the stimuli used during learning and those used during testing, Brooks and Vokey (1991; Vokey & Brooks,

1992) showed that physical similarity is, indeed, important and accounts for roughly half the explainable variance. However, as Knowlton and Squire (1994) reported, it is not whole item similarity that is important here; rather, it is relatively small two- and three-letter chunks that are critical.

This sequence of studies seems to suggest that relatively small chunks are an important aspect of AG learning, but they are not sufficient to explain the full database, because knowledge based on them is not sufficient to support transfer. Both Gomez and Schvaneveldt (1994) and Manza and A. Reber (1997) found that participants who learned an AG by memorizing all of the permissible bigrams but never seeing a complete string failed to show transfer to the well-formedness task when the test strings were instantiated with a novel letter set. Lastly, Knowlton and Squire (1996), in a follow-up to their earlier study, reported that amnesics who had virtually no explicit memory for the specific items used during learning were able to make well-formedness judgments in a standard transfer study using the changed letter set procedure.

Our best guess is that, at least in the AG experiments, implicit learning yields both instantiated and abstract representations. Various aspects of the context for learning and testing will encourage one or another (Whittlesea & Dorken, 1993) and, as A. Reber and Allen (1978) showed, the procedures most commonly in use tend to encourage abstractions. A more direct demonstration of this point was provided by Manza and A. Reber (1997). One group of participants learned an AG by memorizing strings composed with one set of letters (A) while another group learned the same "deep" strings, but half were made up with one letter set (A) and half with another (B). During testing, one-third of the strings were made up using letter set A, one-third used letter set B, and one-third used a letter set, C, new to both. Although both groups showed transfer to novel letter sets, the group that learned with two instantiations performed better on the strings made up with the new letter set, C, than the group that learned using the single letter set A. Clearly, the dual instantiations encouraged the establishment of abstract representations.

When it comes to drawing conclusions about methodologies other than the AG task, there isn't much to go on. In a recent overview of the literature on the SRT task, Hsiao and A. Reber (1997) concluded that participants in SRT experiments are setting up representations based on patterns of covariation reflected in the stimulus sequences. However, it is not clear whether these representations are keyed to the physical form of the sequences or are more abstract. To date, there have been no SRT studies that have used a transfer procedure, so it is not known whether the knowledge gained in the situations tested so far can produce effective performance in a separate domain or under different task constraints.

Interestingly, these findings suggesting deep and partially abstract representations do not fit terribly neatly with the work on implicit *memory*, where transfer is typically not found. Implicit memory, particularly when assessed using priming, has been characterized as being rather concrete in nature (Schacter, Chiu, & Ochsner, 1993; Schacter & Graf, 1986; Squire et al., 1993). Dienes and Berry (1997) have even argued that instantiated and inflexible representations may be a hallmark of implicit systems in general. Why is it that implicit learning appears to yield at least partly abstract representations, whereas implicit memory studies typically report highly concrete and instantiated representations? The answer may be methodological in that procedures such as priming tend to activate specific memories, or it could be more basic than that. We will discuss this issue a bit more in the section on neuropsychological issues.

Individual and Developmental Differences

One of the predictions of the evolutionary stance outlined earlier is that implicit functions ought to show less individual-to-individual variation than explicit functions. The details for this prediction can be found in A. Reber (1992, 1993b), but the proposition depends rather straightforwardly on the recognition that forms and functions that emerge early in any hierarchical system (of which evolution is an example) display less variability than forms and functions that emerge later.

Because this predicted characteristic of implicit processing has only been recently recognized, the empirical evidence for or against it is meager. However, the few studies that have examined this hypothesis show support. A. Reber, Walkenfeld, and Hernstadt (1991) found that young adults showed less interindividual variation on an AG task than they did on an explicit task of equivalent complexity. Recently McGeorge, Crawford, and Kelley (1997) replicated and extended this finding.

The evolutionary model also suggests that the slight interindividual differences found in implicit learning might not be influenced by the same factors that influence explicit learning. This proposition follows from the argument that the evolutionarily newer explicit processes are sensitive to a variety of influences and covary with a number of characteristics that do not influence older structures. The most obvious of these characteristics is the class of skills involved in higher mental processes, as measured by traditional IQ tests. We know of only three studies that looked at the dissociation between implicit learning and IQ scores, but all support the model. The A. Reber et al. (1991) study cited above found that implicit-learning scores were unrelated to IQ, whereas explicit-learning scores correlated .69 with IQ scores. Mayberry, Taylor, and O'Brien-Malone (1995) similarly found that children's IQ scores were not significantly related to number correct on an implicit-learning task, but correlated .37 to .56 (depending on age) with scores on an explicit-learning measure. Furthermore, as with the A. Reber et al. (1991) study, performances on the explicit and implicit tasks were not significantly associated with each other after correction for overall age effects. Finally, McGeorge, Crawford, and Kelly (1997) found the same general pattern both with respect to IQ and age. The one study that found interindividual effects (Kassin & A. Reber, 1979) examined the factor of locus of control and found that participants who were high on the "internal" scale, that is, those who tend to take responsibility for their actions, tended to be better at implicit learning. However, it is not clear whether to attribute this result to true differences in implicit-learning ability or to differences in motivation or attention.

A few studies have examined clinical factors such as mood and anxiety on implicit learning. Abrams and A. Reber (1988) found that a group of psychotics of mixed etiology were markedly impaired in explicit problem-solving tasks but functioned normally on implicit tasks. Parallel findings were reported by Rathus, A. Reber, Manza, and Kushner (1994) in highly anxious participants. Interestingly, depression (at least the nonclinical levels examined by Rathus et al.) had no affect on either mode of processing. These findings generally support the principle that implicit learning displays relatively little variability; they are also coordinate with the robustness argument that implicit learning is less likely to be impaired by factors that disrupt explicit processes.

The evolutionary model also predicts that implicit learning should show fewer age differences than explicit learning. Of course, one would still expect some age differences in implicit learning, particularly in examining early periods of development, because attentional functions, span of apprehension, and information-chunking ability all increase dramatically over the course of early childhood. However, the variations observed in implicit learning are predicted to be less attributable to ontogenetic factors than are the variations in explicit learning. Unfortunately, there are no systematic studies of implicit learning over the entire developmental continuum, with a particular paucity of studies using children. A Reber (1993b) reviewed the available empirical evidence that is consistent with the notion that there are no substantial differences in implicit learning experienced by individuals over the first year of life. One study we are aware of (Mayberry, et al., 1995) found some improvement with age. However, the improvements were small compared to those observed in explicit learning and might well be constrained primarily by attentional factors, change over age. Further, Parkin and Streete (1988) found no differences in implicit memory measures from ages 3 years through young adulthood, whereas differences in explicit memory measures were obtained.

Most studies with older adults have used either the SRT, where participants are exposed to fixed repeating patterns, or implicit memory priming techniques using word lists, rather than using rule-based systems such as AGs. The few studies (Howard & Howard, 1989, 1992) comparing healthy older adults to young adults show no age differences on more implicit, indirect measures of learning (e.g., RTs), whereas older adults are less accurate on more explicit direct measures of learning (e.g., prediction). However, Cherry and Stadler (1995) present evidence that some low-ability older persons might be subtly impaired in implicit learning. On the whole, there is some intriguing evidence that there is less variation attributable to age in implicit learning than there is for explicit learning. The ability to learn implicitly theoretically not only precedes the emergence of explicit processes, but also shows less variation between the age groups studied than does performance on explicit tasks.

Given the interest in both developmental psychology and the issues of aging, it appears to us that this is an area much in need of exploration. We have, at date, precious little understanding of the nature of acquisition of complex knowledge bases in infancy and early childhood, particularly as they function independently from top-down conscious systems. In parallel fashion, we are almost embarrassingly ignorant of how implicit cognitive processes not mediated by awareness are affected by aging.

Neuropsychological Issues

As noted earlier, patients with anterograde amnesia provide a unique opportunity to study the operation of implicit processes with little interference from explicit processes. Perhaps not surprisingly, there is an enormous literature on this general topic. However, most of it focuses on the issue of implicit memory (reviews may be found, e.g., Schacter et al., 1993; Shimamura, 1993). Here we will focus on the work that supports the proposition that implicit learning is mediated by different neuroanatomical structures from those that subsume explicit learning and hence that supports the notion of dissociation between implicit and explicit systems.

First, as noted earlier, amnesic patients exhibit the same artificial grammar learning ability as control participants (Knowlton, Ramus, & Squire, 1992) even when the test is given using a novel letter set applied to the same underlying grammar (Knowlton & Squire, 1996). These patients are unaware of the underlying rule structure and are impaired at recognizing the training strings compared to control participants. This pattern of results has also been observed for amnesic patients in the sequence-learning paradigm. Amnesic patients show normal learning of the repeating sequence but are impaired at recognizing or reporting it (Nissen & Bullemer, 1987; P. Reber & Squire, 1994).

The impaired explicit memory for the training stimuli exhibited by amnesic patients provides valuable support for the dissociation of implicit and explicit learning. In the sequence-learning task, progressively more sensitive tests (e.g., sequence recognition, free generation) have indicated that with practice, most healthy participants acquire some explicit knowledge about a repeating sequence (Perruchet & Amorim, 1992; Willingham, Greeley, & Bardone, 1993). This finding has led some researchers to suggest that the explicit knowledge assessed by these new tests may be the same knowledge that supports the apparently implicit learning exhibited by these participants (Perruchet, Gallego, & Savy 1990; Shanks & St. John, 1994). However, even these more sensitive tests do not detect significant explicit knowledge in amnesic patients (P. Reber & Squire, 1994), suggesting that the implicit-learning performance is supported by a separate system from that which supports the explicit.

Amnesic patients have also been shown to exhibit normal learning on tasks for which it may be difficult to dissociate awareness from performance in control participants. For example, amnesic patients perform normally on the classic Posner and Keele (1968) dot categorization task (Knowlton & Squire, 1993). In this task, participants are shown distortions of a prototypic dot pattern during training and are later able to judge whether new patterns are drawn from the same category (i.e., are derived from the same prototype) as the training items. This task is similar to other implicit-learning tasks in that the participants are not told that they will be learning a category but do so anyway. The normal performance of amnesic patients on this task is accompanied by an impairment in their ability to recognize the items originally seen during training. This finding suggests that explicit recognition of studied patterns depends on the MTL memory system, whereas the intact implicit categorization learning depends on a different brain system that is not damaged in amnesia.

A similar result has been obtained with a probabilistic classification task (Knowlton, Squire, & Gluck, 1994; P. Reber, Knowlton, & Squire, 1996). In this task, participants are shown a set of cues (cards with geometric shapes) that vary in the degree to which they are associated with two possible weather outcomes. Their task is to try to predict whether sunny or rainy weather will follow. Amnesic patients learned the associations at the same rate as control participants, although they showed impaired explicit memory for the training session. In both of these cases, the normal declarative memory function of the healthy controls for the training session and stimuli would have obscured the fact that the categorization and classification tasks are learned implicitly had the amnesic patients not been studied.

One aspect of the implicit-explicit distinction that has emerged recently concerns the extent to which the neurological structures underpinning each allow for flexible representations. Glisky, Schacter, and Tulving (1986) and Winter (1995) have found that with extensive training, amnesic patients could learn the complex cognitive skill of computer operation. The ability of patients to learn this task with extended training itself does not suggest that the skill was acquired implicitly; the explicit memory ability of these amnesic patients was not generally totally impaired. However, Glisky et al. also found that the quality of the patients' learning was different from that of controls. When the amnesic patients were questioned about their knowledge in a manner slightly different from that used in the original learning, their performance was impaired relative to controls. Glisky et al. suggested that implicitly learned knowledge may be "hyperspecific," in that it could not be applied as flexibly as explicitly acquired knowledge.

Because it is possible to measure flexible knowledge use relatively directly using transfer tests, this characteristic lends itself to studies of experimental animals with selective lesions of the MTL memory system. Eichenbaum and colleagues have shown in a number of experiments that rats with damage to the MTL memory system show impaired flexibility in applying acquired knowledge when compared with the performance of control animals (Eichenbaum, Mathews, & Cohen, 1989; Eichenbaum, Stewart, & Morris, 1990). In addition, P. Reber, Knowlton, and Squire (1996) found that amnesic patients who learned a probabilistic classification task at a normal rate showed impairments on subsequent transfer tests that required flexible knowledge use.

The apparent inflexibility of knowledge acquired implicitly should not be interpreted as implying stimulus-specific learning. In fact, as we already noted, several tasks such as AG learning and dot pattern categorization require classification of novel stimuli in order to demonstrate implicit learning of the underlying structure (grammar or prototype). The transfer paradigm within artificial grammar learning is a particularly striking example of successful transfer to novel stimuli that, as noted earlier, strongly suggests abstract representation of the grammar. The findings hinting at inflexibility in the use of implicitly acquired knowledge suggest that there will likely be some transfer tests that participants might be able to perform with explicit knowledge (and associated awareness) that will not be supported when the knowledge is solely implicit.

In addition to the issues of awareness, representational form, individual differences, and neuroanatomical dissociation, there are several other issues we expect to gain ascendance in future years. We will only present them briefly, not because we regard them as unimportant but simply because there has been, to date, less research on them.

Role of Attention

If implicit learning takes place largely outside of awareness, does this entail that it is an automatic process, in the sense that automatic processes are known to use relatively little attentional resources (Hasher & Zacks, 1984)? This issue has been explored intensively in recent years, although unhappily most of it uses a single experimental procedure: the SRT task. A full review of this literature is available elsewhere (Hsiao & A. Reber, 1997); here we merely wish to touch upon the main issues.

Nissen and Bullemer's (1987) initial study suggested that learning in an SRT task required full attention as the introduction of a secondary (tone-counting) task inhibited learning. However, the complexity of the sequence (Cohen, Ivry & Keele, 1990) and the speed of presentation (Frensch & Miner, 1994) are important factors that make simple conclusions unlikely. Reed and Johnson (1994) have shown that with more extensive training, even rather long, ambiguous sequences created by concatenating eight different 12-event sequences can be learned under dual-task conditions. Hsiao and A. Reber (1996) have found that sequences generated by an AG (and that hence do not repeat) can also be learned while engaging in a secondary tone-counting task. Frensch, Buchner, and Lin (1994) reported, not surprisingly, that structural factors are important, with more complex sequences being harder to learn under attentional distraction. Finally, Hsiao and A. Reber (1996) found that timing is important. When the interval between the secondary task and the upcoming target is short (e.g., 50 ms), learning is disrupted considerably more than when the interval is longer (e.g., 150 ms). In all of these tasks, it should be noted, imposing a secondary task compromises learning to some extent. With the exception of Cohen, et al.'s (1990) simple sequences, participants working under dual-task conditions virtually always show slower learning than do controls.

A few studies have examined the role of attention using a task other than the SRT. Hayes and Broadbent (1988) used the process control task in which participants interact with a simulated production plant and attempt to adjust factors such as wages and size of the workforce in order to achieve specific production levels. They reported that the more complex elements of the task, which they argued were acquired implicitly, were not disrupted by the imposition of a secondary task, whereas the simpler were. This result is a bit surprising given the story depicted by the SRT studies. It has also proven difficult to replicate (Green & Shanks, 1993; Sanderson, 1989).

It is difficult to know what to conclude from these studies. It appears, generally speaking, that implicit learning, unlike more primitive processes such as logging simple frequency and location of events, does require attentional resources in that the secondary task invariably slows down learning. Part of the difficulty, as Hsiao and A. Reber (1997) have argued, comes from a lack of a clear understanding of the mechanisms(s) of attention. Is attention some kind of central processor with limited capacity, or do there exist separate modules that handle different tasks? In the former construct compromising attentional resources can be viewed as a bottleneck problem; in the latter it becomes a switching problem. It is not obvious what kinds of data could permit us to disentangle these characterizations.

Implicit Motor Learning

Although the majority of studies of implicit learning have been oriented toward the more compellingly cognitive processes, there has been some work on motor learning. Happily, the results tend to dovetail with those discussed. Pew (1974) first demonstrated implicit motor learning in a pursuit-tracking task. His procedure, which has become the standard for these studies, used a tracking task in which the middle third of each trial was repeated while the other two-thirds were changed randomly. Participants became increasingly more proficient with the repeated segment, although they were unaware of the repetition. Pew (1974) also showed that transfer occurred, in that participants were also more proficient with the repeated segment when it was presented in an inverted fashion than they were with nonrepeated segments.

Wulf and her coworkers (Wulf, Lee, & Schmidt, 1994; Wulf & Schmidt, 1997) have pointed out that motor learning involves at least two processes, one involving timing (the temporal relationships between the various components of the action) and one involving scaling (the magnitude and speed of the action) and have presented evidence that suggests that both components are learned implicitly. In a recent paper, Wulf and Schmidt (1997) reported that these components can be manipulated independently of each other and that both show evidence for abstract representation. When either the timing or the scale of the required response was changed but the underlying structure left intact, participants showed a clear advantage on repeated segments over nonrepeated segments. Interestingly, Wulf and Schmidt also found that learning was enhanced by variable feedback, a factor that, so far as we know, has never been examined in the more cognitively based implicit-learning tasks.

Finally, Masters (1992) has shown that implicitly acquired motor skills show greater resiliency when participants are placed under stress than those acquired explicitly, a finding that is coordinate with results from the AG-learning literature (see A. Reber, 1976). Moreover, Knopman (1991) found that administration of the drugs scopolamine and lorazepan, which block excitatory cholinergic pathways to the hippocampus and hence impair verbal learning, do not impair performance on SRT motor learning. Both findings suggest that implicit motor learning is more robust than is explicit motor learning.

Formal Models of Implicit Learning

The process of implicit learning has attracted a good bit of modeling for obvious reasons. The effects are robust, the database large, and the acquisition process appears (at least superficially) to be relatively simple. All of the models that have been developed are computer-based, formal systems. They use architectures that compute statistically covarying relationships among elements in a complex stimulus display, although they vary in the specifics. Here, we will only touch on the conceptual issues; technical details can be found elsewhere (Cleeremans, 1993; Dienes, Altmann, & Gao, 1995). Note that these models tend to be based on connectionist neural nets that function in a purely bottom-up manner. This is an important point; if a connectionist system can capture the data from the typical implicit-learning experiment, it lends support to the argument that implicit processes can take place independent of a modulating, top-down consciousness.

One of the first successful models was Servan-Schreiber and Anderson's (1990) *competitive-chunking model*. It is based on detecting those elements in a display (such as symbols in an AG) that tend to occur together and building up representations based on groupings, or *chunks*. In this model chunks compete with each other; those with the higher statistical coherency get memorially represented. Dienes's early (1992) model works by representing specific symbols occurring in particular locations in a display and constructing connectionist relations between them. Mathews and his coworkers (Druhan & Mathews, 1989; Mathews & Roussel 1997) used a classifier system that keys in on the encoding of patterns of runs of elements. Cleeremans (1993; Cleeremans & McClelland, 1991) has developed what is probably the most general model, one built on what is known as a *simple recurrent network* (SRN). SRNs, as Elman (1990) has shown, have the capacity to encode complex structures by representing the "next" element in a sequential display. SRNs are connectionist in nature and induce representations by the detection of patterns of covariation between items as they occur in a sequence.

All of these models handle the data from the basic implicit-learning experiments reasonably well, although there are differences in the details (see Cleeremans, 1993, and Dienes, 1992, for reviews). The high level of success is not terribly surprising because, as noted, all of these models are based on the detection and representation of statistical features of the environment that serve as their input and so should, in principle, capture the essential underlying features of the kinds of displays that have been used. However, all of these models, based as they are on the representation of the physical characteristics of the stimulus display, find accounting for the transfer data discussed earlier to be a problem. If learning consists of a sequence of letters generated by an AG, then the models' representations will be based on these letters. If the input is a structured sequence of locations that flash on a computer screen, then so will the underlying encoding that the models will build. However, we know that humans function quite well when the letter set or the modality used to instantiate the AG is changed.

Recently, two models have been put forward that appear, in principle, to have the capacity for abstract representations Mathews and Roussel's (1997) model works by encoding abstract representations such as those reflected by runs of items. For example, a string from an AG such as KVVVVT is coded as "Kvrrr,T" where *r* notes that the preceding letter has been repeated. By using devices such as this, the model can capture some abstract features of a display independent of the physical form of the stimulus. But the more ambitious model is that recently presented by Dienes et al. (1995), which appears, at least in principle, to be able to bootstrap itself into solving the transfer problem. Their model is an extension of the general architecture of Cleeremans's (1993) SRN and functions essentially by introducing an additional hidden layer. Although Dienes et al. (in press) present data that are certainly suggestive of the model's capacity to capture the phenomenon of transfer in an AG-learning experiment, the jury is still out on the model's generalizability. It seems, nevertheless, to be a clear advance over previous models.

Affect and Implicit Learning

Lastly, we want to touch on a new aspect of implicit processing that suggests that implicit acquired knowledge can be used to form preferences for novel stimuli. Gordon and Holyoak (1983) showed some years back that participants in a typical AG-learning experiment developed a marked preference for novel strings that were grammatical over those that contained violations. This basic result has been replicated and extended by Zizak, Manza, and their colleagues in interesting ways. Manza and Bornstein (1995) showed that participants asked to make preference judgments about novel strings in an AG experiment exhibited less evidence of awareness of the rules than those asked to make the more traditional well-formedness judgments. In a similar vein, Manza and Skypala (1996) showed that divided attention disrupts participants' abilities to make well-formedness judgments but does not affect their preference judgments. Manza, Zizak, and A. Reber (1998) have reported that familiarity with the physical form of the symbols used to instantiate the items is important. Basically, the preference for well-formed strings tends not to emerge when novel stimuli, such as Japanese or Chinese characters, are used. Finally, Zizak and A. Reber (1994) have argued that because of the manner in which participants develop preferences for structured items in these experiments, implicit processes have the potential to provide a conceptual foundation for the development of aesthetic judgments. As with the other, less intensively studied areas, there are many fascinating issues here that need both empirical and theoretical exploration.

Summary

We've covered a good bit of ground here, and a quick summary is in order. We will simply list the basic characteristics of implicit learning that we feel have been firmly established by the data and conclude by outlining the boundaries of our current understanding. Specifically, implicit learning (a) operates largely independent of awareness, (b) is subsumed by neuroanatomical structures distinct from those that serve explicit, declarative processes, (c) yields memorial representations that can be either abstract or concrete, (d) is a relatively robust system that survives psychological, psychiatric, and neuroanatomical injury, (e) shows relatively little interindividual variability, and (f) is relatively unaffected by ontogenetic factors.

However, it is clear that there are important areas about which little is known. For example, although the evidence is for developmental continuity, there has been relatively little work on this topic. Although it seems fairly obvious that implicit acquisitional processes play a critical role in infancy and early childhood when natural language learning, socialization, and the like are taking place, there have been few specific studies of how these processes are actually carried out. Further, we have only weak evidence to support the (strong) argument that implicit-learning processes continue to operate unimpeded in an aged population. There is still little understanding about how implicit learning may interact with other factors such as motivation and attention—factors whose role must be understood, particularly if one begins to consider the possibility of applications into domains such as education and remediation. In a similar vein, there has been precious little work carried out on implicit motor learning and how learning in sensorimotor domains interacts with that in the more cognitive. We are fairly confident that we have identified the critical neuroanatomical structure for explicit memorial systems, but to date we have only speculation about which neural structures might be responsible for implicit systems. Interestingly, this issue is relevant for theories that are predicated on modular systems versus those that assume more globally distributed structures. There is the related, vexing question of flexibility—some of the evidence seems to support the notion that implicit knowledge is quite flexible; other evidence suggests that it is not. Are the inconsistencies here due to methodological factors or perhaps to more basic underlying processing mechanisms that are not yet understood? Finally, there is the question of how implicit acquisitional processes fit with other processes that occur largely or wholly outside of consciousness such as implicit (or subliminal) perception, implicit memory, and the role of unconscious motivational and emotional factors. The future looks like it will be fun.

Note

1. This chapter is concerned with the question of implicit learning. However, in places we will discuss issues and findings that have emerged in the study of implicit memory. The division that exists between these two areas is unfortunate, as they are intimately related in the most poignant of ways: implicit learning produces implicit memories. However, the two phenomena are studied using different methodologies. Studies of implicit learning tend to use unfamiliar displays and examine the manner in which participants build up representations of the underlying structure of those displays. Studies of implicit memory tend to use tasks such as priming, where preexisting knowledge is cued in episodic fashion and memory for the cuing episode is subsequently examined. This difference in the traditional methodologies has had the unhappy effect of driving a wedge between the two subdisciplines. Although this chapter is not the place to heal this rift, we will do what we can by bringing in issues and data from studies of implicit memory to help clarify issues that have emerged in the exploration of implicit learning.

References

Abrams, M., & Reber, A. S. (1988). Implicit learning: Robustness in the face of psychiatric disorders. *Journal of Psycholinguistic Research, 17,* 425–439.

Altmann, G. T. M., Dienes, Z., & Goode, A. (1995). On the modality independence of implicitly acquired grammatical knowledge. *Journal of Experimental Psychology: Learning, Memory, and Cognition, 21,* 899–912.

Amaral, D. G. (1987). Memory: Anatomical organization of candidate brain regions. In J. M. Brookhart & V. B. Mountcastle (Eds.), *Handbook of physiology: The nervous system: Vol. 5. Higher functions of the nervous system* (F. Plum, Vol. Ed., pp. 211–294), Bethesda, MD: American Physiological Society.

Bauer, P. J. (1996). What do infants recall of their lives? Memory for specific events by one- to two-year-olds. *American Psychologist, 51,* 29–41.

Berry, D. C., & Broadbent, D. E. (1994). On the relationship between task performance and associated verbalizable knowledge. *Quarterly Journal of Experimental Psychology, 36,* 209–231.

Berry, D. C., & Broadbent, D. E. (1995). Implicit learning in the context of control systems. In P. Frensch and J. Funke (Eds.), *Complex problem solving* (pp. 131–150). Hillsdale, NJ: Erlbaum.

Berry, D. C., & Dienes, Z. (1993). *Implicit learning: Theoretical and empirical issues.* Hillsdale, NJ: Erlbaum.

Brody, N. (1989). Unconscious learning of rules: Comment of Reber's analysis of implicit learning. *Journal of Experimental Psychology: General, 118,* 236–238.

Brooks, L. R. (1978). Nonanalytic concept formation and memory for instances. In E. Rosch and B. B. Lloyd (Eds.), *Cognition and categorization.* New York: Wiley.

Brooks, L. R., & Vokey, J. R. (1991). Abstract analogies and abstracted grammars: Comments on Reber (1989) and Mathews et al. (1989). *Journal of Experimental Psychology: General, 120,* 316–323.

Cherry, K. E., & Stadler, M. E. (1995). Implicit learning of a nonverbal sequence in younger and older adults. *Psychology and Aging, 10,* 379–394.

Claparède, E. (1951). Recognition and "me-ness." In D. Rapaport (Ed.), *Organization and pathology of thought* (pp. 58–75). New York: Columbia University Press. (Original work published 1911.)

Cleeremans, A. (1993). *Mechanisms of implicit learning: Connectionist models of sequence processing.* Cambridge, MA:MIT Press.

Cleeremans, A., & McClelland, J. L. (1991). Learning the structure of event sequences. *Journal of Experimental Psychology: General, 120,* 235–253.

Cohen, N. J., Ivry, R., & Keele, S. W. (1990). Attention and structure in sequence learning. *Journal of Experimental Psychology: Learning, Memory, and Cognition, 16,* 17–30.

DeCasper, A. J., & Fifer, W. P. (1980). Of human bonding: Newborns prefer their mothers' voices. *Science, 208,* 1174–1176.

Dennett, D. D. (1987). Consciousness. In G. L. Gregory (Ed.), *The Oxford companion to the mind* (pp. 161–164). New York: Oxford University Press.

Dienes, Z. (1992). Connectionist and memory array models of artificial grammar learning. *Cognitive Science, 16,* 41–79.

Dienes, Z., Altmann, G. T. M., & Gao, S.-J. (1995). Mapping across domains without feedback: A neural network model of transfer of implicit knowledge. In L. S. Smith & P. J. B. Hancock (Eds.), *Neural computation and psychology* (pp. 19–33). Springer-Verlag.

Dienes, Z., & Berry, D. C. (1997). Implicit learning: Below the subjective threshold. *Psychonomic Bulletin and Review, 4,* 3–32.

Druhan, B., & Mathews, R. (1989). THYIOS: A classifier system model of implicit knowledge of artificial grammars. *Proceedings of the 11th Annual Conference of the Cognitive Science Society.* Hillsdale, NJ: Erlbaum.

Dulany, D. E. (1991). Conscious representation and thought systems. In R. S. Wyer Jr. & T. K. Srull (Eds.). *Advances in social cognition* (Vol. 4). Hillsdale, NJ: Erlbaum.

Dulany, D. E. (1997). Consciousness in the explicit (deliberative) and implicit (evocative) senses. In J. Cohen and J. Schooler (Eds.), *The problem of consciousness.* Hillsdale, NJ: Erlbaum.

Dulany, D. E., Carlson, R. A., & Dewey, G. I. (1984). A case of syntactical learning and judgment: How conscious and how abstract? *Journal of Experimental Psychology: General, 113,* 541–555.

Eichenbaum, H., Mathews, P., & Cohen, N. J. (1989). Further studies of hippocampal representation during odor discrimination learning. *Behavioral Neuroscience, 103,* 1207–1216.

Eichenbaum, H., Stewart, C., & Morris, R. G. M. (1990). Hippocampal representation in place learning. *Journal of Neuroscience, 10,* 3531–3542.

Elman, J. (1990). Finding structure in time. *Cognitive Science, 14,* 179–211.

Frensch, P. A., Buchner, A., & Lin, J. (1994). Implicit learning of unique and ambiguous serial transitions in the presence and absence of a distracter task. *Journal of Experimental Psychology: Learning, Memory, and Cognition, 20,* 567–584.

Frensch, P. A., & Miner, C. S. (1994). Effects of presentation rate and individual differences in short-term memory capacity on an indirect measure of serial learning. *Memory and Cognition, 22,* 95–110.

Glisky, E. L., Schacter, D. L., & Tulving, E. (1986). Computer learning by memory-impaired patients: Acquisition and retention of complex knowledge. *Neuropsychologia, 24,* 313–328.

Gomez, R. L., & Schvaneveldt, R. W. (1994). What is learned from artificial grammars? Transfer tests of simple association. *Journal of Experimental Psychology: Learning, Memory, and Cognition, 20,* 396–410.

Gordon, P. C., & Holyoak, K. J. (1983). Implicit learning and generalization of the "mere exposure" effect. *Journal of Personality and Social Psychology, 45,* 492–500.

Grafton, S. T., Hazeltine, E., Ivry, R. (1995). Functional mapping of sequence learning in normal humans. *Journal of Cognitive Neuroscience, 7,* 497–510.

Green, R., & Shanks, D. (1993). On the existence of independent explicit and implicit learning systems: An examination of some evidence. *Memory & Cognition, 21,* 304–317.

Griffin, D. R. (1981). *The question of animal awareness: Evolutionary continuity of mental experience.* New York: Rockefeller University Press.

Hasher, L., & Zacks, R. T. (1984). Automatic processing of fundamental information. *American Psychologist, 39,* 1372–1388.

Hayes, N. A., & Broadbent, D. E. (1988). Two modes of learning for interactive tasks. *Cognition, 28,* 249–276.

Howard, D. V., & Howard, J. H. (1989). Age differences in learning serial patterns: Direct vs. indirect measures. *Psychology and Aging, 4,* 357–364.

Howard, D. V., & Howard, J. H. (1992). Adult age differences in the rate of learning serial patterns: Evidence form direct and indirect tests. *Psychology and Aging, 7,* 232–241.

Howard, J. H., & Ballas, J. A. (1980). Syntactic and semantic factors in the classification of nonspeech transient patterns. *Perception and Psychophysics, 28,* 431–439.

Hsiao, A., & Reber, A. S. (1996, November). *The role of attention in the SRT task.* Paper presented at the Meetings of the Psychonomic Society, Chicago.

Hsiao, A., & Reber, A. S. (1998). The role of attention in implicit sequence learning: Theories, findings, and methodological issues. In M. S. Stadler & P. A. Frensch (Eds.), *Handbook of Implicit learning* (pp. 471–494). Thousand Oaks, CA: Sage.

Jackson, G. M., Jackson, S. R., Harrison, J., Henderson, L., & Kennard, C. (1995). Serial reaction time learning and Parkinson's disease: Evidence for a procedural learning deficit. *Neuropsychologia, 33,* 577–593.

Jiménez, L., Méndez, G., & Cleeremans, A. (1996). Comparing direct and indirect measures of sequence learning. *Journal of Experimental Psychology: Learning, Memory, and cognition, 22,*

Johnson, S. P. (1996). *Young infants' perception of object unity: Implications for development of attentional and cognitive skills.* Manuscript submitted for publication.

Johnson, S. P., & Nañez, J. E. (1995). Young infants' perception of object unity in two-dimensional displays. *Infant Behavior and Development, 18,* 133–143.

Karmiloff-Smith, A. (1992). *Beyond modularity: A developmental perspective on cognitive science.* Cambridge, MA: MIT Press.

Kassin, S., & Reber, A. S. (1979). Locus of control and the learning of an artificial language. *Journal of Research in Personality, 13,* 111–118.

Kihlstrom, J. F. (1990). The psychological unconscious. In L. A. Pervin (Ed.), *Handbook of Personality: Theory and research* (pp. 445–464). New York: Guilford.

Knopman, D. S. (1991). Unaware learning versus preserved learning in pharmacologic amnesia: Similarities and differences. *Journal of Experimental Psychology: Learning, Memory, and Cognition, 17,* 1017–1029.

Knopman, D. S., & Nissen, M. J. (1987). Implicit learning in patients with probable Alzheimer's disease. *Neurology, 37,* 784–788.

Knowlton, B. J., Ramus, S. J., & Squire, L. R. (1992). Intact artificial grammar learning in amnesia: Dissociation of abstract knowledge and memory for specific instances. *Psychological Science, 3,* 172–179.

Knowlton, B. J., & Squire, L. R. (1993). The learning of natural categories: parallel memory systems for item memory and category-level knowledge *Science, 262,* 1747–1749.

Knowlton, B. J., & Squire, L. R. (1994). The information acquired during artificial grammar learning. *Journal of Experimental Psychology: Learning, Memory, and Cognition, 20,* 79–91.

Knowlton, B. J., & Squire, L. R. (1996). Artificial grammar learning depends on implicit acquisition of both abstract and exemplar-specific information. *Journal of Experimental Psychology: Learning, Memory, and Cognition, 22,* 169–181.

Knowlton, B. J., Squire, L. R., & Gluck, M. A. (1994). Probabilistic classification learning in amnesia. *Learning & Memory, 1,* 106–120.

Knowlton, B. J., Squire, L. R., Paulsen, J. S., Swerdlow, N., Swenson, M., & Butters, N. (1996). Dissociations within nondeclarative memory in Huntington's disease. *Neuropsychology, 10,* 538–548.

Kunst-Wilson, W. R., & Zajonc, R. B. (1980). Affective discrimination of stimuli that cannot be recognized. *Science, 207,* 557–558.

Kushner, M., Cleeremans, A., & Reber, A. S. (1991). Implicit detection of event interdependencies and a PDP model of the process. In *Proceedings of the Thirteenth Annual Conference of the Cognitive Science Society* (pp. 215–220). Hillsdale, NJ: Erlbaum.

Lewicki, P., Czyzewska, M., & Hoffman, H. (1987). Unconscious acquisition of complex procedural knowledge. *Journal of Experimental Psychology: Learning, Memory, and Cognition, 13,* 523–530.

Manza, L., & Bornstein, R. F. (1995). Affective discrimination and the implicit learning process. *Consciousness and Cognition, 4,* 399–409.

Manza, L., & Reber, A. S. (1997). Representation of tacit knowledge: Transfer across stimulus forms and modalities. In D. C. Berry (Ed.). *How implicit is implicit learning?* New York: Oxford University Press. (pp. 73–106).

Manza, L., & Skypala, D. (1996). *Interdependence and implicit and explicit knowledge systems.* Unpublished manuscript.

Manza, L., Zizak, D., & Reber, A. S. (1998). Emotional preference tasks and the implicit learning process. In M. S. Stadler & P. A. Frensch (Eds.), *Handbook of Implicit learning.* Thousand Oaks, CA: Sage. (pp. 201–222).

Masters, R. S. W. (1992). Knowledge, knerves, and know-how: The role of explicit versus implicit knowledge in the breakdown of a complex motor skill under pressure. *British Journal of Psychology, 83,* 343–358.

Mathews, R. C., Buss, R. R., Stanley, W. B., Blanchard-Fields, F., Cho, J.-R., & Druhan, B. (1989). The role of implicit and explicit processes in learning from examples: A synergistic effect. *Journal of Experimental Psychology: Learning, Memory, and Cognition, 15,* 1083–1100.

Mathews, R. C., & Roussel, L. G. (1997). Abstractness of implicit knowledge: A cognitive evolutionary perspective (pp. 13–47). In D. C. Berry (Ed.), *How implicit is implicit learning?* NY: Oxford University Press.

Mayberry, M., Taylor, M., & O'Brien-Malone, A. (1995). Implicit learning: Sensitive to age but not IQ. *Australian Journal of Psychology, 47,* 8–17.

McGeorge, P., Crawford, J. R., & Kelly, S. W. (1997). The relationships between psychometric intelligence and learning in an explicit and implicit task. *Journal of Experimental Psychology: Learning, Memory and Cognition, 23,* 239–245.

Millward, R. B., & Reber, A. S. (1972). Probability learning: Contingent-event sequences with lags. *American Journal of Psychology, 85,* 81–98.

Moon, C., & Fifer, W. P. (1990). Syllables as signals for 2-day-old infants. *Infant Behavior and Development, 13,* 377–390.

Nissen, M. J., & Bullemer, P. (1987). Attentional requirements of learning: Evidence from performance measures. *Cognitive Psychology, 19,* 1–32.

Packard, M. G., Hirsch, R., & White, N. M. (1989). Differential effects of fornix and caudate nucleus lesions on two radial maze tasks: Evidence for multiple memory systems. *Journal of Neuroscience, 9,* 1465–1472.

Parkin, A. J., & Streete, S. (1988). Implicit and explicit memory in young children and adults. *British Journal of Psychology, 79,* 361–369.

Pascual-Leone, A., Grafman, J., Clark, K. Stewart, M., Massaquoi, S., Lou, J.-S., & Hallett, M. (1993). Procedural learning in Parkinson's disease and cerebellar degeneration. *Annals of Neurology, 34,* 594–602.

Perruchet, P. (1994). Defining the units of a synthetic language: Comments on Vokey and Brooks (1992). *Journal of Experimental Psychology: Learning, Memory, and Cognition, 20,* 223–228.

Perruchet, P., & Amorim, M. (1992). Conscious knowledge and changes in performance in sequence learning: Evidence against dissociation. *Journal of Experimental Psychology: Learning, Memory, and Cognition, 18,* 785–800.

Perruchet, P., Gallego, J., & Savy, I. (1990). A critical reappraisal of the evidence for unconscious abstraction of deterministic rules in complex experimental situations. *Cognitive Psychology, 22,* 493–516.

Perruchet, P., & Pacteau, C. (1990). Synthetic grammar learning: Implicit rule abstraction or explicit fragmentary knowledge? *Journal of Experimental Psychology: General, 119,* 264–275.

Perruchet, P., & Pacteau, C. (1991). Implicit acquisition of abstract knowledge about artificial grammars: Some methodological and conceptual issues. *Journal of Experimental Psychology: General, 120,* 112–116.

Pew, R. W. (1974). Levels of analysis in motor control. *Brain Research, 71,* 393–400.

Piaget, J. (1976). *The grasp of consciousness: Action and concept in the young child.* Cambridge, MA: Harvard University Press. (Original work published 1974.)

Piaget, J. (1977). *The origins of intelligence in the child.* London: Penguin. (Original work published 1936.).

Polanyi, M. (1966). *The tacit dimension.* Garden City, NJ: Doubleday.

Posner, M. I., & Keele, S. W. (1968). On the genesis of abstract ideas. *Journal of Experimental Psychology, 77,* 353–363.

Rathus, J., Reber, A. S., Manza, L., & Kushner, M. (1994). Implicit and explicit learning: Differential effects of affective states. *Perceptual and Motor Skills, 79,* 163–184.

Rauch, S. L., Savage, C. R., Brown, H. D., Curran, T., Alpert, N. M., Kendrick, A., Fischman, A. J., & Kosslyn, S. M. (1995). A PET investigation of implicit and explicit sequence learning. *Human Brain Mapping, 3,* 271–286.

Reber, A. S. (1967). Implicit learning of artificial grammars. *Journal of Verbal Learning and Verbal Behavior, 77,* 317–327.

Reber, A. S. (1969). Transfer of syntactic structure in synthetic languages. *Journal of Experimental Psychology, 81,* 115–119.

Reber, A. S. (1976). Implicit learning of synthetic languages: The role of instructional set. *Journal of Experimental Psychology: Human Learning and Memory, 2,* 88–94.

Reber, A. S. (1992). The cognitive unconscious: An evolutionary perspective. *Consciousness and Cognition, 1,* 93–133.

Reber, A. S. (1993a). Personal knowledge and the cognitive unconscious. *Polanyiana, 3,* 97–115.

Reber, A. S. (1993b). *Implicit learning and tacit knowledge: An essay on the cognitive unconscious.* New York: Oxford University Press.

Reber, A. S. (1997). How to differentiate implicit from explicit learning. In J. Cohen and J. Schooler (Eds.), *The problem of consciousness.* Hillsdale, NJ: Erlbaum.

Reber, A. S., & Allen, R. (1978). Analogy and abstraction strategies in synthetic grammar learning: A functionalist interpretation. *Cognition, 6,* 189–221.

Reber, A. S., & Lewis, S. (1997). Toward a theory of implicit learning: The analysis of the form and structure of a body of tacit knowledge. *Cognition, 5,* 333–361.

Reber, A. S., & Millward, R. B. (1968). Event observation in probability learning. *Journal of Experimental Psychology, 77,* 317–327.

Reber, A. S., Walkenfeld, F. F., & Hernstadt, R. (1991). Implicit and explicit learning: Individual differences and IQ. *Journal of Experimental Psychology: Learning, Memory, and Cognition, 17,* 888–896.

Reber, P. J., Knowlton, B. J., & Squire, L. R. (1996). Dissociable properties of memory systems: Differences in the flexibility of declarative and nondeclarative knowledge. *Behavioral Neuroscience, 110,* 861–871.

Reber, P. J., & Squire, L. R. (1994). Parallel brain systems for learning with and without awareness. *Learning & Memory, 1,* 217–229.

Reed, J., & Johnson, P. (1994). Assessing implicit learning with indirect tests: Determining what is learned about sequence structure. *Journal of Experimental Psychology: Learning, Memory, and Cognition, 20,* 585–594.

Rovee-Collier, C. (1990). The "memory system" of prelinguistic infants. *Annals of the New York Academy of Sciences, 608,* 517–542.

Sanderson, P. M. (1989). Verbalizable knowledge and skilled task performance: Association, dissociation, and mental models. *Journal of Experimental Psychology: Learning, Memory, and Cognition, 15,* 729–747.

Schacter, D. L., Chiu, C.-Y. P., & Ochsner, K. N. (1993). Implicit memory: A selective review. *Annual Review of Neuroscience, 16,* 159–182.

Schacter, D. L., & Graf, P. (1986). Preserved memory in amnesic patients: Perspectives from research on direct priming. *Journal of Clinical and Experimental Neuropsychology, 8,* 727–743.

Scoville, W. B., & Milner, B. (1957). Loss of recent memory after bilateral hippocampal lesions. *Journal of Neurology, Neurosurgery and Psychiatry, 20,* 11–21.

Seger, C. A. (1994). Implicit learning. *Psychological Bulletin, 115,* 163–196.

Servan-Schreiber, E., & Anderson, J. R. (1990). Learning artificial grammars with competitive chunking. *Journal of Experimental Psychology: Learning, Memory, and Cognition, 16,* 592–608.

Shanks, D. R., Johnstone, T., & Staggs, L. (1997). Abstraction processes in artificial grammar learning. *Quarterly Journal of Experimental Psychology, 50A,* 216–252.

Shanks, D. R., & St. John, M. F. (1994). Characteristics of dissociable human learning systems. *Behavioral and Brain Sciences, 17,* 367–448.

Shimamura, A. P. (1993). Neuropsychological analyses of implicit memory: History, methodology and theoretical interpretations. In P. Graf and M. E. J. Masson (Eds.), *Implicit memory: New directions in cognition, development, and neuropsychology.* (pp. 265–285) Hillsdale, NJ: Earlbaum.

Squire, L. R. (1992). Memory and the hippocampus: A synthesis of findings with rats, monkeys and humans. *Psychological Review, 99,* 195–231.

Squire, L. R., Ojeman, J. G., Miezin, F. M., Peterson, S. E., Videen, T. O., & Raichle, M. E. (1992). Activation of the hippocampus in normal humans: A functional anatomical study of memory. *Proceedings of the National Academy of Science, 89,* 1837–1841.

Stanley, W. B., Mathews, R. C., Buss, R. R., & Kotler-Cope, S. (1989). Insight without awareness: On the interaction of verbalization, instruction and practice in a simulated process control task. *Quarterly Journal of Experimental Psychology, 41*, 553–578.

Thompson, R. F. (1990). Neural mechanisms of classical conditioning in mammals. *Philosophical Transactions of the Royal Society of London: Biology, 329*, 161–170.

Ungerleider, L. G. (1995). Functional brain imaging studies of cortical mechanisms for memory *Science, 270*, 769–775.

Vokey, J. R., & Brooks, L. R. (1992). Salience of item knowledge in learning artificial grammars. *Journal of Experimental Psychology: Learning, Memory, and Cognition, 18*, 328–344.

Whittlesea, B. W. A., & Dorken, M. D. (1993). Incidentally, things in general are particularly determined: An episodic-processing account of implicit learning. *Journal of Experimental Psychology: General, 122*, 227–248.

Willingham, D. B., Greeley, T., & Bardone, A. M. (1993). Dissociation in a serial response time task using a recognition measure: Comment on Perruchet and Amorim (1992). *Journal of Experimental Psychology: Learning, Memory, and Cognition, 19*, 1424–1430.

Willingham, D. B., & Koroshetz, W. J. (1993). Evidence for dissociable motor skills in Huntington's disease patients. *Psychobiology, 21*, 173–182.

Winter, B. (1995). *Implicit and explicit cognitive functioning in hippocampal amnesia.* Unpublished doctoral, City University of New York.

Wulf, G., Lee, T. D., & Schmidt, R. A. (1994). Reducing knowledge of results about relative versus absolute timing: Differential effects on learning. *Journal of Motor Behavior, 26*, 362–369.

Wulf, G., & Schmidt, R. A. (1997). Variability of practice and implicit motor learning. *Journal of Experimental Psychology: Learning, Memory, and Cognition, 23*, 987–1006.

Zizak, D., & Reber, A. S. (1994, October). *Implicit preferences for novel stimuli.* Paper presented at the meeting of Association for Consumer Research, Boston.

15

Multi-Store versus Dynamic Models of Temporary Storage in Memory

Randall W. Engle and Natalie Oransky

The concept of short-term memory as a distinct type of memory has now become part of our cultural common knowledge. Evidence the Tom Hanks character Mr. Short-Term Memory on the NBC television show *Saturday Night Live*. Mr. STM has good retention of very recent events, but that information is quickly lost and he shows no evidence of long-term retention. However, there has been strong debate throughout the entire era of modern memory research about whether memory for recent events and long-term retention obey different principles. Proponents of multiple memory stores suggest that different memory structures yield distinct memory traces. It seems intuitive that we have several types of memory (e.g., memories that are short lived and others that last for a very long time), but some theorists argue that it is not necessary to posit separate structures to explain different memory traces. According to this unitary approach to memory, differences between memories occur not because they are stored in separate systems, but because of the different processes and modes of representation used to perceive or think about events when they occur. Although the issue of whether or not memory is composed of stages or components is prevalent throughout the memory literature (e.g., implicit and explicit memory; see Roediger, 1990, and Schacter, 1987); this chapter will focus on the contribution of these opposing views to the development of the construct of short-term memory and its younger relative, *working memory*.

In this chapter, we will present a rather cursory history of the ideas about short-term memory along with some of the research findings that were presented to support or refute those ideas. The literature on short-term memory was an important part of the experimental psychology of human memory in the 1960s and early '70s. Early research focused on the nature of forgetting and whether forgetting from short-term memory is a result of decay, displacement, or some other mechanism different from those thought to mediate forgetting from long-term memory. One of the stronger proposals about short-term memory from the earliest theories (e.g., Hebb, 1949) was that the strength of a trace in long-term memory is a function of how long the information is retained in short-term memory. We will see in a discussion of transfer of information to long-term memory that that proposal is quite wrong. Early research also suggested that short-term memory is characterized by a speech-based code, whereas long-term memory is characterized by meaning-based codes. That idea also is likely wrong. These concerns gave rise to a disenchantment with the concept of short-term memory. But the seminal paper by Baddeley and Hitch (1974), along with new ideas in neo-Piagetian approaches to developmental psychology (Pascal-Leone, 1970) and brain-based approaches to memory, led to a renascence that makes working memory one of the core topics in cognitive and developmental psychology today.

Multi-Store Model

The information-processing model proposed by Atkinson and Shiffrin (1968) represents a prototypical multi-store approach to memory. This model distinguished between sensory, short-term, and long-term stores, and it suggested that information is processed through these structurally and functionally independent stages. At the completion of each stage, products are copied to the next stage for further processing. Atkinson and Shiffrin's model combined the attentional system and the temporary storage component of Broadbent's (1958) seminal model into one limited capacity, short-term storage system. Their *short-term store* (STS) has a limited number of slots for holding information,[1] and this information decays rapidly if it is not maintained by control processes such as rehearsal. Support for multi-store models came from data showing differences between the characteristics of the proposed memory systems. For example, Atkinson and Shiffrin characterized STS as having a limited capacity, using primarily verbal codes, and losing information due to decay. In contrast, *long-term store* (LTS) was characterized as having a large capacity, primarily semantic coding, and losing information via interference.

Forgetting

It is difficult to understand the impetus for much of the early work on STS unless you understand that many of the putative characteristics of short-term memory arise from a theory about the physiology of the memory trace put forth by Hebb (1949). Hebb proposed that if two events occur in close proximity to one another, the neural circuits corresponding to those events are active at the same time, and new connections, called *reverberatory traces,* are formed between those two circuits. If given enough uninterrupted time, this new connection will consolidate and become a relatively permanent structural trace. Other events can, however, prevent the consolidation of the new trace so that the connection is lost, or more appropriately, never formed. Hebb envisioned that reverberatory traces and consolidated structural traces are qualitatively different states. The reverberatory trace is time limited and capable of *displacement* by new events. Neither of these traits are true of the long-term structural traces. There was relatively little evidence to support Hebb's ideas at the time and his book was rarely cited in the short-term memory literature that followed, but the influence of those ideas is obvious.[2]

Following Hebb's theory, it is not surprising that the dominant issue in early research on the STS focused on forgetting. Proponents of multi-store approaches demonstrated differences in the mechanisms of information loss from STS and LTS. They suggested that information loss from STS results from one of two types of limitations: temporal persistence and capacity limitations. Some theorists argued that there are limits in *how long* information could be held in STS Brown, 1958; Conrad, 1957; Hebb, 1949; Peterson & Peterson, 1959). That is, if information is not rehearsed, it decays, or fades. Others suggested that there is a limit in the *number* of items that can be held in STS at a given moment and that information is lost because new information replaces or bumps old information out of STS (e.g., James, 1890; Miller, 1956; Waugh & Norman, 1965). Both of these mechanisms of forgetting, time limits and capacity limits, were distinguished from mechanisms proposed to account for long-term forgetting. More specifically, most researchers agreed that information in LTS is long lasting and is lost temporarily through proactive or retroactive interference affecting retrieval rather than through decay or replacement (McGeoch, 1932; Melton & Irwin, 1940; Postman, Stark, & Fraser, 1968).

Brown (1958) and Peterson and Peterson (1959) argued for decay from STS based on the findings that when subjects are prevented from rehearsing, recall quickly declines over the delay. In the Peterson and Peterson experiments, subjects saw trigrams and tried to recall them after a delay period filled with a rehearsal-preventative task requiring backward counting from a number. Recall accuracy of the trigrams dropped dramatically over filled delays of 18 seconds, suggesting that without rehearsal, information in STS is short lived and relatively transient and cannot be transferred to LTS. The rehearsal-preventative task involved numbers, so according to traditional interference theory (McGeoch, 1932), there should not have been material-specific interference for the letters or words in such a task. Further, Peterson and Peterson argued that proactive interference across trials did not occur in their short-term memory task. That is, early trials did not block the retrieval of items on later trials. The rate of forgetting was the same for the first block of 10 trials as for those blocks tested later. However, Keppel and Underwood (1962) showed that the build-up of proactive interference in the Peterson and Peterson task was rapid and quickly reached asymptote within the first 2 to 3 trials of the experiment. Peterson and Peterson had masked this interference by looking only at blocks of 10 trials. These and other results showing interference as a factor in forgetting in short-term memory tasks (e.g., Hebb, 1961; Murdock, 1961) led Melton (1963) to suggest that all memory traces, whether formed 5 seconds ago or 5 years ago, share the same characteristics: namely, they are stable, permanent traces that are susceptible to interference from other traces during retrieval. Speaking to Hebb's reverberatory trace idea, Melton argued for "the fixation of a structural trace by a single repetition of an event without the benefit of autonomous consolidation processes" (p. 19).

Waugh and Norman (1965) used a digit probe task to examine both decay and interference as factors in the loss of information from STS. Subjects heard digits presented at either a one-per-second or a four-per-second rate. At the end of a series of digits, subjects received a probe digit and recalled the digit that had occurred just prior to the probe in the digit series. The number of items intervening between the probe digit and the end of the list was manipulated. Waugh and Norman reasoned that if decay causes forgetting, then recall in the one-item-per-second condition should be worse than recall in the four-items-per-second condition because more time will have elapsed between the presentation of the target and recall. On the other hand, if forgetting is the result of capacity limits, recall of the target digit should be a function of the number of intervening items regardless of presentation rate. Waugh and Norman showed that recall is affected by the number of intervening items and not presentation rate, suggesting that displacement is the critical factor in STS forgetting. Waugh and Norman proposed that STS holds a limited amount of information and once the limit is reached, new information displaces old information, causing old information to be permanently lost. In addition, Waugh and Norman showed that when reinterpreted within their framework, data from other short-term memory tasks (e.g., immediate free recall) support a capacity/displacement interpretation of STS forgetting. This view is consistent with Miller's (1956) conception of STS as containing a fixed number of 7 ± 2 slots or bins for holding information. Thus, Waugh and Norman argued that memory traces in STS are transient because of capacity limitations. However, these traces can be maintained indefinitely in STS and copied to LTS through rehearsal.

Perhaps the most careful analysis of this issue was in two papers by Reitman (1971, 1974). She painstakingly prevented rehearsal over the 15-second filled delay, avoided a ceiling effect for the initial trials she used a task similar to that used by Brown (1958) and Peterson and Peterson (1959) in which each trial presented items for recall followed by a delay before recall,[3] and manipulated the nature of the rehearsal-preventative task, with one task being a tone detection task and the other being a syllable detection task. In the nonverbal but attention-demanding tone detection task, there was a 12% decline in recall, which Reitman attributed to decay. However, the syllable detection task led to a 56% loss in recall. She argued that the predominant cause of forgetting from short-term memory is interference through displacement but that there is evidence also for decay. Thus, there is evidence favoring both time limits and capacity limits as mechanisms for forgetting in STS.

More recent findings also suggest a role for a time-based loss of information. Baddeley, Thomson, and Buchanan (1975) showed that the number of words recalled in a task in which a short list of words list presented for recall in correct serial order depended on the spoken duration of the words in the list, suggesting that time limits are an important component of STS. On the other hand, Glanzer and Razel (1974) found that subjects recalled approximately the same number of items in a STM task regardless of the length of the items (words vs idioms), supporting STS capacity limits. One reason for these contradictory findings may be the use of different tasks. Baddeley, Thomson, et al. (1975) used serial recall of short lists of words that were from a small pool of items sampled with replacement. Glanzer and Razel used the immediate free-recall task in which subjects recalled longer lists of words selected without replacement, so words were never repeated across lists. Time limits may be most important when rote rehearsal processes are used to maintain information: However, when such strategies are less useful, a limitation based on the number of items being represented may be more important.

Transfer of Information to Long-Term Store

In multi-store models, one of the primary functions of STS is to hold information until it can be represented in a more permanent state. Because rehearsal was assumed to be the critical mechanism for this transfer, many researchers attempted to distinguish between STS and LTS by examining the relationship between rehearsal and long-term retention. One line of evidence suggesting that the formation of permanent memory traces depends on rehearsal of information in STS came from the U-shaped immediate free-recall curve (Glanzer & Cunitz, 1966). Typically, recall of the first few items from a list is very high compared to items that occur in the middle of the list. This finding is known as the primacy effect. Glanzer and Cunitz believed that primacy reflects the effect of rehearsal, and studies show that initial items do receive more rehearsal than items from other positions in the list (Rundus & Atkinson, 1970). Recall of the last few items from a list is also very high, even though those items do not receive many rehearsals.

Glanzer and Cunitz argued that this recency effect occurs because the last items have not yet decayed from STS and, therefore, are easily retrieved. In an attempt to show that the recency effect reflects short-term storage, they manipulated the delay between the presentation of the list and the recall of list items. During the delay, subjects counted aloud from a target number until they received a cue indicating that they should recall the items. As expected, this delay reduced the recency portion of the curve and left primacy unaffected. As we will see, however, performance on the recency portion of the immediate free-recall curve[4] does not seem to have any relationship to other measures of short-term memory, so it may not be a *valid* reflection of short-term memory.

Coding

Another distinction between STS and LTS, made by structural theorists, involved the type of coding used in each store. Early evidence suggested that information in STS is coded phonologically,[5] whereas information in LTS is coded semantically. Again, such a dissociation between the two systems supports the existence of two distinct memory structures. For example, in a memory span task, subjects recalled fewer letters when lists were made up of phonologically similar letters (e.g., C, B, G, V, T, P) as compared with lists of phonologically dissimilar letters (e.g., F, J, M, R, L, Y; Conrad & Hull, 1964). Errors made on similar lists are typically phonological confusions (e.g., responding with B rather that D), suggesting that items are coded by their sound even if they are presented visually. Although the phonological similarity effect supports the use of phonological codes in STS, it does not address whether or not semantic, or any other types of coding, can also be used in STS. Baddeley (1966) presented similar and dissimilar lists to subjects for serial recall, but in his study some lists included either phonologically similar or dissimilar words, whereas others included either semantically similar or dissimilar words. Phonological similarity decreased recall performance, but semantic similarity only slightly affected recall performance.

Kintsch and Buschke (1969) used a serial probe task similar to the one used by Waugh and Norman (1965). They found that phonological similarity affected recall for targets at the end of the list (putatively items in STS), but not at the beginning of the list (items in LTS). Further, semantic similarity reduced recall of targets at the beginning of the list, but not at the end of the list. If the recency portion of the list reflects information in STS and the primacy portion reflects information that has been stored in LTS, as already described (Glanzer and Cunitz, 1966), then finding phonemic similarity effects at the end of the list and semantic similarity effects at the beginning of the list supports differential coding and the dual-store approach. That does not mean that all temporary traces, however, are necessarily coded in the same format. It is likely that different tasks used to study human memory encourage or force the use of different codes to represent the information.

Neuropsychological Evidence

In addition to the behavioral data, neuropsychological case studies provided converging evidence for multi-store models. The well-known case of HM suggested that different brain areas may underlie the functioning of proposed memory stores, and thus it supported a multi-store system (Milner, 1966).[6] HM showed normal performance on short-term memory tasks and good recall of events that occurred prior to his surgery. The deficit was clearly in the storage of information in the long-term store. Shallice and Warrington (1970) presented the case of a subject who appeared to be the complement of HM. Their patient showed impaired performance on short-term memory tasks and normal performance on long-term memory tasks. Baddeley and Warrington (1970) compared patients with Korsakoff's syndrome (amnesia resulting from chronic alcoholism) to normal subjects on a variety of short-term and long-term memory tasks. The amnesics showed normal forgetting on the Brown-Peterson task and normal recency in free recall but reduced primacy as compared to control subjects.[7] Together, these results suggested that two separate memory structures, in fact, exist and that performance on short and long-term memory tasks are mediated by different brain areas.

There is now strong evidence that the hippocampus is involved in the temporary storage of information and that bilateral removal of the hippocampus, as in HM, leads to reduced ability to recall information presented more than a few minutes earlier (Kolb & Whishaw, 1990). This reduced ability to store information so that it can be easily retrieved later appears to be specific to what some theorists refer to as *explicit memory.*

HM, for example, learned the backward mirror-tracing task and retained the ability from day to day. Thus, although the research on the hippocampus supports a multi-store approach, it also suggests that the ideas hold for only certain kinds of representations or types of retention test.

Problems with the Multi-Store Model

Support for multiple memory structures based on both behavioral and neuropsychological dissociations seemed fairly strong; STS and LTS appeared to have distinctly different characteristics. However, a great deal of criticism surrounds research that distinguished the characteristics of short-and long-term memory as well as some of the basic features of the multi-store model (cf., Crowder, 1983, 1993). Crowder argued that in postulating distinct memory stores, multiple-memory approaches typically confounds codes and processes.[8] More specifically, he suggested that the distinction between STS and LTS may simply be a distinction between phonetic coding and semantic coding. These codes may be used in different tasks and may affect characteristics of retention, but it is not necessary to hypothesize that different processing systems are involved. In support of this idea, Crowder suggested that characteristics that appear to be unique to STS can be accounted for within a unitary memory framework. For example, as previously discussed, forgetting in the Brown-Peterson task may depend on interference and not on a decay mechanism (Keppel & Underwood, 1962). Similarly, the recency effect found for immediate free recall is also found in long-term memory tasks (Bjork & Whitten, 1974), as is the phonemic similarity effect (Gregg & Gardiner, 1984).

An elaboration on Crowder's point is that much of the early work on STS and, indeed, more recent work on the articulatory loop, made use of a procedure in which subjects were presented a short list of words or letters for serial recall. Further, the list items were generally selected from a small pool of items with replacement from list to list. It is likely that procedures such as the immediate free recall of 12- to 15-item lists in which the items are never repeated gives rise to very different coding and processing. Thus, it is difficult to know how generalizable results are from one task to another, even though both are putative short-term memory tasks.[9] We will further discuss *measurement* aspects of short-term memory in a later section.

Another problem with the multi-store model is the assumption of serial processing through the different stages. First, serial ordering from STS to LTS does not make logical sense. Information is supposed to be held in STS before making contact with LTS, but how can that information be identified without relying on LTS? If you present me with the word *dog* as one item in a list to recall, I certainly recognize the word and have associations with its meaning soon after I see or hear it. Therefore, it must have led to access of some trace in the LTS prior to maintenance in STS. In addition, Shallice and Warrington (1970) pointed out that case studies of patients who have STS deficits without LTS impairments are inconsistent with the serial processing through STS and then LTS. If these processing stages are serial, then deficits in STS should also lead to deficits in LTS because long-term storage is supposed to be dependent on processing information through STS. To circumvent this problem, Shallice and Warrington suggested that information makes contact with STS and LTS in parallel. Most modern theories of short- and long-term memory have eliminated the assumption of serial processing through different stages and assume that STS is a more highly activated subset of knowledge units in LTS.

Further, it is important to think about what really is being learned in a short-term memory task. What is retained in STS is not my knowledge about *dog* but that *dog* was on the list I just saw or heard, that it was near the middle of the list, that it followed the word *table,* and that it, in turn, was followed by the word *aardvark.* That would be the knowledge transferred to LTS or learned through appropriate coding or rehearsal. Correspondingly, that is the knowledge that would be lost either through decay, or interference according to more recent multi-store theories.

Finally, one of the biggest concerns about the multi-store model involved the assertion that strength of the representation in long-term memory is a function of the amount of rehearsal in STS. Rundus and Atkinson (1970) did show that immediate recall is a function of the number of rehearsals given to an item. However, other studies showed that delayed recall of information is not a function of the amount of simple rote rehearsal. For example, Tulving (1966) found that recall of a list of words was not enhanced when subjects repeated the list aloud six times. Similarly, the results of a study by Craik and Watkins (1973) argued against the idea that time spent in STS determines the transfer of information to LTS. Subjects received a target letter and then heard a list of words. They were to retain in memory the first word that began with the target letter until another word beginning with that letter occurred. At this point, subjects could drop the first word and hold the second word in memory. The task continued in this manner until the end of the list, when subjects reported the last word in the list that began with the target letter. By manipulating the number of words between target words, Craik and Watkins effectively manipulated the amount of time a given word spent in STS. At the end of the experiment, subjects were asked to recall all of the critical words from the experiment. Craik and Watkins found no relationship between time spent in STS and the probability of long-term recall. Because the time spent in STS should reflect the amount of rehearsal an item receives, these studies suggested that rehearsal alone is not sufficient to account for the transfer of information to LTS. Problems with serial processing, rehearsal as a mechanism of information transfer, and questions about the distinctiveness of the two stores all contributed to the decline of the popularity of structural models of memory.

In response to many of the problems with multi-store approaches, Craik and Lockhart (1972) suggested that apparent differences in STS and LTS reflect differences in the processes used to analyze information. For example, differences may result because of differential processing demands for tasks used to examine STS and LTS. According to this approach, the time spent in STS is not the factor that determines the strength of the memory trace. Rather, the *level of processing* may be the critical determinant of long-term storage, with "deeper" processing yielding stronger traces. Inconsistent results found in studies examining the relationship between rehearsal and transfer to LTS, then, may be the result of different types of rehearsal processes.

Although Craik and Lockhart (1972) did not propose the existence of multiple memory systems, they did distinguish between information that is currently in consciousness and that which is not. They assumed that a limited capacity central processor (i.e., controlled attention), which operates to provide the different levels of processing, is responsible for keeping information in consciousness and that information which is in consciousness is easily and accurately retrieved. When attention is

directed away from information currently in consciousness, that information decays and is replaced by new information. Craik and Jacoby (1975)
pointed out that the Craik and Lockhart view is not unlike the STS proposed by many multiple memory theorists (e.g., Atkinson & Shiffrin,
1968; Norman, 1969). The difference between the two approaches is that
Craik and Lockhart did not believe that the properties of stored information depend on the structure in which information is held; nor did they
believe that information is transferred between different stores. Consciousness, or *primary memory,* as Craik and Lockhart prefer to call it,
is not a structure; rather, it is the activation of processes used to analyze
information. Limitations in the amount of information that can be "in"
primary memory are due to attentional processing limitations, not structural limitations. As you will see, this view is similar to the concept of
the central executive proposed by Baddeley and Hitch (1974) and the
idea of working memory capacity proposed by Turner and Engle (1989)
and Just and Carpenter (1992).

Working Memory

A number of intellectual influences served to move thought about short-
term memory to what is now called *working memory.* One of these influences was the resurgence of Piagetian constructs relating temporary storage and controlled attention in the developmental psychology literature.
These are most clearly seen in the work by Pascual-Leone (1970) and
Case (1985), who proposed the notion of *M-space,* which is similar to
what later would be called working memory.

   In the experimental psychology literature, Baddeley and Hitch (1974)
proposed a flexible and more complex temporary storage system that
avoids some of the weaknesses of the multi-store model. A major liability
for the multi-store model is evidence that neuropsychological patients
with STS deficits do not have impaired performance on complex cognitive
tasks (e.g., Shallice and Warrington, 1970; Warrington, Logue, & Pratt,
1971; Warrington & Weiskrantz, 1972). This finding posed a problem
for the multi-store model because STS is viewed as the limiting factor in
the information-processing system, and so STS impairments should lead
to impairments in other types of cognitive processing. In a similar vein,

if STS is the bottleneck in processing, then processing on a task that depends on STS should be less efficient when STS is occupied with another task. Baddeley and Hitch examined this hypothesis in a series of studies that manipulated memory load during complex task performance. They showed that although performance on reasoning and comprehension tasks was not affected by a small memory load of two to three digits, performance on these tasks did decrease with a load of six items. These results led Baddeley and Hitch to propose a system of working memory (WM) consisting of three components (see also, Baddeley, 1986, 1996; Baddeley & Hitch, 1994).[10] Two of these components, the *articulatory loop* and the *visual-spatial sketchpad,* are "slave" systems, and the other is a *central executive*. The slave systems are largely responsible for the maintenance of acoustic and visual information, whereas the central executive is responsible for control of information processing. Baddeley and Hitch argued that WM is a unitary system limited in both storage and processing and that there is some flexibility in the allocation of attention to the components. This flexibility accounts for the results of their studies, which found that articulatory suppression and concurrent memory load interfere with the performance of learning and reasoning tasks, more or less independently, depending on the extent to which the task requires the use of phonological information and the extent to which it requires controlled attention for processing. Similarly, their model can account for neuropsychological case studies of patients who have STS deficits but who do not have serious deficits on many complex cognitive skills, by assuming that these individuals have damage to one of the slave systems rather than to the central executive.

Slave Systems

Most of Baddeley's work has focused on the two slave systems, with the articulatory loop receiving more attention than the sketchpad. As with the early work on STS, examinations of WM first focused on issues of coding, rehearsal, and loss of information. Thus, like early models of STS, the two slave systems represent the more rigid, structural aspects of Baddeley and Hitch's (1974) working memory model.

The articulatory loop most closely resembles earlier conceptions of STS because it consists of a limited duration, speech-based representation and is dependent on articulatory rehearsal for the maintenance of information. As previously described, reduced recall with phonemically similar lists suggests that information held in STS may be coded phonologically (Conrad, 1964; Conrad & Hull, 1964). Baddeley and Hitch suggested that because the articulatory loop is responsible for the temporary storage of verbal information, it is the locus of phonemic similarity effects. Further evidence for speech coding and time limits on the articulatory loop comes from studies showing that word length affects recall. That is, recall in a short-term memory task depends on the time it takes to articulate those words; fewer items from lists of long words are recalled than from lists of short words (e.g., Baddeley, Thomson, et al., 1975; Case, Kurland, & Goldberg, 1982; Ellis & Hennelley, 1980; see also, Cowan et al. 1992; Cowan, Keller, et al. 1994; Cowan, Wood, & Bourne, 1994). Further, the importance of articulatory rehearsal for the maintenance of verbal information is demonstrated by the fact that the phonemic similarity effect and word length effect are eliminated under conditions that prevent rehearsal. For example, both effects are eliminated by articulatory suppression, a procedure in which rehearsal is prevented by having subjects vocalize a sequence (e.g., saying "blah, blah, blah") while completing an immediate recall task. The elimination of the effects by articulatory suppression suggests that these effects are the result of articulatory rehearsal (Baddeley, Lewis, & Vallar, 1984; Baddeley, Thomson, et al. 1975; Levy, 1971).

If the phonological loop is to be considered a viable component within the working memory system, it must have functional significance beyond its role in simple short-term memory tasks. Because the phonological loop stores verbal information, it is not surprising that researchers have considered its role in both language comprehension and language acquisition. Results concerning the relationship between the phonological loop and language comprehension have been mixed (Baddeley & Wilson, 1985; Butterworth, Campbell, & Howard, 1986; Caplan & Waters, 1992; Wilson & Baddeley, 1993). However, developmental and neuropsychological studies suggest that the phonological loop may be an important mechanism in language acquisition (Baddeley, Papagno, & Vallar, 1988; Gathercole & Baddeley, 1989, 1990; Papagno, Valentine, & Baddeley, 1991; Papagno & Vallar, 1992).

The other slave system proposed by Baddeley and Hitch (1974), the visuospatial sketchpad, has received far less attention than the phonological loop. The sketchpad functions as a temporary store for holding and manipulating visual and spatial information. Current controversy over the visuospatial sketchpad centers on whether or not there are two interactive visual systems, one that holds visual patterns and the other of which represents spatial information. Both behavioral and neuropsychological dissociations support the dissociation of the sketchpad into two interactive subsystems (Baddeley Grant, Wright, Thomson, 1975; Baddeley & Lieberman, 1980; Farah, 1984; Farah, Hammond, Levine, & Calvanio, 1988; Hanley, Young, & Pearson, 1991; Logie, 1986).

Central Executive

The central executive component of Baddeley and Hitch's (1974) model is the least specified of the subsystems. It was conceived of as a limited capacity processor that is flexibly allocated to processing and/or storage functions. Baddeley (1986, 1996) suggested that the central executive is similar to the concept of *supervisory attentional system* (SAS) proposed by Norman and Shallice (1986). According to Norman and Shallice, actions are carried out via the activation of schemas. Given the appropriate goals and stimulus context, a schema will be automatically activated and initiate a sequence of actions. It is possible that several schemas may be carried out simultaneously (e.g., walking and talking at the same time), but sometimes schemas will conflict with one another or will need monitoring to catch errors. Norman and Shallice proposed two levels of control to activate schemas and resolve conflicts. First, the current goals can lead to the enhanced activation of some schemas and inhibited activation of others, a step that serves to select the most appropriate, or highly activated, schema for action. This complementary process is a result of automatic spreading activation and thus does not require attention unless the procedure is error prone and must be monitored. Second, a limited-capacity attentional control system, the SAS, mediates the scheduling of contending schemas. The SAS is necessary when activated schemas are incompatible with current goals.

Baddeley (1986) suggested that the SAS could account for the results of Baddeley and Hitch's (1974) studies, which showed that some primary tasks were affected by concurrent load while others were not. In several studies Baddeley and Hitch found that concurrent digit load did not affect retrieval accuracy, but did affect retrieval latency. Baddeley argued that neither retrieval nor maintenance of the digit load involves heavy demands on the SAS, so both tasks can be performed accurately. In contrast, retrieval latency was affected by load because performance on the two tasks simultaneously requires more time-consuming contention scheduling than when one task is performed alone. Another set of studies showed that generation of exemplars from a category (e.g., animals) was affected by load. Baddeley reasoned that there are no schemas that can be automatically activated for category generation, so this task relies heavy on the SAS.

Baddeley's reliance on the Norman and Shallice (1986) model to further specify the central executive makes it apparent that the central executive is really a method for allocating attention. So, this aspect of Baddeley's model is similar to Broadbent's (1958) information-processing model in the sense that attentional and short-term storage systems are separated, but highly interconnected.

Baddeley has recently attempted to identify processes that are characteristic of the central executive and has examined executive control by studying neurological patients who appear to have deficits in cognitive control. A series of studies showed that Alzheimer patients exhibited impairments in coordination of slave systems, switching retrieval plans, selective attention, and activation of long-term memory (e.g., Baddeley, Logie, Bressi, Della Sala, & Spinnler, 1986; Baddeley & Wilson, 1988; Baddeley, Bressi, Della Sala, Logie, & Spinnler, 1991). As will be shown, there is now considerable evidence for a view that areas of the frontal lobes, particularly the prefrontal cortex, are important to central executive functioning.

Baddeley and Hitch (1974) set out to create a model of short-term storage that was more flexible than traditional short-term memory systems. According to their model, WM has both storage and processing functions. The slave systems are responsible for the maintenance of information and are similar to traditional STS models. Perhaps because of a rich history of research on temporary storage, these components are fairly well specified and allow for the generation of testable predictions. The central executive is an attentional control system and provides a great deal of flexibility to the WM system. Although the central executive is far less specified than the slave systems, tying it to short-term storage represents an important step toward the understanding of interactions between attention, short-term storage, and complex cognition. Because the model incorporates both processing and storage functions, it can be considered more dynamic than structural models proposed in the past, but it is still structural in nature and it is still a memory system that is distinct from other processing systems.

We should also point out that the two so-called slave systems of the Baddeley and Hitch model are not necessarily structural in nature. It is probable that the human brain has evolved to be especially good at processing speech and visual-spatial information. However, it is also possible to think of articulatory and visual-spatial coding as simply two of myriad other possible ways of coding information. For example, Reisberg, Rappaport, and O'Shaugnessy (1984) taught subjects to code lists of digits by tapping the corresponding fingers and found that the articulatory loop and the "finger" loop are independent of each other. These findings support the notion that the human information-processing system is very flexible in how it can represent information and that each format may have distinctively different characteristics.

Other Approaches to Working Memory

In contrast to Baddeley's (1986) structural approach to working memory, other researchers have described more dynamic or process-oriented models of working memory. Anderson (1983a) proposed a model of cognition in which working memory is simply the set of long-term memory units currently activated above a critical threshold. Schneider and Detweiler (1987) proposed a parallel distributed model of working memory, which, like Anderson's (1983a) model, views short-term storage as activated information. They argued that buffer models have difficulty explaining why temporary interruptions do not destroy performance on a complex task and force the individual to start the task over. In fact, we humans have rapid access to a great deal of information. For example, as I sit here writing this passage, I can quickly think about the previous section I wrote or what I want to say next. If I get interrupted by a student knocking at my door, I can go to the door, open it, greet the person, answer a question, talk about how the student is doing in my class, and so on, and quickly return to the point in my writing where I was interrupted. Miller's (1956) notion of 7 ± 2 items in temporary storage does not say that we can retain 7 ± 2 items in a number of different domains or contexts, but our common experience is that, in fact, we can. The Schneider and Detweiller model is unique in attempting to address this quality of working memory.

In their model, the information-processing system consists of three levels of analysis within many different processing modules. A module is analogous to a brain region that specializes in a class of processing (e.g., visual, motor, or lexical processing). Output units from each module may become activated and transmit activation to other modules or to the next level of analysis. Information in working memory is activated above a critical threshold. There is an active buffer, or short-term store, for each modality or stimulus context. Thus, my writing buffer would not necessarily be interfered with by my student-asking-question buffer. Schneider and Detweiller do not make qualitative distinctions between short and long storage of information; rather, in their model, short- and long-term memory are differentiated by temporal distinctions. So, short-term storage is limited in duration, whereas long-term storage is not.

In addition, there are limitations in the amount of activation that can be transmitted at a given time; these limitations are analogous to capacity limitations in buffer models. Some information can be activated and transmitted automatically, without consuming limited controlled-processing resources. But, control processes at each level of analysis determine what information will and will not be transmitted and the order of transmission. The functions of these control processes are akin to the functions of Baddeley's central executive system; however, Schneider and Detweiller do not invoke a singular executive component that controls processing. Rather, control is distributed among modules and levels of processing within modules. Further, they suggest that there is not a central capacity limitation; processing limitations will depend on the specific modules being used. The most apparent benefit of Schneider and Detweiller's (1987) model is that it allows for a great deal of interaction among different types of processing; thus, it has more power to explain complex processing than do simple buffer models. However, along with the complexity comes a lack of specificity; it is difficult to generate testable hypotheses from their model. Further, there is growing neurological evidence of a central attentional system that is not domain-specific (Posner & Peterson, 1990).

Another comprehensive model of the attention and memory system was proposed by Cowan (1988, 1995). He proposed a dynamic model of attention and memory in which WM is considered an activated subset of LTM. In fact, he suggested that Anderson's (1983a) and Schneider and Detweiller's (1987) models are compatible with his ideas, but he believed that they reflect a different level of analysis. Cowan proposed that there is one storage system that consists of elements and their features in long-term memory (e.g., acoustic, visual, semantic, etc.). At any given time these elements may exist in one of three states of activation. First, they may be inactive, a state that is akin to long-term storage. Next, they may be in a moderately activated state, but outside the "focus of attention." Information in this state is outside conscious awareness, but can influence processing (e.g., semantic priming, subliminal perception, implicit memory). This level of activation represents the passive storage of information in Baddeley's slave systems. The duration of this activation is limited, and without strategies for maintaining activation, information will quickly return to an inactive state. Finally, when information is attended, the level of activation will increase and the information will become the focus of attention, which represents the highest level of activation and is synonymous with conscious awareness. Cowan suggested that there are severe limitations in the amount of information that can be maintained in the focus of attention and that these limitations reflect the capacity of the central executive in Baddeley's model. Cowan eliminated the need for multiple memory structures by invoking different levels of activation that have distinct limitations. Further, he suggested that although much of the evidence supporting short- and long-term stores may actually reflect different processes used for activating information and maintaining activation, there is enough other evidence that supports a qualitative distinction between short- and long-term storage systems to warrant a multiple memory system approach. Cowan suggested that viewing short-term storage as the activation of long-term memory units represents a middle ground between approaches that posit multiple memory structures and completely unitary approaches. Activation approaches eliminate the need for completely separate memory systems while continuing to suggest that short- and long-term storage obey different sets of rules.

In addition to the memory system, Cowan's model includes a limited capacity central processor, or central executive, that is responsible for all control processes. Cowan defined control processes as those processes that are under voluntary control and that require attention for implementation (see Kahneman, 1973; Posner & Snyder, 1975; Shiffrin & Schneider, 1977). Cowan also solved the question of whether forgetting from short-term memory is based on time and decay or capacity limits and displacement. He assumed that the focus of attention is limited in capacity and that newly focused information displaces old information. Information that is activated but outside the focus of attention is lost over time through decay.

The Anderson (1983a), Schneider and Detweiller (1987), and Cowan (1995) views are similar in proposing an active portion of memory. They are different in how they handle the notion of executive control. Anderson proposes controlled attention for maintaining the activation of goals and for resolving conflict, which is similar to Shallice's SAS. Schneider and Detweiller propose that attention, like the memory representations, is distributed across modules. Cowan's view of executive control is, like Anderson's, more in line with Shallice's and with the Baddeley and Hitch central executive.

Working Memory Capacity and the Central Executive

Just and Carpenter (1992) and Engle, Cantor, and Carullo (1992) proposed models to explain individual differences in working memory. As with Anderson (1983) and Schneider and Detweiller (1987), these models assumed that working memory is an activated subset of long-term memory and that individuals differ in the amount of activation available for processing. Work on individual differences in working memory stems from studies that show that unlike traditional short-term memory measures, measures of WM correlate with performance on complex cognitive tasks. For example, Daneman and Carpenter (1980) showed that a measure of WM capacity that involves both storage and processing is related to performance on a higher-level cognitive task. In their reading span task, subjects read a series of sentences and tried to remember the last word of each sentence. The maximum number of final words recalled correlated with reading comprehension and verbal scholastic aptitude scores (VSAT). Other researchers have shown that the reading span and similar WM measures are highly correlated with complex cognitive measures such as writing ability, following directions, logic learning, and vocabulary learning (e.g., Benton et al. 1984; Daneman & Carpenter, 1983; Daneman & Green, 1986; Engle, Carullo, & Collins, 1991; Kiewra & Benton, 1988; Kyllonen & Stephens, 1990). An understanding of why these measures are related and what components of the WM span task are important to individual differences in complex task performance will help to specify those aspects of working memory that are generalizable to real-world cognition and thus are less likely to be peculiar to a specific experimental task.

Daneman and Carpenter (1980, 1983) and Just and Carpenter (1992) argued that individual differences in the level of activation are important to lower-level language processing, such as syntactic parsing and disambiguation of ambiguous linguistic units.[11] They argued that these differences reflect differences in activation available to language processing, but, like Schneider and Detweiller, they assumed domain-specific limitations on activation.

On the other hand, Turner and Engle (1989) and Engle et al. (1992) assumed the central executive reflects a domain-free attention capacity limitation and suggested that individuals with high and low working-memory spans should differ on capacity-demanding tasks, no matter what the processing domain. Like Daneman and Carpenter (1980), they showed that reading-span task performance correlated with global verbal comprehension measures (e.g., VSAT). However, Turner and Engle (1989) also showed that performance on a working memory task that required subjects to solve math problems while remembering words correlated with verbal comprehension as well as did the reading span measure. This finding suggests that the storage component of these span tasks reflects differences in a central attention limitation, not differences due to task-specific processing.

Engle et al. (1992) suggested that WM span differences reflect differences in the overall amount of activation available to the WM system for processing. Individuals with greater WM capacity are able to maintain activation of more LTM knowledge units than individuals with less WM capacity. Thus, high–WM span individuals can keep more units in an active state and available for rapid retrieval and further processing. In addition, Engle, Cantor, and Carullo argued that the amount of activation available is a stable characteristic of the information-processing system and that it changes little with changes in knowledge structure. Cantor and Engle (1993) provided evidence for the general capacity model by showing that working memory capacity and measures presumed to reflect activation of information in LTM are related. In that study, high and low working-memory span individuals learned a series of unrelated sentences. Each sentence consisted of a subject and a predicate (e.g., "The lawyer is in the park"). Further, each subject was paired with more than one predicate (e.g., *lawyer* might be paired with *park* and *boat*). Next, the participants performed a speeded recognition task in which they determined whether sentences belonged to the studied set or not. Typically, in this task, reaction time increases as a function of fan size (fan size is the number of times a given subject appears in the stimulus set with a different predicate; Anderson 1983b) and the increase is attributed to the division of activation among a greater number of knowledge units for sentences with larger fans. Cantor and Engle found that reaction time increased across fan size for both high-and low-WM groups. However, the increase was more dramatic for the low-span subjects, suggesting that it took them longer to activate target sentences because they had less overall activation spreading in the network than did high-span subjects. In fact, when the slope of the fan effect was partialled out of the correlation between span and verbal abilities, this correlation was no longer significant, suggesting that long-term memory activation is an important component of the relationship.

The general capacity model was elaborated by Conway and Engle (1994). They studied whether individual differences in working memory reflect differences in automatic spreading activation, as was argued in Engle, Cantor, and Carullo (1992), or differences in controlled attention, that is, the central executive. Conway and Engle suggested that Cantor and Engle's (1993) task is not sensitive to a distinction between controlled attentional processing and automatic activation, because the fact retrieval task used by Cantor and Engle requires both processes. In the verification phase of the 1993 task, subjects might encode the subject of the target sentence and activate all associated predicates. Next, subjects searched the activated set of information and determined whether the target was a member of the set. Because each sentence in the Cantor and Engle study shared a predicate with another sentence (e.g., "The lawyer is in the boat" and "The teacher is in the boat"), it is possible that there was response competition or conflict that would necessitate a controlled search of the activated information. Thus, differences between high and low WM groups could reflect differences in automatic activation of LTM units, a controlled search of these activated concepts, or differences in both processes. In order to assess differences in these two types of processing, Conway and Engle had subjects retrieve facts from either active or inactive memory.

High and low working-memory span subjects learned an association between items in memory sets of various sizes and a digit set cue that corresponded to the size of the set. Each set contained unique items in one experiment and overlapping items in another. Next, subjects performed a speeded verification task in which they saw a digit and an item and pressed a key to indicate whether the item was a member of the set. In the short-term memory condition, the digit set cue appeared 1 second before the probe. Thus, subjects knew which memory set was being tested and could retrieve the set information into active working memory before the probe appeared. Therefore, recognition only depended on a search of short-term memory. In the long-term memory condition the set cue and probe appeared simultaneously, so the set had to be activated before it could be searched. It was assumed that, in this condition, the subject would need to access the set information from long-term memory, move it into short-term memory, and then do a search of short-term memory. Thus, the two conditions differed in that a retrieval from long-term memory was necessary for the latter condition. Conway and Engle found that the slope of the set size function did not differ for high- and low-span subjects in the no-interference condition, that is, the condition in which there was no overlap in set membership. In the interference condition with overlapping sets and presumed response competition, the slope of the set size function *did* differ for high- and low-span subjects. Under interference conditions, the low-span subjects were much slower to identify the item as belonging to the set. Conway and Engle (1994) argued that this difference between the search functions of high- and low-span subjects resulted from search of activated memory, because the no delay and 1-second delay conditions showed the same slope.

For high-WM subjects, verification times across memory set size were the same for overlapping and unique memory sets. In contrast, set overlap slowed the verification times for low-span subjects. In summary, when unique sets were tested, and thus no response competition was present, the slope functions for high- and low-WM subjects were nearly identical. However, low-span subjects' performance was slowed by overlap between memory set items, but the performance for high-span subjects was *not*. Conway and Engle argued that the verification task in the conditions with nonoverlapping sets could be performed on the basis of automatic spreading activation between the digit probe and the target. In the overlapping sets conditions, however, a conflict would arise when the activation from the target would spread to the correct probe *and* to another probe, hence, a condition that would require the supervisory attentional system of Norman and Shallice. Conway and Engle further argued that this conflict forced the low-span subjects to do a controlled, serial search in that condition. The high spans were argued to use their greater attentional resources to suppress the irrelevant link so they did not need to do a controlled search of the list.

Conway and Engle (1994) argued that working memory capacity is important when retrieval is necessarily or voluntarily achieved through a controlled search, but not when achieved through passive automatic activation. This conclusion was also supported by a set of studies by Rosen and Engle (1997) in which high and low working-memory subjects were instructed to generate as many different animal names as possible over a 10-minute period. In the first study, high-span subjects generated about 40% more animals than low-span subjects. One possible explanation was that low-span subjects relied largely on automatic spreading activation for retrieval but that high-span subjects used controlled attention for search and to suppress previously retrieved responses. This explanation was supported by the finding that doing the retrieval under the workload of an attention-demanding detection task hurt performance for the high-span subjects but had no effect on the retrieval of the low-span subjects.

On the basis of these studies we have proposed that individual differences on measures of working memory capacity reflect differences in controlled attention capability and that those differences will only be reflected in situations that either encourage or demand controlled attention (Conway & Engle, 1994; Engle, Conway, Tuholski, & Shisler, 1995; Rosen & Engle, 1997a). Controlled attention is necessary when task goals may be lost unless they are actively maintained in working memory, where actions contending for the same stage must be scheduled, where conflict among actions must be resolved, where there is value in maintaining some task information in the face of distraction and interference, and where there is value in suppressing task-irrelevant information.

Measurement Issues with Working Memory

As we have traced the history of the literature on short-term and working memory, we have seen that the models have become more complex and more flexible. We have also seen a divergence of methodology from strictly experimental studies to studies of individual differences on hypothesized constructs. This evolution has given rise to some concerns that are novel to most experimental psychologists. Experimental psychologists have, traditionally, not paid much attention to measurement aspects of the tasks they use. Psychometric issues such as task reliability and validity are more often considered in applied areas or areas such as social and personality psychology. Many tasks have been used to study short-term memory and working memory, and because individual differences in working memory have become important, concerns about psychometric issues have increased. Validity as an issue is reflected in such questions as: Does the task measure what you want it to measure? Do different measures of working memory reflect the same construct? Do tasks that putatively measure short-term memory measure the same construct as tasks that putatively measure working memory? and Do working memory and/or short-term memory have construct validity? or Does the construct have some importance or relationship to real-world behavior?

In a review of research on memory span, Dempster (1981) argued that if short-term memory is important to real-world tasks such as reading, and if memory span is an index of short-term memory, memory span should correlate with measures of reading. However, simple span measures, the digit span in particular, do not consistently correlate with measures of reading comprehension. Dempster argued that part of the problem is that simple memory-span scores are simply not very reliable: the same subject can show wide differences in span when different measures are used. The simple word span is typically more reliable than the digit span, which might explain the fact that nearly all of the studies from our lab (Engle et al., Collins, 1991; LaPointe & Engle, 1990; Turner & Engle, 1989) show that simple word span correlates with reading comprehension. We have also found that the digit span does not correlate well with other measures of short-term memory; again, the failure to find such correlations consistently is probably a reliability problem. So, from a simple measurement standpoint, the digit span is probably not a very sensitive measure and, thus, is not a very useful measure of short-term memory; the word span may be a better measure.

Another important measurement issue is whether STM and WM tasks reflect the same underlying construct. We recently addressed this question in a large-scale factor analysis (Engle, Tuholsky, Laughlin, Conway, 1998). The study included tasks traditionally thought of as short-term memory tasks, including forward word span with phonologically dissimilar words, forward word span with phonologically similar words, and the recency score from immediate free recall. Other tasks were chosen to reflect working memory capacity or the central executive. These included the random generation task (Baddeley, 1996), reading span (Daneman & Carpenter, 1980), operation span (Turner & Engle, 1989), and two tasks from the CAM4 battery: continuous opposites and ABCD (Kyllonen & Christal, 1990). Another set of tasks was used because whereas some authors have referred to them as short-term memory tasks, others have referred to them as working memory tasks. These include the backward word span with phonologically dissimilar words, keeping track task, counting span, and recall from all the serial positions in immediate free recall except recency. In addition to the memory tasks, subjects were tested on the Raven's Progressive Matrices Test and the Cattell Culture

Fair Test, both of which are nonverbal tests of general fluid intelligence (*gF*). We tested 133 subjects individually over three sessions and obtained the Verbal and Quantitative Scholastic Aptitude Test scores for them all.

We performed a series of exploratory then confirmatory factor analyses on the memory tasks. These analyses showed that two different factors were necessary to account for the variance in the memory task scores. What we called the short-term memory (STM) factor included the two forward span tests and the backward span. The working memory (WM) factor included operation span, reading span, counting span, keeping track, secondary memory component from immediate free recall, and the two tasks from the CAM4. A partial regression analysis showed that when STM was controlled for, WM correlated with the general fluid intelligence tests, $r = .5$. However, if WM was controlled for, STM did not significantly correlate with *gF*. This finding shows quite conclusively that the STM tasks and the WM tasks reflect different underlying constructs. Both factors, however, contributed significant and independent variance to the Verbal SAT, a measure of verbal skills, including reading comprehension. Our present thinking about these results is that whereas the WM factor reflects controlled attention or attentional resources capability, the STM factor may reflect some basic aspect of speech representation that is also important to the VSAT. An appealing possibility is that the WM factor represents the central executive component of the Baddeley and Hitch (1974) model and the STM factor represents the capability of one of the slave systems, namely, the phonological loop. If this interpretation is correct, then tasks could also be used that reflected the domain-specific capability of the visuospatial sketchpad as well as the phonological loop.

The random generation and recency portion of immediate free recall did not fit with either factor and were dropped from the analyses. This finding calls into question the use of the recency portion of the free recall task for making inferences about short-term memory.

The results of the study fit nicely with work by Kyllonen and Christal (1990), which argues that working memory capacity is an important component of what is commonly thought of as general fluid intelligence. As we will see in the next section, the Kyllonen and Christal conclusions also tie in with work on controlled attention and the functions of the frontal lobes of the brain.

At this point, it might be useful for us to attempt some generalizations about short-term memory and working memory. We would argue, following Craik and Jacoby (1975) and Cowan (1995), that many different processes can be used to maintain the temporary activation of memory units. Certainly phonological, visual, and spatial coding reflect common means of coding, but there are undoubtedly other means as well. It seems reasonable to think of those knowledge elements activated above some threshold as reflecting the contents of short-term memory. Some small number of those activated units may be in the focus of attention. From a measurement standpoint, individuals almost certainly differ in their ability to use speech-based, spatial, and visual coding, and those would be reflected in measures appropriate for each code. The vast majority of short-term memory studies reflect the use of phonological coding of short lists of words and rote rehearsal, using that code, to maintain activation of the representation. As Cowan (1995) pointed out, not all information in short-term memory, that is, activated knowledge, can be the focus of attention, because the focus of attention is quite limited in capacity. We argue that focused or controlled attention corresponds to Baddeley and Hitch's central executive. Individual differences in "working memory capacity" (Just & Carpenter, 1992; Turner & Engle, 1989) are really individual differences in a single component of the working memory system: controlled attention. Further, the differences in working memory capacity are not really differences in *memory* at all. Those differences reflect differential ability to use controlled attention to raise the activation of knowledge units, to maintain or sustain that activation in the face of interference and distraction, and, occasionally, to select among schemes contending for action on the basis of the strength of their activation levels.

Working Memory Capacity and the Frontal Lobes[12]

Research and theorizing about short-term and working memory have benefited considerably from neuropsychological research. As memory models become more complex, we must be mindful of whether the structures and processes proposed for the memory system fit with what is known about the brain.

There is growing evidence that connects the functions we have attributed to the central executive to structures in the frontal lobes, particularly the prefrontal cortex (Duncan, 1995; Duncan, Emslie, Williams, Johnson, & Freer, 1996; Goldman-Rakic, 1987; Kimberg & Farah, 1993; Pennington, 1994; Shallice & Burgess, 1993). Goldman-Rakic (1987), for example, has used a delayed response task in which monkeys are shown a food pellet being placed under one of two objects. Then a screen blocks the monkey's view of the two objects for a period of time, after which the monkey could have the food if it picked the correct object on the first trial. Normal monkeys have no difficulty in representing the correct object in memory over the delay and do well on the task. However, removal of parts of the prefrontal cortex (particularly Brodmann's area 46) leads to an inability on the part of the monkey to retain the information over the delay. This finding suggests that the prefrontal cortex is important to maintaining the temporary representation of the location of the hidden food.

Shallice and his colleagues (Shallice & Burgess, 1993) have argued that the frontal lobes are an important part of the circuitry of the supervisory attentional system, which we previously described. Evidence of this link shows that damage to the frontal lobes, particularly the prefrontal cortex, leads to difficulty in doing tasks that require sustained controlled attention (Duncan et al., 1996; Luria, Karpov, & Yarbuss, 1966; Weinberger, 1993). Duncan (1995) has also made the connection between sustained controlled attention, general intelligence, and the frontal lobes. He argues that frontal lobe damage leads to a substantial decline in general fluid intelligence and the ability to sustain controlled attention. This conclusion, of course, would follow from the research connecting the constructs of working memory capacity, central executive, and gF (Engle, Tuholski, Laughlin, & Conway, 1998; Kyllonen & Christal, 1990).

Although most of these studies used animals or patients with frontal lobe damage, there is at least suggestive evidence linking sustained attention to the frontal lobes in normal, non-brain-damaged individuals as well. For example, individuals with low WM capacity as defined by tasks such as reading span and operations span show similar (albeit less devastating) patterns of performance in comparison to frontal patients on a variety of cognitive tasks. Patients with frontal damage show decreased performance on the verbal fluency task which asks subjects to retrieve as many examples of a category as they can (Benton, 1968; Milner, 1964;

Pendleton Heaton, Lehamen, Hulihen, 1982). Rosen and Engle (1997a) have shown the same pattern for low working memory subjects. Frontal patients also tend to perseverate on a strategy even after it is no longer useful (Drewe, 1974; Luria, 1966; Milner, 1963, 1964). Tuholski & Engle (1997) showed that low working-memory subjects persist in using an ineffective mental model strategy longer than do high working-memory subjects. Finally, frontal patients have been shown, in comparison to normal subjects, to be more vulnerable to interference and less able to suppress irrelevant or inappropriate information (Dempster, 1992; Freedman & Cermak, 1986; Knight, 1995; Knight, Scabini, & Woods, 1989; Leng & Parkin, 1989; Longmore, Knight, Menlus, & Htope, 1988; Shimamura Gershberg, Jurica, Mangels, & Knight, 1992; Stuss, 1991). Similarly, low working-memory subjects have shown greater effects of proactive interference in a Brown-Peterson paradigm (Kane and Engle, 1997). Rosen and Engle (1997b) showed that in an *A-B, A-C, A-B* paired-associate procedure, high working-memory subjects suppressed the list-1 responses during the learning of list 2 but that low working-memory subjects did not. Further, low working-memory subjects made many more intrusions from earlier lists than did high working-memory subjects, suggesting that the former group had not suppressed the intruding items as well as had the latter group. In contrast, frontal patients perform normally on tasks that can be done under proceduralized or automatized processing (Bianchi, 1922; Frith, Friston, Liddle, & Frackowiak, 1991; Fuster, 1980, Penfield & Evans, 1935). Likewise, Conway and Engle (1994) showed that high and low working-memory subjects did not differ in a retrieval task in the absence of response competition.

In summary, there is growing speculation and evidence on the relationship between the central executive and the frontal lobes. It should be noted that Goldman-Rakic's work with monkeys speaks to the storage of the temporary representation itself. The other work cited is more directed at the use of controlled attention to maintain activation of a representation, to suppress interfering representations, or to choose between contending actions. This area of research is particularly vital right now, and we can expect many new findings and ideas on the neuropsychology of working memory, controlled attention, and general fluid intelligence in the near future.

Conclusion

We have briefly reviewed the history of the idea of a temporary memory store distinct from long-term memory starting with Hebb's (1949) physiological theory of the reverberatory trace. The psychological theories that followed were based on the idea that the temporary short-term trace behaved according to different laws than did the structural or long-term memory trace. Unfortunately, these theories were overly simplistic, and the characteristics attributed to short-term memory under the multi-store theories were probably a result of the particular tasks used rather than the inexorable nature of the temporary trace. Modern theories allow for multiple types of representation, each of which may be differentially sensitive to interference and loss over time. Further, controlled attention is important for the maintenance and/or suppression of the representation over time and for resolution of conflict between automatically activated action schemas. The newer theories not only are more content valid, because they show statistical relationships with higher-order or real-world cognitive functions; they also appear to be soundly based in brain science.

Acknowledgments

During the preparation of this chapter, the authors' work was supported by grants F49620-93-1-0336 from the Air Force Office of Scientific Research and RO1-HD-27490-01A1 from the National Institute of Child Health and Human Development. We thank Mike Kane for his helpful comments and criticisms.

Notes

1. Keeping with a useful convention adopted by Atkinson and Shiffrin (1968), we will use the term *short-term store* and the acronym *STS* to refer to the hypothesized temporary memory store, trace, or representation. The term *short-term memory,* or *STM,* will be used when talking about tasks and the phenomena observed from tasks that putatively reflect the underlying STS.

2. Despite the fact that Hebb's idea that the strength of the long-term trace was a function of time in the reverberatory trace has been discredited, the principle is still alive and kicking today in the form of Hebb's rule, which is an integral part of how learning occurs in neural net or connectionist models of cognition (Rumelhart, Hinton & McClellend, 1986).

3. *Ceiling effect* refers to the problem occurring when performance is so high that two conditions cannot be distinguished from each other. If the 100% ceiling did not limit them, one could be higher than the other. A similar problem occurs when performance in two conditions is nearly zero—that is, floor effect.

4. It is likely that modality of presentation is important to whether this generalization is correct. Auditory presentation leads to higher recency than visual presentation, and there is evidence (Cantor & Engle, 1989) that the recency found with auditory presentation is preattentive.

5. There was considerable debate early in this literature as to whether the code used in STM tasks was acoustic (i.e., sound based; Conrad & Hull, 1964) or articulatory (i.e., speech based; Wickelgren, 1966). The issue was never resolved; hence, we will use the neutral term *phonological*. It should be pointed out, however, that articulatory code seems to have won the war because the *articulatory loop* is such an important element of the Baddeley and Hitch (1974) model.

6. HM is more than likely the basis for the Mr. Short Term Memory character.

7. Since Brown (1958) and Peterson & Peterson (1959) both published work using a similar task, the task is typically referred to as the *Brown-Peterson task*.

8. In taking this view, Crowder adopted a position much like that of his mentor, Melton (1963).

9. See LaPointe & Engle (1990) for an example of how sampling with and without replacement in short-term memory studies can differentially affect the results.

10. The term *working memory* had been used earlier (e.g., Douglas, 1967) but, as is often the case in science, the Zeitgeist was not ready for the term until later.

11. There is considerable controversy over this issue, but the debate is beyond the scope of this paper. The reader is referred to papers by Waters and Caplan (1966) and Deaton, Gernsbacher, Robertson, and Miyake (1995).

12. There is an extensive neuropsychological literature on aspects of working memory other than central executive, particularly the phonological loop, but a complete coverage is beyond our scope.

References

Anderson, J. R. (1974). Retrieval of propositional information from long-term memory. *Cognitive Psychology, 6*, 451–474.

Anderson, J. R. (1983a). *The architecture of cognition*. Cambridge, MA: Harvard University Press.

Anderson, J. R. (1983b). A spreading activation theory of memory. *Journal of Verbal Learning and Verbal Behavior, 22*, 261–295.

Atkinson, R. C., & Shiffrin, R. M. (1968). Human memory: A proposed system and its control processes. In K. W. Spence & J. T. Spence (Eds.), *The psychology of learning and motivation* (Vol. 2, pp. 89–95). New York: Academic Press.

Baddeley, A. D. (1966). The influence of acoustic and semantic similarity on long-term memory for word sequences. *Quarterly Journal of Experimental Psychology, 18,* 302–309.

Baddeley, A. D. (1986). *Working Memory.* Oxford, England: Clarendon Press.

Baddeley, A. D. (1996). Exploring the central executive. *Quarterly Journal of Experimental Psychology, 49A,* 5–28.

Baddeley, A. D., Bressi, S., Della Sala, S., Logie, R., & Spinnler, H. (1991). The decline of working memory in Alzheimer's disease: A longitudinal study. *Brain, 114,* 2521–2542.

Baddeley, A. D., Grant, S., Wight, E., & Thomson, N. (1975). Imagery and visual working memory. In P. M. A. Rabbitt & S. Dornic (Eds.), *Attention and Performance* (Vol. 5, pp. 205–217). Hillsdale, NJ: Erlbaum.

Baddeley, A. D., & Hitch, G. (1974). Working memory. In G. A. Bower (Ed.), *The psychology of learning and motivation* (Vol. 8, pp. 47–89). New York: Academic Press.

Baddeley, A. D., & Hitch, G. (1994). Developments in the concept of working memory. *Neuropsychology, 8,* 485–493.

Baddeley, A. D., Lewis, V. J., & Vallar, G. (1984). Exploring the articulatory loop. *Quarterly Journal of Experimental Psychology, 36,* 233–252.

Baddeley, A. D., & Lieberman, K. (1980). Spatial working memory. In R. Nickerson (Ed.), *Attention and Performance* (Vol. 7, pp. 521–539). Hillsdale, NJ: Erlbaum.

Baddeley, A. D., Logie, R., Bressi, S., Della Sala, S., & Spinnler, H. (1986). Dementia and working memory. *Quarterly Journal of Experimental Psychology, 38A,* 602–618.

Baddeley, A. D., Papagno, C., & Vallar, G. (1988). When long-term learning depends on short-term storage. *Journal of Memory and Language, 27,* 586–595.

Baddeley, A. D., Thomson, N., & Buchanan, M. (1975). Word length and the structure of short-term memory. *Journal of Verbal Learning and Verbal Behavior, 14,* 575–589.

Baddeley, A. D., & Warrington, E. K. (1970). Amnesia and the distinction between long-and short-term memory. *Journal of Verbal Learning and Verbal Behavior, 9,* 176–189.

Baddeley, A. D., & Wilson, B. (1985). Phonological coding and short-term memory in patients without speech. *Journal of Memory and Language, 24,* 490–502.

Baddeley, A. D., & Wilson, B. (1988). Frontal amnesia and the dysexecutive syndrome. *Brain and Cognition, 7,* 212–230.

Benton, A. L. (1968). Differential effects of frontal lobe disease. *Neuropsychologia, 6,* 53–60.

Benton, S. L., Kraft, R. G., Glover, J. A., & Plake, B. S. (1984). Cognitive capacity differences among writers. *Journal of Educational Psychology, 76,* 820–834.

Bianchi, L. (1922). *The mechanism of the brain and the function of the frontal lobes.* Edinburgh, Scotland: Livingstone.

Bjork, R. A., & Whitten, W. B. (1974). Recency-sensitive retrieval processes in long-term free recall. *Cognitive Psychology, 6,* 173–189.

Broadbent, D. (1958). *Perception and Communication.* Oxford, England: Pergamon Press.

Brown, J. (1958). Some tests of the decay theory of immediate memory. *Quarterly Journal of Experimental Psychology, 10,* 12–21.

Butterworth, B., Campbell, R., & Howard, D. (1986). The uses of short-term memory: A case study. *Quarterly Journal of Experimental Psychology, 38A,* 705–738.

Cantor, J., & Engle, R. W. (1989). The influence of concurrent load on mouthed and vocalized modality effects. *Memory & Cognition, 17,* 701–711.

Cantor, J., & Engle, R. W. (1993). Working memory capacity as long-term memory activation: An individual differences approach. *Journal of Experimental Psychology: Learning, Memory, & Cognition, 19,* 1101–1114.

Case, R. D. (1985). *Intellectual development: Birth to adulthood.* New York: Academic Press.

Case, R. D., Kurland, D. M., & Goldberg, J. (1982). Operational efficiency and the growth of short-term memory span. *Journal of Experimental Child Psychology, 33,* 386–404.

Conrad, R. (1957). Decay theory of immediate memory. *Nature, 179,* 831–832.

Conrad, R. (1964). Acoustic confusion in immediate memory. *British Journal of Psychology, 55,* 75–84.

Conrad, R., & Hull, A. J. (1964). Information, acoustic confusion and memory span. *British Journal of Psychology, 55,* 429–432.

Conway, A. R. A., & Engle, R. W. (1994). Working memory and retrieval: A resource-dependent inhibition model. *Journal of Experimental Psychology: General, 123,* 354–373.

Cowan, N. (1988). Evolving conceptions of memory storage, selective attention, and their mutual constraints within the human information-processing system. *Psychological Bulletin, 104,* 163–191.

Cowan, N. (1995). *Attention and Memory: An Integrated Framework.* New York: Oxford University Press.

Cowan, N., Day, L., Saults, J. S., Keller, T. A., Johnson, T., & Flores, L. (1992). The role of verbal output time in the effects of word length on immediate memory. *Journal of Memory & Language, 31,* 1–17.

Cowan, N., Keller, T., Hulme, C., Roodenrys, S., McDougall, S., & Rack, J. (1994). Verbal memory span in children: Speech timing clues to the mechanisms underlying age and word length effects. *Journal of Memory & Language, 33,* 234–250.

Cowan, N., Wood, N. L., & Bourne, D. N. (1994). Reconfirmation of the short-term storage concept. *Psychological Science, 5*, 103–106.

Craik, F. I. M., & Jacoby, L. L. (1975). A process view of short-term retention. In F. Restle, R. C. Shiffrin, N. J. Castellan, H. Lindman, & D. Pisoni, (Eds.), *Cognitive Theory* (pp. 173–192). Hillsdale, NJ: Erlbaum.

Craik, F. I. M., & Lockhart, R. (1972). Levels of processing: A framework for memory research. *Journal of Verbal Learning and Verbal Behavior, 11*, 671–684.

Craik, F. I. M., & Watkins, M. J. (1973). The role of rehearsal in short-term memory. *Journal of Verbal Learning and Verbal Behavior, 12*, 599–607.

Crowder, R. G. (1983). The demise of short-term memory. *Acta Psychologica, 50*, 291–323.

Crowder, R. G. (1993). Short-term memory: Where do we stand? *Memory & Cognition, 21*, 142–145.

Daneman, M., & Carpenter, P. A. (1980). Individual differences in working memory and reading. *Journal of Verbal Learning and Verbal Behavior, 19*, 450–466.

Daneman, M., & Carpenter, P. A. (1983). Individual differences in working-memory and reading. *Journal of Verbal Learning and Verbal Behavior, 19*, 450–466.

Daneman, M., & Green, I. (1986). Individual differences in comprehending and producing words in context. *Journal of Memory and Language, 25*, 1–18.

Deaton, J., Gernsbacher, M.A., Robertson, R., & Miyake, A. (1995) Working memory span and lexical ambiguity: problems with lexical access. Paper presented at Midwester Psychological Association, Chicago.

Dempster, F. N. (1981). Memory span: Sources of individual and developmental differences. *Psychological Bulletin, 89*, 63–100.

Dempster, F. N. (1992). The rise and fall of the inhibitory mechanism: Toward a unified theory of cognitive development and aging. *Developmental Review, 12*, 45–75.

Douglas, R. J. (1967). The hippocampus and behavior. *Psychological Bulletin, 67*, 416–442.

Drewe, E. A. (1974). The effect of type and area of brain lesion on Wisconsin Card Sort Test performance. *Cortex, 10*, 159–170.

Duncan, J. (1995). Attention, intelligence, and the frontal lobes. In M. S. Gazzaniga (Ed.), *The Cognitive Neurosciences* (pp. 721–733). Cambridge, MA: MIT Press.

Duncan, J., Emslie, H., Williams, P., Johnson, R., & Freer, C. (1996). Intelligence and the frontal lobe: The organization of goal-directed behavior. *Cognitive Psychology, 30*, 257–303.

Ellis, N. C., & Hennelley, R. A. (1980). A bilingual word-length effect: Implications for intelligence testing and the relative ease of mental calculations in Welsh and English. *British Journal of Psychology, 71,* 43–52.

Engle, R. W., Cantor, J., & Carullo, J. J. (1992). Individual differences in working memory and comprehension: A test of four hypotheses. *Journal of Experimental Psychology: Learning, Memory, & Cognition, 18,* 972–992.

Engle, R. W., Carullo, J. J., & Collins, K. W. (1991). Individual differences in the role of working memory in comprehension and following directions in children. *Journal of Educational Research, 84,* 253–262.

Engle, R. W., Conway, A. R. A., Tuholski, S. W., & Shisler, R. J. (1995). A resource account of inhibition. *Psychological Science, 6,* 122–125.

Engle, R. W., Tuholski, S. W., Laughlin, J. E., & Conway, A. R. A., (in press). Working memory, short-term memory and general fluid intelligence: A latent variable approach. *Journal of Experimental Psychology: General.*

Farah, M. J. (1984). The neurological basis of mental imagery: A componential analysis, *Cognition, 18,* 245–272.

Farah, M. J., Hammond, K. M., Levine, D. N., & Calvanio, R. (1988). Visual and spatial mental imagery: Dissociable systems of representation. *Cognitive Psychology, 20,* 439–462.

Freedman, M., & Cermak, L. S. (1986). Semantic encoding deficits in frontal lobe disease and amnesia. *Brain and Cognition, 5,* 108–114.

Frith, C. D., Friston, K., Liddle, P. F., & Frackowiak, R. S. J. (1991). Willed action and the prefrontal cortex in man: A study with PET. *Proceedings of the Royal Society London B, 244,* 241–246.

Fuster, J. M. (1980). *The prefrontal cortex: Anatomy, physiology, and neuropsychology of the frontal lobe.* New York: Raven.

Gathercole, S. E., & Baddeley, A. D. (1989). Evaluation of the role of phonological STM in the development of vocabulary in children: A longitudinal study. *Journal of Memory and Language, 28,* 200–213.

Gathercole, S. E., & Baddeley, A. D. (1990). Phonological memory deficits in language disordered children: Is there a causal connection? *Journal of Memory and Language, 29,* 336–360.

Glanzer, M., & Cunitz, A. (1966). Two storage mechanisms in free recall. *Journal of Verbal Learning and Verbal Behavior, 5,* 351–360.

Glanzer, M., & Razel, M. (1974). The size of the unit in short-term storage. *Journal of Verbal Learning and Verbal Behavior, 13,* 114–131.

Goldman-Rakic, P. S. (1987). Circuitry of primate prefrontal cortex and regulation of behavior by representational memory. In F. Plum (Ed.), *Handbook of physiology: Section 1. The nervous system: Vol. 5, Higher functions of the brain.* Bethesda, MD: American Physiological Society.

Gregg, V. H., & Gardiner, J. M. (1984). Phonological similarity and enhanced auditory recency in longer-term free recall. *Quarterly Journal of Experimental Psychology, 36A,* 13–27.

Hanley, J. R., Young, A. W., & Pearson, N. A. (1991). Impairment of the visuo-spatial sketch pad. *Quarterly Journal of Experimental Psychology, 43A,* 101–126.

Hebb, D. O. (1949). *Organization of Behavior.* New York: Wiley.

Hebb, D. O. (1961). Distinctive features of learning in the higher animal. In J. F. Delafresnaye (Ed.), *Brain mechanisms and learning* (pp. 37–46). London: Oxford University Press.

James, W. (1890). *The principles of psychology.* New York: Henry Holt.

Just, M. A., & Carpenter, P. A. (1992). A capacity theory of comprehension: Individual differences in working memory. *Psychological Review, 99,* 122–149.

Kahneman, D. (1973). *Attention and Effort.* Englewood Cliffs, NJ: Prentice-Hall.

Kane, M., & Engle, R. W. (1998). *The role of working memory capacity in proactive interference.* Manuscript in preparation.

Keppel, G., & Underwood, B. J. (1962). Proactive inhibition in short-term retention of single items. *Journal of Verbal Learning and Verbal Behavior, 1,* 153–161.

Kiewra, K. A., & Benton, S. L. (1988). The relationship between information processing ability and note taking. *Contemporary Educational Psychology, 13,* 33–44.

Kimberg, D. Y., & Farah, M. J. (1993). A unified account of cognitive impairments following frontal lobe damage: The role of working memory in complex, organized behavior. *Journal of Experimental Psychology: General, 122,* 411–428.

Kintsch, W., & Buschke, H. (1969). Homophones and synonyms in short-term memory. *Journal of Experimental Psychology, 80,* 403–407.

Kintsch, W., & van Dijk, T. A. (1978). Toward a model of text comprehension and production. *Psychological Review, 85,* 363–394.

Knight, R. T. (1995). Escape from linear time: Prefrontal cortex and conscious experience. In M. S. Gazzaniga (Ed.), *The Cognitive Neurosciences* (pp. 1357–1371). Cambridge, MA: MIT Press.

Knight, R. T., Scabini, D., & Woods, D. L. (1989). Prefrontal cortex gating of auditory transmission in humans. *Brain Research, 504,* 338–342.

Kolb, B., & Whishaw, I. Q. (1990). *Fundamentals of human neuropsychology.* New York: W. H. Freeman.

Kyllonen, P. C., & Christal, R. E. (1990). Reasoning ability is (little more than) working-memory capacity. *Intelligence, 14,* 389–433.

Kyllonen, P. C., & Stephens, D. L. (1990). Cognitive abilities as determinants of success in acquiring logic skill. *Learning and Individual Differences, 2,* 129–160.

LaPointe, L. B., & Engle, R. W. (1990). Simple and complex word spans as measures of working memory capacity. *Journal of Experimental Psychology: Learning, Memory, & Cognition, 16*, 1118–1133.

Leng, N. R. C., & Parkin, A. J. (1989). Aetiological variations in the amnesic syndrome: Comparisons using the Brown-Peterson task. *Cortex, 25*, 251–259.

Levy, B. A. (1971). The role of articulation in auditory and visual short-term memory. *Journal of Verbal Learning and Verbal Behavior, 10*, 123–132.

Lockhart, R. S., & Craik, F. I. M. (1990). Levels of processing: A retrospective commentary on a framework for memory research. *Canadian Journal of Psychology, 44*, 87–112.

Logie, R. H. (1986). Visuo-spatial processing in working memory. *Quarterly Journal of Experimental Psychology, 38A*, 229–247.

Longmore, B. E., Knight, R. G., Menkes, D. J., & Hope, A. (1988). The experimental investigation of a case of alcohol-induced frontal lobe atrophy. *Neuropsychology, 2*, 77–86.

Luria, A. R. (1966). *Higher cortical functions in man*. London: Tavistock.

Luria, A. R., Karpov, B. A., & Yarbuss, A. L. (1966). Disturbances of active visual perception with lesions of frontal lobes. *Cortex, 2*, 202–212.

McGeoch, J. A. (1932). Forgetting and the law of disuse. *Psychological Review, 39*, 352–370.

Melton, A. W. (1963). Implications for short-term memory for a general theory of memory. *Journal of Verbal Learning and Verbal Behavior, 2*, 1–21.

Melton, A. W., & Irwin, J. M. (1940). The influence of degree of interpolated learning on retroactive interference and the overt transfer of specfic responses. *American Journal of Psychology, 53*, 173–203.

Miller, G. A. (1956). The magical number seven, plus or minus two: Some limits on our capacity for processing information. *Psychological Review, 63*, 81–97.

Milner, B. (1963). Effects of different brain lesions on card sorting. Archives of *Neurology, 9*, 90–100.

Milner, B. (1964). Some effects of frontal lobectomy in man. In J. M. Warren & K. Akert (Eds.), *The frontal granular cortex and behavior* (pp. 313–334). New York: McGraw-Hill.

Milner, B. (1966). Amnesia following operation on the temporal lobes. In C. W. M. Whitty & O. L. Zangwell (Eds.), *Amnesia* (pp. 109–133). London: Butterworths.

Murdock, B. B. (1961). The retention of individual items. *Journal of Experimental Psychology, 62*, 618–625.

Norman, D. A. (1969). *Memory and Attention*. New York: Wiley.

Norman, D. A., & Shallice, T. (1986). Attention to action: Willed and automatic control of behavior. R. J. Davidson, G. E. Schwartz, & D. Shapiro (Eds.), *Consciousness and self-regulation* (Vol. 4, pp. 1–18). New York: Plenum Press.

Papagno, C., Valentine, T., & Baddeley, A. D. (1991). Phonological short-term memory and foreign-language vocabulary learning. *Journal of Memory and Language, 30,* 331–347.

Papagno, C., & Vallar, G. (1992). Phonological short-term memory and the learning of novel words: The effect of phonological similarity and item length. *Quarterly Journal of Experimental Psychology, 44A,* 47–67.

Pascal-Leone, J. (1970). A mathematical model for the transition rule in Piagets' developmental stages. *Acta psychologia, 63,* 301–345.

Pendleton, M. G., Heaton, R. K., Lehman, R. A., & Hulihan, D. (1982). Diagnostic utility of the Thurstone Word Fluency Test in neuropsychological evaluations. *Journal of Clinical Neuropsychology, 4,* 307–317.

Penfield, W., & Evans, J. (1935). The frontal lobe in man: A clinical study of maximum removals. *Brain, 58,* 115–133.

Pennington, B. F. (1994). The working memory function of the prefrontal cortices. In M. M. Haith, J. B. Bensen, R. J. Roberts, & B. F. Pennington (Eds.), *The development of future oriented processes* (pp. 243–285). Chicago: University of Chicago Press.

Peterson, L. R., & Peterson, M. (1959). Short-term retention of individual verbal items. *Journal of Experimental Psychology, 58,* 193–198.

Posner, M. I., & Peterson, S. E. (1990). The attention system of the human brain. *Annual Review of Neuroscience, 13,* 25–42.

Posner, M. I., & Snyder, C. R. (1975). Attention and cognitive control. In R. Solso (Ed.), *Information Processing and Cognition: The Loyola Symposium* (pp. 55–85). Potomac, MD: Erlbaum.

Postman, L., Stark, K., & Fraser, L. (1968). Temporal changes in interference. *Journal of Verbal Learning and Verbal Behavior, 7,* 672–694.

Reitman, J. S. (1971). Mechanisms of forgetting in short-term memory. *Cognitive Psychology, 2,* 185–195.

Reitman, J. S. (1974). Without surreptitious rehearsal: information in short-term memory decays. *Journal of Verbal Learning and Verbal Behavior, 13,* 365–377.

Reisberg, D., Rappaport, I., & O'Shaughnessy, M. (1984). Limits on working memory. *Journal of Experimental Psychology: Learning, Memory, & Cognition, 10,* 203–221.

Roediger, H. L. (1990). Implicit memory: Retention without remembering. *American Psychologist, 45,* 1043–1056.

Rosen, V. M., & Engle, R. W. (1997). The role of working memory capacity in retrieval, *Journal of Experimental Psychology: General* 126, 211–227.

Rosen, V. M., & Engle, R. W. (1998). Working memory and suppression. (Manuscript submitted).

Rumelhart, D. E., Hinton, G., & McClellend, J. L. (1986). *A general framework for parallel distributed processing* (Vol. 1). Cambridge, MA: MIT Press.

Rundus, D., & Atkinson, R. C. (1970). Rehearsal processes in free recall: A procedure for direct observation. *Journal of Verbal Learning and Verbal Behavior, 9,* 99–105.

Schacter, D. L. (1987). Implicit memory: History and current status. *Journal of Experimental Psychology: Learning, Memory, and Cognition, 13,* 501–518.

Schneider, W., & Detweiller, M. (1987). A connectionist/control architecture for working memory. In G. H. Bower (Ed.), *The psychology of learning and motivation* (Vol. 21, pp. 53–119). New York: Academic Press.

Shallice, T., & Burgess, P. W. (1993). Supervisory control of thought and action. In A. D. Baddeley and L. Weiskrantz (Eds.), *Attention: Selection, awareness and control: A tribute to Donald Broadbent* (pp. 171–187). Oxford: Oxford University Press.

Shallice, T., & Warrington, E. K. (1970). Independent functioning of verbal memory scores: A neuropsychological study. *Quarterly Journal of Experimental Psychology, 22,* 261–273.

Shiffrin, R. M., & Schneider, W. (1977). Controlled and automatic human information processing: Pt. 2. Perceptual learning, automatic attending and a general theory. *Psychological Review, 84,* 127–190.

Shimamura, A. P., Gershberg, F. B., Jurica, P. J., Mangels, J. A., & Knight, R. T. (1992). Intact implicit memory in patients with focal frontal lobe lesions. *Neuropsychology, 30,* 931–937.

Schneider, W., & Detweiler, M. (1987). A connectionist/control architecture for working memory. In G. H. Bower (Ed.), *The psychology of learning and motivation* (Vol. 21). New York: Academic Press.

Stuss, D. T. (1991). Self, awareness, and the frontal lobes: A neuropsychological perspective. In J. Strauss & G. R. Goethals (Eds.), *The Self: Interdisciplinary Approaches* (pp. 255–278). New York: Springer.

Tuholski, S. W., & Engle, R. W. *Individual differences in working memory capacity and the use of mental models.* Manuscript submitted for publication.

Tulving, E. (1966). Subjective organization and effects of repetition in multi-trial free-recall learning. *Journal of Verbal Learning and Verbal Behavior, 5,* 193–197.

Turner, M. L., & Engle, R. W. (1989). Is working memory capacity task dependent? *Journal of Memory and Language, 28,* 127–154.

Warrington, E. K., Logue, V., & Pratt, R. T. C. (1971). The selective impairment of auditory verbal short-term memory. *Neuropsychologica, 9,* 377–387.

Warrington, E. K., & Weiskrantz, L. (1973). An analysis of short-term and long-term memory defects in man. In J. A. Deutsch (Ed.), *The physiological basis of memory.* New York: Academic Press.

Waters, G. S., Caplan, D. (1996). The measurement of verbal working memory capacity and its relation to leading comprehension. *The Quarterly Journal of Experimental Psychology 1996, 49 A,* 51–79.

Waugh, N. C., & Norman, D. A. (1965). Primary memory. *Psychological Review, 72,* 89–104.

Weinberger, D. R. (1993). A connectionist approach to the prefrontal cortex. *Journal of Neuropsychiatry, 5,* 241–253.

Wickelgren, W. A. (1966). Distinctive features and errors in STM for English consonants. *Journal of the Acoustical Society of America, 39,* 388–398.

Wilson, B. A., & Baddeley, A. D. (1993). Spontaneous recovery of impaired memory span: Does comprehension recover? *Cortex, 29,* 143–159.

16

Rational versus Arational Models of Thought

Steven A. Sloman

What do we mean when we say that a person is being *irrational?* Sometimes the phrase is used because of its pejorative connotations or to express the sentiment "I strongly disagree." Let's ignore such pragmatic readings and consider how the phrase might be true or false. The conventional interpretation of an irrational belief or act is that it is incoherent or implies incoherence: it contradicts other beliefs or acts by, for example, violating common sense. In order to be more precise than this, we'll have to consider the multiple forms of rationality.

Forms of Rationality

Rationality sometimes refers to a sound or reasonable thought process. For example, someone engaged in a long division problem might be said to be performing a rational exercise. Rational thinking, in this sense, is logical (Evans, 1993; Evans, Over, & Manktelow, 1993) or at least involves a process that derives valid inferences (Johnson-Laird & Byrne, 1991). Thus, thought can be rational by virtue of the method of inference it employs. Using the Pythagorean theorem to determine the length of the hypotenuse of a right triangle is a rational process because, if applied correctly, it will provide the correct answer. Notice that thinking can involve a rational process even if it generates a wrong answer through an error in calculation.

In this chapter I will focus mainly on a different sense of rationality, which we can call *rationality of response* (cf. Evans, 1993; Evans et al., 1993). I will be concerned with whether or not we get the right answer, without regard to the method used to obtain it. The "right answer" is

the solution to whatever problem is at hand. In other words, I will stipu-
late that you think or act rationally by thinking or acting in a way that
maximizes attainment of your own goals. This is what two of the pioneers
of cognitive science had in mind when they jump-started the computational analysis of human problem solving: rational behavior "is appropriate to the goal in the light of the problem environment" (Newell &
Simon, 1972, p. 53). So rationality of response refers to a harmony between a description of a belief or action relevant to achievement of a goal
and a theory of how that goal is best achieved. Of course, a common
goal is to minimize the time and effort required to perform some task.
Sometimes we'll save time or energy by not performing a task perfectly
but only "well enough." If saving time and energy is part of one's goal,
doing so is by no means irrational.

Three attributes of this definition of rationality are noteworthy. First,
it assumes a goal. The rationality of a system cannot be defined if we
have no idea what the system is trying to accomplish. For instance, if we
don't know where a person is going, then there's no way to judge the
rationality of the person's movement. Second, the definition assumes that
we have some idea of the best way to achieve the goal; this is often called
a *normative* theory. Obviously, we cannot evaluate whether a person is
maximizing attainment of a goal without some idea of how to maximize
it. Sometimes, we do have an idea. If we know that a person wants to
go west, then clearly the person should not go east, assuming that going
around the world is not feasible. But we don't always know the best way
to reach a goal; as we'll see, a normative theory of optimal behavior is
not always available. Finally, rationality refers to a relation between theories: a descriptive (psychological) theory and a normative theory. To illustrate, in several experiments to be described, people were asked to make
judgments of frequency or probability. In such cases, the rationality of
their judgments will refer to the relation between a description of their
judgments and probability theory, a theory of optimal judgment in such
circumstances.

Note that unlike rationality of process, rationality of response does not
imply that a normative theory serves as a basis for thought in any sense. A
person's responses could be rational even if the person had no knowledge
(conscious or unconscious) of the relevant normative theory. The requi-

site consistency between the normative theory and the response could be a result of using some arational procedure that has the effect of producing the right answer (as the natural assessment procedures that will be discussed usually do).

Harman (1995; see also Evans et al., 1993) points out that response rationality has two sides: theoretical and practical. Theoretical rationality entails having beliefs that correspond to reality. The belief that Rhode Island is east of Connecticut is rational in this sense because it is true (whether or not the belief was arrived at using a rational inference procedure). Practical rationality entails acting or intending to act in a way that is most likely to satisfy one's goals. To show that theoretical and practical rationality are not the same, Harman (1995) has us consider Jane. Jane has taken an exam, and before finding out her grade, she concludes and therefore believes she received a good grade because she wanted a good grade. This is clearly an irrational belief (wanting a good grade does not guarantee a good grade) and illustrates the inconsistency between wishful thinking and rational belief—that is, theoretical rationality. However, it would be quite rational for Jane to permit her desire to get a good grade on the exam to influence her studying to make it more likely that she'll get a good grade. Thus, wishful thinking can be perfectly consistent with practical rationality. Hence, desire plays a causal role in practical rationality that it does not play in theoretical rationality.

Limitations on the Assessment of Rationality

Assessing rationality is a difficult and often impossible task. Furthermore, we must be very careful in these assessments because they entail a value judgment. When someone believes something is true or some course of action is optimal, then that person's belief represents not only a description of his or her cognitive state but also, from the person's point of view, a statement of what is normatively justified. If the person didn't consider it normatively justified, then he or she wouldn't believe it.[1] The closest we can come to an independent and disinterested determination of the validity of the normative justification of a belief is to rely on any consensus that can be found in the community of experts (Stich & Nisbett, 1980). The fundamental justification for the belief that the square root of 144 is 12 is that mathematicians agree that it is. So I will limit my ascriptions of irrationality to cases in which a person's responses contradict the overwhelming consensus of a community of experts. In most cases mentioned here, people who provide irrational responses willingly admit the error themselves after consideration of the experts' argument.

Assessing rationality can be difficult because it depends on the goal being pursued. If the goal changes, the rationality of the relevant behavior could change. For example, an apparently irrational play in a poker game could prove quite rational upon realization that the player's goal is not to win the hand but to fool the opponent into the belief that the player is a novice (reminiscent of the familiar "bloodshot eyes" ruse; cf. Cherniak, 1986). Analogously, generals will often lose a battle in order to win a war. Attributing the wrong goal to an individual can be fatal to the accurate assessment of rationality.

A further complication is that on a specific occasion, we might apply the wrong descriptive theory, the wrong normative theory, or both. Descriptive theories are often wrong because identifying reliable psychological phenomena and generating general, empirically valid descriptions of them are notoriously difficult. The study of psychology is hard. Generating normative theories that win reasonable amounts of social acceptance is equally hard; rarely is the optimal way to achieve some goal beyond dispute. Indeed, the study of logic, probability, law, ethics, and other fields constitutes a colossal effort on the part of society to develop valid normative theories. It is clearly a long and ongoing process. So development of normative theory is just as constructive and dynamic a process as is development of descriptive theory.

Moreover, descriptive and normative theory are interdependent. Descriptive theory is often guided by normative theory. For example, some theories of reasoning (e.g., Rips, 1994) posit that everyday inference takes place using rule sets that derive from specific logical inference procedures. Typically, the descriptive theory of reasoning in such cases is composed from a part of a full normative logical theory. Descriptive theory can even include normative theories. Part of a descriptive theory might consist of people's efforts to employ normative principles. For example, the normative theory of probability comprises part of the descriptive theory of (say) weather forecasting to the extent that forecasters deliberately and explicitly employ the rules of probability to derive predictions.

Conversely, normative theories depend on descriptive theories in a number of ways. Descriptive theories provide some of the goals and constraints that normative theories operate under. Without a descriptive theory of what people value, for instance, we couldn't derive a normative ethical theory concerning how people should be treated. More fundamentally, descriptive theories serve as the foundation of normative theories.[2] Some philosophers believe that the ultimate justification for theories such as probability and logic is the basic human intuition that their fundamental principles are sound (cf. Goodman, 1965; Savage, 1972). To illustrate, a basic principle (or axiom) of logic is that the statement x and its complement, *not x,* cannot both be true. Most people agree with this principle even though they cannot justify it; it seems self-evident. Normative theories generally rest on such (apparently) self-evident intuitions—general principles that are psychologically sound.

In many cases, a normative theory doesn't even exist. For example, the optimal strategy for playing poker is unknown and may well be unknowable. A more general example involves how we should change our beliefs when we encounter new information. Optimal belief-updating often depends on assumptions that we make about the situation. Let's say we see someone be helpful to someone else. A rational attribution of helpfulness to the first person presumably would consider the relative authority of the two people. In particular, we would consider the first person less helpful if the second person were his or her boss than if not (cf. Kelley, 1973). But no normative theory can tell us the optimal way to construe a situation. The laws of logic may tell us that new information is inconsistent with our beliefs, but they don't tell us how to revise the beliefs to rectify the inconsistency (Harman, 1995; Stich, 1990); the laws of probability do but in a way that is heavily dependent on prior assumptions (Pearl, 1988). In other words, neither of these theories by themselves can tell us when to ascribe helpfulness to another person and when not to. And whenever a normative theory is unavailable, ascriptions of rationality are too.

Minimal Rationality

Summarizing a body of literature in the philosophy of mind, Cherniak (1986) states, "The most basic law of psychology is a rationality constraint on an agent's beliefs, desires, and actions: No rationality, no agent" (p. 3). Cherniak is referring to the close link that philosophers have established between a person's rationality and our ability to understand that person's plans and purposes—that is, to ascribe intentions to them. Without ascribing rationality to people, we couldn't engage in discourse with them, because we would have no basis for believing they understood our utterances. Imagine that we're taking a walk in the forest together, and an animal you've never seen before comes bounding along and I say, "that's a *dax*." How do you know what *dax* refers to? I could be referring to a part of the animal (its tail or ears, e.g.) or to its manner of movement or to the bush that it is occluding. All these possibilities seem silly, however; the implicit social demand for me to try to make only statements that you can understand (Grice, 1975) seems to require me to refer to this new, bounding creature in its entirety. Discourse inevitably requires a host of implicit assumptions and inferences from context that are licensed by the belief that our interlocuters are rational. If they weren't rational, we would have to spell out every phrase, reference, and allusion. We could not expect our listeners to fill in the smallest detail of our intended meaning. Discourse would grind to a halt, for, in fact, we expect our listeners to fill in a lot (Grice, 1975). We could not collaborate in conversation with those we did not assume were rational, because we could only assume their interpretations were random or absurd. To make matters worse, we could not predict the behavior of people who did not obey rational rules. How could we cross the street if we didn't believe that other people would behave in appropriate ways by, for example, obeying traffic laws? To live with other people and understand them, we must assume that their beliefs are rational (Quine, 1960). For the vast majority of people, the assumption of rationality seems appropriate and actually trivial.[3]

But do we need to ascribe perfect rationality? Cherniak (1986) argues that we need only ascribe *minimal* rationality. We must ascribe enough rationality to allow communication and some predictability of behavior in constrained conditions (such as in traffic), but we need not assume that people never diverge from the dictates of normative theory. By assuming people are like ourselves, we can make educated guesses about how they will interpret us and what they will remember and know. These educated guesses serve to allow communication and prediction by making possible estimates of the degree and kind of rationality people will display. As long as we know how much rationality to expect, we can estimate the minimal amount of rationality that we can assume.

The Value of Error

The first observation made by most students of normal human behavior is the remarkable degree of theoretical and practical rationality that people display. People display more knowledge of the world (theoretical rationality) and perform more varied and complex actions successfully (practical rationality) than any other known entity in the universe. People can adjust themselves to changing environments, derive successful strategies, learn new tasks, imagine other possible worlds, perceive others' intentions, and much more, often rapidly and usually even effortlessly. A classic example of such an intellectual feat is language learning. Almost all children by a few years of age have mastered a huge vocabularly and a syntax too complex to teach any current computer. Another (possibly related) talent is pattern recognition. Even young children are able to distinguish and recognize thousands of objects, displays, and motions, despite variation in orientation, lighting, size, and function.

How do we do these things? This is the most basic question of cognitive science. One of the largest obstacles to answering it is that describing such skilled performance confounds the task performed and the cognitive apparatus performing it. When I see a master chess player plying his trade, I cannot separate what I'm learning about the intricacies of chess from what I'm learning about how humans go about playing chess. Thus most analyses of human behavior concern error—deviations from optimal performance—because errors allow us to separate task factors from psychological factors. This point was made years ago by Newell and Simon (1972). Consider the larger context of their definition of rationality that I provided in the opening section:

[Rational behavior] is appropriate to the goal in the light of the problem environment; it is the behavior demanded by the situation. Now if there is such a thing as behavior demanded by a situation, and if a subject exhibits it, then his behavior tells us more about the task environment than about him. We learn about the subject only that he is in fact motivated toward the goal, and that he is in fact capable of discovering and executing the behavior called for by the situation. If we put him in a different situation, he would behave differently. . . . To the extent that the behavior is precisely what is called for by the situation, it will give us information about the task environment. . . . To the extent that the behavior departs from perfect rationality, we gain information about the psychology of the subject, about the nature of the internal mechanisms that are limiting his performance. . . . A theory of thinking and problem solving cannot predict behavior unless it encompasses both an analysis of the structure of task environments and an analysis of the limits of rational adaptation to task requirements. (pp. 53–55)

Normative theories constitute attempts to describe what people are trying to accomplish in a given task. Points of divergence between what people try to do and what they actually do—errors—are more revealing about mental operation than points of convergence, because when people succeed in accomplishing their goals their performance can be equally well attributed to the structure of the task being performed as the structure of the mind performing the task. As a result, most of our lessons about human behavior come from a focus on error.

Some Deviations from Ideal Rationality

The most transparent and reliable examples of lessons about cognition provided by human error come from the study of visual illusions. One simple example is the moon illusion. The moon appears to be larger when it's near the horizon than when it's overhead, even when the size of the retinal images are identical. A common explanation for this phenomenon (elaborated in Kaufman & Rock, 1989) is that a number of distance cues are available when the moon is near the horizon, which gives the impression that the moon is far away. Because it is perceived as far away, our perceptual system increases its perceived size. When the moon is overhead, fewer distance cues are available, therefore less size correction occurs. Here's a case in which an error in size discrimination (a difference is observed that doesn't exist) provides evidence about the perceptual mechanism of distance perception. It is the deviations from ideal (accurate) size judgments that produce the evidential value.

The 1960s saw the emergence of the study of what are often called, in analogy to visual illusions, *cognitive illusions* (a brief history can be found in Arkes & Hammond, 1986). These were cases in which people's most common responses on tasks involving probability judgment did not conform to the dictates of a probabilistic analysis of the task. These systematic deviations from normative theory are known as biases. For example, Troutman and Shanteau (1977) showed people samples of beads from a box known to contain either 70 red, 30 white, and 50 blue beads or 30 red, 70 white, and 50 blue beads. The samples were replaced after each presentation. After each sample, subjects were asked to estimate the probability that the box was predominantly white. Some of the samples were nondiagnostic; they consisted of either a red and a white bead, two blue beads, or no beads at all. None of these samples should have had any effect on subjects' probability judgments, because they were each equally likely to have come from either box. Nevertheless, each of them caused subjects to reduce their probability judgments (even no beads at all!). Here is a case in which people are clearly not responding in a way that is consistent with probability theory. Demonstrations of systematic error such as this have helped to uncover several general principles of human judgment and reasoning, some of which I will now review.

Reliance on Memory

Are there more words in the English language that end in *ing* or that have the single letter *n* in the second-last position (i.e., that end in _*n*_)? Most people's initial response to this query is that more words end in *ing*. The probable reason for this judgment is that most people try to generate both types of words to answer the question and are more successful generating words that end in *ing* than words that end in _*n*_. A simple heuristic can then be applied: objects and events are frequent to the extent they come easily to mind. This heuristic leads to the conclusion that words ending in *ing* must be the more frequent. Tversky and Kahneman (1973) label this the "availability heuristic" and demonstrate that it is often applied to make judgments of frequency and probability. The heuristic is effective much of the time, especially for rare objects and events, but it does lead to certain errors, as in the example cited. Words that end in _n_ must be more frequent than words that end in *ing*, because every word ending in *ing* is also a word ending in _n_. This is an instance of the *conjunction fallacy of probability*, a case in which people's judgments of frequency violate the conjunction rule of probability: the probability of an event (such as a word ending in *ing*) cannot be greater than the probability of the event's constituents (in this case, the constituent is that the word has *n* in the second-last position). The cause of the conjunction fallacy in this case is that the addition of *i* and *g* to _n_ aids memory retrieval but reduces the set of acceptable words.

A number of other phenomena can also be attributed to the availability heuristic. Our own actions are more available in memory than other people's actions, and tasks that we initiate are more available than tasks others inititiate. This explains Ross and Sicoly's (1979) finding that both husbands and wives tended to give themselves more responsibility for household activities than they gave each other, so the total amount of responsibility they estimated added up to more than 100%. Evidence that this assessment resulted from the availability heuristic and not an attempt by participants to present themselves as responsible is that the effect occurred for negative items (e.g., "Who is responsible for causing arguments"?) as well as for positive items such as household chores.

Events can be made more or less available by the degree to which we are exposed to them. The frequency of events that receive massive media coverage, earthquakes, accidents at nuclear power stations, and electrocutions, for example, tend to be overestimated, whereas the frequency of events that receive little or no coverage, such as deaths due to asthma or heart disease tend to be underestimated (Lichtenstein, Slovic, Fischhoff, Layman, & Combs, 1978).

Past experience serves as our sample of the way the world works and therefore can be a guide for making rational judgments and predictions. Memory serves as our repository of past experience, and therefore memory is central to thinking. But human memory is a mechanism that has certain principles of operation, and those principles make some events easier to retrieve than others. Events that we understand are easier to retrieve than events that are not meaningful (Craik & Lockhart, 1972), and events for which more retrieval cues are provided—such as words ending in *ing*—are easier to retrieve than events not so well cued—such as words ending in _n_ (Tulving & Thomson, 1973). These principles of memory can lead to systematic errors, or biases, in judgment when the cues that ease memory retrieval reduce the size of the set of events whose probability is being judged.

Reliance on Similarity

Here's another example of how human error can lead to insights about how people think:

Linda is 31 years old, single, outspoken and very bright. She majored in philosophy. As a student, she was deeply concerned with issues of discrimination and social justice and also participated in antinuclear demonstrations.

Which of the following two statements is more likely?

Linda is a bank teller. (*T*)
Linda is a bank teller and is active in the feminist movement. (*T&F*)

Tversky and Kahneman (1983) asked this question in a variety of ways and consistently found that most people judged the second statement to be more likely than the first. They attribute this pattern of performance to the *representativeness* heuristic, according to which the probability or frequency of an object or event increases to the extent that it is similar to the category being judged. The paragraph describing Linda is more similar to that of a feminist bank teller than it is to a stereotypical bank teller and therefore we can more easily imagine Linda as a feminist bank teller, which leads us to conclude that she is more likely to be one. Evidence that people use a similarity-based heuristic for this kind of judgment is strong (Crandall & Greenfield, 1986; Smith & Osherson, 1989), although they are also influenced by other factors (Gavanski & Roskos-Ewoldsen, 1991; Shafir, Smith, & Osherson, 1990).

Of course, this is another example of the conjunction fallacy. Statement *T&F* could not possibly be more probable than statement *T,* because it presupposes *T*. A conjunction can never be more probable than one of its constituents. Nevertheless, representativeness overwhelmingly dictates how people respond. The fallacy was committed even by the great majority of a group of doctoral students in the decision science program of the

Stanford Business School, who are highly trained in probability theory (Tversky & Kahneman, 1983).

Another example of too much reliance on similarity to make judgments of probability comes from studies of base rate neglect. Consider Tom W.:

Tom W. is of high intelligence, although lacking in true creativity. He has a need for order and clarity, and for neat and tidy systems in which every detail finds its appropriate place. His writing is rather dull and mechanical, occasionally enlivened by somewhat corny puns and by flashes of imagination of the sci-fi type. He has a strong drive for competence. He seems to have little feel and little sympathy for other people and does not enjoy interacting with others. Self-centered, he nonetheless has a deep moral sense. (Kahneman & Tversky, 1973, p. 238)

Imagine that this sketch of Tom W. had been written by a psychologist, on the basis of projective tests, when Tom was a senior in high school. What field do you think you would find Tom W. in? Rank the following nine fields according to the probabilities that Tom W. is in them: business administration, computer science, engineering, humanities and education, law, library science, medicine, physical and life sciences, and social science and social work. According to Bayes's theorem of probability, your ranking should have considered two aspects of each field: the probability that someone in the field would have Tom W.'s description (case data) and the relative frequency of people in the field (the base rate). The base rate is important because it indicates the proportion of the population that the field includes. To see its importance, consider how much fear you should have about your next airplane trip. No matter how easily you can imagine a fiery crash or other tragedy, the base rate of airplane accidents is so low that you can feel secure about your next flight; tragedies simply hardly ever occur. Analogously, the probability that Tom W. is a computer scientist is a function of both how much he seems like a computer scientist and how frequent computer scientists are in the population. However, in this problem, people pay a lot of attention to the case data and show a relative neglect for the base rates. Rankings of the probability of Tom W.'s being in each field corresponded closely to rankings of the similarity between Tom W. and a typical graduate student in each field and had no relation to judgments of the base rates of students in the fields (Kahneman & Tversky, 1973). Generally speaking, base rates in this type of problem tend to be underweighted although not completely ignored (e.g., Bar-Hillel, 1983). This tendency for people to make their judgments according to the similarity between a description and a representation of a class is another example of the application of the representativeness heuristic.

Errors in reasoning due to reliance on similarity can also be found in tasks that ask people to project unfamiliar properties amongst categories. Sloman (1998) found that people tended to project properties from a superordinate category to a subordinate one in proportion to the extent that the categories were similar. For example, Brown University students were asked to rate the probability of the conclusion of the following argument (that every individual bank manager can use tax form addendum 10–83) given that the premise is true (that every individual white-collar worker can use tax form addendum 10–83):

Every individual white-collar worker can use tax form addendum 10–83.

Therefore, every individual bank manager can use tax form addendum 10–83.

The students gave it a mean probability rating of only .87. They found the conclusion likely but not certain despite agreeing that all bank managers are white-collar workers. Moreover, the argument

Every individual white-collar worker can use tax form addendum 10–83.

Therefore, every individual air traffic controller can use tax form addendum 10–83.

received a mean probability of only .62, even though participants also agreed that all air traffic controllers are white-collar workers. Air traffic controllers apparently have little enough in common with other white-collar workers that they are not automatically ascribed a property held by all white-collar workers, even though they themselves belong to the category. This pattern of response does not conform to set theoretic logic, which dictates that if all white-collar workers have a property then all members of that category must have it. Similarity seems to be playing a role in that the categories of the first argument, which received higher probability ratings, were judged more similar than categories of the second argument (bank managers and white-collar workers were judged more similar than air traffic controllers and white-collar workers). More evidence that similarity plays a critical role in the evaluation of such arguments can be found in Osherson, Smith, Wilkie, Lopez, & Shafir (1990) and Sloman (1993).

In many situations, similarity relations are excellent proxies for probabilistic relations. Generally, instances are more probable if they are similar to a category prototype. The probability of encountering someone whose height deviates slightly from the average—that is, who is similar to the average—is higher than the probability of encountering someone extraordinarily short or tall. Moreover, instances are more probable if they are more similar to the typical outcome of a process. The probability of a snowfall that drops a quantity of snow that's close (similar) to average is indeed higher than a more extreme snowfall. But similarity is determined according to certain cognitive principles such as feature overlap, feature contrast (Tversky, 1977), and feature alignment (Medin, Goldstone, Gentner, 1993), and those principles can lead to such systematic biases in the assessment of probability as neglect of the conjunction rule, of base rates, and of inclusion relations. By focusing on these biases, cognitive scientists have been able to uncover one of the principal means by which people make judgments: on the basis of similarity.

Reliance on Positive Tests

The Sabines were part of (a) Ancient India or (b) Ancient Rome?

Choose one of options (a) and (b), and then state the probability that you're correct. Koriat, Lichtenstein, and Fischhoff (1980) asked subjects to do this using a variety of general knowledge questions of this type. They found their subjects were overconfident in the sense that their probability judgments were too high (cf. Oskamp, 1965). They were *uncalibrated:* the proportion of times they were correct for all questions at each level of judged probability was lower than that probability. For example, considering only those questions that were assigned a probability judgment of .8, the proportion answered correctly was only about .6. In fact, of those questions that subjects assigned a probability of 1 (they were absolutely sure of the answer), they only got about 80% correct. In a subsequent experiment, Koriat et al. had subjects generate reasons either supporting their answer or contradicting their answer (reasons they might be wrong) before generating a probability judgment. Supporting reasons had no effect; subjects were just as overconfident as they were when they generated no reasons. However, generating contradicting reasons reduced the amount of overconfidence observed; judged probabilities moved closer to actual proportions correct. One explanation for these findings is that supporting reasons did not affect judgments, because subjects automatically generated them anyway. Supporting reasons were generated whether or not they were asked for, but contradicting reasons were not. People do not automatically generate reasons contradicting their conclusions, which causes their conclusions to appear to have more support than they do. This leads to overconfidence.[4]

This tendency to generate supporting reasons hints at a more general tendency that has been observed in a number of tasks in which people are required to test hypotheses. People look for reasons that are implied by their hypotheses and examine data to see if they support their hypotheses. They fail to look for reasons that are implied by alternative hypotheses and examine data to see if they support other hypotheses. Klayman and Ha (1987) refer to this as a *positive test strategy:* "people tend to test hypotheses by looking at instances where the target property is hypothesized to be present or is known to be present" (p. 225).

Consider the Wason (1960) rule discovery task, which involves sets of three numbers (triples). The experimenter makes up a rule to which some triples conform and others do not. Subjects are given one triple that fits the rule: 2, 4, 6. Their task is to name other triples, and the experimenter tells them whether or not these other triples fit the rule. When ready, subjects try to guess the rule and test their guess by generating more triples. A common first guess is "three consecutive even numbers." After such a guess, subjects have an implicit choice. They can either try to disconfirm their hypothesis by generating a triple that does not conform to the rule (e.g., 2, 4, 7) or they can try to confirm their hypothesis (a positive test; e.g., 4, 6, 8). Wason found that people tried to confirm their hypotheses much more often than they tried to disconfirm them. This led to trouble in Wason's case because the rule he had in mind was extremely general: any three ascending numbers. As a result, subjects' guesses tended to conform to the experimenter's rule, which led to confirmation of their hypothesis even though it was incorrect. This often caused subjects to develop an unwarranted degree of confidence in their hypothesis. Had subjects used a different strategy, if they had tested their hypothesis using negative instances that did not conform to the rule they had in mind, they would have rapidly disconfirmed it. In sum, use of the positive test strategy gave subjects a mistaken sense of confidence.

One effect of the positive test strategy is to cause people to neglect alternative hypotheses. Such neglect could explain why Troutman and Shanteau (1977), in the experiment described earlier, found that drawing a sample of beads that was unlikely given the hypothesis that subjects believed had the effect of reducing subjects' confidence in that hypothesis, even though the sample was equally unlikely given the alternative hypothesis that they did not believe. Fischhoff and Beyth-Marom (1983) make the point in this way:

A favorite ploy of magicians, mentalists, and pseudopsychics who claim to read other people's minds is to provide universally valid personality descriptions that apply to almost everyone, although this is not transparently so. These operators trust their listeners to assess P(this description given my mind is being read) and not P(this description given my mind is not being read). (p. 248)

This neglect of alternative hypotheses has obvious ramifications for scientific practice and explains why scientists must be reminded of the importance of trying to falsify their hypotheses (Popper, 1959).

Klayman and Ha (1987) demonstrate that the positive test strategy is a useful heuristic that often leads to an optimal information search; that is, it often provides maximum information about the validity of a hypothesis (for a related analysis of the Wason 4-card selection task, see Oaksford & Chater, 1994). However, like any heuristic, it can also lead us astray, as it does when it biases our search for evidence, as in Wason's (1960) rule discovery paradigm, or when it causes us to neglect alternative hypotheses.[5]

I have reviewed only a small sample of the many heuristics that have been posited and the many biases and complexities in judgment and reasoning that have been uncovered. A number of fuller treatments and reviews exist, including Arkes and Hammond (1986); Baron (1994); Kahneman et al. (1982); Nisbett and Ross (1980); Payne, Bettman, and Johnson (1992); and Plous (1993).

Why Do People Make Errors?

Bounded Rationality

Two complementary views of the reason we find systematic error can be distinguished. The older view, made popular by the seminal work of Herbert Simon, is commonly referred to as *bounded rationality*. The idea is that people make errors because they operate with limited cognitive resources. Our short-term memories have limited capacity; we can perform only a limited number of operations at any time; we have limited energy; indeed, we are limited in every way. However, many of the problems that confront us are enormously difficult computationally and sometimes impossible. For example, the world's fastest computer would be unable to consider all the possible sequences of moves in a chess game even if it ran for billions of years. Another example comes from the theory of computation. Some statements about the world are undecidable in the sense that we cannot tell if they are consequences of our beliefs or not. Computational bounds prevent us from knowing whether the desire to maintain consistency amongst our beliefs should cause us to believe these statements. Some problems cannot be solved by unaided humans, and some problems cannot be solved at all. Therefore, instead of deriving optimal strategies that are completely satisfactory, we resort to strategies that are *satisficing*, reasonable but not necessarily optimal (Simon, 1981). We strive to accomplish our main objectives without demanding optimality. We play the best game of chess we can with the expectation that every move won't be perfect, and we accept that some of our beliefs are likely to be inconsistent with others.

This acceptance that trade-offs are made between the efficiency of performing cognitive tasks and the achievement of optimal performance may explain some aspects of mental organization. For example, Cherniak (1986) argues that knowledge is compartmentalized in memory to promote search efficiency. To optimize accuracy, all knowledge would be accessible in memory at all times. But it's not. Knowledge is accessible only in certain contexts. This reduces our ability to make connections between pieces of knowledge stored in different compartments. This inability inhibits discovery as it did in the case of penicillin (Hilding, 1975). Many microbiologists were aware for at least a decade both that molds cause clear spots in bacteria cultures and that bare spots indicate no bacterial growth before Fleming made the critical connection and realized that molds must release an antibacterial agent. This realization led directly to the discovery of penicillin. Cherniak concludes that knowledge is divided into bundles in memory, so only the contents of a single bundle usually need to be searched for a desired trace. The downside of this type of organization is that not all traces will be in the active bundle and therefore will not be accessible when needed.

The observation that rationality is bounded has led to disagreement about the proper definition of it. An extreme view is that human thought and activity *must* be rational because behavior should be judged relative to the constraints under which the behavior is determined. Those constraints are both evolutionary (human behavior has adapted to its environments) and cognitive (human computational resources are necessarily limited). In other words, instead of regarding the constraints as part of a descriptive theory, this view regards them as part of a normative theory of whatever task is being performed. The normative theory thereby becomes much less exacting; people will always come out spectacularly well because any lack of optimality in performance can be attributed to phylogenetic and ontogenetic constraints. An even more extreme view is that all errors in human reasoning are mere performance errors, attributable to constraints on how cognitive systems are forced to operate when resources are limited (Cohen, 1981). According to Cohen, errors do not reflect underlying inferential competence, which is invariably normatively unimpeachable (for reasons already alluded to).[6]

In the words of Bertrand Russell, these extreme views have all the virtues of theft over honest toil by simply defining away the problem of assessing human rationality. By disallowing the possibility of irrationality, they prevent the insights into cognition that error illuminates and they prevent us from trying to improve human performance. To retain content in the notion of rationality, at least some cognitive constraints must be ascribed to descriptive and not normative theory. After all, these constraints do serve to describe the cognitive system. Nevertheless, the alternative view does highlight a critical point. Some tasks, such as beating a grandmaster at chess, are hard. We would not want to label somebody irrational just because he or she failed to win a game against a grandmaster. Our processing is constrained, and our goal is often not to perform a task optimally but to perform it well without too much cost (in time, effort, etc.). If one of our goals is to reduce cost, then the constraint that engenders the cost belongs in normative and not descriptive theory. In sum, optimal performance is often usefully defined as that which could plausibly be expected of a human being with normal human resources. But discrepancies between descriptive and normative theory remain possible (Cherniak, 1986; Dennett, 1995; Evans, 1993). People do make errors.

Natural Assessment Methods

In the early 1970s, the work of Amos Tversky and Daniel Kahneman made popular a second view of the determinants of systematic error. They argued that people make errors because they make judgments and decisions using heuristics (rules of thumb) that are quick and easy for people and that usually provide reasonable and adequate answers but fail under particular conditions. The heuristics they posit draw on the strengths of the human cognitive machinery, and therefore they refer to these heuristics as natural assessment methods. We've already encountered the two most powerful and useful heuristics: representativeness and availability. Representativeness relies on one function at which our cognitive systems excel, similarity assessment. It takes advantage of the ability of similarity relations to approximately map probability distributions. Availability relies on a different cognitive strength, memory retrieval. It takes advantage of the ability of memory to draw on past experience. But these heuristics also lead to certain biases in reasoning and judgment, examples of which we've seen earlier.

The main difference between the two views of error has to do with the rationality of the process people are understood to be using when making judgments. Bounded rationality assumes that people are using a rational inference procedure; they are just limited in their ability to fully exploit it. The natural assessment approach assumes that people are using an arational procedure that approximates rational inference. As we will see in the next section, evidence exists suggesting that people think in different ways, using both rational and heuristic procedures. Given this multiplicity of thought, the two views of error are complementary. Bounded rationality explains error in situations in which people are using a rational procedure, and the natural assessment approach explains why people also use procedures other than rational ones.

Two Types of Thinking

Each of these two views of human error suggests a different way to conceive of the place of normative rules in human thought. Bounded rationality suggests that people are able to follow rules derived from normative theory, although their ability to do so is limited by their limited cognitive resources. The natural assessment approach suggests that thought involves a process in which no rules of any kind are followed. Evidence can be found for both of these suggestions. Human thought seems to have two complementary aspects. These aspects have been distinguished in a variety of ways by a number of theorists over the years. To take only one example, Reason (1992) distinguishes an attentional control mode from an automatic one, which he takes to be the locus of much human error. Following Sloman (1996), I will call the two forms of thought *rule-based* and *associative*.

Rule-Based Thinking

Our ability to use formal systems such as mathematics and logic testifies to our ability to apply rules to perform symbolic manipulations. Our inclination to obey cultural rules (like stopping at stop signs) suggests that not only are we capable of applying rules, but we actually do apply them on a regular basis. This ability to follow rules enables us to follow normative rules, for they are simply rules of a specific kind. We can, for example, apply the rules of probability to derive prescriptions for optimal uncertain inference, as we did to understand the conjunction fallacies introduced earlier. More generally, we have the capacity to strategically adapt to problems in an effort to optimize performance. This type of thinking is flexible and productive and usually involves deliberation and symbolic manipulation (for a fuller characterization, see Sloman, 1996).

Rule-based thinking can lead to error due to bounds on rationality in the way described. Our efforts to follow normative rules may be bounded by the limited cognitive resources at our disposal. Some reasoning problems, for example, require us to maintain more information in working memory at one time than we can handle (e.g., Johnson-Laird & Byrne, 1991). A simple illustration can be constructed using arithmetic. If I ask you to multiply 13 and 9 without the aid of pencil and paper (or a calculator), you are more likely to give the right answer than if I ask you to mentally multiply 138 and 94. The latter problem requires several more intermediate calculations, which quickly overload working memory. You are competent at applying the rules of multiplication, but your performance is constrained by your limited cognitive resources.

Associative Thinking

In contrast to rule-based thinking, thinking compatible with natural assessment methods is guided by principles, such as reliance on memory and similarity, which serve as good approximations to normative principles but are not identical to them. This view of the thinking process has a long history; one tradition it is compatible with is *associationism*. Associationism, especially in its modern guise of connectionism, or parallel, distributed computation, starts from the premise that knowledge is built out of relations based on temporal and spatial contiguity. According to the modern view, an association is a learned tendency for one representation to elicit another when they represent objects that were in the same general vicinity at roughly the same time. Much of the inferential capacity of such systems emanates from their ability to generalize on the basis of similarity. For example, an associative system that has encountered many birds that have wings can automatically infer that a bird it has never seen before also has wings (Hinton, McClelland, & Rumelhart, 1986; Sloman, 1993). Other associative systems are capable of more sophisticated inferences as well (e.g., Barnden, 1994). Associative systems tend to be good at pattern recognition—essentially a form of similarity assessment—and memory retrieval. Not coincidentally, similarity assessment and memory are the two primary functions relied on by the natural assessment approach—in the guise of the representativeness and availability heuristics—to account for patterns of human error. This correlation between the functions that associative systems can serve and those human thought relies on suggests that associationism might serve as one reasonable model of thought.

In conclusion, although the characters of the systems of thought need to be more fully fleshed out (Gigerenzer & Regier, 1996), evidence does exist for both rule-based and associative thought. The best explanation for the available evidence seems to be that human cognition includes both kinds (Sloman, 1996, Gigerenzer & Regier, 1996, provide a contrary opinion). One motivation for this conclusion is the strength of the evidence for each system separately (evidence that people reason using rules is reviewed in Smith, Langston, & Nisbett, 1992). For example, when assigning objects to categories under conditions that demand justification, people tend to base their categorization decisions on rules encoding necessary conditions of the category (e.g., Rips, 1989). But when the demand for justification is removed, people tend to make assignments based on similarity (Smith & Sloman, 1994).

Another form of evidence suggesting two distinct systems of thought is the phenomenon of simultaneous contradictory belief (Sloman, 1996). Sometimes we maintain two contradictory responses to a reasoning problem at the same time, one based on rules and the other on associations. A good example is the "Linda the bank teller" problem described earlier. Even after understanding and accepting the conjunction rule of probability and thus affirming that Linda is more likely to be a bank teller than a feminist bank teller, most people still admit a propensity to believe that she is more likely to be a feminist bank teller. This conviction does not go away despite an equally firm conviction, based on the conjunction rule of probability, that she can't be. She *seems* like a feminist and thus more like a feminist bank teller, even though we *know* that she's more likely to be a bank teller. This phenomenon of simultaneously believing two contradictory statements implies that two systems are operating, each supporting one belief. This assumes, of course, that a system of thought can only maintain one coherent opinion at a time. In conclusion, thought has at least two modes, modes that apparently can operate in the same person at the same time. They are not equals, though. The rule-based system seems to be able, given sufficient time, to overrule and inhibit the associative one.

A variety of evidence suggests that thought consists of at least two systems. Each of these systems offers a solution to the problem of maintaining minimal rationality. The rule-based one does it directly by explicitly following normative rules to the extent that it is able. The associative one does it by operating according to principles that approximate normative ones and by operating quickly while requiring few cognitive resources (cf. Reason, 1992).

Extensional Cues

Can thought and action be made more rational; that is, are there conditions that cause descriptive theory to approach normative theory? The answer is yes. However, the conditions are restrictive: they apply to only certain kinds of problems or can be demanding. I describe two ways to increase the coherence of judgment.

Probability versus Frequency

In some cases, simple cues can serve to make behavior more rational. One cue that has increased the coherence of probability judgments involves asking people to assess frequency rather than probability. Tversky and Kahneman (1983) reduced the incidence of the conjunction fallacy by asking their subjects to estimate the relative frequency of an event given a specified number of possibilities instead of asking for judgments of probability. Similarly, Fiedler (1988) found that only 22% of his subjects violated the conjunction rule using the Linda the bank teller problem when he asked them how many people the statements applied to out of 100 people who are like Linda. However, 91% of his subjects violated the rule when he gave them the standard problem of rank ordering statements about Linda's profession "with respect to their probability." An effective way to understand the conjunction rule is in set-theoretic terms (the set of things with properties T and F is a subset of the set of things with property T). Describing the options in terms of concrete sets seems to make people aware of the subset relation relevant for the conjunction rule in a way that describing the options in terms of combinations of properties does not. Overconfidence can also be reduced by having people assess frequency rather than probability, although the result is sometimes underconfidence (Griffin & Tversky, 1992).

Evaluating relative frequency within a concrete set increases the transparency of relations that are compatible with probability theory.

Evaluating probability directly causes us to rely more on similarity. Unfortunately, assessing frequency rather than probability is not a panacea for irrational judgment, because frequency does not always provide a sensible alternative to probability. For instance, an assessment of the probability that an individual is guilty of murder cannot be transformed into a meaningful assessment of frequency. The desire for rationality (and justice) would hardly be satisfied by substituting the probability question with "How many of 100 people like the accused would have committed the murder?"

Education

Richard Nisbett and his colleagues have amassed a variety of evidence concerning the ability to teach people to apply normative rules (Nisbett, 1993). Because of people's ability to do rule-based processing, if a rule is simple enough, then anybody can be taught to apply it within a given context. Only the rare person cannot be taught the rule "If you are driving and you approach a red sign with the word *STOP* on it, then stop." In consequence, people's ability to learn to apply normative rules must be measured in less transparent ways. One test is whether people can learn to solve a specific rule-based problem through training on an abstract version of the rule (Smith et al., 1992). This test has been applied to a small number of rules, some of which have passed and others of which have failed. Specifically, learning has been demonstrated using statistical rules such as the law of large numbers (Fong, Krantz, & Nisbett, 1986; Lehman, Lempert, & Nisbett, 1988; Lehman & Nisbett, 1990) and the contractual rules of permission and obligation (Cheng, Holyoak, Nisbett, & Oliver, 1986). Learning has not been found for the logical rule of modus tollens (Cheng et al., 1986).

In sum, given sufficient training, people can learn to apply some normative rules but not others. Which rules can be taught? According to Lehman et al. (1989),

A major class of such rules are those that people have induced, though only partially, in the course of their daily existence. Rules about assessing causality, rules for generalizing, rules for determining argument validity, and rules for assessing the probativeness of evidence are the kinds of rules that people must have in some measure in order to live effectively in the world. (p. 335)

As far as these authors are concerned, then, we can learn to apply only those rules that are pragmatically relevant.

Conclusions

People may have a variety of systems for thinking, reasoning, and acting, which are able to serve multiple purposes, singly and collectively. Each system is able to do some things well (i.e., rationally). But this suggests that it won't do other things well. The evidence suggests that some specific functions are not always performed optimally by the system that normally takes responsibility for them. The mere fact that a specific response is irrational in this sense does not condemn a larger more inclusive response repertoire. People may make a specific error because they engage in a form of thinking that is generally well adapted to the activities they engage in and the goals they pursue.

Noting our limitations is part of the process by which society at large can try to relieve them. For example, if people were all born with calculators, then there would be less need to teach arithmetic in school. But we are not; we are naturally limited in our ability to add, subtract, multiply, and divide. By noting this, society has learned that we can benefit one another by teaching arithmetic in school. Likewise, by noting other patterns of thought that can lead to less than optimal responses, we can benefit one another in other ways.

Acknowledgments

I am indebted to David Over, Heather Sloman, and Gideon Forman for their comments on prior versions of this chapter.

Notes

1. At least one philosopher (Cohen, 1981) argues that a person's set of core beliefs is identical to the set of beliefs that person is justified in having; that is, the descriptive and normative theory of an individual's beliefs cannot be distinguished. However, this argument has drawn sharp criticism (see the commentaries following Cohen, 1981) and a detailed rebuttal (Stich, 1990).

2. This proposition supplies a premise to Cohen's (1981) argument that human cognitive competence is necessarily rational.

3. The critical ascription of rationality is not actually to individual beliefs but to systems of beliefs (Stich, 1990).

4. For a review of confidence and its calibration, see Yates (1990).

5. The general conditions under which the positive test strategy does not lead to optimal information gain are discussed in Klayman and Ha (1987).

6. Although the distinction between competence and performance can be found in many flavors, my usage (and Cohen's) corresponds to Chomsky's (1965) original distinction.

References

Arkes, H. R., & Hammond, K. R. (1986) (Eds.). *Judgment and decision making: An interdisciplinary reader*. Cambridge, England: Cambridge University Press.

Bar-Hillel, M. (1983). The base rate fallacy controversy. In R. W. Scholz (Ed.), *Decision making under uncertainty* (pp. 39–61). Amsterdam: North-Holland.

Barnden, J. A. (1994). *Advances in connectionist and neural computation theory* (Vols. 1–3). Norwood, NJ: Ablex.

Baron, J. (1994). *Thinking and deciding* (2nd ed.). Cambridge, England: Cambridge University Press.

Cheng, P. W., Holyoak, K. J., Nisbett, R. E., & Oliver, L. M. (1986). Pragmatic versus syntactic approaches to training deductive reasoning. *Cognitive Psychology, 18,* 293–328.

Cherniak, C. (1986). *Minimal rationality*. Cambridge, MA:MIT Press.

Chomsky, N. (1965). *Aspects of the theory of syntax*. Cambridge, MA: MIT Press.

Cohen, L. J. (1981). Can human irrationality be experimentally demonstrated? *Behavioral and Brain Sciences, 4,* 317–331.

Craik, F. I. M., & Lockhart, R. S. (1972). Levels of processing: A framework for memory research. *Journal of Verbal Learning and Verbal Behavior, 11,* 671–684.

Crandall, C. S., & Greenfield, B. (1986). Understanding the conjunction fallacy: A conjunction of effects? *Social Cognition, 4,* 408–419.

Dennett, D. C. (1995). *Darwin's dangerous idea*. New York: Simon & Schuster.

Evans, J. St. B. T. (1993). Bias and rationality. In K. I. Manktelow & D. E. Over (Eds.) *Rationality: psychological and philosophical perspectives*. London: Routledge.

Evans, J. St. B. T., Manktelow, K. I., & Over, D. E. (1993). Reasoning, decision making, and rationality. *Cognition, 49,* 165–187.

Fiedler, K. (1988). The dependence of the conjunction fallacy on subtle linguistic factors. *Psychological Research, 50,* 123–129.

Fischhoff, B., & Beyth-Marom, R. (1983). Hypothesis evaluation from a Bayesian perspective. *Psychological Review, 90,* 239–260.

Fong, G. T., Krantz, D. H., & Nisbett, R. E. (1986). The effects of statistical training on thinking about everyday problems. *Cognitive Psychology, 18,* 253–292.

Gavanski, I., & Roskos-Ewoldsen D. R. (1991). Representativeness and conjoint probability. *Journal of Personality and Social Psychology, 61,* 191–194.

Gigerenzer, G., & Regier, T. (1996). How do we tell an association from a rule? Comment on Sloman (1996). *Psychological Bulletin, 119,* 23–26.

Goodman, N. (1965). *Fact, Fiction, and Forecast.* Indianapolis, IN: Bobbs-Merrrill.

Grice, H. P. (1975). Logic and conversation. In P. Cole & J. L. Morgan (Eds.), *Syntax and Semantics:* Vol. 3: *Speech Acts.* New York: Academic Press.

Griffin, D., & Tversky, A. (1992). The weighing of evidence and the determinants of confidence. *Cognitive Psychology, 24,* 411–435.

Harman, G. (1995). Rationality. In E. E. Smith & D. N. Osherson (Eds.). *Thinking (an invitation to cognitive science) (Vol. 3).* Cambridge, MA: MIT Press.

Hilding, A. (1975). Letter. *Science, 187,* 703.

Hinton, G. E., McClelland, J. L., & Rumelhart, D. E. (1986). Distributed representations. In Rumelhart, D. E., McClelland, J. L., & the PDP Research Group (Eds.) *Parallel distributed processing* (Vol. 1, pp. 77–109). Cambridge, MA: MIT Press.

Johnson-Laird, P. N., & Byrne, R. M. J. (1991). *Deduction.* Hillsdale, NJ: Erlbaum.

Kahneman, D., Slovic, P., & Tversky, A. (1982). *Judgment under uncertainty: Heuristics and biases.* Cambridge, England: Cambridge University Press.

Kahneman, D., & Tversky, A. (1973). On the psychology of prediction. *Psychological Review, 80,* 237–251.

Kaufman, L., & Rock, I. (1989). The moon illusion thirty years later. In M. Hershenson (Ed.), *The moon illusion* (pp. 193–234). Hillsdale, NJ: Erlbaum.

Kelley, H. H. (1973). The processes of causal attribution. *American Psychologist, 28,* 107–127.

Klayman, J., & Ha, Y. (1987). Confirmation, disconfirmation, and information in hypothesis testing. *Psychological Review, 94,* 211–228.

Koriat, A., Lichtenstein, S., & Fischhoff, B. (1980). Reasons for confidence. *Journal of Experimental Psychology: Human Learning and Memory, 6,* 107–118.

Lehman, D. R., Lempert, R. O., & Nisbett, R. E. (1988). The effects of graduate training on reasoning: Formal discipline and thinking about everyday life events. *American Psychologist, 43,* 431–433.

Lehman, D. R., & Nisbett, R. E. (1990). A longitudinal study of the effects of undergraduate education on reasoning. *Developmental Psychology, 26,* 952–960.

Lichtenstein, S., Slovic, P., Fischhoff, B., Layman, M., & Combs, B. (1978). Judged frequency of lethal events. *Journal of Experimental Psychology: Human Learning and Memory, 4,* 551–578.

Medin, D. L., Goldstone, R. L., & Gentner, D. (1993). Respects for similarity. *Psychological Review, 100,* 254–278.

Newell, A., & Simon, H. A. (1972). *Human problem solving.* Englewood Cliffs, NJ: Prentice-Hall.

Nisbett, R. E. (Ed.) (1993). *Rules for reasoning.* Hillsdale, NJ: Erlbaum.

Nisbett, R. E., & Ross, L. (1980). *Human inference: Strategies and shortcomings of social judgment.* Englewood Cliffs, NJ: Prentice-Hall.

Oaksford, M., & Chater, N. (1994). A rational analysis of the selection task as optimal data selection. *Psychological Review, 101,* 608–631.

Osherson, D., Smith, E. E., Wilkie, O., Lopez, A., & Shafir, E. (1990). Category-based induction. *Psychological Review, 97,* 185–200.

Oskamp, S. (1965). Overconfidence in case-study Judgments. *Journal of Consulting Psychology, 29,* 261–265.

Payne, J. W., Bettman, J. R., & Johnson, E. J. (1992). Behavioral decision research: A constructive processing perspective. *Annual Review of Psychology, 43,* 87–131.

Pearl, J. (1988). *Probabilistic reasoning in intelligent systems: Networks of plausible inference.* San Mateo, CA: Morgan Kaufmann.

Plous, S. (1993). *The psychology of judgment and decision making.* New York: McGraw-Hill.

Popper, K. R. (1959). *The logic of scientific discovery.* London: Hutchinson.

Quine, W. (1960). *Word and object.* Cambridge, MA: MIT Press.

Reason, J. T. (1992). Cognitive underspecification: Its variety and consequences. In B. J. Baars (Ed.) *Experimental slips and human error* (pp. 71–91). New York: Plenum Press.

Rips, L. J. (1989). Similarity, typicality, and categorization. In S. Vosniadou & A. Ortony (Eds.) *Similarity and analogical reasoning.* Cambridge, England: Cambridge University Press.

Rips, L. J. (1994). *The psychology of proof: Deductive reasoning in human thinking.* Cambridge, MA: MIT Press.

Ross, M. & Sicoly, F. (1979). Egocentric bias in availability and attribution. *Journal of Personality and Social Psychology, 37,* 322–336.

Savage, L. J. (1972). *The foundations of statistics (2nd ed.).* New York: Dover.

Shafir, E., Smith, E. E., & Osherson, D. (1990). Typicality and reasoning fallacies. *Memory & Cognition, 18,* 229–239.

Simon, H. A. (1981). *The sciences of the artificial* (2nd ed.). Cambridge, MA: MIT Press.

Sloman, S. A. (1993). Feature-based induction. *Cognitive Psychology, 25*, 231–280.

Sloman, S. A. (1996). The empirical case for two systems of reasoning. *Psychological Bulletin, 119*, 3–22.

Sloman, S. A. (1998). Categorical inference is not a tree: The myth of inheritance hierarchies. *Cognitive Psychology, 35*, 1–33.

Smith, E. E., Langston, C., & Nisbett, R. (1992) The case for rules in reasoning. *Cognitive Science, 16*, 1–40.

Smith, E. E., & Osherson, D. N. (1989). Similarity and decision-making. In S. Vosniadou & A. Ortony (Eds.), *Similarity and analogical reasoning* (pp. 60–75). Cambridge, England: Cambridge University Press.

Smith, E. E., & Sloman, S. A. (1994). Similarity-versus rule-based categorization. *Memory & Cognition, 22*, 377–386.

Stich, S. (1990). *The fragmentation of reason*. Cambridge: MIT press.

Stich, S., & Nisbett, R. (1980). Justification and the psychology of human reasoning. *Philosophy of Science, 47*.

Troutman, C. M., & Shanteau, J. (1977). Inferences based on nondiagnostic information. *Organizational Behavior and Human Performance, 19*, 43–55.

Tulving, E., & Thomson, D. M. (1973). Encoding specificity and retrieval processes in episodic memory. *Psychological Review, 80*, 352–373.

Tversky, A. (1977). Features of similarity. *Psychological Review, 84*, 327–352.

Tversky, A., & Kahneman, D. (1973). Availability: A heuristic for judging frequency and probability. *Cognitive Psychology, 5*, 207–232.

Tversky, A., & Kahneman, D. (1983). Extensional versus intuitive reasoning: The conjunction fallacy in probability judgment. *Psychological Review, 90*, 293–315.

Wason, P. C. (1960). On the failure to eliminate hypotheses in a conceptual task. *Quarterly Journal of Experimental Psychology, 12*, 129–140.

Yates, J. F. (1990). *Judgment and decision making*. Englewood Cliffs, NJ: Prentice Hall.

17

Formal Rules versus Mental Models in Reasoning

P. N. Johnson-Laird

Psychologists are still arguing about how people reason. Some say that it depends on a memory for previous examples, or on principles in the form of conditional rules that capture general knowledge, or even on *neural nets* representing concepts. Such accounts, however, do not extend to the full inferential competence that most of us can display. We can make deductions about matters of which we know nothing:

All zugs squack.
Olp is a zug.
∴ Olp squacks.

Such an inference hinges not on general knowledge, but on linguistic knowledge. The real controversy is accordingly about this sort of deductive reasoning. On one side, there are those who claim that it is a syntactic process that depends on *formal rules of inference* akin to those of a logical calculus. On the other side, there are those who claim that it is a semantic process that depends on *mental models* akin to the models that logicians invoke in formulating the semantics of their calculi. The controversy has been fruitful—it has led to improvements in experimental methodology and in the theories themselves. But it has been going on for a long time, and skeptics have even hinted that it may go on forever. That assessment, however, is premature and pessimistic. It may never be settled to the satisfaction of all parties—controversies in science seldom are—but it is about a major component of human thinking, and it is open to empirical investigation using methods acceptable to all cognitive psychologists. If these methods fail to settle the issue, they are unlikely to be any more successful in any other case.

This chapter is about the controversy. It will describe its background and origins, draw a logical distinction between syntactic and semantic principles, and outline the two sorts of psychological theories and the respective evidence for them. Finally, it will present a new phenomenon— a class of fallacious inferences with compelling conclusions that everyone accepts even though they are totally wrong. These cognitive illusions may resolve the controversy at last.

At this point, I should declare an interest. More than twenty years ago, I published a paper in which I proposed a formal rule theory for one sort of reasoning and a mental model theory for other sorts of reasoning (Johnson-Laird, 1975). I was thus one of the original proponents both of formal rules and of mental models—the two approaches are not necessarily incompatible—but nowadays I am firmly on the side, if not of the angels, at least of mental models. This personal history may disqualify me from giving a fair picture of the controversy, but at least it allows me to sympathize with both sides.

Background to the Controversy

The ability to make deductive inferences is a key component of human thinking. Without it, science and mathematics could not exist, and laws, conventions, rules, and regulations would probably not exist either. Psychologists have long recognized its importance, and they have been investigating it for almost the entire century. Their earliest studies solicited the participants' introspections on reasoning—a procedure that was not very revealing (see, e.g., Störring, 1908). Later, their interests shifted to the causes of error and to the effects of people's prejudices and beliefs on performance (see, e.g., Janis & Frick, 1943; Woodworth & Sells, 1935). What is striking about these early studies is that they were carried out in a theoretical vacuum. There were no theories of how, in principle, individuals could reason correctly. If they had been taught logic, they might fall back on it in a self-conscious way. But, if they had not been taught logic, were they incapable of right reasoning? Of course not. So how were logically untrained individuals supposed to reason? No one knew; more surprisingly, few psychologists seemed to care.

The first theorist to offer any account of deductive competence was the distinguished Swiss scientist Jean Piaget. In a general theory of the psychological foundations of knowledge, he argued that children spontaneously recapitulate the historical development of mathematics (see, e.g., Beth & Piaget, 1966) and eventually arrive at formal reasoning in early adolescence—the so-called stage of formal operations. The formal logic embodied in Piaget's theorizing was idiosyncratic—so idiosyncratic, in fact, that even sympathetic critics have argued that his theory could not possibly account for human logical competence (see Braine & Rumain, 1983). Thirty years ago, the study of deductive reasoning could thus be summarized as follows: psychologists had some ideas about what causes people to make mistakes—though certain dissenters argued that people never make *logical* errors (Henle, 1962)—but they did not know what mental equipment was responsible for logical competence. Even worse, they did not know that they did not know. This extraordinary state of affairs arose from a ubiquitous but tacit assumption: even though Piagetian theory might not be viable in detail, it was right about the "big picture." People could reason because they were equipped with some sort of *mental logic*. The task for psychologists—so they thought—was to carry out experiments that would reveal the principles of this mental logic.

At this point, Wason, the founder of modern psychological studies of reasoning, discovered a disturbing phenomenon. It came in two parts. The first part was that intelligent adults regularly committed a serious logical error (Wason, 1966). He laid out four cards in front of them:

A   B   2   3

The participants knew that each card had a letter on one side and a number on the other side. He then showed them a conditional rule:

If a card has the letter *A* on one side, then it has the number *2* on the other side.

Their task was to select whichever of the four cards they needed to turn over in order to find out whether the conditional rule was true or false about the four cards. The participants in Wason's study, and in replications of it that we carried out together, for the most part selected the *A* card alone or the *A* card and the 2 card. What was puzzling was their failure to select the 3 card: if it has an *A* on its other side, the rule is certainly false. Indeed, nearly everyone judges the rule to be false in that case. Piaget wrote that if individuals have to verify whether *x* implies *y*, then they "will look in this case to see whether or not there is a counter-example *x* and non-*y*" (Beth & Piaget, 1966, p. 181). Yet our adult reasoners were failing to select the *x* and non-*y* cards that falsified an implication of the form "if *x* then *y*."

The second part of Wason's disturbing phenomenon was a discovery that could have been made only by someone not in the grip of the tacit assumption that there is a mental logic. He changed the *content* of the problem, and—much to many people's surprise, including mine—the participants made the correct selections. Wason & Shapiro (1971) used the conditional rule

Every time I travel to Manchester I travel by train

and a set of cards that named a destination on one side and a mode of transport on the other side:

Manchester   Sheffield   Train   Car

Now, at last, the majority of participants correctly selected the *Manchester* card and the *Car* card. Other studies at this time corroborated the result (see, e.g., Johnson-Laird, Legrenzi, & Legrenzi, 1972).

Wason's selection task has launched a vast amount of research, and it still has no generally accepted explanation. It showed, however, that no simple account of mental logic was likely to do justice to human reasoning. Formal rules apply uniformly to expressions of the same form, such as conditionals, without regard to their content. Wason's two-part discovery showed on the contrary that human reasoning was highly susceptible to content. When Wason and I wrote a book summarizing our research, our efforts to develop a theory of logical competence were stymied by the results of the selection task. All that we were able to conclude was that formal logic did not seem a very plausible contender as a psychological theory (Wason & Johnson-Laird, 1972).

So much for the background to the controversy. To go any further into it, the distinction between formal rules and mental models must be made clear. At the root of this distinction is the contrast between syntax and semantics, and so the next section turns to logic in order to elucidate this contrast.

The Distinction between Syntax and Semantics

How people reason is a concern of psychology. Logic, in contrast, is concerned with certain relations between sentences and, in particular, with capturing the relation that holds if a set of sentences implies a conclusion. Readers who have studied logic will know that twentieth-century logicians draw a sharp distinction between syntactic systems of logic (formal proof theory) and their semantic interpretation (model theory). The distinction is easiest to grasp in the case of the *sentential* calculus, which concerns the logic of such connectives as *if, and,* or *or* (conceived in a somewhat idealized way) and negation. Thus, the following inference is an example of the sort of deduction that can be proved in the sentential calculus:

There is a fault in the device or there is no current, or both.
But, there is not a fault in the device.
Therefore, there is no current.

The formal calculus can be specified in various equivalent ways. One way is to use the method of *natural deduction* (see, e.g., Gentzen, 1935/1969). This method renounces axioms in favor of rules of inference. Each logical connective accordingly has its own rules of inference. There are rules that introduce each connective, and there are rules that eliminate it. Inclusive disjunction—as expressed by *or* in the example just given—has the following rules of inference that eliminate the connective:

A or *B*, or both	*A* or *B*, or both
not *B*	not *A*
∴ *A*	∴ not *B*

And it has the following rules that introduce the connective—

A	*B*
∴ *A* or *B*, or both	∴ *A* or *B*

where *A* and *B* can stand for any propositions whatsoever. Natural deduction can yield intuitive proofs, and it had a vogue in logic texts, though it has been supplanted by another still more intuitive method (see, e.g., Jeffrey, 1981).

When you inspect the preceding rules, you naturally allow your knowledge of the meaning of *or* to help you to construe them. It is important to realize, however, that formal rules of inference operate solely in virtue of the form of expressions and that they do not rely in any way on their meaning. The rules allow the formal derivations of conclusions. These derivations are valid—that is, each conclusion must be true if the premises are true—but validity itself is not part of the formal calculus (which logicians contrive to allow only the derivation of valid conclusions). Validity, in other words, is part of the *semantics* of the calculus. This semantics can be made entirely explicit in a separate system. In this system, the meaning of *or* is defined by stating how the truth of assertions containing it depends on the truth of the constituent propositions. Thus, an assertion of the form "A or B or both" is true if both A and B are true, if A is true (and B is false), or if B is true (and A is false). This definition can be laid out in the form of a *truth table:*

A	B	A or B, or both
True	True	True
True	False	True
False	True	True
False	False	False

Each row in the table shows a possible combination of the truth values of A and B, and the resulting truth-value of the assertion that is an inclusive disjunction of the two: A or B, or both.

The formal *sentential* calculus allows you to test the validity of any argument depending solely on the logical properties of *if, and, or,* and *not.* You can derive the conclusion of any valid argument in a proof in which each step is sanctioned by a rule of inference for a connective. Table 17.1 presents a set of rules for the connectives. Consider now the following argument:

1. The circuit is intact.
2. The battery has power.

Table 17.1

Some formal rules of inference for introducing and eliminating the sentential operator *not* and the sentential connectives *and, or,* and *if*

A ∴ not(not *A*)	not(not *A*) ∴ *A*
A *B* ∴ *A* and *B*	*A* and *B* ∴ *A*
A ∴ *A* or *B*	*A* or *B* not *B* ∴ *A*
A ⊢ *B* (i.e., *B* can be derived from *A*) ∴ If *A* then *B*	If *A* then *B* *A* ∴ *B*

3. Current flows or it is not the case that both the circuit is intact and the battery has power.

∴ Current flows.

The conclusion is valid, that is, it must be true given that the premises are true, and it can be proved using the rules in table 17.1. The first step is to conjoin premises 1 and 2 using the first rule for *and* in table 17.1:

∴ The circuit is intact and the battery has power.

Next, we convert this assertion into a double negation using the first rule for *not* in table 17.1:

∴ not(not(the circuit is intact and the battery has power))

Finally, we apply the second rule for *or* in the table to this assertion and premise 3 in order to derive the required conclusion:

∴ Current flows.

The validity of an argument in the sentential calculus can also be demonstrated using the semantic method of truth tables. Table 17.2 shows all the possible combinations of truth values for the three propositions: the circuit is intact, the battery has power, and current flows. We can then eliminate those possibilities that are incompatible with the truth of each premise. Only one possibility survives—the one corresponding to

Table 17.2
Truth table for an argument in the text: each premise rules out one or more possibilities

The circuit is intact	The battery has power	Current flows	
True	True	True	
True	True	False	Ruled out by premise 3
True	False	True	Ruled out by premise 2
True	False	False	Ruled out by premise 2
False	True	True	Ruled out by premise 1
False	True	False	Ruled out by premise 1
False	False	True	Ruled out by premise 1
False	False	False	Ruled out by premise 1

the first row in the table—and in this case it is true that current flows. Hence, the conclusion that follows validity is

∴ Current flows.

Any conclusion that can be derived using the formal rules is also valid using truth tables, and so the formal calculus is *sound* (see, e.g., Jeffrey, 1981). Any conclusion that is valid using truth tables can also be derived using formal rules, and so the formal calculus is *complete*. Moreover, the calculus is *decidable*, that is, one can determine in a finite number of steps whether or not an argument is valid. Logicians have formulated a more powerful system, the *predicate* calculus, which includes the sentential calculus as a proper part but which also deals with quantifiers, that is, with the logical properties of words such as *all* and *some*, which occur in such assertions as

All philosophers have read some books.

The predicate calculus is *not* decidable: valid arguments can be proved in a finite number of steps, but there is no guarantee that the invalidity of an argument can be shown in a finite number of steps. In a higher-order predicate calculus, quantifiers range not just over individual entities but also properties: for example,

Some philosophers have all the qualities of great writers.

This calculus is not even complete in the technical sense just given: it is impossible to frame a consistent set of formal rules of inference from which all valid conclusions are derivable. This result drives a wedge between the syntax of logic and its semantics, and so any attempt to argue that semantics can be reduced to syntax is bound to fail. Semantics has to do with truth (and validity), whereas syntax has to do with form (and derivability). The question is whether human reasoners rely on syntactic or semantic principles. And that is the root of the controversy. The following sections describe the two psychological theories, the evidence in favor of them, and, finally, a possible resolution of the controversy between them.

Formal Rule Theories

In the mid-1970s, several investigators for the first time formulated theories of human logical competence. Notwithstanding the results of the selection task, which I described earlier, these theories assumed that human reasoning depends on formal rules of inference such as those of a system of *natural deduction* (see, e.g., Braine, 1978; Johnson-Laird, 1975; Osherson, 1974–1976). The different theories postulated slightly different formal rules and slightly different procedures for searching for derivations, but they had in common the following point of view, aptly expressed by Rips (1983): "Deductive reasoning consists in the application of mental inference rules to the premises and conclusions of an argument. The sequence of applied rules forms a mental derivation or proof of the conclusion from the premises where these implicit proofs are analogous to the explicit proofs of elementary logic" (p. 38). Since these first efforts, theorists in various disciplines—philosophy, linguistics, and artificial intelligence—have continued to defend the formal point of view (see, e.g., Macnamara, 1986; Pollock, 1989; Robinson, 1979; Sperber & Wilson, 1986; Wos, 1988). In psychology, the two major advocates of formal rules are the late Braine (see, e.g., Braine & O'Brien, 1991; Braine, Reiser, & Rumain, 1984), and Rips (see, e.g., Rips, 1983). Their respective theories are similar, but Rips's (1994) PSYCOP theory is the first formal rule theory in psychology to cope with both sentential connectives and quantifiers and to be implemented in a computer program (written in PROLOG). Hence, this section will concentrate on PSYCOP: it is the most comprehensive theory according to which the mind uses formal rules of inference.

The task for a formal rule theorist is to devise psychologically plausible rules of inference and a psychologically plausible mechanism to construct mental proofs. Following the earlier proposals, Rips adopted the natural deduction method, and a key feature of this method is the use of suppositions—assumptions that are made for the sake of argument and that must be "discharged" sooner or later if a derivation is to yield a conclusion. One way to discharge a supposition is to incorporate it into a conditional conclusion, as done by the first rule for *if* (the rule of *conditional proof*) in table 16.1. Another way to discharge a supposition is to prove that it leads to a contradiction and must therefore be false (the rule of *reductio ad absurdum*, which is not shown in table 16.1). Thus, consider the following proof of an argument in the form known as *modus tollens:*

1. If there isn't a break in the circuit then current flows.
2. Current doesn't flow.
3. There isn't a break in the circuit. (a supposition)

The second rule for *if* in table 16.1 has the form

> If *A* then *B*
> *A*
> ∴ *B*

and is known as the rule of *modus ponens,* a pattern of inference that is ubiquitous and easy for logically untrained individuals. This rule can be applied to premise 1 and to the supposition in order to derive

4. Current flows. (modus ponens applied to 1 and 3)

At this point, there is a contradiction between a sentence in the domain of the premises ("Current doesn't flow") and a sentence in the subdomain of the supposition ("Current flows"). The rule of reductio ad absurdum uses such a contradiction to negate—and thereby discharge—the supposition that led to the contradiction:

5. There *is* a break in the circuit.

Rips could have adopted a single rule for modus tollens, but the inference is harder for logically untrained individuals than is modus ponens, and so he assumed that it depends on the chain of inferential steps illustrated here. A supposition can be made within the subdomain of a supposition, and so on to any arbitrary depth, but each supposition must be discharged for a proof to yield a conclusion in the same domain as the premises.

The two main problems in developing any psychological theory are to ensure that it is computationally viable and that it makes sense of the empirical phenomena. An example of a computational difficulty is that unless the rule for introducing *and* (see table 16.1) is curbed, it can lead to such futile derivations as

    A

    B

∴ *A* and *B*

∴ *A* and (*A* and *B*)

∴ *A* and (*A* and (*A* and *B*))

and so on ad infinitum. Two sorts of rules are potentially dangerous: those that introduce a connective and thereby increase the length of expressions and those that introduce suppositions. One radical solution is to do away with a rule altogether by incorporating its effects within other rules—a method adopted by Braine for *and* and *or* introduction (see, e.g., Braine, 1978). Another solution is to ensure that these rules can be used only in preparation for the use of other major rules (Johnson-Laird, 1975). A lesson from artificial intelligence, however, is that programs can use a rule in two ways: either to derive a step in a *forward* chain of inference from some assertions to a conclusion or to derive a step in a *backward* chain from a conclusion to the subgoal of proving its required premises (see Hewitt, 1972). The problem of curbing rules can be solved by using the potentially dangerous rules only in backward chains. Rips adopted this idea. PSYCOP accordingly has three sorts of rules: those that it uses forward, those that it uses backward, and those that it uses in either direction.

The choice of rules of inference for formal theorists is an empirical matter. The rules should be those that individuals recognize as intuitively sound. Rips has canvassed previous theories to come up with the set of forward and bidirectional rules shown in table 17.3 and the set of

Table 17.3
PSYCOP's forward and bidirectional rules

IF P THEN Q*	IF P OR Q THEN R*	IF P AND Q THEN R
P	P	P
Q	R	Q
		R
P AND Q*	NOT(P AND Q)*	NOT(P AND Q)*
P	(NOT P) OR (NOT Q)	P
		NOT Q
P OR Q*		
NOT P	NOT(P OR Q)	
Q	NOT P	
P OR Q		
IF P THEN R		
IF Q THEN R	NOT NOT P*	
R	P	

Source: Adapted from Rips (1994).
Note: Certain rules, such as the one eliminating *AND*, are shown leading to the conclusion *P*; another version of the rule yields the conclusion *Q* (see Rips 1994).
* Signifies that a rule can also be used backward.

backward rules shown in table 17.4. He allows that individuals may differ in the particular rules they possess, they may acquire new rules, and they may even have idiosyncratic rules that lead them to invalid conclusions. He proves two theorems about PSYCOP and the rules in tables 17.3 and 17.4. First, given an argument to evaluate, PSYCOP always halts after a finite number of steps either with a proof of the conclusion or after having unsuccessfully tried all available derivations. Second, PSYCOP is incomplete with respect to the classical sentential calculus: that is, there are valid arguments that it cannot prove.

PSYCOP can generate its own conclusions by using forward rules to derive them from the premises. In principle, it can use backward rules if it guesses a putative conclusion. However, it is geared to the evaluation of *given* conclusions. The strategy that it then follows is to apply all its forward rules (breadth first) until they yield no new conclusions. It then checks whether the given conclusion is among the sentences that it has derived. If not, it tries to work backward from the given conclusion, pursuing a chain of inference (depth first) until it finds the sentences that

Table 17.4
PSYCOP's rules that can be used only backward, including all rules that use suppositions (i.e., assumptions made for the sake of argument)

$$+P$$
$$\vdots$$
$$\underline{Q}$$
$$\text{IF } P \text{ THEN } Q$$

$$+\text{NOT } P$$
$$\vdots$$
$$\underline{Q \text{ AND (NOT } Q)}$$
$$P$$

$$+P$$
$$\vdots$$
$$\underline{Q \text{ AND (NOT } Q)}$$
$$\text{NOT } P$$

$$P$$
$$\underline{Q}$$
$$P \text{ AND } Q$$

$$\underline{P}$$
$$P \text{ OR } Q$$

$$P \text{ OR } Q$$
$$+P$$
$$\vdots$$
$$R$$
$$+Q$$
$$\vdots$$
$$\underline{\quad R \quad}$$
$$R$$

$$\underline{\text{NOT}(P \text{ OR } Q)}$$
$$(\text{NOT } P) \text{ AND (NOT } Q)$$

Source: Adapted from Rips (1994).
Note: The "+" symbol designates a supposition.

satisfy the subgoals or until it has run out of rules to try. Either it succeeds in deriving the conclusion, or else it returns to an earlier choice point in the chain and tries to satisfy an alternative subgoal. Finally, if it fails all the subgoals, it gives up.

Prior to PSYCOP, formal rule theories did not deal with inferences based on quantifiers, such as:

All philosophers have read some books.
Russell is a philosopher.
∴ Russell has read some books.

The standard treatment of quantifiers in logic is to use rules that eliminate them and then rules that reintroduce them after inferences based on sentential connectives alone have been made. These proofs rapidly become intractable—you are liable to run out of time or memory before you can explore all the alternatives. PSYCOP does not use such rules, but rather transforms quantified assertions into a form in which the work of quantifiers is performed by names and variables. The resulting expressions are akin to those used by automated theorem-provers in artificial intelligence, and Rips invokes rules for matching one expression to another in these quantifier-free expressions.

One final aspect of Rips's theory should be mentioned. Unlike other rule theorists, Rips argues that formal rules of inference underlie not just deduction but thinking in general. Formal rules are accordingly part of cognitive architecture, and they can be used as a general-purpose programming language. This step makes formal rules almost irrefutable. Suppose, for example, that psychologists discover that reasoning depends on a computable procedure, X, which is not part of PSYCOP. The discovery does not jeopardize formal rules in general, because they can be used to write a program that carries out X. When rules are conceived in this general way, they can even simulate the mental model theory. Indeed, the computer programs implementing the model theory depend on purely formal rules because computer programs, at present, do not really understand anything. The controversy about reasoning therefore does not concern formal rules in general but rather current theories of reasoning, such as PSYCOP or Braine's system, which are based on "natural deduction." The issue between them and mental models—as all parties agree—is open to empirical resolution.

Evidence for Formal Rule Theories

The difficulty of a deduction according to formal rule theories depends on two factors: the number of steps in the formal derivation, and the relative availability, or ease of use, of the rules used in the derivation. Modus ponens, for instance, is easier than modus tollens because there is a single mental rule for modus ponens but no single rule for modus tollens, which depends on a chain of inferences. The evidence for formal rule theories, however, mainly comes from studies of large batteries of deductions (for a review, see Evans, Newstead, & Byrne, 1993). In one such study, Braine et al. (1984) tested their theory by asking participants to evaluate given arguments and then to rate them for difficulty. The problems concerned the presence or absence of letters on an imaginary blackboard; for example,

If there is either a *C* or an *H*, then there is a *P*.
There is a *C*.
∴ There is a *P*.

The study examined two potential indices of difficulty—the number of steps in a deduction according to the theory, and the *difficulty weights* of these steps as estimated from the data. Both measures predicted the rated difficulty of the problems, the latencies of response (adjusted for the time it took to read the problem), and the percentages of errors.

In another study of a battery of deductions, Rips (1983) also asked participants to assess the validity of given arguments. Subsequently, he used the PSYCOP program to find the proofs of the arguments and thus to reveal which rules were needed for the derivations. He then estimated the probabilities that the rules were available to the subjects from an examination of the experimental results. When he combined the probabilities for each rule needed in the derivations for the inferences, the theoretical predictions fitted the data reasonably well. It is worth noting, however, that half of the valid deductions in this experiment called for semantic information to be thrown away, because the conclusion was less informative than the premises; that is, the conclusion was consistent with more possibilities than were the premises (see Johnson-Laird & Byrne, 1991). Only 1 out of those 16 problems was evaluated better than chance, with an overall performance of 35% correct evaluations. Conversely, 14 of the other 16 problems, which maintained semantic information, were evaluated better than chance, with an overall performance of 66% correct evaluations.[1] The difference between these two sets of problems was highly significant, corroborating the claim that human reasoners are reluctant to throw semantic information away. Braine et al. (1984, p. 360) have also expressed a methodological worry about the experiment. In commenting on the difficulty of certain deductions, they wrote: "So high a failure rate on transparent problems suggests that the experiment often failed to engage the reasoning procedures of subjects."

In recent work, Rips (1994) found that his theory accounted for the times participants took to understand proofs laid out in explicit derivations and for their memory of proofs: they remembered sentences in the same domain as the premises better than those in a subdomain based on a supposition. Rips has also applied the theory to Wason's selection task, which was described earlier. With abstract conditionals, such as "If there is an A on one side of a card, then there is a 2 on the other side," the program behaves similarly to people: it follows up the implications of a true antecedent, but not a false consequent. It can make modus ponens working forward, but not modus tollens. Rips makes a tentative move to invoke rules from deontic logic in order to explain participants' success with more realistic rules.

In summary, formal rule theories make no surprising predictions, and they have not yet led to the discovery of any striking phenomena. They have been successful, however, in making sense of a body of experimental results. No studies have been carried out as yet to compare different theories based on formal rules.

The Mental Model Theory

Consider the following inference (from Johnson-Laird, 1975):

The black ball is directly behind the cue ball. The green ball is on the right of the cue ball, and there is a red ball between them.
Therefore, if I move so that the red ball is between me and the black ball, the cue ball is to the left of my line of sight.

It is possible to frame rules that capture this inference, but it seems likely that people will make it by imagining the relevant spatial layout. This idea lies at the heart of the theory of *mental models*. Reasoning according to this theory is a semantic process rather than a syntactic one. Reasoners imagine the states of affairs described by the premises—that is, they build mental models of the relevant situations based on their understanding of the premises and, where relevant, on their general knowledge; they formulate an informative conclusion that is true in these models; and they establish its validity by ensuring that there are no models of the premises in which the conclusion is false (Johnson-Laird & Byrne, 1991). A mental model is a representation that corresponds to a set of situations and that has a structure and content that captures what is common to these situations. For example, an assertion such as "The triangle is on the right of the circle" calls for a model of the form

○   △

in which the two referents are represented by two corresponding mental tokens, and the spatial relation between them is represented by the relation between the two tokens in the model.

The first mental model theory was formulated for syllogisms, such as

Some of the artists are beekeepers.
All the beekeepers are chemists.
∴ Some of the artists are chemists.

Several theorists proposed that such inferences might be based, not on mental rules of inference, but on mental representations of the premises that functioned as models of the world. Erickson (1974) suggested that these representations might take the form of *Euler circles*. In Euler circles, each set is represented by a circle (drawn on the plane), and the relations between sets is represented by the relations between the circles. Thus, the premise

All the beekeepers are chemists

calls for two separate Euler circle representations. In one, the circle representing beekeepers lies wholly within the circle representing chemists to show that one set is properly included within the other. In the other representation, the two circles are coextensive to show that the two sets are coextensive. With a pencil and paper, some reasoners do use Euler circles. But one wonders whether they would use them if they had not been taught them or at least seen them as part of the "new math." The circles also cannot deal with assertions containing more than one quantifier. They cannot distinguish between the natural interpretations of

All philosophers have read some books

and

Some books have been read by all philosophers.

My colleagues and I therefore argued for a different sort of representation in which sets of individual entities are represented by mental models containing sets of individual tokens. The theory has developed over the years, but it still reflects this same underlying principle.

In the latest version (Bara, Bucciarelli, & Johnson-Laird, 1995), the premises

Some of the artists are beekeepers

and

All the beekeepers are chemists

call for the following sort of model:

artist	beekeeper	chemist
artist	beekeeper	chemist
artist		
	beekeeper	chemist

. . .

Each row in this diagram denotes a separate individual and the numbers of the different sorts of individual are arbitrary. The first and second individuals are artists, beekeepers, and chemists; the third individual is an artist; and the fourth individual is a beekeeper and chemist. The ellipsis allows for other individuals, and the theory assumes that reasoners have some way to represent that the set of beekeepers has been exhaustively represented in relation to chemists, and so the other possible individuals cannot include beekeepers who are not chemists. The overall model supports the conclusion

Some of the artists are chemists

and no model of the premises refutes this conclusion, which is accordingly valid. Other syllogisms require multiple models. For example, the premises

None of the artists is a beekeeper

and

All of the beekeepers are chemists

yield the initial model

artist		
artist		
	beekeeper	chemist
	beekeeper	chemist

. . .

in which artists and beekeepers are represented exhaustively. This model supports the conclusion

None of the artists is a chemist.

But this conclusion can be refuted by an alternative model of the premises:

artist		chemist
artist		chemist
	beekeeper	chemist
	beekeeper	chemist

. . .

All that follows validly is the conclusion

Some of the chemists are not artists

because it cannot be refuted by any model of the premises.

This account illustrates the fundamental principle of validity: a conclusion is valid if, and only if, it cannot be refuted by any model of the premises. The task of establishing validity is therefore to ensure that there is no model of the premises in which the conclusion is false.

Mental models readily extend to deal with inferences based on multiple quantifiers, spatial relations, and temporal relations (Byrne & Johnson-Laird, 1989; Johnson-Laird & Byrne, 1991; Schaeken, Johnson-Laird, & d'Ydewalle, 1996). But how do they apply to reasoning based on sentential connectives? One possible answer is that the mind uses truth tables akin to the one in table 16.2. This idea occurred to Osherson (1974–1976) in his pioneering study, but he was able to refute it. The truth table in table 16.2 is based on three propositions and has eight rows. If you added a fourth proposition to the argument, the table would have sixteen rows; and, in general, the size of the table doubles each time you add an extra proposition. The difficulty of inferences for human reasoners, as Osherson showed, does not double in this way. The impasse seemed to rule out the feasibility of a semantic theory of reasoning—at least for sentential inferences.

My colleagues and I did not discover a way around the impasse for some years. It rests on the *principle of truth*: individuals tend to minimize the load on working memory by constructing mental models that represent what is true, but not what is false. Hence, given an assertion of the form

There is a king or there is an ace, but not both,

reasoners construct two alternative models to represent the two alternative possibilities:

king

      ace

where this diagram is based on the convention that each row denotes a *separate* model of a separate possibility. Similarly, the inclusive disjunction

There is a king or there is an ace, or both

calls for three models:

king

      ace

king   ace

A conditional,

If there is a king then there is an ace,

calls for one explicit model of the salient contingency and an implicit model that merely allows for other possibilities (in which the antecedent is false) without spelling them out explicitly:

king   ace

   . . .

As a final example, a conjunction,

There is a king and there is an ace

calls for just a single model:

king   ace

One subtlety is that even the explicit models do not contain representations of what is *false*. Consider again the models of the exclusive disjunction "There is a king or else there is an ace, but not both":

king

      ace

The first model represents that there is a king, but it does not explicitly represent that in this case it is false that there is an ace. Similarly, the second model represents that there is an ace, but it does not explicitly

Table 17.5
The mental models and the fully explicit models for five sentential connectives

Connective	Mental models		Fully explicit models	
A and *B*	*A*	*B*	*A*	*B*
A or else *B*	*A*		*A*	¬*B*
		B	¬*A*	*B*
A or *B*, or both	*A*		*A*	¬*B*
		B	¬*A*	*B*
	A	*B*	*A*	*B*
If *A* then *B*	*A*	*B*	*A*	*B*
	. . .		¬*A*	*B*
			¬*A*	¬*B*
If and only if *A* then *B*	*A*	*B*	*A*	*B*
	. . .		¬*A*	¬*B*

Note: "¬" symbolizes negation, and ". . ." a wholly implicit model. The difference between the mental models for *if* and *if and only if* is their associated mental footnotes (see text).

represent that in this case it is false that there is a king. The theory assumes that reasoners make a "mental footnote" to keep track of this information, but that these footnotes are soon likely to be forgotten. In contrast to models based on the principle of truth, *fully explicit* models of the exclusive disjunction would be of the form

king   ¬ace
¬king   ace

where ¬ represents negation. Table 17.5 summarizes the initial mental models for the five main sentential connectives, and it also shows the fully explicit models for these connectives.

One advantage of the mental model theory is that it provides a unified account of logical reasoning yielding necessary conclusions, probable conclusions, and possible conclusions. A conclusion is *necessary*—it must be true—if it holds in all the models of the premises; a conclusion is *probable*—it is likely to be true—if it holds in most of the models of the premises; and a conclusion is *possible*—it may be true—if it holds in at least some model of the premises. The theory thus purports to explain how intelligent, but mathematically ignorant, individuals reason about the probabilities of events from the different ways in which they could occur. Other sorts of judgment are based on the availability of models, that is, how easy it is to construct them (see Tversky & Kahneman, 1973). Still others may call for models to be linked to numerical representations of probabilities.

I have written a suite of computer programs simulating the model theory of reasoning for each of the following domains: sentential, spatial, temporal, and quantified reasoning. Each program is equipped with a lexicon and a grammar. It parses the premises using its representation of the meanings of words and of the semantic import of grammatical structures. The parse yields a representation of the meaning of the premises, which in turn is used to construct models of the situation. The program draws conclusions, and it tests their validity by ensuring that they hold in all the possible models of the premises. These programs merely simulate the theory because they do not really represent the meaning of sentences.

Evidence for the Mental Model Theory

The model theory makes three main predictions about reasoning. First, inferences that depend on only one model will be easier than those that depend on multiple models: reasoners will be faster to reach a conclusion, and they will be more likely to be correct. Second, systematic errors are likely to correspond to initial models of the premises. Third, knowledge can influence the process of inference. If any one of these predictions were shown to be wrong in a robust and replicable series of experiments, then the model theory would be thereby disconfirmed. In fact, all three predictions have been corroborated in a variety of different studies (see, e.g., Johnson-Laird & Byrne, 1991). The following section will describe some illustrative results.

One-Model Problems Are Easier than Multiple-Model Problems   One

example is that exclusive disjunctions, which require only two models, are easier to reason with than inclusive disjunctions, which require three models (Johnson-Laird & Byrne, 1991). Formal rule theories make the opposite prediction because they have no rules for exclusive disjunctions (see, e.g., tables 17.3 and 17.4). Another domain in which this prediction has been confirmed is temporal reasoning. Consider, for example, the following problem:

After the suspect ran away, the clerk rang the alarm.
The manager in the bank was stabbed while the alarm was ringing.
What is the temporal relation between the suspect running away and the stabbing of the manager?

The first premise calls for a model of the form

$r \quad a\text{———}$

in which the time axis runs from left to right, r denotes a model of the suspect running away, a denotes a model of the clerk sounding the alarm, and "———" denotes the alarm ringing for some time. The second premise,

The manager was stabbed while the alarm was ringing,

means that the stabbing occurred at some time between the onset and offset of the alarm:

$r \quad a\text{———}$
$\quad\quad s$

where s denotes a model of the stabbing. This model corresponds to infinitely many different situations that have in common only the truth of the two premises. The model thus contains no explicit representation of the duration for which the alarm sounded, or of the precise point at which the stabbing occurred. Yet, the conclusion

The stabbing occurred after the suspect ran away

is true in this model, and it is not falsified by any other model of the premises.

  Schaeken et al. (1996) carried out five experiments to examine the predictions of the model theory of temporal inferences. They examined problems that call for only one model, such as premises of the following form:

a happens before b
b happens before c
d happens while a
e happens while c
What's the relation between d and e?

The content of the premises concerned everyday events, such as "John reads his newspaper" and "Mary drinks her coffee." The premises above yield a model of the form

a   *b*   *c*
d   *e*

which supports the conclusion

d happens before *e*.

The model theory predicts that this one-model problem should be easier than problems that are similar but that call for multiple models, such as

a happens before *c*
b happens before *c*
d happens while *b*
e happens while *c*
What's the relation between *d* and *e*?

The premises are satisfied by the following models:

a   *b*   *c*   *b*   *a*   *c*   *a*   *c*
       d   *e*   *d*   *e*   *b*
                                                 d   *e*

In all three models, *d* happens before *e*, and so that is a valid conclusion. Schaeken et al. observed that participants make reliably more errors (about 10% more) with these problems than with one-model problems. The second premise in the problem is the one calling for multiple models, because it creates an uncertainty about whether *a* happens before *b*, or after *b*, or at the same time as *b*. Hence, the model theory predicts that individuals should spend more time reading this premise than reading the second premise of the one-model problem. The results also corroborated this prediction: participants took reliably longer (about 2 seconds) to read this premise in the multiple-model problem than in the one-model problem.

Readers should note that theories based on formal rules of inference make exactly the *wrong* predictions about these problems. The one-model problem just discussed calls for a transitive inference to establish the relation between *a* and *c*, which is a precursor to establishing the relation between *d* and *e*. In contrast, the multiple-model problem does not call for the relation between *b* and *c* to be derived, because it is directly asserted by the second premise. Hence, the one-model problem has a formal derivation that contains the derivation for the multiple-model problem, and so according to rule theories the one-model problem should be harder than the multiple-model problem. The irrelevant premise in the multiple-model problem cannot be responsible for its greater difficulty, because one-model problems with an irrelevant premise remain reliably easier than multiple-model problems and no harder than one-model problems without an irrelevant premise. In sum, multiple models do cause problems for the human inferential system.

Systematic Errors Correspond to Initial Models of Premises This prediction has also been corroborated in all the main domains of reasoning (see Johnson-Laird & Byrne, 1991). Thus, a common sort of error in syllogistic reasoning is exemplified by arguing from the premises

All the athletes are bakers

and

Some of the bakers are chemists

to the conclusion

Some of the athletes are chemists.

Such errors used to be described as resulting from the "atmosphere" of the premises (Woodworth & Sells, 1935), where a premise containing *some* was supposed to bias individuals toard a conclusion containing *some*. The model theory, however, provides an alternative explanation. The error arises from a genuine attempt to reason. The initial model of the premises

athlete	baker	chemist
athlete	baker	chemist
athlete	baker	
		chemist

. . .

where each row represents a separate individual, supports the conclusion

Some of the athletes are chemists.

This conclusion is refuted by an alternative model of the premises:

athlete	baker	
athlete	baker	
	baker	chemist
	baker	chemist
		chemist

. . .

But reasoners who fail to construct this alternative model will draw the erroneous conclusion. In fact, the initial model for every syllogism yields a conclusion that matches the mood of one of the premises. Hence, the model theory also explains the tendency for erroneous conclusions to match the atmosphere of the premises. But which account is correct—the atmosphere hypothesis or the model theory?

Several phenomena count in favor of the model theory. If individuals were guided solely by the atmosphere of the premises, then they would never respond, "no valid conclusion." But they do make this response, and they make it correctly better than one would expect by chance. They are also much more likely to draw a conclusion that matches the mood of a premise for one-model syllogisms than for multiple-model syllogisms. The atmosphere hypothesis does not predict this difference. According to the model theory, however, the one-model conclusions should occur more often than the multiple-model matching conclusions, because the latter should tend sometimes to be refuted by the construction of an alternative model. The data from four experiments bear out this prediction: one-model syllogisms yielded 76% matching conclusions, whereas multiple-model syllogisms yielded only 39% matching conclusions (see Johnson-Laird & Byrne, 1991, table 6.1).

Knowledge Influences the Process of Reasoning   If reasoning is a formal process depending on rules of inference, then knowledge can influence the interpretation of premises, but, once their logical form has been mentally represented, it cannot affect the process itself. In contrast, if reasoning is a semantic process based on models, then knowledge can influence the process. Oakhill, Garnham, and I have obtained evidence in favor of the latter prediction from studies of syllogistic reasoning (e.g., Oakhill, Johnson-Laird, & Garnham, 1989). Given the following sort of premises

All the Frenchmen are gourmets

and

Some of the gourmets are wine drinkers,

the majority of our participants (72%) drew the conclusion

Some of the Frenchmen are wine drinkers.

But, given the following sort of premises,

All the Frenchmen are gourmets

and

Some of the gourmets are Italians,

only a few of our participants (8%) drew the equivalent conclusion:

Some of the Frenchmen are Italians.

No participant saw both of these problems, but they each saw a set of problems in which the conclusions based on the initial models were highly believable—as rated by an independent panel of judges—and a set of problems in which these conclusions were rated as highly unbelievable. The results bore out the pattern of response just illustrated.

The phenomenon was predicted by the model theory. In the first case, the theory predicts that reasoners will construct the following sort of initial model,

Frenchman	gourmet	wine drinker
Frenchman	gourmet	wine drinker
Frenchman	gourmet	
		wine drinker

. . .

which yields the conclusion

Some of the Frenchmen are wine drinkers.

This conclusion is highly believable, and so the participants do not bother to search for alternative models of the premises. In the second case, the theory predicts that reasoners will construct the same sort of initial model,

Frenchman	gourmet	Italian
Frenchman	gourmet	Italian
Frenchman	gourmet	
		Italian

. . .

which yelds the conclusion

Some of the Frenchmen are Italians.

This conclusion is highly unbelievable, and so the participants will search for an alternative model. They may succeed in constructing the model

Frenchman	gourmet	
Frenchman	gourmet	
	gourmet	Italian
	gourmet	Italian
		Italian

. . .

If so, they will respond that there is no valid conclusion. The initial conclusion is invalid in both cases, but plausible only in the first case. It is hard to see how a theory based on formal rules of inference could even generate the initial invalid conclusion, let alone account for the effects of believability.

Some formal theorists have seen the force of some of these experimental results. Braine (1990, p. 147), for example, suggested that reasoners often use mental models in reasoning. None of the results, however, has been recognized as decisive in resolving the controversy. The next section describes a new phenomenon that may settle the issue.

Truth and Fallacies in Reasoning

The traditional way to resolve a scientific controversy is to demonstrate a crucial phenomenon that is predicted by one theory but that contravenes the other theory. The more general and the more robust the phenomenon, the more likely it is to be decisive. My colleagues and I have discovered such a phenomenon: human beings are programmed to reason in a systematically fallacious way. This propensity is an unexpected consequence of the principle of truth, that is, of the principle that reasoners construct models of what is true rather than of what is false. This procedure is sensible because it avoids overloading working memory, and it normally yields valid conclusions. But, as a computer program implementing the theory revealed, it can lead to fallacious conclusions for certain inferences.

To understand the phenomenon, readers should make the following inference:

Only *one* of the following premises is true about a particular hand of cards:
There is a king in the hand or there is an ace, or both.
There is a queen in the hand or there is an ace, or both.
There is a jack in the hand or there is a 10, or both.
Is it possible that there is an ace in the hand? (1)

The model theory postulates that individuals consider the possibilities for each of the three premises. For the first premise, they consider three models, shown, as usual, on separate lines, which each correspond to a possibility given the truth of the premise:

king

      ace
king   ace

These models suggest that an ace is possible. The second premise also suggests that an ace is possible. Hence, individuals should respond yes.

Nearly all logically naive individuals drew this conclusion, that is, 99% of responses in two separate experiments (Johnson-Laird & Goldvarg, 1997). Yet, it is a fallacy that an ace is possible, because if there were an ace in the hand, then two of the premises would be true, contrary to the rubric that only one of them is true. The same strategy, however, yielded a correct response to a control problem in which only one premise refers to an ace. The participants also succumbed to fallacies of impossibility that elicited a predicted "no" response. Their confidence in their conclusions did not differ between the fallacies and the control problems. But they were less likely to commit a fallacy of impossibility than a fallacy of possibility. To infer that a situation is impossible calls for a check of every model, whereas to infer that a situation is possible does not, and so reasoners are less likely to make the inference of impossibility. Two studies have corroborated this difference in more difficult control problems than those in the experiment under discussion (Johnson-Laird & Bell, 1997).

If the fallacies result from a failure to reason about what is false, then any manipulation that emphasizes falsity should reduce them. We used the rubric "Only one of the following two premises is false" in a different study, and it did reliably reduce the occurrence of the fallacies, but only by 15% (Tabossi, Bell, & Johnson-Laird, in press). One problem is that individuals do not have a direct access to the cases in which disjunctions, or other compound assertions, are false. They first have to consider the situations in which the assertions would be true and then infer from them the situations in which the assertions would be false (Barres & Johnson-Laird, 1997).

With hindsight, it is astonishing that 99% of the responses to such items as problem 1 were yes, because it seems obvious that the presence of an ace renders two of the premises true. We therefore repeated the experiment, but after half the inferences, we gave one of the two groups of participants a special instruction to check whether their conclusions met the constraint that only one of the premises was true. This procedure had the advantage that the participants did not have to envisage the circumstances in which the premises would be false. They merely had to check how many premises their conclusion rendered true. The results replicated those of the first experiment, except that the group that received the special instruction thereafter showed a striking decline in fallacies. They drew 57% correct conclusions to fallacies of possibility compared to the 0% correct of their previous performance and to the 0% correct performance of the other group. Even with this instruction, however, their performance was far from perfect.

The rubric "One of these two assertions is true and one of them is false" is equivalent to an exclusive disjunction between two assertions, which we can convey more idiomatically as

A or else *B*, but not both,

where *A* and *B* denote the two assertions. This usage leads to still more compelling fallacies that seduce almost everyone, novices and experts alike. Consider this problem:

Suppose you know the following about a particular hand of cards:

If there is a king in the hand, then there is an ace in the hand; or else if there isn't a king in the hand, then there is an ace in the hand.

What, if anything, follows?   (2)

The model theory predicts that the first conditional will be represented by the models

king   ace

. . .

and that the second conditional will be represented by the models

¬king   ace

. . .

An exclusive disjunction, as table 17.5 shows, has as its initial models merely the two sets of possibilities, and so if reasoners interpret *or else* exclusively, they should construct the following models:

king   ace
¬king   ace

. . .

They are likely to forget about the implicit model, and so they should conclude:

Therefore, there is an ace in the hand.

Just about everyone, as Fabien Savary and I have shown in an unpublished experiment, draws this conclusion. Yet, it is a fallacy granted there is a disjunction—exclusive or inclusive—between the two conditional assertions. It then follows that one or other of the two conditionals could be *false*; and if either of them is false, then there is no guarantee of an ace in the hand. Indeed, if the disjunction is exclusive, it follows that there is not an ace; and if it is inclusive, then nothing follows about whether or not there is an ace. The fallacy, like the previous one, rests on the failure to reason about what is false.

Because so many experts have committed the fallacies, we have accumulated many putative explanations for them. For example, the premises of the fallacious inferences may be so complex, ambiguous, and pragmatically odd that they confuse people, who, as a result, commit a fallacy.

This hypothesis overlooks the fact that the participants are highly confident in their responses and that the control problems are often equally complex. Likewise, in another experiment, we have shown that when the fallacies and controls are based on the *same* premises, but different questions, that are all in the form of conjunctions, participants still commit the fallacies but get the control problems correct (Johnson-Laird & Goldvarg, 1997). The other putative explanations depend on special claims about the interpretations of conditionals or disjunctions in problem 2. They offer no account of the results with problem 1 and its cohort.

The fallacies also occur in the case of inferences about relative probabilities (Johnson-Laird & Savary, 1996). Here, for example, is an instructive contrast. Consider the following problem:

If one assertion is true about a specific hand of cards, then so is the other:

> There is a jack in the hand if and only if there is a queen in the hand.
>
> There is a jack in the hand.   (3)

Nearly everyone infers that the two cards are equally likely to be in the hand, but this conclusion is a fallacy based again on representing only the true cases: if both premises are true, then there is both a jack and a queen. But, consider the consequences of both premises being false: there is no jack because the second premise if false, but there is therefore a queen (from the falsity of the first premise). Hence, the queen is more likely to be in hand than the jack. Only 10% of participants made this correct inference. Now consider the control problem, where the failure to represent false contingencies does not yield the wrong conclusion:

If one assertion is true about a specific hand of cards, then so is the other:

> If there is a jack in the hand then there is a queen in the hand.
>
> There is a jack in the hand.   (4)

Nearly everyone drew the correct conclusion that the two cards are equally likely (95% of participants). The two problems are so similar that it is difficult to believe that one is pragmatically odd and the other is not: the only difference between them is that the illusion uses a biconditional whereas the control problem uses a regular conditional.

Many other robust phenomena in reasoning appear to arise from the neglect of what is false. In Wason's selection task, for instance, reasoners fail to represent the false contingencies of the conditional and so go wrong in choosing potentially falsifying instances. Social exchanges were important to our hunter-gatherer ancestors, and thus Cosmides (1989) postulated an innate module for reasoning about cheating. She used a selection task about a potential cheater, and then, as she predicted, most people made the correct choice. Our results suggest an alternative explanation. People construct models of what is true, not of what is false. Hence, any manipulation that helps them to consider false instances of the rule, including their knowledge of cheating, should improve performance. Several studies have corroborated this explanation in selection tasks that do not depend on cheaters (e.g., Green & Larking, 1995; Sperber, Cara, & Girotto, 1995). Likewise, given a conditional, such as

If the experiment continued, then the turbine was generating emergency electricity,

people readily infer that the truth of the antecedent (the experiment continued) implies the truth of the consequent (the turbine was generating emergency electricity). What they have difficulty in inferring is that the falsity of the consequent implies the falsity of the antecedent—a failure that occurs in laboratory tests and that contributed to Chernobyl and other disasters in real life (Medvedev, 1990).

Conclusions

The controversy about whether reasoning depends on formal rules or mental models began some twenty years ago. Both sorts of theory have been formulated in detail, implemented in computer programs, and corroborated experimentally. Although some commentators have argued that the controversy may never be resolved, there are three arguments that favor the mental model theory at the expense of current formal rule theories.

The first argument is that the model theory has a much wider purview than the rule theory. The model theory explains how reasoners reach conclusions that are necessarily true—the conclusions hold in all models of the premises, conclusions that are probably true—the conclusions hold in most models of the premises, and conclusions that are possibly true—the conclusions hold in at least some model of the premises. In contrast, the rule theories have so far been formulated only for necessary conclusions and a small set of possible conclusions.

The second argument concerns judgments of invalidity. The model theory explains these judgments in a simple way: a conclusion is invalid if there is a model of the premises in which it is false. Such a counterexample demonstrates invalidity. However, rule theories have a much more indirect account: reasoners judge that a conclusion is invalid only if they fail to find a formal derivation for it. In contrasting a syntactic and a semantic method in logic, Quine (1974, p. 75) wrote: "[The syntactic method] is inferior in that it affords no general way of reaching a verdict of invalidity; failure to discover a proof for a schema can mean either invalidity or mere bad luck." Barwise (1993, p. 338) has argued that the same problem vitiates psychological theories based on formal rules: "The 'search till you're exhausted' strategy gives one at best an educated, correct guess that something does not follow." If a theory is *incomplete*—as PSYCOP is—the "search till you're exhausted" strategy is particularly dubious because you may fail to find a derivation for a *valid* argument. Thus, when PSYCOP gives up, it may do so because an argument is invalid, or because an argument is valid but it cannot derive the proof with its incomplete rules. In short, incompleteness has a "knock-on" effect: you can no longer decide whether a conclusion is valid or invalid; that is, the failure to discover a proof does not necessarily mean that an argument is invalid. Hence, there is no way to know that an argument is invalid (unless the conclusion contradicts the premises). The theory therefore cannot offer any account of the difference between knowing that an argument is invalid and not knowing whether it is valid or invalid.

The third argument concerns systematic errors. The model theory explains them in terms of the initial models that reasoners construct. Often, as in the case of syllogisms, the result of constructing only a single model of a multiple-model problem is that reasoners will draw a conclusion that is consistent with the premises, though it does not follow from them necessarily. Other systematic fallacies arise because models fail to represent what is false. These errors are compelling; they have the character of cognitive illusions. They are also a crucial phenomenon for deciding between the two competing sets of theories. They were first predicted by a computer program that I devised to simulate the model theory. At first, I thought there was a bug in the program. But there was no bug, and the fallacies were a genuine prediction, subsequently corroborated by our experiments. If the fallacies had not occurred in the experiments, then the model theory would have been disconfirmed. In contrast, these cognitive illusions are counterexamples to current formal rule theories. Such theories contain only logically impeccable rules, and so the only way in which they can yield fallacious conclusions is by a mistake in applying a rule. Such mistakes, however, should be like "throwing a spanner in the works." As Rips (1994) points out, they should occur arbitrarily and have diverse results, not one and the same fallacious conclusion. Indeed, neither PSYCOP nor Braine's system draws any conclusion to problem 1, and neither can accommodate problems 2 and 3.

These three arguments, together with the evidence in favor of the model theory, show that it gives a better account of reasoning than current formal rule theories. They do not, of course, eliminate the possibility that reasoning depends on both mental models and formal rules—only parsimony could count against such an account. Likewise, they do not eliminate the possibility of a new formal rule theory that uses *invalid* rules or principles to deliver systematic fallacies (cf. Jackendoff, 1988). Still less do they rule out the possibility of some entirely new theory. One fine day, someone may formulate just such a theory, one that leads to the discovery of counterexamples to the mental model theory. The theory will be thereby overturned, but it will at least be able to account for its own demise. It argues that counterexamples refute theories.

Note

1. Rips (1994, p. 407, n. 3) claims that only three arguments in his experiment maintain semantic information (arguments *C*, *O*, and *X* in his table 5.1). Consider, as just one counterexample, the following argument (corresponding to argument *E* in Rips's table 5.1):

If p or r, or both, then q
∴ If p or q, or both, then q

There are three possibilities consistent with the conclusion (p and q, q alone, and, where both the antecedent and consequent are false, neither p nor q). Each of these possibilities is consistent with the premise. Hence, this argument does not throw semantic information away. Clearly, there is a misunderstanding here of the sort that often arises in the minutiae of a controversy. Perhaps Rips assumes that the argument throws information away because a term in the premise, r, does not appear in the conclusion. The critical criterion, however, is that information is thrown away only if the conclusion is consistent with more situations than are the premises.

References

Bara, B., Bucciarelli, M., & Johnson-Laird, P. N. (1995). The development of syllogistic reasoning. *American Journal of Psychology, 108,* 157–193.

Barres, P. E., & Johnson-Laird, P. N. (1997). Why is it hard to imagine what is false? In M. G. Shafto & P. Langley (Eds.) *Proceedings of Nineteenth Annual Conference of the Cognitive Science Society* (p. 859). Mahwah, NJ: Erlbaum.

Barwise, J. (1993). Everyday reasoning and logical inference [Commentary on Johnson-Laird & Byrne (1991)]. *Behavioral and Brain Sciences, 16,* 337–338.

Beth, E. W., & Piaget, J. (1966). *Mathematical epistemology and psychology.* Dordrecht, Netherlands: Reidel.

Braine, M. D. S. (1978). On the relation between the natural logic of reasoning and standard logic. *Psychological Review, 85,* 1–21.

Braine, M. D. S. (1990). The "natural logic" approach to reasoning. In W. F. Overton (Ed.), *Reasoning, necessity, and logic: Developmental perspectives* (pp. 133–157). Hillsdale, NJ: Erlbaum.

Braine, M. D. S., & O'Brien, D. P. (1991). A theory of If: A lexical entry, reasoning program, and pragmatic principles. *Psychological Review, 98,* 182–203.

Braine, M. D. S., Reiser, B. J., & Rumain, B. (1984). Some empirical justification for a theory of natural propositional logic. *The psychology of learning and motivation* (Vol. 18). New York: Academic Press.

Braine, M. D. S., & Rumain, B. (1983). Logical reasoning. In J. H. Flavell & E. M. Markman (Eds.), *Carmichael's handbook of child psychology:* Vol. 3. *Cognitive Development* (4th ed.). New York: Wiley.

Byrne, R. M. J., & Johnson-Laird, P. N. (1989). Spatial reasoning. *Journal of Memory and Language, 28,* 564–575.

Cosmides, L. (1989). The logic of social exchange: Has natural selection shaped how humans reason? Studies with the Wason selection task. *Cognition, 31,* 187–276.

Erickson, J. R. (1974). A set analysis theory of behavior in formal syllogistic reasoning tasks. In R. Solso (Ed.), *Loyola Symposium on Cognition* (Vol. 2). Hillsdale, NJ: Erlbaum.

Evans, J. St. B. T., Newstead, S. E., & Byrne, R. M. J. (1993). *Human reasoning: The psychology of deduction.* Hillsdale, NJ: Erlbaum.

Gentzen, G. (1969). Investigations into logical deduction. In M. E. Szabo (Ed. and Trans.), *The collected papers of Gerhard Gentzen.* Amsterdam: North-Holland. (Original work published 1935.)

Green, D. W., & Larking, R. (1995). The locus of facilitation in the abstract selection task. *Thinking and Reasoning, 1,* 183–199.

Henle, M. (1962). The relation between logic and thinking. *Psychological Review, 69,* 366–378.

Hewitt, C. (1972). *Description and theoretical analysis of PLANNER* (Laboratory Report MIT-AI-258). Cambridge, MA: MIT AI.

Jackendoff, R. (1988). Exploring the form of information in the dynamic unconscious. In M. J. Horowitz (Ed.), *Psychodynamics and Cognition.* Chicago: University of Chicago Press.

Janis, I., & Frick, P. (1943). The relationship between attitudes towards conclusions and errors of judging logical validity of syllogisms. *Journal of Experimental Psychology, 33,* 73–77.

Jeffrey, R. (1981). *Formal logic: Its scope and limits* (2nd ed.). New York: McGraw-Hill.

Johnson-Laird, P. N. (1975). Models of deduction. In R. J. Falmagne (Ed.), *Reasoning: Representation and process in children and adults* (pp. 7–54). Hillsdale, NJ: Erlbaum.

Johnson-Laird, P. N., & Bell, V. (1997). A model theory of modal reasoning. In M. G. Shafto & P. Langley (Eds.), *Proceedings of Nineteenth Annual Conference of the Cognitive Science Society* (pp. 349–353). Mahwah, NJ: Erlbaum.

Johnson-Laird, P. N., & Byrne, R. M. J. (1991). *Deduction.* Hillsdale, NJ: Erlbaum.

Johnson-Laird, P. N., & Goldvarg, Y. (1997). How to make the possible seem possible. In M. G. Shafto & P. Langley (Eds.), *Proceedings of the Nineteenth Annual Conference of the Cognitive Science Society* (pp. 354–357). Mahwah, NJ: Erlbaum.

Johnson-Laird, P. N., Legrenzi, P., & Legrenzi, M. S. (1972). Reasoning and a sense of reality. *British Journal of Psychology, 63,* 395–400.

Johnson-Laird, P. N., & Savary, F. (1996). Illusory inferences about probabilities. *Acta Psychologica, 93,* 69–90.

Macnamara, J. (1986). *A border dispute: The place of logic in psychology.* Cambridge, MA: Bradford Books, MIT Press.

Medvedev, Z. A. (1990). *The Legacy of Chernobyl.* New York: Norton.

Oakhill, J. V., Johnson-Laird, P. N., & Garnham, A. (1989). Believability and syllogistic reasoning. *Cognition, 31,* 117–140.

Osherson, D. N. (1974–1976). *Logical Abilities in Children* (Vols. 1–4). Hillsdale, NJ: Erlbaum.

Osherson, D. N. (1975). Logic and models of logical thinking. In R. J. Falmagne (Ed.), *Reasoning: Representation and process in children and adults* (pp. 81–91). Hillsdale, NJ: Erlbaum.

Pollock, J. (1989). *How to build a person: A prolegomenon.* Cambridge, MA: Bradford Books, MIT Press.

Quine, W. V. O. (1974). *Methods of logic* (3rd ed.). London: Routledge.

Rips, L. J. (1983). Cognitive processes in propositional reasoning. *Psychological Review, 90,* 38–71.

Rips, L. J. (1994). *The psychology of proof.* Cambridge, MA: MIT Press.

Robinson, J. A. (1979). *Logic: Form and function. The mechanization of deductive reasoning.* Edinburgh, Scotland: Edinburgh University Press.

Schaeken, W. S., Johnson-Laird, P. N., & d'Ydewalle, G. (1996). Mental models and temporal reasoning. *Cognition, 60,* 205–234.

Sperber, D., Cara, F., & Girotto, V. (1995). Relevance theory explains the selection task. *Cognition, 52,* 3–39.

Sperber, D., & Wilson, D. (1986). *Relevance: Communication and cognition.* Oxford, England: Basil Blackwell.

Störring, G. (1908). Experimentelle Untersuchungen über einfache Schlussprozesse. *Archiv für die gesamte Psychologie, 11,* 1–27.

Tabossi, P., Bell, V. A., & Johnson-Laird, P. N. (in press). Mental models in deductive, modal, and probabilistic reasoning. In C. Habel & G. Rickheit (Eds.), *Mental models in discourse processing and reasoning.* Berlin: John Benjamins.

Tversky, A., & Kahneman, D. (1973). Availability: A heuristic for judging frequency and probability. *Cognitive Psychology, 5,* 207–232.

Wason, P. C. (1966). Reasoning. In B. M. Foss (Ed.), *New horizons in psychology.* Harmondsworth, England: Penguin.

Wason, P. C., & Johnson-Laird, P. N. (1972). *Psychology of Reasoning: Structure and Content.* London: Batsford and Cambridge, MA: Harvard University Press.

Wason, P. C., & Shapiro, D. (1971). Natural and contrived experience in a reasoning problem. *Quarterly Journal of Experimental Psychology, 23,* 63–71.

Woodworth, R. S., & Sells, S. B. (1935). An atmosphere effect in formal syllogistic reasoning. *Journal of Experimental Psychology, 18,* 451–460.

Wos, L. (1988). *Automated reasoning: 33 basic research problems.* Englewood Cliffs, NJ: Prentice-Hall.

18

Cognition versus Metacognition

Thomas O. Nelson

Metacognition is defined as the scientific study of an individual's cognitions about his or her own cognitions. As such, metacognition is more of a subset of cognition than something other than cognition. Put differently, metacognition is a particular kind of cognition.

If this seems a little complicated, it can quickly become even more complicated. The reason is that the difference between an aspect of metacognition versus the aspect of cognition that it is "about" (see the first sentence of this chapter) is *relational* rather than *absolute*. Put differently, there is no particular aspect of cognition that is always at the metalevel in any absolute sense. Instead, we say that if one aspect of cognition is monitoring or controlling another aspect of cognition, then the former aspect is metacognitive in relation to the latter aspect. An elaboration of this idea can be found in Nelson and Narens (1994), and several examples will be given now to help illustrate these distinctions.

In terms of metacognitive monitoring, sometimes you might recall an answer to a question (e.g., to the question "What is the capital of Australia?"), and then I could ask you how sure you are that your answer is correct. Thus you would make a confidence judgment about your recall of that answer. This is an example of your cognition (namely, confidence) about one of your own cognitions (namely, recall). Research has shown that most people tend to be overconfident in such a judgment (e.g., in terms of the preceding question, the answer is not Sydney or Brisbane or Perth or Melbourne but rather is Canberra). Similarly, I could ask you how confident you are about your confidence in your recall of that answer! Then you might respond by telling the size of the confidence interval around the aforementioned confidence judgment; a large confidence rval would represent less confidence about your confidence than ould a small interval. The first confidence judgment that was mentioned in this paragraph would be at the metalevel relative to recall (the confidence is "about" recall) but would be the object of (and therefore is said to be at the object level) for the confidence judgment about that confidence.

Or, instead of your metacognitive monitoring being about an answer you just gave, it might instead be about an answer that you have not yet recalled but on which you will have an upcoming recognition test. For instance, I could ask you, "What is the likelihood that you will recognize the answer that you currently cannot recall?" This kind of metacognitive judgment is called a *feeling-of-knowing* judgment.

Or, your metacognitive judgment might instead be about an item you have recently studied. For instance, I could ask you, "What is the likelihood that you will recall this item approximately 10 minutes from now?" This kind of metacognitive judgment is called a *judgment of learning*. Judgments of learning can be particularly important because they can indicate (either accurately or inaccurately) to the person that he or she should or shouldn't devote additional study to a given item.

This brings us to the second major subdivision of metacognition—in addition to the metacognitive monitoring already described. This subdivision is called *metacognitive control* of one's own cognitions. For instance, as just indicated, one kind of metacognitive control is the control of one's self-paced study. You can devote additional study to a given item if you decide to do so. Or you can decide not to devote additional study to a given item. Either way, that's an example of metacognitive control.

An abstract representation of monitoring and control that arises from this interplay between two levels is shown in figure 18.1. To make this abstract representation more concrete, let's consider examples of metacognitive monitoring and metacognitive control in the area of human learning and memory.

A general framework showing the main components of metacognitive monitoring and metacognitive control during the acquisition or retrieval of information from memory was first formulated by Nelson and Narens (1990; reproduced in part in the book of core readings about metacognition by Nelson, 1992). Figure 18.2 shows an overview of the framework.

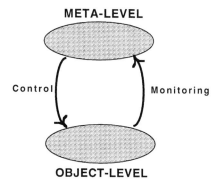

Figure 18.1
Relationship between a component of cognition at the metalevel versus object level in terms of the flow of information from one of those levels to the other level. (Adapted from Nelson & Narens, 1990.)

In figure 18.2 you can see the aforementioned components of meta-cognition, plus additional components. This subvariety of metacognition that pertains to learning and memory is called *metamemory* and refers to the *monitoring and control of one's own memory* during the acquisition of new information and during the retrieval of previously acquired information.

Metamemory has been investigated by psychologists for only about 40 years. Prior to that time, researchers often conceptualized people as blank slates, wherein the learner was considered to be passive and to have little or no control over his or her own acquisition. Since the 1950s, researchers have conceptualized the individual as having substantial control over acquisition and as being active rather than passive, both during the acquisition of new information and during the retrieval of previously learned information (for more discussion, see Nelson, 1996).

An example of the utility of conceptualizing the learner as active is illustrated in table 18.1, which summarizes data collected by Eagle (1967). The percentage of words recalled is shown as a joint function of the strategy the experimenter instructed the subjects to use and the strategy the subjects reported using. Eagle instructed one group of subjects to use rote rehearsal to learn a list of 20 words and instructed another group to use associative organization for the same word list. After study, the subjects verbally described the strategies they had used, and those verbal

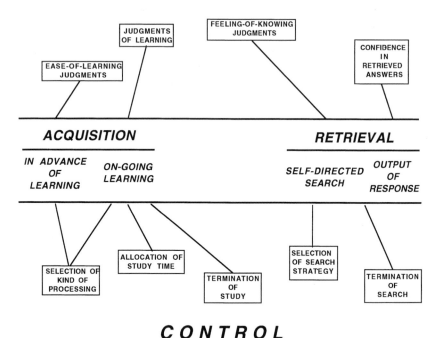

Figure 18.2
A theoretical framework of the metacognitive components involved in acquisition and retrieval. (Adapted from Nelson & Narens, 1990.)

Table 18.1
Mean percentage of words recalled as a joint function of instructed strategy and reported strategy

	Reported strategy	
Instructed strategy	Rehearsal	Associative organization
Rehearsal	48	62
Associative organization	49	65

Source: Data from Eagle (1967).

reports were classified by neutral judges into the categories of rote rehearsal or associative organization. As table 18.1 shows, the effect of various mnemonic strategies are more obvious from knowing the subjects' verbal reports than from knowing the external stimulus condition of the instructed strategy. Thus the traditional effect of instructions on behavior appears to be an indirect one; namely, the experimenter's instructions serve only to influence the subjects' choice of strategy, with the critical factor for predicting the subjects' recall being the strategy that the subjects report using. This is another example—in addition to the above-mentioned example of control of the amount of self-paced study— of how subjects can metacognitively control their processing during learning, in this case by choosing one versus another strategy.

Next, imagine the monitoring and control processes that occur while a student learns new foreign-language vocabulary—say, French/English vocabulary such as *château/castle*—and while the student attempts to retrieve the answers during a subsequent examination. The various kinds of monitoring processes are distinguished by when they occur during acquisition and retrieval, especially in terms of whether they pertain to the person's future performance *(prospective monitoring)* or the person's past performance *(retrospective monitoring)*. Let's consider each of these separately.

Prospective Monitoring

Ease-of-Learning Judgments

When someone is getting ready to learn new information, then even prior to the beginning of acquisition some metacognitive monitoring occurs. An *ease-of-learning judgment* is the person's judgment of how easy or difficult the items will be to acquire. For instance, the person might believe that *château/castle* will be easier to learn than *boite/box*. Underwood (1966) showed that people are somewhat (but not perfectly) accurate at predicting which items will be easier to learn. People's predictions (made in advance of acquisition) of how easy each item would be to learn were moderately correlated with subsequent recall after a constant amount of study time on every item: The items people predicted would be easier to learn had a greater subsequent likelihood of being recalled than items people predicted would be harder to learn.

Judgments of Learning

During or soon after acquisition, the person's *judgment of learning* is the person's evaluation of how well he or she has learned a given item. It is a prediction of the likelihood that the item will be remembered correctly on a future test. Arbuckle and Cuddy (1969) showed that the predictive accuracy of people's judgments of learning is above chance but far from perfect, similar to the situation for ease-of-learning judgments. Subsequently Leonesio and Nelson (1990) showed that judgments of learning are more accurate than ease-of-learning judgments for predicting eventual recall, probably because people's judgments of learning can be based on what the learner notices about how well he or she is mastering the items during acquisition.

Nelson and Dunlosky (1991) isolated a situation in which people's judgments of learning can be extremely accurate, if not perfectly accurate. This occurs when people make the judgment of learning not immediately after studying a given item but rather after a short delay; this is called the delayed judgment-of-learning (delayed-JOL) effect. Dunlosky and Nelson (1992) showed that the delayed-JOL effect occurs if and only if the cue for the judgments is the stimulus alone rather than the stimulus-response pair. For instance, the delayed-JOL effect occurs if the cue for the judgment about *château/castle* is "château?" but not if the cue is "château/castle." This delayed-JOL effect is exciting because it shows that under the proper conditions, people can monitor their learning extremely accurately. Most recently, Dunlosky and Nelson (1997) found that the delayed-JOL effect is not due merely to the situation at the time of the delayed JOL being nominally more similar to the situation at the time of the eventual test. However, exactly what mechanisms underlie the delayed-JOL effect are not yet established (for an example of the controversy, see Nelson & Dunlosky, 1992, and Spellman & Bjork, 1992.).

Feeling-of-Knowing Judgments

These were the first metamemory judgments examined in the laboratory. Hart (1965) found that the likelihood of correctly recognizing a nonrecalled answer was higher for nonrecalled items people said were stored in memory than for nonrecalled items people said weren't stored in memory. But people frequently did not recognize answers that they had claimed that they would recognize, and people sometimes did recognize answers they had claimed they wouldn't recognize. Subsequently, the accuracy of predicting other kinds of memory performance such as relearning was investigated by Nelson, Gerler, and Narens (1964), who also offered approximately a dozen theoretical explanations for how people might make their feeling-of-knowing judgments. However, their and Hart's findings—and more recent ones by Metcalfe, Schwartz, and Joaquim (1993) and by Reder and Ritter (1992)—have led current researchers to conclude that the feeling of knowing is based not so much on the monitoring of nonrecalled information but instead on an inference based on the retrieved aspects of memory (e.g., recognition of the question as having been previously encountered before or recall of some components of the answer such as the first letter or the number of syllables it contains). A currently popular theory of the feeling of knowing that encompasses these ideas was formulated by Koriat (1993).

Retrospective Confidence Judgments

In contrast to the previous metamemory monitoring judgments, in which people attempted to predict their future memory performance, retrospective confidence judgments occur after someone recalls or recognizes an answer and pertain to how confident the person is that his or her answer was correct. For instance, if someone were asked to recall the English equivalent of *château*, the person might say, "castle" (the correct answer) or might say, "red" (the incorrect answer), after which he or she would make a confidence judgment about the likelihood that the recalled answer was correct. Fischhoff, Slovic, and Lichtenstein (1977) discovered a strong tendency for people to be overconfident, especially when the test was one of recognition.

Source Monitoring and Reality Monitoring

In addition to the aforementioned kinds of monitoring that pertain to a person's knowledge of a particular item, people also monitor information about when and where they learned a given item (called *source information*). People who are unable to remember the source of when and where the acquisition occurred are said to have *source amnesia*. One useful distinction in terms of the source of prior acquisition is whether the item occurred externally to the person (e.g., from someone else's saying it to the person) or occurred internally in the person (e.g., in a dream). The ability to distinguish between those two possibilities for a given item is called *reality monitoring* and has been investigated by Johnson and Raye (1981); a quantitative theory of source monitoring is available in Batchelder and Riefer (1990), and potential researchers who need to decide between different measures of source monitoring should see Murnane and Bayen (1996).

Metacognitive Control

That people can monitor their progress during acquisition and retrieval is interesting, but it is little more than a curiosity if it has no other role in the overall memory system. However, as alluded to earlier, people can control aspects of their acquisition and retrieval. First, consider what people can control during self-paced acquisition, and then consider what they can control during retrieval.

Control during Self-Paced Acquisition

A model of how the monitoring and control components interact to form a metacognitive system for the acquisition of new information into memory is shown in figure 18.3. It shows the aforementioned judgments of learning, which are compared to the desired degree of learning (called the *norm of study*). When the person believes he or she has not learned the item as well as desired, then more study time is devoted to the item, and some strategy is employed in an attempt to increase the degree of learning. Consider several empirical findings that are relevant to such a metacognitive system for acquisition.

Allocation of Self-Paced Study during Acquisition   Someone who is learning foreign-language vocabulary can choose to allocate various amounts of study time to each item and can allocate more study time to some items during subsequent study trials. In 1978, the researchers Bisanz, Vesonder, and Voss found that the allocation of self-paced study seems to occur in conjunction with people's judgments of learning. Bisanz

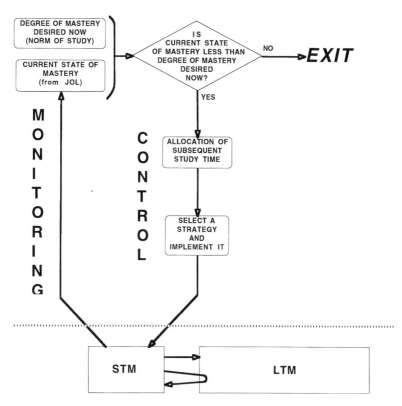

Figure 18.3
Model of the interplay of metacognitive components involved in acquisition of new information into memory. (Adapted from Nelson & Narens, 1990.)

et al. discovered that learners in the early years of primary school make accurate judgments of learning but will not utilize those judgments when allocating additional study time across the items. By contrast, slightly older children will utilize those judgments when allocating additional study time. Whereas older children allocated extra study time to items they judged to have not yet learned and did not allocate extra study time to items they judged to have learned, the younger children were not systematic in allocating extra study time primarily to the unlearned items.

Strategy Employed during Self-Paced Study   There often are strategies that are more effective than rote repetition, but do people know what they are?

People's utilization of a mnemonic strategy for the acquisition of foreign-language vocabulary was investigated by Pressley, Levin, and Ghatala (1984). After people had learned some foreign-language vocabulary by rote and other foreign-language vocabulary by the mnemonic strategy, they were allowed a choice of using whichever strategy they wanted for a final trial of learning some additional foreign-language vocabulary. Only 12% of the adults chose the mnemonic strategy if they had not received any test trials during the earlier phase, whereas 87% of them chose the mnemonic strategy if they had received test trials during the earlier acquisition phase. Thus test trials help people to realize the effectiveness of different strategies for acquisition. When the subjects were children, instead of adults, then they not only needed test trials, but they also needed to have feedback after those test trials to tell them how well they had done on the rote-learned items versus the mnemonically learned items; without both the test trials and feedback, the children were unlikely to adopt the advantageous mnemonic strategy.

Control during Retrieval

Control of Initiating One's Retrieval   Immediately after someone is asked a question and before attempting to search memory for the answer, a metacognitive decision is made about whether the answer is likely to be found in memory. If you were asked what the telephone number is for the current president of the United States, you probably would decide immediately that the answer is not in your memory. Notice that you do not need to search through all the telephone numbers that you know; nor do you need to search through all the information you have stored in your memory about the president. Put differently, you don't even initiate protracted attempts to retrieve that answer. Consider how that situation might differ from one in which you were asked the telephone number of one of your friends.

This initial feeling-of-knowing judgment that precedes an attempt to retrieve an answer was first investigated by Reder (1987). She found that people are faster at making a feeling-of-knowing decision about whether or not they know the answer to a general information question (e.g., "What is the capital of Finland?") than they are at answering that question (e.g., saying "Helsinki"). This demonstrates that the metacognitive decision is made prior to (rather than after) retrieving the answer. Only if people feel that they know the answer will they continue their attempts to retrieve the answer. When they feel they do not know the answer, they don't even attempt to search memory (as in the example of the president's telephone number).

Control of the Termination of Extended Attempts at Retrieval   It is often the case that people who initially believe strongly enough that they know an answer to begin searching memory for it but who after extended attempts at retrieval do not produce it will eventually terminate searching for it. The metacognitive decision to terminate such an extended search of memory was investigated by Nelson, Gerler, and Narens (1984). They found that the amount of time elapsing before someone gives up searching memory for a nonretrieved answer is greater when the person's ongoing feeling of knowing for the answer is high rather than low. As an example, someone might spend a long time during an examination attempting to retrieve the English equivalent of *château* (which the person studied the night before) but little or no time attempting to retrieve the English equivalent of *cheval* (which the person did not study previously). The metacognitive decision to continue versus terminate attempts at retrieving an answer from memory may of course also be affected by other factors, such as the total amount of time available during the examination.

Most of the research articles cited so far in the chapter have been reprinted (with a discussion to tie them together and with additional articles suggested for further reading) in the book by Nelson (1992). Additional research on the above topics can found in the book by Metcalfe and Shimamura (1994).

Neuropsychological Correlates of Metacognition

Neuropsychological Patients

People interested in neuropsychology may be interested in some of the findings that have been discovered in neuropsychological patients concerning various aspects of memory and metacognition. For instance, Korsakoff patients, whose brain damage includes frontal lobe damage

(Shimamura, Jernigan, & Squire, 1988), have deficits in the accuracy of their judgments of learning in terms of predicting their future recall on recently learned items (Bauer, Kyaw, & Kilbey, 1984). In terms of the kinds of dissociations that are the focus of this chapter, patients with less widespread brain damage but with frontal lobe deficits sometimes show normal recall but deficient feeling-of-knowing accuracy (Janowsky, Shimamura, & Squire, 1989). Janowsky et al. concluded, "The frontal lobes make an essential contribution to metamemory ability. Because patients with frontal lobe lesions do not exhibit memory impairment [recall or recognition failure], the present study demonstrates that metamemory deficits can occur in the absence of amnesia" (p. 10). This conclusion provides additional confirmation for the distinction between metacognitive processing (which might be deficient when there is frontal lobe damage) and whatever is being monitored during feeling-of-knowing judgments.

Normal Subjects in Extreme Environments

Research conducted on high-altitude climbers at various elevations on Mount Everest also supports the distinction between metacognitive processing and the cognitive processing that is being metacognitively monitored. Related to the pattern mentioned in the previous paragraph in terms of an effect on the feeling of knowing in the absence of an effect on recall or recognition, Nelson et al. (1990) found that cognitive performance at extreme altitudes, that is, above 6400 meters (relative to lower altitudes such as at Kathmandu or base camp), was unaffected in terms of recall or recognition of the answers to general information questions. However, the magnitude of the feeling of knowing was affected—in particular, was reduced—at the two extreme altitude tests and also on the test one week later back at Kathmandu, relative to feelings of knowing at the initial Kathmandu test or at base camp (Nelson et al., 1990, figure 2).

This finding was important enough that Nelson et al. (1990) decided to examine the individual subjects median feelings of knowing (FOKs) to have a more fine-grained look at the data that gave rise to the overall group performance. Figure 18.4 is a scatterplot matrix (Cleveland, 1985) showing bivariate data wherein each data point indicates one subject's

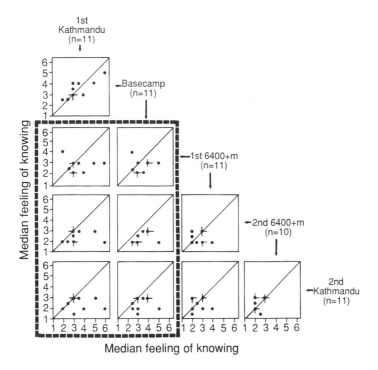

Figure 18.4
Scatterplot matrix showing each individual subject's performance at different test locations. (Reprinted from Nelson et al., 1990.)

median FOK for the row location plotted against that subject's median FOK for the column location. The petals on each sunflower indicate the number of subjects when more than one subject had a given bivariate entry. For instance, the three-petal sunflower in the subplot for the *Base-camp* column and the *2nd Kathmandu* row indicates that three subjects had a median FOK of 4 at basecamp and a median FOK of 3 on the second Kathmandu test. Although an appreciation of the results shown in figure 17.4 may require a little more effort than usual, such an examination is informative: For all six of the subplots comparing any of the first two tests with any of the last three tests—these subplots are enclosed inside the dashed box—the number of subjects who had a lower median FOK after going to high altitude (versus before going to high altitude) is remarkable. For instance, every climber had a lower median FOK at the second high-altitude test than at basecamp. Moreover, there were only two inversions in those six subplots—one in each of the upper two subplots—and both of those inversions came from the same climber. For comparison, notice that there is no trend in one direction or the other for the remaining four subplots that are outside the dashed box. Thus figure 17.4 shows that the group effect mentioned in the previous paragraph is also obvious for the preponderance of individual subjects.

The aftereffects of going to an extreme altitude that Nelson et al. (1990) observed may be due to a relatively long-lasting effect on the frontal lobes. Oelz and Regard (1988) reported that world-class climbers who had repeatedly climbed without supplementary oxygen above 8,000 meters showed subsequent impaired performance on neuropsychological tests at sea level. Those researchers concluded that repeated extreme altitude climbing produces an accumulating and possibly permanent dysfunction in "the fronto-temporal basal brain areas" (p. 86). Similar findings of frontal lobe deficits in climbers returning from high-altitude climbs have also been reported by Cavaletti, Moroni, Garavaglia, and Tredici (1987).

Given that there is a neuropsychological frontal lobe deficit after going to an extreme altitude, the effects *during the expedition* that were observed by Nelson et al. (1990) may have their origin in that same brain area. This pattern of findings represents a nice convergence of neuropsychological data and behavioral data, and both sets of data support a potential dissociation between metacognitive processing and lower-level cognitive processing.

Consciousness and Metacognition

The ideas about metacognition described in this chapter are also related to conceptions of consciousness. Most conceptions (e.g., Kihlstrom, 1984, p. 150) divide consciousness into two major aspects: conscious monitoring and conscious control. The way in which the data from research on metacognition are relevant to theories of consciousness has been elaborated in Nelson (1996), along with additional findings that support the distinction between, on the one hand, the metacognitive aspect of cognition responsible for monitoring and control and, on the other hand, the aspect of the cognitive system that is being monitored and controlled by metacognitive processing.

There is of course plenty of room for modifications to be made in our views of metacognition in comparison with other kinds of cognitive processing. More sophisticated conceptualizations need to be developed, and empirical evidence needs to be collected that refutes or confirms those conceptualizations and that gives us clues about new ways of formulating ideas about metacognition.

Acknowledgments

Preparation of this chapter was supported by grant R01-MH32205 and a career development award (K05-MH1075) from the National Institute of Mental Health.

References

Arbuckle, T. Y., & Cuddy, L. L. (1969). Discrimination of item strength at time of presentation. *Journal of Experimental Psychology, 81,* 126–131.

Batchelder, W., & Riefer, D. (1990). Multinomial processing models of source monitoring. *Psychological Review, 97,* 548–564.

Bauer, R. H., Kyaw, D., & Kilbey, M. M. (1984). Metamemory of alcoholic Korsakoff patients. *Society for Neurosciences Abstracts, 10,* 318.

Bisanz, G. L., Vesonder, G. T., & Voss, J. F. (1978). Knowledge of one's own responding and the relation of such knowledge to learning. *Journal of Experimental Child Psychology, 25,* 116–128.

Cavaletti, G., Moroni, R. Garavaglia, P., & Tredici, G. (1987). Brain damage after high-altitude climbs without oxygen. *Lancet,* 101.

Cleveland, W. (1985). *The elements of graphing data.* Monterey, CA: Wadsworth.

Dunlosky, J., & Nelson, T. O. (1992). Importance of the kind of cue for judgments of learning (JOL) and the delayed-JOL effect. *Memory & Cognition, 20,* 374–380.

Dunlosky, J., & Nelson, T. O. (1997). Similarity between the cue for judgments of learning (JOL) and the cue for test is not the primary determinant of JOL accuracy. *Journal of Memory and Language. 36,* 34–49.

Eagle, M. (1967). The effect of learning strategies upon free recall. *American Journal of Psychology, 80,* 421–425.

Fischhoff, B., Slovic, P., & Lichtenstein, S. (1977). Knowing with certainty: The appropriateness of extreme confidence. *Journal of Experimental Psychology: Human Perception and Performance, 3,* 552–564.

Hart, J. T. (1965). Memory and the feeling-of-knowing experience. *Journal of Educational Psychology, 56,* 208–216.

Janowsky, J., Shimamura, A., & Squire, L. (1989). Memory and metamemory: Comparisons between patients with frontal lobe lesions and amnesic patients. *Psychobiology, 17,* 3–11.

Johnson, M. K., & Raye, C. L. (1981). Reality monitoring. *Psychological Review, 88,* 67–85.

Kihlstrom, J. (1984). Conscious, subconscious, unconscious: A cognitive perspective. In K. S. Bowers & D. Meichenbaum (Eds.), *The unconscious reconsidered.* New York: Wiley.

Koriat, A. (1993). How do we know that we know? The accessibility model of the feeling of knowing. *Psychological Review, 100,* 609–639.

Leonesio, R. J., & Nelson, T. O. (1990). Do different measures of metamemory tap the same underlying aspects of memory? *Journal of Experimental Psychology: Learning, Memory, and Cognition, 16,* 464–470.

Metcalfe, J., Schwartz, B., & Joaquim, S. (1993). The cue familiarity heuristic in metacognition. *Journal of Experimental Psychology: Learning, Memory, and Cognition, 19,* 851–861.

Metcalfe, J., & Shimamura, A. (1994). *Metacognition: Knowing about knowing.* Cambridge, MA: Bradford Books.

Murnane, K., & Bayen, U. (1996). An evaluation of empirical measures of source identification. *Memory and Cognition, 24,* 417–428.

Nelson, T. O. (1992). *Metacognition: Core readings.* Boston: Allyn & Bacon.

Nelson, T. O. (1996). Consciousness and metacognition. *American Psychologist, 51,* 102–116.

Nelson, T. O., & Dunlosky, J. (1991). The delayed-JOL effect: When delaying your judgments of learning can improve the accuracy of your metacognitive monitoring. *Psychological Science, 2,* 267–270.

Nelson, T. O., & Dunlosky, J. (1992). How shall we explain the delayed-judgments-of-learning effect? *Psychological Science, 3,* 317–318.

Nelson, T. O., Dunlosky, J., White, D. M., Steinberg, J., Townes, B., & Anderson, D. (1990). Cognition and metacognition at extreme altitudes on Mount Everest. *Journal of Experimental Psychology: General, 119,* 367–374.

Nelson, T. O., Gerler, D., & Narens, L. (1984). Accuracy of feeling-of-knowing judgments for predicting perceptual identification and relearning. *Journal of Experimental Psychology: General, 113,* 282–300.

Nelson, T. O., & Narens, L. (1990). Metamemory: A theoretical framework and new findings. In G. H. Bower (Ed.), *The psychology of learning and motivation* (pp. 26, 125–173.) New York: Academic Press.

Nelson, T. O., & Narens, L. (1994). Why investigate metacognition? In J. Metcalfe & A. Shimamura (Eds.), *Metacognition: Knowing about knowing* (pp. 1–25). Cambridge, MA: MIT Press.

Oelz, O., & Regard, M. (1988). Physiological and neuropsychological characteristics of world-class extreme-altitude climbers. *American Alpine Journal,* 83–86.

Pressley, M., Levin, J. R., & Ghatala, E. (1984). Memory strategy monitoring in adults and children. *Journal of Verbal Learning and Verbal Behavior, 23,* 270–288.

Reder, L. M. (1987). Strategy selection in question answering. *Cognitive Psychology, 19,* 90–138.

Reder, L. M., & Ritter, F. (1992). What determines initial feeling of knowing? Familiarity with question terms, not with the answer. *Journal of Experimental Psychology: Learning, Memory, and Cognition, 18,* 435–452.

Shimamura, A. P., Jernigan, T. L., & Squire, L. R. (1988). Radiological (CT) findings in patients with Korsakoff's syndrome and their relationship to memory impairment. *Journal of Neuroscience, 8,* 4400–4410.

Spellman, B. A., & Bjork, R. A. (1992). People's judgments of learning are extremely accurate at predicting subsequent recall when retrieval practice mediates both tasks. *Psychological Science, 3,* 315–316.

Underwood, B. J. (1966). Individual and group predictions of item difficulty for free learning. *Journal of Experimental Psychology, 71,* 673–679.

V

Group and Individual Differences in Cognition

19

Culture-Free versus Culture-Based Measures of Cognition

Michael Cole

For almost as long as there have been IQ tests, there have been psychologists who believe it is possible to construct "culture-free" tests (Jensen, 1980). The desire for such tests springs directly out of the purposes for which tests of general intellectual ability were constructed in the first place: to provide a valid, objective, and socially unbiased measure of intellectual ability. Our society, founded upon the principle that all people are created equal, has never lived easily with the recognition of enormous de facto social inequality. We need a rationale for such inequality, and our traditions strongly bias us to seek the causes of inequality in properties of the individual, not society. At the same time, we realize that social and economic conditions, by shaping people's experiences, can be the causes of individual intellectual differences, as well as their consequences. Can't we find universals in human experience and construct a test on this basis?

What would be more ideal than a psychological test that could measure intellectual potential independently of the specific experience provided by sociocultural and economic circumstance? Such a test would provide an excellent tool for insuring that unfortunate social circumstances would not prevent the identification of intellectual potential. Some psychologists have claimed that such tests are not only possible in principle, but have been applied in practice (Herrnstein & Murray, 1994).

In this chapter, I will argue that the notion of culture-free intelligence is a contradiction in terms. I begin by reviewing the historical background of efforts to understand the relation between culture and thought that formed the scholarly background against which IQ testing came into being. After summarizing briefly the strategy developed by the pioneers of IQ testing, I will present a "thought experiment" to help clarify why, by its vary nature, IQ testing is culture bound. I close by offering some comments on how to think about culture and IQ testing given the impossibility of a culture-free test of intellectual ability.

Nineteenth-Century Beliefs about Culture and Cognitive Ability

The several decades just proceeding this century provide a useful starting point from which to trace theories of culture and cognitive development because it was during this period that both anthropology and psychology, the disciplines assigned the roles of studying culture and cognition, took shape. Until this time there was no distinctive body of methods for the study of the "humane sciences"; nor had scholars with different theories been institutionally divided into separate disciplines, each with its own methods of studying human nature.

Obvious differences in technological achievement between peoples living in different parts of the world were common knowledge among European scholars. Their theorizing about sources of these differences had produced rather general acceptance of the notion that it is possible to study the history of humanity by a study of contemporary peoples at different "levels of progress." The "father of anthropology," E. B. Tylor, summarized (in what he called a "mythic fashion") the general course of culture that most of his fellow scholars would have adhered to:

> We may fancy ourselves looking on Civilization, as in personal figure she traverses the world; we see her lingering or resting by the way, and often deviating into paths that bring her toiling back to where she had passed by long ago; but direct or devious, her path lies forward, and if now and then she tries a few backward steps, her walk soon falls into a helpless stumbling. It is not according to her nature, her feet were not made to plant uncertain steps behind her, for both in her forward view and in her onward gait she is of truly human type. (Tylor, 1958, p. 69)

Tylor made another assumption that also won general acceptance: there is an intimate connection between sociocultural progress and mental progress. "[T]he condition of culture among various societies of mankind," he wrote, "is a subject apt for the study of laws of human thought and action" (Tylor, 1874, p. 1). He even adopted the notion of a "mental culture," which he expected to be high or low depending upon the other conditions of culture with which it was associated.

Spencer, writing at about the same time, shared Tylor's belief in the fusion of mental and sociocultural progress. He argued that the circumstances under which the earliest human beings lived provided only a limited number and variety of experiences. "Consequently," he argued, "there can be no considerable exercise of faculties which take cognizance of the general truths displayed throughout many special truths" (Spencer, 1886, p. 521).

Spencer invites us to consider the most extreme case; suppose that only one experience were repeated over and over again, such that this single event comprised all of the person's experiences. In this case, as he put it, "the power of representation is limited to reproduction of the experience" in the mind. There isn't anything else to think about! Next we can imagine that life consists of two experiences, thus allowing at least elementary comparison. Three experiences add to the elementary comparisons and to the elementary generalizations that we make on the basis on our limited (three) experiences. We can keep adding experience to our hypothetical culture until we arrive at the rich variety of experiences that characterizes our lives. It follows from this line of reasoning that generalizations, the "general truths" attainable by people, will be more numerous and more powerful the greater one's experience. Because cultures provide experience, and some cultures (Spencer claimed) provide a greater diversity of experience than others, a neat bond between cultural progress and mental progress is cemented.

Although such evolutionary schemes seemed almost transparently obvious in the enthusiasm following publication of Darwin's *Origin of Species*, events toward the close of the nineteenth century proved that there could be a great deal of disagreement about the relation between culture and thought, despite the compelling story constructed by scholars such as Tylor and Spencer. One set of disagreements arose when researchers started to examine more closely the data used to support conclusions about relations between cultures, especially claims for historical or evolutionary sequences. A different set of disagreements arose around conflicting claims about mental processes.

The source of these disagreements concerning sociocultural sequences can be found in Tylor's own work. The main criteria he used for judging the stage of a culture were the sophistication of its industrial arts (including its manufacturing techniques for metal tools and its agricultural practices) and "the extent of scientific knowledge, the definitions of moral principles, the conditions of religious belief and ceremony, the degree of social and political organization, and so forth." However, in Tylor's words, "If not only knowledge and art, but at the same time moral and political excellence, be taken into consideration it becomes more difficult to scale societies from lower to higher stages of culture" (Tylor, 1874, p. 29).

This undeveloped theme in Tylor's work was taken up by Boas, who submitted the cultural evolution position to a devastating critique at the close of the nineteenth century. On the basis of his own ethnographic work, Boas (1911) concluded that a great deal of the evidence apparently supportive of evolutionary schemes was so deeply flawed that no clear conclusions ranking one culture above another could be accepted. Boas did more than show the flaws in evolutionists' data and arguments concerning culture; he also delighted in showing that examples of the "primitive mind" produced as part of this argument were based on misunderstandings.

Consider the following example from Boas's classic, *The Mind of Primitive Man*, which repeats evidence used by Spencer to make some generalizations about properties of the primitive mind:

In his description of the natives of the west coast of Vancouver Island, Sproat says, "The native mind, to an educated man, seems generally to be asleep. . . . On his attention being fully aroused, he often shows much quickness in reply and ingenuity in argument. But a short conversation wearies him, particularly if questions are asked that require efforts of thought or memory on his part. The mind of the savage then appears to rock to and fro out of mere weakness." (Boas, 1911, p. 111)

Spencer's text goes on to cite a number of similar anecdotes corroborating this point. But Boas produces an anecdote of his own.

I happen to know through personal contact the tribes mentioned by Sproat. The questions put by the traveller seem mostly trifling to the Indian, and he naturally soon tires of a conversation carried on in a foreign language, and one in which he finds nothing to interest him. As a matter of fact, the interest of these natives can easily be raised to a high pitch, and I have often been the one who was wearied out first. Neither does the management of their intricate system of exchange prove mental inertness in matters which concern them. Without mnemonic aids to speak of, they plan the systematic distribution of their property in such a manner as to increase their wealth and social position. These plans require great foresight and constant application. (Boas, 1911, p. 128)

Thus, Boas tells us that the entire scheme was wrong. Cultures cannot be ranked using evolutionary age as a basis for comparison, and "mind" cannot be seen as rank in developmental age. (Boas also demonstrates the total hopelessness of deducing cultural differences from any differences, real or imagined, in genetic makeup.)

Finally, and very importantly, Boas was a leader in a subtle, but essential, change in anthropological thinking about the concept of culture itself. Educated in Germany, Boas had begun his career imbued with the romantic concept of *Kultur,* the expression of the highest attainments of human experience, as expressed in the arts, music, literature, and science. This is the conception of culture that allowed Tylor to talk about "the conditions of culture among various societies." Tylor, like Boas as a young man, conceived of culture as something groups and individuals had more or less of. It was a singular noun: one talked of higher or lower culture, not more or fewer culture. By the same route that led him to deny the basis for ranking cultures in terms of a hypothetical, evolutionary sequence, Boas arrived at the idea that different societies create different "designs for living," each representing a uniquely adapted fit between their past and their present circumstances in the world. This point of view is central to contemporary anthropology, and it clearly has to be taken into account if we want to rank the intellectual achievements (levels of mental development) of people growing up with different cultural experiences. It renders simple more-less comparisons of cultures difficult and restricted, with parallel effects on our inferences about mind.

Enter Psychology

The birth of psychology is usually dated back to 1879, when Wilhelm Wundt officially opened an experimental laboratory in Leipzig. The exact date is not important, because several laboratories opened almost simultaneously in different industrialized countries. But the reasons for these laboratory openings are important for understanding the problems of understanding the relation between culture and intelligence.

Boas's critique of developmental theories, whether of mind or culture, produced controversy in both domains of inquiry. Boas earned the enmity of those anthropologists who believed his criticisms of their general theories unjust; they sought to rescue the more general theories, criticizing Boas and his students for "historical particularism" (Harris, 1968).

While anthropologists generally focused on contents of culture and therefore of mind, psychologists took up the other half of the equation, the problem of specifying mental mechanisms. The major difficulty facing psychologists was to devise methods for specifying pretty exactly what happens in an individual when some sort of "thinking" is going on. Competing claims were evaluated by constructing settings to control as exactly as possible the kinds of events a person experienced and to record the kinds of responses these experiences evoked. Because the presumed processes were not observable (they were, as we say, "psychological"), psychologists spent a great deal of time and ingenuity devising ways to pin down what these nonobservable processes might be.

The rapidly growing ability to control electricity and to build precision machinery was exploited to the fullest; the early psychology laboratories were marvels of inventions. Their instruments allowed psychologists to present people carefully controlled lights and tones for carefully controlled intervals and to measure precisely the time it took to respond. In their search for ways to make mind observable, they used electrophysiological devices to record internal, organic functioning. The discipline of "psychophysics" advanced appreciably in its quest to relate psychological phenomena of an elementary order (discriminating tones, judging hues). There were even hopes of uncovering a "cognitive algebra" by carefully comparing reaction times to stimuli of various complexities arranged to reveal steps in the thought process.

The activities of psychologists and anthropologists soon contrasted very dramatically. Psychologists brought people into the laboratory, where behavior could be constrained, events controlled, and the mind made visible. Whereas the anthropologists continued to concentrate on gathering data that would permit them firm statements about historical relations between cultures, scholars who came to identify themselves as psychologists concentrated on resolving arguments about thinking such as those illustrated in the passage quoted by Boas. Just as anthropology evolved careful field techniques to disambiguate competing claims about *culture*, psychologists developed the laboratory experiment as a way to test competing claims about *mind*.

There occurred, in effect, a division of labor in the "humane sciences," a division that was primarily a matter of scientific strategy in the beginning: progress required some concentrated work on specialized subtopics. The overall task remained the same for everyone: how do human beings come to be the way they are?

Enter Testing

Despite an increasing gulf between scholars who called themselves psychologists and those who called themselves anthropologists, it was not long before those two areas of inquiry were brought together again. At the end of the nineteenth century, Francis Galton, in England, set out to test hypotheses about mental differences among people, using the newly devised psychological techniques. His concern was not differences between people growing up in different cultures. Rather, he studied people growing up in different families. Significantly, his tests were theoretically motivated; he believed that speed of mental processing was central to intelligence, so he created tests to measure the rapid processing of elementary signals. Galton succeeded in finding differences among subjects on such tests as simple reaction time to a pure tone, but he did not succeed in relating these "psychological test" differences to human characteristics of greater interest to him such as scientific excellence or musical ability. Galton's tests, based on an oversimplified model of the human mind and the highly controlled procedures adopted from the laboratory appropriate to testing his theory, were not taken up by society. However, in creating an early precursor of existing IQ tests, Galton did begin the development of the statistical techniques that would be necessary to show how test differences correlate with interesting behavioral differences.

Galton did all of his work in England, but other Englishmen, including Rivers (1901), traveled to the Torres Strait, northeast of Australia, to see if psychological tests could be used to settle disputes over cultural differences in cognition. Rivers was in some senses an antique. He was both anthropologist and psychologist, which meant that he considered both the evidence of his tests and evidence provided by observation of the people he went to study when he made statements about culture and thought. His conclusions were consistent with Galton's data on individual differences; natives differed from each other on such simple tasks as their ability to detect a gap in a line or their recognition of colors. But there were no impressive differences between the natives of the Torres Strait and English people he studied.

It would appear on the basis of this evidence that there are no cultural differences in thinking, at least no differences consistent with the pattern proposed by Tylor, Spencer, and others. However, it could be (and was) argued, that the important ways in which cultural differences cause mental differences were not even tested by Rivers and his associates. After all, Galton had found no relation between responses to his psychological tests and other presumed indicators of intelligence. Why would anyone, then, expect cultural differences in elementary sensory abilities, because these depended on physiological mechanisms common to all people? What seemed necessary were tests of *higher* psychological processes that could be used to compare people from different cultures or different people in the same culture.

This distinction between elementary and higher processes pinpoints a weakness in the basic foundations of experimental psychology, a weakness acknowledged by Wundt, its founder. It is impossible, Wundt believed, to study higher psychological functions in experiments because such functions always depend on prior, culturally organized experience that differs from one individual and society to another, and these differences undermine the purity of the experiment. Wundt believed that scientists should use ethnological evidence and folklore if they want to discover the properties of the mind that get constructed on the basis of the elementary processes he studied in the laboratory.

Wundt's doubts about the experimental method were not accepted, because they put psychologists in a difficult bind. Psychology had been founded on the principle that carefully controlled environments are required to make legitimate statements about how the mind works. But a great many of the questions about how the mind works that interested psychologists and anthropologists alike clearly refer to "higher" psychological processes such as logical reasoning and inference. When Wundt gave up on the idea that such processes could be studied in the laboratory, he was, it seemed, robbing psychology of most of its interesting subject matter. For psychologists, the inability to study higher psychological processes in the laboratory meant that they could not be studied at all.

Binet's Strategy

The major push for a way to measure mental ability apart from culturally conditioned experience came from a source seemingly remote from theoretical disputes among anthropologists about the possibility of reconstructing history through a study of contemporary cultural variation or from issues of cross-cultural experimentation among psychologists. Early in this century, Alfred Binet was asked to deal with a practical, social problem. With the growth of public education in France, there was a growing problem of school failure, or at least severe school underachievement. It seemed not only that some children learned more slowly than others but that some children, who otherwise appeared perfectly normal, did not seem to benefit much from instruction at all. Binet and his colleagues were asked to see if they could find a way to identify slow-learning children at an early stage in their education. If such identification were possible, special education could be provided them, and the remaining children could be more efficiently taught.

The subsequent history of IQ testing has been described too frequently to bear repetition here, but a sketch of the basic strategy of research is necessary as background to understand just how deeply IQ tests are embedded in cultural experience.

To begin with, early test makers had to decide what to test for. The decision seemed straightforward. They wanted to test people's ability to perform the kinds of tasks that are required by schools. They observed classrooms, looked at textbooks, talked to teachers, and used their intuitions to arrive at some idea of the many different kinds of knowledge and skills that children are eventually expected to master in school.

What Binet and his colleagues found was not easy to describe briefly, as anyone who has looked into a classroom can quickly testify (and all of us have done so, or we would not be reading these words). There was a very obvious need to understand graphic symbols, such as alphabets and number systems. So recognition of these symbols was tested. But mastery of the rudiments of these symbols was not enough. Children were also expected to manipulate these symbols to store and retrieve vast amounts of information, to rearrange this information according to the demands of the moment, and to use the information to solve a great variety of problems that had never arisen before in the experience of the individual pupil. Thus, children's abilities to remember and carry out sequences of movements, to define words, to construct plausible event sequences from jumbled picture sequences, and to recognize the missing element in graphic designs were tested (along with many other components of school-based problems).

It was also obvious that to master more and more esoteric applications of the basic knowledge contained in alphanumeric writing systems, pupils had to learn to master their own behavior. They not only had to engage in a variety of "mental activities" directed at processing information; they also had to gain control over their own attention, applying it not according to the whim of the moment but according to the whim of the teacher and the demands of the text.

It was clearly impossible to arrive at a single sample of all the kinds of thinking required by "the" school. Not only was there too much going on in any one classroom to make this feasible; it was equally clear that the school required different abilities from children of different ages. Binet realized that estimates of "basic aptitude" for this range of material would depend upon how much the child had learned about the specific content before he or she arrived at school, but he felt knowing the child's current abilities would be useful to teachers anyway.

In the face of these difficulties, Binet decided to construct a sample of school-like tasks appropriate for each year of education, starting with elementary grades and reaching into higher levels of the curriculum. He would have liked to sample so that all the essential activities were included in his test and that tasks at one level of difficulty would be stepping stones to tasks at the next higher level. But because no firmly grounded theory of higher psychological functions existed, Binet had to rely on a combination of his own common sense and a logical analysis of tasks that different classrooms seemed to require (for example, you have to be able to remember three random digits before you can remember four; you have to know the alphabet before you can read). He also hit on the handy strategy of letting the children themselves tell him when an item selected for the test was appropriate. Beginning with a large set of possible test questions, Binet hunted for items that half the children at a given age level could solve. An "average" child would then be the one who solved problems appropriate to his or her age level. Keeping items that discriminated between children of different ages (as well as items that seemed to sample the activities demanded of kids in their classrooms), he arrived, with help from his colleagues, at the first important prototype of the modern IQ test.

Of course a great deal of work has gone into the construction of tests since Binet's early efforts, but the underlying logic has remained pretty much the same: sample the kinds of activities demanded by the culture (in the form of problems it requires that its children master in school), and compare children's performance to see how many of these activities they have mastered. Children who have mastered far less than we would expect given a comparable sample of kids their own age are those who will need extra help if they are to reach the level expected by the culture.

This strategy is perfectly reasonable, so long as we stay within the framework that generated the item selection procedures in the first place. However, much to the disapproval of Binet, people found new uses for the tests of school-based knowledge that carried with them the seeds of the current disputes over IQ testing.

Although Binet specifically warned against the procedure, his test and tests like it began to be used as measures of an overall aptitude for solving problems in general, rather than samples of problem-solving ability and knowledge in particular. Those engaged in such extrapolations acknowledged that in principle it is important to make certain that everyone given the test has an equal opportunity to learn the material the test demands. But in practice there was no way to guarantee this essential prerequisite for making comparative judgments about basic abilities.

These are important issues in thinking about applications of IQ testing, and they are extensively discussed in the psychological literature. However, it is not until we back up and examine the possible significance of

Binet's work in the light of anthropological scholarship that we can see just how limited an enterprise IQ testing was at the beginning and how restricted it remains today.

A Thought Experiment in Test Construction

A good starting point for this reexamination is to think about what sort of activity Binet would have engaged in if he had been a member of a cultural group vastly different from his own. As a sort of "thought experiment" let us suppose that a "West African" Binet has taken an interest in the kinds of knowledge and skills that a child growing up in his part of the world would need to master as an adult. To make the thought experiment somewhat concrete, I will do my supposing about the tribal groups inhabiting the interior of Liberia, principally the Kpelle people, among whom I have worked and about whom a good deal of relevant information is available.

Following in the footsteps of his French model, our Liberian Binet would want to make a catalogue of the kinds of activities that children are expected to master by their parents and the village elders. People in rural Liberia make their living by growing rice and other crops, which they supplement with meat and fish when these scarce commodities can be obtained. Rice farming is physically difficult work that demands considerable knowledge and planning for its success, but as practiced by the Kpelle, it is not a technologically sophisticated enterprise. It is carried out using simple tools such as a machete to cut the underbrush, fire to burn the dry bush, vines to tie together fence posts in order to keep out animals, and slingshots to harass animals (Gay, 1973). Other aspects of Kpelle material culture are relatively simple, although in every case the proper use of tools requires a good deal of knowledge about how the tools are supposed to be used. There is division of labor among Kpelle adults (men hunt, and women do most of the fishing; men cut the bush on the farms, women plant the seed, and children guard the crops), but far more than is true of contemporary America, everyone pretty well knows what there is to know about adult economic activities. There are some specialists (e.g., blacksmiths, bonesetters, and weavers) whose work is an exception to the generalization, and study of their activities would certainly be important.

Of course, there is more to getting through life as a Kpelle than growing rice or weaving cloth. All descriptions of the social organization of Kpelle life stress that, as in America, knowledge of the social world is essential to adult stature (Bellman, 1975). Kpelle people are linked by a complex set of relations that control how much of the resources available to the society actually get to the individual.

Faced with this situation, how should our West African Binet proceed? Should he sample all the kinds of activities valued by adults? This strategy is almost certainly unrealistic. Even allowing for the possibility that aspects of technology make it reasonable to speak of the Kpelle as a "less complex" society than our own, it is very complex indeed. No anthropologist would claim to have achieved a really thorough description of even one such society. Moreover, like Tylor, he would have to admit the possibility that in some respects Kpelle society provides members with more complex tasks than we are likely to face. Because it is unreasonable in Liberia, as it is in the United States, to think that we can come up with a test that samples all types of Kpelle adult activities, why not follow Binet's example and sample an important subset of those activities? From an anthropological perspective, schools are social institutions for assuring that adult knowledge of highly valued kinds gets transmitted to a society's next generation (it must be transmitted, or there would be no later generations!). Although the school is not likely to contain a random sample of life's tasks, it is certainly a convenient place to sample activities that adults consider important, activities complex enough to make it unlikely that kids would learn what they need to know simply by "hanging around."

So, our Liberian Binet might decide to search for some institutions in his society that correspond roughly with the basic goals of schooling in ours. Not all societies readily manifest such institutions, so anthropologists are led to speak of "socialization" as the broadest relevant category. Fortunately for discussion, in the case of Liberia, he would undoubtedly discover the existence of institutions called *bush schools* in the Liberian English vernacular.

There are no detailed accounts of the curriculum of the bush school. The 3 or 4 years youngsters spend are organized by town elders who are leaders in the secret societies that control a variety of esoteric information. This material cannot, on pain of death, be communicated to outsiders. However, we know enough about aspects of bush school activities to continue our hypothetical research (Bellman, 1975; Gay, 1973): we know that youngsters learn to farm, construct houses, track animals, shoot birds, and carry out a variety of adult economic activities (children live apart from their home villages in something like a scouting camp during their time in bush school). The children are also taught the important lore of the group. This lore is communicated not only in a variety of ceremonies, but in stories, myths, and riddles. So, let us suppose that our West African Binet decided to use successful execution of bush school activities as the abilities he wanted to sample.

Again, like Binet, our researcher would not be able to sample all such activities for his test, nor would he want to. He would not, for example, want to sample activities that all children knew how to accomplish before they got to school; nor would he want to sample activities considered so universally accessible that everyone mastered them well before the end of schooling. This information would not help him pick out those children who needed extra instruction. Instead, he would seek those activities that discriminated among children, activities that some mastered far earlier than others and perhaps activities that some mastered only in later life. Once these Binet-like restrictions had been placed upon the activities selected for study, our hypothetical researcher could begin selecting tasks on which he could base test items.

In considering what sort of test would emerge, it is useful first to consider what activities would be excluded as well as those included. Cutting brush or sowing rice seed probably would not be on the test; everyone knows how to do those tasks before he or she gets to school. Nor would anyone spend time explicitly teaching children common vocabulary. However, there would be explicit instruction in such tasks as constructing houses and identifying leaves that are useful in different kinds of medicine. There would also be some mechanism for insuring that the history of the group and its laws and customs were taught to everyone in the form of stories and dances. Finally, some children would be selected for specialist roles that would require special tests (bonesetter, weaver, midwife, blacksmith, hunter, and so on). These children would receive additional instruction.

Looking at those areas where instruction might be considered important, we can see many candidate activities for testing. We might want to see if children have learned all of the important leaf names for making medicine (Bowen, 1964). Riddles are often important parts of stories and arguments, so we could test to see how many riddles children know and how adept they are at interpreting them (Kulah, 1973). The specialists would be a rich source of test material, especially if we thought that rational testing of ability to perform like adults would improve the quality of our cloth or machetes. In short, it seems possible, in principle, to come up with test items that could perform functions in Kpelle society similar to the way that Binet wanted to use IQ tests.

Could we carry out such a program of research in practice? There is no simple answer to this question, but it is useful to consider the obstacles. For some activities such as naming leaves or remembering riddles, it should be relatively easy to make the relevant observations because the Kpelle have already arranged for them: several researchers have described children's games that embody precisely these activities (Cole, Gay, Glick, & Sharp, 1971; Lancy, 1977). We could also test people's skills at constructing houses, weaving designs, and forging sturdy hoes. However, from a Kpelle point of view, tests of such skills would not be particularly interesting. The real stuff of using one's wits to get along in the world has been excluded.

This point was made very explicitly by a Kpelle anthropological acquaintance of mine who was versed in the more esoteric aspects of Kpelle secret societies and medicine (or magic, according to American stereotypes). We had been talking about what it means to be intelligent in Kpelle society (the most appropriate term is translated as "clever"). "Can you be a clever farmer?" I asked. "No," came the reply.

You can be a hardworking farmer, or you can be a lucky farmer, but we couldn't say that someone is a clever farmer. Everyone knows how to farm. We use "clever" when we talk about the way someone gets other people to help him. Some people always win arguments. Some people know how to deal with strangers. Some people know powerful medicine. These are the things we talk about as clever.

In this bit of dialogue we see an emphasis on activities that require social interaction as the arena where intelligence is an appropriate concept. (Among the Kpelle and many other nontechnological groups, display of a good memory for use in discussions is often considered an important component of intelligence; see Dube, 1977) This usage is quite consistent with Binet's analysis; it is those activities that differentiate among people in terms of the way they manipulate information that the Kpelle, like the French, use to mark intelligence.

However, once we reach this point, we face two important difficulties. First, the situations we have selected for our study of Kpelle intelligence are exceedingly difficult to describe. Second, these contexts are very difficult to arrange. It is not enough to know riddles; everyone knows riddles. What is important about riddles is how they are used to get one's way with other people. Riddles are a resource to be used in a variety of social interactions where people's statuses and rights are at issue.

Consider the first difficulty. Bellman (1978) recounts an occasion when an elder member of a secret society told a long story about how he came to be a high-ranking shaman. He followed this (presumably autobiographical) story with a long riddle, which was also in story form. A novice such as myself would have no way of figuring out what part of the story was true, and I certainly would not have responded to the riddle as if its interpretation depended upon the autobiographical story; the two monologues appear to be about quite different topics. Bellman succeeds in demonstrating, however, that the riddle is closely linked to the autobiography. Not only are there formal, structural similarities (once one understands the basic categories of the relevant Kpelle belief systems); there is a rhetorical link as well. The autobiographical story actually represents a bit of self-aggrandizement by the person who has told it. The man is claiming special knowledge and special power in a covert manner. The riddle reinforces the main point of the story (which raises the teller above his fellow shaman), giving the story "logical" as well as "historical" validity. The fact that listeners are constrained to agree with the riddle also gets them to agree, at least in part, with the message of the autobiographical story.

By almost any account, this man's autobiographical account plus riddle is a clever bit of behavior. It is exactly the kind of thing that our West

African Binet ought to be sampling. But, at precisely this point, our cross-cultural thought experiment in IQ testing comes apart. As I have already pointed out, in order to construct a test Binet needed to be able to select a large number of items. But the "item" we have just described (very loosely) is not easily constructible. The participants in this scene were doing social work on each other; the shaman, in particular, was attempting to establish his preeminence using an account of his past history that would be difficult to check up on, a riddle whose structure was designed to reinforce his account, and his knowledge of his listener's state of knowledge concerning both the shaman's past and Kpelle social structure. This is one item; it was constructed by the subject, not the "tester." It is difficult for me to imagine how to insure that a test includes one or more items of this type. Furthermore, because the example's structure and content depend upon the special circumstances surrounding it, how could I insure that I would be able to present the test to the subject given that it was the "subject" who did a lot of the presenting in the example I have described?

Here the contrast with Binet's situation is strong. Like Binet, we have proceeded by figuring out what sorts of activities differentiate people according to some notion of what it means to behave intelligently. Unlike Binet, the activities we need to sample in West Africa to accomplish this goal lead us into domains that are systematically absent from Binet's tests. These domains involve interactions among people in which flexibly employed social knowledge is of paramount importance. They are not domains of hypothetical knowledge; rather, they always involve some real operations on the world, operations that require a great deal of care simply to describe. We have no good notion of how to make such activities happen in a manner analogous to the way teachers make vocabulary tests and multiplication problems happen. Furthermore, even if we solved all these problems, we would have no real theory of the psychological processes our subject engaged in. Such problems have not been studied by cognitive psychologists.

On both practical and theoretical grounds, then, it appears virtually impossible to come up with a way of testing Kpelle intelligence in a manner really equivalent to what we understand to be intelligence tests in our society. So long as we restrict our attention to Kpelle culture, this conclusion should not cause much consternation. After all, the idea of a West African Binet is rather absurd; Kpelle people have managed to pass on their culture for many years without IQ tests to help them select clever children and give extra assistance to the dull.

Some Implications for the Notion of a Culture-Free Test

Our characterization of what one has to do to be clever in Kpelle culture and what it would take to sample such cleverness in a test must be discomforting for anyone who imagines that one can construct a culture-free test of intelligence. Imagine, for example, that by some quirk it was our imaginary Liberian Binet who constructed the first IQ test and that other West African tribal people had adopted it. Next, imagine that American children were posed items from the West African test. Even items considered too simple for Kpelle 8-year-olds would cause our children severe problems. Learning the names of leaves, for example, has proven too difficult for more than one American Ph.D. Our children know some riddles, but little use is made of such knowledge in our society except for riddling, which would put American children at a severe disadvantage on more "advanced" items.

If our children were forced to take a test constructed by a West African Binet, we might object that these Kpelle-derived items were unfairly biased toward Kpelle culture. If the eventual incomes of our children depended in any way on their ability to interpret Kpelle riddles, we would be outraged. Nor would we be too happy if their incomes depended upon their use of their own riddles as rhetorical devices. At the very minimum, we would want a culture-free test if real life outcomes depended upon test performance. However, what kind of test is a West African Binet likely to dream up that we would consider culture free? It would not involve a set of drawings of geometrically precise figures, because Kpelle, a preliterate group, do not engage in much graphic representation and have no technology for drawing straight lines. It would not be recall of lists of nonsense syllables or even lists of words, because there are no corresponding activities in Kpelle adult life. We might try a memory test such as recalling all of one's family, but here the Kpelle, who teach their children genealogies, would have a distinct advantage: what is the name of your grandmother's father on your father's side of the family? In fact, if we run down the list of presumably culture-free items that our mental experiment on Kpelle IQ testing turned up, we would almost certainly find none of the subtests that have been claimed as culture-free tests of intelligence in our society. The reason is simple; our West African Binet, having scientifically sampled his culture, would have come up with items that reflect valued activities and that differentiate people in his culture, whereas Binet and all his successors have come up with items that do the same job in their culture. They are different kinds of activities.

Our imagined study of cross-cultural test construction makes it clear that tests of ability are inevitably cultural devices. This conclusion must seem dreary and disappointing to people who have been working to construct valid, culture-free tests. But from the perspective of history and logic, it simply confirms the fact, stated so clearly by Boas (1911, p. 133) half a century ago, "that the existence of a mind, absolutely independent of conditions of life is unthinkable."

References

Bellman, B. L. (1975). *Village of curers and assassins: On the production of Fala Kpelle cosmological categories:* The Hague, Netherlands: Mouton.

Bellman, B. L. (1978). Ethnohermeneutics: On the interpretation of subjective meaning. In W. C. McCormack and S. A. Wurm (Eds.), *Language and the mind.* The Hague, Netherlands: Mouton.

Boas, F. (1911). *The mind of primitive man.* New York: Macmillan.

Bowen, E. S. (1964). *Return to laughter.* New York: Doubleday.

Cole, M., Gay, J., Glick, J. A., & Sharp, D. W. (1971). *The cultural context of learning and thinking.* New York: Basic Books.

Dube, E. F. (1977). *A cross-cultural study of the relationship between "Intelligence" level and story recall.* Unpublished doctoral dissertation, Cornell University, Ithaca, NY.

Gay, J. (1973). *Red dust on the green leaves.* Thompson, CT: InterCulture Associates.

Gibbs, J. L. (1965). The Kpelle of Liberia. In J. L. Gibbs (Ed.), *Peoples of Africa* (pp. 197–240). New York: Holt, Rinehart and Winston.

Harris, M. (1968). *The rise of anthropological Theory.* New York: Crowell.

Hernnstein, R. J., & Murray, C. (1994). *The bell curve: Intelligence and class structure in American life.* New York: Free Press.

Jensen, A. (1980). *Bias in mental testing.* New York: Free Press.

Kulah, A. A. (1973). *The organization and learning of proverbs among the Kpelle of Liberia.* Unpublished doctoral dissertation, University of California, Irvine.

Lancy, D. (1977). Studies of memory in culture. *Annals of the New York Academy of Science, 307,* 285–297.

Rivers, W. H. R. (1901). Vision. In A. C. Haddon (Ed.), *Report of the Cambridge anthropological expedition to the Torres Straits* (Vol. 2). Cambridge, England: Cambridge University Press.

Spencer, H. (1886). *The principles of psychology* (Vol. 5). New York: D. Appleton.

Tylor, E. B. (1874/1958). *Primitive Culture.* London: J. Murray.

20

Heredity versus Environment as the Basis of Cognitive Ability

Elena L. Grigorenko

Why do people differ in the way they think? Why are some people smarter than others? Why do children's abilities resemble their parents' abilities? Why do children in one family differ in the way they learn compared with children in another family and, moreover, compared with each other? Why do people vary in intelligence?

The observation of differences in cognitive abilities between people has many explanations, depending on the context and goal of a given discussion. For example, if we discuss differences in people's performance on an IQ test, nutritionists are likely to inquire whether the person had breakfast on the test day and what it was; physiologists will think of differences in serotonin level or nerve conduct velocity; psychologists will look for previous learning experiences, motivation, and ability level. As a psychologist, I will try to address the question of observed variation in cognitive functioning by concentrating on ability level. Moreover, it is not the absolute ability level that is going to be the center of my attention, but rather the causes that lead to differences in abilities.

The goal of this chapter is to explore the problem of sources of observed differences in cognitive functioning. Specifically, I hope to provide a comprehensive overview of how this problem is approached by behavior-genetic research. The design of the chapter is as follows. After describing the phenomenon of individual differences in cognition, I then show how this phenomenon is studied in the behavior-genetic approach. Finally, I summarize the current state of knowledge regarding understanding the sources of individual differences in cognition.

Behavior-Genetic Approach to Studying Individual Differences

The Concept of Individual Differences

If we randomly enter a classroom in any nonspecialized school in any corner of the world and look at the children in this classroom, at first glance we would notice how different these children are. They are different in height and weight, their bodies are formed differently, and their noses and eyes have different shapes. Then, if we look at the class yearbook or talk to a teacher, we will discover that all of these children vary in terms of their academic performance and abilities. In other words, in any randomly chosen group of children (or adults, for that matter), we will find a significant amount of variation in virtually any trait we look at. Almost everything that can be measured or counted in human beings demonstrates variation around the mean value in a given population. The concept traditionally used to refer to such variation in human traits (height, weight, facial features, academic performance, etc.) is that of *individual differences.*

The existence of individual differences in the ways people think, cognize, and learn attracted the attention of philosophers many centuries ago. And along with the questions, theories appeared. The main point of the theories was to reveal the sources of interindividual variation. The assumption made was quite simple: if people vary in the way they think, there should be some explanation of this variation. Two hypotheses appear to be useful: (1) people are born to be the way they are, or (2) people learn to be the way they are. There have been many attempts to verify both hypotheses, and as a result of this massive scientific endeavor, much information has been accumulated. The consensus today, however, is that there is no sole source of individual differences and that the appearance of interindividual variation in any population is the product of a complex interplay of two forces, which are globally referred to as genes and environment.

Genes versus Environment: The Paradigm

How did the idea come about that genes and environments may be relevant to cognition? The idea to look for a link between genes, environments, and cognitive functioning is relatively novel, but its philosophical frame was formulated many centuries ago. The roots of this idea are in the well-known nature-versus-nurture controversy, which has been around for long time. The nature-nurture controversy has many faces, including the nativism-empiricism issue in the psychology of sensation and perception, the issue of maturation versus learning in developmental psychology, and the issue of environmental equipotentiality versus biological preparedness in the psychology of learning and cognition (for more details, see Kimble, 1994). At the end of the last century, British scientist Francis Galton narrowed the nature-nurture controversy down to an opposition between heredity and environment. With the discovery of genes as units of heredity, the controversy took its current form of the "genes-versus-environment" debate. The motivation for formulating such an opposition is obvious—knowing that people differ in the ways they think, scientists wanted to understand why they differ and, subsequently, what (if anything) can be done to minimize (or maximize) these differences. In other words, knowing that there is variation in cognitive functions between people, scientists want to understand the sources of this variation and how to control them.

Studies investigating sources of variability in behavioral traits are being conducted in different fields, among which are developmental psychology, psychology of individual differences, quantitative genetics, molecular genetics, psychiatric genetics, behavior genetics, and others. For the sake of brevity, in this chapter we will refer to all these studies as behavior-genetic studies. Such studies are the focus of attention in this chapter.

Definition of Terms

Definitions are essential at the outset for the following four terms: *phenotype, genotype, components of the phenotypic variance,* and *familial resemblance.*

Phenotype   One of the most important concepts for this chapter is the concept of phenotype. *Phenotype* refers to apparent, observable, measurable characteristics of the individual. Behavior is a phenotype. Cognition is a phenotype. When a given phenotype (e.g., IQ) is measured in a population of individuals and characteristics of the distribution of this measure are obtained, the variance of this distribution is referred to as phenotypic variance. The concept of phenotypic variance is a congruent behavior-genetic concept to that of individual differences used in psychology.

Genotype   Another important concept is the concept of genotype. *Genotype* refers to the genetic composition of the individual. At the present time, there are no known genes that contribute to normal interindividual variation in cognition. Therefore, in the context of this chapter, we will refer to the genotype as an unobservable, latent characteristic of the individual that manifests itself in cognitive phenotypes.

Causal Components of the Phenotypic Variance[1]   The importance of the phenotype-genotype distinction is that it depicts the relation between the observable and unobservable characteristics: an observable trait (phenotype) is not a perfect indicator of the individual's latent qualities (genotype). These differences between the phenotype and the corresponding genotype can be accounted for by environmental influences. For example, monozygotic (identical) twins have identical genotypes, yet one might have a higher IQ than the other because of differences in environment. These relationships between the individual's phenotype (P), the individual's genotype (G), and the environment (E) can be expressed in a simplistic mathematical scheme as

$$P = G + E.$$

This formula signifies that an individual has a given genotype and is exposed to a given environment at a given point of time, so for this person at that point of time there will be one unique value of P. The phrase *at any given time* implies that the individual's environment varies over time. The degree to which environmental changes would influence the phenotypic value depends on what is being measured. For example, whereas a measurement of my height does not depend on daily environment, a measurement of my verbal ability might vary daily, depending on whether it is assessed in Russian, which is my native language, or in English, in which my fluency is magnitudes poorer.

In its somewhat more sophisticated form, this model may also include an interactive term, $G \times E$, referring to possible combinations of genetic and environmental effects. For example, if parental intellectual ability is related to the parents' income and occupation (traits that elate both to genetic and environmental factors), then more able parents will provide a more intellectually stimulating environment. Thus, when the interactive term is included, the formula takes the following form:

$P = G + E + (G \times E)$.

At the individual level, this formula, though being illustrative, is quite meaningless. Unless we know precisely the values of at least two out of the three unknowns [G, E, and $G \times E$], we cannot assign values to any of them.

The situation changes, however, when we look at variation between individuals, quantified by a variety of P values. For example, let us assume that we are measuring IQ in a group of people. Thus, our studied phenotype is IQ. We can calculate the mean value of IQ in this group and then determine where each individual in the group scores relative to the mean. Next, we can determine the variance (V) of IQ in the group, calculated as the sum of individual's squared deviations from the mean, divided by the number of individuals. Thus,

$$V(IQ) = V(P) = V[G + E + (G \times E)]$$
$$= V_G + V_E + 2Cov(G)(E) + V_{G\times E}.$$

In other words, the observed variance in intelligence in a group in which the IQ is measured contains components due to genetic variance (V_G) and those due to environmental variance (V_E). Phenotypic variance also includes components resulting from the covariance (correlation) between genetic and environmental effects [$2Cov(G) \times (E)$], as well as from the interaction between G and E ($V_{G\times E}$). The reader might ask why this formula appears to be solvable at the population level and not at the individual level: what enables us to determine the values of the V_G, V_E, $Cov(G) \times (E)$, and $V_{G\times E}$ at the population level, while they are unknown at the individual level? The answer to this question is provided in the next section.

Familial Resemblance

There are two methods of determining each of the components of the phenotypic variance: measuring response to genetic selection and assessing resemblance between relatives. The first method assumes breeding organisms selectively for a given trait and measuring the outcome of the genetic experiments. The structure of modern human society is such that, due to our ethical norms and values, we do not wish to do it. What we can do, however, is utilize the second method. We can benefit from so-called natural experiments and assess resemblances between relatives, finding spontaneously occurring situations in which (a) genetic influences are either controlled or randomized so the effects of the environment can be studied or (b) environmental influences are controlled so the effects of genes can be studied. So what is the rationale behind quantifying familial resemblance?

Relatives share genes. Monozygotic (MZ; identical) twins share all of their genes. A parent and his or her offspring have half of their genes in common. Two siblings share, on average, half of their genes. Dizygotic (DZ; fraternal) twins, just as regular siblings, also share half of their genes. Half-siblings have a quarter of their genes in common, on average, and so on. Moreover, relatives who live in one home share the family environment. Thus, both genetic and environmental hypotheses predict similarity between relatives living together. This similarity is usually measured by covariance, or correlation, between relatives on a given trait. For example, the correlation of IQs between pairs of unrelated individuals picked at random is 0. Because such individuals share neither genes nor environment, their scores do not resemble each other. Other relationships, however, have both genes and environment in common. For example, the correlation for IQ between identical twins reared together is .86, between fraternal twins reared together is .60, between siblings reared together is .47, and between cousins is .15 (Chipuer, Rovine, & Plomin, 1990). The covariance between relatives could be described as $Cov(P_1)(P_2)$, where P_1 is the phenotype of one relative and P_2 is the phenotype of the other. In the section on causal components of phenotypic variance, we noted that $P = G + E$, so

$$Cov(P_1)(P_2) = Cov[(G_1 + E_1)(G_2 + E_2)].$$

When expressed in terms of components of variance,

$$Cov(P_1)(P_2) = V_G + V_E.$$

In other words, for a given trait (e.g., IQ), the correlation between relatives could be explained by the genetic variance and the environmental variance resulting from genetic and environmental influences shared between relatives.

The simplest illustration of how components of the phenotypic variance can be determined from studying relatives comes from studying identical and fraternal twins. Identical twins reared together share 100% of their genes and 100% of their family environment. Thus,

$$Cov_{\text{MZTwins}} = V_G + V_{E\,\text{MZ Twins}}.$$

Fraternal twins, reared together, share only 50% of their genes but 100% of their family environment. In other words,

$$Cov_{\text{DZTwins}} = 1/2 V_G + V_{E\,\text{DZ Twins}}.$$

Assuming there are no differences in twin environments of identical and fraternal twins (i.e., $V_{E\,\text{MZ Twins}} = V_{E\,\text{DZ Twins}}$), these two equations can be solved for V_G. That is,

$$1/2 V_G = Cov_{\text{MZTwins}} - Cov_{\text{DZTwins}}$$

$$V_G = 2(Cov_{\text{MZTwins}} - Cov_{\text{DZTwins}}).$$

Thus, the components of phenotypic variance can be determined by combining various types of relatives and comparing the measures of their similarity on the trait. Behavior-genetic studies use a variety of methods (e.g., the family method, twin method, adoption/separation method) in which resemblance between relatives of different degrees is assessed.

In this section, I defined the fundamental terms of the chapter. In addition, I summarized the reasoning behind quantifying phenotypic variance and showed how the components of the phenotypic variance can be estimated based on assessing trait similarity in relatives of various degrees. Now, with the necessary background reviewed, the rest of the discussion will center around the following questions:

• What are the factors that determine interindividual variation in cognitive functioning?
• What are the major concepts used to study these factors?
• What is the current state of knowledge regarding relative contributions of genes and environments to variation in cognition?

The Forces in Play

Current behavioral-genetic conceptualization of the forces determining individual differences in cognition distinguish three major groups of factors: genetic, environmental, and interactional. Let us consider each of them separately.

Genetic Influences (G): Types and Effects

Every human cell has two copies of each chromosome, one inherited from the mother and one from the father. Chromosomes are made of genetic material, organized into genes, which are templates for the synthesis of the proteins crucial in the functioning of our organism. Every gene, similar to chromosomes, exists in two copies: maternal and paternal. These gene copies are referred to as *alleles*.

Additive Genetic Effects   Additive genetic effects refer to the combined effects of alleles both within and between genes. If a trait is controlled by a number of genes, the additive genetic effect is calculated as a sum of contributions from every allele, each of which independently contributes a small amount to phenotypic diversity. When alleles do not interact, their effects on the trait is equal to a simple sum of their individual effects. Today's assumption is that human intelligence relies on the effects of the alleles of dozens of genes; thus, many different genes of fairly small effects contribute to the trait of intelligence.

Nonadditive Genetic Effects   The two main types of genetic nonadditivity are *dominance* and *epistasis*. Dominance refers to types of interaction between alleles of the same gene, whereas epistasis refers to types of interaction between different genes. As we will show, both dominant and epistatic effects appear to be important in determining variation in IQ.

Environmental Influences (E): Types and Effects

Behavior-genetic researchers divide environmental variance into *shared* (between-family) and *nonshared* (within-family) components.

Shared Environmental Effects   All children in a family share the same environment to the degree that, on average, psychosocial environmental characteristics (e.g., social class and parenting styles) differ from those in other families. Shared environmental effects make children reared in the same family more similar than children reared in different families. Scarr (1997) suggests viewing between-family differences as differences in opportunities. For example, children from a low socioeconomic status (SES) class are thought of as having fewer opportunities to develop higher cognitive abilities than do children from a higher SES class as a result of both more stimulating home environment and the corresponding school and after-school activities.

Nonshared Environmental Effects   Nonshared environmental variance refers to those aspects of the environment that make children in the same family different. Parents, no matter how hard they try, do not treat all their children in exactly the same way. Examples of within-family environment variance include a wide range of conditions, from prenatal to psychosocial events that affect one sibling differently than another sibling.

It is important to note that decomposition of phenotypic variance, discussed earlier, is carried out under the assumption that the error variance associated, in particular, with measurement error in the phenotype is an indistinguishable part of the nonshared environment component (E) of the total variance (P). In other words, the estimates of E obtained under this model, in addition to reflecting the effects of nonshared environment also contain the error variance, partially attributable to imprecision in the measurement of the phenotype. The significance of this is that, in theory, when the studied trait is influenced by a genetic factor, but the reliability of the trait measurement is less than 1.0, this imprecision in measurement might reduce the estimated size of the genetic effect.

When the Two Are Brought Together: Gene-Environment Effects $(G \times E)$

It has long been realized that the heuristic distinction between "genes" and "environments" is a simplified model that ignores several processes that are important in the appearance of variation between individuals. Thus, three concepts depicting these processes have been suggested.

Gene-Environment Correlations   In most cases (with the exception of children given up for adoption or adverse social circumstances that result in externally caused family destruction), parents bestow upon their children not only their genes but also their related immediate environments and experiences. This phenomenon is referred to as the *passive* gene-environment correlation. One example of evidence supporting the passive gene-environment correlation is the finding that social disadvantage tends to correlate with lower levels of IQ. To take the example a step further, consider the child who inherits the genes that predispose him to a high IQ and who may also experience the stimulating influence of a family environment that promotes reading. It may be that the tendency of parents to read to the child a lot may be associated with the same genes that control high IQ. There are also other types of gene-environment correlations. *Evocative* correlations arise from the fact that the ways people respond to children are influenced by the children's own characteristics (Plomin, DeFries, & Loehlin, 1977). It is possible that high-IQ children elicit different responses from their caregivers than do children of low intelligence. *Active* correlations arise as a result of the increased control over the environment that is experienced by growing children. Children themselves shape and organize their environments. For example, children with lower levels of intelligence tend to spend less time engaged in activities that would further stimulate their intellectual development. Scarr and McCartney (1983) hypothesized that the role of passive, evocative, and active correlations shift in their significance in the course of development, with the passive type declining, the active type increasing, and the evocative type remaining important throughout the lifespan. Effects that are outcomes of gene-environment correlations are bidirectional—the observed differences, resulting from differential levels of intelligence, may in turn influence the later development of intelligence.

Detection of genotype-environment correlations requires large sample sizes. As of today, only one metastudy, combining data from five adoption studies, has sufficient power to conduct an analysis of the importance of passive genotype-environment correlation for IQ (Loehlin & DeFries,

1987). It was concluded that passive correlation may account for as much as 30% of the overall variance in IQ. However, none of the subsequent behavior-genetic studies have yet replicated this finding.

Genotype × Environment Interaction   Gene-environment interaction refers to conditions in which genetically influenced characteristics mediate individual responsiveness to the encountered environment. $G \times E$ refers to the genetic control of sensitivity to environmental differences (Neale & Cardon, 1992). For example, individuals who are genetically susceptible to a disease will be free of the condition as long as the environment does not contain the pathogen; resistant individuals, those who do not have the mutant gene, will be free of the disease even in a pathogenic environment. Thus, the appearance of the pathogen in the environment will have a very different impact on the phenotype of susceptible individuals as compared with resistant ones. In the context of our discussion, if it were found that genetic predispositions for higher levels of cognitive abilities were actualized to a greater extent in some environments than in others, this would be interpreted as genotype-environment interaction.

Although there are many examples of gene-environment interactions in biology and medicine (Rutter & Pickles, 1991), there has been little evidence of $G \times E$ interactions for variation in cognitive abilities within their normal range. For example, a recent publication from the Colorado Adoption Project, a large longitudinal study of adoptive families, reported the number of statistically significant interactions that was actually less than expected by chance (Plomin, DeFries, & Fulker, 1988). There are three possible explanations for this observation. First, most designs have rather weak power for detecting interactions that may be small compared to the main effects of genes and environment (Wahlsten, 1990). Second, it might be the case that genotype-environment interactions for cognitive abilities, if they exist, are not linear and that they have localized effects. In other words, these interactions might be important at extremes, but not around the typical range of environment (Turkheimer & Gottesman, 1991). For example, genotype-environment interactions might be significant within the range of environments thought to impede intellectual development (e.g., undernutrition, poverty, abuse, and authoritarian parenting), but would be virtually undetectable in average nonproblematic families. Most behavior-genetic studies done to date involve middle-class families in which such disadvantaged environments are underrepresented. Third, our statistical apparatus may not be sufficiently developed to detect these interactions (Molenaar, Boomsma, & Dolan, in press).

Assortative Mating   Assortative mating refers to nonrandom pairing of mates based on factors other than biological relatedness. Assortative mating is mostly based on some aspects of phenotype and, correspondingly, influences both genetic and environmental factors. Thus, it may increase homozygosity in a population and affect the transmission, magnitude, correlation, and estimates of both genetic and environmental effects (e.g., Gilger, 1991; Rice, Carey, Fulker, & DeFries, 1989). Positive assortative mating has been demonstrated for a variety of physical, cultural, cognitive, educational, and personality traits and tends to be higher for age, education, ethnic background, and religion and somewhat lower, yet statistically significant, for general and specific cognitive abilities, personality traits, and physical attractiveness (Feng & Baker, 1994; Gilger, 1991; Jensen, 1978; Vandenberg, 1972; Watkins & Meredith, 1981).

The tendency of people to marry others of similar levels of cognitive abilities has been long noticed. Generally, the correlations between spouses on measures of IQ are between .30 and .40 (Dixon & Johnson, 1980). This similarity does not necessarily mean that we intentionally look for partners whose scores on ability tests are similar to ours. Instead, this similarity is derivative of a number of other factors. We tend to marry people of a similar level of educational and socioeconomic status as we are. Moreover, there are correlations between our abilities and both education and economic status (e.g., whether one graduates from college influences the probability than one will marry a college graduate). Thus, it is not difficult to see why spouses resemble each other in ability level. But no matter what the mechanism of assortative mating is, the outcome is that people tend to marry people similar to themselves in ability level. As a result, any given offspring is likely to receive from his other parents genes that are similar. In addition, it may be that assortative mating is stronger at both the higher and lower ends of the IQ range. In other words, correlations between spouses at the higher and lower tails of the IQ distribution are stronger than correlations between spouses of an average level of intelligence. Assuming that intelligence is influenced by genes, such "doubling" of genes increases the proportion of persons who are quite high or quite low, relative to a population mean. Higher assortative mating coefficients at the tails of the distribution might lead to an underestimation of heritability (Simonoff, McGuffin, & Gottesman, 1994).

In the preceding sections I introduced the concept of individual differences; translated this concept into the behavior-genetic concept of phenotype; showed how phenotypic variation on a trait in a population could be described in terms of genetic, environmental, and interactive factors; and described all of these factors. In the next section, I would like to familiarize the reader with two other important concepts: heritability and environmentality.

Major Concepts Utilized in Behavior-Genetic Research

The concepts of heritability and environmentality (Plomin, DeFries, & McClearn, 1990) are used in behavior-genetic studies to quantify the relative contribution of genes and environment to the observed variation on a studied trait in a given population. In other words, heritability and environmentality are the respective measures of G and E.

What Heritability and Environmentality Are . . .

Heritability   The concept of *heritability* (h^2), or the proportion of trait variance (phenotypic variance) due to genetic factors, is used to quantify the genetic contribution. In terms of the components of the phenotypic variance,

heritability (h^2) $= V_G/V_P,$

where V_G represents the sum of additive and nonadditive genetic influences.

Environmentality   Environmentality (e^2) is defined as the aggregate estimate of the proportion of environmental variance in the phenotype (or $1 - h^2$). In terms of the components of the phenotypic variance,

environmentality (e^2) $= V_E/V_P,$

where V_E represents the sum of shared and nonshared environmental influences.

. . . And What They Are Not

Both the heritability and environmentality statistics have a number of frequently misunderstood properties (Plomin et al., 1990; Sternberg & Grigorenko, 1997). In considering the value of these statistics, it is important to remember the following five points.

Heritability and Environmentality Are Estimated Variance Components, Not Measured Effects   Neither heritability nor environmentality estimates point to measurable genetic or environmental effects. In other words, h^2 does not translate into an understanding of the biological mechanisms underlying it; getting a global estimate of the genotypic effect that is reflected by h^2 does not bring us to the discovery of the biological mechanisms behind intellectual development. The same is true for e^2: the estimate of environmentality has yet to be linked to measured characteristics of the environment that can explain the observed variation in cognition.

Heritability and Environmentality Are Not Constants, and Their Estimates Are Not Precise   Both heritability and environmentality refer to a particular phenotype measured in a given population at a given time. These estimates may vary from population to population and from time to time. Both h^2 and e^2 values vary across age: h^2 generally increases with age, whereas e^2 declines with age, changes that reflect both changes in the age-specific breakdown of genetic and environmental influences on the trait and changes in age-to-age genetic effects. Both h^2 and e^2 are estimated with a certain degree of precision involving a range of error that is a function of both sample size and type of relatives from which the estimate is obtained.

Heritability and Environmentality Apply to a Population, Not to One Individual   These concepts apply to populations, not individuals; hence, they do not say anything regarding the strength of either genetic or environmental effects on an individual's intellectual functioning. If we state that IQ has a heritability of .50, that means that 50% of the variation in IQ observed in a given population at this time of the population's history is accounted for by genetic differences among the population's members. It does not mean that an individual whose IQ is 110 got 55 IQ points as a result of his or her genes and the other 55 as a result of the influences of his or her environment. However, if an individual from this population were about 20 IQ points smarter than average, one could estimate (roughly) that about 50% of this deviation is explainable by genetic effects and the other 50% are due to the influence of the environment.

Heritability and Environmentality Do Not Say Much about Means It is important to realize that almost every result and conclusion obtained in the field of behavior-genetic research relates to the *causes* of human differences and does not deal with the processes that account for the development of the typical expression of a trait in a particular population. The field is concerned with what makes people vary around the mean of the group, population, race, or species from which they are sampled, not with what makes people score at a given level.

Suppose, for example, it is found that differences in the ability to write poetry have a significant component only of genetic (and not environmental) variation among citizens of the country Ursulandia. What would this finding tell us about the role of Ursulu culture in determining this ability? This finding could suggest two different meanings. It might mean that the culture is uniform for everyone (i.e., poetry education is either compulsory and equal for everybody or absent for all), so only genetic effects can account for variability in the ability to write poetry. Or it might mean that cultural changes are adopted by everyone so rapidly that environmental effects are not apparent. For example, let us assume that Ursulandia has undergone a war resulting in the simultaneous worsening of the living standards of most of the population; the rapid nature of this change might result in a leveling of the profile of various environments. Perhaps instead of teaching how to write poetry, schools, due to societal hardship, a lack of financial support, and a shortage of teachers, might be forced to concentrate on teaching grammar. In other words, differential levels of poetry education as a source of environmental variability in the ability to write poetry would be absent.

Taking into account this example, it is important to understand the incorrectness of such statements as "The ability to write poetry is genetic," because the precise correct statement based on behavior-genetic analysis would instead be "Individual differences in the ability to write poetry are mainly genetic." It is crucial to be aware of which conclusions are justified and which are not, on the basis of behavior-genetic data.

Heritability and Environmentality Do Not Refer to Modification and Intervention   In early behavior-genetic work, it was assumed that the degree to which a studied trait is inherited carried important implications for the quantification of any environmental intervention (Jensen, 1969). Today, it is, recognized that this assumption is wrong. First, intervention influences the mean of the studied phenotypic variable and can raise the mean and the scores going into it. The mechanism controlling the appearance of individual differences for a given trait might not be altered, however. Second, the causes of variation derived from behavior-genetic studies relate to a particular population of individuals at a given time. Results of these studies might change as a result of the influence of factors altering the gene frequencies in the population, the expression of genes in the population, or frequencies and structures of different environments.

This logic can be easily illustrated by an example from the evolutionary history of the human species. In a given population, gene frequencies have been altered multiple times due to rapid decreases in the size of a population due to wars, hunger, or epidemics. The relocation of a population or rapid changes in climate resulted in changed expression of genes. Cultural developments led to better schooling, reflecting a structural environmental change, which gradually became accessible to the majority of populations, reflecting a change in the frequency of schooling. Third, even when it is shown that genetic effects are important, the possibility of the existence of a rare crucial environmental factor cannot be entirely excluded. An example of such factor is a brain injury that could result in severe mental retardation in an individual with normal genetic endowment for intelligence. Similarly, a rare gene of major effect may hold the key to understanding cognitive development. Due to its rarity, this gene might account only for a relatively small amount of the total variation in cognition, but, when present in an individual, might completely determine the course of cognitive development.

Now, with the measurements of the relative contributions of genes and environment to the phenotypic variation in a given population defined, I would like to review the current state of knowledge regarding the heritability and environmentality of cognitive functions.

What Do We Know about Causes of Variation in Various Cognitive Abilities?

So far in this chapter most of the examples have pertained to general cognitive ability as measured by IQ. There is certainly more to cognitive functioning than the IQ score alone. Regardless of significant correlations between most specific cognitive abilities, the correlations between them are certainly different enough to generate a more detailed analysis of cognitive functioning than is permitted by IQ alone. Even though the number of studies of heritability of IQ is magnitudes larger, there have been a few studies of heritabilities of specific cognitive abilities. In the following section I will provide a brief overview of the behavior-genetic findings regarding heritabilities (and indirectly environmentalities) of (a) general cognitive ability and (b) specific cognitive abilities.

What Have We Learned about Heritability of General Cognitive Ability (IQ)?

The heritability and environmentality estimates of IQ have been obtained by comparing the degree of resemblance of different types of relatives. Three main methodological approaches—family, twin, and adoption/separation methods—are utilized in behavior-genetic research. I will now summarize the results obtained within each of these methods.

Family Studies   Since the late 1920s, when the first studies regarding familial resemblance for IQ were conducted, dozens of studies have been published (for a review, see Bouchard & McGue, 1981). There is a consensus that the data can be divided into two parts, the so-called old (conducted prior to 1980) and new (conducted after 1980) studies. The older studies had relatively small samples, were less sophisticated methodologically, and provided rather high estimates of heritability (with a median correlation of about .42). The newer studies are characterized by larger sample sizes and more sophisticated methodology. The correlations obtained in these studies tend to be lower (e.g., $r = .26$; DeFries, Corey, Johnson, Vandenberg, & Wilson, 1982).

Three explanations of these differences have been suggested. First, the failure of the old data to match the new data may be attributable to environmental and genetic changes in the studied populations that occurred in the time frame between the new and the old studies. This explanation seems plausible for environmental effects (life has changed dramatically since the 1930s), but unlikely for genetic components. Second, there may be restriction of range in the new data (Caruso, 1983). The newer data were collected primarily from middle-class white families, which offer somewhat less variation in IQ than is observed in a normal population and limit the current findings to a group with above-average IQ. The third, most plausible, explanation highlights the role of methodological differences between the old and new studies. The methodological procedures in the newer studies are more standardized. Moreover, whereas the older studies were extended for a longer period of time, the newer studies have involved tests administered to many families at the same time in the same testing facilities.

Twin Studies   The first behavioral-genetic twin study focusing on IQ was conducted by Merriman (1924). Since then, many thousands of twins around the world have served as recruits in studies of general and specific cognitive abilities. Meta-analyses of these data (Bouchard & McGue, 1981; Loehlin & Nichols, 1976) suggest a heritability of about .50 for general cognitive ability. These estimates are not corrected for the effects of either assortative mating or nonadditive genetic variance, but such adjustments are not expected to change this estimate dramatically.

A detailed review of the twin studies of cognitive abilities is beyond the scope of this chapter. However, a number of them have addressed specific issues that are of interest to our broad discussion. For example, cohort changes in heritability of IQ were investigated in a large Norwegian study of approximately 2000 twin pairs born from 1930 through 1960 (Sundet, Tambs, Magnus, & Berg, 1988). The question was whether the implementation of the more egalitarian social and educational policies that took place in Norway after World War II influenced the degree of resemblance between MZ and DZ twins. No clear changes were observed: the correlations for MZ and DZ twins born from 1931 to 1935 were .84 and .51, respectively; after the war, the correlations were .83 and .51. This study is an illustration of the point made earlier—global societal changes tend to influence the mean of the trait rather than the mechanism explaining individual differences.

Another important finding resulted from a study of 300 pairs of same-sex twins and 100 nontwin siblings evenly distributed by gender and ages (from 7 to 12). The pairs were oversampled at the low and high ends of the IQ distribution (Detterman, Thompson, & Plomin, 1990; Thompson, Detterman, & Plomin, 1993). This study indicated, among other findings, that heritability of IQ appears to be different for both high- and low-ability subjects in comparison to each other suggesting that different genetic mechanisms might be involved in the manifestation of individual differences in IQ at different ends of the IQ distribution.

Adoption/Separation Studies   Most adoption studies, like family and twin studies, have also investigated the heritability of IQ. The range of obtained estimates of correlations between biological relatives, though broad (from .22 to .72), results in a mean heritability score of about .50, meaning that genetic differences among individuals account for about half of the differences in their performance on IQ tests.

Some interesting findings regarding the links between IQ and environmental influences were obtained by French researchers. They found that the mean IQ of adoptees reared by parents of high SES was higher than that of children adopted by low-SES parents (Capron & Duyme, 1989). Moreover, children whose biological parents were of high SES scored higher than children of parents of low SES, and school failures of adoptive children were associated with the SES of the adoptive rather than of the biological parents (Duyme, 1988). Thus, the results of the French studies point to the importance of shared environment in IQ variation. Speculating about these and other similar findings, Loehlin (1989) suggested that significant increases in average IQ might occur as a result of radical environmental change due to adoption. However, individual differences remain large and they appear to be mostly genetic in origin. Moreover, a recent review of adoption studies (Locurto, 1990) concludes that they provide modest evidence, at best, for environmental effects on cognitive abilities.

Summary Comments   Four comments should be made regarding the findings resulting from the studies of heritability of general cognitive ability. First, numerous family, twin, and adoption studies have been combined into global analyses using a model-fitting approach (Chipuer, Rovine, & Plomin, 1990; Loehlin, 1989). This approach allows one to analyze simultaneously the data collected in different studies and to obtain more elaborate and precise estimates of genetic and environmental contributions than is possible by comparing simple correlations. The outcome of these analyses places the estimate of heritability of intelligence at 50% to 51% (Plomin & Neiderhiser, 1991), placing it midway between .1 and .9 and indicating approximately equal effects from both genetic and nongenetic influences.

Second, heritability estimates vary depending on the method by which they were obtained. In detail, h^2 appears to be higher when obtained by comparing the resemblance between individuals reared apart than when obtained by comparing the similarity between individuals reared together.

Third, along with showing the importance of additive genetic components arising from summative main effects of a number of genes, researchers (Chipuer et al., 1990) demonstrated the contribution of nonadditive genetic effects, pointing to the importance of gene-gene interaction (i.e., dominance and epistasis).

Finally, behavior-genetic studies of intelligence revealed a number of findings regarding environmental influences. Thus, it has been found that shared and nonshared environmental influences account for approximately the same amount of variance (10%–30%), with the percentage of shared environment contribution being higher for closer relatives (35% for twins, 22% for siblings, and 11% for cousins) and, symmetrically, the percentage of nonshared environment contribution being higher for more distant relatives (38% for cousins, 27% for siblings, and 14% for twins).

These conclusions have been challenged, however, by both those who question the underlying theory and those who question the nature of the data. Theoretical challenges of the global heritability estimates come from (a) those who deny the importance of genetic effects (Schiff & Lewontin, 1986), (b) those who suggest that the magnitude of environmental effects are almost negligible within the normal range of environments (Rowe, 1994; Scarr, 1992, 1997), and (c) those who question the generalizability of these findings (Waldman, 1997).

Researchers who deny the importance of genetic effects point to various inconsistencies in the evidence accumulated from different studies. Supporters of heritability studies counter that when considered as a whole, the evidence is unequivocal in pointing to a substantial genetic effect (Plomin & Neiderhiser, 1991; Rutter & Madge, 1976). Though individual studies are often controversial, and the range of heritability estimates is between .1 (Matheny, Wilson, Dolan, & Krantz, 1981) and .9 (Iskol'd-sky, 1988), if one "mixes" them together and estimates the heritability based on weighted correlations, the estimate comes out to be around .5.

Those researchers who doubt the importance of environmental effects point to the following two lines of reasoning. First, they refer to the failure to account for the 50% of nongenetic effects when the estimated environmental variance is partially substituted by measured environmental variables (Cherny, 1994). In other words, when researchers have tried to incorporate measured variables into their model, dividing V_E into measured and nonmeasured components, the measured variables failed to account for any significant amount of variance in V_E. Thus, even though we have an estimate of the nongenetic effect for IQ, we have no idea what concrete environmental forces are reflected in this estimate. The second point of argument is the "purity" of environmental measures. In detail, researchers have found that many environmental measures, ranging from SES to parenting styles, are still partially under genetic control and therefore not purely environmental (Plomin, 1994, 1995; Plomin & Bergeman, 1991; Posner, Baker, & Martin, 1994). In other words, many of those variables that were nominated as measures of shared environment appear to be, at least in part, influenced by genes, as when parents with genes for high intelligence are led by these genes to provide good environments for their children.

A serious concern regarding the generalizability of findings on heritability of intelligence arises from the fact that most of the data have come from predominantly white, middle-class, North American and European populations. Therefore, the generalizability of these findings is quite limited. With the exception of only a few studies (e.g., Moore, 1986; Scarr & Weinberg, 1978; Scarr, Weinberg, & Waldman, 1993), other populations have not been studied. As has been pointed out earlier, heritability estimates are population specific, and extreme caution is necessary when extending the current knowledge to different populations. Moreover, the vast majority of the relative correlations were derived from samples of individuals between 9 and 20 years of age (Bouchard & McGue, 1981; McGue, Bouchard, Iacono, & Lykken, 1994). Thus, it is unclear whether the obtained heritability estimate of 50% to 51% is applicable to individual variation in IQ at other stages of the life span.

What Have We Learned about Heritability of Specific Cognitive Abilities?

As much as behavior-genetic ideas influence psychology (Waldman, 1997), psychological theories penetrate the field of behavior genetics and influence the heritability-based studies. Even though g (general cognitive ability usually measured by IQ) remains the king or queen ruling the kingdom of h^2 research, attempts have been made to introduce some other cognitive abilities into the kingdom. Although scant, some attention has been given to studying specific cognitive abilities. Researchers have focused on verbal and nonverbal abilities: Thurstone's factors (Thurstone, 1938; Thurstone & Thurstone, 1941) and Guilford's factors (Guilford, 1967), respectively. The general conclusion today is an expected one—specific abilities are differentially heritable (Cardon & Fulker, 1994).

The first assessment of heritabilities of specific cognitive abilities was conducted by Vandenberg (1968a, 1968b). In his twin studies, Vandenberg obtained evidence for the genetic influence on some abilities (verbal, spatial, and language skills) but not on others (memory, numerical, and reasoning skills). This result has been interpreted as evidence that genetic factors play a more significant role in determining individual variation in some cognitive domains than in others. In an attempt to expand these findings, Vandenberg formulated a hypothesis that what is heritable in specific cognitive abilities is the variance that is accounted for by the *g* factor. In other words, he suggested the presence of a genetic *g* with environmental contributions determining specific h^2 to e^2 ratios of various cognitive abilities. A series of Vandenberg's studies was designed to verify this hypothesis. The results yielded evidence both for and against the hypothesis, indicating both a genetic endowment of the correlated components of cognitive abilities (Bock & Vandenberg, 1968; Loehlin & Vandenberg, 1968) as well as unique genetic contributions to various abilities (Vandenberg, 1968a).

Unfortunately, subsequent studies have not clarified the picture. A number of twin studies (Eaves & Gale, 1974; Loehlin & Nichols, 1976; Martin & Eaves, 1977; Martin, Jardine, & Eaves, 1984; Plomin & DeFries, 1979), family studies (DeFries et al., 1979; Spuhler & Vandenberg, 1980), and adoption/separation studies (Horn, Loehlin, & Willerman, 1982; Plomin, 1988; Rice, Carey, Fulker, & DeFries, 1989) presented results suggesting the presence of genetic factors for some specific abilities (most consistently, verbal and/or spatial), but not for others. For example, Scarr and Weinberg (1978), in their adoption study, found significant correlations between biological relatives, whereas the correlations between adoptive parents and their adopted children on virtually all studied measures of specific cognitive abilities are mostly not statistically significant. The exception is vocabulary scores, which appear to be influenced by shared environment in addition to genes. In addition to the ongoing debate on which specific abilities are controlled by genes and which are not, little agreement is present on the magnitude of genetic influence.

Horn (1988) reported results from a behavior-genetic study of eight mental measures mapping Cattell's higher-order factors of fluid and crystallized abilities. (Fluid ability to grasp relationships in novel situations quickly and make correct deductions from them; fluid ability is considered to be relatively culture free. Crystallized ability is the ability to accommodate and assimilate cultural knowledge such as vocabulary, math operations, etc.; crystallized ability is culture and education dependent.) According to Cattell (1941), variability in fluid ability is due primarily to genes, whereas variability in crystallized ability is due primary to environmental factors. In contrast, Horn found that variation in both abilities is approximately 60% heritable, but the genetic variance shared between these abilities is only about 14%, suggesting that, most likely, the abilities are influenced by different sets of genes.

One of the largest studies of specific cognitive abilities, the Hawaii Family Study of Cognition (DeFries et al., 1979), demonstrated another controversy. Fifteen different cognitive tests were administered to over 6000 individuals. Factor analysis yielded four groups of factors: (1) verbal (vocabulary and fluency), (2) spatial (visualizing and rotating objects in space), (3) perceptual speed (simple arithmetic and number comparison), and (4) visual memory (short- and long-term recollection of line drawing). In addition to differences in heritabilities for the four factors, it was found that tests within each factor also demonstrated a wide range in familial resemblance. For example, one spatial test, requiring cutting a figure to yield a certain pattern, showed a heritability of about .60. On the contrary, another spatial test, involving drawing one line and connecting as many dots as possible, showed the lowest familial resemblance (about .27).

Based on the findings of the Hawaii study, in the Colorado Adoption Project (Plomin, DeFries, & Fulker, 1988), an ongoing study of specific cognitive abilities, researchers assessed four broad cognitive domains: verbal comprehension, spatial visualization, memory, and perceptual speed. The results (Cardon & Fulker, 1994) showed that, in part, these different abilities were influenced by the same genes, and, in part, by separate genes, acting independently from each other. Due to the longitudinal nature of their data, the researchers have demonstrated that the ability-specific genes are pervasive throughout young childhood. However, the presence of novel genetic influences was detected at year 7 of the study and have been shown to continue to influence variation in ability at year 9. The environmental analysis showed a large role of nonshared environmental factors, which were found to be important at each age and exhibited lasting effects over childhood. This finding has been interpreted as an indicator that childhood experiences may play an important role for a specific ability at the time of the occurrence, as well as perhaps having a generalized effect on all mental skills. According to these results, educational or childrearing changes that might influence verbal learning at a given age might also influence both verbal and performance abilities in later childhood.

Another dimension of cognition that has been studied is creativity. Creativity demonstrates little genetic influence. A review of 10 studies of twins (Nichols, 1978) presented mean correlations of .61 for identical twins and .50 for fraternal twins. When controlled for IQ, twin correlations for creativity tests become indistinguishable (Canter, 1973). Thus, it appears that the heritability of creativity, estimated at 20%, is primarily due to existing correlations between creativity and IQ.

In summary, tests of some cognitive abilities, primarily verbal and spatial, demonstrate significant and often substantial genetic influence throughout the life span. On the contrary, it appears that memory abilities, perceptual speed, and creativity are influenced by heredity less (if at all). In concluding this discussion, I would like to make four comments. First, whereas the number of behavior-genetic studies of IQ is exceedingly high, there are only a handful of studies on specific cognitive abilities. These studies are characterized by heterogeneity of both underlying theoretical models (e.g., Cattell, 1971, versus Thurstone, 1938) and assessment instruments used. Thus, the observed controversial nature of findings might change when more data are accumulated. Second, a special concern is the diversity of phenotypic definitions utilized in these studies. For example, in studies of creativity, the indicators range from the measures obtained from the Torrance Test of Creative Thinking to raters' evaluations of creativity in the subjects' writings. When there is no agreement on the definition of the studied trait at the phenotypic level, it is unlikely that the results of heritability studies will arrive at a consensus. Third, lower heritability estimates, obtained for specific cognitive abilities, might reflect inadequate redistribution of the phenotypic variance due to considerably less reliable measures used for assessment of these abilities. For example, the fact that behavior-genetic studies of creativity utilize measures whose test-retest reliability is quite (often unacceptably) low might result in attenuation of the genetic factor estimates. Fourth, a distinct characteristic of specific abilities studies is the gap between the richness of psychological theories of cognition existing in modern cognitive psychology and their oversimplified applications in behavior-genetic studies. Thus, the findings might have been more homogeneous were the data obtained in correspondence with modern theories of cognitive abilities.

Concluding Remarks

To understand why people vary in cognitive abilities, one must know what sources contribute to interindividual differences and what the magnitudes of these contributions are. Hence, the problem of heredity and environment and their co-contribution to variation in cognitive functioning has always attracted and will always attract the attention of many psychologists and cognitive scientists.

Many attempts have been made to understand and to theorize about the sources of individual differences in cognition. This chapter presented an overview of only one of those traditions striving to solve the puzzle of individual differences in cognition: the behavior-genetic approach. According to this approach, the phenomenon of individual differences on a studied ability might be translated into the phenotypic variance that can be decomposed into genetic, environmental, and interactive components. These components can be estimated by means of comparing relatives of various degrees. When phenotype is measured in relatives, those who are more closely related genetically are expected to be more similar on the studied ability than those who are genetically more distant.

Behavior-genetic studies of cognitive functioning have investigated both general and specific cognitive abilities. Almost 50 years of intensive research of general cognitive ability (IQ) have revealed a robust estimate of its heritability. It appears that about 50% in interindividual variation on IQ can be explained by genetic influences. Another 50% of the variation is accounted for by environmental factors. Today researchers try to extend their findings beyond the estimates of heritability and environmentality to find specific genes and specific measurable environmental factors that contribute to these estimates.

The field of studying specific cognitive abilities, however, is significantly less explored. Not enough work has been done to warrant firm conclusions concerning the relative contributions of genes and environment to phenotypic variance for specific cognitive abilities. As of today, it appears that variation in verbal and spatial abilities might be under genetic control; however, the significance of nonshared environmental influences also appears to be crucial. Much as with IQ research, even though it has been suggested that the environment plays a significant role in such specific cognitive abilities as perceptual speed and memory, specific environmental components that influence this variation have not yet been identified.

Recent behavior-genetic studies apply sophisticated methodologies in order to go beyond initial heritability and environmentality estimates and to (a) sharpen the existing estimates by minimizing the measurement error, (b) explore sex-specific differences in the ways genes and the environment operate, (c) detect both genetic and environmental influences that will "fit" in the estimated portion of variance, and (d) explore the role of both genotype-environment correlations and interactions. Fifty years of behavior-genetic studies of cognitive functions have brought us to believe that genes are important virtually for every measured cognitive ability. And, when genes are secondary, the leading role belongs to environment. We know that both genes and environments are responsible for individual differences. The next task is to address the questions of *which* (which genes and which environments) and *how* (what biological and social-cultural pathways determine mechanisms of cognitive development). Both are exciting tasks that will be in the center of behavior-genetic research for the next decade or more.

Note

1. For details, see Plomin, DeFries, & McClearn, 1990.

References

Bock, R. D., & Vandenberg, S. G. (1968). Components of heritable variation in mental test scores. In S. G. Vandenberg (Ed.), *Progress in human behavior genetics* (pp. 233–260). Baltimore: Johns Hopkins University Press.

Bouchard, T. J., Jr., & McGue, M. (1981). Familial studies of intelligence: A review. *Science, 250*, 223–238.

Capron, C., & Duyme, M. (1989). Assessment of effects of socio-economic status on IQ in a full cross-fostering study. *Nature, 340*, 552–554.

Cardon, L. R., & Fulker, D. W. (1994). Genetics of specific cognitive abilities. In R. Plomin & G. E. McClearn (Eds.), *Nature and nurture and psychology* (pp. 99–120). Washington, DC: American Psychological Association.

Caruso, D. R. (1983). Sample differences in genetics and intelligence data: Sibling and parent-offspring studies. *Behavior Genetics, 13*, 453–458.

Canter, S. (1973). Personality traits in twins. In G. Claridge, S. Canter, & W. I. Hume (Eds.), *Personality differences and biological variation* (pp. 21–51). New York: Pergamon Press.

Cattell, R. B. (1941). Some theoretical issues in adult intelligence testing. *Psychological Bulletin, 38,* 562.

Cattell, R. B. (1971). *Abilities: Their structure, growth, and action.* Boston: Houghton-Miffin.

Cherny, S. (1994). Home environmental influences on general cognitive ability. In J. C. DeFries, R. Plomin, & D. W. Fulker (Eds.), *Nature and nurture during middle childhood* (pp. 262–280). Cambridge, MA: Basil Blackwell.

Chipuer, H. M., Rovine, M., & Plomin, R. (1990). LISREL modeling: Genetic and environmental influences on IQ revisited. *Intelligence, 14,* 11–29.

DeFries, J. C., Corey, R. P., Johnson, R. C., Vandenberg, S. C., & Wilson, J. R. (1982). Sex-by-generation and ethnic group-by-generation interactions in the Hawaii, Family Study of Cognition. *Behavior Genetics, 12,* 223–230.

DeFries, J. C., Johnson, R. C., Kuse, A. P., McClearn, G. E., Polovina, J., Vandenberg, S. G., & Wilson, J. R. (1979). Familial resemblance for specific cognitive abilities. *Behavior Genetics, 9,* 23–43.

Detterman, D. K., Thompson, L. A., & Plomin, R. (1990). Differences in heritability across groups differing in ability. *Behavior Genetics, 20,* 369–384.

Dixon, L. K., & Johnson, R. C. (1980). *The roots of individuality: A survey of human behavior genetics.* Monterey, CA: Brooks/Cole Publishing Company.

Duyme, M. (1988). School success and social class: An adoption study. *Developmental Psychology, 24,* 203–209.

Eaves, L. J., & Gale, J. S. (1974). A method for analyzing the genetic basis of covariation. *Behavior Genetics, 4,* 253–267.

Feng, D., & Baker, L. (1994). Spouse similarity in attitudes, personality, and psychological well-being. *Behavior Genetics, 24,* 357–364.

Gilger, J. W. (1991). Differential assortative mating found for academic and demographic variables as a function of time of assessment. *Behavior Genetics, 21,* 131–150.

Guilford, J. P. (1967). *The nature of human intelligence.* New York: McGraw-Hill.

Horn, J. M. (1988). Thinking about human abilities. In J. R. Nesselroade & R. B. Cattell (Eds.), *Handbook of multivariate psychology* (pp. 645–685). New York: Academic Press.

Horn, J. M., Loehlin, J. C., & Willerman, L. (1982). Aspects of the inheritance of intellectual abilities. *Behavior Genetics, 12,* 479–516.

Iskol'dsky, N. V. (1988). *Vliyanie social'no-psikhologicheskikh factorov na individual'nye osobennosti bliznetsov i ikh vnutriparnoe skhodstvo po psikhologicheskim parametram* [The role of social-psychological factors in individual and dyadic twin development]. Unpublished doctoral dissertation. Psychological Institute of the Russian Academy of Education, Moscow.

Jensen, A. R. (1969). How much can we boost IQ and scholastic achievement? *Harvard Educational Review, 39,* 1–123.

Jensen, A. R. (1978). Genetic and behavioral effects of nonrandom mating. In R. T. Osborne, C. E. Nobble, & N. Weyl (Eds.), *Human variation: The biopsychology of age, race, and sex* (pp. 51–105) New York: Academic Press.

Kimble, G. E. (1994). Evolution of the nature-nurture issue in the history of psychology. In R. Plomin & G. E. McClearn (Eds.), *Nature, nurture and psychology* (pp. 3–26). Washington, DC: American Psychological Association.

Locurto, C. (1990). The malleability of IQ as judged from adoption studies. *Intelligence, 14,* 275–292.

Loehlin, J. C. (1989). Partitioning environmental and genetic contributions to behavioral development. *American Psychologist, 44,* 1295–1292.

Loehlin, J. C., & DeFries, J. C. (1987). Genotype-environment correlation and IQ. *Behavior Genetics, 17,* 263–277.

Loehlin, J. C., & Nichols, R. C. (1976). *Heredity, environment, and personality.* Austin: University of Texas Press.

Loehlin, J. C., & Vandenberg, S. G. (1968). Genetic and environmental components in the covariation of cognitive abilities: An additive model. In S. G. Vandenberg (Ed.), *Progress in human behavior genetics* (pp. 261–285). Baltimore: Johns Hopkins University Press.

Martin, N. G., & Eaves, L. J. (1977). The genetical analysis of covariance structure. *Heredity, 38,* 79–95.

Martin, N. G., Jardine, R., & Eaves, L. J. (1984). Is there only one set of genes for different abilities? A reanalysis of the National Merit Scholarship Qualifying Test (NMSQT) data. *Behavior Genetics, 14,* 355–370.

Matheny, A. P., Wilson, R. S., Dolan, A. B., & Krantz, J. Z. (1981). Behavioral contrasts in twinship: Stability patterns of differences in childhood. *Child Development, 52,* 579–588.

McGue, M., Bouchard, T. J., Iacono, W. G., & Lykken, D. T. (1994). Behavioral genetics of cognitive ability: A life-span perspective. In R. Plomin & G. E. McClearn (Eds.), *Nature and nurture and psychology* (pp. 59–76). Washington, DC: American Psychological Association.

Merriman, C. (1924). The intellectual resemblance of twins. *Psychological Monographs, 33,* 1–58.

Molenaar, P. C. M., Boomsma, D. I., & Dolan, C. V. (in press). The detection of genotype-environment interaction in longitudinal genetic models. In M. C. LaBuda & E. L. Grigorenko (Eds.) *On the way to individuality: Current methodological issues in behavior genetics.* Commack, NY: Nova Sciences.

Moore, E. G. J. (1986). Family socialization and the IQ test performance of traditionally and transracially adopted black children. *Developmental Psychology, 22,* 317–326.

Neale, M. C., & Cardon, L. R. (Eds.) (1992). Methodology for genetic studies of twins and families. Dordrecht, Netherlands: Kluwer Academic Press.

Nichols, R. C. (1978). Twin studies of ability, personality, and interests. *Homo, 29*, 158–173.

Plomin, R. (1988). The nature and nurture of cognitive abilities. In R. Sternberg (Ed.), *Advances in the psychology of human intelligence* (Vol. 4). Hillsdale, NJ: Erlbaum.

Plomin, R. (1994). *Genetics and experience: The developmental interplay between nature and nurture.* Newbury Park, CA: Sage.

Plomin, R. (1995). Genetics and children's experiences in the family. *Journal of Child Psychology and Psychiatry, 36*, 33–68.

Plomin, R., & Bergeman, C. S. (1991). The nature of nurture: Genetic influence on "evironmental" measures. *Behavioral and Brain Sciences, 14*, 373–386.

Plomin, R., & DeFries, J. C. (1979). Multivariate behavioural genetic analysis of twin data on scholastic abilities. *Behavior Genetics, 9*, 505–517.

Plomin, R., DeFries, J. C., & Fulker, D. W. (1988). *Nature and nurture during infancy and early childhood.* Cambridge, England: Cambridge University Press.

Plomin, R., DeFries, J. C., & Loehlin, J. C. (1977). Genotype-environment interaction and correlation in the analysis of human behavior. *Psychological Bulletin, 84*, 309–322.

Plomin, R., DeFries, J. C., & McClearn, G. E. (1990). *Behavioral genetics: A primer.* New York: W. H. Freeman.

Plomin, R., & Neiderhiser, J. M. (1991). Quantitative genetics, molecular genetics, and intelligence. *Intelligence, 15*, 369–387.

Posner, S., Baker, L. A., & Martin, N. G. (1994). Genetics of social class in Australian twins. *Behavior Genetics, 24*, 525.

Rice, T., Carey, G., Fulker, D. W., & DeFries, J. C. (1989). Multivariate path analysis of specific cognitive abilities in the Colorado Adoption Project: Conditional path model for assortative mating. *Behavior Genetics, 19*, 195–208.

Rowe, D. C. (1994). *The limits of family influence: Genes, experience, and behavior.* New York: Guilford.

Rutter, M., & Madge, N. (1976). *Cycles of disadvantage.* London: Heinemann Educational Books.

Rutter, M., & Pickles, A. (1991). Person-environment interaction: Concepts, mechanisms, and implications for data analysis. In T. D. Wachs & R. Plomin (Eds.) *Conceptualization and measurement of organism-environment interaction* (pp. 105–141). Washington, DC: American Psychological Association.

Rutter, M., & Quinton, D. (1984). Parental psychiatric disorder: Effects on children. *Psychological Medicine, 14*, 853–880.

Scarr, S. (1992). Developmental theories for the 1990s: Development and individual differences. *Child Development, 54*, 424–435.

Scarr, S. (1997). Behavior-genetic and socialization theories of intelligence: Truce and reconciliation. In R. J. Sternberg & E. L. Grigorenko (Eds.), *Intelligence, heredity, and environment* (pp. 3–41). New York: Cambridge University Press.

Scarr, S., & McCartney, K. (1983). How people create their own environments: A theory of genotype-environment effects. *Child Development, 54,* 424–435.

Scarr, S., & Weinberg, R. (1978). The influence of family background on intellectual attainment. *American Sociological Review, 43,* 674–692.

Scarr, S., Weinberg, R, & Waldman, I. (1993). IQ correlations in transracial adoptive families. *Intelligence, 17,* 545–555.

Schiff, M., & Lewontin, R. (1986). *Education and class: The irrelevance of IQ genetic studies.* Oxford, England: Clarendon.

Simonoff, E., McGuffin, P., & Gottesman, I. I. (1994). Genetic influences on normal and abnormal development. In M. Rutter, E. A. Taylor, & L. Hersov (Eds.) Child and adolescent psychiatry: Modern approaches. (pp. 129–151). Oxford, England: Blackwell Scientific Publications.

Spuhler, K. P., & Vandenberg, S. G. (1980). Comparison of parent-offspring resemblance for specific cognitive abilities. *Behavior Genetics, 10,* 413–418.

Sternberg, R. J., & Grigorenko, E. L. (1998). Interventions for cognitive development in children 0–3 year old. In M. E. Young (Ed.), Early child development: Investing in our children's future (pp. 127–156). Amsterdam: Elsevier.

Sundet, J. M., Tambs, K., Magnus, P., Berg, K. (1988). On the question of secular trends in the heritability of intelligence test scores: A study of Norwegian twins. *Intelligence, 12,* 47–59.

Thompson, L. A., Detterman, D. K., & Plomin, R. (1993). Differences in heritability across groups differing in ability, revisited. *Behavior Genetics, 23,* 331–336.

Thurstone, L. L. (1938). *Primary mental abilities.* Chicago: University of Chicago.

Thurstone, L. L., & Thurstone, T. D. (1941). Factorial studies of intelligence. *Psychometric Monographs* (2).

Turkheimer, E., & Gottesman, I. I. (1991). Individual differences and the canalization of human behavior. *Developmental Psychology, 27,* 18–22.

Vandenberg, S. G. (1968a). The nature and nurture of intelligence. In D. C. Glass (Ed.), *Genetics* (pp. 3–58). New York: Rockefeller University Press.

Vandenberg, S. G. (1968b). Primary mental abilities or general intelligence? Evidence from twin studies. In J. M. Thoday & A. S. Parke (Eds.), *Genetic and environmental influences on behavior* (pp. 146–160). New York: Plenum.

Vandenberg, S. G. (1972). Assortative mating, or who marries whom? *Behavior Genetics, 2,* 127–157.

Wahlsten, D. (1990). Insensitivity of the analysis of variance to heredity-environment interaction. *Behavioral and Brain Sciences, 13,* 109–161.

Waldman, I. (1997). Unresolved questions and future directions in behavior-genetic studies of intelligence. In R. J. Sternberg & E. L. Grigorenko (Eds.), *Intelligence, heredity, and environment* (pp. 552–570). New York: Cambridge University Press.

Watkins, M. P., & Meredith, W. (1981). Spouse similarity in newlyweds with respect to specific cognitive abilities, socioeconomic status, and education. *Behavior Genetics, 11,* 1–21.

Contributors

Rhianon Allen
Department of Psychology
Long Island University
Brooklyn, New York

Axel Buchner
Department of Psychology
University of Trier
Trier, Germany

Patricia A. Carpenter
Professor of Psychology
Carnegie Mellon University
Pittsburgh, Pennsylvania

Stephen J. Ceci
Department of Psychology
Cornell University
Ithaca, New York

Michael Cole
Department of Psychology
University of California
La Jolla, California

Eduardus DeBruyn
Department of Human Development
Cornell University
Ithaca, New York

Randall W. Engle
Professor and Chair
School of Psychology
Georgia Institute of Technology
Atlanta, Georgia

Peter Frensch
Department of Psychology
University of Missouri
Columbia, Missouri

Elena L. Grigorenko
Department of Psychology
Yale University
New Haven, Connecticut

Earl Hunt
Department of Psychology
University of Washington
Seattle, Washington

P. N. Johnson-Laird
Department of Psychology
Princeton University
Princeton, New Jersey

Marcel Adam Just
Carnegie Mellon University
Pittsburgh, Pennsylvania

Michael J. Kahana
Assistant Professor
Center for Complex Systems
Brandeis University
Waltham, Massachusetts

John F. Kihlstrom
Department of Psychology
University of California, Berkeley
Berkeley, California

Geoffrey Loftus
Center for Complex Systems
Brandeis University
Waltham, Massachusetts

Valerie S. Makin
Beckman Institute
University of Illinois at Urbana-
Champaign
Urbana, Illinois

Timothy P. McNamara
Department of Psychology
Vanderbilt University
Nashville, Tennessee

Thomas O. Nelson
Department of Psychology
University of Maryland
College Park, Maryland

Raymond S. Nickerson
Tufts University
Medfield, Massachusetts

Natalie Oransky
Department of Psychology
Appalachian State University
Boone, North Carolina

Elizabeth Phelps
Department of Psychology
Yale University
New Haven, Connecticut

Dennis R. Proffitt
Department of Psychology
University of Virginia
Charlottesville, Virginia

Arthur S. Reber
Department of Psychology
CUNY
Brooklyn College
Brooklyn, New York

Paul J. Reber
Department of Psychiatry
Veterans Affairs Medical Center
University of California at San Diego
San Diego, California

Daniel N. Robinson
Department of Psychology
Georgetown University
Washington, DC

Tina B. Rosenblum
Department of Human Development
Cornell University
Ithaca, New York

Brian H. Ross
Department of Psychology
University of Illinois at Urbana-
Champaign
Urbana, Illinois

Steven A. Sloman
Department of Linguistic
and Cognitive Sciences
Brown University
Providence, Rhode Island

Robert J. Sternberg
Department of Psychology
Yale University
New Haven, Connecticut

Author Index

Subject Index

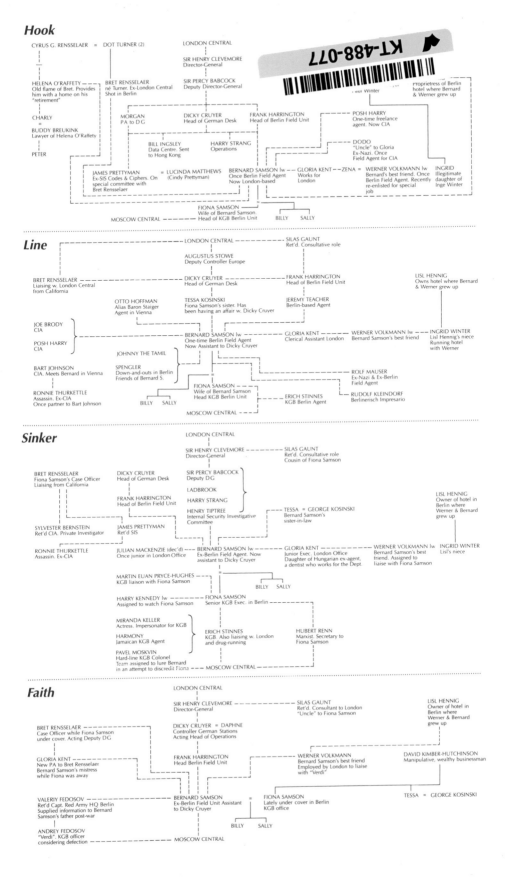

Hook

CYRUS G. RENSSELAER = DOT TURNER (2)

LONDON CENTRAL

SIR HENRY CLEVEMORE
Director-General

SIR PERCY BABCOCK
Deputy Director-General

HELENA O'RAFFETY
Old flame of Bret. Provides
him with a home on his
"retirement"

CHARLY
=
BUDDY BREUKINK
Lawyer of Helena O'Raffety

PETER

BRET RENSSELAER
né Turner. Ex-London Central
Shot in Berlin

MORGAN
PA to DG

DICKY CRUYER
Head of German Desk

FRANK HARRINGTON
Head of Berlin Field Unit

... ur Winter — proprietress of Berlin
hotel where Bernard
& Werner grew up

POSH HARRY
One-time freelance
agent. Now CIA

DODO
"Uncle" to Gloria
Ex-Nazi. Once
Field Agent for CIA

BILL INGSLEY
Data Centre. Sent
to Hong Kong

HARRY STRANG
Operations

JAMES PRETTYMAN
Ex-SIS Codes & Ciphers. On
special committee with
Bret Rensselaer

LUCINDA MATTHEWS
(Cindy Prettyman)

BERNARD SAMSON lw
Once Berlin Field Agent
Now London-based

GLORIA KENT — ZENA
Works for
London

WERNER VOLKMANN lw
Bernard's best friend. Once
Berlin Field Agent. Recently
re-enlisted for special
job

INGRID
Illegitimate
daughter of
Inge Winter

FIONA SAMSON
Wife of Bernard Samson.
Head of KGB Berlin Unit

MOSCOW CENTRAL

BILLY   SALLY

Line

LONDON CENTRAL

SILAS GAUNT
Ret'd. Consultative role

AUGUSTUS STOWE
Deputy Controller Europe

BRET RENSSELAER
Liaising w. London Central
from California

DICKY CRUYER
Head of German Desk

FRANK HARRINGTON
Head of Berlin Field Unit

LISL HENNIG
Owns hotel where Bernard
& Werner grew up

OTTO HOFFMAN
Alias Baron Staiger
Agent in Vienna

TESSA KOSINSKI
Fiona Samson's sister. Has
been having an affair w. Dicky Cruyer

JEREMY TEACHER
Berlin-based agent

JOE BRODY
CIA

POSH HARRY
CIA

BERNARD SAMSON lw
One-time Berlin Field Agent
Now Assistant to Dicky Cruyer

GLORIA KENT
Clerical Assistant London

WERNER VOLKMANN lw
Bernard Samson's best friend

INGRID WINTER
Lisl Hennig's niece
Running hotel
with Werner

JOHNNY THE TAMIL

BART JOHNSON
CIA. Meets Bernard in Vienna

SPENGLER
Down-and-outs in Berlin
Friends of Bernard S.

ROLF MAUSER
Ex-Nazi & Ex-Berlin
Field Agent

RONNIE THURKETTLE
Assassin. Ex-CIA
Once partner to Bart Johnson

FIONA SAMSON
Wife of Bernard Samson
Head KGB Berlin Unit

ERICH STINNES
KGB Berlin Agent

RUDOLF KLEINDORF
Berlinerisch Impresario

BILLY   SALLY

MOSCOW CENTRAL

Sinker

LONDON CENTRAL

SIR HENRY CLEVEMORE
Director-General

SILAS GAUNT
Ret'd. Consultative role
Cousin of Fiona Samson

BRET RENSSELAER
Fiona Samson's Case Officer
Liaising from California

DICKY CRUYER
Head of German Desk

SIR PERCY BABCOCK
Deputy DG

LADBROOK

HARRY STRANG

FRANK HARRINGTON
Head of Berlin Field Unit

LISL HENNIG
Owner of hotel in
Berlin where
Werner & Bernard
grew up

HENRY TIPTREE
Internal Security Investigative
Committee

TESSA = GEORGE KOSINSKI
Bernard Samson's
sister-in-law

SYLVESTER BERNSTEIN
Ret'd CIA. Private Investigator

JAMES PRETTYMAN
Ret'd SIS

RONNIE THURKETTLE
Assassin. Ex-CIA

JULIAN MACKENZIE (dec'd)
Once junior in London Office

BERNARD SAMSON lw
Ex-Berlin Field Agent. Now
assistant to Dicky Cruyer

GLORIA KENT
Junior Exec. London Office
Daughter of Hungarian ex-agent,
a dentist who works for the Dept.

WERNER VOLKMANN lw
Bernard Samson's best
friend. Assigned to
liaise with Fiona Samson

INGRID WINTER
Lisl's niece

MARTIN EUAN PRYCE-HUGHES
KGB liaison with Fiona Samson

BILLY   SALLY

HARRY KENNEDY lw
Assigned to watch Fiona Samson

FIONA SAMSON
Senior KGB Exec. in Berlin

MIRANDA KELLER
Actress. Impersonator for KGB

HARMONY
Jamaican KGB Agent

ERICH STINNES
KGB. Also liaising w. London
and drug-running

HUBERT RENN
Marxist. Secretary to
Fiona Samson

PAVEL MOSKVIN
Hard-line KGB Colonel
Team assigned to lure Bernard
in an attempt to discredit Fiona

MOSCOW CENTRAL

Faith

LONDON CENTRAL

SIR HENRY CLEVEMORE
Director-General

SILAS GAUNT
Ret'd. Consultant to London
"Uncle" to Fiona Samson

LISL HENNIG
Owner of hotel in
Berlin where
Werner & Bernard
grew up

BRET RENSSELAER
Case Officer while Fiona Samson
under cover. Acting Deputy DG

DICKY CRUYER = DAPHNE
Controller German Stations
Acting Head of Operations

GLORIA KENT
New PA to Bret Rensselaer
Bernard Samson's mistress
while Fiona was away

FRANK HARRINGTON
Head Berlin Field Unit

WERNER VOLKMANN
Bernard Samson's best friend
Employed by London to liaise
with "Verdi"

DAVID KIMBER-HUTCHINSON
Manipulative, wealthy businessman

VALERIY FEDOSOV
Ret'd Capt. Red Army HQ Berlin
Supplied information to Bernard
Samson's father post-war

BERNARD SAMSON
Ex-Berlin Field Unit Assistant
to Dicky Cruyer
=
FIONA SAMSON
Lately under cover in Berlin
KGB office

TESSA = GEORGE KOSINSKI

ANDREY FEDOSOV
"Verdi". KGB officer
considering defection

BILLY   SALLY

MOSCOW CENTRAL

CHARITY

BY LEN DEIGHTON

Fiction

The Ipcress File
Horse Under Water
Funeral in Berlin
Billion-Dollar Brain
An Expensive Place to Die
Only When I Larf
Bomber
Declarations of War
Close-Up
Spy Story
Yesterday's Spy
Twinkle, Twinkle, Little Spy
SS-GB
XPD
Goodbye Mickey Mouse
Mamista
City of Gold
Violent Ward

The Samson Series

Berlin Game
Mexico Set
London Match
Winter: A Berlin Family 1899–1945
Spy Hook
Spy Line
Spy Sinker
Faith
Hope
Charity

Non-fiction
Fighter: The True Story of the Battle of Britain
Blitzkrieg: From the Rise of Hitler to the Fall of Dunkirk
Airshipwreck
ABC of French Food
Blood, Tears and Folly

LEN DEIGHTON
CHARITY

HarperCollins*Publishers*

HarperCollins*Publishers*
77–85 Fulham Palace Road
Hammersmith, London w6 8jb

Published by HarperCollins*Publishers* 1996
1 3 5 7 9 8 6 4 2

Copyright © Pluriform Publishing Company, BV 1996

A catalogue record for this book
is available from the British Library

ISBN 0 00 224470 5
ISBN 0 00 225587 1 (Pbk)

Set in Sabon by Rowland Phototypesetting Ltd,
Bury St Edmunds, Suffolk

Printed and bound in Great Britain by
Caledonian International Book Manufacturing Ltd, Glasgow

Author's Note

The first three books of the Bernard Samson story, *Game*, *Set* and *Match*, are set in the cold war period from spring 1983 to spring 1984.

Winter: A Berlin Family 1899–1945 was the next in order of writing. The same places and the same people are to be found in it.

Hook and *Line* take up the story from the beginning of 1987 and through the summer of that same year. *Sinker* uses a third-person narrative focusing on Fiona Samson. It tells the story from her point of view and reveals things that Bernard Samson still does not know.

Faith, *Hope* and *Charity* continue the story. *Faith* starts in California as Bernard's terrible summer of 1987 turns cold. *Hope* follows it into the last weeks of 1987. *Charity* begins in the early days of 1988.

Like all the other books, *Charity* is written to stand alone, and can be read without reference to the other stories.

I thank my readers for their kindness, their generous encouragement and their patience. Writing ten books about the same group of people has proved a demanding labour but certainly a labour of love.

Len Deighton,
Portugal, 1996

1

A BLOATED VAMPIRE moon drained all life and colour from the world. The snow-covered land came speeding past the train. It was grey and ill-defined, marked only by a few livid cottages and limitless black forest grizzled with snow. No roads; the railway did not follow any road, it cut through the land like a knife. I had seen enough of this cheerless country. I tugged the window-blind down, grabbing at a brass rubbish bin to keep my balance as the clattering train argued with a badly maintained section of track.

Sometimes, at night, people also succumbed. Jim Prettyman's complexion, which had always been pale, was ashen under the dim overhead light. Inert on the top berth, a rosary dangling from his white-skinned hand; on the other a gold wedding ring and a massive gold Rolex wrist-watch indicating nine-thirty in the morning. It wasn't nine-thirty here for us. His watch had stopped. Or perhaps that was the right time in Moscow. We were a long way from Moscow, and for us it was still night.

Jim stirred, as if my stare had disturbed his sleep. But his eyelids didn't move. He made a noise; a deep breath and then a stifled groan that ended in a subdued nasal snort as he snatched his arm down under the blanket and resumed his sleep. Jim was tough and wiry but his appearance had never been athletic. Now his white face, with the vestigial eyebrows, made him look like a corpse prettified and readied for the relatives.

Jim had picked up some kind of infection of the liver, or maybe it was the kidneys. The Russian hospital doctors said they could treat it, but, since their diagnosis varied from day to day according to what they were drinking with lunch, no one believed them. Some doctor the American embassy had on call wouldn't give a diagnosis; he just advised that Jim shouldn't be subjected to a plane trip. Rather than have him face any more treatment by Moscow's medics, Jim's American wife had wired the money for him to be evacuated by train and attended by a nurse. Jim's wife was a woman with considerable influence. She had arranged that her father in the State Department sent a night-action fax to make sure the embassy people jumped to it. She wasn't with us; she had to host a Washington dinner party for her father.

Although the paperwork for Jim's passage was being handled by the Americans, someone in London Central ordered that I should accompany him as far as Berlin. I was in Moscow at the time, and their message said it simply meant delaying my return by twenty-four hours. But going from Moscow to West Berlin by air was quite different to doing the same trip by train. By train I was going to encounter whole armies of nosy customs officials, security men and frontier police. Jim had a US passport nowadays, the nurse was Canadian and I was stuck with the German passport that I had used for my entry. With this cosmopolitan party I would have to cross Poland, and then travel across a large section of the German Democratic Republic, before getting to anywhere I could call home. Perhaps the people in London didn't appreciate that. There was sometimes good reason to think pen-pushers in the Foreign Office in Whitehall were still using nineteenth-century maps.

I was looking at Jim, trying to decide how ill he really was, when there came a sudden sound, like a shovelful of heavy mud hitting a wall. The compartment rocked slightly. With no lessening of speed, the express thudded the air and sped between some empty loading platforms, leaving behind no more than an echoed

2

gasp and a whiff of burned diesel. The train was packed. You could feel the weight of it as it swayed, and hear the relentless pounding of the bogies. The compartments of the wagon-lit had been booked for weeks. The cheaper coach seats were all filled and there were people sleeping amid the litter on the floor and propped between baggage in the corridors. Five rail cars were reserved for the army: hardy teenagers with cropped heads and pimples. Their kitbags and rifles were under guard in the freight car. Returning to training camps after playing the sort of war games that didn't include time for sleep. Exhausted draftees. The fighting battalions had forsaken rifles long ago. Rifles were only for clumsy youngsters learning to drill.

Further back in the train there were East European businessmen in plastic suits and clip-on ties; shrivelled old women with baskets heavy with home-made vodka and smoked pork sausage; stubble-chinned black-market dealers with used TV sets crammed into freshly printed cardboard boxes.

Coming half-awake, Jim stretched out a red bony foot so that his toes pressed upon the metal divider that formed the side of a tiny clothes closet. Then he grabbed the edge of the blanket, turned away and curled up small. 'Don't you ever sleep?' he growled drowsily. So he wasn't asleep and dreaming; he simply had his eyes closed. Perhaps that was the way Jim Prettyman had always fooled me. Long ago we'd been very close friends, one of a four-some made up with his petulant first wife Lucinda and my wife Fiona. We'd all worked for the Department in those days. Then Jim had been selected for special jobs and sent to work in corporate America as a cover for his real tasks. He'd changed jobs and changed wives, changed nationality and changed friends in rapid succession. He was not the sort of wavering wimp who let a good opportunity slip past while worrying who might get hurt.

'There's someone standing outside in the corridor,' I told him.

'The conductor.'

'No, not him. Our bad-tempered conductor has assumed

3

tenancy of compartment number fifteen. And he's stinking fall-down drunk and will soon be unconscious.'

'Slide open the door and look,' Jim suggested. 'Or is that too easy?' His voice was croaky.

'You're the one who's dying,' I said. 'I'm the security expert. Remember?'

'Was there someone at the railway terminal?' he asked, before remembering to try and smile at my joke. When I made no move to investigate the corridor noise he repeated the question.

'Yes,' I said.

'Someone you recognized?'

'I'm not sure. It could be the same goon I had sitting in the lobby of my hotel.'

'Go man!' said Jim wearily. He closed his eyes tight, and, with a practised gesture, bound his rosary round his wrist in some signal of benediction.

I went to the door, undid the catch and slid it open, unprepared for the bright moonlit countryside that was painted like a mural along the uncurtained windows of the corridor. There was a man there, standing a few steps away. He was about five feet six tall, with trimmed beard and neat moustache. His woollen Burberry scarf struck a note of affluence that jarred with the rest of his attire: the trenchcoat old and stained, and a black military-style beret that in Poland had become the badge of the elderly veteran of long-ago wars.

We looked at each other. The man gave no sign of friendliness nor recognition. 'How far to the frontier?' I asked him in my halting Polish.

'Half an hour; perhaps less. It's always like this. They are taking us on a long detour around the track repairs.'

I nodded my thanks and went back into my compartment. 'It's okay,' I told Jim.

'Who is it? Someone you know?'

'It's okay,' I said. 'Go back to sleep.'

'You may as well get some shut-eye too. Will the Poles come on and question us at the frontier?'

'No,' I said. Then, changing my mind: 'Maybe. It will be all right.' I wondered if the detour was really because of flood damage the way the press announcement said, or was there something at the frontier that the Soviets didn't want anyone to see?

☆

I was regretting my ready agreement to take this train from Moscow back to my office in Berlin. I didn't have diplomatic status; they had wanted to supply me with a letter with the royal coat of arms at the top, asking everyone en route to be kind to us. That too was a legacy of the FO's nineteenth-century mentality. I had to point out to them that such a missive might look incongruous when carried by someone with a German passport accompanied by an American and a Canadian. I'd not objected to this task of escorting Jim, partly for old times' sake, partly because I'd heard that Gloria would also be in Moscow at that time and the delay would give me two extra days with her. That was another fiasco. Her schedule was changed; she was leaving as I arrived. I'd only had time for one hurried lunch with Gloria, and that was marred by her interpreter arriving to collect her half an hour early, and standing over us with a watch in one hand, a coffee cup in the other, warning us about the traffic jams on the road to the airport. My brief moment with her was made more painful because she was looking more alluring than ever. Her long blonde hair was tucked up into a spiky fur hat, her complexion pale and perfect, and her large brown eyes full of affection, and devoted to me.

Now I had plenty of time to regret my readiness to return by train. Now came the consequences. We were getting close to the Polish frontier, and I was not well regarded in the Socialist Republic of Poland.

I had recognized the man in the corridor as 'Sneaky Jack', one of the hard men employed by our Warsaw embassy. I suppose

London had assigned him to keep an eye on Jim. I had reason to believe that Jim's head was filled with the Department's darkest secrets, and I wondered what Sneaky had been ordered to do if those secrets were compromised. Was he there to make sure Jim didn't fall into enemy hands alive?

'Where's that bloody nurse?' said Jim as I locked the sliding door. He turned over to look at me. 'She should be here holding my hand.' The nurse was a pretty young woman from Winnipeg, Canada. She was spending six months working in a Moscow hospital on an exchange scheme and had welcomed this opportunity to cut it short. She looked after Jim as if he was her nearest and dearest. Only when she was almost dropping from exhaustion did she retire to her first-class compartment along the corridor.

'The nurse has had a long day, Jim. Let her sleep.' I suppose he had sensed my anxiety. Jim had never been a field agent; he'd started out as a mathematician and got to the top floor via Codes and Ciphers. It was better if he didn't know that Sneaky was one of our people. And it was bad security to tell him. But if Jim ran into trouble and Sneaky had to tell him what to do . . . ? Oh, hell.

'In the corridor . . . little fellow with a beard. If we hit problems, and I'm not close by, do as he says.'

'You're not scared, are you, Bernard?'

'Me? Scared? Let me get at them.'

Jim acknowledged my well-rehearsed imitation of my boss Dicky Cruyer by giving a smile that was restrained enough to remind me that he was sick and in pain.

'It will be all right,' I told him. 'With an embassy man outside the door they won't even come in here.'

'Let's play it safe,' he said. 'Get that nurse back here and in uniform, waving a thermometer or a fever chart or something. That's what she's here for, isn't it?'

'Sure. If that's what you want.' I felt that a man in Jim's situation needed reassurance but I was probably wrong about that as I was wrong about everything else that happened on that journey.

6

I went along to find the nurse. I needn't have worried about disturbing her sleep. She was up and dressed in her starched white nurse's uniform, to which was added a smart woollen overcoat and knitted hat to keep her warm. She was drinking hot coffee from a vacuum flask. Bracing herself against the rock and roll of the train, she poured some into a plastic cup for me without asking if I wanted it.

'Thanks,' I said.

'I must look a sight in this stupid hat. I bought it for my kid brother, but I'm freezing cold. They don't have much heat on these trains.'

I tasted the coffee. It was made with canned condensed milk and was very sweet. I suppose she liked it like that. I said: 'I've done this lousy journey a million times and I've never had the brains to bring a vacuum flask of coffee with me.'

'I brought six of these flasks,' she said. 'Vacuum flasks were about the only thing I could find in the Moscow shops that would make a useful gift for my aunts and uncles back home. And they all expect a souvenir. Can you believe that they don't even have fridge magnets? I was looking for something with the Kremlin on it.'

'Moscow is not a great spot for shopping,' I agreed.

'It's a not a great spot for anything,' she said. 'Lousy climate, stinking food, surly natives. Getting out of there early was the best thing that happened to me in a long time.'

'Not everyone likes it,' I agreed. 'Personally there are quite a few towns I'd be happy to cross off my itinerary. Washington DC for a start.'

'Oh, don't say that. I worked in Washington DC for over a year. What parties they have there! I loved it.'

'By the way, the comrades who come climbing aboard at the frontier can be difficult about jewellery. I would tuck that sapphire brooch out of sight, if I were you.'

'Oh, this?' she said, fingering it on the lapel of her coat. 'Mr

Prettyman gave it to me. I wanted to wear it, to show him I appreciated it.' Maybe she saw a question in my face, for she quickly added: 'It was a little present from Mr and Mrs Prettyman. His wife was on the phone. She asked him to give it to me. They are determined to believe I saved his life.'

'And you didn't?'

'I stopped the night-duty man cutting his appendix out, that night when he was admitted. It was a crazy diagnosis but I guess he would have lived.' She paused. 'But that night doctor was very crocked. And he was going to try doing it himself. The things I saw in that hospital, you would never believe. When I think about it, maybe I did save his life.'

'How sick is he?'

'He's bad. These kind of infections don't always respond to drugs . . . The truth is no one knows too much about them.' Her voice trailed away as she fiddled with the pin of her brooch, concerned that she had revealed too much about her patient. 'But don't worry. If anything happened suddenly I could have him taken off in Berlin. The embassy people said Warsaw was not a good place.' She held the brooch in the palm of her hand and looked at it. 'It's a great keepsake. I like the kooky daisy shape; I've always loved daisies. I really appreciate it, but do you really think some Russkie is going to risk his career? He'd look kind of crazy, wouldn't he: snatching from a tourist like me a little silver-plated brooch with plastic sides and coloured brilliants?' She grinned mischievously. 'Want to look closer?'

'I don't have to look any closer,' I said, but I took it from her anyway. 'It's not a flower, not a daisy, it's an antique sunburst pattern. And that's not black plastic, it's badly tarnished silver, with yellow gold on the back. The big, luminous, faintly blue stone in the centre is a top-quality sapphire; maybe thirty carats. It's been neglected: badly rubbed with scratches, but that could all be polished away. All those "coloured brilliants" that punctuate each ray of it are matched diamonds pavé set.'

'You've got to be kidding.'

'The fastening is a simple pin, without safety catches. It's antique . . . well over a hundred years old. It's worth a pile of money.'

'Golly. Are you sure? Where did you learn so much about jewellery?'

'Back in the Sixties, in Berlin, they were tearing down some old houses in Neustadt. The bulldozer pushed a wall down and found a secretly bricked-up part of the cellar. It was full of crates and metal boxes. My father was Berlin security supremo for the British. He had to take charge of it. He tried to get out of it but some of the valuables were marked with labels from the Reichsbank. That opened a whole can of worms . . .' I stopped. 'I'm sorry, I'm being a bore.' I gave her the brooch.

'No, you're not. I want to hear.' She was examining the brooch carefully. 'I don't know anything about the war and the Nazis, apart from what I've seen back home in movies.'

'Gold, silver, coins, foreign paper money including pounds and dollars. And boxes of jewellery and antique cutlery and stuff; most of it solid silver. The Reichsbank labels made it political. The SS had stored their loot in the Reichsbank. So did Göring and some of the others. It could have been the property of the Federal Republic, or it might be claimed by the governments of countries the Nazis took over in the war. Some of the jewellery was thought to be part of the family jewels of the House of Hesse that were stolen by American soldiers in 1945. In other words no one had the slightest idea what it all was. The first job was to have it all listed and itemized, so the descriptions could be circulated. My father had three experienced Berlin jewellers going through it. It was in the old swimming hall in Hauptstrasse in Schöneberg. A big barn of a place, made of shiny white tiles, derelict at that time but still faintly smelling of chlorine and bleach. Folding tables from the army canteen were set up in the drained pool; the jewels and silver and stuff were all arranged on them and there were big printed numbers marking each item. I can see it now. There were cops sitting on the three-metre diving board looking down at us. My Dad told me to keep my eyes open and make sure the jewellers didn't steal anything.' I drank some coffee.

'And did they steal anything?'

'I was very young. I'm not sure if they did or not, but in those days Germans were scrupulously honest; it was one of the aspects of Berlin I took for granted until I went elsewhere. These old jewellers showed me each piece before they wrote out the description. It went on for four and a half days. For me it was an intensive course in jewellery appraisal. But I've forgotten half of it. That stone is cut as *der Achteck-Kreuzschliff*. I only know the German word for it. I suppose it means an octagonal crosscut. The sapphire is a cushion cut; quite old.'

'What happened to all the treasure?'

'I'm not sure. What I remember is having to decipher the handwriting – some of it in old German script – and type it out, with eight carbon copies. It took me a week. And I remember how happy my father was when he finally got a signature for it.'

'That's quite a story,' she said. 'I've never owned real jewellery before. Now if you would kindly turn around and avert your eyes, I shall tuck my valuable brooch into my money belt.'

The express slowed as we neared the frontier, and then, after a lot of hissing and puffing of brakes and machinery, crawled slowly into Soviet Russia's final western outpost, where floodlamps on tall posts swamped the checkpoint area with dazzling light. Like foamy water, it poured down upon the railway tracks and swamped the land. A freight train, caked in mud, was still and abandoned; a shunting engine was steamy and shiny with oil. At its shadowy edge I could see the barrack blocks of the local frontier battalion and their guard towers. Under the fierce lighting, star-shaped shadows sprang from the feet of the sentries, railway officials, immigration and customs men. The lights illuminated every last splash of icy sludge on the army trucks that were awaiting the Soviet draftees. The soldiers alighted first, in a frenzy of shouting, saluting and stamping of feet. Then there came the noise of the army's well-used railway cars being uncoupled and shunted off to a distant siding.

☆

Inside the express train there was an almost interminable processing of paperwork by Soviet officials whose demeanour ranged from officious to witless. They gave no more than a glance at the paperwork for our party. I got a mocking salute, the girl a leer, and Jim's inert form a nod. Eventually the train started again. It slid out of the brightly lit frontier area, and, with many stops and starts, we clanked across the frontier to where the Poles – and another checkpoint – awaited us.

Here the lights were less bright, the armed soldiers less threatening. I stood in the corridor watching the whole circus. Fur hats bobbed everywhere. The soldiers climbed aboard first. Then the ticket inspector came, and then the customs officer, and then two immigration inspectors with an army officer in tow, and a security official in civilian clothes. It was a long process.

An elderly English woman came shuffling along the train corridor. She was wearing a raglan style camel-hair coat over a nightdress. Her greying hair was dishevelled, and she clutched a bulging crocodile-skin handbag tightly to her breast. I'd noticed her on the platform at Moscow, where she'd got into an argument with a railway official about the seats assigned to her and the teenage boy with whom she was travelling.

'The soldiers have arrested my son,' she told me in a breathless croak. She was distressed, almost hysterical, but controlling her emotions in that way that the English do in the presence of foreigners. 'He's such a foolish boy. They discovered a political magazine in his shoulder bag. I want to go with him and sort it out, but they say I must continue my journey to Berlin because I have no Polish visa. What shall I do? Can you help me? I heard you speaking Polish and I know you speak English.'

'Give the sergeant some Western money,' I said. 'Do you have ten pounds in British currency?'

She touched her loosened hair, and a lock of it fell across her face. 'I didn't declare it.' She mouthed the words lest she was overheard. 'It's hidden.' She nervously flicked her hair back, and then with a quick movement of her fingers secured it with a hairclip that seemed to come from nowhere.

'It's what they want,' I said. 'Give them ten pounds sterling.'

'Are you sure?' She didn't believe me. She had become aware of her unladylike appearance by now. Selfconsciously she fastened the top button of her coat against her neck.

'Why else would they let you come here and talk with me?' I said.

She frowned and then smiled sadly. 'I see.'

'The sergeant,' I said. 'Take the sergeant to one side and give it to him. He will share it with the officer afterwards, so that no one sees it. If things go wrong the sergeant gets all the blame. It's the way it works.'

'Thank you.' With as much dignity as she could muster in a frilly nightdress and scuffed red velvet slippers, she hurried off back to her compartment. The door was opened for her when she got there and the sergeant poked his head out and looked at me. I smiled. Expressionless he drew his head back in again.

More uniformed officials came crawling along the train; resolute and unfriendly like a column of jungle ants. But the Polish security man who took me into the conductor's compartment at the end of the carriage was an elderly civilian, a plump man with untidy wavy hair, long and untidy enough to distinguish him from the soldiers. He was wearing a red-striped bow tie and belted brown corduroy overcoat. He scanned my passport with a battery-powered ultra-violet light. There was nothing wrong with my papers – it was a genuine German Federal Republic document – but he ignored the name in my passport and said: 'Welcome to Poland, Mr Samson.'

If they knew who I was, they knew what I did for a living. So they were not to be persuaded that I was an advertising executive from Hamburg.

He didn't give the passport back: instead he put it in his pocket. That was always a bad sign. He questioned me in German and in English. He told me his name was Reynolds and that his father was English, and born in Manchester. The Poles all had an English relative up their sleeve, just as the English like to keep an Irish grandmother in reserve.

I pretended not to understand English. Reynolds told me all over again in German. He was very patient. He smoked cheroots and kept referring to a bundle of documents that he said were all devoted to me and my activities. It was a thick folder, and once or twice it looked as if the whole lot of loose pages would end up cascading to the floor of the train, but he always managed to save them at the last moment.

I told him that it was a simple case of mistaken identity. Mr Reynolds lit a fresh cheroot from the butt of his old one and sighed. Another ten minutes passed in fruitless questions, and then they escorted me off the train. Sneaky Jack did nothing except stand around in the corridor, getting a glimpse of me through the door now and again, and overhearing as much as he could. I didn't blame him. He was no doubt assigned to look after Jim. Solving the predicaments of a supernumerary field agent like me was not something upon which his career would hang.

As far as I could see I was the only person being removed from the train. I jumped down and felt the chill of the hard frozen ground through the soles of my shoes. It was darker now; the moon was hiding behind the clouds. They didn't handcuff me. I followed the two soldiers – a sergeant standard-bearer and a trumpeter, if the badges on their arm were taken seriously. We crossed the tracks, stepping high over the rails and being careful not to stumble as we picked our way through piles of broken sleepers and other debris. Mr Reynolds was breathing heavily by the time we climbed the embankment. We waited for him to catch up.

I looked back at the train. There was lots of noise and steam, and all the squeaky commotion that is the ritual of trains as they prepare to move. The yellow blind of Jim's compartment went up, and the nurse was framed in the window. There was condensation on the glass and she wiped a clear patch with her hand. She looked this way and that, but it was too dark for her to spot me. She wasn't a Departmental employee, just a Canadian nurse engaged to accompany a casualty to London. Having a travelling companion suddenly disappear was no doubt disconcerting for her.

I stood shivering alongside Reynolds and his soldiers and we all watched the train pull away slowly. When it had disappeared the night was dark and I felt lonely. I looked the other way: back across the frontier to the Soviet checkpoint half a mile distant. It was still bathed in light but all the frantic activity there had ceased: the army trucks and the officials had disappeared. The lights were still glistening upon the oval of hardened snow, but the only movement was the measured pacing of a single armed sentry. It was like some abandoned ice-hockey stadium from which teams and spectators had unaccountably fled.

'Let's go,' said Reynolds. He flicked the butt of his cheroot so that it went spinning away in red sparks.

Before I could react the sergeant hit me spitefully in the small of the back with the metal butt of his gun. Caught off guard, I lost my balance. At first I slipped and then, as my knees buckled under me, I tumbled down the embankment with arms flailing. At the bottom there was a drainage ditch. The thick ice cracked and my foot went through it into cold muddy water.

When I got back on my feet I was wet and dirty. There was a wind that shook the trees and cut me to the bone. I wished I'd put my overcoat on before leaving the compartment to go and answer their questions. After five minutes stumbling through the dark, there was the sound of a diesel engine starting and then the headlights of a dark green army truck lit up a narrow road and trees.

☆

They didn't take me to Warsaw or to any other big town. The truck bumped along country roads while the crimson dawn crept out from the woodland. The sky was beginning to lighten as we arrived at the grim-looking castle in Mazury. Without anything much being said they locked me in a room there. It was not a bad room; I had endured worse accommodation in Polish hotels. The worrying thing was our proximity to Rastenburg, where I'd recently shot some Polish UB men and not gone back to feel their pulse. Thinking about that made it a long time before I went to sleep.

The man who liked to be called Reynolds was apparently in charge of me. He came to see me next morning and directly accused me of killing two security officials while evading arrest. Reynolds talked a lot, and continued talking even when I did not respond. He told me I would be held and tried here in the military district headquarters. In the course of the investigation, and subsequent court martial, the army witnesses, prosecutors and judges would go and visit the place where my crime took place. He didn't mention anything about a defence counsel.

The second day was Wednesday. He questioned me all the morning and into the afternoon, and accused me of not taking the charges seriously. I didn't admit to any of it. I said I was German but he didn't believe me.

'You think your government is now strenuously applying for your release through diplomatic channels, do you not?'

I looked at him and smiled. He didn't know much about my government, or its diplomatic service, or he would have known that having them do anything strenuously was far beyond reasonable expectations.

'You've nothing to smile about,' said Reynolds, banging his flattened hand upon a dossier lying on the table.

How right he was. 'I demand to see the consul from the embassy of the German Federal Republic,' I said.

I'd made the same demand many times, but on this occasion he became angry and rammed his cheroot down hard so that it split apart in the ashtray. 'Will you stop repeating that stupid cover story?' There was real anger in his voice. 'We know who you are. The Germans have never heard of you.' Perhaps it was because he'd missed lunch.

They had me in a rambling old fortress that Reynolds called the citadel. It was the sort of fairy castle that Walt Disney would have built on a mountain-top, but this was a region of lakes and marshland and the prominence upon which the castle stood was no more than a hillock.

The buildings that made up the complex provided a compendium of fortification history: twelfth-century dungeons, a keep almost as old, and a seventeenth-century tower. There were three cobbled yards, the one beneath my window crowded with ramshackle wooden huts and other structures that the German army had added when it became a regional school of military hygiene during the Second World War. The walls were thick and castellated, with a forbidding entrance gate that had once housed a drawbridge. The top of the walls provided a path along which armed sentries patrolled as they had no doubt done for centuries. To what extent the poor wretches slapping themselves to keep warm were there because the army thrives on sentry duty and guard changes, or to warn of approaching danger, was hard to decide. But in this eastern frontier region at that time, the prospect of a Soviet invasion was never far from anyone's mind. Some Moscow hard-liners were proclaiming that the Poles had gone too far with their reforms, and the only way to maintain communist power throughout the Eastern Bloc was by a brotherly show of Soviet military repression.

Whether they were reformers, communists or khaki-clad phil-
anthropists, the military government in Warsaw wouldn't
welcome Soviet spearhead armour lunging across the border.
Perhaps that was why this enlarged battalion of Polish infantry
was garrisoned here, and why their day began at five-thirty with
a flag-hoisting ceremony, accompanied by a drummer and that
sort of discordant trumpeting that drives men into battle. And
why the congregation that lined up at the subsequent Holy Mass
was in full battle-order.

They had brought my suitcase off the train. In my presence
they'd unlocked it and searched through its contents and photographed selected items. Now the case was open and placed on a
low table in my room. They found nothing incriminating, but I
didn't like this development. The suitcase, the photos, the polite
questions, and everything else they did, smelled like preparations
for a public trial. Were you ill-treated? No. Were you tortured?
No. Were you properly fed? Yes. Were you given a comfortable
room? Yes. Were these answers given freely and without coercion?
That's the sort of dialogue I smelled in the air, and I didn't like
the prospect one bit.

My third-floor window looked down upon a small inner yard.
Beyond it there was the main courtyard, where the morning and
evening parade took place. My room wasn't a cell. They weren't
giving me the thumbscrews, rack and electric shocks treatment.
They didn't take away my watch and seal off the daylight
to disorient me, or try any of the textbook tricks like that. The
only torture I suffered was when Reynolds blew cigarette smoke
in my face, and that was more because it reminded me of the
pleasures of smoking than because I was overcome by the toxic
fumes.

The room they'd given me high up in the tower also smelled of
ancient tobacco smoke. It smelled of mould and misery too. Its
thick masonry was cold like ice, whitewashed and glistening with
condensation. On the wall a plastic crucifix was nailed and on

the bed there were clean sheets; frayed, patched, hard, grey and wrinkled. A small wooden table had one leg wedged with a wad of toilet paper. On the table half a dozen sheets of notepaper and two pencils had been arranged as if inviting a confession. Fixed to the wall above the table there was a shelf holding a dozen paperbacks; Polish best-sellers, some German classics, and ancient and well-read Tauchnitz editions in English: Thomas Hardy and A. E. W. Mason. I suppose Reynolds was hoping to catch me reading one of the books in English, but he never did. It took too long to get the massive lock turned, and I always heard him coming.

There was a water radiator too: it groaned and rattled a lot, but it never became warmer than blood heat, so I kept a blanket around my shoulders. A great deal of my time was spent staring out of the window.

My small inner yard was cobbled, and in the corner by the well lay a bronze statue. The statue had been cut from its pediment by a torch which had melted its lower legs to prong-like petals. Face down, this prone warrior waved a cutlass in one final despairing gesture. I never discovered the identity of this twice-fallen trooper, but he was clearly considered of enough political significance to make his outdoor display a danger to public order. While only a small section of the main yard was exposed to my view, I could see the rear of the officers' mess where half a dozen fidgety horses were unceasingly groomed and exercised. Early each morning, fresh from a canter, they were paraded around the yard, snorting and steamy. Once, late at night, I saw two drunken subalterns exchanging blows out there. Thus the limited view of the yard and the exposed secrets of the officers' mess was like that provided by the cheap fauteuil seats, high up in a theatre balcony, the obstructed view of the stage made up for by the chance to see the backstage activity behind the wings. I saw the padre preparing for Mass in the half-light of early morning. I saw two men plucking countless chickens so that the feathers blew around like smoke, and during meal-times the mess servants would sometimes emerge for a moment to covertly upend a bottle of wine.

The bigger yard was equally active. For most of the daylight hours it was filled with young soldiers who jumped and ran and reached high in the air at the commands of two physical-training instructors. The trainees were dressed in khaki singlets and shorts, and they moved furiously to keep warm in the freezing air. The instructors ran past my line of vision, shadow-boxing as if unable to contain their limitless energy. When in the afternoon the final company of men had completed their physical training, the sun would come out of hiding. Its cruel light showed up the dust and cobwebs on the window glass. It set the forest ablaze and edged the battlements with golden light, leaving the courtyard in cold blue shadow, luminous and shimmering as if it was filled to the brim with clear water.

My room was no less comfortable than those assigned to the junior officers who shared the same landing with me. Often, when I was on my way to the washroom and toilet, or when Reynolds was taking me downstairs to his office, I caught sight of smartly uniformed subalterns. They looked at me with un-disguised curiosity. Later I discovered that a security company used part of the 'citadel' for training courses, and the officers had been selected for politically sensitive duties supervising municipal authorities. For Poland was a land governed by its soldiers.

I was punched and slapped a few times. Never by Reynolds. Never when Reynolds was present. It happened after he became exasperated by my smartass answers. He would puff at his cheroot, sigh and leave the office for ten minutes or so. One or other of the guards would give me a couple of blows as if on his own account. I never discovered if it was done on Reynolds's orders, or even with his knowledge. Reynolds was not vicious. He was not a serious interrogator, which was probably why he'd been assigned to this military backwater. He wasn't expecting me to reveal any secrets that would raise questions in Warsaw, or even raise eyebrows there. Reynolds was content to do his job. He asked me the same questions every day; changing the order and the syntax from time to time but not waiting too long for a reply. Usually the final part of the day's session would consist of Reynolds telling me about his sister Hania and his lazy good-for-nothing brother-in-law, and the wholesale delicatessen business they owned in Detroit.

On Friday afternoon the wind dropped and the trees were unnaturally still. From under low grey cloud the sun's long slanting rays hit the battlements. A sentry stepped forward and stood fully in the light to capture the meagre warmth. Watching him I noticed a flickering in the air. Tiny golden pin-pricks, like motes of dust caught in a cathedral interior. Snowflakes: the winter had returned. As if in celebration, from one of the rooms along the corridor Tauber burst into a scratchy tenor rendering of '*Dein ist mein ganzes Herz*'. He sounded terribly old.

By morning the snow was no longer made of gold. It had spread a white sheet across the land, and my bronze warrior was dusted with it. It didn't stop. By Saturday evening the snow covered everything. I heard the grinding sounds of the trucks that brought sentries back from guard duty at the nearby radar station. They came in low gear, their engines growling and their wheels intermittently spinning on the treacherously smooth section of roadway that was the approach to the main gate. The snow had blown across my yard, to form deep drifts along the wall, and the bronze warrior was entombed in it. I opened the window and put my head out into the stinging cold. The world was unnaturally hushed with that silence that such snow always brings. Then I heard shouting and saw an agitated sentry aiming his gun at me. I pulled my head in and closed the window. Happy to see such a quick response he waved his gun and laughed so that his happiness condensed on the cold air.

On Wednesday night, after five days in custody, a soldier came for me in the middle of the night. I recognized him as one of the PT instructors. He was a wiry fellow with the inscrutable face that seems to go with gymnasts, as if prolonged exercise encourages the contemplative condition. He led me down the back stairs and through a part of the building I'd not seen before. We passed through the muggy kitchens and a succession of storerooms that had once been cellars. Finally he indicated that I should precede him.

As I bent my head under the low doorway, he hit me in the small of the back. He followed that with another punch that found the kidneys and sent a jolt of pain though my body from heel to head. It was like an electric shock and my mind blanked out as I contended with the intense pain. I fell like a tree.

It was dark, but there was another man in the darkness. He came from the shadows and caught me, giving me a couple of hard jabs in the belly that brought my supper up into my mouth. I tucked my head down and tried to cover myself from their blows but they weren't deterred, nor inconvenienced. These two were experts. They worked on me systematically as if I was a side of beef being readied for the stewpot. After a few minutes one of them was taking my whole weight, holding me up to be punched. When he let go of me I crashed to the stone floor only half-conscious. I couldn't think straight. Every part of my body was singing with pain. Under me I could feel coarse matting, and, reaching beyond its edge, smooth pavement. I moved enough to press my face against the cold stone. I vomited and tasted blood in my mouth.

The two men stood over me watching; I could see a glint of light, and their shoes. Then they went away, satisfied no doubt with the job they'd done. I heard their footsteps fade but I didn't try to get up. I pressed my head against a bag of onions. At the bottom of the sack, rotten onions had fermented to become a foul-smelling liquid that oozed through the sacking. I blacked out and then came conscious several times. Despite the stench I remained there full-length for a long time before very very slowly rolling and snaking across the floor, slowly getting my back against the wall and inch by inch sitting up. No bones were broken; no bruises or permanent marks on my face. Theirs was not a spontaneous act of brutality or spite. They had been assigned to hurt me, but not permanently cripple me, and they'd done their job nicely. No hard feelings, chaps, it's all in a day's work for a soldier serving in a land ruled by generals. Lucky me that they hadn't been told to tear me limb from limb, for I'm confident they would have done it with the same inscrutable proficiency. Having decided that, I lost consciousness again.

Someone must have carried me up to the room in the tower. I don't remember anything of it but I certainly didn't get there unassisted. But why, after a week of Mister Nice-guy, suddenly take me out of my bed and beat the daylights out of me without interrogation or promises? There was only one explanation and it slowly became clear to me. Some higher authority had ordered my release. This was Mr Reynolds's tacit way of protesting that decision, and saying farewell to me.

Higher authority was satisfied, I suppose. The generals in Warsaw were not trying to provoke World War Three. They just wanted to show their opposite numbers in London that they didn't like nosy strangers coming into their territory and doing the sort of things I'd done last Christmas at Rastenburg. They didn't want me demonstrating short-take-off-and-landing aircraft after dark, and kidnapping useful Polish spies. They didn't like me torching shiny new government-owned Volvo motor-cars which were in short supply in Poland in 1987. And they didn't like the way I'd shot and wounded Polish security men who, having failed to stop me, had made sure that arrest-and-detain notices were posted throughout the land.

Well, that was my mistake; I should have killed the bastards.

☆

Reynolds put me on the train the next night. He took me to the station in a car, talking all the time about his sister in America and pretending not to notice that his men had almost beaten the life out of me. It was the same Moscow-to-Paris express train, on the same day of the week. They even put me back into a compartment with the same number. My overcoat – which I'd not seen during my incarceration – was folded and stowed on the rack. Pointedly my passport was balanced on the small basket the railway provides for rubbish. Everything was the same, except that Jim and his nurse were not there.

The train compartment was warm. Outside it was snowing again. Wet dollops of it were sliding down the window glass. I slumped on the berth and stretched out. The pain of my beating had not abated and my clothes still had the sickening odour of putrid onions. My bruises and grazes were at that stage of development when the pain is at its most acute. I closed my eyes. I couldn't even raise enough strength to get up and slide the door closed. From the compartment next door I heard the raised voices of a young American couple arguing with a soldier. 'They say it's a political magazine,' said the woman. She had a nice voice, with the sort of musical Boston accent that the Kennedy family made patrician.

'I never saw it before,' said the man. Then he repeated his denial loudly and in German.

There was a moment of silence, then the woman coughed and the man gave a short angry laugh.

I heard my door slide open. I half-opened my eyes and a Polish officer stepped inside to stare down at me. Then the sergeant joined him and the two of them moved on along the corridor. I suppose the American couple had picked up the local traditions without my assistance.

Some extra railway coaches were shunted and coupled to our train with a rattle and a jarring that shook me to the core. Then, after a great deal of whistling and shouted orders, the train clattered forward. I pulled the pillow over my ears.

2

The SIS residence, Berlin

'THAT BLOODY MAN Kohl,' said Frank Harrington, speaking with uncustomary bitterness about the German Federal Republic's Chancellor. 'It's all his doing. Inviting that bastard Honecker to visit the Republic has completely demoralized all decent Germans – on both sides of the Wall.'

I nodded. Frank was probably right, and even if he hadn't been right I would have nodded just as sagely; Frank was my boss. And everywhere I went in Berlin I found despondency about any chance of reforming the East German State, or replacing the stubbornly unyielding *apparatchiki* who ran it. Just a few months before – in September 1987 – Erich Honecker, Chairman of East Germany's Council of State, Chairman of its National Defence Council and omnipotent General Secretary of the Socialist Unity Party, had been invited on a State visit to West Germany. Few Germans – East or West – had believed that such a shameless tyrant could ever be granted such recognition.

'Kohl's a snake in the grass,' said Frank. 'He knows what everyone here thinks about that monster Honecker but he'll do anything to get re-elected.'

Kohl had certainly played his cards with skill. Inviting Honecker to visit the West had been a political bombshell that Kohl's rivals found difficult to handle. The Saarland premier – Oskar Lafontaine – had been misguided enough to pose with the despised Honecker for a newspaper photo. The resulting outcry dealt Lafontaine's Social Democrats a political setback. This, plus some clever equivocations, patriotic declarations and vague promises, revived the seemingly dead Chancellor Kohl and reaffirmed him in power.

Those who still hoped that Honecker's visit to the West would be marked by some reduction of tyranny at home asked him to issue orders to stop his border guards shooting dead anyone who tried to escape from his bleak domain. 'Fireside dreams are far from our minds,' he said. 'We take the existence of two sovereign states on German soil for granted.'

'Kohl and his cronies have taken them all for a ride,' I said. The 'Wessies' viewed Kohl's political manipulation of the Honecker visit with that mixture of bitter contempt and ardent fidelity that Germans have always given to their leaders. On the other side of the Wall the 'Ossies', confined in the joyless DDR, were frustrated and angry. Grouped around TV sets, they had watched Kohl, and other West German politicians, being unctuous and accommodating to their ruthless dictator, and blithely proclaiming that partition was a permanent aspect of Germany's future.

'It aged Strauss ten years, that visit,' said Frank. I could never tell when he was joking; Frank was not noted for his humour but his jokes were apt to be cruel and dark ones. From his powerbase in Munich, Franz Josef Strauss had proclaimed something he'd said many times before: 'The German Reich of 1945 has legally never been abolished; the German question remains open.' It was not what Honecker wanted to hear. He might have won Kohl over, but Strauss remained Honecker's most effective long-term critic.

We were downstairs in Frank's house in Grunewald, the home that came with the post of Head of Station in Berlin. It was late afternoon, and the dull cloudy sky did little to make the large drawing-room less sombre. Yellow patches of light from electric table-lamps fell upon a ferocious carpet of bright red and green flowers. A Bechstein grand piano glinted in one corner. Upon its polished top, rank upon rank of family photos paraded in expensive frames. Playing centre-forward for this team stood a silver-framed photo of Frank's son, a one-time airline pilot who had found a second career as a publisher of technical aviation books. Behind the serried relatives there was a cut-glass vase of long-stem roses imported from some foreign climate to help forget that Berlin's gardens were buried deep under dirt-encrusted snow. All around the room there were Victorian paintings of a sooty and hazy London: Primrose Hill, the Crystal Palace and Westminster Abbey all in heavy gilt frames and disappearing behind cracked and darkening coach varnish. Arranged around a polished mahogany coffee table there were two big uncomfortable sofas in blue damask, and three wing armchairs with matching upholstery. One of these Frank kept positioned exactly facing the massive speakers of his elaborate hi-fi system, its working parts concealed inside a birchwood Biedermeier tallboy that had been disembowelled to accommodate it. Sometimes Frank felt bound to explain that the tallboy had been badly damaged before suffering this terminal surgery.

Frank was relaxed in his lumpy chair. Thin elegant legs crossed, a drink at his elbow and a chewed old Dunhill pipe in his mouth. From time to time he disappeared from view behind a sombre haze, not unlike the coach varnish that obscured the views of London, except for its pungent smell. After a period of denial, which had caused him – and indeed everyone who worked with him – mental and physical stress, he'd now surrendered to his nicotine addiction with vigour and delight.

'I read the report,' said Frank, removing the pipe from his mouth and prodding into its bowl with the blade of a Swiss army pen-knife. Seen like this, in his natural habitat, Frank Harrington was the model Englishman. Educated but not intellectual, a drinker who was never drunk, his hair greying and his bony face lined without him looking aged, his impeccably tailored pinstripe suit not new, and everything worn with a hint of neglect: the appearance and manner which knowing foreigners so often admire and rash ones imitate.

☆

I sipped my whisky and waited. I had been summoned to this meeting in Frank's home by means of a handwritten memo left on my desk by Frank in person. Only he would have fastened it to my morning *Berliner* doughnut by means of a push-pin. Such formal orders were infrequent, and I knew I'd not been brought here to hear Frank's views on the more Byzantine stratagems of Germany's political adventurers. I wondered what was really in his mind. So far there had been little official reaction to my delayed return to Berlin, and the detention in Poland that caused it. When I arrived I reported to Frank and told him I'd been arrested and released without charges. He was on the phone when I went into his office. He capped the phone, mumbled something about my preparing a report for London, and waved me absent. I resumed my duties as his deputy, as if I'd not been away. The written report I had submitted was brief and formal, with an underlying inference that it was a matter of mistaken identity.

I was sitting on one of the sofas in an attempt to keep my distance from the polluting product of Frank's combustion. Before me there was a silver tray with a crystal ice bucket, tongs, and a cut-glass tumbler into which a double measure of Laphroaig whisky had been precisely measured by Tarrant. He'd put the whisky bottle away again, but left on the table a bottle of Apollinaris water from which I was helping myself. Shell-shaped silver dishes contained calculated amounts of salted nuts and potato chips and there was a large silver box that I knew contained a selection of cigarettes: Tarrant, Frank's butler, had arranged a similar array on Frank's side of the coffee table. Apart from Frank's expensive hi-fi, Tarrant had ensured that the household and its routines were not modified by advances in science or fashion. As far as I could see, Frank did the same thing for the Department.

On an inlaid tripod table, booklets and files were arranged in fans, like periodicals in a dentist's waiting-room. From the table Frank took the West German passport I'd been using when detained in Poland. He flipped its pages distastefully and looked from the identity photo to me and then at the photo again. 'This photograph,' he said finally. 'Is it really you?'

'It was all done in a bit of a hurry,' I explained.

'Going across there with a smudgy picture of someone else in your passport is a damned stupid way of doing things. Why not an authentic picture?'

'An identity picture is like ethnic food,' I said. 'The less authentic it is the better.'

'Can you elaborate on that a little?' said Frank, playing the innocent.

'Because the UB photocopy, and file away, every passport that goes through their hands,' I said.

'Ahhh,' said Frank, sounding unconvinced. He slid the passport across the table to me. It was a sign that he wasn't going to take the matter any further. I picked it up and put it in my pocket.

'Don't use it again,' said Frank. 'Put it away with your Beatles records and that Nehru jacket.'

'I won't use it again, Frank,' I said. I'd never worn a Nehru jacket or anything styled remotely like one, but I would always remain the teenager he'd once known. There was no way of escaping that.

'You are senior staff now. The time for all those shenanigans is over.' He picked up my report and shook it as if something might fall from the pages. 'London will read this. There is no way I can sit on it for ever.'

I nodded.

'And you know what they will say?'

I waited for him to say that London would suspect that I'd gone to Moscow only in order to see Gloria. But he said: 'You were browbeating Jim Prettyman. That's what they will say. What did you get out of him? You may as well tell me, so that I can cover my arse.'

'Jim Prettyman?'

'Don't do that, Bernard,' said Frank with just a touch of aggravation.

If it was a chess move, it was an accomplished one. To avoid the accusation that I was grilling Prettyman I would have to say that I was there to see Gloria. 'Prettyman was more or less unconscious. There was little chance of my doing anything beyond tucking him into bed and changing his bedpans, and there was a nurse to do that. What would I be grilling Prettyman about, anyway?'

'Come along, Bernard. Have you forgotten all those times you told me that Prettyman was the man behind those who wanted your sister-in-law killed?'

'I said that? When did I say it?'

'Not in as many words,' said Frank, retreating a fraction. 'But that was the gist of it. You thought London had plotted the death of Fiona's sister so that her body could be left over there. Planted so that our KGB friends would be reassured that Fiona was dead, and not telling us all their secrets.'

Fortified by the way Frank had put my suspicions of London in the past tense, I put down my drink and stared at him impassively. I suppose I must have done a good job on the facial expression, for Frank shifted uncomfortably and said: 'You're not going to deny it now, are you, Bernard?'

'I certainly am,' I said, without adding any further explanation.

'If you are leading me up the garden path, I'll have your guts for garters.' Frank's vocabulary was liberally provided with schoolboy expressions of the nineteen thirties.

'I'm trying to put all that behind me,' I said. 'It was getting me down.'

'That's good,' said Frank who, along with the Director-General and his Deputy, Bret Rensselaer, had frequently advised me to put it all behind me. 'Some field agents are able to do their job and combine it with a more or less normal family life. It's not easy, but some do it.'

I nodded and wondered what was coming. I could see Frank was in one of his philosophical moods and they usually ended up with a softly delivered critical summary that helped me sort it all out.

'You are one of the best field agents we ever had working out of this office,' said Frank, sugaring the pill. 'But perhaps that's because you live the job night and day, three hundred and sixty-five days a year.'

'Do I, Frank? It's nice of you to say that.'

He could hear the irony in my voice but he ignored it. 'You never tell anyone the whole truth, Bernard. No one. Every thought is locked up in that brain of yours and marked secret. I'm locked out; your colleagues are locked out. I suppose it's the same with your wife and children; I suppose you tell them only what they should know.'

'Sometimes not even that,' I said.

'I saw Fiona the day before yesterday. She annihilated some poor befuddled Ministry fogey, she made the chairman apologize for inaccurate minutes of the previous meeting and, using the ensuing awkward silence, carried the vote for some training project they were trying to kill. She's dynamite, that wife of yours. They are all frightened of her; the FO people I mean.'

'Yes, I know.'

'It takes quite a lot to scare them. And she thrives on it. These days she's looking like some glamorous young model. Really wonderful!'

'Yes,' I said. I would always have to defer to Frank in the matter of glamorous young models.

'She said the children were doing very well at school. She showed me photos of them. They are very attractive children, Bernard. You must be very proud of your family.'

'Yes, I am,' I said.

'And she loves you,' he added as an afterthought. 'So why keep stirring up trouble for yourself?' Frank gave one of those winning smiles that half the women in Berlin had fallen prey to. 'You see, Bernard, I suspect you planned the whole thing – your train ride from Moscow with Prettyman. I think you made sure that there would be no one else available from here to do it.'

'How would I have made sure?'

'Have you forgotten the assignments you arranged in the days before you went away?' As he said this he toyed with his pipe and kept his voice distant and detached.

'I didn't arrange their assignments. I don't know those people. I did as Operations suggested.'

'You signed.' Now he looked up and was staring at me quizzically.

'Yes, I signed,' I agreed wearily. His mind was made up, at least for the time being. My best course was to let him think about it all. He would see reason eventually; he always did. No reasonable person could believe that I'd carefully plotted and planned a way to get Prettyman alone in order to grill him about Tessa's death. But if Frank suspected it, you could bet that London believed it implicitly; for that's where all this crap had undoubtedly originated. And, in this context, 'London' meant Fiona and Dicky. Or at least it included them.

'Did you try one of those fried potato things?' he said, pointing to one of the silver dishes. 'They are flavoured with onion.'

'Curry,' I said. 'They are curry-flavoured. Too hot for me.'

'Are they? I don't know what's happening to Tarrant lately. He knows how I hate curry. I wonder how they put all these different flavours into them. In my day things just tasted of what they were,' he said regretfully.

I got to my feet. When the conversation took this culinary turn

31

I guessed Frank had said everything of importance to him. He rested his pipe in a heavy glass ashtray and pushed it aside with a sigh. It made me wonder if he smoked to provide some sort of activity when we had these get-togethers. For the first time it occurred to me that Frank might have dreaded these exchanges as much as I did; or even more.

'You were late again this morning,' he said with a smile.

'Yes, but I brought a note from Mummy.'

Surely he must have known that I was going to the Clinic every morning; they'd found two hairline cracks in my ribs, and were dosing me with brightly coloured pain-killing pills, and taking dozens of X-rays. I shouldn't be drinking alcohol really, but I couldn't face a lecture from Frank without a drink in my hand.

'Stop by for a drink tonight,' he said. 'About nine. I'm having some people in . . . Unless you have something arranged already.'

'I said I'd see Werner.'

'We'll make it another night,' said Frank.

'Yes,' I said. I wondered if he'd taste one of the 'potato things' and find they were onion after all. I don't know what made me tell him they tasted of curry, except in some vague hope that the hateful Tarrant would be blamed. Perhaps I shouldn't have mixed alcohol and pain-killers.

☆

By the time my official confirmation as Frank's deputy came through I was settled into my comfortable office and making good use of my assistant and my secretary, as well as a personally assigned Rover saloon car and driver. I'd often remarked that Frank had kept the Berlin establishment absurdly high, but now I was reaping some of the rewards of his artful manipulations.

Frank, having resisted appointing a deputy for well over two years, made the most of my presence. He attended conferences, symposiums, lectures and meetings of a kind that in the old days he'd always avoided. He even went to one of those awful gatherings in Washington DC to watch his American colleagues in CIA Operations trying to look cheerful despite the seemingly unending intelligence leaks coming from the top of the CIA tree.

Although in theory Frank's frequent absences made me the de facto chief in Berlin, I knew that his super-efficient secretary Lydia never missed a day without reporting to him at length, even when this meant phoning him in the middle of the night. So I never emerged from Frank's shadow, which was perhaps something of an advantage.

My new-found authority granted me the chance to put my old friend Werner Volkmann on a regular contract. Werner was always saying he needed money, although the fees we paid him wouldn't go very far to meeting Werner's lifestyle. His business – arranging advance bank payments for East German exports – was drying up. Things were becoming more and more difficult for him because the bankers were frightened that the DDR might be about to default on its debts to the West. But being on Departmental contract seemed to do something for his self-esteem. Werner loved what I once heard him call the 'mystique of espionage'. Whatever that was, he felt himself a part of it and I was happy for him.

'Having you here in Berlin, on permanent assignment, is like old times,' Werner said. 'Whose idea was it?'

'Dicky sent me here to spy on Frank.' I said it just to crank him up. We were sitting in Babylon, a dingy subterranean 'club'. It was owned by an amusing and enigmatic villain named Rudi Klein-dorf, who claimed to come from a family of Prussian aristocrats, and was jokingly referred to as *der grosse Kleine*. We were sitting at a hideous little gilt table, under a tasselled light fitting. We had been invited for a drink and a chance to see how everything was coming along. Our inspection had been quickly completed and now we were having that drink.

The club wasn't functioning yet; it was still in the process of being redecorated. The workmen had departed but there were ladders and pots of paint on the stage, and on the bar top too.

There had been stories that it was to be renamed 'Alphonse', but the Potsdamerstrasse was not the right location for a club named Alphonse. Whatever name it was given, and whatever the colour of the paint, and the quality of the new curtains for the stage, and even some new, slimmer and younger girls, it would never be a place that tourists, or Berlin's *Hautevolee*, would want to frequent, except on a drunken excursion to see how the lower half lives. I wondered if Werner had been enticed to put some money into Rudi Kleindorf's enterprise. It was the sort of thing Werner did; he could be romantically nostalgic about dumps we'd frequented when we were young.

Werner reached for the bottle on the table between us and poured another drink for me. He smiled in that strange way that he did when figuring the hidden motives and devious ways of men and women. His head slightly tilted back, his eyes were almost closed and his lips pressed together. It was easy to see why he was sometimes mistaken for one of the Turkish *Gastarbeiter* who formed a large percentage of the city's population. It was not only Werner's swarthy complexion, coarse black hair, large square-ended black moustache and the muscular build of a wrestler. He had a certain oriental demeanour. Byzantine described him exactly; except that they were Greeks.

'And Frank?' said Werner. There was nothing more he need say. Dicky was youthful, curly-haired, energetic, ambitious and devious; while Frank was bloodless, tired and lazy. But in any sort of struggle between them, the smart money was on Frank. Frank had spent a great deal of his long career being splashed in the blood and snot of Berlin, while Dicky was concentrating upon crocodile-covered Filofax notebooks and Mont Blanc fountain-pens. Werner and I both knew a side of Frank that Dicky had never seen. Never mind all that avuncular charm, we'd seen the cold-blooded way in which Frank could make life-and-death decisions that would have consigned 'don't-know Dicky' to a psychiatrist's couch in a darkened room.

34

'What's Dicky frightened of?'

'Nothing,' I said. 'I can truthfully say he's frightened of nothing except perhaps an audit of his expense accounts.' There were voices from behind the tiny stage and then a man came out and played a few bars on the piano. I recognized it as an old Gus Kahn tune: 'Dream a little dream of me'.

'So it was Frank's idea?' Werner asked. Werner was an impressive piano player; I could see he was listening to the music with a critical ear.

'It wasn't anyone's idea. Not the way you mean. The job was vacant; I came.'

Werner said: 'Frank has managed without a deputy for ages. Don't you need to be in London ... somewhere near Fiona and the kids? How are they doing?'

'They are still with Fiona's parents. Private school with extra tutoring as needed, a pony for Sally and a mountain bicycle for Billy, evenings with Grandpa and plenty of fresh fruit and vegetables.'

'What are you going to do?'

'Do? I can't snatch them away from the bastard without providing something better, can I?' I said, curbing my anger and frustration. The piano player suddenly ended his experimental tunes, stood up and shouted that the piano was no good at all. A disembodied voice shouted that there was no money to get another. The piano player shrugged, looked at us, shrugged again and then sat down and tried Gershwin.

'Couldn't they live in London with Fiona?' said Werner.

'It's an apartment – not fifteen acres of rolling countryside ... and Fiona works every hour God Almighty sends. How would we arrange things? I'd have them here if I could think of some feasible way of doing it.' I looked down at my hands; I had clasped one fist so tight that a fingernail had cut my palm, and drawn blood.

Werner watched me and tried to cheer me up: 'Well, you don't have to be in Berlin for ever and I'm sure there's plenty to do here.'

'Enough. A Deputy Head of Station is on the establishment. I suppose Frank was afraid that if the position remained unfilled too long it would be abolished. Anyway it gives Frank a chance to disappear whenever he likes.'

'But it ties you down.'

'The theory is: I get one long weekend in London a month.'

'You'll have to fight for it,' said Werner.

'That's why I'm going this weekend,' I said.

Perhaps he was right to be sceptical. I could see that events were unlikely to make it possible for me to go across to London so regularly. With Frank's frequent wanderings, I would be snatching a day or two as and when opportunities came along. 'This weekend I go,' I promised him again, and in doing so promised myself too. 'I'm booked on the plane; I'm seeing the children. And if World War Three starts at Checkpoint Charlie, Frank will have to handle the opening moves all by himself.'

'You don't think London might have put you on the shelf? Put you here so you don't get access to mainstream material?'

'I handle everything going through here. You need top clearance for that.'

'Except the secrets that Frank handles and keeps close to his chest.'

'Not Frank,' I said, but of course Werner was right. I'd not seen any of the signals about Prettyman, and the questions about moving him, and the complications that arose from his US passport, until I got to Moscow. Who knows if there were other signals expressing interest in my past friendship with Prettyman, or my sometimes indiscreetly voiced suspicions of his role in Tessa's death.

'Frank invited me for happy-hour and then read the Riot Act to me. It must have been prompted by London.'

Werner gave me a told-you-so stare.

36

'Is London sniffing at me? Why me? Why now?'

'Because you keep on about Tessa, that's why. London have sidelined you.'

'No,' I said.

'And this is just the beginning. They'll get rid of you completely. Firing you in Berlin makes sure you can't kick up the sort of fuss you'd be able to do if you were made redundant while working in London Central.'

'Well I'm not going to just forget about Tessa.'

'You said you had forgotten about it.'

'When?'

'You just told me.'

'Don't shout Werner, I'm not deaf.'

Slowly and with exaggerated pedantry Werner said: 'You told Frank you were trying to put the Tessa death behind you. You said the whole business was getting you down. You told me that, Bernie, not half an hour ago.'

'Yes,' I said. 'But I didn't mean I was going to forget about it.'

'What did you mean, Bernie?'

'I mean I will put aside all my previous suspicions and ideas. I will start afresh. I'm going to look into Tessa's death as if I'd come to it for the first time. I'm convinced that Bret Rensselaer is behind it all.'

'Now it's Bret. Why Bret? Bret was in California, wasn't he?'

'If I could get Bret in the right mood, I could get him to spill the beans. He's not like the others.'

'But what would Bret know?'

'Bret had access to a big slice of the Department's dough. It looked as if he'd embezzled it and some idiot tried to arrest him, remember?'

'And you saved him. You saved Bret that time. I hope he remembers that episode when he came running to you in Berlin.'

'He's not likely to forget it. That shooting at the station changed Bret. They thought he would die. His hair went white and he was never the same again.'

'But Bret didn't steal any Departmental money?'

'Bret was up front in a secret Departmental scheme to siphon money away. By koshering a few millions aside they covertly financed Fiona's operations in the East.'

'You told me.'

'But Prettyman was on that committee too. He put some money into his own pocket. They sent me to Washington DC to bring Prettyman back but he wasn't having any.'

'That can't be true, Bernie. Prettyman is a blue-eyed boy nowadays.'

'He did a deal with them. I'd like to know what the deal was; but they bury these things deep. That's why I would like to get Bret talking. Bret was on the committee with Prettyman. Bret was the one who planned Fiona's defection. Bret would know everything that happened.'

'My God, Bernie. You never give up, do you?'

'Not without trying,' I said.

'Give up this one now. The people in London are not going to sit still while you light a fire under them.'

'If no one there is guilty they have nothing to worry about.'

'You sound very smug. If no one there is guilty, they will be even more furious, more angry, more vindictive to find that an employee is trying to hang a murder charge on them.'

'If you are right, Werner. If you are right that they have sent me here as the first step in a plan to get rid of me, I have nothing to lose, do I?'

'If you'd drop it, they might drop it too.'

'Yes,' I said. 'And everything in the garden would be lovely. But I'm going to find out who gave the orders to kill Tessa, and I'm going to find the one who gave the order to pull the trigger that night. I'll face them with proof: depositions and any other kind of evidence I unearth. And well before they pull the carpet from under me, I'm going to have them dancing to the tune I play on my penny whistle.'

'You are just angry. You are just angry that Dicky got the job you should have had. You are just inventing the cause for a vendetta.'

'Am I? Well let me tell you this, Werner. There was a Canadian nurse on that train with Prettyman. She might have been holding hands with him. She has spent many happy evenings in Washington; or so she told me.'

'Prettyman was always like that.'

'She was wearing a brooch that belonged to Tessa.'

'She was what?' He gulped on his drink.

'Oh, I'm glad you still retain the capacity to be surprised, Werner. I was beginning to think there was nothing you wouldn't nod through. Yes, one of Tessa's favourite brooches: a big sapphire set in yellow gold and silver and studded with matched diamonds.'

'How can you be sure that it's not just a brooch that looks like the one Tessa had?'

'It's antique; not a modern reproduction. The chances of finding another one exactly like that are pretty slim. It was Tessa's brooch, Werner. And the nurse told me it was a gift from Mr James Prettyman. Oh, yes, and from Mrs Prettyman too. But nursie seemed to think it was just junk jewellery. Is that what they all thought?'

'Did you ask Prettyman about it?'

'Unfortunately no. I was lifted off the train before I got a chance to beat an answer out of him.'

'Shall I chase it? Where is the nurse now?'

'I've no idea; home with her family in good old Winnipeg, I suppose. Let her be, Werner. She knows nothing. It might pay off better if I surprise Prettyman with the questions.'

Werner looked unhappy. 'Please, Bernie. You are going over the top. I know it's all going to end in disaster. What will you do if they fire you? I'll do anything you want, but please drop this one.'

'You and Frank treat me like I've just got back from a drunken party to report a flying saucer. I'm not going to drop it until I'm satisfied.' I gulped the rest of my drink, then got to my feet and looked around the room again. Werner was determined to play baby-sitter for me, and I wasn't in the mood to be babied. I got enough of that from Frank all week.

'Then don't talk to me about it,' said Werner. 'That's all I ask.'

He didn't say it quickly and angrily; he said it slowly and sadly. I didn't give any attention to that fact at the time. Perhaps I should have done.

☆

'This smell of paint is terrible,' I said. 'When is this bloody idiot supposed to be opening this dump?' I noticed with sadness that the old mural had disappeared under a couple of litres of white paint. It had been an imaginative array of hanging gardens, the great ziggurat and naked women dancing through palm trees, done by a drunken artist who had never travelled beyond the Botanical Gardens in Steglitz. I wondered what would replace it.

'Next Tuesday the builders said, but now they are wavering. The carpenters haven't finished and the painters have hardly started. They will have to finish and clear up completely before anyone can start polishing the floor. It will all take quite a time. Rudi is looking for somewhere else to hold his opening party. Somewhere bigger. Maybe a hotel.'

'I can't just walk away and forget about Tessa,' I said. 'I just can't.'

Werner was closely studying some tiny spots of paint that had been splashed on the table-lamp.

By the time I left, the pianist was playing a Bach partita in a minor key. It wouldn't be easy to dance to.

3

The North Downs, Surrey, England

WHEN SOMEONE ASKS you to make an objective decision that will affect their future, you can confidently assume that they have already decided upon the course they intend to follow. So when my father-in-law phoned to be sure that I would be with Fiona when she visited the children at the weekend, I sensed that there was something else on his mind and I wasn't expecting to hear anything comforting.

But those vague forebodings had faded a little by the time I was with Fiona in her shiny new Jaguar. It was one of the perquisites of her new post. The Department frowned upon senior staff using foreign cars, and a Porsche like the one she'd previously owned would have earned a quiet rebuke.

Fiona was at her magnificent best. She liked driving. Her dark hair was shiny and loose and wavy, and she had let it grow, so that it almost touched her shoulders, and swung wide to frame her face as she turned to smile at me. Her relaxed grin, natural skin texture and rosy cheeks reminded me of the young girl with whom I'd fallen so desperately in love. There was nothing to reveal her long ordeal in East Germany or the demanding workload that she now took upon herself without respite.

Escaping from London's seemingly interminable squalor, and its brooding suburbs, is not easy. The beguiling villages that once surrounded the capital had become small plastic versions of Times

Square. Even the snow could not completely conceal their ugliness. But finally we reached some stretches of open countryside, and eventually the lovely old house where Mr and Mrs David Kimber-Hutchinson made a home for my children. Set in a particularly attractive part of southern England, the house was secluded. There were trees on every side: pines and firs mostly, evergreens that ensured that the scene changed little in winter or summer. The house was Jacobean but successive wealthy owners, and acclaimed architects, had done everything possible to obliterate the original structure. Since my last visit David had squeezed permission from the local bureaucrats to further deform the property with a six-car garage. The new building had a lacquered-brass weather-vane on its red plastic roof, and automatic doors at both ends, so that he could drive right through rather than face the hazards and inconvenience of backing out.

Fiona turned off the road and drove through the entrance where wrought-iron gates entwined the monogram of my in-laws. 'What a horror,' she said as she caught sight of the new garage. Perhaps she'd said it to forestall any rude reaction that might have been my first response. The concertina doors were pushed back far enough to reveal her father's silver Rolls, and the black Range Rover that was her mother's current car. Her mother got through a lot of cars because each time she dented one she 'lost confidence in it'. This latest one had been chosen by David and, on his specific instructions, fitted with massive steel crash bars at front and rear. As if in tacit warning to other road users, it was painted with a livery of formalized flame patterns along its side.

Fiona gave a toot on the horn and parked outside, alongside a battered little Citroën with Paris licence plates and a 'Teachers against the Bomb' bumper sticker. We got out and went into the garage, which was wide enough to take half a dozen Rolls-Royces and still have room for workbench, sinks, neatly coiled hoses and an air compressor. I inspected David's latest pride and joy, a 3-litre Bentley open tourer, one of those shiny green icons of the nineteen twenties. Vintage cars had become his passion since a series of bad falls, and a bitter dispute with the master of foxhounds, had stopped him chasing foxes.

Her father was standing at the workbench when we arrived. He waved her forward, using both hands upraised as if marshalling a Boeing into its slot. He was wearing dark blue coveralls of the sort that garage mechanics favour, but peeping from the collar there was a yellow cashmere rollneck.

'You made good time, darling,' he announced approvingly as Fiona scrambled from the driving seat and kissed him.

'We were lucky with the traffic,' said Fiona.

'And Bernard . . . what have you done to your face, Bernard?' He was sharp, I must say that for him. My face was only slightly swollen and had drawn little reaction from others.

'I walked into a bird-cage.'

'Bernard, you . . .'

Fiona interrupted whatever her father was about to say: 'Bernard fell down the stairs . . . in Berlin. He cracked a rib. He's not fully recovered.'

Fiona knew where I'd got the bruises of course. We'd not spoken of it but she must have read my brief report about the Polish fiasco and guessed the bits I left out.

'Watch yourself, Bernard,' said her father, looking from one to the other of us as if suspecting that the whole truth was being withheld. 'You're not a youngster any more.' And then, more cheerfully: 'I saw you looking at the Bentley. She's one hundred per cent authentic; not a replica or made up from new parts.'

'It's cold, Daddy. Let's go inside the house.'

'Yes, of course. I'll show you later, Bernard. You can sit in her if you want.' He led the way through a doorway that had been cut through a side wall of the original house to gain direct entrance from the garage.

'That frost last night,' he said as he opened the door into his carpeted drawing-room. 'I think it may have killed the eucalyptus trees. I'll be shattered if they go – after all the love and labour and money I've spent on them.'

'Where's Mummy?'

'I have a tree expert coming this afternoon. They say he's the man Prince Charles uses.'

'Where's Mummy?'

'She's resting. She gets up in the small hours and does all that yoga malarkey. Huh! And then she wonders why she gets tired.'

'She says it's doing her good,' said Fiona.

'Six o'clock is far too early. She runs the bath and that wakes me up,' said David, 'and then I sometimes have trouble getting off to sleep again.' He slapped his hands together. 'Now for elevenses, or would you prefer a real drink?'

'It's too early for me,' said Fiona, 'but I'm sure you can persuade Bernard to join you.'

'No,' I said. It was a culture trap. England's holy ritual, of halting everything to sit down and drink sweet milky tea at eleven o'clock in the morning, would be marred by a dissenter guzzling booze, or even coffee.

'I'll order tea then,' said David, picking up a phone and pressing a button to connect him to one of his many servants. 'Who's that?' he asked, and having elicited the name of a servant he instructed: 'Tell cook: morning tea for three in the Persian room. My usual – toasted scones and all that. And take tea to Mrs Hutchinson: Earl Grey, no milk, no sugar. Ask her if she's going to join us for lunch.'

☆

'How lovely to be home again,' said Fiona. I know she only said it to appease her father, but it made me feel as if I'd never provided a proper home for her.

'And you are not looking too well,' her father told Fiona. Then realizing that such remarks can be interpreted as criticism added:

'It's that damned job of yours. Do you know what you could be earning in the City?'

'I thought they were firing people by the hundred after the crash last year,' she said.

'I know people,' said David, nodding significantly. 'If you wanted a job in the City you'd be snapped up.' He leaned towards her. 'You should come to the health farm with us tomorrow. Five days of rest and exercise and light meals. It would make a new woman of you. And you would meet some very interesting people.'

'I have too much urgent work to do,' said Fiona.

'Bring it with you; that's what I do. I take a stack of work, and my tiny recording machine, and do it away from all the noise and commotion.'

'I have a meeting in Rome.'

He shook his head. 'The life you people lead. And who pays for it? The poor old taxpayer. Very well then, it's your life.'

'The children are still studying?' Fiona asked him.

It was not just her way of changing the subject. She wanted me to hear the wonderful things her parents were doing for our children. On cue, her father described the highly paid tutors who came to the house to give my children additional lessons in mathematics and French grammar, so that they would do well in their exams, and be able to go to the sort of school that David went to.

When the tea-tray came, everything was placed on the table before Fiona. While she was pouring the tea David divested himself of his coveralls to reveal a canary-coloured cashmere sweater, beige corduroy trousers and tasselled loafers. He spread himself across a chintz-covered sofa and said: 'Well, what have you done with poor little Kosinski?'

Since David was looking at me as he said it, I replied: 'I haven't seen him for ages.'

'Come along! Come along!' said David briskly. 'You've locked him up somewhere and you're giving him the third degree.'

'Daddy. Please,' said Fiona mildly while pouring my tea.

Pleased that his provocation had produced the expected note of exasperation from his daughter, he chuckled and said: 'What are you squeezing out of the little bugger, huh? You can confide in me; I'm vetted.'

He wasn't vetted, or in any way secure, and he was the last man I would entrust with a secret of any importance. So I smiled at him and told Fiona that I wanted just one sugar in my tea and yes, a toasted scone – no, no home-made strawberry jam – would be lovely and promised that it wouldn't spoil my appetite for lunch.

'I flew to Warsaw to see him,' said David, flapping a monogrammed linen napkin and spreading it on his knee. 'Just before Christmas; at five minutes' notice. No end of bother getting a seat on the plane.'

'Did you?' I said, inserting a note of mild surprise in my answer, although I had been shown a surveillance photo of him and Kosinski there at that time.

'He told me that Tessa was still alive.'

I watched Fiona's reaction to this startling announcement; she just shook her head in denial and drank some tea.

'It was a ruse,' I explained. 'He probably believed it but it was just a cruel attempt to exploit him.'

'And exploit me,' added David. He accepted a buttered scone from Fiona and nibbled at it as he thought about his visit to his son-in-law.

. 'Yes, and to exploit you,' I agreed, although it was hard to imagine how even the wily tricksters of the Polish security service would find ingenuity enough for that. 'Now he is working for us. I don't know any more than that.'

'Don't know or won't tell?'

Fiona got to her feet, looked at the ceiling as she listened, and said: 'I believe the French lesson is ending.'

'Yes,' agreed David, after punching the air in order to expose his gold wrist-watch to view and see the time. 'She doesn't give us a minute of extra time. The French are all like that, aren't they?'

Reluctant to censure French venality in such general terms, Fiona said: 'I'll just go and say hello to her, and ask her how they are coming along.' Clever Fiona; she knew how to escape. It must have been something she learned while working with the KGB. Or with Dicky Cruyer.

'Fifteen pounds an hour she costs me,' David confided to me. 'And she has the nerve to add on travelling expenses from London. The trouble is I can't get anyone from the village. You need the authentic *seizième arrondissement* accent, don't you, huh?'

I drank my tea until, from somewhere upstairs, I heard Fiona trying out her Paris slang on the lady teacher. She hit the spot judging from the sudden burst of hearty feminine laughter that followed the next exchange.

I faced David and ate my scone, smiling between bites. We both sat there for a long time, silent and alone, like a washed-out picnic party, under dripping trees, waiting for the thunder to stop.

Having finished my scone before my host I got up and went to the window. David came and stood alongside me. We watched Fiona tramping across the snowy garden. The teacher was with her, and hand-in-hand with the children they inspected the snowman. The snow had retreated to make icy-edged white islands into which the children deliberately walked. Billy – coming up to his fourteenth birthday – considered himself far too old to be building snowmen. He had supervised the building of this one on the pretext that it was done solely to entertain some local infants who had been at the house for a tea party the previous afternoon. But I could tell from the way they were acting that both Billy and his younger sister Sally were proud of their elaborate snow sculpture. It wouldn't last much longer. A slight thaw had crippled it so that it had become a hunch-backed figure, glazed with the icy sheen that had formed upon it overnight.

'Everybody respects her,' said David.

'Yes,' I said. It was true that everyone respected Fiona, but how significant it was that her father should claim that. Even her mother and father didn't really love her. Their love, such as could be spared, had been lavished on Tessa, the younger sister, the eternal baby. Fiona had too much dignity, too much achievement, too much of everything to need love in the way that most people need it.

My memory went back to the day that I first met Fiona's parents, and to the briefing she provided for me as we drove down here to see them in my old Ferrari. It was my final outing in that lovely old lady. The car was already sold, the deal settled, and the first instalment of the money deposited in my bank. The money was needed to buy Fiona an engagement ring with a diamond of a dimension that her family would judge visible to the naked eye. Tell them you love me, she had advised. It's what they will be waiting to hear. They think I need someone to love me. I told them that. I would have told them anyway. I did love and never stopped loving her.

'You love her,' said David, as if needing to hear me say it again. 'You do: I know you do.'

'Of course I do,' I said. 'I love her very much.'

'She bottles everything up inside,' he said. 'I wish I knew what went on inside her head.'

'Yes,' I said. Many people would have liked to know what went on inside Fiona's head, including me. From what I knew, even the KGB agent – Kennedy – who had been assigned to seduce her, and monitor her thoughts, had failed. He'd fallen for her instead. The wounding fact was that Fiona had taken that sordid little adventure seriously. She'd fooled him of course. She hadn't betrayed her role as a double-agent working for London because Fiona was Fiona – a woman who would no more reveal her innermost thoughts to her lover than she would to her father, her children or her husband.

I watched her with my children; this woman who had bowled me over and from whom I would never escape, this remote paragon, dedicated scholar and unfailing winner of every contest she entered. She might even emerge as the victor in the bitter contest for power in the Department. I suppose my feeling for her was founded upon respect as well as love. Too much respect and not enough love perhaps, for otherwise Gloria would never have turned my life upside down. Gloria was no fool but she was not wise; she was sizzling and street-smart and perceptive and desperately in love with me. I was torn in half: I found myself in love with two women. They were entirely different women but few people would find that an adequate explanation. I told myself it was wrong but it didn't make the dilemma less excruciating.

'That cloud base: it never gets really light these days,' said David, turning away from the window and sitting down. 'I hate winter. I wanted to get away to somewhere warm but there are things here that I must do myself. You can't trust anyone to do their job properly.'

I chose a chair and sat down opposite him. It was a lovely room, the sort of comfortable family retreat that is only found in England and its country houses. So far this room had escaped the 'face-lifts' that David had inflicted on so much of the house. The furniture was a hodgepodge of styles; a mixture of the priceless and the worthless. The Dutch marquetry cabinet, and the collection of Lalique glass displayed inside it, would have fetched a fortune at auction. Next to it there were two battered sofas that had only sentimental value. A lovely William and Mary marquetry mirror reflected an ancient stained and frayed oriental carpet. The log fire made crackling sounds and spat a few sparks over the brass fire-irons. The yellow light of the flames made patterns on the ceiling and lit up David's face. 'He tried to murder me, you know,' he said, and turned to look out of the window as if his mind was entirely given to his family in the garden. 'George,' he added eventually.

'George?' I didn't know what to say. Finally I stammered: 'Why would he do that? He's family.'

David looked at me as if declining to respond to a particularly offensive joke. 'It makes me wonder what really happened to Tessa.' He went and stood by the window, his hands on his hips.

'George didn't kill your daughter, David. If that's what you are driving at.'

'Then why try to poison me?'

Again I was speechless for a moment. 'Why do you think?' I countered.

'Always the police detective, aren't you, Bernard?' He said it with a good-natured grunt, but I knew he had long since categorized me as a government snooper. He said society was rife with prying petty officials who were taking over our lives. Sometimes I wondered if he wasn't right. Not about me, but about the others.

I made a reckless guess: 'Because you suspected him? Because you accused him of being a party to his wife's death?'

'Very good, Bernard.' He said it gravely but with discernible admiration. 'You're very close. Go to the top of the class.'

'And how did George react?'

'React?' A short sharp bitter laugh. 'I just told you; he tried to kill me.'

'I see.' I was determined not to ask him how. I could see he was bursting to tell me.

'That's one of my walking-sticks,' he said suddenly. Following his gaze I saw that out on the snowy lawn Billy was patching up the snowman with fresh snow and had removed the snowman's walking-stick while doing it. I wondered if David was going to lay claim to the snowman's hat too. 'I didn't know they wanted my stick for that damned snowman.'

Billy and Sally patted more snow on to the snowman's belly. I suppose the thaw had slimmed it down a little.

Turning back to me, David said: 'In Poland, I complained of a

50

headache and George gave me some white pills. Pills from a Polish package. I didn't use them of course.'

'No,' I said. 'Of course not.'

'I'm not a bloody fool. All written in Polish. Who knows what kind of muck they take ... even their genuine aspirin ... I'd sooner suffer the headache.'

'So what happened?'

'I brought them back with me. Not the packet, he'd thrown that away; or so he said.'

'Back to England?'

'See that little cherry tree? I buried Felix, our old tom-cat, under it. The poor old sod died from one of those tablets. I didn't tell my lady wife, of course. And I don't want Fiona to know.'

'You think the tablet did it?'

'Three tablets. Crushed up in warm milk.'

'Did the cat eat them willingly, or did you dose it?'

'What are you getting at?' he said indignantly. 'I didn't choke the cat, if that's what you mean. I was dosing farm animals before you were born.' I'd forgotten how highly he cherished his credentials as a country gentleman.

'If it was a very old cat ...'

'I don't want you discussing this with my daughter or with anyone else,' he ordered.

'Was this what you wanted to ask me?' I said. 'The dead cat and whether to report it?'

'It was *one* of the things,' he admitted reluctantly. 'I wanted to ask you to take a note of it off the record. But since then I have decided that it's better all forgotten. I don't want you to repeat it to anyone.'

'No,' I said, although such a stricture hardly conformed to the way in which he identified me with the powers of government. I recognized this 'confidential anecdote' about his son-in-law's homicidal inclinations as something he wanted me to take back to work and discuss with Dicky and the others. In fact I saw this

51

little cameo as David's way of hitting his son-in-law with yet another unanswerable question, while keeping himself out of it. The only hard fact I could infer from it was that David and George had fallen out. I wondered why.

'Forget it,' said David. 'I said nothing, do you hear me?'

'It's just a family matter,' I said, but my grim little joke went unnoticed. He was still standing in the window, and now he turned his head to look out at the garden again. Fiona and the children were heading back. Seeing David profiled, and in conjunction with the snowman at the bottom of the lawn, I wondered if the children had intended it to be a caricature of their grandfather. Now that the belly had been restored and the shoulders built up a little it had something of David's build, and that old hat and walking-stick provided the finishing touches. It was something of a surprise to find that my little children were now judging the world around them with such keen eyes. I would have to watch myself.

'They're growing up,' said David.

'Yes, I'm afraid so.'

He didn't respond. I suppose he knew how I felt. It wasn't that I liked them less as grown-ups than as children. It was simply that I liked myself so much more when I was being a childlike Dad with them, an equal, a playmate, occupying the whole of their horizon. Now they were concerned with their friends and their school, and I couldn't get used to being such a small part of their lives.

☆

'I've got two suitcases belonging to that friend of yours.' David meant Gloria of course. 'When she brought the children over here to us, she left two suitcases with their clothes and toys and things. Expensive-looking cases. I don't know where to contact her, apart from the office, and I know you people don't like personal phone calls to your place of work. I thought perhaps you would be able to take them and give them back to her.'

52

'No,' I said. 'I don't go to the London office, I work in Berlin nowadays.'

'I didn't want to ask Fiona.'

He displayed characteristic delicacy in not wanting to ask Fiona about the whereabouts of my one-time mistress. He didn't really care of course. The question about the suitcases that Gloria had left with him was just a warning shot across my bows. Now he got on to more important matters.

'She's still not well.' He was looking at Fiona and the kids.

'She's tired,' I said. 'She works too hard.'

'I'm not talking about being tired,' said David. 'We all work too hard. My goodness . . .' He gave a short laugh. '. . . I'd hate to show you my appointments diary for next week. As I keep telling those trade union buggers, if I worked a forty-hour week I'd be finished by lunchtime Tuesday. I haven't got even a lunch slot to spare for at least six weeks.'

'Poor you,' I said.

'My little girl is sick.' I'd never heard him speak of Fiona like that; his voice was strained and his manner intense. 'It's no good the pair of you telling each other that she's just tired and that a relaxing holiday and a regime of vitamin tablets are going to make her fit and well again.'

'No?'

'No. Tonight we have a few people coming to dinner. One of the guests is a top Harley Street man, a psychiatrist. Not a psychologist, a psychiatrist. That means he's a qualified medical man too.'

'Does it?' I said. 'I must try and remember that.'

'You'd do well to,' he said gruffly, suspecting that I was being sarcastic but not quite certain. He moved away from the window and said: 'He agrees with me; Fiona will never be fit enough to take charge of the children again. You know that, don't you, Bernard?'

'Has he examined Fiona?'

'Of course not. But he's met her several times. Fiona thinks he's just a drinking chum of mine.'

'But he's been spying on her.'

'I'm only saying this for your sake, and for the sake of Fiona and your wonderful children.'

'David. If this is a prelude to your trying to get legal custody of the children, forget it.'

He sighed and pulled a long face. 'She's sick. Fiona is slowly coming round to face that truth, Bernard. I wish you would face it too. You could help me and help her.'

'Don't try any of your legal tricks with me, David.' I was angry, and not as careful as I might have been.

With an insolent calm he said: 'Dr Howard has already said he'd support me. And I play golf with a top-rate barrister. He says I would easily get custody if it came to it.'

'It would break Fiona's heart,' I said, trying a different angle.

'I don't think so, Bernard. I think without the children to worry about she'd be relieved of a mighty weight.'

'No.'

'Why do you think she's been putting it off so long? Having the children back with her, I mean. She could have come down here as soon as she returned from California. She could have taken the children up to the apartment in Mayfair – there are spare bedrooms, aren't there? – and made all the necessary arrangements to send them to school and so on. So why didn't she do that?' There was a long pause. 'Tell me, Bernard.'

'She knew how much you both liked having the children with you,' I said. 'She did it for you.'

'Rather than for you,' he said, not bothering much to conceal his glee at my answer. 'I would have thought that you would have liked having the children with you, and that she would have liked having the children with her.'

'She loves being with them. Look at her now.'

'No, Bernard. You can't get round me with that one. She likes

54

coming down here to see the children. She's pleased to see them so happy and doing well at school. But she doesn't want to take on the responsibility and the time-consuming drudgery of being a Mum again. She can't take it on. She's mentally not capable.'

'You're wrong.'

'I'm surprised to hear you say that. According to what Fiona tells me you yourself have said all these things to her . . .' He waved a hand at my protest. 'Not in as many words, but you've said it in one way or another. You've told her repeatedly that she's trying to avoid having the children back home again.'

'No,' I said. 'I never said anything like that.'

He smiled. He knew I was lying.

☆

David's dinner party seemed as if it was going to last all night. He was wearing his new dinner suit with satin lapels, and his patent Gucci loafers with red silk socks that matched his pocket handkerchief, and he was in the mood for telling long stories about his club and his golf tournaments and his vintage Bentley. The guests were David's friends: men who spent their working week in St James's clubs and City bars but made money just the same. How they did it mystified me; it wasn't a product of their charm.

By the time the dinner guests had departed, and the family had exchanged goodnights and gone upstairs to bed, I was pretty well beat, but I felt compelled to put a direct question to Fiona. Casually, while undressing, I said: 'When do you plan to have the children living with us, darling?'

She was sitting at the dressing-table in her nightdress and brushing her hair. She always brushed her hair night and morning, I think it was something that they'd made her do at boarding school. Looking in the mirror to see me she said: 'I knew you were going to ask me that.'

'Did you?'

'I could see it coming ever since we arrived here.'

55

'And when do you think?'

'Please, darling. The children's future is hardly something to be settled at this time of night, when both of us are worn out.'

'You can't keep on avoiding it, Fi.'

'I'm not avoiding it,' she said, her voice raised a tone or so. 'But this is not the time or the place, surely you can see that.'

It was obviously going to cause an argument if I pursued it further. I was angry. I washed and cleaned my teeth and went to bed without speaking to her other than a brusque goodnight.

'Goodnight, darling,' she said happily as I switched out the light. I shut my reddened eyes and knew no more until Fiona was hammering at me and shouting something I couldn't comprehend.

'What?'

'The window! Someone is trying to force their way in!'

I jumped out of bed but I knew it was nothing. I was getting used to Fiona's disturbed sleep. I went to the window, opened it and looked out. I froze in the cold country air. 'Nothing here.'

'It must have been the wind,' said Fiona. She was fully awake now. And contrite. 'I'm sorry, darling.' She got out of bed and came to the window with a dispirited weariness that made me feel very sorry for her.

'There's nothing there,' I said, and gave her a hug.

'I think I must have eaten something that upset me.'

'Yes,' I said. She always blamed such awakenings on indigestion. She always said she couldn't remember anything of the dream itself. So now I no longer asked her about them. Instead I played along with her explanations. I said: 'The fennel sauce on the fish, it was very creamy.'

'That must have been it,' she said.

'You've been working too hard. You should slow down a little.'

'I can't.' She sank down at the dressing-table and brushed her hair in a mood of sad introspection. 'I'm directly involved in all the exchanges between Bonn and the DDR. Enormous sums of money are being given to them. I wonder how much of it is being pocketed by Honecker and Co, and how much gets through. Sometimes I worry about it. And they become more and more demanding.'

I watched her. The doctor had given her some tablets. She said they were no more than pep pills – 'a tonic'. She had them on the dressing-table and now she took two pills and drank some water to swallow them. She did it automatically. She always had the tablets with her. I had a feeling that she took them whenever she felt low, and that meant frequently. I said: 'How do you pay them?'

'Depends. It falls into four categories: Western currency payments to the East German State, Western currency payments to private individuals, trade credits guaranteed by Bonn, and a hotchpotch of trade deals that wouldn't be done except that we – or more frequently Bonn – push them along. I don't have much to do with that end of it. We are only really interested in the money that goes to the Church.'

'Is the Department involved in any of the money transfers?'

'It's complicated. Our contact is a man named Stoppl. He's a founder of "the Protestant Church in Socialism", a committee of East German churchmen who negotiate with their regime's leaders and do deals. Some deals involve the Western Churches too – there is a Church trust which arranges the money – or sometimes Bonn. All of these deals are very secret, things are done but never revealed. Sometimes we have Honecker and Stoppl negotiating one-to-one, out at Honecker's Berlin home on the Wandlitzsee.'

'So these deals must be common knowledge among the communist top brass?' Honecker's palatial dwelling was in the Politburo residential compound. The communist leaders had their luxury homes there, together with an abundance of capitalist luxuries from camcorders and laptops to soft toilet paper. The whole site was guarded by armed sentries and surrounded with a chain-link fence and razor wire. I knew that locale very well: it was an intimidating place to visit. The identity of visitors to the sanctum was carefully checked, and their names logged in a book held by the guard commander.

'Oh yes. They all share in the spoils. Our official line is that they may steal a lot of the money but some gets through to Stoppl's people and that money is vital.'

'Vital. Yes.'

'In church halls and vicarages, and church premises of all kinds, ordinary people talk about local social problems, about environmental pollution and injustice. They talk about peace and human rights issues.'

'I get the idea, Fi.'

'The underlying theme is Christian protest.'

'You're playing with fire,' I told her.

'Christian values.'

'You sound just like your father,' I said.

'That's what you always say when you lose an argument with me.'

'I shouldn't have said it.'

She laughed derisively. 'Is that a retraction or just an apology?' But Fiona *was* like her father, there was no denying it. Equally obviously she didn't enjoy that resemblance. I think Fiona dearly loved her mother, but not her father. She was frightened of being too much like her mother; frightened of ending up bullied and silenced as her mother had been over the years. That determination to escape her parents was the key to Fiona's complex personality. For she was also afraid of becoming like her father. At least that's how I saw it, but I wasn't a psychiatrist. I wasn't even a psychologist. In fact I didn't even have a proper contract for my pen-pushing job in Berlin.

'And for how long will the West keep pumping money into Honecker's bankrupt regime?' I asked.

'The communists are extremely good at wining and dining visiting press and TV people. The Leipzig Fair is their show-case.

Ill-informed newspaper articles in the West consistently say Honecker's economy is strong, and getting stronger. You must read the junk that newspaper feature writers produce in return for a first-class ticket and a couple of days of being feasted and flattered. Last month the World Bank had their resident half-wits putting out some crackpot statistics to prove that per capita income in the DDR was higher than in the UK. Yesterday I saw a glowing press cutting from some journalist in Dublin telling her readers that the West could learn a lot from what the East Germans are doing. That sort of bosh is translated and circulated in the East, and it keeps the lid on things back home in Honecker's kingdom.'

'Honecker is cunning. It's a police State, but the East Germans are sheltered from crime, given apartments, cheap food and jobs – no unemployment in the workers' State – cheap holidays, free education, free medical care. It's no good saying it's lousy medical care, or that the jobs are poorly paid, or that the workers are crowded into nasty little apartments. Or that thousands die from the filthy pollution in the air and the rivers and canals are frothing with poisonous scum and belly-up fishes. The citizens of this gigantic prison camp have what the Germans call *Geborgenheit* – security and shelter – and they are not going to fight in the streets to get rid of the regime.'

She sighed. She knew I was right.

'The DDR is bankrupt. The West must chop off all payments without warning,' I said. 'It's the only way to bring change. Let the regime collapse. Show the East Germans that they are living a lie; they are living on handouts from the West.'

'But Washington and Bonn are afraid that Moscow will move in to prop Honecker up if we don't support him,' said Fiona.

'Moscow? Don't start thinking that Gorbachev is some kind of freedom-loving capitalist. He's a dedicated comrade, making a few concessions to the West in order to preserve some semblance of what Lenin created. It will need a braver man than Gorby to reform the USSR. The whole Federation is on the slide. In a few years Moscow will be as bankrupt as Honecker.'

'In a few years, yes. That's why Britain, and the Americans, refused to give Honecker a State visit even when Belgium, France and Spain agreed. How could they do that? And then that silly man Kohl invites him to West Germany. Honecker is shaky, but how long will he last? With such stupid leaders in the West to help him, no one can be sure.'

'If Moscow goes bust, will the West cut Honecker off without a pfennig? That will be worth waiting for.'

Fiona went over to the window. The sky was getting light now. When she spoke it was with a determination that she seldom revealed. 'Yes, and the Honecker regime will collapse. And then the Church groups we've trained will be needed to hold things together.'

'So that's the scenario?'

'It's what I've given half my life to,' she said, as if she was now counting the depth of her sacrifice rather than its duration.

Gently she pulled back the curtain to see the early morning sky. There was a band of mist stretched across the horizon. Dark clumps of treetops floated upon it to make tropical islands in a luminous ocean. I didn't want to challenge her ideas, but every report we saw from agents on the ground said that the Stasi had increased in numbers, and increased in influence, month by month for the last five years. Maybe it was a reaction from a regime that was doomed, but that didn't mean it was less dangerous. The Stasi were penetrating Fiona's precious East German Church groups. In Allenstein bei Magdeburg the pastor was working for the Stasi until, just before Christmas, someone put a bomb under his car. And every month the Stasi – self-styled 'shield and sword of social-ism' – tightened up security. They opposed all attempts to liberalize the regime. The Stasi stamped upon anyone who dared to ask for anything at all. Even Russian publications were banned as too liberal. Now, in what must surely be the ultimate echo of George

Orwell's predictions, East Germans had been forbidden to sing the lyrics of their own national anthem, because its words 'Germany united fatherland' might give loyal communists ideas about co-operating with West Germany.

Perhaps Fiona was thinking along the same sobering lines, for she didn't pursue the matter. 'We mustn't leave it too late,' she said without turning round. 'I hate driving in the dark, nowadays. It's a sign of growing old I suppose. And we're dining with Dicky on Monday.'

'Do you know how to work this gadget?' I was turning all the knobs of the tea-making machine. David had installed them in all the guest bedrooms.

'It's easier to use the electric kettle,' she said. She plugged it in and started it. She switched on the lights too. Then she went back to bed. 'It's too early to get up, darling.'

'We'll have tea in bed,' I said.

'Very well, but if I don't answer your next question for a long while, I may be asleep.'

'I was thinking of ducking out of Dicky's dinner, but I can't think of a convincing excuse.'

'We'll have to go, darling. Everyone will be there. It's not social and it's not optional. Dicky's dinners are just Departmental meetings in disguise.'

'I don't feel strong enough for a whole evening of Dicky's imbecile chit-chat.'

'You don't feel like it!' said Fiona with a sudden burst of resentment. 'How do you think I will enjoy sitting round the table with them all?'

I leaned across and kissed her on the ear. She didn't have to draw a diagram for me. By everyone she meant that Gloria, my one-time lover, would be there. And everyone present would be watching with interest every glance, word and smile that the three of us exchanged. It was difficult for her; but it was no picnic for me either. Maybe Gloria would think of a convincing excuse.

I looked round the room, waiting for the kettle to boil. We'd been installed in the best of half a dozen guest bedrooms. This one was 'the Mozart room' and its walls were hung with framed music manuscripts and some early wooden musical instruments: a concertina, a violin and a mandolin. To save on space, each instrument had been cut in half and mounted on a mirror. It saved on musical instruments too, I suppose.

☆

'Suppose George did try to murder him?' said Fiona calmly, as she sat propped up in bed watching me make the tea. 'It can't be entirely ruled out, can it?'

'For what purpose?' I said, and for a moment regretted confiding the conversation to her. But I couldn't see any way I could avoid reporting it all to the office, and that meant Fiona.

'Does there have to be a purpose? You have always said that not every act has a purpose.'

Actually what I 'always said' was that people 'go mad' or rather act in irrational and inexplicable ways. There was no evidence to suggest that her father was mad. At least no madder than I'd always known him. 'I suppose we could provide it to the interrogation team at Berwick House and see if they can spring it on George to any effect.'

'Felix was very old,' said Fiona.

'Look, darling. If that had really been a lethal poison, the poor old tom-cat would have died in style.'

'What do you mean?'

'It would have shown symptoms of poisoning.'

'How can you be so sure?'

'I've never come across painless poisons,' I said, 'except in books.' I made the tea and took the tray, with teapot and cups and milk jug, to Fiona's bedside table. She was fussy about tea and liked to pour it herself.

'Never?'

'It would have to be from one of the major groups: arsenic, cyanide or strychnine. Any of those would have caused Felix spectacular symptoms.'

'Daddy is not very observant.'

'After feeding it what he suspected was poison intended for himself? He'd be watching every move of that damned cat, you know he would.'

'I suppose you are right,' she said. 'All poisons?'

'Cyanide brings on a desperate breathless choking spasm and convulsions. Strychnine brings even more violent convulsions. But the most likely poison would be arsenic, or one of the other metals. It's the poisoner's first choice.'

'Yes, we had an arsenic case while I was in Berlin. I had to give evidence. It had no security dimension. It was a domestic quarrel – one of the clerks tried to murder his wife. One of the police pathologists told me that, of all the poisons, arsenic produces symptoms most like those of natural disease.'

'Well that's because pathologists don't get to the scenes of crime until life is extinct. Next time you see him, tell him arsenic brings on vomiting, trembling and bloody diarrhoea. If your father had seen the cat succumbing to a lethal dose of arsenic he wouldn't have waited until our next weekend visit to mention it to me.'

'I suppose you're right, you usually are.' She meant of course that I was usually right about vulgar brutal matters that it was better not to know about. 'The pathologist was a her,' she added as an afterthought.

'Your father didn't really believe it was poison.'

'Daddy's not paranoid,' said Fiona, deftly avoiding the question.

No, I thought, he's just a megalomaniac. For people who think of themselves all the time, paranoia is simply a way of confirming how important they are. I said: 'He only had to dig the cat up, and send it along to a laboratory.'

'I think we should suspend judgement.' Her slow smile revealed her true feelings: that my prejudice was unreasonable and unyielding. Of course she might have been implying that there were lots of painless poisons; exotic toxins that chemists concoct in secret government-financed laboratories. But that would have brought us into the world of officially authorized murder; and for the time being, neither of us wanted to believe George could ever have been a party to that kind of killing. 'I'll pour the tea, shall I?'

'Lovely. What are you reading?'

She took her book from the table so that I could see its cover: *Buddenbrooks: Verfall einer Familie*.

'Good grief, Fi, you've been reading that same book for ages.'

'Have I? What's the hurry? Is that enough milk for you?'

'Yes,' I said, taking the tea from her hand. But in fact I don't really like milk in tea; it was one of the many English ideas I never properly adjusted to. 'So Billy got into the football team at school. Well, well, well. I never saw him as an athlete.'

'Yes, that's wonderful,' said Fiona. She didn't like sport of any kind but she tried to sound pleased.

'There was no one trying to get in the window, Fi,' I said.

'It was just the sound of the wind,' she affirmed. 'I don't know what came over me. Listen to it howl in the chimney.'

'Yes,' I said, although I couldn't hear the wind in the chimney nor anywhere else. The night was almost unnaturally calm.

4

London: the Cruyers' home

'NOW THAT BERNARD has finally joined us,' proclaimed Dicky
Cruyer in a voice tinged with impatience, 'we can proceed with
the ceremony.'

Dicky was wearing a navy blue dinner suit. He'd bought it back
in the days when everyone said dark blue photographed better on
television. But Dicky had never been on television, and now his
suit just looked unusual. In response to Dicky's urgent hand signals
someone reduced the volume of the hi-fi from which came Stan
Getz playing the 'One-Note Samba'.

I was the last to arrive only because Dicky had dumped a file
upon my desk just two hours before and I had been working to
complete it before leaving the office. I caught Fiona's eye and she
blew me a kiss.

Bret was there, wearing a new dinner suit. His slim figure looked
good in black. Together with the white hair brushed tight against
his skull, his angular face so carefully shaved and dusted with
powder, he looked somewhat menacing: the sort of gangster figure
that Hollywood invented when George Raft and Jimmy Cagney
stopped doing musicals.

Resuming his brisk parade ground voice, Dicky said: 'I know
everyone here tonight will . . . give Bernard a glass, Daphne darling
. . . will join me in offering Augustus my belated congratulations

65

on becoming Operations supremo. Hurry, Daphne. We are all waiting.'

Daphne Cruyer was pouring measures of champagne from a magnum bottle of Pol Roger. Daphne became nervous at these occasions when her husband brought his colleagues home to a little dinner party. She should not have distributed the empty glasses to the guests before going round with the bottle. Now, as they held their glasses out, she was finding it difficult to pour from the big bottle without spilling some wine each time.

'Thank you, Mrs Cruyer,' said Augustus Stowe, as the champagne overfilled his glass and ran bubbling down his fingers to drip on to his shoe. Stowe had never visited the Cruyers before, and judging by the distracted look on his face was wondering what he was doing here now. He was an efficient, outspoken and extremely irritable Australian. As some of the messenger boys had demonstrated on the wall of the men's toilet, Stowe was remarkably easy to caricature because of the hair that grew from his ears and nostrils, and the fact that his head was shiny, pink and completely bald.

It was of course a contrivance to call this dinner party a celebration of Stowe's appointment. That had all been celebrated, debated and deplored many weeks before. Stowe was reassigned when Dicky was appointed to 'Europe Supremo'. It was only a temporary arrangement. Augustus Stowe, who had held that Europe job for some time, was urgently needed to deal with one of the calamities that were a regular part of life in Operations. Stowe was still there but he wouldn't last much longer. No one held on to Operations for very long. Firing the chief of Operations was the standard act of contrition that the Department offered to the Joint Intelligence Committee each time the politicos lobbed a salvo of complaints at us. And lately those salvos had become a cannonade.

But Dicky was the desk-man par excellence. By having my wife Fiona as his assistant, he'd kept a grip on both the German Desk and the Europe job too. This dinner party was a way of saying to Augustus Stowe – and the world in general – that Dicky was going to fight to hold on to the Europe Desk. It was a way of telling Stowe not to come back this way.

'Now everyone has a glass, I think. So congratulations, Augustus!' said Dicky, holding his glass aloft. With varying measures of enthusiasm and gestures of good will, the assembled company complimented Stowe and then sipped their drink and looked around.

'That's not a ready-made bow tie, is it, Bernard?' said Dicky as he pushed past me to see why the girl with the peanuts and olives was not distributing them quickly enough. She was talking to Gloria and they were comparing the heels of their shoes.

'Come along,' Dicky told the girl. 'You should be doing the hot sausages by now.'

'She forgot the mustard dip,' Daphne told him. 'We haven't used these caterers before. They sent six packets of frozen bite-sized pizzas without asking if we had a microwave. I was hoping they would thaw but they are rock-hard.'

'I can't do the catering too, darling,' Dicky told her in distant tones. 'It's not much to ask: just to make sure these catering people bring the right food. My God, we are paying them enough.'

'It looks ready-made,' I said, 'but that's because I'm good at tying them.'

'What was that, Bernard? Oh, yes. Well, be a good chap and take the olives round, would you?' Then he turned back to Daphne and said: 'Put the pizzas in a hot oven, darling. I'll just keep on serving "shampoo" until they are ready.'

I found the table where Daphne had abandoned the magnum of champagne and poured myself another glass. Alongside the champagne there were two vases crammed with expensive cut flowers. I suppose the other guests had brought them as gifts. I felt guilty about not doing the same until I noticed that a tall bunch of dark red roses held a card saying 'Fondest love from Bernard and Fiona'.

'We love that painting of Adam and Eve,' I heard Dicky saying behind me. I turned and found he was confiding his feelings to Bret Rensselaer and Gloria. I offered them all olives but only Gloria took one. She bit into it with her amazingly white teeth and then handed the pit back to me. There was a certain intimacy to this action and I think she thought so too. I smiled at her. It looked as if this might be the most intimate thing to happen between us for a very long time. Dicky was telling Bret how Daphne had bought the painting cheap in a flea market in Amsterdam. I had heard the story a thousand times, and I clearly remembered Bret standing here in the Cruyers' drawing-room listening politely to Dicky's rambling and rather dubious account of this purchase.

Augustus Stowe was standing by a glass case in the corner studying the contents: Dicky Cruyer's valuable collection of antique fountain-pens. It seemed an appropriate collection for a man who had climbed so far in the world of bureaucrats. Stowe perhaps thought so too, for he pulled a face and moved on to join two people from his Operations section who were talking with Fiona. It didn't really matter whether Augustus Stowe was the guest of honour or just an extra man. The evening had really been arranged so that Dicky could clarify his working relationship with Bret. This was a make-or-break evening. The work at the office might or might not be discussed, but by the time the evening ended these two men would have made their peace or declared war.

Dicky had found it difficult to adjust to the way in which Bret Rensselaer had unexpectedly arrived in London. Unrolled from the magic carpet and into the Deputy's office like Cleopatra for a startled Caesar, he had seized control of the Department. His only real superior, the Director-General, seemed to be giving Bret a more or less free hand.

'Europe can no longer be treated like an odd assortment of people with weird languages and funny costumes,' Dicky was earnestly explaining to Bret. 'Europe together musters more people, more talent and more wealth than the entire USA.'

Bret said nothing. And yet I knew from the long time I had spent with Bret in California that it was the sort of remark that usually produced an acid question about why Europe couldn't afford armed services to defend itself without American military help. Bret was an Anglophile, but that didn't mean he felt European. Bret's infatuation with England and the English made him exceedingly sceptical about life lived by foreigners beyond the English Channel. He smiled at Dicky.

Dicky said: 'Since moving into the Europe slot I have made it my business to visit every one of our European offices. I love Europe. In some ways I think of Paris as my real home.'

'How are you managing to divide authority with Fiona?' asked Bret.

'She hasn't been complaining?'

'She's so busy running around the globe that I seldom get the pleasure of talking with her.'

'She supports me in everything I do,' said Dicky. 'I hardly know how . . .' He paused and wet his lips. I suspect he'd been about to say that he didn't know how he would manage without her but it came out: '. . . how I would replace her.'

'No need to worry about replacing her, Dicky,' said Bret.

'No?' said Dicky nervously and drank some champagne. It was at a previous gathering like this – in Dicky's home – that Bret had announced that he was the newly appointed Deputy D-G. That traumatic experience had left Dicky nervous that Bret might choose this evening for another such bombshell.

But Bret didn't add anything more to this verdict on Fiona's security of tenure. Somewhat pointedly, he moved away from Dicky to speak with her. I heard him say: 'You are looking ravishing tonight, Fiona.' She was wearing a severely cut dark green dress with matching shoes. When Bret started talking to her she frowned and bent her head as if concentrating. Or perhaps she was looking at her silk shoes. She had told me many times that they were difficult to keep in good shape. She never wore them when driving, she slipped them off and operated the pedals in her stockings.

Everyone was in evening dress. Mine was creased in all the wrong places. I'd packed it carelessly when coming back from my weekend with my father-in-law and only got it out of my suitcase half an hour or so before arriving at Dicky's.

As if to cover any confusion he'd suffered at Bret's hands, Dicky turned to me and said: 'Bret's a bit nervous tonight. There was a personal security alert for all senior staff this afternoon. I told Bret he should be armed but he said it would spoil the line of his tuxedo.' Dicky laughed in a way that made it difficult to know if he was scoffing at Bret's foolishness, or memorizing the line for his own use.

'No one told me,' I said.

Dicky sipped his drink and glanced around the room to see who was talking to who. 'Well, you are not exactly senior staff, old boy,' he said with a boyish smile. Dicky was looking young and fresh and energetic this evening. And his hair had suddenly become almost unnaturally curly. I wondered if he had it permed from time to time. 'It's nothing to be alarmed about. The embassy hoodlums have been ordered to provide some sort of back-up. And that's as much as we have discovered. I doubt if it's a hit of any sort. I suspect it's something to do with dissidents. It could be anything. It could be a break-in or a line-tap.'

Daphne came to Dicky's side. She was wearing a long plain dress with large embroidered flowers on it. Daphne had picked up a damaged piece of tapestry in one of the antique markets she frequented, and had removed the flowers from it. 'Will you be able to carve the lamb?' she asked Dicky.

'I told you not to get a leg.'

'A shoulder is so fatty,' said Daphne.

'Get Bernard to carve it,' said Dicky. 'He's good at that kind of thing.'

'Could you, Bernard? I've had the knife sharpened.'

'Of course he can,' said Dicky before I could reply. 'He's my slave, isn't he? He'll do anything I tell him to do.' He put a hand round my shoulder and hugged me. 'Right, Bernard?'

'I'll carve it for you, Daphne,' I said. 'But I'm not an expert.'

'Your poor face,' said Daphne. 'What happened, Bernard?'

'He applied the old powder-puff a bit too energetically,' said Dicky.

'No, really,' said Daphne, looking at me with sympathy.

'It's secret,' said Dicky. 'Let him alone. Bernard is paid to take a few knocks when the job calls for it.'

I knew of course that Dicky was giving me the sort of treatment he would have liked to be giving to Bret. Although I hadn't followed the exact implications of his brief exchange with Bret, his subsequent irritation was enough to tell me that Dicky did not feel entirely secure in his Europe Desk job. I wondered if Bret was about to leap-frog Fiona into becoming Dicky's senior. It was the sort of device that Bret would use to shake up the Department. And Bret had been heard to say that a shake-up was exactly what the Department urgently needed. The trouble was that I was always the one who got Dicky's flak.

'It's mid-life crisis,' said Daphne when we reached the kitchen and I was appraising the roast leg of lamb and putting an edge on the carving knife. 'That's what my doctor says.'

Daphne was wearing a professional cook's white apron of starched white cotton. Her name – Daphne Cruyer – was embroidered in red on its front, in the style of self-acclaim made famous by Paul Bocuse. 'You're young yet, Daphne,' I said.

'Not me; Dicky,' she said, showing a flash of pique. 'Dicky's in mid-life crisis.'

'Your doctor said this?'

'The doctor knows how upset I am,' she explained. 'And he knows how insensitive Dicky can be. It's all those young girls he has around him all day. He has to keep proving his masculinity.' She fetched a large oval plate from the massive shiny steel professional oven she'd had fitted since my previous visit. 'You can carve it in advance, Bernard.'

'I'll do it at the table, Daphne. I know that's how you like to serve dinner.'

'You are a dear man,' she said. 'If all the girls were chasing after you, I would find it easier to understand.'

'Yes, so would I,' I said.

After that the guests sat down and the dinner party continued in the way that Dicky's dinner parties usually continued. Daphne made sure that Gloria and Fiona were sitting as far apart as possible. And for that I was grateful to her.

☆

The next day I made a journey that took me into England's authentic countryside. This was a stark contrast to the cosy toyland which my father-in-law shared with London's stockbrokers, bankers, judges and gynaecologists.

Visits to 'Uncle' Silas had punctuated my life ever since I was a small child. I had always loved Whitelands, his rambling great farm on the edge of the Cotswolds. Even in winter it was magnificent. The house, built of local light-brown stone, its ancient carved-oak front door, and its mullioned windows, provided a perfect image of old England as the Christmas card industry chose to record it. Countless times I had hidden in the cobwebbed attic or sat in the panelled billiards room, on the bench under the cue-rack, looking at the doleful heads of assembled deer, now moth-eaten and threadbare. I couldn't think of Whitelands without smelling the freshly baked scones that Mrs Porter brought from that temperamental old solid-fuel oven. Just as I couldn't remember exploring that vast stone barn without sneezing, or recall the chilly Sunday morning journeys to the church in the village without a shiver.

For me, the highlight of my visits to Whitelands was the perfect roast beef lunches cooked with loving care by Mrs Porter, the housekeeper. On Sundays it was always local game: if not partridge or pheasant, then Silas would be carving and serving hare or rabbit. As I grew up and learned to count, I was permitted to supervise the billiards score-board. It provided an excuse to be there, an opportunity to watch my father, Silas and other luminaries of the Department, smoking Silas's Cuban cigars, drinking his vintage Hine brandy and arguing in a good-natured way about how the world should be arranged and exactly how and when they would do it.

Whitelands had been in the Gaunt family since one of his more affluent predecessors bought it from a beer tycoon who went to something more grandiose. Only after he retired did Silas come to live here all the year round, and his hospitality became legendary. All manner of weird people came here for the weekend; musicians – prominent or penniless – were especially welcomed, for Silas was devoted to music. They were seldom famous people but they were always convivial and interesting. The weekends were an unchanging ritual: a country walk as far as the river, church service, smoky afternoon billiard games for men only, and a formal dinner for which the guests were expected to dress in long gowns and penguin suits.

Silas was a distant relative of Fiona's family, and he became the godfather of my son. Friends became relatives, and relatives became friends. The Department had always been like that; a curious intermingling of bright boys from expensive schools and their otherwise unemployable male relatives. Perhaps it would have been better and more efficient if its personnel had been recruited from a wider spectrum of British life, but it wouldn't have been so amusing, or so frustrating.

Now Whitelands and all it represented was to end for ever. Some

73

of the rooms had already been cleared of Silas's more personal possessions. One capacious white dust sheet had transformed the chairs, and the long polished table of the dining-room, into a wrinkled dirigible. The dining-table, without extension panels, was shorter than I ever remembered it. I was saddened to think that I would never again see that table loaded under food, crowded by visitors and noisy with arguments.

'I'll come back,' said Silas firmly, as if reading my thoughts. 'I'm only leasing this place . . . short lease. And to people I know well. I've told them I will be returning. I'm even trusting them with the key of my wine cellar.'

'I hope so, Silas,' I said. 'What about Mrs Porter?'

'She'll be living nearby. I made that a condition. I need to know there is someone here, keeping an eye on things on my behalf. You'll come and see me?'

I nodded. We were sitting in what Silas called 'the drawing-room'. Most of the light came from the big open fire upon which he had just placed a mossy log. This was the sanctum to which Silas had retired when he first became unwell. Around him he had arranged some of his most cherished possessions: his favourite lumpy sofa and an equally lumpy painting of his grandfather on a horse. Silas was lumpy too. Already big in frame, his indulgence in good food, and complete indifference to his personal appearance, had made him fat and unkempt. His remaining hair was fuzzy, his jowls heavy, his shirt frayed and his woollen cardigan – like Silas himself – slowly coming unravelled.

'You put in the new trees,' I said.

'It broke my heart to lose the elms.'

'They'll soon grow.'

'Canadian maples or some such thing. The forestry people said they grow quickly, but they are sickly-looking growths. I don't like the look of them.'

'Give them a chance, Silas. You mustn't be impatient.'

74

'An apartment,' said Silas. 'What will life be like in an apartment block?'

'I thought it was your idea.'

'It was a compromise,' he said. 'At first it was only my local doctor threatening me. Then the Department joined in. They say it's all for my benefit, but I'd rather stay here and put up with whatever happens. We've all got to die some time.'

'You mustn't talk like that,' I said. 'You've got years of life and work ahead.'

'What about my music?' said Silas. 'I'm taking all my records and tapes. I hope I'm not going to have some wretch banging on the wall just because it's after eleven o'clock.'

'Get well,' I said. 'That's the important thing. Get well and come home to Whitelands again.'

'I'm not sick,' he declared. Although old and somewhat wheezy, he appeared to be in good health and quick-witted too. 'But the Department made me submit to a physical examination by their stupid doctor. It's some new rule about the pension funds. That's what started the fuss. Otherwise I wouldn't have agreed to go away at all. Before you go, you might like to take a last look around, Bernard?'

'Yes,' I said.

'And I want you to take a crate or two of wine with you. Choose whatever you like.' Before I could respond, he added: 'I will never get through it all even if I live to be one hundred.'

I looked at him and waited to hear the reason for him demanding my presence. Silas was a noisy extrovert, a blunt and yet devious old man, and certainly not likely to bring me down here without a specific reason. He got up and closed the door. Tall and plump and untidy, he had many weaknesses, of which gambling was the one most associated with him both at work and at play. 'There are things that were never committed to paper, Bernard. When I go, the facts will go too. You understand?'

'Of course.'

'I've always been a gambler,' said Silas. 'Sometimes I've won. When I've lost I've paid up without complaint. But in all my years in the Department I've never gambled with people's lives. You know that, Bernard.'

I didn't answer. The truth was that I didn't know what was decided in the secret dialogues that men like Silas had on the top floor.

'When I thought we were going to lose Fiona last year, I was worried. They are not like us, Bernard, those people over there. They don't interrogate, explicate and isolate.' He smiled; it was one of the maxims of the Department. 'If they had got wind of what Fiona was doing to their precious socialist empire her end would have been too savage to think about. They put that fellow . . . what's his name . . . into a furnace: alive. At first no one here would believe it, but then we intercepted the official account. It was done in front of witnesses.'

'What is it, Silas? What are you trying to tell me?'

'I didn't know they would kill Tessa,' he said. 'All I was told was that there would be a faked identity. Her identity.'

'Who told you that?'

'We handed the whole project over to the Yanks,' said Silas. 'We needed to be distanced from it.'

'That doesn't fit with what I know,' I told him. 'It was done by a man named Thurkettle, wasn't it?'

'Thurkettle. Yes: an American.'

'An American mercenary. The story I heard is that he was released from a high-security prison to do some dirty work for the CIA. Very dirty work.'

'Perhaps he was,' said Silas. 'I thought he was a bona fide Washington man. I was persuaded to give him a free hand.'

'To do what?'

'Certainly not to murder anyone,' said Silas indignantly. 'I never met him personally of course, but I was assured that he could provide a smoke-screen while we brought Fiona out.'

'A smoke-screen? What did you think he was going to do?'

'It was vital that the Stasi people, and Moscow too, should think Fiona had died. If they had known that she was safe, and in California, giving us a detailed picture of everything they had done . . . Well, they would have simply taken emergency action: changed codes, changed methods, changed agents, changed everything. Fiona's years of courage and jeopardy would have been in vain.'

'But Tessa was killed. And her body was burned to help the deception.'

'What can I say to you? I can't say I wasn't at fault, because I was. I trusted that swine. I thought it was going to be only a matter of paperwork.'

'Without a body? How would that have worked?' I asked him.

'A dead body perhaps. A body taken from a hospital mortuary. That has been done before, and will no doubt be done again. It's not the use of the body, is it? It's the killing.'

'Yes, it's the killing,' I agreed.

'Tessa's death has brought terrible consequences,' said Silas. 'None of us will ever be the same again. Not you, not Fiona, not that poor husband of hers. And certainly not me. I haven't slept one full night since I heard the news. It was the end of my relationship with the Department, of course. The D-G wanted me to continue in my arm's-length advisory role, but I told him I couldn't. It broke my heart.'

'Where is Thurkettle now?'

'He went to Oregon, the last I heard of him. But he may have moved on. Canada perhaps. The Americans had given him a new identity so he could do more or less as he wished. There was talk of having him face some sort of murder charge, but that would have meant negotiations with the Americans. And even if they had agreed we could hardly drag our covert actions through open court. Concealing the fact that Fiona was alive and well was exactly what we had started out to do in the first place.'

'Yes,' I said.

'And to some extent Thurkettle probably feels he did what had to be done.'

'Yes,' I said. 'And to some extent I suspect that's how you feel too.'

Silas frowned. 'I thought you would understand,' he said. 'Your father would have understood.'

'He would have understood all right. He was accused of shooting some Germans named Winter back in 1945. He was innocent. But the Department let the charges stand because they didn't want him to face questioning by American lawyers in another jurisdiction.'

'That's an over-simplification,' protested Silas.

'It ruined his career, didn't it?'

'Your father understood that it was necessary.'

'Very well. But don't expect me to go along with the kind of bloody nonsense my father put up with. My father is not me, and I am not my father. Time has moved on, and so has everything else.'

'I hate rows,' said Silas plaintively.

'Yes, of course you do. So do I, if I can get my way without having them.'

When I left the room Silas leaned back and closed his eyes as if in pain. I sought out Mrs Porter to say goodbye. I was hoping to hear her confidential opinion about Silas and his plans. I found her in the kitchen, and she was determined to keep her own counsel. 'I know what you want to talk about, Mister Bernard,' she said. 'But I know my place. It's not for me to have an opinion about anything.' She took out her handkerchief and wiped her nose. 'I can't seem to shake off this head-cold,' she said. 'And there is so much to do in the house.' She smiled at me. Mrs Porter had helped to create the magical atmosphere of Whitelands. It was difficult to guess how much of all I loved would remain after new tenants moved in.

☆

I got into the car and found myself trembling. I don't know why, perhaps it was due to anger and resentment, or the memories of my father's humiliation. I drove down to the village and stopped at the Brown Bess. It was an unfashionable little pub, sandwiched between a scum-encrusted duck pond and a neglected war memorial. Those villagers who could afford it, and the weekend inhabitants, kept to the other pub, the big multi-mirrored Queen Victoria that faced the village green, where the weekend cricketers and their adoring families could enjoy frozen food with foreign names, and champagne with a dash of blackcurrant juice. The Brown Bess was an intimate gathering place for dart-playing farm-workers. The landlord served me with an excruciating politeness bordering on hostility.

I took my beer and my Cheddar cheese sandwich and sat on the steps of the war memorial to eat it, scarcely noticing the cold. I wanted to think. To be subjected to the devious ways of my father-in-law, and then Silas Gaunt, in close succession was more than anyone should be asked to endure. I rebelled. Afterwards – when it was too late – even my most loyal friends and staunchest supporters said my plan of action had been headstrong and ill-advised. The kinder ones said uncharacteristically so. They wondered why I acted impulsively without taking one of them into my confidence, or giving more thought to the consequences.

It was David's claim upon my children – and Fiona's apparent indifference to it – that worried me most. The problem and possible solutions went round and round in my head. That day, sitting on the war memorial with my pint of beer, I listed on a single page of my notebook every alternative open to me; no matter how absurd or impractical. I went through each answer one by one and rejected only those that stood no chance of success. It looked like this: arguing with David would get nowhere, while fighting him through Britain's expensive legal system would result in custody of the children for him and legal fees that would bankrupt me. With the conversation about arsenic fresh in my mind, I even considered killing him. I might have done it too; but I felt that even undetected it would provide the children with a legacy even worse than having David as a 'father'.

To add another dimension to my predicament, I couldn't forget the warning that an Englishman from the Warsaw embassy had given me recently. He thought the other side might take revenge on Fiona, for the way she had tricked them, by killing off her loved ones one by one and at unpredictable intervals. They had done that to a Russian defector named Simakaitis, and he'd ended up in a mental home. Well, Fiona's sister was dead, and her brother-in-law was in trouble that might well have been contrived by Moscow. Fiona was far from well; sometimes I thought she was on the edge of a breakdown. Perhaps there was some diabolical scheme to take revenge upon the whole family. And perhaps it was working.

☆

I made the most of my extended stay in London. The next day I went to a rendezvous in the basement of one of those second-hand bookshops that crowd the Leicester Square end of London's Charing Cross Road. The meeting was at my request, so I could hardly argue about the venue. I had been to the shop before. It was a useful meeting place – I knew them all – and I picked my way down the narrow wooden stairs to a cellar that became a labyrinth of small rooms. Every room was crammed with old books. Here and there, free-standing racks divided the spaces so that it was a squeeze to get past them. There were books piled on the floor, and more remained unpacked in dusty cardboard cartons.

The subterranean rooms were damp, for London is a basin and we were not far from the river. The books gave off a musty smell. Encyclopedias of all shapes and sizes shared the shelves with the refought battles of wartime generals, the tarnished stars of yesterday's show-business and the memoirs of forgotten politicians, their perceptions polished by hindsight.

Books were scattered everywhere. Some had toppled over, some were pushed sideways on to the shelves and some were on the floor as if discarded. It was as if an unexpected emergency had interrupted work here. As I passed through the low doorways from one shadowy chamber to another, I might have been exploring a prehistoric tomb, and the depredations of robbers long since gone.

I recognized some of the books – they were positioned exactly as they had been when I was here a year or more ago. So was the Swede.

The Swede was a professional pilot. Physically powerful and unquestionably courageous, but by nature cautious. It was the perfect temperament for a man who had landed aircraft in total darkness on unfamiliar terrain, and flown out again. Systematic and serious, he was racked by the chronic back-aches and haemorrhoids that went with the flyer's trade. Once he'd been a beautiful young man – you could see the traces of it – but neglected teeth, a roseate nose and thinning hair now made him just another senior citizen.

He was wearing a new Burberry trenchcoat, a matching tweed hat and tartan scarf: a totemic tribute to the British Tourist Authority. When I came upon him at the appointed spot in the cellar he was standing under a crudely lettered sign, 'Bible Studies'. Although seemingly engrossed in a heavy leather-bound volume, he looked up and pushed the book back on to the shelf.

'Always Bible Studies, Swede,' I said. 'Why is that?'

One hand was in the pocket of his beige trenchcoat until he brought it out to flourish a huge Colt Navy revolver, an antique gun that I knew to be of lethal accuracy. 'Grab air!'

'Don't be a tiresome fool, I'm not in the mood for jokes.'

'Bang, bang. You're dead.' He was short and weather-beaten, his spoken English marked by a nasal intonation that he had acquired in America.

'Yes, I know. Do that to one of our newer kids and they will waste you.'

'It's a replica. I bought it in a store selling model cars and planes. It's a perfect repro. Isn't that neat? Exactly like the real thing. Look.' He offered me the gun. It was a detailed reproduction. Only its light weight betrayed it. I gave it a glance and passed it back to him. I suppose it is in the nature of men who fly that they retain some childish faith in gadgets. Otherwise they might start believing in gravity.

'It went well . . . that pick-up I did for you.'

'Yes,' I said. It wasn't like him to mention past jobs. What was he looking for: a medal? a commendation? a pension? By now he should have learned how much the Department hated anyone they termed 'hangers-on', and that meant anyone who expected proper recompense.

'It was your brother-in-law, wasn't it? That nervous little fellow we brought out?'

'No,' I said.

'That's what I heard.'

'Heard? Heard from who?' I asked. He played with the gun, aiming it at the light bulbs and at the door.

'We aviators get around.' He looked at me: 'Why all this special secrecy? Why London? Why not contact me through your man in Stockholm? Are you in trouble, Bernd?'

'Listen to me, Swede,' I said, and told him briefly what I wanted him to do. A straightforward air pick-up task, the sort of job he'd been doing for twenty years.

'Is this for the Department?'

'Do you think I'm going private?'

'It will cost a lot of money. Whatever way we do it, it will cost.'

'I know.'

'In the old days the Irish Sea was a milk run. But since your Irish rebels started bringing in their Armalites and Semtex, the British have pointed their low-level radar that way, and keep it manned day and night.' He pushed his gun into his pocket. 'Where do I pick up your people? England? Where do I tell flying control I'm going? Don't ask me to drop into some neglected little wartime strip by night, I've given up those jobs where you ground-loop around some pot-holes a mile deep and then hit a combine harvester. Is it worth it, Bernd? I mean, there's no passport control between England and the Irish Republic. Immigration scarcely glance at you. I hear it's a walk-through. What are you doing smuggling people across the water by plane?'

'It's not so easy. Immigration is still intact. Boats are conspicuous, and as soon as you mention Ireland they think you are in the IRA, and get on the phone to the police.'

'Bring a speedy little Irish boat over. No?'

'Even more conspicuous,' I said. 'Outboard motors and other valuable stuff are stolen, so these coastal communities are always watching out for passing strangers who might be about to rip off the boats.'

He scratched his face. 'The smaller the better then. It might be possible to rent a plane from one of those little flying clubs in East Anglia or somewhere. Cash, no questions asked. I don't know. I'll have to enquire into it. How soon are you wanting to set this one up?'

'Soon. As soon as possible.'

'Then clubs are out. They don't get going until the weather brightens a bit. Even renting a decent commercial ship isn't easy at this time of year.'

'Yes,' I said. For him it would be complicated. He would have to do it using bogus identification and all the fake papers needed in Europe to get and fly an aircraft. Lately some rumours had been circulating that the Swede was ready to do all kinds of things that once he would have declined – drugs, arms and gold – and people were saying that he was becoming a lot less discriminating in his choice of clients. That's the sort of nasty things the rumours were saying. I didn't believe them of course, but when freebooters like the Swede grow old you can never be sure which way they will go. And the childish fascination he showed with his imitation gun was not reassuring.

He said: 'It's not for the Yanks, is it?'

'No.'

'Because I won't work for the Yanks any more. They make their detailed plans and then, when the time comes, they turn everything on its tail. I don't work for the Yanks.'

'Yes, I know,' I said.

In fact the man everyone called the Swede was German, a Rhinelander named Franz Bender. In 1944 he was a young civilian pilot working for Messerschmitt at Augsburg. When the war ended, American air force specialists went and grabbed the Messerschmitt jet fighters, the engineers, designers and the pilots too. I can only guess what stories he told them, but the truth was that he was only qualified on light planes. But the Americans believed him. They found American army uniforms to fit them all and smuggled them back to the US. I don't know if he ever had to prove he could fly one of those wartime jets, but they kept him on. He lived on the American base at Wright Field for nearly three years, teaching what he knew about flying and servicing jet planes, and making up the rest. He was good at translating Luftwaffe training manuals into American-style English. They paid him a generous civilian salary; gave him a car and an apartment. He had lots of girlfriends. He was a good-looking kid and his accent delighted them.

Then one night, coming back from a party, a cop pulled him over for speeding. He had no driver's licence, no social security card and, when he admitted he was an alien, not even a passport to prove who he was. The cop was a tough vet from the 82nd Airborne and not sympathetic to Germans in any shape or form. Neither did much sympathy come from the other officials Franz encountered. The war was over and those American pals of his, who might have pulled strings to help him, had become civilians and disappeared. No one was prepared to help him. US Immigration held him in custody for almost six months, but no lawyer stuck with him and he was deported to Germany. Although the charges against him were dropped he was banned from entering the States ever again. He'd never forgiven the Americans for what he regarded as an act of betrayal.

'Perhaps you are making a big production out of it,' I said. 'Couldn't we have a wealthy Swedish national, in a Swedish-registered aircraft, on holiday – flying here and there to amuse his friends?'

Still waving the gun around he suddenly said: 'It's your kids, isn't it Bernd?'

If he had shot a hole in the *Information Please Almanac* for 1965, and made it bleed, he could not have shaken me more. Was it that obvious? Did everyone know so much about my personal life that they could guess what I might do next? 'Give over,' I said.

'They will find them and send them back. It's the Hague Convention: custody hearings always take place in the jurisdiction where children are normally resident. What's more, those stupid judges always send the kids to the country where they have spent most time. I know, my cousin went through that stuff. The judge was a clown, and the social services led him by the nose all the time. They'll get you in the end like they did him.'

'Do you charge for this kind of advice? Or does it go with the air ticket?'

He shrugged: 'Okay. It's no concern of mine, but don't ask me to get involved.'

'Just steer the big bird, Swede.'

'Are you sure you are not in trouble, Bernd?'

'I told you, no,' I said.

'With your people? Or the opposition? You want to disappear, I'll tell you many places a million times better than Ireland.' I didn't answer. He stared at me while his mind whirled. 'Or are you going to run across to Cork and climb aboard that Aeroflot connection that flies direct to Havana?' Slowly he smiled. 'You cunning bastard. And from Cuba where?'

'Why all these questions?' The Swede had always been taciturn and positive, now he had become a garrulous fool.

'Because it all stinks, Bernd,' he said feelingly. 'The way you tell it, it stinks. I've never had worse vibrations than I'm getting now.' He took off his new hat with a sigh, and rubbed the bright red line it had left on his forehead.

'You need a size larger hat,' I said. 'Or maybe a size smaller head.'

He shuffled his feet, gave me a silly smile and then looked at his shoes. We both knew that he'd have to do it. I wouldn't have compromised myself in this way unless I'd been sure of him. Over the years the Department had given him a steady supply of well-paid jobs. Whatever he suspected about this being a private job, he wasn't likely to risk losing a contact like me: 'Look, Bernd. We've known each other a long time and we've both done each other a few favours over the years, so I'm not sure which of us owes what to who. But the only reason I am standing here indulging you in this mad idea is because I know there is not the slightest chance of your getting anyone else to even think about taking it on.'

'Short take-off and landing. Single engine I think; there's not much room at the Irish end. Grass, of course, but it's used by a club so there's no obstructions worse than hedges. I'll get someone to take a close look at its condition when we get nearer the time.'

He didn't reply for a moment, then he said: 'This is not Nintendo; this is not a computer game we are playing: zap the pixels and the screen goes dark. Putting an airplane down on to a garbage dump in pitch darkness is for keeps. Pilots don't benefit from their mistakes, Bernd. Pilots don't benefit from their mistakes because the poor bastards don't live long enough after the first mistake to benefit.'

I'd heard it all before of course. These black-sky pilots liked you to know they were earning their fees. 'Okay, Swede,' I said. 'Put away the violin.'

'I can keep my mouth shut,' he said. 'I flew the plane for your friend Volkmann that night when it all happened. I kept that quiet, didn't I? You didn't know that, did you?'

'No,' I said, and my ears were flapping. I was trying to remember if he had met Werner, and if so where and when. 'Did Volkmann fly that night?'

'Not Volkmann. The plane wasn't intended for him, he was just the one who sent me the order. The plane was for your buddy Prettyman.'

'Prettyman?'

'Don't play dumb, Bernd. Jay Prettyman, the Department's arm's-length hatchet man. The white-faced one – the spooky guy with no eyebrows.'

'Yes, Jay Prettyman. I know him.'

'Of course you know him. He was one of your close buddies, wasn't he?'

'I don't have any close buddies,' I said.

'And I'm beginning to understand why,' said the Swede. 'He briefed me. I was to wait for him to arrive no matter how long. I had a package for him. He was to climb aboard and I would fly him out to England. The timing was important. They found an early-morning slot for me at Gatwick. I didn't want to get there too early and attract a lot of attention with the flight-control people. They are all Gestapo.'

'Yes,' I said. The Swede regarded all authority with contempt. Even the flight controllers were classified as mortal enemies rather than saviours. 'Tell me more.'

'It was almost light before anyone arrived. When the car came it wasn't Prettyman. The arrangement was that Prettyman would be riding a bicycle. I'd take the bicycle with us. It gave him a chance to hide the car away somewhere. I'd taken my seats out to make space for it. I'd even tried a bicycle inside to make sure there was no difficulty getting it through the door.'

Good careful Swede. 'But it was a car that arrived?'

'I guessed something had gone badly wrong. Your wife was being extracted by road, wasn't she?'

'Yes,' I said. 'And who was in the car?'

'A woman. She wouldn't fly with me. She just told me to get out of there as soon as possible. She told me to go home and forget about it. She said I'd be paid a bonus for being kept waiting. I knew that was bullshit. Did you ever hear of those bastards paying a black-sky for being delayed?'

'Who was it? Someone you recognized?'

'I don't know,' he said. 'I gave her the package and I took off out of there.'

'Don't start playing smart-ass with me, Swede.'

'I said I don't know. That means I don't know. Got it?' He was suddenly aggressive as he perhaps realized that he was saying more than he intended.

'You are too old, and too goddamned scarred, and too poor to start handing over packages to people you don't know. How did she identify herself?'

He waved his long-barrelled gun. 'Passport. Mrs Prettyman. Valid UK passport. What was I to do?'

'Don't whine. What was in the package?'

'I don't know. It was sealed. It was a locked case. It weighed a ton. I gave it to her and she beat it right away. Mrs goddamned Prettyman climbed into her car without even a thank-you or good-bye. It was a long time before I got it figured out.'

'What did you figure out, Swede?'

'It was some kind of hit. It was never intended that I should fly Prettyman out of there. What would I be doing with a package for him? Hell, we were on our way to Gatwick. What was in that package that he had to have it on the airplane? His make-up? His vitamin pills?' The Swede laughed. 'No, Prettyman was involved in a hit. I was there to collect the corpse. My guess is that the case contained identity papers for the one they were going to kill. That's why it was all so secret. That's why Prettyman had to get it.'

'Have you seen Prettyman since?'

'I never spoke about it from that day to this. I know how to keep my mouth shut.'

'Until now,' I said.

Swede seemed suddenly to regret his indiscretion. He drew himself up like a soldier getting ready to receive a medal, or be kissed on both cheeks. Or both. 'I will need at least a month to make the preparations,' he said. 'I will need someone to help at the English end. Someone with a bit of authority.'

'I brought some cash for you.' I'd brought a sealed envelope containing two thousand pounds in twenties. Now I handed it to him.

He took the envelope and carelessly pushed it away in an inside pocket. 'I'll need at least five grand up front and I won't be able to give you much of a refund if you cancel. It will have been used by that time. And once I deliver your passengers I take off and that's the end of our deal.'

'Did I ever do it any other way?'

'You're crazy, Bernd.'

'They are my kids,' I said.

'Your passengers,' he corrected me, determined not to be a party to my crime. 'Have you told them what you intend? Don't surprise them at the last minute, will you, eh? I don't want to be struggling with unwilling youngsters. That could make for real trouble.'

'Only four beats to the bar, Swede. You just drive the plane; leave the passenger manifest to me, right?'

'It's the best way,' he said, with a silly smile on his face.

It was only then that it dawned on me. 'You bastard. You're as drunk as a skunk.'

'Naw, naw, naw,' he said.

I stepped forward to slap him, or rattle him, I'm not sure what.

He waved the huge replica Colt at me in a way more comical than threatening. 'Don't shake the pin-table machine, or you won't get your peanuts,' he said.

'If you let me down, Swede, I'll kill you.'

'Yah, yah. I know what you're like.' It didn't sound like warm approval. 'Gabrielle left me,' he said sorrowfully. 'A marketing development analyst, he calls himself. What's that? What the hell does a development analyst do? He's just a youngster. She says he makes a hundred thousand dollars a year. Can you believe it?'

'I can believe it,' I said. I'd never heard of Gabrielle; I didn't know if she was his wife or his girlfriend, or his pet piranha. But whatever she was, I could easily believe she'd want to get away from him.

'Gabi! Gabi!' He said it more loudly to help me remember. 'The one you borrowed the car from.'

'Oh, yes.' I remembered now. Gabi Semmler, a thirty-year-old Berliner who worked as a private secretary to an air charter company with which the Swede wanted to do business. I had in fact seen her in Berlin quite recently. I wondered if that was before, during or after the break-up. But I didn't wonder about it very much.

'Don't worry, my old Bernd. Swede won't spill your beans. Swede never lets you down.'

'Sober up,' I said. 'And make it quick.'

'Yah.' He put the muzzle of the long-barrelled gun against his own temple and shouted 'Bang' loudly enough to make me jump.

'Come along, Swede. Time to go walkies. Put away your toys.' It was terrible weather. We emerged into Charing Cross Road just as a thunderbolt ripped the dark sky apart with a jagged blue line. The crash of its thunder echoed all along the street. Cars, delivery vans, black taxis and the red double-decker buses, glistening with rain, were suddenly frozen by the lightning's flash. Gutters, swollen and turbulent, swept fleets of litter to the maelstrom of the drain. The ferocious downpour made tall stalks on the pavement, and there was a clatter of noise as rain hit the shop-window glass and drenched me. The Swede came into the street and we both huddled in the shelter of a shop doorway, trying to spot an available taxi-cab.

'Sometimes I wonder what goes on in that head of yours, Bernd,' the Swede said. 'Is this a dream of a new life far away?'

'Tell people your dreams, and they never come true,' I said.

'Yah, yah, yah,' said the Swede and laughed. He had an awful laugh; like the bray of an angry mule. Suddenly he spotted a cab. He ran into the street, dodging between the cars as they braked and swerved to avoid him, and all the time he bellowed 'Taxi! Taxi!' to get the driver's attention. 'Heathrow: terminal one,' he shouted to the driver as he climbed inside. He gave me a brief salute of thanks – or was it mockery? – before sliding the cab window closed. I watched him go, suspecting that as soon as he was out of sight he'd tell the driver some other destination.

Then a white Ford Transit pulled away from the kerb and into the traffic. It bore the lettering that proclaimed it to be from a supplier of luxury foodstuffs to restaurants. The driver's face was familiar to me but I couldn't place him. One of the Department's corps de ballet perhaps. If they were tailing the Swede, I wondered if I'd been logged too. I preferred to believe it must be some sidekick of the Swede's. I told myself he was apt to be over-cautious even when meeting old friends. Engaging a minder was usually a sign of bad conscience, or bad company, or carrying too much cash.

I finally got a cab. My next stop was Mayfair and the office of an estate agent. I told the cab-driver I was still looking for the precise address, and let him go round Grosvenor Square twice while closely watching the other traffic. That uncomfortable, unhealthy and neurotic paranoia that had helped keep me alive so long, made me think I was being followed. I wondered if the Ford Transit had not been Swede's man after all, but rather the changeover vehicle for my tail. But if there was someone tailing me now, he was an expert. Or perhaps simply someone who knew what my appointments were, and got there ahead of me.

I was ten minutes late. One of my father-in-law's many lawyers was waiting too, and tapping his fingers on a thick bundle of papers. In 1983, when Fiona suddenly abandoned me and the children, and departed to East Germany, our home was rented to four young Americans. But now the Americans were moving out. Three of them were posted to banks in Singapore and Hong Kong, and the last remaining tenant couldn't find anyone to share the rent. The agent wanted me to sign papers reassigning the property to my father-in-law. I had little alternative, for the major financial investment in the house had been made by him: our investment had been no more than love and labour.

The agent's office was an elegant room furnished with antique furniture, with framed engravings and maps of historic London on the walls. Maps are of course the décor adopted by men reluctant to display their taste in art. The only discordant note was struck by the grey plastic word-processor that occupied a table in the corner and buzzed. 'So good of you to be so punctual,' said the estate agent, as if he'd been warned that I might not show up at all. He smiled reassurance and I smiled right back at him. My father-in-law wasn't a crook; Fiona and I would come out of it with reasonable compensation for our slice of the mortgage, but I hated the way he always did these things through his minions. Why the sudden summons to this office? Why couldn't he have discussed the Duke Street property with us when we were with him at the weekend?

I signed over the pencilled crosses.

☆

When I returned to work Dicky was waiting for me. He was sitting in his office, a large comfortable room with the skins of genuine lions stretched across the floor, and a view across the trees from the two windows. Between the windows he had positioned his lovely rosewood table. The top of it was virtually clear. It was Dicky's oft-stated belief that ordinary office desks, telephones and word-processors were not necessary for work, and for the sort of work that Dicky did, they weren't. He had only one telephone, and the only reason he had a fax machine here was because he had recently been deferring his choice of lunch place until he'd studied the faxed daily menus of his favourite haunts.

'Have coffee,' he suggested. It was a significant offering, and demonstrated that Dicky had something important to ask me. The coffee appeared from the next room, where Dicky stored all the ugly office machinery and the pretty young girls with whom Daphne competed.

'You saw Uncle Silas?'

'Yes,' I said. I was sipping coffee and sitting in the soft white leather armchair that Dicky had recently installed for his visitors. There were new curtains too, and the official sepia portrait of the sovereign had been put into a rosewood frame, so that it matched his table.

'He sent for you?' And in case I didn't understand: 'Silas Gaunt sent for you?' Dicky sat behind his table with his arms folded. He was wearing a blue pinstripe suit of very ordinary style. I guessed he'd been with the politicians.

'There was a garbled message . . .' I explained. I thought he was going to complain about my taking time off to go there without asking his permission.

'He's been refusing to see anyone.' Dicky touched his lips with his fingertips. It was a gesture he often used, but I some-times saw it as some kind of unconscious fear that he was saying too much. 'Silas refused to see the D-G last week. He said he was ill. When Bret tried to meet with him he was extremely abusive.'

I savoured the coffee. It came from the shop of Mr Higgins. Dicky said it was the best coffee in England and Dicky was very fussy about coffee.

'Ye gods, Bernard. Don't just sit there drinking coffee and smiling at me. I'm asking you a question.'

'What are you asking, Dicky?'

'Why you? Why would Uncle Silas send for you while he refuses to see anyone from the top floor? Even the D-G. He told Bret he wouldn't even let the prime minister into his home. He was swearing at Bret like a drunken sailor. Bret recorded the call. He was really insulting. So why you, Bernard? What's it all about?'

'He wanted to talk about my father.'

'Is that all?'

'Yes, that was all,' I said.

'All right, don't go taking offence at every little thing. No reflection on your father.'

Dicky's phone rang. 'It's for you, Bernard.' He handed it to me. It was Bret on an internal line. With that brisk and unmistakable transatlantic accent he had no need to identify himself: 'Bernard.' The accent on the second syllable. 'There's been an irritable female caller on an outside line. Desperately trying to reach Fiona.'

'She's in Rome,' I said. 'The terrorist symposium.'

'Sure, I know that,' said Bret imperiously. 'I sent her there. Do you want to talk to Gloria? She will tell you who took the call.'

'Is it something for Dicky?' I said. I couldn't understand why I should be suddenly handling my wife's day-to-day workload.

'It's not work,' said Rensselaer. 'It's a family matter. Private.' His voice was uncharacteristically concerned as he added: 'You haven't got a car here, have you?'

'No.'

'Take Gloria's.'

'To do what?'

'If you need it, if you need it,' said Bret, almost losing his cool. Then, more calmly, he said: 'Gloria has her car here. She will sort it out, Bernard. She's good at this sort of thing.'

At what sort of thing, I was about to ask, but he had already hung up his phone.

94

I made hurried excuses to Dicky and went to the office I was using. I was looking up Gloria's number in the internal directory when she put her head round the door. She was wearing a crimson suit. Her blonde hair was drawn back and her forehead covered in a neat fringe. The change in her appearance was startling. 'Bernard!' she said. 'Where have you been? I've been phoning everywhere trying to locate you. You don't have a mobile phone; there was no contact number. You just disappeared. I had security go to every room in the building.' She wasn't smiling; she seemed annoyed.

'I do that sometimes,' I said.

She stepped into the room and pushed the door behind her closed as if about to confide a secret to me. 'Did Bret tell you?' Now I could see her more clearly. She appeared to be brimming over with rage. Her face was full and rounded with it, her lips pouting, and her big brown eyes wide open and glistening with animosity.

'What? Tell me what?'

'The school phoned. I phoned them back. It may be nothing.' She stopped before bringing out the rest of it in a rush. 'The school minibus went off the road and turned right over. It's mostly just cuts and bruises but some of the children – five, the matron said – will be kept in hospital overnight.'

'Billy's school?'

'Yes. I'm sorry, I should have said that. Yes, Billy's school. A collision with a motor-cycle ... on the way to a football game with a school in south London. The driver's badly hurt and the motor-cyclist is in intensive care. Oh, Bernard!'

'Where is he?'

She was trying to make it easier for me, I could see that. 'We're not sure that Billy is hurt. There were several ambulances and the children were taken to different hospitals. One of the girls downstairs said it was on the radio. I phoned the BBC but they said it must have been some local news bulletin.'

'Do you know which hospitals?'

'The school said they would telephone again as soon as they hear more about it. But I think it's best we go to the school. Other parents are there already. They will know everything that's happening.'

'It's all right. I know the way.'

'Let me drive, Bernard. Look, your hands are trembling.'

'Don't be silly,' I said, but I found myself pushing my hands into my pockets in case she was right.

'Your in-laws are away. Their housekeeper, or whoever it was I spoke to, said she didn't know how to contact them.'

'They're at a fat-farm. They don't leave contact numbers; they don't like to be disturbed there.'

'I'll leave all this stuff; I'll get you to the school.'

☆

It was a nerve-racking journey, with Gloria driving like a Mexican car thief and the rain beating down and the traffic jams that always result from such storms. Gloria was giving all her attention to the road as an excuse not to engage in conversation, but I couldn't mistake how much the news had upset her.

With other circumstance it might have proved a perfect opportunity to confide in her. I strapped in tight, sat back and looked at her. It was no good denying that I needed her. I needed her now, when the news had brought me low, and I badly needed to hear her say she loved me. I wanted to hear her say that she would gladly exchange her life in England for some lack-lustre penny-pinching life with me. A life in some distant foreign land without an extradition treaty. But I didn't broach any of these complex and far-reaching matters. I sat huddled in her car, an old Saab that she'd got ready for rally-driving but which had blown up on a reconnaissance trip before even starting the first rally. Now it had become her London runabout, a fierce roaring beast which called for endless tinkering and a driving technique that catered to its many vices.

Billy's private school was distinguished more for its high fees and exclusivity than for its academic excellence. It had been chosen by Fiona's father. The school had made its home in a fine old creeper-covered mansion long since adapted, subdivided and bent to the needs of academe. When we arrived its gravel forecourt was crowded with the hastily parked cars of distraught parents. The marques of BMW, Volvo, Mercedes and Rolls measured the aspirations of parents whose faith in the government's oft-promised meritocracy was less than absolute.

The school matron was a plump grey-haired woman in a high-necked white blouse, pleated tweed skirt and flat-heeled shoes. She had been assigned to greet with a weary smile, and copious sweet tea and biscuits, those relatives who had flouted the instruction to stay at home by the phone.

Gloria and I were sitting in the staffroom under a colourful poster depicting the fiercer members of various endangered species of the animal world. I was on my second cup of tea, and selecting a jam-filled biscuit from the plate Gloria offered, when a thin young man in a mauve track-suit told us his name was Hemingway and that he was my son's house master, while studying a clipboard and avoiding our eyes.

'I don't think your son was on the bus,' he said, still looking down at his paperwork. 'He's certainly not in the football team.'

When I replied that I thought he was, Mr Hemingway ran a nicotine-coloured fingertip down the typewritten list on his board and said: 'His name isn't here. So he couldn't have been on the bus. No spectators went along; just the team and two teachers.'

'If he's not on the team and wasn't on the bus, why did you phone?' I said.

'Phone?' He looked up at me.

'My wife's office. Someone called my wife and left a message.'

97

'But not from here,' he said, tucking the clipboard under his arm. 'No one from here phoned any of the parents.'

'But . . .'

'No one from the school phoned. We are responding to calls but we are not alarming people.' He smiled. He was obviously selected as a man who would face irate parents resolutely. 'The Head was saying to me – only half an hour ago – that it was incredible that the word got around so quickly. No parents or next-of-kin have been contacted by us. It was on the radio of course, and parents phone around their friends. It must have been a friend who phoned you, not the school. The Head decided to wait until we had a proper report from the hospital, and a list of who will be held there overnight. It still hasn't come, but as you see there are at least two dozen parents here.'

'How can I be sure about Billy? That he's safe?'

'The little lad must be here. On weekdays no boys are permitted to leave the school grounds without written permission. Why don't I send one of the boys to find him? This afternoon he should be at the social awareness class . . . ah, no, Mrs Phelan is ill. Wait a moment, your son's class were swimming . . . no, I tell a lie: current affairs . . .'

They found him eventually. Billy was in the library, sitting at the back near the heating radiator, memorizing the names of the world's highest peaks for a geography test. He was wearing shorts, long socks and a T-shirt with the slogan 'Bad Spellers of the World – Untie'. He was a different child here in the environment of his school, his hair parted carefully and his shoes polished. And his movements were diffident and restrained. For a moment I found it difficult to recognize him as my little Billy.

'I'm sorry, Dad,' he said.

'We were worried,' I said, embracing him.

He kissed Gloria. She suppressed a little sob and then blew her nose loudly on a small handkerchief that, after some rummaging, she had tugged from her handbag.

'They said I could be a reserve. One of the half-backs had a wisdom tooth seen to. But he got better too quickly.'

'Would you and Mrs Samson like to take your son off for the evening?' said Hemingway, patting Billy on the head and smiling at Gloria. 'He could miss prep, I'm sure.'

'Yes,' said Gloria, assuming the role of Mrs Samson effortlessly, 'we'd like to do that.'

'Wow. Thank you, sir. Would that be all right, Dad? There's a super new Chinese restaurant opened in the high street, where that rotten old second-hand bookshop used to be. It starts serving early: the Pekin Duck it's called – but my friends all call it the Piping Hot.'

'Sounds good,' I said, looking quizzically at Gloria. She nodded. 'It's Gloria's car,' I explained to Billy.

'That great Saab. Yes, you can see where the rally numbers used to be. And a car-phone antenna. It's super. What tyres do you have?'

'Go and get your coat and a scarf,' I said. 'And a sweater, it's cold.'

I looked at Gloria. I didn't have to say anything. It was clear that Billy had seen us arrive, and gone off to hide in the library. 'Who cares if he's in the football team?' I said to Gloria.

'He wants you to love him,' she said. 'He wants to do something to make you pleased.'

'I do love him,' I said testily. Was I such an ogre? It was one of those days when everyone was speaking in riddles.

'And be proud of him.'

'I hate football. I hate all games,' I said, 'even chess.' Mr Hemingway's hearing must have been remarkably acute, for I noticed him stiffen as I said this, although his back was towards me as he stood with other parents on the far side of the room.

'Billy doesn't really like Chinese food,' said Gloria. 'Insist we go to that place on the bypass, it's called The Old Barn or The Manoir or something phoney like that. He can have hamburger and spaghetti and that dessert with apples that they set fire to at the table.'

'So why did he say Chinese?' I hissed. Perhaps I was speaking too loud; people were looking at us.

'You said you liked Chinese one day in Islington when it was raining and we were looking for somewhere to eat lunch before going to a matinee of *Hamlet*. Billy was doing it at school. Remember?'

'Oh, yes.' What a memory she had. I would have given six months' salary to have been able to remind her of what she was wearing on that lovely perfect happy day that I'd entirely forgotten.

'If you two – you and Billy – would just stop trying to do nice things for each other, you . . .'

She never finished what she was about to say, for Billy had made a lightning change of clothes, and was now dressed in grey flannel uniform with the school's Latin motto on the breast pocket. He was running down the stairs swinging his raincoat in his hand.

The fact that we took Billy for a dinner of spaghetti and meatballs did not deprive him of the chance to make jokes, and parade his learning, using the name of the new Chinese eating place. The jokes ranged from oodles of noodles to snub-nosed Pekingese poodles and on to Peking man, and if we didn't laugh enough, Billy explained the reference to us. And he did it in exhaustive detail. He was, in many ways, very like me.

With every last strand of spaghetti devoured and every crêpe flamed, folded and eaten, with jokes all told and Saab tyres examined, Billy was delivered back to his school dormitory. Gloria drove me back to London. It was a perfect opportunity to have the serious talk with her that I had been putting off so long.

Perhaps I didn't choose the most prudent way to begin: 'I'm going to get him away from that bloody school. He'll grow up to be a detestable little snob if he stays there. Did you notice that joke about the slow-witted policeman?'

'Oh, Bernard! Whatever are you on about? You constantly make jokes about people – dim stockbrokers and greedy politicians. Don't be so captious. Billy will never be a snob like that. He is lovely and full of fun.'

'Sometimes I feel like running off with him,' I said, putting a toe into the territory as lightly as I knew how. Gloria Kent, of Hungarian extraction, immediately sensed the danger: you don't grow up a foreign girl in an English school without knowing there is a minefield on both sides of every English social exchange.

'He would never go,' she said.

'You sound very certain.'

'He'd be miserable. He doesn't know you well enough, Bernard.' I could tell from her tone that she was expecting a rush of objections from me, but I let it go and waited. 'He loves you, and he knows that you love him, but you don't know him really well.'

'I know him.'

'You know the child he used to be.'

I thought of Mr Hemingway. Billy had spoken of his house master several times over dinner. I don't say Billy hero-worshipped Mr Hemingway, or even admired him, but any hint of praise from Mr Hemingway was an accolade that Billy was keen to share with us. 'That would come,' I said.

Gloria wasn't so sure. 'He has his friends and a set routine. You can tell that from everything he said tonight. You may regard that school as a factory producing Philistine pin-brained Englishmen of a sort you heartily despise, but it's Billy's only reality. And he likes it.'

'Thanks, Gloria.'

'Did you want me to baby you? You waited too long. Take him back to your fancy Mayfair apartment, but he'll be a stranger. It will all take time, Bernard. Forget any idea about waving a magic wand. He's a young man. He has a mind of his own.'

'I suppose you are right,' I said through gritted teeth.

'Would your wife give her phone number to the school?' said Gloria suddenly, as if she'd been thinking about it.

'No,' I said.

'And not to some other parent?'

'Especially not to some other parent.'

'Then who phoned the office?'

'And why?' I added.

She controlled the car with a manic skill that never quite became frenzy. As we sped along the shiny suburban streets the neon lights made halos of bright pink and blue and green around her blonde hair and painted her face with savage patterns. It didn't seem like the moment to ask Gloria if she'd like to run away with me. But in the event I didn't have to; she read my mind. And she wasn't going to let me out of the car without telling me how well she read it. 'You are not in Berlin, Bernard,' she said as we pulled up in front of my apartment. I reached for the door catch but not too strenuously. 'You can't handle two women in that psychotic way you run from one side of the Wall to the other.'

I didn't answer. I could see she had something she had to say. 'I know you love me, and I love you too,' she said in the speedy perfunctory small-print way that advertisers deal out the mandatory health warnings. 'But you already have a wife and children. Now you must let me alone, and let me make my own life.'

'But Gloria . . .'

She tapped the accelerator just enough to make the engine growl. 'Let me alone, Bernard,' she implored frantically. 'For God's sake, let me alone.'

She stared straight ahead as I climbed out of the car. 'Goodnight, Gloria,' I said. 'I don't want to hurt you.'

She didn't turn her head and she didn't answer; she just drove away.

5

Berwick House, England

I RESENTED BEING sent to London Debriefing Centre to squeeze some reactions out of my brother-in-law George Kosinski. He was being detained on a warrant: which was the Department's way of saying imprisoned without promise of trial. That he was held in a lovely old eighteenth-century manor house, and permitted to wander in its seven acres of lawns and woodland, to say nothing of its rose bushes, orchard and vegetable garden, did not alter the fact that Berwick House was surrounded by a high wall. Or change the fact that the innocuous-looking men working in the grounds were armed. My unease was of course compounded by the fact that I had personally brought George from Poland. And I had submitted a report that described his long-term service as an agent of its communist government. That had been acted upon immediately; my other suggestions were ignored. I'd put aside my personal feelings about George. My anger at his treachery and stupidity had abated. Of course he was small fry by some measures, but even a low-echelon agent such as George could, if handled skilfully, provide valuable information about contacts and safe houses and all the mumbo-jumbo of enemy activities here in Britain. George had not been handled skilfully: he'd been shelved. That was partly because any such vital information he gave us would have to be handed to 'Five', the Department's rivals, and give them a chance to outshine us when the time came to boast to our political masters.

So I wasn't in a happy frame of mind as I turned into the gates of Berwick House. The tyres scrunched on the gravel path as I stopped for the identity check. I pulled my card from my wallet but I didn't need it. The barrier was raised immediately and we went straight through. I suppose the two guards recognized the official car and driver, and one of them seemed to recognize me. He scowled.

There had been a drastic effort to clean the place up since my last visit. The ancient army huts, and their pervading smell of tar preservative, had disappeared from what once had been the croquet lawn. 'Keep off the grass' signs were staked into the mud, erected there in the hope that summer would bring grass enough to hide the huts' broken concrete foundations which had resisted the drills and bulldozers.

The rain had stopped but water was dripping from the trees and there were deep puddles in the gravel drive. Two men in coveralls were fitting cables along the bed of the newly drained moat that surrounded the red-brick main building. The irises, lilies and bulrushes had been ripped out and stacked along the path, ready for the compost heap. As we went over the red-brick bridge to the courtyard, I could see the way the underwater alarms were being replaced with new technology. I wondered what it was costing. It didn't seem as if the Foreign Office cashiers were betting on an early end to the cold war.

The dismal and draughty entrance hall provided more evidence of the many changes that Berwick House had undergone over the years. Its history was to be seen in the notices that defaced the lovely panelled walls. The earliest notice was poster-sized, protected by heavy glass and framed in oak. It declared Berwick House to be a 'prohibited place' by order of the Secretary of State (1911 Act, section three.) The typography was Victorian, its style like a sedate theatre playbill. Amended and supplemented by the Official

Secrets Act of 1920 and 1939, it must have been fixed to the wall soon after Berwick House was taken over by the authorities in that week after war was declared. There were other notices, of varying age, dealing with everything from fire precautions to the playing of transistor radios and not smoking. Now that so many Home Office employees, security men and Special Branch officers were carrying hand-guns, there was a lock-up closet for guns, and bright new notices: 'Strictly No Firearms Beyond This Point'. On one of my previous visits they mislaid the Walther PPK I was carrying and tried to give me a nickel-plated Spanish Astra in its place. It took me an hour to sort it out. Since then I had always made a point of saying I was unarmed.

Having signed the book, and noted that the previous visitor's signature was dated four days earlier, I collected my 'exit chit' and was taken up to see George. I was pleased to find that he had been assigned relatively comfortable rooms. Number five suite was one of the best accommodations, after the staff offices and Governor's apartment. It was large. Its position on a corner of the first floor provided two windows for the drawing-room and extensive views of the grounds. The room was exceptionally tidy; neurotically so. His red velvet slippers were placed along-side his chair, cushions plumped and exactly positioned, even the newspapers were neatly folded as if ready for resale. The book he was reading – *The Last Grain Race* by Newby – had a page marked with a slip of newspaper. The book, and a case for his spectacles, were positioned upon the newspapers with care.

George Kosinski was standing at the window, looking out at the bare trees and the high walls that surrounded the property. He took off his heavy spectacles as if to see me better. 'Bernard. They said you were coming.' His accent – the hard high pitch of London's docklands – revealed his origins, despite his West End clothes.

George Kosinski was forty years old. A stocky, restless Londoner born of Polish parents, he had inherited all the moodiness and poetic melancholy of his forebears. He looked well but dispirited. He'd trimmed his moustache and cut his grey wavy hair shorter. Now, despite the well-cut pants, monogrammed shirt and soft Italian moccasin shoes, I did not see much of the flashy tycoon that I remembered from earlier days.

'I was ordered to come,' I told him. 'I knew that if you wanted to see me, you would have sent a message.'

His quirky smile suggested that, should he ever find himself in need of help or sustenance, my name was not one that would naturally come to his mind.

'Shall we take a walk?' I said. He went across the room to get his coat. 'Wrap up, it's cold outside.'

'I haven't had a breath of fresh air for a week,' he said. It was not true. I had asked that he should not be allowed his daily walk for the two days before I arrived simply because I wanted him to feel a bit cooped up. But I knew from the record that he normally spent an hour outside each day. I knew what he ate, and what he complained about. I even knew how many times a day he went to the toilet. Detainee reports are thorough in some respects. 'I hate this place,' he said.

'I know,' I said. He could hardly hate it more than I did. There was never anything enjoyable about coming down here to hear the contrived fictions of men who saw the error of their ways only after getting caught.

Yet the deeper reason I hated it so much was because of the odour of despair that visits here brought to my nostrils. Berwick House was the end of the trail for the men locked away here. Even those released without officially ordained punishment did not go unscathed. No one escapes the discontent that pitiless self-examination brings to those who try to serve two masters. Of the men I'd seen here, at least four eventually took their own life. Then there were the tragic cases, like Giles Trent, murdered in error when a disinformation plan went wrong. And Erich Stinnes, a KGB man I killed in a messy exchange of rounds that sent his arterial blood gushing into one of my recurring nightmares.

☆

George put on his coat and looked in a mirror to arrange his hat and cashmere scarf. It always encouraged a detainee to be taken away from the rooms where microphones could be hidden. London Debriefing Centre's handling of George had not been done properly. LDC staff never seemed to learn how important the preparation period was, and how much it affected the interrogation. George was not angry, he was not restless and he was not pacing up and down in frustration. It was too quiet and too comfortable here, and he had been given nothing to do. That gave him too much time to think. Thinking at night, when sleep is being lost, is good; but thinking in the daytime is bad. Opportunities for thinking were not desirable when you held a man such as George. Giving him time to reflect gave him time to reconsider, to invent cover stories, weave elaborate lies, suppress guilt and justify his treason. Furthermore I was not an experienced interrogator; I was just a member of George's family.

'I know why you came,' he said. We had walked around the walled vegetable garden in silence, apart from George identifying the dead and dying herbs that had been planted in an elaborate cruciform pattern. 'You want to know if Tessa was a part of it.' He bent to pick some leaves.

'Was she?'

'You don't care about me. It's Tessa you are worried about. Tessa and what she might have been hearing from your wife over the years. What she might have told me and what I might have passed along the line.'

'I can't say I've worried about that angle a great deal,' I told him.

'No? Then you'd better start worrying about it. You can bet that's the part of it your masters are worried about.' He threw away the leaf and pushed his glasses into place with his forefinger.

They were always slipping down his nose. I don't know why he chose such heavy frames.

'Is that what they've been asking you here?' I said. I knew it wasn't; I'd seen the transcripts.

He pulled a face. 'Yes, and no. They go around and around. Yesterday we were talking about my school-days. One of them is a psychiatrist, complete with a slide show. And even a book of those damned ink-blot patterns. I thought those things were ancient history by now.'

'Rorschach test patterns. Yes, well that's normal routine,' I said, in case George had formed some kind of paranoid resentment about it.

'Tess was implicated right from the beginning,' said George.

I didn't respond.

'Sorrel,' said George reaching down to pluck a large green leaf, crushing it in his hand and then sniffing at it. 'I suppose it grows all the year round. I didn't know that. Not much aroma.'

'Where were you at school, George? London I suppose, with an accent like yours. Was it a school in Poplar?'

He swung his head round to stare up at me, hardly able to believe that I was not going to follow up his tempting nugget about the treason of his wife Tessa, and the possible involvement of me and my wife too.

'Yes, good old Poplar,' he said, stressing his cockney accent. 'You knew that of course. But they say a trial lawyer should never ask a question to which he doesn't already know the answer.'

'I'm not a lawyer,' I said.

'But you've done your homework, Bernard. And I admire the way you steer away from the subject of Tessa as if not interested.'

'It's not a matter of being interested, George. It's simply that I recognize it as a bit of bloody nonsense. You'll have to do better than that to get my undivided attention.'

'Will I, Bernard? Well, you deny it. You'll have plenty to deny by the time I've finishing spilling my guts to them.'

'For instance?' I said.

He was getting intense now. That was what I wanted. He pretended to be giving all his attention to the herbs. Upon his open hand he had laid out an array of them, some curled and brittle and blackened by frost, others hard and green and aromatic. He prodded at the leaves with a fingertip, as if giving them all his attention. 'Mint. That one I don't recognize. Marjoram. Bay . . . but its real name is *Laurus nobilis*. Sometimes cookery writers translate it as laurel, but laurel leaves are a deadly poison.'

'And taste like hell,' I said affably, as if I didn't mind his absurd little herb recognition rigmarole.

He looked at me quizzically. 'Like bitter almonds, at least that's what I read somewhere. It's the writers who make all the mistakes, Bernard. The people who worship little pieces of paper with writing on. The cooks and gardeners never get it wrong because they don't care what it's called.'

I grunted. I suppose it was a spontaneous and clumsy attempt to show me how wrong it was to categorize him as an enemy. The truth, as he no doubt saw it, was that decent old George had tried to play some sort of game that wouldn't harm either side. I was able to guess the meaning underlying George's allegory only because nearly everyone locked up here persuaded themselves that the truth was something along those lines.

'"For instance," you ask me,' he said. 'For instance, I could tell them about Tessa's relationship with that fellow Trent, the communist agent. He was one of your people, wasn't he? Then there was your meeting with that CIA maverick Posh Harry . . . a meeting you arranged in my offices in Southwark.'

'That was years ago, George.' I said it as calmly as I could. Locked up here and brooding upon the way I had brought him to book, George had lots of time, lots of motivation, and all the necessary ingenuity, to weave a thousand unconnected incidents into a web from which I wouldn't escape. Perhaps his fabrications wouldn't completely convince the interrogators, the D-G or the

Appeals Board that I was a traitor, but the result might give them an excuse to discharge me as unreliable without feeling guilty about it.

'These interrogators are not fools, George. They have come across spiteful nonsense before. Implicating friends and relatives – it's not unusual in our sort of business.'

He threw the herbs away and rubbed his hands together and looked at me: 'No? How often do you have a prisoner here revealing what he knows about relatives who have top jobs in your "sort of business"? His sister-in-law? His brother-in-law? His wife? Tell me how often, Bernard. Oh, they'll listen. When I start talking, they'll listen. You can bet on that.'

Now it was all coming out: overt threats delivered with malicious intensity. Concealed beneath George's assumed calm there was a desperate drowning man, one whose flailing would pull down with him anyone he could clutch. 'Not often,' I said. 'You're a special case.'

He nodded and smiled grimly. 'Yes, I am. So if it's a servile confession you've come here for, forget it.'

'I'm not your implacable enemy, George,' I said. 'Your wisest course is to tell the truth.' I'd been sent here to Berwick House on Bret Rensselaer's instructions. Bret had told me to start him talking. Well, in that respect my visit certainly seemed to have been a success. The trouble was that George seemed to have focused all his animosity on me.

'You're right, Bernard. It's damned cold out here. Let's go back into the warm.'

There was nothing to be gained from letting George use me as a punching bag for all his frustration and resentment. But while we were still in the garden and away from the microphones I tried to make my own position clear.

'Listen to me carefully, George,' I said. 'I came here today because I was ordered to come. But before coming I put away as much of my personal feelings as I could possibly repress. With great difficulty, I'm still doing that. But you choose to make it personal and threaten me. You threaten me with your lousy rotten lies and fairy stories.' George was looking at me with his eyes open. I think he had never seen me really angry before. 'Listen to me carefully, George. When you face the interrogators you tell them the truth, the whole truth and any excuses you can invent.' I grabbed his upper arm and squeezed as tight as I could. This hurt him I suppose, for he pulled a face but didn't cry out. 'But if you tell lies about me, I will beat you bloody. I won't kill you or even cripple you but I will hurt you, George.' I shook him so that his teeth rattled. I hoped there was no one watching us. 'Even if it costs me my job, my pension or six months in the nick, I will beat the daylights out of you. And I'll get to you even if I have to break down doors.'

As soon as I loosened my grip on his arm he stepped well back from me. My words had been mild enough, but he must have seen the rage that I felt brimming up inside me. He'd seen it in my eyes, and in my face, for now he stared at me as if he was frightened to look away lest I assaulted him. Behind his spectacle lenses his eyes were bright and his cheeks pinched and pallid. 'You're a madman,' he said in a breathless voice. 'You should be put away in psychiatric care, Bernard. What's happened to you? I'm family; I'm family.' He touched his face as if I had slapped him. It was as if the mere thought of the physical beating had brought him pain.

'Don't Bernard me, you bastard.' I'd kept my anger under control for too long, and now I was on the verge of going wild. I took a deep breath and remained rooted there staring at him as I recovered my composure. I told myself that this wasn't the time and place; and that George wasn't really the enemy. George was a nothing, a delivery boy, a kid from the paddling pool who'd fallen into the deep end. George was a child on a visit to the zoo, prodding a finger through the bars of the cage to distinguish moth-eaten fur rug from bad-tempered gorilla. Now he knew. But it was too late to make much difference. I didn't say anything else to him. I returned him to his room, got a 'body receipt' signature from the floor clerk, signed out, called for the car and went home.

☆

I went directly back to London, apart from a brief stop off at a big hotel on London's outskirts. It called itself an inn, and this deception was furthered by the way some architect, who had OD'd on Hollywood Westerns, had provided it with a shiny interior of fake Victorian advertising mirrors and plastic panelling. There were pin-tables too: like glass comic books and flashing and clicking furiously, the sound echoing around the place that was empty of customers other than the driver and me.

The driver stuck to orange juice but I needed a whisky. A large single malt: a Laphroaig. The barman could only find Glenfiddich, so I had two of those instead. Fortified with the smoky taste, I made a couple of calls from the public phone in the lobby. I liked public phones, they were more private than private ones, and the calls more or less untraceable. But none of the calls got any response at the other end. The Swede had not gone home. It made me angry to think he had taken my money and continued his drunken spree. God only knows where he was. His answering machine at his home in Sweden was switched off. There was no answer from the airfield he used, and his contact number in London was giving out the shrill sounds of a line that has been disconnected. I cursed my own stupidity. I'd heard rumours that the Swede went off on melancholy bouts of drunken roving, but I'd not believed them. For years our assignments together had found him a model of competence and sobriety. It was the big bundle of cash that had tempted him of course. But why did it have to be my money?

I hung up the telephone and went into the toilet. The door banged behind me and I looked up. Two men – dressed in leather jackets and jeans – had followed me. Both looked like manual workers, but there was a marked age disparity. The elder man was about thirty-five. He stopped and stood with his back against the door to make sure we were not interrupted. He was a strong man, taller than me, and with calloused hands and battered face. A boxer, judging by the stance he adopted. Boxers can never get out of the habit of standing with their toes turned in.

The younger man was about twenty, with wavy hair and long sideburns. I'd only glanced at them. Now I went to the sink and turned both taps and took liquid soap into my hand as if I was about to wash. Keeping my head down over the bowl, I watched in the mirror as the younger man came up behind me. He thought he had me cold, so he was careless. I turned and slapped the liquid soap into his face. He must have thought it was ammonia or something harmful, for he reared away with his eyes closed and mouth open in a splutter of anger. I hit him hard in the belly, and gave him a jab in the nose as he bent forward. He dropped the knuckleduster he'd been holding and it landed on the tiles with a clatter. But the little guy was tough. He straightened up and shook his head and came at me again. He punched at me with the straight sort of blow that comes from a lot of time at the punching bag, and his fist connected with the side of my face as I ducked aside. It was lucky for me that he'd lost his brass knuckles, otherwise even that glancing blow would have sent me reeling. As it was, the pain of it rattled me. I grabbed at his jacket and held him as I tried to butt my head into his face, but the liquid soap I'd thrown at him was now all over the floor. I slipped on it and only kept my balance by hanging on to his jacket.

There was something absurd about the way we waltzed around the tiled floor, slipping and sliding and punching and clinching with neither of us able to land a decisive blow.

Under my coat, in a shoulder holster, I was carrying a sample of Heckler and Koch's best hardware. I'd been wearing it since the personal security alert. I had taken no notice of Dicky's taunts, figuring that the sort of hard men the other side were using lately might not accurately discern that I wasn't senior staff.

As my feet found a drier piece of floor, I was steady enough to get a better hold on him. I slammed him backwards, pounding him into his partner with enough force to knock the breath out of both of them. As the younger one turned his upper body to avoid my blows, I kicked his knee. The toe of my shoe found the right place, so that his leg buckled and he dropped full-length to the floor. I kicked him again and his face went bloody. It was crude stuff but these were crude people.

It gave me enough time to open my coat and get to my gun. Holding it tight I brought it round to slap the elder man in the side of the face. He was a tough old bird but the gun was heavy steel, and I hit him hard enough to cut him. He gasped with surprise as much as with the pain. It gave me a chance to knee him hard in the balls. As he went down I slammed him again with the gun and took a pace backwards to wave it at them.

The old one put his hands high enough to change the light bulbs. A VP70 is customarily carried with a round in the chamber, and you don't have to be Superman to fire off its eighteen rounds like a machine-gunner.

'Keep still, old man,' I told him. 'I'll waste you and laugh.'

He didn't answer. I frisked him and then bent down to the youngster on the floor and made sure he didn't have a gun. I took his knuckleduster from where it had fallen and stuffed it up his nostrils. 'Next time I'll kill you,' I promised cheerfully. 'If not me, one of my friends will kill you. Either way, you wind up dead. You understand?' Neither of them replied, but I could see they got the idea. 'I should put a bullet into both of you. There is a drain here, and tiles, so it won't make a mess.' I let them think about it for a minute. 'Scram – while I'm in a good mood.'

The old fellow bent and effortlessly lifted his chum to his feet. He said: 'Let me explain, old pal.'

'Shut up.'

'It's not you we are after. It's the Swede.'

'Get out of here before I change my mind.'

I wiped my face and straightened myself out. I put the gun into my coat pocket, so I could get to it quickly, and went back into the bar. I wasn't going to be driving, so I quickly downed another whisky.

Outside it was cold. I checked the car park for strangers but the cars were all empty. My driver was already at the wheel and waiting for me. 'Is there some kind of trouble?' he asked when I got into the back seat of the car. I suppose I was trembling or hyped up or dishevelled. I'm not sure what it was.

'You stupid bastard,' I said. 'You'd sit drinking your bloody orange juice while the opposition wasted me, wouldn't you?'

'What happened?'

'Forget it,' I said. 'Next time stick to Scotch; that citric acid you are drinking is eating up your brain.' The driver was an ex-cop. He was supposed to be guarding the passengers he carried. That's what he was paid to do.

Suddenly all the strength went out of me and I slumped back in my seat. Perhaps I had over-reacted to the two men. I often over-reacted. It was why I had stayed alive so long. But neither of the two had been armed, except for the knuckleduster. I wondered what they intended to do and who might have sent them. If they were really looking for the Swede, what sort of racket were they in with him?

We reached outer London as darkness came. The outward-bound traffic lanes were jammed with commuters going home. I spotted a flower shop still open. On impulse I stopped the car, went in and had them send to Gloria a dozen long-stem red roses. On the greetings tag I wrote 'How can I thank you enough?' I didn't sign it. At the time it seemed like a tender, restrained and appropriate way to say thanks.

☆

The Department had a long-standing regulation about burglars. Any employee finding strange marks around the keyhole of their front door was obliged to call the Duty Officer before proceeding inside. Of course no one obeyed this inconvenient and draconian order. It had been drafted after a female typist left some official papers on the underground train, and invented a story about her apartment in Fulham being broken into. No one believed her story except a simpleton named Henry Tiptree, the investigating officer, who drafted the new regulation as a way to justify the time and money he wasted asking everyone working for London Underground a lot of stupid questions.

I didn't do anything like that when I got back home and found the door was not double-locked. I turned the key very quietly and opened the door very slowly. Poking my head inside the door, I heard a movement upstairs. I closed the door behind me and then tiptoed up the stairs. I moved along the bedroom corridor.

'Oh, you made me jump!'

'Jesus, Fi! I thought you were a burglar!'

'What a lovely greeting, darling. You always know the right thing to say.' Fiona was standing in the doorway of the tiny dressing-room that had become a boxroom and storeroom too. She was holding up a black cocktail dress, as if trying to decide whether to consign it to Oxfam. Behind her, our largest suitcase was balanced on the rollaway bed where her sister had often slept after fighting with her husband George.

I put away my gun and went and kissed her. She smiled and kissed me back, but she did it without relinquishing her hold on the dress. 'Are you all right, darling?' she asked. 'You look funny.'

'I thought you were in Rome,' I said.

'I was. Now I'm off to Düsseldorf. Dicky can't do the European Community Security Conference and Bret says someone has to be there to wave the flag.' She leaned over her suitcase to count the packets of tights and added an extra one.

'When do you have to be there?'

'I came back to get more clothes. And I'm having my rough notes printed out and spiral-bound, to look impressive. I'm going to the office to pick them up . . .' She looked at her watch. 'My God! Is that the time? I'll never catch the plane.'

'Did you hear about the bus accident? Billy's school? The football team.'

'Yes. Billy sent me a fax, and the office sent it on to me. I had my girl phone the office and tell you. Why did you go rushing down there, darling? You had everyone at the office worried. And it's bad for the children if you make a crisis out of every little thing.'

'You phoned?'

'No. I just told you: my girl phoned. I didn't want you to worry.'

'A fax?'

'Billy sent Daddy a fax about the crash as soon as it happened. He often faxes them from the school office. Daddy fixed it up with the house master. And Daddy told Billy that unless he sent me a fax at least once a week he'd get no pocket-money. It's worked wonders, I must say. Daddy's awfully clever with the children.' She picked up a cobalt-blue party dress and held it against her, and then did the same with a dark green one. 'Which one do you think, darling?'

'A bit formal, aren't they?'

'These European people always have a rather grand dinner and ball on the last night.'

'The green one,' I said. 'You looked lovely in that at Dicky's the other night.'

'It is pretty, isn't it? But the shoes that go with it are getting scuffed.' She put the green dress back into the wardrobe and packed the blue dress in her suitcase. 'When are you due back in Berlin?'

'They want me here in London for that meeting tomorrow and another on Tuesday.'

'Unless George says something startling there will be very few items on the agenda,' she said.

'The D-G will be there, and Bret is chairing it. It's a hot potato. I think they want to fix lead weights on it, and drop it into the archives. Dicky is encouraging the idea that the sooner the whole Polish fiasco is forgotten, the better it will be for everyone. And that means forgetting George's activities too.'

'You saw George? Will they release him?'

'Even the D-G can't make that decision alone, but yes I think they'll let him go. "Five" may guess we're holding him but they can't be sure. In any case they probably won't make difficulties, providing he comes clean and then goes straight back to Switzerland and keeps *stumm*.'

'How can you be so confident that Five will agree?'

'I asked around.'

'You know people at Five that well?' From her tone of voice it sounded as if Fiona disapproved of my having friends in the Security Service. I smiled and didn't answer. 'Don't be disloyal to the Department, darling,' she said in that throaty tone that I have always found so seductive. 'Nothing is more important than that.'

'No,' I said. 'Nothing is more important than that.'

'I only asked,' said Fiona quickly and defensively. 'I'm not going to report you to the D-G, or Internal Security,' she added sarcastically. 'Why do they want *you* there? Doesn't Frank usually come over for those policy meetings? Something bad?'

'My role is to say yes to everything. Then, when it all goes wrong, Frank can say I never told him.'

'And will it all go wrong?'

'I don't know,' I said. 'And I don't much care.' I went into the bedroom where I had spotted a cup of coffee Fiona had abandoned. I sipped some of it. For the first time I could say 'I don't care' with all my heart. I'd been suffering agonies of guilt about abandoning Fiona and taking the children with me, but now I shed those penitent feelings in a sudden joyful instant. I wouldn't be here to concern myself with how the review committee disposed of George Kosinski, and swept under the carpet their foul-ups in Poland and elsewhere. I couldn't any longer worry how Fiona, and her egoistic father, arranged their lives. I wouldn't be a part of their lives any longer, and neither would my children.

I know I shouldn't have felt resentment or envy that Billy had been sending a regular fax letter to his mother, but couldn't it have been arranged without the threat of withdrawing his pocket-money? And couldn't there have been a copy forwarded to me? No matter. When I had Billy and Sally to myself I'd make sure I did the right thing for Fiona, and even for her parents. And I would have Gloria too, if everything went according to plan.

I looked at the next room, and at Fiona standing under the merciless bare bulb that lit it. She was trying to close the lid of her suitcase upon a tall pile of beautifully folded clothes interleaved with white tissue paper. She was kneeling on the rollaway bed, pushing down on the lid of the case with all her might, but she couldn't get it closed. Unaware that I was watching her, she gave a scarcely audible sob that combined anger with despair. There were tears shining on her cheeks and her eyes were bright and mad. Was she worn out, just frazzled, angry and bordering on the hysterical due to her worries about the work she did, and her unremitting schedule? Or was this a glimpse into her real mental state?

'Are you all right, darling?' I called from the bedroom without letting her know I had seen her break down and cry.

Slowly she got to her feet and came at snail's pace to the door. She leaned an arm against the door-frame and whispered: 'Would you mind helping me, darling? I never can seem to close it.'

She never could seem to close it because she put ten times as many clothes into the case as it was designed to hold. And like all women, she thought that all it needed was a man's weight and muscle to shut and lock it. It never occurred to her that the hinges were being strained to breaking-point. I got the case and put it on the floor. After a struggle, I got it closed and locked. 'You'd better put a strap round it,' I said. 'You've put far too much into it. One of these days it's going to burst open and scatter your silk panties across the carousel.'

'Don't be silly, darling. I've cut back to the bare minimum; I should have my low-heel shoes, my new hat and some more woollens really. Düsseldorf will be cold at this time of year,' she added with unanswerable logic. Then, on the carpet at her feet, she noticed the fabric flower, a white camellia that must have fallen off her Chanel dress when I was trying to get the case closed. She picked it up, and as she pretended to smell it she looked at me and smiled. She had restored herself, wiped her tears and polished her smile. She picked up a hairbrush and began putting it through her hair in a way she used to do every evening before she went to bed.

What had happened to her after she defected; during those terrible years when she was a double-agent? She seldom talked of it, but once she'd confided that the worst part was the interrogation that took place when she first arrived over there. The Soviets have many skilled interrogators; it is a talent born of their sort of paranoia. And there would be no relaxation of their rigour even when they were questioning 'a heroine of the battle for socialism'. It was a lonely business, she said, and then changed it to being a solitary business. 'But after surviving those endless questions I never felt really lonely again,' she'd told me. 'I often felt isolated and sometimes I felt forsaken, but I never felt lonely. I knew I was lucky just to have survived it.' Poor Fiona.

'A penny for your thoughts, darling,' she said.

'Nothing,' I said, and before I had to invent a lie the phone rang. I was nearest, and when I answered it the night-duty clerk told me that the car was on its way. When I relayed this message to Fiona she emphatically denied that it could be for her.

'I have no car. Bret's driver is taking me to the airport. I think

I'll phone and ask him to bring the typed report with him from the office. No, it can't be anyone for me, darling.'

'Who is the car for?' I asked the duty clerk.

'For you, Mr Samson. Mr Rensselaer and Mr Cruyer will be collecting you in five minutes. Would you please go downstairs and wait for them. It's very urgent, they said. Very very urgent.'

6

Mayfair, London

'WHO IS IT? Bernard? Good! Put your skates on and hurry on down. I'm in a car at your front door and it's urgent. Urgent.'

It was Dicky Cruyer's reedy voice on the apartment's door-phone speaker. I had only put the phone down two minutes before, and now he was at my door. He was taking no chances on my finding a way to escape him.

'What's happened?' I said into the door phone.

'Yes, I know you've had a long day, Bernard. We all have. Jump to it, there's a good chap.'

I felt like pointing out that Dicky's long days were invariably punctuated by leisurely lunches followed sometimes by a post-prandial doze in his office with the 'meeting in progress' sign switched on.

Fiona was toying with the fabric camellia, wondering perhaps whether to ask me to open the case again. She looked at me as I hung up. 'Dicky,' I said. 'He's downstairs, waiting for me.'

'It's late,' she said.

'Do you know what it might be?' I asked. She shook her head. I unlocked my desk and got the VP70 pistol that had proved so useful against the hoodlums. It was a bit on the heavy side, but used with a soft holster it was a nice smooth gun that didn't rip the linings from my jackets. She watched me test it and check the magazine but didn't comment. Things had changed; there was a time when the sight of me packing a gun brought out all her anxieties. I said: 'I'll be off then.'

'Goodbye, darling,' she said. 'I'll miss you.' She held her arms out to me.

We embraced and I kissed her. 'Have a safe trip,' I said. She shivered.

'Oh, I forgot,' she said into my ear as if cooing songs of love. 'That silly girl ... the one Dicky has given me as a temporary secretary, opened one of your letters.'

'Was it anything exciting?' I said, still holding her tightly.

'The bank. You were terribly overdrawn. Three thousand and something ... and four hundred ... I forget exactly how much. I transferred some money from my account to tide you over.'

'You shouldn't have done that,' I said. 'I have back-pay due ... overdue, in fact.'

'We are not so rich we want to pay those bloodsuckers any more bank overdrafts,' she said. 'Or are we?'

'Thanks,' I said.

'There's no need to give me so much housekeeping money. Not while you are in Berlin.'

'You are my wife,' I said doggedly.

'I worry about you,' she said. 'Daddy gives me more money than I need. And it must be terribly expensive for you in Germany with the mark going up and up.'

'I manage.'

'I wish I could be with you.' Her fingers explored my waist. 'You've lost weight.' I turned my head and looked into her moist eyes. It was never easy to know exactly what was in her mind. Perhaps that was why she was able to hold her own among all those inscrutable public-school ruffians. I was not convinced by her wish. Why should she want to be with me? She'd be confirmed as permanent Deputy Europe within a month or two. No woman had ever got that high on the promotion ladder. Perhaps she guessed what was in my mind, for after what seemed ages she said: 'Do you love me, Bernard?'

'Yes, I love you.' It was true. I loved her no less than I had always loved her. The only difference was that now I loved Gloria too and, no matter how I tried, I couldn't stop thinking of her. 'Take care, darling.'

Waiting for me in the street there was a black Rolls-Royce with three whip antennas. It was not a new car; it was tall and angular, built in those days before every Rolls wanted to squat down and look like a Mercedes.

The driver opened the door for me. 'Jump in,' said Dicky, indicating the little folding jump-seat upon which he had been resting his boots. It was warm inside the car, the engine was purring away and the heater was on. Dicky slumped on the black leather back seat with Bret Rensselaer in the far corner.

Bret nodded to me. He was hunched stiffly against the arm rest in a dark suit, charcoal-grey tie, starched white shirt and gleaming black Oxfords neatly laced. His face was dejected and his hands clasped as if in prayer. The sleek Rolls belonged to Bret: elderly, respected, formal and waxen, like the man himself. Like some other American Anglophiles I'd met, Bret had an obsession with renowned old English motor-cars if they had an extra long wheelbase and elaborate custom-made coachwork with brass fittings and silk tassels.

Dicky was wearing scrubbed jeans, and a dark blue cable-knit sweater, the collar of his denim shirt just visible above the neck of it. The way he now rested one leg across his knee revealed the cleated sole of his stylish cross-country boot. Bundled alongside him on the seat he had his leather jacket. It looked as if Bret had picked him up from home at short notice.

'What's the problem?' I asked as the driver started the engine and pulled away.

'You'll see,' said Dicky. 'One of your pals is the problem . . .'

'We don't know,' said Bret, speaking over Dicky's voice with an irritable tone that made Dicky dry up, look contrite, and chew a fingernail energetically, as if trying to press the words back into his mouth.

For a few minutes neither of them spoke.

'Are we driving around the park until the spirits try to contact us?' I said.

Bret gave his famous fleeting smile. But within a few minutes the car had emerged from Park Lane, passed Buckingham Palace and was heading south.

'Special Branch are there. Five are there too. It will be a God-damned circus. I don't want any part of it, unless you need my clout. You and Dicky go inside and look. We'll park around the corner; I'll stay in the car.'

'Look at what?' I said.

'A body,' said Bret. 'They are getting impatient. They will move him as soon as you've had a chance to look. They will have made photos and taken all the measurements by the time we arrive.'

'One of our people?'

'That's what Five claim,' said Bret. 'They say one of their people recognized him.'

'He was carrying a gun,' said Dicky.

'Maybe a gun,' conceded Bret. 'I had conflicting reports about the gun.'

'A field agent?' I asked. I wondered why they wouldn't just tell me all they knew, but I could see they were both disturbed by it. Dicky was wringing his hands with occasional interludes while he chewed his nails. Bret looked drawn, breathless and stiff. The desk people seldom came into contact with the blood and snot of the Department. Any sudden reminder that they weren't working in Treasury or Agriculture came as a nasty shock. 'It's not Harry Strang, is it?'

'Harry Strang?' Dicky's cry was scoffing in tone. 'Why should it be Harry Strang?'

'I don't know,' I said.

'You do come out with some ideas, Bernard. Sometimes I wonder what goes on in that brain-box of yours.' He gave a brief mirthless chuckle and glanced at Bret, who was looking out of the window. 'Harry Strang,' he said reflectively. 'Harry Strang retired ages ago.'

'They are holding someone,' said Bret. 'A youngster. He found the body.'

'They will have to charge him or let him go,' said Dicky. 'We thought you might want to take a look at him. Just in case . . .'

'In case of what?'

'In case you recognize him,' said Dicky. 'You're inside and outside too. You are in Berlin and London. You're always on the go. You know everyone.' He looked at Bret; this time Bret met his eyes. 'Departmental people, I mean.'

'Do I? Perhaps I do.' What sort of people did these two know then? I had the feeling that they had brought me along for some other reason; for some reason they didn't want to admit.

☆

Wimbledon. Once it had been a pretty little village outside London. But when this became the spot where the mighty South Western Railway touched the networks serving London's southern suburbs, Wimbledon ceased to be a village. A frequent train service, season tickets and affordable housing had helped London swallow it up. The big lighted signs we passed offered Thai take-aways, Big Macs, unisex sauna, rented videos and the brilliantly lit products of The Handmade Belgian Chocolate Shop.

Wide and tree-lined, the backstreet in which we came to a stop was quiet. The houses were large with fake-timber façades, front lawns and wide gravel in-and-out drives. They were built for families who enjoyed Assam tea, and heather honey on Hovis toast, in front of a coal fire, until a nanny in a starched apron came and said it was time for the children to take their bath.

But they were no longer family homes, at least not many of them remained as such. Carefully painted noticeboards stared over the privet hedges to tell you that they were nursery schools or 'residential homes'. While in Catholic countries men and women selflessly shared their homes and children with their aged relatives, in Protestant countries equally selfless men and women spent every last penny to lock their aged relatives away to languish in such places as these. Here the warm and well-fed unwanted spent their final years seated side by side watching television with the volume very loud. They were plied with sweet tea and fruit cake and frozen dinners by nurses from the Indian subcontinent where the Assam tea comes from. And spent their final days in refined despair.

Bret remained in his warm car parked out of sight. Dicky walked ahead of me using his flashlight to find the gate of the house we were looking for. The building was dark, and encased in an elaborate builder's scaffolding, like an angular version of the bare trees that framed it. There was a man standing on the doorstep. He was in civilian clothes but his stance, and the quiet way in which he challenged our approach, revealed him as a policeman. When he'd seen our identity cards we went in. Just inside the door there was a uniformed cop who'd found a kitchen chair to perch upon. He was reading a paperback book – *Linda Goodman's Sun Signs* – that he pushed out of sight as we came upon him.

The whole house was in the process of being gutted by builders. Walking through it was precarious. At the front, a part of the floor was missing so that the cellar was visible. Only the staircase remained to show what a lovely old place it had once been. Dicky used his flashlight as we picked our way through the debris: a cement mixer, broken timber, ladders and bent buckets.

There were voices from the back of the house. I recognized the slight, notably refined, Edinburgh accent of 'Squeaky' King of MI5, a prima donna of the Security Service. There were four of them there. The only one I didn't recognize was a tall pale-faced man wearing a soft felt hat, loosened silk scarf and ill-fitting fawn-coloured overcoat. His stiff white collar and dark tie marked him as a senior police officer in improvised disguise. There was a police doctor with him, a man I knew from the old days. I recognized him because of his distinctively worn-out capacious leather bag of the kind that doctors cart around. There was also Keith Golds of Special Branch, a wily old-timer. I winked at Keith. I could see he'd been here a long time putting up with Squeaky, who technically was in charge. Squeaky was wearing his usual winter outfit: a short sheepskin overcoat with its woolly collar pulled up high around his neck. On his head he had a close-fitting checked cap. With his flushed face and squinted eyes he had the look of a racetrack tout.

'Hello, Bernard,' said Squeaky with a marked lack of enthusiasm.

'This is Mr Cruyer,' I said, and introduced Dicky to him. Or maybe I introduced King to Dicky. I always seem to do it the wrong way round; and some people, including Dicky, sometimes take that as a serious blow to their pride.

'Show me,' said Dicky, without spending too much time on polite exchanges of compliments. At the coal-face we always got along well with the workers from Five but Dicky and Squeaky conducted themselves like viceroys, charged with upholding the authority of their tribal chiefs. Squeaky didn't disguise his feelings about Dicky intruding into Five territory, while Dicky treated Squeaky like a judge censuring some pretentious traffic cop.

'Into the breach once more, dear friends,' said Squeaky, leading the way.

Golds rolled his eyes. I suppose they'd all suffered quite a lot from Squeaky while waiting for us to arrive.

He led us into the garage, a separate structure which, until the construction work began, had been connected to the front drive by means of a tarmac area at the side of the house. Temporarily it had become a storage area. They'd taken one of the electric cables the building workers were using, and rigged a bare bulb to illuminate it. There were empty oil-drums and some tea chests and wooden crates all stacked up as high as they could go, and throwing long shadows.

'Here we are,' said Squeaky, like a stage conjuror bringing a rabbit from the hat.

The others had seen it before. They'd had a chance to get ready for it. But even I found it gruesome. Dicky looked away and made a retching noise that became a clearing of the throat and then a cough. He got out his little Filofax notebook and buried his head in it.

The body had been moved. A chalked outline showed where it had fallen to sprawl across an oily drip-tray. Everything had spilled out; the dark ancient oil and fresh blood had grown tacky and made a strange pattern like a map of a mythical country drawn across the floor. The corpse was now laid out nearby, and we gathered round it like a funeral party. The upper part of the head was a bloody mess, wire-frame spectacles smashed into it, and the skull battered brutally. Only the lower part of his bloodied face was recognizable. His thin lips twisted in rictus mortis. 'When a man is born, he cries and others laugh; when he dies he smiles and other cry,' says the old German proverb. But there were no tears from these mourners.

'What's the score, Doc?' I said when no explanation was forthcoming.

'Nasty, isn't it?' said the doctor. 'He took a dozen or more blows with a hammer.'

'We have the hammer,' said Squeaky.

'Cause of death?' I asked.

'The killer wielded the hammer with tremendous force,' said the doctor. 'Right-handed man. You can almost rule out a woman; not many women with that sort of strength.'

'We're looking for a right-handed male tennis champion, are we Doc?'

'I'm only trying to be helpful,' said the doctor.

'Just tell me the cause of death,' I said slowly and clearly. 'Mr Cruyer can write it into his notebook. Then we can all go home and get to bed.'

'How can I be sure what happened or when?' They always start off with a disclaimer. 'Elderly man, viciously attacked: could be heart attack . . .' He gave a quick look at me. 'What the layman calls myocardial infarction. Or perhaps just old-fashioned shock. He has multiple skull fractures of course. One of the hammer blows made a deep puncture over the eye.' He stooped to point. 'That's probably the one that did it. His eye on that side has a blown pupil. That's usually a clincher. But I'm just a pill-pusher. You'd better wait for the post-mortem.'

'He was standing up?'

'Yes. He must have taken a gruesome amount of punishment before he went down. At least five blows. You can see from the blood splashes. More blows while he was on the ground. The top of the crown of his skull is intact.'

'The hands?'

'Fingers fractured and deep cuts. He tried to fight him off. Look for yourself.'

'Who found him?'

The doctor nodded to the police officer from whom he'd heard it. 'A sixteen-year-old kid . . . neighbour, lives three doors away. Kids come here and sniff glue.'

'Where is the kid now?'

'He's with his parents and a woman police constable; he had to have a sedative.'

'Time of death?'

'I've no idea, except that it was today rather than yesterday. It's damned cold in here. Sometime within the last eight hours.'

'Okay,' I said. Boxes and oil-drums were splashed with blood. There was lots of blood but the stains had gone dark and brown like last night's dinner gravy. But most of the spattered stains formed a band of marks along the boxes; at what would have been head level when he was standing up being beaten to death.

'Bloodstains and hairs on the hammer,' said Squeaky. 'It's a straightforward killing. We've done all that Agatha Christie stuff before you arrived.'

'What was in the pockets?' I asked.

'Someone had been there already,' said Squeaky.

'Any idea who it is, Bernard?' Keith asked.

'No papers on the body? Nothing at all?' I asked innocently.

'Good God, Bernard,' said Squeaky in an exasperated voice. 'It's one of your people. Why the hell don't you admit it? Identify him and let these people start clearing up the mess. Try being honest and co-operative for heaven's sake. Bugger about here for another hour, and one of the newspapers will get hold of the story.' He looked at me and more soberly added: 'No, no identification papers on the body. Nothing of any significance on the body. Bus tickets, small change, fifty pounds sterling in tens. Keith is taking the wallet, and odds and sods for Forensic. Whoever did it went through the pockets with great care and attention.'

'Or maybe that was done somewhere else and then he was brought here.'

'We can't rule that out,' said Squeaky. 'But you don't believe it and neither do I.'

Dicky was writing in his notebook and didn't look up.

'It's a German national,' I said. 'About sixty-five years old. Not one of our people. A freelance commercial pilot. We used him from time to time for arm's-length jobs. I don't know his real name. Is that honest and co-operative enough for you, Mr King?'

'It will do for a start,' said Squeaky, appeased perhaps by my polite use of his surname. 'So what do you make of it?'

'Some kind of meeting?' I offered.

'Obviously,' said Squeaky. 'Who? When? And why here?'

'A building site like this is not bad,' I said.

'What about being seen by the workers?'

131

'British building workers?' interjected Dicky. 'In winter? When did you last have any work done, Squeaky? These characters scamper off home right after lunch.'

'But not premeditated,' said Squeaky, ignoring Dicky's levity. 'The killer must have got covered in blood.'

I looked at him. Squeaky was a canny Scot. He might just be leading me on. I said: 'I'd be more convinced it was spontaneous if we knew for certain the killer found the murder weapon here on site.'

The short intake of breath from Squeaky served to indicate exasperation. 'That's really baroque, Bernard. That would be quite a complicated scenario: killer comes along with the hammer, all prepared to get spattered with blood? Why not do it quickly and quietly. Silenced gun? Or a knife? Or bare hands? The victim wasn't armed.'

'You're right, Mr King,' I agreed.

'Any next-of-kin, close friends or business associates that you know of? Wives? Girlfriends?' He smirked. 'Boyfriends?'

'No one,' I said. 'He was a loner.'

'So okay if we clear it all away?' asked Squeaky, looking around. 'By the way, we found this over there in the corner. I don't think it has any bearing on the killing.' He brought a transparent evidence bag from his case. Inside it there was Swede's replica Navy Colt. 'I suppose one of the kids who come here lost it.'

'Sure, clear it all away. That's okay with us, isn't it, Dicky?'

'We appreciate your prompt call to us,' said Dicky, becoming suddenly diplomatic. 'It wouldn't have been much fun having the D-G read it in the *Daily Mirror* and wanting to know what's what.'

Squeaky gave a grim nod. It wasn't going to be in the Daily anything tomorrow morning, or any other morning. That was what Special Branch and the local law were sewing together when we arrived.

Dicky was very businesslike. He made sure they were not going to mess about and make us wait until the post-mortem. Squeaky promised him a copy of the prelims, all the physicals – complete external exam, dental chart, scene-of-crime photos, fingerprints – and anything that Five's Co-ordination people came up with on their data base. And Dicky wanted it all by end of work the following day. 'And the "posting" as soon as it comes,' Dicky added with an authoritative nod. It was almost as if he knew what he was talking about.

'You knew him?' the doctor asked me as the others turned and moved off, leaving me still staring at the body. I suppose he'd noticed I was a bit upset by the way I'd chewed into Squeaky, and then let him have it too.

'Off and on over the years,' I admitted. 'In fact he got me out of trouble . . . a couple of times.'

'If he'd been a bit younger he might have fought his killer off. He must have been a tough old bugger. But at that age the skull becomes thin and osteoporotic.'

'Yes, we lost a tough old bugger,' I said. 'The best pilot in the world and as brave as hell.'

☆

That Bret was sitting in his Rolls and parked round the corner was no great secret. Squeaky was renowned as a rulebook man: not at all the sort of man who would forget to stake out his meeting place with two or three of his instantly recognizable heavy-glove squad. I had no doubt that they were watching us now, their eyes in constant movement and their chins drawn into the collars of their black trenchcoats as they chatted unceasingly into their phones.

'How did it go? Who was there?' Bret asked. He stopped reading his *Economist* and folded the corner of the page to keep his place. I could tell that all Bret wanted was a brief confirmation that nothing catastrophic had happened.

'Squeaky. With Golds to hold his hand,' said Dicky. 'And a

doctor . . . one of Bernard's old drinking companions, I understand. So we have an inside line there if we need it.'

'And what was the conclusion?' said Bret.

'It was the German pilot . . .'

'The Swede,' Bret corrected him gently.

'They call him the Swede,' said Dicky.

Having settled that misnomer, Bret's curiosity seemed to wane. 'No problems?'

'I told you there was no need to come, Bret. They will fax all the medical junk tomorrow if you want to go through it.'

'If there are no problems I don't need to see any of it,' said Bret emphatically. 'I've got a desk that's buried under work.' With that self-assurance that inherited wealth provides, he ended the discussion. He switched off the reading light, tucked his *Economist* down the side of the seat, let his head loll back and closed his eyes.

Dicky said: 'We'll drop you off first, Bernard. You are nearest.' He said it in a whisper in case Bret would be disturbed.

Until now my concern for the Swede had pushed from my mind the effect his death would have upon all my other plans and ideas. Now the consequences fell upon me like an icy avalanche of wet slush. I wasn't going to Ireland or Cuba or South America. I wasn't going anywhere; I would be staying here and putting up with all the crap the Department chose to dump upon me. There was no escape from consequences; that was a fact of life.

'See you in the morning,' said Dicky as he dropped me off at the apartment block.

'Yes,' I said. 'I'll see you in the morning.'

The apartment was dark and cold when I got upstairs. Fiona had left, but not before tidying up everything so that the place was pristine. She'd picked up the pieces of discarded tissue paper, and washed and put away the dishes, milk pan, and a coffee cup and saucer she'd used. The overlay had been taken off our double bed. It had been made up with clean starched sheets, and the pillows were arranged ready for me to go to bed. On the pillow at my side she'd placed the fabric camellia, like a token of love. I was suddenly troubled by the thought that her tears had been shed for our marriage.

☆

You can see right across London from the top floor of our SIS building. Today was hazy, the cloud-filled sky bruised and battered; rain was expected at any minute. Last night I'd watched the steely clouds racing across the sky. This morning they had slowed. Now they were completely still; anchored and threatening like an extra-terrestrial armada waiting for the order to invade.

I was first to arrive in the No. 3 conference room, unless you count the Welsh lady who brews the tea for such gatherings. None of the others were on time. Bret came with the Director-General. Gloria, who was now appointed to a permanent position as Bret's assistant, came with Bret's newly appointed girl secretary. Soon after, Augustus Stowe, the abrasive Australian who used to have Dicky's job, arrived. He was still trying to hold Operations together, and the black marks under his eyes and his general demeanour showed what it was taking out of him. Nevertheless, Stowe was always able to summon up energy in its bellicose form. He came in slapping his hands and shouting: 'What are you idiots all sitting in the dark for? Switch on the bloody lights someone.'

Dicky hurried in breathless, wearing his new Armani trenchcoat. He was the last person to arrive. He obviously hadn't even had time enough to look into his office for the cup of coffee that was awaiting him at ten-thirty each morning. I could see from one glance at his face that missing his regular dose of caffeine had made him resentful, peevish and dyspeptic.

'I wish you had reminded me, Bernard,' he hissed as he hung his raincoat on a wire hanger and pulled out his chair at the conference table. Dicky hated having his precious clothes on wire hangers; he had banished them from his own office, and from his home too.

Although Dicky, like others of the Department's senior staff, sometimes used the No. 3 conference room as a snug hideaway, the rest of us knew it only as a place where we were summoned to give evidence, or be grilled about mishaps or disasters.

Today I wasn't standing on the mat. I was among the eight important people seated at the highly polished coffin-shaped conference table and discussing 'Departmental policy'. Each place was set with a new notepad, a sharpened pencil and a tumbler of water. There was also a copy of the minutes of the previous meeting, and an agenda for this one. My name did not appear on the agenda, but that did not mean anything when Bret was in the chair. And Bret was in the chair. He was seated across the table from me with a gold pencil in position; it was a heavy gold pencil that he clinked against the water glass when he wanted order, silence and attention. His new secretary sat next to him; a dark debby girl wearing a beige-coloured twin-set and pearls and an expensive watch. She was keeping a record of the meeting in longhand. It might have been an impossible task except for the way in which Bret said: 'Don't minute this' frequently enough for her to catch up with the dialogue. In front of her there was an added responsibility: a tray with eight cups and saucers and two plates of biscuits together with milk jug, teapot and so on.

On the other side of Bret sat Gloria. She had come straight from the hairdresser. I could tell, for her hair shone with lacquer, and she never used that at home. Gloria was wearing a dark, rather mannish suit. She had the official black box of documents – orders, regulations, correspondence, carbons and even maps. She was expected to produce the papers Bret needed about two minutes before he knew he needed them. By some miracle, she managed this.

The conference room was all exactly as I remembered it, except that someone had removed the big silver-plated cigarette box that used to be on the table, and all the glass ashtrays too. I remembered that silver box well. Like most other employees, I had often used the need for a smoke as an excuse to defer answering a question, and gone rummaging into that box for as long as possible. I felt sure Bret had banned smoking from the room. Bret was a puritan. When he gave up smoking the whole world had to get in line behind him. When he closed his eyes it was night. Bret was an autocratic do-gooder; a liberal tyrant; a crusading drop-out. The combination of opposing characteristics is what made him so American, and so difficult to understand at times.

This gathering was distinguished from meetings of lesser importance by the attendance of our Director-General, Sir Henry Clevemore. He was accompanied by 'C', his beloved old black Labrador which followed him everywhere. It was the only animal permitted into the building. Once, long ago, a German visitor described Sir Henry as looking like a punch-drunk prize-fighter. The venerable face, long hair and dark complexion easily misled any casual foreign observer. But no one with first-hand experience of the British class system would mistake Sir Henry for anything but what he was: a pre-eminent member of the British establishment. Sir Henry's life story could be written on a postcard: Eton, the Guards, White's Club, Anglican Church, renowned horseman and foxhunting man, married into titled Scottish landowning family with Palace connections. His tall, shambling figure – and the Savile Row chalkstripes that he made look like something from an Oxfam shop – was less often seen in the corridors of the Department since his illness the previous year. But disproving all predictions, his voice was firm and unhesitating and his eyes were quick, like his brain.

Bret had grown older too of course. But Bret was American and they knew how to keep time at bay. He was ageing the way film stars age; preserving all his coil-spring energy and menace. Last night at midnight he looked like hell, but last night he'd been tired, the effects of his rowing machine and vitamins waning.

Sitting in his big car, the harsh light of the tiny reading-lamp cross-lighting his face and bony hands, he was about to turn into a pumpkin. But today, having read the sports pages of the *Herald Tribune*, he was rejuvenated. I could see he was on the warpath and I feared that I was in his sights.

Contributing significant thoughts to meetings like this was not something at which I had ever excelled. I would not have been here, except that Frank Harrington was determined to hold on to the well-established tradition that Berlin should be represented. With Frank now in Berlin, and me temporarily in London, it seemed sensible for Frank to send me to attend in his stead. But I sat through all the exchanges and statistics without doing much more than hold up a hand in assent, and respond to familiar jokes with an occasional smile.

Bret had gone through the meeting at breakneck speed. He turned over the last page of the agenda while Dicky was still talking, and pushed on to the next and final item without pause or apology beyond saying: 'We know all that, Dicky. We've been through it a dozen times.'

I could see Dicky had brought a thick bundle of notes and references, and was only into the first of them. Poor rejected Dicky. In front of the D-G too. Dicky wouldn't like that.

Augustus Stowe, who never passed up an opportunity to rub salt into wounds, especially Dicky's wounds, added: 'You bring too much material to these meetings, Dicky. And a lot of it is time-wasting crap.'

Bret waved a finger aloft to the secretary. 'I don't want any of this on the minutes.'

'No, Mr Rensselaer,' she said.

'So I think that does it . . .' said Bret, leaning over his secretary's notes and making pencilled ticks against agenda items which had not even been brought up for discussion. He looked round the table. 'Unless there is any other business?'

With that tone of voice not even Stowe dared to have other

business. Everyone could see Bret was what he called 'loaded for bear', and they were only too pleased to escape.

Gloria packed up and left, having given me only the briefest possible smile. I was about to follow her when Bret said: 'Could you hold on, Bernard? Dicky too. There are a couple of things . . .'

☆

He waited until the door was closed. 'About last night: the dead man.' He looked down at the neatly arranged contents of his document case. 'I thought you should know that the Soviets had been dealing with that German renegade for years; at least two years.' Bret said this like a sudden and surprise announcement. It was clearly something he wanted over and done with quickly.

Bret looked up at me and waited for this to sink in. I nodded and noted the way in which the Swede, who had risked his life for us countless times, had suddenly become a German renegade. I noted too that Bret had done his homework since last night, when Dicky had had to clarify the misnomer to him. 'Well?' he said, waiting for me to reply. The D-G sat staring into space, as if this exchange was nothing to do with him.

'The Swede was desperately short of money,' I said in his defence. There was a silence. It was of course the wrong thing to say.

'A lot of our people are desperately short of money,' said Bret, and let the implication go unspoken.

'But he wasn't exactly one of our people,' I said. 'Not exclusively. We didn't give him enough money to get his exclusive services. He contracted. He was the best of all our arm's-distance contractors. He was dependable. He never let us down.'

'No,' said Bret. 'He let *them* down; that was the trouble. He tried to sell them what was rightfully theirs; they don't like that kind of freebooting. That was why they wasted him.'

'Could you explain that, Bret, please?' the D-G said.

139

'Killed him,' explained Bret. 'He betrayed the Soviets and they killed him.'

'Ah, yes,' said the D-G.

Hearing his master's voice, 'C' awakened and crawled along under the table until he brushed against my feet, sniffing and snorting. Making sure it was unobserved, I gave the dog a firm push with my shoe, and it retreated a few paces along the table as far as Bret. It sank down with a groan and went back to sleep. Bret guessed what I had done and fixed me with an accusing stare. I suppose he was unhappy to suddenly have the dog resting against his legs, but he didn't complain about it.

I said: 'Am I permitted to hear more detail about this?'

'They brought in a hit man from Dresden,' said Dicky proudly. 'We have been monitoring the whole circus for days. Two local toughs were used. Then the fellow from Germany arrived on an early flight to brief them. He took a rented car to Wimbledon, paid off his two English thugs and was back in Berlin again before the Swede's blood had dried.'

'Two thugs?' I said. 'Where did they clean up?' Squeaky's reasoning had convinced me that it was too clumsy and messy for a contract killing.

'They didn't want it to look like a professional job,' said Dicky. 'That was specified in one of the messages we intercepted. It's new, reformed Gorby-Russia these days. They don't want anyone to know they are still doing the same nasty things they did in the bad old days.'

Then Bret's words sank in. I said: 'You monitored it? You're telling me . . . you let them kill the Swede?'

'We had to let them go through with it,' said Bret. 'We knew they were on the warpath. We thought it was a hit against one of our people from the way the messages sounded. Then we saw what it really was. To have acted on the information would have blown our source to fragments.'

'And you knew all this too?' I looked at Dicky to make it

personal. 'You knew last night when we were talking to Squeaky? You knew about the plan, let it happen, and then leaked it to Five so that they could find the body?'

'I thought you guessed what it was all about,' said Dicky evasively. 'When you told Squeaky you weren't convinced, I thought you must know something. I was thinking how well you handled it.'

'No, that was the real me,' I said. 'Those two came looking for me. They were searching for the Swede. They wanted my help.'

'What happened?' said Dicky.

'I said I'd call them back.'

'You didn't report that,' said Bret very quickly.

'No,' I said. 'I wasn't sure who they were.'

'Really?' said Bret. I could tell from his face that the driver had reported my little fracas. 'And yet by then you knew that the personal security alert was extended to all staff. And you knew the Swede was in town doing business. You had a meeting with him. A meeting in a bookshop on Charing Cross Road.'

Bret was trying to rattle me. 'Routine,' I said.

'I don't think so, Bernard,' said Bret. 'I think it was to discuss some job you wanted done. A flying job?'

I looked at him full in the eyes. 'Tell me all about it,' I said. Bret was in a combative mood but I felt able to take him on.

'We've had you under observation, Bernard,' said Bret. 'It's no good you playing the innocent. You are up to your old tricks. You might just as well level with us.'

'I have nothing to tell you,' I said. 'What evidence do you have? What the hell am I supposed to have done? I fought off a couple of muggers, and I met with one of the people we use. So what?'

Bret remained cool. 'That's just the trouble,' he said softly. 'You've got the fixed idea that we are on trial – the Department. You carry on as if everyone here should be answerable to you.'

The D-G spoke. It was all a little charade acted out for him to watch of course. A play for which I had not rehearsed my role. The D-G said in his deep fruity voice: 'Your brother-in-law is a mischief-maker. Everyone here knows that. But that doesn't mean we can ignore the accusations he brings against you.'

'I didn't know he had brought any accusations against me.' I glanced at Dicky. He looked at me and smiled nervously.

'No. Exactly. Because his wild accusations are not worth repeating,' said the D-G calmly. 'But what have you done to reassure us, Simmons? Very little. Admit it. Haven't you been hinting that the Department had some sort of complicity – however slight, however tangential – in the death of Tessa Kosinski?'

He paused long enough to tempt me into replying. I said: 'We let the Swede die. We knew he was going to be murdered and we just let it happen. Isn't that what we have just heard?'

'That's quite different,' said Bret. 'There was no alternative. That's a ridiculous comparison.'

The D-G ignored both my remark and Bret's too. He said: 'I have decided to extradite this American fellow Thurkettle.' Sir Henry delivered this pronouncement in an august manner that made no reference to other men. Silas was not to be mentioned, let alone my conversation with Silas. 'Any questions that may have formed in your mind,' he said, staring at me, 'will be answered at the Board of Inquiry. It's the fair thing to do. Perhaps we should have done that last year, at the time it happened.' The English have an obsession about fairness, and the D-G was very English.

'Will the Americans extradite Thurkettle?' I asked.

'I have been given assurances at the highest level,' said the D-G. 'But once the process starts there is no telling where it will end. The Americans will protest if they think their man is being treated unfairly. Object on a point of principle.' He sniffed. 'We might end up in open court, with you giving evidence.'

'Yes,' I said.

'You saw the fatal shots fired, didn't you?'

'Yes, I did. Thurkettle killed her. I was there.'

'If it came to a public trial you would be the vital witness – er . . .' The D-G stared at me as if trying to recall my name. Dicky was looking at his raincoat hanging on the rack. I couldn't see Bret's face; still seated, he was bent over, reaching down to the carpet.

'I know what you mean,' I said. He was reminding me that after such a public display I could not be employed by the Department.

'There is an axiom in Bengal,' said the D-G. 'The trackers say that by the time a hunter first sights his tiger, the tiger has seen him one hundred times.'

'I know,' I said. 'But who can rely upon what a tiger claims?' It was a warning of course. He was telling me that any time I thought I was two jumps ahead of him and the Department, they would be three jumps ahead of me.

Outside the window the sky became ever more sombre. All morning London had awaited the rain, but the threatened storm had never arrived.

'Are we going to bury him?' I said. 'The Swede: what will happen now?'

Bret abandoned whatever he was bending down to fiddle with on the carpet, and sat up straight in his chair to face me. He had obviously considered the problem already. He rattled off his reply: 'When the coroner releases the body, if the body isn't claimed, the Department will provide a proper church burial, and a head-stone . . . Somewhere quiet. We'll find a village church in the sticks. We don't let our people down, if that's the thrust of your question.'

I grinned. For a moment I truly believed Bret must be trying out a deadpan joke. I thought it was only in the opening shots of TV movies that eager spooks staged pretty little country funerals to entice out the heavies of the KGB's First Directorate. 'Who's choosing the hymns?' I asked.

'You may go, Simpson,' said the D-G. I got up, glad to be offered an escape.

'Samson,' said Bret, once again bent over and hidden behind the table.

'What's that Bret? Speak up,' said the D-G in the loud voice that is a symptom of deafness.

'His name is Samson,' said Bret, in a voice that revealed his bad mood. I guessed he was trying to brush the dog-hairs from his trouser legs.

'Charity. Charity,' called the D-G in the low firm tenor voice with which he always hailed his dog, taxi-drivers and anyone on the other end of a telephone. 'Charity, come here.'

The dog groaned and shuffled towards its master. I'd always heard him call the dog 'C', and believed it to be named after the D-G's august Departmental predecessors. It shows how easy it is to get things wrong.

7

Hennig Hotel, Berlin

CINDY PRETTYMAN HAD grown older; we all had. The amusing, friendly and attractive girl I once knew was divorced, middle-aged and devoting all her energy to her career. This did not mean she was not still an attractive woman. In some ways the chic confidence she'd acquired with her responsibilities and her travelling had made her more interesting. The gloom of the hotel bar, lit only by a couple of tiny wall fittings, and the flickering light from the TV, flattered her.

Having greeted me, she assumed a pose. One hand held her fur-lined raincoat open to reveal her tailored outfit of black and white check. Pale fingers splayed on her hips, her nails long and red, a selection of rings and bracelets and a fashionable wrist-watch well in evidence. It was a joke, and I grinned to acknowledge it.

Cindy was the epitome of the hard-working and ambitious woman, fighting to survive in a man's world. And her world was peopled by international finalists in the art of self-advancement. No doubt the ability to switch on a sexy provocative come-on was a valuable part of her repertoire.

'Cindy! What a lovely surprise,' I said.

Cindy Prettyman smiled at me and I recognized that expression. She was the indulgent Mother Superior and I was the unwashed choirboy. Her ex-husband had been infatuated with her, and I'd always tried to see her through his eyes. But romantic old Jim was nothing if not a pragmatist. He had gone to other places, other people and other things. Cindy had become a stranger.

The voice of Cindy Prettyman, or Cindy Matthews since she had reverted to her maiden name, had made me jump out of my skin. I was sitting alone in the bar of Lisl Hennig's hotel where I lived, catching up with the German newspapers while waiting for the bartender to come on duty.

'Hello, Bernard. I thought I might find you here.' Big smile.

'Yes,' I said, though Cindy had no reason to think I was in the bar of the Hennig Hotel, or even in Berlin. But Cindy was like that: she combined the instinct of the hunter with the steady pulse of a marksman.

'You haven't changed, Bernard.'

Jim Prettyman had been a Departmental colleague and pal. He taught me to play snooker and billiards too. And helped me learn how to lose with good grace. We all used to play pool back in the old days: Fiona, Cindy and Jim and me. We were all Foreign Office low-life, with few responsibilities and even less money. We went to a snooker hall in south London every week. Usually we followed up with a spaghetti and steak dinner at Enzo's in the Old Kent Road. The winner paid.

They were happy days but they didn't last. Jim's promotions took him up to the top floor, where he was soon rubbing shoulders with Bret Rensselaer on the Special Operations committee. Then he got a new job in America, changed his name from Jim to Jay, found a new wife and made enough money to have his teeth capped. Cindy – who was already becoming a resolute Whitehall *apparatchik* – also left England. She was offered a contract working for the European Community or the European Commission or European Parliament, or one of those well-paid jobs with first-class travel and other lush extras that every pen-pusher in the world dreams about. Meanwhile my wife Fiona had completed her caper in East Berlin, returned and got her name in flashing lights over the Department's marquee. Of the four of us, I was the only one who hadn't changed, the only one who could still be found in the same haunts that I was frequenting in the old days. And wearing the same suit.

She had got older but her salary seemed to be helping her keep time at bay. Her hair, her facial, her gold baubles, and the fashionable fur-lined raincoat that she threw on to a hanger and hung in the closet, told her story. And she had become French enough to believe that expensive outfits, fine perfume and extravagant cosmetics were not worth spending money on unless they were kept well in evidence. She grinned. She was the picture of success. She pulled off her headscarf and shook her head to loosen dark hair that had been streaked and restyled. It was cut in a mannish no-nonsense style that meant a minimum of her valuable time spent with the crimpers.

'I might be coming to Berlin regularly in future,' she said.

'Is that a threat or a penance?'

From her large crocodile handbag she got a silver cigarette case and a gold lighter. She'd been born in a region of England up there near the River Humber where the iron-ore fields stretched conveniently close to the coking coal and the limestone flux. Her father grew up in the time when good steel was precious, and Britain's need for it seemed endless. But nothing lasts forever; not even battleships or empires. Cindy was quick to recognize that. She hadn't entirely lost her accent. Or perhaps she assumed it for my sake, to show me that her achievements hadn't made her forget that she was the same little lass with the beer-drinking left-wing Dad, and the Catholic Mum who worked in the laundry.

'What would you like to drink?' I asked her.

She lit the cigarette with an elegant flourish and, with the cigarette in her mouth, used both hands to close her handbag. She threw her head back and half-closed her eyes as the smoke crawled up her face. Then she removed the cigarette and said: 'Would it be possible to have a glass of champagne?'

She wrinkled her nose in a way that Jim Prettyman once told me was cute.

On the TV screen over the bar two white-coated doctors argued in silence. 'What about the house wine?' I said. 'Hungarian, but not bad. They lock up the best stuff in the chilling cabinet when the barman is off duty.'

I went behind the bar, helped myself to an opened bottle of wine, and returned with a glass for each of us. I poured it carefully, knowing that she was studying me to decide how much older I was looking. '*Gesundheit!*' she said, and smiled before sipping her wine. Then, as if in reaction to the taste of it, she hunched her shoulders. 'When does it get lively?' she asked, looking around at the empty bar. The Hennig Hotel had seen some notably boisterous days and nights, but overall it was a place frequented by less-successful business travellers, tourists who didn't mind going along the hall to find the bathroom, and mysterious men and women who, for reasons of their own, preferred the obscurity such unfashionable accommodation affords. Most abstemious of all there were the elderly long-term residents who eked out their fixed incomes by rationing their eating and drinking. All in all such clientele were not lively in the way that Cindy sought.

'It varies a lot,' I said, sinking down on the sofa next to her.

'It would have to vary quite a lot before getting rowdy,' said Cindy, and laughed, giving a hint of the sort of schoolgirl shrieks that I remembered from the old days.

'I suppose so,' I said.

'Why are you always such a bastard?' she said, without much change of demeanour. She leaned forward, slipped off her shoes and massaged her feet with delicate movements of her long fingers. Through the toe of her stocking I could see that her nails were painted gold.

'Me?' I said.

'Let me see my husband,' she demanded fiercely. 'How can you be such a brute?'

'Jim, you mean? Jim, your ex-husband?'

'You came to Berlin with him. You brought him here. I know. Don't deny it.'

I would have denied even that, but that would have brought more difficult questions, and it would have been bad security to tell her how I'd been hauled off the Moscow Express and locked up by the Polish secret police. 'I was on the same train that he was on,' I admitted. 'But that was just a coincidence.'

'Mother of God: don't lie to old liars, Bernard.' She touched her foot again. Far above us in the gloom, a muscular doctor went running athletically across a field and climbed into a helicopter with a red cross painted on it. The pilot was female and blonde and young.

'I thought that was all over – you and Jim.'

'It is. He bolted off with that American divorcée,' she said with delicate distaste. 'You don't have to be so sensitive, Bernard. You won't make me burst into girlish tears.'

'No,' I said. Envisaging Cindy bursting into girlish tears was something that challenged my imagination. 'So why?'

She bounced to her feet in a manner that demonstrated a seemingly inexhaustible vitality. Still in her stockinged feet, she went to the bar counter and stretched right over it to grab the neck of a bottle of Scotch. She wrenched it from the rack while grabbing glass tumblers with the other hand. Then she got ice from the ice-maker and threw it into the tumblers, expertly, like a bartender. It shouldn't have astounded me that she guessed where everything was kept, and put her hands on it so effortlessly. That's how she'd always been.

'I'll have a proper drink,' she announced while sloshing the Hungarian wine down the sink. 'Scotch for you?'

'No thanks. I'll stick to the wine.'

'I hate wine. I get too much of it where I work. The French have never heard of any other kind of drink. Wine turns to acid in my stomach.' She slid back into her position on the sofa.

'It does that with some people,' I said.

She poured a small measure of Scotch over the ice-cubes, and kept pouring while first they crackled, and then floated. 'Damn you, Bernard,' she said. 'I need help.'

What fuelled her, I wondered. Where did all this energy come from? 'I don't know where Jim is,' I told her. 'He looked very ill when I last saw him.'

'Someone is determined I shouldn't contact him,' she said resentfully.

'Why? Where is he?'

'Are you listening to me, Bernard, damn you? That's what I'm asking you.'

I was on the point of denying that I knew anything about Jim, or where the Department might have squirrelled him away. And that was the truth. But I was curious to discover what Cindy was after. 'I might be able to get a message to him,' I said, without troubling to think where I would start.

'Don't be such a monster, Bernard. This is urgent. There are other people looking for him. They come to me and ask for him, and get nasty when I say I don't know.'

'What sort of people?'

'Pushy Americans from Geneva. Heavies.' She pushed her nose with a fingertip, bending it to show me what sort of plug-uglies they were. 'I can't get them off my back. They say they are acting with authority. I suppose Jim was a partner with them in what-ever it is they do. They hinted they have money for him but they want a box file of business papers they say belongs to them. One of them is a lawyer. He says he has a power of attorney.'

'What did you tell them?'

'I said I didn't know what they were talking about.'

'CIA people?'

'I wondered about that at first.' She sipped her whisky. 'No, I don't think so . . .' She pulled a face. 'Maybe.'

150

'What papers are they talking about? You split up with Jim years ago.'

'This was recent. He phoned me in my office. Right out of the blue and dumped this box file on me. Secret material, he said it was. I was in Brussels. He was on his way to Washington. What could I do? Very secret, he said. He made it sound as if the safety of the free world depended upon me. He said he'd collect it the next time he came to Europe.' She made it into Yurrup; a sarcastic reference to the way Jim had acquired a slight American accent since living over there. 'He never came back for it. I tried all the phone numbers I had for him, but I couldn't get through to him. Then I put the box in store, with some furniture my mother left me. And I forgot about it. Until last month, when I got my things out of store; storage and insurance and all that stuff was costing me a fortune. Last week, when I heard that he'd come to Berlin, and that darling old Bernard was with him on the train . . .'

'Who told you that?'

'Never mind who told me that. Just make sure Jim calls my secretary, and arranges to collect his bloody box file from me. Or says it's okay to let his playmates have it. In writing. I must have his okay in writing. It's in the safe in my office – that's the only place I could think of – and I need the space. And it weighs a ton.'

'When was this? When exactly did Jim bring it to you?'

'A few months back. When was it now? . . . I haven't got my diary with me. Back when there was all that awful trouble in Berlin; yes, last summer. When your sister-in-law got killed in Berlin.'

'Jim is sick, Cindy. Very sick.'

'For richer or poorer; in sickness or in health; yes, that's how I married him. But Jim had other ideas, so I was given the elbow. Jim doesn't give me money, Bernard, not a penny. I earn my own living, and it's not easy. Frankly, I don't care how sick he is, I don't want to be involved.'

'I'll see what I can do.'

'Otherwise I'll just throw the bloody box into the burn bag. Or give it to our security people. Perhaps that's what I should have done at the beginning. I should not have agreed to take it in the first place. The men, his pals, said Jim knew where to find them. They have an office in Geneva. Jim used to work there with them. That's what they said. You can bet it's some kind of deal; you know how keen on money Jim can be. But I'm not going to hand it over to them. If it is secret material I could go to prison.'

Jim Prettyman had always been one for the big numbers. Starting with codes and ciphers, then Special Ops and secret funding. I'd never been officially notified that Jim still worked for the Department, but everything pointed that way. 'Better you hold on to the box file, Cindy,' I said. 'It may have some continuing importance – some bearing on work Jim does for the Department from time to time.'

She narrowed her eyes and said: 'I wondered how long it would take for you to get round to that.' She upended her whisky, looked at her watch and slipped her shoes on. It seemed as if she had decided to leave. 'I should never have let him dump that box on me, the bastard.'

'He knew you were a soft touch, Cindy,' I said.

She didn't smile. 'Phone for a cab, will you, Bernard. I've got a mountain of work that's got to be ready for my policy meeting in the morning.'

☆

I phoned and I watched her as she put on her raincoat and looked at herself in the big mirror behind the bar. So Prettyman had left a box file with her just after that night I pulled Fiona out of the DDR. I knew what she meant by a box file. It was a government-issue steel safety box with combination lock. If it had been a normal office box file she would have been describing its contents to me, not its weight.

If the Swede was to be believed, Prettyman was due to fly out with him that night. But Cindy went instead. Did she fly? Was she in it with the Swede? Never mind all the crap about a bicycle. By my calculation there would have been room for at least two passengers. I suspected that the two seats were for Prettyman and Thurkettle. Or for Mr and Mrs Prettyman. How did the box file fit into the story? And what was likely to be in it; a clean shirt, toothbrush and razor? Used currency notes? Or chopped-up pieces of Thurkettle? Jim's Diner's Club accounts? Or gold sovereigns? The trouble was that Cindy was not renowned as a selfless witness. This yarn might just be her complicated way of locating Jim to put the arm on him for alimony.

Cindy, her coat, her hat and her hair arranged to her satisfaction, the touch of orange lipstick applied, and her lips pressed together for a moment, turned from the mirror to say: 'I saw your blonde bombshell in London. She was looking lovely, I must say. I chatted with her. She worries about you; she wanted to know if I thought you were happy.'

'Gloria? You saw her? What did you tell her?'

'How would I know if you were happy? I told her I never see you nowadays. She must be the only little girl in the world who hasn't discovered that you fell in love with yourself a long time ago, and will never be unfaithful.' She produced a smile to soften this judgement. 'The poor child is crazy about you, Bernard. So I take it that your little fling is still going smoothly?'

'I'm with Fiona,' I said.

'You men!' She looked in the mirror again and flicked her hair with her fingertips. 'I saw Fiona too: in Rome; the big security bash. Chanel suit: Hermès bag. What a woman. Lovely children, desirable husband and gold Visa card. What more could any girl ask for? She had a Commissioner on either arm but she spared a chummy word or two for little me. What a success she is, Bernard. What is it like . . . to have two amazing women desperately, foolishly in love with you?' When I didn't respond Cindy turned to look at me and said: 'Tell me honestly. I would like to know.'

'Give over, Cindy.'

'It's that shy modesty that gets them, Bernard. That and the dimples. Or is it the challenge? The challenge of trying to wring affection from the most selfish egoistical loner in the world?'

'Are you going back to Brussels now?' I asked.

She smiled. I'd been unable to keep from my voice the heartfelt hope that she was speeding directly to the airport and leaving town for ever. 'No, Bernard. I'm staying with Werner and Zena in their gorgeous new home. I'll be in town for a few days.'

'Oh, good,' I said. I'd forgotten that she knew Werner from our times in London together. Cindy was a loyal and conscientious friend to people far and wide. Or a calculating networker who could rally a thousand people to any cause she cared to name, according to whether you heard it from Cindy or Jim.

'And did I say male chauvinist pig?'

'Good luck, Cindy,' I said as she swept out of the bar, her arm upraised in a regal farewell.

I sighed. The blonde doctor had taken off her white coat to reveal black lacy underwear. Her muscular colleague was giving her mouth-to-mouth resuscitation.

Cindy was right: Scotch whisky was better than Hungarian wine.

☆

The presentation portrait of Frank Harrington will be exactly like this, if Gainsborough gets the chiaroscuro right. Frank had pushed his chair close to the window and was reading the *Spectator*. He looked up. In that moment, as his eyes met mine, Frank was his sincere, avuncular and gentlemanly self. His suit – that had doubtless come from the same tailor's workroom as had the suits of his father and grandfather – was in every way perfect. The room was shadowy, with Frank's bony features side-lit by Berlin's grey winter sky. Hair brushed smoothly against that elongated head that is the distinguishing mark of the English among their Continental neighbours. The tall forehead and stubby military moustache made him unmistakably a gentleman.

'I was trying to reach you,' said Frank in a deceptively remote manner. 'All morning,' he added plaintively.

'I was doing a job for Dicky. I still haven't finished.'

'I thought it must be something of that sort.' Frank tapped at the glass window with his fingertip so that it made no audible sound. I followed his gaze. At the other end of the frosty white lawn, near the apple trees, Frank's valet Tarrant was talking to one of the gardeners. They were standing outside the door of Tarrant's workshop, their breath condensing on the cold air. There was a child with them; swaddled up in a white furry hat and coat. He was nursing one of Tarrant's model locomotives.

Tarrant had slowly taken possession of the small brick building at the end of the garden. In my father's time it housed the lawn-mower and other tools, and was a shelter where the gardeners could hide to smoke and eat their lunch. Now the garden tools were relegated to a wooden shed, there was only one gardener and his lunch was usually no more than a curry-wurst on a stick. The brick building had become Tarrant's playroom. It was fitted with an elaborate workbench with a lathe, drills and power tools and everything needed for building and working on his extensive layout of scale model trains. Tarrant took his loco back from the child, and went back to his bench. He spent a lot of time there: he always referred to it as 'the workshop' and claimed to be doing household repairs. Frank called it 'the gingerbread house'.

'I am never quite sure who it is I work for,' I said, becoming defensive when Frank didn't even turn to look at me.

'No one here is,' said Frank. 'Berlin's always been like that. It was the same when your father was doing my job.'

'I wish it could be settled,' I said. It was bad enough to be running around town on one of Dicky's fool's errands without coming back to face Frank's consequential icy mood.

'Now is not a good time,' said Frank, still staring out of the window. He meant of course that Dicky was not yet confirmed in his job, and reluctant to make decisions. While Frank was too old and too near retirement to be picking new fights with anyone in London. Meanwhile I would have to try and work for the uncoordinated wishes of both of them. 'Where do flies go in the wintertime?' said Frank. 'Did you ever wonder about that? In my young days there was a song about it, a music-hall song.'

I didn't know what to make of this quaint entomological digression. It might have been a rhetorical question. Frank was one of those exasperating people who reveal their true feelings only after wrapping them into protracted anecdotes and labyrinthine parables. 'No,' I said after a long silence.

'They end up in these empty spaces between the double-glazing. Look, I'll show you, there are dozens of them here. Dead.' He tapped at the window again. He hadn't been looking at Tarrant and the gardener; he'd been looking at dead flies. Frank was like one of those grand actors who, having devoted time and many performances to understand and assimilate a role, then claim title to it. It was playing the role of quintessential Englishman for a lifetime that enabled Frank Harrington to be convincingly himself. But now, like any great actor nearing the end of his career, his technique had nowhere to go but parody.

'If it's urgent I can put Dicky's little job on hold,' I offered.

'How do the little blighters get in there? That's what I can't make out. Must be the devil of a way to go. Sheets of glass on each side of you, but no way of escape. No way in, and no way out.'

'Do you want me to tell the housekeeping people? The windows all need cleaning up here. The snow dumps all the smoke of that filthy *Braunkohl* down on us.'

Frank ignored my suggestion. Perhaps he thought I was being sarcastic. Perhaps Frank's little two-ways-in, but no-way-out, was intended to have some subtle meaning for me. 'What exactly are you doing for Dicky?' he asked.

'One of the German scientists who defected last month has got them all going with talk about uranium mines.'

'Uranium mines in Germany?'

'About thirty k's south of Chemnitz. Schlema it's called.'

'It's true then? Uranium? I've never heard of it.'

'Tons of it. In the foothills of the Erz mountains. Ore mines. The "ore mountains" the Germans call them. There are ski resorts and lots of thermal springs too. I suppose the spa was a way of getting tourists there when the snow had gone.'

'Uranium?'

'There's a mine there. It's no big secret. Back in the days when it was a fashionable resort, it was called Oberschlema and it was advertised as a *Radiumbad – das starkste Radiumbad der Welt –* guaranteed to lower your high blood-pressure, ease your rheumatism and make you feel young again if you had enough money to stay there. And didn't mind glowing in the dark.'

'What's Dicky's angle?' said Frank, in a voice that suggested that he didn't much care. But I knew Frank better than that: he liked to know what London was doing on his patch.

'There's uranium there all right, and what they dig out all goes to the USSR. At least it used to go there.' I shrugged. 'It might be difficult to confirm what's happening right now. We don't have anyone reliable anywhere near there, as far as I can remember. I'm checking it now.'

Frank sighed. 'Are our masters back to their brawling about whether the Russkies are still manufacturing atomic weapons? I thought all that was settled last year.'

'That was a dispute about bombs; this is a dispute about artillery shells.'

Frank looked at me and nodded as if he was thinking of something else. 'Keep London happy,' he said vaguely. Ordnance was among the things he tried to keep away from. Frank got on well with the army, but he didn't think that providing that sort of intelligence was our province. He called it 'assessment' and maintained the army should be able to deal with that without our help. They had their military attachés, and liaison officers sniffing around the Russian army all the time.

'What was it you wanted, Frank?' I said.

'Wanted?'

'You said you were trying to reach me.'

'Oh, that. Yes, I was thinking about that business in London . . . that poor devil of a pilot who was killed. Your friend.'

I didn't respond to the 'your friend' but I could detect some underlying disapproval in Frank's voice.

'The funeral was yesterday,' said Frank. 'We arranged it. No one claimed the body.'

'So I heard.'

He went on: 'You saw him immediately after it happened? You chatted with Squeaky?'

'Chatted with him? Have you ever tried chatting with Squeaky?'

'Ha!' said Frank mirthlessly. 'I know what you mean. He's always been like that: abrasive. I mean have you been chatting with anyone at all?'

'At the scene of crime?' I said. Frank nodded. I said: 'Is this something Dicky has been saying?'

'He said you hung on there for a few minutes afterwards.'

'I didn't go striding out holding Dicky's hand, if that's what you mean. I know the doctor. I was intending to see him again in some other place in the hope he might be more forthcoming.'

'But you didn't see him again?' Frank opened a brass and ivory marquetry box he kept on a shelf under the window-sill. From it he got his battered Dunhill pipe and his yellow oilskin tobacco pouch. He had reduced his smoking to three pipefuls of his special tobacco per day, and I was going to be on the receiving end of one of them if I didn't get out of here soon.

'No I didn't,' I said.

'London Central has received an official request for us to clarify what we are doing with George Kosinski. Five want him. They are furious.'

'Oh, Jesus! So that's it.'

'I told Dicky that it couldn't have been you who let the cat out of the bag.'

'The doctor is not a part of Five, he's just the doctor. We use him too.'

'Five's official letter went to the D-G of course. So Dicky will have to go into the fire and flame, and explain things, so the D-G can cobble together some sort of servile grovelling explanation.'

'Dicky is good at that sort of thing,' I said.

Frank filled up his pipe bowl with the dark brown muesli that he liked to burn. There came the sudden flare of a match as he set light to it while making little spluttering sounds. Once it was alight, he exhaled smoke, and with a contented smile asked: 'Dicky? Servile grovelling? Or taking the blame?'

'It's no good Dicky trying to dump this one on to me, Frank,' I said. 'I submitted a report after being sent down to see George Kosinski. It's on file. It recommends his immediate release. We won't get anywhere with him by locking him up in Berwick House. You know George.'

'No, I don't know George. Tell me about him.'

'Reflective, self-righteous, single-minded, and with more than a touch of the Old Testament.'

'So why won't locking him up and interrogating him get us anywhere?'

'Because he's sanctimonious. Devout. He goes to Mass early in the morning whatever the weather. Forgives his wife all her many sins. And goes on forgiving her when she sins relentlessly. He won't become anxious or angry or repentant. He'll see Berwick House as a chance to live the cloistered meditative life he's always secretly hankered after.'

'Is that really what you think?'

'Of course it is.'

'I don't know George Kosinski. He's almost family for you of course.'

He was smoking happily now, poking at his pipe bowl with the blade of a penknife, and attending to every strand of burning tobacco with all the loving care of a locomotive engineer. Or a dedicated arsonist. He looked at me. 'This is off the record, Bernard. Strictly *sub rosa*. You tell this to anyone and I'll deny it.'

'Okay, Frank.'

'If you want my theory, it was George who arranged the killing of his wife.'

'George? Had Tessa killed?'

'I didn't mean to upset you, Bernard.'

'I'm not upset. I just can't follow your reasoning.'

He nodded. 'You are too close to it, of course. But George had the motive, the opportunity. And we know he had money enough.'

'To pay a hit man?'

'Of course. You told me, you saw her shot. You said it was some mad American who did it. A professional killer, wasn't he? Or is it your theory that the American killed her for some personal reasons that we are not party to?'

'I don't know,' I said. For a moment I considered telling him about my conversation with Uncle Silas. But it was better kept to myself.

'I've shaken you, I can see. I didn't intend that, old lad.'

'It was certainly a contract killing,' I said doggedly. Then I admitted: 'It could have been something between Tessa and the American. If they were having an affair. I think she might have been getting drugs from him. But . . .' I couldn't get my thoughts in order.

'Come along, Bernard. Forget all those might-have-been excuses. When are you going to start looking soberly at the facts? She had betrayed her husband on a long-term basis. Lover after lover. You've told me this, and it was common knowledge. On the weekend of her death she was betraying her husband with another man, wasn't she?'

'She was sharing a Berlin hotel room with Dicky Cruyer,' I said, to see how Frank responded.

Frank ignored this reference to Dicky. He said: 'How must George have felt? Ask yourself that. Humiliated beyond measure.'

'George is a Catholic.'

'That doesn't make him a saint. It only makes him someone who can't be released from a nightmare situation by means of divorce.'

'No, not George.' And yet . . . Could George have found a way of contacting Thurkettle and paid him to go a whole lot further than Silas wanted?

'No, not good old decent George. Will you start using your brains, Bernard. Your brother-in-law has been deeply involved with Polish spy agencies for years. You saw the effortless way he made contact with that ex-CIA hoodlum Timmermann, and employed him to go prying into the KGB compound in Magdeburg. God knows how much money he paid him.'

'We don't know that George sent him there,' I said, without putting much spirit into it.

'All we know is that Tiny Timmermann died there. We also know that Timmermann was the sort of ruffian who will do anything for money, and we know that George admitted to paying him money . . .' Frank paused. 'You told me that, Bernard. George said he was employing him.'

'Yes. To investigate. To find out what had happened to Tessa.'

Frank took the pipe from his mouth and gave all his attention to the smouldering tobacco: 'I wasn't at the meeting between Timmermann and George. And neither were you, Bernard.'

I didn't answer. I sat there and let Frank blow tobacco smoke across the room at me.

Finally Frank said: 'Reflective, self-righteous, single-minded; and a touch of the Old Testament. Exactly right for someone who would plan a premeditated killing of an unfaithful wife by a third party. The killing to take place during the weekend she was sinning.'

'Yes, Frank. You don't have to draw a diagram for me. Very Old Testament. You are right. It is possible.' I said it in a way that meant I thought it was extremely unlikely. He knew I was unconvinced, but my concession satisfied him.

'Are you thinking of going there?' Seeing my puzzlement, he added: 'To this place, Schlema? For Dicky. The radium place?'

He had put a finger on what was still pushed far into the back of my mind. Dicky was devious. It was only a short step from 'What do you think about Schlema?' to 'Why don't you step across and take a look at it, Bernard, old boy?'

'No,' I said firmly. 'I wasn't thinking of going there personally.'

'It's always bad luck to be good at something you don't want to do.' He looked out of the window. 'Or to be good at something dangerous. My brother-in-law Alistair suffered like that. He was a pilot in Bomber Command in the war. Pathfinders; showered with medals. God knows how many bombing raids he did. He was the best, so they kept sending him. Again and again and again, long after he was worn out. He didn't enjoy it.'

'I don't remember meeting your brother-in-law.' I'd known Frank almost all my life, and yet I'd never heard about his brother-in-law until this moment. How strange it is that some intimate aspects of those we know so well remain a firmly closed book. And yet perhaps in this case not so strange. Spending your life here in Berlin with German friends would not encourage anyone to recount stories about close relatives who had excelled in bombing their cities to rubble. 'Is that why your son wanted to fly?' I asked. Against Frank's advice his son had become an airline pilot. His promising career came to a sad and dismaying end some years later, when he failed his medical.

'Yes. My boy lapped up all those flying yarns he read at school.

It was my fault as much as anyone's. I was always telling him stories about Alistair. Alistair was a lovely man. No, you never met him, Bernard. He bought it in that big raid on Nuremberg – March forty-four. A massacre for Bomber Command. My sister married again within the year: a man from the same squadron. She was only a child; she lived only for Alistair. When the telegram came she almost died of grief. I think she was trying to find some fragment of Alistair in the man she married. Perhaps she found it, I don't know. They are still married.'

'How can you be sure your brother-in-law didn't enjoy his bombing? Some men enjoy being heroes.'

'Not Alistair. He left a diary in a locker in his room. His batman had the key: he sent the diary to me. Thank God he didn't send it to Emma. It was a chronicle of concealed torment. Not just for himself, but for the men he sent out each night. Poor Alistair. I burned it eventually.'

'If someone has to go over there, it had better be me,' I said as I reflected upon the alternatives. 'At present there is no one else I'd feel happy to send.'

'You'll stay here,' said Frank. 'I'll make that clear to Dicky, and anyone else in London who argues. You are more useful here. I don't want you schlepping around their bloody uranium mines. It's too dangerous and you've done your share – far more than your share – of those jobs.'

'There is no one else to use. You know that.'

'What did that wretched woman want?'

'Woman?'

'In the bar at Lisl's last night. Come along. No one is spying on you. I just happened to be passing as she was coming out. She didn't recognize me, thank God. I know everyone says she's hard-working and amazingly efficient, but I simply can't stand her.'

'Mrs Prettyman?' It was something of a relief to know that Cindy's networking didn't extend into Frank's office.

'She's been sniffing around Berlin for almost a week. What is she up to, Bernard?'

'She wants to talk to her husband.'

'What husband? Ex-husband? If you mean that fellow Prettyman . . .'

'Yes, she wants to talk to him. She says she has a box of papers belonging to him.'

'I'd treat that with a certain amount of reserve. She has a reputation as a trouble-maker. And this is a domestic quarrel.' He pursed his lips. 'What the devil is she doing here?'

'She said she was sent here to work,' I said. 'Only for a few days.' I could see that Frank was getting worked up and I wanted to defuse his anger. I didn't tell him she was staying with the Volkmanns. Werner had enough trouble fitting into Frank's domain without that.

'You know she went to the funeral of your pilot friend?'

'No, I didn't know that,' I said.

'In England. She talked to everyone there. Asking questions and making a nuisance of herself. Dicky sent someone along to make a video of all the mourners . . . everyone who attended. She was the only surprise, Dicky said.'

'I see.'

'You persist in thinking that Dicky is a complete fool. You made a joke about him setting up a funeral to discover who would attend. But sometimes such obvious devices prove valuable.'

'Yes,' I said, feeling deflated.

'What was her motive? What could be her interest? Was she close to the pilot? Is there a security aspect?'

'As I say, she is very keen to make contact with her husband. I suppose she heard about the Swede's funeral – she always seems to know what's going on – and was hoping Prettyman would turn up there too.'

'I don't like the sound of it. I don't trust that woman. Find out what she's up to.'

'I'd rather go after the *Radiumbad*.'

'Of course you would,' said Frank. 'So would anyone.'

'What about the report for Dicky?'

'Dicky's uranium mine can go on hold for the time being. I'll get Werner on to it. We have other tasks more urgent. I shall tell Dicky that.'

'Yes,' I said.

'My son has decided to go and live in Melbourne.'

'Has he?'

'Australia.'

'Yes.' I looked at Frank. He doted on his son. To be told he was planning to go to Australia must have been one of the worst things that had ever happened to him.

'I'll miss him.' It was the ultimate understatement. Frank's relationship with his wife had dwindled to a point where she was spending most of her time in England. He lived only for his son.

'It's a small world nowadays,' I said. 'People fly across the world, backwards and forwards all the time.'

'My boy told me the same thing.' Frank opened a brown file and looked down at the letters that were waiting to be signed.

☆

Thus dismissed, I went back to my office to check my incoming afternoon work. The dark skies of Berlin's winter were oppressive. I switched on the desk lights, the overhead fluorescent lights and every other light I could find, including the ones in the corridor. My secretary watched me do this. If she was surprised she gave no sign of it.

'Don't you ever feel like going off to live some place where the sun burns the skin off you all year round?' I said.

'Oh, no, Herr Samson. That would be carcinogenic.'

She had opened everything already. When I sat down, she came and stood by my desk to make sure I didn't toss the difficult ones into the pending box. She was very German.

I went through it quickly. At the bottom of the tray there was a bulging brown manila envelope. It was not internal mail. It had been posted in London using a long strip of Christmas commemorative postage stamps. The cover was already slit open, so I tipped the contents out. A shower of rose petals fell upon my desk. They were crisp and brown and dead, and there was a brittle piece of stem and a curly leaf with charred edges. I looked inside the envelope. There was nothing else. Just the remains of my roses. They had not died a natural death; there hadn't been time enough. These were petals from red roses that had been scorched, or perhaps rescued at the last moment from an open fire. I wondered what my German secretary thought of this tacit message. I looked at her but she gave no sign of what she was thinking.

I dictated my way through the daily stuff from London. When we were finished I said: 'Did we ever get the police reports I asked for? The ones for the night Mrs Tessa Kosinski died?'

'I thought you had finished reading them.'

'Was that all?'

'I will bring the file,' she offered.

'Don't bother. There was almost nothing. I'd like to spread the net wider.' I went to the map on the wall of my office. 'Look at all these jurisdictions . . . The shooting took place here. Assume someone left the Autobahn at any one of these exits. Here, here or here.'

'Each jurisdiction? Towns and villages too? Every one?'

'Yes.'

'May I ask you what we seek?'

'I don't know exactly. Drunks. Dangerous driving. Trucks illegally parked. Accidents. Wrecks. Property lost and found on or near the highway. Anything unusual in even the smallest way.'

She wrote it down.

I thought about Thurkettle's possible movements. 'What would I have done had it been me?'

'I don't know, Herr Samson.'

I had spoken aloud without realizing it. I wouldn't drive eastwards, would I? It would be too dangerous to go East after a shoot-out that had wiped out a couple of important Stasi men. What fugitive would head towards a land brimming with cops, and endless demands for signed papers with rubber stamps? No, I would drive along the Autobahn westwards. It would be cold and dark. How do I feel? I feel lousy. I'm driving fast, but not fast enough to get a ticket or to get noticed by other road users. I'm hyped up but I feel lousy. I stink of fear and sweat and dirt and spilled blood. I need somewhere to hide for five minutes while I collect my wits. But there is no one I can trust. So I want an empty house, not an apartment, a house, an isolated house. Because I like to do the hard bits first, I would want to get across the border before stopping. I would choose a lonely spot just across the border in the Federal Republic and near an exit from the Autobahn. Why near an exit? Because I might choose to get back on the Autobahn. It's night; I might decide to put as many miles behind me as I can. But then another thought came to me. If I was dirty and bloody and conspicuous I might want to have somewhere to clean up before going through the checkpoint.

There would have to be a rendezvous with my paymaster. I will be paid off and change my clothes and my ID and pick up my tickets or whatever I needed. Hits were always like that. There was always someone waiting at a rendezvous. If not a someone, a somewhere, a place of refuge. I had never heard of a hit man working without back-up. And I'd never heard of a hit man being paid one hundred per cent in advance. Somewhere that night there had been a contact. And that meant the chance that some cop or nosy neighbour had seen it happen. There had to be some clue somewhere, but I had no idea what it might be.

And then a likely solution came to me. 'It's got to be one of those camper vehicles,' I told her. 'That's the sort of thing I'm looking for.' That could be placed wherever it was wanted. He could use it to wash and change. Then he could use it as a vehicle in which the journey could be resumed under a different name, and with all the necessary papers. 'A camper,' I said aloud. That's why he used a motor-cycle to get to and from the killing. His plan was beginning to make sense to me.

'I will require a person to help.'

'Parked overnight on some isolated stretch of road near one of the exits, but not on the Autobahn where a cop might stop and check it.' Stopping on the DDR's Autobahn was verboten. 'Talk to all the West German cops who were riding in cars that night, riding anywhere in the vicinity of the exit ramps. Asking for written reports was the wrong way to do it. Talk on the phone. Talk to them in person.' I would have to tackle the DDR side myself.

'How near to the Autobahn? One kilometre? Five kilometres?' she asked.

'I don't want to extend it too far or it will give you too many cops to contact. Tell them we are after a serial killer, I don't want them to think we are chasing up parking tickets.'

'I will require help.'

'Five kilometres. Start right away. It's the night-shift cops you want. Take anyone you need . . . within reason,' I added quickly in case she did something crazy, like demanding help from Frank's secretary. Or Frank.

8

Horrido Club, Berlin-Tegel

TEGEL, WEST BERLIN'S third airport, was built in a hurry. In a vindictive attempt to squeeze the Anglo-American armies out of the capitalist 'island' that defaced their communist domain, the Russians suddenly blocked the road links with the West. They cut off everything, even the long-standing delivery of Swedish Red Cross parcels for hungry Berlin children. The US Air Force, the RAF and a varied assortment of civilian fliers supplied the city by air. In that feverish climate of resentment and hatred a new airport was built. It materialized here on the flat land of Tegel on the edge of a sector of town that the Americans and British had given to the French so they could play conquerors. The airfield was operational after little more than eight weeks, built with American engineers directing German labourers, almost all of whom were female. Without notice, two Red Army radio masts in line with the approach were blown away. Angry Russian generals demanded an explanation. The French Commandant disarmingly replied that it was all done with dynamite.

That was in 1948. Now, almost four decades later, we were sitting in what had been the site-manager's office during the construction work. At least we were sitting in a hut of which one badly scarred wall, and the concrete base block, had been its final remains. The old hut had remained abandoned and neglected on the edge of the Tegel runway until Rudi Kleindorf came and preserved it. Rudi was an oddball, a one-time professional soldier and self-advertising patriot who declared a sentimental attachment to this place. He'd put up a notice on the wall claiming that it was the last remaining trace of a miracle of construction work. Now, said Rudi's notice, it was almost completely forgotten, even by those who came here.

'So what is going on in Frank's mind?' said Werner, after I'd told him about Cindy, and about Frank's reaction to her sudden intrusion into what Frank always considered his own personal fiefdom. When I shrugged Werner rephrased it: 'What was the implication? Does Frank think she's going to kill Jim Prettyman?' Werner's heavy irony seemed to be as much directed at me as at Frank. With Cindy as his house guest he felt defensive on her behalf. He got up and went to the refrigerator to find a bottle of carbonated water. He held it up: I shook my head. It was clubby enough, and German enough, for that sort of self-help and payment on trust system to survive. Perhaps that was what attracted Werner to this large prefabricated shack, half-hidden in the trees of Jungfernheide.

'Kill Jim? Good God no,' I said, pretending not to notice the little dig at me. 'Why do you say that?'

'It was a joke,' said Werner.

'Yes, well Jim Prettyman knows where all the bodies are buried,' I said. 'And there are not many people left who might know the true story behind what happened on that night Tessa died.'

'Is that what Cindy says?'

'Cindy? She knows nothing about it, except that Jim left a box of papers with her the next day.'

'So what did she want then?'

'She wants more space in her office safe. I think she was hoping that I would ask her for the box file, and pay her a reward or something. You know what she's like.'

'Why didn't you?'

'Not with Cindy,' I said. 'Nothing is simple with her. You can bet it was some kind of baited trap. I take the box file from her, and she hits us with a demand for official recognition as Jim's wife.'

'Jim remarried.'

'In Mexico. Cindy has been advised that Mexican marriages are not recognized under English law. She would like to see it annulled. It would give her the green light for a legal action against the Department.'

'Yes, I remember now. And where would that leave Prettyman?'

'Exactly. She's a devious woman,' I said.

'You used to like her.'

'Did I?'

'You were always saying how clever and attractive she was. You used to say that she was the brains behind everything that Jim Prettyman did.'

'Not Cindy,' I said.

'You don't like any of your old friends these days, Bernie. What's happened to you? Why are you so caustic? Why so suspicious of everything and everyone?'

'Am I? Well I'm not the only one afflicted with that,' I said. 'There is an epidemic of suspicion and distrust. It's contagious. We are all in its grip: you, me, Fiona, Gloria and the whole Department. Frank has got some crackpot idea that George had his wife killed because the Church wouldn't give him a divorce. Even when my father-in-law's superannuated moggy rolls over dead, I have to listen to some half-baked conspiracy theory.'

'Yes, but cats have nine lives,' said Werner. 'There must have been eight other serious attempts.'

'I must tell him that,' I said. 'It would be something more for him to worry about.'

The conversation stopped while a British Airways jumbo trundled along the perimeter and revved its fans loudly enough to rattle the bottles on the bar counter, and shake the moths out of the fur collar of Werner's ankle-length black overcoat. There were soft thuds on the roof as the snow was shaken out of the trees above us.

I suppose all airports have hideaways like this: places where staff on duty can escape from work for as long as it takes to swallow a drink or two and smoke a couple of cigarettes. But this prefabricated cabin was not content to be a ramshackle refuge for airport staff. It pretended to be a club. The décor was contrived to make it seem like a private and exclusive spot for intrepid birdmen to gather to exchange stories about Richthofen. Its name was enough to tell you what it was – The Horrido Club. The word Horrido had gone into German folklore as being the word used by old-time Luftwaffe fighter pilots to proclaim an enemy aircraft shot down. Children's comics and romantic military historians endorsed it. So did Rudi, who enjoyed nothing better than reading books about the war. But as I told him, none of the Luftwaffe fighter pilots I had asked could remember anyone ever saying Horrido: they simply said *Abschuss!* Rudi had just grinned. Like so many people who had fought in the war, Rudi had developed a possessive attitude towards it. He was apt to dismiss anything I said about that period as an example of the English sense of humour, which he much admired.

Rudi had decorated the 'club' with all kinds of junk. There were model aircraft, baggage labels and sepia reproductions of old photos and posters. On the ceiling there were tacked two large sections of fabric bearing RAF roundels and one with a black German cross insignia.

Sitting in the corner, nursing beers, there were two policemen and two engineers from Lufthansa. Rudi was there too. They'd been arguing about the football game they'd seen the previous Saturday. Now the argument ended with that suddenness with which such conversations can become exhausted. They downed their drinks, looked at the clock – an old RAF Operations Room clock with coloured triangles – and left.

Rudi came over to say hello to us and offer us a drink. He was at least one hundred years old, a craggy-faced giant, with broken nose and battered cheekbones. His hair he could call his own, and his upright military bearing went well with the card he gave me advertising his new club. Since he had not yet decided upon a name for it, the card just had Rudi's name on it – Rudolf Freiherr von Kleindorf – and the address and phone number. Small type under his name claimed him to be a retired Colonel of Infantry, *ausser Dienst*. Many times I had vowed to check up on the old rogue, and blow away these pretensions to aristocratic title and military rank. But Rudi was very old: one day soon I might be glad that old men are so often indulged in their petty vanities.

We listened to Rudi's extravagant description of his new club, the hard-sell message being larded with amusing gossip and the scandals that were a permanent part of Berlin's high society. When Rudi finally departed, the club was empty, apart from me and Werner.

☆

'How often do you come here, Werner?' I wondered if it was somewhere he came to take refuge from Zena; and from Cindy too.

'You come here too,' said Werner.

'Not often. I've never liked this part of the city.' Through the window I could see the forest. At this time of day in winter there was always a white mist threaded through the trees.

It made me remember that day long ago when, as a schoolboy, I came here on a trip. One of our teachers, Herr Storch, an unrepentant Nazi, told the class about the vast dump of artillery shells that had been hidden under the trees of Jungfernheide during the final weeks of the war. It must have been a misty winter day exactly like this one. The dump was guarded by a dozen or so Hitler Youth boys. They were in their uniforms, and proud of the new steel helmets they'd got from the Spandau army clothing depot, together with ten *Panzerfaust Klein 30* anti-tank rockets that were effective only when used as close as thirty metres. Accompanying the boys there were three elderly brothers named Strack. They were local men: foresters who had been given Model 98 rifles and Volkssturm armbands. Ruined by rifle-grenade training, the guns were virtually useless for shooting.

Also here that fateful day, there was a broken-down three-ton ambulance – an Opel Blitz. Its transfer lever had jammed halfway into the four-wheel-drive position, and the vehicle had become inextricably stuck in the overgrown ditch from which the driver had been trying to reverse. The driver was a female civilian volunteer. Herr Storch described her vividly: she wore a fashionable hat and coat and chamois gloves, and was distinguished only by her *Im Dienste der deutschen Wehrmacht* armband. Standing round the ambulance there were eight nurses of a surgical unit, none them warmly clad.

At this point in his story, my teacher Herr Storch kicked the ditch at the place the Opel had stuck as if to convince himself it had all happened.

The nurses were on their way to a *Feldlazarette* of Busse's 9th Army at Storkow. It was all futile, for Busse's men were no longer there: tanks of Koniev's First Ukrainian Front wheeling north had flattened and forgotten the Mobile Field Hospital. Storch had never been the sort of man to take orders, or even suggestions, from a woman. So there was little chance of the unit's nursing sister – a grey-haired woman, long past retirement age – commandeering Storch's own vehicle, a six-wheel truck that he was loading with rations and rifle ammunition. Storch was, at the time, a lieutenant of a Luftwaffe signals regiment that had been pressed into service as infantry. He wouldn't let the nurses have his truck. To take such a step would have been to invite execution at the hands of the 'flying court martials' that were to be seen roving the streets, interrogating the old and the young, the high and the low, with equal ferocity.

While Storch was arguing with the nurses, unwelcome strangers stepped out of the mist. They were the 'point' of an armoured reconnaissance battalion of the 12th Guards Tank Corps. This was the other prong of the attack: Marshal Zhukov's army heading south to cross the canal and descend upon the industrial complex of Siemensstadt. A large proportion of the foot-soldiers were fighting drunk on plundered schnapps. Some were injured and others burdened under incongruous assortments of looted domestic treasures. They were all hungry, and now they pounced with glee upon the unexpected bounty of German army rations. They also pounced upon countless tons of munitions hidden under camouflage netting. And with even greater glee they pounced upon the nurses.

Storch had jumped down into the ditch to show us how he had survived. From there he had watched the killing of the Volkssturm men, the cruel deaths of the Hitler Youth boys and the repeated brutal raping of the nurses. He told the story with an intensity that horrified me and my classmates. 'Defeat is shame,' he yelled at us as the tears rolled down his cheeks. 'And shame is having to watch barbarians defile your women while you do nothing – nothing – to defend them. Shame and fear. I did nothing, do you hear me: Nothing! Nothing! That is defeat.'

What was he trying to tell us? We schoolboys watched Storch with consternation that did nothing to aid our understanding. I was the only foreign barbarian in the class, and his wet wide-open eyes stared at me for so long that the boys who had at first turned their heads to look at me turned away in confusion and embarrassment. I never did fully understand what motive he had for inflicting upon us the emotional trauma we all shared that day, but for ever afterwards even the name of this place was enough to bring upon me an ache of apprehension and misery.

☆

'Are you listening?' Werner said loudly enough to bring me out of my reverie.

'Yes,' I said as the voice of Storch echoed in my memory and faded away.

'I like aeroplanes,' admitted Werner. 'Remember all those models I built?'

'I thought you bought them from that woodcarver,' I said.

'Black Peter?' said Werner, showing great agitation. 'What are you talking about? My models were immensely better, and far more detailed than those Flying Fortresses he made. His crudely carved models were just for selling to the American soldiers.'

'Were they?' I said innocently.

'Don't be stupid, Bernie. My Dornier X had all the engines in it. You could lift up the cowlings and see the details inside.' He was passionate now, his voice quivering with indignation. It was so easy to crank him up, but I always felt guilty afterwards. It's only our very closest friends who are so immediately vulnerable to our teasing.

'The big flying boat? Yes, that was a good one, Werner. I remember that one. You kept it for years.'

'What are you going to do about the Matthews woman?' said Werner, as if trying to get even with me.

'Nothing,' I said. 'Frank expects you to follow up on her. He'll ask you what's happening.'

'I can't start cross-questioning her. She's a guest, and very close to Zena. He's dumped the radium mine problem on my desk. He told me you were doing something urgent for him. I thought he meant about Cindy.'

Clever old Werner. But I fielded that one. 'Frank doesn't know she's staying with you.' I drank the drink Rudi had so kindly pressed upon me and then said: 'Not so long ago, Werner, I looked up at the stars in the night sky, and wondered how they had come into such harmonious configuration. Everything seemed to be going perfectly. I was foolishly in love with Gloria, and I was beginning to believe – against all reasonable expectations – that she was deeply in love with me. My kids seemed to have recovered from the shock of their mother's departure. Gloria and me and the children all shared our sleazy little suburban love nest in the sort of foolish happiness I had never known before. Of her own choice, Fiona had defected. Given average luck, it seemed like I would never see my father-in-law again. My brother-in-law George was packing his bags to become some kind of rich tax exile in Switzerland, and I was happy to say *auf Wiedersehen* and good luck to him. My job seemed secure. I was in London, and that elusive pension for which I was not officially eligible was almost within my grasp. You were here in Berlin, as happy as a lark, fixing up the hotel in conjunction with your lovely Ingrid. Can you remember those days, Werner? Those Elysian days.'

'The Elysian fields were the dwelling of the blessed after death,' said Werner, who could always find a way of dampening my euphoria.

'I said, can you remember those days?'

'No. What did Rudi put in your drink?'

'Look at the situation now, Werner. Gloria hates me. Fiona is eating most of her meals on planes, and is too busy to stop work for five minutes to talk to me. My children have been kidnapped by my father-in-law. My job is on the line. The chance of my getting into any sort of pension scheme is zero. My father-in-law thinks someone is trying to poison him. My brother-in-law is being held as an enemy agent. . . '

'And me?' asked Werner, when my voice trailed off. I suppose he guessed I was trying to find some acceptable way to describe his reconciliation with his wife, the fiery Zena.

'No news is good news, Werner,' I said.

'You're right,' he said grimly. He'd given up trying to persuade me that Zena wasn't as bad as I thought.

'Where is Jim Prettyman? What have you heard?'

'Am I your friend?' said Werner.

'Sometimes I think you are my only friend.'

'That would be paranoid,' said Werner. 'You have hundreds of friends – too many – even if they are mostly low-life specimens. And more supporters than I can count. Your wise words are endlessly quoted and your deeds recounted. Seriously, Bernard. You have many friends.'

'I don't think so.'

Werner looked at me, took careful aim, and then hit me in the eye with a mossy clump of Schiller:

> *'Freudlos in der Freude Fülle,*
> *Ungesellig und allein,*
> *Wandelte Kassandra stille*
> *In Apollos Lorbeerhain.'**

'I don't need poetry, Werner,' I said.

Werner said: 'For the sort of work you do, you have an instinct that I envy. And over the years I have seen you combine that instinct with powers of deduction, and pull off the impossible.'

'Now for the down side.'

'But you make little effort to see things from the other point of view. Maybe that's why you bring such powers to your work: that unyielding single-minded determination. But at times like this, it cripples your reasoning.'

'Is that what I'm doing now?'

'You have become obsessed with discovering some dark secret about the death of Tessa Kosinski. At least, you seem to be obsessed with it. You drag it into the conversation every time I see you. But who was present at that shooting? You were.'

'Not only me, Werner.'

---

*   Joyless there, where joy abounded,
Friendless and misunderstood,
Walked Cassandra, fear-surrounded,
In Apollo's laurel wood.

'Cassandra' by Friedrich von Schiller. Translation taken from *Treasury of German Ballads* (Frederick Ungar Pub. Co. Inc., New York, 1964).

'Fiona has repressed her memories of that night,' said Werner. 'She remembers nothing. A hundred analysts working day and night wouldn't dredge it up into her conscious memory in a hundred years.'

'Who says so?'

'The shrinks said so. You said so. You told me that Bret said exactly that to you in California after one of the debriefing sessions.'

'Oh, yes,' I said. 'I thought I recognized Bret's flowery syntax. I remember now. But you've got to allow for the way Fiona was traumatized at suddenly finding herself in the middle of a shoot-out. She's worked behind a desk all her life. She wasn't ready for that especially nasty little blood-letting.'

'No one is ever ready for it. But you handled it with your usual superhuman efficiency. You wrote out a detailed report and answered questions about it for weeks.'

'I don't see what you're getting at, Werner.'

'It was dark. Chaos. You were worried about Fiona, and about Tessa too. There was a lot of shooting. Men were killed. You shot and killed that KGB man Stinnes, and the man he brought with him.'

'Kennedy; Fiona's lover.'

'Kennedy, yes. And then you pushed Fiona into the van and drove away and escaped. But no one, not even you, comes out of a shooting completely unscathed. When you arrived in the West you were in a state of shock. You told me that.'

'There was a lot of blood. Fiona was covered in blood. Having Fiona there was what made it terrible for me. You are right, I wasn't prepared for it.'

'The British army doctor sedated you?'

'I was hyped up. He said I needed some magic pills if I was to fly across the Atlantic.'

'So you remember the pills?'

'Of course I do. Didn't I tell you about them? How would you know else?'

'Where's the gun you used?'

'It was my dad's Webley Mark VI.'

'Yes, where is it?'

'I don't know. I'd never used one of those old wartime guns before. The rounds come out in slow motion, and tip on impact. They land like an artillery shell and tear a big hole in a man, Werner. It worked okay, but it was pretty damned grim to watch.'

'How many rounds did you fire?'

'I can't be sure.'

'One? Two? Three? Four?'

'I said I don't know!'

'Don't get excited, Bernard.'

'I know what you're thinking.'

'What am I thinking?'

'You're going to pretend I shot Tessa.'

'Well, isn't it possible? It was dark: just the headlights of the cars. And then someone shot the headlight out. Dark and muddy. People running. Confusion. . . Try and remember.'

'You weren't there, Werner. Thurkettle shot Tessa. I saw him.'

'Slow down, Bernard. Play let's suppose. Many shots were fired that night, but we don't know who fired which. You fired, Thurkettle fired, and maybe the others fired too. You depart in the van with Fiona. Thurkettle leaves on his motor-bike, and goes to London and tells them what he saw. How will his account fit to yours?'

'Is Thurkettle in London?'

'He might well be. I'm playing let's suppose.'

'Jesus Christ, Werner! I don't care what Thurkettle is telling them in London. No one is going to railroad me into confessing that I killed Tessa. I loved Tessa. She was always wonderful, supportive and full of life. When Fiona went, Tessa helped me with the children. I wouldn't think of killing her.'

'You wouldn't think of it? Couldn't think of it? Never? Not

even if she died as the result of a perfectly understandable accident? We are talking about an accident, Bernard.'

'Is this what Thurkettle said?'

'Tessa was stoned. . . drugged to the eyebrows that night. She was dancing through the mud, twirling around in her silk dress and singing. These are your words, Bernard.'

'I'm not sure. . . ' I said.

'You took Tessa there in that van,' said Werner. 'But for that, she wouldn't have been there for anyone to kill.'

I jerked as if I had taken a slap in the face. It was true. Tessa had climbed into the van I was using that night. I had driven her to the shooting and thus to her death. It was the guilt that came from that fact that gave me no rest. She had come to Berlin with Dicky, and shared his bedroom at the hotel. But I could not free myself from the feeling that her death was my responsibility.

'Bernard. If you killed Tessa, you must come to terms with it. No one is going to charge you with anything. London would give a big sigh of relief. Everyone knows it wouldn't have been done intentionally.'

'Who's got my Webley?'

'I don't know.'

'But someone has? It was my father's gun. Have the DDR been playing games with phoney ballistics?'

'I heard that Thurkettle brought your Dad's Webley back with him,' said Werner.

'Why the hell would he do that?'

'You used it to kill Russians. It was a British Army pistol with marks leading straight back to your father. Leaving it at the scene of the shooting would have been madness.'

'Is this what the Department think happened? That I killed them all?' I looked at Werner; he often got to know what people were saying long before I did.

'I don't know what they think,' said Werner. 'Probably they are as puzzled as I am: they don't know what to think.'

'Where is Thurkettle now?'

'I don't know.'

'The Department is going after him. They want to bring him face to face with me.'

'Bernard. If Thurkettle is in hiding it's because he's frightened.'

'Frightened of me, you mean?'

'Of course. See it from his point of view.'

'That I killed Tessa?'

'And he is the only witness. Yes. What chance would he stand, with you challenging him in a Departmental inquiry? That's how he will see it.'

I sat back and rubbed my hands together. My palms were sweaty and I could feel that my face was flushed and burning. I must have looked as guilty as hell. 'It's bullshit, Werner. I don't know who you've been talking to, but it's all bullshit. In any kind of inquiry I can clear up all the details. I remember everything as clearly as if it happened yesterday. Everything important anyway. When they bring Thurkettle in I'll tackle him. I'll show you what is really what.'

'I wouldn't count on finding Thurkettle,' said Werner. 'When a man like that wants to disappear, there is no finding him again.'

☆

I sat there for a long time.

'I was going to run away,' I said finally. Werner nodded. 'I was going to grab the kids and Gloria too. I had planned everything. The Irish Republic and the Aeroflot connection: Shannon to Cuba. From Havana a ship to. . . I'm not sure where.'

Werner stared at me. 'Have you gone mad, Bernie?'

'It would have worked,' I protested.

'Did you ask the children?' He didn't wait for a reply; he knew I hadn't taken them into my confidence. 'It would have been a fiasco,' he said softly.

'I don't think so,' I said.

'And what about Gloria? Did you talk it over with her?'

'No,' I said.

'That's all over, Bernard. I saw Gloria in London. She's happy. No men in her life. Sometimes she has dinner with Bret; I suppose they both get a bit lonely sometimes. But I could tell she's content living her own life on her own. She brought you into the conversation. She said how pleased she was that you were working in Berlin. She said you were brilliant and that she hoped you would make a big splash. She meant it. There was no bitterness, no ill-feeling in her, Bernie. But you are not a part of her life any more. And not a part of her future. You'd better face up to it.'

Werner's words drained the life from me. I felt sick. 'You don't know her, Werner,' I said desperately. 'And anyway. . . ' I sipped at my drink and recovered my composure. 'Gloria and me; yes, that's all over. Very much all over. Now tell me something I don't know.'

'So what is it all about, Bernie? This madness of yours. Is it some deep-down resentment and envy of Fiona's success?'

'Envy? Really, Werner.'

'Or hatred? Do you hate Fiona? Perhaps without even really understanding that you do. She loves you very much. She's like me, she's not good at saying things, but she loves you, I know.'

Werner's calm voice and considerate tone made me cautious. This was Werner the world-famous children's psychologist. I answered him in the same calm manner: 'I don't think she does,' I said. 'Fiona is in love with her work. She would be happy to see me run away with Gloria and the children too. It would give her more time for meetings and writing reports.'

'Frank guessed you were going to run,' said Werner.

'Frank did? How do you know he guessed?'

'He sent for me. And you know what a surprise that must have been. Frank and I have never got along. Frank said he'd be wanting me to go over to London and talk to you. He didn't say what about. Then, when he heard from Bret that you'd been meeting with the Swede, Frank told me to be in Leuschner's Café next morning. I got there early and Frank was waiting for me. I don't know how long he'd been waiting, he had already downed a couple of coffees and bread rolls and stuff. He was very agitated: filled his pipe with tobacco and put it away without smoking it. You know what he's like when he's jumpy. He said the Swede was dead, and that there was no need to talk to you after all. He said you'd be okay.'

'Frank's known me a long time.'

'That's the trouble,' said Werner. 'We all know each other too well.'

'I'm not going to sit still for this one, Werner,' I said. 'I didn't shoot Tessa. And you can go back and tell anyone who asks you about it.'

Werner stood up, huge and threatening. I'd never seen him like this before. He didn't raise his voice above a whisper, but for the first time in my life I found him intimidating. 'Very well,' said Werner. He made it sound like the final curtain to a Chekhov play.

I didn't move. Werner walked across the room to a photograph of Richthofen standing amid a group of scruffy pilots in front of an Albatros biplane. Werner took his time studying the picture, as if trying to recognize which one was Göring. Werner was walking with a limp. Long ago he had his leg broken by some thugs from the other side of the Wall. The leg bothered him sometimes: in cold weather like this, or when he was emotionally unsettled. I said nothing. Werner stood with his back to me, looking at the photo and bending his leg slightly, as I'd seen him do when it pained him. It was better to let him calm down.

Eventually Werner turned to look at me. Perhaps he'd been counting to ten. He said: 'You spoke with Silas Gaunt?' He spoke in a casual voice, but could not conceal his interest in the meeting. 'Did he add anything?'

'Yes, he added to my confusion,' I said.

Werner continued quietly: 'Well, perhaps it hasn't occurred to you, Bernie, that if the Department was desperate to cover up the judicial slaughter of that poor woman – bringing along a highly paid hit man who came in, did his job, and disappeared – they wouldn't be forging documents, wriggling and lying, and going to all the other absurd lengths that you ascribe to them. Now would they?'

'Maybe,' I said.

'No . . . They would simply kill you. If that's the way they did things, they'd do it to you. That way they'd get it over with neatly and quickly. And relatively cheaply.'

I still didn't move. He looked at me for what seemed like a long time. I stared back at him and finally he stalked out, his terrible anger seemingly unabated. His long black overcoat, and his infirmity, added an extra and sinister aspect to his somewhat theatrical exit.

☆

Soon after Werner had departed, a man named Joschi, I never knew his family name, suddenly appeared behind the bar. He was a small melancholy individual who had lost both parents in the war. He spent his childhood in a Silesian orphanage. In the final weeks of the war, Joschi, with the other inmates, trekked westward with the Red Army close behind. He had worked in a communist-run chinaware factory in Dresden until he escaped from the DDR two years ago. Now he insisted upon thanking me for his job working for Rudi in the Horrido. In fact I'd done no more than mention his name at a time when Rudi was looking for an honest and uncomplaining slave who would work the clock around for starvation wages.

'Schnapps, Herr Samson?' He was standing holding a glass and a bottle ready to pour.

'No thanks, Joschi. I've had enough.'

'Scotch? Cognac: seven years old?'

'Thanks, but I mustn't.'

'You are looking well, Herr Samson.'

'You too, Joschi.' I appreciated his encouraging remark, as from what I had heard from several outspoken friends I was looking decidedly timeworn.

'Can they make a hand-gun from plastic, Herr Samson?' I hesitated and looked at him. 'The customers were arguing about it around the bar, the night before last. One of the airport cops – the noisy argumentative young fellow with the trimmed beard. The one who shows everyone his paper targets from the pistol range. I think you may know him. He bet fifty marks that it was possible to make a plastic gun. They couldn't agree. I said I knew someone who knew about these things.'

'How did it start?' I asked.

'A package came for Mr Volkmann. . . long time ago. . . A courier-service delivery. It was a plastic gun. I said it was a toy.'

'Sounds like a toy to me,' I said. 'Maybe I will have that schnapps.'

He poured my drink and I sipped it. He held up his glass in a toast of good health. I could see that I was being told something important. This was Joschi repaying something of the debt he thought he owed me. But I wasn't quite sure how far I was permitted to go in asking questions. I said: 'A long time ago?'

'That time when there was all the fuss, and you went off somewhere to recuperate.'

'This cop who thinks they make plastic guns: what does he say?'

'He says he's seen them. American plastic pistols, with triangular plastic bullets that fit tightly into the breech. They are made to get through the airport security machines.'

'What would Werner want with it?' Werner had no special interest or need for a hand-gun, let alone a special-purpose one. I worried lest he was involved in something that would get him into trouble. There was a secretive side of his nature; I'd known that since we were kids together. But I felt sure that there was nothing he would not confide to me, just as I had no secrets from him.

'We get a lot of funny packages behind the bar here, Herr Samson. The boss looks inside sometimes; he likes to make sure it's not drugs. Of course Herr Volkmann's name was never spoken.'

I nodded. Any of the arriving airline crew members could walk across the airfield, and come through the same broken wire fence that all the on-duty engineers and office staff used when they dropped in for a furtive drink. In a way I had played into Joschi's hands. He now knew that the gun had not been handed on to me, or gone to Werner with my knowledge or blessing.

'Don't mention it to anyone, Joschi,' I said. 'It's a toy I'm sure. Talk about it and you might spoil a nice surprise for someone.'

'I'll say it's impossible then?'

'Yes, you can take my word for it. The poor fellow has lost his money.'

9

Colnbrook, England

IT WAS A STRANGE place to find the grievously sick Jim Prettyman. Jim was rich. He was an unnamed 'exceptional business
and financial adviser' according to an article about one of his
clients that had appeared in the *Wall Street Journal*. Jim liked
numbers, and his mathematical talent enabled him to adjust
effortlessly to computerized management. He was a sought-after
man nowadays, a consultant to half a dozen international companies, as well as condescending to occasional jobs for the
Department. I would have expected to find a sick Jim Prettyman
hidden behind diagnosticians, pretty nurses and grim-faced
specialists in white coats. I would have looked for him in a
big private suite of the Mayo Clinic, the top floor of a Harley
Street infirmary with three-star cuisine, or one of those fancy
hospitals in Switzerland where the best rooms have a view of
the Alps.

As it was, he had chosen a suburban house in Colnbrook, not
far from Heathrow, London's major airport. Heathrow's claim to
be the world's most active airport was disputed, but surely its role
as the largest must be uncontested. Aircraft hangars and repair
sheds, service areas, high-security car parks, transport depots and
freight warehouses, and offices for the legions who flew the word-
processors, sprawled for miles in every direction.

Not so long ago, the airport's vociferous neighbours were continually staging demonstrations protesting about the noise and inconvenience they suffered. But eventually they discovered that their houses had become very desirable as accommodation for well-paid airline employees. Soon specialist rental agents took interest in this area, conveniently close to central London, where houses could be made available on short leaseholds for wealthy foreigners. Now Jim Prettyman – born a Londoner – found himself in this wealthy foreigner category: a weary wealthy visitor looking for a place to rest his head.

His rented house was typical of those built in southern England between the wars, but it had been furnished and equipped to meet the more stringent requirements of foreigners. The house was served by a heating system that dispensed warmth. The furnace could be heard somewhere in the cellar, roaring like an antique jet engine and shaking the whole house. The other facilities included two German dish-washers, a gleaming chest freezer and a two-door refrigerator with ice-water dispenser. The kitchen was like the flight deck of a spaceship, with an array of whippers, mixers and blenders, a coffee-maker that dispensed steam for frothy milk, and a complex of ovens that would microwave, turbofan or radiant-heat your dinner at the touch of a button.

'I'm so glad you came, Mr Samson. Jay needs cheering up.' From some unseen speaker system there came a soft but spirited performance of *The Merry Widow*.

I had seen photos of Mrs Prettyman. I remembered how 'Jay' had large coloured portraits of her in expensive frames around his Washington DC office. The photos had always shown her smartly dressed in simple shirt-style dresses that were right for Washington's hot summers. In the pictures she had a wide film-star smile, and athletic pose. Her wealthy family, and her father who was something important in the State Department, had taken Jim to their heart and helped his career. No wonder that in the photos Jim was always smiling too.

As she took my coat and hat she said: 'Of course he's doped up. I have coffee brewed; will you take some?'

'Is he? Coffee? Yes, please.'

'He has to be on medication. I have a nurse come in three times a day. She's a lovely person: Australian. The clinic wouldn't discharge him to my care except on condition a real good qualified nurse attended him.'

'But he's on the mend?'

She frowned at me. 'No, he's not on the mend, Mr Samson – may I call you Bernard? I thought you knew that.'

'No,' I said. 'I mean yes, do call me Bernard.'

'And my friends call me Tabby, it's short for Tabitha.'

'Tabby. That's a pretty name. So he's not on the mend?'

She made a movement of her hand to invite me to sit on one of the high padded stools that were alongside the breakfast counter. An 'open-plan kitchen' was the sort of amenity estate agents like to mention on their prospectus.

There was a glass pot of coffee sitting on the hot-plate of the coffee-maker. She took two decorative mugs from a shelf and poured coffee into both of them. My mug had a brightly coloured pre-Raphaelite woman drowning in a pale blue river. Ophelia I suppose. The coffee was watery too.

'He's not expected to live above three months,' she said.

'I had no idea. I knew he was sick of course . . . I was on the train with him.'

'He wanted to be in England again. North London, he said, but this was the best I could do at short notice.'

'Three months?'

'At most. Jay doesn't know that of course. He thinks he's recovering strength enough for his treatment to resume. But I think it's better that you should know the score.'

'Thank you. Are you telling all his friends?' I wondered if Cindy was a party to this alarming prognosis.

'He hasn't seen any friends. Few people know where Jay is.'

She gave a little chuckle, as if hiding him away was good fun. 'I was surprised when you tracked us down and said you wanted to come.'

I smiled and nodded. We drank coffee.

'Jay goes up and down,' she said. 'Today seems to be one of his good days.' She was very restrained, very understated: no make-up, no ornaments, not even a watch; cotton dress, and hair cut like a schoolgirl. Yet she had a natural effortless elegance that gave her authority and importance. It was, I suppose, a product of her affluent background. Bret had the same sort of aplomb.

'The nurse will be down in a moment,' she said. 'She goes through a routine. She takes about twenty minutes usually. Tell me about yourself, Bernard. Are you married?'

'Yes, I am,' I said.

'That's wonderful,' she said. In theory – and on paper – the second Mrs Prettyman was everything I usually ran fast to escape, but I have to admit that I found her both clever and charming, the way Werner told me I used to see Cindy. I decided that Jay was lucky to find such a loyal and generous lifetime companion, for Tabby told me that, despite two failed marriages and grown-up children, he was 'the real thing at last'.

'We understand each other, you see,' she told me. 'My previous husbands were not too particular about telling the truth: to me or anyone else. But Jay is just wonderful. We tell each other everything.'

'Do you really?' I said. Jim Prettyman was entrusted with some very dark Departmental secrets. It was hard to believe that Tabby had been made a party to all of them. And in any case Jimjay was not noted for his unwavering veracity.

She leaned over to see that my coffee cup was empty and poured more for me. 'I'm not saying it wasn't the religion that did it. But Jay says that has nothing to do with it.'

'What religion?' I said.

'He went back to the Church. You didn't know that?'

'The Catholic Church?' I remembered the rosary he clutched constantly on the train.

'Yes, I'm not a Catholic. I was brought up a Presbyterian. What are you?'

'I'm not sure,' I said. 'It depends what sort of trouble I'm in.'

'Jay felt bad at discouraging his first wife from attending Mass. He was born a Roman Catholic. His folks were Catholic. Catholic childhoods seem to take a grip on people, don't you find?'

'Yes, I suppose so.'

'It's a comfort. It has helped him endure this terrible sickness. He can't go to Mass, of course, but the local priest calls in frequently. He's a lovely Scotsman. Jay looks forward to the visits, and the father likes a glass of whisky. They chat for hours.'

'That's nice,' I said. But it wasn't nice. I didn't like anything I was hearing. I didn't enjoy the idea of Prettyman confiding secrets to his wife, nor chatting for hours with his priest over a glass or two of whisky.

Perhaps my reservations showed on my face, for she said: 'Have you seen Jay's first wife recently?'

'As a matter of fact I have.'

Tabby seemed distressed at this: 'You are not here because of her?'

'No, I'm not.'

'She's blackmailing Jay, you know that, do you, Bernard?'

'Blackmail is a serious accusation, Tabby. I hope you know what you are saying.'

She smiled: 'I should do, Bernard. I have a PhD in International Law and ten years' experience as an attorney in Washington.'

Touché. 'So what kind of blackmail?'

'You'd best level with me, Bernard. What's your angle? You say you are not acting for the first Mrs Prettyman?'

'I certainly am not,' I said.

'But you have spoken with her. Is she seeing you again?'

'Not if I see her first.'

'Okay. I'm convinced. I was all prepared to be friendly with her. I'm sympathetic. But she's nothing but a trouble-maker.' She held up the coffee pot and I shook my head.

'So what kind of blackmail?' I asked again.

'Maybe you should ask Jay,' she said. 'It's his ex-wife.'

☆

Tabby had warned me that the injections, and whatever other dope they were feeding him, left him in a euphoric mood, but I wasn't prepared for the transformation. I'd last seen him on the Moscow express stretched out like a corpse and only half as lively, but I found a Jim who was full of fight.

'Bernard, you son of a gun. Where have you been?'

'Trying to find you,' I replied.

'England is wonderful, Bernard.' He had a plate of grapes by his side, and he was popping one into his mouth between every few words. 'Green and fresh and friendly. I didn't realize how much I'd missed it until I came back this time.'

I looked out of the window. It didn't look so great to me: too many bricks and cars and not enough trees and grass.

'We are not bothered by the planes,' he said. 'They take off the other side; unless the wind is that way we hardly hear them.' He offered me his grapes but I shook my head.

The bedroom was equipped with an assortment of expensive medical equipment of the sort that glitters in the windows of medical suppliers in London's Wigmore Street. Jim was not in bed. He was dressed in a striped cotton dressing-gown and sitting in a chair, a soft cream-coloured blanket draped over his legs. Despite his lively manner his complexion was, as always, chalky. On his knee he had an open notebook, its pages covered with scribbled numbers. He saw me looking at it: 'I can't seem to concentrate on reading these days, Bernie. I started doing number games ... it started me off remembering old times.' He tapped the notebook. 'I was thinking of the way we cracked the one-time pad,' he explained. 'That was the high point of my days in the Department.' He stared at me. His eyes were bright and unnaturally active. I suppose it was the medicine.

'I heard about that,' I said.

'They all said that the Soviet one-time pads were unbeatable, didn't they? No one wanted to know. I said it was worth tackling, but no one wanted to know.'

He held up his notebook so that I could look at the lines of numbers he'd written, but it was difficult for me to understand what he'd been doing. Was it gibberish or genius? I couldn't even read it properly. Perhaps his scrawling writing was also something to do with his drugs.

'Consider the problem,' said Jim, as if to the world at large, rather than to me. 'Forty-eight five-digit groups. Every page of every pad different, with the sole exception of the corresponding leaf of the pad at the other end. Impossible to crack. Bret told me that. He said: "In two words, Jim, Im possible."'

'Yes,' I said. 'Bret has always had a great sense of humour.'

Ploughing on without pause: 'Where do one-time pads, and all their clever constantly changing codes, come from? I asked them that. They are not handwritten, are they? They are all printed, and if they are printed that must be done on a printing machine. They don't have thousands of Russian machinists standing there, turning a handle to change the numbers one by one, do they? They use a printing machine that automatically changes the numbers or letters. That printing machine has to be programmed. And that order – the sequence in which the machine changes the ciphers – can be cracked, just like any other code can be cracked.'

'It was quite a triumph,' I said. There was no way of stopping him; it was better to let him go on. While he talked I looked round the room at the electrically controlled bed and the stainless steel bedpans, the medical trolley and racks for medicines and syringes. It all made me wonder if Tabby was that kind of woman who, late in life – after charity committees, piano lessons and the history of Renaissance painting – discovers a need to play Florence Night-ingale with any relative within reach. Well, maybe that's the way it was, and maybe it suited both of them.

'And later on I found that it had been done before; back in the war,' Jim was saying. 'Of course I went back through the *American Mathematical Monthly*. I found the copies published in the sum-mer of 1929 when the idea was first being mooted at Hunter College in New York. But then a chance remark from one of the old-timers put me on to what our own Denniston and his Diplo-matic Section had done in Berkeley Street, Piccadilly, right here in London in the war. The German pads had eight lines of six five-figure groups. Of course that set me thinking.' He gave me a quizzical stare.

'Of course,' I said, trying to look like someone who would know how many lines of six-figure groups a German wartime one-time pad always had. And figure it the way Jim had figured it.

'It was obviously using 240 wheels,' he said.

'Yes,' I said.

'When I went to the old man and showed him the way that the diplomatic OTPs had been cracked in the war, he wouldn't believe it at first. When I talked to him about it, he gave in.'

'I can imagine,' I said.

'The old man was ecstatic: he gave me everything I asked for.'

'It was a triumph, Jim.'

'It came together neatly. The Americans went wild; Langley opened a whole new department to handle it. Millions of dollars went into it.'

'It restored their faith in us,' I said.

'I would have got an OBE – maybe something even grander – had we not been so covert. The old man told me that, and later on Bret told me the same.'

'Maybe even a K,' I said.

'Not a K, Bernie,' he said, coming to earth with a bump. 'You don't have to overdo it.' He looked at me. 'Now what did you really come here to ask me?'

'Does there have to be anything?'

'Come along, Bernard. You don't pay social calls and you don't like grapes. When you come out here, to the wrong side of the airport, it's because you are after something.' Perhaps he felt he was being a shade too offensive, for he added: 'No one in the Department pays social calls. It's not in the training manual, is it?'

'Cindy dropped in on me. She said you left a box file with her. She wants to get rid of it.'

He swallowed the grape he was chewing and pushed the rest of them aside. 'Get rid of it?'

'She says she's looked after it long enough,' I said.

'Is that what she told you?'

'Yes. That's what she said. It's not true?'

'She's a lively one, isn't she?'

'Yes, she is,' I agreed emphatically.

'She stole it. She stole that box file. I gave her a lift to her apartment in Brussels, and when I helped her carry her bags from my car boot into the building she took the box file along with her other baggage. I didn't notice until I got to the airport. I called her from the transit lounge but her line was busy.'

'You didn't do anything about it?'

'What am I going to do? Tell the Department that I let my ex-wife steal a secret box file? Jesus, they would have ripped my balls off. If they find out what's happened, they still will. You've got to get it back for me, Bernard.'

'Okay. You think she will just hand it over?'

'Not Cindy. Nothing comes free with Cindy. Where is she keeping it?'

'In her office safe, she said.'

'In Brussels?'

'How many offices does she have?'

196

'What did you think? When you saw her, what did you think of her?'

'She looked fine,' I said cautiously. Experience told me that no matter how much men criticized their ex-wives, it was not an invitation to join in. 'Very glamorous; very attractive.' And yet making ex-wives sound too attractive also held its dangers, so I added: 'Of course we are all getting older.'

'Is she still using all that make-up? Fluttering those false eyelashes; rouged cheeks like a tart. And dousing herself in scent? I told her she was overdoing it: she smelled like the perfume room in Harrods.'

'You told her that, did you?' It sounded like a dangerous conversational ploy.

'We've got to get that box back,' he said.

'What's in it?' I asked him.

'I'm not sure.'

'You're not sure? I thought it would be something you wanted and needed.'

'I was told to open it only after getting the order to open it. I figured it contained orders of some sort.'

'It's big and heavy,' I reminded him.

'And maybe a gun or something. I had the key and the combination but I lost both. And then I thought what the hell.'

'I see.'

He looked at me. 'Have you reported this?'

'Reported what?'

'Don't be dumb, Bernard. Have you reported what Cindy told you? That she has the box file.'

'Of course I haven't. I wanted to talk to you about it first.'

'I always said you were the smartest one there,' he said. 'More cunning, more devious and more far-sighted than any of the rest of them.'

'Spread it around,' I said. 'Or maybe not.'

He was smiling, and perhaps there was some margin of

admiration in this trenchant description but I don't know how much. He was resentful. Indignant in the way that I would have been if he had tried on me the trick I was pulling on him. 'No,' he said. 'If you had reported it you would have nothing to threaten me with, would you?'

'Don't be that way, Jim.'

'So now I've got two of you twisting my arm. You and Cindy: the two who were closest to me in the old days.'

'Oh, sure. *Et tu, Brute*. But Caesar hadn't mislaid a box file, old buddy.' I gave him back his notebook and his numbers. 'I'd get that box back from her, Jim. If I were you, I really would get it back from her. Even if it means paying her some alimony. In the long run it might prove cheaper. The Ides of March are come, Jim. This is a bad time of year.'

'But not gone. Yes, well I don't give a damn. Go back and tell them all you know. And tell Cindy to go to hell. I don't work for the Department any more. I don't give a damn what happens to any of you.'

'Cindy said two men came to her asking for it. Americans from Geneva, she said. Business associates of yours.'

'And you believed her? Jesus Christ, Bernard. How can you let her make such a fool of you? That was my lawyer and his partner. I sent them along to talk with her, but she played little girl lost with them. She is too cunning to say anything that a lawyer might use.'

'I wish you two would get your stories straight,' I said. 'Surely you don't enjoy all this hassle.'

'I've got no money to spare for Cindy. Do you know how much it costs to be sick nowadays? A fortune!'

'You should have taken time out to be sick back when we could afford it.'

'Yes, that was my big mistake,' he said ruefully. 'Why are you so interested in that box file? What are you expecting to find inside it? Give it to me straight.'

'Once upon a time there was a man named Thurkettle, a rent-a-gun who killed my sister-in-law . . .'

'Hold it . . .'

'No hold-its, Jimmy. I was there; I saw it. He shot Tessa Kosinski on the Autobahn, and then came to meet you and catch a plane to safety. Knowing the way the Department do things, I know that he must have been debriefed by someone . . .' Seeing that Jimmy was about to start interrupting again, I quickly added: 'And that someone was you.'

☆

Jim wet his lips. I thought he was going to say something interesting but he picked up a glass of water and sipped some. 'Go on.'

'Cindy drove to the plane and got the box from the Swede. Meanwhile you paid off Thurkettle and helped him do his disappearing act.'

'No, Bernard.'

'Don't tell me no. You gave him his money and his new ID. He was so pleased that he made you a present of the sapphire brooch that he had ripped from the dead body of Tessa Kosinski.'

'You've got it wrong.'

'Oh, sure. Well, you'll be able to explain how wrong I've got it to a Board of Inquiry. Washington has agreed to extradite Thurkettle. So don't imagine you will be able to run back to America and escape their clutches.'

'Extradite Thurkettle!' He laughed scornfully. 'How are they going to do that? Resurrection? Thurkettle is dead. Very very dead. Yes, I went to the rendezvous – the Ziesar exit ramp – and saw Thurkettle. But he was dead.'

'If Thurkettle is dead you killed him. Where did you get Tessa's brooch? You must have stolen it from his body after you wasted him.'

'I didn't steal anything from him. I didn't touch him.'

'Let's play it your way, Jim. You arrive to find your contact is dead. Of course you would touch him. You'd have to be crazy not to check his pockets. London would want proof that someone had hit the right target. You would need to know if he had a gun in his pocket. A gun could get you into a lot of trouble in that jurisdiction. Or get you out of it.'

'Okay, I looked in his pockets.'

'And found the sapphire brooch?'

'Yes. Yes, I did. In his pocket. That was a silly mistake.' Prettyman suddenly stiffened. Sometimes throwing a scare into a suspect makes them freeze like that. 'I've got the brooch here,' he said in a whisper. 'You didn't say anything to Tabby, did you?'

'Say anything? How would I start? You are such a complicated double-dealing crook I wouldn't know how to tackle it.'

'I didn't know the brooch belonged to your sister-in-law. I swear I didn't.'

'That would have made a difference, would it? You are the bastard who had her killed. And then killed her hit man.'

'I tell you no.'

'No, not you. You just waited for Thurkettle to arrive at the rendezvous and have heart failure.'

'I was just a contact man. Let me explain. The first I heard was that Silas Gaunt wanted to talk to some sort of hit man. It was not such a surprising request. The Department often use me to make contact with hard-to-find people or esoteric institutions. So I set up the meeting. I didn't know what it was all about.'

'Silas Gaunt actually talked to Thurkettle? When? Where?'

'How was I to know that Silas was going nuts? No one told me he was a crazy man. His name was whispered like he was about to be canonized. They told me he was an infallible old hero. They told me that nothing important was decided until word had come from this oracle in the Cotswolds.'

'How do you know he's going crazy?'

'Right! It came as a surprise to me too. Everyone said it was the D-G who was going nuts, didn't they? Now it becomes clear that it was Silas Gaunt who was running out of control: the D-G was just on a damage-limitation exercise.'

'What is out of control?'

'All the signs were there ages ago but no one would face up to it. First I heard that Silas Gaunt was sick and bed-ridden. Then he gets some sort of brain-storm because the local district council tells him to chop all his elm trees down. Maybe there were other signs of physical deterioration. Who knows what was hatching in his brain? All we know for sure is that now they have locked him away.'

'Silas is alive and well and living at Whitelands,' I said.

'They are keeping it very need-to-know.'

'You say Silas briefed Thurkettle? Are you sure?'

'Sure? Sure? I arranged it. I took Thurkettle to the Hilton Hotel in Park Lane. I wasn't allowed to sit in at the meeting of course.'

'Silas Gaunt would never have revealed his identity to a hit man.'

'What did he have to lose? He was arranging for Thurkettle to be killed too. And anyway, as I say: Silas was crazy.'

'I don't believe you. I've known Silas Gaunt all my life. I saw him recently . . .'

'I don't care what you believe. If you go chasing after him, like you chased after me, you won't get to him. Because they finally slammed him into some special funny farm the Department uses for people who have State secrets in their heads.'

'It shouldn't be difficult to check out,' I said.

'Not difficult at all,' he agreed. 'Check it out. And you'll find I'm telling you the truth.' He craned towards me and stared: 'I swear to God.'

'Look, Jim. Thurkettle killed Tessa Kosinski; I was there, I saw it. But you killed Thurkettle. You took the gun that Werner Volk-mann delivered to you; a special plastic gun. You waited at the rendezvous for Thurkettle to arrive on his BMW motor-bike. No one pays a hit man in advance, so he would have had to meet you somewhere to collect his payment. You wasted Thurkettle, grabbed the money, abandoned the motor-bike, dumped the gun and drove away. My guess is that you drove away in some kind of camper vehicle.'

'This is your theory, is it? It's not something you saw on late-night TV?' Prettyman narrowed his eyes. Perhaps he wasn't staring; perhaps he was in pain.

'And that's not all of it,' I said. 'Your Cindy was there. I sometimes suspect that this knock-down, drag-out brawl the two of you like displaying to everyone is a cover-up. I think you two have been in cosy agreement until now. She took you to your rendezvous with Thurkettle in a car. You had to have someone drive you there, because after killing Thurkettle you have to drive his car away somewhere. Cindy maybe helps you with your murder and then drives on to meet the Swede and his plane. She collected the box file from the Swede and took it away with her. Now you have some kind of fight about who owns it. Or maybe you don't have a fight; maybe that's a scam too.'

'Maybe there's not even a box file,' he said.

'The thought had occurred to me,' I agreed.

'Very good, Bernard. Very logical, but too baroque for a Hollywood movie. Cindy help in a murder? Are you serious?'

'You took the payoff money to Thurkettle. A lot of money, because professional hits like that cost a lot of money. You would have had to bring back some kind of receipt, however disguised that paperwork might have been. There would have to be a piece of paper, for some cashier somewhere in Whitehall to do his sums. And somewhere too there would be a debriefing report.'

'And is that what you think you'll find in the box file?' He forced a little laugh. 'You're a card, Bernard, you really are. You'll be sorry you ever started this nonsense.'

'Let's not play truth or consequences, Jim. Threats leave friendships in tatters.'

'So you've noticed that, have you, Bernard? It took you a long time, didn't it? And cost you a lot of tattered friends.'

'Too late now to worry about that, Jim old pal. Right now I'm more interested in the box file Cindy wants to sell you.'

'Are you? You are very clever, Bernard. And very nearly right. But no cover-up. Cindy and I don't get along and that's for real. Your biggest error is thinking that I killed Thurkettle. You're right too about him leaving a camper in place. I was told not to let him drive off in it, so Cindy was with me to drive the camper away. But when I found Thurkettle dead I sent her to the plane instead. Wrong about the money too. I didn't have any money for Thurkettle, I had an arrest warrant. Thurkettle had been told we would fly him to a spot he'd chosen in Germany. But my orders said I was to fly with him to England, to a military strip in Dorset. They were going to put him on ice. I had no money for him: that was how I was going to get him on the plane instead of letting him drive away. And I wasn't told to debrief him. In fact I was told not to talk to him about any work he'd done, or let him tell me anything about his operation or his orders.'

'Why try to wriggle out of the Thurkettle killing?' I asked him. 'It's got your prints all over it.'

'Of course you don't believe me. The truth doesn't fit into your theory, does it? Well, you can go on disbelieving for as long as you like. The truth is that I was fooled. We were all fooled. Thurkettle was more fooled than any of us: fooled to death. But Cindy knew nothing of it: she was waiting back on the Autobahn. I didn't tell her I'd found Thurkettle dead. Yes, I searched Thurkettle's body to get his car keys. I took his VW camper and went through the checkpoint and drove all night to a safe house I knew in Düsseldorf. I went to earth and waited for instructions. I think that's what the manual says is the right drill.' He smiled. How these bloody office people always liked to play field agent. 'Two days after that, the alarm bells started to ring in London. With me sitting in Düsseldorf, and the Swede arriving in England with empty seats in his plane, Silas Gaunt knew his pet scheme had fallen apart. Nothing had gone the way he planned. From the Department's point of view it was a total disaster.'

☆

I nodded as I ran it through my mind. Prettyman's story would have a strand of truth woven into it. Good cover stories always do. But I noticed that Cindy could not be called in to corroborate his version of the Thurkettle death.

Was it a cock-up or a triumph of concealment? Never mind the way he now wanted to bend the truth. Prettyman was concocting a story that got him off the hook. I suppose he didn't want to go along to Mass and explain that gunning down a colleague in cold blood was a part of his misspent past. But look at it another way and Jim had done more or less what he was told, and the Department had got more or less what they wanted out of it. Silas had fixed it so that no one knew the whole story. Only a maniac or a genius could have programmed such a complex operation, and Silas was a mix of both. Congratulations Uncle Silas. Disaster? A couple more disasters like that and they'd be giving Jim the medal he so desperately craved.

Perhaps he saw what sort of doubts I had. He said: 'Maybe it was all planned that way.'

'Was his payoff waiting in the camper?'

'No. I went right through it next day. The camper was obviously arranged by Thurkettle himself. He planned to take the money and run, but I had no money for him. Inside the camper I found a wallet with an Amex card and Visa and some other plastic, small change and odds and ends. It was all in some Scandinavian name – not Thurkettle – so I guess he was going to change identity. No passport; he must have hidden that somewhere else. He'd made all the arrangements to escape, but he had reckoned without the arrangements that someone else had made for him.'

'You're a cold-blooded bastard,' I said. 'You go through his

204

pockets, and you steal a brooch and give it to some girl you take a fancy to. It stinks; you stink.' I wondered what else he'd stolen from the body and I would never know about. I couldn't help wondering if Prettyman disobeyed orders and killed Thurkettle in order to steal the payment for the hit. I wouldn't put it past him if he became desperately short of money. And the fee for a tricky and dangerous job like that might have gone into six figures.

'The stink comes from the Department,' said Prettyman. 'And it didn't even work.'

'Didn't it?'

'They thought they could foist off the burned body of Tessa Kosinski as being that of your wife, while you two escaped. That was a stupid idea. I could have told them that if they had consulted me. You can't burn a body properly in a car fire with a few gallons of petrol.'

'Why?'

'You need a temperature of about one thousand degrees centigrade to reduce the big bones to ash.'

'It doesn't have to become ash to be beyond identification,' I said.

'No it doesn't, but that wasn't the problem. They wanted a corpse that *was* identified, a corpse that would resemble another specific person. What Thurkettle did was useless. It didn't burn properly. You've got to take into account all the water in the guts of a human body. I saw the East German report on the Kosinski body.'

'Where did you get hold of that?'

'The Department. Did they never show it to you?'

'No,' I said.

'The skin and flesh was blackened, the legs were burned, but the abdomen and the internal organs – lungs and liver and so on – were virtually intact, and that had prevented the upper body burning properly . . . Is this affecting you, Bernard?'

'No,' I said. 'Go on.'

'It's your sister-in-law, I know.'

'Go on, I said.'

'The failure of the upper body to burn meant that the skull was too preserved to fool them. The top of the skull had gone, but the frontal sinus was intact. Fiona had been treated for a sinus problem. They had X-rays of her skull.'

'A substitute skull was burned with the body. The prepared skull had had its dentistry specially done to be like Fiona's.'

'It wouldn't fool them for a moment. The sinus cavities are just as identifiable as teeth. And anyway, much of that clever dentistry was a waste of time and effort. The lower jaw detached from the skull and was burned away; the upper was less easy to match.' He rubbed his hands together. 'No, it was all for nothing.'

'What happened to you, Jim? Back in the old days you would never have considered becoming a part of a dirty business like this.'

'That was the old days,' he said, looking at his hands. They were bent and pale and spotted; the hands of a sick man. 'We live in a different world now, Bernard. In the old days it was all an amusing game, and we were good at playing it. But the world has gone professional, Bernard. You tell me I stink, and maybe I do. It's because the Department called me in to do their dirty work. I do it so that people like you, and Bret and Sir Henry and Silas Gaunt and all the rest of the sanctimonious time-servers, could keep your hands clean, and keep your conscience in good shape, by telling me I stink.'

'You can't rationalize murder,' I said.

'I've never killed anyone,' said Prettyman. 'I draw the line at that. And at the drug dimension too. I never knew that Thurkettle was supplying Tessa with dope to keep her under his spell. But I'm through with all that. I have made my peace with God. I will meet my maker and I will be free.' He reached into the top pocket of his dressing-gown and found the sapphire brooch. 'Take it; give it to Fiona or to George. I don't want it.' He passed it to me. It was carefully wrapped into a white silk handkerchief. He must have already decided to give it to me, and put it in his pocket before I arrived. I suppose he'd been sitting here all morning rehearsing his story. I wondered how much he had changed in the face of my questions.

I unwrapped the brooch and looked at it. The sapphire was scratched but its faint blue cast was luminous and liquid, like a glass of mountain water. The sparkle from the diamonds was quite different; a very hard light, like the beam from a carbon arc-lamp. It was easy to see why people became obsessed by such stones. The brooch suddenly reminded me of Tessa and I could hear her voice. I wrapped it up and put it in my pocket. 'I'll send it to George; he's next-of-kin I suppose.'

'The pretty little Canadian nurse told me what you said to her.'

'She thought you'd got it out of a bran-tub.'

'I didn't know it was that valuable. Or where it had come from. I just wanted to empty Thurkettle's pockets. I don't know why I didn't just throw it away at the time. I wanted to give the Canadian kid something. She was a nice little girl.'

'They all are, Jim. But don't tell Tabby, is that it?' I said.

He gave me a man-to-man smile. I was sorry for him, in the way I would be sorry for anyone living out his final days near London's airport. But he was a creep and he was using me as an anvil upon which to beat his newly heated memories into a shape that suited him. I'd had enough. I got up and said goodbye. From the downstairs hi-fi a soprano was singing exuberantly. Under the circumstances, I'm not sure that Tabby's *Merry Widow* was a felicitous choice of background music.

'Was that all?' he said with evident relief. Despite my denials, he still thought the Department had sent me to check him out.

'You've told me all I need to know, Jim,' I said. 'You did okay. You are well on the way to a medal.'

He smiled suspiciously.

How much of it could I believe? Was Thurkettle really dead? I wasn't even totally convinced that Jimjay was sick. If next week I happened upon Jim and Thurkettle playing a strenuous game of squash, Jim would just give me a shy smile and another long explanation.

10

An Autobahn exit. The German Democratic Republic

THE BEST WAY to test Prettyman's story was to go to the exit ramp he'd specified and see what could be found there. It was forbidden to leave the Autobahn, so I didn't tell Frank what I intended.

I took Werner with me. I hadn't told him about my meeting with Prettyman, but he knew I'd been pursuing every lead I could find. By the time we reached the Ziesar exit ramp I had formed a clear idea of what Thurkettle would need for an inconspicuous rendezvous.

'This would be good, Werner,' I said as I lowered the window and looked around. This was Germany at its most rural. There was the smell of freshly dug lignite on the air. Since the oil crisis of 1973 the Soviet Union had become more possessive about its oil. The German Democratic Republic was producing its own energy and paying the price in dozens of open-cast *Braunkohl* workings. They scarred the landscape, and this low-grade solid fuel polluted the air, both before and after being burned.

Werner didn't reply. He seemed to think we were engaged on a wild-goose chase, although he was too polite to say so in those exact words. But this was a perfect spot for a secret rendezvous of any kind. The junction was wide and hidden from view, protected from the weather and yet very close to the Autobahn. I ran the car – it was Werner's ancient Mercedes – up on to the grassy verge and used my binoculars to scout the surroundings. Two or three fields away I saw two farm-workers forking over a manure heap. 'Let's go, Werner,' I said, getting out of the car. I buttoned up tight against the steady downfall of wet snow that had continued ever since we left Berlin. It was better to walk over to the men. Until I had sniffed out the situation in this sleepy little backwater, I preferred that they didn't see the West Berlin licence plates on the car.

The temperature seemed to be below zero, but that was hard to reconcile with the sleet. It fell steadily and was whisked into little tempests that whipped my face painfully, like shaving with a rusty razor-blade. The wind was from the north, the most unkind wind, for north of here the world was flat; as level as a vast sea-bed, which it had once been. From here to the Baltic Sea there stretched the north German plain. This was Europe's battlefield, an arena where invading armies had manoeuvred and fought since Germans stood firm against the Slavs, and their recorded history began. Little wonder that the wall dividing the Soviet Empire from the forces of NATO was so near to this place.

As we walked towards them, the two men stopped work. They rested upon their long-handled forks and watched us approach, viewing us with that cool suspicion that country-dwellers save for visitors of urban appearance. Werner's long black overcoat was not the sort of garment to be encountered frequently in the German countryside unless he had been the proprietor of a travelling circus – a few mangy lions, a zebra and a trapeze act – the sort of family enterprise still to be found touring round Eastern Europe from one small town to the next.

'Good day,' I said. Both men nodded with an almost imperceptible movement of the head. Reaching into my pocket I brought out a half-bottle of schnapps. I twisted the cap from it and offered them a swig. Only after they had drunk some did I gulp at it myself. It warmed my throat. I gave it to Werner, who pretended to drink some. Werner was not keen on booze and particularly hated apple schnapps.

Taking my time with some preliminaries about the weather and the changing seasons, I asked them to remember the previous June. Had they seen a car or any kind of van or camper . . . left parked in the next field? Or anywhere near the Autobahn. Some time last summer. I didn't give them the exact date; it was better to reserve one known fact against which to test the information.

'Yes,' said the elder of the two men. 'Dark green: a sort of van.'

The younger one added: 'It was there two days and nights. There was no one inside it. We went and took a close look at it. It had a cooking stove, and a soft bed inside. No one went near it. Then, a couple of days later, it had gone. Gone in the night.' The younger man's voice was keener and he seemed more accommodating than his father. They looked alike, except in stature. The elder man was short, his unshaven face deeply lined, and his manner resigned.

The younger man was freshly shaven, his hair cropped in a style that Germans thought was American. His clothes, although equally old, were cleaner than his father's. Under his waterproof jacket the boy had Western-style denim pants. He said: 'We thought it might have been damaged on the Autobahn and waiting for the tow-truck. But it seemed to be in perfect condition.' The boy was unafraid, almost defiant in his willingness to help us. The two Germans personified the history of their land. The wary old man was a typical product of wartime rationing, postwar shortages and the rigours of the police State. The confident boy was tall and fit, a beneficiary of State welfare but restless and discontented.

'It sounds like what I'm looking for,' I said.

'Are you the police?' said the young man. He had been studying my English trenchcoat and waterproof hat with the close interest that comes from living in a society where imports are virtually unobtainable. He was about eighteen, and strong enough for the toil of a farm with few mechanical implements.

'I work for an insurance company in Stuttgart,' I said. 'I'm a claims adjuster. I make sure my company doesn't get swindled by false claims.' That explanation seemed to satisfy them that I wasn't dangerous. The most dangerous visitors were of course the avid communists from the West: trade union officials and activists and busybodies. These were the ones that were likely to report any lack of enthusiasm they encountered in citizens lucky enough to live in a workers' paradise. 'I'm a capitalist,' I said. It was usually the best way of being reassuring.

'That's where it was,' said the boy, pointing a finger.

So Thurkettle had parked his camper under the trees. He'd pulled off the feeder-road to where the silver birches sprang from the unruly gorse. This was a land of sand and birch and beech; the sort of landscape in which I had grown up and felt at home. 'A Volkswagen. Not new. West Berlin licence plates.' The younger one sensed there was money in it; I could tell by the way he looked at me. He was trying to introduce the subject of payment. In the West he would have asked directly. Such reticence here was not only a legacy of the socialist State, it went right back to the old Germany where any mention of money carried with it a stigma. Nowadays such niceties had long since been forgotten by hotel staff, and others who came into regular contact with Westerners. But here in the countryside such manners remained.

'Did you see anything else over there?' I asked. 'Anything at all?' They looked at each other and then said no with rather too much emphasis. I let it go. 'He's claiming for a wrist-watch, an expensive wrist-watch,' I said. They nodded but seemed unconvinced. I suppose they were wondering why the insurance company had waited so long before investigating the claim. Fortunately there is a prevalent view in the East that Western-style capitalism moves in strange inexplicable ways.

'We don't go over there near the road,' said the younger man. He smiled, revealing uneven and overcrowded teeth. He might have been a handsome youth but for that. Eastern Europe had not yet discovered orthodontistry. With no proper elections to contest, its leaders did not need teeth and hair. 'The land is the property of the State,' he added. At one time it would have been the 'property of the people', but now only party members were clinging to such starry-eyed notions. All pretence had gone: land and people were the property of the State, and woe betide anyone who forgot it. Soon the State would make a more immediate claim upon the boy. He was obviously waiting for the summons that would take him for the compulsory couple of years of military service.

I nodded. The three long Autobahnen that linked West Germany to Berlin were subject to complex laws and international agreements. Westerners were permitted to use them, subject to checks at each end of the journey. But even to wander a few yards from the road was a serious offence. The sort of offence that I was now committing.

'We keep away,' said the old man to further endorse his son's statement. It was apparent that they were tenant farmers, which was as near to capitalism as the German Democratic Republic was likely to get. The State remained the sole owner of the tiny plot of land they farmed, while they were permitted to work it and sell its produce for gain. But one had only to look at them to see that, after taxes and rent, the gain was very small. The government wanted to ease the food shortages but they didn't want anyone to start thinking that such capitalism was widely desirable.

'Oh, yes,' I said, as if searching for something to say. 'I forgot to mention it: there is a reward.'

I passed the apple schnapps to them for a second round, and we stood there looking at the endless flat land, at the occasional truck and car that went whizzing past on the Autobahn, and at the smoke rising from the chimney of what must have been their lop-sided little brick farmhouse. There was no shelter. The sleet stung my face and reddened my hands. I blew on my fingers to get the circulation going but the two men seemed hardly to notice the wind or the wet ice that dribbled down their faces.

'Reward?' said the son.

'Two hundred West Marks,' I said.

'For what?' said the father, his caution signified by the way he laid his hand upon his son's arm.

'For any material thing . . . for any piece of solid evidence that will convince my company that the thief came here.'

The two men looked at each other. I got out my wallet and flipped it open casually to reveal a lot of West German paper money.

'There was a motor-cycle,' said the son. 'The remains of one . . . It is badly burned, so not much of it is left.'

'Find me a piece of it, and one hundred marks is yours,' I said.

☆

They took me to a ditch near where they said the camper had been parked. It would have taken hours, perhaps days, and a properly organized search party to find it. 'We saw it burning,' said the boy.

'We found it after it was burned,' said his father in flat contradiction to his son. 'It was just like this when we found it.'

I could see why the old man changed his account. The bike had been stripped. It was bereft of any valuable part that could be carried away and concealed. Perhaps the burning had been a way of disguising the extent of the theft.

'Have you got time to help me?' I said. 'I pay twenty West Marks per hour.' Neither man answered me. By that time we all knew it was a rhetorical question. 'I want to search the ditch.'

The two men used their potato hooks and began to stab into the hidden depths of the ditch to find anything that had broken free from the bike.

'Now do you see what happened, Werner? Thurkettle came here on his motor-bike, dumped it here and left in a camper.'

I looked down into a drainage canal to see the motor-bike better. Over time it had settled deeper into the earth. I climbed down to examine it more closely. Although its remains were damaged to the point of being virtually worthless the frame was not old. I pulled some brambles away to see the engine; all the electrical accessories had been stripped out. The motor-bike was wide and squat-shaped: one of those high-powered BMWs. And it wasn't the costly sort of Western luxury that citizens of the DDR would be likely to spend their precious hard currency on. Or abandon by the roadside.

'It's a beauty,' I said. The two men looked down at me without changing their dour expressions. Werner smiled. Despite the way I was trying to remain cool and composed, I suppose he could see how pleased I was. Werner liked to tell me that I frequently behaved like a schoolboy. No doubt at some future time he would quote today's doings as evidence of it. 'A beauty!'

'You're getting mud all over you,' said Werner.

When new it had been an impressive machine, its chrome bright and paintwork glistening. Its engine must have made it as powerful as many a small car. Now the frame was twisted and blistered with burning. Its fuel tank had held enough to make a ferocious blaze. Both wheels had disappeared, and every part of the engine not caked in mud was ravaged by fire. Only the tiniest pieces of heavy plastic remained to show where the rivets had fixed saddle and panniers to the frame.

I took out my Olympus camera and took some photos of the wreck. The camera was tiny, and over the years of using it I had found that pictures could be taken, and the camera hidden again, before anyone really noticed what you were doing. That's how it was now.

'Probe the ditch all the way along to the ramp,' I said.

'Let's get out of here while we can,' said Werner softly in English.

It made me angry. Although he said it in English the tone of his voice was enough to create anxieties in the two locals. Luckily the thought of the money seemed to keep them going.

Each man carried a three-pronged *Kartoffelhacke*, which they had been using to turn over the manure. They dragged the prongs through the drainage canal, twisting them to disentangle the roots and brambles and dislodge clods of sandy earth. They knew about clearing ditches and automatically assumed positions as a pair: the old man in front and the boy behind digging deeper. To account for the need for such meticulous searching, I explained to them again that we were looking for the wrist-watch. Werner grunted. He was about to say something but changed his mind, and smiled instead.

Any more sardonic remarks from Werner were silenced when the old man's fork struck the leather case. By now the two farm-workers had caught the fever of finding buried treasure. 'Fifty marks,' I said as he pulled it up for me to inspect. I handed the money over.

It was a Samsonite metal-framed document case. The frame was only slightly corroded and its imitation leather exterior was little affected by the months it had spent in the ditch. Apart from a long gouge and a bad dent on the underside, it could have been cleaned up to look no worse than the average item of luggage seen on commuter trains every morning. It was not locked but there was enough corrosion on the hinge fittings to make it stiff to open. It was slimy inside with a coating of fuzz. All kinds of grubs, worms and squrming animal life had made a home in it. I ran my hand around the rotting cloth lining. Werner watched me. There was nothing there until I scratched at the lining with my fingernails. I peeled a label from where it had stuck, tearing it as I pulled. The 'label' was a small piece of a US fifty-dollar bill. I held it under Werner's nose. 'How does that grab you, Werner?'

'You did it, Bernie,' said Werner with as much enthusiasm as he could muster. 'How did you know?' Then it clicked. 'You talked to Prettyman?'

'Yes,' I admitted.

'How was he?'

'Too late for sweets; too early for flowers,' I said.

'Is there something wrong?' said the elder man, who had been trying to follow our conversation in English.

'This gentleman is my business associate from Dresden,' I said. 'We had a disagreement and a small wager about the solution of this mysterious business. Now he is angry to find that my theory was right. He is a bad loser.'

'Look,' said the younger man. He had continued prodding into the ditch while I examined the document case. He was about ten metres away from me. He held up the hook. On the point of the prongs there was a large section of rotting fabric: striped like shirt material. 'There is something here! *Gott!*'

Farmers are used to life and death, but none of us were prepared for the human remains that he found at the tip of his fork. Dump a side of beef into a ditch on a warm day in June. Within a week it stinks. Flies descend upon it, and so do rats and all the other scavengers of the countryside. Eventually the worms move in. 'It is Thurkettle,' I said. He had been there a long time.

'How do you know who it is?' said Werner.

'We'll get him out,' I said. 'And you'll see.'

'No,' said Werner. 'It's too risky.'

I ignored Werner's caution. It was very heavy. An old dried-out cadaver like that would normally have been as light as a feather, but Thurkettle was heavy. His coat had become one with the earth, so that a massive weight of mud was clinging to him. Had the corpse not been clad in tough ballistic nylon coveralls we would never have lifted it intact. But the heavy-duty nylon had defied the attacks of the rodents, and the degradation of nature. The woven plastic was as stout and intact as the day the coveralls were made. With all four of us combining our utmost efforts, we gripped the plastic of his arms and legs, and lifted Thurkettle's earthly remains out of the ditch like a sack of coal. Puffing with the exertion we dumped it on the embankment. The two locals looked at each other and then they looked at me. The elder man made the sign of the cross. I kneeled down. In places the body had been gnawed to the bone. Half of one arm was missing entirely; little was left of the face, so that the teeth were bared.

Closing my mind to the disgust that human remains always bring, I pushed my folding knife into the body to locate the spine. I'd seen such remains before, but always on a properly drained mortuary slab, with hot black coffee and a cigarette not far away, and a pathologist to do the tricky bits. Now I had to do it on my own. The juicier parts of the internal organs had long disappeared. The rats had gone first for the delicacies: the liver, kidneys and stomach, and for the eyes too.

The position of the body was that of a man cowering from a blow; that defensive posture that some bodies assume in death. Now I could see what time had brought. Some of the muscle was still intact; dried and as hard as granite. Muscular contractions had distorted the skeleton. I probed deeper. What a way to go. No man deserves to be reduced to such a horrifying bundle of old bones and leather.

'You have found what you were looking for,' said Werner without pleasure. 'Let's go.'

'I must know the cause of death,' I said.

'It wasn't old age,' said Werner.

'No,' I agreed. 'And if he was shot, I might find evidence of that on the skeleton.' I looked up at the farmers. The discovery of the dead body had frightened them. What had started off as an amusing way to get their hands on some Western currency had turned into a nightmare that was likely to end with them facing interrogation by the Stasi. I could see what was going through their minds.

'Give me one more minute,' I said, closing the knife and putting it away. I shut my eyes and thrust my hands right into the remains.

It was hard and bony. My fingers found and felt the spine, and the pelvis and the shoulder-blades. 'Yes, Werner. Yes, Werner, Yes.' I said. I could feel what I was searching for: the rough edges on the bones. It wasn't the gnawing of rats. 'He's been hit by a fusillade of bullets,' I said.

When I examined the coveralls again more closely I found the bullet holes in corresponding positions. There were at least six of them, very close together, the surrounding burn marks still just visible. 'I'll settle for that,' I said. I got to my feet.

'Gunshot?' said Werner.

'Six rounds, maybe more: two of them probably high enough to find the heart.' With my foot I rolled him over. Nothing would have persuaded me to touch the body again except with the toe of my shoe. I was about to give it a final shove that would roll it back into the ditch when I spotted there at the bottom of it what looked like a bright green patch of patterned fabric. 'What is that?' I said aloud. But even as I said it I knew what it was. The corpse had been resting upon a fortune in dollar bills. Dozens upon dozens of fifty-dollar bills. Protected by the weight, and by the nylon coveralls, the money had remained fresh and new-looking. I glanced at the others. No one wanted to grope through the worms to get the money. We had all had our fill. With no more hesitation I kicked the corpse gently. It flopped back into the ditch with a squelching sound, a protest that seemed to come from the dead man's mouth.

'All gone. All finished,' I said to the two men. I gave them the rest of my West German money: three hundred marks. 'Go home,' I said. 'Don't go spending the money and attracting attention to yourselves. You understand? Forget everything. Don't tell your wife. Don't tell your neighbour. Don't tell anyone. We will drive away now. And we will never come back.'

For a moment they stood there transfixed. I thought they were going to make trouble for us. I invented a story for them: 'It was his wife who did it,' I said. 'She is not a bad woman. He beat her.

Now she is trying to collect his life insurance. Go home and forget it all. In the West this happens sometimes.'

It seemed ages before the two men looked at each other and without speaking turned and began to walk back to their home and their fields. I had a feeling that they were going to walk until we were out of earshot and then discuss it. While I was still trying to decide what to do, Werner went after them. I watched him as he stopped and talked with them. I couldn't hear what he said but they both nodded assent. When Werner returned he said: 'It will be okay.'

By that time I was so hyped up that I didn't care about anything except the proof of my theory. 'Look, Werner,' I said. I had already spotted the most conclusive discovery of all. 'I didn't want the farmers to see this.' I climbed down into the ditch again and used a twig to hook up my find. I wanted to show Werner what it was, but I didn't hold it up high in case the farmers were looking back at us.

'What is it?' said Werner. 'Is it a gun?'

'It's the final link with Prettyman,' I said. 'This is the gun that killed Thurkettle.'

'Funny-looking gun,' said Werner. 'It looks like a toy.'

'Yes, it does. We live in an age when toy guns look like the real thing, and the real guns look like toys. But a plastic gun like this is deadly. Expendable and non-ferrous so it goes through airport security checks. Hatchwork all over the grips so that no finger-prints can ever be found on one. The triangular cartridge cases fit tight, and are supplied in short strips. Rapid fire: pull the trigger and it goes like a machine gun. I should have guessed what it would be, when I saw the gouge marks in the bottom of the document case.' I laid the white plastic gun alongside the document case. 'When fired, the metal bullet snaps out of its triangular polyethylene cartridge casing. One round must have nicked the bottom of the case. The whole story is right here before us, Werner.'

'Are you going to take the gun along?' asked Werner.

'It's evidence,' I said. 'You can see what happened. Prettyman came here to meet Thurkettle and pay him. Perhaps they quarrelled; about the payoff or about going to the plane instead of letting Thurkettle drive away. Prettyman holds the case like this . . . like a tray. He holds it high and with one hand to conceal the gun he's got under it. I remember you doing that, Werner, when we got into that little problem in Dresden back in . . . oh I forget when . . . Prettyman fired the gun at point-blank range. Prettyman is no kind of marksman, but with the muzzle almost touching Thurkettle's guts he didn't have to be. Thurkettle drops instantly, and he tips the body into the ditch. Prettyman must have had it figured in advance. I think he enticed Thurkettle to a position near the ditch, so that he didn't have to drag the body over here.'

'You make him sound very cold-blooded,' said Werner, as if unconvinced.

'Prettyman. I know him very well, Werner. He is cold-blooded. We're talking about a bastard who went through Thurkettle's pockets and took Tessa's sapphire brooch. And then gave it to his fancy girlfriend in Moscow.'

'If it was the same brooch.'

'I don't make mistakes like that, Werner. I recognized Tessa's sapphire as soon as I clapped eyes on it. And Prettyman admitted taking the brooch. He puts it in his own pocket, tosses gun and document case into the ditch, jumps into the camper and drives back on to the Autobahn and into the West. Cold-blooded? He's cold-blooded all right.'

'Very clever, Bernie. But aren't you forgetting one little thing?'

'What?'

'He drives away in the camper. What about the car he arrived here in? The farmers didn't see any other car parked here. If there was no car, how did Prettyman get here?'

'Mrs Cindy Prettyman. That's the answer to that one, Werner. Everything has fallen into place for me. I talked to the Swede before he was killed. He said a woman came to him that night. She collected from him the box file she's been talking about. It was intended for Prettyman: his payoff, no doubt. Swede asked her for ID and she showed him a UK passport in the name of Mrs Prettyman. I'd say that was conclusive enough, wouldn't you? She brought Jim here and then drove off to the plane, while Prettyman drove away in the VW camper.'

'Jesus,' said Werner.

'Yes, your friend Mrs Prettyman. You think she's all sweetness and bright light, but she's always been able to look after herself.'

'You can't prove any of that.'

'The camper's not here now, Werner,' I said sarcastically.

'The Swede is dead. You can't get anything more from him.'

'I don't need him,' I said. 'I know just about everything I need to know. I know Uncle Silas briefed Prettyman and Prettyman sent Thurkettle on his mission.'

'If you take that plastic gun back to London I'll bet you anything you care to bet that London will accuse you of the killing.'

'Me?' I said.

'Bernie, they already suspect that you are deeply involved in all this. I've told you once, and I'll tell you again: they think that your wild accusations are made to cover up your guilt. You take that gun and tell them where we found it and they will say you arranged the killing of Thurkettle. They will say that you left the gun here and planned this excursion so that I would witness the "discovery" and so back you up.'

'Frame me?'

'No, Bernie. I'm not saying that London Central would frame you. But to them it will make you look guilty. I believe your theory about Prettyman. At one time I thought you were going crazy but now I believe you. But you won't make your case any more convincing by taking this document case and plastic gun back to show them. You need people to give evidence. Failing that, you need signed and witnessed statements. A gun without fingerprints, and your story about where you found it, won't mean much. Let it go, Bernie. We know what happened. Now let it go.'

Maybe Werner was right. He was sober and level-headed in a way that I would never be. He was often able to see things more clearly than I could. I dropped the gun and the document case back into the ditch and kicked them well down and out of sight. I could see another metal artefact there too. Werner hadn't seen it. I didn't prod at it, or dig it out from where it was half-hidden in the earth. It was my father's Webley pistol. 'Let's get out of here,' I said. 'I've had enough of this for one day.'

☆

'You did it, Bernie,' said Werner to cheer me up.

We reached the car and Werner slid behind the wheel. I got in the passenger seat and Werner started the engine. 'Do you think those two farmers will report us?' I asked him.

'No,' said Werner. 'It will be all right.' As we got to the top of the ramp, and joined the traffic on the road back to Berlin, there was a sudden fierce downpour of sleet that obscured the glass. Werner flicked the control to increase the speed of the wipers.

'What did you say to them?' I asked.

'I told them you were a trouble-making foreigner but that they could take your Western money and keep it. I told them that I was a secret policeman, assigned to keep watch on you. I told them that if they mentioned anything they had seen, I'd make sure they went into a prison camp.'

'A foreigner? Did they believe that?' I looked at him. His face was solemn as he stared at the road and at the blizzard that obscured the windshield and buffeted the car.

'You think your German is perfect,' said Werner. 'But you have an English accent that you can cut with a blunt knife. Any German can hear it.'

I aimed a playful swipe at his head. He knew how to goad me. 'How can you be sure they believed you were a secret policeman?'

'Don't I look like a secret policeman?'

'I suppose you do.'

'I demanded one of the fifties back and put it in my pocket. That convinced them. They know a Stasi man's technique when they encounter it.'

'Brilliant, Werner. That was a stroke of genius. And don't forget you owe me fifty marks.'

No sooner had I said it than a police car with flashing light came speeding along the Autobahn towards us.

'They must have phoned,' I said anxiously.

'Watch to see if it goes down the ramp,' said Werner.

'I can't see. He's too far back and there's too much snow.'

'I'll put my foot down.'

'It won't help, Werner. If those two bastards have sounded the alarm they will be waiting to lift us at the checkpoint.'

'It will be all right,' said Werner. In the old days we would have enjoyed the danger of it, but the old days had gone. Werner was sweating and I was swearing. We didn't say much but we were both thinking of what kind of gruesome and incriminating exhibits were going to be produced in court before the prosecutor got his unchallenged verdict. If the guards at the checkpoint had plucked us out of the car and grilled us, I'm not sure how composed we would have been.

As it was, they waved us through without coming out of the box. One pressed his nose against the glass and made a thumbs-up sign. There was something to be said for the blizzard and the freezing cold after all.

I don't know which of the two of us gave the deepest sigh of relief as we rolled across the checkpoint into Nikolassee, so close to Werner's new home. He stopped the car near the station. 'I promised Zena I would buy oranges and milk,' he said. Zena was a health freak. 'Why not come back to the house?' he suggested. 'We'll have coffee and relax.'

'I'd rather get back to my place and shower,' I said. The heat in the car had made me aware of my dirt-caked hands, and the stinking offal into which I'd been groping.

He looked at me and my soiled coat and hands. 'I'll run you back there,' he said.

Before he started the engine I said: 'You haven't been entirely frank with me, Werner.'

'What's wrong?'

'That gun. That plastic gun. You had it.'

'What gun?'

'Don't play the innocent with me, Werner. We're friends, aren't we?' He grinned nervously. I said: 'You received a package containing that gun.'

'I can't answer that, Bernie. It's official business.'

'That plastic gun that you were pretending you'd never seen in your life before – you handled it. You acted as a letter-box. You took the gun and delivered it to Jay Prettyman.'

'Who says so?'

'I say so.'

'No,' said Werner.

'What do you mean: no? What are you – Prettyman's lawyer? What's got into you? Why don't you tell me the truth? That plastic gun is the last remaining link that puts Prettyman there at the Autobahn meeting and killing Thurkettle.'

'You know how these thing work,' said Werner in an unnaturally calm and lowered voice. 'It's need-to-know, Bernie. I can't confirm it without breaking every promise I made.'

'Screw you, Werner. You're a sanctimonious bastard.'

'You've put it all together with superhuman skill,' said Werner, without reflecting any of the anger I'd shown him. 'Be content.'

'I'll get a cab,' I said, and climbed out of the car and walked away.

'You're forgetting your binoculars,' called Werner.

I went back and climbed into the car. Werner started the engine without saying a word. He drove me into the centre of the city

225

and to Lisl Hennig's hotel. I didn't speak to him again, except to say thanks when I got out of the car.

I knew it was as far as I was going to get with him. I would have to be content with that grudging affirmation. Werner had a stubborn streak that was unassailable. He'd always been like that, ever since we were at school together.

11

The SIS offices, Berlin

EVEN BEFORE THE First World War, the joke about 'count the dumplings, and divide by ten' had been doing the rounds. The dispositions of Rommel's Afrika Korps had several times been betrayed by a 'dumpling count', and no doubt all the belligerents had, at some time or other, infiltrated spies into the enemy catering arrangements to equal effect. So I suppose I should not have been surprised when London's questions about the radium diggings at Schlema were solved by means of an intelligence method even older than blowing trumpets at the walls of Jericho.

Larry Bowers, a long-term Department employee, had brought it in to me. Bowers was an enigmatic fellow. A young good-looking Oxbridge graduate who always landed buttered side up. For a long time I had regarded him as someone on a postgraduate fling, someone doing his stint of service to the Crown before leaving to start his real career, someone who would eventually wind up with a dozen undemanding directorships and a Rolls-Royce with a personalized licence plate. But I was proved wrong. Larry Bowers fell desperately in love with Germany and stayed on. It was a fatal attraction, as I knew to my cost. And for people like Bowers, who went freely from West to East, protected by his military identification, Berlin had no rivals. Here was the only city in the world with three renowned opera houses, a dozen symphony orchestras, theatres of all shapes and sizes, countless cabaret clubs, three universities and even two zoos.

Larry Bowers put the report on my desk on Tuesday afternoon. Some agent unnamed had reached Schlema and gained access to the kitchens of the ore miners' canteen and even survived the eating arrangements. Bowers had had the report beautifully typed. He'd bound it with a bright yellow cover, and put his name on the front in a typeface large and clear enough to be read from the far side of the office. Bound into the back of the report, there were photocopies of documents from the mine cashier: food accounts, the licences, ration documents and delivery manifests. The report was as comprehensive as can be, apart from not mentioning the name of Werner Volkmann, who had supplied a considerable part of the material and been the principal contact for the informant. I liked Larry Bowers, but he could be very show-biz when it came to screening the credits.

I read the report carefully. Flour, coffee and potato consignments for the month of November were all that we needed. There were no records of beer or mineral water, but the figures were enough to convince anyone that there were no more than thirty or forty men and women eating at the miners' canteen each day, and that included the kitchen staff. The uranium mine was obviously on an upkeep and maintenance schedule. Safety men to work the pumps and the fans, keep the conveyor belts lubricated and operate the lifts from time to time. The German Democratic Republic was not noted for its labour-saving mining technology. Even if it had been, a mine like that can't be worked by shifts of a dozen or so men.

At noon Frank came steaming into my office as I knew he would. He was waving his abbreviated copy of the report. 'I'll tell London there is nothing doing there?' he said, holding the paper up to his face, so he could read it without his glasses.

'That's it,' I said, passing some additional sheets of figures to him.

'You file them,' he said, without taking them to look at. Frank was a cunning old fox. He wasn't going to tell London that his belief that the Schlema workings were not producing uranium was based upon any kind of 'cold dumpling estimate'. And making sure that I filed the notes away would enable him to deny that he knew the source. Should the estimates prove incorrect, I would face London's angry questions about the source.

'Going to Werner's housewarming party?' asked Frank.

'Yes,' I said.

'You don't have to answer in that guarded manner. I'm going too. At least, I was thinking of going. I was wondering what sort of a gathering it will be. Big? Small? Very formal? Dinner suit? Sit-down? What's he planning?'

It took me a moment to digest this shattering turnabout in the always turbulent social history of the Berlin office. Frank Harrington had long pursued what I had heard described as a 'vendetta' against Werner. An additional obstacle to the relationship came from the short but intense love affair that Frank had had with Zena. Not one of Frank's pull up your pants and run affairs. It had been very earnest. He'd even found a love nest for her: a comfortable house tucked away in the leafy northern Berlin suburb of Lübars. 'It's not entirely a housewarming,' I said.

'I thought . . .'

'Rudi Kleindorf's new club. This is a launch party for it. The decorators are not finished at the club premises. Rudi persuaded Werner to hold it at his house and combine it with a house-warming.'

'I noticed Kleindorf's name in small print. So that's it?'

'Gold-edged invites with colour . . . you can bet a lot of them have been sent out. I can't imagine a printer wanting to do that kind of job a dozen at a time.'

'Always the detective, Bernard,' said Frank, without putting too much breathless admiration into it.

'I try, Frank.'

'You were right to bring Werner back, and put him on the payroll,' said Frank. 'I had doubts at first – especially about him having an office – but I decided to let you do it your way.' He provided a significant pause during which I could worry about what was coming next. 'And it's worked out very well, hasn't it?'

'Yes,' I said. I was tempted to point out the way that Werner's bare, bony and much-calloused hands had pulled the Schlema chestnuts out of the embers. And wonder aloud why his name was nowhere to be found in that report. But I didn't.

'I don't want to offend him,' said Frank vaguely. I could tell he was seeking an excuse to go to the party. Frank loved parties. He loved planning them, giving them and attending them. He loved talking about them and hearing about them. It was an element of what made him so influential and effective in Berlin, for this was the greatest party town in the world. Forget New York or Paris or London. You had only to see the elaborate fancy costumes in the Berlin stores when *Fasching* celebrations brought party time around, to know that this was the place where the party had been refined to an art form for big spenders. Party time was always the highlight of Frank's year. I remember a German visitor to his office asking Frank what they did in England at *Faschingszeit*. Frank replied: We eat pancakes; it's what we call pancake day. The German visitor laughed heartily. Too heartily. I knew him well: both his parents had died in the RAF firestorm raid on Dresden in 1945. I knew Germany well enough to know that for some Germans Shrove Tuesday was best remembered as the anniversary of that night.

There was another reason for Frank's interest in the Volkmanns' party. It would provide an opportunity for him to see Zena again. She'd been away in Switzerland for quite a while; perhaps he still carried a torch for her. Frank was practised in the alchemy that transmuted lovers into friends. 'You heard that Rensselaer and his entourage are in town? At least, on their way,' he amended, looking at his watch. 'They are finished in Frankfurt.'

'Bret? You mean here, in Berlin?'

'I wish I didn't mean here in Berlin; I wish I meant there in Timbuktu. This city is packed with visitors right now. Do you know how long my secretary Lydia spent on the phone, pleading for hotel rooms for them all? Pleading.'

'How long?' I said in innocent enquiry.

'Instead of returning to London directly he suddenly decided he had to detour this way and bring his entourage with him. I suppose he intends it as a display of Yankee methodology, but I call it a pointless waste of time and effort.'

'He eats too much sugar,' I said.

Frank nodded without hearing what I said. 'The Steigenberger. Bret specified the Steigenberger; Dicky demanded the Kempi.' He gestured with his pipe. 'They will have to put up with what hotels they can get. And they might end up in a bed and breakfast in Rudow.' Frank always saved his most caustic contempt for Rudow, an unremarkable residential neighbourhood that formed the southeastern tip of capitalist Berlin. I wondered what caused this antipathy. Was Rudow associated with one of Frank's unhappy love affairs?

'Dicky Cruyer too?' I asked. Dicky would not be happy with the sort of bed and breakfast typically on offer in Rudow. Frank nodded.

'Yes. How am I supposed to entertain such a crowd at short notice? My cook is visiting her married daughter, and Tarrant is still recovering from this damned gastric influenza that is doing the rounds. I can't entertain them all at the house.'

'So you are taking them along to Werner's party?'

Frank looked at me; I met his eye solemnly. Frank said: 'It would solve a problem for me.'

'They will love it,' I said. 'Music and dancing and champagne. Wonderful food. Werner has been talking about nothing else.'

'I thought he was away,' said Frank, who didn't miss everything of what went on in the office.

'He went away. Only one day. He's back now.'

Frank said: 'Bret's NATO conference was scheduled to go on through the weekend, with a formal dinner on Sunday. But the French delegation made a fuss about the agenda and walked out yesterday morning. The Yanks released some woolly press statement about continued meetings of the secretariat – you know what bullshitters they are – and that ended the whole get-together.'

'Most people will guess it was a French walk-out. There was an argument with them last time,' I said. 'Fiona was there.'

Frank sighed. Moscow's protracted political operation that levered France out of NATO was the KGB's finest battle honour. It was never mentioned without a resonance of our failure. 'Yes. There must be better ways of plastering over the cracks.' Frank was renowned for his expertise at patching over administrative disasters. 'They will all have dinner suits and so on,' he said, as if putting his case to me.

'It's brilliant, Frank,' I said. 'Take them to Werner's party.'

☆

When I got back to my own office there was a fax in my tray. It was the copy of another police report about traffic movements on the West Berlin Autobahn on the day after Tessa was killed. It described traffic accidents and abandoned vehicles and mysterious strangers wandering in the vicinity of Autobahn exits. Campers' tyre marks and picnic remains. I had of course found everything I'd been looking for at Autobahn exits. But I didn't want to circulate a message cancelling my requests. I didn't even want to confide to my secretary the fact that I'd found what I was looking for. There was no way I could call off my search without being asked questions I didn't care to answer. I put the reports and faxes in my drawer and shuffled them so it looked as if I'd been studying them.

Then I went back to my room in Lisl's hotel to change and make myself ready for Werner's party. It would be a dressy affair. Werner had moved into one of those grand old houses in Wannsee.

A house of any shape or size was a conspicuous mark of success in a city where most people lived in apartments. This one was truly remarkable. From its terrace there was a view of the waters of the Wannsee and as far as the pretty little island of Schwanenwerder where Goebbels, the Nazi propaganda minister, lived during the war. I knew these Wannsee houses and I had visited many of them. I liked them. Sometimes I've thought how happy I would have been in a career such as architecture. I had mentioned that to my father during my time at school, but my father said an architect's life was precarious. To him a government job was the epitome of security. I wondered what he might have said if he were still alive.

But my interest in buildings remained with me. More than once, being able to guess where an upstairs landing emerged, or the fastest route to the roof, and where to find a fire-escape back to ground level, had helped me out of serious trouble. Tonight I had no difficulty guessing the layout of Werner's new home. I drove past a no-entrance sign, and found a place to park at the back. I let myself in through a service door on the terrace.

Werner had chosen this house not just because it was so spacious and light but because of its history. Like many of the houses in that street so near the lake, there were rumours about its history. Berlin's real estate men had discovered that having a top-level Nazi as a one-time resident was unlikely to deter their prospective clients. It wasn't something to be included in the prospectus, of course, but a whispered word about some notorious blackguard of the Third Reich could sometimes conclude a sale.

The stories said this particular house had once been occupied by Reinhard Heydrich. As well as being the evil spirit behind Himmler, Heydrich was a notable athlete and a fencing champion. Support for the contention that this was his former home was to be seen in the extended room that gave on to the terrace. It was said to have been built to satisfy Heydrich's need for a fencing hall. The large room had been restored to something like its nineteenth-century origins, and could be divided in two by ornate folding doors. Or, as tonight, the whole ground floor could be made into a room into which a hundred guests could dance without knocking over the tables loaded with luxury food, or blundering into the massive flower arrangements, or getting poked in the eye by the elbows of any of the musicians. I mean: it was big.

In line with Rudi's intention to offset part of its cost against tax, the party was described as being a celebration for the opening of Rudi Kleindorf's new club in Potsdamerstrasse. There were signs advertising the club, which was now named *Gross und Klein* – 'high and low', or 'adults and children'. It was also a reference to Rudi Kleindorf's nickname: *der grosse Kleine*. Personally I preferred the place when it was a shady dump called the Babylon, but Werner never liked that name. He said Babylon had bad associations for a Jew. I wondered what the associations were. Or how those associations could be more disturbing than living in Wannsee, a stone's throw from the place where the infamous conference was held, and living in a house where coming downstairs for a midnight snack you might rub shoulders with a natty-uniformed blond ghoul with blood on his hands.

I wondered if the club's change of name was an indication that Werner had invested money in the new venture. I hoped not. The old Babylon had gone bust, owing money to most of its suppliers. I couldn't see how the new one was likely to do much better. It was all right for Rudi: he used the club as a hangout for his cronies, and a base for his murky business activities. In the front hall there was an artist's impression of what the new club would look like. Rudi was standing alongside it, telling anyone who would listen about his new place.

I could see all this as I stepped through the terrace window, and hear it too. The five-piece band – veterans of Rudi's previous excursions into Berlin nightlife – was expanded by a few white-haired musicians. They were indulging themselves by playing kitsch Thirties music more in accord with their advanced age, and more in line with my dancing lessons, than their usual repertoire at the Babylon. As I closed the terrace door behind me, they were moving into the final chorus of 'Sweet Lorraine'.

Once inside the main room, I looked around. The decoration that had been installed for this party took my breath away. I knew that the house was wonderful. Werner had shown me the photos, and the surveyor's report, and discussed his offer and counter-offer. I was ready for the house but I wasn't ready for the decorations. They had obviously been installed solely for the party, and would be torn down tomorrow. That was what I called conspicuous high living.

The theme of the party, as stated on the printed invitations, was 'The Golden Twenties'. Its ambivalence had left the German guests uncertain of whether to respond with a fancy dress suited to Berlin in the Weimar years, or simply to wear gold. Many had done both. There were plenty of gold lamé gowns, and gold jewellery was in abundance, for this was Berlin and flamboyant ostentation was *de rigueur*. There was even a gold lamé evening jacket – although that was worn by a tenor from the opera and so didn't count as a surprise of any kind – and there was a glittering outfit of gold pyjamas worn by a skinny old lady who did cooking lessons on TV.

Gold wire and gold foil and gold ornaments of many kinds were liberally arranged on the walls. Gold ceiling hangings echoed in shape the antique glass chandelier that Werner had bought in an auction, so that it could become the centre-piece of the room. The moving beams from clusters of spotlights were directed upwards to patch the false ceiling with their light, and create golden clouds that floated overhead.

Looking around at all this I began to understand what the extravagant Zena did for Werner. Zena was the catalyst that enabled Werner to waste his money in the ways he secretly enjoyed. Such symbiotic relationships were not uncommon. Any number of middle-class husbands bought a big Volvo or Mercedes saying its impact-proof construction would protect their families. They installed top-of-the-range computers because it would help their kids at school, ear-shattering hi-fi equipment to play 'good' music. To help their kids' history lessons they went first class to Egypt and made sure the Pyramids were still on the Nile. So did Zena provide for Werner a rationale for his intemperate lifestyle.

There was a time when I would have been concerned at Werner spending money so recklessly. For Werner periodically confessed to me that he was on the verge of financial collapse. At first I was flattered by these confidences, as well as alarmed on his behalf. But over the years I had come to understand that Werner's measure of poverty was not like mine. Werner became alarmed when the interest on his capital was nibbled by inflation, or when he suffered some other financial malady that periodically scourged the rich. For people like me, just getting enough in my savings account to stave off impending bills gave me a heady feeling of opulence. It was not so with Werner. Right from the time he first got a car, Werner always went into a petrol station and filled his tank to the brim. And he had the oil checked too; and frequently asked if his tyres were worn enough to need changing. Werner simply didn't know there were people who bought petrol, beer or milk one litre at a time. Or managed with tyres that were down to the wire.

The dance floor was full and there were crowds arriving but I spotted Werner and Zena by stepping up on to a wooden pot in which a monster-sized fern plant was growing. I could see over the heads of the dancers to the front lobby. Werner and Zena were in the large oval-shaped hall, formally greeting the guests one by one as they were ushered through the front door. It made a theatrical scene. The second massive chandelier – in the hallway – had been hung in such a way that the wide staircase curved around it, following the wall up to the interior balcony on the upper floor.

Werner waved and bent down to whisper to Zena. She looked

up with fire in her eyes. She didn't approve of guests letting themselves in by the back door. She wanted guests to arrive two by two, like animals boarding the Ark. And she wanted them at the front door, where she could inspect them closely, make sure they had washed their hands and face, and tell them how lovely it was to have them with her.

They were both looking good. Zena had her dark hair coiled up and studded with jewels. She was wearing a simple cream-coloured silk dress: long and low-cut so that her diamond necklace and matching bracelet sparkled against her bronzed skin. Zena liked being sun-tanned. The darker she was, the better she liked it. She had grown up in the days when foreign travel was a sought-after rarity. But a complexion like a Malibu lifeguard was incongruous for someone dressed as a delicate Meissen figurine.

Werner was wearing a cream-coloured, slubbed-silk jacket, black pants and frilly evening shirt with a big black bow tie. I suppose he knew he looked like a band-leader from the sort of old Hollywood film they show on TV in the afternoons. This effect was further endorsed when the band struck up 'Laura', the schmaltzy old Mercer number. Werner looked at me again and gave a self-conscious smile. I waved an imaginary baton at him.

☆

It was while I was moving through the dancers, to the tables where the food was arrayed, that I was suddenly grabbed from behind by two hands and someone said: 'You don't get away as easy as that, you bastard.'

I turned to see who it was, and came face to face with Gloria at very close range. My amazement must have shown on my face, for she laughed. 'Didn't they tell you? I'm with Bret. We were all at the NATO conference. Frank Harrington brought us here.' She grabbed me round the waist and said: 'Dance. Hold me tight and dance.'

'Gloria . . .'

'Shut up. Don't say anything. Just hold me very tight. Dance . . . and don't blunder into anyone.'

We stepped out on to the dance floor. If we had on occasions blundered into other couples, it wasn't due solely to my clumsiness but also because she always danced with her eyes tightly shut.

A vocalist sang in uncertain English: *She gave your very first kiss to you . . .*

'Is it supposed to be fancy dress?' asked Gloria.

'The Golden Twenties.'

'I wish I'd known and had had time to dress up.'

'You are the Golden Twenties,' I said. It was true. Her hair against her dress was shiny gold and she was looking younger than ever.

She gave me a broad tight-lipped smile. 'I've missed you, Bernard.'

'It's no use pretending any more. I must talk to you. We must . . .'

She reached up and pressed her hand to my lips. 'Don't spoil it. Just for this evening let's pretend. No talking: just pretend.'

'Okay.'

We danced. She was soft and warm and fragrant and slim and lovely. By some miracle my feet hit all the right places at the right moments. Neither of us spoke.

I would be dancing there still, but the music eventually ended: *You see Laura on a train that is passing through . . .* I held on to her with a desperation that I couldn't contain. *That was Laura but she's only a dream.* As the music stopped my reverie came to an abrupt end, but I remained close to her: very close.

Bret Rensselaer gave no sign of noticing my despair as he approached us, balancing his own glass against two glasses of champagne for us. 'Isn't this a phenomenal party? What a surprise. I was just telling my old buddy Werner that this has got to be the bash of the year.' Bret was looking ten years younger. Those golden threads in his silver hair reminded me of the blond tough guy who had almost died after that shooting in an abandoned Berlin train station. So did the grin and the radiant self-confidence. I suppose his new Deputy's job had given him a fresh lease of life. Or maybe he was still floating on the euphoria that came after sneaking across the Atlantic for a weekend and front seat at the Super Bowl. Or maybe he was eating too much sugar.

Bret pointed towards the food-filled tables now, since the music stopped, obscured by eager guests piling up their plates. 'Did you taste those home-made poppy-seed cakes?' said Bret. 'Wow. Looks like they are home-made. What do they call them in German?'

'Are they called *Mohnklösse*?' said Gloria.

'Yes, but here in Berlin they call them *Mohnspielen*,' I said pedantically. 'Werner is very keen on them. They say they were Hitler's favourite snack.'

'Yeah, well I always said he had taste,' said Bret. 'Werner, I mean.'

'What does it mean: *Mohnspielen*?' said Gloria, childishly put out by my correction.

'*Mohn*; *Mond*. Moon; poppy. It's some kind of Berlin double-meaning that makes it into the moon's plaything.'

'You are a living encyclopedia,' said Gloria.

Having no immediate ambition to be a living encyclopedia, I sipped my champagne and nodded and smiled. And marvelled at the way in which life can go from heaven to hell in such short measure.

'And he's working with you now, Bernard?' said Bret, to demonstrate the way he had his finger on the Department's pulse. 'On the payroll?'

'Werner?' I said. 'Yes.' And I perversely added: 'It was all Frank's idea.'

'Quite a bash,' said Bret, who knew very well how strenuously Frank had opposed Werner's employment. 'And the kind of old-timers' music I like.' I suppose it was a nice surprise for anyone expecting an evening of shoptalk and passive smoking with Frank Harrington. But there was no mistaking the bench-mark change in Werner's fortunes. Twenty-four hours ago I would have bet a million pounds to an old shirt-button that Bret didn't remember that Werner Volkmann existed. Now he's Bret's old buddy, and getting three-star accolades for his home-made *Mohnspielen*.

Werner old pal, you made it, I thought. Frank might pretend this was some half-hearted reconciliation, a rehabilitation or a convenient place to dump unwanted visitors. The fact was that Bret Rensselaer – the Deputy D-G no less – was giving Werner the coveted guarantee of Good Housekeeping handwritten on parchment. And doing it in public, in a manner I had seldom witnessed.

While we were talking, Frank had approached us. He listened to Bret's continuing appreciation of Werner's party but, judging from Frank's smile and nods, he thought it was Bret's tactful way of thanking him for bringing the errant souls of Frankfurt to this golden Berlin evening.

Frank said: 'I hear the Frogs were playing up again.'

'It wasn't entirely the fault of the French,' said Bret diplomatically. 'One of my countrymen started the row.'

'It was filthy weather,' said Gloria with feminine insight. 'They were all in a bad mood.'

Bret said: 'One of the London people had an Irish name, and our little German interpreter with the beard made a joke about the Irish Republic not being a member of NATO. One of the CIA crowd didn't understand that it was a joke, and got defensive. He said something about France not being a member of NATO either ... There was a bitter row. All bathed in smiles and nods, but they became damned spiteful. Afterwards I even heard one of the Italians saying the only way to define a Frenchman was someone who knew the difference between Hitler and Napoleon.'

The music began again, and Bret asked Gloria to dance. 'You don't mind me taking her away, do you, Bernard?'

'Where did you say the poppy-seed cakes were, Bret?'

Gloria gave me a brief consolatory smile.

Isn't it a lovely day to be caught in the rain; I always liked that melody. Astaire and Ginger Rogers dancing in the rainswept bandstand where no one could get to them. I went to eat. I didn't waste too much time watching Gloria and Bret dancing. I didn't want to pursue her, and if I was old enough to be Gloria's father, Bret was old enough to be her grandfather. Anyway, she knew we could not go on. She knew it and I knew it. Her unexpected appearance had unbalanced me. I was frightened that I might do the wrong thing here; do something or say something that, instead of healing the wounds, would cripple both of us for ever.

☆

'Aal grün,' called Werner from the other side of the table as I reached for potato salad. 'Not smoked: fresh.' He knew I liked eel. I put some on my plate, trying to keep it separate from the pan-fried slices of ham dumpling with wild mushrooms. It was a buffet dinner. Real plates and real cutlery, but wobbly tables and gold-painted chairs supplied by the catering company.

'Come and sit over here,' said Werner. 'I haven't seen you all evening.'

'I was dancing.' I looked around to see where Gloria was, and caught a glimpse of her golden head and Bret's white hair. They made a nice couple. They would have looked like father and daughter, had they not been dancing so close.

'With Gloria?' said Werner. 'Oh yes, I saw you and Gloria dancing. Wonderful, Bernard. You looked very happy, like a kid in love.'

'Any objections?' I said.

'No, I suppose not. But love is like the measles; the later in life it afflicts you, the more severe the consequences.'

'Is there anything you can take for it?'

'Only wedding vows.'

'Is that what Zena told you?' I asked politely.

He gave a tiny smile to show that he forgave me for my bad temper. 'Zena believes in marriage,' he said. 'All wives believe in marriage.'

'I suppose so,' I said. 'I don't see Cindy Prettyman anywhere. Has she gone back to Brussels?'

'She's up in her room,' said Werner. 'She's in a bad way. I took some food up to her but she won't eat a thing. She said eating would make her vomit.'

'Why is she in a bad way?'

'Something happened at her job. A robbery. She was on the phone to her office and suddenly burst into tears. She's been stretched out on her bed sobbing. I've given her a sleeping pill but it doesn't seem to have any effect. Zena said it's better to leave her alone.'

'Maybe a whole bottle of sleeping pills?'

'You don't have to be a bad-tempered pig all the time, Bernard,' said Werner stiffly. 'You can take an evening off, and try being human.'

'I tried it once; I didn't like it.'

'If you must be your usual obnoxious self, go and be obnoxious to the soldiers sitting around in my kitchen all dolled up in shiny belts and guns. They are getting in the way, eating all the *petits fours*, and annoying the people from the caterers.'

'Soldiers?'

'Redcaps. Do you think I should ask Bret to send them away?'

'Not if they are redcaps,' I advised. 'Bret is a top-of-the-range spook nowadays. He has to be given a military and civil police escort in this sort of situation. You probably have a busload of uniformed Kripo parked on the front drive.'

'What for? Who's going to assassinate him?'

'It's not only that. They can't risk anything happening. Suppose he was picked up by a cop . . . for being drunk or something. And he's not on home ground. Your house is in the American Sector.

If there was any kind of wrangle – if he got punched on the nose – all concerned might get dragged down to the barracks, and held in US military custody while IDs were examined and charges drawn up, and it was sorted out. That would be a major embarrassment for everyone concerned.'

'Is that why you are not going to punch him on the nose tonight?'

'Very funny, Werner,' I said.

Werner led the way to the terrace.

Tonight the bitter winter weather was being defied in a manner typically *Berlinerisch*. Flowers and sunny colours recreated the outdoor parties of summer. The terrace – where now bench-style tables were arrayed – had been roofed over. It was a cleverly designed temporary structure supported by Roman columns made from hardboard faced with golden-foil. From the low ceiling, leafy creepers and real blooms trailed, reaching down to table-tops to become table-decorations. Hidden heaters made it warm enough for bare shoulders, and hidden loudspeakers brought soft, vaguely classical music.

'Don't mention the redcaps to Zena,' he said. 'I promised I'd get rid of them.'

'No, of course not,' I said, and took a deep breath as I saw that he was guiding me to where Zena was sitting with an elegant selection of their friends.

'Bernard! How lovely!'

'You're looking ravishing,' I told her, and nodded while she told everyone at the table that I was a very old friend of her husband's. It was the nearest she could get to completely disowning me.

'Beside me,' said Zena. 'I must have a word with you.' I sat down at the empty seat that had obviously been reserved for Werner, while Werner squeezed himself on to a bench that was the seating arrangement for the other side of the table. I said hello to the other guests, who nodded acknowledgements. There was a 'mergers and acquisitions man' from Deutsche Morgan Stanley and a high-powered woman dealer from Merrill Lynch. There was a bearded man who designed costumes for the opera, the wife of Werner's wine merchant, and a young woman who owned a fur shop on Ku-Damm. I struggled to remember their names, but I am not good at the social graces: Fiona and Gloria agreed on that.

I tried the eel. It was very good. 'You should eat salad,' said Zena.

'I do normally,' I said. 'But these dumplings looked so delicious.'

'That Berlin food was all Werner's arrangement,' she said. Werner caught my eye and nodded. 'It's not healthy – all those heavy old-fashioned German dishes. And Werner is far too fat.'

'It's a lovely house, Zena,' I said. A waiter was pouring wine for everyone at the table. He looked at Zena to make sure that he was doing it right. She had them all well trained.

'You can see the water from here,' said Zena.

'Yes,' I said. I couldn't actually see the lake. There was condensation on the windows so that the lights in the garden became coloured blobs. There were more distant lights too: lights from across the water, or they might have been boats. In daylight the view would be wonderful.

'Cindy is here,' said Zena. It was almost a hiss.

'Where?'

'She's in bed.' The way Zena said it, you would have thought that I knew all about Cindy and her indisposition.

'Is she sick?' I asked.

'In a way. She's very angry, Bernard. Very very angry.'

'I'm sorry to hear that,' I said. Perhaps this expression of condolence was marred by the overlarge mouthful of *Schinkenknödel* I was chewing. Or perhaps Zena wasn't listening to my replies.

'Yes, I know all about that,' said Zena. She gave me a look of fierce dislike before smiling at everyone around the table and asking Werner to go and get another plate of lobster salad for the elderly banker. Turning to me again she said into my ear: 'She's upset about what you have done.'

'I haven't done anything,' I said. 'At least not to Cindy Prettyman.'

'Her name is Matthews. She's not married to that ghastly friend of yours any more.'

'Matthews, I mean . . . Look, Zena, I don't know what Cindy has been telling you . . .' I said.

'When Cindy is angry . . . really angry, she is likely to do something desperate.'

'Yes, I can imagine that.'

'You must go up and talk to her. Say you're sorry. Make amends. Give her back whatever it is her husband stole from her office.'

'I'll take her some eel.'

'Finish your food and I'll show you to her room,' said Werner, who had come back with a plate of sliced wurst instead of the lobster, and now looked as if he was keen to escape being asked about this failure.

I abandoned the rest of my meal and got to my feet. As we went across the crowded floor, Werner said: 'Rudi was looking for you.'

I said: 'You haven't put money into that damned club, have you, Werner?'

'Only pennies,' said Werner. 'Rudi said he wanted a bigger number of shareholders this time. He said more people would come along and support the place if they had a stake in it.'

'And did he find people?'

'They all bought shares in the club,' said Werner, waving his arm in the air. 'Almost everyone here tonight bought at least one share. The invites went out only to special friends and to people who bought a share.'

'You're a genius, Werner,' I told him as he was waving and

smiling to his appreciative guests. 'Is that why Tante Lisl isn't here?'

'You are in a filthy mood tonight, Bernie. You know I wouldn't leave Tante Lisl uninvited. She wasn't feeling well enough. And it's her evening for playing cards.'

A string quartet had been playing Mozart while the meal was eaten. It had provided a change of pace that relaxed the eaters, and encouraged them to chew every mouthful twenty times before swallowing. But now the dance band were returning from wherever they'd been to eat dinner. There was a riff on a trumpet and it was every stomach for itself.

While the musicians were settling themselves down for an evening of hard work, the waiters were clearing the trestle tables and folding them up to make more room for dancing. The guests stood around talking and laughing and smoking and drinking and planning all kinds of other things that are bad for you. Several times Werner was buttonholed by guests who wanted to congratulate him on the party, so it took a while to cross the dance floor. With a drink in my hand, I followed Werner from the large ballroom to the brightly lit front hall, and its wide and curving staircase. Understandably reluctant to hurry in his visit to Cindy, he frequently stopped to talk, but eventually he started ascending the main stairs and I followed him.

From halfway up the staircase I looked down. I spotted Frank Harrington near the band. He was standing with Zena: she looked ravishing tonight, her dress and jewellery transforming her into a fairy princess. Not a real princess: Berlin was well provided with such nobility, and none of them looked like Zena. Zena had all the glitter of Hollywood, and she had the imperious bearing of a film star that made her the centre of attention. Frank was laughing with her. She was showing him the palm of her hand as if it was something to do with fortune-telling. I wondered what she was telling him. Frank didn't usually laugh like that.

'What a crowd,' said Werner.

'It's like the last reel of *Sunset Boulevard*,' I told him in a meaningless attempt to think of something to say to someone who is watching his wife so obviously enjoying the company of another man.

'What?' said Werner.

'Nothing,' I said.

Then, as if in fulfilment of my remark, a woman started down the staircase, stepping with the slow and deliberate manner of someone under the eye of a movie camera.

'*Scheisse!*' said Werner.

☆

Then I recognized her. Her hair looked like hell but it was no more untidy than hair I'd seen coming out of expensive hairdressers. Her nightdress was thin and frilly and filmy with an elaborate pattern of orchids. It could easily have passed as the most expensive of evening gowns. She was barefoot but I'd seen at least one guest dancing without shoes. Even the sleepwalking manner of this woman's movements was not unique to her. The only thing that distinguished her from the other guests was the shiny pistol she was holding high in the air as she came down the stairs.

'Cindy!' said Werner.

'Get out of my way,' called Cindy. Her voice was croaky. She waved the gun at him. It was a Walther. I recognized it as a Model 9 that Werner had bought for Zena but never given to her. That model was always in demand because the smart alecs in the Ku-Damm bars sold them to credulous tourists together with all kinds of cleverly forged documentation to prove that this one was the gun that had once been owned by Eva Braun.

'Put it down,' Werner called to her.

She was at the top of the stairs. Beyond Cindy's shoulder I could see guests standing along the upper-floor balcony. Sensing danger, they began to move back out of sight. Below, in the hallway, guests were also alarmed at the sight of Cindy brandishing the gun. From the corner of my eye I saw the crowd crushed back upon one another, as they sought the protection of the wall or doorways.

I halted and froze. So did Werner. Cindy brought the gun to eye level with care and precision. It was only a handbag gun, but I've looked down more gun barrels than the Lone Ranger, and I knew that a hole measuring only 6.35 mm could, at this range, end a promising career. 'You, and that damned husband of mine, got together, did you?' Cindy yelled at me.

Werner moved closer to the wall, trying to get to the side of her, so that he could grab the gun. But she wasn't going to let that happen. She put her back against the wall and was moving down the stairs a step at a time. I moved down a step too. Werner did the same. We all moved together. I would have thought it comical had I not been almost scared to death.

Without warning she pulled the trigger. I had hoped it wasn't loaded but it fired, and there was a crash of broken glass somewhere below and behind me.

'You've got what you want now, have you?' Cindy shouted hoarsely. Her eyes were red and bloodshot. She looked ferocious now that I was closer to her. She had lots of make-up on her face but the paint-job wasn't completed. Tears had made the mascara run, so that her lower face was marbled with grey and black wavy streaks. 'You thief! Are you satisfied now? You swine. I'll kill you.'

'Listen, Cindy . . .' said Werner. She swung round to him and pulled the trigger. He was close to her but she was too hasty and the shot missed him. The round hit the wall alongside him and broke off a large chunk of moulding. The plaster shattered and its pieces went spinning away to land with loud noises on the marble floor of the hall below. I heard a distant scream, a man's shout and the soft sounds of a woman sobbing hysterically.

Without taking proper aim, I threw the glass in my hand at her. My action was completely instinctive, and like most completely instinctive actions it was ineffective. The ice-cubes bounced out, and the whisky came splashing over me. The glass didn't cut Cindy, but that was because she saw it coming and ducked to avoid it before firing again.

That next shot still scored. It hit Werner in the head. He cried out and grabbed at his skull. His cry was very loud, and very close. The impact knocked him backwards. He lost his balance, to fall full-length. He curled up and went head over heels down the stairs past me. 'Werner!' I tried to grab him as he tumbled past but it was all happening too fast for me. Foolishly I turned my head to see him falling. His eyes flicked open wide as he fell, his face was clenched in pain and I saw anger in his eyes. His cry was shrill. It ended in a choking sound as he landed at the bottom and kicked his legs in the air.

Realizing that my back was exposed to this madwoman's marksmanship, I swung round in time to see a big man in a khaki uniform leaping down the stairs. His red-topped cap fell off, and went bowling down the staircase. The cap created a diversion: everyone's eyes followed it as the soldier jumped. With arms spread wide apart, he tried to grab her and pinion her arms. But Cindy was too quick for him. As he came towards her she jumped aside, smashing her back against the wall with an audible slap. She brought the gun up and fired again. Having misjudged his leap the soldier's arms were flailing, his hands trying to grab carpet or banister to save himself from falling all the way down the stairs, as Werner had done. But what he grabbed was Cindy's lower legs. He held on to her. He was a heavy man and he held on tightly. His weight was enough to pull her with him as he continued his fall. Her legs dragged from under her and Cindy buckled at the knees. Letting out a yelp of pain and fear, she toppled like a tyrant's statue.

She could not escape the policeman's grasp as, twisting and turning, they grabbed at stair-carpet, and at each other, in the panic that free-fall produces. They came bumping past me, crashing against the wall, against the wrought-iron and against the stairs, until they both ended heaped upon Werner. They were still; the three of them dumped at the bottom of the stairs like a big bundle of laundry waiting to be ironed. Werner's head moved, emerging from the confusion of limbs and bodies. He was still holding his head in his hands; his hair, face and fingers so bloody that it was difficult to distinguish between them. Blood was everywhere on the soldier's face and all over Cindy's nightdress.

For a moment the whole house was silent. Then everyone began talking at once. Two agile waiters ran to help the injured, while a couple of quick-thinking soldiers ushered others away. As more soldiers crowded around the bodies they were hidden from view. The band started playing 'Mister Sandman' very softly. The lights went down to a glimmer so that the only illumination was a spotlight trained on Frank Harrington. He came sauntering across the floor, cigarette drooping from his mouth, clapping his hands in a warm, appreciative way. Others joined in the applause. Then the music stopped with a little drumroll and Frank was standing on a chair making a speech saying that the 'most original entertainment' was a truly splendid surprise but typical of Mr and Mrs Volkmann's imaginative gala setting. There were calls of approval and more scattered applause. An English voice shouted 'Hear! Hear!'

Frank seemed to enjoy his improvised role of master of ceremonies. He looked around, beaming at the upturned faces, for by now he was the centre of attention. He continued talking. Frank was good at after-dinner speeches, and now he used fragments from ones I'd heard many times before. It was all delivered in Frank Harrington's version of German. You couldn't exactly fault the syntax, but his old-fashioned German had the flavour of years long past. If there was anything that could persuade the guests present that they had really witnessed a charade, rather than a shooting, it was Frank doing his spiel in his weird *Kaiserliche* German. Then someone propelled Zena forward, and Frank told everyone how lovely the hostess looked and Zena smiled with grim satisfaction and everyone applauded. Some of those present knew of Frank's affair with Zena, and I had the impression that most of the jocular cheering came from them.

By the time Frank had finished his eulogy there was no sign of poor Werner or Cindy or the injured military policeman. The band were playing louder and faster than they had ever played before; the waiters were pouring larger measures than before, both activities probably done at Frank's instigation. The guests were dancing and laughing and flirting. Only the broken section of moulding was there to prove that the evening's 'most original entertainment' had ever taken place.

They didn't let me see Werner until past one o'clock in the morning. He was in the Steglitz Clinic, in the hospital of the Free University. It was dimly lit and silent and there was that unmistakable smell of anaesthetics, antiseptics and disinfectant that mingles and hangs on the air in all such medical establishments. By that time, I was the only one in the waiting-room. Frank had squeezed an optimistic prognosis out of one of the senior medical staff, and then taken Zena back to her home before going to the office to phone Bret and other people who would expect to be kept informed. Frank would be blamed for this silly fiasco. It was not his fault, but that was how the system worked. It could even hasten Frank's retirement.

I waited. The surgeon finished his needlework and finally took pity on me because I had been there so long. He came out and gave me a detailed account of the surgical job he'd done on Werner's skull. Bad concussion, extensive cuts, but probably no fractures. Head-scan in the morning: then he would have more to go on. The surgeon had the sort of unmistakable Berlin accent with which Bavarian comics get laughs in Munich nightclubs. Hearing his accent I responded using the soft gees and clickety voice I had acquired as a streetwise Berlin schoolboy. He responded with a more pronounced accent as he told me that Werner's upper body was badly bruised and that he had damaged his ankle too. Perhaps a tiny fracture there. After another exchange of ever-broadening dialect he smiled and said: 'Five minutes; no more. He's a lucky man to be alive.'

Werner was sitting up in bed. He'd had a local anaesthetic while they stitched up the furrow that the bullet had torn above his ear. Now that they had cleaned away all the blood from his hands and head, he looked much better than I had dared hope when I saw him at the bottom of the staircase. But his face was seriously bruised and beginning to swell. According to the doctor it would be some time before he was allowed out of bed. They had shaved the hair from the side of his head to get to the wound. Half bald, he had his stitches covered with no more than a small rectangular dressing, secured by strips of pink tape.

'You had me worried, Werner,' I said. 'I didn't know whether to bring the girlie mags or a wreath.'

'When I go, it's not going to be from a handbag gun.'

'Don't be macho, Werner.'

'What happened to Cindy Prettyman?'

'She's here in the Clinic. Asleep. One of the soldiers gave her a hefty sedative in the ambulance and forgot to write it down for the hospital reception. The doctor who examined her gave her another dose. She's well away. The doctor says she won't be fit enough to question until late tomorrow. Maybe the day after.'

'I blame myself,' said Werner.

'You couldn't have known she was going to run amok like that.'

'She thought you and Jim Prettyman had organized the robbery in her office. She thought you had the box file.'

'No, I don't have the box file,' I said. 'Jim Prettyman must have organized it. He played it very cool but it was his box. I shouldn't have told him she had it in her office. My fault. He must have got

252

on the phone right after I left him. Jim knows where to find hoodlums and thieves. Seems like it's his speciality.'

'Jim has it?'

'I'm sure he does. But I can't help wondering if it was official. I wonder if he talked to someone in London about it. It's an official box and the Department must have an interest in it.' I looked at Werner quizzically. It took a long time for him to respond. 'I went to Brussels. I stole the box file from her safe.'

I smiled blankly.

'Did you guess?'

'It took time. But when Cindy started shooting I could see what had really happened. And you were the one who knew where Cindy was all the time. You knew that while she was in Berlin she would not be in her office. And you had a perfect opportunity to take an impression from her keys.'

He gave a grim smile. We knew each other too well. 'Why lead me on about Jim Prettyman stealing it?'

'I wanted to see how good you are at telling lies.'

'What do you mean, you could see it when she started shooting?'

'Cindy was on the stairs. At that point maybe she thought it was Jim Prettyman who did it. Then she saw you and me together on the stairs in front of her. She had told me that the file was in her office safe. You'd been away from Berlin for a day. She figured that I had told you to go and steal the box.'

'She intended to shoot me?' said Werner, frowning as he tried to decide whether he preferred the role of injured innocent bystander or target. He touched his head with a fingertip. I suppose the frowning had caused him pain; or maybe it was the thinking.

'She aimed that shot at you. Sure she did,' I said cheerfully. 'That's why I am still in one piece and you have a hole in your skull. She was going to plug me. But then all her anger was redirected . . at you. You'd actually invaded her office and stolen her nest-egg. It was personal.'

'What will happen now?'

'If it was left to Frank she'd be locked away for ever.'

'I know. He hates her,' said Werner and nodded.

'That is something of an understatement. Frank regards the shooting fracas as a personal affront. But you know how Frank works. He won't let her be charged with attempted murder, or common assault or party-pooping. He'll pull strings in Brussels and try and get her fired. Frank feels he was humiliated by it happening while Bret was here in the city.'

'They won't get away as easily as that. Those people who were there last night will work out what really happened.'

'Maybe. But it will take time. And news editors spike timeworn stories.'

'Is that redcap in one piece?'

'He won't be going back to the gymnastics team. A bad compound fracture of the ribs, and mild concussion. He'll be all right. They will fly him home tomorrow. The surgeon thinks it will be a straightforward job. Military policemen are all bone.'

'And Cindy Prettyman too?'

'Drunks bounce like rubber balls, Werner. She was lucky. For security reasons none of those redcaps had been told who they were guarding. They were just told that there was a political VIP in the car Bret was using. They figured that any kind of shooting was likely to be an attempt on the life of the man they were guarding. If that cop's flying tackle had not done the trick, there was a sniper lining her up, and about to shoot Mrs Prettyman dead.'

The door opened and the surgeon came in and said I mustn't make his patient tired. He was taking a personal interest in Werner's well-being. I wondered what Frank must have told him.

'They wouldn't let Zena in to see me,' said Werner as I was putting on my overcoat.

'Yes, well, Zena doesn't speak Berlin German as well as I do,' I said in my heaviest possible accent.

The doctor nodded. I think he was beginning to think he was the butt of my humour instead of a part of it.

'You haven't asked me if I got the box open,' said Werner as I moved to the door. 'You don't know what might be inside it.'

'Don't try opening it, Werner. I know what's inside it, believe me.'

'Tell me.'

'That would spoil the fun,' I said.

'What fun?'

'The fun of seeing if what you hand over to Bret fits my guess.'

Werner looked at me and said: 'It is the same box file. I haven't substituted it for another. Take the keys of my desk. It's in the office; in my big filing cabinet.'

'Let it stay there,' I said.

'I'm sorry about what happened . . . and tearing you away from the party,' said Werner. 'I know you wanted to take Gloria back to her hotel.'

'She had Bret and *Mohnspielen*,' I said. 'You can't have everything.'

'It's over, isn't it?' said Werner. I only wish I could always see into Werner's head with the ease with which he sees into mine. 'You and Gloria: it's all over.'

'Try to get some sleep, Werner,' I said. 'That crack on the head is making your brains rattle.'

☆

It was very late by the time I got back to the hotel but Lisl was still awake. She was sitting up in bed in a frilly jacket, reading newspapers and playing her old records. She seemed to like sleeping in the downstairs room to which she had moved. It not only saved her going up all those stairs to bed, it was a way of being at the centre of everything, of all the hotel's comings and goings.

Even while I was coming through the main door I heard the immortal Marlene singing: *Das war in Schöneberg*. Lisl's new record-player had revived all her nostalgia and enthusiasm for the music she grew up with. Werner had bought the player for her; it was becoming too difficult for her to wind up by hand the ancient machine she preferred. He had searched everywhere before finding an electric machine that would play her scratchy old 'seventy-eights'. I went in to her room to say goodnight. No matter how much her hearing deteriorated, she was always able to hear me tiptoeing past her door should I attempt to go upstairs without paying my respects.

'Was it a good party, *Liebchen*?'

'They missed you, Lisl. Everyone was asking where you were.'

'You tell lies not so well, my darling. Perhaps it's better you stick to the truth. Give your poor old Tante Lisl a proper kiss, not one of those English pecks.' She puckered her mouth and closed her eyes like a child.

'A big band and dancing and real German food,' I said as I took her bony shoulders in my hands and bent low to give her a kiss. 'But without you it was nothing.'

'I let him borrow Richard, my clever young cook.'

'That was very kind, Tante Lisl,' I said. 'Everyone was talking about the food.'

'Zena wasn't sure about it,' said Lisl. 'She wanted to get prepared dishes from Ka-De-We. But lovely food costs lovely money. Werner should be more careful with his money.' She looked at the time. 'Did it go on so late?'

'Werner tripped on the stair carpet,' I told her. 'They had to take him for tests.'

'Oh, my God. The times I've told him not to drink. When you are the host, Werner, keep a clear head. I've told him that over and over again.'

'Calm down, Lisl. He wasn't drunk. You know Werner; he never drinks. Almost never. He stumbled on the stairs. He twisted his ankle. It's nothing, but Zena wanted to play safe so she made him go for an X-ray. He's in the Steglitz Clinic overnight. That's all.' I thought I should mention Werner's condition rather than risk her hearing it from elsewhere.

'The Steglitz Clinic? I must go. Get my dressing-gown from the door, there's a darling.' She twisted in bed so that she could inspect her face in the mirror, and decide if her make-up was suited to a visit to the hospital in the middle of the night.

'He's asleep,' I said. 'They gave him pain-killers and something to make him sleep. You wouldn't be able to see him. Anyway, it's nothing.'

'If it's nothing will he still be coming for coffee and *Kipferl* tomorrow?'

I didn't know Werner had promised to visit the next day. I tried to think of a reason he wouldn't be here.

She said: '*Nit kain entfer iz oich an entfer*.' The Yiddish proverb – No answer is also an answer.

'I'm sure he'll be here tomorrow,' I said without much conviction.

'I can always detect when you tell me lies, *Liebchen*. It's something I can see in your eyes. Your Lisl can always tell. Why didn't the foolish boy phone me? When it happened: why didn't you phone me?'

'He's all right, Lisl. It's just a little sprain. Zena makes too much of a fuss about Werner. She worries about him too much.'

'He should have phoned,' Lisl said petulantly.

'He made me promise that I would tell you as soon as I got back here.'

'Even one little drink can be too much. And Werner can't drink; he knows that.'

'I must go to bed, Lisl. Goodnight. See you at breakfast.'

'Yes, I know it must be boring for you to be talking to an ugly old woman.'

'You are a darling,' I said. I gave her another kiss and started to make my escape.

257

Lisl looked at me. 'Very well, then. I shall phone the hospital first thing in the morning.'

'Goodnight, Lisl.'

'Oh, I'm forgetting, Bernd darling. There is a fax message for you. The telephone went during dinner. The girl was serving some people who came late so it was difficult for her. The people calling spoke no German. I had my friend Lothar take the call, and deal with them. He speaks the most beautiful English. We were playing cards here. Was that all right?'

'How is Lothar?'

'Not so wonderful, darling. He has had to stop smoking.'

'That's too bad,' I said. But since Lothar Koch was about two hundred years old, a prohibition on smoking seemed a minor restriction and long overdue.

'He gave the foreign lady the fax number here. I know you have told me never to give that number as a way to reach you, but Lothar said this was an emergency.'

I took the printed message slip from her. As was to be expected of a man who had loyally served in the Nazi Party's Interior Ministry, Lothar Koch had neatly entered the date and time and his initials on the covering sheet and written 'Herrn Bernd Samson' in the appropriate place. 'Dear Herr Samson, the attached fax was sent to you this evening at 21.30 hours. Your caller said it was an emergency. I hope this is in accord with your wishes.'

The fax consisted of one sheet. It was from Mrs Prettyman, and handwritten in a good firm hand with big looping school-book letters that were characteristically American.

Dear Bernard,

I have to tell you the terrible news that my darling Jay died yesterday morning. The doctor and the priest were both with him. It was a peaceful end to his pain, and in some ways for the better. He so enjoyed your visit with us. I think it made him recall happy times you had spent together. He wanted to see you again very much. I told him you were coming back to see him and he died with that thought. He made me promise that I would send this message to you without delay. He wanted me to tell you that you were right in what you said. You guessed what happened. He was all alone that night in Germany. He did everything as you described: there was no one else with him. I hope you understand this message. I have written it exactly as Jay asked.

Would you also please pass news of his condition to any of his friends or relatives with whom you are in touch.

Yours truly,

Tabby Prettyman

I read it through twice. 'Thanks Lisl.' Until now I had felt certain that Prettyman had killed Thurkettle. But this death-bed confession to it jarred me. It made me wonder if this was Prettyman's final gesture of earthly compassion: pleading guilty to a killing he hadn't committed.

'A friend has died?' Lisl was rummaging through her precious collection of records, her fingers flicking against the corners of the dog-eared paper sleeves. Finally she found what she was looking for. She looked up at me. 'Is it someone I know?'

I had no doubt that together with Herr Koch she had given the fax message her earnest scrutiny.

'Yes, a death. He was very ill. No, it was no one you know.'

'Was he very religious?'

'As religious as only a repentant sinner can be,' I said. She nodded sagely. I held her tight and kissed her again. I loved her very much. I said goodnight. As I went upstairs, Marlene began singing *Durch Berlin fliesst immer noch die Spree*. All those unforgettable Berlin cabaret songs had an underlying melancholy. I wondered if that's what Berliners liked about them.

12

The SIS residence, Berlin

'THIS IS NOT going to become an inquest,' said Bret, standing
at the end of the dining-table in Frank Harrington's residence.
Bret rested his fingers lightly upon its polished surface, so that the
reflections looked like big pink spiders. Behind me I heard Frank
Harrington give a deep sigh. Werner, across the table from me,
shrank a few inches into his collar. He looked like hell. The clinic
should never have released him. The others also looked glum. We
all suspected that an inquest was exactly what Bret intended that
it should become. 'It's not official, and nothing anyone says will
be on the record.' Bret smiled grimly. He had his jacket hanging
on the back of his chair and his waistcoat was unbuttoned. Experience had taught me that such dishabille was a bad sign: a warning
that Bret was restless and belligerent. As he looked round at us
all he added: 'Or even remembered. You'll notice that this is a
need-to-know gathering.'

Bret sat down. Dicky Cruyer fingered his wrist to look at his
watch. Dicky had remained in Berlin to attend this meeting at
Bret's request. Dicky wanted everyone to know that he had urgent
and pressing business elsewhere. Dicky's attire had lately taken
a nautical turn: a dark blue Guernsey seaman's sweater and a
red-spotted kerchief tied at his neck. He sat well back from the
table, a sharpened wooden pencil in his hand. His head was tilted
and his eyes fixed, like a sparrow listening for the approach of

some distant predator. Augustus Stowe was there too: swollen to bursting with impatience and importance. Rumours said that he was trying to arrange that he swap jobs with Dicky. There were notepads and pencils at each place. A small table behind me held a tray with glasses and a bottle of fizzy mineral water for those who wanted such Spartan refreshment. No one did. At the centre of the table there were two potted plants that had been brought indoors for the winter. There were no blooms on them; just dark green leaves. It was going to be one of those sessions that Bret called 'informal' because he honestly didn't know that for everyone else these rough-tongue exchanges, with Bret in the driving seat, were white-knuckle rides.

As if Bret had arranged it in advance, the tension created by his serious mien was relaxed for a moment while the coffee was poured and a plate of digestive biscuits circulated. An essential component of the Englishman's diet, various brands of digestives, the coarseness of their oatmeal content, their thin or thick coatings of plain or milk chocolate, are a subject of animated discussion at almost any Departmental gathering. And sometimes the most memorable one.

'We are looking at ongoing success,' said Bret, continuing his leadership role from the seated position. No one spoke. Bret continued: 'We are all party to some aspect of the long-term plan in which Fiona Samson played such a vital part. Maybe none of you know the full story, and that's just the way it should be.' Bret waved away the biscuits, poured cream into his coffee and drank some. His offhand self-assurance in respect of digestive biscuits revealed his transatlantic origins. 'But there were hiccups . . . hiccups and tragedies. I won't name names, and I don't want to apportion blame. But I know that some of you have glimpsed ugly episodes. Many others may have guessed at them. Some of you have encountered questions to which you have no answer. I want to say how much I appreciate the trust and dedication you have provided to the Department in the face of painful doubt.'

The gathering remained silent. It was an opportunity for private worry. Dicky began biting his nails. I took another couple of biscuits, reasoning that the plate might not come back down the table again.

'Things went wrong,' Bret continued. 'In the field we contend with disaster and learn to live with it. But when flaws are traced to London; when catastrophe is built into any operation due to faulty planning, and even fundamentally wrong strategy, we have to put the blame right where it was born: London Central.'

Bret drank some coffee, and let us all catch our breath, clear our throats, and wonder which way he was going. Frank reached out to push a coaster across the table to where Augustus Stowe was about to put the hot antique silver coffee-pot down on the polished surface. It was all right for Bret to talk about London's disasters. Bret had been resident in California – debriefing me and Fiona – long enough to stay out of the firing line. He had chosen just the right time to return and assume the role of prosecutor, judge, juror and probation officer too. But no one said anything like that. We all chewed on our digestives, and guzzled our coffee, and thought our thoughts in a silence broken only by murmured rituals of coffee drinking.

If Bret hadn't started speaking again I think we would all be sitting there still. 'I know that there is no one in this room who can truthfully deny owing a debt of gratitude to Silas Gaunt. Silas was never a glory hunter. Nothing better shows his character than the way he left the Department without recognition of any sort. No knighthood, no CBE, not even the standard letter of recommendation that we give to lower ranks. And yet, with a little lobbying, there is no question that he could have obtained the recognition he deserved. But as you may or may not know, Silas Gaunt asked that he be given nothing, so that he could continue to be in close association with the Department. And for obvious reasons connection would have to be severed with any ex-employee the Department permitted to be honoured in any way.'

There were non-committal noises from the assembled party while Bret took a deep breath. 'And so Silas worked at arm's length for us. And continued to work at arm's length even when he was old and unwell. It is everyone's fault. Dozens of people were in regular contact with him. Any one of them could have shouted stop. Any one of them might have pointed out that Silas was no longer the omnipotent far-sighted strategist he'd once been. But Silas was never content with past glories: he was always look-ing to the future. In hindsight it's obvious that Silas Gaunt thought the Department was languishing and slipping ever further back in our war with the Soviets. He said we hadn't kept up to date. He said it to me, he said it to everyone he could influence. Unfortu-nately he didn't sufficiently distinguish between being up to date and becoming more operational. Our traditional role of intelli-gence gatherer – and nothing beyond – became in his eyes an unendurable restriction. He wanted the Department to be more assertive, even if that meant sometimes being more violent.'

Bret put his hands into the praying position and sat back for ten seconds to let us think about it. Bret had gone as near to the brink as I'd ever heard a senior official go in personalizing the Department's shortcomings.

'I've now put into play checks and balances that would preclude this ever happening again,' said Bret. 'Even senior staff will no longer be able to give off-the-record briefings to anyone engaged in a task that could go operational. Silas Gaunt's contacts with the Department are now severed . . . a thing of the past. We have now cleared up the remnants of every stratagem that Silas Gaunt had access to. Now we start afresh.'

Bret looked around to see how this monologue had been received. Augustus Stowe moved about on his chair, as if suffering cramp. It was difficult to be sure how many people present fully understood what Bret was telling us. Werner looked half-asleep; probably as a result of all the pain-killers he was taking. Frank was anxiously fingering the leaves of the potted flowers that had been brought indoors for the winter. I think he'd noticed black spot. Dicky sat with both hands in his trouser pockets, as if in a resolute attempt to stop nail-biting. Bret said: 'Bernard has had personal involvement in this whole episode. No one blames him for breaking a few rules in his need to find out the answers to questions that kept him awake at night.'

Bret looked at me and said: 'When you went out to the Ziesar ramp last week, and found Thurkettle's decomposing body, you fitted into place the final piece of jigsaw puzzle.'

They all turned to stare at me. 'Who told you I went out there?' I said, keeping my voice pitched in a way that reserved the right to deny that it was true.

'Don't blow a fuse, Bernard. It's standard procedure. Werner is under strict orders to keep me informed of any serious development ... No, no, no. He's a loyal friend of yours, I'll tell you that. But he's also a loyal employee of the Department.'

Werner looked at me and shrugged. Bret knew I could hardly go ape right now. This wasn't the moment to beat Werner over the head, or start arguing the finer details of the Tessa killing. And Bret had set it up so well. He had us all convinced that his only desire was to come up with the truth. And here he was inviting me to say anything I wished.

☆

'Prettyman killed Thurkettle,' I said.

Bret hesitated for a long time. Then he said: 'Yes, I see. But can you tell us why he did it?'

'Prettyman did what Silas Gaunt ordered him to do.'

'But ... Even killing?'

'Not so long ago you sent me out to Washington DC to sweet-talk Prettyman into coming back to London to face an inquiry ... money had gone astray and Prettyman knew the score.'

'Afterwards ...' said Bret.

'Sure,' I said, interrupting him. 'Afterwards it was all smoothed

264

over. No money had gone missing. It was a slush fund. It was just some creative accounting to kosher away money for Fiona's operations in the East.'

'But I can see that you don't believe that,' said Bret.

'I'm guessing. I think Prettyman made sure that a few pennies ended up in his own pocket. I think Silas Gaunt faced Prettyman with evidence of his crime, and used it to blackmail him into doing whatever the Department needed doing.'

'Hold the phone,' said Bret. 'Are you hinting that Prettyman was stitched up? If that's what you think, let's hear it.' Bret knew all the tricks of chairing a meeting, and the number one trick was to remain on the side of the angels.

'That Prettyman was tempted, deliberately tempted, into stealing so that he could be trapped?' I said. 'Yes, that's what I think. Prettyman was perfect for what they wanted: intelligent, quick, unscrupulous and greedy. Yes, I'm sure he was targeted. But there had to be a cut-out point. Blackmailers have to give their victims a look at the light shining at the end of the tunnel.'

'And what was that?'

'On the instructions of Silas Gaunt, Prettyman sought out Thurkettle – a hit man he'd heard his CIA friends talking about – and set up the killing of Tessa Kosinski. Prettyman arranged to pay off Thurkettle in person. But Prettyman was waiting out there with a gun; he killed him instead.'

Bret made a noise: 'Sounds like a damned stupid hit man who gets killed by his client. Wouldn't a contract killer suspect that his employer might try to kill him? And take precautions?'

I said: 'Prettyman made it clear that he was no more than the go-between. It wasn't Prettyman's money and it wasn't Prettyman's chosen target. Prettyman was just the middleman. That way of working would reassure a hit man like Thurkettle. Remember that, as far as anyone knows, Thurkettle had always worked arm's length for organizations. That's how Prettyman heard about him in the first place. He'd always been paid, and always found himself dealing with an intermediary. You don't go off and make a hit for the CIA, or the British government, and come back worrying about being gunned down.'

'Don't you?' said Bret.

'If Uncle Silas is running wild, maybe you should,' I agreed. 'But you know Prettyman, he was quite a wimp, and looked even more feeble than he was. It's not easy to think of a white-faced pen-pusher like him gunning down a hit man in cold blood. It took me a little time to adjust to that idea. But of course that's just what made it all so easy for him.'

'So for you the story is complete, Bernard,' said Bret.

'Almost,' I said. Bret made a movement of his hand urging me to continue. 'There was always the mechanism of getting Tessa Kosinski to the place on the Autobahn where she was killed. From the party in Berlin, she went in the van I was driving. But how was she persuaded to get into it? I did all I could to make her get out. The second mystery is how she came to be in Berlin in the first place.'

'She was with Dicky,' said Bret. 'That's correct, isn't it, Dicky?'

Dicky came bolt upright in his chair and said: 'Yes, Bret' in a whisper.

'But why?' I persisted.

Bret said: 'I'll save Dicky the embarrassment of revealing all the details. Tessa was given two free round-trip air tickets London to Berlin: first class. They were supposed to have come with the compliments of British Airways. In case more inducement was needed a friend of hers, called Pinky, was told to send her some desirable opera tickets. At that same weekend Dicky was told to attend a meeting in Berlin. Dicky was spending a lot of time with Tessa and it all worked out.'

'Was Dicky ordered to take Tessa to Berlin?' I persisted.

Bret looked at Dicky. Dicky's face went a bright red. He said: 'Yes.' I suppose he couldn't say anything else; I'm sure Bret knew the correct answer already.

'That still leaves the question of why she got into my van,' I said.

Dicky, pleased to move on to something other than the hotel room he'd shared with Tessa, said: 'That was a coincidence. She was pretty high by the time she climbed into your van. I tried to get her out but you punched me in the face, Bernard.'

'I'm sorry about that,' I said. 'The van started and my hand slipped.' Dicky had never mentioned my one and only assault upon his person until now. There were times when I even thought he might have forgotten it.

Dicky decided not to pursue it. 'But soon after you left, the Thurkettle man arrived at the party. He was looking everywhere for Tessa. He'd arranged that she should ride on the back of his motor-bike. When he became convinced that she was in your van, he got on his bike and raced off after you.'

'Okay,' said Bret. 'Now tell us, Bernard. What was Prettyman's light at the end of the tunnel?'

'The Swede was waiting at the plane with a box that would solve all Prettyman's problems. This was to be Prettyman's final job for Silas Gaunt. And it was.'

'The evidence of his malfeasance; the accounts or whatever?'

'I've got my own theory about what was in the box,' I told him.

'I sent Werner to get it for us,' said Bret.

'Steal it from Mrs Prettyman, you mean,' I said. 'And use Cindy Prettyman's own keys. That was neat, Werner.' Werner smiled. He didn't mind how sarcastic I was, he knew it was a successful operation. And he knew that, measured in need-to-know brownie points, he outranked me.

'Bernard knows what's in the box file,' said Bret with an edge of sarcasm. 'The rest of us mortals have to guess. I asked London to look up the reference number in Registry but they say there is no record of that box file ever having been issued.'

Never been issued. Clever old Uncle Silas. 'How are you going to look inside it then?' I asked.

'We are cutting the lock off,' said Bret. 'Then we'll settle what's inside. Good old Yankee know-how; isn't that what I'm noted for?'

I had said something along those lines from time to time to all kinds of people, so I wasn't in a position to deny it now. 'I wouldn't cut into that box, Bret,' I said.

'I already have,' said Bret with a smug grin. 'Tarrant has it in his workshop. I'm waiting for him to bring it up here and show us the contents.'

'No, Bret, no,' I said. I jumped to my feet so hurriedly that I knocked my chair backwards, and heard it hit the little table holding the tray of glasses. Everything fell to the floor with the sound of breaking crystal.

'Where are you going?' shouted Bret.

☆

Like all such old Berlin houses this one had a staircase at the back so that servants could move about unobtrusively. Access to the stairs was through doors without doorknobs or locks; doors designed to conform with the wall decoration and be unnoticed by the casual observer. I knew this house well, and I went through the door to find the landing at the top of a narrow wooden staircase. I wasn't expecting to find an elderly man sitting there in regal style on the draughty upstairs servants' landing. Neither was this tall stranger ready for my sudden eruption through the wall. 'Oww!' he shouted as he sprang to his feet, responding to the way my booted foot had landed on his arthritic knee, and the jolt from my outstretched hand when it steadied itself upon his neck.

I didn't stop to strangle him. There was no time. I ran down the stairs, and was at the next landing by the time I realized that the man I had stumbled over was the Director-General. He had been seated on an antique chair, with a woollen blanket over his knees and headphones clamped over his ears. Listening of course to everything that Bret and the rest of us were saying. We were being bugged by the Director-General in person! So that was how it was done; and no one had even been told the D-G was making one of his rare excursions to this outpost of Empire. That bloody Frank and his potted plants. And I thought he was finding black spot on them.

From above I heard a distant yell as the D-G recovered himself from where he had been sent sprawling across the floor. But by that time I was going down the stairs as fast as I could run. My brain had become alive. What was I doing, I asked myself. Why was I running frantically through the house, so concerned about Tarrant? I hated and despised Tarrant. He had always shown aloof hostility to me and everything I did and said. But how could I stop right here on the stairs, go back up to the others and tell them I'd changed my mind? I remembered Frank's words at an earlier meeting: It's always bad luck to be good at something you don't want to do – or something dangerous. Well, Frank old daddy, you said it all.

I rushed down the final flight of stairs, pushed the door open and emerged into the hall. I slid on the loose carpet so that I almost fell full-length across the floor. Then, recovering my balance by grabbing the hall table, I ran through the drawing-room and burst out of the garden door and into the long conservatory. Rows of potted plants were lined up near the light and the whole place smelled of the onions and apples that were stored there in winter. I pulled the outside door open with such force a glass pane cracked. Then I was out into the biting cold air and the garden. I ran along the path, skirting round a wheelbarrow, the ice and gravel crunching and cracking underfoot. 'Tarrant, stop!' I shouted as I ran.

I wrenched open the door of Tarrant's sanctum. He stood at his workbench. One hand was raised as he brought the lever of a power drill down to make another hole in the steel box file that was gripped in the vice.

I grabbed Tarrant's shoulders to spin him around. Then I used both hands on the small of his back to propel him through the door and out into the garden. He went flying, his feet scarcely touching the ground. I was following behind him, thinking all the time of what a fool I would look if my calculations proved wrong.

But I had no need to worry on that account. As Tarrant and I hit the frosty lawn, and rolled over in the snow with Tarrant shouting his objections, the bang came.

Tarrant's brick-built play-pen was just what the Semtex needed. It constrained the force of the explosion enough to make sure it really went with a noise that echoed round the neighbourhood. The workshop door was already open, but the force wrenched it off its hinges and sent it bowling across the grass like a rectangular wheel. The window disappeared in a red flare and became broken glass and firewood.

'Oh my God,' shouted Tarrant. 'I'm dying.'

I stayed where I was on the cold ground. Now that it was over I was shivering, and it wasn't entirely due to the weather. I also felt an almost overwhelming need to vomit. Getting angry and screaming abuse at Tarrant enabled me to overcome these symptoms.

☆

'How did you guess?' Bret asked me after I'd had a stiff drink, and been checked over by Frank's tame doctor. It was just Bret and me. And we were not sitting near any of Frank's potted plants.

'There was no other explanation.'

'Ah, yes, Sherlock Holmes: when you have eliminated the impossible, the remaining improbable explanation must be right.'

'Something like that,' I said. Bret was not a Sherlock Holmes fan: his favourite reading matter was the sports pages of the *International Herald Tribune*.

'But why wait so long before confiding it to us?' said Bret. He was distressed. He was good at hiding his emotions, but Bret was always dismayed by the cadenzas of violence that brought discordant counterpoint to the formal harmonies of office life in Whitehall.

'I needed to know who else was in on the secret,' I explained. 'I had to see how you and Werner and Frank saw it all coming undone. And I wanted to see how you all reacted to the prospect of opening the box file. I wanted to find out who was in this with Silas.'

'And did you find out?'

'Well, I bumped into the Director-General,' I said.

Bret acknowledged this joke with one of his well-known flickering smiles. 'Did Prettyman know what was in the box?'

'I wonder. He must have had some strange sort of worry about it. But what could he do?'

'He could hope his wife forced it open,' said Bret.

'It's tempting to think that he wanted her to steal it and break into it. But when you see how difficult it was to open without a key it's clear that if someone got blown away opening it, it wouldn't be Mrs Prettyman but some poor bloody technician in Brussels. And I'm not sure Prettyman would try that on his ex-wife. I was surprised that he found the nerve to kill Thurkettle.'

'Well, ex-wives sometimes generate considerable motivation along those lines,' said Bret, who had suffered chronic ex-wife angst. 'What made it explode?' he said. 'Tarrant had been struggling with it for half an hour.'

'Some sort of composite fuse. A trembler wouldn't have been suitable. It had to be a fuse that could take rough treatment. My bet would be a light-sensitive fuse: a photo-electric cell, set so it would be triggered by light.'

'I've never heard of a gadget like that.'

'The Luftwaffe used them on time-delay bombs dropped on London during the war. They were put into the delay circuit as a back-up. If the time-fuse failed, the light-sensitive one would explode when the bomb disposal team dismantled it to look inside.'

'A secondary fuse?'

'Two fuses would be in keeping with the purpose of the device.'

'Would it?'

'It was designed to make sure the Swede, his plane and Pretty-man would disappear for ever. With Thurkettle already dead, that would have eliminated any possibility of the truth ever coming to light.'

'Silas Gaunt,' said Bret sadly. 'Don't let's be mealy-mouthed about it. Silas Gaunt set up the Kosinski killing and the Thurkettle killing. And then wanted to make certain the killers were all dead too. It was almost the perfect . . .'

'The perfect crime?' I supplied.

'The perfect solution,' said Bret.

'What will happen now?'

'No one was hurt,' said Bret. 'What do you want to happen? Do you want to sue Silas Gaunt?' he asked caustically.

'He wasn't the only one,' I said. 'He is simply the one who will get all the blame. They will dump every mistake and crime the Department committed on to Silas Gaunt. They did the same with my father.'

'He'll never be released.' Bret didn't argue with my verdict.

'I think he knows that,' I said.

'He is seriously disturbed,' said Bret.

'He seemed quite rational when I saw him.'

'I know. Sometimes he seems absolutely normal. No one suspected the truth for a long time. He simply lost all sense of right and wrong. I blame the D-G in some ways. He put far too much on to Silas's shoulders at a time when Silas should have been resting and having counselling.'

'You said you wanted to see me, Bret,' I reminded him. 'Was there something else to tell me?'

Bret looked at me in a very solemn way and said: 'Last weekend I asked Gloria to marry me.'

'Congratulations, Bret.'

'She told me yes.'

'That's great.' So that look in his eyes hadn't just come from eating too much sugar.

'This is it, Bernard. No fancy weekends in country hotels. Nothing sneaky. I want this to be the one thing I do just right. Love and cherish; for better or for worse; happy ever after, and all that.' He looked at his hands. In what was probably some significant signal of what was in the deepest recesses of his mind, he twisted his gold signet ring round, so it looked like a wedding band. 'Freud said that a man can be in love with a woman for many years without realizing that he's in love.'

'Yes, well, when you read those books of his, you can tell he had a lot of things on his mind.'

'I figured I should clear our plans with you first. Gloria thought the same. One of the reasons I came here to Berlin was so that I could see you and make sure it was okay by you.'

'I'm not your prospective father-in-law, Bret. You do it the way you want. She deserves a break.'

'I told her that I didn't want a wife who was yearning for some other guy. I had one of those wives the last time around. Gloria said there was no one else.'

'She's right as far as I'm concerned. It was obvious from the start. I knew it would never work: we both knew.' I gave a sincere smile and reached out and shook his hand in a grown-up, calm and dignified way. 'Congratulations, Bret. It will be just fine. You're a lucky man; she's quite a girl.'

'Whatever she is, I love her, Bernard. I need her.'

'I'm a married man, Bret,' I said, to stem his confession.

'I know. It will all work out for you too, Bernard. Fiona's something special. All marriages go through a really bad patch some time.'

'How long does it last?'

'If it's any help, I can tell you that the Department plan to offer you a proper contract . . . pension and so on.'

I nodded.

'The Department owes you that at least. And I owe you a great deal too.'

'Do you? What?'

'Have you forgotten that night I came to you at the Hennig place? That night when Five sent a K7 man to caution me and put me under house arrest. I phoned the D-G . . .'

'And the D-G just happened to be on a train to Manchester,' I supplied. 'Yes, I remember. The D-G becomes conveniently restless when a bitter row is in the offing.'

'I was desperate. You were the only one I knew wouldn't turn me in, Bernard.'

'You were taking a chance,' I said.

'No, I wasn't. I knew you would go out on a limb for me, Bernard. You are your own man. I've cursed you for that many times. But I admire it too. That's why I want to do everything right by you.'

'Okay, Bret.'

'I'll pull out all the stops to get Frank's job for you when he goes. Not because I owe you a favour but because you are the best man for the job. My guess is that he will resign, and go out to Australia with his son. You know how Frank feels about him.'

I nodded my thanks.

'I can't promise of course. They might have bowler-hatted me by then. I'm on a handshake arrangement. When they get someone younger and more suited for the Deputy's job, I will go back to California.'

'With Gloria?'

'Oh, sure. I will always have my home there. She's never been, but I know she will love it. There's a real big age disparity but . . .'

'Forget it. You'll be very happy together,' I said. 'Gloria likes older men.'

'You have all the answers, Bernard.'

'Us people with all the answers always get a few of them wrong.'

'You don't have to get all of them wrong. You are the luckiest man in the world, Bernard. You're married to Fiona.'

'She's married to her work,' I said.

'You two just don't communicate at all, do you? You couldn't be more wrong about Fiona. Look, I have spent a lot of time worrying about this . . . worrying whether I should show it to you. But I can't see any alternative.'

☆

Bret took a sheet of writing paper from his pocket. The letterhead was La Buona Nova, the California estate where Fiona and I had spent so long being debriefed by Bret. The note was creased, as if it had been read, re-read, folded and refolded many many times. It was Fiona's handwriting:

Dear Bret,

I can't go on day after day of talking about my past. At first I expected it to become a sort of therapy that would heal me and make me whole. But it's not like that. You are considerate and kind but the more I talk the more dispirited I become. I've lost Bernard. I realize that now. And when I lost Bernard, I lost the children too, for they adore him.

It's not Bernard's fault, it's not anyone's fault except my own. I should have known that Bernard would find someone else. Or that someone else would find him. And I should have known that Bernard was not the sort of man who can jump into bed and out of it again. Bernard is serious. Bernard would never admit it but he is a romantic. It is what made me fall in love with him, and stay in love. And now he's serious and romantic and madly in love with Gloria, and I know I will never be able to compete with her. She's young and gorgeous and sweet and kind. And clever. She loves our children and from what I hear, she says only complimentary things about me. What can I offer him that is better? Bernard hungers for her all the time, and

275

perhaps he's right to love her. I know him so well that I can see every thought that is written in his face. And it devastates me. He's desolate at being separated from her. He gave me some money the other day and there was a tiny photo of Gloria folded inside. He keeps it with his money so that I never see it, I suppose. I placed it on the floor in the dressing-room and he found it there and thought I'd never seen it.

It was my affair with Kennedy that destroyed our marriage of course. I was a fool. But Kennedy could never have become a 'Gloria' in my life. He was in love with Karl Marx. I soon guessed that he was spying on me, and that everything was secondary to his 'duty'. And I knew that if he discovered that I was still working for London Central he would turn me in without a flicker of hesitation, or a moment of remorse.

I learned that life's unendurable tests come in the shape of memories, not experiences. That night when Tess died and when I saw Bernard shoot Kennedy . . . the confusions and the shouting, the dimly lit roadside and my fears. These all anaesthetized my emotions and feelings. For a few days I felt able to deal with it. But when the memories of that night visited me I saw it for the first time. For the first time, I felt the warm blood that spattered upon me. For the first time the hatred and despair was so evident that I could smell the emotion. And each time the memories return they are more fearful. Like all intruders they come unexpected in the night. They drag me slowly from deep drug-induced sleep, to an interim state of half-awake nightmare from which I struggle to awaken.

After the nightmares started, I saw Bernard in a new way. Bernard gave me everything he had to give. Throughout our married life I had blamed him for not being demonstrative, at a time when I should have been thanking him for never burdening me with the hell he'd been through. Bernard has spent all his life doing a job for which he was never really suited. He is not tough. He is not insensitive. He is not violent. His brain is quicker and more subtle than that of anyone I've ever met. And this is why he decided he must keep his nightmares all to himself. Now I have discovered how much it costs to be alone with such terrors. But for me it is too late.

How can I ever make Bernard love me again? Don't say I can't. Life without Bernard would not be worth living. No one will ever love him as I have. And do. And always will.

Goodnight, Bret. Thank you for more than I can ever say.

Fiona

I folded up the letter and handed it back to Bret. It had disturbed me very much. 'I'm grateful, Bret,' I said.

'You still don't understand, do you?' said Bret. 'Can't you read?'

'Yes, I can.'

'When I got to her room she had taken a whole load of tablets. She got them from the doctor two or three at a time, and saved them up. And she drank half a bottle of vodka.'

'Fiona had? Vodka and pills?'

'You were away in Santa Barbara that night. I pushed her into the car and got her to the hospital. They were great. They did all the things they do, and they saved her. I knew the director there. We told everyone she was there for tests.'

'I remember when she was having tests. Jesus Christ! Why didn't you tell me the truth?'

'I promised her I wouldn't. She left a note for you; I burned it. I promised I'd never tell you. Now I'm breaking that promise. But how can I stand by and let the pair of you tear each other apart? I'm too fond of you both to permit it without doing something.'

'I love her, Bret. I've always loved her.'

'You are a callous brute. Forget all that stuff about you being a romantic; that's just a measure of how much she loves you. You are brutal.'

'Towards Fi?'

'Can't you see what you do to her? She's not married to her

work, Bernard. She'd give it up tomorrow if you gave her the kind of love and understanding she needs. She's a woman, Bernard, she's your wife. She's not a drinking buddy. She works non-stop because you drive her out of your life. Can't you see that, Bernard? Can't you see that?'

'How do you know? . . . know what she feels?'

'She talks to me because she can't talk to you. You're a smart talker, Bernard, a beau parleur. You can talk your way through any situation if you have a mind to. Fiona is not like that. The more important it is to her, the more tongue-tied she becomes. She can't express her deepest feelings to you. She would love to have the children with her all the time. But you've got to be with her too. Not time-wise but with her in spirit. How can you expect her to commit herself to you, while you are still sending long-stem red roses to Gloria?'

'I hope you're right, Bret,' I said. 'Last night I wrote to Fiona: a long letter. I want to start again.'

'Good! That's good, Bernard. Let's make at least one good thing come out of this mess.'

'I asked her to come and live with me in Berlin. And send the children to a German school. Have them grow up the way I did.'

'She will jump at it, Bernard. I know she will.'

Fiona was right: and happiness too comes more often from memories than from experiences. My happiness came in the shape of a perfect day long ago. I was with my schoolfriends, Werner and Axel. We were running down to the canal, and then along it to Lützowplatz. I ran and ran until I got to Dad's office on Tauentzienstrasse. What a hot summer day it was: only Berlin enjoys such lovely days. I opened Dad's desk and found the chocolate bar, his ration, that he left there for me. He always saved it for me. Today there were two bars: that's why I remember it so vividly. We shared the chocolate between us and then climbed up the mountain of rubble. It filled the middle of the whole street, as high as three floors. From the top – sitting on an old piece of box

278

– we went sliding down the steep slope, bumping in clouds of dust. The next stop was the clinic where the salvaged bricks, bottles and pieces of timber were cleaned and sorted and arranged with a care that only Germans could give to such things. We worked there for an hour each day after school. Then we would go swimming. The sky was blue and Berlin was heaven.

'I hope she will,' I said.

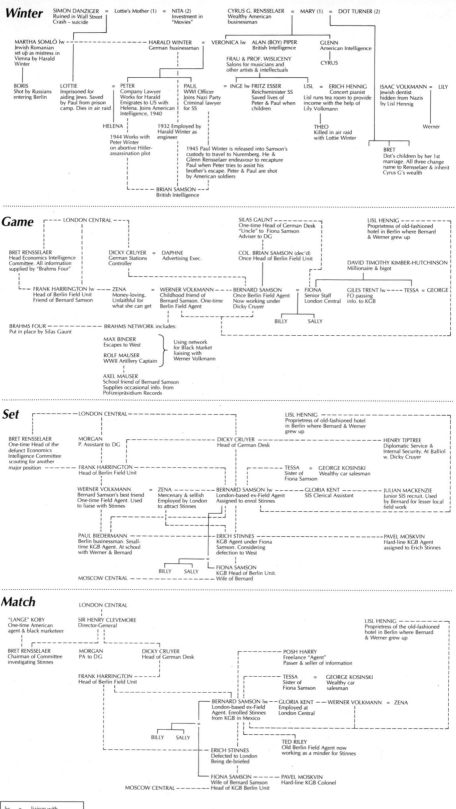

Winter

SIMON DANZIGER = Lottie's Mother (1) = NITA (2)
Ruined in Wall Street | Investment in
Crash – suicide | "Movies"

CYRUS G. RENSSELAER = MARY (1) = DOT TURNER (2)
Wealthy American
businessman

MARTHA SOMLÓ lw = = = = = = = = = = = = = HARALD WINTER =
Jewish Romanian | German businessman
set up as mistress in
Vienna by Harald
Winter

VERONICA lw   ALAN (BOY) PIPER   GLENN
British Intelligence   American Intelligence

FRAU & PROF. WISLICENY   CYRUS
Salons for musicians and
other artists & intellectuals

BORIS   LOTTIE   PETER   PAUL   = INGE lw   FRITZ ESSER   LISL = ERICH HENNIG   ISAAC VOLKMANN = LILY
Shot by Russians   Imprisoned for   Company Lawyer   WWI Officer   Reichsminister SS   Concert pianist   Jewish dentist
entering Berlin   aiding Jews. Saved   Works for Harald   Joins Nazi Party   Saved lives of   Lisl runs tea room to provide   hidden from Nazis
    by Paul from prison   Emigrates to US with   Criminal lawyer   Peter & Paul when   income with the help of   by Lisl Hennig
    camp. Dies in air raid   Helena. Joins American   for SS   children   Lily Volkmann
        Intelligence, 1940

HELENA   1932 Employed by   THEO   WERNER
1944 Works with   Harald Winter as   Killed in air raid
Peter Winter   engineer   with Lottie Winter
on abortive Hitler-
assassination plot   1945 Paul Winter is released into Samson's   BRET
    custody to travel to Nuremberg. He &   Dot's children by her 1st
    Glenn Rensselaer endeavour to recapture   marriage. All three change
    Paul when Peter tries to assist his   name to Rensselaer & inherit
    brother's escape. Peter & Paul are shot   Cyrus G's wealth
    by American soldiers

BRIAN SAMSON
British Intelligence

Game

LONDON CENTRAL   SILAS GAUNT   LISL HENNIG
    One-time Head of German Desk   Proprietress of old-fashioned
    "Uncle" to Fiona Samson   hotel in Berlin where Bernard
    Adviser to DG   & Werner grew up

BRET RENSSELAER   DICKY CRUYER = DAPHNE   COL. BRIAN SAMSON (dec'd)
Head Economics Intelligence   German Stations   Advertising Exec.   Once Head of Berlin Field Unit   DAVID TIMOTHY KIMBER-HUTCHINSON
Committee. All information   Controller   Millionaire & bigot
supplied by "Brahms Four"

FRANK HARRINGTON lw = = = ZENA   WERNER VOLKMANN = = = BERNARD SAMSON = FIONA   GILES TRENT lw = = = TESSA = GEORGE
Head of Berlin Field Unit   Money-loving.   Childhood friend of   Once Berlin Field Agent   Senior Staff   FO passing
Friend of Bernard Samson   Unfaithful for   Bernard Samson. One-time   Now working under   London Central   info. to KGB
    what she can get   Berlin Field Agent   Dicky Cruyer

BRAHMS FOUR = = = = = = = BRAHMS NETWORK includes: BILLY   SALLY
Put in place by Silas Gaunt

MAX BINDER   Using network
Escapes to West   for Black Market
    liaising with
ROLF MAUSER   Werner Volkmann
WWII Artillery Captain

AXEL MAUSER
School friend of Bernard Samson
Supplies occasional info. from
Polizeipräsidium Records

Set

LONDON CENTRAL   LISL HENNIG
    Proprietress of old-fashioned hotel
    in Berlin where Bernard & Werner
    grew up

BRET RENSSELAER   MORGAN   DICKY CRUYER   HENRY TIPTREE
One-time Head of the   P. Assistant to DG   Head of German Desk   Diplomatic Service &
defunct Economics   Internal Security. At Balliol
Intelligence Committee   w. Dicky Cruyer
scouting for another
major position   FRANK HARRINGTON   TESSA = GEORGE KOSINSKI
    Head of Berlin Field Unit   Sister of   Wealthy car salesman
        Fiona Samson

WERNER VOLKMANN = = = ZENA = = = BERNARD SAMSON lw = = = GLORIA KENT   JULIAN MACKENZIE
Bernard Samson's best friend   Mercenary & selfish   London-based ex-Field Agent   SIS Clerical Assistant   Junior SIS recruit. Used
One-time Field Agent. Used   Employed by London   Assigned to enrol Stinnes   by Bernard for lesser local
to liaise with Stinnes   to attract Stinnes   field work

PAUL BIEDERMANN = = = = = = = = = = ERICH STINNES = = = = = = = = = = PAVEL MOSKVIN
Berlin businessman. Small-   KGB Agent under Fiona   Hard-line KGB Agent
time KGB Agent. At school   Samson. Considering   assigned to Erich Stinnes
with Werner & Bernard   defection to West

BILLY   SALLY   FIONA SAMSON
    KGB Head of Berlin Unit.
MOSCOW CENTRAL = = = = = = = = = = = =   Wife of Bernard

Match

LONDON CENTRAL

"LANGE" KOBY   SIR HENRY CLEVEMORE   LISL HENNIG
One-time American   Director-General   Proprietress of the old-fashioned
agent & black marketeer   hotel in Berlin where Bernard
        & Werner grew up

BRET RENSSELAER   MORGAN   DICKY CRUYER   POSH HARRY
Chairman of Committee   PA to DG   Head of German Desk   Freelance "Agent"
investigating Stinnes   Passer & seller of information

FRANK HARRINGTON   TESSA = GEORGE KOSINSKI
Head of Berlin Field Unit   Sister of   Wealthy car
    Fiona Samson   salesman

BERNARD SAMSON lw = = = GLORIA KENT = = = WERNER VOLKMANN = ZENA
London-based ex-Field   Employed at
Agent. Enrolled Stinnes   London Central
from KGB in Mexico

BILLY   SALLY   TED RILEY
    Old Berlin Field Agent now
    working as a minder for Stinnes

ERICH STINNES
Defected to London
Being de-briefed

FIONA SAMSON = = = = PAVEL MOSKVIN
Wife of Bernard Samson   Hard-line KGB Colonel
MOSCOW CENTRAL = = = = = = Head of KGB Berlin Unit

lw   =   liaison with
= = =   =   connected by family